CORPVS POETICVM BOREALE

GUDBRAND VIGFUSSON

F. YORK POWELL

CORPVS POETICVM BOREALE

THE POETRY

OF THE

OLD NORTHERN TONGUE

FROM THE EARLIEST TIMES TO THE THIRTEENTH CENTURY

EDITED

CLASSIFIED AND TRANSLATED

WITH

INTRODUCTION, EXCURSUS, AND NOTES

BY

GUDBRAND VIGFUSSON, M.A.

AND

F. YORK POWELL, M.A.

VOL. II

COURT POETRY

New York

RUSSELL & RUSSELL

1965

FIRST PUBLISHED IN 1883
REISSUED, 1965, BY RUSSELL & RUSSELL, INC.
L.C. CATALOG CARD NO: 64-23469

PRINTED IN THE UNITED STATES OF AMERICA

ADDENDA AND CORRIGENDA TO EXCURSUS I, VOLUME II.

(The reconstructed texts involve some addenda and emendenda in Excursus I, vol. ii, pp. 447-486.)

Page 452. **Mouth**—*add*, frœða-salr, Sonat. 22, Skíða R. 375; óðar-grunnr, Sonat. 11; hiarta strönd, Sonat. 10.

Tongue—*add*, óðar lokarr, Sonat. 21; rýnis rœði, Sonat. 12.

454, l. 16, *read*, 'thong, garter, or necklace of the woods.'

457. **Heavens**—*dele*, Mistar mar, Helgi i. 192.

458. **Porpoises**—*add*, brim-svín, Hym. 104; and *dele* the same word in paragraph above.

461. **Woden, Lord of Soma**—*add*, farma-goð, Sonat. 9; and *dele*, 'forns hrosta hilmir . . .'

462, l. 3, *insert*, **Lord of the Wolves**—skoll-blœtr, Hlt. 9.

After **Earth** *insert*, The **World-tree**—Yggjar galgi, Sonat. 74; Yggdrasils askr, ut infra.

Poetry—*add*, Farma-goðs hrosta-brim, Sonat. 10.

l. 6 from bottom, *read*, Alfoðrs hrosta-*brim*.

463, l. 1, *dele*, 'Forniótz hrosti?'

466. **Human kind**—*add*, Yggjar galga alþióð, Sonat. 74.

Balder—*add*, Gráta goð, Vsp. 65.

After Heimdal add, **Hœni**—Fetmeili (step-meter), Haust. 13; cp. Aur-konungr, Langi-fótr, I. 575.

479. **Pontiff**—*dele*, ve-frömoðr, Rogna hrœrs fromoðr, Skiald blœtr.

480. **Icelanders**—*dele*, elgjar galga alþioð.

Henchmen—inndrott, *add*, Hornkl. 26.

ERRATA TO VOLUME II.

Bragi 9, *read* bœti-þrúðr.

„ 46, *read* Iarðar reist.

Haustlong 28, *read* hollz.

Þd. 52, *read* gnípo.

p. 37, foot-note to l. 44, *read* spörom.

p. 54, l. 3 from bottom, *read* skæ.

p. 62, top, *read* svellz.

Kormak 3, *read* fári.

„ 16, *read* Hagbarðz . . . starði.

p. 80, l. 30, *read* gína.

p. 98, l. 16 from bottom, *read* was about to make *for* made, *and* ere he sat out *for* on his return.

p. 115, l. 10, *read* Alpta-firði.

Sighvat iv. 8, *read* konungs.

„ iv. 40, *read* elld.

„ v. 23, *read* varr glœstr.

„ vii. 15, *read* mörgo; foot-note, *dele* or viva.

„ vii. 44, foot-note, *read* stóðo.

„ x. 71, *read* rán mun.

Ott. i. 29, *read* Yngvi.

p. 136, l. 8 of transl., *read* black *for* blue.

p. 176, l. 39, *dele* fröm.

Arnor vi. 2, *for* fen *read* brim.

p. 188, l. 59, *read* runs down Meiti's cliffs with his sea-skate *for* plows the main with his galleys.

p. 195, l. 1 of transl., *for* 'Duncan' *read* 'Hundason' [Macbeth].

Arnor vi. 60, *read* drakk.

Thiod. i. 28, *read* munðot.

„ iii. 78, *read* él-kers.

„ iv. 11, *read* sæ-fang.

„ viii. 21, *read* Hitt hefig heyrt.

p. 215, l. 15 of transl., *insert* the king raised the mast in a heavy sea.

p. 218, l. 3, *read* brynnir.

Mark. i. 3, *read* orðz-tír.

„ i. 49, *read* sungo.

„ v. 6, *read* slíðr-áls.

p. 229, l. 1 of transl., *read* journey *for* hasten.

p. 247, l. 5 of transl., *read* lassie *for* darling.

p. 250, ll. 15–17 of transl., *read* as it told that of yore kings' sons took service with the wise Kraki's kinsman.

p. 268, l. 10 of transl., *read* fir-shaw *for* fire-shaw.

p. 269, l. 3 of transl., *read* I have heard that fiv? kings.

p. 270, l. 20, *read* óra.

p. 273, l. 9 of transl., *read* Thou didst break the eagle's *fast*.

p. 277, l. 12, *read* leikara.

Geisli 32, *read* lærðrar.

„ 152, *read* fyrða; *dele* brackets.

„ 195, *read* snyrtiss.

Rekst. 86, *read* strangr.

Iomsv. 54, *read* frœkn at.

p. 326, l. 12 of transl., *read* morsels *for* mortals.

p. 337, l. 31, *read* Hlébarðr.

p. 361, l. 20, *read* grip þo ek gamall verði.

Merl. i. 152, *read* gollor-hallir.

Skíða R. 144, *read* kappa gilda.

Thulor, l. 17, *for* Sölsi *read* Sölvi.

„ 477, *for* rai *read* rati?

„ 588, *read* Andhrimnir.

„ 657, *read* Skolm.

„ 667, *read* Solund.

p. 440, l. 20, *read* Hísing.

p. 450, *read* Blöndo-skald.

p. 529, l. 13 from bottom, *read* Hreid-marr *for* Hreidarr.

p. 577, l. 10 from bottom, *read* truck *for* trunk.

p. 580, l. 7, *read* like *for* as.

p. 591, l. 16 from bottom, *read* 62 *for* 162.

p. 637, l. 13, *read* cleft *for* cleaft.

Note that the piece of verse paraphrased here is probably by the author of the poem on *Hell*, paraphrased p. 546, both of which pieces were originally in the Dialogue-metre.

p. 646, l. 9 from bottom, *read* elilenti *for* elilenfi.

BOOK VII.

HEATHEN POETRY IN COURT METRE.

THE various poems in this Book represent the antique heathen age of court poets. They are hard to group, but have here been roughly arranged according to subject. They range, with one important exception (Bragi), from c. 930–995.

SECTION 1. *Mythical.* Contains the Hesiodic Shield-songs, poems on the Labours of Thor and the like; addressed to kings and nobles.

SECTION 2. *Historical.* Early *royal* court poetry of heathen time, of the days of King Hacon to Earl Hacon.

SECTION 3. Fragments of *private historical* compositions, poems on the sea, on Icelandic heroes, and the like in court metre, but not composed on Kings or Earls.

SECTION 4. Stray verses of *lyrical* cast. *Improvisations* on a variety of subjects, many relating to incidents of Icelandic feuds.

§ 1. MYTHICAL COURT POEMS.

BRAGI'S SHIELD-LAY (RAGNARS-DRÁPA).

THERE are two Bragis; with one, a mythical divine being (originally perhaps Woden himself, in his character as the arch-poet), we have nothing to do here; but the other, Bragi, the son of Boddi, surnamed the old (Gamli) to distinguish him from a son or younger kinsman possibly, is a real historical personage. He is mentioned in Landnama-bok, Snorri's Edda, Skaldatal, Ynglinga, Egil's Saga, etc. We must base our views of his date and position in Northern poetry upon what we can gather from the poems ascribed to him by Snorri, and from Ari's genealogy of his family in Landnama-bok. The more important of the poems is a Shield-Song (Ragnars-drápa) upon a shield sent by King Ragnarr (Reginhere), son of Sigrod (Sigfred), to Bragi by the hand of Hrafnketill (Ravenkettle). The genealogy runs thus—

Bragi Bodda son, *m.* Lopthæna daughter of *Erp lútandi*
|
Astrid Slækidreing, *m.* Arinbiorn the elder (of the Fiords)
|
┌─────────────────────────┴─────────────────────┐
Arnthrudr, *m.* Thori Hersi   Lopthæna, *m.* Thorstein
| |
Arinbiorn Hersi, d. 976   Hrosskel of Acreness, a settler
                                           |
                                        Hallkel
                                           |
                       ┌───────────────────┴──────────────┐
                  Tind, c. 990–1010   Illugi Swarti
                       | |
                  Thorwald   *Gunnlaug Ormstunga,*
                       | c. 984–1008
                  Illugi
                       |
                  Gisl, 1100

The two Arinbiorns and Thori were nobles of the district of the Friths in Western Norway. The date of Bragi has been hitherto thrown too far back. Counting from Arinbiorn, Egil's friend, and remembering that the two generations between, being of women, are probably short, we might safely make Bragi's life to lie between c. 835 and 900. This date does not forbid our identifying the Ragnar Sigrod's son, Bragi's patron, with the famous Ragnar Lodbrok. Snorri says, 'Bragi the old spoke of Sorli and Hamtheow in the Encomium he made in Ragnar Lodbrok;' and again, in reference to the Everlasting Fight,

' According to this story Bragi the poet made his verse in his Encomium of Ragnar Lodbrok (Ragnars drápa loʒbrókar).'

The legend as preserved in the North tells of a king Ragnar, Sigrod's son [Reginhere Sigfredsson], surnamed Lodbrok [probably *eagle*, as hábrok means *hawk*], coming to England, where he was slain by a king Ella. Lodbrok's sons then invaded England and conquered part of it. The first ships of the Northmen from Harethaland are noted in the English Chronicles, and seem, according to Mr. Howorth's hypothesis, to have come in 793. A king Ella of Northumberland is known to the English authorities, and dated c. 867.

In the poem itself we find that the shield is *sent* to Bragi, which implies, one would fancy, a distance between the king's seat and the poet's homestead. This agrees with tradition and the genealogies, which place Bragi on the N.W. coast in the Friths and make Ragnar reign in the Wick and Westfold, near Drammen. See Introduction to Book ix, § 1. Consistent with this are the two or three mentions of Bragi as connected with Eystein Beli, king of the Swedes, a foe of Ragnar Lodbrok and his sons (see Skaldatal), and the incident alluded to by Arinbiorn in Egil's Saga, when he advises Egil to calm Eric's anger by a poem of praise, ' for so did Bragi, my kinsman [the true reading is ' minn ']. When he had drawn down on him the wrath of Biorn o' Howe, king of the Swedes, he made an Encomium [drápa] of twenty stanzas upon him, in one night, and so ransomed his head.' A story which, by the by, seems the nucleus of the legend that has descended upon Egil, and is given as the ground for the title Head-Ransom of his rhymed Encomium on Eric Bloodaxe. However this be, we may safely take it that all chronological requirements will be satisfied by taking Bragi to have been a poet famous in the last generation of the Norwegian polyarchy and living into the days of Harold Fairhair.

Bragi has left a great name behind, and his poems, if we had them in their original form, would be a most precious monument of the speech and thought of a famous age in the North. But it is not so. It cannot be too often insisted on, that the remains of his verse that have reached us have been so completely *metamorphosed*, that save for a line here and there *we cannot rely upon word, metre, or meaning;* and any version which may be given of them must be more or less different from what Bragi composed. No amount of critical ingenuity can possibly do more than recover a genuine phrase here and there in these old poems.

Nor are the reasons of this metamorphosis far to seek. Bragi composed at a time when, under some foreign influence, a new school of poetry was rising in the North. The common old four-measured alliterative metre was changed into a more regular six-measured line. A new ornament—consonantic correspondence (*consonance* as we may call it)—was brought *into* the line, the poetical synonyms were developed to a very extraordinary degree, the wide field of mythology being ransacked for apt and ingenious allusions, and lastly the loose varying periods of the old poetry were replaced by a new unit—the four-lined stanza (itself a doubling of the two-lined couplet), and these stanzas were combined into regular strophes. Bragi himself probably took no mean part in introducing these new forms, which were gradually perfected by successive generations of court poets, till in St. Olave's and Harold Hardreda's time we see the court metre in perfection, with strict six-measured lines (sometimes even eight-measured), consonance, full line-rhyme, fill-gaps (stál), strict syntactic arrangement, and elaborate strophic form.

During nearly nine generations, almost three centuries, Bragi's verses must have suffered many changes in his reciters' mouths, even by the time that Ari received them; but these changes, though no doubt modernising grammar, substituting newer for older words and phrases, were not of the radical character which, we believe, those of a later date were. In the North French Chansons de geste, we see the old 'assonantic leashes' replaced by rhymed couplets, and these by Alexandrines, as successive editions of a poem are adapted to successive generations, and we take it, that either deliberately, as in France, or by degrees, many of Bragi's rough lines were in the generations between Ari and Snorri polished into more or less strict court-metre of Harold Sigurdsson's day; a line here and there being left almost untouched, where tradition spoke too strongly in its favour, to give us some glimpse into the real state of the case. A line, one half blank, one half with a fairly pure consonance, is, we think, the true Bragian line, still extant in the *burdens* —

þat sék fall á fögrom, etc. þá má sókn, etc.;

and the lines we have been able to recover—

iofrom vulfs of sinna með valgifris lifro;

and—

fyr Veniris víðri val-rauf fiogor havfuð.

Many of the lines yield as they stand either no meaning at all, or a forced commonplace platitude. This must not be put to the poet: on the whole, we believe that two-thirds of the verses in Bragi's remains are either maimed or metamorphosed so that we cannot be sure of a word in them, in the remaining third a word or phrase occurs with the genuine 'Bragian' ring.

The old Hamtheow's Lay must have been known to Bragi. We have noted the parallelisms in the margin. Egil seems to have known Bragi's poems. We may fancy that such characteristic and peculiar words as 'enni-tungl' (Egil's 'enni-mani') were coined by Bragi, and passed from him to the younger poet.

Most if not all of Bragi's verse that has reached us are from a *Shield-Lay*, viz. the introduction, and two sections (the Everlasting Fight and the Struggle in Eormanric's Hall). Part of a third section (on Gefion's Draught), and an epilogue (on the King's Guerdon), may have belonged to the same poem, as we have arranged it here. As also the fragments depicting Thor fishing for the Earth-Serpent, and a few lines on the same god's exploits against the three-headed monster Thriwald and the giant Thiazzi (which it is possible may have belonged to a separate Thors Drápa), together with a line on Woden.

The little verse ascribed by Snorri to Bragi, see Book vi, Ditties No. 1, is given by Saxo to Bersi and Groa. See Notes.

The *shield* which Bragi describes, may have been not unlike those of Homer and Hesiod. Like them too, it was probably of foreign design and make. The lively fancy of a poet would identify the struggling monsters on an eastern target with Thor and the Beast (just as he would no doubt have, had he seen a Greek vase, identified the sack of Troy with the vengeance of Gudrun's son on Eormanric, or Herakles and Geruones with Thunder and Thriwald), as we know that Warangian tradition declared the statues in the Hippodrome at Constantinople to be the images of their own Wolsungs and Giukungs.

The *story* of the *Everlasting Battle* is a wide-spread tradition in the North, localised in many places. Saxo the Dane fixes it in Hethinsoe,

the German author of Kudrun lays the scene at Wülpensand or Wül-
penwert, at the Scheldt-mouth, Bragi the Northman (see l. 14 and in
our reading l. 17) in Hod, an island off Northmore in Norway, while
Snorri, whose information on these matters is, we take it, drawn from
the Western Islands more or less remotely, places it at Hoy in
the Orkneys, where also it is fixed by the late legend in Flatey-bok,
where King Olaf Tryggvason is made to break the spell that bound
the doomed kings.

Snorri tells the tale in Skaldskapa-mal thus:—"A king who is called
Högni (Hagena) had a daughter whose name was Hild. The king,
whose name was Hedin, the son of Hiarrand, carried her off as captive.
Hagena was away at the time at the Kings'-Moot, but when he heard
that his realm had been harried and his daughter carried away, he set
out with his men of war to seek Hedin, having heard that Hedin had
sailed northward up the coast; but when King Hagena came to Norway,
he heard that Hedin had sailed west across the main. Then Hagena
sailed after him as far as the Orkneys, and when he came to the island that
is called Hoy, there he found Hedin with his men of war. Then Hild
went to meet her father, and offered him on Hedin's behalf a Necklace
for peace, but her words were otherwise, for she said that Hedin had
made ready to fight, and that Hagena could look for no mercy from him.
Hagena answered his daughter stiffly, but when she came back to
Hedin, she told him that Hagena would have no peace, and bade him
make ready for battle. So the two kings did, and landed on the island
and set their warriors in array. Then Hedin called to Hagena his
father-in-law and offered him to make peace and give him much gold as
boot. Then answered Hagena, Thou makest this offer too late, if thou
wishest for peace, for now I have drawn Dains-loom which the Dwarves
wrought, that is fated to be a man's death every time it is made bare,
and never swerves in its stroke, and its wound never heals, if it be but a
scratch of it. Then answered Hedin, Thou shalt brag of thy sword but
not of the victory. I call that a good sword that is true to its master.
Then they begun the battle which is called the *Heathnings' Fight*, and
fought all the day, but in the evening the kings went off to their ships.
But Hild went by night to the slain, and woke to life by her enchantment all them that were dead. And the next day the kings went
to the field of battle and fought, and with them all they that had
fallen on the former day. So that battle went on day after day, and
all they that fell and all their weapons that lay on the field of battle,
and their bucklers likewise, turned to stone; but in the dawning all the
dead men arose and fought and all their weapons then became of use
again. And it is told in Lays that the Heathnings shall in this wise abide
the Doom of the Powers."

The 'stone weapons' look as if the necessary correspondence in shape
between weapons of bronze and stone had been noticed by some early
observer, and theorised upon with a curious inversion of the development theory.

Bragi takes up the story when the two kings are lying at the island
ready for war, and that guileful witch, the fair Hild, is going from one to
the other with the necklace.

The *Eormanric story*, as told by Bragi, begins with the Gothic king's
evil dream and waking under the swords of the avenging brethren. The
scene in the hall must have been of great power in the original form.
The death of the brethren closes the strophe. Snorri's prose here
follows Bragi rather than Hamtheow's Lay:—'But when they came to

King Eormanric's by night, when he was sleeping, and cut off his
hands and feet, then he awoke and called to his men and bade them
awake.' Nor does Snorri know of Woden's interposition, but with our
poem ascribes to Eormanric himself the command to stone the brothers.

The *Gefion story*, a geographic legend, is told in Ynglinga Saga,
where the lake from which the island Zealand is dragged is called
Mælar (by a mistake which would easily occur to foreigners at a time
when maps were not). However, the poem itself contains the real name
(which one glance at the shape of the lake makes evident) concealed
under the senseless 'uineyiar ualrauf.' There must have been another
like story about Gotland and Mælar lake, one would think. The four
heads and eight eyes recall the old chariot scenes of Assyrian and
Egyptian sculpture, and incline one to put this section to the Shield Lay.

The next morsel, *Thor and the Serpent*, if we read 'sent' as 'seen,' an
archaic form (and it can hardly be from 'senna' the meaning of which
'to banter' would not fit), would be also a section of a Shield-Lay.

We should thus get a round target of four sections, each containing a scene of a separate subject. The sections of this shield may
even have led to the strophic division of the drápa, which was possibly a
development of the Shield-Lay, and Bragi, the earliest Northern Shield-
Poet, may have been the creator of this metric form.

Bragi's fragments are found in Edda, Codex Wormianus as usual
yielding the best text. But the Eormanric section, not found there, is
best given in 1 e β, which, for instance, has preserved the right reading
'öl-skalir,' confirmed by Hamtheow's Lay, where Cd. *r* is wrong.
Gefion's bit is also seen in Ynglinga Saga. Sinfitela's death is alluded
to in a 'kenning.'

Contemporaries of Bragi are *Flein Hiorson, Erp Lowting (Lutandi)*, and
Wolf Uargi.

'Thorwolf the son of Hariwolf Horn-breaker, and Olaf (Anlaf) his
brother, were kings in the Uplands. With them was FLEIN HIORSON the
poet, who was bred up north in More, in an island a little off Borgund,
which is called Iosurheath, where his father dwelt. Flein went to Denmark to meet King Eystan, and gat great honour there for his poesy, so
that the King gave him his daughter to wife. Thrasi was the name of
Thorwolf's son.' *Landnama-bok*, (H b) V. ch. 1.

ERP LOWTING was the father-in-law of Bragi the poet. See *Landnama-bok*.

'WOLF UARGI was a noble baron in Norway, in Naumdale, the father
of Hallbiorn Half-fiend, the father of Kettle Hæing. Wolf made a
Praise-song in one night, telling his valiant deeds, and was dead before
daybreak.' *Skaldatal*. He was Kveld-Ulf's mother's father. *Landn.*

We take 'uarge' to be simply 'wærg,' cursed, wicked; the epithet
applied to any of the bigger beasts of prey, lion, etc. It probably
implies something like 'hamramr' and 'ofreskr.'

No verse of these men remain, but there is a *metre* called Flein's.

I. *Introduction.*

1.   VILIT, Hrafn-ketill, heyra hve hrein-groit steini
        Þrúðar skal-ek ok þengil þiófs ilja-blað leyfa?

I. *Prologue.* Hearken, O Ravenkettle, to my praise of the brightly-
painted Shield and of the king, *that gave it me:* so that the son of

2. ok] om. W.

2. Nema svá at góð ins gialla giæld baug-navar vildi
meyjar hióls enn mœri mœgr Sigræðar Hœgna.

II. *Hilda and Hogni.*

3. Ok um 'þerris œða' ósk-rán at þat sínom   5
til fár-huga fœri feðr veðr 'boða' hugði:
Þá es hristi-sif hringa hals in bœls of fyllda
bar til byrjar dræsla baug œrlygiss draugi.

4. Bauða sú til bleyði bœði-þrúðr at móti
malma mœtom hilmi men dreyrogra benja: 10
svá lét ey þoat etti sem orrosto letti
iœfrom Vulfs of sinna með valgifris lifro.

5. Letrat lýða stillir landa vanr á sandi
(þá svall heipt í Hœgna) Hœð Glamma 'mun' stœðva
es þrym-regin þremja 'þróttig Heðins sótto'   15
heldr en Hildar svíra hringa þeir of fengo.

6. Ok fyr Hœð í holmi hveðro brynjo Viðris
feng eyðandi flióða fordæða nam ráða:
Allr gekk herr und 'hurdir' Hiarranda 'fram kyrrar,'
reiðr at Reifniss skeiði raðalfr af mar bráðom.   20

7. *Þá má sókn a Svelniss sal-penningi kenna
(Ræs gáfomk reiðar mána Ragnarr) ok fiölð sagna.*

III. *Hamtheow and Sorli in Iormunrek's Hall.*

8. Knátti endr við illan Iœrmunrekr at vakna
með dreyr-fár dróttir draum í sverða flaumi:

Sigrod [Sigfred] may learn the song I have made in return for the
ring-naved buckler.
II. *The Everlasting Battle.* *The sense beneath the 'overlaid' words and
phrases seems to be*—And in dire mood she plotted her father's death,
when she maliciously brought him the Necklace down at the ships. It
was not for peace sake she brought it him. She made ever as if no
bloodshed would come of it, while she was egging them on to the
company of the corse-greedy Wolf's sister [Hell].
Hageno, with furious heart, brought his ships to land on the sand of
the isle of Hod, and the host of Hedin came forth to meet him, having
received Hilda's necklace. Yea, the fatal sorceress prevailed on them
to fight in the isle of Hod, and the whole host of Hiarrandi's son
[Hedin] marched straightway down to the sea. . . . *Refrain.* This
Battle and many tales more may be seen on the Shield that Ragnar
[Reginhere] gave me.
III. *The Avenging of Swanhild.* In days of yore Eormenric and his . . .

---

3. -navaðs, 748.   4. Sigurðar, W.   6. boða] miswritten in W.   11. ætti,
W.   12. Vulfs . . . valgifris] emend.; Ulfs . . . algifris, Cd.   14. Read, mar ?
15. Read, -reginn . . . þróttigr Heðin sótti ?   17. Höð] emend.; hond, W.
19. Réad, und hialmom Hiarranda fram burar.   21-22. Moved four lines down.
23. endr] eðr, r; áðr, 1 e β.

aH108. arósta varð í ranni Randvéss hœfuð-niðja 25
　　　þa es hrafn-blair hefndo harma Erps of barmar.
9.　Flaut of set við sveita, sóknar-alfs, á golfi
bH113. hræva-dœgg þar es hœggnar bhendr sem fóetr of kendosk :
cH109. cFell í blóði blandinn brunn dœl-skálir runna
dH108. —þat-es á Leifa landa laufi fátt—at hœfði. 30
10.　Þar svá at gœrðo gyrðan golf holkvis sá fylkiss
　　　'segls naglfara siglor saums' andvanar standa :
eH39. urðo snemst ok Sœrli esam-ráða þeir Hamðer
　　　hólom herði-mýlom Hergautz vino barðir.
11.　Miok let stála stœkkvir stydja f'Bikka' niðja 35
fH85. flaums þá es 'fiœrvi næma Fogl-hildar' mun vildo :
　　　ok 'bla serkjar birkiss bœll fagr-gœto allir'
gH117. enni-hœgg ok geggiar Ionakrs sonom launa.

12.　Þat sék fall á fögrom flotna randar botni
　　　(Ræs gáfomk reiðar mána Ragnarr) ok fiölð sagna. 40

IV. Gefion ploughing Seeland out of Lake Wenereu.

13.　Gefion dró frá Gylva, glœð diúp-rœðul, œðla,
　　　(svá at af renni-rœknnom rauk) Danmarkar-auka :
　　　Bóro œxn ok átta enni-tungl þar-es gengo
　　　fyr Veniris víðri val-rauf fiogor hœfuð.

V. Thor fishing for the Earth Serpent.

14.　Þat eromk sént; at snemma sonr Alda-foðrs vildi 45
　　　afls við úri þafðan Iærðar reist of freista.
15.　Vaðr lá Viðris arfa vilgi slakr, enn rakðisk
　　　á Eynefiss œndri Iormun-gandr at sandi.

---

host woke out of an evil dream to battle. There arose a tumult in the
hall of Randve's kinsman *Eormenric* what time the raven-black brothers
of Erp avenged their wrongs. The benches were swimming in blood,
the king's hands and feet lay lopped on the floor, the ale-beakers were
shivered, and he fell headlong in his gore. This is painted on my
Shield. One might see the hall all stained with blood, the . . . , till
at last the two single-hearted brethren Hamtheow and Sarila were
stoned with the rolling bowls of the earth [stones]. Bikki's men stoned
the brothers who came to avenge Swanhild's death, and they paid back
the blows and wounds *they had got* from Ionakr's sons.
　The Fall of these men and many tales more I see upon the fair field
of the Shield. Ragnar gave it me.
　IV. *The Hire of Gefion.* Gefion the rich dragged the Increase of Denmark out of Gylve's domain, her ox-team steamed : four fair heads they
bore and eight eyes, while they drew the broad Spoil of Lake Wener.
　V. *Thor and Leviathan.* Moreover I see how Thor would try his might

---

28. þar es . . . kendosk] I e β.　29. Emend. ; aulskali, I e β.　31. gyrðan]
i. e. gœrðan, *gory.*　35. Bikka] emend. ; Giuka, W ; see Höm. 85.　36. Fogl-
hildar = Svanhildar ?　44. Veniris] emend. ; Vineyjar, Cd.

16.   Hamri fórsk í hœgri hœnd, þá-es allra landa
       eygir œflog-barða endi-seiðs of kenndi.   50
17.   Ok borð-roins barða brautar-hringr inn lióti
       á haus-sprengi Hrungniss harð-geðr neðan starði.
18.   Þiokk-vœxnom kvað þykkja þikkling firin-mikla
       hafra-niótz at hœfgom hætting megin-drætti:
       Þá-es forns litar flotna á fang-boða œngli   55
       hrœkkvi-áll of hrokkinn hekk Volsunga drekko.
19.   Vildit vrœngom ofra 'vágs hyr-sendir' ægi
       hinn es mió-tygil máva mœrar skar fyr Þóri.
20.   Vel hafit yðrom eykjom aptr, Þrívalda, haldit
       simli sumbls of mœrom sundr-kliúfr nio hœfða!   60
21.   Hinn es varp á víða vinda Öndor-dísar
       yfir manna siœt margra munnlaug fœðor augom.

                        VI. On Woden.

22.   Þars es lofðar líta lung váfaðar Gungnis.

                        VII. The End.

23.   Elld of þák at iœfri œlna bekks við drykkjo;
       þat gaf Fiolniss fialla með fulli mer stillir.   65
24.   Þann áttak vin verstan vazt-rœdd, enn mer baztan
       Ála undir kúlo óniðraðan Þriðja.

HAUST-LÖNG; or, THE HARVEST-LAY OR SHIELD-SONG.

WE have already made some mention of this poet in Book iv, § 2,
when we dealt with his poem Ynglingatal. He came from the little
dale of Hwin, still known as a valley west of Lindisness (Naze).
The patron, for whom he made the poem with which we are con-

---

against the wave-washed Earth-Serpent. His line was strained hard on
to the gunwale while the Leviathan writhed in the sand. He grasped
the Hammer in his right hand when he felt the monster on his hook,
and the horrid serpent glared up at him. The burly giant *Hymir* said
he thought that Thor had made a parlous haul, when he beheld the
venomous snake hanging on the ogre-grasper's hook. He would pull
no more, and he cut the slim line for Thor.

O thou that clove asunder Thriwald's nine heads, thou hast brought
thy team safe back.

He who cast the eyes of Thiazzi up into the wide dome of the winds,
above all the habitations of men.

VI. Here one may see the steed of Woden, *Sleipni* . . . .

VII. I got gold at the king's hands in return for my song. He (*the
king*) was the worst friend to gold and the best to me.

---

53. firin] farin, W.   62. föðor] fiogor, W.   64. at] af, W.   66.
vaz rọð, W.

cerned, was the great lawyer and constitution-maker Thorleif the
Wise, the organiser of Gula-thing (see King Hakon's Saga, cap. 11), and
the counsellor of the Icelanders in their establishment of one General
Constitution, 'which' (as Ari tells in Libellus) 'was made for the most
part according to the law of Gula-thing as it then stood, and by the
advice of Thorleif the Wise, the son of Hordakari, as to the additions or omissions or changes to be made.' Thorleif was the adviser
of King Hakon the Good, Æthelstan's foster-son, and probably died
about 960. He was the ancestor of the later Orkney Earls, of the
twelfth century. (See their pedigrees, vol. i. of Orkney Saga, Roll Series.)
It was for some member of his family that Hyndlu-liod was made.
As the poem tells us, he gave Thiodwolf a shield painted with figures,
and it is as a return for this bounty that Thiodwolf made the Shield-
Song called *Haust-long* (Harvest-long). The exact meaning of the
title is not certain, but it would seem to show that the poem was meant
to while away the long autumn evenings. It is a brighter, but at the
same time a more religious poem than any other of its kind. The *text*
rests only on two Edda MSS. (W & r), and chiefly Wormianus.

Thiodwolf's poems have suffered far less than Bragi's from the hand
of the improver, chiefly we believe because he is of a more modern type
as regards metre. His verses come possibly two generations after
Bragi's, and these intervening years are most important ones as regards
possibilities of foreign, western, and especially Celtic influences; hence
we may readily admit that Thiodwolf employed a more elaborate
metric expression than Bragi. Bragi's characteristic line, as we have
seen, probably contained no ornament save the old alliterative syllables
in the first half, but had a line-consonance in the second half. From
this Thiodwolf seems to have gone a step further and sometimes used
a full line-vowel rhyme in the second half, while he put a line-consonance in the first half, thus in all probability, for we have no earlier
examples of it than his, originating the normal court-metre line. But
there were still Bragian lines in his genuine poems (many more than at
present no doubt), and the *burdens* especially are after the older model,
and lines with the line-consonance in *both* halves are frequent.

Thiodwolf uses a rich vocabulary, and has many lines of great force.
The opening of the second section of Haust-long, where the Thunder-
god comes storming through the sky englobed in fire, is very fine,
recalling Milton.

Thiodwolf's poem is a fountain to the mythologist, both as regards
the story and, even more, the allusive synonyms.

There are but two sections of Haust-long preserved as citations in
Edda, but they seem fairly perfect. The *first*, with the prologue, tells
the tale of the *Rape of Idwyn* and the death of Thiazzi, thus paraphrased
(from the poem) by Snorri, in the beginning of Bragi's Teaching:—

"He began the story there, how three of the Anses set forth from
home, Woden and Loki and Honir, and journeyed over fell and forest,
and were badly off for food. And when they came down into a certain
dale, they saw a herd of oxen there and took one ox and fell to seething
it. And when they thought that it must be sodden, they tried the meat,
and, lo, it was not done; and a second time, when an hour had gone
by, they tried it again, and it was not done yet. Then they fell to
talking among themselves as to what might be the cause thereof, when
they heard a voice up in an oak above them, and he that sate there told
them the reason why the meat was not done. They looked up, and it
was an eagle, and no small one, that was sitting there. Then the eagle

spake, If ye will give me my fill of the ox, then the meat will be done. They consented so to do. Then he let himself stoop down out of the tree, and sate down to the meat, and straightway caught up both the thigh of the ox and both the shoulders.

"Then Loki grew wroth, and snatched up a great staff, and brandished it with all his might, and hit the eagle on the back. The eagle started at the blow, and flew up, and, lo, the staff was fast to the back of the eagle, and Loki's hands *fast* to the other end. The eagle flew so high that Loki's feet grazed the rocks and stocks and tree, and he thought that his arms would be torn from his shoulders. He cried out and begged the eagle hard for quarter; but he said that Loki should never get loose, till he set him a day on which he would bring Idwyn with her apples out of Ansegarth. And Loki did so, and straightway he was loosed and went off to his companions; and nothing more is told of their journey before they got back home. But at the appointed hour Loki enticed Idwyn out of Ansegarth into a certain wood, telling her that he had found some apples, which she would think treasures, and bidding her take her apples with her, so as to be able to set them against these. And thither comes Thiazzi the giant in his eagle-skin, and takes up Idwyn and flies away with her into Thrym-ham to his dwelling. But the Anses became distressed at the vanishing, and soon began to grow hoary and old. Then the Anses held a moot, and enquired one of another what was the last seen of Idwyn; and the last seen of her was, that she was going out of Ansegarth with Loki. Then Loki was taken and brought before the moot, and they promised him death or torture. And when he grew fearful thereat, he said that he would go and seek after Idwyn in Giant-land, if Freya would lend him the hawk-skin she had. And when he had put on the hawk-skin he flew northward into Giant-land, and reached Giant Thiazzi's in one day. He had rowed out to sea *fishing*, and Idwyn was at home alone, *so* Loki turned her into the shape of a nut, and took her into his talons and flew off as hard as he could. But when Thiazzi came home and missed Idwyn, he took his eagle-skin, and flew after Loki, and flapped his eagle-wings in his flight. But when the Anses saw how the hawk was flying with the nut and the eagle flying after him, they went out in front of Ansegarth bearing thither loads of plane-chips. And when the hawk flew in over the fortress, he let himself alight just behind the fortress-wall; and immediately the Anses kindled the plane-chips, but the eagle was not able to stay himself when he missed the hawk, and the fire caught in the eagle's plumage and stopped his flight. Then up came the Anses and slew the eagle that was giant Thiazzi inside *the wall of* Ansegarth, and this slaying is far famed."

The second, the tale of *Thor's Wager of Battle* with the monster Rungnir, is also paraphrased by Snorri in Skaldskaparmal in the following words:—

"Then Bragi told Egir that Thor was gone into the Eastern quarters to smite giants. But Woden rode Slipper into Giant-land, and came to the house of a giant whose name was Rungnir. Then Rungnir asked, who was the man that wore a golden helmet and was riding over sky and sea, and said that he had a wonderful good horse. Woden said that he would wager his head that there was not a horse in Giant-land as good. Rungnir said that it was a good horse, but that he had a bigger stepper, whose name was Goldmane [Gollfaxi]. (*Something missing here.*) Rungnir was angry, and leapt upon his horse and rode after him, and thought to pay him for his proud speech. Woden rode so hard that he was only just in sight; but Rungnir was in such mighty giant-wrath that he never stayed till he galloped inside the gates of the Anses. And when he came into the doors of the hall the Anses bade him to the drinking; he went into the hall *therefore* and called for drink to be brought him. Then they took the bowls that Thor was wont to drink out of, and Rungnir emptied them one after another. Now when he was drunken there was no lack of big words *in him;* he boasted that he could take up Walhall and carry it into Giant-land, and sink Ansegarth, and slay all the gods save Freya and Sif, whom he would carry home *captive* with him. Freya was the only one that dared to bear drink to him, and he boasted that he would drink up all the Ale of the Anses. But when the Anses were tired of his bragging, they called for Thor. Forthwith Thor came into the hall; he was holding his Hammer aloft, and was very wroth, and asked by whose counsel it was that dog-minded Giants should be drinking there, and who it was that had given Rungnir safeguard to be in Walhall, and why Freya should be his cup-bearer, as at a guild-feast of the Anses. Then Rungnir answered, beholding Thor with no friendly eyes, saying that Woden had bidden him to the drinking, and that he was under his safeguard. Then Thor said that Rungnir should rue that bidding ere he left *the hall.* Rungnir says that it were little glory for Thor *the Champion* to slay him weaponless as he was; it were greater prowess if Thor dared to fight with him on the march at Rockgarth, and it was the greatest foolishness, said he, for me to have left my shield and hone at home, for if I had my weapons here we would try wager of battle now; but as it stands now I charge thee with a craven's deed if thou slay me weaponless. Thor would by no means fail to come to the wager of battle, now that a battle-place was pitched for him, for no one had ever dared to challenge him before. Then Rungnir went his way and rode mightily till he came to Giant-land, and his journey was widely famed among the Giants, and especially that he had set a day for him and Thor to meet. The Giants thought there was great risk which of them should win the day. They feared evil from Thor if Rungnir should fall, because he was the strongest of them all. Then the Giants made a man at Rockgarth of clay; he was nine leagues high and three broad under the arms, but they could not get a heart for him big enough to fit, so they got one out of a mare, and it was not steady within him when Thor came. Rungnir, as it is said, had a heart of hard stone, and pointed into three horns, and according to it is made the figure [fylfot] which is called Rungnir's heart; his head was also of stone, his shield was of stone *too*, broad and thick, and he held this shield before him as he stood at Rockgarth and waited for Thor, and for a weapon he had a hone which he bore on his shoulder, and was not a man to cope with. On the other side of him stood the Giant of Clay, who was named Muck-calf, and he was very frightened, yea, it is said that he . . . . when he saw Thor. Thor went forth to the set place of battle, and Thialfi [Delve] with him. Then Delve ran forward to where Rungnir stood and spoke to him, 'Thou art standing unwarily, O Giant, with thy shield before thee, for Thor hath seen thee, and he is going down into the earth and will come against thee from below.' Then Rungnir thrust the shield under his feet, and stood upon it, and took hold of his hone with both hands. And straightway he beheld lightnings and heard great thunder-peals, and saw Thor in his god's wrath. He came on mightily, and brandished his Hammer, and cast it at Rungnir from afar. Rungnir caught up the hone with both hands, and threw it against the Hammer, and it met the Hammer in its flight, and the hone broke

asunder, and one half fell to earth, whence came all the rocks of hone,
the other half crashed into Thor's head so that he fell forward to the
earth.   But the Hammer Milner lit on the middle of Rungnir's head
and broke the skull into little morsels, and he fell forward over Thor,
so that his foot lay athwart Thor's neck.   And Delve fought Muck-calf,
and he fell with little ado.   Then Delve went to Thor, and tried to
take Rungnir's foot off him, but could not even stir it.   Then all the
Anses, when they heard that Thor was fallen, tried to take the foot off
his neck, but could not stir it.   Then came (Magni) Main, the son of
Thor and Ironsax, he was at that time three nights old, he cast Rungnir's
foot off Thor, and said, 'Little harm may it do thee, father, that I am come
so late, I think that I would have smitten the Giant to death with my fist
if I had met him!'   Then Thor stood up and welcomed his son heartily,
and said that he would be a big man of his hands; 'and,' said he, 'I will
give thee the horse, Goldmane, that Rungnir owned.'   Then spake
Woden, saying that Thor did wrong to give that good horse to a giantess'
son rather than to his own father.   Thor went home to Thrudwong
with the hone still in his head.   Then there came a Sibyl whose name
was Groa, the wife of Orwandil the Brave [Orion], she chaunted spell-
songs over Thor, till the hone began to loosen.   And when Thor felt
this and began to think it likely that the hone would soon be out, he
wished to repay Groa for her leechcraft and make her glad, so he told
her this news, that he had waded over Sleet Bay [Elivoe] from the North
and had borne Orwandil from the North out of Giant-land in his basket
on his back, and for a token thereof that one of his toes had stuck out
of the basket and so got frozen, so that he, Thor, had broken it off and
cast it up into the heaven and made the star with it that is called
Orwandil's toe [Orion's toe, the star Rigel in Orion?].   Thor said that it
would not be long before Orwandil would be home, and Groa was so
glad that she could not go on with her spells, and so the hone never got
looser, and it is still fast in Thor's head.   And that is why it is forbidden
to cast a hone across the floor, because it makes the hone turn that
is in Thor's head.   According to this tale Thiodwolf of Hwin made
Harvest-long."

It is said in the Saga of Harold Fairhair (chs. 26, 37) that Thiodwolf
was a dear friend of that king and foster-father to his son Godfrid Gleam;
but it will not do to build too much on such tales as are told of him and
these princes, for fixing the poet's age or date.   They are popular tales,
and must go for what they are worth.   The king, sitting at a banquet
of mead, mutters as he looks down at the long row of men drinking,
'My men are eager over their mead.   Ye are over many here.'   Up
spake the poet, 'When we were with the king in the battle we were
none too many then.'   The story is repeated with reference to King
Hakon Æthelstan's foster-son and his men (Fagrsk.).   And again as
occurring to King Magnus Bareleg and Kali the Wise (the descendant of
Thiodwolf's pátron Thorleif).   Another time, when Godfrid was wishing
to put to sea, Thiodwolf is said to have improvised this stave, 'Go not
hence, Godfrid, till the sea grows calm!   The billows are dashing the
rocks aloft.   Wait for a fair wind! stay with us till the fine weather
comes!   The surf is running off Iadar!'   But the young man would
not be stayed, and off Iadar his ship sunk in the storm with all hands.
We have added these verses as interesting, though not like to be
Thiodwolf's.

W = Cod. Worm. (ll. 1–43 and 53–80), r = Regins (ll. 44–52).

I. *The Rape of Idwyn by Giant Thiazzi.*

1. HVE skal galla giœldom gunn-veggjar brú leggja
. . . . . . radd-kleifar Þorleifi!—
Týframra sé-ek tiva trygglaust of far þriggja
á hrein-gero hlýri hildar-véss ok Þiaza.

2. Seggjondom fló sagna Snótar-ulfr at móti   5
í gemliss ham gœmlom glamma afyr skœmmo:
settisk œrn þar-es Æsir ‘ár gefnar’ mat bœro
(vasa byrgi-týr biarga bleyði vendr) á seyði.

3. Tor-miðlaðr vas tivom tál hreinn meðal-beina;
hvat kvóðo hapta snyrtir hialm-faldinn því valda: 10
marg-spakr of nam mæla már val-kastar bœro
(vasat Hœnis vinr hónom hollr) af fornom þolli.

4. Fiall-gylðir bað fyllar Fet-meila ser deila
hlaut af helgom skutli Hrafn-Ásar vin blása:
Ving-rœgnir let vagna víg-frekr ofan sígask   15
þar-es vél-sparir vóro varnendr goða farnir.

5. Fliótt bað foldar dróttinn Fárbauta mœg ‘vára’
þekkiligr með þegnom þrym-seilar hval deila:
enn af breiðom bióði bragð-víss at þat lagði
ósvifrandi Ása upp þiór-hluti fióra.   20

6. Ok slíðr-loga síðan svangr (vas þat fyr lœngo)
át af eiki-róto ok-biœrn faðir Morna:
áðr diúp-hugaðr dræpi dolg ballastan vallar
hirði-týr meðal herða her-fangs ofan stœngo.

7. Þá varð fastr við fóstra farmr Sigynjar arma,   25
(sá-es œll regin eygja) Öndor-goðs (í bœndom):

I. *Prologue.* How can . . . my mouth render thanks to Thorleif for the
bright-ringing shield!

The story of Thiazzi. Yea, I see the hapless journey of the three gods
and Thiazzi painted on the polished cheek of the shield. In days of yore
Giant Thiazzi flew in an ancient eagle's feather-skin towards the Anses.
He alighted where the Anses were boiling their meat (no coward was
he). The gods' dinner was long a preparing. 'What is the cause of it?'
quoth the helm-hooded one [Woden]. Up spake the wise eagle from
the ancient tree; (no·friend of his was Loki.) He prayed Honir for a
share from the·hallowed dish. Loki had hard work to blow the fire.
The greedy Giant stooped down to where the guileless gods were
gathered. *Woden*, the lord of the earth, bade Loki to portion out the
ox, and the wily foe of the gods took the four quarters up out of the
huge cauldron, and then the hungry Giant out of the tree ate of the ox
(it is an old tale) till the deep-plotting god, *Loki*, struck him between
the shoulders with a staff. And forthwith Loki (whom in bonds all the

---

2. Blank in W; kleif at, W?   3. of] ok, W.   4. vez, W.   8. seiði, W.
10 Read, hvat kvað?   14. helgu, W, *r*.   laasa, W.   17. faar-, W.
19. Emend.; breiðo, W.   20. osviprandi, W.   21. sliðrliga, *r* (better?).
23. ballaðan, W.

loddi rǽ við ramman reimoð Iǫtun-heima,
enn hollr vinar Hœniss hendr við stangar enda.

8. Fló með 'fróðgom' tíva fang-sæll of veg langan
sveita nagr, svá-at slitna sundr Ulfs fœðr mœndi: 30
þá varð Þórs of rúni (þungr vas Loptr) of sprunginn
málo-nautr hvatz mátti miðiungs friðar biðja.

9. Ser bað sagna hrœri sorg-eyra mey fœra,
þá-es elli-lyf Ása, átt-runnr Hymiss, kunni:
Brunnakrs of kom bekkjar Brísings goða dísi   35
girði-þiófr í garða griót-niðaðar síðan.

10. Urðot brattra borða byggvendr at þat hryggvir;
þá vas Ið- með Iǫtnom -unnr ný-komin sunnan:
Gœrðosk allar áttir Ingi-Freyss at þingi
(váro heldr) ok hárar (ham-liót regin) gamlar: 40

11. Unz 'hrun sæva hræva' hund Ölgefnar fundo
leiði-þir ok læva lund Ölgefnar bundo:
Þú skalt véltr, nema vælom (Veoðr mælti svá) 'leiðar'
mun-stœrandi mæra mey aptr, Loki, teygir.

12. Heyrdak svá þat síðan (sveik opt Áso leikom)   45
hug-reynandi Hœniss hauks flaug bialba aukinn:
ok lóm-hugaðr lagði leik-blaðs reginn fiaðrar
ern at œglis barni arn-súg faðir Mornar.

13. Hófo skiótt, en skófo skǫpt, ginn-regin brinna;
enn son biðils sviðnar (sveipr varð í fœr) Greipar.   50

Powers fear) was fast to Thiazzi; the staff clave to the mighty denizen
of Giant-land, and Loki's hands clave to the end thereof. Rejoicing in
his prey, the eagle flew a long way with the god of wiles, so that he was
like to have been torn asunder; he was well-nigh riven, for he was
heavy, and was forced to beg for quarter. The monster bade him
bring him the sorrow-healing Maiden, who knew the gods' Elixir of
Youth: upon which the Thief of the Brising-girdle, Loki, brought the
Fairy of Bourn-acre, Idwyn, to the hall of the giant. Joyful were they
that dwell in the rocks, *the Giants*, when Idwyn first came among them
from the south: but all the kindred of Ingwi-Frey, *the gods*, became old
and hoary: very withered of form the gods showed at their moot: till
they found him that had cruelly carried off the goddess, and bound the
betrayer of Idwyn. 'Thou shalt surely pay it dear, thou guileful Loki,'
so Thor spake, 'save by thy cunning thou bring back the blessed heart-
renewing Maiden.' I have heard that after this, Loki (who had often
betrayed the Anses by his tricks) took flight in the hawk-skin guise,
[bearing Idwyn with him,] while the false-hearted Giant-eagle flapped
his eagle wings in *hot* chase of the hawk. In haste the gods gathered
wood-shavings and kindled a fire, and the Giant was scorched and his
journey brought to an end.

---

29. fróðgom] *r*; miswritten in W.   41. seva, W.   42. ok] at, W.
43. vælom] W leaves a blank for ll. 44-52.   44. teygir] by guess, blank in *r*.
45. Áso] emend.; asa, *r*.

Þatz of fát á fialla Finnz ilja brú mínni.
Baugs þák bifom fáða bif-kleif at Þorleifi.

II. *Thor's Wager of Battle.*

14.　Eðr of sér es Iœtna ótti lét of sóttan
hellis bur á hyrjar haug Griótuna baugi :
Ók at ísarn-leiki Iarðar sunr ; enn dunði　　　　55
(móðr svall Meila bróðor) mána-vegr und hánom.

15.　Knátto œll, enn Ullar (endi-lág) fyr mági
(grund vas grápi hrundin) ginnunga vé brinna :
þá-es húf-regin hafrar hóg-reiðar fram drógo
(seðr gekk Svolnis ekkja sundr) at Hrungnis fundi.　60

16.　Þyrmðit Baldrs of barmi berg-folgnom sak-dolgi
(hristosk biœrg ok brusto ; brann Rán-himinn) mána :
miœk frá-ek mœti hrœkkva myrk beins Haka reinar,
þá-es vígligan vogna vátt sínn bana þátti.

17.　Brátt fló biarga gæti (bœnd ollo því) randa　　　65
[imon] fœlr und iljar íss [vildo svá dísir] :
varðat hœggs frá hœrðo hraun-drengr þaðan lengi
trióno trollz of rúna tíðr fiœllama at bíða.

18.　Fiœr-spillir lét falla fialbrs ólágra gialbra
bœl-verðungar Belja bolm á randar-holmi :　　　70
þar hné grundar gilja gramr fyr skœrpom hamri ;
enn berg-Dana bagði briótr við iœrmun-þrióti.

Refrain. Lo, this is painted on my shield. I received the coloured buckler from Thorleif's hands.
　II. *The story of Rungni.* Next I see, how the Terror of the Giants, *Thor*, visited the cave-dweller, *Rungni*, at Rock-garth, in a ring of flame. The son of Earth drove to the battle (his heart was swelling with wrath), and the moon's path [heaven] thundered beneath him. The whole ether (City of the Ginnungs) was on fire about him, and the flat, out-stretched ground below him was beaten with the hail : yea, the earth was rent asunder, as the goats drew the chariot-god on to his tryst with Rungni. Thor spared not the mountain-abiding foe of the moon [giant] ; the mountains quaked and the dominion of Ran [ocean] blazed. I have heard that the denizen of the dark cliffs shrunk wondrously when he espied his slayer, the god of the Car ; the yellow shield he flung beneath the soles of his feet, the Powers ruled it so, the War-fairies willed it so ; the haunter of the wilderness had not long to wait for a stroke from *Thor*, the wielder of the life-crushing snout-ogre [Hammer]. He that spoils the wicked Giant-host of their lives felled the monster of the loud-roaring ocean-caverns on the lists [shield-holm] : the Lord of the glens bowed there before the sharp Hammer, what time the Giant-killer struck down the

---

53. es] of, W.　　54. bur] borua hyriar haugs, W ; bror, *r* (badly).　　59. *r* ; hófregin höfðu, W.　　60. seðr] seið, W.　　61. Emend. ; solgnum, Cdd. 61–62. Thus W ; þar dolgi . . . brann upp himin manna, *r*.　　67. hörðo] thus W, *r*.

19.   Ok harð-brotin herjo heim-þingoðar Vingniss
       hvein í hiarna mœni hein at Grundar sveini:
       þar svá eðr í Óðins ólaus burar hausi   75
       stála-vikr of stokkin stóð Einriða blóði:
20.   Áðr or hneigi-hlíðom hárs œl-gefjon sára
       Reiði-týs ið rauða ryðs heili-bœl gœli:

      Görla lít-ek á Geitiss garði þær of ferðir.
      Baugs þá-ek bifom fáða bif-kleif at Þorleifi.   80

      LAUSA-VÍSOR (for translation see the Introduction).

                I.

King.   Miok ero mínir rekkar til miœð-giarnir fornir,
       ok her komnir hárir,—Hví erot avar-margir!
Thiodolf. Hœfðo ver í hœfði hœgg at eggja leiki
       með vell-brota vitrom—Vóroma þá til margir.

                II.

Thiodolf. Fariða ér áðr fleyja flat-vœllr heðan batnar,
       (verpr Geitis vegr grióti) Goðrœðr of sió stóran:
       vind-bysna skaltu vísi víð-frægr heðan bíða;
       vesið með mer unz verði veðr, nú es brim fyrir Iaðri!

EILIF GUDRUNSSON (ÞÓRS-DRÁPA).

OF this poet we know nothing but his mother's name, which might imply his posthumous birth, and his date; he is mentioned as one of Earl Hakon's poets in Skaldatal (see § 3). And it is certain that he lived into the Christian times, as he made an Encomium on Christ. Besides this, which, like his poem or poems on Earl Hakon, is lost (save one citation in Edda), he composed *a poem on Thor* (Þórs-drápa), of which we have a long fragment. It deals with the popular and interesting stcry of Thor's adventures with the volcanic Giant Garfred (Geirrod), whose daughters raise the river Wimmer against the god, while the Giant assails him with a glowing mass of iron off his forge, which Thor catches and returns with deadly effect upon the huge Smith's head.—A primitive myth, dealing with the weird gigantic forces of nature, water and fire, and quite in keeping with the half-humorous, half-fanciful spirit of the poets who loved to sing of Thor.

Eilif has dealt well with the legend. Through the confused corruptions of parts of what is left to us of his Thors-drapa, and in spite of the intricacy which he affects to a far greater degree than any poet of his

---

mighty defaulter. Yet the hard-quarried hone from the Giant's hand struck into the brain-pan of the son of Earth; yea, the steel-grinding stone stood fast in Thor's skull, sprinkled with his blood: till the Healeress of wounds [Giantess Groa] chaunted the hone, the ridder of rust, out of the chariot-god's head.

Refrain. Clearly I see all these adventures on the shield. I received the coloured buckler at Thorleif's hands.

---

76. *r*; um stokkvi, W.   78. heyli-, *r*.   80. bifom] bifa, W.

day, we see the mighty stream roaring and rattling over its rocky bed, the yellow water beating on the broad shoulders of the god, while the heavy boulders are dashed against his feet, as he staggers through it with the help of his trusty staff and his belt of strength, to which the little Delve, his servant, hangs, like a sheath-knife, pressed tight and flat to his master's side by the water's force. The Struggle in the Hall is more briefly told, but there is a certain grandeur throughout the poem which carries one over its entangled phrases and massed synonyms.

The story of Garfred has also been treated in a lost poem which Snorri knew, and of which the two remaining verses are given in Book ii, p. 126. Wolf Uggason knew the tale, calling Thor the 'Hero of Wimmer-ford,' and there is an incident in King Harold Hardrede's story, which shows the wide fame of the legend, c. 1060:—The king and his poet Thiodwolf are walking out one day, when they come upon a tanner and a blacksmith fighting: says the king, 'Put those fellows into verse under the names of Thor and Garfred,' which the poet does. 'Now speak of them as Sigfred and Fafni,' which again was obeyed. For the verses made on this occasion see Book viii, § 3. Snorri's paraphrase, taken partly from our poet, partly from the poem of Book ii, is as follows :—

"*Then answered Eager:* That was a tale worth telling, when Thor went to Garfred's-garth. At that time he had not the Hammer Milner, nor the Girdle of Strength, nor the Iron Mittens; and that was Loki's doing, for he went with him. Because it had happened to Loki, when once upon a time he was flying in Frigg's hawk-skin for a pastime, to fly for the sake of amusement into Garfred's-garth; and there he saw a great hall, and lit down and looked in at a window. But Garfred espied him and bade 'take that bird and bring him to him,' but the man he sent had hard work to get to the top of the wall, so high was it. And Loki thought it sport for the man to be taking such trouble to get at him, and he would not fly away before he had got over all the difficulties. But when the man came up to him he spread his wings and thrust against his feet, but then he found his talons were fast, and Loki was taken prisoner there and brought to Giant Garfred. But when the Giant saw his eyes, straightway he suspected that it was a man, and bade him answer him, but Loki held his peace. Then Garfred locked Loki up in a chest, and there he starved him three months. And when Garfred let him out and bade him talk, then Loki said who he was, and swore this oath to Garfred as a ransom, that he would bring Thor into Garfred's-garth without his Hammer or his Girdle of Strength.

"Thor took up his quarters with a Giantess whose name was Grith, she was the mother of Widar the Silent. She told Thor the truth about Garfred, that he was a cunning Giant, and bad to deal with. She lent him a girdle of strength and mittens of iron, which she had, and her staff which is called Grith's-rod. Then Thor set out to the river which is called Wimmer, the biggest of all rivers. And he girt himself with the Girdle of Strength and struck the Rod of Grith against the stream, but Loki held on by the girdle of strength. And as soon as Thor was got to the midst of the stream the river swelled so mightily that it broke on his shoulders. Then Thor said these words :—(See vol. i, p. 126.)

"Then Thor beheld a certain glen, and Yelp [Gialp], Garfred's daughter, standing there across the river and causing the river to swell. Then he took up out of the river a great stone, and cast it at her, and said that 'One must dam a river at its mouth.' He never missed when he cast at anything. And with that he drifted up to the bank and got a grip of a certain rowan, and so came up out of the river; wherefore it has become a proverb that 'rowan is Thor's rescue.' And when Thor came to Garfred's they were turned into a goat-house for shelter, he and his fellows. And there was a stool for a seat, and Thor sat him down thereon, and straightway he found that the stool under him was being raised up towards the roof. He thrust the Rod of Grith up against the rafter and bore hard down on the stool, then there was a great crack, and after it a great shriek heard. Garfred's daughters Yelp [Gialp] and Grip [Greip] had been under the stool and he had broken both their backs. Then said Thor:—(See vol. i, p. 126.)

"Then Garfred had Thor called into the hall to play. There were great fires down the hall lengthwise, and when Thor came into the hall over against Garfred, Garfred caught up a glowing mass of iron with the tongs, and cast it at Thor; but Thor caught it with his iron mittens, and swung it up, and Garfred ran behind an iron pillar to save his life. Thor cast the mass, and it went through the iron pillar, and through Garfred, and through the wall, and so out into the earth. According to this tale, Eilif Gudrunsson has sung in Thors-drapa."

This poem was originally, and of set purpose, hard and intricate in its circumlocutions, and it has since, through corruption, fallen into a sad jumble, inasmuch that any attempt to give a word-for-word rendering of it or do more than paraphrase as closely as is well, is not to be thought of.

The *text* is preserved in Edda, W and *r*.

1. FLUG-STALLA réð fellir Forniótz goða at hvetja
   (driúgr vas Loptr at liúga) lœg-seims faðir heiman:
   geð-reynir kvað grœnar Gautz her-þrumo brautir
   vilgi tryggr til veggjar viggs Geirrœðar liggja.

2. Geð-strangrar let gongo Gamm-leið Þórr skœmmom   5
   (fýstosk þeir at þrýsta Þorns niðjom) sik biðja:
   þars giarð-venðir gœrðisk Gandvíkr Skottom ríkri
   endr til Ymsa landa Iðja setrs frá Þriðja.

3. 'Gerr varð í fœr fyrri farmr mein svara 'ns arma'
   'sóknar haptz með svipti sagna galdrs an rognir'   10
   þyl-ek gran-strauma Grimnis gall-mann tælir hallar
   opnis ilja gaupnom Endils á mó spendo.

4. Ok gangs vanir gengo gunn-vargs himin-tœrgo
   'friðar vers til flióða frum-seyris kom dreyra:'
   þá bœl kvettir brióta bragð-mildr Loka vildi   15
   brœði vændr á brúði bág sefgrisnis mága.

LOKI, the Earth-Serpent's father, ready liar as he was, egged Thor the Giant-killer to set out, saying that green paths would take him to Garfred's Hall. Thor soon yielded to Loki's prayer; they were eager to beat the giants; what time Thor set out from Woden's town (Ansegarth) for Giant-land .... (*unsafe text*). I go on with my song, how they [Loki and Thor] strode on their feet across the Mountain Path. And .... the bloody Foes of the Sun [the Giants] were sore afraid

---

1. *r*; Fiornatz, W.   3. Gautz] om. W.   7. þau, W.   giarðvenioðr, *r*.
12. apnis, W.

5.   Ok veg-þverrir værro vann fet runar nænno
     hialltz af hagli oltnar hlaup-ár um ver gaupo :
     miok leið or stað stækkvir stik-leiðar veg breiðan
     urðar þriótz þá-es eitri œstr þióð-ár fnæsto.   20

6.   Þar í mærk fyrir markar mál-hvettan bor setto
     (ne hvel-vœlor hálar) háf skot-naðra (svǽfo) :
     knátti hreggi hœggvin hlym-þél við mæl glymja ;
     enn felli-hryn fialla Feðjo þaut með steðja.

7.   Harð-vaxnar let herðir hall-landz of sik falla   25
     gataði maðr niótr en neytri niarð- ráð fyr ser -giarðar :
     þverrir let nema þyrri Þorns barna ser mærnar
     sneri-blóð til svíra sal-þaks megin vaxa.

8.   Óðo fast enn friðar flaut eið-svara Gauta
     setrs víkinga snotrir sverð runnið fen gunnar ;   30
     þurði hrænn at herði hauðrs runn kvika nauðar
     iarðar skafls af afli áss hret-viðri blásin.

9.   Unz með ýta sinni (afl-raun vas þat) skaunar
     á seil himin-sióla sialf-lopta kom Þialfi :
     aðo stáli stríðan straum Hrekk-mímis ekkjor ;   35
     stop-hníso fór steypir stríð-lundr með væl Gríðar.

10. Né diúp-akarn drǽpo dolg-vams firom Glamma
     stríð-kviðiændom stæðvar stall við rastar falli :
     ógn-diarfan hlaut arfi eiðs fiarðar hug meira ;
     skalfa Þórs né Þialfa þróttar-steinn við ótta.   40

11. Ok sifuna síðan sverðz lið hattar gerðo
     hlífar borðz við Hærða harð gleifnir dyn barði :

---

now that Thor in his wrath was coming to fight them. And Thor the
Giantess-destroyer strode over the wilderness across the swoln rivers
that rushed along with a hail-like avalanche of stones. Thor the Giant-
killer sped on a good way, crossing the ford, while the mighty streams
spurted venom. They [Thor and Loki] put forth [resting on] their
steel-shod mountain staves; nor did the slippery round boulders sleep.
The staves rattled against the stones, whilst the stones clashed in the
storm-beaten mountain-stream. Now Thor beholds the mountain-
stream beat upon his burly shoulders, yet the wearer of the Belt of
Strength put forth his whole might. He cried out that unless the
rapid waters went down his strength would wax sky-high. They waded
stoutly, but the river ran on, the troubled waters tempest-stirred
rushed over Thor's shoulders. Now Delve [Thor's page] lifted himself
up and clung fast to the Belt of the King of heaven [Thor]. The
Giant-maidens made the stream swell high, whilst sturdy Thor the
Giantess-slayer strode on, the Staff of Grith in his hands. Nor did
their hearts quake within them at the strong rush of the stream.
Thor's courage rose, nor did Thor's or Delve's heart quake for fear.
     *The Second Section, the fight in the Giant's Hall, is very obscure, but the
sense of most of the verses can be gleaned. Thor and his companions reach*

---

     18. ver] v', W.   20. þioðar, W.   21. bur, W.   22. hallar, W.
     26. Read, mar?   35. Read, óðo?   42. kyn, W.

áðr hylríðar heiði hrióð-ruðr fiæro þióðar
við Skylld-Breta skytjo 'skaleik Heðins reikar.'

12. Dreif með dróttar kneyfi dolg Sviþióðar kolgo 45
(sótti ferð á flótta) fles-drótt (Ivo nesja):
þá es fun-ristis fasta flóð-rifs Danir stóðo,
knátto Iolnis ættir út-véss fyrir lúta.

13. Þeirs í þróttar bersa þorn rans hugom bornir
(hlymr varð hellis Kumra) hrin-balkar fram gengo: 50
listi feðr í fasta (frið-sein vas þar) hreini
snípo hlœðr á greypan gran hœtt Res kvánar.

14. Ok hám loga himni hall fylvingom vallar
tróðosk þer við troði tungls brá-sólir þungo:
húf-stióri braut hværo hreggs vafr-æyða tveggja 55
hlátr-elliða helliss hund-fornan kiæl sprundi.

15. 'Fá-tíða nam frœði' fiarð-epliss kon Iarðar;
merar leggs ne mugðo menn æl teiti kenna:
alm-taugar laust œgir angr-þiof 'sege' tœngo
Óðins afli soðnom átt-niðr í gin Suðra. 60

16. Svá at ... skyndir handa hrapp munnar svalg gunnar
lypti-sylg á lopti lang-vinr sio þrongvar:
þá es aurþrasis esjo ás hrimnis fló drósar
til þrá móðnis þrúðar þióst af Greipar briosti.

17. Bifðisk hœll þá es hœfði Heiðreks of kom breiðo 65
und flet-biarnar fornan fót-legg þrasis veggjar:
ítr gulli laust Ullar iótr veg-taugar þrióti
meina niðr í miðjan mez bigyrðil nezo.

18. Glaums niðiom fór gœrva gramr með dreyrgom hamri
of sal-vanið synja sigr laut arin bauti: 70
komað tvíviðar tími tollur karms sá es harmi
brautar liðs of beiti bekk fall iotuns rekka.

19. Hel-blótinn vá hneitir hóg-brotningi skógar
undir fialfrs at alfi Alfheims bliko kalfa:

Giant-land, and attack Garfred and his fellow-giants. The fiendish
host of Giant-land was turned to flight, and gave way; before the onslaught of the Fire-Hurler they fled. There was an uproar among the
Cave-dwellers, when Thor and his men came into the hall. There
was an end of peace, when Thor struck the Giantess' head with his
lightning. The flashes crossed beneath the roof of the Cavern, and
Thor, the Chariot's Lord, broke the aged backs of both the Giantesses
[Yelp and Grip]. Little joy was the Giant's; he hurled a mass of
glowing iron, caught off the anvil, at the son of Woden. Thor caught
the bar in his hands as it flew, when the lord of the forge, Garfred, threw
it. The Hall rocked to its fall, when Garfred's head was crushed
under the ancient pillars, when Thor dashed the bar down on the head
of the Giant. Thor made utter destruction of the monsters with his
bloody Hammer, and won the day. The rod of Grith .... The

---

43. hrióðendr, r.   59. Read, sega?   71. tími] W, though indistinct.

ne lið-fæstom Lista láttrs val Rygir mætto   75
aldr-minkanda eldar Ello steins of bella.

LAY ON CHRIST (*from Edda*).

SET-BERGS kveða sitja sunnr at Urðar brunni;
　　svá hefir ramr gramr remdan Róms banda sik lœndom.

HÚS-DRÁPA; OR, THE LAY OF THE HOUSE.

By WOLF UGGASON (ULFR UGGASON).

OF Wolf's family we know nothing; though his wife Irongerth, the
daughter of that Thorarin Corni (the cairn-dweller we had the ditty
about, Book vi, ditty 22), is named by Ari in Landnama-bok. Wolf
himself lived in the south of Iceland, and one of the few incidents of
his life is his refusal to make satires on the missionaries who brought
Christendom into the island; the verses he then made we print below in
§ 4. His greatest claim rests on this poem, of which Snorri has preserved several fragments, and Laxdæla the following account :—

Olaf Peacock, the son of Hoskold, the husband of Thorgerd, Egil's
daughter, the mightiest man of his day in Iceland, "made a hall in
Herd-holt, bigger and finer than men had ever seen. There were
drawn on it famous Stories, on the wainscot and on the roof; it was
also so well built that it was thought fairer when the hangings were
down. At the coming of winter there was a multitude bidden to Herd-
holt, for the hall was finished by that time. Wolf Uggason was bidden,
and he made a poem on Olaf Hoskuldsson, and upon the stories that
were written in the hall, and he delivered it at the banquet. This poem
is called Hus-drapa, the Praise of the House, and is a fine poem. Olaf
requited the song well."

Snorri, to whom we owe the fragments of Hus-drapa, says that
"Wolf Uggason made a long section about the story of Balder." Again
he says, "Heimdal, *the God*, is the owner of Goldcrest, he is also the
Visitor of Voe-skerry and Singastone, there he and Loki contended for
the Brisings' necklace. He is also called Windler. Wolf Uggason made
a long piece about the story of these two in Hus-drapa, where it is told
that they were in the likeness of seals."

Parts of three sections, and the prologue, are preserved (all in citations from Edda and Skalda). They touch on the subjects of some of
the carvings, the *Bale-fire of Balder*, *Thor fishing for the Serpent*, the *Fight
at Singastone*. We should add to these a line or two of a fourth section
dealing with the *Story of Garfred the Giant*, miscited, we think, as Eilif's.

---

god slew all the Ogres with his staff, nor could the fires of the Lord
of the Rocks harm the mighty Monster-slayer.

Lay on Christ. They say that he, *Christ*, sits on a mountain throne at
the Weird's brook, so has the mighty Lord of the Powers [angels?]
strengthened himself with the land of Rome.

---

75. Read, hval Rygja (hval-láttrs Rygja), Cd.

The poem was made use of by Snorri for his prose paraphrasis of the Legend of Balder, etc. It is a poetic work, with some touches of skill and picturesqueness of detail.

The *metre* is still of an antique type, and reminds one of Bragi and Thiodwolf. The poem was in regular sectional Drapa form, with a cloven burden of two lines, the first line of which is lost. The bearing of which we take to have been, ' Thus is the roof inside painted with old stories.'

The *age* of the poem would seem to be fixed roughly by the fact that while the frequent echoes of Egil's Hofudlausn and Lay of Arinbiorn (complimentary no doubt to Egil's daughter, who must have listened to the poem at the feast) form a very marked feature of Wolf's verse, Egil's greatest poem Sonatorrek is nowhere imitated. This would in- cline one to put the composition of Hus-drapa c. 975–980; and to fancy that the hall was built and the banquet (its house-warming pro- bably) held rather earlier than the Saga implies, at the time when Olaf was yet young and rising in power, a year or so *before* Egil's Sonatorrek was made.

The *text* is from citations in the Edda; ll. 13–14 from W Appendix. It is in a fair state of preservation, yet ll. 28–29 at least have suffered from retouching. The figures on the margin mark parallelisms with Egil's Lays on Arinbiorn and Hofudlausn.

I. *Introduction.*

1.　HODD-MILDOM ték hildar hug-reifom Áleifi
　　　　(hann vil-ek at giæf Grimniss) geð-fiarðar lá (kveðja).

II. *The Balefire of Balder.*

2.　　Ríðr á bœrg til borgar bœð-fróðr sonar Óðins
　　Freyr ok folkom stýrir fyrstr golli byrstom.

3.　　Kostigr ríðr at kesti kyn-fróðs þeim-es goð hlóðo　5
　　Hrafn-freistaðar hesti Heimdallr at mœg fallinn.

4.　　Ríðr at vilgi víðo víð-frægr (en mer líða)
ªA 56.　Hropta-týr (of hvápta ª hróðr-mól) sonar báli:
　　þar hykk sig-runni svinnom sylgs Valkyrjor fylgja
　　heilags tafns ok hrafna;—' *hrót' innan svá minnom.*　10

I. *Prologue.* I set forth my song to the generous Anlaf, pledging him in Woden's gift.

II. *The Burning of Balder.* First rides Frey, the king of men, on his boar with golden tusks to the bale-fire of *Balder*, Woden's son. The goodly Heimdal rides his horse to this pile that the gods had cast up for the dead son of the wise Friend of the Ravens [Woden]. The wide- famed God of Soothsaying [Woden] rides to the huge wooden bale-pyre of his son. (The Song of Praise is gliding through my lips.) I can see the Walkyries and the Ravens following the wise God of Victory, the Lord of the Holy Draught. *Burden:* Thus, within, the roof *is adorned* with memories.

The mighty Giantess launched the ship, while the champions of Woden felled her charger, *the wolf.*

---

7. blido, W.　　10. hrót] emend. ; hlaut, Cd. (here and l. 20).

5. Full-æflug lét fialla fram haf-sleipni þramma
hildr, en Hroptz of gildar hialm-elda mar feldo.

III. *Thor fishing up the Earth-Serpent.*

6. [a]Inn-máni skein enniss øndóttr vinar banda;
[a]A 19. óss skaut [b]œgi-geislom orð-sæll á men storðar:
[b]A 20. enn stirð-þinull starði storðar-leggs fyr borði   15
fróns á folka reyni frán-leitr ok blés eitri.

7. Full-æflugr lét fellir fiall-gautz hnefa skialla
(ramt mein vas þat) reyni reyrar-leggs við eyra.

8. Við-gymir laust Vimrar-vaðs af frónom naðri
hlusta grunn við hrønnom ;—*hrót innan svá minnom.*   20

IV. *Loki and Heimdall fighting about the Brising necklace at Singastein in the shape of Seals.*

9. Ráð-gegninn bregðr ragna-rein at Singa-steini
frægr við firna slœgian Fárbauta mœg-vári :
móð-æflugr ræðr mœðra mœgr haf-nýra fœgro
[a]A 54. (kynni-ek) áðr ok einnar átta ([a]mærðar þóttom).

V. *Thor and Giant Garfred.*

10. Þrœngvir gein við þungom þangs rauð-bita tangar   25
kveld-runninna kvenna kun-leggs alin-munni.
Vreiðr vas Vrœsko bróðir vá gagn faðir Magna.

VI. *The End.*

11. Þar kœmr á (enn æri endr bar ek mærð at hendi)
[a]H 69. ('ofra ek svá') til sævar ([a]'sverð-regns' rofi þagnar).

III. *Thor and the Serpent.* The eye of the Gods' friend *Thor* shone fiercely, the beloved God darted awful glances at the Serpent of Earth, and *the Serpent*, the Stout Girdle of the World, glared over the gunwale at the Friend of Man, spirting venom the while. Then the mighty Giant-slayer smote the monster with his fist on the ear; it was a deadly blow. The Champion of Wimmers-Ford struck the head off the cruel Snake *as it rose* above the sea. *Burden :* Thus within the roof, etc.

IV. *The struggle of Loki and Heimdall.* The skilful renowned Warder of the Path of the Powers [*rainbow-bridge*] wrestled with Loki, Faarbaute's most wily son, at Singastone, before the sturdy Son of Nine Mothers [Heimdall] won the fair necklace of stones. I set this forth in my song.

V. *The Fight with Garfred.* Thor, the Destroyer of the Giantesses, grasped the red mouthful of the tongs [*the red hot mass*] with his hands. Wroska's brother [*Delve*] was wroth, the father of Main [*Thor*] won the victory.

VI. *Epilogue.* Here the river reaches the sea [my Song ends]. I have delivered my Song of Praise, till the silence [*hearing accorded me*] was broken.

---

12. *r*; hialm ǫldom, W.   13. Emend.; ondottz, W.   18. logs, W.
21. rogna, W.   22. faar- . . . vaari, W.   29. Emend.; lofi þegna, W.

MYTHICAL FRAGMENTS IN COURT-METRE.

THERE were other Shield-Songs and Thor-Lays, the authors of which, less fortunate than Eilif or Thiodwolf, have only survived in fragments kept by Snorri (Sk.), who no doubt made use of their poems in his paraphrases of the Thor-myths.

First of these comes OLWI SNUB (Olver Hnúfa),—in Norwegian law 'hnúfa' is the bondmaid whose nose has been cut off for theft thrice repeated; as a nickname it must refer to some hurt that Olwi, like Michael Angelo, had suffered,—a poet of Harold Fairhair's, according to Skaldatal, of whom some mention is made in Egil's Saga. In one passage, which is worth comparing with Hornklofi's Raven-Lay, it is written, 'Of all his henchmen the king set most store by his Poets; they sat on the opposite bench [next in honour to the high seat of the king]. Inmost of them sat Eadwine Ill-poet (Audunn Illskælda); he was the eldest of them, and had been the poet of Halfdane the Black, the father of King Harold. Next to him sat Thorbiorn Hornklofi, and next to him sat Olwi Snub, and the next to him was Bard (Barfred) seated. He was called Bard the White, or Bard the Strong.' Somewhat is also told about Olwi and Bard's quarrels and adventures, but no certain or important fact. There is, however, in chap. 3 the following passage, which is worth citing:—

" Atli the Slim was then Earl in Firth, he dwelt at Gaul. His children were Hallstan, Holmstan, Herstan, and a *daughter*, Solweig the Fair. It happened one harvest-tide that there was a great company at Gaul at the Harvest-Sacrifice. It was then that Olwi saw Solweig, and fell in love with her. Afterwards he asked for her hand, but the earl did not think him a good enough match, and would not give her to him. After this Olwi made many Love-Songs *about her*. He was so much in love with her that he left off going a-wicking (buccaneering)." Afterwards, for the sake of these songs, "the sons of Atli attacked Olwi in his house, wishing to slay him. They had so many men with them that Olwi could not withstand them, and only got off by flight. He went north to More, and there found King Harold and became his liegeman .... and came into the greatest friendship with the king; and was with him long afterwards and became his poet."

The bit of Olwi is evidently part of a poem on Thor and Hymi and the fishing for the Serpent,—perhaps a Shield-Song. A second fragment of his, quoted in Skalda, is subjoined: it seems part of a longer poem.

EYSTEIN WALDASON, a tenth-century poet, is nowhere spoken of. The fragment he has left also relates to the Fishing Adventure of Thor. It is bold and realistic, and leads one to regret the loss of the rest. Snorri, with his eye ever open to the good points of a story, has used the incident of Thor's hands being dashed against the gunwale by the jerk of the Snake he had hooked.

WINTERLID (Vetrlidi), a son of Summerlid, a contemporary of Wolf Uggason's, who was not wise enough to abstain from satire on the missionaries, but, as Ari tell us in Kristni-saga and Landnama-bok, " made libellous verses upon Thangbrand and many others. But when they [Thangbrand and his fellows] came west into Fleetslithe, Godlaf, the son of Ari of Reek-hills, was with them also; they heard that Winterlid the poet was out turf-cutting with the men of his household. And Thangbrand and his company went thither and slew him. . . . . .

Thence they went westward to Grimsness and found Thorwald Veili
there at Hestbrook, and slew him there." The Melabok (Landnama)
tells the story thus:—" Winterlid made a Libel on Thangbrand, who
therefore slew him whilst cutting peat. He (Winterlid) defended
himself with the peat-cutter against Godlaf of Reekness, but Thangbrand run him through with his spear. Song-Chaps (Liodarkiopt)
made an Encomium on Godlaf."

The bit of Winterlid's which remains is from a poem in praise of
Thor, telling over his exploits.

This THORWALD VEILI is the poet of whom Snorri speaks in Hattatal,
talking of a variety of the court-metre called Skialf-henda. " This
metre Veili first invented, when he was lying upon a certain sea-reef,
saved from a shipwreck, and they were badly off for clothes, and the
weather was cold. It was then that he made the poem which is called
the 'Shivering Poem,' or the 'Burdenless Poem,' wherein he follows
the story of Sigfred."

THORBIORN DISAR-SKALD, the poet of the Goddesses, of whom nothing more than the name is known, must have made a poem like that
of Winterlid's on Thor, reciting his great deeds; of this song two morsels remain.

Of GAMLI nothing is known.

The *text* of all these fragments is from Edda (ll. 2–3 from Skalda).

ÖLVI HNÚFA.

I. *On Thor.*

ŒSTISK allra landa um-giœrð ok sonr Iarðar . . .

II. *From Skalda.*

Maðr skyldi þó moldar megja hverr of þegja
kenni-seiðs þó at kynni klepp-dœgg Hárs lœggvar.

EYSTEIN VALDASON (*on Thor*).

1. SÍN bió Sifjar rúni snarla fram með karli
        (horn-straum getom Hrimnis hrœra) veiðar-fœri.   5
2. Svá brá við at sýjor seiðr, rendi fram 'breiðar'
    Iarðar út at borði Ullz mágs hnefar skullo.
3. Leit á brattrar brautar baug hvassligom augom
    (œstisk áðr at flausti 'augrs búð') faðir Þrúðar.

Olwer Snub. I. The Girdle of all lands began to rage, and the Son of
Earth . . .
II. Yet every man should know how to hold his peace even though . . .

Eystan Waldason. Sif's mate and the churl [Hymi] made ready their
fishing tackle. Let us stir the stream of Hrimni's horn [begin our song].
The tackle ran out. The Snake pulled so hard against the gunwale, that
Thor's fists were dashed against the streaks. Thor looked on the Serpent
[lit. the rock's-ring] with piercing eye. The wave, *churned up by the
struggling snake*, was raging against the boat the while.

---

9. avg's, W ; read, ægis brúdr.

VETRLIÐI (*on Thor*).

LEGGI brauztu Leiknar, lamðir Þrívalda,
steypðir Starkaði; stéttu of Gialp dauða!

ÞORBIÖRN DÍSAR-SKALD (*on Thor*).

1. ÞÓRR hefir Yggs með ǿrom Ásgarð af þrek varðan.

2. Gall í Keilo kolli, Kiallandi brauztu alla,
áðr draptu Lut, ok leiða léztu dreyra Buzeyro; 5
heptir-þú Hengjan-kiǣpto; Hyrrokkin dó fyrri;
þó vas snemr en sáma Sivǣor numin lífi.

GAMLI (*on Thor*).

MEÐAN gramr (hinn es sitt samði snart) Bilskirnis (hiarta)
grundar fisk með grandi gliúfr-skeliungs nam riúfa.

---

§ 2. ROYAL COURT POEMS.

HORNKLOFI (GLYM-DRÁPA).

IN Book iv we have given early poetry in the *old metres*, dealing with
historical subjects and genealogy, by men who lived at the courts of
Harold Fairhair and his sons. In this Book we shall give the work of
the first generation of the long line of court-poets who composed in the
new metre and the *new style*. Among them are men whose poems in the
old style have already been noticed above, such as Hornklofi and
Eywind; see the Introduction to their poems in Book iv.

With reference to these early Encomia in court-metre, it will be
necessary to give here certain facts and their explanation, which, while
bearing special reference to *Hornklofi*, *Eywind*, and *Guthorm Cindri*,
must be borne carefully in mind by the student of the whole mass of

---

Winterlid. Thou brakest the legs of Leikn [an Ogress], didst crush
Thriwald, didst pull down Starkad [the Giant], and didst overcome and
slay Yelp.

Thorbiorn, the goddess-poet. Thor, with the champions of Woden, has
mightily defended Ansegarth.

There was a clatter on Keil's skull, thou didst crush every limb of
Kialland [giantess], ere that thou didst slay Lout, and make the loathsome Buzear bleed. Thou didst put an end to Hanglip before Hyrrokin
died, yet ere that was the swarthy Swiwor [Ogresses all three] reft of
life.

Gamli. While the lord of Bilskirni [Thor's hall], *Thor*, he of the
dauntless heart, smote the Serpent with his Hammer.

---

8. sitt] emend.; sirk, W.

court poetry throughout the whole length of this and the following Book.

When we look at the morsels of Encomia scattered up and down in the Lives of Harold and his sons, we find an extraordinary paucity of incident, a most marvellous flow of empty words, and an almost complete absence of fact; while for regularity and even monotony of metre, these verses might vie with the most perfect productions of Snorri's and Sturla's days. Now these are all features totally unlike those we have observed in the undoubted work of men of Harold's age, and if we had no further light to throw upon the question, we should be absolutely driven to conclude that these verses are of far later date, attributed by some error to early poets. But, curiously enough, we have in the King's Lives distinct categorical statements relating especially to *names, places, and dates,* all sober facts, in proof of which appeal is made to these very verses, which not only do not support them, but often apparently contain no allusion to them or to any fact whatever.

How is this to be explained? One can only answer, *the verses are in their present state corrupt;* they once did give the facts for which the historian made use of them, they were in their original state the foundations upon which Ari himself rested for sober annalistic facts, for names and places. One thing is certain—the *paraphrasing* and the *inserting* were not contemporary, but a long time must have intervened, during which the poems were 'inked over,' all their original roughness polished away, and with it their whole worth and truth. The 'irregularities' of the old verses no doubt shocked the purist poetasters of the twelfth and thirteenth centuries, the names and places they celebrated were so forgotten that they had become unintelligible; new words, new grammar, new metre were therefore substituted for them, and now it is barely possible through their smooth vapidity to distinguish the blurs that mark some deeply bitten trait of the original design. Yet these poems were the means of preserving information of a kind that could have been preserved in no other way, till a wise historian like Ari made use of them. After this they were half forgotten, then 'restored,' and at last inserted in the text of the Kings' Lives in their sorry condition; so that now we have to seek in Ari's prose paraphrase for the very meaning and contents of the verses upon which it is founded.

We have now and then been able to replace a vanished word, to restore a name, or date, or place, underneath some commonplace platitude, an epithet or 'kenning,' often *resembling in sound* the name required; but there are still many instances where we are sure that there were words in the text, of which not the faintest indications are left. As an *example of corruption,* in Guthorm's poems we may give the line 'Undan allar kindir Eireks á haf snekkiom,' which we see from the prose, ch. 20, Hakon's Saga, must have contained the word Jutland. Beneath the 'undan' here, we can dimly see that 'Iotlandz' must have stood. Again we are told in the text, chs. 23–26, Hakon's Saga, of Egill Wool-sark (Ullserkr), Hakon's standard-bearer, killing King Gamli Ericsson in flight at Rastarkalf, by Frodarberg. The verse cited does not give a name of any kind, but we can see that beneath the 'rád-sterk' lies 'Ullserkr,' and that at least the names of Gamli (beneath 'Gramr,' l. 26) and the place of his death must have also occurred though they have left no trace. In ch. 9, Hakon's Saga, we want in the verse cited the names of the Scots and of King Tryggwi, and though they do not now appear, we can have little doubt but that under the words 'hraustan' and 'skiðom' (ll. 14–15) are buried 'Trausta' and 'Scottom.'

The same kind of corruption marks the verses of succeeding poets, though in continually lessening degree, but it is very bad in the poems relating to King Olaf and to Cnut the Great, where it is more to be deplored, for Ari's excerpted statements are not so full with reference to them. So that for verses relating to doings in England we must grope for the facts with the help of the Maps and the English Chronicles, which, however, sometimes fail us too, and pass over in silence things which the poems seem to have told of. As an instance of corruption in these verses we find that under 'Sundvigg' is hidden 'Sandwich.' Many more instances will be noticed in the text and notes.

We can see that Ari cared not for the poems, their figures of speech, or inanities, only for their *facts;* having extracted them he left the verses like the husks of thrashed corn; yet his wonderful sagacity enabled him to make the right use of them, and were they still perfect they would in many cases merely confirm his statements. But here and there, as in Hallfred's case noticed below, we can still dimly see that other views and facts (unnoticed rather than deliberately rejected by Ari) than those the prose preserved must have been contained in the verses, and one might have gleaned from them some fresh information of value which is now for ever lost.

GUTHORM SINDRI. Of *Guth-thorm Cinder,* whose name has not been noticed earlier, we know little. He is however the hero of a charming story told in the Kings' Lives. King Harold and his son Halfdan had quarrelled and taken up arms against one another. "Guth-thorm Cinder was the name of a nobleman who was in the host of Halfdan the Black and had formerly been with King Harold and was a dear friend of both of them. He was a great poet, and had made poems both on the father and on the son. They had offered him guerdon therefore, but he would not take it, but asked them to grant him a boon; and they had promised to do so. Accordingly he now went to see King Harold and bore messages of peace between him and his son, and besought each of them to give him as his boon that he would make peace with the other. And the two kings set so much store by him that they made peace at his request. It is upon this story that Iorun the Poetess made a section of Sendibit," see Book viii, § 5.

The *name* of Hornklofi's poem GLYM-DRÁPA is not explained. It is quoted by Snorri (in a corrupt state).

A verse ascribed to Gundhild herself, in Fagrskinna, is added last.

GLYM-DRÁPA.

(Verse 1 from Edda, the rest from Lives of Kings.)

1. HRIÓÐR lét hæstrar tíðar harð-ráðr skipa bœrðom
   báro-fáks ins bleika barn-ungr á lœg þrungit.

2. Hilmir réð á Heiði 'hialdr-skíðs þrumo galdra'
   óðr við 'œski-meiða ey vé-brautar' heyja:
   áðr 'gnap-salar gripnis gný-stœrandi' fœri   5
   'rausnar-samr til rimmo riðvígs lagar skíðom.'

Glym-drapa. In happy hour the king launched his grey billow-steeds on the sea. He fought at the Heath with the O . . . before he went in his barks to war against the . . . . The judge of men went against

4. Read, Orkndœli?

3.   Gœrðisk Glamma ferðar gný-þróttr 'ioro' dróttar
     hel-kannandi hlanna Hlymræks um 'trud' glymja.
     Áðr út á mar mætir mann-skœðr lagar tanna
     ræsi-maðr til rausnar rak vé-brautar Nokkva.   10

4.   Þar svá at barsk at borði; borð-holkviss rak norðan
     hlífar valdr til hildar hreggs dœglinga tveggja:
     ok all-snœfrir iœfrar orða laust at morði
     (endisk rauðra randa rædd) 'dyn-skotom' kvæddosk.

5.   Háði gramr, þar-es gnúðo geira hregg við 'seggi,' 15
     rauð (fnýsti ben blóði) bryn-gœgl í 'dyn Skœglar'
     þá-es á rausn 'fyr ræsi' (réð egg-litoðr) seggir
     [œfr gall hiœrr við hlífar] hnigo fiœr-vanir (sigri).

6.   'Grennir þrœng at gunni gunn-más' fyr haf sunnan ,
     (sá vas gramr) ok gumnom (goð-varðr) und sik iœrðo: 20
     ok hialm-tamiðr hilmir 'holm-reiðar' let olman
     lindi-hiœrt fyr 'landi lund-prúðr' við stik bundinn.

7.   Ríks þreifsk reiddra œxa rymr; knátto spiœr glymja;
     svart-skygð bito 'seggi' sverð þióð-konungs ferðar:
     þá-es hug-fylldra 'hœlda' (hlaut annskoti Gauta) 25
     ár vas sœngr of svírom (sigr) flug-beittra vigra.

8.   'Men-fergir bar margar marg-spakr niðar varga'
     lundr vann sókn á sandi 'sand-mens' í bý randir:
     áðr fyr 'eljan-prúðom allr herr' Skotta þverri
     lœgðis seiðs af láði læ-brautar varð flœja.   30

. . . .

GUTHORM SINDRI (HÁKONAR-DRÁPA).

1.   BIF-ROKNOM trað bekkjar blá-rœst konungr œrom;
         mætr hlóð mildingr Iótom mistar-vífs í drífo:

the Irish, and fought a sea-fight at Limerick before he thrust Nokkwi
out of the land.   Then he drove his vessels from the north to meet the
Two Kings, and the princes fought each other at the *Isle of* Solskel.   He
gladdened the mail-birds (*ravens*) at . . . . *place*, what time the storm of
spears broke on . . . ., when men fell life-reft in the forecastle before
. . . .; the dyer of the sword-edge won the day.   The greedy sword
screamed against the bucklers.   He hastened to battle south over the
sea (he was god-protected), yea, the helm-wont lord of the Holm-
Rygians moored his mad sea-deer to the stakes of . . . .   The noise of
the axes waxed 'high, the spears rattled, the black-polished sword of the
high-king bit . . . .   The foe of the Gauts won the day, what time
there was a song of keen-cutting spears above the necks of the bold-
hearted . . . .   The waster of the Manx carried the shield into the town
of . . . . and fought a battle on the sand of the isle of Man, ere that his
foes were forced to fly the land before the valiant harrier of the Scots.

Hakon's praise.   The king trod the blue mile [sea] with his foam-
splashed oars and slew the Jutes in battle, and drove them to flight into

7. Read, Íra?   14. Read, við Solskel?   21. Read, Holm-Rygja?
27. Read, Manverja bar myrðir?

svan-gǿðir rak síðan 'sótt Ialfaðar flótta'
'hrot giljaðar hyljar hrafn-víns at mun sínom.'

2.   Alm-drosar fór eiso él-runnr mǽrom sunnan   5
trióno tingls á grǿna tveim einom Sel-meina :
þá es ellifo allar all-reiðr Dana skeiðar
val-sendir hrauð vandar, víð-frægr at þat síðan.

3.   Selund náði þá síðan sókn-heggr und sik leggja
'vals ok' Vinda frelsi við Skáneyjar síðo :   10
skatt-gilda vann skyldir skaut Ialfaðar Gauta ;
goll skyflir vann giǽflastr 'geir-veðr' í fǽr þeiri.

4.   Ok sókn-hattar setti svell-ríóðr at því flióði
Ónars eiki-grǿno austr geð-bǿti 'hraustan :'
þann-es áðr frá Írom 'ið-vandr' of kom 'skíðom'   15
sal-brigðandi Svigðiss svan-vangs liði þangat.

5.   Val-þǽgnir lét 'vegnom víg-nestr saman bresta
handar-vafs of hǽfðom hlym-mildingom gyldir :'
þar gekk Niǫrðr af Nirði naddz há-mána raddar
'val-brandz víðra landa vápn-undodom sunda.'   20

6.   Alm-drœgar vas œgiss opt sinn (enn ek þess minnomk),
barma ǫld fyr Baldri ben-síks vita ríkiss :
bǫð-sǿkir hélt bríkar brǿðr síns ok rak flǿðar
'undan' allar kindir Eirekks á haf snekkjom.

7.   Hræddr fór hiǫrva raddar herr 'fyr malma þverri'   25
'róg-eiso gekk ræsir ráð-sterkr' framar merkjom :
Gerra gramr í snerro geir-vífa ser hlífa,
'hinn es yfrinn gat iǿfra os kvánar byr mána.'

A STRAY VERSE, attributed to Queen Gunnhild, in
Fagrskinna, p. 15.

Há- reið á bak bǿro borð-hesti -kon vestan ;
skǫrungr lét brim bíta bǿrð, es gramr hefir Fiorðo.

---

the land as he chose.   He came from the South with only two ships
towards the green Sealand, and, henceforward famous, cleared eleven
ships of the Danes.   Then he put Sealand under him and beat the
Wends on the coast of Sconey : he made the Gauts pay tribute, and
won much gold in this campaign.   And he put the Trusty Chief
[Tryggwi] over the oak-green wife of Woden eastward [Ran-rick], him
that came here formerly over sea with a fleet from the Irish and Scots.
The king let . . . . at . . . . he left his enemies weapon-wounded at . . . .
The followers of his brother [Eric] often, as I remember, suffered many
a defeat before him ; he drove all the kindred of his brother Eric out
into the Jutland sea.   At Froda-berg Woolsark fell in front of the
standard, ... fighting against Gamli . . . . he that . . . .

HAKON rode over the billows on his wooden horse from the west, he
makes his timbers cleave the sea, he lands at the Firths.

---

14. Read, Trausta.   15. Read, Skottom.   24. Read, Iótlandz.
25. Read, fyr Frodarbergi?   26. Read, víg-eiso fell œsir Ullserkr fr. m. ?
27. Read, Gamli ?

CORMAC OGMUNDSSON (SIGRŒÐAR-DRÁPA).

A WILD, wandering, ill-fated Bard this, throwing his life away by recklessness and lack of purpose. His life, and many verses ascribed to him, are found in a separate Saga, one of the oldest, preserved only in one vellum, AM. 132, but in an obscure and corrupt form.

Cormac's father, Ogmund, came out to Midfirth, probably from the Western Islands, and settled at Melar 'Sands.' There is a curious tale, which seems to foreshadow the lucklessness of his son, told of his laying the foundations of the house there. When a man had laid out his house "it was the belief in those days, that as the meteyard fitted, when it measured a second time, so the man's luck should fit. So that if the meteyard showed too little, his luck would shrink too, but if the meteyard showed something over, his luck would be fair. And *here* the measure was found too short every time it was tried, and they tried three times." Cormac bore an Irish name (his mother, Dalla, was a daughter of Anwind Sioni, and may have been of Gaelic family), and there was something foreign in his features: 'he had black curly hair,' which his mistress counted his only blemish, 'a white skin, was somewhat like his mother, big and strong he was, and of passionate nature.'

The central fact of his life was his love for Steingerd, to which nearly all the verses in his Saga refer, being either *love-songs* to her or *satires* on her successive husbands Bersi and Tintein, with whom he fought wagers of battle, in the former case unsuccessfully. Of these verses we shall treat in § 4.

Like other Icelandic poets of his day, Cormac went abroad to Norway, where he is said to have made an Encomium on King Harold Grayfell, which is lost, while bits of his Sigrod's Praise, which is not mentioned in his Saga, are extant. After a number of adventures, the story of which is difficult to follow from the confusion of his Saga, Cormac is said to have died in Scotland from the hurts he got in a struggle with a giant Scot. His bones therefore, like Hallfred's, lie in British ground.

As a court poet, Cormac chiefly interests us by the curious *mythological burdens* which are wedged into his poem at short and regular intervals. In these curt phrases we have mention of the tale of Thiazzi, of Sigfred and Fafni, of Woden charming Wrind (an otherwise unknown tale), of Weird at her Brook, of Woden's spear Gungni, and of Thor's car. The *historical contents* of the poem are also noteworthy, referring to Earl Sigrod's sacrifices, about which we have the following statement in Hakon's Saga, ch. 16. The earl was a great man for sacrifices, and so was Earl Hakon his father. He was the King's representative at the solemn sacrificial feasts in Thrond-Law. " It was the old custom when a sacrifice was to be held, that all the franklins should come to the place where the temple was, bringing their victuals with them to eat while the feast lasted . . ., but the Earl was the most generous of men; he did a deed which was talked of far and near, he made a great sacrificial feast at Hlathe, and bore all the cost. Cormac Ogmundsson mentions this in his *Sigrodar-drapa*, saying etc."

Like Eywind, Cormac makes the Earl spring from Frey. It is a great pity that so much of this poem (composed c. 960–970) is lost. Its curious refrains are imitated in another good poem, also a fragment, by Illugi Bryndola-scald in Harold Hardrede's day, see Book viii, § 3.

SIGRODAR-DRAPA.

I. *Introduction.*

1. HEYRI sonr á Sýrar sann-reyniss fen tanna
    (aur greppa lætk uppi) iast-Rín Haraldz mína!

2. Meiðr es mœrgom œðri morð-reins í dyn fleina;
    hiœrr fær 'hildi-bœrrom' hiarl Sigrœði iarli.

II. *The Staves.*

3. Hafit maðr ask né eski afspring með ser þingat   5
    fé-særanda at fœra Freyss.—*Véllo goð Þiazza:*
    Hver mani véss við valdi 'vægja' kind of bægjask?
    því-at 'fun-rœgni fagnar fens.'—*Vá Gramr til menja.*

4. Eykr með 'enni-dúki iarð lutr' dia fiarðar
    'bræyti hún sá es beinan' bindr.—*Seið Yggr til Vrindar.*   10

5. Svall, þá-es gekk með giallan Gautz eld hinn es styr belldi
    glað-fœðandi gríðar, gunnr.—*Komsk Urðr at brunni.*

6. All-gildan bið-ek aldar allvald of mer halda
    ýss bif-vangi Yngva ungr.—*Fór Hroptr með Gungni.*

7. Hróðr gœrig of mœg mæran meirr Hákonar fleira;   15
    hapt-sœnis galt-ek hánom heið.—*Sitr Þórr í reiðo.*

EYWIND'S IMPROVISATIONS.

OF Eywind the Plagiarist we have already given the two most famous poems in Book iv, but it remains to give some brief account of his Life and Family. The following Genealogy shows his kinship to the Haleyia-Earls, and gives some means of fixing his date.

Sigrod's praise. Prologue. Let *Sigrod* the son of Harold's friend [Hakon] listen to the rock-nymph's yeasty River [poetry] which I bring. I deliver the poet's draught. *Burden:* The warlike Earl is foremost of all in the shock of spears. The sword wins land for Sigrod the 'warrior' Earl.

Staves: One need neither take bowl nor basket with one thither to the generous kinsman of Frey. *Refrain:* The gods beguiled Thiazzi. Who can vie with the lord of the sanctuary in his welcome? *Refrain:* Grani [Sigfred's sword] won the hoard. The Earl ekes . . . the Brewer of the Divine Nectar, *poet*, with *gold. Refrain:* Woden charmed Wrind. The battle waxed high where the war-stirring wolf-feeder [Sigrod] went with whistling brand. *Refrain:* Weird came to the Brook. I, a youth, beg the goodly ruler of Yngwi's folk to hold his hand over me. *Refrain:* Woden carried Gungni. I go on with further praise on the famous son of Hakon. I pay him a fee [wages] of Divine Nectar [Soma]. *Refrain:* Thor is sitting in his Car.

---

4. Sigurði, W.   6. Freyss] emend.; fress, Cd.   10. bræyti hún] W.

Earl Griotgard

```
        ┌──────────────┴──────────────┐
   Earl Hakon I                      Haward
        │                               │
   Earl Sigrod          Ingibiorg, m. Eywind Lambi, brother
        │                          of Olwir hnúfa
   Earl Hakon II, d. 995                └──┐
        ┌──┘                     Finn Skialg, m. Gundhild, grand-
   Earl Eric, d. c. 1023, m. Cnut's sister   daughter of Harold Fairhair
        │                               │
   Hakon, the doughty Earl, d. c. 1029,      Eywind
   m. Gundhild the noble wife,                 │
        Cnut's niece             Harek of Thiotto, d. c. 1036
```

To his connection with the Haleyia family, and with the friend of
that family, King Hakon the Good, we owe his poems *Haleyia-tal* and
Hakonar-mal. In the evil days, when his two powerful patrons, Earl
Sigrod and King Hakon, were slain, he composed several *stray verses,*
cited in the Lives of Kings, which give glimpses into his life. These
we have given below. Verses 1–4 refer to the battle of Stord. Verse 6
is a palinode as it were, composed in opposition to a verse of Glum.
Verses 7–8 recount the miseries of the present in contrast with the
happiness of the past, 'once every man had his gold ring on his arm, but
now folks hide their treasures in the earth.' This open championship
of the dead brought down on him an accusation of treason, which he
repels (v. 9), and a fine for which he was obliged to pay his great ring,
Mould, which had been dug up at Thursaby long ago (v. 10). The hardships of the *famine year,* 976, are the subject of the two following verses
(11–12): first the terrible weather which caused it, snow in midsummer:
then the call to his men to betake them to the sea, and take advantage
of the shoaling of the herrings, which alone, it seems, preserved great
part of the Norwegians from starvation. The last stave (13) recounts
an anecdote of the famine, mentioned in the Kings' Sagas:—

"He made a Song of Praise on all the Icelanders, and they gave him
this guerdon for it: every franklin gave him one scot penny, worth
three pennies of silver in weight, and white money by essay. And when
the silver was got together at the Great Moot they took counsel to get
a smith to purify it, and then there was a Cloak-brooch made out of it,
and the smith's fees paid also. Now the cost of the brooch was fifty
marks, and they sent it to Eywind. But Eywind had it cut in pieces,
and bought stock with it."—But even the ring was gone at last, and
Eywind was obliged to barter his arrows for herrings, as the last two
lines of the stanza relate.

Eywind survived the Iomswicking battle. Haleyia-tal, which mentions that event, is the last poetry of his which we know of, but there
is no likelihood of his having survived to King Olaf Tryggvason's days.
He left a sturdy son, *Harek of Thiotto,* a bit of a poet too, see Book viii,
§ 2, who played a distinguished part at Sticklestead against St. Olaf, lived
down to 1036, and had a son he named Finn (after his own grandfather).
After him we hear nothing more of the family. Eywind's father's
sister Ranweig was married to a settler in Iceland, Sighvat, from whose
family came Mord, the Iago of Nials Saga.

Eywind's verses are fresh and genuine, and full of incident, and but for
the *metre* we should have put them along with his other poems. As the
sole Norwegian contemporary testimony to the 'swiðe mycla hungor,'
which went all over Northern Europe, they have high value. Other

references to this famine are found in Niala, the tale of Swadi and Arnor
Kerlingarnef in Flateyar-bok, vol. i, 435–439. Ari's account on lost leaves
of Hawks-bok, printed in the Appendix to Landnama-bok, is as follows:
"There was a great winter of famine in Iceland in the heathen days, at
the time that King Harold Grayfell fell, when Earl Hakon took the rule
in Norway. It was the worst of famines in Iceland: men ate ravens and
foxes, and much that was not meet for food was eaten, and some slew
old folks and paupers, hurling them over the cliffs *into the sea*, many men
were starved to death, and some took to the waste and robbed, wherefore many were outlawed and slain: and it was made law by Eywolf
Walgerdsson, that he who slew three of those men should clear himself
thereby." The English poet mentions both the comet of 976 and the
famine:—

> Wæs geond werðeode
> Waldendes wracu wide gefrege
> hungor ofer hrusan, etc.—*Winchester Chronicle.*

Eywind's verses have been better preserved than those of other poets
of his day, but still, as in line 37 (where the innocent-looking 'skeria
foldar' covers the palimpsest 'Mold,' the name of the poet's Ring), or in
the following more opaque line, telling how the ring had been taken
out of the earth (the image the same as in preceding verses), we have
several instances of the rewriter's hand.

Neither Eywind nor any other poet of his day made pithless platitudes,
and wherever we find a respectable-looking commonplace verse with
nothing new or fresh or ingenious about it, we may be certain that
it is altogether corrupt.

From the Lives of Kings. Snorri in Edda cites ll. 21–22, 25–26, 29–32.

1.   BLÓÐ-ŒXAR tiá beiða bryn-þings fetil-stinga
       (oss gœrask hnept) ens hvassa hefnendr (setu-efni):
     heldr es vant (enn ek vilda veg þínn, konungr), segja
     [fǽom til fornra vápna] fliótt her-sǽgo dróttni.

2.   Samira niǿrðr en norðar nadd-regns hvǽtom þegni   5
     (ver getom bili at bǿlva) blá-mǿrar skæ fǿra:
     nú-es þat-es rekr á Rakna rym-leið flota breiðan
     (grípo ver í greipar gunn-borð) Haraldr norðan.

3.   Baða val-grindar vinda veðr-heyjandi Skreyjo
     gumnom hollr né golli gefnar sínni stefno: 10
     ef sǿk-spenni svinnan sigr-minnigr vilt finna,
     fram haltu, niótr, at nýtom Norðmanna gram þannig.

Before Stord. The avengers of Bloodaxe are bent on battle, they give
us little leisure for rest. It is a risk to tell our king the news of war,
though I mean it for thy welfare, my lord. Let us grasp our old
weapons. It does not beseem brave men to put north the head of the
steed of the black moor [*the ocean*], now that Harold from the north
is driving a broad fleet along the roaring path of the Sea-king. We
scorn to fear! Let us grasp the shields in our hands!

After Stord. The warrior king, that spares men, not gold, bade
Skreya hold on his course. 'Keep straight on there, if thou wouldst
meet the lord of the Northmen.' I remember how the double-handed

---

6. Cod. Acad. ii; borð-, Cd. Acad. i.

4. Veit-ek at beit inn bitri byggving meðal-dyggvan
   bulka skíðs or bǽðom ben-vœndr konungs hœndom:
   ófœlinn klauf Ála él-draugs skarar hauga   15
   goll-hiœltoðom galtar grandaðr Dana brandi.

5. Fyrr rauð Fenriss varra flug-varr konungr sparra
   (malm-hríðar svall meiðom móðr) í Gamla blóði:
   þá-es óstirfinn arfa Eireks of rak (geira
   nú tregr gæti-Gauta grams fall) á siá alla.   20

6. Lítt kvǽðo þik láta, land-vœrðr, es brast, Hœrða,
   benja-hagl á brynjom (bugosk almar) geð falma:
   þá-es úfolgin ylgjar endr or þínni hendi
   fetla-svell til fyllar full-egg, Haraldr, gullo.

7. Bǽrom Ullr um alla imon-lauks á hauka   25
   fiœllom Fyris-valla frǽ Hákonar ævi:
   nú hefir folk-stríðir Fróða fá-glýjaðra þýja
   meldr í móðor holdi Mello-dolgs of folginn.

8. Fullar skein á fiœllom fall-sól brá-vallar
   Ullar kióls of allan aldr Hákonar skœldom: 30
   nú-es alf-rœðull elfar Iœtna dolgs um folginn
   (ráð ero ramrar þióðar rík) í móðor líki.

9. Einn dróttinn hefi-ek áttan, iœfurr dýrr, an þik fyrri;
   (bellir bragningr elli) biðkat-ek mer ins þriðja:
   Trúr vas-ek tyggja dýrom; tveim skiœldom lék-ek aldri; 35
   fylli-ek flokk þínn, stillir; fellr á hœnd mer elli.

---

stroke of the keen wound-wand bit the traitorous skipper *Alf;* the
desolator of the Danes clove the hair-hill of the pirate with the gold-
hilted brand.

The golden age of Hakon. Of yore the flight-hating king dyed the gag
of the Wolf's lips, *the sword,* red in the blood of Gamli: what time the
gracious chief drove all the heirs of Eric out to sea: men's wrath
swelled high. But now all men are grieving over the prince's fall.

Apology to Harold. They say that thy courage never flinched, thou
warden of the Hords' land, when the wound-hail clashed on the mail,
and the bows were drawn: what time the bare full-edged spear whistled
out of thy hand to fill the she-wolf's maw.

The evil days of Harold. We bore, my friend, the seed of Fyrisfield,
the gold, on the hawk's cliffs, *our wrists,* all the days of Hakon: but now
the tyrant has buried the flour of Frodi's joyless bondmaids, *gold,* in the
flesh of the giant-slayer's dam, *Earth.* The snood-sun of the nymph's
brows, *the gold,* beamed on the shield-hills, *arms,* of the poets all through
the life of Hakon: but now the stream's light, *gold,* is buried in the body
of the mother of the monster-destroyer, *Earth.* The distress of the
people is great.

Apology. I have had one lord, O king, before thee, and I wish for no
third one. Age pursues me. I have been true to my dear lord, I have
never played with two shields, I stand by thee faithfully, O prince. Age
is overcoming me.

---

15. draugs] draug, Cd.   34. bið ek eigi, Cd.

10.   Skylda-ek 'skerja foldar, skíð-rennandi,' siðan
Þursa bóes 'frá þvísa þínn góðan byr finna:'
ef 'val-iarðar verðom veljandi' þer selja
lyngva mens þat-es lengi láttr mínn faðir átti.   40

11.   Snýr á Svolnis vǽro. Svá hǽfom inn sem Finnar
birki-hind of bundit brums at miðjo sumri.

12.   Lǽtom langra nóta lǫg-sóta ver fótom
at 'spá-þernom,' sporna sporð-fiǫdroðom norðan :
vita ef 'akkar-mutur iokla' 'eld-gerðr,' falar verði   45
ítr, þær-es upp um róta unn-svín, 'vinom' minom.

13.   Fengom feldar-stinga fiǫrð, ok galt við hiǫrðo,
þann-es Ál-himins útan oss lendingar sendo :
mest selda-ek mínar við mǽ ǫrom sævar
(hall-ærit veldr hvǽro) hlaup-sildr Egils gaupna.   50

THE SONS OF GUNDHILD AND THEIR POETS.

(c. 970–976.)

GLUM GEIRASON.

WE have (Book iv) noticed the reigns and fates of Eric Bloodaxe and
of Hakon the Good, his supplanter. Hakon in his turn was to fall before
a combination of the old party in Norway and the Danes, set on foot by
the Queen-dowager Gundhild, the sister of the Danish King Harold
Bluetooth, as one Chronicle tells us (Historia Norwegiæ): and no doubt
it is true. The recurrence of the names Gundhild, Gorm (Gundhild's
two sons), so characteristic of the Skioldings; the course of contemporary politics; the English Chroniclers, who, from this marriage,
call Eric 'King of the Danes'—all confirm it. The rule of the young
kings was far from joyful; to the unhappiness of civil strife was added
the terrible misery of famine and disease. These evils have made the

His ring Mould. I am obliged to pay thee my ring Mould, that was
long ago dug out of the earth at *Thursaby,* and give thee for thy favour
the necklace that my father long owned.

The famine. It snows on Woden's bride, *Earth:* we, like Finns, must
house the does of the birch-buds, *goats,* at midsummer.

The herrings. Let us from the north make the long-netted sea-steeds
spurn the sea with their feet, *oars,* in quest of the fine-feathered shafts
of the sea, *herrings:* let us see if we can get these arrows of the waves
which the sea-swine are rooting up so freely.

The brooch. Last year, I got a cloak-pin, which the Icelanders sent
me from beyond the sea, and I paid it away for stock, for I had sold
clean out all the leaping herrings of Egil the archer's hands, *my arrows,*
to buy the slim shafts of the deep, *herrings.* Famine will make a man
do anything.

37. For foldar read Moldá.   38. týs, Cod. Acad. ii.   44. Read, spiörum . . .?
45. akkar] akur, Cd.   Thus Cod. Acad. i.   Here is a great blank in Acad. ii.
46. Read, at mun sínom.

name of Gundhild as infamous as Jezabel, and probably coloured her character (a sorceress, they say, brought up among the Finns) and the rule of her sons in darker colours than the true. What we know of Harold Grayfell, the most prominent of them, is not altogether unfavourable; of great bodily strength, and master of twelve accomplishments, he seems to have lacked neither valour nor energy, but sadly good luck. Perhaps we may liken him and his father to Eric XIV of Sweden. But the old prejudice, which led the heathen Northmen to sacrifice their kings for good seasons, and the patriotism which could not brook the suzerainty of the Danes (for there seems little reason to doubt that the sons of Gundhild were vassals of the Danish king), have blasted the rule of these kings beyond the power of apology. We hear tales too of the lust and cruelty of a younger brother, Sigrod Sleva, which seem to be well-founded. Particulars of the few years of their rule are few. We hear of an expedition to Perm-land in the Arctic Ocean, and of a foray across the main to the Western islands, wicking expeditions, perhaps, necessitated by lack of food. Ari would make their power last sixteen years, but we cannot, according to English chronology, give them much more than seven; the one fixed date in their period being the great European Famine of 976. At last the suspicious Danish suzerain wiles Harold to Limfirth, where he falls; and Earl Hakon, whose noble father he and his brothers had put to death, entered, under the protection of the Danes, upon the heritage they left.

To Harold Grayfell are ascribed two Poets in Skalda-tal—*Cormac*, of whom we treat elsewhere, for none of his poem on Harold has survived, and GLUM GEIRASON. Glum was a remarkable man, son of one of the latest of the Settlers, who took up his abode in the north of the island, whence, with his sons, as Landnama-bok tells us, he was driven away, in consequence of a feud and manslaughter in which they were involved. There must have been a Saga about Glum, for in Islendinga Drapa we are told how he fought at Fitjar, and 'got speech out of a dead man;' neither of which feats are mentioned elsewhere. He appears as the rival of Eywind, Hakon's faithful poet, and the champion of Eric and his sons, whose henchman he had been. In the Kings' Lives the two poets are brought in, capping verses with each other. One line only of his *Eric's Praise* remains, but there are several stanzas remaining of *Grayfell's Praise*—a Dirge, made when the news of Harold's death was still fresh, and apparently addressed to the two surviving Gundhildssons, as the heads of their party and avengers of Harold.

This poem has been dreadfully maltreated. It must have contained in the verses we have many names of persons and places, which are now washed out, and their space filled by silly commonplace of a late type, so that at first sight, from its smoothness and over-regularity of rhyme, the poem appears, in parts, at least two generations later than it is. We cannot, of course, recover all that is lost; but we have pointed out where the text is unsafe, and indicated the places of some of the missing names in the translation, which it is obvious, from the state of the text, can only be tentative. Among such restorations as appear pretty certain are 'Hallandi' for 'Scotlandi,' l. 5; 'Gauta' for 'Gauti,' l. 6; 'Skotta' for 'flotta,' l. 9; 'Hakon' for 'heppinn,' l. 34.

The *Poem on Eric* is described in Fagrskinna, chap. 28.

The fine *improvisation* seems to be stuffed up with 'stals,' and may have been an old-metre couplet.

I. Glum.   (Grafeldar-drapa, c. 976.)

(From the Lives of Kings; vv. 5, 9 from Fsk.; vv. 1, 3, 13, 14 from Edda; the Stef from Landn., Mb.)

1.   HLÝÐI! (hapta beiðiss hefk) mildingar (gildi)
     því biðjom ver þøgnar þegna tjón at fregnom.

2.   Hafði før til 'ferio' fróðr Skáneyjar góða
     blakk-ríðandi bakka barn-ungr þaðan farna:
     Róg-eiso vann ræsir ráð-vandr á 'Skotlandi,'   5
     'sendi seggja kindar' sverð-bautinn her 'Gauti.'

3.   Hilmir rauð und hialmi heina-laut á Gautom,
     þar vas í gný geira grundar vørðr of fundinn.

4.   Dolg-eiso rak dísar (drótt kom mørg á 'flótta')
     gumna vinr at gamni gióðom Írskrar þióðar: 10
     Foldar rauð ok felldi Freyr í manna dreyra
     sunnr 'á sigr of hlynninn' seggi mækiss eggjar.

5.   Braut við brynjo nióta bág 'rifiunga Ságo,'
     nadd-skúrar vas nœrir Noregs konungr stóra:
     val-galtar let vélta varg-fœðandi marga   15
     (of vægjom réð iœfri) iafn-borna ser þorna.

6.   Austr-lønd um fórsk undir allvaldr, sá-es gaf skøldom
     (hann fekk gagn at gunni) 'gunn hørga sløg' mørgom:
     slíðr-tungor let syngja sverð-leiks reginn ferðir
     sendi 'gramr' at grundo goll-varpaðr snarpar.   20

7.   Austr rauð iœfra þrýstir 'orð-rakkr' fyr bœ norðan
     brand, þar-es Biarmskar kindir brennandi sá-ek renna:
     Gótt hlaut gumna sættir geir-veðr í før þeiri
     (øðlingi feksk ungom orð) á Vino-borði.

8.   Mælti mætra hialta malm-Óðinn, sá blóði,   25
     þróttar-orð, es þorði þióðom vøll at rióða:

I. *Prologue.* Listen, I begin my song. I beg the *two* kings for a silent hearing, now that we have news of this disaster [the fall of Grayfell] ...
His Eastern forays. When yet in childhood he sailed to Sconey, he fought a battle in *Halland,* and smote with the sword a host of Gauts. ... He reddened his blade on the Gauts, and was found in battle there.
His Western forays. Then he battled with the *Scots* and the Irish, and victorious south in ... smote ... with the edge of the sword. Norway's king fought with ... and defeated princes of like rank to himself.
His Northern exploits. The king who gave *treasure* to poets subdued the eastlands, he made the sheath-tongues [blades] sing at . . . He burned eastward north of O ... by, where I saw the Perms running from the flames; and battled on the banks of the Dwina. The young Etheling won fame there.
His last battle in Denmark. He spake a word of courage, yea, Harold

---

5. Read, Hallandi.   6. Read, Gauta.   9. For flótta read Skotta ?
24. Read, Dvino borði ?

víð-lendr of bað vinda verðung Haraldr sverðom
(frægt þótti þat flotnom fylkiss orð) at mørði.

9.　　Hioggosk hvárir-tveggjo 'heggir' mækiss eggja;
'varð í gœgn at ganga geir-drótt' Haraldr þeiri.　　30

10.　　Varð á víðo borði viggjom hollr at liggja
gætir glamma sóta garðz Eylima-fiarðar :
sendir fell á sandi sævar báls at Halsi ;
olli iœfra spialli 'orð-heppinn' því morði.

11.　　Féllomk hølf þá-es hilmiss hiœr-drífa brá lífi　　35
(réðat oss til auðar) auð-ván (Haraldz dauði) :
enn ek veit at hefir heitið hans bróðir mer góðo
(siá getr þar til sælo segg-fiœlð) hvaðar-tveggi.

12.　　Kunni tolf sá-es tanna tíðom Hallin-skíða
ógnar-stafr um iœfra íþróttir fram sótti ; . . . . .　　40

13.　　Hein-þynntan lét hvína hryn-eld at þat brynjo
foldar-vœrðr sá-es fyrðom fiœr harðan sik varði :

14.　　Þar vas þrafna-byrjar þeim styrðo goð beima
sialfr í sœki-alfi Sigtýr Atals dýra.

The Stef.—Víg-eiso tekr vísa val-fall Haraldz alla.　　45

II. On Eirik Bloody-axe (from Skalda).

The Stef.—Brandr fær logs ok landa landz Eiriki banda.

III. Lausavísa (from Lives of Kings).

Vel hefir hefnt (en hafna hiœrs-ben-draugar fiœrvi)
[folk-rakkr of vant, fylkir, framligt] Haraldr Gamla :
es dœkk-valir drekka dolg-bandz fyr ver handan
(roðin frá-ek rauðra benja reyr) Hákonar dreyra.

---

bade his men 'draw swords for the battle.' The king's words pleased
the warriors! The two namesakes, Harold *and Gold Harold,* cut at each
other with the edge of the sword. He (the king) was doomed to lie on
the broad bank of Lim-firth, at Halse on the sand he fell. It was . . .
[Hakon] that planned that slaughter.

His glory. Half my hope is gone, now that the battle has reft the
king of life. Harold's death was no blessing to me, yet I know that
both his brothers have given me fair promises ; the court looks to them
for solace now. Harold was the master of twelve accomplishments . . .

Fragment. He made the hone-thinned blade whistle as he defended his
life against his foes. Woden himself was with him, and the war-god
steered his course.

Burden. Harold's hand makes a great slaughter all . . .

II. Dirge on Eric Bloodaxe. His brand wins Eric land and
gold.

III. Improvisation after Stord. Well has Harold avenged Gamli
[his brother] now that the ravens over sea are drinking Hakon's
blood !

---

30. Read, Haraldar?　　34. for heppinn read Hakon.　　43. þeim er stýrðo beima, W.

EARL HAKON'S POETS (976–995).

HAVING driven the sons of Gundhild out of the kingdom, Earl Hakon ruled Norway for nearly twenty years, when he in his turn fell before the young Olaf Tryggvason.   Hakon was the scion of a famous family, whose genealogy and exploits were given by Eywind in Haleyia-tal, Book iv.   The first Hakon, Earl of Yriar, his grandfather, was known as ' the friend of Harold Fairhair,' whose faithful helper and counsellor he was; his father Sigfred, a notable man in his day for his Law-making and organisation, was the fast friend and adviser of Hakon Æthelstan's foster-son.   Of Earl Hakon himself we hear a good deal in the Kings' Lives.   Succeeding to the rule of Norway after a time of famine and misery, the country recovered under his rule; and the favour of the gods was signally manifested to the man whose ritualistic piety to them was a contrast to the careless iconoclasm of Gundhild's sons, by a succession of good seasons and unchecked prosperity.   His cult of the gods won him the renown of a sorcerer, and the name of the 'sacrificing earl' from his Christian foes.   There may have been in truth something of the Waldstein character about him, but we can hardly doubt that his memory has somewhat suffered at the hands of the party which overthrew his dynasty.

The chief exploits of his life were the Avenging of his father, burnt in his house by the crafty treason of the Sons of Gundhild.   As a vassal earl of Harold Blue-tooth's of Denmark he fights against the great crusade of the German Emperor, Otho II, 975, where he shares Harold's ill-fortune.   On his return through Gautland he makes a sacrifice, ' casting the Divining Rods.'   In Norway he twice fights the wicking Reginfred (said by the Sagas to be a son of Gundhild).   Feeling himself now firm in his seat, he shakes off the Danish suzerainty, which had boasted of making Norway its 'hawk island.'   The Danish king, failing to reduce him, sets the Wickings of Iom, his formidable and turbulent allies, upon the stubborn Earl, who gains a glorious victory over them at Hiorunga Bay, off South More (Norway).   This battle must not be placed at the end of his career, as the Kings' Lives seem to do, but rather as the 'crowning mercy' which put him for many years in safety.   More grateful than ever to the gods, who had saved him from such peril, he restores the fallen Temples, and celebrates their feasts with all the ancient pomp and circumstance.   His daughters marry into the best families of Norway, and there is hardly a noble house in the two following centuries which cannot trace up to the ' wicked Earl.'   At last a sudden rising, in which his good fortune failed him at last, put him to flight and hiding, and he met his death at the hand of a treacherous slave.   Of his son Eric we shall have somewhat to say later.

Hakon had many poets about him.   Eight are named in Skalda-tal; of two of these, Skapti the Lawman and Hvannar-Kalf, no line is left, though Skapti's life is well known from the Sagas. Of Eywind the Poetspoiler and Eilif Gudrunsson we have already spoken.   Of Einar Skalaglamm, the poet of his early years of power, Tind Hallkettleson, the poet of his zenith, Thorleif Redcloakson, and Thorolf Mouth we must now speak.

The following passages will give the best account of EINAR HELGASON :—

" There was a man named Einar, son of Helgi Othere's son, son of Biorn the Easterling, who settled in Broadfirth.   Einar's brother was

Oswif the Wise (*the father of* Gudrun the heroine of Laxdæla Saga). Einar was even in his youth big and strong, and a very accomplished man. He took to making *poetry* when he was yet young, for he was a man eager to learn. It happened one summer at the Moot that Einar went into Egil Skalla-Grimson's booth, and they fell to talking, and their talk soon turned to the craft of poetry. Both of them thought talking on this head the best of pastime. After that Einar would often turn in to talk with Egil, and great friendship sprung up between them."— *Egil's Saga*, ch. 82.

The poet, like other young Icelanders of family, went abroad to the court of Norway and took service with Earl Hakon, where he got his nickname ' Rattle-scale' in the following way:—

" On one occasion Einar, fancying that he was not well treated, grew angry and would not come near the earl. The earl, finding that Einar was displeased with his treatment of him, sent to bid him come and speak with him ; then he took a fair pair of Scales made of pure silver, and all gilt, and with them there went two weights, one of gold and the other of silver, that were made after the likeness of men, and were called 'lots.' And this was the power that was in them :—The earl would lay them in the scales and say which of them should come up, and if the one that he would came up, it would shake in the scale so that ' it made a rattle.' The earl gave Einar the scales, and he was very pleased with them, and was ever afterwards called *Einar Rattle-scale*."—*Iomswikinga Saga*.

Of another famous gift which the generous earl bestowed on his poet we are told in Egil's Saga :—

"Einar made an Encomium on Earl Hakon, which is called Lack-Lucre; and for a very long time the earl would not listen to the poem because he was wroth with Einar." Einar threatened to leave him, "but the earl would not have Einar go abroad, and listened to the poem, and then gave Einar a shield which was the greatest jewel. It was engraved with tales of old, and all between the engravings it was over-laid with bosses of gold, and set with precious stones." Einar comes home, and in the harvest rides over to Borg and guests there. Egil was away from home at the time. Einar waited for him three nights. "And it was not then the custom to stay longer than three nights on a visit. So he made ready to go ; and when he was ready he went into Egil's room, and there he fastened up the precious shield, and told the household that he gave the shield to Egil. Then he rode away. That same day Egil came home, and when he came into his room he saw the shield, and asked who owned that jewel. They told him that Einar Rattle-scale had been there, and had given him the shield. Then spake Egil, What, is he making *me* a gift, most miserable of men that he is! Does he think I am going to sit awake and make poetry over his shield? Go and catch my horse. I will ride after him and slay him. Then they told him that Einar had ridden away early in the morning. He must have got to Dale by now. Afterwards Egil made a poem, of which the beginning is—[here a spurious verse is inserted]. Egil and Einar kept up their friendship as long as they were both alive. And it is told as follows of the fortunes of the shield afterwards, that Egil had it with him when he went on the bridal-way, when he went north to Wood-Mire with Thorkettle Gundwaldsson and the sons of Red-Biorn, Treevle and Helgi. Then the shield was spoilt, having fallen into sour milk. And afterwards Egil had the mounting taken off it, and there was twelve ounces of gold in the bosses."—*Egil's Saga*, ch. 82.

The end of Einar is thus told in Landnama-bok, ii. 11: "Helgi [Einar's father] harried in Scotland, and there took captive Nidborg, daughter of King Beolan, and Cathleen the daughter of Ganger Rolf [Rollo]. He married her; their sons were Oswif the Wise, and Einar Rattle-scale, who was drowned on Einar's-reef [Einarssker, now called Einars-bodi, near Hrappsey in Broad-fiord] in Seal-sound, and his shield came ashore on Shieldey and his cloak on Cloak-holm [Feldar-holm]. Einar was the father of Thorgerd, the mother of Herdis, the mother of Stein the poet."

Einar's most famous work was *Vell-Ekla* (*Lack-Lucre*), which is quoted in the Kings' Lives and also in Edda. It was no doubt one of the chief sources for the early career of the earl. It is very antique in spirit, akin in feeling and treatment to Thiodwolf's poems, but, curiously enough, without any trace of Egil's influence. As a dated work, before 980, on such a man as Hakon, the poem is of high interest to the historian. It was in Drapa-form, and each section treated of a separate exploit of the earl's; thus, had we the whole, there would be a complete annalistic account of his life, beginning with his revenge for his father's death, down to the eve of the Iomswicking battle. We have parts of sections relating (1) to Fighting the sons of Gundhild and Gritgard's fall; (2) the Expedition in aid of the Danish king Harold against Otho II; (3) a Campaign in Gautland; (4, 5) the first and second Campaigns against Reginfred; (6) the Re-establishment of peace and good rule and the heathen ritual in Norway.

Vellekla's text is in a fearful state, whole lines *rotten* and *overlaid* by Philistine folly—once a fine poem, rich in parallelisms, and variations on a single theme, stern, almost religious, full of condensed facts—but now, names and facts that Ari once found there lie buried beneath the stucco of jingle, e. g. the name of Griotgard in v. 6 concealed under 'harda loptz vinar barda,' the 'three winters' in v. 1, the name of the emperor in v. 11, and the name of Othere [Ottar] in v. 13. In l. 62, stod and byrjar where Ari read Stad and Byrda; in ll. 65–66, Ari read þinga nes. In l. 44, for 'fior Gauta' Ari read 'sker Gauta;' farther we have been able to restore the reading 'he enquired of the oracle by the divining rods' to the form in which we believe Ari read it.

The arrangement of the sections is determined by the German chronicle, which forbids us to allow Hakon's rule to have been estab-lished *before* the Danish expedition, as indeed was *à priori* unlikely. Ari or his editors have been misled here in some way.

There is a peculiarity which marks many genuine verses of Einar— *consonance* between the last measure of the first half and the first measure of the second half of the line. This ornament characterises a whole poem *on Hakon* 'different from Vellekla' cited in Edda and Fagrskinna, but of which the name is lost; and even the text is not safe in parts. This metrical form was imitated and pushed to extremes by later poets.

TIND HALLKETTLESSON, one of Bragi's descendants (see Book vii, p. 2) and kinsman of the poet Gunlaug Snake's-tongue, was a man of adventurous life. There are traditions relating to him in the Heidar-viga Saga, where we are told of his smithy, and of his part in the Heath-slaughter feuds. The verses ascribed to him in that Saga are of doubtful authenticity. There are fragments of a *Hakon's-drapa* in the Kings' Lives, and in the Iomsvikinga-vellum, AM. 510, is a long snatch of the same poem in a terribly corrupt state, published first by Dr. Petersens, Lund 1880. This Encomium relates to the Iomswicking battle, and contains particulars and names (such as Godmar in the

Wick, the site of some engagement of the year 980) which are not contained elsewhere, and we must regret the impossibility of doing much to restore these verses to their original state.

THORLEIF REDCLOAKSSON is told of in Landnama-bok, where we find the story how he and his brother killed Klaufi who insulted them; a ditty Thorleif made on the occasion is given in Book vi, Ditty 19. He is told of also in Swarfdæla Saga. He has become a legendary person, and a story (known already to Hawk Waldisason and hinted at in his Islendinga-drapa) sprung up of his having composed a bitter satire on Earl Hakon, who sent a ghost to slay him. The ghost did his work at the Great Moot, where Thorleif was buried. It is on his cairn that the shepherd sat, as is told in the pretty story, parallel to our Cædmon legend, in Flatey-bok, to be found in the Reader, p. 146.

THORWOLF MOUTH is only known from Skalda-tal, as Hakon's poet.

EILIF GUDRUNSSON. We have noticed this poet in the introduction to his Thors-drapa, above, § 1 of this Book.

EYIOLF DADI'S POET. What is known of this poet is noted below in Book viii, § 1. His poem is inserted here, belonging more fitly, as a heathen composition of Hakon's days, to this Book than the next.

I. EINAR (VELLEKLA, or LACK LUCRE).

(From the Lives of Kings; vv. 30–32 from Edda.)

1. OK odd-neytir úti eið-vandr flota breiðan
   'glaðr í Gœndlar veðrom gramr " svafði bil " hafði:'
   ok rauð-mána reynir róg-segl Héðins bóga
   upp hóf iœfra kappi 'etjo-lund at setja.'

2. Vasat of byrjar œrva odda-víffs né drífo   5
   sverða sverri-fiarðar svan-glýjaði at frýja:
   brak-rœgnir skók bogna (barg uþyrmir varga)
   hagl or Hlakkar seglom (hiœrs rakkliga fiœrvi).

3. Mart varð él áðr Ála 'Austr-lœnd' at mun banda
   randar lauks af ríki rœki-lundr of tœki.   10

4. Ber-ek fyr hefnd þá es hrafna 'hlióms lof toginn skióma'
   þat nam vœrðr at vinna vann síns fœður hranna: . . .

5. Rigndi 'hiœrs á hersa hríð-remmis fiœr víða'
   (þrym-lundr of iók Þundi þegns gnótt) meil-regni:
   'ok hald-viðorr hœlda haf faxa' lét vaxa   15
   laufa veðr at lífom líf-kœld Hárs drífo.

6. 'Hialm-grápi vann hilmir harðr' (Loptz vinar) barða
   (þá kom vœxtr í 'vino' vinheims) fiándr sína:

I. *He revenges his father.* The oath-fast earl had a great fleet on the sea for three winters waging war against the kings [Gundhild's sons]. No one could question his courage in battle. He shook the bows' hail, *arrows*, out of the sail of the Walkyries, *his shield*, and feasted the wolves. There was many a hard struggle ere he won the lands of his heritage by the gods' will. I set forth his praise for his avenging of his father. Iron-rain was showered at . . . He strengthened the host of Woden. He made the life-chilling sword-storm at . . . wax high.

2. Read, þriú Svafnis böl.   9. Read, ætt-lönd.

ok for-sniallir fello fúrs í Þundar skúrom
(þat fær þióðar snytri) þrír iarls synir (tírar).   20

7.   Hvarfat aptr áðr erfðan odd-stafr fœður hafði,
her-forðaðr réð harða hiœr-veðrs konungs fiœrvi:
varðat Freyr sá-es fœri folk-skíðs né man síðan
(því bregðr œld við aðra) iarls ríki framm slíko.

8.   Hitt vas auk es eykir aur-borðz á vit norðan   25
und sig-runni svinnom sunnr Danmarkar runno :
ok holm-fiœturs hialmi Hœrða valdr of faldinn
Dofra 'Danskra iofra' Dróttinn fund of sótti.

9.   Ok 'við frost' at freista fé-mildr konungr vildi
myrk-hloðynjar markar morð-alfs þess es kom norðan :   30
þá-es val-serkjar Virki veðr-hirði bað stirðan
fyr hlym-niœrðom Hœrða 'Hagbarða gramr' varða.

10.   Vasat í gœgn þótt gœrði garð-rœgnir styr harðan
gengilegt at ganga geir-ásar her þeira :
Þá-es með Frísa fylki fór 'gunn-viður' sunnan   35
'kvaddi vígs' ok Vinda vágs blakk-riði Frakka

11.   Þrymr varð logs es lœgðo leik-miðjungar þriðja
(arn-greddir varð 'oddom' andvígr) saman randir :
sund-faxa kom Sœxom sœki-þróttr á flótta
þar 's svá-at gramr 'með gumnom' Garð yr-þióðom varði.

12.   Flótta gekk til fréttar felli-niœrðr á velli   41
(draugr gat dolga Ságo dagráð) 'Heðins váða'
ok hald-boði hildar hræ-gamma tvá ramma;

He slew Gritgard. There was fresh company for Woden's hall. Three earls' sons fell; it was a glory to the furtherer of the people. He turned not back till he had kept the arval over his father, having slain the king, *Erling*. Neither before nor after has there been an earl who showed such earl's power; all talk of it.

II. *Expedition against Otho.* Next the ships sped under him southward to Denmark, and the lord of the Northmen, hooded in helm of awe, went to meet the Danish prince; for the Danish king coming from the north wished without fail to do battle against the *Emperor*, the ruler of the Dark-woodland, *Holstein, Germany;* he bade the prince of the Hords, *Hakon*, defend the Wall against the king of the Longobards. However bravely he fought, it was no easy task to meet this host, when the emperor came from the south, ready for battle, with a great company of Frisians, Saxons, Wends, and Franks. It was a hard fight when they joined shields; the earl faced Otho bravely, he turned the Saxons to flight. Thus he guarded the Wall against the army of the Southerners.

III. *Sacrifices in Gautland.* He enquired of the oracle on the . . . field, and he got *for an answer that there was* a fair chance of a victory,

---

28. Read, Dana iöfri?   29. Read, *some place*?   32. Read, Langbarða gramr?   36. Read, *Saxa* ok Vinda.   38. Read, Odda?   43. tvá] sá, Cd.

týr valði sá tírar tein hlautar við sker Gauta.

13. Háði iarl þars áðan engi mannr und ranni 45
hyrjar-þing at herja hiœr-lautar kom Sœrla:
bara maðr lyngs en lengra 'lopt varðaðar' barða
(allt vann gramr um gengit Gautland) frá siá randir.

14. Val-fœllom hlóð vœllo varð ragna konr gagni
hríðar áss at hrósa (hlaut Óðinn val) Fróða. 50

15. Enn reið œðro sinni iarl borð-mœrom norðan
(sókn-herðir lét sverða sótt) Ragnfrœði at móti.

16. Hóf und hyrjar kneyfi (hraut unda fiœld) Þundar
[þat sleit vígi á vági] vandar-dýr at landi:
né fiœl-nenninn fyrri fé-mildr konungr vildi 55
(vægðit iarl fyrir iœfri) Yggs niðr fríðar biðja.

17. Buinn létzk valdr ef vildi val-mey konungr heyja
hœlða morðz at halda (herr fell um gram) velli.

18. Hitt var meirr at Mœra morð-fíkinn lét norðan
folk-verjandi fyrva fœr til Sogns of gœrva: 60
ýtti Freyr af fiórom folk-lœndom sá branda
'ullr "stoð" af því' allri yr-þióð 'Héðins "byrjar."'

19. Ok til mótz á meita miúk-hurðom fram þurðo
með svœr-gœli svarfa siau land-rekar randa.

20. Glumði allr þá-s Ullar egg-'þing' Heðins veggiar 65
(gnótt flaut nás) fyr 'nesjom' Noregr saman fóro.

21. Varð fyrir Vinda myrði víð-frægt (enn gramr síðan
gœrðisk mest at morði) mann-fall við styr annan:
hlym-narfi bað hverfa hlífar-flagðs ok lagði
ialks við œndurt fylki ondur-vœrp at landi. 70

22. Strœng varð gunnr áðr gumnar gammi nás und hramma
þrœngvi-meiðr of þryngi þrimr hundruðom lunda:

---

and he beheld two ravens. Yea, he cast the divining rods at the Gauta Skerries. He fought *against* Othere where none had ever come helmed before; no wicking had ever borne shield farther from the sea. He covered the field with slain; won a victory: Woden gained by the dead.

IV. *Fight with Reginfred.* A second time the earl rode his sea-horses from the north to meet Reginfred. The ships hove towards land, which cut short the battle in the bay: the earl would not ask the king for peace, the earl did not give in to the king. The earl said that he was ready, if the king would, to fight on land.

V. *Second fight with Reginfred.* Again another time the earl went from the north to Sogn; he had with him the full levy of four folk-land between Byrda and Cape Stadt. Seven earls sailed to battle with him, and all Norway resounded when they joined in fight off Thinga-Ness. There was a famous slaughter before the slayer of the Wends in his second battle *with Reginfred;* the earl laid his ships to land, and drew

---

44. Emend.; vildi . . . tyna tein lautar fior Gauta, Cdd. 62. Read, Stað. 63.
Read, frá Byrðo. 65-66. Read, þinga . . . nesjom? 70. vorp, Fms.; þorf, Cd.

knátti hafs at hꜹfðom (hagnaðr vas þat) bragna
folk-eflandi fylkir fang-sæll þaðan ganga.

23.   Siau fylkjom kom 'silkis snúnaðr vas þat brúna'   75
'geymir grundar síma grand-varr' und sik landi.

24.   Hver sé if nema iꜹfra ætt-rýri goð stýra.
Ramm-aukin kveð-ek ríki rꜹgn Hákonar magna.

25.   Nú liggr 'allt' und iarli (imon-borðz) fyrir norðan
('veðr-gꜹðiss' stendr víða) Vík (Hákonar ríki).   80

26.   Öll lét senn inn svinni sꜹnn Einriða mꜹnnom
herjom kunnr of 'herioð' hofs lꜹnd ok vé banda
at Veg-Ióta vitni valfallz um siá allan
(þeim stýra goð) geira garðz Hlórriði farði.

27.   Ok her-þarfir hverfa Hlakkar mótz til blóta   85
'rauð-bríkar fremsk rꜹkir' ríki ás-megir slíko:
nú grꜹr iꜹrð sem áðan aptr geir-bruar hapta
auð-rýrir lætr ꜹro ótryggva vé byggva.

28.   Engi varð á iꜹrðo ættom góðr nema Fróði
gæti-niꜹrðr sá-es gꜹrði geir-bríkar frið slíkan.   90

29.   Hvar viti ꜹld und einom iarð-byggvi svá liggja
(þat skyli herr of hugsa) hiarl ok sextán iarla?
þess ríðr fúrs með fiórom folk-leikr Heðins reikar
log-skundaðar lindar lof-kendr himins endom.

30.   Né sigbiarka serkir sóm-miðjungom rómo   95
Hárs við Hꜹgna skúrir hlꜹðut fast um sꜹðir . . .

31.   Odda gnýs við ꜹsi odd-netz þindl setja . . .

32.   Hnigo fiándr at glym Gꜹndlar grams und arnar
hramma . . .

---

up his men in array. There was a hot fray ere three hundred warriors
fell, and he walked thence over the dead to his ship again victorious.
He became the lord of seven counties, from . . . to . . .
  VI. *Establishes peace, restores the Gods' worship.* Who can doubt but
that the gods guide the upsetter of kings! Now all the Wick north of the
Wethereys is under his sway; Hakon's realm stretches far and wide. He
restored the temple glebes of Thor and the holy places of the gods,
driving the Jutes into the sea with slaughter by the gods' help. And all
the people turn back to sacrifices; such might do the gods grant him:
the earth yields crops as of yore, and he makes men joyfully people again
the sanctuaries of the gods. Never was there prince save Frodi that
made such peace as he.
  I say that the gods strengthen Hakon's sway. Was there ever a land
and sixteen earls lying so under one ruler? His glory soars high under
the four ends of the heaven.
  VII. *Fragments.* Nor could the firm-sewn mail shirts shelter the men
in the battle . . .
  To set the sword against the rearer of war *no one dared.*
  The foemen sank in battle underneath the talons of the eagle.

79–80. Read, öll . . . Veðreyjar.   82. Read, hérod?   86. ásmegui, Fms.

II. Fragments of a later Drapa on Earl Hakon.

(Verses 1-8, 10, 11 from Edda, verse 9 from Fagrsk.)

1.   Nú es þat es Boðnar bára berg-Saxa tér vaxa;
gœrvi í hœll ok hlýði hlióð 'fley'-iœfurs þióðir.

2.   Hug-stóran bið-ek heyra (heyr iarl Kvásiss dreyra!)
foldar-vœrð á fyrða fiarð-leggjar brim dreggjar.

3.   Hlióta mun-ek (né hlít'k) hiœr-týs (of þat frýjo)   5
fyrir œr-þeysi at ausa austr vín-gnóðar flausta.

4.   Því at fiœl-kostigr flesto flestr ræðr við son Bestlo
tekit hefik morðz til mærðar mæringr an þú færa.

5.   Goll-sendir lætr (grundar glaðar þengill her-drengi)
[hans mæti kná-ek hlióta] 'hliót' Yggs miaðar nióta.   10

6.   Eisar vágr fyrir vísa, verk rœgnis mer hogna,
þýtr Óðreriss alda aldr hafs við fles galdra.

7.   Ullar gengr of alla ask-sœgn þess es hvœt magnar
byrgiss bœðvar sorgar bergs grunn-lá dverga.

8.   Né ætt-stuðill ættar ógn-herðir mun verða   15
(skyldr em-ek hróðri at halda) Hilldi-tannz in mildri.

9.   Bygði lœnd (enn lunda lék orð á því) forðom
Gamla kind sú-es granda (gunn-borðz) véom þorði:
nú es afrendra iœfra Ullr geir-vaðils þeira
sóknar hvatr at setri setrs hveim gram betri.   20

10.   Hialm-faldinn bauð hildi hialdr-œrr ok Sigvaldi
hinn es fór í gný Gunnar gunn-diarfr Bui sunnan.

Prologue. It is now that the wave of Bodn [poetry] begins to wax
high, may the prince's courtiers give ear in the hall and listen to the
Giants' beverage, *poetry*. I pray the brave lord to listen to the Liquor of
the Giants. Hearken, earl, to Quasi's blood. I must pour out blame-
lessly before thee, prince, the bilge water of Woden's wine-vessel, *verse*.
No ruler rules more in accordance with the son of Bestla, *Woden*, than
thou. I have begun my poem. I know how to make the ruler of the
land enjoy Woden's holy Mead. The prince gladdens his men, I get
gifts of him. The wave of Woden foams . . . . the billow of Odreari
thunders . . . The cliffs' surf that the Dwarves own, *my poetry*, praising
him, spreads among all men. Never shall be a more goodly scion of
Hildi-tand [War-tusk] the generous. I must set forth his praise.
Hakon revenged. The kindred of Gamli [Gundhild's sons], who dared
to defile the sanctuaries, ruled this land of yore; all men's report witnesses thereto: but now there is set in the seat of those mighty lords
an earl better than any king.
Iomswicking fight. The helm-hooded Sigwald and the daring Bui, who
came from the south, offered battle. The warrior fed the ravens on

---

2. Read, veig *or* lið?   9. Read, gollsendi-lætk?   10. hliót = hlaut?
14. grynn-, W.

11.   Fiall-vœndom gaf fylli (fullr varð) [enn spiœr gullo]
       her-stefnandi hrœfnom (hrafn á ylgjar tafni).

III. STRAY VERSES.

(Verse 1 from Edda, verses 2, 3 from Iómsvíkinga Saga.)

1. BAUGS getr með þer þeygi þýðr drengr vesa lengi
       (elg búom flóðs) nema fylgi, frið-stœkkvir, því nœkkvað.
2. Gœrða-ek veig of 'virða' Viðris illrar tíðar,
    þat vann ek meðan aðrir œr-vávaðir svœfo :
    komkat-ek þess þar es þótti þing-sættis fé betra   5
    (meiðr sparir hodd við hróðri hverr) enn skald in verri.
3. Sœkjom iarl þannz auka ulfs verð þorir sverðom
    (hlœðom borð-roinn barða baug-skiœldom) Sigvalda :
    drepr eigi sá sveigir sár-linnz es gram finnom
    (rœnd berom út á andra Endils) við mer hendi.   10

TIND HALLKELSSON.

(Verses 1, 2, and ll. 15, 16 from Lives of Kings, the rest from AM. 510.)

1. VARÐA gims sem gœrði Gerðr biúg-limom herða
       (gnýr óx Fiolnis fúra) farlig sæing iarli :
    þá es hring-fœm hanga hryn-serk Viðorr brynjo
    (hruðosk rið-marar Róða rastar) varð at kasta.
2. Vann á Vinda sinni verð-bióðr Hugins (ferðar)   5
    (beit sól-gagarr seilar) sverðz-eggja spor leggja :
    áðr hiœr-meiðar hrióða (hætting vas þat) mætti
    leiðar langra skeiða liðs halfan tœg þriðja.
3. Gat ohræðin ædra odd galdrs en Sigvaldi
    vítt saukk næti niotar viðr nám Bua 'kvanti'   10
    aðr mót-rœðuls mattu 'magrendr' Grimnis vagna

---

the wolves' quarry, and the spears rang; yea, he gave the mountain-
ranging ravens their fill.
To Hakon. I cannot stay with thee, Earl, any longer save I get some
good by it. I shall make my ship ready *to leave.* In an evil hour
I brewed Woden's draught [my Song] for this Earl, yea, alas, when
other men were asleep. I never came to any place where more store
was set by money and less by poets! Every one here grudges the fee
to pay for his praise. Let us seek Earl Sigwald, the wolf-feeder.
Should we meet him, he will not wave us off with his hand. Let us
dress our oar-fitted bark with the ringed shields! Let us bear the
targets out on to the sea-king's car [ship]!

Tind. It was not as if the damsel were making a bed for the Earl
in her arms when he had to throw off his ring-stripped mail-coat. The
battle grew hot: the ships were won. He laid the prints of his sword-
edges on the Wends [the Iomswickings] before they (*his men*) could
clear twenty-five ships of war. The sword bit the warriors: a dangerous game it was. *The rest of the lines are untranslateable, so corrupt*

---

3. viðis, Cd.   10. Read, kvámo?

saung at sverda þingi sorla Þrœnskum iarli.

4.   Dreif at Viðris vedri vargi grim a margan
verð aud kundu virðri vagll agls timis hagli:
þars í sundr á sandi Sœrla 'bles' fyr iarli   15
(þess hefir seggja sessi) serk hring-ofinn (merki).

5.   Forrad iarl enn aara hendr her maurum kendi
gvndlar dóms at glaumi geirs tírar fœr meiri
undz þa er hrauð en hauðri hialldr ræsi eg þat giolldum
nunnar fús 'á mæti morðr' vikinga skeiðar.   20

6.   Giorðuzt gœndlar borda glaumr óx þar at er naumu
'auði grims at eyðiz' oll lond Dana brandi
kent hefir 'hægr' at hœggua 'hræber birtingum senar'
veðr eggi undum uiggiar ueggurs nidz um þat skeggi.

7.   Saddi iarl þars odda of þing saman geingu   25
'van hugda valt hungri hranna' byrgis nafni
mord skyar vard monnum mistar gott til vista
heiðins doms at hada 'œlld uann markar síðu.'

8.   Þat uill olld medan alldir 'yngs kueðiu menn' byggja
gnogt-þess er goglum veitti 'glaum' Hakonar æfi   30
þui hyck bitrum beita baund at villdu landi
hyck lar reiði lyda lætr huerium gram betri.

9.   Hraud (en Hroptr um nádi) hialldr skya (ual nýum)
þar uar lindz fyr landi leidangr Dana skeidar.

10.   Þa er fyr bord a Barda i brudar fang at ganga   35
ueðr magnanda uiðris uirdendr Bua kendu.

11.   Mikin giordi her hiorua 'hliomur' Bui sunnan
bauga skerdur at breidu balldur Hakonar valdi.

12.   Undr er þreytt ef þrindi þann kendi ual er sendir
gulli safnadar gumna 'godinnar' hræum fiarri.   40

---

are they; we can however make out a few broken lights. Verse 3, we have
Sigwald *and* Bui. Nor could the Wicking vie with the Throndish Earl.
In verse 4, we can only see descriptions of battle and the mention of the
mail-coat blown to pieces in the war-storm. *In verse 5, the Earl is
mentioned clearing some number of* Wicking ships at More. *In the next he*
teaches his Danish foes to veil their beards in the dust. *Verse 7, must
have given the account of some battle* on Denmark's coast. *Verse 8.* As
long as men dwell on Earth, so long the joy Hakon's heir gave the
birds of prey will be held in mind. I deem him the better of any
king ... *The* clearing of the Danish ships *is told of in verse 9. Bui's
going overboard when he despaired of victory,* into the embraces of Ran's
daughters, *is in verse* 10. Great was the Sacrifice [human] at the
Launch of the ships, when Bui set out from the south and hastened to
Hakon's broad domain, *says verse* 11. *Verse 12 tells of a fight at* God-
mere *in East Wick.*

---

15. Read, hiosk?   20. Read, á Mœri meiðr.   22. Read, auði grimmr
at eyða?   23. Read, heggr ... hræ-birtingom sævar?   26. Read, vann
hanga valr hungri hafna.   28. Read, hríð Danmarkar síðo?   29. Read,
yggs ... man (*earth*).   30. Read, glæ.   37. Read, hlunn-roð.   40. Read,
Goðmarr.

ÞORLEIFR RAUÐFELDARSON.

(Verse 1 from Lives of Kings, verse 2 from Skalda.)

1. HÁKON! vitom hvergi (hafisk hefir runnr af gunni)
fremra iarl und ferli (folk-Ránar) þer mána:
þú hefir æðlinga Óðni (etr hrafn af ná getnom)
(vesa máttu af því vísi víð-lendr) nio senda.
2. Hæfðo ver í þer, Hákon, es at hiœr-rógi drógomk 5
(þú rautt Skœglar skýia skóð) forosto góða.

ÞÓROLFR MUÐR (from Edda).

SAGÐI hitt es hugði Hliðskialfar gramr sialfom
hlífar-styggr þá es hœggnir Háreks liðar váro.

EILIFR (§ 1) cited in Edda.

VERÐI þer allz orða oss grœr um kon Mœrar
á sef-reino Sónar sáð vin-giœfom ráða. 10

EYIOLFR DADASKALD. (BANDA-DRÁPA.)

(From the Lives of Kings.)

1. FOLK-STÝRIR vas fára finnz œl-knarrar linna
suðr at siávar naðri set-bergs gamall vetra:
áðr at Yggjar brúði el-hvetjandi setja
hildar hialmi faldinn hodd-mildingar vildo.
2. Meita fór at móti miœk síð um dag skíði 5
ungr með iœfno gengi Útvers frœmom hersi:

Thorleif Redcloaksson. O Hakon, I know nowhere under the moon's path [heaven] a greater earl than thou. Thou hast grown mighty by war. Thou hast given nine Ethelings to Woden; and hence mayest well be a far-ruling lord. O Hakon, thou wert a good captain to us whenever we went forth to battle . . .

Thorwolf Mouth. The king of Lith-shelf [Woden] spoke out when the followers of Harek were cut down . . .

Eilif Gudrunsson. May gifts of friendship come to me in return for the seed of Sôna which grows in our breast respecting the famous prince of the land, *i.e. I want a fee for my Song.*

Eyiolf, Banda-drapa. The Burden. Joyful in battle, Eric draws under himself the land, by the will of the gods, and wages war. Yea, the war-glad earl rules the god-protected land since that day.

Introduction. The prince was but a few winters old when the earl [his father] put him over the land. Late one day he went in his ship against a proud baron; yea, he slew Skopti at Utver [island]. Thou

---

9. Read, verði mer.   Read, iarðar.   Read, mæran?

þá-es rið-loga reiðir rand-vallar lét falla
(ulf-teitir gaf œto opt blóð-vœlom) Skopta.

3.   Hodd-sveigir lézk hníga harða ríkr þá-es barðisk
(log-reifiss bráttu lífi land-mens) 'Kiar sanda.'   10

1.   Stál-œgir nam stíga stafn flet-balkar hrafna
af dyn-sveigi dauðom.—*Dregr land at mun banda*—

4.   Mærr vann miklo fleiri malm-hríð iœfurr síðan
áðr frœgom þat aðra—*Eirikr und sik geira*—
þá es garð-vala gerði Gotlandz vala strandir   15
Virfils vítt um herjat.—*Veðr-mildr ok semr hildi.*

5.   Stœrir let at Stauri stafn-viggs hœfuð liggja,
gramr vælti svá gumna.—*Gunn-blíðr ok réð síðan*—
sleit at sverða móti svœrð víkinga hœrðo
unda-mœr fyr eyri.—*Iarl goð-vörðo hiarli.*   20

11. 6.   . . . .

.   . . . . .—*Dregr land at mun banda*—

7.   Frá-ek hvar fleina-siávar fúr-herðir styr gœrði
endr í Eyrar-sundi.—*Eirekr und sik geira*—
Rauð fúr-giafall fiórar folk-meiðr Dana skeiðar
ver frœgom þat, vága.—*Veðr-mildr ok semr hildi.*   25

8.   Áttuð hialdr þar es hœldar hlunn-viggs í bý runno
gæti-niœrðr við Gauta.—*Gunn-blíðr ok réð síðan*—
Her-skildi fór Hildar (hann þverði frið manna)
áss um 'allar Sýslor.'—*Iarl goð-vörðo hiarli.*

9.   Odd-hríðar fór eyða óx stríð at þat síðan   30
log-fágandi lœgiss land Valdamars brandi :
Aldeigio brauzt œgir (oss numnask skil) gumna
(sú var hildr með hœlðom háðrð) ; komtu austr í Garða.

---

madest thine adversary to bow at K . . . , where thou didst fight, taking
his life.

Stave I. Thou didst stand over his dead body. A second battle, and
many more afterwards, Eric fought, when he harried all Gautland. He
set his ship's prow towards Staur [Staver, south point of Femern], off
the point the ravens devoured the Wickings' carcases.

Stave II. I have heard how he battled in Eyre-sound, taking four
Danish ships. He fought against the Gauts and sacked the town
of . . . , and went with war-shield over all the Adal-sysla [Adal-sysla =
Curland].

End part. He harried Waldemar's land [Russia] with fire ; stormed
Aldega-borough [Ladoga], that was a hard fight : thou camest eastward
into Garda [territory of Novgorod].

---

29. Read, Aðal-sýslo.

§ 3. POEMS OF INCIDENT.

SAILOR POETS.

The Sea-Walls' Song. This account is given in Landnama-bok: "Heriwolf the Younger went out to Greenland (c. 986–990), when Eric the Red was settling the land. On board his ship was a Southern Islander [Hebrides man], a Christian, who made the 'Sea-walls' poem,' in which this burden occurs." These 'hafgerdingar' or 'sea-walls' are noticed in the Speculum Regale (King's Mirror) about 1250, where they are described as great waves of the Arctic Sea, which wall round the whole ocean 'higher than mountains, like steep cliffs.' These huge rollers are coupled with the Northern Lights, as the two wonders of the Arctic Ocean; but we may accept the acute conjecture of Japhetus Steenstrup, of Copenhagen, who believes them to have been the 'earthquake waves,' which have been repeatedly observed and described in modern days (in 1755 for instance). So this poem is the earliest Northern record of subterranean disturbance, and therefore of interest. The eruptions of the beginning of the thirteenth century would arouse fresh interest in the subject, and account for the name and mention in the Norwegian 'King's Mirror.' The poem appears to have been of a votive character. Besides the *burden*, one line, the *beginning*, is also quoted in Landnama, v, ch. 14.

Norðseta-drapa, by Swein. This poem is curious as having been composed by one of the settlers in a fishing-place, Northset, in Greenland, far to the north beyond the Arctic Circle, whence its name, the Norsetman's poem. It is, perhaps, the most northern in locale of all known poems. The few lines that remain describe with some force the icy storms of the North, but the end seems addressed to a lady. The final words 'the river at length winds down to the sea' are prettily expressed. One would like to have more of this sailor poet.

Snæbiorn. We have in Book vi, Ditty 20, set a verse on Snæbiorn, one of the earliest Arctic adventurers of the tenth century, a predecessor of Eric the Red, a seeker for the unknown land, 'Gundbiorn's reef,' a sailor poet. Parts of a poem of his on the Sea are quoted by Snorri. They are of note as containing the only allusion, outside of Saxo, to the Hamlet story, the sea being called 'Amlodi's quern.'

Snæbiorn's life, the nucleus for an interesting Saga, is given in Landnama-bok. He was of a good family, that of Eywind the Easterling; his mother's name was Kialwor. He was fostered by Thorodd at Thingness, and was nicknamed 'Galti.' Hallbiorn married a daughter of one of his kinsmen, Hallgerd, who had the most beautiful hair of any woman in Iceland, and murdered her in a fit of jealousy. Snæbiorn slew the murderer, and then went off on a pioneering expedition; but one of those deadly quarrels, so frequent in the histories of early explorers, broke out between the adventurers, and Snæbiorn was killed.

Orm Barreyiar Skald. Poet of Barra in the Hebrides. At the banquet of Reekholar in 1120, among other entertainments, 'Priest Ingimund told the story of Orm, the Barrey Poet, with many verses, and at the end of the Saga a short poem of his own making. Many wise men therefore hold that it is a true Saga' (Sturl. ii, ch. 10). This Saga is lost. Nothing further is known of Orm. The fragments are cited in Edda.

HAFGERÐINGA-DRÁPA; or, THE SEA-WALLS' SONG
(c. 986–990).
(From Landnama ; verse 1 from Hb.)

Beginning :

1. $\mathbf{A}$LLIR hlýði osso fulli Amra fíalla Dvalins hallar!

Burden :

2. Mínar bið-ek Munka-reyni meina-lausan farar beina: heiðiss haldi hárar foldar hallar Dróttinn yfir mer stalli.

SVEINN: NORÐSETA-DRÁPA (NORSET SONG).
(Verses 1–3 from Edda ; verse 4 from Skalda.)

1. $\mathbf{T}$ÓKO fyrst til fíúka Forniótz synir liótir.

2. Þá-es el-reifar ófo Ægiss dœttr ok tætto ('fats' við frost of alnar fiall-garðz) rokor harðar.

3. . . . . . Hléss dœttr á við bléso.

4. Þar kœmr (lyngs en løngom lind vanði mik strindar leika leyni-síka lævi) á til sævar.

SNÆBIÖRN.
(Verses 1, 2 from Edda ; verse 3 from AM. 738.)

1. $\mathbf{S}$TIÓR-VIÐJAR lætr styðja stáls buðlunga máli hlemmi-sverð við harðri húf-langan sæ dúfo.

2. Hvatt kveða hrœra Grotta her-grimmastan skerja út fyr iarðar skauti Eylúðrs nio brúðir:

The Sea-Walls' Song. Prologue. Let all hearken to the cup . . . of the dwarves' halls [poetry]. *Burden.* I pray the guileless Friend of the Monks [Christ] to forward my voyage. May the Lord of Earth's lofty hall [heaven] hold his hand over me.

Norset Song. First the horrid Sons of Forniot [gales] began to drive the snow : what time the storm-loving Daughters of Eager wove and ripped the cruel foam, nursed by the frost of the mountain-ranges. The daughters of Lear [ocean] blew on the ship. Here comes the river to the sea. [I. e. here my song ends.]

Snæbiorn. He plunges the broad blade of the beak of his long-hulled bark into the hard wave. Men say that the nine Maidens of the Island-Mill, *the ocean,* are working hard at the host-devouring Skerry-quern [the sea] beyond the skirts of the earth : yea, they have for ages past been

þær es (lungs) fyr længo lið-meldr (skipa hlíðar)   5
(baug-skerðir rístr barði ból) Amlóða mólo.

3.   Svá at or fitjar fiætri flóðs 'Ásynjom blóði'
(ræst byrjask ræmm) en systra rýtr Eymylrir snýtir.

ORMR BARREYJAR SKALD.

UTAN gnýrr á eyri Ymiss blóð. Fara góðra!

Hvergi es Draupnis drógar dís (ramman spyr ek vísa)
(sá ræðr valdr fyr veldi vagn-brautar) mer fagnar.

HROMUND AND HIS SONS.

ROMUND the Lame came of a Northern family living at Fagra-
brekka (Fair-brink), in Ramfirth, in the middle of the tenth century.
He is lying in the early dawn awake in his bed, when there comes a
raven on the luffer of the hall, and screams loudly.   Romund breaks
into verse and declares this token to presage death to warriors (v. 1).
His son Thorbiorn Thyna (axe) answers him (v. 2) and Romund replies
(v. 3).   Hardly had he finished, when certain Easterlings, pirates, break
into the court.   The sons of Romund rush out to meet their foes, but
the women try to stay Romund, saying he is too old to fight; he answers
them (v. 3).   Hastan and his brothers win the day, though Romund is slain
and his grandson Thorleif wounded to death, but seven of the twelve
Easterlings were left dead on the field.   The women ask the men what
has happened when they see them coming back to the house, and
Hastan answers (vv. 4–11).   The Easterlings that escaped were wrecked
on Helgi's reef and drowned the same day.   Hastan afterwards went
out to Norway, took service with King Olaf Tryggvason, and died aboard
the Long Serpent, at Swold.   The tale of Romund, germ of a good
Saga, and the poem are found in Landnama-bok.   It is also told in a
diluted form in Flatey-bok.   The story of the wound that Iokul, Ingimund's son, gave him with that famous heirloom, the sword Ættar-tangi,—
whereby he was lamed,—and of his outlawry from Ingimund's settlement,
is told in Vatzdæla Saga.   The whole family are good specimens of the
fierce spirit of the settlers.   Eywind, the father of Romund, on hearing
of his foster-brother Ingimund's death, fell upon his sword, refusing to
outlive his friend.—From Landnama.

There is something antique about the *style* and *metre* of all the lines,
and the first verses are markedly poetic and weird.   It is, though now
maimed like its author, a fine old Wicking Song.

---

grinding at Amlodi's meal-bin, *the sea*.   Let us furrow the waves with
the prow of my ship.

So that the Daughters of the Island-grinder [sea] spirt the blood of
Ymi [brine]; and the Sisters of the Miller of Islands, *sea* . . .   We are
coming into a mighty current.

Orm the Barrey-poet.   The blood of Ymi, *the sea*, is surging out there
on the Tongue.   A happy voyage!

. . . Wherever the lady welcomes me.   I know the king of the realm
of the Wain-path, *Christ*, is mighty.

---

7. Read, Ymis bloði?

Romund:

1.   Ú TI heyri-ek svan sveita sára-þorns es mornar
         (bráð vekr borgin-móða) blá-fiallaðan gialla:
     svá gól .fyrr þá-es feigir folk-nárungar váoro
     Gunnar haukr, es gaukar Gautz bragða spáo sáogðo.

Thorbiorn :

2.   Hlakkar hagli stokkinn (hræs) es kœmr at sævi   5
     (móðr krefr morgin-bráðar) máor val-kastar báoro :
     Svá gól endr þá-es unda eiðs af fornom meiði
     hræva gaukr es haukar hildinga miæð vildo.

Romund :

3.   Vasa mer í dag dauði (draugr flat-vallar bauga)
     (buomk við ilmar ialmi) áðr ne gœrr of ráðinn :   10
     Rœki-ek lítt þó-at leiki lit-vændr Heðins fitjar
     (oss vas áðr of markaðr aldr) við rauða skiæoldo.

Hastein :

4.   Her hafa 'sex' þeir es sævask sút-laust bana úti
     svip-niæorðungar sverða sár-teins á brú-steinom :
     hygg-ek at halfir liggi heptendr laga eptir ;   15
     egg-skeindar lét-ek undir óbíðingom svíða.

5.   Vaskat-ek fyrr með fleiri fetla stígs at vígi,
     fyrir váorom þar fiórir frændr ofstopa vændir :
     enn tolf af glað Gylfa gunn-þings hvatir runnar
     kæold ruðo váopn, þeir-es vildo várs fundar til skynda. 20

6.   Siau hafa sœki-tívar Svolniss garðz til iarðar
     (blóð fell varmt á vera, val-dæogg) næosom hæoggit :
     munat fúr-viðir fleiri Fiolniss þings an hingat
     út um Ekkils brautir Ialks mœrar skæ fœra.

7.   Her mego hœli-bæorvar hlióms dal-tangar skióma   25

Romund. Outside in the morning I hear the croak of the raven [black-skinned swan], he wakes to the prey : so in times of yore, when the Shepherds of the people were death-doomed, the war-hawks were wont to scream before a fray, auguring the Game of Wodin, *battle.*

Thorbiorn. The eagle, dew-sprinkled, screams when he comes to the sea, craving his morning meal : so in the days of yore the eagles were wont to scream out of the ancient tree when they thirsted for the blood of kings.

Romund. It was not to-day nor yesterday that my death-hour was fixed for me. I care not though brands play on red shields, for my life was long ago marked out for me.

Hastan. Seven pirates have met their death out on the causeway, the half of the law-breakers are lying on the field. I made them smart with the wound the edges gave. I was not on the bigger side : there were four of us kinsmen, when twelve wickings from the ship met us in fight. Seven of them have struck the ground with their faces, the dew of the slain is on them ; the greater half of them shall never launch

---

13. Read, siau, cp. v. 6.

dýrs hvat drýgðo fiórir dag-verks siá merki:
enn ek, hyr-brigðir, hugða (hrafn sleit af ná beito)
Gunnar-ræfrs, at gæfim grið-bítom frið lítinn.

8.   Unnom auði-mœnnom (á-ek þunnan hiœr) [Gunnar
drógomk vær at vígi verk] dreyroga serki: 30
hœfðo herði-lofðar Hildar borðz und skildi
(þvarr hangr-vœlom ' hengi' hungr) ' vesæri' tungor.

9.   Harðr vas gnýr þá-es gœrðom griót-varps loto snarpa;
gengo sverðz at sœngvi sundr grá-klæði Þundar:
áðr á hæl til hvílðar (hluto þeir bana fleiri)   35
[hialdrs kom hríð á skiœldo] Hœkings viðir œki.

10.   Heyri svan, þar-es sárir sigr-stallz viðir gialla,
(ben-skori drekkr bœro blóð-fallz) of ná gialla:
þar fekk œrn (enn erni ero greipr hræjom sveipðar)
sylg, es Sleito-Helgi ' segð auðigr' félt rauðo.   40

11.   Bœro upp af ára all-þekkligom blakki
ýtar oss at móti alm-þingsamir hialma:
enn á braut þeir-es bœro beiðendr goðom leiðir
hlíðar herði-meiðar hauðr-mens skarar rauðar.

THORARIN THE BLACK: MÁ-HLIDINGA-VÍSOR.

THERE is in Eyrbyggia (chaps. 15–22), among other episodes of which
that Saga is made up, the story of Thorarin and his famous Feud, without which lucky interpolation we should know nothing about him, except
his name and a line of quotation in Snorri's Hattatal.   His character is
thus drawn in Eyrbyggia: "At that time there were living at Mew-side
Geirrid, the daughter of Thorwolf Shankfoot, and Thorarin the Black,
her son; he was a big, strong man, ugly, and speechless, but usually
good-tempered.   He was known as a peacemaker.   He was not very
rich, though he had a well-stocked farm.   He was so easy to deal with,
that his foes said he had more of a woman's nature than a man's; he
was a married man, and his wife's name was Aud."   A quarrel arose
between Thorarin and Ord Kettleson, and they came to blows in the
yard at Mewside.   Aud rushed out to part them, and the fight was
stayed, when a woman's hand was found on the spot.   It was the hand
of his wife Aud.   When Thorarin knew of this (though the brave

their ship hence for sea.   The marks of the day's task we four have
won are here to be seen, for I know we gave the truce-breakers little
grace.   We gave the rievers bloody shirts, they bore . . . under their
shields.   There was a grim clatter of stone-casting, and the gray sarks
of Woden rove asunder at the song of the sword, ere the Wickings gave
way, the most of them being slain.   Hearken to the eagle screaming
over the carcases; the erne gets his fill of blood, and his talons are foul
with carrion, where the traitorous Quibble-Helgi won a red hood [a
bloody pate].   They bore white helmets up to meet us, but they carry
away ruddy locks, the accursed ones [dyed in their own blood].

---

26. Read, drygðom.   32. Corrupt.   40. Read, sekð-auðigr?

woman, wishing to spare further bloodshed, tried to conceal it), and heard the laughter of his foes, who mocked him as being himself the man that had wounded his own wife, the fighting spirit woke in him, and he rushed out at once and fell upon his enemies, slaying the ring-leader Thorbiorn, and pursuing the rest so that one, Nail, a thrall, went mad with terror and cast himself into the sea.   This victory, while it wiped off all the reproaches of his enemies, drew down deadly hate on Thorarin; but with the help of his mother's brother, one of the heroes of Eyrbyggia Saga, Arnketil, the antagonist of Snorri the chief, whose brother-in-law Thorarin had killed, he wins through it all.   The verses which Thorarin made upon the various incidents of this feud were known as the *Mewsiders' Verses*, and form together a kind of history of it, upon which the prose tale in Eyrbyggia seems to be partly founded.   This piece is in the ancient vein, and not devoid of vigour and poetry in spite of its intricate phrasing.   It forms a 'flokk' addressed to Arnkettle and Wermund.

The text is from Eyrbyggia, edit. 1864, emended and re-arranged in parts; for, like most of the older court-metre poems, these verses have suffered a good deal from corruption, the plain phrases of the original being put out to make way for elaborate and unmeaning circumlocutions here and there throughout; thus, 'fyrir einni' probably stands for 'fyrir Enni,' 'fran Vikinga mána' conceals beneath it 'á fundi hlídinga Máva,' and under the name 'Froda' must be the place 'Frodá,' *Froda-water*, where Thorbiorn lived.

1.   VARÐAK mik, þars myrðir morð-fárs vega þorði,
      (hlaut ørn af ná neyta nýjom) kvenna fryjo:
    barkat-ek vægð at vígi val-naðrs í styr þaðra
    (mæli-ek hól) fyr hœli hialdrs-goðs (af því sialdan).

2.   Myndit vitr í vetri vekjandi mik sekja   5
    (þar ák líf-hvøtuð leyfðan) løg-ráns [of þat vánir]:
    ef ek nið-bræði næðak nás val-fallins Ásar
    (Hugins létom nið nióta ná-grundar) Vermundi.

3.   Skal-ek þrym-viðom þremja (þegi herr meðan !) segja
    [vœn es ísarns Ásom ør-leiks] frá því gœrva: 10
    hve hialdr-viðir héldo haldendr við mik skialdar
    (roðin sá-ek hrundar handar hnig-reyr) løgom (dreyra).

4.   Sóttumk heim þeir-es hætto hiœr-nirðir mer fiœrvi
    (gný-liómi beit geymi geira-stígs) at vígi:
    Svá gœrðo mer (sverða) sókn-'niðiungom' þriðia   15
    (sleitka) líknar (leiki lostigr) fá kosti.

Mewsiders' Verses.   I have cleared myself in the fray from the women's reproach.   I showed no mercy to him, *Thorbiorn*, in the bicker, I seldom boast of it.   My adversary, *Thorbiorn*, would not have wrested the suit against me last winter, if I could have got the help of Wermund the Warrior.

Now I will set it forth clearly to all men.   Give ear the while ! how they held a Leet-court against me, *and how* I saw my lady's hand stained red in gore.   They visited me with armed force, threatening my life;

---

5.   Urðo ver at verja (vas ǫ́r drifin sára)
     [hrafn naut hræva] (gefnor hialdr-skýja) mik frýjo:
     þá es við hialm (á holmi) hrein míns fæður sveini
     þaut andvaka unda (unnar ben-lœkir runno).   20
6.   Knátti hiǫrr und hetti (hræ-flóð) bragar móða
     (rauk um sóknar sœki) slíðr-beitr staðar leita:
     Blóð fell, es vas váði víg-tjalldz nær, skialdi
     (þá vas dœmi-salr dóma dreyra-fullr) um eyro.
7.   Knátto 'hialmi hættar hialdrs' á mínom skialdi   25
     'þrúðar vangs ins þunga þings spá-meyjar' syngva:
     þá-es biúg-rǫðull bóga baugs fyr óðal-draugi
     (giǫll óx vápns á-vǫllom) varð blóð-drifinn Fróða.
8.   Vas til hreggs at hyggja (hrafn-víns) á bœ mínom
     (þurði eldr um aldir) uggligt Munins tuggo: 30
     þa-es á fyrða fundi fran 'víkinga mana'
     lind beit logðis kindar liðo hǫgna vé gœgnom.
9.   Reka þóttomk-ek (Rakna) remmi-skóðs við móða
     (kunn-fáka hné kennir) klám-orð af mer borða:
     hvatki-es (hildar gotna hrafn sleit af ná beito   35
     síks) við sína leiko sælingr of þat mælir.
10. Kveðit man Hroptz at heiþðom hyr-skerðir 'mer' verða
     ('kannak áðr fyr "einni" Yggs teiti svá leita'):
     es hlaut-viðir héto (hlœkiendr, þeir-es skil flœkja,
     eggjomk hófs) at ek hiœggja Hlín guðvefjar mína.   40
11. Ná-gǫglom fekk Nagli nest dáliga flestom;
     kaf-sunno ríð kennir klœkkr í fiall at stœkkva:
     heldr gekk hialmi falldinn (hialdrs) 'at' vápna galdri
     (þurði elldr um aldir) Alfgeirr af hvǫtt meiri.
12. Grátandi rann gætir geira-stigs frá vígi;   45
     (þar vasa grímo geymi góð vǫ́n friðar hǫ́nom):
     svá at mer-skyndir mœndi mein-skiljandi vilja
     (hugði bióðr á bleyði bif-staups) á sió hlaupa.

---

yea, they gave me little hope of mercy. I had to defend myself from
reproach, when the sword whistled about the head of my father's son,
me. The sword struck the poet [me] below the helmet, the blood flew
about the bard's ears; the moot-place was full of gore. The ... rung on
my shield ... Froda was blood-stained. It is dreadful to think of the
fight at my homestead when sword clove shield at Mewside. I cleared
myself of railing accusation, and slew him [Thorbiorn], whatsoever the
lord [Snorri] may say to his sister [the widow of Thorbiorn]. I had to
call on the moon against their cursed reviling, when the wretch, that
wrested the law, said that I had wounded my own wife. Nagli fast
ran whimpering to the hills, and Alfgeir made still greater haste to be
away. Weeping he [Nagli] fled from the fray, so that he was on the
point of leaping into the sea, out of pure cowardice.—I remember, Wer-

---

31. Read, hlíðinga Máva?   37. Read, mána; see vol. i. p. 15, l. 37.   38.
Read, Enni.   43. at] read, af or frá.   48. Or bifr-staups?

13.   Muna muno ver at vórom, Vermundr, glaðir stundom,
       auðar-þollr, áðr ollom auð-varpaðar dauða: 50
       Nú siǿmk hitt at hlǿgi hǿr-gerðr munom verða
       (leitt eromk rauðra randa regn) fyr 'prúðom' þegni.

14.   Héto hirði-niótar hauka-ness til þessa
       (heptandi vas-ek heiptar) hóg-lífan mik drífo:
       opt kœmr (alnar leiptra æfi-fús) or dúsi   55
       (nú kná iǿrð til orða) œði-regn (at fregna).

15.   Skalat ǫl-drukkin ekkja (ek veit at gat beito
       hrafn af hræva-efni) hopp-fǫgr at því skoppa:
       at ek (hiǿr-dǿggvar) hyggja (her es fión komin lióna)
       [haukr unir hǿrðom leiki hræva stríðs] á kvíðo.   60

16.   Láta hitt at hljóta haldendr mynim skialdar
       (sækjom ráð und ríkjan) rómo-samt or dómi:
       nema Arnketill órom, æ-góðr við lof þióðar,
       (vel truik grímo geymi galdrs) sak-mǿlom haldi.

17.   Esat sem grepp fyr glǿpi grund fagr-vita mundar   65
       fúra fleygi-ára frænings lǫgom ræni:
       ef sann-vitendr sunno (sé-ek þeira lið meira)
       [oss megni guð gagni] Gautz þekjo mik sekja.

ORD AND THE SONS OF HEALTI.

It is told in Landnama-bok that Healti came out and 'settled Hof in
Healti's dale [in the N.]. His sons were Thorwald and Thord, noble
men. It was the noblest arval that ever was in Iceland, the arval they
made over their father; there were 1400 guests bidden, and the men of
quality among them were given parting-gifts. At that arval Ord the
Broad-firther delivered a Song of Praise, which he had made upon
Healti. Before this, Glum Geirason [the poet] had summoned Ord to the
Thorskafirth-moot, and now the Sons of Healti set out from the north
in a ship to Steingrim's firths, and thence went southward over the
Heath, by the place now called Healtdale-bait. And when they came
to the Moot, they were so well dressed that men thought that it was
the gods that were come there, whereon this verse was made' [see
verse II, p. 62 below].

<hr>

mund, how often we were merry together, before I slew him; but
now I fear lest I become a laughing-stock to the wise one [Snorri].
Hitherto folks have called me peaceful: a furious rain-storm often comes
out of a sultry sky. The fair-hipped lady [Snorri's sister], merry with ale,
shall not make mock of me, that I ever trembled at what was to come
[that I lacked courage]. Men say that I shall have the verdict dead
against me, unless the ever-kindly Arnkettle, in whom I put all my trust,
upholds my cause bravely. It will not be for crime of mine, if they outlaw me. They have the bigger party. May the gods strengthen my
cause.

<hr>

51. hlǿgi] emend.; hlauia and hlaupa, Cdd.   52. Read, fróðom (i. e. Snorri).
58. Read, skaupa?

Of this Ord's poem (*Hialta-drapa*) nought is left; but in Eyrbyggia there is a fragment of a Praise-Song, on Illugi the Black (the father of Gunlaug the poet), touching certain law dealings of his, ascribed to Ord the poet. We take this to be our Ord of Broadfirth.

Of the Healtissons, 'from whom there came,' as Landnama-bok says, 'a great and noble race,' we have no particulars, save in the Tale of Styrbiorn the Champion of the Swedes. In Flatey-bok we have, in an account of the Battle of Fyrisfield, the following notice :—'King Eric [the Victorious] was standing on Upsala brink, and he bade him that could, to make a verse, promising a guerdon for it. Thorwald Healtisson made these verses [given below, verse III]. Thorwald got for his guerdon a ring of half a mark for every verse, and he never made a verse before or since that any one knows of.' This is confirmed by Skalda-tal, which names Thorwald as a poet of the Swedish king, Eric the Victorious.

OGMUNDAR-DRAPA, by GUEST THE WISE and SIBYL-STEIN. It is told in Landnama-bok that Guest Ordlafsson, whom we know from Laxdæla Saga, 'was bidden to a harvest feast at Leot's, and thither came Egil, Sibyl-Stein's son, and prayed Guest to take some counsel, whereby his father might be comforted in his deadly grief that he was in for Ogmund his son. Guest thereupon made the beginning of Ogmund's Praise.'

We have in Edda the beginning of this Ogmundar-drapa, but ascribed to Sibyl-Stein himself, and it may be that Ari means to imply that Guest began the poem for Stein to finish. There are two distinct echoes of Egil's in the four lines left us, 'Mims vinar' and 'Thundar fundr,' which would confirm the chronology of the incident, a half-dozen years later than *Sona-torrek* (Book iv). This Sibyl-Stein was the son of Thurid Sound-filler, a Sibyl, who came, as Landnama-bok further informs us, from Haloga-land to Bolungwick, in Waterness, in Iceland. 'She was called Sound-filler, because in Haloga-land, during a famine, she worked her charms so that every sound was filled with fish. She also made Fold-bank in Icefirth-deeps, and got thereby a humble-ewe *as fee* from every franklin in Icefirth.'

STEINTHOR. The beginning of a Song of Praise, ascribed by Snorri to Steinthor, of whom nothing else is known, but the scrap has the true early ring about it. The second fragment, though anonymous, is clearly part of the same poem.

UNNAMED POET. BARRODAR-DRAPA. One verse is left of a Praise of Barrod [Barfred], who is mentioned in Wiga-Glum's Saga.

ORD.   I. *Illuga-drápa* (from Eyrbyggja).

1. VESTR vas þrøng á þingi Þórsness með hug stórom
     hæppom studdr þar-es hodda hialm-raddar stafr kvaddi:
snar-ráðan kom síðan (sætt vasa gœr með létta)
Forna sióðs und fœði farmr dolg-svœlo barma.
2.   Drótt gekk sýnt á sættir, svellendr en þar felĺo   5

Ord. Illugi's Praise. There was a throng in the west on Thorsness Moot, when the lucky Illugi claimed the hoard: it was not easy to come to a decision: and at last it came to pass that the verdict gave him the purse of Forni. The people clearly broke the agreement: three men

þremja svellr fyr þolli þrír andvaðko randa :
áðr kyn-framaðr kœmi kvánar hreggs við-seggi
(frægt gœrðisk þat fyrða forráð) griðom Snorri.

II. *On Healti's Sons.*

Mangi hugði manna morð-kannaðar annat
ísarn-meiðr an Æsir al-mærir þar fœri :   10
þá-es á Þorska-fiarðar-þing með enni-tinglom
holt-vartariss Hialta harð-fengs synir gengo.

III. *Thorvald Healtason.*

Fari til Fyris-vallar folka tungls hverr es hungrar
verðr at virkis garði vestr kveld-riðo hesta :
þar hefir hræ-dœggvar hœggit (hóllaust es þat) sólar ⸗ 15
elfar gims fyrir ulfa Eirekr í dyn geira.

VÖLO STEINN. *Ogmundar-drápa* (from Edda).

Heyr Míms vinar mína (mer es fundr gefinn Þundar)
við góma-sker glymja, Glaumbergs Egill! strauma.
Man-ek þat es iœrð við orða endr Myrk-Danar sendo
grœnnar grœfnom munni gein Hlóðynjar beina.

STEINÞÓRR (from Edda).

Forn-gœrvom á-ek fyrnom farms Gunnlaðar arma
horna fors at hrósa hlít-styggs ok þó lítlom :
Bæði á ek til brúðar berg-iarls ok skip Dverga
sollinn vind at senda sein-fyrnd gœto eina.

BÁRRŒDAR-DRÁPA (from Landnama-bók).

Bárrœðr of rístr bœro braut land varar andra.

---

fell before him, ere that Snorri, the glory of his family, brought about
a peace between them. This management of Snorri's became very
famous among men.

The improvisation on the grand array of Healt's sons. No one doubted
that the all-glorious Anses were coming in person, when the sons of
Healti, in helm of awe, marched on the moot of Thorskafirth.

Thorwald Healtisson. On the battle of Fyris-field, where he fought.
Let every charger of the ogress [wolf] that hungers go to Fyris-field.
There (it is no vaunt) Eric has cut down in battle quarry enough for
every one of them.

Sibyl-Stein. Ogmund's Praise. Prologue. Listen, O Egil of Glamberg,
to the river of Woden singing against the reefs of my gums. Woden's
Find [the gift of poesy] is granted to me. I remember that . . . rocks.

Stanthor. I boast of Woden's horn-rapid [mead of Poesy]; old brewed
it is, but there is little of it. By the same path I have to send the swollen
gale of the Giantess [thought] and the everlasting ships of the Dwarves
[verses].

Barrod's Praise. Barrod is cutting the path of the billow's-land with
his sea-sledge.

§ 4. IMPROVISATIONS.

CORMAC AND BERSI'S STRAY VERSES.

THE Stray Verses (Lausa-vísor) of Cormac are given here. What we know of his regular compositions and of his life is said above in § 2. They rest upon a Saga only, for not one of them is cited by Snorri though there are so many of them, while the Sigrodar-drapa is quoted several times; nay even, strange to say, Olaf gives one line, v. 42, which is *not* found in the Saga. At first sight there are several suspicious points in them; for instance, the repeated use of the word 'borda,' embroider, a modern kind of sentiment, many 'half-kennings,' and the too perfect metre. But one is loath to give them up; there is an extravagant but passionate force about some of them, especially those addressed to Steingerd, which makes one accept *them* as genuine at any rate. And on closer examination one sees that there are evident marks of 'over-working' and 'repainting' about the greater number of them. Even well-known verses like 8 have suffered, for under 'handan' must stand some synonym for Norwegian, 'Heina' or 'Horda,' and surely under 'svinna' lies 'Svia,' for otherwise 'ok' has no raison d'être in the verse. We can see here and there that Cormac's lines must have been like Thiodwolf's or Bragi's rather than Sighwat's, and that these irregular lines have often been remodelled.

Those verses which are absolutely corrupt or meaningless have not been printed here; but the rest are given, with such translation as seemed most tenable. Were they perfect, they would probably be the finest of all Northern classic love-poetry.

BERSI the Duellist, the scarred old veteran, whose coolness and trained courage is contrasted with the violence and rage of the young Cormac, is a good specimen of the heroic age, and no mean poet. There is a simple straightforward force in his verses which makes them tell, and heightens one's interest in their author. There must have been a separate Saga on him, but we only know him from that part of it which is wedged into Cormac's Saga and from a few scattered notices elsewhere. The way he got protection from Olaf the Peacock when he was harassed by his enemies in his old age, and the verse he made on himself and his baby foster-son, will be found in the Reader; the ditty we have given in Book vi, no. 25.

Several of Bersi's verses deal with his life of combat, some are laments over his declining strength and the loss of friends, and recall Egil's feelings in like case, though they are not so thoughtful or pathetic. The Editor has only given those which bear most marks of authenticity (for many have been tampered with, some may even be forged); these have a rougher and more unsophisticated appearance than Cormac's. Edda and Skalda cite three lines of Bersi (5, 6, 15). A new edition of Cormac's Saga in which all these verses are found would be welcome.

1. NÚ varð mer í míno, men-reið, iœtuns leiði
      réttomk risti snótar ramma œst fyrir skœmmo:

The first sight of Steingerd. I saw the lady's feet just now, mighty

þeir muno fœtr at foári fall-gerðar mer verða
(allz ekki veit-ek ella) optarr an nú svarra.

2. Brunno beggja kinna biœrt liós á mik drósar 5
(oss hlœgir þat eigi) eld-húss of við felldan :
enn til œkla svanna ítr-vaxins gat-ek líta
(þrœ monat oss um ævi eldask) hiá þreskeldi.

3. Brá-máni skein brúna brims und liósom himni
hristar hœrvi glœstrar hauk-fránn á mik lauka : 10
enn sá geisli sýslir síðan goll-hrings Fríðar
hvarma tungls ok hringa Hlínar óþurft mína.

4. Hófat lind (né ek leynda) liðs hyrjar (því stríði)
[bandz man-ek beiða Rindi] baug-sœm af mer augo :
þá-es húm knarrar hiarra happ þægi-bil krappra 15
helsis sœm á halsi Hagborðz á mik storði.

5. Eitt lýti kvezk ' íta eld bekks' á mer þykkja
eir um aptan-skæror all-hvít, ok þó lítið :
hauk-mœrar kvað hári Hlín vel-borin míno
(þat skylda-ek kyn kvinna kenna) sveip í enni. 20

6. Svœrt augo ber-ek Sága snyrti-grund til fundar
þykkir erma Ilmi all-fœlr ' er la sœlva :'
þó hefi-ek mer hiá meyjom men-grund komit stundom
hrings við Hœrn at manga hagr sem drengr in fegri.

7. Öl-Sœgo met-ek auga annat beðjar Nœnno, 25
þat es í lióso líki liggr, hundraða þriggja :
þann met-ek hadd es (hodda) hœr beiði-Sif greiðir
(dýr verðr fægi-Freyja) fimm hundraða snimma.

8. Allz met-ek auðar-þello Islandz, þá-es mer grandar,
Húna-landz ok ' handan' hug-sterkr sem Danmarkar : 30

---

love is roused within me; those ancles of hers will some day be a
stumbling-block to me; though when, I know not. The bright beams
of both of her cheeks shone on me from behind the plank [shutter], it
bodes no good to me; I saw the feet of the fair-formed damsel on the
threshold, I shall never lack pain therefore as long as I live. The
keen stars of her brows shone on me from the heaven of her face; this
beam from her eyes will hereafter work my woe. The ring-dight one
never raised her eyes from me, nor do I hide my pain : what time the
maid of the house looked on me in the dusk from behind Hagbard's
neck [the pillar carved caryatid-wise]. Fair in the even-gloom, she said
that I had but one blemish in me, and that a small one : she declared
that there was a curl in the hair on my forehead. Black are my eyes
and very pale she thinks me. Yet I have won favour with ladies, for I
am as skilled to please them as any fairer man.

Her worth. One eye of hers, that lies in her fair face, I value at three
hundreds. The locks she is combing (she is a costly thing) I value at
five hundreds. The whole body of her that makes my misery I value
at Iceland, Hunland, the land of the Hords [Norway], and Denmark.

---

15. hún, Cd.   20. *Or* sveipt, Cd.   24. fagri, Cd.   30. Read,
Horða.

verð-ek Engla iarðar Eir há-þyrnis geira,
sól-gunni met-ek Svia sundz ok Íra grundar.

9.   'Heitast' hellor flióta hvatt sem korn á vatni
(enn em-ek auð-spæng ungri óþekkr) enn biæð sœkkva,
fœrask fiæll in stóro 'fræg' í diúpan ægi: 35
áðr iafn-fægr 'tróða' alin verði Steingerði.

10.   Létt-fœran skaltú láta (lióstu vendi mar Tosti)
'móðr of' miklar heiðar mínn hest und þer renna:
makara es mer at mæla, an mórauða sauði
of afrétto elta, orð mart við Steingerði.   40

11.   Braut hvarf or sal sæta (sunnz eromk hugr á gunni)
[hvat merkir nú] (herkis) hæll þverligar alla:
rennda-ek allt ið iðra Eiri gollz at þeiri
(hlíns erom hærn at finna) hús brá-geislom (fúsir).

12.   Sitja sverð ok hvetja sín andskotar mínir   45
eins karls synir inni, eroð þeir banar mínir:
enn ef á víðom velli vega tveir at mer einom
þá-es sem ær at ulfi óvægnom fiær sœki.

13.   Sitja menn ok meina mer eina Gnæ steina,
þeir hafa víl at vinna es mer varða Gnæ borða: 50
því meira skal-ek þeiri es þeir ala stœri
æfund um okkrar gængor unna sœrva Gunni.

14.   Sitja menn ok meina mer eina Gnæ steina,
þeir hafa 'lægðis loddo' linna fœtr at vinna:
þvi-at upp skolo allar æl-stafns áðr ek þer hafna   55
lýsi-grund í landi linnz þióð-ár renna.

I value her at England, Sweden, and Ireland too. The slates shall
float as light as corn on the water, and the earth shall sink, the huge
mountains shall drop into the deep sea ere a lady so fair as Steingerd
shall be born. Yet she loves me not!

To his friend. O Tostig, strike thy steed, and let the swift horse
speed panting across the wide heaths. I had sooner hold long parley
with Steingerd, than chase black sheep over the pasture.

On Steingerd. My lady is clean vanished out of the hall; eager to find
her I have scoured the whole house with the glances of my eyes.

His constancy. My enemies, the sons of one man, sit within and whet
their swords, but should they come against me in open field, it would be,
as it were, ewe sheep seeking the life of a fierce wolf. They sit on the
watch and forbid me her company, they have a hard task to win, for
the more they nurse envy of our meetings, the more shall I love her.
They sit on the watch and forbid me her company: they might as
well fit legs to a snake! Every river in the land shall run backward ere
I forsake thee.

---

32. Emend.; svína, Cd.   38. Read, móðan?   43. eirar, Cd.
44. Read, Hlín . . . horns?   48. ouiæknom, 162; oræknom, Cd.   51.
stœri] meira, Cd.   52. varar, Cd.; . . . solva, Cd.

Kormak :

15. Hvern mundir þú 'grundar' Hlín skap-frœmuð líno,
'líkn sýnir mer lúka,' liós þer at ver kiósa?

Steingerð :

Brœðr munda-ek 'blindom' baug-lestir mik festa,
yrði goð sem gœrðisk góð mer ok skœp, Fróða.   60

16. Brott hefir Bersi setta (beiðisk hann áreiða
val-kiósandi at víso víns) heit-kono mína :
þá-es unni mer manna (mist hef-ek flióðs ins tvista)
[þá kysta-ek mey mióva] mest [dag-lengis flestan].

17. At em-ek Yggjar gauta ullr at Svœlnis fulli   65
um reiði-sif ríóða runnr sem vífl at brunni : . . .

18. Dýrt verðr dœggvar kerti Draupnis mart at kaupa,
þrimr aurom skal þetta Þórveigar skip leiga : . . .

19. Þú telr liós of logna lín-gefn við þik stefno ;
enn ek gœrða miœk móðan mínn fák um sœk þína :   70
heldr vildag hœlfo, hring-eir, at mar spryngi
(sparða-ek ió þannz œttom all-lítt) an 'þik grafna.'

20. Máka-ek hitt of hyggja, hve þú skyldir verða
goll-hlaðz geymi-þella gefin Tin-dráttar manni :
traulla má-ek of tœja tanna silki-nanna   75
sízt þik fastnaði frægja faðir þínn blota-manni.

21. Þarftattu hvít at hœta Hlín skrautligrar líno
(ver kunnom skil skepja) Skíðunga mer níði :
nadd-hríðar skal-ek níða niót 'sva-at steinar flióti ;'
nú hefi ek íllan enda Eysteins sonom leystan.   80

22. Skaka verðo vit, Skarði (skald á búð til kalda),

To his love. Whom wouldst thou choose for a husband, fair lady ?
Her answer. Were the gods and the Fates duly propitious I would
wed the *black-eyed* lad, the brother of Frodi (Cormac).
Loss of her. Bersi has taken away my betrothed, she that loved me
best. I have lost the maid I kissed many a long day.
I am like a bucking-bat at the brook, I . . . my song.
I must pay dearly for much. I am forced to take Thorweig's ship
and pay three ounces for my berth.
To Steingerd. Thou sayest, lady, I have broken my tryst with thee ;
the truth is, I have foundered my steed for thy sake. I would far rather
my steed should fall dead than miss thee. I have not spared my horse.
On her wedding. I cannot think of it, how thou, lady, couldst be
given to a tin-drawer ! I can hardly smile since thy father gave thee
to a loon. Thou needst not threaten me with the Skidung's libels (I
know the poet's craft), I will lampoon them so that . . . I have made
an ill knot for Eystein's sons to loosen.

---

59. Emend. ; braðr, Cd.   72. Read, an ek þer hafna ?   75. tẹia, Cd.
81. verð ek við, Cd.

[fiǫll ero fiarðar 'kelli' faldin] hrím af tialdi:
vilda-ek 'at ræðar' valdi væri engo hæra,
hann es 'latr fra' lióssi lín beðjar gná sinni.

23.   Uggi-ek lítt þó leggi land vǫrðr saman randir   85
. 'varat' virðar stœri vell-auðigr mer dauða:
meðan sker-iarðar, Skarði, skorð man-ek fyr norðan
(hvǫss of angrar sú, sessi, sótt) Þorketils dóttor.

24.   Skiótt munom, Skarði, 'hernir,' skolom tveir banar þeira,
allz andskotom 'hrinda hiǫr-drífr' nio fiǫrvi: 90
meðan goðleiðom gáða grunnleit, sú-es mer unni,
gengr at glœstom bingi goll seim-niorunn beima.

25.   Brim gnýr bratta hamra blálandz Haka strandar,
'allt gialfr' eyja þialfa 'út líðr í stað víðiss:'
mer kveð-ek heldr of hildi hrann-bliks an þer miklo   95
svefn-fátt, sǫrva gefnar sakna mon-ek es ek vakna.

26.   Esa mer sem Tinteini (trauðr es vásfara kauði)
['skiarrer' hann við þys þenna] þriótr myk-sleða brióti:
þá es al-sniallir allir odd-regns stafar fregni
í Sólunda-sundi sund-faxa rá bundinn.   100

27.   Veit hinn es tin tannar, trauðr sæfara inn blauði,
(stǫndomk Ilmr fyr yndi) ógǫrva þat sǫrva:
hvar eld-faldin alda opt gengr of skǫr drengjom,
hann á vífs at vitja varma búð á armi.

28.   Svǫfom hress í húsi horn-þeyjar við Freyja,   105
fiarðar-leygs ins frægja fimm nætr saman grimmar:
ok hyr-ketils hverja hrafns ævi gnoð stafna
lags á lítt of hugsi lá-ek andvana banda.

29.   Svá ber mer í mína men-gefn of þat svefna,

On a voyage, to his brother Skardi. We two have to shake, Skardi, the
frost off the awning. The poet has a cold berth, the firths are hooded
with ice. I would he were no better off that is slinking to his lady's bed.

I care little though they threaten me with death, Skardi, as long as I
think on the daughter of Thorkettle in the north (that is the sickness
that ails me). We shall be hard put to it, Skardi; we two must be
fighting nine men, while the fair lady that loves me is going to the
bed of the god-accursed loon, *Tintein.*

The surf is dashing on the steep cliffs, the brine [lit. the trench of
the islands] is stirred . . . I sleep less than the . . . and miss her
when I wake.

The yard springs in a gale. It is not as if a slave broke the pole of
Tintein's dung-sled, when our sail-yard snaps in Solund-sound. The
vile Tin-gnawer little knows how the fire-tipped wave breaks over
the men's heads, where he, the wretch, lies warm in his wife's arms.

To Steingerd. We two slept five cruel nights together . . . I lay . . .
It comes before me in my dream, lady, unless I am much mistaken,
that your arms, fair one, shall at last be clasped about my neck.

---

82. af] á, Cd.   84. Read, latrar at?   88. hvess, Cd.   93. brattir
hamrar, Cd.   96. samna, Cd.   es] ef, Cd.   101. Read, veitat.
104. baud, Cd.   Read, inn armi?   109. svá] sv, Cd.

nema fági dul driúga drengr ofraðar lengi :   110
at axl-limar yðrar auð-Frigg mani liggja
hrund á heiðis landi hlíðar mer um síðir.

30.   'Digla bauð-ek við dregla dagtála því mali'
'mer vasa dagr sa es dugði dríf-gagl af því vífi'
enn blíð-huguð bæði 'bauð gyls' 'maran' (auðar   115
mítt víllat fé fylla) fingr-goll gefit trollom.

31.   Vilda-ek hitt at væri vald-eir gæmul ialda
stœri-lát í stóði Steingerðr, enn ek reini :
væra-ek 'þráða þrúði þeiri stæðvar geira'
gunn-æorðigra garða gaup-ellz á bak hlaupinn.   120

32.   Seinn þykki mer sœkkvi snyrti-niótz or Fliótom
sá-es· átt-grennir unnar orð sendi mer norðan :
hring-snyrtir þarf hiarta 'hafærr' í sik fœra
þó es 'men gunnar' manni merar vant or leiri.

33.   Ek verð opt þviat þikkjom æorróttr af mer þerra   125
(gollz hlítk af þer þella þraut) á mæottuls skauti :
því láttu í set snauta saur-reiði bragar greiði
(mér hefir steypt í stúro Steingerðr) bana verðan.

34.   Hefik á holm um gengit hald-eir um þik fæoldo
(hvat megi okkrom æostom) annat sinn (of renna?) :   130
ok víg-sakar vakðar Vár hefk um þik bæoro
(því skal mer an Tin-teini) tvær (unnasta in næri).

35.   Hins mun hæor-gefn spyrja, es ið heim komit báðir
'með blót-roðin beiði ben-hlunnz' sú-es mer unni :
hvar es nú baugr enn brendi ; bæol olítið hefir   135
hann nú sveinn inn svarti, sonr Ögmundar skaldit.

36.   Baugi varð-ek at bœta brún-leggs hvaðran tveggia
'guldot fe fyrir biartrar' hals-fang 'myils spangar'

I offered the lady gold as a recompense ; but the merry lady would
not take my gift, and wished my ring were given to the Trolls, *fiends*.

I would the proud Steingerd were an old mare, and I a stallion, I
should soon be on her back.

At his wager of battle for Steingerd with Tintein. He of Fleet, that sent
me word out of the north, is slow of coming : the huge Mud-man has a
mare's heart in his breast. (See p. 12.)

I have often to wipe my face in the skirt of my mantle ... Steingerd
has put me in sore stead. I have fought a second wager of battle for
her sake. After two deadly combats for her sake she should be nearer
me than Tintein.

He sells a sacrificial bull for a ring of Steingerd's. The lady will ask
when we both come back with the sacrificial bull, Where is now the
ring of pure gold ? What has he done with it, the swarthy lad, the
son of Ogmund the poet ?

He pays for kissing Steingerd. I had to pay a fine for both of my kisses;
there never were costlier kisses. I have lost by my love.

---

119. þeiri er, Cd.   121. sœkkva, Cd.   124. merar] emend.; meira, Cd.

gǽtoð 'giallar mæta gollz laufgoðom þolli'
(tál hefik teiti-mála) tveir kossar fé-meiri.   140

37.   Víso mon-ek of vinna áðr ver til skips gangim,
senda sǫrva Rindi til Svínadals mína :
koma skolo ǫll til eyrna orð mín Skǫgul borða,
betr ann-ek silki-Sǽgo an siǫlfom mer hǿlfo.

38.   Fekk sa-es fǫgro vífi fór nær an ver stórom   145
hœgg af hialmar skíði í hattar-stall miðjan :
Eysteins hratar arfi á Elliða stafni ;
styrðu ekki á mik, Steingerðr, þótt þú steigorliga látir.

39.   Drengr ungr stal mik dalki þa-es drakk á mey rakka,
við skolom dalkinn deila sem drengir tveir ungir :   150
vel hefir Vigr of skepta, varð-ek í gríót at skióta,
víst es at mannzins misstag, mosinn varð upp at losna.

40.   Runno randar linna rógendr at mer gnógir,
þa-es ver of fen fórom flokkom, díkis bokkar :
Gautz mondi þá gáttar gunn-svellz ef ek þar féllag   155
lundr kom-ek lítlo sprundi lǫngom munar ǫngom.

41.   Þvi at mál-vino minnar mildr Þorketill vildi.
42.   Vasa sem flióð í faðmi þá es fangremi 'mǿtask'
við streng-mara stýri Steingerði mer hefðak :
myndag ǫl at Óðins iǫndugi drekka   160
(skiótt segig til þess skǿtnom) ef mer Skrymir lið veittið.

43.   Vasa með mer í morgin maðr þinn konan svinna
roðinn vas hiǫr til hodda hand-fǫgr á Irlandi :
þá es slíðr-dregin Sága sǫng um mínom vanga
Hlakkar trafr, enn hrafni heitr fell á nef sveiti.   165

Again on a journey. I will make a verse ere I go aboard, and send it to
my lady in Swinedale. All my words shall reach her ears! I love her
twice as much as myself.

_Cormac strikes Tintein with the tiller, upon which Steingerd grasps the
rudder._ He, that goes nearer to the fair wife than I may, got a stroke
in the middle of his pate ; see how Eystein's son, _Tintein_, staggers in the
bows of his bark. Do not steer athwart me, Steingerd, though thou
bearest thyself so proudly.

His brooch is stolen. The young fellow stole my brooch while I was
drinking with my love. My spear, Wig, was ... I shot into the rock ...

As he wades, eels wind round his legs. The eels swarm at me ...

Of Steingerd. Because the goodly Thorketill _father of_ my love ...

Of his last battle. It was not as if I had my lady Steingerd in my
arms, when I grappled with the champion, the sea-steed's steerer.
I should have been drinking ale in the high seat at Woden's, if Skrymi,
the sword, had not lent his aid. It was not like playing with a fair-
handed lady this morning when we fought in Ireland, when the sheath-
drawn blade whistled about my cheeks and the hot blood fell on the

156. muns or, Cd.   158. Read, mǿttag.

44.   . . . .
Forðomk vætr, þviat verða víg-naðrs stafar aðrir
(snertomk hiœrr við hiarta) helnauð 'ok,' kœr dauða.

HOLMGONGO-BERSI.

1.   HVERR es biarnar barði á bekk kominn rekka?
    ulf hafa 'órir niðjar' œgiligr und bœgi:
glíkan hefir of gœrvan, Glúmr es nefndr eða Skúma,
'fœrom til mótz at morni' mann Steinari þenna.

2.   Þótta-ek þá-es œri (ár-sagt es þat) várom   5
hœfr í Hlakkar drífo hyr-runnom vel Gunnar:
nú vilja mik mínir (minz dyljom þess) hylja,
[þat hefik sótt] í sléttom Saurbœ frændr auri.

3.   Mer hafa frændr at fundi (fersk ván gleði) þessom
[rœði-ek heldr fyr hœlðom hugat mál] í því brugðisk: 10
Torogætir ro (teitan tók hrafn á ná iafnan)
[ek-em við ógnar-rekka óhryggr] vinir tryggvir.

4.   Mer helzt yggr und eggjar all-sterkr 'gois' vallar
(nauðr hagar nú til frœða) naðrs, enn hlífðir œðrom:
svá fara rœð; enn reiðask róg-linnz 'sumir' minna;   15
nú læt-ek þar þrióti, Þórrœðr, vinon óra.

5.   Nú hefik, enn tel tanna Tann-gnióst vegit manna
(þau beri menn frá morði mín orð) tigar fiorða:
koma manat Ullr þótt elli optar mara þopto
(litak blóði svan sveita), setrs í heim at betra.   20

6.   Ben-gióði hio-ek bráðir blá-fiðroðom skára
(kendr vas-ek miœk við manna morð) halfan tog fiorða.
Troll hafi líf, ef laufa litag aldregi bitran;

---

raven's beak ... We cannot escape death. The sword stands in my heart; other men suffer the pains of death and a wasting agony.

Bersi on a guest. Who is this grim bear-cloak come into men's benches? He bears a wolf under his arms, *a savage fellow.* He looks like Stanhere, though he calls himself Glum or Scum.

Faithless friends. When I was young I was thought fit for the fray (that is an old tale), but now my kinsmen think to hide me away in the earth, here in Sourby. This is what I have come to. My kinsmen have failed me at this tryst; all my hope of joy is gone; I speak it from my heart. Faithful friends are hard to find ... Thou heldest me under the sword-edge while thou didst shelter my enemy. This is my sad tale. So things turn. Now I proclaim, Thorrod, the end of our friendship.

His feats. I have slain this Tusk-gnasher, first of the fourth ten [he is the thirty-first I have slain]. Let men bear my words in mind ... I have cut down thirty-five men as quarry for the black-feathered raven.

---

167. hiörr] havfuð, Cd.   8. sléttan, Cd.   13. helt, Cd.   15. Read, stafar?   16. Read, vinom órom?   21. ben-giða . . . skrara, Cd.

beri þá brynjo-meiðar briót í haug sem skiótast.

7.   Veit-ek at Vali beitir veg-stórr tꜹðor órar   25
oss vill heldr enn hvassi hialm-niótr troða und fótom:
opt hefig ýfsk þá es heiptir unn-sólar galt-ek runnom
rauð-ek á brynjo beiði benja linn of minna.
8.   Kominn es Ullr við elli ꜹlna-griótz at fótom;
mart verðr gæti-gautom geir-fitjar nú sitja: 30
þótt 'skiald-viðir' skaldi skapi aldr í græf kaldan,
(fyrr 'rýð'-ek hialms á holmi hríð-vænd) 'en ek því kvíða.'

EGIL'S IMPROVISATIONS.

BESIDES the three great poems in old metre in Book iv, the Ditty
No. 26 in Book vi, and the stray staves in Torf-Einar metre in Book vi,
§ 2, Nos. 3-6, the whole Saga of Egil is studded with verses in court-
metre, which would naturally find their place here. But a close examination of these scattered verses leaves one with the firm conviction that most
of them are *spurious*. That Egil made verses in an early form of court-
metre is, we think, proved from the quotations by Snorri and Olaf; but
if we look at the proportion their quotations from Egil's old-metre
poems bear to the whole poems, viz., about one-twelfth (some thirty lines
out of four hundred), and find that, in spite of their fondness for court-
metre, they only cite five lines as Egil's in that metre, it will be at all
events fair to suppose that they did not know more than ten or twelve
stanzas in all—say fifty lines.

We can identify but a few of these, and as for the others (some
fifty stanzas), we can only keep or reject them on grounds of internal
evidence. A certain number bear the marks of thirteenth-century verse,
and may, we believe, be credited to Lawman Sturla, who would naturally
take an interest in Egil, and whose hand (or Snorri's) we trace in editing
his Saga. They are not entirely valueless, for they contain echoes and
imitations from Egil's undoubted compositions, such as Arinbiorn's Praise
(e. g. Eromka leitt, and Svart-brúnum lét siónum . . .). Among the most
striking proofs of the *impossibility* of these verses being genuine, is the
weary *sameness* in which Kweldwolf, Skalla-Grim, and Egil are made to
improvise; and the palpable fact that the staves on Brunan-burh battle are
not the foundation for the prose, but, on the contrary, founded upon it.

Guided by these considerations we have picked out all those we have
any grounds to suppose genuine; they are but few and in a mangled state,
though one would not pledge oneself to the authenticity of even all these.
Edda and Skalda cite ll. 6, 25, 28–29. (45 *not* in the Saga.)

I have got me a name for man-slaying. May the fiends take me when
I am no longer able to wield my sword! Let men bear me into
my barrow then, the sooner the better.

Wali has been grazing his flocks in my land, he tries to tread me
beneath his feet. I have often bristled up for less reason and reddened
my sword. I am crippled by old age, and must sit under much ill-usage
from others now. I care not though the Fates have decreed me a cold
grave. Once I could dye the sword in battle . . .

---

31. Read, skuldir.   32. Read, rauð.

1. RISTOM rún á horni, rióðom spiæll í dreyra
   'þau vel-ek orð til eyrna óðs dýrs viðar róta'
   drekkom veig sem viljom vel-glýjaðra þýja
   vitom hve oss of eiri æl þatz Bárrœðr signdi.

2. Knǽtto hvarms af harmi hnúp-gnípor mer drúpa   5
   nú fann-ek þann-es ennis ósléttor þær rétti:
   gramr hefir gerði-hæmrom grundar upp um hrundit
   'sa er ygr' af augom ár-síma mer grímor.

3. Okunni vensk ennis ungr þorðag vel forðom
   hauka-hlifs at 'heyra' Hlín þver-gnípor mínar: 10
   verð-ek í feld þá es foldar faldr kœmr í hug skaldi
   Berg-Oneris brúna brátt mið-stalli at hvatta.

4. Svá skyldi goð gialda (gram reki bænd af lændom)
   [reiðr sé Rægn ok Óðinn] rán míns fiár hǽnom!
   folk-mýgi lát flýja, Freyr ok Niærðr, af iærðo!   15
   leiðisk lofða stríði Land-áss þann-es vé grandar.

5. Veiztu ef ek ferr með fióra, fœra-þu sex þá-es víxli
   hlífa 'hveiti-krupom' hialdr-goðs við mik roðnom:
   enn ef ek em með átta, eroð þeir tolf es skelfi
   at sam-togi sverða svart-brúnom mer hiarta.   20

6. Þel hœggr stórt fyrir stáli stafn-kvígs á veg iafnan
   út með éla meitli and-ærr iætunn vandar:

Let us cut the runes on the horn, let us paint the characters red with blood. These signs I choose for the root of the tree of the fierce beast's ear [the horn]. Let us drink as we will the draught the merry slave-girls serve. Let us see whether the cup that Barrod blessed will harm us.

His sorrows ended by King Æthelstan's kindness. The crags of my brows were drooping for sorrow, but now I have found him that was able to smooth the frowns of my face. The king . . . has thrown open the jutting rock-wall that covered my eyes.

His love-pain. I have become unsociable. When I was young I dared to carry the steep of my brow high, but now, when the lady's name comes into my mind, I hasten forthwith to hide the high place of my forehead under my cloak.

His curse on Eric Blood-axe. May the gods requite thee for the robbery of my goods! May the Powers drive thee from the land! May the Holy Ones and Woden be wroth with thee! O Frey and Niorth, let the oppressor of the people fly from the country! May the god of the land [Thor] loathe the tyrant who defiles the sanctuaries!

His prowess. If I have four men with me, there will not be found six men that will dare to redden swords with us. If I have eight men with me, there are not twelve alive who can make the heart of the swarthy-browed one [myself] tremble.

Of the wind at sea. The sturdy giant of the forest, *the wind*, cuts a deep

---

4. Barðr of, Cd.   5. harms, Cdd.   10. Read, hefja? heyrna?

enn sval-buinn seljo sverfr eirar vanr þeiri
'Gestils alfraðr gvstv' gandr yfir stál ok brandi.

7.   'Vrungo' varrar Gungniss varrar lungs um stunginn.   25

8.   Hvarfa-ek blindr of branda, 'bið-ek eirar Syn geira'
þann ber-ek harm á hvarma hvít-vøllom 'mer sitja.' . . .

9.   'Vals' hefi-ek váfor 'helsis vá;' føllomk rǿ skalla;
blautr eromk bergis fótar borr; enn hlust es þorrin.

WIGA-GLUM AND HIS FELLOWS.

THE Saga of Battle-Glum has been preserved. It gives a fine account
of his life, and is accessible to English readers in Sir Edmund Head's
translation; see Prolegomena.   It contains some fifty lines of verses, all
of which appear genuine; six of them (ll. 27–28, 35–38), as many as we
should expect in proportion, being quoted in Edda.   Glum was a hard
fighter like Bersi, but of weird fancy, and gloomy brooding mind,
with bursts of frenzied passion; hence his nickname, the murderous
Glum. Most of his improvisations, and there is no proof of his ever
having composed a long poem, are on his dreams, which he interprets
as prognostications of his wishes, or else evoked by the over-mastering
anger that was boiling within him.   The despondency of old age, as in Egil
and Bersi, is shown in one stanza.   The Saga exists but in one vellum
(AM. 132); that the verses are not in good state appears from the citation in Edda.   In v. 9, at a junction of two leaves, the beginning words
are lost.

WIGFUS, Glum's son, who wielded his club at the battle with the
Wickings of Iom, like the valiant Spanish knight in the ballad, also
improvised a couple of stanzas, which we add.   Wigfus slew Bard, the
son of Hall the White, on whom a dirge was composed called *Bard's
Praise*, of which the burden is given in Landnama-bok, see § 3.

BRUSI, Bard's brother, another personage in the Saga of Glum, composed a couple of lines, also given below.   He may be the author of
Bardar-drapa.

HAWARD THE LAME of Icefirth is the hero of a Saga that contains
some fourteen verses which we do not believe to be genuine; but there
are two lines (not found in the Saga), quoted in Edda, which may
well be his. We may take this as another proof of the way Saga editors

---

groove on either side before the beak of the ship, with the chisel of the
tempest : and the cold-clad devourer of the woods, *the gale*, mercilessly
sweeps the spray above the sea-king's swan, *like chips before the chisel as
it were*.

Of a spear-cast.   The lips of the spear are twisted . . . ships . . .

His old age.   I grope in blindness round the fire.   There is a cloud on
my eyes.   This is the ill that sits upon the white fields of my brows.

My gait is tottering as that of a . . .   The forest of my head, *hair*, is
falling, desire has failed me, and my hearing is dried up.

---

25. *Or* vrǫngo.   28. Obscure? föllomk rá skaila] emend. ; vafallr em ec
skalla, 132.

went to work. It was known that Haward was a poet, therefore his Saga must have poetry in it. If none were known it was easy to make some which would fit the peripeteia of the tale, and ornament it in the accepted way. It is thus that Sagas got filled with spurious verse.

1. NÆR gengr mer ok mínom, men-dœll, hiúm œllom
(þverr við glaumr) enn grœni garðr, an oss of varði :
verðr hróðr-skotað harðla (her tíni-ek þat) mínom
[munak enn of styr stála starf-lauss] fœðor-arfi.

2. Fara sá-ek holms und hialmi hauks í miklom auka   5
iœrð at Eyjafirði isungs firin-dísi :
þá sva-at dóms í draumi dals ótta mer þótti
felli-guðr með fiœllom folk-vandar biœð standa.

3. Halfs eyriss met-ek hverjan hrís-runn fyrir œ sunnan ;
vel hafa víðir skógar vargi opt um borgit.   10

4. Eigi sofna-ek ofniss ys-heims í bœ þeima
(munat eld-viðom œldo auð-bœtt við mik) sœtan :
áðr grind-logi Gœndlar gellr í hattar felli
(opt vá-ek mann of minna) meirr nokkorom þeira.

5. Hard-steini lét húna 'harð-gerðr' Limafiarðar   15
(þat sák) dóms í draumi dyn-niœrðr mik barðan :
enn ek þrá-dráttar þóttomk þiósti keyrðr of liósta
sævar hrafns í svefni snarr beinanda steini.

6. Men-stiklir sá mikla (man sverða brak verða)

Wiga Glum. After his father's death, the neighbours encroach upon the land of the widow and orphan; young Glum, seeing their wanton trespasses, breaks out. The green turf-wall is shrinking about me and my household closer than I care for, lady, (*O mother.*) My patrimony is being roughly docked. There is strife in store for me.

Glum dreams that he sees a Giantess walk to his homestead, whom he welcomes in. He believes her to be the fetch of his grandfather Wigfus. I saw a mighty hooded Fairy of great stature walking under the sky at Eyafirth ; as it seemed to me in my dream, she stood on the ground with her shoulders even with the hill-tops.

Glum lurking in the bush. Every brake south of the river is worth half an ounce to me. The wide woods have often saved the wolf.

Glum panting for revenge. I shall never get sweet sleep at home before the sword clashes into the skull of one of them. They will not easily be able to recompense me. I have often slain a man for less *than their offence.*

Glum dreams that his foe and he, like Rungni and Thor, are fighting with hones ; he awoke with the crash of the stones meeting, which presaged feud as far as the sound could be heard. My grim adversary struck me with the hone (I saw it in my dream), but I, angered, thought that I smote him back with another stone.

Glum dreamed he saw a troop of women with a trough full of blood, which they were sprinkling over the country. I saw a great troop of spirit-

---

4. munat, Cd.   6. fira-, Cd.

[komin es grára geira] goð-reið of træð [kveðja] :   20
þá-es Ásynjor jóso egg-mótz of Fiærð tveggja
(vinir fagna því) vegna víg-móðar framm blóði.

7.   Virkiss spyrr at verkom víns hirði-Sif mínom
(esat at manna máli) morð vóro þau forðom :
'liggr þeim-es hrafn of huggar hær' van-talið gærva   25
. . . .

8.   Rudda-ek sem iarlar (orð lék á því forðom)
(meðr veðr-stæfom Viðriss vandar) mer til landa :
Nú hefik Val-þægniss vegna varrar-skíðs um síðir
breiða iærð með bærðom bendiss mer or hendi.   30

9.   . . . (munat enn sælo men-briótandi hlióta)
[oss kom breiðr í búðir bæggr] af eino hæggi :
þá-es ('fleymarar') fióra fúll-kátir ver sátom
(nú es mógrennir minna mítt) sextigi vittra.

10.   Lattisk herr með hætto Hanga-Týs at ganga   35
(þóttit þeim at hætta þekkiligt) fyrir brekko :
þá-es dyn-fúsar dísir dreyra más á eyri
(bráð óx borgin-móða blóðs) skialdaðir stóðom.

Einar :
11.   Þrœngvir varð af þingi þremja linnz at renna
(vasat) í Ála eli (auð-lættr) fyrir mel brattan :   40
þá-es má-stéttar máttit Mævils við þræm sævar
geira niótr á grióti Gestils klauf of festa.

---

women over the paddock. There will be a swording: there will be a
greeting of grey spears. The goddesses were sprinkling blood over the
Firth in front and on both sides.
Glum is asked how many fell in one of his frays. He answers: The lady
asks about my day's work of yore: it is not commonly known what the
number of the dead was. The score is clearly under-reckoned . . .
Glum's reflection. Like earls of yore I won land with the sword, it
was famed among men: but now in turn I have fought my own heritage
out of my hand *by unseasonable manslaying.*
His last troubles. Grief has come upon me from one death-stroke of
mine. I shall never know joy again! I have got a stumbling-block in
my house after having sat in peace sixty winters. I am going to the
wall at last.
Glum's vaunt over a bicker. They shrunk from going down the brink
in arms; they deemed it no pleasant venture: when I stood shielded on
the shore below.
Einar's account of the same incident. Glum had to run from the moot
down the sand-hill, and could not get a firm hold with his shield among
the pebbles on the slope by the sea.

21–22. Emend.; of fior seggja . . . vagna, Cd.   25. van-] emend.; veig, Cd.
26 and 31. . . .] blank in Cd.   38. blóð, Cd.

Brúsi:

12.   Hǿfom 'ver' af vígom (veit-ek orð á því) borða
      stóðs við stýri-meiða stafn-Gǫndul hlut iafnan :
      þó hykk fúr-viðo fóro fley-garðz an mik varði   45
      beiði-Hlǫkk fyrir brekko bliks harðara miklo.

Glum :

13.   Íllt es á iǫrð of orðit ; aldr bǫlvar miǫk skaldi ;
      liðit es mest it meira mítt líf Heðins dríſo :
      ef óvægins eigi Eyrar-leggs fyrir seggjom
      Gríms í Gǫndlar flaumi 'gefnar' mák of hefna.   50

VIGFUS, THE SON OF GLUM (Fagrsk. and Jomsvik. S.).

1.   VARÐAT hǿgt þá-es hurðir hiǫr-klofnar sá-ek rofna
     'hátt sǫng Hǫgna geitis hregg' til Vagns at leggja :
     þar gengo ver 'þrǫngvar þunn íss boði Gunnar'
     (strǫng vas Danskra drengja darra flaug) til knarrar.

2.   Oss es leikr (enn lauka liggr heima vinr feimo)   5
     [þryngr at Viðriss veðri vandar] góðr fyrir hǫndom :
     hlýss kveð-ek hæla bossa (hann væntir ser annars)
     vífs und vǫrmom bǿgi [ver skreytom spiǫr] neyta.

HÁVARÐR HALTI (Edda).

NÚ es ió-draugom ægiss arnar-flaug of bauga
    (hygg-ek at heim-boð þiggi Hanga-goðs) of vangi.

Brusi's tale of the same adventure. Our lots were even, as far as the
slaughter went ; though I think they [Glum and his men] ran faster down
the brink than I looked for.

Glum's last verse. It has grown evil on earth. Old age is a curse to
the poet [me] ; my better life of warfare is past, if I shall not be able to
avenge the innocent Eyre-leg [his murdered brother-in-law] on them.

Wigfus, Glum's son, of the Iomswickings' battle at which he fought. It
was not easy to reach Wagn, where the shields were being cloven. We
boarded the ships, there was a strong flight of darts from the Danish
men. We have a hard game to play, while the gallant is lounging at
home. The storm of Woden is a gathering. The lover is seeking shelter
in the warm arms of his mistress—his is another sport—while we are
handling our spears.

Haward the Halt, seeing the eagles flying above him. There is a flight
of eagles over our shoulders. I hold it to be Woden bidding us home.

---

43. Read, vegs ?   7–8. Read, hlýss meðan h. bossi ... neytis ... ver skreytom.

SATIRES BY ICELANDERS.

TIORWI THE MOCKER. As Landnama-bok says: "Tiorwi the Mocker
and Gunnar were sisters' sons of Roar (Rodhere). Tiorwi asked for the
hand of Anstrid Manwit-brink, Modwulf's daughter, but her brothers
Kettle and Rodwulf refused him, and gave her to Thori Kettlesson. Then Tiorwi drew their likenesses on the gong-wall, and every
evening ... he would spit upon the likeness of Thori and kiss that of his
sister, till Roar scraped them off the wall. Then Tiorwi carved them
on the haft of his knife, and made this verse [1, below] ... And from this
came the slaying of Roar and Tiorwi." Roar was a man of mark, he had
married the sister of Gunnar of Lithend, the hero of Niala, and his son
Hammond the Lame is renowned.

THE TWO HELGIS. In Landnama-bok it is written, that Olaf Twin-
brow, a settler who lived at Olafsfield, between Thwartwater and
Sandbeck, died, and was buried at Brunishowe, under Wardfell, leaving
a widow, Anshild, and three sons, Helgi Trust, Thori Drift, and Wade.
Thorgrim Scarleg, an old veteran, foster-father of Thorgils, set his heart
on Anshild, "but Helgi forbade him her; he lay in ambush for Thorgrim on the cross-path down below Anshild-moor. Helgi bade him
stay from his visit. Thorgrim said he was not to be treated like a child.
They fought, and Thorgrim fell there. Anshild asked where Helgi had
been." He answered in a verse [2, below]. "Anshild said that he struck
his own death-stroke," and so it turned out. Hering Thorgrimsson and
Teit Gizursson his friend slew Helgi by Helgis-hurst, on the way to
Einars-haven. Helgi's sons were Sigrod the Land-dweller, and Skevill
of Hawkdale the father of Helgi Deer, who fought a wager of battle
with Sigrod's son, Liot Longback, on Axwater-holm at the Great Moot;
whereon Helgi [Deer] made this verse" [3, below].

HALLBIORN ORDSSON (see p. 93). Of Hallbiorn, who was slain by
Snæbiorn, it is written in Landnama-bok, that he and his wife Hallgerd
did not get on well. He got ready the first year against his journey
home at the Flitting-days, when he determined to leave his father-in-
law's house. "And while he was getting ready, Ord, her father, went
from the house to the baths at Reekholt, where his sheep-house was, for
he did not want to be there when Hallbiorn started, for he suspected
that Hallgerd would not be willing to go with him. Ord had always
tried to make peace between them. When Hallbiorn had saddled their
horses, he went into the bower, and there sat Hallgerd on the dais
combing her hair, which fell all over her down to the belt; for she had
the best hair of any woman in Iceland, as fine as Hallgerd the Tall.
Hallbiorn bade her stand up and come; she sate still and held her peace.
Then he took hold of her, but she never stirred, and this happened
three times; then Hallbiorn took his stand in front of her and said
[4, below]. Then he twisted her hair round his hand and tried to drag
her from the dais, but she sat still and did not budge. Then he drew
his sword and cut her head off, and went out and rode away." Snæbiorn
was sent after him by Ord, and came up with him and killed him at the
place called Hallbiorn's heaps, now called Sælu-hus, a cold-harbour on
Blue-shaw heath, between Borgfirth and the Moot-field. It is a most
beautiful and romantic place on a balmy summer's night, with an amphi-
theatre of glacier before the eyes on the one side, and the wide heath
on the other. Here died Bishop Widalin on 31 Aug., 1720 (as we hear
from his chaplain Olaf Gislason, afterwards Bishop of Skalholt, who

gives a touching account of his death), on his way to his kinsman's funeral. Widalin, who had often passed there on his journeys, said that it was the fairest spot he knew.

THE POETS AND THE NEW FAITH.   There is in Kristni Saga a series of verses connected with the early missions into Iceland.   When, in 981, the Saxon bishop Frederick and THORWALD KODRANSSON preached the Gospel (and encountered such libellous satires as the one we have noticed in Book vi, Ditty 57), they came into West-firth Quarter to Hwam, about the time of the Great Moot, to Thorarin's house; he was away, but his wife Fridgerth was at home and their son Skeggi. "Thorwald preached the faith before the house, and Fridgerth was in the temple the while sacrificing, and each could hear what the other was saying, and the boy Skeggi laughed at them both." Then Thorwald spake a verse [5, below].

In 996, STEPHEN (Stefnir), the son of Thorgils, and great-grandson of Earl Helgi Beolan, the Christian settler of Keelness, came out tó 'set forth God's errand.' He was not well received; but when he saw that he had no success he took to breaking down idols and wrecking temples, so that the Heathen rose against him and he was driven to Keelness. "His ship lay up at Gufwater-oyie, and was torn away from her moorings by the rising of the sea and a great storm; whereupon the Heathen made these verses [below]. But the ship came ashore little injured, and Stephen had her mended in the spring. That summer it was made law at the Great Moot that the kindred of Christians being nearer than fifth cousins and farther than first cousins, should indict them for blasphemy; and that summer Stephen was prosecuted for Christianity . . ." Stephen's death at Sigwald's hands for his satire is noticed in Book vi, Ditty 59.

In 997–999, Thangbrand, who had been sent by King Olaf Tryggvason, was in Iceland, and while he was teaching the faith 'many men took to making lampoons on him.' THORWALD VEILI (whom we know from p. 26) did so; he lived at Wick in Grimsness: he made poetry upon Thangbrand and recited this verse to WOLF (ULF) THE POET, the son of Uggi [7, below]; but Wolf answered in another verse [8, below]. When Gudleif helped Thangbrand to slay Winterlid and Thorwald Veili for their satire, this verse was made [9, below].

When Thangbrand went into the West, "STEINUNN the mother of Poet Ref went to meet him; she preached heathenism to Thangbrand and spoke at length before him. Thangbrand was silent while she was speaking, but made a long speech afterwards, and turned all she had said upside down. 'Hast thou ever heard,' said she, 'how Thor challenged Christ to a wager of battle, and that he dared not fight with Thor?' 'I have heard,' says Thangbrand, 'that Thor was nothing but dust and ashes save God were willing to let him live.' 'Dost thou know,' says she, 'who wrecked thy ship?' 'What dost thou know about it?' says he. 'I will tell thee that,' says she." And she explained in two verses that it was Thor [vv. 10–11, below]. After that Thangbrand and Steinunn parted, and he and those that were with him went west to Bardstrand.

LIBEL ON KING HAROLD.   It is told in the Kings' Lives, that Harold Gormsson, King of Denmark, was once about to make an expedition to Iceland, to revenge himself for the satires they made on him. "For there was a law made in Iceland that one verse of satire should be made upon the Danish King for every poll on the island. And this was their case, that a ship that certain Icelanders owned was wrecked in Denmark and the Danes took all the cargo under the name of '*Wave-wreck*,' and he that brought this about was the King's steward, whose name was Byrgi." And there was a satire made upon both of them ; and in it the following lines come [verse 12].

"And EYWULF WALGERDSSON made this verse when he heard that his henchman had bartered his axe for a grey cloak, having just heard the news of the quarrel with King Harold" [verse 13]. This passage is found in Iomswikinga Saga.

THE STONE AT OLAND. On a Runic-stone in Oland in Denmark (now Sweden) is found the only court-metre verse met with out of Iceland. Possibly the composition of some traveller. It appears to mark the grave of a prince [verse 17].

1. VÆR hœfom (þar sem Þóri þat vas sett við gletto)
     auðar unga brúði áðr á vegg of fáða :
nú hefig rasta karms ristið (réð-ek einn fyrir því meini)
hauka skoptz á hepti hlín ' œl ' bœkis mína.

                                Landn. iv. 4.

2. Vas-ek þar-es fell til fyllar (fram sótti vinr dróttar),— 5
Erro-beinn þa-es unnar útr-tungor hátt sungo :
Ásmóðar gaf-ek Óðni arfa þróttar diarfan,
guldom Galga-valdi Gautz tafn enn ná hrafni.

3. Band es á hœgri hendi (hlaut-ek sár af tý bœro)
[lýg-ek eigi þat] (leygjar) [linn-vengis Bil] minni.   10

                                Landn. v. 10.

4. Öl-karma lætr arman eik (firromk þat) leika
Lofn fyrir lesnis stofni lín-bundin mik sínom :
Bíða man-ek of brúði (bœl gœrir mik fœlvan)
[snertomk harmr í hiarta hrót] aldregi bótir.

                                Landn. ii. 30.

5. Fór-ek með dóm inn dýra, drengr hlýddi mer enginn ; 15
     gœtom háð at hreyti hlaut-teins goða sveini :

Tiorwi's painting and sculpture. I first painted the semblance of the young bride on the wall, 'twas done in mockery of Thori. Now I have carved my lady's hair (face) upon the beechwood haft of my knife. I planned the scoff alone.

Helgi the Trusty. I was by when Scar-leg fell to earth, what time the swords sung high. I gave Thormod's gallant son to Woden, a sacrifice for the gallows-god, and a carcase for the ravens.

Helgi the Deer. There is a bandage on my right hand. I got a wound from him. I lie not, lady !

Hallbiorn Ordsson. The linen-veiled lady lets me stand as a poor beggar before her face. *He slays her and then finishes the verse.* I shall never be recompensed for my lady's loss. Grief makes my face pale. Woe touches me to the very roof of my heart.

Thorwald Kodransson. I went *in procession* with the halidom, and no man listened to me. I got mockery from the sprinkler of the divining

---

4. Read, skopt . . . minnar ?   12. stafni, Cd.

enn með enga svinno aldin rýgr við skalði
(þá kreppi Goð gyðjo!) gall um heiðnom stalla.
Kristni S., ch. 2.

6. Nú hefir stafn-valinn Stefniss (straumr ferr um hol knerri)
    felli-veðr af fialli fiall-rœnt brotið allan: 20
    heldr geto ver at valdi (vesa muno bœnd í landi)
    [geisar ǽ með ísi] Áss ríkr gný slíkom.
                                                Kristni S., ch. 6.

7. Uskelfom skal-ek Ulfi ein hendis boð senda
    (mer es við stála stýri stygglaust) syni Ugga:
    at geir-hríðar gœðir goð-varg firin-argan,   25
    sá-es við Rœgn of rignir, reki hann; enn ver annan.

8. Tekkat-ek, sundz þótt sendi, sann-reynis, boð, tanna
    hverfs við hleypi-skarfi Hagbarðz véa-fiarðar:
    esa rá-fáka rœkis (rœng ero mála-gengi)
    [sé-ek við miklo meini] mínligt flugo at gínad.   30

9. 'Ryð-fiónar gat reynir randa suðr á landi'
    'bœðs' í Boðnar smiðjo Baldrs sig-tólom haldit:
    sáð reynir lét Sónar sniallr morð-hamar gialla
    hauðrs í hattar steðja hialdrs Vetrliða skaldi.

10. Þórr brá Þvinnils dýri Þangbrandz or stað lœngo;   35
    hristi blakk ok beysti brandz ok laust við sandi:

---

rods, the priest's son, while the old house-wife rudely shrieked to me
from the heathen altar. May God cripple that priestess [her]!

The Heathens scoff at Stephen. Now a mountain hurricane from the hill
has broken Stephen's ship to pieces, the stream is pouring through the
hold of the bark. Surely it was the mighty Thor that made such a
wreck. The gods are in the land indeed. The river is rushing down
ice-laden.

Thorvald to Wolf. I will send a message straight to Wolf Uggi's
dauntless son (for I love him well) that he may drive away the reprobate
outcast of the gods, that blasphemes the Powers. I will deal with his
mate.

Wolf's answer. I will not take the fly in my mouth, though my
friend, the warden of Woden's holy mead [Thorwald the poet], sends
it me. It is not for me to gulp down the bait. The case is wrongeous;
I can see the great evil that will come of it.

Thangbrand the Missionary Priest and Gudlaf slay Winterlid the Poet.
The bearer of the Rood [Thangbrand] ran his battle-tools, *sword*, into
the mind's smithy, *breast*, of the master of the Blood of Bodn [Poet]:
the keeper of the seed of Soma [the poet Godlaf] made his axe clash
into the skull of Winterlid the bard.

Steinunn the poetess. Thor hurled Thangbrand's bark far from her
moorings; he tossed and battered her and crushed her upon the sand.

---

22. Áss ríkr] as ríki, Cd.   25. fyrir argan, Cd.   26. sva at við, Cd.
31. Read, Róðo . . .   gat] gekk, Cd.   32. Read, blóðs?   Baldrs] Baldr,
Cd.   33. Emend.; sið-reynir, Niala; sigð-reynir, Cd.

muna skíð á siá síðan sund-fœrt Atals grundar;
hregg þviat hart nam leggja, hánom kennt, í spáno.

11.   Braut fyrir biœllo gæti (bœnd ráko val strandar)
      mœg-fellandi mello mó-stallz vísund allan: 40
      hlífðit Krístr, þá-es kneyfði knœrr, mál-feta varrar;
      lítt hygg ek Goð gætti Gylva hreins it eina.
                                              Kristni S., ch. 8.

12.   Þá es sparn á mó mornar morð-kunnr Haraldr sunnan
          (varðat Vinda myrðir vax eitt) í ham Faxa:
      enn 'berg-Saxa' Byrgir bœndom rækr at landi   45
      (þat sá œld) í iœldo óríkr fyrir líki.
                                        Konunga Sogor, O. T. ch. 36.

13.   Selit maðr vápn við verði (verði dynr ef má sverða),
      verðom 'hœft' at herða hlióð; eigom spiœr rióða:
      ver skolom Gorms or gœmlo Gandvíkr þoko-landi
      (hœrð es vœn at verði vápn-hríð) sonar bíða.   50
                                        Iomsvikinga S., ch. 13.

14.   Folginn liggr, hins fylgðo (flestr vissi þat) mestar
          dáðar, dolga Þrúðar draugr í þaimsi haugi:
      munat reið-viðurr ráða róg-starkr í Danmarko,
      Vandils iarmun-grundar, œr-grandari, landi.
                                              Runic Stone, Oland.

The ship will never be sea-worthy again, since the mighty gale he [Thor] sent shivered her into splinters.

The Feller of the giantess-brood broke up the sea-bison [ship] for the bell-ward [priest Thangbrand]; the Powers wrecked the hawk of the shore [ship]. Christ did not guard the charger of the main when she was crushed; God, I ween, kept little watch over the sea-king's reindeer [ship].

Lampoon on King Harold Bluetooth and his Steward. When the murderous Harold galloped from the south to Giant-land [the desert waste] in stallion-shape, the butcher of the Wends was no wax-heart then; the weakling Byrgi, god-accursed, ran before him to the mountain-folk's land in the likeness of a mare. All men saw it.

The warning of Eyawolf. Let no man sell his weapon for a price, there may soon be a clashing of swords. Let us temper our blades, let us have our axes ready. Let us abide *the onslaught of* Gorm's son in the old Fog-land of the Arctic Main. There is like to be a stubborn shock of weapons.

The Epitaph at Oland. The warrior, whom every one knows as the man of most exploits, lies buried in this barrow. The strife-strong forayer, the rider of the car of the main, shall never lord over the land in Denmark [i.e. he is dead].

---

45. Emend.; berg-sala, Cd.   at] í, Cd.   49. or] af, Cd.

BOOK VIII.

CHRISTIAN COURT POETRY.

THIS Book covers the whole of the classic age of Court Poetry, and falls into divisions according to the leading kings at whose courts the successive generations of poets flourished.

SECTION 1, 995–1015, the poets of Olaf Tryggvason's day, amongst whom the leading figure is *Hallfred*. The poets of Earl Eric are also placed here.

SECTION 2, 1015–1040, the poets of the courts of St. Olaf and Cnut the Mighty, a period which really closes with the end of the career of *Sighvat*, perhaps the finest poet of this Book.

SECTION 3, 1040–1075, the poets of Magnus the Good and Harold Hardrede, Earl Thorfin of Orkney and their generation, closing with Sweyn Wolfsson's death. *Thiodolf* and *Arnor* are the most prominent of these.

SECTION 4, 1076–1130, the poets of Magnus Bareleg and his sons, to the death of the Crusader King Sigurd. The foremost man of this period is *Mark Skeggison*.

SECTION 5, 1130–1200, the poets of the Gille-crist family and Magnus Erlingsson down to Swerri. The representative poet of this period of declension is Einar Sculason.

SECTION 6. Poems by men of the twelfth century referring to *past historical deeds and men*, on Tryggvason, St. Olaf, Iomswickings. Konunga-tal (c. 1190) forms as it were a poetical index to the whole of the seventh and eighth Books.

SECTION 7. Scraps of court-poetry, dream-verses, ditties and other pieces belonging to the times covered by this and the preceding Book.

§ 1. OLAF TRYGGVASON (995–1000).

THE greatest of all the Northern kings, his life is an epic of exceeding interest. Coming out of the darkness, he reigns for five short years, during which he accomplishes his great design, the Christianising Norway and all her colonies; and then, in the height of his glory, with the halo of holiness and heroism undimmed on his head, he vanishes again. But his works do not perish with him. He had done his work, and though maybe his ideal of a great Christian Empire of the Baltic was unfulfilled, he had single-handed wrought the deepest change that has ever affected Norway. His noble presence brightens the Sagas whenever it appears, like a ray of sunshine gleaming across the dark shadowy depths of a Northern firth. All bear witness to the wonderful charm which his personality exercised over all that were near him, so that like the holy king Lewis (who however falls short of Olaf), he was felt to be an unearthly superhuman being by those who knew him. His singular beauty, his lofty stature[1], golden hair, and peerless skill in bodily feats, make him the typical Norseman of the old heroic times, a model king.

The facts of his life must be gathered from *two* distinct bodies of documents. The *first* and most trustworthy, derived from the oral traditions handed down to the faithful keeping of *Ari the historian*, and embalmed in the poetic prose of Snorri, gives us the national, northern, and historical account of him, which is comprised in the original draft of his life in the Book of Kings.

The *second*, legendary, ecclesiastical, and tinged with foreign-medieval influence so deeply as to give false impressions of his character and doings, seems to owe its start to the Latin Chronicle of *Sæmund*, and is found in the interpolations and additions intertwined into the MSS. of his Life, and in the legendary (Latin) chronicles which deal with him. It is in these that we find him, agreeably to the medieval ideal, turned into a Charlon, a *malleus paganorum*, who would shrink from no cruelty in his desire to spread the faith. From them came such horrible and incredible legends as the torture of the demoniac by fire; the slaying of Raud by the snake that was forced to eat into his heart; the exposure of the keen-eyed Sigurd naked to the hound Vigi, echo of the Swanhild legend; the wholesale Jehu-like massacre of the wizards by fire in the hall at Nidarnes (Sæmund given as authority); and of the warlocks by water on the Reef of Wailing. The neglect of *distinguishing* the two distinct sources for Olaf's history has bred great confusion in past historians, even Keyser and Munch, and set a brand on the king's name, which it is a duty to help to efface. The clear and patent difference of these classes of narrative, which can no more mix than oil and water, admits of their certain separation.

---

[1] A cross of Olaf's height was borne in the procession at the Althing in 1000; last heard of in Ari's time at East Skard, a farm since 1391 hidden under the ashes of Mount Hecla.

Of the king's youth we have little to depend on but notices in the Western Chronicles, telling of his forays, and his confirmation, such as the famous entry in the English Book, telling how he came with a fleet of 450 ships to Stone, and harried there, and then went to Sandwich, and thence to Ipswich, and so to Maldon, where he fought with and beat the good Alderman Byrthnoth, whose death is worthily sung in the best of old English war-poems. The English Chronicles also tell of his coming with Swain to London on the Nativity of St. Mary, how God's holy mother by mercy saved the town, and how, after harrying Essex, Kent, Surrey and Hampshire, the host wintered at Southampton, and took 16,000*l.* from the English king. Then the king sent Ælfheah the bishop and Æthelward the alderman to King Olaf, and they led him with them to Andover, where the English king took him 'at the bishop's hands, by the teaching of Sigric, Archbishop of Canterbury, and of Ælfheah, Bishop of Winchester,' and gifted him royally, 'and then Olaf made him a promise, *which he also kept,* that he would never more come to England with war.' This is confirmed by the list of Olaf's early exploits given by Hallfred in II,—the poem the king, and no wonder, would not listen to,—who notices him as warring in the East, Friesland, Saxony, Brittany, England, Wales, Cumberland, Scotland, Ireland, Man, and the Islands (Orkneys). In the Western islands the king seems to have married, though the stories concerning this marriage are apocryphal; but his wife was probably dead before he came to his own country.

The legends of Olaf's youth in the lost Latin Sæmundian books (which we can see were the originals of the account in the Kings' Lives of his flight, persecution by Gundhild, adventures in Russia and Wendland, and like) are full of echoes of the Josiah and Jezebel of the Bible, and perfectly incredible. That he came from the West is certain; that he was born there seems likely from his name, borne by the famous Anlaf Cuaran, the little we know about his father Tryggwi, and stray hints in poems and chronicles. Up to this time Olaf's career has been that of a wicking prince, but we are now to see him as a man with a great purpose before him, spending his life in working to fulfil it, and reaping even before his death the reward of his labours. What influence he underwent during this period of his life we cannot tell; but underneath the bare words of the English Chronicle may there not be a lurking hint of a crisis having passed over the man when he was in England? The English Churchmen were at that time under the fresh impulse of that revival which manifested itself in such men as Odo and Oswald and Dunstan; and may it not have been one of the North English clergy, Northmen or Danes themselves by race, or even one of those half-Welsh monks whose influence may be traced on the Southern English of Edgar's day, that turned his thoughts to a higher ideal than Reginhere or Thorgisl, and to labours worthier of David than of Saul?

Suddenly he appears in the heart of Norway. All welcome him that was to restore the realm and laws of Harold Fair-hair; and the 'wicked Earl' and his supporters can make no stand against the popular impulse which lifts the hero to the throne. And now he starts on a missionary *Circuit* in Norway (not unlike a Swedish *Erics Gate*), first to the *Wick*, where by his preaching and persuasion the people (among whom a little germ of Christianity was already struggling into life) are converted to his faith, and the nobles attached to him by the marriage of his two step-sisters. Thence he bends his way to the *South-west,* to the great moot at *Moster-Island,* when the graphic scene, which Snorri tells so

well, took place; where, after the king's speech, the franklins are unable
to answer him, one after another getting up and being forced to sit down
without getting a word out, so that it seemed miraculous, and the moot
was half-convinced at once of the power of his gospel. Popular fancy
dwelt on the story; and the foot-print of the king, and the prints made
by the 'shoes' of his followers' spears, were shown in the rock of the
moot-hillock. Here, too, Olaf did not neglect to join the chiefs to him
by the ties of marriage, and Erling Skialgsson, grandnephew of Thorleif
the Wise, the law-giver and creator of Most-moot (Thiodwulf's patron),
weds Olaf's sister, Anstrith.

Hence he turned north to a moot at *Dragsheath*, on the Tarbert
behind Cape Stadt (Sæmund has an account of his speech and the proceedings here), after which he sets forth his errand among the Hords at
their *Moot of Gula*. Thence he was minded to preach the faith in *Haloga-
land*, in the far north, and so complete the circuit of the coast; but the
heathen party was yet strong in the wilder and more pagan parts of the
land, and the chiefs were forewarned of his intentions, so that he was obliged
to abandon his work there for the present. A hard struggle awaited him
on his return to his own people; the Thronds were a stubborn set, and
for the only time there is a stain of blood on the record of his missionary
career. Ironbeard was slain in the half-rebellious, half-heathen resist-
ance which was offered to his projects, but 'the heart' of Norway was
now 'as his heart.' The summit of his Hill Difficulty was reached in
two years. There remained only the baptism of the *Uplanders*, which
is connected with the name of Gudbrand o' Dale. Curiously enough
(as we can prove by the retention of Olaf Tryggvason's bishop's name
Sigfred) this part of Olaf's history has, like several other less important
incidents, been bodily transferred to St. Olaf's Life, where it is plainly
out of place, and causes such manifest contradictions as the reconver-
sion of Gudbrand, whom we know from the context, from an episode in
Tryggvason's Saga, and from Sighvat's testimony, to have been a devoted
Christian and a friend of the king.

Haloga-land now submits; and the home-lands being all christened,
the king meant to evangelise the *Outlands* and *Colonies* also. First
winning over by his personal influence such western and northern emi-
grants as visit his new merchant town at Nidaros, he engages them as
his disciples to carry the faith to their homes. Sigmund Brestisson
wins over the Færeys at the cost of his own life. Thangbrand, the hot-
headed Saxon priest, is employed to take the Good News to Iceland;
and though he does not meet with all the success the king had hoped,
Gizur and Healti, Icelanders born, succeed in carrying the law which
established the Christian Faith in their commonwealth. Not even
Greenland is forgotten; Leif the Lucky, son of the old pioneer, Eric
the Red, the discoverer of the American continent, is the king's ambassador to the most northern Teuton colony. The Orkneys Olaf had
already converted on his way to Norway, according to Orkneyinga Saga.
So he had now planted the Faith firmly in the 'five folklands' that afterwards formed the province of Nidaros, his own town, 'Norway, Iceland,
Greenland, Færeys and Orkneys' being the sees of suffragans.

That during the last three years of his reign, while thus engaged in
completing his scheme of missionary labour, Olaf was also bent on some
great political design, we can hardly doubt. The statesmanlike instinct
which had led him to found the *first city* in Norway on Nidaros, a standing witness to his foresight, was not likely to have stopped at such
designs. That it was his hope to found a Christian Empire of the Baltic

(Sweden, Denmark, Norway, and her colonies) is clear from the whole context, τὰ πράγματα, of his last years. Amid the pagan state of Sweden (note what Sighvat found it twenty years later) and the half-heathendom of Denmark under Sweyn Forkbeard's rule, his own wooing of the Swedish Queen-dowager Sigrid, his final marriage with a Wendish princess, and the close league of the two kings against him point this way. To this too we must ascribe the building of the three war-ships year after year, the 'Crane,' the 'Short Serpent,' and the 'Long Serpent,' the most splendid ship which had ever floated in northern waters; and still more surely the gathering and training of that crew of heroes, whose names comprise so many men of mark, and who were a fitter instrument of conquest than even the buccaneers of Iom, who formed in after days the lever with which Cnut was able to win and rule the widest empire any northern prince had ever swayed; even the marriage of his last sister to the Earl of Gautland—all seem to give hints of his plans; and it is some belief of this sort which underlies the popular stories of the Angelica stalk and the like in the traditional narrative of Snorri.

Nor with all this was law or order neglected. From a hint in Sighvat's Bersoglis-visur we may gather that Olaf had claims to notice as a law-giver, and this is but what we should expect from him.

Then comes the end. Overtaken by his enemies at Swold (off Stralsund, west of the spot that legend had hallowed as the scene of the Everlasting Battle), Olaf fought his last fight.

No day is more famous in Northern story, no battle more stirring than this of Swold. Legends grew up about it pathetic, marvellous, and miraculous. It was impossible for his surviving followers to believe that the holy king, their invincible leader, was really dead; and the fond popular belief which has in its own dogged faithfulness conferred on such men as Frederic Red Beard, Arthur, and Charlemagne an immortality of hope, dealt also with the memory of Olaf. The Confessor knew of his death as a hermit by miracle, but the people believed that he would yet come back to rule in his own land. It is certain that no such king or man was to appear again in the North till the great Gustavus, with whose life and character that of Olaf has many striking resemblances.

The age of Olaf is uncertain. It is commonly believed that he was born in 969 and that he came to Norway at the age of twenty-eight (that of Hannibal) and died in his thirty-second year. Looking, however, to the length of his warfare in the West, when he was a real commander, not a boy-king, the maturity of his plans, and the character of his work, one would incline to put his age at his death as five or six years older in the absence of positive information on the subject, for the legends of his connection with the Emperor Otto II, etc., cannot of course be credited. About the date of Swold itself there is a doubt. The battle and the taking of Christianity to Iceland did *not* happen in the same year, hence we must put Swold at 1000, if we take the vote of the Althing to have been passed in 999; but if we hold that court to have taken place in 1000, then the king must have fallen in 1001. No Icelander of note was with the king when he fell. Skuli, who is the only Icelandic eye-witness we have, was in Eric's following [his account will be found in the Reader], the reason being that Olaf, desirous of giving the greatest support to the Christian party in Iceland, had, in the preceding autumn, given his Icelandic henchmen leave to go home, and they had not had time to join him again before he fell. In a passage in the Great Life of Olaf it is said that the battle took place on 'Monday the day after later Marymass,' the 9th of September, 1000. This statement we believe to come from some verse of a poet, most probably Hallfred, in whose Olaf's Drapa it may lurk under some commonplace 'fill-gap phrase' or 'kenning,' as in ll. 43–44, which has taken its place.   We incline to accept this date.

HALLFRED VANDRÆDA-SCALD.

To Olaf Tryggvason, curiously enough, Skaldatal only gives two poets, Biarni and Hallfred.   Of the former no mention is made in the King's Life, but Skaldatal is confirmed by Hallar-Steinarr in Rek-stefia, when he says that Hallfred and Biarni formerly made Encomia on Olaf, and that he will now make a third; and in Islendinga-Drapa we have it recorded, doubtless from a lost Saga of Biarni's, that when this poet's courage was challenged, he struck Earl Hakon in the face with a drinking-horn.

Of Hallfred details abound; we have a separate Saga of him, which gives a good picture of his life and character.   Born in the north of Iceland, he took to trade in his youth, and coming out to Norway, is said to have become the henchman of Earl Hakon, and to have made an Encomium on him.   In the autumn of 997, on the King's first return from Haloga-land, he met King Olaf and entered his service.

"One day King Olaf went out into the street, and there met him certain men, the foremost of whom greeted him.   The King asked him his name.   He said his name was Hallfred.   'Art thou the poet?' asked the King then.   'I know how to compose,' said he.   Then spake the King, 'Thou must be minded to become a Christian, and then thou shalt be my man.'   'I will let myself be baptized,' says he, 'on condition that thou, O King, be my god-sir.   I will not accept that office from any other man.'   'I will do so,' says the King.   Then Hallfred was baptized and the King held him up in his baptism.   Then he asked Hallfred, 'Wilt thou be my man?'   'I was formerly a henchman of Earl Hakon's, and now I will not become thy liege or any other chief's, save thou promise me that no matter what I do, thou wilt never drive me from thee!'   'But I am told of thee,' says the King, 'that thou art not so wise or careful but that it is likely that thou wilt do something that I could not by any means suffer to be passed over.'   'Then slay me,' says Hallfred.   'Thou art a troublesome poet, but thou shalt be my man.'   Quoth Hallfred, 'What wilt thou give me, O King, as a name-gift if I am to be called the troublesome poet?'   The King gave him a sword without a sheath, and bade him see that no man got hurt by it for three days and three nights, and told him to make a verse on the sword, and let the word 'sword' come into every clause.   Hallfred did so [see p. 97].   Then the King gave him the sheath and belt and said, 'The word sword is not in every clause, though!'   'No, but there are two swords in one clause,' answered Hallfred.   'So there are,' said the King."   In another place it is told of him, "And now Hallfred was with the King for a time and made a short poem on him and prayed him to listen to it.   But the King said that he would not hearken to him.   Hallfred answered, 'Thou shalt have thy way, but I shall cast off all the stories [the Creed, Lord's Prayer, etc.] thou makest me learn, if thou wilt not listen to my poem, for those stories thou makest me learn are no whit more poetic than the poem I have made on thee.'   Said King Olaf, 'Thou art truly called the troublesome poet, and I will listen to thy poem.'"

But with the poetic feeling as to the old gods clinging round him, we are told that Hallfred did not very easily put off his old faith, and it seems to have been more love for the King than the creed that kept him a Christian. 'Hallfred would never speak ill of the gods, though other men railed at them, saying that there was no need to speak evil of them, though they would not believe in them.' And once he spoke this verse in the King's hearing, 'We used formerly to sacrifice to Woden. Our life is changed now.' 'That is very bad verse, and you must unsay it.' Then Hallfred sang, 'We used to sing of the gods, but now I must put away Woden's service though I loved it, and serve Christ.' The King said, 'Thou lovest the gods too well, and it will not profit thee. That verse is no better, and must be mended.' *Then Hallfred renounces the gods*, and the King said, 'That is well sung and better than any, but go on.' *And Hallfred added another verse witnessing to his faith.* While he was with the King he made a Poem on him, and when sent on an embassy to the east to Earl Reginwald of Gautland, about the marriage of Olaf's sister, he seems to have made the Earl's Encomium, of which also we have fragments. He went back to Iceland the year before Olaf's death, and so was not present at Swold.

There is a touching account of the way in which he came to hear the tidings of his master's fall. He was just about to fight a wager of battle with Gris, the husband of Kolfinna, his love, and he dreamed the night before that King Olaf appeared to him and told him not to fight in an unrighteous cause, and that he should go to the wood where the cross-roads meet, and that there he would bear tidings which would touch him more nearly than this matter of the wager of battle. So he went, and lo, men in red coats riding from the ships, and from them he heard the news that was shocking the whole north. 'Hallfred was as if he were stunned with a stone.' He settled his suit, went out at once to Norway to hear what he could of the King, and then he made the dirge Olaf's Drapa. A piece of a fragment on Earl Eric is ascribed to him about this time, but he seems to have composed no more afterwards, for he was never happy or at rest after the King's fall, 'the world was empty,' as he says; and though he went out to Sweden, where he had a wife and son, he could not stay there in peace, but was minded to go back to Iceland, and on that voyage he died, as the Saga tells us.

"Hallfred was then about forty years of age when he set out to Iceland to fetch his property. His son Hallfred was with him. They had a bad voyage. Hallfred pumped in his turn, and yet he was very ill. And one day as he came from the baling, he sat down on the boom, and at that moment a wave struck him down on the deck with the boom on the top of him. Then cried Thorwald, 'Art hurt, brother?' and he answered him *in a verse*. They thought they could see that he was in a fever, and laid him aft along the deck, and made up his berth, and asked him what he thought of himself. He answered in a verse. And lo, they saw a woman walking after the ship; she was tall, and clad in a mail-coat, and walked over the billows as if she were on dry land. Hallfred looked at her, and saw that she was his Fetch, and said, 'I renounce thee altogether.' She said, 'Wilt thou take me, Thorwald?' but he refused. Then said Hallfred the Young, 'I will take thee.' Then she disappeared. Then spake Hallfred, 'I will give thee, my son, the sword, King's-gift, but my other treasures thou shalt lay in the coffin with me if I die on board,' and he spake this verse [see p. 98] ; and a little later he died, and was laid in his coffin with his treasures, the mantle, the helm, and the ring; and they were all cast overboard together. The coffin came ashore in Holy Island (Hy) in the Sudreys, and the Abbot's servants found it. They broke up the coffin and stole the goods and

sunk the body in a great marsh. But lo, in the night the Abbot
dreamed that King Olaf came to him; he was very angry, and said that
he had evil servants, that had broken his poet's ship, and stolen his
goods, and bound a stone about his neck. 'Now do thou enquire diligently of them the truth of these matters, or there shall marvellous
things befall thee.' Then the servants were taken and they confessed,
and were pardoned. And Hallfred's body was brought to the church
and buried worshipfully; a chalice was made out of his ring, and an
altar-cloth of his mantle, and a candlestick of his helmet." [See the
Reader for this story, p. 109.]

Besides the poems noted above, there is an Uppreistar Drapa (or
Song on the Creation) of his mentioned, which is now lost. In Codex
Birgianus, there is an Olaf's Drapa set down to him, but wrongly, for
the following reasons. The author of this poem speaks modestly of
himself (not a characteristic of Hallfred's); says that famous poets
have sung already of Olaf, but that he also presumes to do so; and talks
of hearsay information, 'I have heard of a king named Olaf,' which
Hallfred had no reason to do. Secondly, he uses late phrases, such as
stol-konungr, βασιλεὺς καθέδριος, a synonym brought, we fancy, by
Harold Hardrede from Byzantium, and certainly not used before his
day. Thirdly, the *metre* and *cadence* is not that of Hallfred, but of
some thirteenth-century poet, presenting striking resemblances, especially to those of one named 'Hallr Skald,' whose poem, *Brand's Drapa*,
is quoted in Sturlunga, c. 1246. The similarity of the names 'hallr'
and 'hallf.' would easily lead to a copyist's mistake, as Hallfred was
well known as Olaf's friend and poet.

Of Hallfred's own characteristics as a poet, we may call him the first
of the second school of court-poets;—nothing antique or deeply thought
out in his verses, though a real devotion and affection breaks out in
his dirge on the King. Of Hallfred's improvisations, those which occur
in his first interviews with the King, and in the last hours of his life,
are genuine to our mind; but those which are given to him in the
course of his love for Kolfinn and quarrel with Gris are coarse and
commonplace and spurious. Like Thormod and Cormac, his love was
an unlucky one; he seems, like them, to have been of a wayward Irish
temperament, hot-headed and ready-handed, and passionately devoted
to his lord. Like theirs, too, his life was more romantic and imaginative than his verse.

Hallfred's poems have suffered not a little, for it is clear that whole
lines have been irretrievably 'improved' away, chiefly in the Swold
section: better are vv. 17–25; though there are a few places where one
sees that behind a banal phrase or word there once stood a statement
or proper name; thus in II. 7 'val-kera' stands for 'Wal-Breta,' so
'Hedinsmeyiar' (I. 11) is really 'Hedins-eyiar,' as the 'sundi' preceding shows. Again, 'Hedins rekka' (I. 10) is Hedin's 'swirl' or 'race,'
not 'warrior;' 'rekka' being the common Slav word for current, which
translates Swold here, for Swold 'swelchie' is not an island at all, and
the nearest island is Hedinsey. 'We fought before the mouth of Swold,'
says Skuli, and Skioldunga twice mentions Swold, and enables us to fix
its place. There are reasons for doubts respecting II. See notes.

Hallfred helps one to several details in the battle of Swold, which
differ from the prose account. He hints at some stratagem (vel) in
the fight, followed by some breach of discipline (such as that of Senlake
we may fancy) committed by the crew of the Serpent, which he takes
to have lost the day for Olaf. '*Eric would never have won the Long*

Serpent, as long as the King's men kept the shield-wall within the ship.'
The popularised version of this is that Olaf's men went mad with Bear-
sark rage, and leapt overboard. The forecastle seems to have been
deserted by the crew, who had, contrary to Olaf's orders, boarded one
of the ships that lay alongside, so that Eric was able to throw his men
on board, and once an entry gained the force of numbers must have
prevailed. Hallfred's reflection on the Thronds (ver. 20) does not seem
to be, as might be guessed, an accusation, but simply the thought that if
all Northmen had stood together, the King would have been invincible.
Unfortunately both lines 15 and 79 have been tampered with; who is
meant by 'committed treason' is obscure. Respecting Sigwald (to whose
treason Stephen's verse witnesses Book vi, Ditty 59) Hallfred says
nothing, but Skuli speaks to his accompanying Eric against the King,
though the popular prose account slurs over his behaviour. Whether
his treason consisted, as one might guess, in some Themistoclean message to Olaf, or in more open treachery, we cannot tell. Hallfred's
poem is touching where he hovers between hope and despair, as he
hears the varying reports 'from the East' as to the fate of his lord,
and finally is assured of the worst. The last stanzas, however, have
a triumphant ring; his grief, great as it is, has the greatest comfort,
the proud remembrance and assurance of the dead King's glory.

I. Óláfs-drápa; *or,* Olaf's Dirge.

(Verses 2–3, 13, 16–18, 20, 21 from Kringla; lines 1, 2 from Þiðr. S.;
lines 3, 4, and 89, 90 from Fagrsk.; the rest from Ólafs S.)

Stef. a. N*ORDR ro öll of orðin auð lönd at gram dauðan:*
    allr glepsk friðr af falli flug-styggs sonar Tryggva.
  b. Grams dauði brá gleði góðs ófárar þióðar
    allr glepsk friðr af falli flug-styggs sonar Tryggva.
  c. Eigi látask ýtar enn þeirs víða nenna   5
    fremra mann of finna folk-reifom Áleifi.
  d. Hverr vas hræddr við örvan hug-dyggvan son Tryggva
    (óðosk malm-þings meiðar) maðr und sólar-iaðri.

  1.   Flug-þverrir nam fyrri frægr aldregi vægja
     heldr lét hauka skyldir hug-rekki ser þekkja.   10
  2.   Geta skal máls þess es mæla menn at vápna senno
     dolga-fangs við drengi dáð-œflgan gram kvǽðo:

Burdens. a. All the Northern lands are made desolate, all peace is
confounded by the fall of Tryggwi's steadfast son.
  b. The death of the good king has bated the joy of many a people.
All peace is confounded by the fall of Tryggwi's flight-scorning son.
  c. Men that have travelled far declare that they have never met
a man like the doughty Olaf.
  d. Every man underneath the course of the sun trembled before the
stout-hearted son of Tryggwi, yea, his foes feared him.
  The king's orders before the battle. The famous king that spurned flight,
that never turned his back, said that all his mind was set on good
courage. Now I will tell the word the king spake to his men at the
clash of weapons. He bade his followers 'never think on flight.' These
words of prowess shall never die.

baðat her-tygðar hyggja hnekkir sína rekka
(þess lifa þióðar sessa þróttar-orð) á flótta.

3.   Þar hygg víst til miøk misto (mørg kom drótt á flótta)   15
gram þannz gunni framði gengiss Þrœnzkra drengja:
næfr vá einn við iøfra allvaldr tvá snialla
(frægr es til slíks at segja siðr) ok iarl inn þriðja.

4.   Hept vas lítt á lopti (liðo ørvar fram gœrva)
brodda flaug áðr bauga briótendr skyti spiótom: 20
orð vas hitt at harðast hvar-kunnr fyr løg sunnan
mest í malma gnaustan mínn dróttinn framm sótti.

5.   Sótti herr þar es hætti hund-margr drasil sunda;
'enn hialm-spiotom' hilmir harð-fengr Dønom 'varði:'
fello þar 'með þolli' þeim skævaðar geima   25
(mein hlaut ek af því) mínir meirr holl-vinir fleiri.

6.   Her-skerðir klauf harðan (hann gekk reiðr of skeiðar)
svarðar-stofn með sverði sunnr eld-viðom kunnom:
kunni gramr at gunni gunn-þinga iarn-munnom
(margr lá heggr of hœggvinn) hold-barkar rǿ sarka.   30

7.   Varð um Vinda myrði víg-skýs (enn þat lýsig)
ramr und randar himni rymr, knǿtto spior glymja:
hirðir stóðsk við harðan hnit-vegg með fiølð seggja
víðiss velti-reiðar varg-hollr þrimo marga.

8.   Upp søgðo løg løgðar 'líf skiótt firom' hlífa   35
gnóg til gumna feigðar gølkn við randar bølko.

9.   Leitt hykk Leifa brautar log-nǿrungom vǿro
geirs við 'gumna' stióra geigor-þing at eiga:
þa-es fák-hlaðendr frǿknir farligs at vin iarla
húfs með hamri þœfðar hring-skyrtor fram gingo.   40

Then I ween the king missed the Thronds' backing sorely. A great
people was put to flight. Alone he withstood two mighty kings and an
earl the third. It is a glorious feat to tell of.
The first attacks. There was little space between the arrow-flight and
the spear-hurling; the story goes that my lord fought foremost of all,
south over sea. A mighty host beset his ship, he *defended himself against*
the Danes *and Swedes.* Many a good friend of mine fell there on board
in the king's crew, whereby I grieve. The king clove the skulls of his
foes with his sword, and made many a man's locks bloody with the lips
of the iron. Many a warrior was cut down at that war-moot. There
was a grim clatter of shields about the slayer of the Wends [Olaf], he
and his men withstood the onslaught of many foes. The swords spoke
out the law of death to the Swedes from the tables of the shields. They
[the Danes and Swedes] became weary of holding the dread parliament
of spears against the lord of the Grenes, where the good crew with
their hammer-clenched ring-shirts charged following their king.

---

24. Read, med . . . Sviom.   Read, varðizk.   29. iarn-munnom] Edda 748;
a hior þunnom, Cd.   30. Emend.; holdbarkat rá, Cd. and 748.   35. Flb.;
lagðiz, Cd.   Read, líf-skiörr Sviom.   37. Emend.; let it hygg, Cd.   38.
Read, Grena?

10. Firðisk vætr sa es varðisk víð-lendr Breta stríðir
'bleyði firðr' við breiðan bekk dóm Heðins Rekka:
hann lét 'of sœk sanna' (sverð-ialmr óx þar) verða
'skilit frá-ek fyrir skylja skóð mær roðin blóði.'

11. Harð-gœrvan lét 'hiœrvi' holms verða týr sverða   45
vind á víðo sundi víg-þey 'Heðins meyjar:'
áðr an Ormi næði Eirekr eða hlut meira
mœrg óð bitr í blóði ben-kneif fyrir Áleifi.

12. Mœndit Lung it Langa læ-síks und gram ríkjom
(blóð kom á þrœm þíðan) þióð varliga hrióða: 50
meðan ítrs vinir œtto innan-borðz (at morði)
(sú gœrðisk vél) varða (verðung) iœfurs sverðom.

13. Sukko niðr af naðri nadd-fárs 'í bœð' sárir
baugs gœrðot við vægjask 'verkendr Heðins serkjar'
vanr man Ormr 'þó at' Ormi all-dýrr konungr 'stýri,'   55
þars hann skríðr með lið lýða, lengi slíkra drengja.

14. Itr-fermðom réð Ormi orð-sæll iofurr norðan
(snœrp varð at þat sverða snót) Eiriki á móti:
enn húf-iœfnom hefnir hlýrs þeim gota stýrði
(áðr óx um gram góðan gunnr) Hákonar sunnan.   60

15. Gótt es gærva at frétta (gunnr óx) fyr haf sunnan
[sverð bito feigra fyrða fiœr-rœnn] orð at mœnnom:
hvern rakklegast rekka rand-láðs viðir kvœðo
(Surtz ættar vinn-ek sléttan sylg) Áleifi fylgja.

16. Ógrœðir sá auðan orm-griótz Trana flióta   65
(hann rauð geir at gunni glaðr) ok báða Naðra:
áðr hialdr-þorinn héldi hug-framr or bœð ramri

The assault of Eric. The fearless foe of the Welsh did not refuse to
plead by the broad bank of Hedin's Race. He defended himself bravely.
He fought a hard fight on the wide sound at Hedinsey, till Eric won
the Serpent and got the upper hand of Olaf. He would never have
won the Long Serpent from the mighty king as long as the king's men
stood on their defence on board. That stratagem [of Eric] wrought
their death.

The king's men on the Serpent sunk down wounded into the
swelchie of Hedinsey, not sparing themselves. Never again shall the
Serpent have such a crew, whatever king steer the Serpent.

The fame-blessed king launched the Serpent from the north to meet
Eric, but the avenger of Hakon [Eric] steered the even-hulled bark
from the south again.

Thorkettle's bravery. It is good to enquire diligently into the report
men gave from the south, as to whom they say followed him most
bravely of all his men; I go on to this in my song: Thorkettle the
wise saw the Crane and both the Serpents drifting crewless before
he turned away on his ship out of the fierce fray.

---

41. Emend.; varði víð lond, Cd.   42. bráðan, Cd.   43. Read, fyr sæ
sunnan?   46. Read, Heðins eyjar.   51. vin, Cd.   54. Read, Heðins
rekka?   55. Read, þar es ... styrir?   59. Emend.; hý iofnum, Cd.   62.
orð at] emend.; at þvi, Cd.   65. auða Tröno, Cd.

Snotr á snœris vitni sundz Þorketill undan.

17. Veitkat-ek hitt hvárt Heita hungr-deyfi skal-ek leyfa
dyn-sæðinga dauðan dýr-bliks, eða þó kvikvan :   70
allz sannlega segja (sárr man gramr at hvǫro)
[hætt es til hans at frétta] hvárt-tveggja mer seggir.

18. Sumr vas ǫrr of ævi 'odd-flagðs' hinn-es þat sagði
at lofða gramr lifði læ-styggs sonar Tryggva :
vesa kveðr ǫld ór éli Áláf kominn stála ;   75
menn geta máli sǫnno (miǫk es verr an svá) ferri.

19. Sagðr vas mer (enn meira munoma stríð of bíða)
lýðom firðr ok láði land-vǫrðr fyr siá handan :
væri oss þo-at 'ærir elldz þeim' svikom belldi
heila líkn ef hauka há-klifs iǫfurr lifði.   80

20. Mœndot þess, es Þrœndir þrótt-harðan gram sótto,
('frá-ek með lýða liði' land herðar) skǫp verða :
at mund-iǫkuls myndi marg-dýrr koma rýrir
(geta þikkjat mer gotnar glíkligs) or styr slíkom.

21. Enn segir óðar kenni austr or malma gnaustan   85
seggr frá sǫrom tyggja sumr eða braut of komnom :
nú hefk sann-fregit sunnan siklings or styr miklom
(kannka-ek mart við manna) morð (veifanar-orði).

22. Norðmanna hygg-ek nenninn (nú-es þengill fram genginn)
[dýrr hné dróttar stióri] dróttinn und lok sóttan. 90

23. Illt vas þatz ulfa sultar of þverri stóð-ek ferri
mest þar-es malmar gnusto mein, þo at smátt sé und einom :
skiliðr em-ek við skylja ; skalm-ǫld hefir því valdit ;
vætti ek virða dróttins (víl est mest) of dag flestan.

Olaf's end. I know not whether I am praising a dead or living king,
as people tell me both things for certain. However, he is at least
wounded, for there are no news of him. One there was that told me
of the fate of Tryggwi's son, that he was alive ; men are saying that
Olaf came alive out of the battle ; but they guess far beside the truth :
it is much worse than that ! I have been told the king lost life and
land over the sea : though it were a great mercy to me if the king
were yet alive, in spite of . . . committed this treason. Fate would
not have turned it so, that he should have escaped out of such a battle
. . . . . . Still there is one that tells me that the king was wounded,
or has escaped from the fight in the east ; but at last I have got the
true news of the king's death in the great battle in the south : I set no
store by the wavering reports of men. I believe that the doughty king
of the Northmen has come to his end. The prince is gone, the dear
captain of the Guard has sunk in death.

The poet's grief. 'Twas pity that I was far away from the king, where
the iron rang, though there is small help in one man. Now I am
parted from him : the sword-tide has wrought this. I yearn for my

---

68. á] af, Cod. (badly).   73. Samr, Cd.   79. Corrupt text.   85. auðar, Cd.
94. Emend. ; ok dul flestom, Cd.

24.   Hef-ek þannz hverjom iœfri heipt-fíknom varð ríkri   95
und nið-byrði Norðra norðr goðfœðor orðinn:
bíða man-ek þess es breiðan borð-mána vann skarðan
marg-aukanda mækiss mót, aldregi bótir.

25.   Fyrr man heimr ok himnar hug-reifom Áleifi
(hann vas menzkra manna mest gótt) í tvau bresta: 100
áðr an glíkr at góðo gœðingr moni fœðask.
—Kœns hafi Christr inn hreini konungs œnd ofarr lœndom!

II. The Older Praise of Olaf.

(From the Lives of Kings.)

1.   TOLF vas elldz at aldri ý-setrs hati vetra
hraustr þa-es her-skip glæsti Hœrða vinr or Gœrðom:
hlóðo Hamðes klæðom hiœrva gnýs ok skyjom
hilmis menn sem hialmom hlýr-vigg, enn mól stýri.

2.   Hilmir let at Holmi hræ-skóð roðin blóði   5
(hvat of dyldi þess hœlðar?) hœrð ok austr í Gœrðom.

3.   Svá frá-ek hitt at háva hœrg-briótr í stað mœrgom
(opt-kom hrafn at heipta) hlóð val-kœsto (blóði).

4.   Endr let Iamta kindir all-valdr í styr falla
(vanðisk hann) ok Vinda vé-grimmr (á þat snimma):   10
Hættr vas hersa dróttinn hiœr-diarfr Gota fiœrvi,
goll-skerði frá-ek gœrðo geir-þey á Skáneyjo.

5.   Bœð-serkjar hió birki bark-laust í Danmœrko
hleypi-meiðr fyr Heiða-, hlunn-viggja, -bý sunnan.

6.   Tíð-hœggvit let tyggi Tryggva sonr fyr styggvan   15
Leiknar hest á lesti liót-vaxin hræ Saxa:
vin-hróðigr gaf víða vísi margra Frísa
blœkko brúnt at drekka blóð kveld-riðo stóði.

---

lord every day! It is the height of woe! I had him to my godfather
who was mightier than any king under the burden of the Dwarves
[heaven]; I shall never get a recompense for his loss. Earth and
heavens shall be rent in twain, ere there shall be born a lord like to
Olaf. He was the best of earthly men. May Christ the pure keep the
king's soul in paradise [lit. above the lands].

Olaf's wicking exploits. He was twelve years old, the Friend of the
Hords [Anlaf], when he launched his war-ship out of Garth [Nov-
gorod territory]. They loaded her with Hamtheow's clothes [mail-coats]
and shields' and helms, then the rudder churned *up the sea.* He dyed
his spear red in blood at Holm [Borgund-holm?], and east in Garth.
Who knows it not? I have heard how the Breaker of high-places
piled heaps of corpses in many a place. The Hater of the Fanes made
the kindred of the Iamts and Wends to fall in battle. He was trained
early to that. He was a danger to the lives of the Gots [Gotland folk],
and I hear that he fought at Sconey. He hewed the mail-coats with
the sword in Denmark, and south of Heathby Tryggwi's son cut down
the coarse-grown carcases of the Saxons for the witches' chargers
[the wolves], and gave the blood of many a Frisian to the steeds of the

7. Rógs brá rekka lægir ríkr Val-Breta líki;
    her-stefnir lét hræfnom hold Flæmingja goldit.   20

8. Gœrðisk ungr við Engla of-vægr konungr bægja;
    nadd-skúrar réð nœrir Norðymbra því morði:
    Eyddi ulfa greddir ógn-blíðr Skottom víða;
    gœrði seims með sverði sverð-leik í Mæon skerðir.

9. Ýdrogar let œgir Eyverskan her deyja   25
    (týr vas Tiorva dýra tírar giarn) ok Íra:
    Barði Bretzkrar iarðar byggvendr, ok hió tyggvi
    (gráðr þvarr geira hríðar gióði) Kumbrskar þióðir.

III. On Earl Rognwald (or, Earl Hakon?).

(From Edda.)

1. ASK-ÞOLLOM standr Ullar austr at miklo trausti
    rœki-lundr inn ríki rand-fárs brumaðr hári.

2. Ráð lukosk, at sá síðan sniall-mæltr konungs spialli
    átti enga dóttur Ónars viði gróna.

3. Breiðleita gat brúði Báleygs at ser teygja   5
    stefnir stœðvar hrafna stála ríkis-málom.

4. Sann-yrðom spenr sverða snarr þiggjandi viggjar
    barr-haddaða, byrjar, bið-kván und sik Þriðja.

5. Því hykk fleygjanda frægjan (ferr iœrð und men-þverri)
    itra eina láta Auðs systor miœk trauðan.   10

6. Grams rúni lætr glymja gunn-ríkr, hinn-es hvœt líkar,
    Hœgna hamri slegnar, heipt-bráðr, um sik váðir.

7. Ok geir-roto gœtvar, gagls, við strengja hagli
    hungr-eyðondom hanga hlœðot iarni sœðar.

---

night-hags [wolves]. He fed the wolves on the bodies of the Gaulish
Bretons [lit. Wal-Brets], and gave the flesh of the Flemings to the
raven. The young king waged war against the English, and made
a slaughter of the Northumbrians. He destroyed the Scots far and
wide. He held a sword-play in Man. The archer-king brought death to
the Islanders [of the Western Islands] and Irish; he battled with the
dwellers in the land of the British [Wales], and cut down the Cumbrian
folk.

On Earl Rognwald. This doughty tree of war, budded with hair, is
a mighty refuge for men in the East. The agreement was concluded
that the eloquent friend of kings [earl] should wed the only Daughter of
Woden, green-with-wood [the land]. With mighty covenants he allured
to him the broad-faced Bride of Woden; with true compacts he wiles
to himself the harvest-haired Spouse of Woden. And now that the
land is his, he is very loath to put away the beautiful Sister of Aud [i. e.
he has gained the land, and will not part with it].

His battle. The earl made the hammer-beaten weeds of Hagena
[mail-coat] fall about him. Yea, the iron-sewn mail-coat did not

---

19. Emend.; valkera, Cd.

8. Ólítið brestr úti unn-dýrs sumom runnom   15
    hart á Hamðis skyrtom hryn-gráp Egils vápna.

9. 'Þaðan' verða fœt 'fyrða' (fregn-ek gœrla þat) Sœrla
    [ríóðask biœrt í blóði ben-fúr] meil-skúrom.

IV. On Earl Eric.

Stef. Bœrr ert hróðr at heyra, hialdr-œrr, um þik gœrvan!

V. Improvisations.

(From Hallfred's Saga.)

Hallfr. FŒROM festar órar; ferr sæ-roka at knerri,
        svœrð tekr heldr at herða; hvar es Akkeris-frakki?

Olaf. Enn í ólpo grœnni ek fæk dreng til strengja
    þann-es hnakk-miðom hnykkir. Her es Akkeris-frakki.

2. Veit-ek at víso skreyti víð-lendr konungr sendi   5
    nœkðan brand af nokkvi; nú ák Sýrar mey dýra:
    verða hiœlt fyr herði (hœfom, gramr, kera framðan
    skœlkving um þá-ek skialga) skrautlig konungs-nauti.

3. Fyrr vas hitt es harra Hlið-skialfar gat-ek sialfan
    (skipt es á gumna gipto) geð-skiótan vel blóta.   10

4. Öll hefir átt við hylli Óðins skipat lióðom
    all-gilda man-ek aldar iðjo várra niðja:
    enn trauðr (þvi-at vel Viðriss vald hugnaðisk skaldi)
    legg-ek á frum-ver Friggjar fión, þvi-at Kristi þiónom.

---

protect them [his foes] against the hail of the bowstrings [arrows]. And the hail-grape of Egil's weapon [arrows] burst hard upon the shirts of Hamtheow [mail-coats]. The raiment of Sarila [mail-coat] was beaten by the iron shower. The bright blades are dyed red in blood. Yea, I heard it of a truth.

Burden. It beseems thee to listen to the song I have made upon thee.

Hallfred to Olaf. Let us shift our moorings, there is a gust from the sea coming upon our ship. The cable is overstrained. Where is the anchor-man?

Olaf to Hallfred. Here in a green jacket is the anchor-man. I will get a lad for the cable who shall move the buoy.

The king's gift. I know that the wide-ruling king gave the poet a naked sword for a certain thing [for his song?]. I have a precious jewel now. The hilts of the king's gift are costly mounted. A fine sword I have; I got a brand from the king.

Hallfred's conversion. It was of old that I worshipped the swift-thoughted Lord of Lithshelf [Woden]. Men's conditions are changed now. All men once set their song to the praise of Woden; I can remember the honoured compositions of our ancestors; and therefore, now that we serve Christ, I unwillingly renounce Frigg's Spouse, because his rule suited me very well. It is the rule of the Lord of Sogn [Olaf]

---

17. Read, slegin verða?   6. nokkva nu flaustr burar Austra, Fs.

5.   Sás með Sygna ræsi siðr at blót ero kviðjot;   15
      verðom flest at forðask forn-haldin skœp Norna:
      láta allir ýtar Óðins ætt fyr róða;
      verð-ek neyddr frá Niarðar niðjom Krist at biðja.

6.   Hœfnom hœlða reifnir Hrafn-blœtz goða nafni
      þess es ól við 'lof' lýða lóm í heiðnom dómi.   20

7.   Mer skyli Freyr ok Freyja (fiorð let-ek aðul Niarðar),
      [líknisk grœm við Grímni] gramr ok Þórr inn rammi:
      Krist vil-ek allrar ástar (eromk leið Sonar reiði),
      [vald á frægt um foldar] Feðr einn ok Goð kveðja.

8.   Eitt es sverð þat-es sverða sverð-auðgan mik gerði;   25
      fyr svip-niœrðom sverða sverðótt mun nú verða:
      muna van-sverðat verða; verðr em-ek þriggja sverða,
      iarðar-mens ef yrði umgiœrð at því sverði.

9.   Hnauð við hiarta síðo hregg-blásin mer ási
      (miœk hefir) uðr (at œðro aflat bœro skafli):   30
      marr skotar mínom knerri; miœk em-ek vátr af nækkvi;
      munat úr-þvegin eira aldan síno skaldi.

10.   Rind mun hvítri hendi hœr-dúks um brá miúka
      (flióð gat fremðar œði) fiœl-errin ser þerra:
      ef dauðan mik meiðar morð-heggs skolo leggja   35
      (áðr vas-ek ungo flióði) út um borð (at sútom).

11.   Ek mœnda nú andask (ungr vas-ek harðr í tungo)
      senn, ef sœlo minni, sorglaust, vissa-ek borgit:
      veit-ek at vætki of sýtig (valdi Goð hvar aldri),
      [dauðr verðr hverr] nema hræðomk Helvíti (skal slíta).   40

---

that the sacrifices are forbidden. We are forced to forsake all the time-honoured ordinances of the Norns. All men now cast to the wind the kindred of Woden [the old gods]; I am forced to renounce the children of Niord [Frey and Freya] and to pray to Christ.—I renounce the divine name of the Raven Sacrificer, him that nursed deceit to the hurt of mankind, in heathendom. May Frey and Freya and the mighty Thor be wroth with me! I forsake the son of Niord. May the fiends find a friend in Woden! I will call on Christ, one Father and God, with all my love. I can bear no longer the wrath of the Son, who rules gloriously over the earth.

The Sword-Verse. There is one sword that makes me sword-rich in swords; among sword-bearers there will now be a sword-bounty; there will be no lack of swords now. I am worthy of three swords. Would there were but a sword-sheath to the sword!

Hallfred's Death-Verses. The tempest-blown billow, with a mighty sweep, rushed my heart to my ribs with the boom. The sea tosses my ship and I am wet; the brine-washed roller will not spare the poet. The linen-clad lady will wipe her soft eyelids with her white hand, if they have to throw me overboard, though formerly I caused grief to her. I would gladly die now if I knew that my soul were safe. I was sharp of tongue in my youth. I feel that I am troubled about nothing save that I fear the pains of Hell. Every one must die! May God fix whither my soul shall pass!

EARL ERIC HAKONSSON (1000–1014).

Of Eric's birth we are told in the Kings' Lives that his mother was an Upland woman of low estate. Having named and 'sprinkled' her child she took him to Hakon, who acknowledged the boy and gave him in fosterage to Thorleif the Wise, who dwelt up in Medal-dale (Meldal). Eric was soon of ripe growth, most fair to look on, and soon grew big and strong. Hakon did not care much about him. The remarkable beauty which he afterwards transmitted to his son Hakon was a family characteristic.

Eric's life is full of stirring scenes. Born about the time of Eric Bloodaxe (after whom he may even have been called), he was at his father's side during the chief events of his rule, for example, at the Iomswicking battle, c. 980. After his father's death, he fled from Olaf Tryggvason to the Baltic, where we hear of him as a wicking leader harrying the coasts. He is one of the confederates at Swold. At the division of the spoil which followed, Eric and his brother Sweyn were, as vassals of the Danish and Swedish kings, given the earldom of Norway 'from Weggerstaff to Agde,' the whole west coastland from Finmark to Cape Naze; Earl Sweyn also taking Ranriki from Swine-sound to Gota River as a fief from the Swedish king. Both were bound to fidelity to their allies by marriage, Eric wedding Gundhild, king Sweyn's daughter, and Sweyn Holmfrid the daughter of Olaf the Swedish king. After twelve years (as it seems from the passage in Thorrod's poem, which mentions 'the kings,' i.e. Sweyn and his son Cnut), Eric is sent for by his suzerain and father-in-law to England to help in the conquest of that kingdom. Leaving Norway and his son Hakon in charge of his brother Sweyn, he sets out with a fleet, sailing into the 'mouth of the Thames at the springtides,' as Thorrod seems to say; meets Cnut at Greenore (Greenwich, as we take it); lands and fights a campaign in the interior of the island, at several places now obscured in Thorrod's poem, but to be partly recognised by the maps and the English authorities; is present at battles west of London against Wolfkettle the Brisk (Æthelred's son-in-law), and at Ringmere-heath. His subsequent career after Eadmund's death, when Cnut is sole king, we learn from English authorities. He is made earl in Northumberland, and signs charters as Dux Ericus down to 1023. Of his end we have a tradition in the Kings' Lives, that he made a pilgrimage to Rome, and that on his return he was unskilfully operated upon by a doctor for quinsy, and died of hemorrhage. The person who told the luckless leech to cut deeper while he was using his knife is variously given as Cnut himself or an old friend of Olaf's who had survived Swold.

Like his father Hakon, Eric was a patron of poets, and no less than seven 'makers' are recorded as his panegyrists; the works of four of these, Eywolf Dadi's poet (p. 51), Thorrod Siareksson (§ 3), Gunlaug Wormstongue (p. 109), and Hallfred (p. 96), we have given elsewhere.

Eric had the good fortune to take a secondary part in three great actions which brought fame to all concerned in them,—the defeat of the Iomswickings, the confederacy against and defeat of Olaf, and the campaigns which led to Cnut's power in England. His fame rests on these events, and his poets may be classed chronologically according to the part of his life they have celebrated. Indeed of the rest of his life we know little, no single action of his during his twelve years' rule can be mentioned, save (if we accept the authority of Gretti's Saga as possibly derived from Ari) the abolition of wager of battle in Norway (though more like to be St. Olave's legislation), while of his personal traits, save the mercy and generosity which is traditionally ascribed to him as a set-off to his father, we are wholly ignorant.

EYWOLF DADASCALD, the singer of the Earl's youth before the Swold. His poem is of heathen times with a heathen burden; we have therefore set what remains of his *Banda Drapa* by the works on Earl Hakon in Book vii. Of Eywolf's life and family nothing is known; he was probably an Icelander, and he must have won his by-name by his eulogy on some one called Dadi, a rare name which only occurs once in Landnama-bok, where it is held by a person of the Western Family (perhaps a Gaelic name). His poem may have got its name Banda Drapa from the word böndom in the *burden,* or else from the curious structural peculiarity it exhibits; its burden being cut up into five half-lines, which are inserted one by one into the body of the poem, thus as it were 'banding' or 'linking' it together. It is, one would think, a further development of the insertion of sentences such as Cormac puts into his Encomium.

For the *battle of Swold* Hallfred is of course the chief authority, but here he is supplemented by Eric's two poets Halldor and Skuli.

HALLDOR THE UNCHRISTIAN composed his *Encomium on Eric,* of which eight stanzas remain, the next year after the great fight, if we may trust the 'fiord' of line 13. He gives the number of Olaf's ships, seventy-one; relates the boarding of the Long Serpent, when Eric laid Beardie, his galley, beside her; and mentions the final fight 'on the benches' in the waist and after-part of Olaf's ship, and how she was at last carried by the Earl. Of this poet's name, nation, or life, we know nothing. His verses are preserved in the Kings' Lives.

SKULI THORSTANSSON the grandson of Egil, whom he seems to have resembled more closely than his father. His *Eric's Praise* was composed apparently in his later days. He says that he followed Sigwald and the Terror of the Frisians [Earl Eric most likely] to the battle, showing that Sigwald was regarded by his followers as Olaf's open foe. There is rather a fresh stirring air about his verses, and he is distinctly original and Homeric, when he describes a sunrise in verses worthy of his grandfather. He is the one poet of his day who had eyes for aught save the glory of the tempest-tossed galley, or 'the splendour of spears,' and as such deserves special mention.

The *English Campaigns of Cnut* are told by three noted poets, Sighvat, Othere, and Thorrod Kolbeinsson; the first of whom relates St. Olaf's career in England before Æthelred's death, and the second and third tell of Cnut's campaigns, completing the story as it were. We also have an unnamed poet, who sings the *Siege of London;* and Hallward Harek's-blesi, who mentions Cnut at Fleet and Sandwich (as we read it).

We deal with Sighvat, Othere, and Hallward in their more appropriate positions in the following section, but THORROD KOLBEINSSON is essentially Eric's poet, and the best authority for his life. Luckily a good piece of his *Eric's Praise* is preserved; but it is by no means in a perfect state. Again and again we can trace obliterated names, of men and places, beneath the commonplace phrases which the Kings' Lives' text gives us; once or twice we have succeeded in finding what we take to be the original wording. Thus in the strophe on the Division of Norway, 'Veiga-staf' was hidden under 'Veigo .... styr,' 'svárr,' l. 29, under 'vôr.' In the following verses English local names lie beneath the corrupt 'Grunni,' 'uarr lǽð,' 'herferd,' 'glaum skerss bæi,' 'áttstorr,' etc., which even with the help of the MSS. and the English Chronicles, our prime authority and staff here, we cannot identify. An important chronological point seems to underlie 'miss-long,' which exhibits a striking coincidence with the Chronicles.

It is possible this poem was composed in England. Thorrod was a notable trader and traveller, and his lively description of the place where Cnut met Eric tells of local knowledge, as do the numerous place-names which must have been derived by the prose historian of the Kings' Lives (Ari) largely from him, though unfortunately he has not cared to excerpt verses touching England so carefully as he does those dealing with Norway, so that in the work of restoration we are not so much helped by the prose here, as in the case of other poets. It is not likely that Thorrod composed his poem on Eric in Norway, where his enemy St. Olaf was then in power, so that we should conclude that he either sent it from Iceland, or more likely composed it for the Earl in England.

Thorrod's life and travels are told of in the Saga of Biorn the Hitdale champion, where however he is subordinated to that hero, and somewhat unfairly handled. The greater part of the *Improvisations* there ascribed to him are spurious, those which *may* be genuine we give below, along with the fragment of his *Dirge on Gunlaug Snakestongue*. He is mentioned also in Landnama, where his genealogy is given. He was the father of a more distinguished poet, Arnor Iarla-scald (see § 3), who in the earlier part of his Drapa, when he told of his Western wanderings and early life, may have said something about his father, but whose extant remains yield no notice of him.

Thorrod's poem was once terse and full of facts, with something of the antique ring in it, rather taking after Einar than Hallfred.

Lines 5–6, 31–32 are cited by Snorri in Edda, with the same errors as in the Lives of Kings.

THE LITHSMAN'S SONG, a 'flokk' which was, as Skioldunga says, 'made by the Lithsmen [men of the levy],' not, as Olaf's Legendary Life and Flatey-bok have it, 'by Saint Olaf,' is an interesting record of the siege of London, 1016. In the form of a love poem addressed to a lady, Steinwor, the wife of one Gall, living at Stone, north of Cape Stadt, in Norway, it gives a lively account of the besiegers lying at Southwark by the Dyke (which is mentioned in the English authorities), looking across the river up at the higher city lying on the hill of St. Paul's. It mentions Thorkettle (the friend of Æthelræd and Cnut, the whilom Iomswicking, the captor of Ælfheah) and his men, and tells how Wolfkettle plucked up courage to meet 'the wickings,' but was forced to give in. The close is a triumphant stave, ' Here we sit at our ease in fair London,' which speaks to the date 1016, according to the English Chronicles, with which it agrees.

The love verses are in the stanzas 3, 10, 11, and have little to do with the main subject of the poem.

HALLDOR ÚKRISTNI ON ERIK (c. 1001).

(From Kringla; verse 5 from the great Olafs Saga.)

1. UT bauð iæfra hneitir él-móðr af Svíþióðo
    (sunnr helt gramr til gunnar) gunn-bliks liði miklo:

HALLDOR. He levied great forces out of Sweden. He held southward

hverr vildi þá hꜵlða hræ-geitunga feitir
(mꜵr fekk á siá sára sylg) Eireki fylgja.

2. Œna fór ok einni (unn-viggs) konungr sunnan   5
   (sverð rauð mætr at morði meiðr) siau tigom skeiða :
   þá es hún-lagar hreina hafði iarl of krafða
   (sætt gekk seggja ættar sundr) Skánunga fundar.

3. Gœrðisk snarpra sverða (slito drengir frið lengi)
   [þar es gollin spiꜵr gullo] gangr um Orm-inn-Langa :   10
   dolgs kvꜵðo fram fylgja fráns legg-bita hꜵnom
   Sœnska menn at senno sunnr ok Danska runna.

4. Fiorð kom heldr í harðan ('hnito reyr saman dreyra '),
   [tungl skꜵrosk þá tingla tangar] Ormr-inn-Langi :
   þá-es borð-mikinn Barða bryn-flagðs reginn lagði   15
   (iarl vann hialms at Holmi hríð) við Fáfniss síðo.

5. 'Hykkat-ek vægð at vígi,' vann drótt iꜵfur sóttan
   (fiorð komsk iarl at iꜵrðo ; ogn-harðan sik sparðit) :
   þá es fiarð-myvils fœrðut folk-harðr á trꜵð Barða
   (lítt vas Sifjar sóti svangr) við Orm-inn-Langa.   20

6. Hét á heiptar nýta hug-reifr (með Áleifi)
   (aptr stꜵkk þióð á þoptor) þengill sína drengi :
   þá es 'haf-vita' hꜵfðo Hallandz um gram sniallan
   (Varð fyr Vinda myrði vápn-eiðr) lokit skeiðom.

7. Drógosk vítt at vági Vinda skeiðr ; ok gínðo   25
   þriðja hauðrs á þióðir þunn 'galkn iarn-munnom :'
   Gnýr varð á siá sverða ; sleit ꜵrn gera beito ;
   dýrr vá drengja stióri ; drótt kom mꜵrg á flótta.

8. Hialm-faldinn bar hilmi hrings at miklo þingi
   (skeiðr glœsto þá þióðir) þangat Ormr-inn-Langi :   30

---

to the battle. Every man wished to follow Eric. *Olaf*, the lord
of the Oyns [people in Throndheim], stood from the south with
seventy ships and one, while the Earl was holding his levy among the
Sconey-folk. There was a tryst of swords about the Long Serpent.
There followed Eric to the battle Swedish and Danish warriors. Year
gone the Long Serpent came into hard straits (spears were clashing,
shields were cloven), when the Earl laid his high-bulwarked Beardie
alongside the Dragon. He won the day at the Island [Hedinsey].
There was little quarter in the battle. Year gone the Earl won the
land, what time he brought Beardie broadside to the Long Serpent.
The Earl called on his men, while Olaf's men gave back to the benches
[i. e. gave up the forecastle and retreated aft to the waist], while the
lord of Halland [the Danish king] blocked in the king [Olaf] with his
ships. The weapons clattered round the slayer of the Wends. The
Wends' ships [Sigwald's squadron] spread over the bay, and the thin
beaks gaped with iron mouths upon the warriors ; much people turned
to flight. The Long Serpent brought the helm-hooded king to the

---

5. einni] emend. ; eino, Cd.

enn sunnr at gný Gunnar glaðr tók iarl við Naðri
(áðr varð egg at rióða) ætt-góðr Hemings bróðir.

SKULI ÞORSTEINSSON.

(Verse 3 from the Lives of Kings; the rest from Edda.)

1. VAKI-ek þar-es 'vell-eiðs ekka' víðiss ár ok síðan
    'greppr hlýðir þá' góðo gallopnis vel spialli.

2. Mœndit efst, þar-es undir ár-flogni gaf-ek sárar,
    hlæokk í hundraðs flokki hvítinga mik líta :
    þá-es ræfr-vita Reifniss rauð-ek fyr Svolð til auðar   5
    her-fylgins 'bað-ek' Hœlga haug-þæok 'sama' baugom.

3. Fylgða-ek Frísa dolgi (fekk-ek ungr) þar-es slæg sungo,
    [nú fiðr æld at ek eldomk] (aldr-bót) ok Sigvalda :
    þá-es til mótz við mœti malm-þings í dyn hialma
    sunnr fyr Svolðar mynni sár-lauk roðinn bæorom.   10

4. Margr of hlaut of morgin morð-elldz þar-es 'ver' feldom
    Freyjo tæor at fleiri fár-bióðr at þar várom.

5. Glens beðja veðr (gyðjo) goð-blíð í vé síðan ;
    (liós kœmr gótt með geislom) ; grán setr ofan mána.

THORROD KOLBEINSSON (EIREKS-DRÁPA).

(Verse 5 from Fagrsk.; 12–15 from Skiöldunga; the rest from O.T. and O.H.)

1. OK sannliga sunnan (sásk Vík-buendr haska)
    stríð of stála meiða stór her-sæogor fóro :

---

great moot of war, but in the south the Earl, that nobly-born brother
of Hemming, took her in fight.

Prologue. Awake.... in the winter.... Listen to the good tidings of
the poet!

Swold battle. The lady would not have seen me in the rear of the array
of the hundreds, when of yore I gave the raven drink, when I reddened
my sword off Swold in adventure. I won gold and rings there. I followed
the terror of the Frisians [Earl Eric] and Sigwald, when the swords
sung (I won glory in my youth, now men find that I am aging): what
time south of Swold Mouth we bore the bloody sword to meet the
Judge of the iron-moot [Olaf] in battle. In the morning many won....
gold when we made havoc....

Sunrise. When the wife of Glen, *the Sun,* wades into the heaven,
the blessed light of the goddess comes with beams, and the grey moon
sinks down (vanishes).

I. *The Iomswickings' battle.* And verily there came alarm of war from
the south, the dwellers in Wick were in dread, the Earl heard that in

---

1. Read, vall-seiðs ekki.   2. Read, grepps hlyðit ér?   6. Read, bar-ek
... saman?   11. Read, val.   14. W; gran serks, *r.*   1. *Or* vit
uendr, Cd.   2. Read, stríðan ... meiðar?

súð-lœngom frá-ek Sveiða sunnr af dregnom hlunni
vangs á vatn um þrungit 'vigg meiðr' Dana skeiðom.

2.   Miok lét margar snekkjor mærðar-œrr sem knœrro 5
(óðr vex skalds) ok skeiðar skiald-hlynr á brim dynja :
þá-es ólítill útan odd-herðir fat gerða
(mœrg vas lind fyrir landi) lœnd síns fœðor rœndo.

3.   Setti iarl, sa-es atti ogn-fróðr á lœg stóði,
hremnis háfa stamna hót Sigvalda at móti : 10
margr skalf hlumr, enn hvergi huggendr 'bana' uggðo
þeir-es gœto siá slíta-sár-gamms blœðom ára.

4.   Enn í gœgn at gunni glæ-heims skriðo mævar
(renndi langt með landi leiðangr) Dana skeiðom :
þær-es iarl und 'árom œrins gollz' á Mœri 15
(barms rak vigg und vœrmom val-kesti) hrauð flestar.

5.   Œfri varð, enn urðo all-hvatt Danir falla,
blóð-helsingja bræðir, brœðr Sigrœðar œðri.

6.   Mein-rennir brá (manna margs fýsa skœp) varga
lióða lítlo síðar læ Hákonar ævi : 20
enn til landz þess-es lindar láð-stafr vegit hafði
hraustr þa-es her fór vestan hygg-ek kómo son Tryggva.

7.   Hafði ser við sœri (slíks vas vœn at hœnom)
auðs an upp um kvæði Eirikr í hug meira :
sótti reiðr at ráðom (rann eingi því manna) 25
(þrá-lyndi 'feksz' Þrœndom) Þrœnzkr iarl konung Sœnskan.

8.   Þar vas hialmaðs 'herjar' Hroptz við drœrgar toptir

. . . .

---

the south the sea was thronged with long-streaked Danish galleys
launched off the drawn rollers. He in his turn crowded many a sloop,
buss, and galley into the deep (My song swells high), and made a shield
fence about the land of his father. There was many a linden buckler
there. The Earl set his high-stemmed bark straight against Sigwald
[the leader of the Iomswickings], many an oar-loom swayed when they
clove the sea with the oar-blade. They did not fear the Danes. The
fleet ran far down the coast to encounter the Danish galleys, most of
which the Earl boarded and took south of Mere. The well-born
brother of Sigrod [Eric] won the day, and the Danes fell fast.
II. *The Death of Hakon.* The treason of men cut short Hakon's life.
The changes in men's fates are many! Then to the land which Hakon
had conquered the brave son of Tryggwi came, I ween : what time
the Host came from the West. But Eric had more in his mind than he
put forth (as was to be looked for in such a man). The Throndish Earl
sought forthwith furtherance from the Swedish king. The Thronds
were stubborn [i. e. stood fast by him].
III. *The Fall of Olaf at Swold and the Division of Norway.* There was
a fierce battery upon the bloody tofts of Woden . . . . Hyrning, the

---

4. *Or* viggo leið, some place?   7. úti, Cd.   11. Read, Dani.   17. Emend.;
iofrom, Cd.   18. Sigurðar, Cd.

orð fekk gótt sa-es gœrði grams svárr blǽm hiǿrvi,
hǿll bilar hára fialla, Hyrningr, áðr þat fyrnisk.   30

9.   Enn ept víg frá Vægi- (vel-ek orð ðat) -staf norðan
land 'eða lengra stundo' lagðisk suðr til Agða:
enn Sveinn 'konungr sunnan sagðr es dauðr enn auðir'
'fátt bilar flestra ýtra fár hans byir váro.'

10.   Ítr þrifosk iǿfra hleyti 'egg-veðrs' í fǿr 'seggja,' 35

11.   Veit-ek fyr Erling útan ár at hersar váro
('lofak fasta tý') flestir ('far-landz') vinir iarla:
all-valdz nuto aldir (una líkar vel slíko),
skyldr lézk hendi at halda hann of Noregs mǿnnom. 40

12.   Enn hefsk leyfð þar-es lofða lof-kenda frá-ek sendo
at hialm-tǿmom hilmi hiarls 'dróttna' boð iarli:
at skyldligast skyldi ('skil-ek hvat gramr mun vilja')
endr at ásta-fundi Eirekr koma þeira.

13.   45
skeið hélt mǿrg í Móðo 'miss lǿng' sem ek vissa:
brim-dýrom hélt bǿro brandz svá nær landi
Ullr at Enska vǿllo 'átt stórr' siá knátti.

14.   Enn at 'eyrar grunni' endr brim-skíðom renndi,
hinn-es kiǿl-slóðir kníði, Knútr lang-skipom útan: 50
varð, þar-es 'vildo fyrðar' 'varrláð' kómo báðir
hialmaðs iarls ok hilmis hǿgr fundr á því dǿgri.

15.   Gengo upp þeir-es Englom ár-hrafn-gefendr váro
langa stund á landi leiðir upp af, skeiðom:

King's brother-in-law, won a good report that day; the hall of the high
hills [heaven] shall fall ere his fame shall grow old. But after the battle,
the land from Weggerstaff in the north, south to Agde, along the coast,
came under Eric's sway: I tell the story. But under Earl Sweyn *came
Ranriki from Swine Sound to Gaut river.* Both the Earls flourished by their
affinity [marriage-bond] with the Kings. I know that, save Erling only,
most of the barons were the friends of the Earls. I praise him. The
people rejoiced in him, and he held his hand over the men of Norway.
IV. *The Meeting of Kings.* Next I raise my pæan, *telling* how the song-
famed Kings of the Danes [Sweyn and Cnut] sent word to the helm-wont
Earl [Eric] that he should dutifully come to the friendly interview.
V. *Exploits of Eric in England.* Many a galley stood into the Mouth
[of Thames] with the spring tides, as I have heard. The Earl held his
course so near the land that he could see the English fields at *Sturry,*
while Cnut brought his war ships from the sea to Green-ore [Greenwich],
furrowing the keel-track with his ocean-cars. It was a joyful meeting
on that day when the helmed Earl and the King met at W.... lade. They
landed from their galley far into the land against the English ....

29. svárr] emend.; vörr, Cd.   31. Emend.; Veigo ... styr, Cd.   orðat, Cd.
32. Read, með langri ströndo?   33. Corrupt; read, Enn Sveinn iarl .... Svína-
sundz .... elfar Gauta ....?   42. hialm-sömom, Cd.; read, hiarls Dana? read,
beggja.   46. Read, miss-göng?   48. Read, at S ....?   49. Read, eyrar
Grenni.   51. Read, W ...?   koma, Cd.

enn í gœgn þeir-es 'gáðo Glaumskers' bœi verja   55
(galt hialmað lið hialta) 'herferð' buendr gœrðo.

16. Goll-kennir lét gunni (græðiss hestz) fyrir vestan
(þundr vá leyfðr til landa) Lundun saman bundit:
fekk 'regn þorinn rekka ronn' af Þinga-mænnom
ýglig hœgg þar-es eggjar Ulfkell blár skulfo.   60

17. Hvatr vann Freyr 'á flotna folkstafns' sa es gaf hrafni
sollit hold né sialdan sverðz eggja spor leggja:
sniallr lét, opt ok olli Eirekr bana þeira
'rauð' Hringmara-heiði her Engla lið þverra.

II. Dirge on Gunlaug.

(From Gunnl. S.)

HLÓÐ áðr Hrafni næði hug-reifom Áleifi
Gœndlar þeys ok Grími Gunnlaugr hiœrvi þunnom:
hann varð hvatra manna hugmóðr drifinn blóði
Ullr réð ýta falli unn-viggs bani þriggja.

III. Lausa-vísor.

(From Biarnar S. AM. 551.)

Thorrod. 1. ÚT skaltu ganga; illr þykki mer
gleymr þínn vesa við grið-konor:
sitr-þú á œptnom es ver inn komom
iafn-auðigr mer. Út skaltu ganga.

Biorn.   Her man-ek sitja ok hátt vel kveða   5
skemta þínni þióð-vel kono:
þat manat okkr til orðz lagit;
em-ek heill í hug. Her man-ek sitja.

Thorrod. 2. Út skaltu ganga; oss seldot miœl
rautt at liti, rug sagðir þú;   10
enn þegar virðar vatni blendo
vas þat aska ein. Út skaltu ganga!

---

but the franklins defending . . . . when they were guarding . . . . by.
They joined battle west of London, and Wulfkettle gat ugly blows
from the Thing-men's weapons at . . . . The Earl laid many sword-prints
on the English, he minished the English host at Ringmere-heath.

Before Gunlaug got at Raven he laid low Grim and Oleif with his
thin blade. He was sprinkled with the blood of three men.

Thorrod. Get thee gone, I mislike thy fooling with the handmaids;
thou sittest in the evenings, when we come home, as proud as myself.
Get thee gone!—*Biorn.* I shall sit here and sing aloud and entertain
thy lady. It shall never be a reproach against either of us. I am whole-
hearted. I shall sit here.
Thorrod. Get thee gone! Thou didst sell me red [bad] flour, saying
that it was rye; but when they mixed it with water it was but dust. Get

---

56. Read, Hord Hertford? 2. hiörvi] með hior, Cd. 7. þat man okkr eigi, Cd.

Biorn. Kyrr man-ek sitja. Kom-ek á hausti;
　　　hefik fornan mær fullo keyptan;
　　　feld gáfut mer fagr-ræggvaðan　　　　　　　　15
　　　kapps-vel dreginn. Kyrr man-ek sitja.

3. Sextán vas hugr hióna, hverr lifði ser þverrir
　　auðs í óro húsi, auð-lín, at mun sínom:
　　áðr garð-vita gerði grundar einn fyr stundo
　　stríðri stækr í búðom stór-geðr liði óro.　　　　20

4. Öllungis bið-ek allar atgeirs eða goð fleiri
　　(rétt skil-ek) rammar vættir rand-óps þær es hlýrn skóput:
　　at styr-bendir standi stál-galdrs, enn ek valda
　　blóðigr ærn of Birni bráð-rauðr hæfuð-snauðom.

5. Hvert stefni þer hrafnar hart með flokk inn svarta?　　25
　　farit lióst matar leita land-norðr frá Klif-sandi:
　　þar liggr Biærn (enn Birni blóð-gægl of skær stóðo)
　　(þollr hné hialms) á hialla Hvítings ofar lítlo.

6. Móðr verð-ek mítt hross leiða (miúk verðra for siúkri
　　[reið vara fliótt] und fríðri fiarg-vefjar) dag margan:　　30
　　því at . . . . borgar hvergi Hlækk unði sér dækkva
　　(mikit stríð vas þat móða merki-skins) fyrir verkjom.

THE LITHSMEN'S SONG.

(From Flatey-bok iii. 237 ff. and O. H. L [less good text]; verses 1, 2 also
in Skioldunga.)

1. GÖNGOM upp, áðr Engla ætt-lænd farin rændo
　　　morðz ok miklar ferðir malm-regns stafar fregni:

thee gone!—*Biorn.* I will sit quiet. I came here last autumn; I bought
old [stinking] lard full dear; I gave thee in return a cloak of fair skins,
beautifully furred. I will sit quiet.

Thorrod on Biorn. There were sixteen in the household, all of one
mind, and every one in the house lived at his ease, till a short while ago
one man raised discord in our dwelling.

Thorrod's prayer. I pray all the mighty spirits and the gods that
made the heavens, that the bloody eagle, fresh from the carrion, may
stand over the headless Biorn by my act.

Fulfilment of it. Ravens, whither go ye so fast, ye black bevy! Go
straight to seek your meat north-east of Cliff-sand: there Biorn lies, a
little above the shelf of Whiting [a hill in Hitardale]. He fell, and the
birds of blood stand over his head.

Illness of his wife. Many a day in sorrowful mood I have to lead
my horse; the journey is not easy for my sick wife, for the dark lady
could find no rest anywhere from pain. It was a great grief to me.

SONG OF THE SIEGE OF LONDON. Let us march inland, ere that the
people learn that the heritage of the English is ravaged, or get news of

15. Read, gaf ek þer.　　　16. drepinn, Cd.　　　17, 18. þverrir auðs]
emend.; þverri rus, Cd.　　20. Emend.; strið' stokkvi buðom, Cd.　　29.
verð-ek] verðr, Cd.　　31. Blank in Cd. (hauk?).

vesom hug-rakkir Hlakkar hristom spiót ok skiótom!
leggr fyrir órom eggjom Engla gnótt á flótta.

2. Margr ferr Ullr í íllan odd-senno dag þenna　　5
Freyr þars fœddir vórom fornan serk ok bornir:
enn á Enskra manna œlom gióð Hnikars blóði
'vart' mun skald í skyrto 'skreiðaz' hamri sœéða.

3. Þollr mun glaums of grímo giarn síðarla árna
randar-skóð at rióða rœéðinn sá es mey fœéðir:　　10
berr eigi sá sveigir sára lauk í ári
reiðr til Rínar glóða rœnd upp á Englandi.

. . . .

. . . .
rýðr eigi sá sveigir sára lauk í ári
hinn-es Griótvarar gætir, gunn-borðz, fyrir Stað norðan.

4. Þóttot mer, es ek þátta, Þorkels liðar dvelja　　15
(sásk eigi þeir sverða sœng) í folk at ganga:
'áðan er "haurða heiði" hríð víkingar kníðo'
ver hlutom vápna skúrir (varð fylkt liði) 'harða.'

5. Hár þykki mer hlýra hinn iarl es brá snarla
mær spyrr vitr ef væri val-kœst ara fœsto:　　20
Enn þekkjondom þykkir þunn-blás megin-ásar
hœrð su-es hilmir gœerði hríð á Tempsar síðo.

6. Ein-ráðit lét áðan Ulfkell þar-es spior gullo
'hœrð óx hildar garða hríð' Víkinga at bíða:
ok slíðr-hugaðr síðan sáttu á oss hve 'matti'　　25
byggs við 'bitran skeggja' brunnz tveir hugir runno.

7. Knútr réð ok bað bíða baug-stallz Dani alla;

---

the great Host. Let us be of good courage. Let us shake and shoot
the spears of the Walkyria. The multitude of the English will take
to flight before our sword-edges.

Many a man in the land where we were bred and born is wearing his
old coat to-day, while the poet, who is drenching the swans of Woden
with the blood of the English, clothes himself in the hammer-sewn shirt.
The laggard, who is caressing his lady by night *in Norway*, will be slow
to redden the spear, he will not bear his shield into England this year,
or, he, the husband of Stanwara, north of Stadt, will be slow, &c.

Thorkell's men, when I espied them, seemed as if they would not
hold back from the fray. They feared not the song of the Sword:
meanwhile they drew up in stern battle-array at Ringmere-heath. The
Wickings won the day. . . .

Seems to me . . . . the earl's brother. It was a hard battle. The king
fought a hard bout on Thames-side, as all can tell. Wolfkettle made up
his mind to abide the Wickings, but afterwards it was seen that he
changed his purpose at . . . . (*place*).

Cnut commanded and ordered the Danes to make a stand, and went

---

8. Read, ört . . . . skrýðaz.　　11. aari, Cd.　　13-14. We have transposed
these two lines (a duplicate?).　　17. Read, á Hringmara heiði.　　18. Read,
harðar?　　25. Read, motti.　　26. Read, at Branda furðo?

lundr gekk ræskr und randir ríkr; vá herr við Díki:
nær var sveit 'þar es sóttom sýn með hialm ok brynjo'
'elldz sem olmom heldi elg-rennanda kennir.'   30

8.   'Út man ekkjan líta' (opt gloa væpn á lopti)
(of hialm-tæmom hilmi) hrein ꜱu-es býr í Steini:
hve sigr-fíkinn sœkir snarla borgar karla
(dynr á Bretzkom brynjom blóð-íss) Dana vísi.

9.   Hvern morgin ser horna Hlœkk á Tempsar bakka   35
(skalat hanga-má hungra) hialm-skóð roðin blóði:

   .   .   .   .

10.   Bœl es þatz lind í landi land-rifs fyrir ver handan
golli merkt við Galla Griót-œlniss skal fœlna:
þann mœnda-ek við vilja val-klifs meðan ek lifða
(alin eromk biœrk at bœlvi bandz) al-grœnan-standa.   40

11.   Ár stóð enn en dýra iarla-dóms með blómi
harðla grœn sem Hœrðar hvart misseri visso:
nú hefir bekkjar tré bliknat brátt mardallar gráti
'lind hefir laufi bundit líno-iœrð í gorðom.'

12.   Dag var hvern þat es Hœgna hurð rióðask nam blóði   45
ár þars úti vórom ilmr í fœr með hilmi:
Knegom ver, sízt vígom varð ný-lokit hœrðom,
fyllar dags í fœgrom fit, Lundunom sitja.

BIORN THE HITDALE CHAMPION.

Biorn's Saga, like Gretti's Saga, has been adorned with spurious
verse, attributed to him and Thorrod Kolbeinsson, but none of them
can be supposed genuine, save two satirical staves, one in court-metre,
which has been maimed by the copyist, for its coarseness, and one called
Gramaga-flim, the Rock-perch-flyting, which is in a rhyming-ditty metre.
It may here be noted that in Eyrbyggia Saga there is a group of
verses of the same type as that in Biorn's Saga, but of rather higher

---

himself into the array. The Host fought by the Ditch [London Dyke].
The Host was near the place where . . . . passed with his ships.

The lady that dwells at the Stone will hear how the conquering lord
of the Danes [Cnut] attacked the churls of the city [London]. The
blades glow aloft over the head of the helm-wont hero, the swords clash
on the British mailcoats. Every morning the lady on Thames-bank sees
the sword dyed in blood.

It is a pity the lady Steinwara over sea should wither away with Gall
[there is a play here on gall, a blemish, and Gall, a man's name].
Would that she might ever stand green. I was born to sorrow after
her. She was wont to stand every season like a linden tree in full
blossom, but now she is like a faded leafless tree. She has . . . .

Every day the buckler was stained red with gore when we were out
on the foray with our prince [Cnut]; but ever since the hard fight
[Assandun] was fought we sit merrily in fair London.

---

31. Read, ört man e. spyrja?

poetic merits, but they are plainly late: such a line as 'Spurðusk *vár*
und vörðum verk' settles the whole question, for the other verses are
consonant in style, and must all stand and fall together. But, even if
we had not the proof, it would be hard for any one that knows the
genuine tenth-century verse to allow their authenticity. The first satire
deserved comparison with the libel on Harold Gormsson, and with the
flytings of the heroes in the Helgi Lays.

I. Níð-vísa.

S TANDA stýri-lundar, staðar es leitað í miðjo,

. . . .

glíkr es geira sœkir gunn-sterkr at því verki
(stendr af stafna-lundi styrr) Þórrœði inn fyrri.

II. Grámaga-flim.

1. Fiskr gekk á land, en flóð á sand,   5
   hrognkelsi glíkr, vas á holdi slíkr,
   át einaga ylgr grá-maga
   mein-blandit hræ. Mart es illt í sæ.

2. Óx brúðar kviðr frá bríósti niðr
   sva at gerðo eik gekk heldr keik,   10
   ok aum í væmb, varð heldr til þæmb.

3. Sveinn kom í liós, sagt hafði drós
   auðar-gildi at hon ala vildi:
   henni þótti sá hund-bítr þars lá
   iafn-sniallr sem geit, es í augo leit.   15

GUNLAUG SNAKESTONGUE AND RAVEN.

ONE of the descendants of Bragi and the nephew of Tind, Gunlaug,
was also a poet. His luckless love for Helga and his tragical death have
made his name and story famed. To his Saga we may refer the reader
for all detail. But most interesting to us for our present purpose is the
vivid account it gives of his poetical Circuit, from which, whether it be
historically true or not, we may judge of the kind of lives the Court-
Poets of the heroic age led.

Setting sail from Norway, where he had got into some trouble by his
bold tongue and ready hand, he came to London Bridge, and found
King Æthelred Eadgarsson ruling in England. He goes before the king,

I. *Biorn's Lampoon.* The *two men* .... with a space between them.
The foremost of them at this work is like Thorrod.

II. *Biorn's Stone-perch Lampoon.* A fish, like a stone-perch, soft of
flesh, came ashore with a tide on the sand. She ate the venomous
grey-maw. There are many poisonous things in the sea! Her belly
grew big down from the breasts, so that she walked with jutting
paunch, and sore in the womb and swollen in the guts. A boy came
to light. She had told her husband that she was to give birth to a
child. She thought the babe looked but a currish morsel, where he
lay, as cowardly as a wild goat, when she saw his eyes.

2. Purposely left blank in the vellum.

who asks him whence he came and who he was. Gunlaug answers and adds, "and I have come to see you, my lord, because I have made a Poem about you, and I should like you to listen to it. The king said that he would, and Gunlaug delivered his poem in a fine, bold way." The *burden* of this poem is in verse 1. The king thanks him and gives him a scarlet cloak, lined with the finest fur, and laced down the skirt, for his poet's fee. He then goes to Dublin. "At that time King Sigtrygg Silk-beard, the son of Anlaf Cuaran and Kormlaith, was ruling over Ireland, and he had been ruling but a short while. He received the poet well, and Gunlaug said, 'I have made a poem on you, and I should like to have silence.' The king answered, 'No man before up to this time has done this and brought me a poem,—thou shalt surely be heard.'" Then he delivered his Song of Praise, of which one of the burdens and a few more lines remain. It is in Egil's *rhyming* metre, and composed in imitation of him. "The king thanked him for his poem, and called to his treasurer, saying, 'How shall this poem be repaid?' 'How do you wish to repay it, my lord?' answers he. 'How will it be paid,' says the king, 'if I give him two ships of burden?' The treasurer answers, 'That is too much, my lord,' says he; 'other kings give goodly gifts as poets' fees,—good swords, or good gold rings.' The king gave him his coat of new scarlet, a laced kirtle, a cloak of noble fur, and a gold ring of great price." And Gunlaug, after a little while, went on to the Orkneys. There he recites a short poem, 'Flokkr,' before Earl Sigrod (who fell at Clontarf). None of this poem is left. Gunlaug then went on to Sweden, where King Olaf the Swede, son of Eric the Victorious and Sigrid the Proud (the Termagant Queen), was ruling at Upsala. Here he met a fellow Icelander, Raven, his rival in poetry and love. "One day Gunlaug asks the king to listen to his poem. 'And I want to deliver mine too, my lord,' says Raven. 'But mine must come first, if it be your will, my lord!' 'Nay, I should deliver mine first,' answered Raven, 'for I was the first to come here to you.' Said Gunlaug, 'Where were our fathers ever together, when my father was after-boat to yours? Never anywhere! and so shall it be with us.' Raven proposes that the king shall settle it. Then said the king, 'Gunlaug shall deliver his first, for he will not be quiet if he does not have his turn first.' When he has finished his poem, the king turns to Raven, 'How is this song composed?' 'It is well composed, my lord, but it is full of big words, and not elegant, and there is something stiff about it, as there is in Gunlaug himself.' Then Raven recites his song. Says the king, 'What do you think of that, Gunlaug?' Says Gunlaug, 'It is well composed, my lord. The poem is pretty, like Raven himself, but rather common-place. But (turning to Raven) why didst thou make a short poem on the king? didst thou not think him worth a full Song of Praise?' 'Let us talk no more about this matter,' says Raven." But the insult was not forgotten, and was the beginning of jealousy between the two poets. This criticism recalls that of The Frogs, but it is not borne out by the remains of the two poets, for the three verses of Raven Anwindsson that remain have something antique, spiritual, and weird about them, which is lacking in Gunlaug's verses.

Raven is twice mentioned in Landnama-bok, which calls him Skald-Hrafn, 'Raven the Poet,' telling us that he had a *sister* called Helga. We have some seven stanzas of Gunlaug's in the Saga, two lines of which (a fair proportion) are quoted in Edda. All the verses are taken from the Saga.

A short account of this fine Saga is given in Prolegomena, § 9, pp. 51-52.

I. Praise on Æthelræd.

Stave.   Herr sésk allr inn ærva Englandz sem Goð þengil
          ætt lýtr grami gumna gunn-brǽðom Aðalráði.

II. Praise on Sigtrygg, King of Dublin.

Stave. 1.   Elr svǽro skæ Sigtryggr við hræ.

2.   Kann-ek máls of skil; enn ek mæra vil
     konung-manna kon; hann es Kvarans son: 5
     mona gramr við mik (venr hann giǫfli sik)
     [þess man grepp vara] goll-hring spara:
     Seg hilmir mer, hvǽrt heyrðot ér
     dýrligra brag; þat es drápo lag.

III. Improvisations.

1.   Koma skal ek víst at vitja viggs dǽglinga þriggja   10
     (því hefig hlut-vǽndom heitið) hiarls ok tveggja iarla:
     hverfka-ek aptr áðr 'arfi auð veital fyrir leita'
     'orma-borð fyrir ermar odd gefnar mer stefni.'

2.   Segit ér frá iarli odd-feimo stafar þeima
     hann hefir litnar . . . . hár karl es sá báror: 15
     Sig-reynir hefir sénar sialfr í miklo gialfri
     austr fyrir unnar hesti Eirekr blár fleiri.

3.   Rǽki-ek lítt þo-at leiki (létt veðr es nú) þéttan
     austan-vindr at ǫndri ann-ness viko þessa:
     meirr siámk hitt (enn hodd-stríðandi bíðit)   20
     orð, at ek eigi verðag iafn-rǽskr taliðr Hrafni.

I. ÆTHELRÆD'S PRAISE. *Burden.* All the host reverence the generous
King of England like God himself. All men pay homage to the valiant
Æthelræd.

II. SIGTRYG'S PRAISE. *Burden.* Sigtryg feeds the ogress-charger with
carrion. I know the distinctions of speech. Now I will praise a scion
of kings, he is Cuaran's son. The king will not grudge me a gold ring,
he trains himself to liberality. This I know. Tell me, O king, if thou
hast ever heard a more costly poem. It is all in Encomium Metre.

III. *To Æthelræd.* I am going to visit three kings and two earls, I
have promised so to do; I shall not come back till . . . . fame and
money.

On Earl Eric. You speak of this Earl . . . . but Eric has seen greater
waves dancing in front of his sea-steed.

On the loss of his love. I care not though the Eastern wind play
against my ship this week, I fear more for the report that I shall not be
reckoned an equal match for Raven [his adversary].

1-2. Emend.; ens . . . Guðs þengils . . . grams ok g. gunnbráðs, Cd.   4. enn]
hvern, Cd.   8. Emend.; segi siklingr mer ef hann heyrði ger, Cd.   19.
andra, Cd.   20. biði, Cd.

4. Munat 'háð-værom hyrjar' hríð-mundaðar þundi
'hafna' hœrvi drifna hlýða iœrð at þýðask:
þvi-at 'lausikjar' leikom lyngs es vórom yngri
'alnar gims á ymsom ann-nesjom því landi.'   25

5. Orms-tungo varð engi allr dagr und sal fialla
hóegr sízt Helga in Fagra Hrafns kvánar réð nafni:
Lítt sá hœlðr inn hvíti hiœr-þeyss faðir meyjar
(gefin vas Eir til aura ung) við minni tungo.

6. Væn á-ek verst at launa, vín-gefn, fœðor þínom   30
(fold nemr flaum af skaldi flóð-hyrs) ok svá móðor:
þvi-at gœrðo Bil borða bæði senn und klæðom
(herr hafi hœlðs ok svarra hag-virki!) svá fagra.

7. Gefin vas Eir til aura orm-dags in lit-fagra
(þann kveða mann né mínna mínn iafn-oka) Hrafni: 35
allra nýztr meðan austan Aðalráðr farar dvaldi
('því es men-rýrir minni mál-gráðr') í gný stála.

8. Nú em-ek út á Eyri Al-vangs buinn ganga
(happs unni Goð greppi) gœrt með tognom hiœrvi:
hnakk skal Helgo lokka (haus vinn-ek frá bol lausan)   40
loks með liósom mæki lyf-svelgs í tvau kliúfa.

9. Alin vas rýgr at rógi (runnr olli því gunnar),
[lóg vas-ek auðs at eiga óð-giarn] fíra bœrnom:
nú-es svan-mœrar síðan svart-augom mer bauga
landz til lýsi-Gunnar lítil þœrf at líta.   45

HRAFN ONUNDARSON (SKALD-HRAFN).

1. HUGÐOMK orms á armi ý-dœggvar þer hœggvinn,
væri brúðr í blóði barmr þínn roðinn míno:

It will not do for Raven to take my love, for when young we had
many a merry game together.

No day under heaven has ever been sweet all through to Snake's
Tongue, since Helga the Fair was wedded to Raven. The White
Franklin, her father, did not take my tongue into account *when he gave
her to another*. She was given away for the sake of money.

My lady, who takes my joy away, I have the worst of scores to wipe
out against thy father and mother, that they both of them, beneath the
coverlet, wrought thee so fair. The fiends take this masterpiece of man
and wife. The fair one was given away for money to Raven, though he
was neither her match nor mine. She was given away to him while
Æthelræd delayed my journey from the East in warring.

Before the Wager of Battle. Now I am ready to go to the Allfield eyre
with drawn sword. God give me victory. I shall split the head of Helga's
paramour with my bright sword, severing his head from the trunk.

On Helga. The proud lady was born to cause strife to the children
of men. I was very eager to win her, but now it is no use for me, the
black-eyed bard, to look on her.

POET-RAVEN. *Raven's Dream, to his wife Helga.* I dreamed I was

---

23. Read, Hrafni?   41. Read, liúf-svelgs?   44. Emend.; svart augo mer.
45. lýsi-] lægi-, Cd.   líta] i. e. vlíta.

knættit endr of undir æol-stafns niorun Hrafni
'lík getr þat lauka lind hagðyrnis' binda.

2.   Samira okkr um eina, Ullr brim-loga, Fullo,   5
fægir folka Sǽgo fangs, í brigð at ganga:
miǫk ero margar slíkar mót-runnr fyr haf sunnan
('ýti ek sævar sóta') sann-fróðr konor góðar.

3.   Veitað greppr hvárr greppa gagn-sælli hlýtr fagna;
her es ben-sigðom brugðit, búin es egg í leggi: 10
þekk man ein ok ekkja ung mær, þó-at vit særimz,
þorna spǫng at þingi þegns hug-rekki fregna.

ÞORKEL ON HELGA'S DEATH.

L AGÐA-ek orms at armi orm-góða mer tróðo
    Guð brá ley[f]ðrar líns andaða mína:

.   .   .   .

þó es beiðondom bíða bliks þungara miklo.

GRETTI THE STRONG AND OTHER ICELANDERS.

THE Saga of Gretti (on which see Prolegomena) is full of verses
scattered up and down it; but of all these, two pieces only are, we believe,
genuine; the first is quoted also in Edda, the second is found in Landnama-bok. The rest of the verse, much of which by such line-rhymes
as 'var-ek' and 'þeirra,' 'hræddr' and 'blœddi,' must be at once pronounced as of the late thirteenth century. But besides this group of late
spurious verse, there is another lot of more poetic worth which, with
Arni Magnusson, we have no hesitation in ascribing to Sturla. There is
undoubted proof that Sturla's edition of Landnama-bok was the sole
source of the verses known to the Saga editor, and one curious example
of his procedure may be instanced. He found in his Landnama-bok
text *five* lines beginning 'Rídkat et.' This would never do; all court-
metre verse must be in *four* lines, so he cuts out line 4, and concludes
his stanza with line 5 (thus Grettis Saga in AM. 556). But when we
turn to the other text in Hawk's Landnama-bok, we find two whole
eight-lined stanzas perfect, and see that line 5 is really the *beginning* of

wounded in thine arms, and that thy breast was red-stained with my
blood, and that thou didst bind up my wounds . . . .
To Gunnlaug. It ill beseems us to enter upon deadly strife for this one
woman's sake. There are many other such noble damsels, south over
sea. Neither of us can tell, now that the swords are drawn, who will gain
the day; but though we wound one another let the young damsel hear of
my valour in the combat.

THORKETTLE, *Helga's second husband, on Helga's death.* I laid my
dead lady in my arms. God took her life . . . . Yet it is worse for *me*
to abide *death, than for her to die.*

---

3. knettinn, Cd.   4. Read, líkn?   hagðyrnis] AM. 557; hagdreyrins, Cd.
11. þekk] emend.; þat, Cd.   12. at] read af.

the second set of four lines and not the supernumeral end of the first. In another instance the two genuine lines 'Heldo Hlakkar, etc.' have been filled up by a spurious continuation by the same editor.

GEST THORHALLASON. The lost part of Heidaviga Saga was, as John Olafsson testifies, studded with verses of Gest, the slayer of Styr, Snorri's father-in-law ; the Cod. Worm. Appendix has preserved two morsels which may be genuine. One would have liked to have the Likewake story and the verses there, for § 5 of this Book.

THORMOD TREFILSSON is mentioned in Landnama. 'His (Trefil's) son was Thormod who made *Raven's Speech* (Hrafns-mal), on Snorri's Godi.' A few verses are preserved in Eyrbyggja, a bald, barbaric poem, though the later poets laid store by it, for we find that Lawman Sturla, 250 years later, borrows name and metre for his Song on King Hakon's Expedition into Scotland.

SKAPTI, the famous Lawyer and Speaker (1004–1031), is in Skalda-tal said to have composed poems on Earl Hakon and St. Olave, one in the heathen Era, one in the Christian; of neither is anything left. But Edda has preserved two lines of a Praise on Christ (Christ-drapa) of his in court-metre. Interesting are those notions of Christ as the Builder of Rome, the Holy City.

1. HÉLDO Hlakkar tialda heféndr saman nefjom
    Hildar-veggs ok hioggosk hregg-nirðir til skeggjom.

2. Ríðkat-ek rœki-meiðom randar hótz at móti,
    skœput es þessom þegni þraut, ferr-ek einn á brauto:
    vilkat-ek Viðriss balka vinnendr spaka finna ;   5
    ek man þer eigi þikkja œrr, leita-ek mer fœra.

3. Hnekki-ek frá þar-es flokkar fara Þóriss miœk stórir ;
    esa mer í þys þeira þerfiligt at hverfa :
    forðomk frægra virða fund, á-ek veg til Lundar ;
    verð-ek Heimdala at hirða hiœr; biœrgom svá fiœrvi. 10

GESTR ÞORHALLASON.

(From Cod. Worm. Appendix.)

1. VASAT um sœr (enn sáran sá-ek Víga-Styr hníga)
    bœndom þœrf at binda; beit hialma-stoð þveita :
    þa-es or brúnar beinom bág-lundz Goða mági

Gretti the Strong, on his enemies plotting. The fellows were putting their noses together and wagging their heads into each other's beards.

The odds are against him. I shall not ride to meet them, now that I am in such stress. I will go off alone, I will not meet them. I will be no such fool as that. I seek for a place of safety. I keep out of the way when the big flocks of Thori are passing. It is not safe for me to turn into the throng of theirs. I seek to escape from meeting them ; my way leads to Lund. I mean to save my head. So I save my life.

Gest splits the head of Styr, his father's murderer. I saw Wiga-Styr fall wounded : it was needless to bind up the wound, the axe bit the head, when I saw the red stream of blood gush over his eyes out of the temples

unda sœg í augo all-rauðan sá-ek falla.

2.   Gestr hefir Geitiss rastar galdrs miðiungi skialdar   5
(dunði diúpra benja dœgg) rœskligast hœggit.

ÞORMÓÐR TREFILSSON.

HRAFNS-MÁL ON SNORRI-GOÐI, comp. c. 1012.

(From Eyrbyggja S.)

1.   FELLDI folks-valdi, fyrst ins goll-byrsta
vellti val-galtar, Vígfús þann héto:
slito þar síðan sára ben-skárar
brœð af bœð-nirði Biarnar arf-nytja.

2.   Fekk inn folk-rakki (framðisk ungr sigri)   5
Snorri sár-orra sverði gnógs verðar:
laust í lífs-kœsto, Leifa má-reifar,
unda ialms eldi, es hann Arnkel felldi.

3.   Svaddi svan-greddir sára dyn-bœro
œrn á ulfs virði í Aptafirði: 10
þar lét þá Snorri þegna at hiœr-regni
fiœrvi fimm numna.   Svá skal fiándr hegna.

4.   Meirr vá inn móð-barri menn at hiœr-senno
týnir tiœr-Rínar tvá fyr ó sunnan:
lœgo siau síðan (slíks ero iartegnir)   15
Gífrs- á -grand-nesi gumnar fiœr-numnir.

5.   Bœð varð í Bitro, brœð hykk þar fengo
gœrvi gnógs styrjar gióðom sigr-flióða:
lœgo lífs vanir leiðendr haf-reiðar
þrír fyr þrek-stœri.   Þar fekk Hrafn væri.   20

SKAPTI ÞÓRODDZSON: (KRIST-DRÁPA.)

(From Edda.)

MÁTTR es munka Dróttins mestr; aflar Goð flesto;
Kristr skóp ríkr, ok reisti Róms hœll, verœld alla.

---

of the father-in-law of the wily Priest [Snorri the Priest].   He has struck
him a most daring blow . . .   (The blood gushed from the deep wounds.)

Thormod Trefilsson.   Snorri's Praise.   First he felled the warrior whose
name was Wigfus, the son of Biorn.   Snorri gave the raven a full
quarry, and the sword struck home when he felled Arnkettle.   The
warrior fed the eagle on wolf's food at Alfta-firth.   There Snorri
took five men's lives.   Then he overcame two men south of the River
[Whitewater].   After which, seven lay life-reft at the Ness of Ogress-
queller [Thorsness].   There was a fray at Bitter [Frith of].   Three were
left dead there.   Raven won his rest there [i. e. was one of the three].

Skapti the Lawyer, on Christ.   The might of the Lord of monks
[Christ] is the greatest.   Christ the mighty reared the City of Rome,
and made all the world.

---

14. Conj. tioreinar, Cd.

§ 2. ST. OLAF AND CNUT.

ST. OLAF HAROLDSSON (1014–1030).

THE son of Harold, King of Grenland or Grænd, a county in South Norway, whence he was surnamed Grenzki, and of Asta daughter of Gudbrand, a Norwegian noble. Harold met with a tragical death on a journey to Sweden, leaving Asta a widow, pregnant with the boy who soon was to be St. Olave. Asta, many years later, married Sigrod the Farmer-King of Ringerik, and by him became the mother of another future king, Harold Hardrede.

We have the testimony of the poets, that as early as twelve years old, the boy Olaf, under the charge of his foster-father Rani, was put aboard a Wicking fleet, under his nominal leadership, and that henceforth he led the life of a sea-king. Thirteen battles of his are mentioned. The Baltic coast, Denmark, Jutland, Holland, England, France were each in turn visited by his pirate squadron; from the Wistula to Poitou he won his way by the sword.

But at last there came an opportunity for the young buccaneer to win a richer prize than the gold of Gaul or the silver of England. In Normandy, where he seems to have had friendly relations with the great Duke, Olaf meets with Æthelred, and heard of the death of Sweyn, with whom he had perhaps served. The English, tired of foreign rulers, offer to take their King again on the promise of good rule. It was Olaf's fleet that in Lent, 1014, bore the exile back to his realm. And now he sees that there is an opening before him. Cnut had his hands full for years to make good his hold upon the land his father had not been able totally to subdue. The North was emptied of troops, who flocking to Cnut's call, or eager for the plunder of the richest land they knew of, had followed Earl Eric, or joined Thorkettle in England.

In the late summer, 1014, Olaf crossing the sea in two ships of burden, overtook the young Earl Hakon unawares, who swore strong oaths to him to leave the land and never fight against Olaf. The following winter the Uplanders joined Olaf, and on Palm Sunday, 1015, he vanquished Earl Sweyn (Eric's brother, left by him in charge of Norway), which battle gives Olaf the crown of Norway. His youth, his renown as a leader, his mother's energy which won him the help of the Uplanders, and even his name, helped to smooth his way. But he was no Olaf Tryggvason come back, as the people hoped, this short, thick-set, ruddy young man, that carried his head slightly stooping, like the hard thinker he was. Here was a lover of order, who drove the courts, enforced the laws with the strong hand, and who, as other kings in like case, ruled through poor men he could trust rather than the nobles whom he suspected; who was the organiser of the public and the church-law and the severe scourge of those that broke it; in short, as a man of Henry II's type rather than that of Tryggvason, essentially a secular, business-like, hard-working man,—such was Norway's Saint that was to be.

Ten years he passed as an undisputed sovereign; he swiftly quelled a dangerous plot of the Upland Kings who had once joined him, but now, like the Horse in the Fable, found out their mistake; settled a treaty and marriage with Sweden; made the Orkney earls his liegemen.

But now, c. 1025, when Cnut had made firm his seat in England, and a new generation of Englishmen faithful to the new dynasty, Godwine and Siward and Leofric, sat in the seats of Eadmund Ironside and Wolf-kettle, the mighty Dane sent, like some Assyrian emperor of old, to bid Olaf acknowledge his suzerainty. Olaf refused, and then the storm, that had been gathering for some years at least, broke upon his head: the nobles who had felt the weight of his unswerving justice, the franklins who feared for their free moots and allods, and resented his inquisitorial proceedings with regard to the smouldering embers of heathendom, which were still to be found here and there among them. Their discontent was fed by the fair promises and more tangible money of Cnut, who, like Louis XI, thought that gold was a better weapon than steel. Olaf attempted to strengthen himself by an alliance with his namesake of Sweden, which led to the *Holy River battle* [near Christianstad, South Sweden], 1026; but, like the Jewish kings' league with Egypt, availed him little. When Cnut's fleet made its progress up the Norwegian coast, Olaf was obliged to fly, and after a sharp stroke of revenge, the slaying of Erling (Dec. 21st, 1028), he left his fleet, and marching by land across Norway and Sweden, he sought refuge in Russia.

In 1030 he determined to make an effort to regain his throne, and pushing across Sweden he came over Iamt-land into Norway. But it was too soon; the remembrance of his harshness and the sweetness of Cnut's gold were still strong, and he comes face to face with his angry subjects at *Sticklestead*. The result of the battle must have been almost certain, but calmly and bravely, even cheerily, the King and the little knot of gallant followers, who had shared his good and evil fortunes with unshaken faith, meet the overwhelming host that were arrayed against them.

The day of Sticklestead (July 29, 1030), when Olaf fell, stands next to Swold in the Kings' Lives, and in the popular mind as the most memorable day of Northern history, and poetry gathers about it. The nobility of the man, who, though of a less heroic mould than his namesake, was yet very marked and real (Sighvat and Thormod would not have loved a king who was not worthy of their jealous affection), the tragedy of his death, the feeling that in the people's mind ever follows such an event, the superstition which the horrifying phenomenon of a total eclipse on the battle-field a month later (Aug. 31st), could hardly fail to excite,—all contributed to canonise Olaf. And when the unfortunate reign of Cnut's lieutenant, the alien Sweyn Ælgyfu's son, with its bad seasons, its disappointments and degradations, and finally Cnut's death, had wrought such a revulsion of feeling that the very nobles who had slain the father sent for the son Magnus, a boy in his eleventh year, from Russia to be their king, it is not wonderful that it became almost a political creed and stamp of loyalty to regard Olaf as a martyr, and to cry up the miraculous efficacy of his relics. Soon, too, the missionary labours of the earlier Olaf were attributed to the later king, and the stern politician was transformed into the martyr missionary.

It is a remarkable proof of its credibility and early date, that the Icelandic Life of Olaf, when we remove foreign accretions and appendices, is free entirely from any legendary views of his character. It draws him as a *secular* person, law-giver, justice, and financier. Hall of Hawkdale, Ari the Historian's foster-father, was King Olaf's partner in trade. Olaf the Stout (Digri) is the name he bore in his lifetime. Sighvat, repeatedly, and the Poets address his son Magnus as 'the son of the Stout;' even Ari the historian, in Libellus, still names him Olafr Digri.

We can even account for the one mistake the Icelandic Life makes, the identifying the day of the battle, July 29th (fixed by his Saint's day), with the day of the eclipse, August 31st; for Sighvat, who was in Rome at the time these events took place, must have heard of both *together*, and his words, though not quite clear, may be well construed to favour such an identification, so agreeable to oral history.

St. Olaf's exact age at his death is not recorded; he would have been about twenty or twenty-two at his arrival in Norway, thus, thirty-six on the day of Sticklestead. Sighvat, in December 1028 (straitened, it is true, for rhyme on Tungor), speaks of him as *young :* yet every page of his Life impresses on one's mind the image of a man ripe in years and judgment. Kings of the olden time in the North, from their early youth in camp and on the sea, must have aged wonderfully fast.

OLAF AND ANWYND THE SWEDISH KINGS.

OLAF THE SWEDE, son of Eric the Victorious, fought at Swold and got a share of the spoil, whence arose diplomatic complications with the Norwegian King, Olaf Haroldsson. He had two daughters, Ingigerd and Anstrith, and one son, Eanwynd (Onund) or James. He married his eldest daughter to the Russian king Iaroslaw, instead of to Olaf, upon whom the second daughter was palmed off, though she too proved a noble-minded lady. By her St. Olaf had one daughter, Ulfhild, married to a Duke of Brunswick, through whom St. Olaf is the ancestor of almost all the Royal Houses of modern Europe, that of England among the rest.

The Swedish King loved flattery, and we hear of poets at his court, and of embassies to him in which poets were employed. He died c. 1024, and was succeeded by his son JAMES, the foe of Cnut at Holy River, but his friend later on. He is known as the preserver of the English Æthelings, whom he sent into Hungary. He helped Magnus after Cnut's death, and lived on to 1054. Sighvat is put down as his poet in Skalda-tal. After his days Swedish history is almost blank. The house of Steinkell succeeds, who also seem to have encouraged poets to their court.

THE POETRY: SIGHVAT THE POET.

THE first half of the eleventh century in the days of St. Olaf, Cnut the Mighty and Olaf the Swede, was the heyday of Court-Poetry. There are counted nearly twenty poets who were at one time or another at these kings' courts. Of all these, SIGHVAT was incontestably the first; there is no one since Egil who can be put in comparison with him; he is indeed the only one of the court-poets who, in our acceptation of the term, could be called a poet; he alone has burst through the chief difficulties of the metre which bound all the others, and is able to express himself almost as freely and pointedly as if he were making blank-verse; with him sense must come first, he has a meaning and must set it forth plainly; and in several instances it is amusing how he contrives to do this, by putting in *an aside*, often a proverb, scorning the inane kennings and fill-gaps of the poetasters. One cannot but regret that Sighvat was forced to compose in court-metre; but it is certain that he is able to convey more in that straitened vehicle than many another poet could in plain rhymeless verse. To this end, too, he often *dislocates* his sentences, throwing object or subject into the centre of the next period; but as his use of kennings is so sparing, the isolated word is at once referred by the mind of the listener to the right place, and the sense is not obscured. His *vocabulary* is remarkably rich, and we meet with many foreign words (indices of Northern culture of that day) in his poems, especially those of Romance origin, which first appear in them. Happily more of Sighvat has reached us than of any other court-poet, although no long poem of his is complete, over 600 lines in all.

Sighvat's character is also very different from the troubadour-type of court-poet, of which we had several examples. He was a thoughtful, gentle, peace-loving man; a man to be trusted in matters of state and affairs of consequence; a steady, wise and bold counsellor and friend, and not ashamed to stand before kings. A man of true valour, though in warfare the Nesia Battle is his *only* feat in arms.

He was dark-haired and dark-eyed, as almost all the Icelandic poets were, and his speech was hesitating, but he could improvise verse as fast and clearly as another man could talk.

Sighvat's father was Thorfred (Thorrod) Sigwald's poet, an Icelander who had been in the service of the Iomswicking Sigwald and his brother Thorkettle the Tall (who is well known from the English Chronicle). Thorfred is said to have taken to trade on his first patron's fall, and to have met King Olaf in the Baltic and entered his suite. The boy Sighvat is said to have been brought up at Apewater in South Iceland, and to have come out to seek his father when yet a youth. He himself says, 'I was *beardless quite* when I met Cnut and Olaf first.' This was probably in the year 1014–1015, but as he was old enough to compose a poem, *Olaf's Praise*, for which he got a good fee, and to be enrolled in the king's guard, and as we find him fighting in the Nesia Battle in 1015 for certain, and a few years later (1018, if we trust chronology, which is never quite safe) trusted to carry on some important negotiations, we cannot place his birth later than 995. On the *Nesia Battle* he made a *short poem*, addressed to a comrade, Teit. We are told of his doings at court in connection with the troublesome blind King Rorek (Roderick) also about this time.

The high consideration and friendship with which he was held by such a king as St. Olaf, often touchingly referred to in his verses, is a signal proof of his worth. He was the king's ambassador in a journey which supplied him with material for his '*Journey to the East*,' a poetical report on a diplomatic errand to Earl Reginwald then in Garth [Novgorod], to whom Olaf Tryggvason had sent Hallfred twenty years earlier. In the first part of this poem he bids farewell to Olaf, and then goes on to tell of his adventures, giving his opinion on the Earl's character, and his attitude towards the Norwegian King.

About 1025, an incident is recorded in which Sighvat plays a prominent part. "Alfhild, the king's handmaiden, bore a son one night, and for a time it was uncertain whether the babe would live, and the priest begged Sighvat, who was present, to tell the king. 'I dare not wake him,' said the poet, 'for he has strictly forbidden any one to wake him before he wakes of himself.' 'But the child must be baptized, for it looks very poorly.' 'I would rather risk your baptizing the child at once, than wake the king; and I will bear the blame and give it a name.' So they did, and the boy was baptized and called Magnus. In the morning, when the king was awake and clothed, he was told all that had happened. Then he sent for Sighvat to him, and said, 'Why wast thou so bold as to have my son baptized before

I heard of it?' 'Because,' answered Sighvat, 'I would rather give two people to God than one to the Devil.' 'What dost thou mean by that?' said the king. Sighvat answered, 'The child was at the point of death, and would have been the Devil's if he had died, but now he is God's. Moreover I knew this, that if thou wert wroth with me, I could lose no more than my life. Moreover, if thou shouldst order that I lose my life for this cause, I hoped that I should belong to God.' 'Why didst thou call the boy Magnus?' said the king. 'That is not one of our family names.' 'I called him after King Carla-Magnus (Charlemain), whom I knew to have been the best man on earth.' Then the king said, 'Thou art a man of great good fortune; and it is no wonder for fortune to follow wisdom; it is rather a marvel, when, as sometimes falls out, good fortune follows fools, and foolish counsels turn out luckily.'"

In 1026 we find Sighvat travelling to the West with his partner Berg to Rouen in Normandy, and from thence to England, where he went up at once to see Cnut, for he wished to get leave to go to Norway, and he found an embargo laid on all ships, for the king was minded to lead a great host across the North Sea to enforce his suzerainty on Norway. He made an Encomium on Cnut at this time (1026–1027), called *Tog-drapa* (afterwards imitated by Thorarin Praise-tongue), in a peculiar metre, *four measured, with line rhyme*, in which, amongst other things, he records that monarch's journey to Rome, apparently still fresh in men's minds, an additional confirmation of the view that with regard to that event even the English Chronicle is a few years wrong.

From England (autumn 1027) Sighvat sailed to Norway, and went to King Olaf at Borg on the Raum-Elbe (Glommen), a favourite resort of his, 'and, entering the hall, greeted him, but Olaf looked at him and said nothing.' Sighvat then improvised a verse, 'Tell me, lord, where am I to sit, I have been away and all the benches are full.' Then was proved the truth of the old saw, 'The king has many ears,' for Olaf had heard all about his journey, how he had been to see Cnut, and he said to him, 'I know not whether thou meanest now to be my marshal or whether thou hast become Cnut's liegeman.' Sighvat answers in verse : 'Cnut asked me to be his liegeman as I was yours; but I said that one lord was enough for a man, and I think I have set a good example in this answer.' Then the king bade him go to the seat he was wont to have before, and Sighvat soon grew into the same friendship with him which he had enjoyed before. Of this voyage Sighvat made a poem, *Journey to the West*, which he addresses to his partner Berg.

But it would seem that Olaf never quite forgave the poet, for Sighvat anyhow was not with the king in the last days of his career, and the death of Erling Skialgsson, 21 Dec. 1028, drew from him a feeling little poem, *Erling's Dirge*, on the generous Baron, Tryggvason's brother-in-law, who had been so cruelly slain. And now the catastrophe, which ever since his voyage to England Sighvat had probably seen and deplored, came, and Olaf was obliged to fly. Sighvat remained in Norway, which he would hardly have done if the two had been on the old familiar footing of friendship; but not for long, for he was determined to throw away the sword and take the staff and pay a pilgrimage to the holy places at Rome, and there he was when Sticklestead fight was lost, and there the news reached him. An affectionate poem, *Olaf's Dirge*, 'Erfi drapa Olaf's,' attests his sore distress at the sad tidings, nor does the impression ever seem to have worn off; there is a deeper and more pensive strain in all his later compositions than we find in his earlier works.

A few *improvisations* of regret and disgust mark his feelings at the degradation of Sweyn's alien sway : but in 1036 (according to Sæmund's chronology), to his great delight, his godchild Magnus is called to his father's throne.   His fatherly affection for the boy is shown in all his dealings with him.   About 1039 we get the highest proof of this; the young king, led astray by evil counsellors, was beginning, contrary to the agreement of Wolfsound, upon which he was raised to the crown, to wreak unlawful vengeance upon those who had been in the battle against his father.   The franklins called for the laws of Hakon the Good, and murmured loudly.   At last the king's true friends met, and twelve of them took counsel together, and agreed to throw lots among them for one of them to go and tell Magnus what men were murmuring against him, and it was so managed that the lot fell upon Sighvat.   So he made the poem called *Bersoglis Visor*, the *Plain-Speaking Verses*.   'A king should keep his word.   He is a friend that warns a man in time.   There is one tale all tell, that you are laying your hand on your thanes' allod-lands.   This they will call robbery.   Be warned in time, my lord,' are a few of the salient phrases of this striking poem.   It may be compared with the Grand Remonstrance of Simon's Partisan after Lewes, but it was more successful; to Magnus' honour he listened to the good advice, and it seems to have been a kind of crisis in his life, for a Norse Code of Laws called Greygoose was in the tradition known as the Law of Magnus, Sighvat's godchild—in fact, some codification of St. Olaf's Law.

This is the last noticed act of the poet; he died within a little time, 1040-1043, but exactly when we cannot say.   His body was laid in Christ Church at Nidaros, as the pretty account of his death in Flatey-bok informs us.   He had one daughter, Tova, to whom King Olaf stood godfather, but of her subsequent fortunes nothing is known.

There must have been a *Saga* of Sighvat, from which some of the stories about him are taken; for instance, that of Ivar the White, a gentleman of good family and a baron of King Olaf's.   One day, when he had heard Sighvat recite a poem in the king's honour, he said, 'It would be wise for you poets to make poems on other great men, and not only on the king, for he may grow tired of giving you gifts, if you keep on making poetry on him.'   'Such men as thou art,' says Sighvat politely, 'are well worthy of a poet's praise.'   A little time afterwards Sighvat, remembering Ivar's words, goes to visit him, and tells him that he has made a poem on him.   The king had warned him that Ivar was a fitful and changeable man, so Sighvat was not surprised to find him by no means pleased to see him.   'It is often the way of you poets, when the king gets tired of your noise, to come down, and seek how to draw money out of us franklins.'   Sighvat answered this welcome warily in verse, 'You saw the king sit quiet enough while I sang in his honour, you can surely do the same.'   'You are right, poet,' says Ivar; and he listened quietly to the poem, and paid for it handsomely when he had heard it out.

Taking Sighvat's poems one by one :—

I. *Olaf's Drapa* (of c. 1014), a 'flokk' or short encomium.   It is of type originated probably by Sighvat himself or his father, a *chronological list* of engagements in regular order, told in a conventional way, which does not show such skill as he afterwards exhibited. It is, however, very valuable as an authentic account of St. Olaf's early life, and may be used to check the prose accounts. In the English stanzas we have an interesting notice of the Dyke at London, and mention of the Port-reeves and Port-men of Canterbury: a place-name is concealed beneath 'Nya-modo,' perhaps 'Lea-mouth.' In the French stanzas a good many names are corrupt, and not yet identified. 'Hæli,' 'Grislapoll,' 'Earl William of Wi...,' 'Fetla-firth,' 'Gundwald's borough,' and the Earl thereof, 'Geirfrid.' Verse 15 is not by the poet of the rest. See Notes.

II. The *Nesia Visor* (of 1016), a 'flokk.' The poet is here for the first time seen in his characteristic style. He delights in having been with his sharp sword and his Poitevin helmet, by the golden banner-staff, when Carle-head [Olaf's ship at that time] was laid alongside the Earl's galley, on that glorious Palm Sunday. He describes the rattle and confusion of the fight, the wounded crew tumbling overboard in their panic when the day was lost, the order of Sweyn (whom he treats with chivalrous courtesy throughout) to cut away the stems, so that the ships, chained together by head and stern, might get loose quickly. The mention of the Upland men confirms the accounts in the Life of Olaf, of the king having got hold of Norway mainly by the Upland counties' help.

III. The *Austr-fara Visor* (c. 1023), in very confused order in the Saga. We have tried to put it into order, according to their subjects, under three heads: the sailing and riding to Rognwald in Gard [Novgorod]; the arrival at Rognwald town; the wearisome journey back on foot through Sweden, among inhospitable heathens, told with humour; and, lastly, the results of the embassy. This seems the only practicable plan, for it, at all events, yields a consistent story and does not go counter to any fact we know; some order it is evident they must be put into. The names 'Strinda fiördr,' 'Listahaf,' 'Eikunda sund,' 'Eygota land,' 'Gardar' mark the points of his journey (though two of them are restored words). In his journey Sighvat found Rognwald in Garth, not in Upsala as the prose makes out, and we thereby learn that he had already left Sweden, and was in that universal refuge for princes, the Swedo-Slavonic state of Novgorod. There are some fine touches in Sighvat's best style in this poem and the *improvisations* which we have put in their places in its course. It is a pity the political part of the poem (vv. 19–23) is partly corrupt, partly lost.

IV. With the remnants of *West-fara Visor* (journey to England and Normandy) we have put the *Stray Verses* which deal with his return after the journey which he has celebrated in that poem. His *frequent* trading journeys are spoken of in stanza 1. The political allusions in some of these verses are to be noted; the grandeur of Cnut's court (at Southampton probably); the splendid presents with which he sought to win his rival's friends; the submission of the Scottish princes 'North of the middle of Fife' (a fact recorded in the English Chronicle as happening the year after he came home from Rome); the warning to Olaf of the way Cnut was using his riches; and we must not overlook the poet's proud repudiation of any treachery to his lord and friend, though, poet as he was, he had been dazzled by Cnut's greatness, and even requited Cnut's kindness by an Encomium.

V. *Tog-drapa* (autumn 1027?). This metre is here met with for the first time. Thorarin's copy was produced next year, so that it may have been a new and admired invention of Sighvat himself. The stanzas on the English King's pilgrimage, meeting with the Emperor, and favour

with him and the Pope, confirm (though they are a little corrupt, and
we cannot be sure of the readings) the conclusions of modern chrono-
logists. The autumn of 1027, before the poet left England, seems the
right date of this poem. There is no reason to suppose that this poem
was a Dirge, though some MSS. read 'Cnutr *was* und himnom,' instead
of '*es* und himnom,' but the tenor of the whole is against its being composed after Cnut's death. Nor can we find any probability of Sighvat's
making a Dirge on Cnut, in the circumstances in which he was then
placed as trusty adviser of the young Magnus and spokesman of the
Norwegian baronage. The allusion in ll. 1–2 shows the light in which
the Danes regarded Cnut, as the successor of Ragnar rather than the
peaceful ally of Eadmund.

VI. *Erling's Dirge* (January 1029). It is a chivalrous tribute to one
whom he must have loved, to risk his patron's favour in praising. For
Olaf, though a just, was not a 'forgiving man,' and Sighvat could have
remembered his anger at the *Tog-drapa*. This poem has suffered sorely.
The prose of the Kings' Lives contains statements that certainly were
drawn from the poem, and are not now found in it. We may be sure,
for example, that the date Thomas-mass occurred here, and can point
out the line from which it is missing. One statement as to Sighvat's
being at Wick we can see underneath a common phrase. The stanza
(10) respecting Erling's wealth and power has been turned into a
commonplace eulogium on his glory in war. His glory was that of a
great lord and husbandman, and there is no proof that he ever was
in battle till the day he fell.

VII. *Erfi-drapa Olaf's* (c. 1031). This poem is full of noteworthy
features. We have put into order, according to subject, all the stanzas
which we have of Sighvat on the dead King, irrespective of their order
in the Kings' Lives. Thus we have put to the end the stanza which
speaks of the Eclipse, 31 Aug. 1030 (as Hanstein has calculated), because,
though in accordance no doubt with popular belief, the prose makes the
words 'That day' refer to the battle-day, and inserts the verse there;
it is not certain that Sighvat thought so. He certainly knew 'Olaf's-
mass,' 29th July, a date which was by all analogy fixed on because it was
the day of the King's martyrdom. In the account of the battle itself, we
have tried to restore the poet's text from the old extracts in the Saga,
the number of the combatants, the order of battle, etc., for which due
account will be given in the Notes. The early established sanctity of
the King is attested by this poem, composed within a year or two of his
death : the two miracles (beside the Eclipse) being the giving of sight
to the blind and the incorruptibility of the Saint's body, upon which the
hair and nails grew. Thorarin's imitation of these stanzas (at most a
year or two later, c. 1033–4) in Sweyn's days adds to these the ringing
of the bells of the shrine, and the big bells in the tower pealing
without mortal hands, and sets forth Olaf plainly as the patron saint of
Norway. Verse 7 we would ascribe to Othere. See Notes.

VIII. A collection of Stray Verses, some composed before, some after
the date of the last poem (1030–32), put together in order as here. They
form a little poem as it were, in which the poet sets forth the grief with
which he remembered the past when he heard the sad news on the
Alps in the morning, and repels the accusation of having abandoned Olaf.
'I was in Rome in jeopardy,' he says (sickness probably), and laments
the evil hungry days of Sweyn, all the more dreary by their contrast with
the smiling happiness of Olaf's reign. One would like to have Sighvat's
impressions of Rome, but they have perished.

IX. Verses on Magnus' Restoration (c. 1035–36), in *praise of Anstrith* his good step-mother, 'the wise counsellor, the deep-thoughted lady, the daughter of Olaf, whom the Stout One wedded.' The exhortation to Alfhild, 'the king's bond-woman,' Magnus' mother, is put here as analogous in subject.

X. The *Bersoglis Visor* (c. 1039–40) open and close with an exhortation to speedy action, for the danger is pressing. But the tenor of the whole is to set forth the grievances which caused the disaffection, and to counsel the young king, for his own sake, to amend them and cleave to his coronation oath. 'A noble king should hold fast to his word.' The vindication of the poet's own position, the enumeration of the faithful service which gives him a right to speak and be listened to, are nobly simple and pathetic. We have set the verses in order as well as we could, but any arrangement must, in absence of more evidence, be tentative. In the Norwegian laws we find the notice of an Atli, speaker of the law in Gula-land, who won certain 'novels' from King Magnus, his name is almost certainly hidden under the 'ætlak' of l. 65 and 'lattan' of l. 1, cf. Agrip. cap. 29. The compiler of Magnus' Saga did not understand the verse. [See Dict. sub voce ætla, 769 a.] There are many more corrupt verses in this poem, which stands alone among the compositions of the court-poets.

XI. The *Occasional Verses* have been thrown together at the end. We do not take ver. 10 to refer to the King's death, but rather to some petty incident of Sighvat's life. The verse, p. 148, seems to be a fragment of a saint's Encomium, perhaps founded on some story the poet heard in Rome.

The poems of Sighvat have suffered a great deal, though with this distinction: his 'Visor,' or more informal poetry (III–V, VIII–XI), have, like the Wolsung-lays in our vol. i, undergone decomposition from faulty memory and indifferent MSS., but no revision. These may in time be restored. Here we often meet with a whole suite of verses in Sighvat's pure strain without a single kenning; even through the faulty mangled lines the sense gleams, often pathetic, always loyal. Worse is the case in the more historical Encomia of I, VI, VII; especially the battle section of Sticklestead. Here whole sets of lines are painted over by a later re-modeller; the lines stuffed with inane sentences mostly in Cambyses' vein, unworthy of Sighvat. The facts as they once stood, and as Ari read them, we have now to glean from the prose narrative of the Saga, which too is often diluted by a thirteenth-century historian. Yet the annalistic, realist sentences of Ari gleam out of it, and the lines in the poem whence these statements of fact were drawn can be marked out with certainty in many cases.

The great bulk (always, unless the contrary be stated) of this section is drawn from St. Olaf's Saga (in the foot-notes A, A¹, or Cd. = Cod. Holm.; A² = Kringla; B = the text in Fms. vols. iv, v, AM. 61).

I. THE FIRST PRAISE OF OLAF (1006–1014).

1.   LANGR bar út enn unga iœfra kund frá sundi
        (þióð ugði ser síðan) siá-meiðr (konungs reiði):
     (kann-ek til margs) enn manna minni *fyrsta* sinni
     hann rauð œztr fyrir austan ulfs fót við sker Sóta.

The East Baltic. The long-ship bore the young king out of the Sound (many a thing I can remember); and for the *first* time he

2.   Þat vas enn ok *önnor* Áláfr (né svik fǫ́losk)   5
odda þing í eyddri Eysýslo gekk heyja :
sítt ǫ́tto fiœr fótom (fár beið or stað) 'sára'
'enn þeir-es undan runno allvaldr,' buendr gialda.

3.   Hríð varð stáls í stríðri strœng Herdala gœngo
Finnlendinga at fundi fylkiss niðs en *þriðja* :   10
œnn 'austr við lá' leysti leið víkinga skeiðir
Bala-garðz at borði brim-skíðom lá síða.

4.   Enn kvǫ́ðo gram gunnar galdrs upp-hœfom valda
(dýrð frá-ek þeim-es vel varðisk vinnask) *fiorða* sinni :
þá-es ólítill úti iœfra liðs í miðli   15
friðr gekk sundr í slíðri Suðr-vík Dœnom kuðri.

5.   Víg vantu, hlenna hneigir, hiœlmom grimmt it *fimta*
(þolðo hlýr) á hári (hríð) 'Kinnlima-síðo :'
þá es við rausn at ræsiss reið herr ofan skeiðom,
enn í gœgn at gunni gekk hilmiss lið rekkom.   20

6.   Rétt es at sókn en *sétta ;* snarr þengill bauð Englom
at þars Áláfr sótti, Yggs, Lunduna-bryggjor :
sverð bito Vœlsk, enn vœrðo Víkingar þar Díki,
átti Sumt í slétto Suðvirki lið búðir.

7.   Enn lét *siaunda* sinni sverð-þing hait verða   25
endr á Ulfkels-landi Áláfr, sem ek ferr máli :
stóð Hringmara-heiði (her-fall var þar) alla
Ello kind, enn olli arfvœrðr Haraldz starfi.

8.   Veit-ek at víga mǿtir Vindom hættr enn *átta*
(styrkr gekk vœrðr at Virki verðungar) styr gerði :   30

---

reddened the wolf's paw off Soti's reef [off the Swedish coast]. That was the *second* when Olaf brought about a sword-moot in the wasted Island Osel; nor was treachery lacking there, they owed their lives to their feet, the runaways, none dared make a stand. The *third* was a hard fight on the Herdale-raid, where he met the Finlanders: a great gale overtook the wickings' ships, the Balagard coast lay alongside his ships.

North German Coast. They say that he brought on a battle for the *fourth* time, when peace was broken between the king's armies in the broad Southwick [Suderwijck in Pelworm] known to the Danes. Thou didst win the *fifth* battle off the high [sic] Kinnham-side [North Frisian coast], when the host rode down to the ships and the king's men went up to meet them in fight.

England. The *sixth* battle, it is true, the king offered to the English, when he beset London-bridges; the Gaulish sword bit, and the wickings guarded the Ditch; some of the host had better [quarters] in Southwark. And for the *seventh* time Olaf let there be a sword-moot on the land of Wolfkettle [East Anglia], as I go on to tell: the kin of Ælla [the English] took their stand all of them at Ringmere-heath; many men fell there, the heir of Harold set them a hard task. I know that the . . . . of the Wends began an *eighth* battle: the mighty master of

---

7. Read, sárir.   11. Read, laust veðr ok leysti.   12. borði] B.
18. Read, Kinnheima siðo.

sínn mǿttoð bǿ banna borg Cantara sorgar
mart feksk prúðom pœrtom port-greifar Áleifi.

9. Vann ungr konungr Englom ótrauðr skarar rauðar
('endr fell brúnt á branda blóð') 'Nyja móðo:'
Nú hefik orrostor austan 'ogn diarfr' nio talðar,   35
'herr fell Danskr' þar es dœrrom dreif mest at Áleifi.

10. *Tœgr* var fylldr í fœgrom (folk-veggs drifa hreggi)
(hélt sem hilmir mælti) Hrings-firði (lið þingat):
ból lét hann á Hœli hátt Víkingar átto
('þeir bǿðot ser síðan slíks skotnaðar') brotna.   40

11. Áláfr vantu, þars iœfrar, *ellifta* styr, fello
(ungr komtu af því þingi þollr) í Grislo-pollom:
þat frá-ek víg 'at vitto' Vilialms fyr bœ hialma
'tala minz' es þat telja tryggs iarls hait snarla.

12. Tann rauð *tolfta* sinni tír fylgjandi ylgjar   45
(varð) í Fetla-firði (fiœr-bann lagit mœnnom).

13. *Þrettánda* vann Þrœnda (þat vas flótta bœl) dróttinn
sniallr í Seljo-pollom sunnarla styr kunnan:
upp lét gramr í gamla Gunnvaldz borg um morgin,
'Geirfiðr' hét sá, gœrva gengit, iarl um fenginn.   50

14. Malms vann Mǿra hilmir munn-rióðr, es kom sunnan,
gang þars gamlir sprungo geirar, upp at Leiro:
varð fyr víga Niœrðom Varrandi siá 'fiarri'
brendr á bygðo landi (bœr heitir svá) Peito.

---

the henchmen went to the Work; the Port-reeves could not keep their
town, Canterbury, against Olaf, many a sorrow befell the proud port-
men. The bold young king gave the English red pates in .... New
Mouth [?   ]; the brown blood dripped on the brand. Now I
have counted nine battles *beginning* from the East; wherein the darts
drove about Olaf ....
France. The tale of *ten* was filled in fair Rings-firth [?   ],
whither at the king's command they wended their way; he stormed a
lofty pirate hold on Hæli [?   ] .... never after enjoyed such
booty as they won there. Thou foughtest the *eleventh* fray, where
princes fell, in Grisla-pool (thou wert young, Olaf, when that battle
ended); I heard of the victory by the trusty Earl William's town at
Wi ....; so I count. The *twelfth* time he reddened the wolf's
tusks in Fetla-firth [?   ], where there was loss of life to many
men. The lord of the Thronds won a well-known *thirteenth* fight
south in Selia-pool [?   ]; early in the morning the king bade
his men march up into the old Gundwald's borough, and *took* prisoner
an earl called Geifrid [Geffrey]. The Prince of the Mores, when he
came from the South, made an inroad up the Loire, where the
old spears sprung: Warrand [Guérande], so the town is named near
to the sea in Poitou-land, was burnt by his host.

---

32. paurtom, A.   34. Read, Lea móðo?   50. Read, Geifriðr?
53. Read, nærri.

[15.   'Ríkr kvað ser "at sœkja"' Sauðungs- konungr 'nauðir'
'fremðar giarn' í 'forno' fund Hákonar -sundi: 56
'Strangr hitti' þar þengill þann iarl es varð 'annarr'
œztr, ok ætt gat bazta, ungr á Danska Tungo.]

II. Nesja Vísor (1015).

(Verses 1, 4, 14 from Fagrsk., the rest from O. H.)

1.   FÓR ór Vík á vári válaust konungr austan
(þeir kníðo blœ́ báðir borð) enn iarl kom norðan:
kann-ek sigr-viðom segja sundz, hve þeira fundir,
œrin skil, þvi-at órom, at bœ́rosk, þar, váro.

2.   Veitti sókn þar-es sótti siklingr firin-mikla   5
(blóð féll rautt á róða rein) í hœfn at Sveini:
sniallr hélt at þar-es olli eirlaust konungr þeira
(enn Sveins liðar) sýnom (saman bundosk skip) fundi.

3.   Þat erom kunnt hve kennir Karlhœfða let iarli
odda frostz fyr austan Agðir nær of lagðan   10

4.   Hirð Áláfs vann harða hríð (enn svá vark bíða)
[Peitneskom félt-ek] (Páska) Palm-Sunnudag [hialmi].

5.   Vasa 'sig-mana' Sveini sverða sverða gnýs at flýja
gióðs ne gœrrar hríðar gunn-reifom Áleifi:
þvi-at 'kvistungar kosto' (kom at herr í stað verra)   15
'œ́tto sín þar es sóttosk' seggir hvárir-tveggjo.

6.   Teitr sá-ek okkr í ítro allvaldz liði falla
(gœrðisk harðr) um herðar (hiœr-dynr) svalar brynjor:
enn mín at flug fleina falsk und hialm inn Valska
(okkr vissak svá, sessi) svœrt skœr (við her gœrva).   20

Norway. The king stood from the island Selja toward Hakon at
Saudungs-sound; there the earl swore strong oaths to that young king
who was by far the highest and best in race of all the Danish
Tongue . . . . [See Notes.]

Nesia Verses. The king went from the East out of the Wick in
the spring, and the Earl [Sweyn] came from the North; they both plied
the black oars: I can tell men point by point how their meeting went
off, for I was there myself. The king [Olaf] made a very fierce attack
on Sweyn in the haven; the king openly brought about the battle and
held sharply to it, and Sweyn's men lashed their ships together. I
know how the king had Carle-head laid alongside the earl East off
Agd. Olaf's henchmen made a hard onset on Palm Sunday. I myself
kept the Easter vigil hooded in a Poitevin helmet. The brave Sweyn
could not be challenged for his behaviour in the battle, nor the warlike
Olaf for his fighting; for on both sides the men had . . . . saplings . . . .
when they made at each other. I saw the cold mail coats, Tait, fall
over our back in the king's army, and I covered my black hair under
the helmet of Gaul in the shaft-shower. So we were indeed equipped,

---

55. Corrupt, or Seljo.   57. Read, Ströng heit vann þar þengli þeim iarl es
vas allra . . . ?   4. þeim er, Cd.; for váro read hváro?   13. svinn-huglom, B.

7.   Stœng óð gylt þar es gengom Gondlar serks und merkjom
gnýss fyr gœfgom ræsi greiðendr á skip reiðir :
þági vas sem þessom þengils á ió strengjar
miœð fyrir malma kveðjo mær heið-þegom bæri.

8.   Ölld vann ossa skiœldo (auð-sætt vas þat) rauða   25
(hlióms) þa es hvítir kómo (hring-miðlendom) þingat :
þar hykk ungan gram gœngo (gunn-sylgs), enn ver fylgðom,
(blóðs fekk svœrr þars slœðosk sverð) upp í skip gerðo.

9.   Vær drifom hvatt (enn heyra hátt vápna brak knátti)
[rœnd klufo roðnir brandar] reiðir upp í skeiðar :   30
enn fyr borð þar-es bœrðomk (buin fengosk skip) gengo
[nár flaut œrt fyr eyri ófár] buendr sárir.

10.   Sialfr bað svartar kylfor Sveinn harðliga skeina ;
nær vas áðr í óra auðván 'roit' hánom :
þa-es ('til góðz enn gióði') gœrt ('fengosk hræ svœrtom') 35
(Yggs) lét herr um hœggit (hrafni) skeiðar stafna.

11.   Þess get-ek meirr at missi morð-œrr sá-es kom norðan
harða margr í hœrðom heim-kvœmo styr þeima :
sœkk af syndi-blakki sunno margr til grunna,
(satt es at Sveini mættom) sam-knúta (ver úti).   40

12.   Frýr eigi oss í ári Inn-Þrœnzk, þoat lið minna,
(gœrt hugðak svá) snerto, snotr mær, konungs væri :
brúðr mun heldr at háði hafa drótt þa-es 'framm sóttit'
feld 'ruðom skers,' ef skyldi, skeggi, aðra-tveggjo.

13.   Afli vex, þvi-at efla Upplendingar sendi   45
(Sveinn fundot þat) þenna þil-blakks, konungs, vilja :

---

mess-mate. The golden banner-staff waded on, when we, in our mail-coats, dashed aboard the ships under the standard before the noble king's face : on board the prince's ship in the fight it was not at all as when the damsel is bearing mead to the henchmen. Our shields, that came white thither, were made red, it was easy to see that; and the young king boarded the enemy's ship, and we followed him : I remember it well. We soon stormed on sharply aboard their galleys (one could hear the loud clatter of weapons, the red brands clove the shields), and overboard went the wounded crew, when we rushed on in the fight; corses untold floated out upon the shore. Sweyn himself, in his sore distress, bade his men cut away smartly at the black clubs [the figure-head beams], and his men hewed the figure-heads of their galleys clean off. Many a man, I ween, that came from the North, will in this hard fray have lost his hope of coming home again. Many a man sunk overboard to the bottom from the ships that were knit together when we met Sweyn off the land. The proud In-Throndish damsel will not surely challenge our gallantry in the battle, though we, the king's men, were the fewest : the lady should rather make mock of them who wrapped their bearded faces in their cloaks, if either side are to be blamed. The king's might grows apace, ever

---

34. Read, kōmit (cōit).   44. feld] emend. ; fold, Cdd.   45. vex] A².
vætt, Cd.

raun es hins at Heinir (hræ-linnz) mego vinna
(þeir átto flug) fleira fiøl-rekks an øl drekka.

III. AUSTRFARAR VÍSOR; or, EASTERN TRAVEL VERSES.

1. Á ÐR hefek gótt við góða grams stallara alla
   átt, þá-es ossom dróttni ógn-diarfs fyr kné hvarfa:
   Biørn, faztu opt at árna, íss, fyr mer at vísa
   góðs megot gótt of ráða, gunn-rióðr, þvi-at vel kunnot.

2. Nú sittu heill, enn hallar her finnomk meirr þínnar, 5
   at unz ek kem vitja, Áláfr, konungr mála:
   skald biðr hins at haldi hialm-drífo stafr lífi
   (endisk leyfð) ok landi [lyk-ek víso nú] þvísa.

3. Bua hilmiss sal hiølmom hirð-menn, þeir es svan grenna
   (her sé ek) bens, ok brynjom (beggja kost á veggjom): 10
   því á ungr konungr engi (ugglaust er þat) dyggra
   hús-búnaði at hrósa; høll es dýr með øllo.

4. Kátr vas-ek opt þa-es úti ørðigt veðr á fiørðom
   vísa segl í vási vind-blásit skóf Strinda:
   hestr óð kafs at kostom; kilir risto haf Lista 15
   'út' þars eisa létom 'undan skeiðr at sundi.'

5. Sniallz letom skip skolla skiøldungs við ey tiøldut
   fyrir 'agetu' úti øndurt sumar landi:
   enn í haust es hestar hag-þorns á mó sporna

---

since the Upland-men have given him help, Sweyn found that to his cost. It is now clear that the Heins [Heathmark folk] are good for more than ale-drinking.

Prologue. Before starting, to Biorn the Marshal. I have ever been on good terms with all the king's marshals, who walk before his knees. Biorn, thou hast often won favour for me with the king, for thou art well skilled to counsel, I will follow thee.

Farewell to Olaf. Abide in peace, O King Olaf; when I come back to make my report I shall see thee again. The poet prays this, that the king may keep his life and land safely. May thy glory endure. So I end my verse at this time.

On his return the Poet makes his report. As he enters the hall he says, The king's henchmen have dressed the walls with helms and mail-coats, I see a choice of both on the walls: no young king, verily, can boast of such fine house-furniture. The hall is right precious withal!

Incidents on the journey up. I was often blithe enough in the wet when a stiff breeze swept the king's sail on the firths of Strind. The sea-steed waded gallantly on, the keels plowed the Sea of Lister when we made the galley speed at Eker-Sound. We let the gallant king's ship with awnings pitched hover out off the Isle of Gotland ere the summer ended, and in the harvest-tide when the sea-king's chargers are launched on the hawthorn's mere [hoisted up on land] then I had to

---

16. Read, at þ. e. l. Eikunda- skeið -sundi?   18. Read, Eygota landi.

tekk (ymissar ekkjom iðir hlýtk) at ríða.   20

6.   Iór renn aptan-skæro all-svangr gœtor langar
      (vœll kná hófr) til hallar [hœfom lítinn dag] (slíta):
      nu es þatz blakkr of bekki berr mik 'daunum' ferri;
      fákr laust drengs í díki (dœgr mœtask nú) fœti.

7   Út muno ekkjor líta all-snúðola prúðar   25
      (flióð siá reyk) hvar ríðom Rœgnvalldz í bý gœgnom:
      keyrom hross, svá-at heyri harða langt or garði
      hesta rœs or húsom hug-svinn konan innan.

8.   Oss hafa augo þessi Íslenzk, konan, vísat
      biartan stíg at baugi brœttom langt en svœrto: 30
      siá hefir, miœð-nannan, manni mín ókunnar þínom
      fótr á fornar brautir full-drengila gengit.

9.   Hug-stóra bið-ek heyra 'hress fors' iœfurs þessar
      (þolða-ek vás) hve vísor, verðung, um fœr gœerðak:—
      Sendr vas-ek upp af œndrom austr, (svaf-ek fátt) í hausti 35
      til Sviðióðar síðan svan-vangs í fœr langa.

10.   Átt hafa ser, þeir-es sótto, sendi-menn fyr hendi
      Sygna grams, við sagnir siklinga, fœr mikla:
      spœrðomk fæst (enn fyrða fœng ero stór) við gœngo;
      vœrðr réð nýtr því es norðan Nóregs þinig fórom.   40

11.   Lét-ek til Eiðs, þvi-at óðom aptr-hvarf, dreginn karfa
      ver stilltom svá valtan vátr til glœps á báti:
      taki hlœgi-skip hauga herr (sákað-ek far verra)
      lét-ek til heims á hrúti hætt, fór betr en ek vætta.

---

take to horseback: I will tell the ladies of my various fortunes. The
slim steed gallops over the long roads in the even-gloom towards the
hall. The hoof cuts the turf! The day is short! And now it is
that my steed bears me over the brooks, far from the ships; my horse's
feet light on the Dyke; day and night are meeting [it is twilight].
The proud ladies, seeing the dust, will look out on us as we ride right
gallantly into Reginwald's town. Let us spur our steeds, so that the
gentle ladies in the town may hear afar off the din of the horses coming
towards the city. Those black Icelandic eyes of mine have brought
me from far up a steep path to a bright ring [he had had a ring given
him at Reginwald's court], these feet of mine have sped sturdily over
ancient ways where thou hast never been!

The journey back. Gentle King, I beg thy henchmen to listen to these
verses which I made on my journey. I suffered from the wet. In the
autumn I was put ashore in the east from the ships back to Sweden for
a long journey. I gat little sleep! The messengers that the Lord of the
Sogn-folk sent on his business had a great journey before them. We
spared not to walk. It was the Norse king that sent us thither from the
North. I had a rickety smack drawn towards Eid [the isthmus], for I
feared lest I should never get back, we were in such jeopardy in the boat.
The host of the barrows [fiends] take the mock ship; I never saw a worse
boat. I risked my life on the old sea-ram [smack], yet things went better
than I thought likely.

---

23. Read, knörrom.

12.   Vasa fýst; enn ek rann rastir reiðr of skóg frá Eiðom   45
      (menn of veit at mættom meini) tolf ok eina:
      hykk á fót, enn flekkom fell sár á il hvára,
      hvasst gengom þó þangat þann dag, konungs manni.
13.   Réð-ek til Hofs at hœfa; hurð vas aptr; (ek spurðomk)
      inn settak nef, nenninn (niðr-lútr fyrir útan):   50
      orð gat ek fæst at fyrðom; (flœgð bað-ek) [enn þau sœgðo]
      hnekðomk heiðnir rekkar, [heilagt] (við þau deila).
14.   Gagkattu inn, kvað ekkja, armi drengr, in lengra,
      hræðomk-ek við Óðins (erom heiðnir ver) reiði:
      rýgr kvazk inni eiga óþekk, sú-es mer hnekði,   55
      alfa blót, sem ulfi, 'otvín' í bœ sínom.
15.   Fór-ek at finna bœro, friðs vættak mer, síðan
      briót þann-es bragnar héto bliks vildastan miklo:
      grefs leit við mer gætir gerstr, þá es illr enn versti
      (lítt reiði-ek þó lýða last) ef sá es inn bazti.   60
16.   Nú hafa hnekt, þeir-es hnakka hein-fletz við mer setto,
      (þeygi bella þollar) þrír sam-nafnar (tíri):
      þó siœmk hitt at hlœéir haf-skíðs myni síðan
      út, hverr es Œlvir heitir, allz mest reka gesti.
17.   Mista-ek fyr austan Eiða-skóg á 'Leiðo'   65
      Ásto burs, þa-es æstag ókristinn hal vistar:
      Ríks fauka-ek son Saxa, saðr vas œngr fyrir, þaðra;
      út vas-ek eitt sinn heitinn innan fiórom sinnom.
18.   Driúg-genginn vas drengjom (drengr magnar lof þengils)

It was not for my pleasure that I had a smart walk of twelve leagues
and one through the wood from Eid. Look you, I met with trouble
enough! Yet I went briskly forward on foot all that day: though
sores fell thick on the soles of the feet of the king's men. I made my
way gallantly to Hof [Temple]; the door was shut, but I put my nose
in and I asked for lodging from outside, downcast enough. I got no
answer from them. The heathen-folk turned me away, saying it was
hallowed. I prayed the fiends to deal with them! Go not in further,
quoth the goodwife, thou miserable man! for we fear the wrath of
Woden; we are heathen folk! The surly housewife that turned me
away like a wolf said that they were holding a Sacrifice to the Elves
within her homestead. Then I went to find the man whom the people
spoke of as the most hospitable, hoping for peace; but the wretched
digger [farmer] looked grimly on me. I am no slanderer; but if this be
the best, the worst must be bad indeed!

Three namesakes have now turned their back upon me, they have
acted very churlishly, and I fear that every one whose name is Olwi
drives his guests *from his door*.

I missed the son of Asta [King Olaf] when I asked the heathen man
for quarters east of Eidwood. I did not find a son of Saxi [an hospitable Earl Reginwald] at home there! There was no kindliness to be
met with there, I was turned away four times in one evening!

It was hard walking for us east [from the east?] towards the king

---

45. fyrst, Cd.   51. at] en, Cd.   65. Name of place?

'austr' til 'iœfra þrýstiss' Eiða-skógr a 'leiðo:'   70
skyldit mer, áðr mildan mínn dróttinn kom-ek finna
hlunnz af hilmiss runnom hnekkt dýr-loga bekkjar.

19.   Lét-ek við yðr es ítran, Áláfr, hagat mœlom
rétt, es ríkjan hittag Rœgnvald, konungr, haldit:
deilda-ek mœlom mildan malma-vœrð í Gœrðom   75
harða mœrg, ne ek heyrða heið-mannz tœlor greiðri.

20.   Þik bað sólar sækkvir sínn halda vel Rínar
hvern es hingat árnar húskarl nefi iarla:
enn hverr es austr vill sinna (iamn-vist es þat), Lista
þengill, þínna drengja, þar á hald und Rœgnvaldi.   80

21.   Folk réð um 'sik' fylkir flest es ek kom vestan
ætt 'sem áðr of hvatti' Eireks 'svika' þeira:
enn þvi-at iarla frændi eins því es tókt af Sveini
yðr kveð ek iœrð es nœðot Ulfs bróðor son stóðosk.

22.   Spakr lét Ulfr meðal ykkar Áláfr tekit mœlom   85
(þítt fengom svar) sætta [sakar leggit it] beggja:
þer let þiófa rýrir þær sem œngar væri
ripta reknar heiptir Rœgnvaldr gefit aldar.

23.   Fast skaltú ríkr við ríkjan Rœgnvald, konungr, halda
(hann stendr þýðr af þínni þœrf) nœtt ok dag sœttom: 90
þann veit-ek, þinga kennir, þik baztan vin miklo
á Austr-vegom eiga allt með grœno Salti.

24.   Nú ero mælt, enn mála meir kunnom skil fleiri,

on the road through Eid-shaw. I go on with my song on the king.
May I not, when I come back to my lord again, be turned away by his
henchmen!

   At Reginwald's court. I delivered your weighty message faithfully, O
Olaf, when I reached the mighty Reginwald. I held much talk with
the generous Earl in Garth [Novgorod], nor have I ever heard fairer
speech from any noble. The Earl bade thee to take good care of any of
his house-carles that might turn hither, and any of thy men that will go
to the east shall be in likeway treated by Reginwald. All men when I
came from the west spoke of thee, my lord, according to the promptings
of the son of Eric, the Swedish king. But as for the land of the Earl's
which . . . . the brother's son of Wolf [Reginwald] acknowledged
thy title also to the land thou tookest from Earl Sweyn. The wise
Wolf [Reginwald's son] received kindly your offers of treaty. We got a
kind answer, ye put away your feuds: the . . . . Reginwald . . . . and
made as if there were no vengeance to be wreaked for breaches of the
peace *between you.* Hold fast, O Mighty King, by day and night, thy
covenant with the mighty Reginwald, for he is helpful to thee at need.
He is, I very well know, the best friend by far that thou hast in the
East-Way, all along the green Baltic.

   Epilogue. Now, O King, I have delivered all the words that most

70. Read, austan?   73. Read, hugaz malom.   75. mal ens milda . . .
vörðz, Cd.   76. mörg] A²; margr, Cd.   81. Read, þik?   82. Read,
Svia?   86. þau, Cd.; þétt, A².   88. Emend.; riptar, Cd.

orð þau-es oss um varða allz mest, konungr, flesta :
Got láti þik gæta, geð-harðr konungr, iarðar   95
(víst hefi ek þann) þvi-at, þínnar, þú ert til borinn (vilja).

IV. Vestrfarar Vísor ; or, Western Travel Verses.

(Verse 9 from AM. 75 c.)

1.   BERGR, hæfom minnzk hve margan morgon Rúðo-borgar
     bæorð lét-ek í fæor fyrða fest við arm in vestra.

2.   Útan varð-ek áðr an Ióta and-spilli fekk-ek stilliss
     (melld sa-ek her fyr hæolði hús-dyrr) fyrir spyrjask :
     enn eyrendi óro átt-runnr í sal knátti   5
     Gorms ('ber-ek opt á armi iarn-stúkor') vel lúka.

3.   Örr tegask Áláf gœrva 'allt hefir sa er' fiæor-valtan
     (konungr dauða mon-ek kvíða) Knútr ok Hákon úti :
     haldizk væorðr, þoat vildit varla Knútr ok iarlar,
     'dælla es fyrst á fialli fundr' ef hann sialfr kœmsk undan.   10

4.   Átti iarl at 'sætta all-framr' buendr gamla
     ok þeirs optast tóko Áláf at því máli :
     'þeir hafa fyrr af fári framt es Eireks kyn meira'
     hæofðom keypt an heiptir Hákon saman mœndi.

5.   Knútr hefir okkr enn ítri all-dáð-gæofugr bæoðom   15
     hendr, es hilmi fundom, Húnn, skrautliga búnar :
     þer gaf hann mæork eða meira, marg-vitr, ok hiæor bitran
     gollz (ræðr gœrva æollo Goð sialfr) enn mer halfa.

6.   Hafa all-framir iæofrar út sín hæofuð Knúti
     fœérð or Fífi norðan (frið-kaup vas þat) miðjo : .   20

---

concern us all, though I have much more which I could tell. May God give thee, good King, thy land to which thou wert born! Surely that is my wish !

How many a morning, Berg, we have been talking over how on my voyage I moored my ship fast to the western side of Rouen.

I had to enquire outside the hall before I could get speech of the lord of the Jutes [Cnut]: I saw the doors barred before me by a host of men. But once within the hall, the scion of Gorm graciously discharged my suit.

Cnut and Hakon threatened to take the life of Olaf. I fear lest he should die. May he be kept safe, even though Cnut and the Earls would have it otherwise. It would be well if he escape with life. The Earl has been bribing the old franklins to betray Olaf, and now they have pledged their heads to it. Eric's kin are eager.

To Bersi. O Cub, Cnut decked the arms of both of us when we visited him. He gave thee a mark of gold and a keen sword, and to me half a mark. God himself rules all things.

The foremost princes [Macbeth and Iehmarc], away north of Fife, have brought their heads to Cnut, to buy peace from him. Olaf never

---

4. sa er, Cd.   14. Read, sama mœndi ?

seldi Áláfr aldri (opt vá sigr inn Digri)
haus í heimi þvísa hann œngom svá manni.

7. Heim erom hingat komnir (hygg-þú at iæfurr skatna)
[menn nemi mǽl sem ek inni mín] stallarar þínir:
seg-þú hvar sess hafir hugðan seims þióð-konungr beima   25
(allr es þekkr) með þollom (þínn skáli mer innan).

8. Knútr spurði mik mætra mildr ef ek hónom vilda
hendi langr sem hringa hug-reifom Áleifi:
einn kvað-ek senn at sænno (svara þóttomk vel) dróttinn
[gœr ero gumna hverjom gnóg dǿmi] mer sǿma.   30

9. Eið láta-þú ýtir einn, þó ek vera seinni,
iarðar alla verða, auðar mildr, an ek vilda:
esa fyrir mál þat-es mæla mann þu lætr her vándan
' læng þœrf mun gram' gengit, gestr Knútz vas-ek flestom.

10. Fiándr ganga þar þengils (þióð býðr opt) með sióða   35
(hæfgan malm fyrir hilmiss haus ófalan) lausa:
sik veit hverr, es harra hollan selr við golli
(vert es slíks) í sværto, sínn, Helvíti innan.

11. Kaup var daprt þatz diúpan dróttin rækt of sótto,
þeir es, heim á himni hǽm ellz, svikom belldo.   40

12. Gœrðisk hilmiss Hærða húskarlar þá iarli
es við Áláfs fiærvi of vægir fé þægi:
hirð esa hans at verða háligt fyrir því máli;
dælla es oss ef allir erom ver of svik skírir.

---

yielded his neck to any one in this world; the Stout One often won
a victory.

His return to Norway. Behold, O King, we are come home again, we
thy marshals. Let men listen to what I am saying. Tell me where thou
hast settled a seat for me among the men in the hall. Thy whole house
withal is agreeable to me [*or* thy hall is all full of men].

The King distrusting him. Cnut asked me if I would serve him as I had
served Olaf, and I told him (and I thought I had answered well and
given a good example to all men), that it was fit for me to have but one
lord. O King, let not one oath cover all [i. e. because others are traitors
do not suspect me], though I am later *back* than I wished. The accusation which wicked men have brought before thee has not been sifted
to the bottom, ... although I was Cnut's guest.

The traitors. The king's enemies are walking about openly with bags
of gold, offering gold for his priceless head. Every man that sells his
good lord for gold knows that he deserves to be in the midst of black
Hell-pain. It was a sorry bargain when the traitors, who betrayed their
lord, sold their homes in the high heavens for a place in the fire of the
deep pit. It were a sad thing for house-carles of King Olaf to take
money of the Earl against King Olaf's life. It is not honourable for
his henchmen to lie under such a charge. It would be well if we were
all clear of treason.

---

25. beimom, Cd.   26. þaktr, *some.*   30. *Or,* góð dœmi.   39. rækt]
emend ,—red *or* rett, Cdd.   40. hás, Cd.

13.	Út býðr allvaldr sveitom Englandz ; enn ver fengom	45
	(lítt sé-ek lofðung óttask) lið færi ok skip smæri :
	ráöð ero liót, ef láta landz menn konung þenna
	(lætr einæorð fé fyrða ferð) lið-þrota verða.
14.	Flœja 'getr' enn frýjo fiándr leggr oss til handa,
	verð-ek fyr œðro orðs 'allvaldz en fé gialda :'	50
	hverr skal þegn (þótt þverri þengils vina gengi)
	[upp 'hvolfra' svik] sialfan sik lengst hafa miklo.

V. Tog-drapa ; or, Stretch-Song on King Cnut.

(Verse I from Ragnars S. ; verses 2 and 11 from Fagrsk. ; verse 2 from Skioldungr S.)

1.	OK Ello bak at lét hinn es sat
	Ivarr ara Iorvik skorit.

2.	Ok senn sono sló hvern ok þó
	Aðalráðs, eða út flœmði Knútr.

1.	3.	Knútr es und himnom—Hygg ek ætt at frétt	5
	Haraldz í her hug vel duga :—
	Lét lýr-gæoto lið suðr or Níð
	Áláfr iæofurr ár-sæll fara.
4.	Þurðo norðan (namsk þat) við gram
	til sléttz svalir Silunz kilir :	10
	enn með annan Onundr Dæonom
	á hendr 'at há' her Sœnskan ferr.
5.	Lét um land lokit liðs gramr saman
	mar-beðjom með mæorg nef-biæorgom

The King of England is calling out a levy, but we have fewer men and smaller ships; yet our king fears not. It will be an ugly case if the people of this land let their king be short of men. Bribes foil their honour. *Obscure. Some counsel not to make a stand, the odds are too great, and the country not to be trusted, treason smouldering underneath.* Let every man take heart, *he said*, let us not be the laughing-stock of our enemies. It is better to fight than ransom oneself. The king's friends are getting few; yet every man must always take count with himself [he cannot evade his conscience]. Treason will out.

And Iwar that ruled at York cut an Eagle on the back of Ælla. And then Cnut slew or exiled one and all of Æthelred's sons. *The Burden.* Cnut is the foremost suzerain under heaven. *Staves. Attack on Cnut.* I know that heart was not lacking in the son of Harold [Olaf]. King Olaf, blessed with fair seasons, let the fleet speed over the sea from Nith in the south. The cold keels went from the north to flat Sealand against the king [Cnut]: while Eanwynd brought a Swedish host against the Danes on the other hand. The king [Cnut] fenced the land in with many helmets.... (*The hostile fleet hanging*

---

12. hanom *or* heyja, *others.*

'þar es gráðr fyrir gnóð grá hialmom lá' 15
'þorn heims þrumo þundr of fundr.'

6. Gǽtoð dróttnar Danmørk spanit
undir sik søkom snarir herfarar:
þá lét skarpla Skáney Dana
hlœðr herjaða—*höfuð-fremstr iöfurr.* 20

II. 7. *Knútr es und himnom*—Herr austan ferr
fríðr fylkiss niðr frán-eygr Dana:
skreið vestan viðr varr-glœstr, sa-es bar
út andskota Aðalráðs þaðan.

8. Ok bǽro í byr blǽ segl við rǽ 25
(dýr vas døglings før) drekar landreka:
enn þeir-es kómo kilir vestan til
um leið liðo Lima-fiarðar brim.

9. Létað af iǽfurr (ætt manna fansk)
Iótlandz etask ílendr (at því): 30
vildi foldar fæst rán Dana
hlíf-skiøldr hafa—*höfuð-fremstr iöfurr.*

III. 10. *Knútr es und himnom* . . .

. . . .

11. Kómo fylki far-lystir, es bar
her-víg í hug, hafanda staf: 35
raufræsir af Rúms veg 'suman'
kær keisara Clus Petrúsi.

12. Svá mun fár feril fetom suðr metinn
hring-drífr hafa—*höfuð-fremstr iöfurr.*

---

all about the coast.) The two kings could not wile Denmark out of his,
Cnut's, hands into their power. Upon which, the Vanquisher of the
Danes [Olaf] severely ravaged Sconey.
  Burden. Cnut etc.
  Stave. The muster of Cnut's forces. The keen-eyed son of the Danish
king [Hardacnut] brought a host from the East. From the West sped
the fleet that shone on the sea, bearing the enemy of Æthelræd [Cnut]
thither. And the king's dragons carried blue sails on their yards.
Goodly was the king's voyage, and the keels that came from the West
sped over the sea-path to Limb-frith. Men said that the King of
Jutland would not take the smallest mess. The Buckler of the Danes
[Cnut] would have no plundering of his land.
  The Pilgrimage. Over the war-minded king came the longing for
travel, bearing a staff; the Lord of the Cumbrians sped on the way to
Rome, dear . . . . Emperor . . . . Key-Peter. No other king will have
thus measured the southward path with his feet.

VI. Dirge on Erling.

(Verse 8 from Flatey-bok iii. 244.)

1. UT réð Erlingr skióta eik ('sá-es rauð enn bleika')
['if-laust es þat'] iœfri ('arnar fót') at móti:
Skeið hans lá svá síðan siklings í 'her miklom'
(snarir bœrðosk þar síðan) sí-byrð við skip (fyrðar).

2. Rakkr þengill hió rekka, reiðr gekk hann of Skeiðar; 5
valr lá þrœngt á þiljom; þung vas sókn fyrir Tungom:
bragningr rauð fyrir breiðan borð-vœll Iaðar norðan;
blóð kom varmt í víðan (vá frægr konungr) ægi.

3. Öll var Erlings fallin (ungr fyrir norðan Tungor)
(Skeið vann skiœldungr auða) skip-sókn við þrœm Bóknar:
einn stóð sonr á síno snarr Skialgs vinom fiarri 11
í lyptingo lengi læ-trauðr skipi auðo.

4. Réð eigi grið gygjar geð-stirðr konungs firða
skers þó at skúrir þyrrit Skialgs hefnir ser nefna:
enn varð-kers virðir víð-botn ne kœmr síðan 15
glyggs á gialfri legðan geirs ofrhugi meiri.

5. Öndurða það iarðar Erlingr (sa-es vel lengi
geymði) hann lystr, (ne lamðisk land-vœrn) kloask œrno:
þá-es hann at sik sœnnom (sá var áðr buinn) ráða
(atz) við Útstein hitzig Álafr um tók mœlom. 20

6. Erlingr fell (enn olli allríkr) 'scipat slico'
[bíðrat betri dauða] (bragna konr) með magni:
mann veit-ek engi annan all-brátt at fiœr-láti
enn sá-es allan kunni aldr fullara at halda.

7. Áslákr hefir aukit (es vœrðr drepinn Hœrða) 25
[fair skyldo svá] (foldar) frænd-sekjo [styr vekja]:

ERLING had his ship brought broadside to the king, that is certain. His galley lay alongside the king's ship in .... The king [Olaf] cut down the warriors, he soon boarded the galley; the dead lay thick on the deck; there was a tough fight off the Tongues. The king dyed red the broad ship-field [sea] north of Iadar. The warm blood fell on the wide main, the famous prince won the day. Off the side of Bokn all Erling's crew fell; the young king cleared the galley north of the Tongues. Skialg's gallant son stood long alone on the forecastle of his empty ship. The avenger of Skialg [Erling] did not care to ask quarter of the king's men. There was never, nor shall come again, on the wide surf-girt plain of the dome of the winds [earth], a braver heart. Erling, who long bravely defended his land and never failed, cried out that 'eagles should use their talons face to face,' when Olaf accosted him there in battle south of Out-stone. Erling fell *on Thomas' day;* the king caused it. Never shall a better lord die! I knew no other man who, till his death, could hold his own like him. Anslak committed parricide when

---

5. Read, Skeiðo. 14. þyrrit] A²; berðiz, Cd. 16. lœgðan, A².
20. Ólāf, Cdd. 21. Read, E. fell ogn-hress ... Thomas messo?

ætt-vígi má hann eigi (á líti þeir) níta;
[frændr skyli bræði bindask bornir] (máol in forno).

8.   Drakk eigi ek drekkjo dag þann es mer sæogðo
Erlings fall at Iólom all-glaðr 'þess er reð Iaðri'   30
hans mun dráp um drúpa dýr-mennis mer kenna
hæofuð bæoróm þá hæra (hart morð vas þat) forðom.

9.   Erlingr 'vas sva at iarla átt' es Skioldungr máttit
Áláfs mágr 'svá at œgði' all-dyggs sonar Tryggva:
Næst gaf sína systor snarr bú-þegna harri   35
Ulfs feðr (vas þat) aðra (aldr-gipta) Rognvaldi.

10.   'Erlingi vas engi annarr lendra manna'
'æorr sá-es átti fleiri orrostor stoð þorrinn:'
'þrek har seggr við sóknir sinn, þvi-at fyrst gekk innan'
'mildr í marga hildi mest enn or á lesti.'   40

11.   Einn vissa-ek þer annan ialks-brík-tæopuð glíkan
(vítt réð gumna gætir) Goðbrandr hét sá (læondom):
ykkr kveð-ek iamna þykkja, orm-láðs hati, báða;
lýgr hinn at ser lægir legg-setrs es telsk betri.

VII. OLAF'S-DRAPA. OLAF'S DIRGE.
(Verse 2 from Flatey-bok.)

1.   ÁLÁFR reð it œfra and-prútt hæofuð landi
fulla vettr áðr felli fimtán á því láni:
Hvar hafi hers inn nœrðra heims enda ser kendan
(skiæoldungr hellzk an skyldi skemr) landreki in fremri?

2.   Upplænd vann til enda 'óss gneista,' ok þar reisti   5
Kristni hald, þat es héldo 'hvers veitir sverðs beita:'

---

the defender of the Hords was slain: no man should wake such war *as
this between kinsmen.* He cannot deny that he has slain a kinsman.
Born kinsmen should abstain from feud; let them look to the legends
of old. I did not drink merrily the day that I was told, *over in Wick,*
of the fall of Erling at Yule. His death will make me droop my head,
which I carried high before: his was a cruel death! Erling, the brother-
in-law of Olaf Tryggvason (that was a stroke of fortune), ruled over Agd
in spite of the Earls .... He [Olaf Tryggvason] gave his next sister
to Reginwald, father of Wolf. *There was none of the Barons that had so
much rent (revenues) as Erling. He drew the half of the dues from the south
to Sogn, from the west to Rygiar-bit.* I never knew but one other like unto
thee: his name was Gudbrand; he ruled broad lands [Godbrand of the
Dales]. I declare you both evenly matched, he who says he is better lies.

His Glory. OLAF, the proud of soul, ruled the upper land full fifteen
winters, ere he fell on his own fief. Wherever was there a greater
ruler known under the northern skirts of the earth! would that he had
reigned longer! He conquered the Uplands from end to end, and set
up Christendom again; formerly *five* kings had held sway thereat

---

30. Read, í Vík þaðra.   34. Read, at Agðom?   37-40. All corrupt
and painted over, see O. H. ch. 21.   Read, stoðir runno undir . . . frá Sogni sunnan
. . . til Rygjarbitz vestan.

áðr stýrðo því eyðar 'ellifo' fyrr 'hella'
'mildings mals' en guldo menn vísliga gísla.

3. Lyngs bar fiskr til fengjar flug-styggs sonar Tryggva
giolnar golli mælno (Goð vildi svá) roðnar:　　10
annan lét á unnir Áláfr buinn hála
(lœgr þó driúgt) inn Digri (dýrs horn) Vísund sporna.

4. Vissi helzt, þat-es hvæssom hund-mærgom let grundar
værðr með væpnom skerða, víkingom skær, ríkiss:
mildr let mægo valdit Magnúss faðir gagni;　　15
fremð Áláfs kveð-ek fræmðo flestan sigr ens Digra.

5. Goll buðo opt, þeir es ollo út-hlaupom, gram kaupask
rautt enn ræsir nítti, rík-lundoðom, undan:
skær lét hann með hiœrvi (herland skal svá verja)
[ráns biðo rekkar sýna refsing] firom efsa.　　20

6. 'Fœddi' mest sa-es meiddi marg-dýrr konungr 'varga'
hvinna ætt ok hlenna; hann stýfði svá þýfðir:
þýðr let þermlask bæði þióf hvern konungr erna
(frið bœtti svá) fóta (fylkir landz) ok handa.

[7. Tolf frá ek tekna elfar tállaust viðo bála　　25
olli Áláfr falli eirlaust konungr þeira:
Svia tiggja leit-ek seggi sokn-stríðs fyrrum ríða
(bœl vas brátt) til Heljar (buit mest) Sigars hesti.]

8. Lopt-byggvir, mátt leggja land-rétt þann es skal standask
unnar, allra manna, eiki-hliðs, á miðli.　　30

9. Þorð frá ek þat sinn 'herða (þreifsk sókn') með Áleifi
[góð 'foro þar'] 'geirom' gœrt víg [saman hiœrto]:

.... paid hostages .... The Heath-Fish [Serpent] with gills of ground
gold bore Tryggvi's son to the battle. So God willed it. But a second
Olaf, the Stout One, let the well-rigged Bison tread the waves; the
billows drenched the Beast's horns.

His Law. It was a proof of his stern rule, that the warden of the land
had the heads of many Wickings [pirates] cut short with keen weapons.
The gentle father of Magnus has wrought many a gainful deed *for
the land.* I can tell how many a victory made Olaf the Stout glorious.
They that made armed trespass ofttimes offered gold to the stern king
for ransom; but he refused it, and commanded their heads to be chopped
off with the sword. The blessed king maimed the race of robbers and
reivers, thus he cut short theft; he made every thief lose hands and feet,
so he bettered the peace of the land. Nor did treason, I know well,
thrive .... towards the king. [There were twelve men taken; Olaf had
them all put to death without mercy. I formerly saw the messenger of
the Swedish king ride on Sigard's steed [the gallows] to hell.] Thou didst
lay down that Constitution which shall endure among all men ....

The battle of Sticklestead. I heard that Thord Folason fought alongside King Olaf (a brave heart was his). Ogmund's gallant brother
[Thord] bore the fair gilt Banner-staff high before the lord of the Ring-
folk. The king himself marched next to his standard, the banner-staff

24. friðr bættiz sva, Cd.　　32. Read, Fólason *or* viva.

stœng bar hátt fyrir Hringa hialdr-móðom gram bróðir
(fullt vann) fagrla gyllta, fram-lundaðr Ogmundar.

10.   Mest frá-ek merkjom næstan mínn dróttinn framm sínom
(stœng óð fyrir gram) gengo ['gnógr styrr vas þar'] fyrri : 36
'œld vann Áláf feldan œflgan sigr' enn Digri
gekk sókn-þorinn sœkja sinjór framm í brynjo.

11.   Sumir trúðo á Goð gunnar, grein vas liðs á miðli,
'folk-orrostor fylkir fram-ráðr tiogo háði:'   40
frægr bað hann á hœgri hœnd Kristið lið standa
'feðr Magnus bið ek fagna flótt skiœrrom Goð dróttinn.'

12.   Enn þeir es austan nenna ('óx hildr') með gram mildom
['mart segik bert'] í 'biarta blóð-rœst' Sviar 'óðo.'

13.   Olmr eromk harmr sa es hilmir hafði (golli vafðan)   45
(ioforr kreisti) sá austan afl-fátt (meðal-kafla) :
gagn fengo því þegnar þeir at hœlfo fleiri,
'hvœtoð tælði þat hildar,' hvœrongi frá-ek váro.

14.   Fór í fylking þeira framm [iðrask nú] miðri
(snarir fundosk þar) Þróenda (þess verks) ' buendr ' merki. 50

15.   Vítt varð fold und fótom (frið-bann vas þar) mœnnom
[þá réð í bœð bráða brynjað folk] at dynja :
þá-es árliga ærir alms með biarta hialma
(mikill varð á stað Stikla stál-gustr) ofan þusto.

16.   Ekl vas ógn á Stikla óblíð stœðom síðan . . .   55

17.   Geirs hykk grimmligt váro gunn-reifom Áleifi
log-rœtondom líta lións í hvassar siónir :
þorðot Þrœnzkir virðar (þótti hersa dróttinn
œgiligr) í augo orm-frœn siá hœnom.

---

waded on before the prince.   Olaf the Stout carried his sword Hneiti ;
the *Senior* went forth in his mail-coat in quest of a great victory.   Some
of his men believed in God, he made a distinction between them.   The
king had thirty companies *of a hundred* [3,600] in that battle.   The
famous prince bade the Christian band to stand on the right hand, ...
but the Swedes who followed the king from the East stood on his
left hand.   It is a great sorrow to me that the king who clasped the
gold-wound hilt had too few men from the East.   The thanes got the
victory because they were more by half.   I am told the whole of both
hosts numbered a hundred times a hundred [14,400] : i. e. *they were
three to one.*

The Banner.   The standard of Calf went forth in the midst of the array
of the Thronds.   They repent this deed now !   The earth did thunder
far and wide under their feet as the mail-coated people marched on to
battle.   The peace was broken there when the warriors with the bright
helmets charged down upon the yeomen.   Great was the storm of steel at
Sticklestead !   There was no lack of terror on Sticklestead . . . .   It was
dreadful for the franklins, I ween, to look into the fierce lion eyes of

---

38. Read, folk . . . fylkir . . . þriá togo . . .   40. Overworked text.   41.
Overlaid text.   44. All corrupt ; read, stáðo?   48. hvar tveggi, B.
Read, huudraða tölðosk hundroð.   50. Read, Kalfs?

18. Rauð í rekka blóði rænd 'með gumna hœndom' 60
dreyrog sverð þar es dýran drótt þióð-konung sótti:
ok at ísarn-leiki Inn-Þrœndom lét finnask
rœkinn gramr í reikar rauð-brúnan hiœr túnom.

19. Mildr fann gœrst hve galdrar gramr sialfr megin-rammir
fiœl-kunnigra Finna full-stórom barg Þóri: 65
þá es hyr-sendir Hundi húna golli búno
(slœtt réð sízt at bíta) sverði laust um herðar.

20. Þollr dylr saðrar snilli seims, en þat veit, heiman
(hverr sæi Hundz verk stœri?) hug stórs er frýr Þóri:
'en' þver-garða þorði þróttr hinn-es framm of sótti 70
glyggs í gegn at hœggva gunn-rannz konung-manni.

21. Biœrn frá-ek ok af œrno endr stallorom kenndo
hug hve halda dygði (hann sótti fram) dróttinn:
fell í her með hollom hann verðungar mœnnom
(leyfðr es) at hilmiss hœfði hróðr-auðigs (sá dauði). 75

22. Hœrð es, sízt her-menn gœrðo (hlíf raufsk fyr gram) lífi,
auðn at Engla stríði, ómiúk, konung siúkan:
œr brá Áláfs fiœrvi œld, þar es herr klauf skiœldo,
('folks odda gekk fylkir fund') enn Dagr hélt undan.

23. Áðr vito eigi meiðar ógnar skers ne hersa 80
(þióð réð þengils dauða) þann styrk buand-manna:
es slíkan gram sóknom sár-elldz viðir felldo
(mœrg lá dýr í dreyra drótt) sem Áláfr þótti.

24. Gœrt es þeim es gótt bar hiarta goll-skrín of 'veg' mínom
(hrósa-ek helgi ræsiss) [hann sótti Goð] dróttni: 85

Olaf. The Thronds dared not meet the serpent-keen eyes of him. The gory swords reddened the shields in men's hands, when the people attacked their dear king, and at the iron-play the king let the red-brown blade meet the heads of the In-Thronds. The gentle prince found for himself how the strengthful charms of the wizard Fins saved the sturdy Thori, what time the king struck with the gold-mounted blade on the shoulders of Hound [Thori], the blunt sword did not bite at all. He who denies that Thori brought from home a full stock of courage lies. Who ever saw a bolder feat for a Hound than when he dared to smite the king. I hear that Biorn taught the marshals how to keep a true heart towards their lord. He fought in the van! He fell at the head of the glorious king, with his fellow-henchmen. That was a death to be praised!

There is a great void ever since the men of the host made the foe of the English sick of life [i. e. slew Olaf]. They took Olaf's life, but Dag got away .... Never before was such strength known in the barons and franklins, as that they should be able to fell such a king as Olaf was known to be.

Olaf's Sanctity. They have made a golden shrine for my lord who ever bore a good heart; I praise his saintliness. He has gone to be with God. Soon many a man, that came blind to the famous tomb

---

69. Read, hugar stórs?   70. en] read, es.   73. Read, dróttins?

ár gengr margr frá mæro meiðr þess konungs leiði
hreins með heilar siónir, hrings, es blindr kom þingat.

25. Lýg-ek nema Áláfr eigi ýfs, sem kvikir tivar,
(gœði-ek 'helzt' í hróðri hár-vœxt konungs) árar:
enn helzk (þeims sun seldi) svœrðr (þanns óx í Gœrðom), 90
[hann fekk læss] á liósom [lausn] (Valdamar), hausi.

26. Oss dugir Áláfs messo (iœfur magnar Goð) fagna
meina laust í míno, Magnúss fœðor, húsi :
skyldr em-ek skilfings halda, skoll-laust (þess es bió golli)
helgi (handar tialgor) harm-dauða (mer rauðo).   95

27. Dánar dróttni mínom dœgn of sent at hendi . . .

28. Dróttinn ! hialp þú þeim-es dóttor (dýrr es þínn vili) mína
heim ór heiðnom hóf, ok nafn gaf Tófo :
hélt und vátr enn vitri (varð-ek þeim feginn harðla
morni) míno barni móð-rakkr Haraldz bróðir.   100

29. Lát auman nú nióta Nóregs ok gef stórom
(mœl halt) svá sem sælan, sinnjór, laga þínna !

30. Undr láta þat ýtar eigi smátt es máttit
skæ-niœrðungom skorðo skýlauss rœðull hlýja :
driúg varð á því dœgri (dagr náðit lit fœgrom)   105
[orrosto frá-ek austan atburð] konungs furða.

---

of the pure king, goes away with his eyes whole. I lie if I deny that
Olaf's hair and nails grew like a living being's. I exalt the king's
holiness in my song : and the growth still stays on the bright head of
him, who sent his son, that grew up in Garth [Novgorod territory],
to Waldhammar [Waldimar]. He has won freedom from corruption !
The Poet's Prayer. It beseems us, especially in my house, guilelessly
to celebrate the mass of Olaf [29th July] the father of Magnus, this
king whom God magnifies. I am bound to keep duly the holiday of
him who was grieved for, who formerly adorned my hands with red
gold. The day of death allotted to my lord . . . . O Lord, Thy will
be done, help thou him who lifted my daughter out of heathendom,
and gave her the name of Tova ; for the wise and brave brother
of Harold held my child at the font. I was mightily glad on that
morning. O Lord of Norway [Olaf], let the poor as well as the rich
profit by thy Law and keep thy promise.
The Eclipse. It is thought a great wonder, that the cloudless sun
could not give warmth to men. On that day there happened a great
miracle concerning the king : the day could not yield its fair hues. I
learnt from the East the details of the battle.

---

88. ys, Cd.   89. Read, Helgi.   árar] áro, Cd.   91. á] af, Cd.
97. mínni, Cd.

VIII. Pilgrimage, etc.

1. RÚMS lét-ek ok hélt heiman her-móðr á fœr góðri,
   giallar vœnd, þann-es golli gaf mer konungr vafðan :
   Sult þá es silfri hialtað ʻsverð dyrt viðir þverðo'
   lœgðom vápn, enn vígðom ver ʻylgjar' staf fylgðom.
2. Stóð-ek á Mont, ok mintomk mœrg hvar sundr flaug targa
   breið ok brynjor síðar, borgom nær of morgon :   6
   munða-ek, þar es unði, œndurðan brum lœndom
   (faðir mínn vas þá) þenna (Þórrœðr) konungr forðom.
3. Fúss lœzk maðr, ef missir meyjar faðms, at deyja ;
   keypt es óst ef eptir of látinn skal gráta :   10
   enn full-huginn fellir flótt-styggr sa-es varð dróttinn
   (várt torrek lízk verra) víg-tór (konungs órom).
4. Hrafna sé-ek til hafnar (hræs minnask þeir) sinna,
   þar-es flaut und nið nýtom Norðmanna skip forðom :
   gialla hátt fyrir Hillar hvern dag frekir ernir   15
   endr þeir-es Áláfr grenndi, innan, mœrgo sinni.
5. Geng ek um þvert frá þengils (þroask ekki mer) rekka
   [emk sem bast í briósti bleikr] verðungar leiki :
   minnomk ek hvar manna mínn dróttinn lék sínna
   opt á óðal-toptom, orð-sæll, ok ver forðom.   20
6. Hafa láti mik heitan Hvíta-Christr at víti
   elld, ef ek Áláf vildag (emk skirr at því) firrask :
   vatn-œrin hefi-ek vitni, vask til Rúms í haska,
   (œld leyni-ek ʻþví' aldri) annarra þau manna.

Regrets and Pilgrimage. WAR-WEARY I left the gold-wound battle
rod, which the king gave me, and set out from home on a blessed
journey to Rome, when the king . . . . at Sult. I laid down the
silver-hilted weapons and took up the consecrated staff. I stood on
the Mount [Alps] near the cities in the morning, and it was brought
back to me how many broad targets and long mail-coats were riven
asunder; and at that early hour I was minded of the king, who formerly
sat in the land when my father Thorrod was alive. Lo, a man who
has lost his mistress's embraces is eager for death (love is dear bought
when one must weep over the dead!): and the brave soldier, who has
lost his lord, lets fall cruel tears. Yet the loss, we king's men have
suffered, seems the greater *of the two.* I see the ravens speeding
to the Haven, mindful of carrion, where formerly the ships rode
under the goodly King of Northmen. The greedy eagles scream
every day inside Hillar, whom of yore Olaf fed full many a time. I
go indoors from the games of the king's henchmen. Sorrow waxes
high within my breast; I am as white as bast : I remember how often
in his own land my glorious lord and I joined in sport in old days.
May the White Christ appoint me the hot pains of fire if I wished to
abandon Olaf. I am clear of this accusation! I have overflowing
witness of other men (I hide nought) I was in Rome in jeopardy. The

---

3. sverð dyrt þat er viðir þverðo, Cd.   10. oblati, Cd.   11. sa er ann
dróttni, B.

7.   Há þótti mer hlœgja hœll um Nóreg allan   25
     (fyrr vas-ek kendr á Knœrrom) klif meðan Áláfr lifði :
     nú þikkja mer miklo (mítt stríð es svá) hlíðir
     [iœfurs hylli varð-ek alla] óblíðari síðan.

8.   Alfífo mon ævi ungr drengr muna lengi
     þá es oxa mat œtom inni skaf sem hafrar :   30
     annat vas þa-es Áláfr ógn-bráðr réð láði,
     hverr átti þá hrósa hialmr korns frævi borno.

IX. MAGNUS AND ANSTRID.

(From Kringla.)

1.   E NN lystir mik austan (erot um spœrð) or Gœrðom
         frá œðlingi ungom (opt 'byrjoð' lof) spyrja :
     frétti-ek smás ' þa-es ' smæstir smoglir ástar foglar,
     ('þing hœgjomk ') fœr fliúga fylkiss niðs á miðli.

2.   Hrein getom hála launa hnoss-fiœlð lofi osso   5
     Áláfs dœttr, es átti iœfur sigr-hvatastr Digri :
     þings beið herr á Hœngrom hund-margr Svia grundar
     austr, es Ástríð lýsti Áláfs sonar mólom.

3.   Máttit hon við hættna heil-ráð Svia deila
     meirr þótt Magnús væri marg-nenninn sonr hennar :   10
     olli hon því, at allri átt-leifð Haraldz knátti,
     mest með móttkom Kristi, Magnúss konungr fagna.

4.   Mildr átt menzko at gialda, Magnús, enn því fœgnom,
     (þat gœrði vin virða víð-lendan) Ástríði :

---

high cliffs all over Norway seemed to me to be laughing while Olaf was
alive (I was formerly known at Cnear) ; but ever since the mountain-
sides seem to me much less joyful.   This is my woe, now I have lost
my beloved king.   I shall always remember the days of Ælgifu's young
son when we ate oxen's food in our houses—bark scrapings, like goats.
It was different when the valiant Olaf ruled, every rick boasted of
ripe corn.

I LONG to get news of the young Etheling east in Gard [Russia].
Oft-told praises of him are not lacking !   I ask for every bit of news
whenever the wee inquisitive birds of love [letters] fly between the
king's son and myself.   I cannot appear in person !   I will repay with my
song of praise . . . . the daughter of Olaf [Swedish King] whom the victorious Stout One wedded.   Many of the Swedes waited for the Moot
at Hanger in the east, where Anstrid put the case of Olaf's son [Magnus].
She, the giver of good counsel, could not have pleaded more warmly with
the Swedes though Magnus had been her own son.   She was the chief
one, next to the mighty Christ, in bringing it about, that King Magnus
should enjoy the heritage of the son of Harold.   Thou hast to thank
Anstrid, Magnus, for her manly dealing, which made thee, friend of

---

28. iofurs falli kann ek illa, B.   29. From Fms. v. 209 Cod. L ; cp. Fb. ii.
393.   32. Emend. ; hialmr þorn fræri borinn, Cd.   3. Emend. ; þoat . . .
fliúgi, Cd.   4. Read, þing- liúgomk -för.

hon hefir svá komit sínom (sœnn) at fáo mon œnnor   15
(orð gœri-ek drós til dýrðar) diúp-ráoð kona stiúpi.

5.   Ástríði láttu œðri, Alfhildr, an þik sialfa,
þer þótt þínn hagr, stórom, (þat vildi Goð) batni.

X. Bersœglis Vísor, c. 1039.

(From the Lives of Kings, especially Kringla, Hulda, Flatey-bok iii. 267-269.)

1.   FREGN ek at suðr með Sygnom 'Sighvattr hefir
gram lattan'
folk-orrosto at fresta 'ferr' ef þó skulom berjask:
'fœrom í vapn' ok verjom vel tvist konung lystir
'hve lengi skal hringom hans grund' til þess fundar.

2.   Sighvatz hugir ro hitzig Hœrða-Knútz i garði;   5
mildr man miœk vel skaldi, Magnús, Haraldr fagna:
fór-ek með fœðor þeira (fékk ungom mer tunga)
(gollz) [var-ek enn með œllo óskeggjaðr þá] beggja.

3.   Vas-ek með gram þeims gumnom goll bauð dróttin-hollom,
('namn' fekk hann enn hrœfnom hræ) þess konungs ævi : 10
'full-kœrskom sá-ek falla frán-eggjom son gránom'
'gaf margan val vargi verðung konungs sverðom.'

4.   Fylgða-ek, þeim-es fylgjo fé-mildom gram vildi
(vóro þegnar frið fegnir) feðr þínom vel, mína:
vasat í hœll (enn húsa) hlið, þars ek stóð í miðjom   15
(hróesinn skal með hrísi) hans flokki (við þiokkva).

5.   Gekk við móð inn mikla, Magnus, allt í gœgnom

---

men, the ruler of broad lands. She, the lady of deep thoughts, has
done for her stepson what few other stepmothers would have done.
I tell the truth to the lady's praise.

Addressing Alfhild. Alfhild, set Anstrid ever higher than thyself,
though God willed that thy condition should be the better! [thou shouldst
have a son and she not.]

The Plain-speaking Verses. *To the king.* I hear of a movement
among the Sogn-folk in the South, how Atli has egged them on to try
battle, so that we shall have to fight. Let us take up our weapons
and heartily defend our lord in this encounter. How long shall the
land be unsettled?

O Magnus, Sighvat's thoughts lie yonder towards Hard-Cnut's palace;
the generous Harold will welcome the poet well. I followed the father
of them both [Cnut]; I was altogether beardless when I first won gold
by my tongue [came as a poet to court]. I was with the generous
prince, who gave gold to his faithful followers and . . . . I remember
his days. I saw the keen-eyed son of Harold . . . . I followed the
open-handed king thy father; he was pleased with my service; all
men lived in peace. There was no gap in the hall where I stood in
the midst of his guard: even the proud rafter needs be wattled with

---

1. Read, s . . . hvatta hefir Atli?   2. Read, freista . . . ferð.   6. Emend.;
mildr nema m. v. s. M. kgr. fagni, Cd.   7. fekk ek mer ungan, Cd.   10.
Read, mank?   14. vóro] nu ero, Cd.   15. Emend.; varat a hæl með
hiörvi, Cd.

ferð þar es flokkar bœrðosk, faðir þinn liði síno:
varði hart, enn hiœrto hug-full við þat skullo,
Áláfr réð svá iœfra erfðir framm at hverfa.   20

6.   Áláfr lét mik iœfra órýr framast dýrða
urðo driúg ens Digra dróttins þing með hringom:
goll bar-ek iamnt um allan aldr ok her-verk sialdan
hrygg á hvárri-tveggja hendi flotna sendiss.

7.   Hét sá-es fell á Fitjom fiœl-gegn ok réð hegna   25
heiptar rœn (enn hœnom) Hákon (firar unnu):
þióð hélt fast á Fóstra fiœl-blíðs lœgom síðan
(enn ero af því minni) Aðalsteins (buendr seinir).

8.   Rétt hygg-ek kiósa knœtto karl-folk ok svá iarla,
af því at eignom lofða Áláfar frið gœfo: 30
Haraldz arfi lét haldask hvar-dyggr ok son Tryggva
lœg þau es lýðir þœgo lauk-iœfn at þeim nœfnom.

9.   Heim sóttir þú hættinn hœnd, enn vel mátt lœndom
(þinn stoða-ek mátt) sem mœnnom, Magnus konungr, fagna:
'fœra ek vist því at várom' vœrðr með þer í Garða   35
skri .... skíri-nafna skript þióð-konungr 'niptar.'

10.   Ungr vas-ek með þer þengill þat haust es komt austan,
'einn stillir mátto alla iœrð hegna svá fregnisk:'
himin þóttosk þá heiðan hafa es landa krafðir,
lofðungs burr, ok lifðir, land-folk tekit hœndom.   40

11.   Mínn hug segi ek mœnnom, Magnus, at ek fagna
(góðs 'lán' es þat) þíno þing-drífo vel lífi:

---

faggots [i. e. even I filled a place usefully] .... Thy father, Magnus,
with his company pierced right *through* his enemy's ranks with high
courage. Olaf's brave heart did not quail.

Olaf gave me rank and rings; the favours of the Stout king were
lasting. I ever bore gold of his giving on both my arms all his days.

The glorious examples of former kings. He that fell at Fitiar and
punished robbery was named Hakon, and folks loved him: and the
people have held fast to the Laws of the well-beloved Foster-son of
Æthelstan, and the franklins are slow to let his memory die.

I am sure that both the gentry and the yeomanry were right in
choosing both the Olafs; because they both protected men in their possessions. The heir of Harold and the son of Tryggwi kept upright as a
leek the laws which the people had accepted at these namesakes' hands.

O King Magnus, when thou didst come home to thy land .... I was
thy stay. I went to thee to Gard ....

Lo, here is a sharp shrift from thy godfather!

I was with thee, thou young king, that autumn when thou camest
from the East; and all the people rejoiced in thee. The people of
the land thought that they held the bright heaven in their hands [i. e.
thought the golden age had come] when they heard that thou wast
alive and laying hold on thy heritage.

I tell all men my mind, Magnus, that I rejoice that thou shouldst live

---

28. þvi er minnir, Cd.   36. Read, skorpnar?   38. Read, ... knátto allir, ...
þegnar þer fegnir.   42. Read, ván *or* vánir.

ætti drengja dróttinn dýrðar son, ef yrði
(þióð mætti fá fœða) feðr glíkr (konung slíkan).

12.   Fœður Magnúss let-ek fregna folgin iœfurs dolga   45
orð þau es eyro heyrðo ór á svik hve fóro :
mál bar-ek hvert af heilom hug, því at eigi brugðomk ;
ek vissa þó óssom ótta lánar dróttni.

13.   Skoloð ráð-giœfom reiðask (ryðr þat) konungr yðrom
(dróttins orð til dýrðar) dœglingr, við bersœgli :   50
Hafa kveðask lœg, nema liúgi land-herr, buendr verri
endr í Ulfa-sundom œnnor an þu hetzk mœnnom.

14.   Hverr eggjar þik, harri heiptar-strangr, at ganga
(opt reynir þú) þínom ('þunn stœl') á bak mœlom ?
fast-orðr skyli fyrða feng-sæll vesa þengill ;   55
hœfir heit at riúfa, hialdr-mœgnuðr, þer aldri.

15.   Hverr eggjar þik hœggva, hialdr-gegnir, bú-þegna ?
ofrausn es þat iœfri innan-landz at vinna :
œngr hafði svá ungom áðr bragningi ráðit ;
rœn hygg-ek rekkom þínom (reiðr es herr), konungr,
leiðask.   60

16.   Gialtu var-huga véltir viðr þeim-es nú ferr heðra,
þiófs (skal hœnd í hófi) hœlða kvitt (of stytta) :
vinr es sá es varmra benja vœrnuð býðr ; enn þú hlýði
tár-mútariss teitir, til hvat bú-menn vilja.

17.   Hætt es þat es allir ' ætla ' ' áðr skal við því ráða '   65

---

well and sway the moots. It is of good augury. The people would have a
glorious lord, if the son were like his father. Folks find few such kings.

I used to tell thy father, Magnus, the secret words that reached
my ears and were bruited around me. I told him every word with
a true heart, whenever I knew of any peril to my liege lord; for I
never failed him.

Ye should not be angry with your councillors, O king, for their
plain speaking. What I am now telling thee, my lord, is for thine own
good. Unless the multitude are lying, the franklins declare that they
have other and worse laws than those thou formerly didst promise
thy people in Wolf Sound.

Who is egging thee, king, to go back from the oath thou hast
sworn? A worthy king of men should be true to his word. It can
never beseem thee, my lord, to break thine oath.

Who is egging thee, prince, to slaughter the cattle of thy thanes?
It is tyranny for a king to do such deeds in his own land. No one
has ever before advised a young king so. This open robbery is most
hateful to thy henchmen, I know. The people are angered, O king.

Take heed of the murmuring of men, which is now bruited hither
and thither. A man should not stretch his hand too far. He is a
friend that warns one. Listen therefore to the complaint of the
franklins.

There is one danger I have heard of, that the men .... of Atli are

---

44. fœðaz, Cd.   46. Read, svig.   63. enn ek hlyðs, Cd.   65. Read,
Atla.

'hárir menn es ek heyri hót' skiǫldungi á móti:
greypt es þat es hǫfðom 'hneypta' heldr, ok niðr í felda
(slegit hefir þǫgn á þegna) þingmenn nǫsom stinga.

18. Eitt es mǫl þat es mæla, (mínn dróttinn leggr sína
eign á óðul þegna); ǫfgast, buendr gǫfgir; 70
raun mun seggr, hinn es sína selr út, í því telja
flaums at felli-dómi, fǫður-leifð, konungs greifom.

19. Syni Álǫfs bið-ek snúðar (síð kveða aptans bíða
óframs sǫk); [meðal okkar allt es háligt svá] mála:
erom, Magnus, mer vegnir, vilda-ek með þer mildom 75
(Haraldz varða þú hiǫrvi Hauk-ey) lifa ok deyja.

OF A SACRED POEM (from Edda).

Endr reð Engla senda Iórdanar gramr fióra
fors þó hann á hersi heilagt skopt or lopti.

ANOTHER FRAGMENT (from Edda).

Þat frá ek víg á vatni verðung iǫfurs gœrðo
nadda él en nýla næst tel ek eigi en smæzto. 80

XI. LAUSA VÍSOR.

(Verses 1, 3, 5-6, 8 from O. H.; verse 4 from Hulda; the rest from Fb. ii.
and iii. 240-244, cp. O. H. L.)

1. FISKR gekk oss at óskom eitrs sem ver hǫfom leitað
lýso-vangs or lyngvi leygjar orm at teygja:
at-rennir lét annan ǫngul-gripinn hanga
(vel hefir œrriða at egna) agn-galga (mer hagnat).

---

rising against the king; some counsel should be taken against it. It
looks ugly when all the thing-men [franklins] are *gloomily* bowing
their heads and thrusting their noses under their cloaks [brooding
vengeance]. Silence has fallen upon the thanes.

It is one phrase that all the noble franklins are using: 'My lord
claims his thanes' free-land as his own.' The man that has to deliver
the heritage of his fathers to the king's reeves under some sham sentence
against him will call it robbery by violence.

I pray for the success of Olaf's son in his suit; for between us
two all is ever friendly. The laggard's case waits till the evening *when
it is too late to get it heard.* [Make up your mind now.] I am willing to
live and die with thee, Magnus, who guardest Harold's hawk-island
[Norway] with thy sword.

OF yore the lord of Iordan [God] sent four angels out of heaven,
when he [?] washed the holy hair of the baron.

Some Battle *on a lake* . . . .

Out fishing. THE poison-fish comes as I wish, for I have sought to
draw the sea-serpent out of the ling-bed; my fellow-fisherman has

---

67. Read, knippa.   76. varðar, Cd.

2. Heðan sé ek reyk es riúka rœnn of fiski-mœnnom 5
    (stór ero skaldz um skæror skelli-brœgð) or helli :
    nú frýra mer nýrar nenningar dag þenna
    hlyta ek fyrir hvíta horn-straums dœgurð naumo.

3. Hlýð mínom brag 'meiðir myrk blás!' þvi-at kannk yrkja,
    (all-tíginn máttu eiga eitt skald) drasils tialda : 10
    þótt œllungis allra, allvaldr, lofan skalda
    (þer fæ-ek hróðrs at hvœro hlít) annarra nítið.

4. Eigi sœtoð ítrom, Ivarr, megin-fiarri,
    orð þá es ossom fœrðak (at sóttisk lof) dróttni :
    þer es, allz hann réð hlýða hróðr sínn, lofi þíno 15
    (hlióðs hefig beitt á báða bekki) vant at hnekkja.

5. Ek tók lystr, né ek lasta (leyfð íð es þat) síðan
    sóknar-niœrðr við sverði (sá es mínn vili) þíno :
    þollr féktu húskarl hollan (hœfom ráðit vel báðir)
    láttrs, enn ek lánar-dróttinn, linnz 'blóða,' mer góðan. 20

6. Gœr-bœnn mun-ek gunnar gamm-teitondom heita,
    áðr þœgom ver ægis eld, ef nú bið-ek felda :
    land-aura veittú 'lýro láð-þverrandi' af knerri,
    'enn af ganga engi,' ek hefi sialfr mœrk halfa.

7. Þrœngvisk ér um ungan ítr-menni gram þenna ; 25
    bægisk œld sva-at eigi Áláfs náig máli :

---

another fish caught on his angle. A sea-trout bait has served me well.
Hence from the cave I can see the smoke which rolls from the houses
over the fishermen. The poet has many a trick in the gloaming.
Now no one could challenge my day's work, if I could but win the
white damsel before breakfast.

To Olaf, who will not listen to him. Listen, O king, to my song, for I
know how to make verse. Thou mayst well keep one poet, though thou
refuse the praise of all other poets. I can make thee songs of praise
enough.

To Iwar, who will not hear him. Thou wast not sitting far from
the king, Iwar, when I delivered my song before him. It was received
well. Since he listened to the whole of the poem on him, it is not
fit for thee to refuse my Encomium on thee. I have asked both
benches for a hearing.

To Olaf, when he took him into his guard. I willingly received the sword
from thee, king, nor shall I ever repent it. We have both made a good
bargain : thou hast got a good house-carle and I have got a good
liege-lord.

To Olaf, pleading for a fellow-countryman to be excused landing-duty.
I shall be called greedy for begging pelts, having already received gold
of thee. Give up the half-mark landing-duty of his ship to the Icelander, I cannot pay it myself. *The duty was paid in kind, here by pelts.*

When the court was crowded. Ye are thronging about the good
young king, and elbow each other so that I cannot get a word from

---

8. hvítan, Cd.   23. Read, lýra láð-þaks-veri.   24. A²; of fanga aungi,
A¹.   mörk] emend. ; krafit, Cd.

mer vas orð at órom auð-sótt frœmom dróttni
þá-es óðom miœk móðir miœll á Dofra-fiœllom.

8.   Sverð standa þar [sunda sárs leyfom ver árar],
(her-stilliss þarf-ek hylli hollost) buin golli: 30
við tœkja-ek (víka vas endr með ´þer sendir
elldz), ef þú eitt hvert vildir, allvaldr, gefa skaldi.

9.   Muno þeir es mest um skynja mun-veig Dains kunno
síðr at Sighvatz hróðri svinnir brag-lœsto finna:
sik vill hverr, es hnekkir, hald-orðr boði skialdar   35
éls, því es allir mæla, iflaust gœra at fífli.

10.   Seinn þykki mer sunnan sókn-diarfr Haraldz arfi
(Langr es) at 'lýða þengils lífs sorg' (konungs morgin):
hvatki es´ heiðis gotna hyr-tælanda sælan
(nú hefik 'vætt í dag' Dróttins) dvelr ('bíð-ek' hans or Seljo) 40

11.   Sendi mer hinn mœri mann-þengill siá drengi
(síðan mun-ek heldr at hróðri) hnœtr þióð-konungr (snytrask):
opt, enn okkr bað skipta, Óttarr, í tvau dróttinn
(enda-ek mál) sem mundom, mann-diarfr, fœðor-arfi.

OTHERE THE BLACK.

THIS poet was a near relation to Sighvat, who once got him out of a serious scrape into which his poetic fervour had led him, according to the popular story told in one of the insertions in King Olaf's Saga. Whilst at the Swedish Court he made a love poem on Anstrid, daughter of Olaf the King of the Swedes, which displeased her husband King Olaf Haroldsson, who took him when he came to Norway and put him in prison, being minded to put him to death. Sighvat went one night to his dungeon and made him repeat the poem. 'It is very strongly expressed,' he said when he had heard it; 'no wonder the king was angry about it; but now we must soften down the strongest expressions, and

---

Olaf. Formerly I got easier speech of my lord, when we were very wearily wading through the snow-drifts on Dover-fell.

To Olaf. Swords gold-mounted are standing there; I would gladly take it, if thou wouldst give me any one of them; I have served thee long.

A retort. Wise men, those who can judge the Dwarf's Drink [poetry] best, will find least fault with Sighvat's song. He that carps at what every one else values, certainly makes a fool of himself!

Waiting. The warlike heir of Harold seems slow in coming from the South. 'A king's morning is long.' Whatever it be that hinders him, I have been all Sunday waiting for him in Seal-island [Selia].

On receiving a gift of nuts from King Olaf's table. The king sent me down some nuts, bidding Othere and myself to share them as if they were our heritage [fairly].

---

33. mun-veigurs, Cd.   34. svinnz, Cd.   36. Read, meta.   40. Read,
nu hefek ... dag Dróttins beðit hans or Seljo.

then you must make a poem on the king, and make that as full of praise as you can. And when the king asks to hear the poem on the queen, directly you have finished the one, you can begin the other.' During the three days he lay in the dungeon, Othere worked at his poems; and when he was led out to recite his verses on the queen, the king grew red as he listened to it. But as soon as they were finished he began the other; the henchmen called out, seeing the king's anger, that Othere should stop; but Sighvat said, 'The king will do as he likes of course, whether he allows Othere to finish his poem or not; but it cannot hurt us to hear our king's praise.' So they were silent, and when he had finished Sighvat praised it highly. So the king forgave Othere, saying, 'Take your head as your guerdon.' 'A good guerdon too, my lord,' said he, 'though the head is not a fair one.' But the queen drew a ring off her hand and gave it him. Then the king said to her, 'Are you still giving love-gifts to Othere?' Anstrith answered, 'You cannot blame me, my lord, for wishing to reward his praise of me, as you did his praise of you.' 'Well, let it stand as it is,' said the king. The king's poem (for the queen's is lost), of which there is a part remaining, was called *Head-Ransom* (Flatey-bok iii. 241), a title which, we suspect, gave rise to the whole story, which we have already in various forms seen ascribed to Egil, Bragi, and others.

Othere was in high favour with the Swedish king. We hear of him and Gizur standing before the king, introducing Icelanders to him with their recommendation. 'They were often with the king; for they were very bold, and often sat by the king's high seat by day in high honour.'

Of Othere and Cnut it is told, that the poet went to England and came to the king's hall, probably at Winchester. "After evensong the king came into the hall and said, 'I see a man here who is not of this country. He looks like a poet, and I would sooner have him to second me in a wager of battle than any one else, but I would not trust him alone with my wife.' And now Othere entered the hall and addressed the king in a verse [see IV. 1 below], and forthwith asked to be allowed to recite a poem on the king. Cnut answered, and the poem was delivered to a great gathering at the next day's moot, and the king praised it, and took a Russian cap off his head, broidered with gold and with gold knobs to it, and bade his chamberlain fill it with silver and give it to the poet. He did so, and reached it over men's shoulders, for there was a crowd, and the heaped-up silver tumbled out of the hood on the moot-stage. He was going to pick it up, but the king told him to let it be. The poor shall have it, thou shalt not lose by it." *Hofudlausn* may be dated c. 1020; the poem on Cnut c. 1027, the last event it mentions being the Holy River battle; and it was certainly *spoken* to the king, and proves the poet's being at the English court.

There is also a fragment of an *Encomium on the Swedish King Olaf*, and a few *Improvisations*, one on a gift of nuts from St. Olaf one day at dinner, the other on some hangings with the story of Sigfred slaying the Dragon on them. Othere's style is even, resembling Sighvat at times, though never rising to his level.

I. *Olaf's Drapa*, of which parts of six strophes remain, comprises some valuable lines on English and French history, but they are precisely the worse treated. We have obelised the most un-sound passages, and in a few instances have been able to suggest emendations, e. g. 'att siclinga' should read 'at siclingom,' at Silling, near Canterbury. Tuska-land stands for some name of Touraine, 'Tursa-land' probably. The name of a Northumbrian port, perhaps

Shields or the like, lurks under the corrupt line 44. The curious 'fore Wald,' p. 154, we have not identified. We might expect to find Selia in the unsafe line 51.

The restoration of Æthelræd by Olaf's ships 'in Lent,' as we read it, is to be noticed. This verse has been transposed, in accordance with the English Chronicle, to the place it originally occupied, we believe. The stress laid on the Colonial empire of Olaf is to be noticed.

II. *Cnut's Drapa* completes and supplements Thorrod Kolbeinsson's poem, as Olaf's Drapa does Sighvat's Olaf's Drapa. Here again the names of place and person have been covered up by empty phrases here and there. 'Castala verda' is plainly a mistake for some 'H . . . worth' or the like. The drowning of Eadmund's men is probably concealed under the unsafe verse 10. The flying of the Swedes at Holy River is a piece of flattery, if we trust the plain sarcastic words of the English Chronicle.

III. *The Swedish King's Encomium* is in a peculiar metre, with double line-rhymes, in a 'stumped' line, which is perhaps his own invention. A metre too difficult to admit of much information being conveyed in it.

IV. The Improvisation in old-metre is to be noted as containing the very titles the Chroniclers give Cnut, as confirming the evidence of the coins struck at Dublin, and illustrating Cnut's own language respecting his Empire.

I. HŒFUÐ-LAUSN, C. 1020.

(Verse 1 from Fms. v. 174; verse 2 from Edda.)

1. HLÝÐ 'mann-gæofigr' minni 'myrk-bals' því ek kann yrkja:
   finnom yðr ok annan all-valdr konung fallinn:
   þat tel-ek grams ok Gauta 'glað sistanda' mistag
   dœglings verk at dýrka dýr þengill mik lengi.

2. Góð-menniss þarf-ek gunnar glóð-briótanda at nióta;   5
   her es al-nennin inni inn-drótt með gram svinnom.

3. Ungr hrattu á vit vengiss víg-rakkr konungr blakki,
   (þú hefir dýrom þrek drœra) Danmarkar (þik vanðan):
   varð nýtligust norðan (nú ert ríkr af hvæt slíkri)
   [frá-ek til þess] es fórot fœr þín, konungr [gœrva].   10

4. Öttoð æorom skreyttom austr í Sallt með flaustom;
   bæoroð land af landi, land-væorðr, á skip randir:
   neyttuð segls, ok settoð sund-varpaði stundom
   (sleit miæok roin) mikla (mæorg æor und þer bæoror).

5. Drótt vas driúglegr ótti, dólg-linnz, at fœr þinni;   15

I. OLAF'S PRAISE. *Prologue.* LISTEN, my lord . . . . I can compose . . . . I tell of the king's deeds. I need the good favour of the king and the intercession of those within the hall . . . .

The Baltic. Young, thou didst set thy ship towards Denmark; the voyage thou madest from the North, O king, was very splendid, I know it all clearly. Ye did row the shrouded ships with the oars eastward in the Baltic, ye did carry the shield from land to land, ye used the sail and the oar by turn. Many an oar clave the billows below thee. The people were in great fear for thy voyage. Afterwards thou didst

---

1. mannig, Cd.   12. lind, Cd.

svan-bræðir, namtu síðan Svíþióðar nes hrióða.

6. Gildir komtu at gialdi Gotneskom her flotna;
    þorðot þer at varða þat land, iæfurr, brandi:
    rann (enn maðr um minna margr býr um þrek) [varga
    hungr frá-ek] austr (inn yngri) Eysýslo lið [þeyja].   20

7. Enn brauztu, éla kennir Yggs gunn-þorinn, bryggjor
    ('linnz' hefir lønd at vinna) Lundúna (þer snúnað):
    hæfðo hart um krafðir (hildr óx við þat) skildir
    gang, enn gamlir sprungo, gunn-þinga, iarn-hringar.

8. Þengill frá-ek at þunga þínn herr skipom ferri   25
    rauð Hring-mara heiði (hlóð val-kæsto) blóði:
    Laut fyr yðr, áðr létti land-folk, í gný randa
    Engla ferð at iærðo ótt, enn mærg á flótta.

9. At-gæongo vant Yngri 'átt siklinga' mikla,
    blíðr hilmir, tóktu breiða borg Kantara um morgin: 30
    Lék við rænn af ríki (réttu, bragna konr, gagni);
    [aldar frá-ek at aldri] eldr ok reykr [at þú belldir].

10. Máttið Enskrar ættar æld, þar-es tókt við giæoldom,
    vísi, vægðar-lausom, víð-frægr, við þer bægja:
    guldot gumnar 'sialdan goll dæglingi hollost;'   35
    stundom frá-ek til strandar stór-þing ofan fóro.

11. Næðot ungr at eyða, ógn-teitr iæfurr, Peito;
    reyndot, ræsir, steinda rænd á 'Tuska-landi' . . . .

12. Komtu 'í land' ok lendir láð-værðr Aðalráði,

---

harry the Ness of Sweden. Thou broughtest the Gotland folk to pay
tribute, they dared not to guard their land against thee, sword in hand;
and the people of Osel in the East fled before thee.

England. Next thou didst break down London Bridge; thou hast had
good hap in gold-getting. The shields cracked, and old iron rings of the
mail-coats sprung under the strain of battle. I have heard how thou
didst redden Ringmere-heath with blood; there thy host did pile a heap
of corses. The people of the land fell to the ground before thee, and
many Englishmen were turned to flight. Thou didst make a great raid
at *Silling,* thou didst sack broad Canterbury one morning. Fire and
smoke played mightily against the houses, thou hadst the victory; I
have heard that thou didst make havoc among the people. The English
race could not withstand thee, and thou didst receive a merciless ransom
from them. The English paid thee the fine gold 'by force.' I know that
oftentimes great treasures were borne down to the strand to thee.

France. Ye did lay waste Poitou, and tried the stained shield in
Touraine.

Back in England. Ye came back in Lent, and landed Æthelræd, O
king. He profited by thy help therein. It was at Iung-firth that ye
brought back the kinsman of Eadmund from his refuge [Normandy] to the
land which he had ruled before. *The sons of Æthelræd, meeting opposition
from Cnut's men, resolve to go back to Rouen (says St. Olaf's Life, paraphrasing*

---

20. ungi, Cd.   29. Read, Siclingom?   38. Read, Tursa-landi. . . . .] *lost
half-verse.*   39. Read, í Lent?

þín naut rekka rúni ríki efldr at slíko: 40
'harðr vas fundr þa-es fœrðot' frið-landz á vit niðja,
réð átt-stuðill áðan, Iatmundar, þar grundo.

13. Val-fasta bióttu vestan veðr-œrr tvá knœrro;
hætt hafit ér 'í otta opt, Skiœldunga-þopti :'
næði straumr ef stœði strangr kaup-skipom angra   45
innan borðz um unnir erringar lið verra.

14. Eigi hræddosk ægi, ér fóroð siá stóran;
allvaldr of getr aldar engi nýtri drengi:
opt vas þars (enn forsi flaust hratt af ser brœttom)
neytt áðr Noreg beittoð, 'niðiungr Haraldz,' miðian.   50

15. Blá-gióða tóktu bræðir ben-gialfrs 'ok þá sialfa'
skatti gnœgðr með skreytto skeið Hákonar reiði:
ungr sóttir þú, Þróttar þings-má-grennir, hingat
(máttið iarl) þau-es áttoð átt-lœnd (fyr því standa).

16. Lýtandi hefir liótar land-ráðondom branda   55
um-stillingar allar ifla 'follz' um goldit:
Hafa léztu Heiðska iœfra, her-skorðandi, forðom
mundangs laun, þá-es meinom, mœtr gramr, við þik sætto.

17. Braut hafit, bœðvar-þreytir branda 'rióðr,' or landi
(meirr fansk þínn an þeira þrekr) dœglinga rekna: 60
stœkk, sem þióð um þekkir, þer hverr konungr ferri;
heptuð ér enn eptir orð-reyr þess-es sat norðast.

18. Nú ræðr þú fyr þeiri (þik remmir Goð miklo)
fold, sem forðom heldo fimm bragningar (gagni):

---

a lost verse of Ottar's),—['Then Olaf parted with them and would not go
to Walland (France), he sailed north along all England till he came to
Northumberland; he made a haven there called Fore Wald, and fought
there with the townsmen and chapmen, and gat there victory and much
goods.']

The Gale. Thou didst set out with two ships of burden from the west,
thou wast in great peril . . . . the mighty current would have wrecked
the merchantmen, had there not been such a doughty crew aboard them.
Thou didst not fear the sea, but met the mighty main; never had king
a better crew. The ship kept throwing off her steep-falling billows; ye
had to try your vessels oft and hard ere ye could make the midst of
Norway *at Cape Stadt.* Thou didst take the well-rigged galley of
Hakon, and the Earl himself. Thou camest young hither to the land of
thy heritage, which thou shouldst have; the earl could not hinder it.

The Upland Kings. Thou hast paid the kings for all their dark plots.
Thou hast given the Heath-*mark* kings meet reward, who devised thy
destruction. Thou didst drive *four* kings out of the land, as all men
know; every one of them fled far from thee; and afterwards thou didst
hobble the word-rearer of him that ruled farthest to the north [i. e.
maimed his tongue?]. Thou art now ruling over the land which five
kings ruled of yore; God strengthens thee with great increase. The

---

41. Read, Iung furðo?   44. Corrupt, some place, Shields?   50. Read,
Nóreg . . . . at Staði miðjan?   59. Read, fiora?

breið ero austr til Eiða ætt-lœnd und þer, 'Gœndlar'   65
(œngr sat) 'elda þrœngvir' (áðr at slíko láði).

19.   Gegn ero þer at þegnom (þióð-skiœldunga góðra
haldit hœft á veldi) Hialtlendingar kenndir:
eigi varð á iœrðo, 'ógn-bráðr, áðr þer náðom,'
austr sá es Eyjom vestan Ynglingr und sik þryngvi.   70

II. KNUTZ-DRAPA, C. 1027.

(Verses 1, 2, 4–11 from Skioldunga; verse 3 from Edda; verse 12 from O. H.)

1.   HRATSTU lítt gamall lýtir lœg-reiðar fram skeiðom;
fócað fylkir œri, folk-sveimaðr, þer heiman:
hilmir bióttu, ok hættir, harð-brynjoð skip, kynjom;
reiðr hafðir þú rauðar randir, Knútr, fyr landi.

2.   At fylgðu þer Iótar, auð-mildr, flugar trauðir;   5
skaut-hreina bióct skreytir Skánunga lið-vánir:
váðð blés of þer, vísi; vestr settir þú flesta
(kunnt gœrðir þú 'þenna' þítt nafn) í haf stafna.

3.   Skócrot skœfno stýri (skaut) sylg-hár bylgior;
(lék við hún á hreini hlunnz, þat-es drósir spunno.)   10

4.   Her-skiœld bartu, ok héldut hilmir ríkr á slíko;
hykkat-ek, þengill, þekðosk þik kyrr-seto mikla:
Ætt drap Ióta dróttinn Iát-geirs í fœr þeiri;
þveit rakt (þrár ert heitinn) þeim, stillis-konr, íllan.

5.   Brunno bygðir manna, buðlungr, fyr 'þer ungom;'   15
opt léztu 'hús ok heiptir her-kall buendr gerva.'

6.   Gunni léztu í grœnni, gramr, Lindisey framða;
'beldu viðr því-es vildo víkingar því ríki:'

broad land of thy fathers *from Gandwick* east to Eid is under thee; never king, ere thee, had such domain. Thou hast the sway of an overlord *or* emperor. The Shetlanders are now acknowledged thy thanes; never, *since the day of Fairhair*, was there Yngling in the East that subdued the Western Islands under him.

II. CNUT'S PRAISE. THOU wast of no great age when thou didst put forth in thy ship; never younger king set out from home. Thou, prince, didst equip the hard-mailed ships, and put them in jeopardy, and heldest red shields before the land. The Jutes followed thee out, thou didst call out the levies of the Sconey-folk; the canvas blew over thee; thou didst turn all the stems of thy ships to the main, making thy name famous. Thou didst score with thy smooth-shaven oarage the high-swelling billows; the pennon, the ladies spun, floated from the mast-top. Thou barest a war-shield without ceasing, O king; thou didst not long enjoy a quiet seat at home, I ween. The Jutes' lord on this voyage slew the kindred of Eadgar; thou didst strike them [the English] a deadly blow. Thou art called 'the steadfast.' The dwellings of men burnt before thee, thou hast often .... Thou didst play the war-game in green Lindesey .... the wide Bay [Wash] .... Thou madest the English people to suffer sorrow in

65. For Göndlar . . . read Gand-víkr?   69. Corrupt; . . . dag ens Harfagra?
6. bio, Cd.   11. á] af, Cd.   18. Read, víð vík . . .?

Bíða léztu í breiðri borg 'Heminga' sorgar
œst fyr Úso vestan Engst folk, Svia þrœngvir. 20

7. Bióðr, vantu brynjor rauðar, blíðr stór-giafa, síðan
(lætr-þú ænd áðr þrek þrióti þínn) fyrir Norðvík innan.

8. Fram gekkt enn þar-es unnot (almr gall hátt við malma)
'knattuð sæ' þar-es sóttuð 'sverð castala verða:'
unnut eigi minni (ulfs gómr veit þat) rómo, 25
hnekkir hleypi-blakka hlunnz, á Tempsar grunni.

9. Ungr fylkir léztu Engla all-nær Theso falla;
flǽði diúpt of dauðra dík Norðymbra líkom:
svefn brauzt sværtom hrafni sunnr, el-hvætuðr gunnar,
(olli sókn enn snialli Sveins mægr) at Skorsteini. 30

10. 'Fiorlausa hyr Frisa' frið-skerðir þik gerðo
brauztu með bygðo setri Brandfurðo þer randa:
Iatmundar 'laut undir átt-niðr gæfugr hættir;'
Danskr herr 'skaut þá dœrrom drótt' es þú rakt flotta.

11. Skiœldungr vantu und skildi skæro-verk inn sterki 35
(fekk blóð-trani bráðir brúnar) Assatúnom:
váttu (enn val-fall þótti verðung), iœfurr, sverði
nær fyr norðan stórom nafn (gnógt) Dána-skóga.

12. Sviom hnekktir þu 'sœkkva siklingr orr' enn mikla
ylgr þars A'-in-Helga ulfs beito fekk heitir: 40
héltu þar-es hrafn ne svaltað (hvat-ráðr ertu) láði,
ógnar stafr, fyr iœfrom ýgr tveim við lið beima.

---

broad *Nottingham*, west of the Ouse, thou crusher of the Swedes. Thou
madest the mail-coats red, blithe bounty-giver, west of Norwich. Thy
breath will cease ere the fame of thy exploits shall end! Thou didst go
forth to where . . . . what time ye attacked *Hazelworth*; ye won no less
fame on the shallows of Thames. Young king, thou madest the English
fall near Tees, the Dyke of the Northumbrians flowed deep over the
bodies of the dead. Thou brakest the fast of the black raven at Scorstan
[Shirstone]; Sweyn's brisk son fought there. Thou . . . . didst make
a slaughter; thou didst storm Brentford, a settled place. Edmund
the noble king's son's men *were drowned there*; thou didst put the
people to flight. The Danish host shot at them with darts. O thou
Shielding, thou didst win under shield a mighty work of war at Assatun
[Assandun] : again thou didst fight with the sword, and win fame
enough near to the north of Dean forest.

Sweden. Thou didst put the Swedes to flight at the Holy River,
and didst hold thy land against two kings [the kings of Sweden and
Norway].

---

19. Read, Snotunga? 24. Read, H. . . . furðo? 28. dauða, Cd.
29. gunnar hvotoðr, Cd. 31. Read, hykk. 33. Read, hlaut . . . undir
hættar? 38. Storo . . . gnóg, Cd.

III. On Olaf, the King of Sweden.

(From Edda.)

1. IÖFURR heyri upphaf (ofrask mun konungs lof)
    (hátto nemi hann rítt hróðrar míns) bragar síns.

2. Fold verr folk-Baldr; fárr má konungr svá;
    ærno reifir Áleifr; es framr Svia gramr.

3. Örn drekkr undarn; ylgr fær af hræm sylg;   5
    opt rýðr ulfr keypt; ari getr verð þar.

4. Þengill vas þegar ungr þrek-gœrr, víg-ærr;
    haldask bið-ek hans aldr; hann tel-ek yfir-mann.

5. Braut (en breki haut) borð (óx viðar morð),
    (meðr fengo mikil veðr) mió fyr ofan sió.   10

6. Vísi tekr Víg-freys víst austr mun-laust
    (aldar hafi all-valdr) ósk-víf (gótt líf!).

IV. Improvisation.

(Verses 1 and 3 from O. H. L.)

1. SVÁ skal kveðja konung Dana
    Ira ok Engla ok Ey-bua:
  at hans fari með himin-kræptom
  lændom ællom lof víðari.

2. Hnetr sendi mer handan hrandaðr alun-branda   5
    (áðr væntisk mer meiri mín þing) konungr hingat:
  Miór es (markar stióri meirr seamk þar til fleira
  'niðr attu oss í æðro' Islandz) mikils vísir.

3. Geisli stendr til grundar 'gunnar iarðar munna'
    'ofan fellr blóð á báða ben-seiða, konungr reiðisk:'   10

III. Olaf of Sweden's Praise. Let the king hearken to the beginning of my verse; may he catch the metre of it aright. He defends his land as few can; Olaf feeds the eagles; the lord of the Swedes is foremost. The erne drinks his supper; the she-wolf laps the blood; the wolf stains his jaws; the eagle gets his meal there. Already in his youth the king yearned for exploits, was eager for battle; I pray for his life. Captain I call him. The slender weather-boards above the sea were broken, the waves waxed, the gale grew, the crew encountered a great storm. The king wins land east of the sea. May he live in prosperity.

IV. Cnut's Praise. Let us so greet the king of the Danes, Irish, English, and Island-dwellers, that his praise may travel wide over all lands as far as the pillars of heaven.

On a gift of nuts, to St. Olave. The king [Olaf] sent me nuts hither; I used to look for greater things than this.ˈ The seed-sprout of a big tree is small; I hope for more . . . .

On the hangings with Sigfred slaying Fafni on them. The blade stands in the mouth of the dragon; the blood falls down both edges; the king

---

12. hafir, Cd.

hristisk hiœrr í briósti hringi grœnna lyngva,
en folk-þorinn fylkir ferr við steik at leika.

THORARIN PRAISE-TONGUE, AND HALLWARD HAREK'S-BLESI.

"THERE was a man called Thorarin the Flatterer; he was an Icelander by race, a good poet, and had been much with kings and other princes. He was with King Cnut the Mighty, and had made a Short Poem (flokk) on him. But when the king knew that Thorarin had made a Short Poem on him, he grew very angry, and bade him make a full Encomium on him by the next day when he should sit at table. But if he did not, the king said that Thorarin should be hanged for his presumption in making a Short Poem on King Cnut. So Thorarin made a refrain and thrust it into his poem, and eked it out with some more verses. And this is the refrain, 'Cnut watches his land just as God guards heaven.' King Cnut gave him fifty marks of silver as his fee for this poem. It is called 'Head-Ransom.'

"He made a second poem on King Cnut, which is called *Tog-drapa* [in imitation of Sighvat's doubtless], in which he tells of the voyage of Cnut when he went northward from Denmark to Norway; ... and boasts therein that he was there on that voyage with Cnut when he went to Norway."

The first poem must have been made before the other, after 1028. The refrain of the second poem, of which one line, 'Cnútr es und solar,' remains, has been happily completed by Dr. Egilson, 'setri hveim betri.'

A later and curious poem of Thorarin's is the *Glælogns-kviða*, composed between 1032–1034, and addressed of all men to Sweyn, Ælfgifu's son, on his accession, describing the shrine and cult of St. Olaf; noticing the bells that ring of themselves over his unchanged body, whereon the hair and nails grow as on a living man; and asserting that the blind beggars come to his shrine to return whole. He further recommends Sweyn to pray to Olaf, 'for he is a man of God.' This poem is in the old metre, simple in style, and imitates Sighvat's dirge very closely. The title we take to be *Shrine Song*, Glelogn = Glœ-long, Glœ-lung (Glow-ship-song).

All Thorarin's work is fairly preserved, a few emendations only are admissible. The word 'Weg-Iota' is only found in Thorarin's Tog-drapa and in Vellekla. Skalda-tal does not know Thorarin as Olaf's poet, so that the verse about Thormod [below, p. 175] looks extremely suspicious, and may refer to some other king and be by another.

HALLWARD HAREK'S-BLESI. Of him we know nothing, and have but a fragment of an Encomium on Cnut, made about 1028; the king has won England and Denmark, and now is winning Norway. Hallward's verses are somewhat intricate in style. There are a few lines out of the seventeen remaining which are not quite unaltered, 'svikol-giardar' stands for the English 'segel-gyrd,' sail-yard. The doubtful 'Ullr-Ello' is like a phrase of Sighvat's. 'Sund-viggs' is, we have little doubt, 'Sandwich.'

[Sigfred] is wroth. The sword quivers in the breast of the coil of the green ling [the snake], and the gallant prince begins to roast the steak [its heart] for pastime.

I. Tog-drapa.

(Verse 8 from Edda; verse 7 from Skioldunga.)

1. K*NÚTR es und sólar*—Sið-næmr með lið
   fór miøk mikit mínn vinr þinnig:
   fǿrði or firði- fimr gramr Lima-
   út ólítinn otr-heims flota.

2. Ugðo Egðir øor-beiðiss føor   5
   svans sigr-lana søok-ramir miøk:
   allt vas golli grams lið framið
   vǽromk sión søogo slíks ríkari.

3. Ok fyr Lista lið fram viðir
   Hádyri um haf hart kol-svartir: 10
   byggt vas innan allt brim-galtar
   suðr sæ-skíðom sund Eikunda.

4. Ok fyr fornan frið-menn lið
   haug Hiør-nagla hvast grið-fastir:
   þar-es stóð fyr Stað stafn-klifs drifo;   15
   vasat eyðilig øor-beiðiss føor.

5. Knǽtto súðir svangs miøk langar
   byr-røomm bera brim-drif fyr Stim:
   Svá lið sunnan sval-heims valar,
   at kom norðr í Nið nýtr her-flýtir.   20

   .   .   .   .   .   . [*setri hveim betri.*]

6. Þá gaf sínom sniallr gǿrvallan
   Nóreg nefa niótr Veg-Ióta:
   sá gaf sínom (segi-ek þat) megi
   dals døkk-salar Danmøork svana.   25

7. Giøld hefi-ek marka malm-dyns fyr hlyn

I. THE STRETCH-SONG ON CNUT.
Burden. CNUT is *the best of kings* under the sun's *seat*.
The voyage to the North. My noble patron went thither out of
Limfirth with a great following. He stood to sea with a mighty
ocean-fleet. The guilty Agd-folk dreaded the king's voyage greatly.
His fleet was all gold-decked; the sight of it seemed grander to me
than all report of it [i. e. I saw it myself]. And the coal-black barks
sped fast over the Lister-sea, doubling Highdoor [a point west of Cape
Naze]. All Eikund Sound in the South inwards was thronged with the
war-galleys: and the sworn henchmen swept by Hiornails' old howe
[Hornelen] when the ships drove past [Cape] Stad: the king's voyage
was not fruitless. The sea-surge carried the long-streaked hulls of the
ships off Stim [Stem-hesten]. So the sea-hawks glided from the South,
till the good speeder of the host reached River Nith in the North.
The Division of the Empire. Then the brisk ruler of the Weg-Jutes
[Cnut] gave all Norway to his nephew [Hakon]; and to his son he gave,
I say it, Denmark, the dale of the dark halls of the swan [Sea-land].
Epilogue. I have gotten fifty marks of the king as a fee, which he

---

10. A²; hafdyrs, A.   18. brimdyr, Cd.   22. Iotᵂ, Cd.

fram fimm tigo for-vist borit,
þeirra es veitti víg-hagr brag
mer morð-stœrir mann-Baldr es ek fann.

8.   Gat-ek goll-skata (gœrva leygs um bœr   30
gœto gunn-vita gráps) Tog-dráopo.

II. Hœfuð-lausn.

(From O. H.)

Stef. Knútr verr grund sem gætir Gríklandz himin-ríki.

III. Glælogns-kviða.

(Verse 1 from Fagrsk.)

1. Þat vas dullaust at Danir gœrðo
dyggva fœr með dœglingi:
'þar vas iarl fyrst at upphafi;'
ok svá hverr es hánom fylgði
annarr drengr œðrom nýtri.   5

2. Nú hefir ser til sess hagat
þióð-konungr í Þróndheimi:
þar vill æ ævi sína
bauga-brjótr bygðom ráða.

3. Þar-es Áláfr áðan bygði,   10
áðr hann hvarf til himin-ríkiss:
enn þar varð, sem vito allir,
kvikva-settr or konung-manni.

4. 'Hafði ser harðla ráðit'
'Haraldz sonr til himin-ríkiss:'   15
áðr seim-brjótr at set[ti varð]
[Clement-kirkjo konungr grafinn].

---

gave me for my Song that I delivered on him. I made the Stretch-Song on the Gold-giver [King].

II. Head-ransom. *On Cnut. Burden.* Cnut guards his land as the King of Greekland [God] keeps the kingdom of heaven!

III. Shrine Song: *to Swein Ælfgifu's son!* It was manifest how the Danes made a noble voyage following the prince; there went an earl, Harold, son of *Thorkettle* the High, and every man, one good warrior after another in order, followed him. Now the high king [Sweyn] has prepared a seat for himself in Throndham, there the ring-breaker [Sweyn] will ever dwell all his life; where Olaf dwelt before, ere he passed away into the kingdom of heaven; and from a king became, as all men know, an enshrined saint. Harold's son [Olaf] had been laid in the sand at . . . . before that *he was buried at Clement's Church.* So that there the pure king lies glorious with a

---

30. gœrva] gœr es, Cd.   3. Read, þar var Haraldr iarl Háva borinn?
15–16. Read, Hafdi í sandi . . . legit hilmiss lík . . .?   17. Blank in A and A².

5. Þar svá at hreinn með heilo liggr
   lof-sæll gramr líki síno:
   ok þar kná sem á kykom manni   20
   hár ok negl hánom vaxa.

6. Þar borð-vegs biøllor knego
   of sæing hans sialfar hringjask:
   ok hvern dag heyra þióðir
   klokkna-hlióð um konung-manni.   25

7. Enn þar upp af altari
   of kisto konungs kerti brenna:
   svá hefir Áláfr áðr hann andaðisk
   synda-lauss sœlo borgit.

8. Þar kœmr hverr, es heilagr   30
   konungr sœfr, kryppr at gangi:
   enn beiðendr blindir sœkja
   þióðan máls, en þaðan heilir.

9. Bið-þú Áláf at hann unni þer
   (hann es Goðs maðr) grundar sínnar: 35
   Hann um getr af Goði siølfom
   ár ok frið øllom mønnom.

10. Þar-es þú rekr fyr regin-nagla
    bóka-máls bœnir þínar.

HALLVARD (KNÚTZ-DRÁPA).

(Verse 4 from Skioldunga; verses 1 and 6 from O. H.; the rest from Edda.)

1. KNÚTR verr iørð sem ítran allz Dróttinn sal fialla.

2. Vestr léztu í haf, hristir harð-viggs sikol-giarðar
   umbandz allra landa íss, fram-stafni vísat.

---

whole body; and hair and nails grow on him as on a living man. There the bells do ring of themselves over his coffin-bed; and every day the people hear the pealing of the big bells over the king. And there above the altar over the king's coffin the candle burns; for the sinless Olaf before he died had saved his soul. Every cripple comes walking to where the holy king sleeps, and blind suppliants seek to get audience of the king and go away whole. Pray thou to Olaf that he grant thee his land; for he is a man of God, and he can get good seasons and peace for every man of God himself, when thou puttest forth thy prayers before the mighty pillar of the scriptures [the Saint].

CNUT'S PRAISE. *Burdens.* Cnut defends his land as the Lord of all does the glorious hall of the mountains [heaven].
Cnut's attack on England. Thou didst turn the prows of thy sail-yard-steed westward to the main. Thou, the victorious son of Sweyn,

---

27. kristi þæg, Cdd.   31. sialf, Cdd.   33. þioðar, Cdd.   35. A and A³; þinnar, B.

3.   Súð-læongom komt Sveiða (sundz liðo dýr frá grundo)
      sig-rakkr Sœlsa bekkjar Sveins mœgr, á trœð hreinom.   5
4.   Knútr léztu framm til Flióta (frægr leið vœrðr um ægi
      heipt-snarr hildar leiptra) harð-brynjoð skip dynja:
      Ullar léztu við Ello ætt-leifð (ok má reifðir
      sverð-mans) snyrti-gerðar 'sund-viggs' flota bundit.

5.   Esat und ('iarðar hœslo œrð-briótr Dœnom forðar')   10
      mold-reks munka valdi mæringr an þu nærri.
6.   Englandi ræðr Yngi einn (hefsk friðr at beinni
      bœð-rakkr bœnar nœkkva bark-rióðr), ok Danmœrko:
      ok hefir odda leiknar ialm-Freyr und sik (malma
      hialdr-œrr haukom þverrir hungr) Nóregi þrungit.   15

7.   Rauð-liósa sér ræsir (rít brestr sundr in hvíta)
      baug-iœrð brodda ferðar (biúg-rennd) í tvau fliúga.

BIARNI GULLBRA (KALFS FLOKKR).

OF this poet nothing is left but an *Ode on Calf Arnisson*, a well-known Norwegian noble, the chief opponent of St. Olaf, the franklins' Commander at Sticklestead, and later the restorer of Magnus. Succeeding in some degree to the position of the murdered Erling Skialgson, Calf entered into alliance with Cnut, who despatched Hakon Ericsson, 'the Doughty earl,' to his aid against Olaf; but even without foreign aid he managed to carry out his wishes. Cnut's promises to Calf, whom our poet tells us he endowed with a fief, are represented as false wiles by the historian of the Kings' Lives; but we get a more favourable view in this poem, both of Calf and the English King. That Calf was made Earl of the Thronds is not unlikely, though we do not find express mention of it. Calf is here by his own poet made out a Northern king-maker, and celebrated as the restorer of Magnus. 'It was by thy doing he got his kingdom.' The envy of the courtiers, which procured Calf's disgrace and exile, though Magnus gained nothing by it, and was himself little to blame, is also clearly set forth here; then the Western adventures of Calf are told, down to the death of Earl Reginwald. who was overcome by his help. Earl Thorfin of Orkney was nephew-in-law of Calf, having married his niece Ingibiorg, Fin's daughter, 'Mother of Earls.' The Arn-modlinga-tal (Fagrskinna) gives their genealogy, etc.

Calf came back to Norway in Harold Hardrede's days, and was

---

didst go with the long-hulled flock of the sea-king [ships] on the sea, the ships sped South from the land. Thou, Cnut, didst make thy hard-mailed ship to go in array to Fleet, speeding over the sea, and didst moor thy fleet by Ælla's land, at Sandwich . . . .

Epilogue. There is no greater king than thou underneath the sway of the Lord of the Monks! the prince . . . . Danes!

The Yngwi rules England alone (peace has begun) and Denmark, and has now crushed Norway under him . . . . He sees the shield fly in twain.

---

9. Read, Sandvik.

by stratagem (Uriah-message) sent to death, a murder which angered
his brother Fin so much that he left the country.

We have put this poem with the rest of the poems on Cnut and
Olaf, as it gives a view which is certainly more true than that of the
Olaf's Saga, and is in contradiction to the Reynard-like character
which the Icelandic historians give King Cnut.
The reading in l. 20 is necessary for the context; l. 8 is a correction
of a manifest mistake.

The little *Epigram* of COLGRIM (from Hulda) exemplifies the poet's
assertion, that envious men sowed hatred between King Magnus and
Earl Calf. Here they are using the sharp-tongued Icelander as a cat's-
paw. For Colgrim, see Magnus Saga, cap. 20.

1.　VASTU, þar es vígs bað kosta vápn-diarfr Haraldz arfi
　　　(kynnisk kapp þitt mǫnnom) Kalfr við Bokn austr sialfa:
　　gǫtoð Gríðar sóta gólig fǫng til Ióla;
　　kendr vastu fyrstr at fundi flétto-griótz ok spióta.

2.　Öld fekk illt or deildom, Erlingr vas þar finginn　　　　5
　　(óðo biǫrt í blóði borð) fyr Útstein norðan:
　　'Liós es raun at ræsir' ráðinn varð frá láði;
　　'lagðisk lǫnd und Egða;' 'lið þeira frá-ek meira.'

3.　Austr réð all-valdr þrýsta ótála haf-stáli;
　　varð at vitja Garða víg-móðr Haraldz bróðir:　　　　10
　　enn (um iðnir manna emkat-ek tamr at samna
　　skrœkvi), at skilnað ykkarn, skiótt leztu Knút um sóttan.

4.　Áttu Engla dróttni ogn-rakkr giafar þakka;
　　iarls niðr, komtu yðro ótála vel máli:
　　þer lét fold áðr fœrir (frest urðot þess) vestan　　　　15
　　[líf þítt esa lítið] Lunduna gramr fundna.

5.　Iǫrð réttu vígi at varða víg-reifr fyr Áleifi;
　　brauztu við bragning nýztan bág; þat kveð-ek mik frǫ́go.
　　Fyrr gektu á stað-Stikla stór-verkr (enn óð merki);
　　satt es at sókn um veittir sniallr unz gramr vas fallinn. 20

BIARNI GOLDBROW. *Calf Arnisson's Praise: Erling's death.* Thou
wast there, O Calf, east at Bokn when Harold's heir summoned men
to fight. Ye gave the Wolf a good promise for Yule-tide; thou wast
foremost where sling stones and spears crossed. It was an evil case;
Erling was caught there north of Outstone. It is clear that the
lord of the Rugians [Erling] was betrayed. The Agd's warden [Erling]
was laid low; their [the king's] force was the greater I heard.
Sticklestead. Then the war-weary brother of Harold went to the
East to Gard in ships. After you parted, thou didst soon go to seek
Cnut. I do not lie. Thou hast to thank the lord of the English for
his gifts; thou didst plead thy case well. Ere thou wentest from
the West, the lord of London found land for thee [gave thee a fief];
there was no delay over it. Thy state is no small one! Thou didst
guard the land against Olaf, and grappled with him; I have heard it;
thou wast foremost at Sticklestead, and didst not cease from the battle
till the king fell.

7-8. Read, Lióst es at Rygja ræsir *and* lagðisk land-vörðr Egða?　　15.
Emend.; urðo, Cd.

6. Hafa léztu unga iœfra erfð sem til réð hverfa
satt es at ‘sitja knátti Svein’ at Danmœrk einni:
kendot, Kalfr, til landa kapps-fúsom Magnúsi
(olloð ér at stillir iœrð of fekk) or Gœrðom.

7. Þer frá-ek Þorbergs hlýri (þess gœrðosk ér verðir)   25
(hélt því unz ‘hann’ of spillti) Haraldz bróðor son góðan:
vœkðo œfund-menn ykrir iðula róg í miðli;
óþœrf lízk mer arfa Áláfs í þeim mœlom.

8. Frágom Finnz hve mági fylgdot, Kalfr um dylgjor;
ok léztu á siá snekkjor snarla lagt at iarli: 30
‘Áræði váttu eyða ófúss’ syni Brúsa
hlœði-rædr, enn tœðut heipt-minnigr Þorfinni.

KOLGRIM: Her-stillis þarf ek hylli, hœlf ero vœld und Kalfi.

ÞORÐR SIAREKSSON AND SKÁLD-REFR.

Thord Seawrecksson. He made a dirge on St. Olaf, which is called
Roda-drapa, *the Rood-Song.* There is a story that he went on a
pilgrimage to Jerusalem, and that in Syria he met a tall man in a cowl,
as he and other palmers went out of a certain city, who accosted
them in Danish, and asked if there were any Northmen among them.
‘We are Northmen’ they said, ‘but I am an Icelander’ says Thord.
‘I know where that is; how is it with Healti Skeggisson?’ ‘I am his
son-in-law.’ ‘Where are you going?’ ‘To Jerusalem.’ ‘Turn back
then, for the road is unsafe.’ ‘Who is king in Norway?’ again the
unknown asked. ‘Olaf Haraldsson.’ ‘Bear my greeting to Healti
when you get back to Iceland.’ ‘Whom shall I tell Healti it is that
sends the greeting?’ ‘The man who spoke with him at Lathe, when
I was holding a sword, and Healti put his hands between my hands
the last time I saw him.’ So their talk ended. But when Healti heard
Thord's tale he knew that Thord had spoken with Olaf Tryggvason.

Thord made a *poem in praise of Thorwolf Skolmsson,* the strong man
that fell at Fitiar (Book iv. § 3 and vii. § 3), a few lines of which are

---

He restores Magnus. Thou madest the young kings have their due
heritage, according to law. It is true, that thou didst seat Sweyn alone
in Denmark [sendest him away to Denmark], and brought Magnus
out of Gard to be king in the land. It was thy doing that he got
his kingdom. I have heard, thou brother of Thorberg, that Harold's
brother's son [Magnus] was good to thee, and deservedly; and this
lasted till wicked people spoilt it. Envious men were constantly
sowing strife between you; though the heir of Olaf to my mind gat
little profit from this.

Calf in Orkney. We have heard, how thou didst follow Fin's
son-in-law [Earl Thorfin]. Thou foughtest against [Reginwald] Brusi's
son, but succoured Thorfin.

Colgrim's complaint against Calf. I need the king's protection, half
the realm is Calf's.

---

22. Read, se:ja knáttir Svein?   26. Read, herr?

given in Kringla; he also made a curious *legendary poem*, a fragment of which is given in Skalda, the peculiarity of which is that the first half-line must be construed with the fifth half-line, the second with the sixth, and so on. The only verse we have of it deals with the Tale of Gudrun's egging her sons to avenge Swanhild, and brings in as intercalary the story of Scathe and Niord, and the lost legend of Woden drawing the sledge. It is an exaggeration of the verses of Cormac and Illugi.

I. Róða-drápa.

(Verse 1 from Edda; verse 3 from Skalda.)

1. SVEGGJA lét fyr Siggjo sól-borðz goti norðan,
    gustr skaut Gylfa rastar glaumi suðr fyr Aumar:
    enn slóð-goti síðan sæðings fyrir skut bæði
    (hestr óð lauks fyrir Lista) lagði Kœrmt ok Agðir.

2. Átti Egða dróttinn Áláfr þrimo stála   5
    við ágætan Ióta œðling þann-es klauf hringa:
    skaut nær skarpt at móti Skánunga gramr hánom;
    Sveins vasa sunr at reyna slær (þaut ulfr of hrævi).

3. Hlakkar stofns at hefna herðendr at því sverða.

II. On Thoralf Skolmsson.

(From Kringla; lines 20-21 from Fagrsk.)

1. ÞAR-ES bœð-harðir bœrðosk bandz ió-draugar landa   10
    (lystr gekk herr til hiœrva hnitz) á Storð á Fitjom:
    ok gim-slœngvir ganga gífrs hlé-mána drífo
    nausta blakks it næsta Norðmanna gram þorði.

2. Varði varga myrðir vítt (svá skal frið slíta)
    [iœfur vildo þann eldask] œndurt folk [at lœndom]:   15
    starf hófsk upp þar-es arfi ótta-vanr á flótta
    gollz es gramr vas fallinn Gunnhildar kom sunnan.

3. Þrot vas sýnt þar-es settosk sinn róðrs við þrœm stinnan
    (maðr lét œnd ok annarr ófár) buendr sárir:
    ok 'hior-krafðir' hœfðo 'huggendr' Munins tuggo   20

THE ROOD-SONG. He made the ships swing past Sigg [island] from the north. The gust drove the bark past Aumar [isles], and the vessel showed her stern to Kormt and Agd, doubling Listi between. Olaf, lord of the Agd-folk, fought a battle against the noble Etheling of the Jutes. The lord of the Sconey-men shot sharply against him. Sweyn's son was no sluggard to deal with. The Walkyria's . . . to revenge . . .

ON THOROLF THE STRONG, *the son of Skalm*. When they fought at Fitia on Stord, he [Thorolf] dared to stand beside the king of the Northmen. The king, whom the people wished to grow old in the land, fought in the van: the havoc began when the king was struck down and the son of Gundhild from the south turned to flight. It was a manifest defeat when the wounded franklins sat themselves at the stiff rowlocks, and the

---

20. Read, hiör klufðrar . . . hœggvendr?

gauks við gialfr um leikna grunno sand í munni.
4.   Afreks veit þat es iœfri all-ríkr í styr slíkom
    gœndlar niorðr sa-es gœrði gekk næst, Hugins drekko.

III. An unknown Song.

VARÐ sialf suna	Nama snotr una
Kialarr of tamði	Kvóðot Hamðe
Goðrun bani.	goð-brúðr Vani.
heldr vel mara.	hiœr-leik spara.

GIZORR AND HOFGARÐA REFR.

GIZUR GOLDBROW POET'S fragment of an Encomium on King Olaf
Haroldsson is the only piece left of this poet, who fell with his master.
He is also mentioned as being at the court of Olaf the Swedish king.
His *Gold-brow* was doubtless his love, like Thormod's *Coal-brow*.

HOF-GARTH REF. The son of Steinunn the heathen poetess who
opposed Thangbrand. We know nothing of his life, but we have part of
a poem on *Thorstein Egilson* (the poet's son), of a *Dirge* on his foster-
father Gizur Goldbrow the Poet, who was slain at Sticklestead, a bit of
a *Shield Song* in court-metre, and part of a poem on a *sailing voyage*. We
find an echo of Hus-drapa (on Thorstein's mother's father Olaf Peacock)
in the first line of his Thorstein-drapa.

GIZORR GULLBRÁR-SKALD.

On St. Olave? (Edda).

FYLKIR gleðr í folki flakk ok svan Hlakkar;
    Áláfr of viðr élom Yggs gœgl fegin Skœglar.

SKALD-REFR.

I. On Thorstein Egilsson? (Edda).

1.   GRIÓT-ALDAR ték gildi geð-reinar Þorsteini;
        berg-Mœra glymr bára; bið-ek lýða kyn hlýða.

---

sword-cut corses drifted, with the sand in their mouth, on tne sea-
washed shores. It was a sign of great prowess that in such a deed of
arms he marched next to the king.

A myth-blending.

a. Herself of her sons	*c.* The gentle goddess [Scathe]
b. Kialar [Woden] broke	*d.* Hamtheow never was
a. Gudrun was the death.	*c.* did not love the Wane [Niord].
b. his horses well.	*d.* sparing of sword-play.

GIZUR GOLDBROW *on St. Olaf.* The king gladdens the roving wolf, and
the swan of the Walkyria, Olaf, battens the Walkyria's fowl in the
gale of Woden.

HOF-GARTH REF. *Thorstein Egilsson's Praise at his Wedding Feast.*
Prologue. I deliver the Banquet-drink of the Rock-men [poetry] out
of my mind-field to Thorstein. Lo, the Wave of the Hill-dwellers

---

1. ték] rer, Cd.

2. Allz bœð-gœði bióða (bœr ræðr til þess hiœrva)
    ógn-stœðvar hefik ægi ein-ráðit Þorsteini.
3. Gekk í golli stokkna giœf-rífr Hárs-drífo   5
    askr við œrinn þroka ' es freyr ' sæing meyjar.
4. Enn hodd-vœnuðr hlýddi (hlunn vitnis em-ek runni
    hollr) til hermðar spialla (hein-vandil) Þorsteini.

II. Dirge on Gizor Gullbrár-skald.

(Verses 1, 2, 4 from Edda.)

1. OPT kom iarðar leiptra ' es ' Baldr hniginn skaldi
         hollr at helgo fulli Hrafn-Ásar mer stafna.   10
2. Þær eigo ver veigar Valgautz salar brautar
    fals hrann-vala fannar framr valdi tamr gialda.

3. Einn háði gný Gunnar gall bál Hárs stála
    rimmo askr við rœskva regn-bióðr tvá þegna :
    dal-steypir hió Draupniss dœgg-Frey bana hœggvi   15
    (hann rauð iarn) enn annan, ár-strauma, vann sáran.
4. Dagr vas fríðr sá-es fœgro fleygendr alin-leygjar
    í hang-feril hringa hlýr-tungli mer þrungo.

III. Of a Voyage (Edda).

1. VÁG-ÞRÝSTA berr vestan (vætti-ek landz fyrir brandi)
         [hval-mœni skefr] húna hóg-dýr of lœg bógo.   20
2   Fœrir biœrn, þar-es bára brestr, undinna festa
    opt í Ymis kiœpta úr-svœl Gymiss vœlva :
    enn siá-gnípo Sleipnir slítr úr-drifinn hvítrar
    Ránar rauðom steini runnit brióst ór munni.

[my song] is roaring. I ask men to listen; for I mean to offer the sea
of the *mind of Woden* [poetry], that I have devised, to Thorstein; he
asked me to do so.
    Stave. He went in the bloom of youth into the maiden's bed ... and
the prince listened to Thorstein ...
    Dirge *on Gizur Goldbrow, his master.* The dear dead poet often
brought me the holy toast-cup of the Raven-God [taught me song-craft].
I have to requite thee for these bowls of Woden, thou master of the ...
    Of his bravery at Sticklestead. Alone in the battle he bravely en-
countered two men. To one he gave a death-stroke, the other got
a wound.
    On the gift of a shield. It was a happy day when they placed the fair
shield on my arm.
    On sailing. The gentle mast-beast is bearing her wave-beaten bows
from the west. I see land ahead, the whale-roof [sea] is splashing. The
ice-cold Sibyl of Gymi [Ran] often drags the bear of the twisted cable
[ship] down to the jaws of Eager [ocean] where the billow breaks, but
the foam-flecked steed of the sea-ridges tears her breast, painted with
red earth, out of the mouth of Ran's husband.

---

6. Read, osk freyr?   11. Valgautr, Cd.

3.   Hrynja fiǫll á fyllar framm œsisk nú Glamma   25
     skíð Vetrliði skeiða skaut-biǫrn Gusiss-nauta.

4.   Borð-ristinn nemr bríósti borð-heim drasill skorðo ;
     nauð þolir viðr ; enn víði verpr inn of þræm stinnan.

5.   Sæll es hinn es hranna há-dýra vel stýrir
     (tíð eromk Vitniss váða vín-gerð) unir síno.   30

IV. Riddle (Skalda, Edda Lauf.).

S ODS ok síðra heðna sundr fœrir tré grundi.

MINOR FRAGMENTS.

Bersi, the son of Poetess Torwa (Skald-Torfoson), made a short Song of Praise on King Olaf Haroldsson, as is told in Olaf's Life. "Bersi was on the forecastle of Earl Sweyn's ship *at Nesia battle;* and when his ship withdrew from out of the rest of the fleet, King Olaf called out aloud when he caught sight of Bersi,—for he was easy to know, being a very handsome man, wonderfully well-weaponed and clothed,—'Farewell, Bersi!' He answered, 'Keep well, King!' so he says in a short poem which he made when he was come into King Olaf's hands and was sitting in fetters."

He was once with King Cnut, who gave him two gold rings, each worth half a mark, and a mounted sword withal. There is an allusion to these gifts in a verse of Sighvat's, who complains that he did not fare so well himself.

St. Olaf's Praise. A morsel of a poem on St. Olaf, and a fragment on Klæng, both by unknown authors.

Iokul Bardsson, a gallant Icelander from Waterdale, an enemy of St. Olaf, cruelly put to death c. 1028. His dying words are here preserved.

Harek of Thiotto, the son of Eywind the poet, a sturdy North-man of the old franklin type. His clever escape from the great Danish Armada, 1027, must have given the Haloga-lander a laugh at the Danes for many a day. 'I am not used to walking,' he said, when after the Holy-River battle King Olaf abandoned his fleet, and every one else had to go ashore and return to Norway overland, not daring to pass Ore Sound. 'I am too old and heavy!' So he dressed his ship like a herring-boat and slipped through the Sound past the Danish fleet, till he got out far enough to feel the wind, and then 'hoisted his sails and showed his gilt-vanes; the sails were white as snow, and striped white and blue,' in defiance of the whole fleet. So that the chagrined

---

O Winterlid, the sea-mountains [rollers] dash upon the ship. . . .

And the sea takes hold of the bows of the shores' steed, the timbers strain, and the water comes pouring in over the stiff gunwale.

Blessed is the steersman of the big billows' beast [ship], that is content with his lot. I am wont to make the wine of the Wolf's foe [Woden : Song].

Riddle wholly dark to us.

---

26. Emend.; skeið . . . skíða, Cd.

Danes, to cover their disappointment, declared that he had been allowed to get by under a secret agreement with the king.

The POETS AT STICKLESTEAD, see the introduction to Thormod Coalbrow's poet below.

BRYNIOLF ULFALDI [camel], his ditty on the king's gift.

HELGI THE POET, of whom there was a lost Saga, see Proleg. § 23.

The FRAGMENT ON TRYGGVI. A man calling himself Tryggvi, and pretending to be the son of Olaf Tryggvisson, came to Norway to claim the throne in 1033, but was defeated and slain by Sweyn Ælfgifuson. He had, however, friends who mourned his death in such poems as the one we have a piece of, by some man who was in the battle. One of Sweyn's eulogists made a short poem on the same subject, of which a verse also remains.

ST. OLAVE. There are several verses ascribed to St. Olaf himself, which, though probably wrongly ascribed to him, are of his day, and therefore to be given here. The *first* may even be the king's, it is not by a practised poet; the *second* may be by the author of the anonymous 'flokk' upon him; the *fourth* is by a courtier after Erling Skialgsson's death.

BERSI SKALD-TORFOSON (a Flokk on St. Olaf).

1. H RÓÐRS baðtu heilan líða hag-kennanda þenna ;
    enn snar-reki slíko svarat unno ver gunnar :
orð seldom ver elda út-hauðrs boða trauðir
knarrar haptr, sem ek keypta kyn-stórs at við brynjo.

2. Sveins raunir hef-ek sénar (snart rekninga biartar)   5
(þar-es sval-tungor sungo saman fóro ver) stórar :
elgs mun-ek eigi fylgja út hríð-boða síðan
'hellzt' at hverjom kosti hranna dýrra manni.

3. Krýp-ek eigi svá, sveigir sára linnz, í ári
(buom ólítinn Áta æondor) þer til handa :   10
at ek her-stefni hafna heið-mildr eða ek þá leiðomk
(ungr kunna-ek þá þrœngvi þínn) holl-vini mína.

ON ST. OLAF (Fragment).

Áláfr knýr und æorom orð-sniallr Vísund norðan,
brýtr annarr gramr úti unn-heim Dreka sunnan.

BERSI, *Poet Torf's son, on St. Olaf, at the Nesia battle.* Thou didst hail me and I answered, paying back word for word as I got them from him. I have seen the great woes of Sweyn, for we were together in the battle. I shall never follow a better man to battle. I am not cringing to thy hand, O king, to renounce my lord or turn away from my faithful friend, for I was with thy foe from my youth up.

UNNAMED POET *on St. Olaf.* Olaf plies the Bison under oars from the north; the other king [Cnut] from the south to seaward cleaves the wave-world with his Dragon.

---

8. Read, hæstr.   10. Áta] úti, Cd.

ON KLONG BRUSASON.

Brunno allvaldz inni (eldr hygg-ek at sal feldi)   15
[eimr skaut á her hrími] half-gœr við Níð sialfa.

IOKULL BARÐARSON.

1. Hlaut-ek frá Sult (enn sæta síð fregn at ek kvíða)
    [vǽn eromk hreggs at hreini hlýrs] því skipi stýra :
    es ý-stéttar átti Áleifr funa kleifar
    (gramr vas sniallr) á sumri (sigri ræntr) inn Digri.   20
2. Svíða sǽr af mǿði ; setið hef-ek opt við betra ;
    und es á oss su-es sprændi ótrauð legi rauðom :
    býss mer blóð or þessi ben ; ték við þrek venjask ;
    verpr hialm-gǿfugr hilmir heið-særr á mik reiði.

HÁREKR OR ÞIÓTTO.

1. Ráðit hef-ek at ríða Rín-leygs heðan mínom   25
    láðs dyn-mari leiðar lǫngom heldr an ganga :
    þótt legg-fiǫturs liggi lundr í Eyrar-sundi
    (kann þióð kerski mínni) Knútr her-skipom úti.
2. Lékkat-ek Lundar ekkjor (Læ-baugs) at því hlægja
    (skiótom eik fyrir útan ey) ne Danskar meyjar :   30
    iǫrð, at ek eigi þœrðak, ifla flaustz, í hausti
    á flat-slóðir Fróða fara aptr vali krapta.

THE POETS AT STIKLASTAD.

Gizur :

    Skala óglaðan ifa (orð fregin þat) [borða]
    [buomk við þrœng á þingi] þegns dóttir mik fregna :

ON KLÆNG. The king's half-built houses were burnt on the banks of
the Nith. The fire, I ween, broke down the hall, and the smoke spread
soot on the people.

Iokul Bard's son. Death Song. My lot last summer was to steer the
ship [the Bison] from Sult, which was once Olaf the Stout's, who was
deprived of victory. My wounds smart ; I have often fared better. I
have a wound that spirts red fluid freely ; the blood gushes out of my
wound ; I keep a stout heart. The wage-paying king casts his wrath
on me.

Harek of Thiotto. I have made up my mind to ride my ship rather than
walk, though Cnut with his war-ships is lying out in Ore Sound. I
will not make the damsels of Lund or the Danish maidens laugh
because I dared not go home over the flat roads of Frodi. Let us clear
Wetherey !

The Poets at Sticklestead. Gizur. The thane's daughter shall not hear
that I was sorry for the battle. The word is spoken. Let us make

23. þessu beni, Cd.

þótt sig-runnar svinnir segi váon Heðins kvánar   35
(vesom í Ála eli) austr (bragningi at trausti).

Thorfinn Mouth :
Rœkkr at regni miklo randar-garðz ins harða;
vill við vísa sniallan Verdœla lið berjask:
verjom allvald œrvan; œlom teitan má sveita;
fellom Þrœndr í Þundar (þess eggjomk ver) hreggi.   40

Thormod :
Ála þryngr at éli œr-stiklanda miklo;
skyldo eigi skelknir hœldar (skalm-œld es nú) falma:
buomk við sókn, enn slœkin seggr skyli orð um forðask,
es at geir-þingi gœngom gunn-reifom með Áleifi.

BRYNIOLF ULFALÐI.
Bragningr gaf mer brand ok Vẹttalandir.   45

SKALD-HELGI.
(From AM. 738.)
(Megot iarna fet fyrnask) friðar skepjanda miðjom.

TRYGGVA FLOKKR.
Tír-eggjaðr fór Tryggvi (tóksk morð af því) norðan;
enn Sveinn konungr sínni sunnan ferð at gunni:
nær vas-ek þausnom þeirra; þat bar skiótt at móti;
herr týndi þar Hœrða (hiœr-gǫll vas þá) fiœrvi.   50

ANOTHER (Anonymous).
VASA Sunno-dag, svanni (seggr hné margr und eggjar)
morgun þann sem manni mær lauk eða œl bæri:

---

ready for the crowded shield-moot.   Though the people say in the east
that there is a battle to come, let us stand true to the king.
Thorfinn Mouth. The great tempest is darkening over the hard shield-
wall. The Werdalesmen are going to fight against our king. Let us
defend our lord, and fell the Thronds in Woden's storm. So we egg
one another on.
Thormod Coalbrow's poet. The battle is gathering fast, men must
not fumble now for fear. Let us make ready now for the fray, and let
no cowardly word be spoken. Now we go forward with the brave
Olaf to the court of spears.
BRYNIOLF. The king gave me a sword and Wettaland.
POET HELGI. The sword-prints will not grow old . . . .
TRYGGVI'S VERSES. Tryggvi came from the north, and Sweyn from
the south. I was present at the fray which broke out suddenly. A host
of the Hords lost their lives.
ON SWEYN *Ælfgifu's son* [perhaps by the same poet]. That Sunday

---

44. gunn-reifr, Cd.   50. harða, Cd.

es Sveinn konungr sína saman tengja bað drengi
(hrátt gafsk hold at slíta hrafni) skeiðar stafna.

OLÁFR HELGI.

(Verses 1-3 from Flatey-bok iii. 241 ; verse 4 from O. H. L.)

1. Segið ér Karla es kœmr hingat   55
    nýtom þegni fyrir norðan haf:
    at fleira skal í fœrom vinna
    an hylda hval hvœssom knífi.

2. Nær es sem upp or eiso (innar lít-ek til kvinna)
    [snót hver svá miok láti seg þu mer] loga bregði :   60
    mik hefir mála sykninn mest á skœmmo fresti
    (gekk-ek um golf at drekka) Gramr ok Brattir-hamrar.

3. Fagr stóð-ek, es bar brúi blakkr, ok sák á sprakka,
    (oss lét ynðiss missa aug-fœgr kona) á haugi :
    keyrði gerðr or garði góðlát vala slóðar   65
    eik, enn ein glœp sœkir iarl hvern, konor allar.

4. Lítt man hœldr inn hvíti (hrafn etr af ná getnom)
    [ver unnom gný gunnar] glaðr í nátt á Iaðri :
    svá hefir œllungis ílla (ek gekk reiðr of skeiðir)
    [iœrð veldr manna morði] mítt rán getið hánom.   70

THORMOD COALBROW'S POET.

IN a very charming Saga, that of the 'Foster-brothers,' we have the
story of a poet whose life was as wild and adventurous as any of the
long list of Northern poets. Like the others, Cormak, Gunlaug, and
Hallfred, he was unlucky in his loves. There is an amusing tale told
of one of his poems in his Saga which is worth giving here.

---

morning it was not as when the maid is serving men with leeks or ale,
when King Sweyn bade his men lash the prows of the galleys together.

Ascribed to King OLAF. Tell Charles the good farmer, north over sea,
that there is better work to do here than cutting up a whale with
a whetted knife.

A love ditty. It is like a fire breaking out of the glowing embers—
my love. I am looking at the ladies *passing;* tell me, who so proud as
she! I am going to drink in the house. Ingibiorg [lit. King-Hill, a
word-play] has made me speechless in a little space.

I stood on the howe when the steed bore the lady away. She seemed
fair to me. She went out of our sight. She turned her horse out of the
yard. Every man has his madness.

After Erling's death. The White One of Iadar will not be merry
to-night. His plundering of me has turned out altogether ill for himself.

---

65. gorðom, Cd.

" He made a poem of praise *on his love*, Thorbiorg Coalbrow, which
he called Coalbrow's verses; and when he had made it he delivered it,
so that many men heard it. Katla, Coalbrow's mother, drew a great
and fair finger-ring off her hand and said, ' This finger-ring I will give
thee, Thormod, as a poet's fee and as a name-gift; for I will give thee a
name, thou shalt be called Coalbrow's poet.' But Thormod was fickle,
and went off to stay with Grima, the mother of Thordis, another of his
loves, at Ogur. Grima welcomed him kindly, but Thordis bridled a little
and looked askant at him, 'as is women's wont when they are not quite
content with a man.' Thormod, 'remembering the old saw, that it is
easier to land your fish if you keep the line a bit slack,' tries to soothe
her by calling to mind former love-passages between them; and at last
she explains her behaviour. 'I have heard tell that thou hast got a new
love, and hast made a song of praise on her.' Thormod, *innocently*, 'Who
is this love of mine that thou sayest I have made a poem on?' Thordis,
' It is Thorbiorg, west in Ernedale!' Thormod, *boldly*, 'It is not true
at all that I made a poem on Thorbiorg; what is true is, that I made a
song of praise on *thee* when I was in Ernedale; for it came into my
mind how much difference there was between thee and Thorbiorg in
beauty, and in behaviour also; but now I am here I will recite the poem
to thee.' So he recited Coalbrow's verses to her, turning to the praise
of Thordis the expressions that were of the most personal bearing in his
poem on Thorbiorg. This had the desired effect, and Thordis took him
back to favour again. But one night, when Thormod lay at home in
Long-boll, he dreamed that Thorbiorg Coalbrow came to him and
asked him whether he was waking or sleeping. He said he was waking.
Said she, 'Thou art asleep, but what happens to thee in thy sleep shall
be fulfilled when thou wakest. But what is this? Hast thou given to
another woman the poem thou didst make for me?' Thormod answered,
readily, 'It is not so.' Said Thorbiorg, 'Aye, but it *is* so, thou hast
given my song to Thordis, Grima's daughter, and turned to her the love-
phrases that thou didst make for me; for thou didst not dare, thou
craven, to tell the truth, and say for whom thou hadst made it. But I
will pay thee for thy leasing and lie, thou shalt be seized with such great
and dire pains in thine eyes, that both thine eyes shall start out of thine
head, save thou publish before all men thy shameful dealing in taking
my Song of Praise from me and giving it to another woman. Thou
shalt never be hale again till thou cast out those verses which thou hast
turned to Thordis' praise, and put back those thou didst make on me;
and do not call thy poem by any woman's name but mine, for whom it
was made.' He awoke terrified, with a pain in the eyes so bad that he
could hardly help crying out, and got no more sleep or rest. His father
Bersi went to see him, and when he heard of his dream he said, ' Thy
loves bring thee no good; through one thou gottest such a wound as thou
wilt never be a sound man again [when Thormod was set upon by
Colback Grima's·thrall], and now thou art like to lose thine eyes by the
other. I counsel thee to obey thy dream as soon as may be.' And so
Thormod did, and his eyes got well again."

His friendships brought him almost as much trouble as his love. His
first friend and foster-brother, Thorgeir Hawarsson, was slain, and
Thormod went out to Greenland and avenged him in the most sweeping and dauntless way, at the hazard of his life, lying out on the desert
reefs, cold and hunted about, and after the most hair-breadth escapes
getting away from the Arctic regions and coming to St. Olaf, with
whom he was in high favour. But this second friendship cost him

his life, for he fought and fell with his master at Sticklestead, as the fine passages in the Kings' Lives tell us.

When the king had set his men in array in a 'shield wall' or phalanx, he called to his poets and bade them come inside the shield wall. 'Ye shall be here,' said he, 'and see what things shall betide, then shall ye have no hearsay tales to tell, for ye shall set forth all these things in tale and poems afterwards.' There were there that day Thormod Coalbrow's poet, Gizur Goldbrow, the foster-son of Hof-garth Ref, and the third of them was Thorfinn Mouth [Sighvat being away on a pilgrimage in Rome]. Then spake Thormod to Gizur, 'Aye, let us not stand too close for Sighvat to take his place when he comes; he will want to be next the king, and the king will like him to be there.' The king heard this, and answered, 'There is no need to sneer at Sighvat for not being here, he has often followed me closely; and he is praying for us now, and we shall have no small need of his prayers.' Said Thormod, 'Maybe, O king, that ye need his prayers; but the ranks round the banner-pole would be thinned if all thy henchmen were now on the way to Rome; and it is true, that we often used to say, that through Sighvat there was no room for a man who wished to speak to thee.' Then the poets spake among themselves, saying that it would be very meet that each should make a memorial verse concerning those things which were near at hand and like to befall. These three verses have survived and are given above, pp. 170–171.

Again it is written, how in the night before the battle Olaf was sleepless and awoke in the early dawn, and thought it too early to rouse his host, and called for Thormod. He was near at hand, and asked what the king wanted with him. 'Recite us a poem now.' Thormod got up, and recited in a very loud voice, so that he was heard by all the host; and the poem he recited was the old Lay of Biarki. [See Book iii. § 3.] Then the host awoke, and when the poem was ended men thanked him for his poem, and thought highly of it, holding it very well fitted to the time, and they called the poem the 'Guard's call.' The king thanked him too, and gave him a gold ring worth half a mark. Thormod thanked him for his gift and said, 'We have a good king, but who knows how long he may live? This is my prayer, O king, that we two shall never part alive or dead.' The king answered, 'We will never part by my will.' Then Thormod said, 'I hope that I may be found near thee, O king, in good hap or ill, as long as I may have my will, no matter where Sighvat may be roaming with his gold-hilted sword.'

Thormod had his wish; he got a deadly hurt from a javelin, and after the fight went to a barn where the wounded lay, and there improvised two or three verses in answer to those who asked for news of the battle [see p. 177]. The nurse, seeing his pale face, said, 'Why wilt thou not let me search thy wounds?' He replied in verse, and before he could speak the last word; fell dead to earth, like a nightingale shot in the midst of its song. And it is told that King Harold Sigurdsson filled up the half-finished line with the word 'svida,' saying, 'That is what he must have meant to put!'

The jealous love and passionate irony of Thormod are well brought out in the fine scene—too long to quote here—in the Kings' Lives. Thormod's real poetry was rather in his deeds than in his words. Of his person, we hear from himself that he was dark-haired, left-handed, and had an impediment in his speech.

The dirge *Thorgeir's-drapa* in the Saga is spurious, the *Coalbrow's verses* have been lost, and most of the *Greenland improvisations* are not authentic; but the verses relating to the last scene of the king's and his own life, some twenty stanzas in all, especially those cited in the Legendary Saga of St. Olaf or in the Kings' Lives, may in part be genuine, and have a real and peculiar beauty of their own. As to the verse spoken to Loftung, it can hardly be Thormod's, for Thorarin was not a poet of St. Olaf, but of Cnut and his son; so, believing as we do, that the piece is genuine, it must have been spoken by some poet of the Danish king's court.

Verses 3–6, 12–19 are taken from O. H. L.; verses 1, 7–11 from Fbr. S.

1. ILLA réð-ek því es allar (ey-draupniss) gaf ek meyjo
(mer barsk dóms í drauma dís) Kolbrúnar-vísor:
þá tók-ek þorna Freyjo (þrúðr kann mart in prúða)
[líknomk heldr við Hildi hvítings] á mer víti.

2. Þarf sa-es þer skal hverfa, þengill, fyrir kné lengi   5
(svarar-þu hógliga hverjo) hug-borð (konungr orði):
fair ero ver (enn frýjo frændr órom þó vændir),
[minnomk meirr á annat mítt starf] konung-diarfir.

3. Þer man-ek enn unz œðrom allvaldr nair skaldom
(nær vættir þú þeira?) þing-diarfr fyrir kné hvarfa   10

4. Loftungo gaftu lengi láttr þat-es Fáfnir átti
þú lézt mer, inn mæri, merkr frán-œluns vánir . . . .

5. Flestr of ser hve fasta fagr-búnar hef-ek túna
báðar hendr or brendom barðz þióð-konungs garði:
eld á-ek iœfri at gialda ungr, þeim-es bregðr hungri   15
diúps (berr-ek goll á greipom) gráðogs ara (báðom).

6. Hafa þóettomk ek, hættinn happ-sœkjandi, ef tœkir
hreins við haldi míno 'hvert land' þegit, branda:
ríkr vil-ek með þer rœkir randar-linnz ok Finni
(rœnd berom út á andra ey-baugs) lifa ok deyja.   20

7. Örvendi trezk undir (opt finnomk þess minni)
[œll es fremð of fallin fiœr-nepps í strá greppi]:

His apology to Coalbrow. I did ill when I gave all Coalbrow's verses to the maid; she [Coalbrow] appeared to me in a dream. I got a punishment in my body from her.

To King Olaf. He need have a stout heart [lit. a high freeboard] who would stand long beside thy knee, O king; few of us kinsmen are bold before kings.

His constant faithfulness. Till thou get other poets, king, I will be ready at thy knee . . . .

[*His jealousy.* Thou hast given Praise-Tongue gold, thou hast let me hope for gold too. Every man can see that I have both my arms adorned with burnt gold. I must repay the king for it. I have gold on both hands. I should think that I had grasped heaven in my hands if thou wouldst receive me. I am ready to live and die with thee and Fin (Arnisson).]

His biography. All my honour is perished. My left-handedness must

---

18. Read, hreggland (heaven)?   21. Read, tésk?

ef hregg-boða hœggit hef-ek vart í skœr svarta
nadda-borðz þvi-at nirði nættings bana veittag.

8.   Undr es hví ekki kendo él-bœrvar mik gœrva   25
stáls; hefig mark á máli mart ok skopt it svarta:
burgomk, langs þvi-at lengra líf vas tý skapað drífo,
þremja svellz, enn þolli þeim aldr-tili seima.

9.   Matka-ek hefnd (enn hrafni hrings fekk-ek bráð á þingi)
[Baldrs lét-ek vígi valdit varga setrs] við marga: 30
gný-þolli lét-ek gialla, gœrt hefek fyrir mik svartan,
meirr hefni þó þeira Þorgeirs vinir fleiri.

10.   Skopta-ek þa es uppi undarlegr á sundi
hrókr dó heimskr við klœki hans raza klof ganði:
alla leit-ek á Ulli egg-veðrs hugar-glœggom   35
(setti gaurr, ok glotti) goð-fión (við mer siónir).

11.   (Els) hefig íllan díla (Ekkils) þeim-es mik sekðo
(geig vann-ek gœrvi-draugom) Grœnlendingom brendan:
sá manat sœki-tívom sverð-éls frœm frœmom verða
hrings á hryggjar tanga hóg-grœddr nema mer lógi.   40

12.   Sex hefig allz, es óxo ón hialta mer fiónir,
(kendr er-mik við styr stundom) stál-regns boða vegna:
nú em-ek enn (ok mank manna morð) varliga (forðom)
[ver létom þó þeira] þrítœgr [skarar bíta].

13.   Brennom œll fyrir innan Inney þau-es ver finnom   45
(lœnd tegask herr með hiœrvi) Herbiœrg (fyr gram verja):
(ýss) hafi allra húsa Inn-Þrœndir kol sinna
(angr man kveykt í klungri) kœld, ef ek má valda.

14.   Ála þryngr at éli . . . . . . [see p. 171].
15.   Ört vas Álafs hiarta; óð gramr í styr blóði;   50
rekin bito stœl á Stikla-stœðom, kvaddi lið bœðvar:

---

be in fault if I have struck a slack blow on his black head, for I meant to
kill him outright. It is a wonder they did not know me, for I have a
blemish in my speech, and black hair.   I escaped, because much longer
life was fated to me, and destruction to them.   I have not trusted others
with my revenge.   I have struck his black pate, let other friends of
Thorgeir do more.

Satirical verses. I floated up, etc.

His vaunt. I have branded the Greenlanders who outlawed me; I did
them deadly hurt; this spot on their back will not easily heal as long
as they leave me alive.   I have been the death of six enemies, though I
am barely full thirty years old.

Before Sticklestead. Let us burn all the houses inside Herbiorg and
Inney. The In-Thronds' houses would be lying in cold ashes if I had my
will.   Let the flames be kindled within their walls.

At Sticklestead. The battle is gathering fast, etc.   See above, p. 171.

After Sticklestead. Proud was Olaf's heart; the damasked steel bit at

---

45-46. innin . . . Hverbiorg, Hauksbok.

ý-þolla sá-ek alla Ialfaðrs nema gram sialfan
(reyndr varð flestr í fastri flein-drífo) ser hlífa.

16.   Á ser at ver várom víg-reifir með Áleifi;
sǫ́r fekk-ek, hildr, at hvǫ́ro, hvítings, ok frið lítinn: 55
'skínn' á skildi mínom; skald fekk hríð til kalda;
nær hafa eski-askar ǫrvendan mik gœrvan.

17.   Haraldr sá-ek at vel varðisk víg-reifr með Áleifi;
þar gekk hárra hiǫrva Hringr ok Dagr at þingi:
réðo þeir und rauðar randir prútt at standa   60
(fekk ben-þiðorr blakkan biór) dǫglingar fiórir.

18.   Undrask œgliss landa eik at ver sém bleikir;
fár verðr fagr af sǫ́rom; fann-ek ǫrva-drif, svanni:
mik fló malmr enn dœkkvi magni keyrðr í gœgnom
hvast beit hiarta 't næsta hættligt iarn, es ek vætti.   65

19.   Emkat-ek ríóðr né rauðom 'ræðr' grǫnn kona manni
hauka-setrs in hvíta; hyggr fár um mik sáran:
hitt veldr mer at meldrar morð-venjandi Fenjo,
diúp ok Danskra vápna Dags-hríðar spor svíða.

Sticklestead.   I saw them all spare themselves save the king.   Many a
man was hard put to it in the shaft-shower.

It can be seen that we were with Olaf: I got wounds and little mercy;
my shield is scored; they have nearly done for the left-handed poet.

I saw Harold fighting fiercely by Olaf's side, Ring and Day went up to
the high sword-moot; they stood gallantly under their red shields, those
four Ethelings.

His last verses. 'Why art thou so pale?' says the lady. The maiden
marvels why I am so pale. I was in the arrow-shower, lady. Wounds do
not make a man fair. The black iron, hurled amain, has pierced me;
the deadly steel has bitten me keenly to the heart's core, as I can feel.

I am neither red nor ruddy of hue, lady; no one cares for me, a
wounded man. What ails me, maiden, is that the deep prints of the
Danish weapon and of the storm Day raised are—smarting.

---

56. Read, skeina es.   61. þiðors blakkr, Cd.   66. Read, né rauðom
ræðk...   67–69. iarn stendr fast it forna fen-stigi mer benja | þat veldr mer in
mæra marglóðar nú tróða | draupnis dýrra vápna D. s. svíða, Hauks-bok; um
hættinn ... þat veldr mer en mæra mót eggiaðra spióta draupnis dyrra, O. H. L.

§ 3. THE COURT POETRY OF MAGNUS AND HAROLD HARDREDE.

(C. 1040–1070.)

ABOUT the time of Cnut's death, probably in the summer following, 1036, Magnus (in the eleventh year of his age) was recalled from Russia, and put on the throne; and, as he was a child, and the nobles formed a regency which ruled successfully, prosperity returned to Norway. The young king grew up into a good ruler under the hands of his friends and tutors. There was matter for bloodshed in the heritage of Cnut; but some kind of agreement was come to between Magnus and Harda-Cnut, giving the survivor the right to both crowns of Denmark and Norway.

In March, 1042, Harda-Cnut died, upon which young Magnus (now seventeen) set sail for Denmark to take possession of his kingdom. Here a sorry inheritance awaited him:—A Wendish invasion into Jutland, which Magnus defeated in a fierce battle near Hetheby (Sleswick near Lurschau), Sept. 28th, 1043 (age then eighteen), and again at Scotborg water (two battles within a few days). Here Sweyn Wolfsson, the young Danish 'Earl,' fought by Magnus' side. Soon, however, Sweyn rebelled, but was defeated in four successive battles (all in Jutland), fought in one year (Magnus' twentieth); after which Magnus chased Sweyn across Funen, Sealand, and Sconen, clean out of Denmark into Sweden.

Meanwhile, Harold, the young half-brother of St. Olaf, had fought and been wounded at Sticklestead when he was only fifteen years old; and after adventures in the woods, hiding from his enemies, he escapes from Norway and gets to Russia, where St. Olaf's sister was married and where he had friends and kinsfolk. Soon after we hear of him as captain of the Warangian guard at Constantinople; and wonderful stories of his exploits in their service afterwards reached Norway and are told in our Lives of him, how he slew a dragon, how he fought in eighty engagements, how he had love-passages with Greek princesses, shared twice in the imperial largesse at the Emperors' death, and finally broke from an imprisonment which he had earned by his adventures, and came home with his hoard of money, and his repute as a great captain, to claim his share of his family's restored good-fortune. Magnus agrees to accept him as fellow-king (1046).

The reason why Magnus, in the height of his good luck and in prime of youth, should consent to accept a joint king has never been duly given, and one cannot believe the puerile account given in the Saga. There are manifest marks that weighty plans were brewing, Magnus, now king of Denmark and Norway, meant to reconquer Cnut's empire; and to this end Harold's experience and treasure were serviceable. Even the Saga gives hints, how Magnus, like Cnut of yore to his father, wrote a letter to King Edward to yield up his kingdom. The Chronicles mention about this time an incursion led by Yrling and Lodin (Erling Skialgson's son and grandson?). But the young king Magnus' sudden death in Sealand (Denmark) gave things another turn. Saxo relates the accident. His horse took fright in a forest at a hare crossing the path, and the king struck (his head?) against a jutting stump of a tree, of which he died 25th Oct. 1047, in his twenty-fourth year. The Saga makes no mention of the *accident*, but speaks of the young king's dying in a strange and mysterious way, as though from fever or concussion of brain; probably he was not killed on the spot, but died from the effects of the blow; and so but half the story was told. Thus by an untimely end was the heroic son of St. Olaf cut off in the prime of life.

In Norwegian Law Traditions, Magnus is the mender and betterer of St. Olaf's law. He, they say, gave the Thronds their code Greygoose. Hence he was called the 'Good,' the Debonair. Upon his death Danish Sweyn took heart, and the Danes rose afresh to shake off the rule of Harold, whose reign of nineteen years is filled up by troubles at home and by expeditions, victorious but fruitless, into Denmark; by preparations for an English expedition, and the establishment of a somewhat tyrannical power in Norway. Here he was driven, by his policy of keeping down the great houses, to the murder of Einar, the veteran of Swold, and of Calf Arnason, the captain of Sticklestead, which bred much evil feeling. In 1062 he at last made peace with Denmark, giving up the game; then followed an insurrection of the borderers in the Uplands in Norway (1065).

When Harold at last went out on his forlorn fatal errand he was in his fifty-second year, worn by toil, too old one may safely say.

Early in 1066 the news came of the Confessor's death, and in that year Harold sets sail with 360 ships to the west, picks up the Orkney Earls and their force, engages other hireling troops, and coasting southwards, meets Tosti with his twelve ships full of Flemings (the remains of a squadron of sixty), who is glad to join him. After a temporary success and the surrender of York, Harold Godwinesson hurries northwards, and by some means, not explained in our authorities, Harold and Tosti, with a part of their force, are brought face to face with the whole English army. The details of the battle in the Kings' Lives are of course, as pointed out by Mr. Freeman, apocryphal, and even the verse said to have been sung by Harold would seem to be part of an earlier poem; but after a sharp engagement, in which the king's personal following and Tosti's Flemings seem to have borne the brunt (the Norsemen would have suffered less, for we find only *one* mention of men 'falling with the king at Stamford Bridge,' Brand an Icelander), it is certain that Harold, his marshal Eystan Gorcock, and Tosti were slain, and the whole expedition thus brought to nought.

There are fewer verses on the battle and its circumstances than we should expect from the king being a poet himself and a great patron of poets, and we get little help from them. One verse by Thiodwulf (who was present at the battle), which is made by the prose Chronicles to be spoken before the king's fall, must refer to the despondency felt immediately after that event, for the word 'avengers,' i. e. 'sons,' is only used of near of kin whose relations have met with bloody deaths, and the first line must be mended in consequence. Harold Godwinesson's leniency after the battle and the wise policy of William, who feared Denmark and therefore favoured Norway, seem to have brought about a friendly feeling between Englishmen and Northmen during Olaf the Quiet's reign, and the rise and growth of his merchant town at Bergen is a memorial of increased trade and intercourse between the two countries, which brought in the new medieval fashions and ways of life, so that Harold's death marks the beginning of a fresh era of culture in Norway.

The name Hardrada (Tyrant) is never given by the Icelanders to Harold; whatever he may have been to his subjects, to them he was ever favourable, helped them in the famine of 1056, sent timber for a church at Thingwalla; and though we hear of his cynical speeches, and his somewhat cruel sport of setting his sensitive and jealous poets to use their gifts one against the other, we should only get a good character of this king from them. It was the Norwegians who gave him the name, in contrast to the debonairté of Magnus; that it was extant in his day, the corruptions of the English Chronicle 'Harfayera' etc. show. In Northern authorities it only appears in the superscription to three chapters in Fagrskinna, which was written in Norway, whence, through Torfæus, it has passed into modern use.

Harold composed a short poem, recounting some of his exploits to his lady; and several stray verses, which we still possess, but probably more of his work is lost. Of all the Northern kings, he took most interest in the craft and minutiæ of the court-poetry, which had the same fascination for him as the Provençal *sirventes* and *tensons* had for the sons of Henry II.

THE ORKNEY EARLS.

THERE is unfortunately no list of the Orkney Earls and their Poets in Skalda-tal, though even English kings and Norwegian barons and their bards find place there. This is a pity, for the Earls themselves were many of them poets; and as we cannot but believe that many of the finest Northern poems were composed within their domains, we should no doubt have found in such a list the names of their authors. Such a one as the author of Darrad-liod was certainly closely connected with the Stout Earl whom he mentions. Nor have we an *Iarla-tal;* that there was one, known as late as the composition of Iarla Saga, seems very likely from the way in which the deaths and burial-places of the first Earls are recorded, quite in consonance with similar notices drawn from Ynglinga-tal.

The history of the Northern Earls of Orkney is a curious and instructive chapter in the tale of the colonisation of the Western isles, illustrating the enormous influence of the Celts upon the Northern immigrants.

In the necessarily imperfect accounts that are left us in the Earls' Saga, the first part of Orkney Saga, we have a series of brilliant and tragic episodes with long blanks of dead silence between, broken only now and again by a line or two in an Irish or Scottish Chronicle. There is a picturesque character about the scene, the men, and the motives, which makes the Orkney Saga one of the most fascinating of the series of Northern histories. Reginwald the Mighty and Wise, the friend and counsellor of Harold Fairhair, and his name-giver, we have met with above. To him, as weregild for his son Inwar, slain in an enterprise (undertaken, we should suppose, in Harold's interest) in the Orkneys, Harold gives the Island-Earldom. He, choosing to live in Norway, bestows it upon his brother Sigfred the Mighty, who, followed by a short-lived son, held it in Alfred's days, according to Ari's synchronism.

But it is by his successor, TURF-EINAR, Reginwald's bastard son according to the tradition, that the Earldom is consolidated and its history takes on its distinctive character. By his days the turbulence of the Wicking settlement was settling down into regular lines of commerce, migration, and buccaneering. His revenge of his father upon Fairhair's son, Halfdan Highleg, is commemorated in his verses which we have given in Book vi. § 2. A goodly husbandman, poet, and peat-digger, who taught his Norsemen in the wood-lorn islands to dig and use turf-fuel, his memory should be ever green in the islands he ruled so long ago.

His sons Thorfinn, Arnkettle, and Erlend are mixed up with the Ynglings and Shieldings by their connection with Eric Bloodaxe and his wife Gundhild. It was by Eric's side that two of the brothers fell at Stainmoor, c. 954. But Thorfinn lived on to win his ghastly by-name 'skull-splitter,' to wed the Celtic lady Grelod, and to bring up a brood of wild reckless sons, who are plunged in fratricidal strife and murder by the wicked wiles of Ragnhild, Gundhild's daughter, which brings death to the two eldest. Hlodwe, whose name points to some Frankish connection of his father, succeeds to the earldom, and weds Aithne, daughter of the Irish king Cearbhal of Leinster.

Hlodwe had the rare misfortune to die in his bed, and left his earldom to his eldest son SIGROD THE STOUT. This earl's life was eventful. His battle with Finnlach the Scottish marmaor, his forced conversion by Olaf Tryggvason (according to a shaky tradition), his marriage with the daughter of Malcolm the Scottish king, a fact which points to the policy pursued so successfully by his mighty son, and finally his ill-fated alliance with Sigtrygg Silkbrow, then king of Dublin, and fall at Clontarf, April 23rd, 1014, make up what is known of his history. He appears before us in a more romantic aspect, as the friend of Icelanders, the host of Gunlaug the poet, and the patron of Flosi the Burner.

The eldest son of Sigrod is unable to hold the heritage, and Brusi, the next, is too easy-natured and void of ambition to take the first place. The earldom therefore practically soon falls into the hands of the youngest, THORFINN THE MIGHTY, the greatest of his race. He submits to St. Olaf, who seems to have aspired to rule 'the whole empire as Harold Fairhair held it,' and seized the occasion of the disputed succession to have his suzerainty acknowledged, and to get Rognwald, Brusi's son, as a hostage of its rights being preserved. But Thorfinn, 'mightily strengthened by his Scottish kinsfolk,' pursued his path unchecked, and as the death of Olaf, the anarchy in Scotland, and the absorption of Cnut in other projects left him scope to act, he succeeded in making himself master of half Scotland. 'Nine earldoms he ruled,' says Arnor with a reminiscence of the Vellekla pæan-notes, and his sway was felt from Dublin to Giant-skerries; the Isle of Man and the Isles and Galloway (or rather Cumbria) being also under his influence. At last, however, Magnus was restored to his father's seat, and he determined to pursue his father's colonial policy, for he had a ready instrument at hand. Rognwald, Brusi's son, had been his foster-brother, had fought at Sticklestead where his father fell, had gone into exile with him to Russia, and there entered upon the career of arms. Magnus sent him to the islands to share Thorfinn's power as the liegeman of the king of Norway. The rivalry, as usual in the Orkneys, soon turned to a tragedy. It is as the poet of these two kinsmen and historian of their deadly feud that ARNOR won his name of *Earls' poet*. His finest verses were made for them. He was the friend of Rognwald, whose defeat at Redburgh he deplores, and the panegyrist of Thorfinn, whose dirge he composed.

After Redburgh, c. 1045, Rognwald fled to Norway, but soon made a
fresh dash at his opponent, which all but turned the tables and put an
end to Thorfinn's career. But the 'great earl's' luck never left him, and
he was more fortunate in laying hands on his nephew, who was put to
death in 1046. Thorfinn had been largely helped by his Norwegian
uncle-in-law, the exiled Calf Arnison, who gave him a steady support
against Magnus' friend and nominee. This alliance is alluded to in the
Dirge on Calf, see p. 164. Thorfinn's later years are unruffled. Magnus'
death relieved him of possible trouble, for Harold had his hands full and
would not, we think, alienate such a useful ally on the brink of his
great enterprise, the conquest of England. Just before the expedition,
which was to effect this, sailed, Thorfinn had died full of years and
honours.

The Earl's two sons by Ingibiorg, Fin's daughter, Mother-of-earls
(as she is often styled by an echo of Gundhild's appellation), lived
together long in peace and amity unexampled in their race. Paul
marrying back into the old stock by wedding the daughter of Hakon, son
of that Iwar of the Uplands whom Sighvat compelled to listen to him.
Erlend wedded Thora, daughter of Somerlid Ospac's son. Magnus Bareleg
appeared in the west in 1098; he sent both the brothers to Norway,
where they died. But, between the two brothers' sons, Hakon, Paul's
son, and Magnus, Erlend's son, this thirty years' peace of their fathers
was not long to remain unbroken. A deadly feud arose among the
cousins, and the murder, which gave Magnus a place among the Northern
Saints, was the upshot of their struggle. They had a poet, whose name
is not given, but who is called upon in Orkney Saga, ch. 49, as witness to
certain events in their career, the slaying of Dubhniall, the burning of
Thorbiorn the Shetlander, before 'wicked men brought strife between
them.' Hakon was a man of mark, a pilgrim, and a lawgiver. The
career of Sweyn Asleifsson, 'the last of the Wickings,' which would have
afforded ample material for a poet, is now only preserved in prose. He
is said to have been the captor (year 1135) of Paul, Hakon's son, the
last heir on the spear-side of the 'race of Reginwald.' As in Norway,
a new line arose on the spindle-side. Coll, a descendant of Thorleif the
Wise, the well-known lawman, married Gundhild, St. Magnus' sister, and
his son Cali was enfeoffed of the earldom by Sigurd the Crusader (in
pursuance of the old policy) in rivalry with Paul, Hakon's son.

It was now that he assumed the respected name of ROGNWALD. A
poet himself, and a man of romantic character and remarkable career,
this earl comes before us as a patron of poets. With his friend Hall he
composed 'Hatta-lykill;' many of his improvisations are preserved in
Orkney Saga (see § 5). Rognwald completed the work of Coll, the
splendid cathedral of Kirkwall, which was raised in pious memory of his
uncle, St. Magnus. With Rognwald, who was murdered in Caithness,
Aug. 20th, 1158, winning a saint's name in the Islands, the right line of
the old lawman, Thiodwolf's patron, ended, for he left only a daughter.

The half-Gaelic line of Harold, Maddad's son, in close affinity with
the Scottish king, now comes in, but our interest with the earldom now
ceases. Swerri's long arm was felt here as at home in Norway, and he,
a Western Islander, himself asserted his suzerainty over the earldom.
It is indeed merely as the nurse of doubtful pretenders that the Islands
had lately influenced the politics of Norway, and soon, when the temporary revival of the imperial ideas had shown their hollowness, and
Hakon's ill-success had disgusted the home government of Western
enterprise, the earldom falls into a barony of the Scottish kingdom.

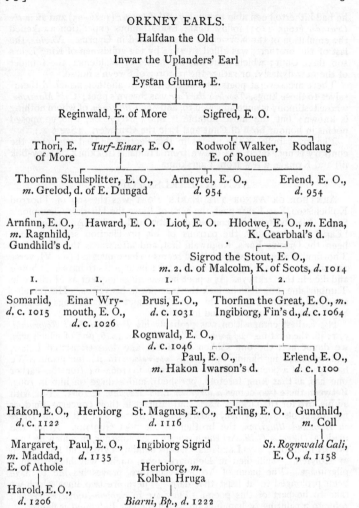

ORKNEY EARLS.

Halfdan the Old

Inwar the Uplanders' Earl

Eystan Glumra, E.

Reginwald, E. of More   Sigfred, E. O.

Thori, E.   *Turf-Einar*, E. O.   Rodwolf Walker,   Rodlaug
of More   E. of Rouen

Thorfinn Skullsplitter, E. O.,   Arncytel, E. O.,   Erlend, E. O.,
  m. Grelod, d. of E. Dungad   *d.* 954   *d.* 954

Arnfinn, E. O., Haward, E. O. Liot, E. O. Hlodwe, E. O., *m.* Edna,
m. Ragnhild,   K. Cearbhal's d.
Gundhild's d.

                           Sigrod the Stout, E. O.,
                    m. 2. d. of Malcolm, K. of Scots, *d.* 1014

  1.   1.   1.   2.

Somarlid,   Einar Wry-   Brusi, E.O.,   Thorfinn the Great, E.O., *m.*
d. c. 1015 mouth, E. O., *d. c.* 1031   Ingibiorg, Fin's d., *d. c.* 1064
             d. c. 1026
                           Rognwald, E. O.,
                           d. c. 1046
                             Paul, E. O.,   Erlend, E. O.,
                           m. Hakon Iwarson's d.   *d. c.* 1100

Hakon, E.O., Herbiorg St. Magnus, E.O., Erling, E. O. Gundhild,
d. c. 1122   *d.* 1116   *m.* Coll

Margaret, Paul, E. O., Ingibiorg Sigrid   *St. Rognwald Cali*,
m. Maddad, *d.* 1135   E. O., *d.* 1158
E. of Athole   │
  │   Herbiorg, *m.*
Harold, E.O.,   Kolban Hruga
d. 1206   │
                        Biarni, Bp., d. 1222

SWEYN ESTRITHSSON AND HIS SONS.

SWEYN, Cnut's nephew, son of Ethelwolf and Cnut's sister Estrith,
to whom we owe in all probability the preservation of England from
invasion during the Confessor's reign, was king till 1076, surviving all
his rivals. He and his five sons, succeeding one after another,
founded a dynasty, which lasted for ninety years (1044–1134): *Harold
hone*, a quiet ruler (1076–80). *Cnut the Saint* (d. 1086), who prepared
to invade England in 1086, but was slain by his own men in church,
thus enabling the Conqueror to disband his hired forces, and by means
of the Survey to devise better means for defending his kingdom than

he had hitherto been able to employ. *Olaf hunger* (1086–95) and *Eric the Crusader* (1095–1103) follow next; Eric's famous expedition awakened the emulation of the Norwegian king; he died in Cyprus. *Nicolas*, the last of the brothers, was killed in 1134 by the guildsmen of King Eric's son, duke Cnut; which Cnut was the father of Waldemar, the founder of the new dynasty, or rather the restorer of Sweyn's house.

There are several poets who at one time or another attached themselves to those kings. *Thorleik the Fair* was Sweyn's poet; *Calf Manisson*, whose testimony is once appealed to, and *Skuli Illugason*, of whom nothing is known; but the most notable is *Mark Skeggisson*, who composed poems in honour both of Cnut and Eric the Crusader. (See § 4.)

The great bulk of the poems in this Section, indeed wherever the contrary is not stated, are drawn from Hulda (Hrokkinsk., Flatey-bok iii) and Kringla, a few from Fagrskinna.

ARNOR EARLS' POET.

ARNTHOR OR ARNOR THE EARLS' POET was the son of Thorrod Kolbeinsson, Earl Eric's poet, the hero of Biorn the Hit-dale Champion's Saga. Like Sighvat, he combined poetry and trade. As his by-name 'Earls' Poet' implies, the patrons of his predilection seem to have been the Orkney Earls, Rognwald first, and afterwards the great Earl Thorfinn, whose relative he indeed seems to have married (see VI. verse 22), so he must have been a man of mark; he appears to have kept house and died in the Orkneys. As a poet he was magniloquent as Marlowe in Tamburlaine, nor does he lack the true fire in his verses. His remains are considerable, scattered through Hulda and the Iarla Saga (Orkney Saga), and a few are also cited in Edda.

His earliest composition was probably his *Dirge on Earl Rognwald*, c. 1046, the next his *two poems on King Magnus*, 1046, one of which was, we doubt not, the one spoken of in the anecdote translated below, and criticised in Skalda by Olaf as *macrologic* in its inception. We have part of a poem *on Harold* of Norway in 1062–64 (for the earlier one has, as that king foretold, perished), and a dirge on him in 1067. Between these two comes *a dirge on Earl Thorfinn*, c. 1065. But with all his love for the Orkney Earls, and interest in their concerns, he does not forget his countrymen, and there is a morsel still left of his *Dirge on Hermund Illugisson*, the brother of the poet Gunlaug. Arnor also made a *Dirge on Gelli*, Ari the historian's grandfather, in which he ' expressly mentions,' says Laxdaela, ' Gelli's building a great and fine church at Holyfell.' Gelli died in Denmark, 1073, on his way home from a pilgrimage. The poem of Arnor's, therefore, proves his life to have been prolonged to at least that date. There are two lines which we take to be part of this poem. They are in *eight-measured metre*, and refer to a painting or hangings on which the last Judgment is figured.

Arnor is remarkable as the only court-poet who quotes from the early poems, citing Volospa in one line. Upon our theory his close connection with the West would account for this.

The following story gives perhaps the most characteristic traits of Arnor's character:

" It happened once upon a time, that the two kings [Magnus and Harold] were sitting in one hall over the table north in Chipping, and Arnor the earls' poet was come to the town. He had made a poem for each of the two kings. And one day, while Arnor was tarring his ship, the king's messengers came to him, and bade him come and deliver his poem. He went off at once, without washing the tar from his hands, and when he came to the hall, he called to the door-ward, Room for the kings' Poet! and in he went before them and cried, Hail, emperors both! Said King Harold, Whose poem shall be said first? He answered, The younger's. The king asked, Why his first? My lord, said he, it is a saw that 'Young men are impatient.' But every one thought it most honour to him whose poem was said first. Then he began to recite his poem; and first he treated of the earls west of the main, and then he came to his own voyage. And when he had got thus far, Harold said to King Magnus, Why sit here, my lord, over this poem, which he has made about his journeys and the earls in the Western island? Let us wait, kinsman, answered King Magnus, I fancy that you will not think me in need of praise before the poem is ended. Then he came to the verse (3) in which he calls Magnus 'the greatest of all kings.' Then King Harold said, Praise this king as thou wilt, but do not despise other kings. Then he went on till King Harold said again, This man makes the lordliest kind of verse, I do not know where he will get to. And when the song was ended, straightway Arnor began the poem on Harold, which is called *Blue cocks-drapa* [Raven's praise], a fine poem. But when it was finished, King Harold was asked which he deemed the better poem. I can easily see, said he, the difference between the two poems; my poem will soon fall to the ground, so that no man shall know it, but this Song of Praise, which is made on King Magnus, will last as long as there is a man in the lands of the North. Harold gave him a gold-bound spear, and Magnus a gold ring, and the poet went out of the hall, holding up the ring on the spear, crying, So shall the two kings' gifts be borne aloft. Harold said to him ere he went, He did not come for nought, the wordy fellow! When thou comest again bring me another poem. Arnor promised to do so, and when he heard of Harold's death he set to work and made a dirge upon him."

Arnor's poems have been spared to a greater extent than any other man's, save Sighvat only. There is a magnificence and dash about them which no doubt won him many admirers, and his perfect form and rich metre pleased even the later critics, like Snorri and Olaf. The sea and the golden-headed galleys, marching like God's bright angels over the waves, the savage triumph over the 'roasted heathen,' the horrors of the Day of Doom (where he is inspired by Volospa), these are his themes, tricked out in glittering if sometimes borrowed sheen. The dirge on Thorfinn, his kinsman by marriage, shows feeling and loyalty that are to be admired.

It is, as we have seen before, in poems relating to England and foreign lands that the worse corruptions of text are to be looked for, and Arnor's poems have suffered the common fate. It is in the *Dirge over Harold* that we find 'the Dyke by Ouse' buried under 'tok fusa;' 'Fulford' under 'fell at fundi;' the famous mail-coat 'Emma,' which 'could not protect him from the spear points' that fatal day at Stamford Bridge, hidden in the phrase 'hlenna sæfi hoddum,' etc. But in the *Dirge on Thorfinn* matters are worse still; 'af skeidom' conceals 'a Skidi' on Skye; 'trura tyggia' is the unmeaning substitute of 'Tyris tyggi,' lord of Tyrist. The battle in Anglesey Sound is hidden beneath the commonplace 'Ein uas su-es Engla minnir,' rightly 'Endr was i Onguls sundi.' Some verses we can see are wrong, but cannot put right, such a line as VI. verse 11 suggests some place-name beneath 'milli borga.' Even the lines quoted in Edda seem corrupt, and to refer to the Redburgh fight in which Rognwald fell, VI. verse 17. The poet's mention of Tyrfing is to be noted III. 2.

I. Hrynhenda (1047).

(From Kringla, Hulda, Hrsk.; verses 1, 2, 21 from Edda and Skalda.)

1. KLIÚFA lét-ek í kaupfœr dúfo knarra mínn við borð in stinno
2. Seinkon verðr þá es hlébarðz hanka hnika ár in lióta bára.

3. Magnús, hlýð til máttigs óðar! manngi veit-ek fremra annan;
yppa ráðomk yðro kappi, Ióta gramr, í kvæði flióto :
haukr réttr es-þú, Hœrða dróttinn ; hverr gramr es þer stórom verri;
meiri verði þínn an þeira þrifnoðr allr unz himininn rifnar.
4. Her-skip vantu af harða stinnum hlunni geyst í Salt-it-Eystra
(skiœldungr stéttu á skœrom hveldan skeiðar-húf) með Girzko skrúði:
vafðir lítt, enn vendir bifðosk; (verða hrœkk) enn ' niðr nam sœkkva,'
[geystisk 'hlýr,' enn hristizk bára] (hrími stokkin) búnar grímor.
5. Rauðar bórot randir síðan, rimmo Yggr í Sœnskar bygðir ;
eigi gaztú liðs kost lágan ; landz-folk sótti þer til handa :
austan þurður, ulfa ferðar œldum kuðr, við hvíta skiœldo,
tungo rióðr, til tírar þinga ' teknir menn' ok dœrr in rekno.
6. Austan komtu með allra hæstom, Yggjar más, í Þrœnda bygðir,
fiðri-rióðr (enn fiánd-menn yðra falma kvóðo) œgis-hialmi :
' breiðast' visso, blá-gamms fœðir benja kolgo, yðrir dolgar
(hræddir urðo fiœrvi at forða fiánd-menn þínir) vesœld sína.
7. Ungan frá-ek þik, eyðir þrœngva ulfa gráðar, þeira ráði
(skiœldungr stœkk) með skœðan þokka (skeiðar-brandz fyr þer or lan<

Magnus' Praise. *Introduction.* I made my stiff-timbered buss cleave
the billows .... There comes .... when the ugly wave .... the oars
of the leopard of the tackle [ship] ....
I. *The Praise.* Magnus, listen to my mighty song ! I know none better
than thee ; I will exalt thy prowess, thou dread of the Jutes, in my swift
verse. Thou art a true hawk, lord of the Hords ; every king is far
behind thee. May thy glory ever be greater than theirs, until the
heavens are rent. Thy war-ship thou didst dash off the strong rollers
into the East Baltic, with her Russian rigging ; and didst go on board
the hollow-straked hull thereof. Little didst thou shrink though the
masts quivered, the ice-sprinkled bulwarks shrank, and the waves made
the fair figure-heads rattle ; ocean boiled and the billows were tossing.
Thou didst bear the red shield into the Swedish land. No little company
didst thou gather, for the people of the land sought thee as their liege.
Ye sped from the east to battle with your homagers ; they bore white
shields and inlaid darts. Thou camest from the east to the Throndist
land in helm of terror, and your enemies trembled, it is said. Soon th*
foes felt their evil plight ; yea, thine enemies fled fearing for their lives
Thou young king, thou didst put them to straits in thy wrath. Before
thee the prince [Sweyn Wolfsson] fled out of the land. Thou didst

---

9. Read, uðr . . . nam klœkkva.   10. Read, Hlér.   14. Read, tekn
menn?   17. Read, bráða.

8. Eignask namtu óðal þegna, allan Noreg gotna spialli　　21
(mangi es yðr mildingr annarr mœri gramr) til landa-mœri.

9. Síðan vas þat es suðr með láði, siklingr, ýtti flota miklom;
skíði vas þá skriðar of auðit skorðo; renndi Vísundr norðan:
samnazk 'bað' til hverrar hœmlo; hræðazk menn við ættar klæði　　25
Giúka 'þótti' gœfugt eiki Girzkan malm ok Peito hialma.
10. Lióto dreif á lypting útan lauðri (bifðisk goll it rauða),
[fastligr hneigði furo glœstri fyris-garmr] um skeiðar stýri:
Stirðom héltu um Stafangr norðan stólom (bifðosk fyrir álar),
[uppi glóðo él-mars typpi eldi glík] í Dana-veldi.　　30

11. Heyra skaltu hve her-skiœld bórot, hilmis kundr, til Vinda grundar
(heppinn dróttu af hlunni sléttom hélog borð) í STEFJA-MÉLI:
12. Aldri frák (enn, vísi, valdit Vinda sorg) at dœglingr spendi
[flaustom vas þá flóð of ristit] fleiri skip til óðals þeira.
13. Skiœldungr, fórtu um óþióð eldi (auðit vas þá flotnom dauða)　　35
[hæstan kyndot, hlenna þrýstir, hyrjar lióma] suðr at Iómi:
hvergi þorði hallir varða heiðit folk í virki breiðo
(buðlungr, unnot borgar-mœnnom) biœrtom eldi (stall-dræp hiœrto).
14. Skiœldungr, lézt við skíra valdit Skotborgar-á Vinda sorgom
(Yngvi vas sá frægr es fengot fœrnoðr þinn) við helming minna:　　40
vœrro lá þar val-kœstr hæri (vas þer sigr skapaðr grams ins Digra)
'virðom' kunn an víða runnin varga ætt of klífa mætti.

---

take hold of the freelands of men, yea, all Norway up to the borders of
the land. No king is more glorious than ye *two*.
Warfare in Denmark and the Baltic. Then it came to pass that ye
stood southward, prince, with a great fleet; the ships sped apace, the
Bison ran from the North. Thou badest men gather to every rowlock-
strap; they went on board the goodly bark with mail-coats, Russian
metal [steel swords], and helmets of Poitou. The grim foam dashed in
upon the forecastle over the captain. The red gold *figure-heads* quivered,
and the stiff gale made the shining ship dip. Thou didst stand from the
North past Stavanger, thy prow towards the realm of the Danes; the
deep was stirred; the tops of the ships gleamed like fire above.
II. *Staves.* Now thou shalt hear in the STAVE-PIECES, O prince, how
thou didst bear the war-shield into the land of the Wends, having
launched the frozen bark off the smooth rollers. I never heard of a
king leading a greater number of ships towards their heritage. Ye did
work woe to the Wends. The sea was furrowed by vessels! Thou,
king, didst carry fire south to Iom among the barbarians; they were
death-doomed. Ye kindled the lofty flame of fire. The heathen in their
great fortress dared not guard their hall against the bright flame, for
thou didst make their hearts shake within them. With the smaller army
thou didst bring sorrow on the Wends, by the clear Scot-borough Water;
great was the victory ye won. There lay there a pile of corses so high
that the wood-haunting, wide-roving pack of wolves could not climb it.

---

25. Read, baðtu.　　25-26. Read, hlœðask . . . þopto . . . Girzkan malm.
33. Read, voldut.　　42. Emend.; virðum, Cd.　Read, viðom.

15. Keppinn vantu þatz æ man uppi Yggjar veðr meðan heimrinn byggisk
(val-gammr skók í vápna-rimmo) við Helganes (blóðokt fiðri):
Yngvi, féktu öll með hringom (iarl vissi sik foldar missa)   45
þióðom kuðr, [enn þú tókt síðan] þeira flaust [við sigri meira].

16. Hefnir, fengot yrkis-efni Áláfs; (gœri-ek slíkt at mǽlom)
[Hlakkar lætr-þú hræ-lǫg drekka hauka]; nú mun kvæðit aukask:
fiórar hefir-þú, randa rýrir reyrar setrs, á einom vetri
(allvaldr est þú of-vægr kallaðr) ǫrva hríðir frœkn of gœrvar.   50

17. Ótti, kunnot elgjom hætta œði-veðrs á skelfðan grœði,
fengins gollz, eða fœðit ella flestan aldr und drifno tialdi:
glíkan berr þik hvæossom hauki, holl-vinr mínn, í lypting innan
(aldri skríðr und fylki fríðra farligt eiki) Vísundr snarla.

18. Eigi létot, iæofra bági, yðro nafni mann-kyn hafna   55
(hvárki flýr-þú, hlenna þreytir, hyr né malm) í broddi styrjar:
hlunna es sem ræoðull renni reiðar búningr upp í heiði,
(hrósa-ek því) es her-skip glœsir, hlenna dolgr, eða vitar brenni.

19. Mæonnom lízk es mildingr rennir Meita hlíðir sævar skíði,
unnar iamnt sem 'osamt' renni Engla fylki himna þengils.   60

20. Eyðendr frá-ek at elska þióðir (inn-drótt þín es hæofð at minnom)
græði lostins Goði it næsta geima vals í þessom heimi.

21. Skiæoldungr man þer annarr aldri œðri, gramr, und sólo fœðask.

Thou didst in champion-wise win that battle at Holy-Ness, that shall
ever be remembered while there are men on earth. The eagle shook
her gory wings in the fray. Glorious king, thou didst take also their
ships with all their crew. The earl [Sweyn] lost his land and thou didst
gain a great victory.

III. Thou hast given me matter of song, Avenger [son] of Olaf. I will
exalt thy deeds. Now I will come to the EKING of my song. Thou hadst
bravely fought four battles in one winter, O king. Thou art wont to
risk thy ships on the tumbling sea, or else thou art spending thy life
under the driven awnings [in port]. The Bison bears thee in her forecastle like a keen hawk, my good lord; never sped more famous ship
under more glorious king. Thou wilt never let men miss thee in the
van. Thou fleest neither for fire nor sword. The ornaments [figure-
heads] that glitter on thy war-ships (I boast thereof) are to look on as it
were the sun rising in a clear sky, or glowing beacons. When the king
plows the main with his galleys, it seems to men as if legions of angels
of God were marching along over the waves.

   Burden. I know that the people cherish thee next to God in this
world; thy household is far-famed!
   A greater king than thee will never be born under the sun.

---

55. Read, látið.   61. Eyðendr, i. e. the *two* kings, objective case.

II. Magnus-drápa (1046–47).

1. NÚ hykk rióðanda reiðo róg-ærs, þvi-at veitk gœrla,
   (þegi seim-brotar!) segja seggjom Hneitiss eggja:
   vasat ellifo allra orm-setrs hati vetra
   hraustr þá-es herskip glœsti Hœrða vinr or Gœrðom.

2. Þing bauð út enn ungi egg-rióðandi þióðom;   5
   fim bar hirð at hœmlo her-væðr ara bræðiss:
   Salt skar húfi héltom hraustr þióð-konungr austan
   (bóro brim-logs rýri brún veðr) at Sigtúnom.

3. Gekk á Sviþióð sœkkvi Sveins, es fremð vann eina;
   fýstizk Áláfs austan af kárt sonar hiarta: 10
   nótt beið ok dag dróttins dygg ferð Iaðar-byggva:
   'fyst' bað gramr í geysto gífrs veðri 'ser' hlífa.

4. Flýði fylkir reiði framr þióð-konungs rama,
   stœkk fyrir otvín okkrom arm-svellz hati gerla:
   létat Noregs nióta nýtr þengill gram lengi;   15
   hann rak Svein af sínom sókn-diarfr fœðor-arfi.

5. Afkárlig vas iarla orð-gnótt su-es hlaut dróttinn;
   fylgði efnd því-es ylgjar angr-tælir réð mæla:
   at framm í gný grimmom grafnings und kló hrafni
   fúss lézk falla ræsir feigr eða Danmœrk eiga.   20

6. Segja mun-ek hve Sygna snar-fengjan bar þengil
   (hallr vas hrími sollinn hlé-borðz) Vísundr norðan:
   setti bióðr at breiðo (bryn-þings) fetil-stinga
   (fús tók œld við œsi) Iótlandi gramr branda.

7. Náði siklingr síðan sniallr ok Danmœrk allri   25
   (móttr óx drengja dróttins dýrs) Nóregi at stýra:

MAGNUS' PRAISE. Now I must tell the deeds of the king, for I know them well. Be silent, men! The patron of the Hords was not full eleven years old when he launched the ships from Garth [Novgorod]. The young king called out a levy, and the men in mail stood to the row-lock-straps. He furrowed the Baltic in a fresh gale from the east with his curved hulls toward Sigton. Sweyn's victorious adversary landed in Sweden, Olaf's brave-hearted son hastened from the East. They that dwelt in Iadar waited night and day for their lord, begging Christ to defend him in the battle. The prince [Sweyn] fled the king's wrath, and ran out of the land. The king would not let him enjoy Norway long, but chased Sweyn from the heritage of his father [Olaf].

War in Denmark. Marvellous was the boast of the lord of Earls [Magnus], and fulfilment followed his words: that he would gladly fall, doomed, in battle under the raven's claws, or win Denmark for himself. I must tell how the Bison bore the Sogn-folk's lord from the North. Her sides were thick with ice; he steered his ship's bows towards broad Jutland, and the people welcomed him. Then he came to rule Norway and all Denmark. Never has any child-king won him so

---

7. I. e. hveltom.   12. Read, Christ bað grami ... hverr?   26. dyrr, Cd.

œngr hefir annarr þengill áðr svá gnógo láði
(bráskat bragnings þroski) barn-ungr und sik þrungit.

8. Vann, þá-es Vindr um minnir, vápn-hríð iæfurr síðan
(sveið of ám) at Iómi (illvirkja hræ stillir):   30
búk dró bráðla steikðan blóðogr vargr af glóðom ;
rann á óskírð enni all-sterkr bani hallar.

9. Óð með œxi breiða ódæsinn framm ræsir,
(varð um hilmi Hœrða hiœr-dynr) enn varp brynjo :
þá-es um skapt (enn skipti skap-vœrðr himins iœrðo), 35
(Hel klauf hausa fœlva) hendr tvær iæfurs spendo.

10. Svá hlóð siklingr hávan snarr af ulfa barri
(hrósa-ek hug-fullz vísa) hræ-kœst (tírar-ævi) :
at á-leggjar Yggjar all-nátt-fœrull máttið
(œld lá vítt), þótt vildi, víf-marr yfir klífa.   40

11. Fúss lét á Ræ ræsir ramm-þing háit Glamma ;
Valska rauð fyr víðo Vestlandi gramr branda.

12. Títt hefi-ek heyrt at héti Helga-nes, þar-es elgi
vágs enn víða frægi varg-teitir hrauð marga :
Rœkkr œndurt bað randir Reggbuss saman leggja ; 45
róg-skýja hélt rýgjar regni haust-nótt gegnom.

13. Dœrr lét drengja harri driúg-spakr af þrek fliúga
(glœddi eldr af oddom) almi skept á hialma :
Létat hilmir Hneiti (Hœgna væðr í gœgnom
iœrn flugo þiokt sem þyrnir) þél harðara sparðan.   50

14. Skeiðr tók Biarnar bróðor ballr Skánungom allar
(þióð rœri þeirar tíðar þingat) gramr með hringom.

15. Upp-gœngo vann Yngvi ítr-lógandi gnóga
(gœrði hilmir Hœrða hiœr-þey) á Skáneyjo.

---

much land. He was soon of full power. He fought a battle at Iom, the
Wends will remember ; he singed the dark carcases of the heathen; the
bloody wolf dragged the half-roasted trunks out of the embers, and the
fierce fire raged over their unchristened brows. The king went in front
with his axe, casting off his mail-coat, when he grasped the shaft with
both his hands. The sword-clash rose round the lord of the Hords.
Hell [Magnus' axe] clove the yellow skulls. The Lord of heaven
shared out the earth. Such a high carrion-heap of wolf's food did the
king raise, that the night-roving steed of the mate of the giants could not
climb up it. Men's bodies lay far and wide. He fought on Rae [Rugen]
and reddened the Welsh [Gaulish] blade off the wide Westland [Meck-
lenburgh].

I have heard it called Holy-Ness, where he won many ships. Regbus
bade them lock their shields early in the twilight, and the battle lasted
all through the autumn night. Our king made the elm-shafted darts
to fly fiercely on the helmets. The fire sprang off their points. He
did not spare Hnit [St. Olaf's sword] that is harder than the file. The
Sconey folks forsook all the galleys of Biorn's brother [Sweyn Wolfsson]
with all thereon. The Hords' lord made a raid into Sconey and fought

---

38. firar-ævi, Cd.   49. veðr, Cd.

16.   Svik réð eigi eklo all-valdr Dœnom gialda;   55
lét full-hugaðr falla Falstr-byggja lið tyggi:
Hlóð (enn hála tœðo hirð-menn ara grenni)
auðar-þorn fyr œrno ungr val-kœsto þunga.

17.   Enn bar framm á Fióni (fold sótti gramr dróttar)
(ráns galt herr frá hánom) hring-serks litoðr merki: 60
minnisk œld, hve annan iafn-þarfr blóm hrafni
(œrt gat hilmir hiarta) her-skyldir tog fylldi.

III. PRAISE OF HAROLD.

(Verse 4 from O. H.; verses 6, 7 from Edda.)

1.   R AUÐ (enn rýrt varð síðan) [rann eldr of siœt manna]
    fróna egg á Fióni (Falstr-byggva lið) tyggi.

2.   Hialm-óro léztu heyra hnitz, es rautt fyrir Nitzi
tyggi, Tyrfings eggjar tvœr áðr mann-fall vœri:
Naðrs borð skriðo norðan nýs at allvaldz fýsi;   5
hlaut til Hallandz skióta hrafn-þarfr konungr stafni.

3.   Hrauð, sá-es hvergi flýði, heið-mœrr Dana skeiðar
glaðr und golli roðnom, geir-ialm, konungr hialmi:
skiald-borg raufsk, enn skúfar (skaut hodd-glœtoðr broddom)
bragna brynjor gœgnom buðlungr of ná sungo.   10

4.   Gekkat Sveinn af snekkjo saklaust inn for-trausti
(malmr kom harðr á hialma) [hugi mínn es þat] sinni:
far-kostr hlaut at flióta fliót-mœltz vinar Ióta,
áðr an œðlingr flýði, auðr, frá verðung dauðri.

5.   Gengr í ætt þat-es Yngvi Upplendinga brenndi,   15
(þióð galt ræsiss reiði) rann sá-es fremstr 'vas' manna:
vildot œflgar œttir (áðr vas stýrt til váða)
[grams dolgom feksk galgi] gagn-prýðanda hlýða.

---

there. He paid the Danes back unstintingly for their treason, and
smote the dwellers in Falster. His henchmen helped him. He bore
forth his banner to Fion [Funen], and all remember how he fulfilled his
second tale of ten years.

HAROLD'S PRAISE. *War in Denmark.* Fire ran over the seats of men,
the king reddened the keen edge on Fion [Funen], and the dwellers
in Falster withered away.

The Niz River Battle. Thou lettest men hear thou didst dye both
Tyrfing's edges red off Niz [1062]. The Snake sped from the North to
Halland. In his golden helmet the king, that never fled, chased the Danish
galleys; the shield-wall was broken. Sweyn did not leave his ships without
doing any harm. The ship of the patron of the Jutes was cleared before
the Etheling fled, all his guard being dead.

Rising of the Uplanders [1065]. It runs in the king's family for the
king to burn the Uplanders' houses [his brother St. Olaf had done it
before him]. The good people would not obey him. The people had
to pay for his wrath. The gallows were the portion of his enemies; ere

---

61. hver annan, Cd.   16. Read, es.

6. Œmðit ráóð við Rauma reiðr Ey-Dana meiðir,
    heit ðvinoðo Heina; hyrr gœrði þá kyrra.   20

7. Siklinga venr snekkjor siá-lútar konr úti;
    hann litar her-skip innan (hrafns góð es þat) blóði.

IV. ERFI-DRÁPA ON KING HAROLD (c. 1067).

1. ÞUNG rauð iœrn á Englom eir-laust (ne kœmr meira)
    vísi vel nær Úso (val-fall um her sniallan).

2. 'Féll at fundi stilliss framm óðo vé móða'
    'œrt fló gríót á gauta glóð-heitr ofan sveiti:'
    'þióð hykk þaðra náðo þúsundom tok fusa'   5
    '(spiót flugo) líf at láta (laus í gumna hausom):'

3. Gagn fékk giaf-vinr Sygna (gekk hildr at mun vildra)
    hinn-es á hæl fyr mœnnom 'hrein-skialdaðr' fór aldri:
    Dynðo iarlar undan (eir fékka lið þeira)
    [mann-kyn hefir at minnom morgin þann] til Borgar.   10

4. Upp-gœngo bauð Yngvi ítr með helming lítinn,
    sá-es á sínni ævi sásk aldregi haska:
    Enn um England sunnan œflugr herr at berjask
    fór við fylki dýran; fundosk þeir af stundo.

5. Olli of-rausn stilliss, orma-láttrs, þat-es máttit,   15
    stáls í strœngo éli, stríðir elli bíða:
    hinn-es aldregi 'aldins' ótams litoðr hramma
    viggs, í vápna glyggvi, varð-rúnar, sik sparði.

6. Hafðit bríóst (ne bifðisk bœð-snart konungs hiarta)
    í hialm-þrimo hilmir hlít-styggr fyr ser lítið: 20

---

this it had been well-nigh a revolution. The foe of the Island-Danes dealt roughly with the Reams, the threatenings of the Heins fell low. Fire silenced them. The king ever keeps his sea-swaying ships out at sea.

DIRGE ON HAROLD. *Fulford Fight.* The king reddened the heavy irons [axes] on the English hard by Ouse without mercy. There shall never be a greater slaughter among gallant men! *At Fulford the king's army marched down the Dyke, his banner went forth in the van.* The spears flew. I know that the people rushed by thousands into the Dyke by Ouse. One could pass over upon the heads of men. The fair-shielded friend of the Sogn-folk [Harold], he that never turned on his heel in the face of his foes, won the day: the earls [Eadwine and Morcar] marched back to the Borough [York]: their side had the worst of it. Men hold that morning in remembrance.

Stamford Bridge. The noble king, that never feared danger in his life, made an inroad with a little band; but from the south of England there came a mighty host to battle with the good king. They met forthwith. The king's rashness in battle prevented him from awaiting old age, that king who never spared himself in fight, the dyer of the giant good-wife's charger's [Wolf's] paws. His was a steadfast breast in battle; the bold

---

3-6. The whole verse is over-painted. Read, at Fulla-furðo . . . Móðo . . . ofan sveitir.   5. Read, díki Úso.   8. -skialdaðr] thus Hrokk.

'þars til þengils hersa, þat sá herr, at skatna'
'blóðogr hiœrr ins barra beit dœglinga Hneitiss.'

7. Eigi varð ins ýgja auðligr konungs dauði;
    hlífðot 'hlenna sœfi hoddom reknir oddar :'
    Heldr kuro meirr ens mœra mildings, an frið vildi,   25
    of folk-snaran fylki falla liðs-menn allir.

8. Vítt fór Vœlsungs heiti ; varð marg-lofaðr harða
    hinn-es skaut or Nið nýtla norðan her-skips borði.

9. Myrkt es hverr meira orkar mer, allz greppr ne sérat,
    (harðr es) í heimi (orðinn hrafn-grennir) þrek iœfnom :   30
    'ert' gat óslætt hiarta eljon-fims und himni
    'mest hefir mildingr kostoð minni hvers grams vinnor.'

10. Haraldr vissi sik hverjom harð-ráðr und Miðgarði
    (dœglingr réð til dauða dýrð slíkri) gram ríkra :
    Hefir afraka ens œfra átt-stýrœndom dýrri   25
    (hnígrat hilmir frægri) heilœg fold (til moldar).

V. Rögnvaldz-drápa.

(Verses 1–5 from Iarla Saga ; verse 6 from Edda.)

1. DEILDISK af svá aldri, él grafninga þélar
        gunnar niœrðr í Gœrðom gunn-bráðr tio háði.

2. Em-ek sízt ýtar hnekðo iarla sætt, es ek vætti,
    ('iœfn fengosk hræ hrœfnom') hegjo trauðr at segja :
    sleit fyr Eyjar útan allvaldr blá tialdi,   5
    hafði hregg-svœl dúfa hrími 'fast um' líma.

3. Oskepnan varð uppi endr þá-es mœrgom kendi

---

king's heart never trembled when the bloody brand bit the lord of
barons [Harold]. His death was not according to fate [it was too
early]! His . . . . mailcoat *Emma* did not save the king from the
spears. Sooner than take quarter of the people [English], his men
rather chose all of them to fall with the king.

Far did his name travel ; many were the poems on the king that
doughtily launched his war-ships out of Nith in the north. It is dark
to me, and I can never see king on earth that was his match in deeds
of prowess . . . . the greatest prince under heaven.

Harold the Stern seemed to men the mightiest king on earth, so
great was his renown till his death . . . . Never sank to earth more
glorious captain.

EARL ROGNWALD'S PRAISE. *In Russia.* His life passed in such wise
that he fought ten battles in Gard [Novgorod territory].

Battle of Redburgh. I am grieved to tell what happened. I know,
after men broke the peace between the earls [Rognwald and his
brothers], the prince struck his awnings and put to sea outside the
Islands [Hebrides] . . . . ice cold . . . . [it was still winter]. A dire fate was

---

24. Read, hlífðit Emma iöfri oddom . . .?   35. Thus Thulor ; afreki, Cd.
6. Read, föstom ?

'háligt' róg at hníga hæorð þar-es iarlar bæorðosk:
nær réðosk ást-menn órir, 'elld-hríð,' enn varð síðan
(æld fékk mein in milda mæorg) fyrir Rauða-biæorgom.	10

4.	Hvárn-tveggja sá-ek hœggva hirð á Pettlandz-firði
(ór þrifosk mein at meiri) mínn auð-giafa sína:
siár blézk, enn dreif dreyri dœkkr á saum-fæor klœkkva,
skaut á skiald-rim sveita, skokkr vas blóði stokkinn.

5.	Gramr mundi sá gæomlo gunn-bráðr und sik láði	15
(hann fekk miklo minni mann-spiæoll) koma æollo:
Ef ílendra Endils ætt-stafr hafa knætti
(vélti herr um Hialta) hialm-þrótta lið (dróttinn).

6.	Saðr stillir hialp þú sniæollom sól-tialda Rognvaldi!

VI. ÞORFINNZ-DRÁPA.

(Verses 3–14, 26 from Iarla Saga, Orkn. S., chs. 22–38, Rolls Ed.; verses 1–2,
16–25 from Edda; verse 15 from Skalda.)

1.	NÚ hykk slíðrs-hugaðs segja (síð léttir mer stríða)
[þýtr Allfæoðrs] ýtom iarls kosto [fen hrosta].

2.	Nemi drótt, hve sæ sótti snar-lyndr konr iarla!
eigi þraut við ægi of-vægjan gram bægja.

3.	Hilmir rauð í hialma hreggi skelkings eggjar;	5
fór áðr fimtán væri fet-ríóðr hugins vettra:
gœrr lézk grund at verja gunn-frœkn ok til sœkja
œrri Einars hlýra.—*Ongr mannr und ský-ranni.*

---

ruling when the earls fought of yore, their great feud brought many a man
low that morning. My beloved patrons fought at Redburgh [Rattar-
brough, East of Dunnet Head]. I saw them, both my patrons, hewing
down each other's men in Pentland Firth. Very great was my sorrow.
The sea was stained, the dark gore was dashed on to the fine strakes,
the blood flew on to the rim of the shields [round the waist of the war
galleys], the hull was splashed withal. The prince [Rognwald] would
have won all the ancient land for himself (he lost far fewer men), if he,
the scion of Endil [the sea-king], had had the help of the Islanders
[Hebrides people]; the people betrayed the lord of the Shetlanders.
Prayer. O true king of the sun's awnings [heaven], help thou the
gallant Rognwald!

EARL THORFINN'S DIRGE. *Burden.* No man under the hall of the
clouds *was greater than Thorfinn.*
Now I am going to tell of the deeds of the great-hearted earl. The
yeasty draught of Woden is bubbling; [my song is running through
my lips]; my sorrow grows no lighter. Hearken, O men! how the
prince of earls [Thorfinn] put to sea; he was not afraid to face Eager
[the sea-giant].
Scotland. He fought and went forth to sea before he was fifteen
years old; the younger brother of Einar was ready to defend his own
and to win other men's land to boot. I know he battled with Karl

---

8. Read, hættligt.	9. Read, odd-hríð.	16. mínna, Cd.	3. kgr, Cd.

4. Endr hygg-ek Karli kendo 'kyndom lofut brynjo'
(land vasa lofðungs kundar laust) fyrir Dýrsnes austan :　10
fimm snekkjom ıéð frammi flug-styggr við hug dyggvan
rausnar-maðr at ræsiss reiðr ellifo skeiðom.

5. At lægðo skip skatnar skilit, fell herr á þiljor ;
svǽmo iǫrn í ǽmo óð-hǫrð Skotta blóði :
Stall drapa (strengir gullo ; stál beit, enn rann sveiti ;　15
broddr fló, bifðosk oddar biartir) þengils hiarta.

6. Þrima vas þvigit skemri, þat vas skiótt at spiótom
mætr við minna neyti mínn dróttinn rak flótta :
gól 'áðr grams menn fæli' gunn-már um her sǽrom,
hann vá sigr fyrir sunnan Sandvík, 'ruðu branda.'　20

7. Ulfs tuggo rauð eggjar, eitt þars Torfnes heitir,
(ungr olli því þengill ; þat vas Mána-dag) fránar :
sungo þar til þinga þunn fyrir Ekkial sunnan
sverð, es siklingr barðisk snarr við Skotlandz harra.

8. Hátt bar Hialta dróttinn hialm at geira ialmi　25
(ógn-stǿrir rauð Írom odd) í ferðar broddi :
mínn dróttinn naut máttar mildr und Brezkom skildi,
hendi Hlǫðvess frændi her-menn, ok tók brenna.

9. Týndosk ból þar-es brendi (bráskat þat dǿgr haski)
[stœkk í reyr en rokno rauðr eldr] Skotta-veldi :　30
morð-kennir galt mǫnnom mein ; á sumri eino
fengo þeir við þengil þrim sinnom hlut minna.

10. Veit-ek þar-es Vatz-fiǫrðr heitir (vask í miklom haska)
míns (við mannkyns reyni) merki dróttins verka :
þióð bar skiótt 'af skeiðom' skiald-borg Friá-morgin,　35
gœrla sá-ek at gínði grár ulfr of ná sǽrom.

[Duncan] off Deerness [Orkney] in the east .... the earl attacked him
with a stout heart, his five ships against the king's eleven galleys. They
laid their ships together ; the keen weapons swam in the black blood of
the Scots ; the bow-strings rang, the steel cut, the blood flew, the shaft
sped, the bright points quivered, the prince's heart trembled not. Long
they fought with spears ; but soon my lord with his small force drove
them to flight. He won the day in the south of Sandwick [Orkney].
The young earl reddened the keen edges of the Wolf's morsel [sword]
at the place called Torfness [Tarbatness?] ; it was a Monday. The thin
swords sung at the meeting south of Ekkial [R. Oikel] when the earl
fought with the lord of Scotland [King Duncan].
Ireland. The lord of the Shetlanders fouзht the Irish, carrying his
helm high in the van of his host. Hlodwe's kinsman [Thorfinn] showed
his prowess under the British [Welsh] shield, and burnt the land. Many
a homestead perished when he burnt the realm of the Scots. Three
times in one summer they were defeated by him. I know the tokens
of my lord's prowess at the place called Water firth [isle of Skye] ;
I was in jeopardy there with my lord. Briskly did men foım up in the
shield-wall at Skye on a Friday morning.

11.   'Margr' varð 'milli borga,' mildingr þrœng at hildi,
horna-blástr, þar-es hristosk hug-stórs iɔfurs merki:
'vatr bra' es víg-lióst þótti 'varg-steypis her greypom'
(skulfo iarn, enn ulfar) Yggs morgin (hræ tuggo).   40

12.   'Ymist vann sa er unni' Irsk felı drótt þa-es sótti
'balldrs eðr' Brezkar aldir, brá eldr Skotta veldi.

13.   'Ein er su er Engla minnir' egg-hríð, ne mun síðan
hár með helming meira hring-drífr komit þingat:
bito sverð (enn þar þurði) þunn-gœr, fyrir Mɔn sunnan   45
(Rɔgnvaldz kind und randir 'ramlig' folk ins Gamla).

14.   Stɔng bar iarl á Engla ætt-grund, enn rauð stundom
(vé bað vísi knýja verðung) ara tungo:
hyrr óx, hallir þurro, 'her-drótt' rak flótta,
eim hratt, enn laust lióma lim-dolgr nær himni.   50

15.   . . . . . . Sumar hvern frekom erni.

16.   Harri fekki í hverri Hialtlandz þrimo branda
(greppr vill grams dýrð yppa) gagn, sa-es næstr es bragna.

17.   Svalg átt-boði ylgjar ógóðr, enn varð blóði
græðir grœnn at 'rauðom' grand 'auknom' ná blandinn.   55

18.   Ungr skiɔldungr stígr aldri iafn-mildr á við Skialdar;
þess vas grams und gɔmlom gnóg rausn Ymiss hausi.

19.   Hrafns fœði varð hlýða herr fra Þursa-skerjom
('rétt segig þióð hve þótti') Þórfinni til Dyflinnar.

20.   Orms felli drakka allan all-kostigr fen hrosta   60
(rausn drýgði þá ræsir) Rɔgnvaldz niðr í gœgnom.

England and Wales. There was much horn-blowing 'between the
boroughs' [sic] when the earl's banner swayed . . . . at daybreak . . . .
Wednesday morning. The earl . . . . the Irish people fell . . . . the British
[Welsh]; he carried fire over the realm of the Scots. There was a
battle fought in *Anglesey Sound;* never shall prince come there with
a greater fleet. The son of Rognwald the old [Thorfinn] stood under
shield; the thin swords bit a multitude of men in the south off Man.
The earl bore his banner upon the Englishmen's fatherland, the fire waxed,
the halls fell together, the smoke poured forth, and the flame rose
up to heaven. The prince drove the people to flight. Every summer *he
fed* the greedy erne.

The lord of Shetland, doughtiest of men, gained every battle. The
poet [I myself] will exalt the prince's praise.

The Battle of Redburgh. The wolf swallowed the carrion, the green
sea was blent with blood at Redburgh [Caithness].

Never shall such a generous young prince step on Shield's timber [the
ship]: great was his renown under the ancient skull of Ymi [heaven].
All men obeyed Thorfinn from Giant-skerries [the reef east of Orkney]
to Dublin.

Lost Verse. [He won nine earldoms in Scotland and all the Sudreys.]

---

43. Read, Endr vas í Önguls sundi?   49. Read, hár dróttinn.   55. Read,
at Rauða-biorgom.

21. 'Het ek' þa es hvern vetr sǽtom hrafns verð-giafa iafnan
     (líð drakk gramr á góðar) gagn-vert (skipa sagnir).
22. Réð Heita konr hleyti her-þarfr við mik gœrva;
     styrk lét oss of orkat iarls mægð af því frægðar.   65
23. Bera sín (en 'mik minir' morð-kendz taka enda)
     (þess of þengils sessa) þung mein synir ungir.
24. Bǿnir hefi-ek fyrir beini bragna fallz við sniallan
     Grikkja vǿrð ok Garða; giǫf launag svá iǫfri.
25. Ǽtt-bǿti firr ítran all-ríks (enn ek bið líkna)   70
     ('trúra' tyggja dýrom) Torf-Einars, Goð, meinom!
26. Biǫrt verðr sól at sortna; sœkkr fold í mar dœkkvan,
     brestr erviði Austra, allr brunar sær með fiǫllom:
     áðr at Eyjom fríðri (inn-dróttar) Þórfinni
     (þeim hialpi Goð geymi!) gǿðingr moni fǿðask.   75

VII. DIRGE ON HERMUND (from Edda).

HIALP þú dýrr konungr dýrom dags grundar Hermundi!

VIII. DIRGE ON GELLI (from Edda).

MIKKJALL vegr þat-es mis-gœrt þykkir, mannvitz fróðr, ok
     allt it góða;
tyggi skiptir síðan seggjom sólar-hialms á dœmi-stóli.

IX. IMPROVISATION (from Iarla Saga).

DRENGR es í gegn at ganga (gótt es at fylgja dróttni)
     [ǫld leynig því aldri] ófúss syni Brúsa:

Rognwald's kinsman [Thorfinn] drank of the yeasty pool [ale] all the
winter through (such was his state). I used to sit over against the earl
every winter, and he used to toast his good men. The kinsman of Heiti
[Thorfinn] contracted affinity with me [he gave me his kinswoman in
marriage]. This marriage kinship gave me rank. The earl's young sons
bear up against their heavy sorrow. Lo, now my memories of the earl
are fast tending to an end.

Epilogue. I offer prayers for the valiant earl [Thorfinn] to *God*, the
ready Patron of the Greeks and Gard-folk [Russians]; thus I repay him
his gifts. O God, deliver the goodly furtherer of Turf-Einar's mighty
race from woe! I pray mercy for the good lord *of Tyree.*
The bright sun shall turn black, the earth shall sink into the dark
sea, the burden of the Dwarf [heaven] shall be rent, the whole sea
shall rush up over the hills, ere there shall be born in the Isles a better
prince than Thorfinn. O God! help the lord of the henchmen!

HERMUND ILLUGISSON'S PRAISE. Help thou the good Hermund, thou
dear King of the land of Day [Heaven]!

GELLI'S DIRGE. The wise Michael weighs men's misdeeds and good
works; then the King of Heaven, sitting on His judgment-seat, sepa-
rates men *into two companies.*

IMPROVISATION. *Before Redburgh Battle.* I will never hide it. I am

---

62. Read, Hlaut-ek hvern v. sitja?   66. Read, enn miök minni.   71.
Read, Tyris?   74. fríðom, Cd.

oss es, ef iarlar þessir ógn-bráðir til ráðask,
(hœrð mun vin-raun verða) vandligr kostr fyrr hœndom.

FRAGMENTS (Edda Lauf.).

Bekks lá eldr ok axla ulf-liðs Dœnom miðli
ek sá 'orm ruð þakka' eitt Skánunga hánom.
Kreysti knúto lostna klifs bein fiœro-steina.   3

THIODOLF ARNORSSON.

THIODWOLF, the poet of Harold par excellence (as Arnor was of the
Earls and Magnus), was a prolific poet, and so much of his work has been
preserved that we might construct a little Chronicle from it of the
reigns of his patrons, even of Magnus; for he followed that king in his
campaigns in Denmark, and has left vivid pictures of the scenes he
beheld; he carefully tells us of the spoils he bore home, a Gautland
shield, a mail-coat, sword and helm. He talks, too, of Harold's benefac-
tions to him, and of other personal reminiscences.

He was an Icelander, son of a poor man (if we may credit the court
gossip preserved in the story of his quarrel with Hall, provoked by the
king), but of his family and quarters we know nothing. He seems to have
been in Norway as early as 1043, he was present at Stamford Bridge,
and survived Harold at least.

His career, as traced in his poems, begins with *Improvisations* on
Magnus' campaigns, 1043-45; and encomiums on both kings, *Magnus
flokk*, and a *Welcome to Harold*, in 1046. The *Dirge on Magnus*, the
Launch of the Dragon, seem to belong to 1048, and the short poem on the
Levy against Sweyn to 1054. The longest poem, *Six-Stave*, containing a review of Harold's whole career down to the quelling of the Upland
Rebellion, which he says was put down after three years, cannot be
earlier than 1065. The *Improvisations* on the morrow of the fight at
Stamford Bridge and the *Dirge of Harold*, of which we have a fragment,
would belong to 1066. A fragment of a *poem on an Earl* [Thorfinn?]
we cannot date; nor of course the *comic lines* composed for Harold,
who delighted in his impromptu verses. The tale of Thiodwolf in
Flatey-bok, iii. 415, is a mere inflated version of the Hulda story, stuffed
out and garnished with additions and forged verses.

Thiodwolf's poems have undergone serious injury, as can be seen by
comparison with the prose drawn from his verses; but, as usual, it is in
those lines where reference is made to foreign places (e.g. Denmark) that
the dilapidation is the worst.

In the *Magnus Ode* we have been able to restore 'Iota' for 'iöfra,'
'Fion' for 'i folk,' 'solar-dag at Iolum' for 'Sunnudag of unnin,' and
'þridia vé,' Woden's home, i.e. Odensé, for 'þordir bæ,' etc.

It is in the *Improvisations* on Magnus' Danish campaigns in Denmark
that the corruption and rottenness of the present text is most manifest. After the repeated defeats in Jutland (that of Helganes was the
finishing stroke), Magnus gave chase, pursuing Sweyn over Fünen,
Sealand, and Sconen into Sweden; for from the places named in Sealand

---

unwilling to march against the son of Brusi [Rognwald]. It is good to
follow one's lord. A hard choice is before me if these two earls come
to blows. It will try their friends sharply.

---

3. Some Danish name of place? Orms-ruð?

it is manifest the hunt ran *eastward*, and not, as in the Saga, over Sealand to Fünen . . . . Under ' auŏtrodu, saur stokkinn ' lurks 'And-word skog ' and ' Saurar,' the famous Sorö. 'Hrokaland' is nonsensical, and stands for 'Hnikars-lund,' i. e. Woden's grove, that is, Odensé in Fion ; ' at ærno ' marks some place-name in Sconey, as do ' locuanar ' and ' suia collom.'—The fire of youth is in these rough cruel verses.

In *Six-Stave* we can trace sections : 1. *On Sticklestead*, where Bolgara brennir is a notable synonym for Harold.　2. *On Harold's Eastern war-fare*, where the curious Gaelic ' cras ' occurs, and the blinding of the Emperor is mentioned.　3. His return to Norway.　4. The battle at the mouth of the river Niz, in Halland, 1062, when the number of Sweyn's ships is given.　There are several rotten places here.　5. The remaining strophes on the Swedish quarrel.　6. The Upland rebellion.　7. The law-keeping of Harold.　8. Seemingly the End Piece : his generosity and glory, where the poet uses the metaphors (peculiar to himself) of the harvest-field and the reaping.　The concluding Epilogue is preserved.

The *Launch of the Dragon* is Thiodwolf's best work (as he calls the king *young*, so we have put it as early as we could, in 1048 Harold was thirty-three). It is a good dashing picture of the fine new galley of Harold, steered out of Nith river down to the Firth on a bright day, while the ladies of the city are looking out with wonder at the quick even stroke of the oarsmen (seventy oars) and the glittering jaws of the Dragon figure-head.　Thorodd the Grammarian cites l. 9.

The *Levy Ode* and the Ode on the *Tryst with Sweyn* are anonymous, but so entirely consonant with Thiodwolf's work and age that we do not hesitate to put them among his works.

The *Stamford Bridge* verses convey the feeling that the expedition was ill-advised from the beginning; which, as such legends as the *Dream Verses*, § 7, relate, was the impression left on the popular mind.

The *Dirge on Harold* contained, like Arnor's short poem, a rapid calendar or summary of the king's exploits, imperfect now.

The *Comic Verses* are corrupt, and we could not mend them. All through Thiodwolf's poems we can see that he knows and admires Sighvat's works, but of course beyond *form* and *place* there is no direct imitation or echo.　Thiodwolf is at his best in his impulsive emotional verses and short odes, some of which, as the Launch, are not surpassed by any court-poet.

I. Magnus-flokkr (c. 1046).

(Verse 1 from Edda.)

1.　VASTU, Oláfs son, austan efldr á vatn it skelfŏa.
2.　Út réttu, allvaldr skióta (eikin dúŏisk rá) snekkjo ;
enn þrítœg skip ' þrauta ' þann tíŏ í haf skríŏa :
vægŏit vendi sveigŏom veŏr ótt um þer, dróttinn ;
hlóŏo hirŏ-menn prúŏir hún-skript í Sigtúnom.　　5
3.　Aur spornaŏot arnar il-rióŏr frá Sví-þióŏo

I. Magnus Flokk. *Return to Norway.* Thou didst come in strength, O son of Olaf, over the troubled water.　Thou didst thrust out thy bark, the oaken yard was tossing ; thou didst run out to sea in a thirty-oared ship ; the gale did not spare the creaking mast above thee, king. The proud crew furled their mast-scroll [sail] at Sigtun.　Thou didst tramp over the clay out of Sweden from the east to Norway.　A trusty

(herr fylgði þer, harri hraustr) í Nóreg austan:
flýði Sveinn, enn síðan sann-ráðinn frá láði,
erlendiss, frá-ek undan Alfívo son drífa.

4. Diarft neyttir-þú, dróttinn dolg-strangr skipa langra;   10
af því at ýtar hœfðo austr siau tigi flausta:
suðr gnauðoðo súðir segl-hind á stag 'ryndo;'
Vík skar vand-langt eiki; Vísunðr hneigði þrœm sveigðan.

5. Sialfr vas austr við Elfi Ulfs mœgr, ok hét fœgro;
þar réð Sveinn at sverja sínar hendr á skríni: 15
réð Áláfs sonr eiðom (átt hafa þeira sáttir
skemra aldr an skyldi), Skánunga gramr, hónom.

6. Hykk í hundraðs flokki Haraldz bróðor son stóðo
(hrafn vissi ser hvassast hungr-bann) framast manna:
vítt lá Vinda flótti; varð þar-es Magnus barðisk   20
hœggvinn valr at hylja heiði rastar breiða.

7. Mínn vá sigr fyrir sunnan sniallr Heiða-bý spialli
(Nær frá-ek skarpa skæro Skotborgar-á) gotna:
undi ótal Vinda Ello konr at fella;
hvar hafi gumnar gœrva geir-hríð fregit meiri?   25

8. Lœgðo (græðiss glóða) gramr ok iarl fyrir skœmmo
(þar kom bitr á bœrva brand-leikr) saman randir:
sva-at man-þinga mœndot merkendr Heðins serkjar
(herr knáði gný gœrva geirs) orosto meiri.

9. Skotið frá-ek skepti-flettom skiótt ok mœrgom spiótom   30
(bráð fekk hrafn þar-es háðisk hildr) á breiða skiœldo:
neytto mest sem mœtto menn at vápna senno
(baugs enn barðir lógo bœrvar) griótz ok œrva.

---

host followed thee, O king! and then Sweyn fled abroad, deserted, from
his land. I know that the son of Ælfgifu hastened away.
War in Denmark. Thou didst take boldly to thy long ships, standing
east with seventy ships. The barks went scudding on, the sail-hind
[ship] raced ahead; the tall-masted oak [ship] clave the Wick (Bay); the
Bison ran her gunwales under. The son of Wolf himself [Sweyn] met
thee at the Elbe [Gaut-Elf] and promised fair; yea, Sweyn [Sweyn the
Earl] swore with his hand on a shrine. Olaf's son, the lord of the
Sconey-folk, gave out the oath; yet their covenant lasted a shorter
while than it ought.
Magnus defeats the Wends. Harold's brother's son [Magnus] stood
foremost I know in his host of hundreds [battle array]; far and wide
the flying Wends lay; where Magnus fought the slain covered a league-
wide Heath. In the south my patron won a battle at Heathby
[at Lürschau near Sleswick]; there was *another* hard fight near Scot-
borough water [border of Jutland and Sleswick]. I know the kinsman
of Ælla [Magnus who claimed the English crown] slew Wends untold.
Sweyn vanquished. The King and Earl fought a short time ago [at
Aros = Aarhuus in Jutland] a greater battle . . . . the wearers of Hedin's
shirt [mail] . . . . I heard of the swift shooting of staff-slings and spears
on the broad shields; men used their stones and arrows as fast as they

10.   Bǿrot bœslar fleiri bog-menn af hæʀ tognom;
mœndit þann dag Þrǿndi þreyta fyrr at skeytom: 35
svá þiokt flugo síðan snœri-dæʀr um 'skæro,'
(æʀt vas æʀ-drif látið) ílla sáttu í milli.

11.   Miǫk bað Magnuss rekka mannr rǫskliga annan
(hæʀð 'þrífosk' borð þar-es bæʀðomk) bæð-ský framar knýja.

12.   Væʀðr gekk meirr at morði Magnus kialar vagna   40
(þat vas frægt) í fagran fram-stafn varrar hrafni:
gœrðom þar sva-at þurði (þengils enn óx gengi)
[skeiðr nam herr at hrióða] húskarla lið iarli.

13.   Áðr svan-foldar seldi sól-rýrandi inn dýri
(iarls lá ferð á ferli) fiǫr-grið stǿfom hiǫrva.   45

14.   Rǫmm vas hildr, su-es hramma harð-éls viðir bæʀðosk,
(herr gekk snarr at snerro) 'Sunno dag of unnin:'
flaut, þa-es feigir léto fiǫr gný-stafar hiǫrva,
(þióð sœkk niðr af Næðrom) nár á hverri bǿro.

15.   Náði iarl at eyða 'iǫfra' settr á vettri;   50
lézt eigi þú lítla land-vǫʀn af þer standa.
máttir Magnus hætta mildr 'í folk' und skildi;
nefa Knútz vas þá nýtom næʀ sem ráðinn væri.

16.   Rǫnd bartu, ræsir Þrǿnda, reiðr 'þorðir bæ' meiða;
hús namtu hvert ok eiso hyr-felld gefa eldi: 55
gœrr vildir-þú gialda, gǿðinga konr, skǿðar
(æʀt rendo þeir undan) iarls fylgiorom dylgjor.

17.   Hizig laut, es heitir Helganes, fyrir kesjom
(sukko sárir rekkar) Sveins ferð (bana verðir):
mætr hélt mǫrgo spióti Mǿra gramr í snǿri   60
(odd rauð aski studdan æʀr land-reki) dæʀrom.

---

could. The archers never sped more [arrows] off their strings. The
Thronds did not fall short in shooting that day, the thong-darts flew so
thick one could hardly see between them at . . . . Every man of Magnus'
host was cheering on his neighbour to the attack. Magnus went forward
in the battle; we lessened the number of the Earl's house-carles; the
king began to board the galleys before he gave quarter to the earl's
men. Hard was the battle on the Sunday before Yule. The people
sunk dead from out of the Snakes [dragon ships]. The earl left the
land of the Jutes in the winter; Magnus crossed under shield to Fion
[Funen]; Cnut's nephew [Sweyn] was then, as it were, done for. Thou
didst bear the shield, O lord of the Thronds, and sack Woden's grove
[Odensé], giving every house to smoke and flame; thou wast eager to
pay the earl's people for their evil words of hate.

Final Battle of Helganes. Sweyn's men fell before the javelins at
Holyness [Helganes in East Jutland]; the lord of the More-men swung
many a thong-dart. The earl fled from his empty ship where Magnus

---

39. Read, rufosk.   42. þengill . . . fengi, Cd.   47. Read, Solar dag at
Iólom?   50. Read, Ióta.   52. Read, á Fión?   54. ronn lézt, Cd.
54. Read, þriðja vé?

18.   Flýði iarl af auðo, otvín, skipi síno
morð, þar-es Magnus gœrði mein-fœrt þaðan Sveini :
réð her-konungr hrióða Hneitiss egg í sveita ;
sprændi blóð á brýndan brand ; vá gramr til landa.   65

19.   Háðisk heilli góðo hildr sem Magnus vildi ;
selr of slíkt at þylja sókn-stœrir mer fœri :
brand rauð buðlungr Þrœnda ; berr íðula síðan
hann ept her-víg þrennin hæra skiœld or giœldom.

II. Vísor (1044–45).

(Verse 3 is in Hulda wrongly given to Arnor.)

1.   H RAUÐ Áláfs mœgr áðan (iœfurr vá sigr) ens Digra
[fregnat slíkt or Sogni] siau skip [konor hnipnar].

2.   Misst hafa Sveins at sýno, sverð-gautr, fœro-nautar
(hœrð es heldr um orðin) heim-kvœmo (fœr beima) :
hrœrir hausa þeira hreggi œst ok leggi   5
(siár þýtr auðs of œrom) unnr á sanda grunni.

3.   Sveins manna rekr sunnan sœndog lík at strœndom ;
vítt sér œld fyrir útan Iótland hvé hræ flióta :
vitnir dregr or vatni (vann Áláfs sonr bannat)
[búk slítr vargr í víkom] val-kœst (ara fœsto).   10

4.   Hrindr af 'Hroka lundi' hregg af eiki-veggjom
(sunnr leikr eldr of innom) óðr í lopt upp glóðom :
bœr logar hœlfo hæra hiónom nær á Fióni ;
ræfr þola nauð ok næfrir ; Norðmenn sali brenna.

5.   Menn eigo þess minnask manna Sveins at kanna   15
víga-Freys sízt váro, vef-gefn, tvinnar stefnor :
vœn es fagrs á Fióni flióðs, dugir vœpn at rióða,
vesom með fylkto folki framm í vápna glammi.

---

wrought woe to Sweyn ; the king won the land, wielding Hnit [Olaf's
sword]. The battle turned as Magnus hoped. The lord of the Thronds
bore ever his shield highest three times over at their settling.

II. *His own exploits when following Magnus. Jutland.* The son of Olaf
the Stout cleared seven ships [carried them]. The ladies of Sogn will
not grieve at such tidings. The men of Sweyn have lost their hope of
getting home ; the storm-stirred water tosses their heads and legs on the
sandy shoals. The sandy corses of Sweyn's men are floating off the
strand at Jutland. The wolf drags his prey from the water, and tears it
in the Wicks. Olaf's son won the day.

Funen. The storm-wind throws up the glowing embers of the oak
walls at Woden's grove [Odensé]. The furious fire plays over the houses ;
the rafters and black thatch are in evil case, the farms at Fion [Funen]
were aflame over the households. The Northmen burnt the hall.
S weyn's men will remember those two battles. There is no lack of fair
maids in Fion [Funen]. It is seemly to redden one's weapon ; let us go
forth to battle in array !

---

11. Read, Hnikars lundi.   12. unnin, Cd.

6. Gœr sá-ek grióti stóro (gein hauss fyrir steini)
[fóra fylking þeira fast] harðliga kastað :   20
ofan keyrðo ver (orðom iœrð mana Sveinn of varða)
[staðar hefir stafn í 'miðjo'] strand-hœgg [numit 'landi'].

7. Spurði eino orði (œld blóð-roðna skiœldo)
(satt es at 'sva' mœrg átti) Siálandz mær hverr vé bæri :
'audtrodu' varð auðit yfir um 'skóg' at spróga ;   25
títt bar tý-margr flótti til Hring-staða 'iljar.'

8. 'Saur,' stokkinn berr svíra snarr Skánunga harri,
undr es nema allvaldr Lundar 'aldr prúðr fyrir haldi : '
gœr flugo mold ok mýrar merki iarls ens sterka,
slóð drap framm at flœði flaugar 'dorr' um Hauga.   30

9. Bauð Áláfs sonr áðan upp á land at standa ;
gekk við mann-dýrð mikla Magnús reiðr af skeiðom :
snarr biðr hilmir herja (hark óx í Danmœrko)
[fleygir hart of Hauga hestr] or Skáni vestan.

10. Nú taka Norðmenn knýja (nær gœngo ver stœngo)   35
[berkak] Magnús merki [mínn skiœld á hlið sialdan] :
Skýtr skeifom fœti Skáni yfir sláni
(fár vegr es mer fegri fundinn) suðr til Lundar.

11. Bǽrom iœrn at 'œrno' ískœld á hlið vísa
skiótt ríða nú skeyttar Skánunga 'lokvanir : '   40
rauðr leikr of bý 'breiðom' bráðr at óro ráði'
eldr, enn œrnir valda at-blásendr því vási.

12. Svíðr of seggja búðir siklingr 'í her' miklom
(eyðir bygð sem bráðast biartr eldr) Dana-veldi :
móðr berr halr of 'heiði hialdrs' Danmarkar skiœldo ;   45

Sealand. Yesterday I saw big stones thrown crashing into men's skulls. We drove cattle down to the shore. With words alone Sweyn cannot guard his land. The stem of the ship had come to land in . . . . The maid of Sealand asked who bore the standard. The . . . . They had to hasten through the Andwordwood to Ringstead. The lord of the Sconey-folk marked to Sora. The king . . . . Lund . . . . Yesterday the strong Earl's banner flew over field and fen . . . . at the Howes.

Sconey. Olaf's son bade us land, Magnus came ashore in great state. Ever grows Denmark's danger. The king bade us harry Sconey from the west. The horse flies over the Howes. The Northmen carry Magnus' banner, I walk by the pole. They are trampling over Sconey, southward to Lund.

He bore the ice-cold irons [swords] after the king at A . . . . The Sconey-folks' houses at . . . . are tumbling in, the red fire plays over the broad tower [Lund] at our command, and many fan the flames at . . . . With a mighty blaze he wastes the houses of men in the realm of the

---

22. Corrupt, some place ?   24. Read, sía ?   hverr] hve, Cd.   25. Read, Andverðo skog.   26. illra, Hulda.   27. Read, Saura ?   28. vatr sem veigðo skauti valdruðr fyrir haldi, Hrokkinsk.   30. Read, kiörr, *or* Kiœgr, Kœgi ?   40. Some place ?   43. Read, hyr ?   45. Some place ?

ver hlutom sigr, enn sárir Sveins menn fyrir renna.

13. Fiorð lét fylkir verða forn-traddan mó spornat
(leynomk lítt) á Fióni (liðs skiœldunga miðli) :
muna fyrir Magnús synja menn Sveins, þeir-es nú renna,
(upp fara mœrg í morgin merki) stórra verka.   50

14. Ekki hef-ek at drekka annat an sió þenna
(sýg-ek or sœltom ægi sylg) es ek iœfri fylgi:
Liggr fyrir oss, enn uggom all-lítt, Svia 'kollom'
(driúgt hœfom vás fyrir vísa) víð Skáneyjar síða.

15. Skiœld bar-ek heim frá hialdri (hlauzk mer til þess)
Gauzkan   55
[ramr varð suðr á sumri sverð-dynr] ok þó brynjo :
vœpn gat-ek fríð; enn flióði fyrr sagða-ek þat kyrro;
þar fekk-ek hialm es hilmir harð-ráðr Dani barði.

16. Nú es val-meiðom víðiss (veit drótt mikinn ótta)
[skeiðr hefir hann fyr hauðri] hætt góðs friðar vætta : 60
mildr vill Magnús halda morðz hlym-gotom norðan
ítr enn œnnor skreytir unn-vigg Haraldr sunnan.

III. Sex-stefja on King Harold (1065).

(Verses 23, 25–29 from Edda; verse 24 from Skalda.)

1. HVAST frá-ek Haugi it næsta hlíf-él á gram drífa,
enn Bolgara brennir brœðr sínom vel tœði :
skilðisk hann, ok hulði hialm-setr, gamall vettra
tyggi tolf ok þriggja trauðr við Áláf dauðan.

Danes, the bright fire swiftly wastes the houses .... heath .... Denmark .... Sweyn's men run wounded before us.
Last year the king stepped on the paths Funen trod of yore. Sweyn's men cannot deny Magnus' great deeds. Many a banner landed that morning.
I have nought save the sea to drink as I follow my lord. I suck my draught from the salt Ocean. There lies before us the broad coast of Sconey ....
I bore home a Gautish shield, that was my luck, and a mail-coat too. There was hard fighting this summer in the south. I got a fair weapon. I told the gentle lady. I got a helm also where the Stern King beat the Danes.
Harold's first appearance in Norway. There is now scant hope of peace, there is great peril ahead. The king has his galleys ready; Magnus is going to stand south with his ships, but Harold is bringing another fleet northwards.
III. Six-stave. *Before Exile.* I heard that the sharp war-gale burst upon him close to Howe [Olwi's howe near Sticklestead]; and the burner of the Bulgarians backed his brother well. He parted from the dead Olaf against his will, when he was twelve years old and three [fifteen], and hid his head.

2. Togo má tekna segja (tand-rauðs) á Serklandi   5
    (ungr hætti ser) átta (orm-torgs hœtuðr) borga :
    áðr her-skorðuðr harðan Hildar leik und skildi
    Serkjom hættr í sléttri Sikleyjo gekk heyja.

3. Dolg-lióss hefir dasi darr-latr staðit fiarri
    endr þa-es eljo Rindar ómynda tók skyndir :   10
    vasat Afrika iœfri Ánars mey fyrir hánom
    hag-faldinni at halda hlýði-samt né lýðom.

4. Lét, þa-es lypt vas spiótom, liðs hœfðingi kviðjat
    (enn þeirs undan runno) ulfs gráð (friðar bœðo) :
    Hann hefir fyrir Siá sunnan (svá finnask til minni)   15
    opt með oddi keyptan auð, þars leitt vas blauðom.

5. Þióð veit at hefir háðar hvar-grimmligar rimmor
    (rofisk hafa opt fyrir iœfri) áttián Haraldr (sáttir) :
    hœss arnar rauðtu hvassar, hróðigr konungr, blóði
    (imr gat krœs hvar kómot) klœr áðr hingat fœrir.   20

6. Stól-þengils lét stinga (styrjœld vas þá byrjoð)
    eyðir augo bæði út heiðingja sútar :
    lagði allvaldr Egða austr á bragning hraustan
    gráligt mark, enn Girkja gœto illa fór stillir.

7. Sá-es (við lund) á landi Langbarða réð ganga.   25

8. Reist eiki-kiœlr austan œrðigt vatn or Gœrðom,
    (Sviar tióðo þer síðan) sniallr landreki (allir).
    Gekk með golli miklo (glygg féll ótt um tyggja)
    hœll á hlé-borð sollin Haraldz skeið und vef breiðom.

9. Vatn lézt, vísir, slitna, víð-kuðr, und skœr þuðri   30

Warfare in the East. Eighty conquered towns may be counted in Saracen-land ; the young king went through much danger, ere he, the periller of the Saracens, began to wake war on the flats of Sicily. The laggard, slow to handle the dart, stood afar off when he took to himself the ripe rival of Wrind [land]. The king of Africa could not keep the grass-hooded maid of Woden [the land], nor his people, against him. Our leader stayed the wolf's hunger, the foe ran away praying for peace. He has often bargained treasures with his spear south of the Sea, where cowards dare not come. I know that King Harold fought eighteen fierce battles, the grey-wolf got 'cras' [dainties] where he went. Before he came hither [to Norway again] the king stabbed out both eyes of the Enthroned King [κάθεδρος βασιλεύς]: the lord of the Agd-folk set a cruel mark on the prince in the East. The ruler of the Greeks went an evil way .... He that bravely marched on the land of the Lombards [South Italy].

Back to Norway. The oaken keel breasted the steep water from Gard in the East. All the Swedes, O gallant king, backed thee there. Harold's galley, carrying the great hoard, went gunwale under beneath the broad canvas, while the sharp gale blew over the king. Thou far-famed prince, thou didst cleave the waters with the strakes of thy ship from

---

(dýr klufo flóð, þars fórot, flaust) or Danmœrk austan:
bauð hœlf við sik síðan sonr Áláfs þer hála
(frændr hygg-ek þar fyndisk fegnir) lœnd ok þegna.

10.　Þegn skyli hverr sem hugnar hialdr-vitjaðar sitja
dolg-stœranda dýrom dróttin-vandr ok standa.　　　35

Stef.　*Lýtr folk-starra feiti* (*fátt es til nema iálta*)
(*því sem þá vill gotnom*) *þióð öll* (*konungr bióða*).

11.　Lét vin-giafa veitir varg-hollr Dreka skolla
lystr fyrir leiðangrs briósti (liðs oddr vas þat) miðjo.

12.　Fast bað fylkir trausta frið-vandr iœfurr standa　　40
hamalt 'sýndosk mer hœmlo hildings viðir skildir:'
ram-syndan lauk rœndom ráðandi mann-dáða
nýtr fyrir Nizi útan Naðr, sva-at hver tók aðra.

13.　Alm dró Upplenzkr hilmir alla nátt inn snialli,
hremsor lét á hvítar hlífar landreki drífa:　　　45
buand-mœnnom smó brynjor blóðogr oddr, þars stóðo
(flugr óx) Fáfniss (vigra) Finna giœld í skiœldom.

14.　Sogns kvóðo gram gegnan glœst siau tigi it fæsta
senn á svip-stund einni Sveins þióðar skip hrióða.

15.　Sveinn 'att sigr at launa' sex 'þeim er hvot vexa'　50
'innan eina gunni œrleiks' Dana iœrlom:
varð sa-es vildit forða víg-biartr snœro hiarta
í fylkingo finginn Fiðr Arna son miðri.

16.　Öld vas su-es iarli skyldi ógn-teitom lið veita
(sterkr olli því stillir) Steinkels gefin heljo:　　　55

---

the east out of Denmark. The goodly ship climbed the flood. The son
of Olaf [Magnus] offered thee half his land and people along with him.
The kinsmen [uncle and nephew] met with joy I ween.

Burden Verse. Every loyal thane of the king should sit and stand at
his will. The whole nation bows to him; there is nothing for it but to
submit to what the king commands his people.

Battle of River Niz, 1062. The king hove his Dragon before the
breast of the levy in the midst thereof, at the point of the column [at
the apex of the battle-wedge of ships]. The prince bade his men stand
fast. I saw his rowlock-beams [ships] drawn up in wedge-shaped array:
the king commanded them to fence his mighty Adder [his ship], outside
off Niz, with shields, so that one touched the other all round it. The Upland king was drawing his elm-bow all that night, making the arrow-heads
hail on the white bucklers; the bloody points pierced the franklins' mail,
what time the Fins' tribute [arrows] stood *thick* on the Serpent's shields.
They say that the lord of the Sogn-folk, in one swoop, cleared and
carried seventy [17?] of Sweyn's ships. Sweyn *was followed by* six
warlike Danish earls. Fin Arnisson, who would not turn his brave heart
out of the fight, was taken in the midst of their array.

The Swedish quarrel with Hakon and Steinkel. The people of Steinkel

---

41. skilda, Cd.　　48. Read, siautian?　　51. Corrupt.

enn, þvi-at ílla reyndisk afls væn þaðan hánom,
fyrir lét Hákon hæorfa; hvat segir hinn es þat fegrir?

17. Nú es um verk þau es vísi vand-mælt, sva-at af standisk,
auðan plóg at eiga Upplendingom kendi:
ok því ráði þióðar þeim bruto troll, es ollo, 60
hæls í hleypi-kióla hrís, andskotom vísa.

18. Tók Holm-bua hneykir harðan taum við Rauma,
þar hykk fast ins frǽkna fylking Haraldz gingo:
eldr vas gœrr at gialdi, gramr réð, enn þá tœði
hár í hóf at fǽra hrót-garmr buendr arma. 65

19. Gagn brann greypra þegna, glóð varð fæst í tróði;
laust hertoga hristir Heina íllom steini:
lífs bæðo ser Líðar; logi þingaði Hringom
nauðgan dóm áðr næðisk niðr-fall Halfs galla.

20. Fœrði fylkir Hæorða (friðr namsk) ár it þriðja 70
[rendr bito stæl fyrir strændo] starf til króks (at hvarfi).

21. Áræðiss naut eyðir all-dyggr Selundz-byggva;
Hugr ræðr hæolfom sigri (Haraldr sannar þat) manna.

22. Refsir reyndan ofsa ráð-gegn Haraldr þegnom;
hykkat-ek hilmiss rekkar haldi upp þvi es valda: 75
sverðz hafa slíkar byrðar (sannz nýtr hverr við annan)
[Haraldr skiptir svá heiptom] hliótendr, es ser brióta.

23. Útan bindr við enda elg-vers glætuðr hersa

[King of the Swedes], who ought to have helped the earl [Hakon Ivars-
son], were given to hell; the King [Harold] wrought this; and as the
hope of help from them failed, Hakon turned away. What can he say
who would put a fair face on this?

The Rebellion in the Upland, 1063–65. Now it is hard to tell, so that
it all be in right order, how the king taught the Uplanders to have an
empty cart. The king's head has gained such glory these three seasons
[years] that it will last for ever. The unruly churls of the land would
not consent to their king's law, and committed crimes in the country;
and now the fiends broke rods over the legs of the ring-leaders of the
king's enemies. Harold, the enemy of the Holm-dwellers [Danes], had
a tight trace over the Reams, the king's array went forth fast. They
were paid with fire; the king ordered that the high roof-wolf [fire]
should teach the wretched franklins their meet course. The wicked
thanes' crops burnt, the embers took hold of their roof-trees. The
dukes' lord struck the Heins [Heathmark people] a deadly blow [lit.
with an evil stone]. The Liths people prayed for pardon, but the flame
passed sentence on the Ring-folk [Ringrick people] before Half's scathe
[fire] was quenched. The third year the lord of the Hords brought
the matter to the haven; peace ensued at last . . . .

Fragments hard to place. The waster of the dwellers in Sealand was a
man of dash. A good heart is half the battle. Harold is a proof of it.

His law. The orderly king punished the proved transgressions of his

---

57. Read, hvat sé?

'hreins við húfi rónom hafs botni far gotna.'

24. Gera vas gisting byrjoð gnóg (enn ulfr or skógi) 80
     sonr (á sǽr at spenja) Sigorðar kom norðan.
25. Lét hræ-teina hveiti hrynja gramr á brynjo ;
     vill at vexti belli val-bygg Haraldr Yggjar.
26. Blóð-orra lætr barri bragningr ara fagna ;
     Gautz berr sigð á sveita svans ǿrð konungr Hǿrða : 85
     geirs oddom lætr greddir grunn hvert stika unnar
     hirð þá es hann skal varða hræ-gamms ara sævar.
27. Örð sær Yrso burðar inn-drótt iǿfurr sinni
     biart-plógaðan bauga bratt-akr vǿlo-spakra :
     eyss landreki lióso last-varr Kraka barri 90
     á hlé-mildar holdi hauks kalfor mer siǿlfom.
28. Mǿrk lét veitt fyrir verka vekjandi mer ' snekkjo '
     (hann lætr hylli sinnar) hialdrs (til-gerðir valda).
29. Hár skyli hirðar stióri hug-reifr sonom leifa
     arf ok óðal-torfo (ósk mín es þat) sína. 95

IV. Vísor (from Hulda).

1. SKEIÐ sá-ek framm at flǿéði, fagrt sprund, í ǿ hrundit ;
    kenndu hvar liggr fyrir landi lǿng súð Dreka ins prúða :
    Orms gloa fǿx und farmi frǿn, þvi-at ýtt vas hǿnom
    (bǿro búnir svírar brunnit goll) af hlunni.
2. Slyngr Laugardag lǿngo lið-Baldr af ser tialdi, 5
    út þá-es ekkjor líta Orms súð or bǿ prúðar :

---

people. The prince's subjects, I know, cannot do as they please. Men
must carry the loads they cut. Fair play is kept between man and man,
so Harold stops feuds.

Fragments. The King's valour and liberality, etc. The lord of barons
moors his ship . . . .
The she-wolf got food enough, and the wolf out of the wood drunk
of the wound-wells when Sigurd's son [Harold] came from the north.
Harold lets blood sprinkle the mail, and wishes the harvest of slain to
grow thick. The Hords' king makes the eagle enjoy the crop of the
blood-bird, and puts Woden's sickle into the raven's harvest. He makes
his men fence the land with a stockade of spears . . . .
His gifts. He sows the crop of Yrsa's son [gold] on the fresh-plowed
steep acres of the wrist-rings [arms], and scatters the seed of Kraki
[gold] on my warm flesh paddocks of the hawk [arms].
He gave me a mark for my song, he metes out his favour according
to merit.
May he leave to his sons their heritage and patrimony, that is my
wish.

IV. THE LAUNCH OF THE DRAGON, 1048. A galley I see, fair lady,
launched into the river [Nith river] seaward ; look where the long
hull of the proud Dragon is riding off the shore : the bright Serpent's
mane is gleaming under her *golden* weight ; her neck is ornamented with
burnt gold, now that she is launched off the rollers. On Saturday the
king furls the long awnings, while the ladies of the city look out upon

vestr réð or Níð næsta nýri skeið at stýra
ungr, es árar drengja, allvaldr, í siá falla.

3. Rétt kann rœði slíta ræsiss herr or verri;
ekkjan stendr ok undrask ára-burð sem furðo: 10
ært man snút áðr snerto sæ-fangs í tvau gangi
('þæll' leggr við 'frið fullan') fer-kleyf (á þat leyfi).

4. 'Sorgar veit,' áðr slítisk sæ-fang or mar stræongom,
herr þar es heldr til varra, hár, siau tigom ára:
Norðmeðr roa Naðri negldom straum inn heglda;   15
út es sem ekkjan líti arnar-væng or iarni.

V. Vísor.

1. E IGOT skiól und skógi skafnir snekkjo stafnar,
læsir leiðangrs vísi land her-skipa brœndom:
almenningr 'liggr' innan (eið láta ser skeiðar)
(há-brynjaðar hlýja) hverja vík (í skerjom).

2. Hléseyjar lemr hávan hlym-garð konungr barði;   5
neytir þá til þrautar þengill snekkjo strengja:
eigi es iarni biúgo inn-dæll skaði lindiss
(gnegr af gaddi digrom griót) ok veðr in lióto.

VI. Vísor.

H ARALDR þeysti nú hraustla helming sinn at Elfi,
náttar Nóregs dróttinn nær at landa-mœri:

---

the proud Serpent's hull. The young king is steering his new galley westward out of Nith river, while the oars of the crew dip into the sea. The
king's crew pull the oars out of the water in time. The lady stands
and wonders at the oars' stroke as a marvel. They must pull briskly
indeed ere the four-square blade-looms fly in two. The damsel praises
. . . . The rowlock is sorely tried at each pull, before the blade
is slashed out of the strong sea, when seventy oars smite the sea with
one stroke. The Northmen are rowing the nailed Dragon on the
stricken stream. It seems to the ladies as if she had eagles' wings of
iron upon her sides.

V. *The Levy*. The polished galley stems find no shelter in the
forest; the king is fencing his land about with the stem-beams of
the war-ship of the levy; the whole levy of the land locks in every
bay, and the necks of the skerries shelter the high-mailed galleys.
The king smites the high surf wall of Hlesey with his prow; he tries
the strength of his cable to the utmost, the scathe of the linden [the
wind] and the ugly storms are not easy for the iron bows [anchor-bows]
to bear, when it gnaws the rocks with its thick flukes.

VI. *Levy against Sweyn*, 1054. Harold is now moving his forces to
Elbe [Gauta-Élf]; the king of Norway takes a berth near the Marches.

---

11. I. e. snuið; snot, Cd.   12. Some place?   3. Read, lykr.

gramr á þing við Þumla, þar es ein-dagaðr Sveini
'hrafni skyldr' (nema haldi) hans fundr (Danir undan).

VII. Vísor.

FRÁN hefir sveit við Sveini sinni skipt (at minnom)
dǽð ok dróttni góðom (dreng-spell es þat lengi).

VIII. Vísor.

1. NORÐR lykr gramr sa-es gerðir grund frá Eyrar-sundi
    (hrafn-gǿlir sparn hæli hǽfn) lang-skipa stæofnom :
    rísta golli glǿstir gialfr (enn súðir skialfa)
    hvast und her fyr vestan Hallandi fram brandar.

2. Gerðir opt fyr iæorðo, eið-fastr Haraldr, skeiðom ;   5
    Sveinn skerr ok til annars ey-sund konungs fundar :
    út hefira lið lítið lof-sniallr Dana allra,
    hinn es hvern vág sunnan hrafn-grennir lykr stæofnom.

3. Sýstot suðr þar-es ǿsto, sniallr gramr, Danir allir
    (enn sér eigi minni efni) mæltrar stefno ;   10
    Sveinn tekr norðr at nenna nær til landa-mǿri
    (varð fyr víðri iæorðo vindsamt) Harald finna.

4. Telja hitt, es hittask, hvárs-tveggja miæok seggir
    orð, þau es angra fyrða, all-mæorg, buendr sniallir :
    láta þeir, es þræta þegnar, allt í gǿgnom   15
    (svellr ofr-hugi iæofrom) eigi brátt við sæottom.

5. Ofreiði varð iæofra all-hætt ef skal sættask ;
    menn þeir-es miðla kunno mǽol æoll vega í skǽolom :
    Dugir siklingom segja slíkt allt es her líkar ;
    veldr, ef verr skolo hæoldar, vili girnðar því, skilja.   20

The prince holds a moot at Thumblie [Thumla off the Gauta-Elf],
where Sweyn is to meet him on a given day, unless the Danes fail him.

VII. *The Danes take Sweyn for King*, 1054. The Danes have bartered
their honour and their good lord for Sweyn [the son of Wolf]; this
villany will long be held in mind.

VIII. *The tryst with Sweyn*, 1063? The king locks the whole land north
of Eyra Sound [Ore Sound] with the long-ships' stems, he treads the
havens with his rudders' heel [starts from the haven]. The gold-glitter-
ing prow-coursers cleave the sea swiftly eastward off Halland. Harold
the faithful often walls in the land with his galleys. Sweyn is cutting
through the island sound to meet the other king; he has no small levy
of Danes out in the sea, shutting up ·every bay *as he comes* from the
south with his ships. Ye hastened south, where all the Danes had
fixed the trysting-place . . . . while Sweyn is travelling north to meet
Harold at the Marches. On both sides the franklins count over, when
they meet, all their grievances; they are not very easy to bring to
agreement, for they push their case to the utmost; the kings are
puffed up too with pride. The anger of the kings is dangerous, if they
are to come to terms at all; men who can mediate will have to

6.   Hitt hefi-ek opt at setti Haraldr ok Sveinn við meinom
(Goð sýslir þat) gísla glaðr hvárr-tveggi œðrom:
þeir haldi svá sœrom (sœtt lauksk þar með vóttom)
ok œll í frið fullom ferð at aldri skerði.

IX. Improvisation.

1.   SKALKAT-EK frá, ' þótt fylkir falli sialfr ' til vallar
(gengr sem Goð vill) ungom grams erfingjom hverfa :
skínnat sól á sýnni snar-ráðs, an þá báða,
(Haraldz ero haukar gœrvir hefnendr) konungs efni.

2.   Öld hefir afráð goldit íllt; nú kveð-ek her stilltan ; 5
bauð þessa fœr þióðom þarflaust Haraldr austan :
svá lauk siklings ævi sniallz, at ver rom allir
(lofðungr beið inn leyfði lífs grand) í stað vœndom.

X. Rímhenda on Harold.

(Verses 1, 2 from Edda.)

1.   VEX Óláfs feðr Iarn-sœxo veðr,
harð-ræðit hvert, svá at hróðrs es vert.

2.   Iarizleifr of sá hvert iœfri brá,
hófsk hlýri frams ens Helga grams.

3.   Eitt hœfðosk at Eilífr þar es sat,   5
hófðingjar tveir, hamalt fylkto þeir.
Austr-Vindom ók í œngan krók,
vasa Læsom léttr Liðs-manna réttr.

---

weigh all the charges in scales [fairly]. If they part . . . . it is passion
that is the cause thereof. Now I have heard that Harold and Sweyn
have, by God's help, given hostages to each other against future out-
rages. May they and all the people keep their oaths and keep full
peace, so that no damage be done. The peace was concluded there by
the sworn witnesses.

IX. *Stamford Bridge, Sept.* 25, 1066. I shall not forsake the king's
young heirs, though the prince himself is now fallen on the field. All
goes as God wills! The sun shines on no finer king's sons than both of
them. Harold's avengers are true hawks.
The people have paid a terrible price, the army is trapped, I know.
It was ill-devised when Harold bade his levy sail from the east. We
are all at a parlous point, now that the good king has lost his life. Yea,
the famous king is dead.

X. *Dirge on King Harold the Stern.* The giantess storm [courage]
rose in Olaf's father in every danger worthy of song. Iarisleif saw after
whom he took, the brethren of the holy king [Olaf] waxed well. The
two princes, he and Eilif, had one intent, they formed the wedge of
battle together. He drove the East Wends into a narrow pass. The
lord of the Lithsmen did not deal lightly with the Lechs. Now dead

---

1. Read, þótt sé fylkir fallinn sialfr til vallar, *or* þótt fylkir fallinn sé til vallar.

4.   Andaðr es sá, es of alla brá,
hauk-stalla konr, Haraldz bróður-sonr.   10

XI. Comic Improvisations.

1.   SIGURÐR eggjaði sleggio snák 'váligrar' brákar,
enn skap-dreki skinna skreið of leista-heiði:
menn sásk orm aðr ynni il-vegs buinn kiljo
nauta-leðrs á naðri nef-langr konungr tangar.

2.   Varp or þræto þorpi Þórr, smið-belgja stórra,   5
hvatt eldingom hœldnom, hafra-kiœtz, at Iœtni:
hlióð-greipom tók húða hrœkkvi-skafls or afli
glaðr við galdra smiðjo Geirrœðr sio þeiri.

3.   Fœrðr sýndizk mer frændi Frísa kyns í brynjo,
gengr fyrir hirð í hringum hialm-faldinn kurfaldi: 10
'flýrat elld í ári' út-hlaupom vanr Túta;
sékk við síðo leika sverð rug-hleifa skerði.

XII. Fragments (Edda and Skalda).

1.   Iarl lætr odda skúrar opt herðir gœr verða,
hrings áðr hann of þryngvi hœrð él und sik iœrðo.

2.   Snart við sæ-þráð kyrtat síkr, lá blær á díki.

ODDR KIKINA-SKALD, etc.

EIGHT small poets, one (Ord) on King Magnus, and one (Thorleik) on King Sweyn, the rest on Harold, especially the earlier part of his reign.

is he that surpassed all, the noble king, Harold's brother's son [Magnus the Good, nephew of Harold].

XI. *Improvisations. On the fight between the Blacksmith and Tanner.* Sigfred of the sledge-hammer challenged the horrid Serpent of the brakes, and the Dragon of the hides wriggled out of Last-heath [the tan pit where the shoemakers' leather was tanning]. Men feared the Serpent of the boots ere the long-nebbed King of the tongs got the better of the Adder of the neat leather.

The same figured as Thor and Giant Garfred. Thor of the he-goat flesh cast out lightnings against the Giant of the big smithy bellows, and the Geirrod of the brake caught the glowing bar in his speech-smithy [mouth].

The Dwarf in the King's mail-coat Emma. The Frisian is clad in a mail-coat. Cuttiecoat walks helm-hooded before the host. Tout strides about in the mail-coat Emma; I see a sword by the side of the carver of the rye-loaf.

XII. *A Fragment.* The earl [Thorfinn?] had fought many battles ere he could win the land.

A Fishing Scene. The seak [a kind of salmon] touched the sea thread gently, there was a calm over the sea.

11. Read, flœrat Emmo . . . ?

ORD, KITCHIN'S POET. Part of a dirge on Magnus, composed about 1047, which must have been a beautiful and affecting poem, is all that remains of this poet: his name was probably derived from some patron, a foreigner, whom he had eulogised. One of the verses (5) is in Skalda given as Thiodwolf's, erroneously we think.

The exact date of the battle of Aros was contained in these verses, and we have been able to restore it. A verse which we believe to be his is added here.

BALEWORK (Bolverkr), brother of Thiodwolf, recounts in order, in a *drapa* of about 1055, the exploits of King Harold in Russia, Byzantium, Sicily, Africa, his return to Norway and his wars with the Danes.

His encomium is of the regular type of Harold's court-poets, and corrupt in many places. The date of the levy-song by Thiodwolf is fixed by the last verse to 1048.

WALGARD O' FIELD (Valgardr af Velli) bears a name which would connect him with the home and family of Fiddle-Mard, the traitor of Niala. He also runs over Harold's early exploits (a theme which the king seems to have never tired of hearing), and goes to tell of his doings in Sigtun, Sweden, Selund, Funen, Roskild, and winds up with addressing him as king of all Norway. This encomium must date after Magnus' death, 1047.

Walgard's poem, which is one of the best of those on Harold, is very unsafe in places. King Harold's fleet seems to have anchored at Fredriksværk, mouth of Roskeld-firth, harrying cruelly on both sides. We recognise under the cover of inane appellatives, names such as Hramnlausa = Ramlösa, Helsinge, Skylda-laif (?), in north point of Sealand; by the forest the people fled into is meant Gribskoven, still the ornament of Sealand.

ILLUGI THE BRYNDALE POET. An Icelander from the south-west, of whom there exists a morsel, containing as a kind of burden a series of allusions to the Wolsung story, wedged into the body of the poem, which is in praise of Harold after the manner of Cormac and his imitators. One of these burdens we have not been able to make out. The name of the Greek emperor, Michael, occurs in the fragment.

GRANI. We know nought of him save the fragment in which he celebrates Harold's Danish wars: the captivity and ransom of Dotta, daughter of a Danish noble, Thorkell Geysa, who had satirised Harold and the Northmen.

THORARIN SKEGGISSON. He sung of Harold's eastern exploits, as the two lines left of one of his poems testify. We take him to be the brother of the well-known Mark Skeggisson (§ 4), whose elder he would seem to have been by several years.

We have mended these lines in accordance with the indications furnished by the prose derived from them when they were perfect.

SHUTTLE-HALLI (Snœglo-Halli). This poet, like Thorwolf, a poor man's son, is always described as having a very marked individuality; there is something of the Falstaff about him; but his sharp wits and bitter tongue always bring him out of the scrapes he is thrust into, and he gets the better of Thiodwolf in their quarrel. It is of him and Edward the Confessor that the Herodotean story is told in Hulda. The king graciously hears his poem, on his visit to the English court, and when assured of its goodness by Raud, his own poet, promises Hall as much silver as will stick on his hair when a money-bag is emptied over his head. Hall puts tar on his hair and manages to catch the greater part of the money, and then hurries off with his fee. When he is gone and they begin thinking over his poem, they find that it is nothing but nonsense-verses.

One fragment of his, in old metre, remains on Harold.

THORLAK THE FAIR (Thorleik Fagri). King Sweyn Wolfsson's poet, whom we have mentioned above. His *Praise-Song* on that king, of which a fair part remains, composed c. 1055, deals with Harold's inroads and escapes in Denmark, and with negotiations not yet successful. He congratulates his lord on still, in spite of the northern king's power, remaining sole king of Denmark and Jutland. It gives some notable historical details, the number of Sweyn's ships, etc., and, when in a perfect state, no doubt contained more. Lines 18, 22, 27, 34–36 are unsound and overlaid certainly.

ODDR KIKINA-SKALD.

(Verse 5 from Skalda.)

I.

1. VAS fyrir Mikjals-messo malm-grimm hain rimma;
    féllo Vindr, enn vœndosk vápn-hlióði miok þióðir:
    Enn fyrir Iól varð œnnor 'óhlítulig' lítlo
    (upp hófsk grimm með gumnom gunnr) fyrir Árós 'sunnan.'

II.

2. Felldo menn, þa-es mildan, mœrg tœr, í grœf bœro   5
    (þung byrðr vas sú) þengil (þeim-es hann gaf seima):
    deilðisk hugr, svá-at heldo húskarlar grams varla
    (siklings þióð enn síðan sat opt hnipin) vatni.

3. Má-ek, sízt Magnuss œvi móð-fíkins þraut góða
    (Odd hafa stríð of staddan) stilliss, harða ílla: 10
    hvarfa-ek hvers mannz þurfi; harmr strangr fœr mer angrað;
    þióð es at dœgling dauðan dœpr, því fœro ver aprir.

4. Nú fara heim í húmi her-kunn fyrir lœg sunnan
    daprar skeiðr með dauðan dýr-nenninn gram þenna:
    œld hefir illa haldit, esa stríð-vana síðan;   15
    hult hafa hirð-menn skylja hœfuð þat-es fremst vas iœfra.

ODD, KITCHIN'S POET. I. *Dirge on Magnus.* There was a cruel battle fought before Michaelmas; the Wends fell, and on Sunday a little before Yule a second fight off Aros [the river mouth by Aarhuus in Jutland].

II. When they bore the gentle king to the grave, there fell many a tear, it was a heavy grief to his henchmen: their minds were so distraught that the house-carles could scarce withhold their tears, the prince's followers have often sat bowed down since then. I feel very sorrowful since the good life of Magnus came to its end. Affliction has overtaken me. I wander about helpless, strong sorrow is oppressing me. The people are sore distressed since the king's death, and I go joyless.

[Now the drooping galleys have borne the beloved king over the sea in the dark from the south. The land has suffered sorely. There is no lack of woe ever since the henchmen covered the head that

---

3 and 4. Read, ohlítin, dag . . . . Sunno.

5. Leiða langar dauða limar illa mik stilliss;
bøprot menn inn mæra Magnús í grøf fúsir.

BÖLVERKR.

1. MILDINGR strauktu um mækiss munn, es lézt af gunni;
holdz vantu hrafn um fyldan hrás, þaut ulfr í ási:
enn, gramr, (ne ek frá fremra, frið-skerðir, þer verða)
austr vastu ør in næsto ørðig-lyndr í Gørðom.

2. Hart kníði svøl svartan snekkjo brand frá landi   5
skúrr, enn skrautla børo skeiðr brynjaðar reiði:
mætr hilmir sátt malma Mikla-garðz fyrir barði;
mørg skriðo beit at borgar barm-føgr høm armi.

3. Sniallr rautt í styr, stillir, støl ok gekkt á mála;
háðisk hvert ár síðan hildr sem sialfir vildot.   10

4. Súð varð, þar-es blétt blóði, (borð rendosk at iørðo)
[váttu drengiliga, dróttinn] dreyra-full ‘við eyri:’
fann und ser fyrir sunnan Síkley (liði miklo)
sand (þar-es sveiti skyndi) sokkit lík (of stokka).

5. Réttu við rausn at hætta, reið-mæltr iøfurr, skeiðom   15
(prýddr lá byrr at bræddo) Blálandz á vit (stáli):
laust (enn lauka reisti lofðungr við sió þungan)
skúrr á skiald-rim dýra skokks miøll á þrøm stokkinn.

6. Gramr nenninn hefir gunni (gekk ferð ok hió sverðom)
[snørp háðisk þá síðan snerra] gagn or hverri.   20

7. Ok hertoga hneykir her-fengnom létzt stinga
leyfð frá-ek hans or høfði ‘hauks’ skyndaði augo.

---

was the highest among the kings. Sorrow has struck deep roots into
me! All unwillingly, men bore Magnus to the grave. *Unnamed, but
probably Odd's.*]

BALEWORK, KING HAROLD'S PRAISE. *After Sticklestead.* Thou,
king, didst wipe the mouth of thy sword when thou didst pass from
the battle, and wast in the east in Gard the years after.
Warring in the East. The cold shower blew the black prow-stems
of the ship from the land, and thou didst see the towers of Micklegarth [Constantinople] before thee, and broughtest many a fair-bosomed
bark to the high city side. Thou didst dye the steel in battle and take
a covenant [enter the Emperor's service]; every year after thou didst
fight at thy will. The hull was full of gore off the . . . . shore the sunken
carcases grounded on the shoals south off Sicily. Thou didst jeopard
thy ships, O ready-spoken king; the gale blew proudly on the tarry
bows, towards Blackland [North Africa]; the shower fell on the costly
shield-rim, and the foam drove upon the bulwarks. Thou didst win
every battle . . . . and didst put out the two eyes of the prisoner-
emperor's head.

---

7. sá, Cd.   9. rauð . . . gekk, Cd.   12. Some place?   14. Read,
skokka?   16. breiddo, Cd.   21. let, Cd.

8. Heimol varð, es ek heyrða, hodd-stríðir, þer síðan
grœn, enn goll bautt hánom, grund es Magnus fundot:
endisk ykkar frænda all-friðliga miðli   25
sætt, en síðan vætti Sveinn róm-œldo einnar.

9. Leiðangr biótto af láði (lœgr gekk um skip fœgro)
[gialfr-stóðom reistu græði glœstom] ár it næsta:
skokkr lá dýrr á dœkkri (Danir váro þá) bœro
[skeiðr sá herr fyrir hauðri hlaðnar] (illa staðnir).   30

VALGARÐR Á VELLI (C. 1047).

(Verse 1 from Fagrsk.; verses 2–5 from Edda.)

1. 'HELMINGI bauttu hanga' hilmiss kundr, af stundo;
     Skipt hafit ér, svá at 'eptir ero' Væringjar færi.

2. Skilfingr héltu (þar-es skulfo skeiðr) fyrir 'lœnd in breiðo'
(auð varð) suðr (um síðir Sikley) liði miklo.

3. Biartr sveimaði brími, bruto víkingar fíkjom   5
vísa styrks of virki 'varp sorg á menn' borgar.

4. Snarla skaut or sóti 'svek of hus' (enn reykir
stóðo stopðir síðan) stein-óðr logi glóðom.

5. Skauztu und farm inn frízta (frami veitisk þer) beiti;
fœrðir-þú goll or Gœrðom grunnlaust, Haraldr austan: 10
stýrðir hvatt í hœrðo, hug-dyggr iœfurr, glyggvi
'sáttu þa es sædrif létti Sigtún en skip hnigðo.'

6. Eik slœng und þer, Yngvi, ógn-blíðr í haf síðan
(rétt vas yðr of ætlat óðal) frá Sviþióðo:

Back in Norway. The green land became thy own, and thou gavest
him thy gold, when ye found Magnus, as I heard. Then came to pass
a very peaceful agreement between you two kinsmen, and Sweyn had
only war to look for afterwards.

King alone. Thou didst call out a sea-levy the next year; the costly
galley lay on the dark billow; the Danes were in evil stead.

WALGARD O' FIELD. KING HAROLD'S PRAISE. *In the East.*
Thou didst order the half of them to be hanged forthwith. Ye
have had the Largesse few Warings ever had. Thou didst hold
thy course with a great fleet to the south of the 'broad land.'
Sicily was wasted there. The bright flame flickered. The king's
wickings stormed the town [of . . . .]. The violent fire poured glowing embers out of the sooty reek, and the smoke went up like pillars
from the burning houses.

Home again. Thou didst launch thy ship with the costliest cargo,
and didst carry gold without end out of Gard from the east; thou didst
steer thy ship through a sharp gale, and when thou didst furl thy
canvas thou didst see Sigtun. The oak sped under thee next over

---

3. Name of place.   6. Some place.   12. Corrupt; read, . . . Sigtúna
skript húna?

hind bar rif, þars renndi rétt á stag fyrir slétta 15
skeið (enn skelkto brúðir) Skáney (Dœnom nánar).

7. Gekk á Fión (enn fekkat) fiœl-meðr konungr (hiœlmom)
[brast ríkula ristin rít] (erviði lítið).

8. Haraldr gœrva léztu herjat (hnyggr-þú andskotom tyggi)
[brátt rann vargr at vitja val-fallz] Selund alla : 20

9. Brann í bœ́ fyrir sunnan biartr eldr Hrois-keldo ;
rœnn lét ræsir nenninn reyk-vell ofan fella :
lœ́go landzmenn gnógir ' lo hel sumom frelsi ;'
drósk ' harm vesalt ' hyski hliótt til skógs á flótta.

10. ' Dvalði daprt ok skilda ' (drifo) þeir es eptir ' lifðo ' 25
' ferð ' [enn fengin urðr fœgr sprund] (Danir undan) :
láss hélt líki drósar ; leið fyrir yðr til skeiða
(bito ' fíkula ' fiœtrar) flióð mart hœrund-biarta.

11. Inn vas í sem brynni ið-glíkt siá miðjan
eld þar-es yðrom heldot, orms-munn-litoðr, sunnan : 30
skeið bar skolpt inn rauða ; skein af golli hreino ;
dreki fór dag-leið mikla ; dúfo braut und húfi.

12. Lauðr vas lagt í ' beði,' lék sollit haf golli ;
enn her-skipom hrannir hœfuð ógorlig þógo :
ræðr-þu (enn ræsir œ́ðri rístr alldri siá kaldan) 35
[sveit tœ́r sínom dróttni sniœll] Nóregi œllom.

---

the main from Sweden ; thy birthright land was duly given thee ; the
galley sped straight ahead, doubling the flats of Sconey ; the Danish
maidens were in fear.
War in Denmark. Funen. Thou didst land on Fion [Funen].
Sealand. Thou didst harry all Sealand thoroughly. The bright fire
burnt in the town of Hroe's well [Roskeld] in the south. The
Ramnlosa people fled to the woods. The Helsings [men of Helsinge,
the Neck of Sealand] lost their freedom. At Skyldelow we got fair
bondmaids, the Danes were put to flight. The cords were tight on the
ladies' bodies ; many a fair-skinned damsel was driven down to the
ships. The fetters bit sore.
Voyage home. Your gilded galley-head was to look on like a serpent
breathing fire, when ye sailed from the south ; she bore a dragon's
head, she shone with pure gold ; she went a long day's journey, breaking
the waves with her breast. The foaming waves lay in ridges, the swollen
billows played against the gold, and the rollers washed the grim heads of
the war-ships. Thou rulest all Norway ! Never shall greater king
cleave the cold sea !

---

23. Read, lósk Helsingjom frelsi. 24. Read, Hramnlauso. 25. Corrupt ;
read, Skylda-leif ? in the point between Roskeld-firth and Ice-firth.

ILLUGI BRYNDŒLA-SKALD.

(Verse 1 from Edda; verse 2 from AM. 748.)

1. VARGS vas munr þar es margan—*Men-skerðir stakk sverði*
    myrk-örriða markar—mínn dróttinn rak flótta.
2. Enn hélt ulfa brennir—*Eiskaldi framm beisko*
    mildr réð Orms of elldi—austr-fœr þaðan gœrva.
3. Opt gekk á frið Frakka—'*Fliotrent at by snotar*'   5
    '*vara doglingi duglom*'—dróttinn minn fyr ótto.
4. Brauztu und Mikjál mestan—*Mágom heim sem frágom*
    sonr Buðla bauð sínom—Sunn-lœnd, Haraldr, rœndo.

GRANI-SKALD.

(Verses 2, 3 from Edda.)

1. LET aldregi úti osvífr Kraka drífo
    hlœkk í harða þiokkom Hornskógi brá þorna: 10
    Fila dróttinn rak flótta fiánda grams til strandar
    auð varð út at greiða all-skiótt faðir Dótto.
2. Dœglingr fekk at drekka Danskt blóð ara ióði,
    hœrð veit-ek hilmi gœrðo Hugins Iól við nes Þiólar:
    ætt spornaði arnar all-vítt um val-falli;   15
    hold át vargr sem vildi (vel nióti hann þess!) Ióta.
3. Glœéðr hygg-ek, Glamma slóðar (gramr eldi svá), feldo.

ÞÓRARINN SKEGGJASON.

NÁÐI '*gœrr*' enn glóðom Gríklandz iœfurr '*handa*;'
    stól-þengill gekk strœngo stein-blindr aðal-meini.

ILLUGI BRYNDOLA-SCALD. The Wolf's joy was when my lord drove many a foe to flight. *Refrain:* The king [Sigfred] stabbed the Serpent [Fafni] with the sword.—He also made a foray thence eastward. *Refrain:* The king held the bitter heart of the Serpent to the fire.— My lord often fought with the Franks in the morning watch. *Refrain:* The doughty prince had not . . . .—Thou didst subdue the most of the southern lands, O Harold, for Michael. *Refrain:* We have heard how Budli's son Attila bade his brothers-in-law to his house.

GRANI THE POET. *Harold's Danish Campaign.* May the ungentle gold-decked lady [lit. Walkyria of Kraki's scattering] of Horn-shaw [Jutland] never have dry eyes. The lord of the Fiala-folk drove his foes captive to the coast. The father of Dotta [a Danish lady] was forced to pay down a ransom forthwith. The king gave the young eagles Danish blood to drink at Thiolar-ness [Jutland]. He gave the ravens a merry Yule: the erne's white brood stood above the slain Jutes, the wolf ate flesh as he would: may he enjoy it well! He gave gold, the king . . . .

THORARIN. The prince bound forthwith the King of Greece's hands; the throned-king, stone-blind, suffered a terrible outrage.

---

18. Read, hondom.

SNŒGLO-HALLI, *or* HALLI STRIÐI.

(From Skalda.)

SVÁ lét und sik seggja dróttinn
    lœnd œll lagin liðs oddviti.

THORLEIK FAGRI (FLOKKR).

(Verses 1, 10 from Skioldunga; verses 4, 5 from Fagrsk.; verses 11–13 from Edda.)

1. FÚR-SENDIR vann fiándom fiœr-spell í gný hiœrva
    (brœð fekk hrafn) fyr Heiða-, hauk-storða, -bý, norðan:
    Rœkosk Vindr (enn vakar vals gino þeim of halsa)
    [dauðr lá herr á heiði hund-margr] fair undan.

2. Vœn eromk vísa kœnom vígs á Rakna stígo   5
    œrr í odda snerro Inn-Þrœnda lið finni:
    þó má enn, hvárr annan œndo nemr eða lœndom,
    (lítt hyggr Sveinn á sættir siald-festar) Goð valda.

3. Fœrir reiðr, sá-es rauða rœnd hefir opt fyr lœndom,
    breið á Buðla slóðir borð-rœkn Haraldr norðan: 10
    enn lauks of siá sœkja Sveins fagr-buin steini
    glœsi-dýr (þess es geira) goll-munnuð (rýðr) sunnan.

4. Fiœrs mun flestom hersi feng-sæll Dana þengill
    (reiðr hefir hann fyr hauðri há-brynjoð skip) synja:
    es hún-ferils hreina hlunn-tamða rekr sunnan   15
    við Hœrða gram harðan, hundrað sex, til fundar.

5. Stýrir Úlfs til Elfar ósk-mœgr skipom fœgrom,
    'sá-es hræ-kœsto hæsta hleðr í Gunnar veðri:'
    Skullo vé, þar es vœllo vápn-lauðri drífr rauðo,
    (regn drepr Gautz í gœgnom) goll-merkt ('Halfs' serki). 20

SNEGLE'S HALL.   So the king brought all lands under him.

THORLEIK THE FAIR. *A Flokk on King Sweyn.   Battle with King Magnus against the Wends at Sleswick, Lurschau.* He put his enemies to death north of Heathby [Sleswik]; few of the Wends escaped, a countless host lay dead on the Heath.

Rising and Battle against King Harold. We may look for a battle on the sea between our king [Sweyn] and the In-Thrond's patron [Harold]. But God will rule which of the two will take the other's life and land. Sweyn puts little store by covenants that are seldom kept.   Harold is bringing his broad timber-teams [ships] over Budli's tracks [the sea] from the North, while the fair-eyed, gold-jawed, glittering mast-beasts [ships] of Sweyn speed from the South.   The victorious king of the Danes will take the life of most of the *Northern* barons; he is driving north six hundred billow-wont reindeer of the mast [ships] to meet the king of the Hords.   The beloved son of Wolf [Sweyn] stands with his fair ships to the Elbe [Gaut Elf].   The gold-marked banner waved,

---

20. -morkuð, Cd.   Read, Hamðés.

6. Hví hefir til Heiða-býjar heipt-giarn konungr árnat,
    folk-rœgnir getr fregna fylkiss sveit hinn es veitað:
    þá-es til þengils bœjar þarf-laust Haraldr austan
    'ár þat-es án of væri' endr byr-skíðom rendi.

7. Bauð, sá-es baztrar tíðar borinn varð und Miðgarði,   25
    ríkri þióð at rióða randir Sveinn á landi:
    Þó lézk heldr, 'ef "héldi" hvat-ráðr konungr láði,'
    á byrjar-val berjask bil-styggr Haraldr vilja.

8. Allt of frá-ek, hve ellti Austmenn á veg flausta,
    Sveinn, enn siklingr annarr snar-lundaðr helt undan: 30
    Fengr varð Þrœnda þengils (þeir létto skip fleiri)
    allr á éli sollno Iótlandz-hafi flióta.

9. Sætt buðo seggja dróttni siklings vinir mikla
    'svæfðo hialdr þeir es hœfðo hug-stinnir lið minna:'
    'ok snar-ráðir síðan sókn es orð um tókosk'   35
    '(œnd vas ýta kindom ófœl) buendr dvœldo.'

10. Hætt hafa ser þeir es sótto Sveins fundar til stundom;
    lítt hefir 'þer' at þreyta þrim bragningom hagnat:
    þó hefir hœld-vinr haldit (hann es sniallr konungr) allri
    Ióta grund með endom ógn-starkr ok Danmœrko.   40

11. Kastar gramr á glœstar gegn val-stœðvar þegnom
    (ungr vísi gefr eiso arm-leggs) dígul-farmi.

12. Hirð viðr grams með gerðom goll-vorpoðr ser holla.

13. Siár þýtr, enn berr bára biart lauðr of við rauðom,
    grans þar es golli búnom gínn hlunn-vísundr munni.   45

Woden's rain [missiles] pierces Hamtheow's sarks [the mail]. Why
the cruel king has come to Heathby .... can easily be known, when
Harold wantonly steered his ships to .... by .... Sweyn, who was
born under the best augury on earth (Midgarth), proffered him to fight
on land, but Harold would rather fight on sea than give battle ashore. I
have heard how Sweyn chased the Eastmen over the sea, whilst the
other king fled. The booty of the Thronds' lord was floating about
on the shower-swollen sea of Jutland [Cattegat]. They prayed for
peace [*seven* ships of the Norway levy of Wick whom he had captured
at Hlesey] .... the franklins ....
Fight with Stankel the Swedish King. Those who have encountered
Sweyn have jeoparded themselves. The three princes [Magnus, Harold,
Stankel] have gained little by it, for he has in the end kept all the land
of the Jutes and Denmark withal.
His generosity. The king gave his thanes gold.
His ship. The sea roars and the waves dash the white spray over the
red-painted timbers, while the water-bison gapes with golden jaws.

---

27. Read, hildi.   36. The verse is all painted over.   38. Read, við þik.

STUF (STUMP) THE BLIND AND STEIN HERDISSON, ETC.

BOTH poets of the Stamford Battle and the next following events.

STUMP. In a chapter of the Book of Kings the following account of Poet STUMP occurs:—

" There was a man named Stump, the son of Thord (Thorfred) Cat, whom Snorri the Chief fostered. Thorfred Cat was the son of Thorfred, the son of Glum Geirason, *the poet*. Thorfred's mother was Gudrun, Oswif's daughter (*the heroine of Laxdæla Saga*). Stump was blind; but he was a wise man and a good poet. He went to Norway, and lodged with a franklin in Upland. One day when men were standing out of doors on his farm, they saw a number of richly-dressed men riding up. ' I did not look to see King Harold here to-day, but I should not wonder if it were he.' And as they drew near, they saw that it was he. The franklin greeted the king, and then said, ' We cannot treat you as ye should be treated, my lord, for we did not know of your coming.' The king replied, ' We would not give any trouble; we are only going on our way through the country; my men shall tend their horses themselves, and look after the horse-gear; but I shall go into the house.' The king was in a merry mood, and the franklin followed him into the parlour to his seat. Then the king said, ' Go about, franklin, as thou wilt, and treat us in all things as thou art wont to do every day!' ' Well, I will do so,' says the franklin. So he went out, and the king looked about on the bench and saw a big man sitting below on the bench, and asked him who he was. ' My name is Stump,' says he. ' What a name,' says the king; ' whose son art thou?' ' I am Cat's son,' said he; ' That is no better.' . . . Then said the king, ' Come up near me on the bench and let us talk together.' So he did, and the king found him no fool, and took pleasure in talking with him. When the franklin came back, he said that the king must have been dull. ' Not at all,' says the king, ' for this winter-guest of thine has entertained me finely, and he must be my partner at the drinking to-night.' And so it was. The king talked a good deal with Stump, and he answered him wisely; and when folks went to bed, the king bade Stump come into the room where he slept to amuse him. Stump did so; and when the king was got to bed, Stump began to entertain him, and recited a Short-Poem (flokk), and when it was ended the king told him to go on again. The king kept awake a long while, and Stump kept reciting to him, and at last the king said, ' How many poems hast thou recited to-night?' Answers Stump, ' I thought you would have reckoned them up.' ' So I have,' says the king, ' and there are now thirty; but why dost thou only say Short-Poems? knowest thou no Long-Poems [Encomia]?' ' I know as many long poems as short,' answers Stump; ' and I have many which I have not yet given.' ' Thou must be very learned in poetry,' said the king; ' but whom wilt thou entertain with thy long poems, since thou givest me only short poems?' ' Thyself,' says Stump. ' But when?' says the king. ' When next we meet.' ' Why then rather than now?' ' Because,' said Stump, ' I would have it so with my recitals as with all else in me, that thou shouldst like me the better the longer thou knowest me and the better we are acquainted.' ' Well, let us sleep now,' says the king." Next morning he grants Stump three wishes, and receives him afterwards into his

guard, and Stump became his liegeman and was with him some time,
'and made a dirge upon him, which is called Stump's Praise-Song or
Stumpie.'
We have fragments of this Dirge. For Stump's family and kindred
see the table given below, p. 228.

The prose shows that a stanza has been dropt out between those we
have, which are not quite uncorrupt. The little reminiscence in the
last lines is natural and pathetic.

STEIN HERDISSON. There are two poems of his—a *Poem of Praise*
(flokk), called *Nizar Visor*, on his cousin, Wolf the Marshal, and the battle
of the River Niz, about 1062. He here imitates Sighvat's Nesia Visor.
Surviving the fall of Harold, he made a long poem to *King Olaf the
Peaceful*, in which he glosses over the defeat of Stamford-bridge, and
declares that the English will never forget the defeat of Fulford.
This poem is imitated by the author of Rekstefja. Several verses are
unsafe. We have restored the mention of the 'Fleet;' the verse about
Morcar is strange: it has suffered corruption. The mention of Chipping (Nidaros), Olaf's town, and the confidence in St. Olaf are to be
remarked.

THORKELL HAMMER POET. The son or poet of Skalli, but of his
family nothing is known. He made a *Dirge on Earl Waltheow*, whom
he may have met in England on one of the expeditions of Asbiorn or
other leaders which harried England in the Conqueror's days. He is
mentioned in Skalda-tal as a poet of Magnus Bareleg, and we have part
of a *Dirge* of his on that king, and a fragment of a *Poem in Old Metre*.
'The son of the Wolsungs sent me a gold-mounted weapon over the
cold ocean,' alluding to the gift of a weapon from some king. The
first verse seems to refer to Waltheow's exploits at York; the second
shows the general impression as to the execution of the Earl, which led
to the belief in his sanctity.

ANONYMOUS. Four lines of a '*Stikki*,' a small poem or sonnet on King
Harold's victory at Fulford, mentioning 'Waltheof's men,' which seems
to be used as a synonym for 'Northumbrians,' which may have led to
the misunderstanding in Harold's Life as to Waltheof's presence or
leadership in the Stamford-bridge campaign. If this be so, the poem
must date from 1076 rather than 1067.

STÚFR BLINDI (STÚFA).

1. FÓR ofr-hugi (in œfri) egg-diarfr und sik leggja
   [fold vas víga valdi virk] Iórsali [ok Girkjom]:
   ok með œrno ríki óbrunnin kom gunnar
   heimol iœrð und herði—*Hafi ríks þars vel líkar.*
2. [Lost verse. . . .]—*Haraldz önd ofar löndom.* 5
3. Stóðosk rœð af reiði (rann þat) svika-mœnnom

STUMPIE. *Burden.* May the soul of the mighty Harold have a pleasant dwelling above the earth with Christ for ever.

In the East. The king went to conquer Jerusalem-land, and the
upper country welcomed him and the Greeks; the whole land came un-
burnt into his possession with mighty dominion. *The lost verse here, as
the prose tells us, must have read,* 'He offered at the grave of the Lord and at
the Holy Rood, and at other holy places in Jerusalem-land, so much in gold
and jewels that it is hard to count in marks.' The lord of the Agd-folk

Egða grams á ymsom (orð) Iordanar borðom:
enn fyrir afgœrð sanna ílla 'gat' frá stilli
þióð fekk vísan váða — *Vist um aldr með Christi.*

4. Mœgð gat all-valdr Egða ógnar-mildr þá-es vildi; 10
gollz tók gumna spialli gnótt ok bragnings dóttor.

5. Autt vas Falstr 'at fréttom,' fekk drótt mikinn ótta,
gladdr varð hrafn, enn hræddir hvert ár Danir vóro.

6. Flýðo þeir af Þióðo þengils fund af stundo;
stórt réð hug-fullt hiarta—*Haraldz önd ofar löndom.* 15

7. Tír-eggjaðr hió tiggi. tveim hœndom lið beima
(reifr gekk herr und hlífar) hizig suðr fyr Nitzi.

8. Gekk sem vind, sá-es vætki varðandi fiœr sparði
geira-hreggs, í gegnom glaðr orrostor þaðra:
gramr flýðit sá (síðan sœm ero þess of dœmi 20
éls und erki-stóli) eld né iarn it fellda.

9. Vissa-ek hildar hvessi (hann vas nýztr at kanna)
af góðom byr Gríðar gagn-sælan mer fagna:
þá es ben-starra bræðir baugom grimmr at Haugi
giarn með gylldo horni gekk sialfr á mik drekka. 25

STEINN HERDÍSARSON. I. NIZAR VÍSOR.

(Verses 7, 8 from Skioldunga.)

1. SAGÐI hitt es hugði hauk-lyndr vesa mundi,
(þar kvað þengill eirar þrotna vón fyr hónom):
heldr kvazk hvern várn skyldo hilmir frægr an vægja
(menn bruto upp) of annan (œll vópn) þveran falla.

.... brigands .... on both banks of Jordan, and for their proved
crimes .... paid heavy fines to the prince. He won the match he
wished, getting gold enough and the king's daughter.

War in Denmark. Falster was made waste, and every year the Danes
were full of fear. They fled from Thiod [in Jutland] before the king
forthwith.

Niz Battle. He hewed down his foes with both hands there, south
off Niz.

In England. He went like the wind through the battle there, the
king that never fled for fire or sword; there are many glorious proofs of
that on earth [lit. under the wind's cathedral *or* archbishopric].

The King's Hall. I remember how he graciously welcomed me (he was a
good friend to know), when he himself drank to me in a golden horn at
Howe (in Throndham).

NIZ VERSES. The king spoke his will, he said that every one of us
should fall one across the other before we gave way; the men brought
out their weapons. Wolf, the king's marshal, when the high javelins
were being brandished, and the oars pulled for the attack out on the

---

8. Read, galt? 20. sæm ef þ. ero dæmi, Cd.

2. Hét á oss, þá es úti, Ulfr, há-kesjor skulfo,   5
(róðr vas greiddr á græði) grams stallari alla:
vel bað skip með skylja skel-eggjaðr framm leggja
sítt; enn seggir iátto, sniallz landreka spialli.

3. Hætti hersa dróttinn hug-strangr, skipa langra
hinn es við halft beið annat hundrað, Dana fundar :   10
næst vas þat-es réð rísta reiðr at-seti Hleiðrar
þangs-láð-mœrom þangat þrimr hundroðom sunda.

4. Vann fyr móðo minni mein-fœrt Haraldr Sveini
'varð, því at vísi gœrði viðr-nám, friðar biðja:'
Herðu hiœrvi gyrðir Halland iœfurs spiallar   15
(heit blés und) fyr útan atróðr (á lœg blóði).

5. Nýtr bað Skiœldungr skióta (skamt vas liðs á miðli)
hlífar styggr ok hœggva hvárr-tveggi lið tiggi :
Bæði fló (þá-es blóði brandr hrauð af ser rauðo),
[þat brá feigra flotna fiœrvi] griót ok œrvar.   20

6. Undr es ef eigi kendo œr-mótz viðir gœrva,
bœrðomk ver, þeir-es vœrðo víða grund, of síðir :
þá-es her-skildi héldo (hrafn fekk gnótt) í ótto
nás fyr Nizár-ósi Norðmenn, Harald, forðom.

7. Oss dugir hrafns ens hvassa hungr-deyfi svá leyfa   25
linnz at lastim annan láttr-sveigjanda eigi :
aldregi kvœddozk oddom (annat hverjom manni
tál es um tiggja at mæla) tveir full-hugar meiri.

8. Eigi mundi undan all-valdr Dana halda
(oss dugir satt um snotran sælinga kon mæla):   30
ef menn fyr siá sunnan (sverð reiddosk at ferðir),
þeir-es her-skildi héldo, hrafns-fœði vel tœði.

II. OLAFS-DRÁPA.

(Verse 1 from Edda; the rest from Hulda.)

1. HÁS kveð-ek helgan ræsi heim-tiallz at brag þeima
(mærð tésk fram) an fyrða fyrr, þvi-at hann es dýrri.

---

sea, he, the king's friend, bade us lay his ship in the forefront of the battle,
by the side of the king's, and his men assented. The King [Harold]
ventured on meeting the Danes with a third half-hundred of ships [180],
while the dweller in Hlethra [Leire] led three hundred [360] vessels.

Harold beat Sweyn at the mouth of the river [Niz] .... The king's
men, sword-girt, attacked off Halland. When there was little space
between, both kings bade their men shoot; both stones and arrows
flew. It is a wonder that they did not .... when we the Northmen
held the shield about Harold in the morning-watch, off Niz-mouth.
Let us praise one of the kings, so that we do not blame the other.
Never did two more stout-hearted men greet each other with the spear-
point. The king of the Danes would not have given way (we must
speak the truth of him), if the men from the south of the sea had fought
well for him.

OLAF THE QUIET'S PRAISE. *Prologue.* I first call on the holy King of
the World-tent [Heaven], for he is more glorious than the king of men. My

2.   Veit-ek hvar Óláfr úti óslœkinn rauð mœki
     (deilask mer til mála minni) fyrsta sinni:
     Hlaut til hafs fyrir útan Halland konungr branda   5
     (fœgr sverð ruðo fyrðar) fiœl-góðr litoð blóði.
3.   Gengo Danskir drengir (dynr vas gœrr) með brynjor
     útan-borðz til iarðar 'uríks' malms ok hialma:
     sukko sárir rekkar sunnan hafs til grunna;
     hár varp hausom þeirra hrann-garðr á þrœom iarðar.   10
4.   Ungr vísi léztu Úso all-nær buendr falla,
     sótti herr þar-es hætti hiœr-diarfr konungr fiœrvi:
     þess man þangat-kváma þengils vesa Englom
     enn sem eptir renni iflaust es þá lifðo.
5.   Féllo vítt um vœllo (vargr náði þá biargask)   15
     benja regn, enn bragna blóð Víkingar óðo.

I. 6.   Þióð fórsk mœrg í Móðo (menn druknoðo sokknir)
     drengr 'lá ar of' úngan ófár Morokára:
     Fila dróttinn rak flótta framr, tók herr á ramri
     rœs fyr rœskom vísa.—Rík-lundaðr veit undir   20
7.   Fylkir lét 'in flioto' flaust, es leið at hausti;
     skaut í haf, þars heitir Hrafnseyrr, konungr stafni:
     tróðo borð-vigg breiðan brim-gang (skipa langra)
     (óðr fell siór um súðir).—sik baztan gram miklo
8.   Austr helt Engla þrýstir, ótvín, liði síno   25
     stóran (braut um stýri straum) sæ konungr Rauma:
     Glaðr tók herr, þá-es heðra hring-lestir kom vestan,.
     allr við œflgom stilli.—Óláfr borinn sólo.

II. 9.   Heldr sízt hárri foldo heipt-bráðr iœfurr náði

song sets forth! I know where Olaf first reddened his sword out in the
sea off Halland. My memories fall into speech. The Danish men
went overboard in the mail-coats, sinking to the bottom, their bodies
drifting ashore in heaps.

In England. O young king, thou madest the franklins fall hard by
Ouse. The coming of the king will be to the English who escaped
alive a memorable thing. The Wickings waded in blood. They (the
English) fell wide over the field.

Burden. The mighty-minded Olaf knows himself to be by far the best
king under the sun.

His English Foray. Stave 1. Many people fell in the mouth [of Humber],
many a man lay about the young Morcar. The Fiala-folk's lord drove
the fliers forward.

Return. The king put his ships in the river, and ran out at harvest-
tide to sea by the place called Ravensore; the timber steeds trod the
long sea-paths, the mad waves fell on the strakes of the long ships.
The enemy of the English [Olaf], the king of the Reams, held his course
over the great deep, the mighty stream broke around him. All the
people welcomed the noble prince when he came hither from the west.

His good-will. Stave 2. Now since the king [his brother Magnus, who

18. Read, orof.   21. Read, í Flióti.   23. bordveg, Cd.

(ætt þreifsk Egða dróttins) ólaust konungr stóli : 30
mætr hilmir rauð malmi (man-ek skiœldungs lof) kœldom
Rauma grams ok rœndo.—*Rík-lundr borinn undir*

10. Öll biðr Egða stillir egg-diarfra lið seggja
sund fyrir síno landi sókn-œrr stika dœrrom:
iœrð mun eigi verða auð-sótt Fila dróttins 35
sókn-herðondom sverða.—*sik baztan gram miklo*

11. Lœnd vill þengill Þrœnda (þat líkar vel skœtnom)
œll við œrna snilli egg-diarfr í frið leggja:
hugnar þióð, es þegna þrá-lyndr til frið-mála
kúgar Engla œgir.—*Óláfr borinn sólo.* 40

III. 12. Óláfr gefr svá iœfra, allz engi má sniallra
hœggvit goll til hylli hildinga konr mildri :
Gramr veit heiðom himni, hann es fremstr konung-manna,
[spyr-þu hverr glíkt man gœrva] *giöf-lundr borinn undir*

13. Gefr átt-stuðill iœfra œrr ok steinda knœrro 45
(hann vill hnœggvi sínnar) há-brynjoð skip (synja):
þióð nýtr Óláfs auðar (annar konungr mœnnom
se-þú hverr slíkt-fé reiðir).—*sik baztan gram miklo*

14. Her-þengill gleðr hringom hodd-œrr sa-es rýðr odda,
bekk-sagnir lætr bragna bragningr giœfom fagna: 50
Norð-mœnnom gefr nenninn Nóregs konungr stórom;
œrr es Engla þverrir.—*Óláfr borinn sólo.*

15. Enn-at gœrva gunni gramr biósk við styr rœmmom,
her-skildi bað halda hraust-geðr konungr austan :
út fœrðot lið lítið lœng borð fyrir Stað norðan; 55
trœðot tún-vœll reyðar tveir dœglingar meiri.

16. Sín óðul mun Sveini sókn-strangr í Kaupangi,
þar es heilagr gramr hvílir (hann es ríkr iœfurr), banna :

---

died young] won heaven, he [Olaf] holds his throne firmly (the race of the
Agd-folk's lord thereon). The good king of the Reams defends his land
with cold iron and shield. I set forth his praise. The lord of the Agd-
folk makes his men fence in every creek of his land with darts, so that
the Fiala-folk's king [himself] cannot be easily attacked. The Thronds'
prince wishes his land to lie in peace, and the people are well pleased
that he, the terror of the English, forces them to peaceful dealings.
His open hand. Stave 3. Olaf gives so much gold to his men that no
other king can do the like. He gives them helmets and mail-coats as if
it were nothing. 'King's clothes look so well.' .... [*The two verses*
have been amplified out of one we think, the rendering of which we
give.] He gives them also painted busses and high-mailed war-ships, for
he despises miserliness. He gladdens his henchmen with rings, and his
courtiers with gifts. The minisher of the English is generous indeed.
War is at hand, but the poet is confident in the patron saint of his master.
The brave king [Olaf] bade his men make ready for battle, for another
prince [Sweyn] was coming with war-shield from the East. He [Olaf]
is standing to sea north of Stad with his fleet. Never did two better

---

42. mildi, Cd.   43. veit] es, Cd.

ætt sínni man unna Áláfr konungr hála;
Ulfs þarfat því arfi allz Nóregs til kalla.　　　60
17.　Varði ógnar-orðom Óláfr ok frið-máolom
iǫrð sva-at engi þorði allvalda til kalla.

ÞORKELL SKALLASON (VALÞIÓFS-FLOKKR).

1.　H UNDRAÐ lét í heitóm hirð-menn iǫfurr brenna
sóknar yggr, enn seggjom (sviðo-kveld vas þat) elldi:
frétt vas, at fyrðar knáotto flagð-viggs und kló liggja;
im-leitom fekksk áta ǫls blakk við hræ Frakka.

2.　Víst hefir Valþióf hraustan Vilhialmr, sás rauð malma,　5
(hinn-es haf skar sunnan hélt) í trygð um véltan:
satt es, at síð man létta (snarr enn minn vas harri)
[deyr eigi mildingr mæri] mann-dráp á Englandi.

HARALDZ STIKKI.

L ÁGO fallnir í fen ofan
Valþiófs liðar váopnom hœggnir:
svá at gunn-hvatir ganga knáotto
Norðmenn yfir á náom einom.

OCCASIONAL VERSES AND IMPROVISATIONS.

KING HAROLD SIGURDSSON. *A Love-Song,* of which six stanzas out of sixteen are imperfectly preserved, is attributed to the king himself, who was quite capable of composing it. It is addressed to the lady of the gold-ring in Gardric, of whom we know nothing. The allusion to Olaf and the wicking exploits of Harold's youth are quite consonant with what we know of the buccaneer king. The verse on his accomplishments is a copy of that on Earl Rognwald, but there was, we take it, a stanza in the original on the subject, which, being lost or corrupt, some copyist has filled up for the better-known Rognwald's verses. The list is interesting: Earl Rognwald knows—tables, runes, book-reading, harping, smithying [carpentry], shooting, rowing, snow-skating, and poetry. Harold Greyfell had 'twelve royal accomplishments,' says Glum Geirasson, but the verse he counted them up in is lost. Olaf

kings tread the whale-path. He will keep Sweyn off his heritage at Chipping [Nidaros], where the holy king [St. Olaf] lies. King Olaf [the saint] will protect his race to the utmost. [Sweyn] Wolfson's claim to all Norway shall be of no effect. Both against threats and soothing words Olaf protected his land so that no king durst lay claim to it.

THORKETTLE SKALLASON ON WALTHEOW. *His exploits.* He burnt in the hot fire a hundred of the king's henchmen; it was singeing-time for men [the day they singe the fresh slain sheep in the autumn]; prey was given to the grey-wolf from the corpses of the French.

His death. Surely William, that reddened swords and clave the icy sea from the south, has dealt treacherously with the gallant Waltheow in full truce. Verily, slaughter will not soon be stayed in England. Brave was my lord, a better prince never died.

HAROLD'S SONNET. *Fulford.* Waltheow's weapon-slain men lay down in the Dyke, so that the brave Northmen could walk across on their bodies!

Tryggvisson, we learn (no doubt from a verse now perished), knew climbing, swimming, juggling with knives, was ambi-dexterous, and could walk along his galley on the bows of the oars which the men were rowing. These passages recall the list of feats in the Irish Tales. We have added the King's *Improvisations* on the *Death of Fin* and *Capture of Einar* (the veteran from Swold); the verses before *Sticklestead* and *Stamford Bridge* battles; and the *Dialogues* with his poets Thiodwolf and Hall. The Thiodwolf and Fisherman lines existed apparently in two versions, one of which replaced Fisherman by a Salt-burner.

KING MAGNUS. A little scrap out of a love-song is ascribed to this prince, it refers to some unnamed lady.

WOLF THE MARSHAL. A great friend of Harold, one of his old comrades in the East. He died in 1066, just before the English Expedition. His kinsmanship to Stein and Stump, his contemporaries at Harold's court, and other men of mark before and after, will be clear from the following table:

King Beolan *m.* Cathlin d. of Rodwolf Duke of Normandy

Helgi, *m.* Nidbiorg

Einar Skalaglam	Oswif the Wise	*Glum* Geirasson
Thorgerd	Ospak Gudrun *m.* Thorkell *m.* (2) Thorrod	
Herdis *Wolf* the Marshal, *d.* 1066 Gelli, *d.* 1073 Thorrod Cat		
Stein John of Rayfield Thorgils *Stump the Blind*		
Erlend Himaldi ARI the Historian, *d.* 1148		
Eystein the Archbishop, *d.* 1188		

How Harold missed him may be guessed from his eulogy at his grave:
' Of all men he was the truest to his lord.'
The stave of his, given below, alludes to the report of Harold God-winesson's house-carles, 'that they were a match for any two Northmen.'

I. MANSÖNG.

1. FUNDR vas þess at Þrœndir; þeir hœfðo lið meira;
    varð sú es ver of gerðom víst errileg snerra:
    skildomk ungr við ungan all-vald í styr fallinn—
    Þó lætr Gerðr í Görðom goll-hrings við mer skolla.

2. Sneið fyr Sikley víða súð, vórom þá prúðir;   5
    brýnt skreið vel til vánar vengis-hiœrtr und drengjom:
    vætti-ek miðr at motti moni enn þinig renna—
    Þó lætr Gerðr í Görðom goll-hrings við mer skolla.

I. KING HAROLD'S LOVE-SONG. *Battle at Sticklestead.* We met the Thronds: they had the greater host. It was a sharp bicker we had. I was young when I parted with the young king [Olaf] fallen in the fray.—*Refrain :* Yet Gerd Gold-ring in Gard holds me in scorn.
In the East. The bark sped to broad Sicily; we were proud *of array* then. The galley went fast under her crew. I do not think the

3. Senn ióso ver, svanni, sextán, enn brim vexti,
  (dreif á hlaðna húfa húm) í fiórom rúmom: 10
  vætti-ek minnr at motti moni enn þinig renna—
  Þó lætr Gerðr í Görðom goll-hrings við mer skolla.

4. Íþróttir kann-ek átta :—Yggs fet-ek líð smíða ;
  fœrr em-ek hvasst á hesti ; hefi-ek sund numit stundom ;
  skríða kann-ek á skíðom ; skýt-ek ok rœk svá-at nýtir— 15
  Þó lætr Gerðr í Görðom goll-hrings við mer skolla.

5. Enn monat ekkjan finna ung ne mær at værim,
  þar-es gœrðom svip sverða, síð í borg of morgin:
  Ruddomk um með oddi ; ero merki þar verka—
  Þó lætr Gerðr í Görðom goll-hrings við mer skolla.   20

6. Fœddr vas-ek þar-es alma Upplendingar bendo ;
  nú læt-ek við sker skolla skeiðr buœndom leiðar.
  Vítt hefi-ek sízt ýttom ey-garð skorið barði—
  Þó lætr Gerðr í Görðom goll-hrings við mer skolla.

II. Lausa Vísor.

1. Þora mun-ek þann arm verja (þat es ekkjo munr) 'nokkut'
  [ríóðom ver af reiði rœnd] es ek í hlýt standa :
  Gengr-a greppr inn ungi gunn-blíðr, þar-es slœg ríða,
  (herða menn at mórði mót) á hæl fyr spiótom.

2. Nú læt-ek skóg af skógi ... (see Book vi, § 1, vol. i. p. 365). 5

The King :

3. Láto ver, meðan lirlar lín-eik veri sínom,
  Gerðr, í Goðnar-firði 'galdrs' akkeri halda.

---

laggard would hasten thither. Yet, etc. We baled sixteen of us in four berths. And the sea grew high and the dun wave drove over the laden hull. I do not think, etc. I know eight accomplishments: I can brew Woden's draught [poetry], I am nimble on horseback, I have at times taken to swimming. I know, etc. [*See Earl Rognwald's verse*, p. 276, *from which these have been at all events mended.*] The young damsel shall never find us late in the town of a morning when sword strokes are to be given. We broke our way with the point of our spear. There are marks of our deeds. Yet, etc. I was born where the Uplanders bear the bow, but now I make the galley, the franklins hate, hover off the skerries *like a wicking's.* I have cloven the main far and wide with my prow since first I put out to sea. Yet, etc.

II. Improvisations. *Before Sticklestead.* I shall be bold enough to guard the wing in which I stand. The young poet in his war-joy will not turn his back to the spear, where the missiles are flying.

Sticklestead. See Book vi, § 1, no. 42.

At Sea. King: We make the anchor of the galley take hold in Godnar-firth [Guden-firth in East Jutland], while the lady Gerd is

---

1. Read, nokkur?

Thiodwolf:
Sumar annat skal sunnar (segi-ek eina spá) fleini
[ver aukom kaf króki] kald-nefr furo halda.

4. Skáro iast or osti Eybaugs Dana meyjar 10
(þat of angraðit þengil þing) akkeris hringa:
nú sér mœrg í morgin mær (hlær at því fœri)
œrnan krók or iarni all-valldz skipom halda.

King: 5. Logið hefir Baldr at Baldri:
Thiodwolf: Bryn-þings fetil-stinga
linnz sá-es land á sunnan láð-briótr fyrir ráða: 15
þó es siá niœrðr inn nerðri norðr glym-hríðar borða
(gramr es-þú frœkn ok fremri) fast-málari hála.

King: 6. Hvert stillir þú Halli?
Halli: Hleyp-ek fram at skyr-kaupom.
King: Graut muntu gœrva láta?
Halli: (Gœrr maðr es þat) smiœrvan.

7. Her sé-ek upp inn œrva Einar (þann-es kann skeina 20
þialma) Þambar-skelmi (þangs) fiœl-mennan ganga:
Full-afli bíðr fyllar (finn-ek opt at drífr minna)
hilmis-stóls (á hæla huskarla-lið iarli).

8. Rióðandi mun ráða randar-bliks or landi
oss, nema Einarr kyssi œxar-munn inn þunna. 25

9. Nú emk ellifo allra (eggjom vígs) ok tveggja
(þau ero sva-at ek mani inna orð) ráð-bani vorðinn:
'ginn enn gráleik inna gollz ok ferr með skolli;'
lýtendr kveða lítið lauki gæft-at auka.

---

fondling her husband *at home.—Thiodwolf:* I utter a prophecy. Another
summer Cold-nose [the anchor] shall hold the bark with his fluke
farther south still. We make the anchor-bows dive!
In Jutland. The Danish maids carved anchor-rings out of yeasting-
cheese. That did not vex the king. But this morning many a maiden
may see how the huge iron flukes hold the king's ship. None of them
will laugh now!
Sweyn would not keep tryst or truce. Harold: King has lied to king.—
Thiodwolf: Warrior to swordsman. I saw the King of the South; but
the King of the North is truer to his word. Thou art the better king.
King: Whither art thou slinking, Halli?—*Halli:* I am running off to
buy curds.—*King:* Thou wilt be having porridge?—*Halli:* With butter
—dainty food!
At the Capture of Einar. Here is the bold Einar gut-shaker with
his company; he knows how to plow the sea. In his pride he looks
forward to filling the throne. I have often seen a less number of
retainers at an earl's heels. He will scheme us out of the land, unless
he kiss the thin lips of the axe.
Harold at Calf's death. Now I have caused the death of eleven men
and two, that I can remember. These men are showing treason,
schemes, and plots. Little makes the leek grow, they say.

---

27. orð] morð, Cd.

10.　Kriúpo ver fyr vápna (val-teigs) bræokon eigi　30
　　　(svá bauð hildr at hialdri hald-orð) í bug skialdi:
　　　Hátt bað mik (þar-es mǿttosk) men-skorð bera forðom
　　　(Hlakkar íss ok hausar) hialm-stall í gný malma.

Fisher :　　　III. KING, THIODWOLF, AND FISHER.

1.　ÓFÚSA dró-ek ýso, átta-ek fang við laungo,
　　　vann-ek of hæfði hennar hlæomm—*Enn þat var skömmo :*
　　　þó man-ek hitt at hrotta hafðak golli vafðan,
　　　dúðom dæorr í blóði drengs—*Vas þat fyr lengra.*
King :
2.　Hioggo harða dyggir hirð-menn Dani stirða,　5
　　　sótti ferð á flótta framm—*Enn þat vas skömmo :*
　　　Hitt vas fyrr es fiarr: fóstr-landi rauð-ek branda,
　　　sverð í Serkja garði sæong—*Enn þat vas löngo.*
Thiodwolf :
3.　Mildingr rauð í Móðo, (mót íllt vas þar) spiótom ;
　　　Dæonom váro goð geira græom—*Enn þat vas skömmo :* 10
　　　Setti niðr á slétto Serklandi gramr merki,
　　　stóð at stillis ráði stæong—*Enn þat vas löngo.*
Fisher :
4.　Heyr-þú á upp-reist orða, otvín, konungr, mína,
　　　gaf mer goll it vafða gramr—*Vas þat fyr skömmo :*
　　　Saddir æorn, ok eyddir æorom Blámanna fiæorvi,　15
　　　gall styr-fengins stilliss strengr—*Vas þat fyr lengra.*
King :
5.　Hlaut-ek af hrauðung skióta hlýri, mær in skýra,
　　　skeið gekk felld á flǿði framm—*Vas þat fyr skömmo :*

At Stamford-bridge.　We do not crouch behind the hollow of our shields in the crash of weapons.　The faithful lady bade me be bold in battle.　Of yore she bade me bear my head high where swords and skulls met.　*Hardly genuine.　Another verse attributed to him (quoted from an old song paraphrased in Saxo,* Book i) *is given in* Book vi, no. 45.

III.　*Fisherman :* I pull up the struggling haddock, and grapple with the ling.　I beat its head in with my club, a short while ago.　But I remember how I held a gold-wound Hrunting [sword] ; we dipped our darts in men's blood, a long while ago.—*King :* My gallant guard cut down the stubborn Danes, they fled away, a short while ago.　But before that I made my sword sing in the Saracen's city, a long while ago.—*Thiodwolf :* The king dyed his spears at the Mouth *of Niz.*　The gods of the lance were angry with the Danes, a short while ago.　The king planted his banner on the flats of the Saracen land, and the staff stood still by his command, a long while ago.—*Fisherman :* Hear my song's beginning ! The king gave me the twisted gold, a long while ago.　Thou didst rob the Blackamoors of life, a long while ago.—*King :* I launched my ship in haste, O lady, and the well-payed galley ran out to sea, a short while

Enn fyr 'England' sunnan '6ð' borð und mer norðan,
ristin skalf í ræstom ræng—*Enn þat vas löngo.*   20
Fisher :
6.   Víg létzt Vinda mýgir virðom kunn of unnin,
Þrœndir drifo ríkt und randir, ræmm—*Enn þat vas skömmo :*
Enn fyr Serkland sunnan snarr þengill hió drengi ;
kunni gramr at gunni gœng—*Enn þat vas löngo.*
Cod. Fris. adds—Salt-burner :
7.   Fer-ek í vánda verjo, 'ver nauð' of mer snauðom ;   25
kausungr fær víst í vási vœmm—*Enn þat vas skömmo :*
Endr vas hitt at hrundi hring-kofl of mik Inga,
gœgl báro sik sára svœng—*Enn þat vas löngo.*
8.   Brendom brúk á sandi, bauð-ek hyr þara rauðom,
reyk-svælan tók riúka ræmm—*Enn þat vas skömmo.*   30

ULFR STALLARI.

E SA stallarom stilliss stafn-rúm Haraldz (iafnan)
(ónauðigr fekk-ek auðar) innan þœrf at hverfa :
Ef, hœr-skorðan, hrœkkva hrein skolom tveir fyr einom
(ungr kendak mer) undan (annat) Þinga-manni.

KING MAGNUS THE GOOD (BARELEG?).

M ARGR kveðr ser at sorgom sverð-rióðr alin verða
(uggi-ek all-lítt seggja ótta) bú-karls dóttor :
Enn ef einhver bannar eld-gefn fyrir mer svefna,
víst veldr siklings systir svinn andvœko minni.

---

ago. But south of Sicily the ship tossed under me from the north, its
ribs rattled in the swirl [off Messina], a long while ago.—*Fisherman :*
Thou didst fight far-famed battles ; the Thronds flocked under shield,
a short while ago ; but south off Saracen-land thou didst cut down
warriors, a long while ago.

Salt-burner. Another version. I go in a poor frock, a smock covers
me in my need. A jacket covers me in the wet, since a short while ago.
But of yore the ring-cowl of Ingwi clothed me, a long while ago. I
burnt weed on the sand, I set fire to the red tang, the bitter smoke
began to reek, a short while ago. . . .

Wolf the Marshal before Stamford-bridge. It is no use for the king's
marshals to turn into the forecastle, if two of us, lady, are to fly before
one 'Thing-man' [guard of the English king]. I did not learn this in
my youth.

King Magnus in love. Many a man complains that a cotter's daughter
was born for his sorrow ; but if any woman banishes sleep from me, it
is the king's sister.

---

19. Read, Sikley . . . sveif?   25. Read, vesl.   1. alin] read, alna.

§ 4. KING ERIC THE GOOD OF DENMARK, AND MAGNUS BARELEG AND HIS SONS (1093–1130).

THE Danish King ERIC THE GOOD—Eirikr Gódi, as the Annals call him (1095–1103), whose poet Mark heads this section—for him and his father and brothers, see Introduction to § 3.

But as for the Norse kings of this period—

The quiet reign of Olaf Haroldsson (1067–93, died Sept. 22, 1093) was not marked by such deeds as the court poets loved to sing. His motto, 'Farmers and Peace' (see the Ditty 46, Book vi), was not one to please them. His son Magnus, on the other hand, took after his grandfather Harold, and was the last king of the real old type, adventurous as Charles XII himself, and not without dreams of a mighty sea-empire, the realisation of which was impossible. His pleasure in the storm in the North Sea, when the 'seventy feet wand' was swaying in the ship and bending to the force of the gale, shows the same spirit that breathes through the Helgi Lays.

Twice in his ten years—first in 1098 and again in 1102—'Fighting-Magnus' (like Fairhair two centuries earlier) crossed the main and harried in the Islands. He dressed like the half-Gaelic chieftains of the Irish and Scotch coasts, in the saffron-dyed pleated shirt and long mantle, whence he got one of his nicknames, 'Bareleg.' It was his deadly aim that slew the doughty Norman earl off Anglesey, his exultant shout that marked his enemy's fall. All through his short career he lived up to the device he had chosen—'Kings should live for glory rather than grey hairs.' But like his grandfather, he perished by a blow from an unknown hand, for he fell on the 24th August, 1103, in an ambush set for him by the wild Irish, near Downpatrick, where he is buried. Yet his plans, the restoration of Harold Fairhair's colonial empire over the Isles (Orkney, Sudrey, Anglesea, the Isle of Man, for he laid claim on all the isles, including Cantyre), did not quite fail. He was long after his death a bugbear to the Scots, still remembered in Ossianic ballad. Shock-head's [see vol. i. p. 258] expedition was the first, but the third and last, pompous and badly managed, was that of King Hakon in 1263, who meant to restore Fairhair's and Bareleg's empire.

And now the Norse colonies, memorials of the great wickings and kings of old, fell off óne by one. By the Treaty of Perth, 1266, Man and the Hebrides were lost. Two centuries later, in 1468–9, Orkneys and Shetland were pledged and never redeemed. All trade with Iceland, Greenland, Faroe ceased. The Greenland colony, deserted by the mother country, perished in the fifteenth century [by famine and plague?]; trading in Iceland passed into English hands (fifteenth century); though the Norse fishermen remained what they have always been, the best seamen and boat-builders ever known.

Magnus left three young sons who reigned together, and with them died out the true line of Harold Fairhair, the Ynglings whom Thiodwolf had traced to the gods. The youngest, *Olaf*, died in his youth (1116); *Eystan the Lawyer*, who stayed at home like his grandfather the

Farmer-King, died 29 Aug. 1122; and the third, *Sigurd the Crusader*, who chose the other path and went abroad and accomplished the crusade of which Northmen long boasted, but when he came home he fell into a mischievous madness, and died 26 March, 1130, aged forty years.

Except Mark's poem, taken from Skioldunga, the poems of this Section, like those of the preceding, are, where there is no statement to the contrary, taken from Hulda, Kringla . . . .

MARK SKEGGISSON THE LAW-SPEAKER. A man, on Ari's testimony in Kristni Saga, ' The wisest of all the Law-speakers next to Skapti.' ' From his narration,' he also says in Libellus Islandorum, ' has been written down the lives of all the Speakers of the Law in this book [referring to the lost Liber Islandorum in which they must have existed]; all those, I say, which were before our memory. But he was informed by Thorarin his brother [the poet, we think], and Skeggi their father, and other wise men, of the life of those that were before his memory, according to the narration of Bearni the Wise, their father's father, who could remember Thorarin the Law-Speaker and six more after him.' Mark is mentioned in the Laws, as Gaius or Ulpian are cited in the Digest, and his decisions were looked on as authoritative. His Speakership lasted from 1084 to 1108; died 15th Oct. [1108?]. He had a daughter Walgerd; for her offspring, see Sturl. ii. 489 (Table).

As a poet he is high in the rank of court-poets. His ' hryn-hend' *Dirge on Eric of Denmark* (1103) is interesting from its tone, which rings to a nobler chord than Arnor's glowing but boisterous work. It praises the king for deeds of Peace and Order, derives his epithets from law and peace rather than war, and is a welcome relief from the monotonous strain of most of Harold's poets, whose delight is in the shedding of blood, setting banquets for the wolves, dying their blades in the rain of the tempest of Woden, and the like,—though something must be set to the remodeller's score. Nor is Mark a mean craftsman. He has all the melody which one expects from poets of his day, and he was highly esteemed for his skill by such exacting critics as Snorri and Olaf.

We have bits of longer poems of his on *Christ*, on Eric's brother *King Cnut the Saint* of Denmark, and a morsel of a *Sea Song*, and a *Satire*.

The long poem on Eric the Good is of high value, not only from its style, but from its contents. It is addressed to Nicholas, the last of ' the five kings,' whose brother Eric was; [unlike Saxo and Knytlinga, Mark seems to count Harold, Cnut, Olaf, *Biorn*, Nicholas.] Its successive strophes deal (1) with *Eric's Visit to Gardric;* (2) his glorious rule, generosity, good law, upholding of canon law, memory, learning, and knowledge of tongues; (3) recounts his pilgrimage to Rome (1093), with the splendid reception he met with, and its happy results—the founding of the archbishop's see at Lund, which was for many years afterwards the centre of Danish culture and Christendom. His *War with the Wends* takes up strophe 4, the apostacy of these heathens rousing the anger of the pious king and the lawyer-poet. In the next strophes (5–6) he recurs to the *defensive measures* and *ecclesiastical work* of Eric, the Danish St. David, who founded ' five stone minsters,' ' head churches.' The *Visit to the Emperor* (7), the lord of Franconia, when final arrangements were probably made with regard to Lund. The *Consecration of Ozur* (8) was not Eric's doing (it took place in the year following his death), nor does the poet imply this; he merely turns aside to pay a compliment to the archbishop, who was sitting, we may fancy, by Nicholas's side when the Encomium was delivered. Strophe 9 tells of Eric's *Second and final pilgrimage to Palestine* (1102), which was the forerunner of the exploits of Sigurd of Norway (1107-1109) and Earl Rognwald of Orkney (1151-1152). His visit to the Emperor of the Greeks, from whom he received a royal robe and 'half a last' of gold, and to whom he gave fourteen war-ships, is to be noted. Part of a strophe on Eric's death in Cyprus (10), and bits of other lost stanzas, complete all we have of the poem, which is very well preserved. The *Improvisation* on the ship as a Bear is one of the best examples of the 'conceits' of Mark's day.

I. HRYNHENDA, *or* EIRIKS-DRÁPA, c. 1104-1108.

(Verses 1-3 and 27 from Edda.)

1. HARRA kveð-ek at hróðr-gœrð dýrri hauk-lundaðan Dana grundar.

2. Eireks lof verðr œld at heyra, engi maðr veit fremra þengil; (Yngvi hélt við orðrz-tír langan iœfra sess) í verœld þessi.

3. Fiarri hefir at fáðisk dýrri flotna vœrðr á él-kers botni (háva leyfir hverr maðr ævi hring-varpaðr) gialfri kringðom. 5

4. Fœðir sótti fremdar ráða foldar vœrðo austr í Garða; auði gœddo allvald prúðan ítrir menn þeir-es hnœggvi slíta: Stillir varð um Austr-veg allan einkar tíðr inn mærðar blíði; hinn vas engr es hans nafn kunnit heiðar-mannz í lofi reiða.

5. Vár œndurt bió Vinda rýrir vegligt flaust or Gœrðom austan (hlýrom skaut á hola bœro helmings oddr) í sumars broddi: 11 hlýðo studdi borð-við breiðan bróðir Knútz í veðri óðo; síðan knátti svik-folks eydir snilli-kendr við Danmœrk lenda.

6. Drengir þœgo auð af Yngva, œrr fylkir gaf sverð ok knœrro (Eirekr veitti opt ok stórom arm-leggjar rœf) dýrom seggjom: 15 hringom eyddi harra slœngvir hildar ramr, enn stillir framði fyrða kyn, svá-at flestir urðo, Fróða stóls, af hónom góðir.

7. Vœrgom eyddi Vinda fergir, víkingom hepti konungr fíkjom; þiófa hendr lét þengill stýfa, þegnom kunni hann ósið hegna:

I. ERIC'S PRAISE. *Prologue.* I call on the gallant king of the Danes [Nicholas] to listen to my precious song.

People shall hear the PRAISE OF ERIC, no one knows a better king in this world. He held his throne to his lasting fame; never shall a goodlier king be borne on the surf-ringed floor of the wind's chalice [earth]. Every one praises his lofty life.

His visit to the East. The nourisher of mighty schemes visited the kings east in Gard; they, generous, gave him wealth, he became famous all over the East-way. There was no one but praised his name. Early in the spring, at the point of summer, the dread of the Wends made ready his gallant ships to sail West from Gard; the captain launched his barks on the hollow waves; Cnut's brother strengthened his broad bulwarks with weather-boards in the mad storm, and at last landed in Denmark.

His glory. He gave swords and ships to his good lieges. Yea, the lord of Frodi's Throne helped his people so that all got good from him. The Terror of the Wends thoroughly purged the land of Wickings [pirates]; he cut the hands off thieves, he knew how to punish breach of law. Thou hast never heard of Eric's wresting righteous judgment;

alldri fréttu at Eirekr vildi all-réttligom dómi halla;   20
hála kunni ser til sælo sigrs valdari Goðs lœghalda.

8. Hróðigr átti bryn-þings beiðir biartan auð ok frœknligt hiarta,
minni gnógt, ok man-vit annat mest, fylgðo því hvergi lestir :
alla hafði ꜵðlingr snilli, ungr nam hann margar tungor;
Eirekr vas, svá at mátti meira, mestr ofr-hugi, iꜵfri flestom. 25

9. Lýst skal hitt, es lofðungr fýstisk langan veg til Róms at ganga
(fylkir sá þar frið-land balkat Feneyjar-líð) dýrð at venja :
Bróðir gekk í Bár út síðan (bragningr vildi goð-dóm magna)
[hylli Goðs mun hlífa stilli] hꜵfuð-skiꜵldunga fimm [at
giꜵldom].

10. Stóra sótti Haraldz hlýri helga dóma út frá Rómi ;   30
hringom varði átt-konr Yngva auðig skrín ok golli rauðo :
mildingr fór um Munka-veldi móðom fœti sꜵl at bœta ;
sveitir kníði all-valdr austan ; Eirikr vas til Róms í þeiri.

11. Eirekr náði útan at fœra Erki-stól um Saxa-merki
(hliótom ver þat-es hag várn bœtir) hingat norðr (at skiꜵld-
ungs orðom) :   35
Eyðisk hitt at iafn-stórt ráði annarr gramr til þurftar mꜵnnom ;
leyfði allt sem konungr krafði Kristz unnandi Pávi sunnan.

12. Veldi þorðot Vindr at halda (villan gœrðisk þeim at illo),
[sunnan kom þá svíkdóms manna sátta-rof]þat-es buðlungr átti ;
Yngvi hélt í óða-strꜵngom ꜵldo-gangi skipom þangat,   40
hlýðan skalf, enn hristo græði hélog bꜵrð, fyr Vinda gꜵrðom.

13. Rꜵndo lauk um rekka-kindir risno-maðr svá at hver tók aðra ;
hamalt (knꜵtto þá hlífar glymja) hildingr fylkti liði miklo :

---

he upheld to the utmost the laws of God [the church law] to his own
profit. He had bright wealth, a bold heart, a good memory, and other
gifts of mind to the utmost, and all without blemish ; he had all kinds of
knowledge, he learnt many tongues in his youth. Eric was the most
high-minded, the best of all kings beside.

His Pilgrimage. It shall be told how the king went the long-path to
Rome to win a share in its glory; there he saw the fenced land of
refuge. After this the brother of five kings went on to Bari to the glory
of the Godhead ; and God's grace will keep his soul safe therefore.
Harold's brother visited the great halidoms [relics, etc.] in Rome ; he
adorned the rich shrines with rings and red gold ; he went with weary
feet round the realm of the monks [Rome] for his soul's good ; he passed
on from the East and came to Rome withal. Eric carried from abroad
an archbishop's see over the Saxon March hither in the North [the
archiepiscopal see of Lund]. Our *spiritual* state is the better by his act.
It is impossible that another king should do as much for our *souls'*
needs. The pope, Christ's friend, in the south granted all that he asked
of him.

His war with the Wends. The Wends durst not keep the realm that
was his. Their apostacy cost them dear. When the traitors' rebellion
was heard from the south, he sailed with his ships in a swelling sea
thither, the weather-boards shivered, and the cold timbers troubled the
sea off the Wends' land. The king arrayed his men in a great shielded

Styrjæld óx um stilli ærvan; stengr bǽro framm vísiss drengir;
mildingr gekk at miklom hialdri malmi skrýddr ok faldinn
hialmi.   45

14. Hǽrga varðisk herr í borgom; hialdr-ganga vas snæroð
þangat;
harðir kníðosk menn at morði; merki blés um hilmi sterkjan:
Eirekr vakði odda-skúrir; eggjar týndo lífi seggja;
sungr iærn, enn sǽfðosk drengir; sveiti fell á val-kæst heitan.

15. Blóðit dreif á rand-garð rauðan; rógs hegnir drap ótal
þegna;   50
framði sik, þar-es folk-vǽpn glumðo, fylkir ungr, enn brynjor
sprungo:
Heiðinn vildi herr um síðir hæmlo vígs ór porti gæmlo;
urðo þeir es virkit værðo vangi næst á hænd at ganga.

16. Heiðin vóro hiærton lýða hrygðar-full í Vinda bygðom;
eldrinn sveif um ótal hælða; Eirekr brendi sali þeira: 55
eisor kyndosk hátt í húsom; hallir nǽðo vítt at falla;
ótto leið; enn uppi þótti elris grand í himni standa.

17. Eirekr vas með upp-reist hári; undan flýðo Vindr af stundo;
giæld festo þá grimmir hælðar; gumnar vóro sigri numnir:
Yngvi talði erfðir þangat; alþýða varð stilli at hlýða;   60
veldi réð því ást-vinr aldar; einart lá þat fyrr und Sveini.

18. Flaustom lukði folka treystir foldar síðo brimi kníða,
ærr vísi bað oddom læsa úrga strænd ok svalri rændo:
hlífom keyrði hersa reyfir harðla nýtr um land it ýtra;
hilmir lauk við hernað stóran hauðr Ey-Dana skiald-borg rauðri.

19. Víða setti vísdóms grǿðir virki skrýddar hæfuð-kirkjcr 66
gœrva let þar holl-vinr herjar hrein musteri fimm af steini:
vóro þau með trygðar tíri tíða flaustr, es gramr lét smíða
bæðvar sniallr ok baztr at ællo, borði mest fyr Saxland norðan.

---

war-wedge, so that target touched target. The fray waxed high about
the gallant prince. The host of the fanes [heathen] defended themselves
in their strongholds, the banner blew over the strong king. Eric waked
the war, he slew men unnumbered. The heathen host tried to sally
out of the ancient town. Heathen hearts were sorrowful in the country
of the Wends. Eric kindled the lofty flame in their houses; Eric had
great good fortune, the Wends fled away forthwith; that gruesome folk
paid ransom, being reft of victory. The king claimed his heritage there,
it had formerly lain under Sweyn's sway.
His defensive measures. He bade them guard his watery shores with
spear and cold shield. He locked the land of the Island-Danes with a
red shield-fortress against great raids.
His good works. The nurse of wisdom [king] raised walled head-
churches [cathedrals] in many places; the patron of men built five
polished minsters of stone; these ships of services [naves horarum], which
this most gallant king and noblest built to his true glory [devoutly], were
the loftiest north of Saxony [Germany].

---

69. mest] emend.; merkt, Cd.

20.   Blíðan gœddi biœrtom auði Biarnar hlýra Frakklandz stýrir;
      stórar lét ser rand-garðz rýrir ríks keisara giafar líka: 71
      Hánom lét til her-vígs búna harra spialli láð-menn snialla
      alla leið, áðr œðlingr næði Ióta grundar Cesars fundi.

21.   Dróttom lét í Danmœrk settan dœglingr grundar skamt frá
      Lundi
      Erki-stól þann-es œll þióð dýrkar, elion-þungr, á Danska
      tungo: 75
      Hildingr framði heilagt veldi; hvar-gegnan má Otzor fregna
      (hónom vísar hœlda reynir himna-stíg) til byskops vígðan.

22.   Lýst skal hitt, es læknask fýstisk lið-hraustr konungr sœr
      in iðri;
      norðan fór með helming harðan hersa mœðir sœl at grœða:
      harri biósk til heims ens dýrra; hann gærði fœr út at kunna.   80
      (buðlungr vildi biart líf œðlask) bygð Iórsala í friði trygða.

23.   Bóro menn or borgom stórom bleyði-skiarrs á móti harra
      (sungit vas þá-es herr tók hringja) hnossom gœfgoð skrín ok
      krossa:
      Aldri fær í annars veldi iœfra ríkir metnað slíkan;
      eitt vas þat es iafnask mátti engi maðr við Dana þengil.   85

24.   Hildingr þá við hæst lof aldar hœfgan auð i golli rauðo,
      halfa lest af harra siœlfom, harðla ríkr, í Miklagarði:
      áðan tók við allvaldz skrúði Eirekr þó-at gefit vas fleira;
      reynir veitti her-skip hánom, hersa máttar, sex ok átta.

25.   Andar krafði út í lœndom allz-stýrandi konung sniallan;   90
      elli beiðat of-vægr stillir; aldr-stríð es frægt es víða:

The interview with the Frankish Emperor. The lord of Frankland [Fran-
conia] gratified Biorn's brother [Eric] with bright wealth, and he was
pleased with the great gifts of the mighty Emperor, who gave him good
guides all the way till the Etheling of Jutland reached Cæsar.
    The founding of the province of Lund. The king founded an archbishop's
throne a short way from Lund, which all men of the Danish Tongue
should reverence. He forwarded the holy province. The wise Ozur
was consecrated as bishop there, to whom the Patron of men [Christ]
shows the pathway of heaven.
    His Pilgrimage to Palestine. It shall be told how the gallant king
prepared to heal his inner wounds [his soul's hurt]. He went from the
north with a brave company to heal his soul; he made him ready for
the Dear World [heaven]; he went his way to seek Jerusalem-land in
fair peace; he wished to win a life of light [in heaven]. Men bore
splendid jewelled shrines and roods out of the great cities to meet him;
they sung to the pealing of bells. Never gat king such honour in
another king's dominion. It is certain that no other man could match
the king of the Danes. He received a weight of wealth in red gold, half
a last from the mighty lord of Micklegarth [Constantinople] himself,
and the praise of all men withal. He received a king's robe and more
beside *of the Emperor,* and gave him six and eight war-ships in return.
    His death. The Ruler of all [God] required the king's soul in a

Síðan harma siklings dauða sniallir menn um heims-bygð alla ;
drúpir herr at dolga steypi dyggvan ; þótti verøld hryggva.

26.   Hvergi stóðosk hiørva borgar hristi-meiðar konungs reiði ;
raunar varðat rønd við hánom reist, gœrðot þess iøfrar freista :
ógnin stóð af iarla meiði ; engi þorði kapp at strengja   96
(flestir ugðo fold-vørð hraustan) fylkir snarr við Dana harra.

27.   Ræsir lét af roðnom hausi Rínar sól á mar-fiøll skína.

II. On St. Knute? (from Skalda).

1. HIART-FŒRRA veit harri hrein-vazta sik baztan
2.   Ríkr es harra hneykir, heldr Goð iøfurs veldi,
sann-dyggs vitoð seggir Sveins brœðr konung œðra.

III. Christ-drápa (Skalda).

Stef.: GRAMR skóp grund ok himna glygg-rannz sem her
dyggvan ;
einn stillir má øllo alldar Kristr of valda.

IV. Of a Voyage (from Edda).

FIARÐ-LINNA óð fannir fast vetrliði rastar ;
hlióp of húna gnípor hvals-rannz iugtanni :   2
biørn gekk framm á fornar flóðs haf-skipa slóðir ;
skúr-ørðigr braut skorðo skers glym-fiøtor bersi.

V. Some Libel (from Skalda).

SŒGS man-ek síðr an eigi (sá es fllr es brag spillir)
sólar sverri-málan glíðr-áls Regin níða.

---

foreign land ; this public sorrow has been noised far and wide. Good
men, all over the inhabited earth, bewail his death ever since ; the world
mourns.
   His prowess. No man durst withstand the king's wrath, no prince
even tried to do so. Terror was shed from him ; no prince ever dared
to match his prowess with the king of the Danes.
   His ships. He let the gold shine from the red figure-heads down upon
the mountains of the sea.
   II. On St. Cnut. .... best of kings. Mighty is he ; God supports
his power ; men know no king greater than Sweyn's brother.
   III. On Christ. *Burden.* The king of the winds' hall [heaven]
created earth, and heaven, and all men. Christ, the lord of men, alone
rules all things.
   IV. Improvisation. The bear of the stream waded through the waves ;
the mast-bear ran over the peaks of the whale-abode ; the flood-bear
wended forward through the old track of the ships [sea] ; the high-
headed bear of the waters clove the roaring sea.
   V. Satire. I am far from lampooning him. He that wrests a song
is a bad man.

2. Emend.; hliop ok huna gnipor hval iugtanni hranna, W.

GISL ILLUGISSON AND HIS FELLOWS.

A DESCENDANT of Bragi, as may be seen by his pedigree (p. 2). His highly romantic career may be read in Magnus Barefoot's Life. He came to Norway when seventeen years old, and slew his father's slayer, Giafald, one of the king's henchmen, for which he was condemned to death; and was only saved by the wisdom of John (since Bishop of Holar), who, with the rest of the Icelandic colony in Norway (Nidaros), interceded with the incensed king. He was with the king on his Anglesey expedition. His Poem on *Magnus Bareleg* is in plain old metre, almost perfect, in four sections, which deal with the *Rebellion of Egil and Thori*; the *Western Foray*, when Hugh was slain, ll. 49–53; the *Gale* on the way back to Norway; and the *Gautland Campaign*. There are many fine touches and noteworthy passages in this poem. We have besides an improvisation of his in prison.

BIORN CRAMPHAND. A *Poem on King Magnus* by this poet, of whom nought else has reached us, is rich in names of Western Islands,—Lewes, Uist, Tyrvist, Mull, Sandey, Santire [Cantyre], Man; it mentions the slaying of Hugh the Proud in Anglesey Sound, and runs parallel to Gisli's, which it supplements.

KING MAGNUS BARELEG. A *Love-Song on Mahthild* is ascribed to this king in Frisbok and Fagrskinna, but they appear to belong to a later time, and there is '*r*' for '*s*' (hvat'r) in the fifth line, which makes one hesitate to believe it his. It has, however, been very badly treated, so that it is hard to judge of it definitely. Another *verse on an Irish love* is far better, and one would like to think it his.

The *Improvisation on Giffard*, the cowardly French knight, is also his.

ELDIARN OF CONSTANTINOPLE. He is known from his rebuke to the cowardly Giffard, who stowed himself away during the battle at Foxern, and lay helpless in the ship which brought him back to England. When they landed, Giffard went to the city and complained to the reeve of the lampoons of Eldiarn. 'The reeve was a young man, and had but lately taken up his office, and he said he would listen to his plea, according to the state of the case as he should find it.' A moot was called, and the Northman summoned, and the case came on. Eldiarn denied that he had libelled Giffard, and offered to recite the poem if the reeve liked. The reeve said, 'I have not yet had much experience of law, but I know still less how to deal with what you call poetry, nevertheless let us hear it.' So Eldiarn, in high-sounding words, praised Giffard for his noble deeds at Foxern, where he had run away. And the reeve said, 'I don't understand poetry, but I can see that this is not libellous but laudatory, and I can give no other judgment.' Giffard could not explain the true state of the case for very shame.

ANONYMOUS. Popular verses on the pretenders and rebels of Magnus' days, especially on Thori, vv. 1, 2, 3. The fourth is a fine verse on a ship plunging in the gale, a noble bit of Sea-Poetry.

1. UNGR framði hann sik, þá-es alendr vildo
        lof-sælan gram landi ræna,
    Imðar faxa; enn iœfurr sótti

GISL ILLUGISSON. *Magnus' Praise. The Rebellion of Egil and Thori of Skye.* He fought in his youth when they wished to rob him of his land [lit. Woden's bride], but he sought them with the black blade.

Báleygs 'viðo' með blám hiœrvi.

2. Ýtti or Osló til Egils fundar   5
    lofðungr liði landz at krefja :
    fylgðo ræsi ok Rygir sunnan
    linnz láð-gefendr ór lœgom tvennom.

3. Siá knátti þá siklings flota
    vel vígligan vanan sigri :   10
    þá-es fyr Yrjar í aga miklom
    óþrotligt lið árar kníði.

4. Átti hilmir hús-þing við sió,
    þat vas fyr innan Örva-hamra :
    biósk at brenna, enn buendr flýðo   15
    stór-ráðr konungr af Staði útan.

5. Raufsk við rosto, rymr varð í her,
    helmingr Egils við Hlaðir útan ;
    mœttoð hersar við Haða-dróttni
    láð-gœfgoðom landi ráða.   20

6. Hyrr sveimaði, hallir þurro,
    gekk hár logi um hérað þeira :
    siá knátti þar es salir fello
    land-ráð konungs um liði Þóriss.

7. Sœttisk síðan, siðr batnaði,   25
    hug-fullr konungr við hatendr sína :
    þann gat bragningr, es buendr œtto,
    rétt ráð-spakr rekkom launat.

8. Gramr vann gœrvan, enn glatað þiófom,
    kaup-mœnnom frið þannz konungr bœtti :   30
    sva-at í Elfi œxom hlýddi
    flaust fagr-buin firom at skorða.

9. Tók fyr Skíði, enn Skottar flýðo,
    iœfra œgir Ivistar gram :

He set forth out of Oslo to meet Egil to claim his land, and the Rygs [of Rogaland] followed him and the men out of two laws [Gulalaw and Heithlaw]. His fleet was very warlike, and victorious to look on, when they plied their oars with great power away off Yria [mouth of Throndham-firth]. The king held a husting at sea, off Arrow-Hammer, and made ready in his anger to burn all north from Cape Stad. The franklins fled. Egil's company broke up north of Lather; there was a murmuring in their host; the barons could not prevail against the lord of Hada-land. The fire wandered wide, the halls were consumed, and the high flame walked over their land. The king's anger was shown when the halls fell about Thori's men's heads. Then the king made peace with his rebels, and they repented, and he gave back to the franklins the rights they had before. The king punished thieves, but kept the peace for the merchants, so that they could safely shore up their fair busses with their axes on the Elbe [the *Gaut Elb*]. *The first land-foray* (1098) *to the West.* The king took the lord of

---

4. Read, bruði or vino.   19. mattoð, Hrokk.

hafði fylkir, sá-es frami tœði,   35
Lœgmann konung í liði síno.

10. Ætt-lœnd um vann Eyja dróttar
folk-vœrðr und sik fiórom þrungit:
áðr an hitti, sá-es hamalt fylkti,
veðr-smiðr Viðors Valska iarla.   40

11. Háðom hildi með Haraldz frænda
Önguls við ey innan-verða:
þar-es af reiði ríkis-vændir
konungr ok iarlar kapp sítt bruto.

12. Margan hœfðo Magnús-liðar   45
biœrtom oddi baug-vang skorit:
varð hertoga hlíf at springa
kapps vel skipoð fyr konungs darri.

13. Bœð-kennir skaut bœðom hœndom
allr vá hilmiss herr prúðliga: 50
stukko af almi, þeims iœfurr sveigði,
hvít-mylingar áðr Hugi félli.

14. Hœfðo seggir, þá vas sókn lokit,
heim-fœr þegit af hœfuðs-manni:
land-menn lito yfir liði gœfgo   55
segl siá-drifin sett við húna.

15. Vágr þrútnaði, enn vefi keyrði
stein-óðr á stag storðar galli:
braut dýrr dreki und Dana skelfi
hrygg í hverri hafs glym-brúði.   60

16. Blár ægir skaut búnom svíra,
gialfr hlióp í gin gollno hœfði;
skein af hœfðom sem himins-eisa
dœglings dreka diúps val-fasti.

Uist off Skye; the Scots fled; he kept King Lawman in his company.
Four heritages [four provinces, Hebrides, Orkneys, Shetlands, and Man]
of the Island people the king subdued by force before he met the Welsh
[French] earls. I fought beside Harold's kinsman [grandson] inside
Anglesey, when the ambitious king and earls tried their prowess fiercely
together. Magnus' men scored many a target with their bright spear-
points. Many a well-made buckler of the duke's was sprung by the
king's dart. The king shot with both hands, and all his men fought
gallantly; the white arrow-heads sped from the bow he drew, ere
Hugh fell.

The voyage back. When the battle was over, the king's men got home-
leave from their captain. The men of the land saw the sea-bleached sai'
hoisted to the top over the noble crews. The wave rose high, and the
mad gale drove the canvas forward of the stays. The goodly dragon
bearing the dread of the Danes, broke the back of every daughter o'
Ocean [billow]. Black Ocean struck the carven neck, and the sea
leaped into the jaws of the golden figure-head; the gold shone like the
fire of heaven [the sun] from the heads of the king's dragon-ships.

17. Framðisk síðan á Svia dróttni   65
     austr frá Elfi Upplanda gramr:
     Lið-skelfir tók or lægom Gauta
     fimmtán héroð fránni eggjo.
18. Reið folk-hvætoðr fyrst í gœgnom
     safnað Svia sigri hnugginn: 70
     malmr dreyrogr varð á meðal hlaupa
     hauss ok herða hans andskota.
19. Hel-merki bles, enn huginn gladdisk,
     fráno hæfði feðr Sigurðar:
     Þann sá-ek fylki með frama mestom.   75
     snærpo sverði til sigrs vega.
20. Fylgða-ek frœknom seṁ ek framast kunna
     Eysteins feðr í Atals drífo:
     opt brá-ek hiœrvi með Haraldz frænda
     vanr vás-fœrom þars vega þurfti.   80

II. Improvisation.

KÁTR skal-ek enn, þótt ætli aldr-rán viðir skaldi
     (iœrn taka oss at orna) unda-teins (at beinom):
Hverr deyr seggr (enn svarri) [snart es dreng-skapat hiarta]
(prúðr skal-ek enn í óði) eitt sinn (á þrek minnask).

BIÖRN KREPPIL-HENDI.

(Verse 4 from Morkinskinna.)

1. VÍTT lét Vorsa dróttinn (varð skiótt rekinn flótti)
     [hús sveið Hœrða ræsir] Halland farit brandi:
     brendi buðlungr Þrœnda (blés kastar hel fasta)
     [vakði Visk-dœlsk ekkja] víðz mœrg héroð síðan.

Expedition to Gautland. After this the lord of the Uplands won fame over the king of the Swedes, east by *Gaut*-Elbe. He took with his keen sword-edge fifteen hundred out of Gautland. He went foremost through the vanquished herd of Swedes. His gory steel passed between the necks and shoulders of his foes. Hell-mark [his standard] blew over the head of Sigurd's father. Then with greatest glory did I see the king win victory with the sharp sword. I followed the bold father of Eystan in the battle as well as I could. Wont to wet travelling wherever a fray was at hand [on the sea], I often swung the sword beside Harold's kinsman.

Gisli in prison. The irons begin to burn into my legs. I shall be cheery still, even though they mean to put the poet to death. A man can only die once, and, lady, I shall still remember my exploits in my song. A warrior's heart is stout.

BIORN THE CRIPPLE-HANDED *on King Magnus. The War in Halland, Denmark.* The lord of the Wors-folk [from Wors], the prince of the Hords, had Halland burnt. The Thronds' king burnt many hundreds more. The Wisk-dale [Wiskærdal in Halland] lady waked *in fear.*

2. Snarr rauð Sygna harri sverð á úthlaups ferðom   5
    (vítt rann vargr at slíta varma bráð) á Harmi:
    Fráttu hve fylkir mátti (fór svá at hengðr vas Þóri)
    [fœr varð Gunnar gœrviss greið] dróttins svik leiða.

3. Hrafn-greddir vann hrædda hlífar-stygðr, í bygðom,
    Þrœnska drótt, es þótti þeim markar bœl sveima :   10
    hygg-ek at hersa tveggja her-Baldr lyki aldri;
    (sinjór vesa sóro); svangr flaug œrn til hanga.

4. Víkinga lætr vengiss vall-baugs hati falla
    (vítt ryðr iarn á ýtom) Óláfs mœgr (in-fœgro).

5. Lék of Lióðhús fíkjom lim-sorg nær himni;   15
    (vítt bar ferð á flótta fús) [gaus eldr or húsom]:
    œrr skiœldungr fór eldi Ivist; buendr misto
    (róg-geisla vann ræsir rauðan) lífs ok auðar.

6. Hungr-þverrir lét herjat hríðar-gagls á Skíði;
    tann rauð Tyrvist innan teitr vargs í ben margri :   20
    Grætti Grenlandz dróttinn (gekk hátt Skotta stœkkvir);
    [þióð rann Mylsk til mœði] meyjar suðr í Eyjom.

7. Vítt bar sniallr of slétta Sandey konungr randir;
    Rauk um Il, bá-es ióko all-valdz menn á brennor:
    Sanntíris laut sunnar seggja kind und eggjar;   25
    sigr-gœðir réð síðan sniallr Manverja falli.

8. Hætt vas hvert, þat-es átti, hvarf Goðrœðar arfi;
    lœnd vann lofðungr Þrœnda Lœgmanni þar bannat:
    nýtr fekk nesjom útar naðrs-bing-tœpoð finginn,
    Egða gramr, þar-es umðo, ungr, vætt-rima tungor.   30

9. Líf-spelli réð laufa lundr í Önguls-sundi
    (broddr fló þars slœg snuddo snúðigt) Huga-ins-Prúða :

The Rebellion. The lord of the Sogn-folk fought the rebels at Harm [Haloga-land]. Thou hast heard how he made them smart for their treason: it came to pass that Thori was hanged. He frightened the Thronds, when he made the fire walk over their dwellings : he put to death two barons, I ween ; the 'senior' had them hanged. Olaf's son destroyed the robbers.

His voyage to the West (1098). Fire played fiercely to the heavens over Lewes ; he went over Uist with flame ; the yeomen lost life and goods. He harried Skye and Tyrey. The terror of the Scots was in his glory. The lord of Grenland made the maidens weep in the Southern Islands ; the people of Mull ran for fear. Far over the flats of Sanday he warred. There was a smoke over Ila: the king's men fed the flame. Further south, men in Cantyre bowed beneath the sword-edge. He made the Manxmen to fall. Every way of escape was stopped for Godrod's son ; the lord of the Thronds banished Lawman from the land. The Agd-folk's prince caught him off the Nesses [of Skye]. He quickly caused the death of Hugh the Proud in the Sound of Anglesey. The slayer of the Irish [Magnus] has

---

20. tonn, Cd.   25. Thus, the elder form.

aull hefir 'Iota' fellir Ey-lænd farit brandi
(vítt liggr 'dyggs und' dróttom dœglings grund) of stundir.

THORKELL HAMAR-SKALD.

I. *Magnús-drápa.*

1. VÍTT dró sínar sveitir saman stór-hugaðr Þórir
   (heldr vórot þau hœlðom haglig ráð) með Agli:
   snœrp frá-ek á þar, es urpo, endr Skialgs vinom, lendir,
   menn við morð-hauks brynni, mein, um afl ser steini.

2. Orð frá-ek Agli verða, unnar dags, á munni,   5
   sól! við siklings þræla satt einarðar latta:
   Hvern þeira kvað hæra (hialdr-bliks) an sik miklo
   (beið of mikit eyðir angr) makligra at hanga.

3. Vestr lét varga nistir (vann hilmir frið bannat)
   [hrœnn bruto hlýr in stinno] hug-prúðr fœro snúðat. 10

4. Dunði broddr á brynjo; bragningr skaut af magni;
   sveigði all-valdr Egða alm; stœkk blóð á hialma:
   strengs fló hagl í hringa; hné ferð, enn lét verða
   Hœrða gramr í harðri hiarl-sókn banat iarli.

5. Eggendr bað at ugga óhlífinn gramr lífi   15
   hvegi es lét inn lióti land-garðr fyrir barði:
   satt vas at all-valdr átti ógn-snart borit hiarta
   (súð varð í gný græðiss geyst) far-sælo treystask.

6. Hraustr lét Elfi austar all-valdr saman gialla
   (vitr stillir rauð vœllo) Valskan brand ok randir: 20
   Varð á víg, þar es 'Herðir,' vell-mildr konungr, fello,
   (bolr lá Gauzkr und gulri grás arnar kló) þrási.

---

carried fire over all the Islands for a while. The broad . . . . lies in the king's power.

THORKETTLE HAMMER-POET. MAGNUS' PRAISE. *The Rebellion.* Thori and Egil in their pride drew men together; ill-fated was their plan. It was evil for the friends of Skialg when the barons cast 'a stone beyond their strength.' Egil, I ween, spoke a true word to the king's slaves [his executioners], when he said that each of them was worthier to hang than he. He, Egil, met too sad a fate!

Western expedition. He hastened on his warlike way to the West. He shot amain, the lord of the Agd-folk drawing his bow; the bow-string's hail flew on the mail-rings; the lord of the Hords slew the earl in fight.

The voyage back. He bade them not fear for their lives, however the sea might roar at the bows. The king's brave heart was proved; he believed that his voyage would be prosperous.

The War in Gautland. He made the Welsh sword scream on the targets east of the *Gaut*-Elbe; he warred where the Herds [people of Härad?] fell and the Gauts died.

---

33. Read, Ira?   21. Read, Herðir, people of Gautland (Härad).

7.   Upp-gœngo réð Yngvi ítr með helming lítinn;
     áræði hygg-ek áðan Eysteins fœðor treystask:
     Hátt gall hiœrr; enn sótti (hneit egg við fiœr seggja),   25
     [malm-sœkir rauð mæki] Magnus lið í gœgnom.

II. *Another Drápa* (from Edda).

M ER réð senda um svalan ægi
     Vœlsunga niðr vœpn goll-buin.

STRAY VERSES.

I. *Anonymous.*

1.   U NGR kom Hákon hingat (hann es baztr alinn manna)
     frægðar mildr á foldo fór með Steigar-Þóri:
     syni Óláfs bauð síðan sialfr upp Nóreg halfan,
     mildr enn Magnus vildi mál-sniallr hafa allan.

2.   Breðr í Biarkey miðri ból þatz ek veit gólast,   5
     tœra þarft af Þóri (þýtr vandar-bœl) standa:
     Ioan man eigi frýja elldz né ráns es kveldar,
     svíðr biartr logi breiðan bý, leggr reyk til skýja.

3.   Spurði Ull-strengr orða (at rendosk skip hvatla)
     [sverð bito snarpra ferða sætt] hve Þórir mætti: 10
     Lundr kvazk heill at hœndom hiœrs (frágom þat gœrva)
     [gœrðisk glamm á borðom griótz] enn hrumr at fótom.

II. *Anonymous.*

4.   Vegg blæss veðr um tyggja; viðr þolir nauð í lauðri;
     læ tekr klungrs at knýja keip; enn gellr í reipom:

His death in Ireland. He made an inroad with a small company; the son of Eystan trusted in his boldness. Magnus went through the foe, the sword sung shrill.

Fragment of a Praise-Song on King Olaf (?). East over the swollen Ocean the son of the Wolsungs [King of Norway] sent me a gold-mounted weapon.

STRAY VERSES. I. *Unnamed Poet on Magnus' cousin Hakon's death.* Hakon, the best-born man on earth, came over here young and joined Sty-Thori. He offered half Norway to Olaf's son, but Magnus wished to have it all.

On Thori's rebellion. In the midst of Bearkey high burns the merriest homestead I know; the ill is Thori's doing. John will have enough of fire and plundering this evening; the bright flame burns the broad town, the smoke climbs up to the clouds.

Sigurd and Thori. Woolstring asked how Thori did, when the ship drew near. 'Hale in the hands,' said he, 'but tottering on the feet.' We tell the truth.

II. *A Storm at Sea.* The wind blows round the king's ship; the

---

26. í lið, Cd.

miór skelfr (Magnús stýrir; móð skerr eik at flóði)
[beit verða siá slíta] siau-tœgr vœndr [und rœndom].

III. King Magnus' Love-Verses (Fagrsk.).

1.　EIN er su er mer meinar Makthildr, ok vekr hildi,
　　　(már drekkr suðr or sœrom sveita) leik ok teiti:
sá kennir mer svanni, 'sín lond er ver rondo'
(sverð bito Hœgna hurðir) hvít-iarpr sofa lítið.

2.　Hvat 'r í heimi betra (hyggr skald af þrœ sialdan)　5
[miok er langr sa er dvelr drengi dagr] an víf in fœgro:
þungan berr-ek af þingi þann harm, at ek skal svanna
(skreytazk menn at móti) minn aldregi finna.

3.　Iœrp mun eigi verpa orm-hlín á glœ sínom
(orð spyr-ek goll-hrings gerðar) góðom skald (í hlióði):　10
ann-ek, þótt eigi finnak opt, goð-vefjar þopto;
veit menn at ek hygg hennar hála rœktar-mœlom.

4.　Hvatt skal heim-fœr kvitta, hugr er minn í Dyflinni,
enn til Kaupangs kvenna kem-ek eigi austr í hausti:
unik því at eigi synjar Ingjan gaman-þinga;　15
œrskan veldr því er Irskom ann-ek betr an mer svanna.

IV. The Norman Knight.

King:　1. VILL hann eigi flokk várn fylla, falsk riddarinn
　　　　　Valski.

Eldjarn: 2. Hví samir hitt at dúsa hirðmanni geð-stirðom;
　　　　　vestu nú, þo-at kiœl kosti knárr, riddari 'nn hári:

---

timbers labour hard in the foam. The gale tries the rowlocks, and
screams in the rigging; the slim seventy-foot stick [mast] is quivering;
Magnus is steering, and the angry bark cleaves the flood; the shielded
ship cuts through the sea.

III. KING MAGNUS BARELEG. Love-Song. Mahthild alone grieves me,
forbidding me joy or pleasure. That fair brown lady lets me have little
sleep. What is better on earth than a fair woman? The poet never
ceases to pine; long is the day that keeps her away. I carry this heavy
grief home from the moot, that I shall never meet my lady again. The
brown lady will not have cast on the sea her good words about me
which I have heard. I set great store by her loving speech, though I
seldom see her. [Grammar of original is bad and twisted, but the sense is
clear.]
The Irish lady. The King's last Verse. Why should we think of going
home? My heart is in Dublin, and I shall not go back in the autumn
to the ladies of Chipping [Nidaros]. I am glad that the darling does not
deny me her favour. Youth makes me love the Irish girl better than
myself.

IV. On Giffard the Coward. King: He will not take a place in our
band. The Welsh [French] knight hides himself.—Eldjarn: Quit thee
well now, noble knight. Why shouldst thou now be lagging when the

þat-es satt at ek býð bytto (breið-húfoðom) reiða
(austr es til hár á hesti hval-iarðar) Giffarði.   5

Variation of the same.

Spurði gramr hvat gœrði Giparðr þar er lið barðisk,
ver ruðom vápn í dreyra, varat hann kominn þannog:
fram-reiðar var fnauði full-trauðr á ió rauðom.
Vill hann eigi f. v. f. . . .

3.   Frá-ek at flótta rǿkot (falsk annat lið manna),
[þar vas harðr sem ek heyrða hernoðr] á Foxerni:
varð hialm-þrimo hilmiss hárr, þars staddir várom,
gangr, es Gautzka drengi, Giffarðr, í hel barðir.

V. *King and Kali* (Orkn. S.).

Kali :   HVE launa þer þínir þing-ríkir hæfðingjar
(vestr bifask rengr í ræstom) [reyndu oss, konungr]
hnossir?

King :   Auð hef-ek minn, þanns mænnom marg-teitom reð-ek veita,
(húf læt ek klœkkvan klífa kolgor) illa folginn.

HALLDOR SQUALLER; or, HALLDOR SKVALDRI.

THE author of a *Pæan on Sigurd the Crusader's Voyage*, recounting the
taking of eight galleys, the fighting at Cintra, Lisbon, Alkassi, Gibraltar,
the Caves of Algiers, and the expedition to the Balearic islands Iviza
and Minorca, and storming a 'heathen' castle on the coast. He also
made a *poem on Harold Gilli-Christ*. (See § 5.)

THORWALD BLEND-POET. Fragments of two poems of his are preserved. We only know his date from Skalda-tal.

THORARIN CURT-MANTLE (STUTT-FELDR). An Icelander, who
made a *poem* in Tog-metre *on Sigurd's Crusade*, the fragments of
which add to our knowledge of it. He mentions his sixty ships, his
worshipful reception in England, his Formintera and Cave Exploits,
and his reaching the Jordan and visiting 'God's grave.' The poem
runs parallel to that of Halldor. Of the improvisations (1) refers to
the origin of his nickname; the others (2–3) are satirical.

EINAR SCULASON. We treat of him in the introduction to § 5.
We here insert pieces of two of his poems, one on the Crusade of
Sigurd, which tells of his wintering in England, the first winter; in

---

keel is straining? Verily, I offer the bucket to Giffard to hand up,
for the bilge-water is very high in the broad-hulled steed of the whale's
land.

In England before the Port-reeve. I heard that ye drove the flying
host at Foxerne, while other men were hiding away : it was a hard battle,
I heard. It was a mad fray where you were, Giffard, beating the Gauts
to death.

V. *Kali :* How do thy mighty chiefs requite thy gifts? Try me, O
king. The ship is tossing in the current.—*King Magnus :* I have put
the money I gave my men to little profit; I make the crank hull climb
the billows.

Galicia, with an Earl, the next; his passage over the Greek Sea to Acre; his arrival at Jerusalem, and bath in the white water of Jordan. KING SIGURD THE CRUSADER. One verse to his lady—'I have struck a blow in the Saracen's land: let thy husband do the same!'—is attributed to this king.

HALLDÓR SKVALDRI.

(Verses 11, 12 from Edda.)

1. OK fá-dýrir fóro (Fiolniss-hrótz) at móti
    (víg-ǽsom hlóð vísi) víkingar gram ríkjom:
    Náði herr at hrióða (hlaut drengja vinr fengi
    fyrðom hollr; enn féllat fátt lið) galeiðr átta.

2. Stór skal-ek verk, þau-es vóro (Vánar-dags) á Spáni,   5
    (prútt lét slœngvir sóttan Sintra) konungs inna:
    Gœrðisk heldr við harða her-menn gramr berjask
    grátt, es gœrva nítto Goðs rétti ser boðnom.

3. Suðr vannt sigr inn þriðja sniallr við borg, þa-es kalla,
    lofðungs kundr, es lendot, Lissibón, á fróni.   10

4. Út frá-ek yðr, þar-es heitir Alkassi, styr hvassan
    folk-þeysandi fýsask fiórða sinn at vinna:
    unnit frá-ek í einni eyddri borg, til sorga
    (hitti herr á flótta) heiðins vífs (at drífa).

5. Treystosk egg fyr austan (yðr tióði Goð) rióða   15
    [ná-skári fló nýra] Nœrva-sund [til unda].

6. Bœð-styrkir lézt-þú barka (bragnings verk á Serkjom
    fræg hafa gœrsk) fyr gýgjar gagn-stíg ofan síga:
    Enn í hall at helli her-nenninn fiǫl-mennom
    Gœndlar þings með gengi gný-þróttr neðan sótti.   20

7. Náði folk, þar-es flýði ferð skundliga undan,
    (illr varð hreimr í helli) heiðit konungr meiða:
    Lífs bauð 'enn' þá es unnot, af-tig gamall, vígi
    (kvǫl beið ǫld í eldi ósæl) Diǫfuls þrælom.

HALLDOR SQUALLER. *King Sigurd's Crusade.* And the wicked Wickings [Moorish corsairs] attacked the good king, and he was able to carry eight of their galleys. I will tell the great deeds he wrought in Spain. He took Cintra; the warriors who altogether deny God's law offered to them, found it grim work to fight against the king. The *third* victory he won at the city which is called Lisbon, coming ashore. Ye won a *fourth* victory at the place called Al-Kassir, I ween, and caused grief to the heathen women in a certain waste city. Ye did redden your sword-edge east of the Narrow-Sound [Straits of Gibraltar]. God helped you. Thou didst let down barks over a giantess-stair [precipice], (the king's dealings with the Saracens have become famous,) and fought victoriously from below against the crowded cave of the rock. The king destroyed the heathen: there was an evil howling in the cave. He, when *only* nineteen years old, made life hard for the Devil's slaves,

---

22. heimr, Cd.   23. Read, önn.   af-tig] thus; cp. Lat. un-de-viginti.

8. Marg-dýrkaðr kom merkir morð-hióls skipa-stóli   25
    (fúss vas fremðar-ræsir frið-slitz) til Ivitzo.
9. Knátti enn ina átto odd-hríð vakit síðan
    (Finnz rauð giœld) á grœnni (grams ferð) Manork verða.
10. Borg heiðna tókt bræðir benja-tíkr af ríki
    (háðisk hver við prýði hildr) enn gaft af mildi.   30
11. Ér knáttuð þar þeira (þú vast aldregi) [skialdar
    leygr þaut of siðt] (sigri sviptr) gœrsemom skipta.

12. *Orkit Ála serkjar él-festir þrek mestom;*
    ætt berr grams ok gumna gagn-prúðr Sigurðr magni.

ÞORVALDR BLENDO-SKALD.

I. (From Edda.)

KONUNGR heill! ok svá sniallir, sókn-œrr við her gœrvan
    (óð hafa menn í munni mínn) húskarlar þínir!
Goll-striðir verpr glóðom (gefr auð konungr rauðan)
[óþióðar bregðr eyðir] orm-leggs [Grana farmi].

II. (From Edda.)

NÚ hefik mart í miði geipat
    burar Bors Bura arfa.

THORARIN STUTTFELD.

1. DREIF til handa herr framr grami
    hollr hauk-sniœllom hvaðan-æva svá:
    sem fyrr í fœr frétt hœfðo rétt
    konunga kyn Kraka marg-spœkom.
2. Svá kom fylkiss framt lið saman   5
    marg-spaks mikit mildingi vilt:

---

when he took their stronghold, and the cursed folk perished in the fire.
The king came with his fleet to Ivica. He woke the *eighth* fray there
on green Minorca . . . . He took by force a heathen city [Acre], and gave
it up in kindness [to Baldwin] . . . . when he shared out the precious
things there.

Burden. Ye wrought the greatest deeds! Sigurd the gallant out-
does all kings and men in might.

THORWALD BLEND-POET. *On King Sigurd.* Hail, O king, and all
thy gallant house-carles: men have my songs of praise in their mouth!
The prince casts the rings away, and gives the red treasure, and distri-
butes Grani's burden [gold].

End of another Poem. Now I have talked freely in the mead of the
son of Bor, Buri's heir.

THORARIN CURT-CLOAK. *King Sigurd's Crusade.* They drove
together from all parts to take service with the good king, as of yore it
is told that on his journey the people sought service with the wise Kraki's
kinsman. A great host devoted to the king came together, so that

at skip, við skœp, skar-fœgr um lœg,
hreins grams hímins, hnigo sex tigir.

3.   Óðo at Engla ætt-iœrðo bœrð
skaplig skipa skafin vestr um haf: 10
þótti Þrœnda þar-landz sem hvar
yfir-maðr iœfurr allz-herjar sniallr.

4.   Varð fyr stafni styrjar-giœrnom
frið-raskaði Formintera:
þar varð eggjar ok eld þola   15
Blá-manna lið áðr bana fengi.

5.   Það gramr guma gunn-hagr draga
byr-varga á biarg blá-svarta tvá:
þá-es í reipom ram-dýr þrama
sigo fyr helliss hlið-dyrr með lið.   20

6.   .... Herr hauk-snœrom harð-mœðigr varð ....
Ey man uppi Endils meðan stendr
sól-borgar-salr svœr-gœðiss fœr:
þú hefir í vatri vegsamr þvegizt,
geirs gný-stœrir gráns, Iorðánar.   25

7.   Varðir Hœrða hvatr fylkir at
grœf Gods .... kvik-sáttar:
Á skínn æva Yggs fiœl-dyggra
sól svan-gœli, siklingr, an þik.

II. IMPROVISATIONS.

1.   HYKK at her megi þekkja heldr í stuttom feldi
oss, enn ek læt þessa óprýði mer hlýða:
værir mildr, ef mæra mik vildir þú skikkjo
(hvat hafim heldr an tœtra?) hildingr muni vildri.

there went, at God's order, sixty fair-timbered ships over the sea. The
shapely-smoothed ships rode west over the sea to the fatherland of the
English; the Thronds' lord there, as anywhere else, was held the most
gallant of kings. . . . Formintera was before the king's bows, the Blackamoors had to suffer sword and fire before they died. The king
commanded two blue-black wind-wolves [boats] to be drawn up the
mountain and to be let down filled with men in ropes before the doors
of the cave . . . . The people were angry with the gallant . . . . As long
as the hall of the city of the sun [earth] endures the king's voyage shall
be spoken of. Thou hast bathed, O glorious king, in the water of
Jordan. Thou, lord of the Hords, didst endow the grave of God [Holy
Sepulchre] and the shrines of the saints with gold in plenty. The sun
shall never shine on a better king than thou, my lord!

Improvisations. I daresay thou knowest me in my very scant cloak,
but I have to put up with my shabby attire. Thou wert a right gracious king, if thou wouldst give me a little better mantle. What have
I but tatters now?

8. himins, emend. ; heðan, Cd.

2. Þú vændir mer, Þrœnda þengill, ef ek stef fengja   5
    frænda Serks at fundi folk-rakkr gefa nakkvat:
    lét-þú at Hákon héti, hildingr inn fé-mildi,
    (enn samir mer at minnask) Mœr-strútr (á þat gœrva).

3. Full-víða hefir frœðom Fiœro-skeifr of her veifat
    lystr ok leiri kastað last-samr ara ins gamla: 10
    ok vantú eina kráko orð-vándr á Serklandi
    Skeifr (bartu Hœgna húfo hræddr) varliga brædda.

EINARR SCULASON (SIGURÐAR-DRÁPA).

1. VÁS-ÖFLUGR réð vísi vestr helmingi mestom;
        óð at Ensko láði Ægiss marr und harra:
    Stœl lét hilmir hvílask heipt-glaðr ok vas þaðra
    (ne gramr á val Vimrar) vetr-lengis (stígr betri).

2. Ok, sá-es œzt gat ríki, ól þióð-konungr sólar   5
    œnd á Jacobs-landi annan vetr und ranni:
    þar frá-ek hilmi herjar (hialdrs) laus-mæli gialda
    (gramr svan bræddi snemma snar-lyndr) frœmom iarli.

3. Húf lét hilmir svífa haf-kaldan (lof skaldi
    esat um all-valdz risno ein-fallt) í Grík-salti: 10
    áðr við einkar-breiða auð-lestir skip festi
    (œll beið œld með stilli) Akrs-borg (fegins-morgin).

4. Get-ek þess es gramr fór vitja (glyggs) Iorsala-bygðar
    (meðr vitoð œðling œðra) ógn-blíðr (und sal víðom):
    ok leyg-hati laugask (leyft ráð vas þat) náði   15
    hauka-setrs í hvíto hvatr Iórdanar vatri.

5. Sætt frá-ek Dœla dróttinn (drengr minnisk þess) vinna;
    tóko hvasst í Hristar hríð val-slœngor ríða:
    Sterkr braut váligt virki vargs-munn-litoðr gunnar;
    (fœgr ruðosk sverð); enn sigri snarr bragningr fagnar.   20

A Satire. Thou wilt have me make a stave on Serk's kinsmen, promising to give me something for it, telling me that his name was Hakon
Suet-paunch (Pot-belly). I must not forget thee.
A Satire. F. has scattered libels far and wide, and cast about the
droppings of the old eagle [satire]. Thou didst hardly feed one crow in
Saracen-land, thou slanderous Wry-leg, coward in armour!
EINAR SCULASON. *King Sigurd's Crusade.* The sailor-king went
westward with a great force, and Ocean's steed galloped under him
towards the English shore. He let his ships rest there, and stayed there
all the winter. Never better king ever stepped aboard Wimmer's
charger [ship]; and a second winter he passed in James' land [Galicia],
where, I ween, he paid the bad earl [?   ] for his breach of covenant.
He made the sea-cold hulls sweep into the Greek sea [Levant], and at last
moored his ships off the full broad town of Acre. All the people
welcomed the king that morning. I tell how the king went to see
Jerusalem-land, and was able to bathe in the white water of Jordan, a
noble deed. The lord of the Dalesmen won Saietta [Sidon], I ween;
the war-slings did sharp work in the fight; the strong captain stormed a
huge stronghold and won a victory.

SIGURÐR IORSALA-FARI.

1. VILLIR hann vísdóm allan, veldr því karl í feldinom.

2.   Skiótt bar-ek skiœld inn hvíta (skald biðr at Goð valdi)
ár til odda skúrar auðigr, enn frá rauðan:
þar hefek hœgg of hœggit handlaust á Serklandi
(Goð ræðr sókn ok sigri), svanni, þínom manni.

GULL-ÆSO ÞÓRÐR.

NÚ tekr ygr at œgja of-kúginn mer driúgom;
þinn hefir hœlðr of hlannat hialdr gegninn mik tialdi:
trautt mun-ek lausan láta linnz . . . . giafi at sinni
vísan þióf, þo-at váfi ván mín und hlut þínom.

---

§ 5.   THE GILCHRIST FAMILY AND LATER KINGS (1130-1200).

UP to the death of Sigurd the Crusader Norway had been ruled by a series of vigorous and talented kings, following each other by a rough, but well-understood and acknowledged, rule of succession. But from henceforward the power fell from the crown to the barons, who were divided into factions, and ruled under cover of *rois faineans*, impostors set up, as occasion required, by the opposing parties. A nominal king was necessary, that was all, and there was little difficulty or back-wardness shown by the heads of the factions in supplying themselves with one that would suit their views.

The insanity of Sigurd gave opportunity for the first contrivers of this kind of imposture to act. They seem to have plotted against Magnus, the young prince, and his friends, and to have worked on the mad jealousy of the distraught king, to induce him to look with favour upon the man who declared himself the son of Sigurd's father. 'Towards the end of Sigurd's reign' (in 1129?) a certain Gilchrist was discovered in Ireland by a Norse noble, and carried over the sea to Norway. 'The worst import ever brought to Norway,' says a later historian. Arrived there he took the name of Harold. Like the following impostors, he does not pretend to be the son of an acknowledged concubine such as Alfhild or Thora, but merely the offspring of a chance amour. He does not come forward till twenty-six years after his supposed father's death (1103). He brings no proof of his assertions, as far as we know, but merely offers to undergo the ordeal of 'bearing the iron,' which he accomplished safely, thanks no doubt to his clerical supporters.

KING SIGURD THE CRUSADER. *To Curt-cloak.* He confounds all wisdom. The churl in the cloak is the cause!

A Love-Song. I tore my shield white to battle, and red back again. I pray God to keep me. I have cut a sure stroke now here in Saracen-land for thy husband, lady, to match. God orders battles and victories.

ASA-THORD. *Complaint to Ingimar of Ask.* The tyrant is threatening me, but thy vassal has stolen my tent. I shall not give up a red-handed thief, though thou art richer than I.

The party that are behind him, however, manage to gain such a hold on the country before the death of Sigurd (in March, 1130) that they are able to seat their claimant on the throne as joint-king with *Magnus Sigurdsson.* Ere long a quarrel, premeditated or not, arises between the colleagues. Magnus is defeated, blinded, mutilated, and sent helpless to a monastery. This is the first instance in Norway of the foul cruelty which breaks out again and again in the Orkney Saga, and in the histories of Scotland and Ireland. It is not, however, the last ; the civil wars which go on for a century are, like our Wars of the Roses, red with butcheries and barbarities.

The path Harold Gilchrist had trodden was still open, and Magnus had a few supporters left. A new claimant, *Sigurd Slembi-diakn,* appears next (in 1135), a reputed son of Magnus Bareleg, a man whose romantic life and cruel death awake an interest in him, which few of the actors in this wretched epoch of Norwegian history can arouse. His mother was a Norwegian lady, Thora, of the great Arnmodlinga family, and we should guess that it was her ambition which led her to put the fanciful claim forward on behalf of her son, who may very well have believed it. He is in character above the adventurers that follow his track ; a true Northman, second only to Swerri, and a man who had proved his worth before he started to claim the throne. The foster-son of a priest, Athelberht, in the Western Islands, he had taken minor orders in his youth,—hence his name ' Ill *or* Sham-Deacon,'—had served in the court of David of Scotland, and made the pilgrimage to Jerusalem, where he had found five bishops to go through the ordeal and thus give the required proof of his claim to be Magnus' son, before he appeared as king in Norway. Gilchrist tried to do away with Sigurd, but he escaped and murdered him Dec. 14th, 1136 [1]. However, Gilchrist left two or three sons born in Norway : Sigurd-Gilchrist, born 1133 ; Ingi-Gilchrist, a cripple, born 1135 ; and Magnus (?) ; from whom in after time sprang a fresh brood of claimants.

The Hords and men of Sogn and Haloga-land helped the pretender Sigurd, but he never could secure a hold on the heart of the country, nor the clergy, so as to be admitted to the ordeal. After adventures among the Fins in the north, and on the Baltic in the south, he obtained help from Denmark, and sailed back to put his fortunes to the touch in a pitched battle. But his Danish auxiliaries fled, and he was defeated, taken, and tortured to death by the partisans of the *Child-Kings,* Harold's sons, *Ingi* the crippled baby and *Sigurd,* Nov. 12th, 1139.

His failure did not discourage fresh pretenders, the most impudent of all being *Eystan,* who claimed to be the son of Harold Gilchrist by a Western Island woman, whom he had met before he started on his career in Norway. Eystan was acknowledged by the partisans of the young kings whom he claimed as half-brothers. But this did not prevent civil war between them. Sigurd was slain by Simon Scalp in a treacherous way in 1155. Eystan fell in a brawl with Ingi, in 1157. Gregory Daysson, the king-maker, to whose protection Ingi owed his life and realm, was killed in January, 1161 ; and in a few weeks afterwards, Ingi the crippled king is vanquished and slain, Feb. 2nd, 1161, against a fresh claimant put forward by Einrid the Young (known from Orkney Saga), who, falsely no doubt, was represented as the son of Sigurd Gilchrist.

This pretender, *Hakon Broadshoulders,* a mere boy, did not long

---

[1] Sigurd's life should be compared with that of his contemporary claimant Wigmund (Malcolm McEth).

enjoy his position, for Erling Shank, the most energetic of the barons, decided upon an innovation in the succession, and set up his son Magnus.

Magnus Erlingsson was an undoubted scion of the Ynglings however, and born (1156) in wedlock. His mother Christina, Erling's wife, was the daughter of Sigurd the Crusader; but still, to trace descent through a woman was an entirely new phenomenon in the history of Norwegian claimants, and it was only by securing the aid of the Church and paying a high price that Erling secured the seal of a solemn coronation, hitherto unknown in the Northern kingdom (1164), for his son's claim (an eight years' child). But in return for this a regular acknowledgment that Norway was held as a fief of St. Olaf was required by the Church.

In spite of these precautions the 'first crowned king' did not escape the fate of so many of his predecessors. A pretender, *Eystein Meyla*, rose against him and was put down (1174), but his followers, the Birchlegs or Birkbones, lit upon a man who was to put an end to this era of confusion and anarchy. This time the Faro Islands, a poor outlying colony, proved a Corsica to Norway, her mother country:—A Faro franklin, named Unas the Comber, a brother to Roi the Faro Bishop (d. 1162), had, by his wife Gundhild, a Norse lady, a son named *Swerri*, who was brought up for the Church and ordained priest. In 1176 he appears as a pretender, as a son of Sigurd Gilchrist. Watchful, untiring, sober, persevering, and full of confidence and zeal, this man was of a very different mould to any of his contemporaries in the North. That he was the son of Sigurd is on the face of it impossible, and may be set down as the necessary fiction which entitled the man best fitted to rule to claim the crown. We know that Sigurd Gilchrist's son was two years older than Ingi, and born therefore in 1133. As far as we can judge, Swerri, who first appears in 1176, *must* have been over fifty at his death (1202). This would put his birth about 1150, when his reputed father was seventeen. But everything we know would rather incline us to put his birth at a few years earlier, and so tend to increase the *impossibility* of the story. The character of Swerri is however the weightiest proof that he was no chip of the Gilchrist block. The reticence displayed in his own narrative on his early career is easily accounted for.

It cannot be denied that the time was ripe for a destroyer. Material prosperity had sapped the frugality and energy of the Northern character, at least in the leading families. Seamanship even was being neglected; drunkenness, to a phenomenal degree, had become an unpleasant national peculiarity; lazy gluttony, bold perjury, selfishness, and cruelty are seen in the most prominent men of the day. Brave they are, but they have lost the power of combination, or of foreseeing the danger to come. Swerri swoops down upon the Earl and his son in the midst of their drunkenness (June 19th, 1179), and though Magnus escapes, his father is killed. Defeat follows defeat, till at last Magnus, after a swift voyage from Denmark, overtakes Swerri in Sogn. But Swerri breaks fiercely through the toils that have been spread for him and inflicts a crushing defeat upon the royalists on June 15th, 1184, slaying the king and most of his adherents. This wonderful and unlooked-for victory threw the country at his feet. For eighteen years he ruled alone, all the party-risings against him being put down. The *Cowlings* were quelled; the *Island-Beardies*, a formidable fleet from the Western Islands, were smitten and broken by the terrible king (April 3rd, 1194). The toughest tustle, that with the *Croziers* headed by a fierce Bishop, took up Swerri's last years. The powerful position of the clergy (which drew from him the famous *Anecdoton*, a protest against the encroachments of the Roman power), the difficulties which only a longer peace and leisure could have smoothed, concurred to prevent him from showing his constructive power. As with Cromwell, his work was undone when he died (March 9th, 1202), and he was not lucky enough to have his plans and wishes carried out by his successors.

His only son, Hakon, died suddenly after less than two years' reign, perhaps by poison (Jan. 1st, 1204), leaving, as far as we know, no son. Two rival makeshift kings are set up by the *Birchlegs* and *Croziers*, each ruling part of the country. Earl Hakon Galin, the Regent, now brings forward as a candidate a boy whom he declared to be the son of Hakon Swerrisson. His mother, Inga, bears the iron as proof of his birth, and the party accepted the child. The Editor's impression is that the Earl himself, his foster-father, was the *father* of this Hakon. The sour looks and harshness of Lady Christina, the Earl's wife, and the fond doting of the Earl himself towards the orphan boy, so naively told by the historian, gives a hint of the true relationship of the parties. This boy, *Hakon Hakonsson*, grew up and survived in the struggle which went on as usual with the pretenders who cropped up against him. He ruled Norway for forty-six years, restored the country to prosperity and peace, and gained a hollow, paste-board glory, such as that of the Second Empire. The test of war shows its real value. A skirmish at Largs and the shock of a storm drives the dream of conquest away for ever; and the king dies, worn out and disappointed, at Kirkwall, in the Orkneys, Dec. 15th, 1263. His only success was the subjection of Iceland, his life-aim, planned and schemed for through long weary years (1262); it took him some thirty years, and coming too late, brought little good to either country[1].

Magnus the Law-mender, Hakonsson, b. 1238, d. March 6, 1280, Sturla's friend, succeeds his father in regular orthodox fashion. His sons *Eric* (d. 1299) and *Hakon Highleg* (d. 1319), who follow him, are the last males of the line. The son of Hakon's daughter and the Swedish duke carry on

---

[1] In the following list the first column gives the name of the claimant, the second that of the person of whom he claims to be the son, the third the date of the claimant's appearance, and the fourth the number of years elapsed since the death of the supposed father. Nowhere, save from the history of some Slavonic or Eastern dynasty, could such a list as we append be compiled. We have omitted some of the more insignificant fungi, but there are enough given to prove the character of the age, which produced but one man of mark, Swerri, and even he could do nothing but cut away as much as he could of its shams, without being able to begin the work of regeneration.

Harold Gilchrist . .	Magnus Bareleg	1129	. . 26.
Sigurd Slembidiakn .	Magnus Bareleg	1135	. . c. 32.
Eystan	Harold Gilchrist	1142	. . c. 6.
Hakon Broadshoulders	Sigurd Gilchristsson . . .	1159	. . c. 4.
Eystan Meyla . . .	Eystan pseudo-Gilchristsson .	1174	. . c. 17.
SWERRI	Sigurd Gilchristsson . . .	1176	. . c. 21.
Eric	Sigurd Gilchristsson . . .	1181	. . c. 26.
John the Cowling . .	Ingi Gilchristsson	1185	. . c. 24.
Sigurd Brennir . . .	Eystan pseudo-Gilchristsson .	1188	. . c. 27.
Broadbeard	Eystan pseudo-Gilchristsson .	1191	. . c. 34.
Sigurd	Magnus Erlingsson . . .	1192	. . c. 8.
Erling Stonewall . .	Magnus Erlingsson . . .	1205	. . c. 21.
HAKON	Hakon Swerrison	1205	. . 2.
Beni	Magnus Erlingsson . . .	1218	. . 34.
Sigurd Ribbung . .	Erling Stonewall	1221	. . 15.

Gilchrist appeared in 1129, Ribbung perished in 1226, making ninety-seven years.

the blood of Hakon in the new line, whereof the last scion, a boy, died in 1387. In 1380 Norway and Denmark were united. The Hanseatic Company, with true Carthaginian policy, soon forced their 'celibate tyranny' upon the sea-coast towns; the Norwegian shipping, sailor-life, and commerce disappeared. And such had been the force of Swerri's strokes, so completely had the upper and middle classes been swept away, so dead was the stupor which the Hanse Towns' thraldom had laid upon the towns, from which some fresh element might have been looked for, that Norway slept a 'bear's sleep' of hybernation through centuries, not even waking at the Reformation, or stirring when the Hanse fell.

Norway is the most modern and the oldest of all European countries; her new semi-American constitution and her Old World life, half yeo-man's, half fisherman's, are quite exceptional phenomena. In no country have the medieval spirit or institutions left so few traces. The coarse healthy animal existence, which she led for so long with-out a ray of spiritual light, gave place after 1814, when the deadening bond of foreign supremacy was snapped, to a vigour and energy which has, under a new Royal House and in a happy union with Sweden, brought the kingdom to a happy issue.

At the final separation from Denmark in 1814, Iceland and the Faroes, the ancient colonies of Norway, were left behind, forgotten and un-claimed by the rising Norwagia Rediviva and her new king.

THE GILLUNG COURT POETS.

IVAR INGIMUNDARSON, the author of *Sigurd's Baulk*, was an Ice-lander, of whose life we know little, save the pretty story (printed in the Reader, p. 144) which tells of his despairing love for his brother's wife, Ordny, and shows him to have been a favourite of King Eystan the Law-giver, who died Aug. 29, 1122. In Skalda-tal Ivar stands as the poet of Eystan and Magnus Bareleg and Sigurd the Crusader, but no line of his on these kings survives. His *Praise of Eystan* one is sorry to miss. After the death of the Crusader, Ivar appears as the poet of Sigurd Slembidiakn the Claimant (whose own improvisations are given in Book vi, Nos. 51–52), and it is from the *Dirge* the poet made on his patron that the Chronicler has drawn the chief facts of the Ill-deacon's life.

It is fairly complete, in distinct stanzas, but in the old epic metre. It contains several clear echoes from the old poetry of the Western Islands (Sigurd's birthplace), which we have pointed out in the margin. In two or three instances (ll. 129, 135), one seems to hear the cadences of the Helgi Lays. There is a love of the sea (characteristic of the hero), and a certain simplicity of tone about it, which relieve its tale of war.

It is found imbedded in the Hryggiar-Stykki of Eric Oddsson in the Morkinskinna MS. of the Book of Kings. (See Prolegomena, § 13.)

There is a notable Ingimund in the Sturlunga, a poet, story-teller, and priest, but the dates forbid us to assume him as the father of our poet.

HALLDOR SKVALDRI. All that is known of this poet is told in the preceding section in the introduction to his poems on pp. 248–9.

EINAR SCULASON. The favourite poet of the twelfth century, a Western Islander, as we know from Presta-tal (see Sturlunga, vol. ii,

p. 502), and according to an interpolation in Gunlaug's Saga he was of the Myre-men family. 'Wise men [historians] say that many of the house of the Myre-men, who come from Egil, have been very handsome men, albeit it went by extremes among them, for some of that house have been called the ugliest of men. In this house there have also been many men who were accomplished in every way, as was Kiartan Olaf Peacock's son, and Battle-Bard, and Skuli Thorsteinsson [the poet, see p. 102]. Some of this house were also great poets—Biorn the Hitdale champion, Einar Sculason the priest, Snorri Sturlason, and many others.' But we do not know Einar's pedigree, though the very name of his father is one that is met with in the family. He seems to have passed most of his life in Norway, and we can trace him there by his poems, from the days of Sigurd the Crusader to the death of Gregory Daysson. There are a good many anecdotes about him in the Kings' Lives, witnessing to his remarkable powers of improvisation. These bits are given p. 277. Einar's death-year is not known ; we might guess that he died abroad shortly after 1160. His earliest poem, *Praise of Sigurd*, one of the parallel poems on the Crusade, composed during Sigurd's last years, we take to have been one of his first poetical flights. Next came *Tog-drapa*, and a parallel *Poem* in *epic metre* on Harold Gilchrist, c. 1135. In his *rhyme-metre Praise of Eystan*, the frays of the pseudo-Gilchristsson are recounted, and especially his raid upon England in 1151. It was about c. 1154 that his most famous poem *Geisli*, the Beam, on the patron saint of Norway, was composed and recited in Throndham Cathedral before the three brethren. (See § 6, p. 283.) To Sigurd, whose marshal he was, he was especially beholden ; and after his death (1155) we have from Einar, who was still with the other brothers, a long *Encomium on the Gillungs*, of which there are many fragments, here patched together and arranged as well as the materials allow.

The last of his dateable poems are the *Verses on the Gaut-Elbe Battle* (1159), in imitation of Sighvat's *Ness*-verses. Besides his *Improvisations* there is a curious composition on the *Gift of an Axe* from one of his royal patrons, in which Einar has set himself to emulate Bragi's Shield Song. It is a poem of his later years, full of conceits. The bits of *Love-Songs*, one to *Solborg* and one to *Ioreid* (on whose name he puns), cannot be dated. The *Thulor* (see Book x) fill the list of his known works.

Prolific and industrious, Einar has left more behind him than almost any one save Sighvat ; but the quality is not high, though the perfect mastery of metre can be clearly felt. It was this quality which especially raised him in the eyes of his followers, the Sturlasons. But the paucity of idea and the absence of any reality in his phrases make his work tiresome and in many cases unworthy of translation. In *Geisli* he reaches his highest mark. Its mechanical finish is very remarkable, and it provoked a crowd of imitations.

We have a grave suspicion that Einar was the person who re-edited and polished and veneered many of the poems we find in the Kings' Lives and Snorri's Edda. Ari knew them in their perfect state ; Snorri seems to have received them in their 'newly-restored' state, for we can hardly impute the restoration to *him*. Einar's verses are always smooth and flowing, and so are the restorations ; while Snorri's verses are all hard and wooden. As it must needs be some poet *between* Ari and Snorri, and as Einar was a ready poet, a 'collector,' as the Thulor show, and master of a style which is as like to that of the re-edited verses as egg to egg, we take it that Einar collected the old verses, which no doubt were in a more or less corrupt state from one to two centuries of oral tradition, and polished them up, as Percy did his Ballads, so that they might 'obtain the favour of an elegant and critical public.' This is no proved case, of course, but, we think, one in which there is some reasonable presumption of Einar's guilt.

The Kings' Lives, Edda, and Skalda give the foundation for the text of Einar's poems.

BODWAR THE HALT appears in Skalda-tal as poet of Sigurd, where he is called 'balti,' *belt*, instead of 'halti,' *halt*, which may be right. There is a like name found in the Western Islands. The fragment is from a *Praise of Sigurd*.

COLL THE PROUD. Another of the Gillung poets. The fragment of his work is from a *Praise of Ingi*.

THORBIORN SHANK'S POET. The bard of the king-maker, Earl Erling Shank. His poem on his patron's exploits would be c. 1165.

ASGRIM KETTLESSON. He is named as Swerri's poet in Skalda-tal, with twelve others; hence the verse remaining may be the only remains of the Encomia of the thirteen poets of the terrible king.

STYRKAR ORDSSON. The Law-speaker of Iceland (1171–1181), at which last date he died. We cannot identify the subject of his verse.

CLONG, BISHOP OF SKALHOLT. A fragment of his on sailing, in 'alhenda' court-metre, is preserved in Edda. We have a life of this prelate in Hungrwaka, which testifies to his high worth and ability. 'He was a fair man to look on, and of middle size, active and bright, very accomplished and a good scribe, and a man of great learning.' And again, 'Bishop Clong was a great advocate, when he was taken as counsellor, for he was, both for the sake of his wisdom and his eloquence, a great chief. He was also learned in every point of the constitution.' Bishop John's Life tells a story of his youth. 'It is told that he [Bishop John] found out that Clong Thorsteinsson (he who was afterwards bishop of Skalholt, but was then a novice and a boy) was reading the verse-book which is called *Ovidius de Arte*. Now in this book Master Ovid treats of the love of women, and shows how men may beguile them with all kinds of devices and get their will of them. When the blessed John saw and understood what he was reading, he forbade him to study that kind of book, saying that man's frail nature was well inclined to lustful living and fleshly love, without a man's irritating his mind with filthy and sinful books.' Bishop John, a worthy man, was the founder of the school at Holar, of which Clong was a pupil. Clong, in spite of his love of Latin and native poetry, turned out well. Among other things he built the church at Skalholt (a ditty on which see p. 282), and died aged 71; Hungrwaka winding up his life with, 'And it seems to us now that there has never been in Iceland a man of such manifold accomplishments as was Bishop Clong, and we may likewise be sure that his fame will last as long as Iceland is inhabited.' In his last few years he was bed-ridden, owing to his penances, walking barefoot in winter on the snow, and Thorlac, abbot of Thickby, was chosen as his suffragan and substitute. His death-day was Feb. 27, 1176. His name means 'Clawing,' i. e. Raven—a rare name.

With this group of poets the COURT POETRY really expires; the talents of Einar himself are those of a dying art, like those of the Italian Improvisatori of the last century. Thought had grown more and more vapid, metre had been polished up to the highest degree, the synonym system had multiplied in stereotyped lines till every understandable paraphrase had been employed. There was also no longer a hero to sing to. The crippled Ingi, the swash-buckler Eystan, the wanton Sigurd could hardly inspire the enthusiasm necessary to carry even a court-poem through, and this difficulty, which Landor too felt, as he plainly told Southey, was not to be surmounted. Even Einar only shows at his best when he is chanting the praises of the worthy dead. Swerri, who was a man indeed, was as little fitted for flattery as Cromwell himself; and the praises his poets sung on him are happily lost. There is not likely to have been a Milton, no, nor a Cowley, among them. And even in Cromwell's case, we feel the few earnest words of the chaplain more deeply than all the praise that authors have given him since. And Swerri was a man of distinctly lower type than Cromwell.

To go on with court-poetry after Swerri was to galvanise a corpse; the thing was dead. But the Sturlungs, Snorri, a great poet in prose, but a bad praiser in verse, and his two nephews Sturla and Olaf, also men of talent, attempted it. Snorri sings his wonderful Hatta-tal, *ordo metrica*, to Hakon and Earl Skuli, his patrons. Sturla hymns the praises of Hakon Hakonsson, and Magnus his son. Sturla's verses of him are all preserved in Islendinga and Hakon's Saga, like flies in amber, and Snorri's Hatta-tal fills a useful place in giving examples to his Poets' Handbook. Some of Olaf's are to be found in Sturlunga. We have not reprinted them here, for they are mere laboured book-poetry, Chinese-puzzle verses, full of echoes, imitations, citations from the older spontaneous poetry; and they themselves were never really genuine court poets, but just would-be revivers of an old perished fashion. Medieval poetry and medieval subjects were attracting every one in Norway, and the poet was set aside for the 'translator from the French.' We have, from Sturla's own hand in Islendinga, a scene which may fitly wind up this sketch, showing us, as it does, the last court-poet face to face with his last king-patron.

In 1263, Sturla, flying from foes at home [see Prolegomena for his life and those of the other Sturlungs], came to Norway to seek refuge at King Hakon Hakonsson's; but the king had gone on his last voyage, and the young king Magnus, like his father, was no friend to the Sturlungs. However, he gave him shelter, and Sturla found the means of rousing his interest and winning the goodwill of the kindly queen Ingiborg (daughter of the 'holy king' and granddaughter of the Danish king, Waldimar II) by his fine telling of the Tale of Hold the Giantess. When he had ended the Tale "Sturla thought he could see that the king's whole behaviour was more favourable than on the former day. Then he told the king that he had made a poem on him and likewise on his father. 'I would fain have thee hearken to them.' The queen said, 'Let him recite them, for I am told he is the best of poets, and his poem will be wonderfully good.' The king bade him recite if he liked 'what thou pretendest to have made upon me.' Then Sturla recited it to the end. The queen said, 'I think this, that the poem is very well composed!' The king said, 'Dost thou indeed understand anything of it?' She said, 'I should like you to think so, my lord!' The king said, 'I have heard that Sturla knows how to make verse.' Sturla saluted the king and queen and went to his room. The king got no fair wind that day, and in the evening, before he went to sleep, he sent for Sturla. And when he came he greeted the king, and then said, 'What wilt thou with me, my lord?' The king bade them give him a silver beaker full of wine, and drank some of it, and then gave it to Sturla, saying, 'Friends should drink wine together.' [There is a play of words in the original here, 'Vín skal til vinar drekka.'] 'God be praised that it is so!' said Sturla. 'So it shall be,' said the king. 'And now I wish thee to recite the poem that thou hast made on my father.' Then Sturla recited the poem, and when it was finished men praised it highly, but most of all the queen. Said the king, 'I think thou art a better composer than the pope!' [After a little more talk the king says], 'I have now heard thy poem, Sturla, and I think thou must be the best of poets. Now I will give thee for thy reward, that thou shalt come home with me in quiet and good peace! But my father will judge of what is between you, when ye two meet, but I will do my best for thee.' The queen thanked the king and said she thought Sturla was a very good man. The king treated Sturla well, and kept him liberally. The queen was exceedingly kind to him, and all the rest followed her example."

IVARR INGIMUNDARSON (SIGURÐAR-BꝊLKR).

1. ÓX í œsko við Aðalbricti.
    . . . . . .

2. Vas með iarli afkár-lyndom
    vargs verð-giafi vestr í Eyjom:
    unz siklingar sóknar hvattir
    Fóstra Þorkel . . . rufo.   5

3. Sótti síðan Sigurðr af Eyjom
    dýrr at rꜵðom Dávid konung:
    vas með vísa Vilialms-bani
    flein-þinga-samr fimm misseri.

4. Þótti dýrom Dáfinnz liðom   10
    œngr maðr kominn œðri þangat:
    bꜵetti vísi verðungar lið,
    hafði ungr konungr almanna lof.

5. Ól hertogi hrafna í Fiꜵrðom,
    (skulfo skeyti) í Skotta blóði: 15
    þars fyr iꜵfri austan komnom
    morð-als metendr merki bꜵro.

6. Bar Sigurði sigr at hendi
    ór orrosto inn frá Stauri:
    Háði hilmir her-víg fiogor,   20
    skýrstr at ꜵllo, í Skotta-veldi.

Sigurd in the Western Islands. He grew up in his youth with Æthel-briht. ... He was with a noble earl [Harold] west in the Islands [in the Orkneys] till they slew Thorcytel Fosterer. Then Sigurd went from the Islands to seek help of King David. The slayer of William [Skinner] stayed five years with the king. David's men thought that no such man had ever come thither, the young king won all men's praise. He, the duke [Sigurd], fed the ravens in the Firths [Minch]; the missiles were shaken in the blood of Scots, as they bare the standard before him. Sigurd won a battle inside Staur. He won four victories in the Scottish realm [probably *against Malcolm the rebel claimant*].

7. Vann Róms gœto ræsir Þrœnda
    fœti farna, sá-es frama drýgði:
    sótti síðan, ok synðom hrauð,
    hers odd-viti helga dóma.   25

8. Sótti breiða borg Iórsala
    œrr odd-viti út í lœndom:
    áðr í vatni, því-es vígði Goð,
    Sigurðr af ser synðir þvægi.

9. Gœrðo skírslo um skiœldungs kyn   30
    fimm byskopar, þeir-es framast þótto :
    svá bar raunir, at ríks konungs
    þess vas enn mildi Magnús faðir.

10. Léto síðan súð-vigg buin,
    (œstisk ægir) útan or Girkjom :   35
    sótti Frakka fremðar ræsir,
    áðr Saxa siœt Sigurðr kannaði.

11. Hélt snarr konungr snekkjo einni
    vígligr um ver vestr í Eyjar :

12. Tóko síðan Sigurð til landa   40
    Hœrðar ok Sygnir at Harald fallinn :
    svœrðosk margir menn á þingi
    buðlungs syni í bróðor stað.

13. Riso við vísa vestan komnom
    Þrœndir ok Mœrir, þeir-es þrifom nítto :   45
    brugðosk hœlðar í huga sínom
    menzko mildom Magnuss syni.

14. Drifo til reipa í roðo-veðri
    reyndir at risno ræsiss þegnar :
    urðo seggir segls at gæta,   50
    (þá vas svalt á sæ) enn sumir ióso.

Pilgrimage. The lord of the Thronds went on foot over the road to
Rome; and there he stripped off his sins and sought the holy places.
He sought the great city of Jerusalem, far from home, and then he
washed off his sins in the water, God-hallowed [Jordan]. Five bishops,
the greatest known, went through the ordeal; the proof came out that
Magnus the Generous was his father. Now his ship was bound *home-
ward* out of the land of the Greeks [Byzantine Empire]; he sought
the Franks' land [Franconia], and then the home of the Saxons
[Saxony]. With one cutter he came over the sea westward to the
Islands [Orkneys].

Pretender in Norway. The Hords and Sygns took Sigurd *as king* over
the lands at the death of Harold; many men swore to brotherhood with
him at the moot [Gula-thing]. The Thronds and More-men did not
know their own good, and rose against the prince that came from the
West; they turned their hearts away from the gallant son of Magnus.

Voyage to Denmark. The king's men ran to the ropes in wicked
weather, some to get in the sail, some were a-baling; it was cold at sea.

15.   Skók veðr-vita í vátom byr
      golli glœstan um grams skipi :
      klœkkar urðo (enn konungr stýrði)
      snekkjo sneisar of Sigurði.   55
16.   Hratt hvast skipi í hvœto veðri
      rœst ríðandi ok ramir straumar :
      festo seggir snekkjo langa
      kyn-stórs iœfurs við Kalmarnir.
17.   Ser framliga friðar leitaði   60
      il-rióðr ara við Ióta gram.
18.   Mœtti Vindom, sá-es vega þorði,
      sókn-diarfr Sigurðr suðr við Erri.
19.   Hrauð ungr konungr átta snekkjor
      (vargr gein um val) Vinda ferðar :   65
      hné fyr eggjo óþióðar lið.

      .   .   .   .

20.   Enn lét aðra austr fyr Mœri
      gramr geir-þorinn gunni háða :
      neytti vápna, þá-es Vindr hnigo,
      œrr odd-viti œðro sinni.   70
21.   Vann í Elfi, þar-es iœfurr barðisk,
      fall folk-starra til fœðor-leifðar :
      skulfo skeyti, skot magnaðisk,
      hnigo hring-viðir hvárra-tveggjo.
22.   Vann leyfðr konungr af liði Þóriss   75
      þriú skip hroðin í þeirri fœr :
      setto undan Óláfs liðar,
      þeir-es or Elfi eltir vóro.

23.   Hélt á Lista lofðungr skipom
      œrr fyr Agðir austan af Nesjom :   80

The weather-vane, glittering with gold, on the king's ship rattled in the wet gale. The cutter's spars bent, the king was at the helm. The rolling race and the mighty currents drove the ship sharply along in the sharp gale. The crew moored the king's long-cutter off Calmar. He sought refuge with the lord of the Jutes. *Adventures in the East.* The bold Sigurd met the Wends south off Arroe. The young king cleared eight smacks, the barbarian crew sunk before the sword. And he had a second battle east of More [More hundred by Calmar], when the Wends fell a second time. He made a slaughter for the eagle in the Elbe [Gaut-Elbe] when he fought for his father's heritage, men fell on both sides. In this cruise he won three ships of Thori's fleet which he cleared. Olaf's men sailed off when they were chased out of the Elbe. *Again in Norway.* He held his course along List in his ships in Agd east of the Naze ; the baron's kin fell ; the homesteads burnt before

59. Emend.; Kalmarnes, Cd.

hné hersa lið ; herr vas í landi;
brunno bygðir fyr buðlungi.

24. Dreif til skógar fyr skiœldungi
land-manna lið, þar-es logar brunno :
vœkðo drengir með dœrr roðin   85
blóð Benteini, áðr bana fengi.

25. Þann vas enn næsta naðra deyði
hug-fullr konungr með Háleygjom :
olli falli feðga þriggja
ulfs angr-tœpoðr út í Vœgom.   90

26. Þat vas et næsta norðr í Vœgom
vápna-skipti es Vilialmr féll.

27. Mœtti síðan suðr við Byrðo
gramr gunn-þorinn Glœsi-rófo :
olli stillir Styrkars bana ;   95
bar ben-þiðorr blóðga vængi.

28. Veitti vísi fyr Valsnesi
sókn snarpliga Svína-Grími :
hann lét missa mildings nefa
hœgri handar, áðr hialdr lykisk.   100

29. Mœtti Finni fremðar-giœrnom
œrr odd-viti austr á Kvildrom :
léto nýtan nadd-veðrs boða,
Ulfs arf-þega, œndo týna.

30. Vann fyr Mœri mildingr tekinn   105
Héðin með hœndom ok hans liða :
hann lét Kalfi Kringlo-auga
heldr harðliga heiptir goldnar.

31. Her-skildi fór harri Sygna
allt ið ýtra eyjar ok strandir.   110

.   .   .   .   .   .

---

him; there was a host in the land. The country folk fled to the woods
when the flames were blazing. They wounded Bentein with reddened
darts before he got his death-blow. The next serpent-death [winter] he
was with the Haloga-men, and slew *a father and two sons*, three of a kin
[Swain the priest and his sons], out in the Voe. The next action was
north in the Voe, where William [William Skinner] . . . . *and Thorald
Chap fell*. Then south off Byrd, the king met Glitter-tail ; yea, he brought
about Styrcar's death. By Walsness he gave Swine-Grim a sharp bout,
cutting the right hand off the king's nephew before the fray ended. He
met the gallant Fin east of Quilder. Sigurd's men caused Wolf's brave
heir to lose his life. By More he took Hedin and his men prisoners, and
paid a heavy score off on Calf Cringle-eye. He went with war-shield,
the lord of the Sygns, the whole way outside the islands and the coasts
[outside the Skerries in the green sea]. You might see the bitter brands

---

32.   Siá knátti þar fyr Sigurði
       bitra branda, brynjor hœggnar,
       skarða skiœldo, skœpt blóð-roðin,
Gkv. 12.   veðr-blásin vé of vegœndom.

33.   Fýstisk sunnan Sigurðr á lesti   115
       með lítið lið lœnd at sœkja:
       biósk með hánom til her-farar
       margs andvani Magnús konungr.

34.   Hélt þrim togom þióð-nýtr konungr
       snekkjom sunnan við sókn buinn: 120
       uggðo lýðir lið Sigurðar;
H. 105.   lék skiœldr við skiœld a skipom vísa.

35.   Fóro leyfðir með liði miklo
       Haraldz hróðr-synir her-stefno til:
       þá-es at mildom Magnús-syni   125
       at-róðr á siá Ingi kníði.

36.   Hraut í stœngom þar-es hildingar
       við víg vanir vápna neytto:
H. 51.   friðr slitnaði frænda á millom,
       guðr geisaði, gekk hildr saman.   130

37.   Stunðo seggir, stál roðnoðo,
       skaut biartr konungr báðom hœndom:
       hœrð spiót bito, benjar svíddo,
       her-skip hruðosk hvárra-tveggjo.

H. 49.   38.   Flugo hundroðom her-stefno til   135
       sár-gœgl um siá sveita at drekka:
       eyddo oddar iœfors full-trúom,
       morð miklaðisk þá-es Magnús féll.

39.   Flýðo Iótar átján skipom

---

hewing the mail-coats before Sigurd, the blood-sprinkled shafts scored
the shield, the gale-tossed banner waved over the fighters.
  His final defeat at Grey-Holm, off Frederick-hall. At last Sigurd hastened
from the south to seek his lands. There went with him on the expedition the hopelessly maimed king Magnus. Sigurd stood from the
south with thirty ships; they dreaded his fleet. Shield played against
shield [they were ready for action] on his ships. The renowned,
noble sons of Harold came with a mighty fleet to the war-tryst, what
time Ingi rowed out against the generous son of Magnus. There was a
clash in the forecastles, *or* the banner-staves groaned, as the war-wont
princes handled their weapons. The peace was shattered between the
kinsmen, the fray raged high, the battle was joined. The warriors
shouted, the steel was made red, the bright king [Sigurd] shot with both
hands; the hard spears bit, the wounds smarted, war-ships were cleared
on either side. The ravens flew by hundreds to the war-moot to drink
the blood. The spear-heads swept away the king's true friends, the
murder grew to its height when Magnus fell. The Jutes fled, eighteen

---

126. knvði, Cd.

þeir-es Sigurði sunnan fylgðo: 140
raufsk ræsiss lið, þá-es ríkr konungr
vanr vás-færom vápna neytti.

40. Hrauðsk und iœfri austan komnom
(bito slœg suðrœén) snekkja með stœfnom:
þá-es skiœldungs son af skipi síno   145
sókn-fœérr á siá sundz kostaði.

41. Varð á vatni víkingr tekinn,
sá-es manna vas mestr full-hugi.
.   .   .   .

42. Þat tel-ek ílla, es iœfurr skyldi
kyn-stórr koma í kvalar slíkar: 150
tekr Sigurði síðan engi
maðr rœskvari um meðal-kafla.

43. Sœng Saltara, meðan Sigurð píndo
iœfurs óvinir, ýta dróttinn:
bað fyr brœgnom bœð-frœékn iœfurr,   155
þeim-es vell-skata veitto píslir.

44. Frá-ek at léti líf sítt konungr
þá-es Saltara sungit hafði:
vildi ganga gramr til skriptar,
enn því þióð-konungr þeygi náði.   160

HALLDORR SKVALDRI (on Harold Gilchrist).

(Verse 5 from O. H. L.; verse 6 from Morkinsk.; verse 5 from Fagrsk.)

1. M AGNUS fekk (þar es miklo margs gengis naut hann) lengri
[valr nam vœll at hylja varmr] fylkingar arma.

2. Harð-éla léztu herðir Haddings á ió tradda
(glaðr tók gramr við hauðri) grund til Eireks fundar:
fekk, sa-es fremstr vas miklo, fliót-mæltr konungr Ióta   5
(réð Hollseta hræðir) hraust gengi þer drengja.

3. Ásbiœrn varð, sa-es orðom ílla hélt við stilli,
(gramr fœéðir val víða vígs) í Sarp at stíga:

---

ships of them, that had followed Sigurd from the South. The king's array was broken where the sailor-king handled his weapons. The southern missiles bit ;. the cutter of him that came from the East [Sigurd] was cleared from stem to stern, when he sprang from his ship into the sea to try swimming. He was taken in the water, the Wicking who, of all men, had the bravest heart.

His cruel death. It is ill to tell that a king should come to such torments. Braver man than Sigurd never gripped a sword-hilt. He sang the psalter while his enemies tortured him; he prayed for the men that ordered his torments. I know that he died when he had sung the psalter through; he wished for shrift, but it was denied him.

Halldor Squaller. *Harold Gilchrist's Praise.* Magnus' battle-array had the greater wings. He [Harold] sailed the sea on the horse of Harding steed [ship] to meet Eric. The swift-spoken king of the Jutes gave thee a fine company of warriors. Asbiorn, who kept his word

Nereið lét gramr á grimman grand-meið Sigars fiánda
(hús-þinga galt) hengja (hrann-báls-glœtoðr mála).   10
4.   Fékk meira lið miklo mildr an glœggr til hildar,
hirð þa-es hugði forðask heið þióð-konungs reiði :
Enn vinlausom vísa varð, þeim es fé sparði,
(háðisk víg fyrir víðom vangi) þunnt um stangir.
5.   Máttit œld, þa-es ótta ógn-fýstr konungr lýsti,   15
(hlióp fyrir hilmiss vápnom her-flótti) bý verja.
6.   Nu es auð-sendir undir allr Nóregr þik fallinn ;
þín liggr gipt á grœno (Goðs ráð es þat) láði.

EINARR SCULASON. I. Tog-drápa.

(Verses 4, 5 from Mork.)

1.   SÓTTI á slétt seiðs hryn-leiðar
iœrð él-skerðir ungr Skánunga :
fann fiœl-nenninn freks landreka,
gífr-skæs gœfugr gran-rióðr, Dana.
2.   Luko vág viko, vara kostr fara   5
brýns Biœrgynjar braut há-skrautom.
3.   Allz varð Ello ungr geitunga
lofaðr líf-giafi landz ráðandi.
4.   Vann val-grennir viðr 'rá fiðris'
Hveðn 'há mœðro hroðit vápn boða :'   10
flugo framliga, fekk svan-bekkjar
snarr sól-þverrir sigr, fal-vigrar.
5.   Eyddi oddom ey ben-þeyjar
Hléss- hel-fýsir hungr gollunga :
líkn gefi læknir lofaðr frið-rofa   15
húms haf-lióma hár lausnari.

II. Haraldz-drápa.

ÓTRYGGOM lezt-þu eggjar elion-þrár und hári
Hveðn á hœldom roðnar hrafns munn-lituðr gunnar :
átti sókn við slétta serk-rióðr Hárs merki
harða (þar-es hregg of virðom) Hless-eyjar þrœm (bléso).

---

badly to the king, had to step over Sarp [the water-fall] ; but the prince
had Nereid hung on the cruel deadly tree of Sigar's foe [Hagbard].
The stingy one [Magnus] could gather a much less force than the
generous one [Harold], and thin was the array before the banner of the
friendless king.   It is God's will . . . . could not defend the city [Ber-
gen] against the . . . .   Now all Norway is fallen to thee.

EINAR SCULASON. I. *Dirge on Harold Gilchrist. Stretch-Song.* The
young king sought the . . . . he met the lord of the Danes. They locked
the bay of Bergen, so that there was no means of getting away. He that
feeds Ella's wasp [the eagle] became ruler of all the land . . . . He
fought at Hwedn [in Ore-Sound] and at Hlesey [Cattegat]. May the
Redeemer, the great Healer of Heaven, grant the king his mercy.

II. PRAISE OF HAROLD GILCHRIST.   He fought a battle at Hwedn
and another by the shore of Hlesey.

III. Eysteins-drápa (Rímhend).

1. VÍKVERJOM galt, (varð þannog hallt)
    gœrræði gramr giæf-mildr ok framr:
    flest folk var hrætt áðr fengi sætt,
    enn gíslar tók sá-er giæ̨ldin iók.

2. Funi kyndisk fliótt, enn flýði skiótt   5
    Hísingar herr sa-er hafði verr.

3. Vann siklingr sótt við snarpa drótt
    (leyfðr er lýðom kær) Leikbergi nær:
    Remir flýðo ríkt, ok reiddo slíkt
    (æld festi auð) sem æ̨ðlingr bauð.   10

4. Frétt hefig at fell, (folk brusto svell)
    [iæfurr eyddi frið] Apardiánar lið.

5. Beit buðlungs hiærr (blóð féll á dærr)
    [hirð fylgðisk holl] við Hiartapoll:
    Hugin gladdi heit (hruðosk Engla beit)   15
    [óx vitniss vín] val-kastar Rín.

6. Iók hilmir hialdr (þar var hiærva galdr)
    [hiósk Hildar ský] við Hvítabý:
    ríkt lék við rann (rauðsk ylgjar tann)
    [feksk firom harmr] fyri-skógar garmr.   20

7. Drap dæglingr gegn (dreif strengjar regn)
    við Skorpo-sker skiald-kœnan her:
    rauf styrjar garð þá er stœkkva varð
    randæ̨lom sótt reið-manna gnótt.

8. Rauð siklingr sverð (sleit gylðiss ferð   25
    prútt parta lík) í Píslavík:
    vann vísir allt fyrir vestan salt
    (brandr gall við brún) brent Langatún.

9. Skar-ek súðom sund fyr sunnan Hrund
    mín prýddisk mund við mildings fund.   30

III. Eystan's Praise. *Forays in the South.* He paid the Wick-dwellers
for their treason. Many a man was in fear; ere peace was made, he
took hostages and laid fines on them. Fire was kindled, and the people
of Hising [on Gota-river mouth] fled fast in defeat. He had a sharp
struggle near to Leikberg; the Rems fled [people of Rimaland], they
submitted to pay what the king ordained.

Cruise to the West. I know that many fell of the Aberdeen array: the
king broke the peace. His trusty guards followed him: he fought at
Hartlepool. The English ships were stained with blood. The king
raised war at Whitby. The fire-shaw's hound [fire] wrought men woe.
He slew a shield-keen host at Sharpreef [?   ]. The war-fence
was broken when the knights fled. The sword tore the bodies of proud
Portmen [citizens]: the prince crimsoned his blade at Pillwick [?   ].
He won all west of the Main: he burnt Langton. I clave the waves south

10. Brýnd vóro dœrr, boga fylgði hœrr,
    sparn rastar knœrr rá-dýris vœr.

IV. Praise on the Four Brothers.

1. FRÁ-EK við Holm at heyja hildingar fimm gingo
    (lind varð grœn) inn Grána (geir-þings í tvau springa).

2. Auð gefr Eysteinn lýðom, eykr hialdr Sigurðr skialdar,
    lætr Ingi slœg syngja, semr Magnus frið bragna :
    fiœl-dýrs hafa fiórir (folk-tiald) komit aldri   5
    (rýðr bragnings konr blóði) brœðr und sól in œðri.

3. Snild berr, snarpa elda sár-flóðs þess er rýðr blóði,
    (gefit hefir Goð sialfr iœfri gagn) Sigurðar magni :
    svá's es Rauma ræsir reið-mæltr tœlor greiðir
    (rausn viðr gramr) sem gumnar (glað-mæltr) þegi aðrir. 10

4. Vóro Sogns með (sára) syni Maddaðar staddir
    (má-grennir fremsk) manna (máttigr) tigir átta :
    þrim skútom tók þreytir þann iarl drasils hranna ;
    hraustr gaf her-skúfs nistir hœfoð sítt frœmom iœfri.

V. Dirge on Sigurd.

1. ALLZ engi þarf Inga arn-grennir þat kenna
    (hverr spyri satt frá snerro seggr) at gram bito eggjar :
    bœð gatat stillir stœðvat styrjar mildr þoat vildi,
    fús var fiœr-spell vísa fylkiss sveit at veita.

2. Út let stœng á stræti sterkr dýrligra merkja   5
    (dúðosk dœrr af reiði) Dags-sonr bera fagra :
    hnigo menn í gný gunnar gagls fyrir strengjar hagli,
    brœðr hafa barsk í víðri Biœrgyn fyr ósynjo.

3. Myndi eigi seima-sendir svá skiótt hafa látið

---

of Hrund [island in South More]. My hand was decked when I met
the king [i. e. he gave me a guerdon]. Darts were whetted, etc.

IV. *On the Gillungs.* I have heard that the kings went forth to battle at
Grey-Holm, the green linden-wood [shield] sprang in two in the fight.
    Eystan gives men riches, Sigurd makes the shield-fray to rise, Ingi
lets the arrows ring, Magnus brings peace to men. Four such noble
brethren of royal blood have never come beneath the sun's canopy.
Sigurd's valour is surpassing, God gives him victory. When the Lord of
the Reams speaks, all other men may hold their peace.
    Of Eystan. There were eighty men with the son of Maddad
[Harold, Earl of Orkney], and the king attacked the earl with three
small ships, and the earl bowed to him.

    V. Dirge on Sigurd. Ingi cannot be blamed in that the edges bit
the king [Sigurd]. Let the truth be told. He could not stop the
slaughter of the king though he would, for his men were too eager to
kill him. Daysson bore the banner up the street, the brothers fought
untimely in the midst of Bergen. The king would not have died so

(spiót flugo langt í liótri) líf sítt (boga drífo):   10
ef all-kostigs austan Eysteins flota leysti
beinn at Biœrgyn sunnan byrr tveim dœgom fyrri.

4.   Mun, sa es morði vanðisk marg-illr ok sveik stilli,
síð af slíkom rǽðom Simon Skalpr of hialpask.

VI. (From Edda.)

1.   L EYG rýðr ætt á ægi Oláfs skipa sólar
     (ylgr brunar hvatt) ins Helga (hræ-giörn í spor örnom)
2.   Snáks berr fald of frœknom fold-vörðr (konungs Hörða)
     (frama kveðr greppr fyr gumnom) geð-sniallr skarar fialli.
3.   Glym-vindi lætr Göndlar (gnestr hiörr) taka mestom   5
     Hildar segl þar er hagli, hraustr drengr, drífr strengjar.
4.   Verja hauðr með hjörvi hart döglinga biartir
     (hialmr springr opt fyr olmri egg-hrið) framir seggir.
5.   Dolg-skára kná dýrom dýr-magnaðr stýra
     Hugins fermo bregðr harmi harmr blik-sólar garmi.   10
6.   Enn við hialdr, þar er hölðar, hug-þrútið svellr, lúta,
     (Muninn drekkr blóð or benjom blá-svartr) konungs hiarta.
7.   Sám-leitom rauð sveita (sleit örn gera beito)
     [feksk arnar matr iarnom] Iarn-söxo grön faxa.
8.   Lögr þvær flaust, (enn fagrir) flóðs vaskar brim glóðom,   15
     þar er sær á hlið hvára hlymr (veðr-vitar glymja).
9.   Kaldr þvær marr und mildom mart dœgr viðo svarta
     (grefr él-snuin) iöfri (alm-sorg Manar-þialma).
10. Ne fram-lyndir fundo fyrr (hygkat lá kyrðo)
     þar er siár á við vörro vini ára féll stórom.   20
11. Viknar ramr í Rakna rek-saumr fluga-straumi;
     dúks hrindr böl þar er bleikir bif-grund á stag rifjom.
12. Harðr hefir ört frá iörðo él-vindr (svana strindar
     blakk lætr í sog sœkkva Snæ-grund) skipi hrundit.
13. Margr ríss, enn drífr dorgar dyn-strönd í svig löndom   25
     (spend verða stög stundom) stirðr keipr fira greipom.
14. Grans bera gollna spáno (göfug ferð er sú iöfri),
     [skýtr holm-fioturr Heita hrafni] snekkjo stafnar.
15. Haustköld skotað heldom holm-rönd varrar öndri.
16. Sundr springr svalra landa sverri-giörð fyrir börðom.   30

VII. Elfar-vísor on Gregorius.

1.   M ARGR fell maðr af dreyrgo mar-blakks á kaf saxi;
     gnógt elði fekksk gýgjar glaum; rak ná fyrir straumi:

---

soon, if a fair breeze had borne Eystan's fleet to Bergen but two days
earlier. The wicked Simon Scalp, who betrayed him, will be long ere
he is helped out of torment [i. e. will be in hell for ever].

VI. *Fragments of Encomia. Battle.* St. Olaf's kinsmen redden the
sword at sea. The king of the Hords bears a serpent-hood [helm].
Their men defend the land with the sword .... The king's heart
quakes not ; he feeds the wolves.

Sea. The sea breaks on both bows; the weather-vanes gleam fairly.
The cold sea washes the black timbers; the whirlwind cuts the sea ....
The tree-nails spring in the fierce race. The gale drives the ship on from
the Snowland. The ship .... The wind tries the stays .... The stems
of the galley bear gilded chips of pine.

VII. ELBE-VERSES *on Gregory Daysson.* Many a man fell from ship to
sea. The poison-cold Elbe [Gaut-Elbe] was dyed with bloody foam, and

Elfr varð unda gialfri eitr-kœld roðin heito;
vitniss féll með vatni varmt œldr í men Karmtar.

2. Mœrg fluto auð [á úrga] (alm sveigði lið) [hialma]   5
[rauð flugo stœl] í stríðri stafn-blóðog skip Móðo:
áðr á grund af grœðiss gœðinga lið flœði
(sveit varð í rym rítar rýr) Hákonar dýrom.

VIII. LAY ON AN AXE.

(From Edda ; verse 5 from Skalda.)

1. HRÓÐR-BARNI kná-ek Hörnar (hlutom dýran grip) stýra,
brandr þrymr gialfrs á grandi goll-vífiðo hlífar:
sáðs berr sinnar móðor svans unni mer gunnar
fóstr-gœðandi Fróða Freyss nipt brá-driptir.

2. Nýt buðomk Niarðar dóttor ʻnálægt var þat skála'   5
vel of hrósag því vísa ʻvarn siávar öl' barni.

3. Gaf sá er erring ofrar ógn-prúðr Vana-brúðar
þing-vávaðar þrœngvir þrótt-öflga mer dóttor:
ríkr leiddi mey mækiss mót-valdr á beð skaldi
Gefnar glóðom drifna Gautreks svana brautar.   10

4. Ráð-vöndom þá-ek rauðra randar ís at vísa
(grand berom hialms í hendi) hvarm-þey drifinn Freyjo.

5. Hring-tælir gaf Hálo hlvr-sólar mer dýra,
oss kom hrund til handa hræ-pollz drifin golli:
sótt þá-ek Herjans hattar   15

6. Næst sé-ek orm á iastar ítr-ʻserki' vel merkðan,
nemi bióðr hve ek ferr flœðar fiarð-báls of hlyn máli.

7. þar er Mardallar milli (megin-hurðar) liggr skurða
(Gautz berom galla þrútinn) grátr (dal-reyðar láttra).

8. Eigi þverr fyrir augna Óðs beð-vino róða   20
ræfrs (eignisk svá) regni ram-svell (konungr elli).

9. Blóð-eiso liggr bæði biargs tveim-megin geima
(sióðs á-ek sœkkva stríði) snær ok eldr (at mœra).

10. Siá mego rétt, hve, Rævils ríðendr, við brá Gríðar
Fiorniss fagrt of skornir fold-viggs drekar liggja.   25

11. Frá-ek at Fróða meyjar full-góliga mólo
(lætr stillir grið golli) grafvitnis beð (slitna).

the warm blood flowed down into the sea. Many an empty ship with
bloody bows was floating on the rapid river-mouth ere the warriors of
Hakon *Broadshoulders* betook themselves to flight.

VIII. *The axe Hnoss*. I own the child of Horn [Hnoss], a precious
possession decked with gold. The king gave me Frey's niece adorned
with the corn of Frodi. The child of Niord's daughter . . . . He
provided me with a wife, the daughter of the Wane's bride ; he led her
to my bed, the daughter of Gefn, sprinkled with the embers of the sea
[gold]. I received an axe adorned with Freya's tears. He gave me a precious shield-devouring ogress. I got a helmet-crusher studded with gold.
Next I see a well-carved serpent on the willow-bane [axe]. I praise the
king. Lo, a target-breaker heavy with Mardall's tears and the dragon's
litter. There was no lack of the eye-rain of Od's spouse on the blade.
Silver and gold lie on both cheeks of the axe. Thou mayest see the
dragons lying fairly carved about the face of the blade. I know that
Frodi's maids did merrily grind the serpent's bed, and the cheeks of my

16. Read, -herkio or verki?

12.   Miúks bera mínnar œxar meldr þann við hlyn feldrar
       (konungs dýrkar fé) Fenjo fögr hlyr (bragar-stýri).

13.   Dœgr þrumir hvert (enn hiarta hlýr-skyldir ræðr mildo)   30
       Heita blakks of hvítom haf-leygr dígol-skafli :
       aldri má fyr eldi áls hryn-brautar skála
       (öll viðr folka fellir fram-ræði) snæ bræða.

14.   Hvargi er Beita borgar bál-grinmostom skála
       hárr of hnoss-vin órom heims vafr-logi sveimar.   35

IX. Love-Song (on Solborg and Ioreid).

(Verses 1, 3 from Skalda ; verse 2 from Edda, W. App.)

1.   HARÐAN þrýtr á hvítom harm Sólborgar armi.
2.   Hrynja lét in hvíta haus-miöll ofan lausa
      strind örriða strandar stallz *af skarar fialli.*
3.   Víst eromk Hermð á Hesti hefir flióð ef vill góðan.

BÖÐVARR HALTI (on Sigurd).

(Verse 1 from Mork. ; verse 4 from Edda.)

1.   NÚ skal lýst hve Lista læ-skiarr konungr harra
         (gœrðisk afreks orða efnd) þíns fœðor hefndir :
      létoð hialms at Holmi (hríð-spurðisk sú víða)
      [ofkúgi dó iœfra] allvaldr, Sigurð falla.

2.   Magnus varð at morði mál-sniallr í bœð falla ;   5
      réð fyrir ræsiss dauða ríkr þióð-konungr slíkom :
      meirr rak þik til þeirra, þrek-sterkr konungr, verka
      (flagðs hest hafit flestan fylldan) nauðr an skyldi.

3.   Þar féll allt ok œrvir (ulfr rauð á her dauðom
      teðr) í tognings veðri tveir iœfrar lið þeira.   10
      Allz engi verðr Inga undir sólar grundo
      böðvar havir né betri, brœðr, landreki in œðri.

KOLLI PRÚÐI (on Ingi).

1.   UNNOT austr fyrir Mynni odd-hríð (ok brátt síðan
         hilmir fekkt und hialmi hrafns verðar lið) sverðom :

---

axe are fair with plenty of this meal. The sea-fire [gold] lies on the
snow of the crucible [silver] on my weapon, but that fire will not meet
that snow. The generous king's gift makes the poet proud. Wherever
the world's flame [sun] swims may he, my Hnoss-giving patron, be
happy.

IX. *To Solborg.* Deep grief vanishes in the white arms of Solborg.
She lets her hair [the white meal of the skull] fall down from her head
to her shoulders.

To Ioreid. Verily I love Ioreid [lit. horse = io + wrath = reid] if she
will have me.

BODWAR THE HALT. *Sigurd's Praise.* Now I will tell how thou
didst revenge thy father. Ye made Sigurd to fall at Holm ; the cower
of kings died. Magnus the eloquent was slain there. It was a greater
need than was meet that drove thee to this. There fell two kings and
all their host.

Burden. There is no king better than Ingi's brother underneath the sun.

COLL THE PROUD. *Ingi's Praise.* Ye fought a battle in the east off

lægðot ér, enn eirar ǫrr synjaðir brynjo
(ungr varðir-þú, þengill þítt land) saman randir.

2. Fyrr lá hans, an harri hring-mildr þaðan vildi, 5
verðung ǫll á velli—*Vig-fimr konungr himni* :
sundr klauft siklingr Þrœnda (sókn-fúss an Magnúsi
þer féksk hǫlfo hæri) her-skriptir (iǫfurr gipta).

3. Lýsa man-ek hve liósa (laut hrafn í ben Gauta)
[ǫrn fylðit sik sialdan] sár-ísa rauð vísi : 10
goldit varð þeim-es gœrðo glaum herðondom sverða
(raun er at ríki þíno) róg á Króka-skógi.

4. Rauðri dreif (þá er riúfa réð ǫld of gram skiǫldo)
miǫll, áðr Magnús félli morð-giarn, þrumo iarna :
harmar œngr (þvi-at, Ingi, áttu ráða vel láði) 15
[dœgg fell driúgt á skokka] dráp Sigurðar [vápna].

5. Syndi sialfr at landi sniallr (enn þú brátt allri)
[vel um hrósak því] vísi val-kǫst (ara fǫsto) :
ulfs bǫrnom varð arnar einkar tíðr í víðo
(borð ruðo frægir fyrðar) fundr Langeyjar-sundi. 20

ÞORBIÖRN SKAKKA-SKALD (on Earl Erling Skakki).

(Verse 2 from Edda.)

1. HIŒGGO œxar eggjom ugg-laust hvatir glugga
(því var nennt á nýjo) Norðmenn í kaf borði :
eyðendr sá yðrar arnar hungrs (á iǫrnom)
(vág-fylvingi) vélar (víg-skǫrð) ofan (bǫrðot).

2. Haf-reiðar var hlœðir hlunnz í skírnar brunni 5
Hvíta-Kristz sa-es hæsta hodd-sviptir tók gipto.

3. Greitt frá-ek gumna dróttinn (gríðar fáks) í víðo
(trauðr erat tenn at rióða) Túnsbergi þer snúna :

---

the Mouth [southern outlet of Lake Miösen]. All his men were lying on
the field before he turned to flight.
Burden. . . . Gallant king, *greatest* under heaven.—The Thronds' king
clave the war-scrolls [shields]; ye had better luck than Magnus. Now
I will tell how the prince dyed his bright blade. The raven stooped to
the gashes of the Gauts : the evil they wrought was repaid them on Crook-
shaw. There was a snow-fall of blood ere murderous Magnus fell. The
slaying of Sigurd no man is sorry for, because thou, Ingi, wilt have the
rule of the land. Thou didst break the eagle's feet. There was a feast
for the wolves in Langey-sound.

THORBIORN SHANK'S POET. *Sigurd and Erling's Praise. The drome-
dary taken in the Mediterranean.* The brisk Northmen cut a clean dead-
light into the timbers at the water's edge with their sharp axes. It
was a cunning trick. The pirates [Saracens] could not see your stratagem
from above. Ye cut a scarp with your iron upon the ship.
Pilgrimage. The earl had the bliss of bathing in the baptismal font
of the White Christ [Jordan].
Fight in Tunsberg. I heard of thy success at Tunsberg ; the townsmen
feared the bright spears and fire and the bow bent, *and submitted.*

hræddosk biartra brodda bǿjar-menn við renno;
ugðo elld ok sveigðan alın dyn-viðir malma.   10

4.   Urð dró austan-fiarðar Erlingr at víkingom
(mein fekk margr af Kǿno maðr) er hann fór þaðra:
fǿrðr var fleinn meðal herða Friðreks ofar nœkkvi
skolldi óþarfr ǫldom ill-giarn við tré Biarni.

ÁSGRÍMR KETILSSON (on HAKON HERÐI-BREID).

(From Edda.)

SIGR-GŒÐIR var síðan seim-ǫrr í Þróndheimi
(þióð veit þínar iðir) þann orms-trega (sannar).

STYRKARR ODDASON (on MAGNUS ERLINGSON).

(From Edda.)

OK ept ítrom stœkkvi ók Hǫgna lið vǫgnom
hlunnz á heiða fannir hyrjar flóðs af móði.

KLŒNGR BISKOP (ALHENDA).

(From Edda Ht.)

BAÐ-EK sveit á glað Geitiss, gœr er ið at fǿr tíðom;
drǫgom hest á lǫg lesta; lið flýtr, enn skrið nýtom.

OCCASIONAL VERSES.

WE have placed here a number of Occasional Verses of interest, all,
save one or two, between 1130–1202, contemporary with the events
treated of in this section; a pendant to the Improvisations in Book vi,
though they are of a less spontaneous character. They are arranged
roughly in chronological order.

The first set belongs to EARL ROGNWALD the Crusader, whose life and
deeds have been already touched on. They are selected from a number
of verses in the Rolls Series' edition of Orkney Saga, where the rest will
be found. They refer to Rognwald's stay at Grimsby in his youth (No. 1),
to his accomplishments (No. 2), to his exploration of the Doll's Cave
in one of the islands off South More in Norway (No. 3), to Hall his

---

Hanging of Biarni and Frederick. East of the Wick Erling piled stones
over the Wickings ere he left. Many a man had fared ill at Kona's
hands. A fluke lashed to Frederick's back was cast overboard, but the
wicked Biarni was whipped up to the gallows-tree *ashore.*

ASGRIM KETTLESSON. *On Swerri.* This winter thou didst stay in
Throndham. Men know thy deeds of renown.

STYRKARR ORDSSON. *On Swerri* (?). The host chased him in
Hogni's wains, making a hot pursuit over the snow-heaps of the surges.

CLONG. *A Cruise.* I call my crew aboard my ship. I am often
busy a-journeying. Let us launch the cargo-horse on the water. The
galley speeds; let us carry on.

friend and poet's introduction to him (Nos. 4, 5), to the Earl's crusading exploits (Nos. 6, 7), and to his escape from his enemies when they were foiled by the clever misdirection of Botolf the Icelander (No. 8). The poem which the Earl and his friend Hall (the author of verse 4) made together as a *Clavis Metrica*, 'Hatta-lykill,' must be dealt with elsewhere.

The next group gives stray verses of the prolific *Einar Sculason*, whose powers of making impromptu epigrams were remarkable. One (No. 9) refers to the scant welcome he got from the Danish king Swain, who preferred the new-fashioned music to the Encomia, which he could not understand. The next three (Nos. 10–12) were made at the court of the Northern kings, to whom he was marshal. One when he was fined for being late for dinner, having been on a visit to the Abbess of Bank. One made while Earlman the fiddler was being flogged for theft, it being understood that he was only to be beaten till the poet had made a verse. It is said that he finished the couplet ere more than five stripes had fallen. The last is on a fair lady sailing out of harbour in her ship, and was completed before the ship reached a certain point in the bay.

Thorward, Hall, Biarni, Mani, Nefari, and others are the composers of the next group, which deals chiefly with events in Norway, chiefly from Swerri's time. To be noted is the greeting from Thorward in Iceland to his brother Ari in Norway at the king's court; and Mani's complaint that poetry is going out of favour.

The next two sets (Nos. 30–42) deal chiefly with Icelandic men and things. *Eyiolf* tells of the famous Gudmund's voyage, and refers to a certain Botolf the skipper. *Kolbein Tumason* (died 1208, see Prolegomena, cxxiii–iv) complains that, like Henry II, he has made a mistake, Gudmund his minister has turned out like Thomas à Becket. Kolbein's prayer, inspired by the Psalms, is not to be passed over.

In the last group we have *Runolf* talking with pride of the cathedral of Holar, built by Arni and Biorn, under the orders of his own father Clong (No. 43). *Amund Arnison*, the architect of Paul bishop of Skalholt, who may be the son of Runolf's Arni, made a dirge on his patron. He had already composed a blessing (No. 44) on Paul's four children. The fortune of these children did not come up to all that the good poet wished. Loft (the puffin-bone picker of Book vi, No. 70) lived long enough to play the spy for Snorri Sturlason's murderers, dying 1261: see Sturlunga Saga. Of Kettle we know but this, a wit said of the two brothers, that Loft had always a good word to spare, but that Kettle bore good will to all; one preached what the other practised. Halla, still a girl, was drowned with her mother whilst crossing a river, May 17, 1207 (see the pathetic story in the Reader, p. 225); when the whole burden of the Bishop's household fell on Thora (called after her great-grandmother, the Royal Thora of p. 319), who, as the author of Paul's life tells us, though a mere child, managed everything exceedingly well. What afterwards became of her we do not know. The Bishop was the son of John Loptsson, of whom below, p. 309.

The hangings in Holar cathedral bore on them the verse, No. 46. They were in existence in the last century.

Hall of Madderfield, the popular chief praised in the ditty, No. 45, was one of those who signed the Act of Resignation in 1262, which transferred the sovereignty of the Commonwealth of Iceland to the king of Norway.

Both these last verses may be by the same man, the metre (called dun-hent) is the same, and both are from North of Iceland.

I. Rognwald and his Friends.

1. VER hœfom vaðnar leiror vikor fimm megin-grimmar
    (saurs vara vant þar er várom viðr) í Grímsbý miðjom:
    nú es þat-es márs of mýrar megin-kátliga lǿtom
    branda-elg á bylgjor Biœrgynjar til dynja.

2. Tafl em-ek œrr at efla—íþróttir kann-ek nío;—   5
    týni-ek trauðla rúnom; tíð erom bók ok smíðir:
    skríða kann-ek á skíðom; skýt-ek ok ræ-k svá-at nýtir;
    hvárt-tveggja kann-ek hyggja, harp-sláttr ok brag-þótto.

3. Her hef-ek hávan reistan harð-geðjoðom varða
    Dollz í dœkkom helli draug; leitak svá bauga: 10
    eigi veit nær ýtir unn-skíða kœmr síðan
    langa braut ok lióta leið yfir vatnit breiða.
                                         Orkney S., chs. 61, 63.

4. Senda-ek son þínn, Ragna (sœnn koma mǿl fyrir bragna)
    hans var hagleg iðja hirð-vistar mer biðja:
    hafa kvezt hodda rýrir, hinn-er hæstom veg stýrir,   15
    (neitti hann grúpans granna) gnótt víglegri manna.
                                         Hall Breiðmagi, Orkney S., ch. 85.

5. Aldr' hefek frétt þat-er féldo frán-stallz konor allar
    (verðrat menja-myrðir miúk-orðr) hǿfoð-dúkom:
    nú tér Hlœkk um hnakka hauk-strindar ser binda
    (skrýðisk brúðr við bræði ben-gagls) merar tagli.   20
                                         Orkney S., ch. 85.

6. Vill eigi vinr minn kalla (varð allr í drit falla)
    [nær var í því œrin úgæfa] midævi:

I. Earl Rognwald. *The mud at Grimsby.* I have been plodding
through the muck in the middle of Grimsby for five awful weeks. There
was no lack of mud when we were there; but at last with great joy I
am making the prow-elk (ship) run over the billows of mew's moor [sea]
to Bergen. [c. 1125.]

His prowess. I am strong at table-play. I know nine accomplishments.
I never mistake a rune. I am used to book-learning and carpentry.
I can stride on snow-skates, and I can shoot and row as well as needs be
[very well]. I understand both harp-playing and poet-craft.

The Giant's Cave. Here I have reared a high cairn to the grim ghost
in Doll's dark cave where I came seeking for treasure. No one can tell
how long it will be ere another man shall pass over the long road and
ugly way over the broad water [inside the cave].

Hall's rejection. I sent thy son Ragna, of a truth, to seek quarters for
me, but the Earl said he had no lack of better men, and refused the
Sausager [Icelanders were so nicknamed from their mutton sausages].

On the new fashion. I always heard that ladies were wont to wrap
their heads in kerchiefs, but here is a lady who binds her hair with a
mare's tail. [c. 1140.]

In the Eastern city. My friend would not cry 'midhæfi' [μεταβῇθι,

---

lítt hykk at þá þcétti þengils mágr, er hann rengðisk,
(leir fell grár of geira) góligr í Imbólom.

7.   Ríðom Rævils vakri (rekom eigi plóg af Akri)   25
[erjom úrgo barði] út at Mikla-garði :
þiggjom þengils mála, þokom framm í gný stála,
ríóðom gylðis góma, gœrom ríks konungs-sóma.
Orkney S., ch. 96.

8.   Ferr at foglom harri, firar neyta vel skeyta,
vǽn á heiðar-hœna hnakka-dytz und bakka :   30
þar lætr almr, er olmir unn-linnz stafar finnask,
(lǫnd verr lofdungr brandi) lyng-hœsn vegin kyngjom.
Orkney S., ch. 193.

II. EINAR SCULASON.

9   Eigi hlaut af ítrom Einarr giafa Sveini
(ǫld lofar ǫðlings mildi œðro-styggs) fyrir kvæði :
Danskr harri metr dýrra (dugir miðlung þat) fiðlor
[ræðr fyr ræsiss auði Rípa-Ulfr] ok pípor.
Skioldunga (Knytl. S., ch. 108).

10.   Oss lét abbadissa angri firð um svangann   5
(dygg þoli víf in vígðo víti fyr þat) gyrða :
enn til átz með nunnom (ógnar-rakks) á Bakka
(drós gladdit vin vísa) varat stallarinn kallaðr.

11.   Austr tók ílla kristinn Iarlmaðr frá bú-karli
(gráðr var kiǫtz á kauða) kiðling, hinn er slær fiðlo :   10
vǫndr hrœkk, vámr lá bundinn vesl-máll 'á sk . . .' þíslar,
sœng leikarn lengi límí harðan príma.

12.   Hola bǽro rístr hlýri hreysti-sprund at sundi
(blæss él-reki of Ási) Útsteins (vefi þrútna) :

---

make way]. It was a great mishap, he fell into the dirt. I do not think
that he was very gay to look on, the king's son-in-law, when he was
rolling in the mire in the city [ἔμπολιν?]. [1152.]

In the Archipelago. Let us ride Refil's steed to Micklegarth. Let us
plow with our wet prows from Acre [Constantinople]. Let us enter
the service of the Greek Emperor.

Botolf the Icelander. The earl is a-fowling, the men are plying their
shafts. The heath-hen may look out for a blow on her neck. The
bow is making terrible havoc of the heath-cock. [1154.]

II. EINAR SCULASON. *Swain's stinginess.* Einar got no gifts from king
Swain for his song; the Danish king cares more for fiddles and pipes.
Ripe-Wolf rules his treasury. [c. 1155.]

The Abbess' poor fare. The abbess left me starving. Let the holy
wives suffer for it. The marshal was not called to dinner with the nuns
at Bank. The lady did not treat the king's friend [me] well.

The verse on Earlman. The heathen Earlman, greedy fiddler, stole a
kid from a cottager. The rod is swung, the thief is sized to the gratings,
the minstrel sings a long-drawn note under the stick.

The fair Ragnhild sailing round the Naze at Bergen. The proud lady

---

6. þoli] emend. ; þótt, Cd.

varla heldr und vildra vík-marr á iarðríki   15
breiðan við brims-gang súðom barmr lyptingar farmi.
Morkinskinna, pp. 227, 228.

III. NORWEGIAN INCIDENTS.

13.   Berit hildingi hœlða, harð-geðr Ari, kveðjo
(þeim-es lætr í bœð bíta bryn-þing) ok Erlingi :
at lang-viðris lengi lifi þeir, ok sé meiri
allri þióð, í œllom óttlaust friði Dróttins.

14.   Gramr hefir suðr á sumri snar-fingr með Erlingi   5
bróðir mínn und breiðar brand-éls staðit randir :
víg-garðz hefir varðat veðr-eggjandi beggja
okkart rúm, þar-es ámir, ungr, bœð-koflar sprungo.
Gudmundar Saga, Bk. i. 410, 411.

15.   Önundr kvask eigi mundo við orrosto kosta,
fyrr an sunnan sigldi Sigurðr iarl með húskarla :   10
miœk fara Magnúss rekkar mætir upp at stræti,
enn Hákonar haukar hart skundoðo undan.
Hulda, Kings' Lives.

16.   Fylgðo ræsi Rygir ok Hœrðar,
Filar ok Sygnir, sem Firða lið,
Mœrir allir, menn Raumdœlskir,   15
Erki-biskop, œll Þrœnda-lœg.

17.   Glym-vœllo rístr, golli (góð er stilliss fœr) Róða
Óláfs-súð und auði (auð-grimms) buin rauðo :
Nú er œgr or fœr frægri (fellr húfr í svig dúfo
svelldr) með sœmð ok mildi siklingr kominn hingat.   20

ʃ 8.   Berr fyrir Holm, þar-er harri hlýrs fagr-gota stýrir
(stœl bruna rauð á reyðar rym-vœll) und gram sniœllom :

---

plows the hollow billows in her ship over Utstein's Sound, the gale blows
upon the canvas on the yard. Never ship on earth held prouder lady,
nor broad hull bore costlier burden over ocean. [c. 1150–55.]

III. *Thorward Thorgeirsson to his brother Ari, Ingi's henchman.* Greet for
me, good Ari, the King and Erling, that they may live a long life many
a day in the peace of the Lord. My brother stood stoutly under shield
this summer with Erling, when the dark war-cowls were split. He has
filled his place and my own. [1160-67.]

Anonymous. Tunsberg Battle. Anwynd would not fight till Earl Sigurd
and his guard came from the south. Magnus' men are marching swiftly
up the street, but Hakon's war-hawks are flying fast away. [1162.]

The Norwegians. The Rugians and the Hords followed the king, the
Fils and Sogn-folk, and the men of the Friths, all the Mores, the
Reamsdale men, the Archbishop and all Thrond-law. [1180.]

Hall Snorrisson. Olaf's galley, adorned with the red gold, furrows the
roaring plain of Rodi, beneath her costly load. The king's cruise is
prosperous. The king has come off his famous journey, the big hull is
dipping into the lap of the billows. The goodly ship fetches Holm ; the
king is steering ; the red prow speeds over the thundering whale-path
beneath the king. The famous prince is come hither with fame and
victory, for he has won a battle. [1182.]

frægr er með fremð ok sigri (folk-bráðr konungr háði
darra-þing við drengi) dœglingr kominn hingat.

19.　Fant sé-ek hvern á hesti (her er nú siðr inn versti)　25
[leið eigo ver langa] enn lendir menn ganga:
hirð-menn skolo hlaupa (her erat gótt til kaupa)
[munka-ek mœrgo kvíða], enn mat-sveinar ríða.

20.　Byr gefðu brátt inn œrvi Biœrgynjar til mœrgom
(þess biðjom ver) þióðom, þung-stóls konungr sólar:　30
angrar oss þat-er lengi út-nyrðingr heldr fyrðom
(vindr er til seinn at sundi sunn-rœnn) í dys Unnar.

21.　Slœgr ferr gaurr með gígjo (ginn er her komit inni)
[meiðr hefir skialdar-skóða skrípa-lát] ok pípo:
rekkr lætr rauða bikkjo (rekkit skvaldr!) fyrir aldir　35
[skolot hlýða því þióðir; þat er skaup] yfir staf hlaupa.

22.　Gígjan syngr, þar-er ganga (grípa menn til pípo)
[fœra fíflsko stóra framm] leikarar bleikir:
undr er hve augom vendir umb sa-er þýtr í trumbo,
kníðan lít-ek á kauða kiapt ok blásna hvápta.　40

23.　Týnom Birki-beinom! Beri Sverrir hlut verra!
látom rand-hœing reyndan ríða hart ok tíðom:
hœlomk minzt í máli, metomk heldr at val feldan,
látom skipta Guð gipto, gœrom hríð þa-er þeim svíði.

24.　Reisom vé fyrir vísa, verom þungir Kuflungom,　45
látom brýndan hiœr líta, bolom tafn und kló hrafni:

Bearni Calfsson. We have a long way to march. There is a most evil custom observed. Every rascal footman is on horseback, but the barons are walking; the guard must run, while the sutlers ride. This is a bad bargain, but I shall not worry over it. [1182.]

Mani the Icelander. For a fair wind. O thou King of Heaven, give us a fair wind to Bergen, we pray thee. It grieves us that the north-west keeps us here so long at Unnar-dys. The southern wind is too slow in coming from the Sound. [1184.]

The same. Jugglers preferred to Poets. The crafty rascal comes with pipe and fiddle. The conjuror has come. The chattering impostor is beginning his mummery. He is making a red bitch jump over a stick for a show to the people. What folly! People ought not to listen to it. Cease this din! The fiddle sings out as the pale players walk along; they grasp their pipes, they carry on the greatest foolery. It is won-derful how the man that blows the trumpet rolls his eyes. Behold the wry chaps and puffed out cheeks of the zany! [1184.]

Nefari. Curse on the Birchlegs. Let us destroy the Birchlegs; may Swerri be crushed; let the shield-snake strike hard and swift. Let us not boast in our speech; let us tell over the score when the battle is over. God give the victory! Let us fall upon them and make them smart. [1186.]

Blank's answer. Let us hoist the standard before the king, and bear hard on the Cowlings. Let the keen blade bite, and let us hew a sacri-fice beneath the raven's talons. Let us hobble our enemies' bands.

hnekkjom fiánda flokki, friðom land iæfurs brandi
rióðom dœrr í dreyra, drepom meira hlut þeira.

25. Öld man heldr, at hœldosk (hvatir guldo þess skatnar)
fyrr (or flokki þeirra) forráðs-tungor Koflunga: 50
nú kná bergs í biœrgom (búk reiðir lǽ siúkan)
[mettr varð hrafn í Hrótti] hótz annan veg þióta.

26. Biœrt kveða brenna kerti Breið-skeggs yfir leiði,
lióss veit-ek at mun missa meirr hœfðingi þeira:
.   .   .   .
vitom at vánir betri (verr hugðomk því) brugðosk.   55

27. Hafði her meðan lifði hvárt-tveggja Breið-skeggi
(nu er frið-spillir fallinn) fæst gótt ok dul hæsta.

28. Mánadag kvaddi mildingr sína, menn drifo hart til vápna
unno;
Inga hirð enn upp réð ganga ár morgin til Sverris borgar:
ýtar reisto merki at móti margar stengr, ok bœrðosk lengi; 60
Baglar stóðo í brodda hagli, brunno skip þa-er kappar runno.

29. Mánadag kvaddi 'níðingr' sína menn g. h. til v. s.
(Þúfo-skítr þrífisk aldri!) þann morgin t. S. b.
ýtar r. m. at m. m. st. ok b. lengi
Baglar standa í banni allir, brunno sk. þ. e. k. r.   65

Verses 16–29 from Sverris Saga.

Let us win peace for our lord's land with the sword. Let us dye our
darts in blood. Let us slay the most part of them.

After the battle. Men remember well how the slanderous tongues of
the Cowlings boasted. Now they have paid for it in person. There is
another sound heard in the hill [berg] of Tunberg, [the wind has turned]
now that their corpses are washing in the shallow, and the raven was
sated at Rott [island]. [1187.]

Broadbeard the Rebel. They say that bright candles are burning over
Broadbeard's grave, but I rather think that this chief of theirs will turn
out a lack-light. Better hopes have failed than his; I believe the case is
a far worse one.

Burden of a mock dirge on Broadbeard. All the while he lived here
Broadbeard was both of smallest good and greatest damage. Spill-
peace is dead at last. [1191.]

The Croziers' lampoon. On Monday the king called on his men, and
soldiers rushed swiftly to battle. Ingi [the Croziers' king] marched up
to Swerri's stronghold early in the morning. They raised many a staff
over against the standard and fought long. The Croziers stood in the
arrow-hail. The ships burnt when the champions fled.

The Birchlegs' answer. On Monday the Niding called on his men, and
soldiers rushed swiftly to battle in the morning to Swerri's stronghold.
Plague upon him, that dung-heap! They raised many a staff over
against the standard and fought long. The Croziers stood all under
one curse. The ships burnt while the champions fled. [1198.]

IV. *Grim and his friends sailing with the bishop-elect, Gudmund, to Norway, July 14th, 1202, are driven out of their course to the Orkneys, where they
hear the news of Swerri's death. On the storm there are the following verses.*
Eyiolf: The ship was driven eastward out of Ireland. God gave them

IV. Gudmund's Friends.

30. Báro austr frá Íra ætt-landi skæ branda
hregg óð, himna tiggi heit-byr firom veitti.

31. Sér á sigling óra Suðreysk kona (þuðri
súð gærask nú nauðir) nám-giœrn, er hryðr stiœrnom.

32. Her hefir beitt á brattri Bótolfr skipi flióto   5
(áðr fell sær um súðir) Sandeyjo skæ branda :
reisti sialfr (ok sýsti) snarr félagi harra
hafnar-mark fyrir hrefnis (happs-verk) gota sterkan.

33. Her náðom val víðis víg-lundr með Guðmundi
sterkr at stœðva merki stefno, biskops-efni :   10
frágom áðr á Eiði einni nótt fyrir Dróttins
(trauðr man glaum at gœða grams herr) bana Sverris.

34. Eisandi veðr undir uðr (nú er hvast or suðri)
[stœrir sterkar báror, starf erað smátt] fyrir Hvarfi :
klœkkr verðr kiœlr, enn rakkan kemr hregg í stað seggja,   15
nu ero fiœll á sæ sollin, súð gengr æ sem prúðast.

Hrafns S., ch. 11.

35. Klasi nam kalla þrysvar, komi menn ok renni !
(iœrð bifast œll und fyrðom) undan biskops fundi.

Bisk. Sogor, i. 513, v. l.

V. Kolbein Tumason.

36. Báls kveðr hlynr at Hólom hvern mann vera í banni
Gylva láðs þann er greiðir geð-rakkr fyrir mer nakkvat :
trautt kann hóf, sá-er háttar hodd-lestir vel flesto,
(meðr ero at því aðrir ósælir) stór-mæla.

37. Bannar biskop mœnnom (berr stríð af því víða   5
lýða kind á láði lœngom) kirkjo-gœngor :
geystr man gegn at flesto Guðmundr fara um stundir,
trautt má-ek enn fyrir annan enda siá hvar lendir.

---

the wind they desired. *Grim :* The maids of the Isles look on our proud sailing. The wave dashes up to the stars. Here Botolf has laid his ship on steep Sanday. He had a harbour-mark raised for the strong ship. We have now reached the harbour-mark. At Eid, one night before the Lord's day, we first heard of King Swerri's death. [Swerri died March 9th, 1202.] The surge is boiling off Cape Wrath. The ship goes on as proud as may be. [1202.]

Anonymous Ditty, in a fight. Clasi called out thrice, 'Come and let us run away from facing the Bishop. The earth is quaking beneath our feet.' [1220.]

V. Kolbein Tumason's *troubles with Gudmund.* The bishop of Holar proclaims every man under his ban who does me any kindness. He knows no measure in his curses. He forbids men's going to church, he carries his head high; I cannot tell what end it tends to. God has made Gudmund like Thomas in power, he lies close to our ears, he

---

3. Read, fæsto ?

38.   Guð hefir Guðmund gœrvan glíkan Thoma at ríki,
      nær liggr okkr við eyra erfingi hœfðingja: 10
      rœðr Guðs laga geymir geð-biartr snœro hiarta ;
      hræðisk himna prýði hann, enn vætki annat.

39.   Mundi mer fyrir stundo mikit orða-lag þykkja
      of elg-renni unnar eyrom slíkt at heyra.
                    Bisk. Sogor, i. 490, 491 (verse 39 from *Skalda*).

40.   Heyrðu, himna smiðr, hvers er skaldit biðr;   15
      komi miúk til mín miskunn þín:
      því heit-ek á þik, þú hefir skapðan mik ;
      ek em þrællinn þínn, þú ert Dróttinn mínn.

41.   Guð heit-ek á þik at þú grœðir mik ;
      minnstu, mildingr, mín, mest þurfom þín: 20
      ryttu, rœðla gramr rík-lyndr ok framr,
      hœldz hverri sorg or hiarta borg.

42.   Gættu, mildingr, mín (mest þurfom þín)
      hœlzt hverja stund á hœlda grund :
      sentu, Meyjar mœgr, máls-efnin fœgr   25
      (œll er hialp af þer) í hiarta mer.
                    Bisk. Sogor, i. 568.

VI. On Icelandic Subjects.

43.   Hraust er hœll su-er Kristi hug-blíðom lét smíða
      (góð er rót und ráðom) ríkr stiórnari (slíkom):
      gipta var þat-er gœrði Guðs rann Ígultanni,
      Pétr hefir eignast ítra Arna smíð ok Biarnar.
                    Runolfr, Hungrvaka, ch. 17.

44.   Lopt efli Guð gipto (gangi fæst af því) hæstri !   5

---

has a proud heart; he fears God and nought beside.   A long time ago
I should have thought it strange to hear such language from him.
[c. 1206.]
      Kolbein's prayer.   Listen, O Maker of the Heavens, to the poet's prayer.
May thy gentle mercy reach me.   I call upon thee, thou hast made me,
I am thy servant, thou art my Lord.   I pray thee, O God, to heal me.
Remember me, O Lord, I am in sore need of thee.   Do thou, King of
the Sun, mighty and great, take every sorrow of mine from my heart.
Keep me, O Lord, I am in sore need of thee every hour on this earth:
send a fair hope into my heart, O Son of the Virgin; all help is from
thee. [c. 1206.]

      VI. *Runolf, Bishop Clong's son, on his father's new-built Cathedral at Skal-
holt.*   Proud is the hall that he [the Bishop] raised to Christ.   Such a
plan springs from a good root.   It is of good omen that Bearn built this
house of God.   Peter [the saint to whom it was hallowed] has acquired
the noble handiwork of Arni and Beorn [the architects]. [c. 1170.]
      AMUND ARNASON, *the cleverest carpenter in all Iceland, who made the
steeple of Holar Cathedral, that for carpentry bore the palm over all that had
ever been done in Iceland.   His blessing on Bishop Paul's children, two boys
and two girls.*   May God magnify Loft with the highest and most

---

5. Emend.; eflir, gengr, stýðr, liær, Cd.

kœnn styði krapti sínom Ketils lán iœfurr mána:
œztr leai ævi baztrar allz Dróttinn þer, Halla!
dýrr magni þrif Þóro þengill hœfuð-Engla.

Amundi, Pals S., ch. 12.

45. Öll unna hiú Halli, Hallr er blíðr við alla;
getr eigi slíka í svcitom, sveit þo-at víða leiti: 10
kynnist mœrgom manni mann-baldr sa-er fremr aldir;
full er œlbærð œllom, œll a Mœðro-vœllom.

Bisk. Sogor, i. 593.

46. Gramr skóp hæstr heima, heims fegrð ok kyn beima;
frægr hefir sett með sigri sigr-valdr skipan aldar:
spenr í sælo sína sín bœrn iœfurr stiœrno,   15
því er al-stillir allra all-sannr faðir manna.

---

§ 6. TWELFTH-CENTURY POEMS ON PAST EVENTS.

GEISLI, or ÓLÁF'S DRÁPA, by EINAR SCULASON, 1154.

THE following statement is found in Morkinskinna:—"Einar Sculason
was with the brothers Sigurd and Eystan; and King Eystan was a great
friend of his, and bade him compose an Encomium on Olaf; and he
did so, and delivered it at Throndham in the North, in Christ Church
itself; and this took place in the midst of great tokens, and there came
a sweet savour into the church. And men say that this was a sign from
the king (St. Olaf) himself, that he was pleased with the poem."

The time of this occurrence is fixed between 1152, (the establishment
of the archbishop's see spoken of in the text,) and the beginning of the
quarrel between the brothers which led to Sigurd's death in 1155 (10th

---

unstinted gifts. May the King of the Moon increase Kettle's estate
by his power. May the Lord of all bestow a most blissful life on Halla.
May the precious Ruler of the archangels make Thora thrive mightily.
[c. 1200.]

On Hall of Madderfield. Anonymous. All the household love Hall.
Hall is blithe with all. You will not find such a man though you seek
far and wide through the counties. He is well known to many men,
this chief of men who helps every one. There is hearty hospitality for
all in Madderfield. [c. 1260.]

Embroidered on the hangings in the Cathedral Church of Holar in Iceland.
The high King of the worlds, he created the beauty of the world and the
children of men; the glorious Prince of victory has victoriously ordained
the estate of mortals. The Ruler of the stars draws his children into his
bliss; whereby he, the Lord of all, becomes a true father to all men.

---

12. I. e. olværð.

June). Still nearer we can get by the mention of Eindrid the Young, a crusader who had been with Earl Rognwald in the Holy Land. He could not, we should think, have been home before the spring of 1153; and it must have been on St. Olaf's day, July 29th, of 1153 or 1154 that Einar delivered his composition before the three kings, Eystan, Sigurd, and Ingi, the new archbishop John, the Guild-Brothers of St. Olaf, and the general congregation of Thronds. There is a blank in the Gillungs' Saga covering these two years 1153 and 1154, so that we are dependent on the poem itself for the record of this great meeting and ceremony.

The *text* is founded on the two vellums, Birgis-bok (Codex Holmensis) with the better, and Flatey-bok (vol. i) with the worst text. A skilful edition of this poem by Cederschiold, Lund 1874, has been consulted.

The *title* is given as GEISLI in Flatey-bok. In the other MS., and when cited, as in Morkinskinna, it is headed *Olaf's drapa*. The title 'Geisli' is taken from the word for 'saint' in lines 3 and 25.

The poem is planned on the lines $17 + 1 + (9 \times 3) + 26 = 71$, and the internal arrangement is fairly symmetrical.

The interest of the poem lies in its historical notices and associations, for which alone it can be read; for the long-winded and sanguinary synonyms mixed up with grotesque religious 'kennings,' and the tiresome repetitions of the 'stal,' will quickly weary the hearer or reader. There is however that musical rhythm for which Einar is well known.

The old church of Throndham, built by Olaf the Quiet, is the scene of the first recital; portions of it are still imbedded in the magnificent pile which the piety, zeal, and art of Eystan (the archbishop who followed John) raised over the shrine of the patron saint. Eystan's cathedral is of interest to every Englishman, as it contains a 'crown' imitative of that of Canterbury, which Eystan would have seen and copied in his exile in England (1179–83) from the power of Swerri. Munch's splendid volume tells the tale of the succeeding churches which occupied the place of Magnus' wooden fane.

I.

1. EINS má (óð ok bœnir) allz-valdanda ens snialla
    (miœk er fróðr sa er getr greiða) Guðs þrenning mer kenna:
    gœfugt liós boðar geisli gunn-œflugr miskunnar,
    ágætan býð ek ítrom Óláfi brag sólar.

2. Þeirrar er (heims) í heimi, heims myrkrom brá þeima, 5
    (ok liós meðan var vísi veðr- kallaðisk -hallar):
    sá lét biartr frá biartri berask mannr und ský-ranni
    (frægr stóð af því flœéðar (fœrnoðr) rœðull, stiœrno.

3. Síðar (heilags) brá sólar setr (var þat fyr betra),

I. OPENING. *Verses* 1–6, *the* CREED. It becomes me here to set forth the Trinity of One God Almighty. Wise is he that knows the song [Litany] and prayers [the Mass]. The mighty Beam, *that shines* from the Sun of Mercy, forebodes a glorious light,—I offer my poem to Olaf.

The Incarnation. From that Sun *I say*, who, when he was in this world, scattered the darkness of the world, and though he was the King of Heaven, called himself the Light of the world. In all his brightness he chose to be born a man of a bright Star of the Sea [Mary].

The Passion. Afterwards setting darkened the light of that Sun, that

---

1. óð] orð, Fl.   2. greiða] goða, Fl.   8. stiornur, Cd.

(auð-finnandom annars ómióss ræðuls) liósi: 10
œztr þrifnaðr nam efnask oss þá-er líf á krossi
iarðar allra fyrða ónauðigr tók dauða.

4. Upp rann (Engla skepno ið-vandr) of dag þriðja
(Kristr ræðr) krapti hæstom kunn réttlætiss sunna:
veit-ek at mildr frá moldo megin-fiœlði reis hœlða,   15
(iflaust má þat efla ossa væon) með hánom.

5. Sonr sté upp með ynði auðar-mildr frá hauðri,
iœfra baztr, til œstrar allz-ráðanda hallar:
lofaðr sitr œllom œfri (œðlinga hnígr þingat
dœglings hirð) á dýrðar, dag-bóls konungr, stóli.   20

6. Veitti dýrðar dróttinn dáð-vandr giafar Anda
(mœl sanna þau) mœnnom máttigs (framir váttar):
þaðan reis upp sú-er einom al-þýð Guði hlýðir
(hæstr skiœldungr býðr hœlðom himin-vistar til) Kristni.

7. Nú skolom gœfgan Geisla Guðs hallar ver allir,   25
ítr þann-er Óláfr heitir, all-styrkan vel dýrka:
þióð veit hann und heiða hríð-blœsnom sal víða
(menn nemi mœl sem ek inni mín!) iartegnom skína.

8. Heyrðu til afreks orða, Eysteinn konungr, beinna!
Sigurðr, hygg at því snœggjom, sókn-sterkr, hve ek fer verka!
drengr berr óð fyrir Inga; yðarra[r] bið-ek styðja   31
mærð, þat-er miklo varðar, máttigt hœfoð áttar.

9. Yfir-manni býð-ek unninn (upp er mœrð komin) lœrðrar
[Ioan kalla-ek] allrar alþýðo, brag hlýða:
hœfom hróðr, enn leyfa hygg-ek vin ræðuls tiggja   35
(stóls vex hæð þar-er hvílir heilagr konungr) fagran.

10. Oss samir enn at þesso (orð-gnóttar bið-ek Dróttinn

---

we might gain another light [win life everlasting]. It was the greatest
blessing for us when the Life of all mankind received death on the cross
of his own will.

The Resurrection. On the third day Christ, the Sun of Righteousness,
who rules over the angel creation, arose in his glory; I know that a
noble multitude of men arose with him from the earth; this must
strengthen our hope.

The Ascension. The Son ascended from the earth to the highest hall
of the Lord of all, and sitteth there above the angels on a throne of
glory, and the host of God bow before him . . . .

Sending of the Holy Ghost. Then God granted to men the gifts of the
Mighty Spirit; blessed witnesses speak to it. Hence arose the commu-
nion of Christendom, that obeys one God . . . .

Dedication. Now let us all worship that bright beam of God's hall,
who e name is Olaf. All men under the storm-tossed hall of the hills
[heaven] know that he shines brightly with tokens of power [miracles].
Hearken, King Eystan, to my song; and do thou, Sigurd, mark how I
carry it on. Before Ingi I deliver my poem; I pray the mighty head
of your race [St. Olaf] to strengthen my Song of Praise. To John, the
head of the clergy [archbishop of Throndham], I offer my Song of
Praise. I am about to celebrate the fair friend of the Lord of the Sun.

aldar) Óláfs gilda ítr-geðs lofi kveðja :
fann-ek aldri val vildra vall-rióðandi allra
(raun dugir rétt) í eino ranni fremðar-manna.   40

11.   Þrek-lyndz skolo Þrœndir þegn-prýðis brag hlýða,
      (Kristz lifir hann í hæstri hǫll) ok Norðmenn allir :
      dýrð er ágæt orðin elion-hress í þesso
      þióð (né þengill fœðizt því-líkr) konungs-ríki.

12.   Sighvatr frá-ek at segði sókn-bráðr iǫfurs dáðir ;   45
      frétt hefir ǫld at orti Óttarr um gram dróttar :
      þeir hafa þengils Mœra (því er sýst) frama lýstan ;
      [helgom lýt-ek] er héto hǫfoð-skald [fira iǫfri].

13.   Réð ok tolf, sá-er trúði tír-bráðr á Guð, láði
      (þióð muna þengil bíða) þriá vetr konungr (betra) :   50
      áðr full-hugaðr félli folk-valdr í dyn skialda
      (hann speni oss) fyrir innan Ölvis-haug (frá bǫlvi)!

14.   Móðr vann margar dáðir munn-rióðr Hugins kunnar
      (satt var at siklingr bœtti sín mein) Guði einom :
      leyndi lofðungr Þrœnda lið-gegn snara þegna   55
      (fæstr gramr hefir fremri fœzk) háleitri gœzko.

15.   Fregit hefi-ek satt at segði sniallri ferð áðr berðizk
      (drótt nýtr dœglings máttar) draum sínn konungr Rauma :
      stiga kvað standa fagran styrjar-fimr til himna
      (rausn dugir hans at hrósa) Hǫrða-gramr frá iǫrðo :   60

16.   Ok hagliga hugðisk hrœkkvi-baugs ins dœkkva
      lyngs í lopt upp ganga láttr-stríðandi síðan :
      lét, sá-er land-folks gætir, lík-samr himin-ríki
      um-geypnandi, opna, allz heims, fyrir gram sniǫllom.

17.   Vakit frá-ek víg á Stikla- (víð-lendr) -stǫðom síðan   65
      (Inn-Þrœndom lét undir alm-reyrs litoðr dreyra) :

The renown of the see, wherein the holy king rests, shall wax high. It
beseems me next to address my lay to the noble Guild-Brethren of
St. Olaf. Never have I met a fairer assembly of worthies in one hall.
The Thronds and all the Northmen shall hearken to my Encomium on
the glory of the Saint, who is now living in the Hall of Christ. His
renown is become very precious in this kingdom. No such king shall
ever be born again *among us.*
   The King's holy life. Sighvat, I know, has told the deeds of the king ;
Ottar has sung of his works. These two master-poets have praised the
lord of the Mores, the holy king, to whom I bow. Fifteen winters he
ruled over the land, ere he fell in his holiness in the battle within Olwi's
howe. May he deliver us from evil. Many mighty deeds the prince of
the Thronds accomplished, known to God alone, hiding them from men,
to the healing of his soul. I know of a truth that the king of the Reams
told his dream ere the fight began ; that he, the lord of the Hords, saw
a fair ladder reaching from earth to heaven, and he dreamed that he
climbed aloft, and that the merciful Encompasser of the World opened

---

50. konungs, Cd.

heims þessa frá-ek hvassan (hvatir felldo gram skatnar)
[þeir drýgðo bœl] brigðo baug-dríf numinn lífi.

II.

Stef. :
18.   Fúss em-ek, þvi-at vann vísi (var hann mestr konungr) flestar,
[drótt nemi mærð] ef ek mætti, mann-dýrðir, STEF vanda : 70

*Greitt má gumnom létta Guðs ríðari stríðom ;
hraustr þiggr allt sem œstir Óláfr af gram sólar.*

I. 19.   Náðit biartr, þá-er beiðir baug-skialdar lauk aldri,
(sýndi sal-vœrðr grundar sýn tœkn) rœðull skína :
fyrr var hitt er harra, hauðr-tialda brá aldri,   75
hept (nýtask mer mætti mál-tól) skini sólar.
20.   Giœrðozk brátt, þar-er barðisk brodd-rióðrvið kyn þióðar,
(gramr vanðit sá synðom sik) iartegnir miklar :
liós brann líki ræsiss (lœg-skíðs) yfir síðan,
(því at œnd með ser syndis) sam-dœgris (Guð framði). 80
21.   Dýrð lætr dœgling Hœrða (dyljask meðr við þat) gleðja
ítr [munat œðlingr betri] allz grœðari [fœðask] :

*Greitt má gumnom létta Guðs ríðari stríðom ;
hraustr þiggr allt sem œstir Óláfr af gram sólar.*

II. 22.   Drótt þó dýran sveita dœglings ríks af líki   85
(vœn gleðr hug) með hreino hans (batnaðar) vatni :
satt er at Sygna dróttinn særendr Guði kæran,
hrings, (skolo heyra drengir hans brœgð) í grœf lœgðo.
23.   Þar kom blindr (enn ek byrja blíð verk) muni síðarr
auðar-niótr, er ýtar iœfurs bein þvegit hœfðo :   90

---

the kingdom of Heaven unto him. Afterwards the battle of Sticklestead
was fought, and the prince of the In-Thronds was reft of his life. An
evil deed they did that struck him down.

II. STAVE.   Fain would I, if I could, work out the STAVES of my
Praise of the glorious king.—*Refrain :* Verily God's knight is able to
lighten the sorrows of men. The brave Olaf can get all that he desires
from the King of the Sun !

The sun was not able to shine the day the king lost his life. God
showed forth manifest tokens ! So, long ago, when the Lord of the
Heavens died, the sun's light was stopped.

After the battle great signs and wonders were made manifest. A light
burned over the king's body the day that he died. The Saviour of all lets
the lord of the Hords enjoy his glory.—*R. :* Verily God's knight . . . .

The blind man's sight restored. The people washed the precious blood
from the body of the king with pure water, and laid the lord of the
Sogn-folk in the grave. Hearken to his miracles ! Soon afterward
there came a blind man where they had washed the king's body; he

---

76. mætr, Cd.   78. vanðit] firði, Cd.   80. syndizt, Cd.   81. meðr] m', Cd.

sión-brautir strauk sínar seggjom kunns í brunni
árr, þeim-er Óláfs dreyra, orms-landa, var blandinn.

24.   Sión fekk seggr af hreino (sú dýrð munat fyrðom)
[fœrnoðr var þat] (fyrnask) fiœl-góðs konungs blóði.

Greitt má gumnom létta Guðs ríðari stríðom;   95
hraustr þiggr allt sem œstir Óláfr af gram sólar.

III. 25.   Tolf mánoðr var týnir tand-rauðs huliðr sandi
fremðar lystr ok fasta, fimm nætr, vala strætiss :
áðr an úpp or víðo ulf-nistanda kisto
dýrr lét Dróttinn harra dáð-milds koma láði.   100

26.   Mál fekk maðr, er hvílir marg-fríðr iœfurr, síðan
áðr sá-er orða hlýðo af-skýfðr farizt hafði :
frægð vinnr fylkiss Egða folk-sterks af því verki ;
iœfurs snilli þreifsk alla ungs á Danska Tungo.

27.   Fœðor skolo fulltings biðja (fremðar þióð) enn góða   105
(mœéðir mart á láði) Magnúss hvatir bragnar !

Greitt má gumnom létta Guðs ríðari stríðom;
hraustr þiggr allt sem œstir Óláfr af gram sólar.

IV. 28.   Gekk sínom bur sœkkvir sólar-straums í drauma ;
valdr kvezk fylgja foldar fram-lundom gram mundo :   110
áðr á Hlýrskógs-heiði harð-fengr iœfurr barðisk
(góðs elðiss fekk gylðir gnótt) við heiðnar dróttir.

29.   Lét iarp-litan áto (arnar-ióðs) enn Góði
(munn rauð mildingr innan) Magnús Hugin fagna :
hrætt varð folk á flótta (frœn beit egg) at leggja ;   115
sorg hluto víf [en vargar] Vindversk [of hræ gínðo].

30.   Raun er at sigr gaf sínom sniallr Lausnara spialli
(hrósa-ek verkom vísa víg-diarfs) frœmom arfa :

Greitt má gumnom létta Guðs ríðari stríðom;
hraustr þiggr allt sem œstir Óláfr af gram sólar.   120

---

washed his eyes in the stream that was mingled with the blood of Olaf,
and received his sight.—*R. :* Verily God's knight . . . .
A man gets back his speech. Twelve months and five days the king's
body was shrouded in sand, till God made his coffin to come out of the
earth. A man, whose tongue had been cut out, got back his speech afterwards on the spot where the king rests. The prince of the men of Agd
won renown through this mighty work ; he became famous throughout
the Danish Tongue. Men should pray for help to the noble father of
King Magnus.—*R. :* Verily God's knight . . . .
Magnus' Dream. He appeared in a dream to his son before he fought
the heathen-folk at Lurschau-heath, and promised to help him. Magnus the
Good gave a meal to the grey wolf ; the people were soon turned to flight.
Upon the Wendish women a sorrowful lot fell [they were widowed].
The king gave his son the victory.—*R. :* Verily God's knight . . . .

---

91. í] or, Cd.   94. -goðr, Cd.

v. 31. Reyndi Guthormr grundar (gat hann rétt) við þræm
slèttan
(áðr) hvat Óláfs tœðo al-kœns við Guð bœnir :
dag lét sínn með sigri sókn-þýðr íœfurr prýðask,
þa-er í Önguls-eyjar- und-reyr bito -sundi.

32. Víst hafði lið lestir linnz þrimr hlutom minna   125
heiptar-mildr at hialdri (harðr fundr var siá) grundar :
þó réð hann at hvœro (hónom tióði vel móðor)
[hár feksk af þvi hlýri] (hœgnuðr) or styr gagni.

33. Öld hefir opt enn mildi unnar-bliks frá miklom
(Kristz mæri-ek lim) leysta, lit-rauðs, konungr nauðom : 130

Greitt má gumnom létta Guðs ríðari stríðom ;
hraustr þiggr allt sem æstir Óláfr af gram sólar.

vi. 34. Satt er at silfri skreytta seggjom hollz ok golli
her lét Guthormr gœrva (grams hróðr er þat) róðo :
slíkt hafa menn at minnom meirr iartegna þeirra ;   135
mark stendr Kristz í kirkjo (konungs niðr gaf þat) miðri.

35. Menn hafa sagt at svanni sunnr Skáneyjom kunnir
oss at Óláfs messo ómildr baka vildi :
enn þá er brúðr at brauði brenn-heito tók leita,
þat varð grión at gráno grióti Danskrar snótar.   140

36. Hildings hefir haldin hátíð verit síðan
(sann-spurt er þat sunnan) sniallz of Danmœrk alla :

Greitt má gumnom létta Guðs ríðari stríðom ;
hraustr þiggr allt sem æstir Óláfr af gram sólar.

vii. 37. Gœfog skar Hœrn or hœfði hvítings of sœk lítla 145
auðar aumom beiði (ungr maðr var siá) tungo :
þann sœm ver, þá-er vœrom, válaust nominn máli

Earl Guthorm's deliverance. Guthorm [St. Olaf's nephew] found out
how the king's prayers prevailed with God. Olaf caused his day to be
celebrated in Anglesey sound. Guthorm had three times less men, and
yet, by the help of his mother's brother, he carried the day. The king
[Olaf] has ofttimes delivered men from evil straits.—*R.:* Verily God's
knight .... [29th July, 1052].

Guthorm had a rood made, inlaid with gold and silver. Such tokens
all men may remember ; it stands right in the middle of Christ's church;
the king's kinsman gave it.

The miracle of the loaves. Men have told how a misbelieving woman
of Sconey would bake upon the feast of Olaf ; but when she looked
for the burning-hot bread to be baked, lo ! the Danish damsel's loaves
were turned into grey grit. The king's feast has been kept ever since
throughout Denmark.—*R.:* Verily God's knight ....

The maimed man healed. A noble lady, for a slight cause, cut out a
poor young man's tongue. I saw him a few weeks since entirely bereft

---

130. Kristz] Krist, Cd.   133. ok] of, Cd.   140. grænu, Cd.

hodda bríót, þar-er heitir Hlíð, fǽm víkom síðarr.

38.   Frétt hefi-ek, at sá sótti síðan malma stríðir
      heim, þann-er hialp gefr aumom, harm-skerðanda ferðom:
      hér fekk hann (enn byrja hátt kvæði skal-ek) bæði   151
      (snáka vangs of slœngvi slungins) mál ok tungo.

39.   Dýrð er ágæt orðin œðlings ríks af slíko
      (mærð nemi mildings Hœrða mest!) of heims bygð flesta:

      Greitt má gumnom létta Guðs ríðari stríðom;   155
      hraustr þiggr allt sem æstir Óláfr af gram sólar.

VIII. 40.   Veit-ek at Vindr fyrir Skauti (verðr bragr af því) skerði
      gialfrs nið-branda grundar (greiddr) sárliga meiddo:
      ok endr frá trú týndir tírar-sterks or kverkom
      auð-skýfanda óðar ór grimmliga skóro.   160

41.   Sótti skrín it skreytta skíð-rennandi síðan
      (orð finnask mer) unnar Óláfs dreka bóli:
      ok þeim, er vel vakði (veit-ek sœnn) Hugins teiti,
      máls fekk hilmir heilso heilagr (á því deili).

42.   Hás lætr helgan ræsi heims dómari sóma   165
      (fyllir fram-lundr stillir ferð himneska) verðan.

      Greitt má gumnom létta Guðs ríðari stríðom;
      hraustr þiggr allt sem æstir Óláfr af gram sólar.

IX. 43.   Hneitir frá-ek at héti hialdrs at vápna galdri
      Óláfs hiœrr, þess-er orra il-bleikom gaf steikar: 170
      þeim klauf þengill Rauma þunn-vaxinn ský gunnar
      (rekin bito stól) á Stikla-stœðom val-basta rœðli.

44.   Tók, þá-er fell inn frœkni fylkis kundr til grundar,
      sverð, hinn er sœkja þorði, Sœnskr maðr af gram Þrœnzkom:
      sá var hiœrr ins háva hring-stríðanda síðan   175
      golli merktr í Girkja gunn-diarfs liði fundinn.

45.   Nú fremr, þann er gaf gumnom, gœfug dýrð konung fyrða,
      (slœng Einriði Ungi) arm-glœðr (í brag rœðo):

---

of his speech at a place called Lith. Afterwards, I have heard, he visited
him who gives help to the wretched, and there he got back both speech
and tongue. By this the king's renown was spread all over the world.—
R.: Verily God's knight . . . .
   The mangled man made whole. I have heard how the Wends, off
Sheet, sorely mangled a man. Yea, the miscreants cruelly shore the
tongue out of his throat. Afterwards he sought the shrine of Olaf, and
the holy king healed him. The Judge of the World grants much
glory to the holy king.—R.: Verily God's knight . . . .
   The Saint's sword. Olaf's battle-sword with which he, the Reams'
prince, fought at Sticklestead was named Hnit [Cutter]. When he fell to
earth, a Swede picked up the sword, and it was afterwards found in the
warlike troop of the Greeks [Warangian guard]. Eindrid the Young

---

171. Read, þunn-varin?   174. svænskr, Cd.

Greitt má gumnom létta Guðs ríðari stríðom;
hraustr þiggr allt sem æstir Óláfr af gram sólar. 180

III.

46. Mer er (enn mærð skalk stœra mildings þess-er gaf hringa
styrjar sniallz) of stilli styrkjan vant at yrkja:
þvi-at tókn þess, es lið læknir, lofðungs vinar tungla
(liós verðr raun of ræsi) rannz ferr hvert á annat.

47. Gyrðisk hála herðom heldr náliga at kveldi 185
glaum-vekjandi grímo glaðr vett-rimar naðri:
drengr nam dýrr á vangi (dagr rofnaðisk) sofna
ítrs landreka undir ógn-fimr berom himni.

48. Misti maðr, er lýsti, (morgin var þá) borgar
styrks mundriða steindrar styr-sniallr roðins galla: 190
þátti sínn á sléttri seim-þiggjandi liggja
grundo gylðiss kindar góm-sparra ser fiarri.

49. Þriár grímor vann þeima þióð-nýtr Haraldz bróðir
rœkn-stefnandi Reifniss ríkr bendingar slíkar:
áðr þrek-hvæssom þessar þing-diarfs firar Yngva 195
(biœrt ero bauga styrtiss brœgð) iartegnir sœgðo.

50. Más frá-ek iarðar eiso allvalld fyrir hiœr gialda
(slétti-ek óð) þann-er átti Óláfr (bragar-tólom):
yfir-skiœldungr lét iœfra odd-hríðar þar síðan
Garðz á golli vœrðo grand altari standa. 200

51. Tákn gœrir biœrt, þau-er birta brand-él, á Girklandi
(mærð finnsk of þat mœnnom) mann-þarfr Haraldz arfi:
fregn-ek allt; ne ógnar innendr megoð finna
(dýrð Óláfs ríðr dála dag-ræfrs) konung hœfra.

52. Háðisk hildr á víðom (hungr slœkði vel þungan 205

---

has now forwarded my poem [Eindrid told me this].—*R.:* Verily God's
knight . . . .

III. END-PIECE. It is hard for me to *work out* my poem on the
king, for his miracles pass from one place to another.
Olaf's sword. One evening the man girt on the sword and fell asleep
on the field beneath the open sky. When he awoke he missed the
weapon and saw it lying some way from him on the ground. Three
nights running Harold's brother wrought this marvel, before the men
told the emperor of the miracle. The emperor bought the sword of
Olaf for gold, and had it laid ever afterwards upon the high altar in
Garth [Constantinople]. Harold's glorious heir showed forth tokens
in the battle in Greece. I set forth his praise.
Battle in Wallachia. A battle was fought on the broad Petzina-plain
[Wallachia]; the people fell in thousands by the sword; the Greeks

---

185. hǫla, Cd.

gunnar márr í geira gæll) Petzina-vællom:
þar svá at þióð fyrir hiœrvi þúsundom laut undan
(hríð óx Hamðes klæða hialm-skœð), Girkir flœðo.

53. Mundi mest und fiœndom Miklagarðz ok iarðar
hryggs (dugðit lið) liggja lagar eld-brota veldi: 210
nema rænd í byr branda (barð-rœkns) fáir harða
(rœðuls bliko vœpn í veðri) Væringjar fram bæri.

54. Héto hart á ítran hraustir menn af trausti
(stríð svall ógn) þá-er óðosk, Áláf í gný stála:
þar-er of einn í œrva (und-bœro) flaug váro.   215
(roðin klofnuðu Reifniss rœnn) sex tigir manna.

55. Var sem reyk (af ríki regn dreif stáls) í gegnom
hialm-niœrðungar harðan heiðingja lið gengi:
halft fimta vann heimtan hundrað brímiss sunda
nýztan tír þat-er nœra Norðmanna val þorði.   220

56. Eyddo gumnar gladdir (gœfogr þengill barg drengjom)
vagna borg, þar-er vargar vápn-sundroð hræ fundo:
Nennir œll at inna œngr brim-loga slœngvir
dœglings verk þau er dyrkar dáð-sniallz verœld alla.

57. Nú er oss þau-er vann vísi verk fyrir þióð at merkja   225
nauðr í nýjom óði næst; ríðra þat smæstom:
krapt skolom Goðs (enn gipto) geð-styrks lofi dýrka
(lér hialdr-frœmom hárar heims læknir gram þeima).

58. Angr-fyldrar varð aldar (illr gœrisk hugr af villo)
mildings þiónn fyr (manna marg-faldr) œfund kaldri: 230
lýgi hefir bragna brugðit (brýtr stundom frið) nýtra
(hermðar kraptr) til heipta (hialdr-stríðr) skapi blíðo.

59. Lusto sundr á sandi seggs marg-litendr eggja
(hœrð grœr fión af fyrða) fót (alldr-trega rótom):
ok prest, þeir-er lœg lesto líknar krœfð, or hœfði   235
(hætt mál var þat) heila himin-tungl þegar stungo.

were fleeing. The realm of the king of Micklegarth [Byzantium] must
have yielded to the enemy, had not the few shield-bearing Warangians
attacked them in the fight. They called loudly upon the good king Olaf.
There were sixty heathens to one of them in the fray. They went
through the heathen host as through smoke. The four hundred and
fifty Northmen won fame in that place. They destroyed the heathens'
waggon-fort. No one can count the wonders the king wrought; they
are famed all over the world.

The injured priest healed. Now I must needs, in a fresh strain, last not
least, make mention before men of the deeds the king did, and praise
the might of the saint.—A priest fell under the cruel wrath of wicked
men. Slander has often turned a kindly nature to hatred. Out on the
sand they brake the priest's legs, and, against the laws of mercy, thrust
his eyes out of his head. Twice was his tongue drawn out with
tongs and cut with a knife; they left him lying there cruelly scalped

---

234. Read, grœri.   235. leyfðar krofð (better?), B.

60.   Tunga var með tangar tír-kunn nomin munni
      (vasa sem vænst) ok tysvar (viðr-líf) skorin knífi :
      œr-skiptir lá eptir (œnd lætr maðr) á strœndo
      (margr of minni sorgir) meinsamliga hamlaðr.   240
61.   Leyfðr er, sá er lét ok stýfðrar lamiðs fótar, gramr, nióta
      ungan þegn, sem augna út-stunginna, tungo :
      hœnd Óláfs vann heilan hreins grimmligra meina
      (gœr muno giœld þeim-er byrja) Goðs þræl (œfog-mæli).

62.   Bíðr allz-konar œðri (œruggt mæli-ek þat) sælo   245
      dýrðar-váttr með Dróttni dyggr an þióð of hyggi :
      ef Lausnara lýsir (liðs valdr) nominn aldri
      vinr (firði sik synðom) slík verk á iarð-ríki.
63.   Heðan var ungr frá angri (allz mest vini flesta
      Goð reynir svá sína) siklingr nominn miklo :   250
      nú lifir hraustr í hæstri himna-valdz (þar-er aldri)
      fár-skerðandi (fyrða) friðar-sýn (gleði týnisk).
64.   Hverr er svá horskr at byrjar hás vegs megi segja
      lióss í lífi þesso lofðungs giafar tungla :
      þær-er heims ok himna heit-fastr iœfurr veitir   255
      (skreytt er of skatna dróttinn skrín) dýrðar-vin sínom.
65.   Heims hygg-ek hingat kómo hœfoðs menn í stað þenna
      (snarr tyggi bergr seggjom sólar) erki-stóli :
      hér er af himna gœrvis heilagr viðr (sem biðjom
      yfir-skiœldungr biarg aldar oss) píningar-krossi.   260
66.   Öld nýtr Óláfs mildi (iœfurs dýrð hœfom skýrða
      þróttar hvass) at þessom þrek-sniœll frama œllom :
      Lúti landz-folk ítrom lim sal-konungs himna!
      sæll er hverr, er hollan hann gerir ser, manna.
67.   Talða-ek fátt ór fiœlða frið-gegns af iartegnom   265

upon the shore. Little life was left in him; many a man has lost his life
by less hurts. Praised be the king that gave the young man the use of
his lamed feet, stumped tongue, and his stabbed-out eyes. Olaf's hand
healed God's servant of his grievous wounds. They who set the slander
afoot must pay for it.

Verily, the precious martyr must be enjoying bliss not to be told of
with the Lord, if after death he can show forth such mighty deeds. He
was taken away in his youth from much evil,—so God tries them that
love him ;—now he lives in highest peace before the face of God, where
is joy that never shall cease. Who is so wise that he can tell all the
gifts which the Lord grants to his beloved one? His shrine is fairly
adorned! The Ruler of the earth [Pope] set an archbishop's see
here, where is the holy wood of the cross of the Lord's passion.
Herein all men profit by the blessing of Olaf, whom I have been praising.
Let the folk of this land bow to the Limb of the Lord. Blessed is he
who makes a friend of him.

The End. I have counted up but a few of Olaf's Miracles. May every

---

254. tungla] emend.; tungna, Cd.; tunga, F.

(ber koma orð frá órom) Óláfs (bragar stóli):
bóls taki seggr hverr-er, sólar siklings, þess-er Goð miklar,
hilmis óst ens hæsta heið-biartrar lof greiðir:

68. Svá-at Lausnara leysi lang-vinr frá kvøl strangri
nýta þióð ok nauðom nagl-skaddz við trú stadda: 270
víga-skýs þar-er vísa veljendr glaðir telja,
øflogs Kristz af óstom al-nennins, brag þenna.

69. Bragr mundi nú brøndom baug-ness vera þessi
(man-ek rausnar skap ræsis) raun-dýrliga launaðr:
ef lofða gramr lifði leik-mildr Sigurðr hildar   275
(þess hrósa-ek veg vísa vellom grimms) enn ellri.

70. Óláfs høfom iøfra orð-hags liði sagðar
(fylgði hugr) ens Helga happs dáðir (því ráði):
laun fæ-ek holl ef hreinom hræ-síks þrimo líkar,
gøfugs óðar lér góðir Goðs bletzon liðs þessa.   280

71. Bóen hefi-ek, þengill, þína, þrek-ramr, stoðat framla;
iflaust høfum iøfri unnit mærð sem kunnom:
Ágætr segit ítran, Eysteinn, hve ek brag leystak:
Hás elskit veg vísa vagn-ræfrs!—Enn ek þagna.

HALLAR-STEINARR (REKSTEFJA, or DRAPA TVI-SKELFÐA).

OF this man, save that his fore-name seems to be derived from a
farm, Hall, in the West of Iceland in Borgar-firth, we know nothing;
and it is in accordance with the internal evidence afforded by his poems,
which present a most remarkable likeness to those of Einar Sculason,
that we place him here. One might even guess at a relationship between
the two.

Rekstefia, his famed poem, is in the great Olaf Tryggvason's Life
ascribed to 'Hallar-stein;' under which form the Rimur on Skald-
Helgi also cite this author: and Dr. Egilsson believed that Hallar-Stein
was no other than Stein-Herdisarson (§ 3), and urges that a refrain of
Stein-Herdisarson is copied in Rekstefia. But we find our poet's full
name to have been, not Stein, but Steinar (in Bergs-bok); under which
form he is once or twice quoted in Edda; and we can have little doubt
that Hallar-Stein is merely a shortening of this. The style and bearing

---

man that spreads these praises of the king whom God magnifies, win
the love of the high King of Heaven; so that the friend of the nail-
pierced Saviour may save men from torment and evil, whenever they
shall joyfully recite this praise of the king for the love of Christ. This
Song would have been richly rewarded were the generous king, Sigurd
the Elder, still alive. The MIRACLES OF ST. OLAF I have told before
the kings. I shall surely get a noble fee for my Lay in the blessing of
the saint, if my verse please him.

I have accomplished that which thou didst desire of me, O king:
I have wrought the praise of the king [Olaf's Encomium] as well as I
could. Tell me, O Eystan, how I have acquitted me of my Lay. Love
ye the Lord. Now I will hold my peace.

---

270 -skaddz] emend.; nagl-kvaddr, Cd.   280. let, Cd.

of the whole of Steinar's work is decidedly that of the twelfth century, or Einar Sculason's age. Notice that Steinar calls the 'stone' bokar sol, a pun or image drawn from illuminating (staining) manuscripts. Rekstefia is a poem in praise of Olaf Tryggvason. Its title, given it by the poet, of *Inlaid* or *Set-Stave*, is derived from the 'cloven burden,' cut into three, and wedged bit by bit into the stanzas of the stave-strophes. He also calls it *Twi-skelfda Drapa*, or the *Two-stress Encomium*, from the occurrence of a measure of double stress at the beginning of each line. There are a few exceptions to this (possibly corruptions), as hátto, l. 44; sidan, l. 90; hegio, l. 90; eigi, l. 137; others, as heidinn, blodogr . . . . , may pass as double stressed. The metre, as Steinar says, 'is not often met with.'

In *form* the poem, as we have it, follows the scheme $(1 + 7) + (5 \times 3) + (10 + 2) = 35$.

The historical worth of Rekstefia is not small. It gives in some instances the life of Olaf according to a tradition, followed only by Agrip, and differing from that of the Book of Kings altogether. Thus it praises Olaf for avenging his father (on the rebellious men of Ranrick). It also gives fresh details as to Swold; the Swedes attack first with *fifteen* ships, then Swain with *sixty*, lastly Earl Eric with *five*, an order and number which does not tally with the received account. He alone gives the stratagem by which Eric wins the Serpent, viz. casting big beams on to the big ship's deck, to crush and hamper her defenders. One cannot help recalling the gallant Sir Andrew Barton of our Ballad, and his famous ship 'brass within and steel without'—

'With Beams for his Topcastle : that is both huge and high.
There is neither English nor Portingale : can Sir Andrew Barton pass by?
Said the merchant, " If you do so, take counsel then I pray withal ;
Let no man to his Topcastle go, nor strive to let his Beams down fall."'

Steinar is also the primary poetic authority for the miracles of St. Olaf and his great bodily feats. The mention of Hallfred and Biarni and their Drapas on Olaf is also to be noted.

There is a bit of a *Love-Song* of Steinar's (in Einar's very vein) cited in Edda, wherein is an echo from Egil. Steinar also made a *Dirge on Helgi the poet*, a hero of his own district (see Prolegomena, § 23). A piece of it which has survived is given below.

The text, like that of Geisli, is from Bergs-bok. Many verses, in a less good text, are cited in O. T. Saga, A. M. 61 (B). We have consulted Cederschiold's Edition, Lund, 1881.

I.

1. HERS-DRÓTT hœlða sléttom hlióðs kveð-ek mer at óði;
   rand-hvels remmi-Þundi REKSTEFJO tek-ek hefja :
   ský-runn skialdar linna skal-ek fríðom lof smíða
   þing-Baldr' þróttar-mildom, þeim-er fremstr var beima.

2. Veg-mildr víðrar foldar vœrðr þá fóstr í Gœrðom;   5
   vell-bióðr vísar dáðir vann, sá-er hæst gekk manna :

THE OPENING. I call on men to listen to my song. I am beginning my SET-STAVE (Rek-Stefia). I shall smithy a Song of Praise upon a king that was the first of men.

---

3. ský-runn] emend.; skurumz, Cd.

Blik-runnr brigða-miklom brátt réð hann þeims átti
all-prútt éla-Þróttar Óláfr skipa-stóli.

3. Óláfr allra iœfra óttlaust ok nam bríóta
varg-hollr Vinda borgir, vestr hernað rak mestan : 10
hræ-linnz hverjo sinni, hlióm-váttandi, knátti
sókn-bráðr sigri ráða, Svolniss dóms, í rómo.

4. Senn œll síðan runno snekkjo bœrð or Gœrðom
her-mœrg hála tiœrgoð hildings und gram mildom :
Vestr-lœnd virða kindir ver-fœkom lét herjat 15
all-dyggr arfi Tryggva Áláfr ok klauf stœlom.

5. Full-snart frœkno hiarta fríðr þengill lét síðan
(hiœrr gall, hœlðar féllo) hefnd síns fœðr efnda :
blóðogr bragnings þióðar brandr gall á Englandi,
ó-trautt Enskrar dróttar aldr-spelli frá-ek valda. 20

6. Ugg-laust Íra bygðir úkvíðinn lét síðan
él-Freyr Ullar kióla endr fíkula brendar :
Skot-land skœfnom brandi skiald-frýðr of nam ryðja
(oddr beit) [ulfar sœddosk] ódeigr (Skotta feiga).

7. Frón-bandz fœri-œndrom fríðr til Nóregs síðan 25
sker-Baldr Skœglar elda skiald-búnom lét haldit :
heiðinn heiman flýði (hildingr ne þar vildi
' áðr an' Óláfs bíða) iarl af síno hiarli.

8. Hauk-ióðs harða víða (hœtt) Norœnar dróttir
(Þund-regns heim of vandak þengil) á bý gengo : 30
ó-ráð illri þióðo Áláfr of galt dála ;
víg-runnr velja kunni víkingom hlut slíkan.

II. Stef.

1. 9. Fé-miidr fylkir vildi firna mœrg ok hœrga,
blót-hús, brenna láta ; bað hann heiðin goð meiða :
sigr-brandz síðan kendi sann-hróðigr trú góða 35

Olaf was fostered at Garth, he was soon the leader of a fleet. Olaf
betook himself to storming the strongholds of the Wends, raising war in
the West; every time he fought he won the day. Many a well-manned
smack ran out of Garth at his command; Olaf, Tryggwi's heir, harried
the Western lands [south Baltic coasts].

Soon he avenged his father. His bloody blade whistled in England, he
wrought the death of English folk. Then he burnt the dwellings of the
Irish, and cleared Scotland with his whetted blade.

Then he held his course in his ships towards Norway. The heathen
earl [Hakon] fled from his land, afraid to abide Olaf's coming. The
Northern people [Norwegians] took him as king. He requited evil-
doers heavily, he paid the buccaneers for what they had done.

II. THE STAVES. Refrain: Olaf was the mightiest and best of kings
beneath the sun's path.

He busied himself in burning many a fane and high-place, and the

7. -ruðr, Cd. 18. hefnt . . . efndi, Cd. 20. Odd-rióð Enskra lýða, B.
23. frýðr] B ; prúðr, Cd. 30. I. e. þengli ; þengils, Cd.

her-lundr hǫlða kindom.—*Hann var ríkstr konung-manna*
10. Þióð-lǫnd þremja skyndir þrenn kristnaði ok tvenni ;
hilding hǫppom valda (hans ríki frá-ek) slíkom :
mærings mǫnnom skírisk merki fremðar-verka
egg-mótz ekki lítil.—*Óláfr und veg sólar*   40
11. Ísland éla skyndir ítr lista vann kristnað,
goll-mildr, Grœna-veldi, gǫndlar-þeyss, ok Eyjar :
hand-víst Hialta grundar hann, sem Nóregs manna
'hátto' hilmir bœtti.—*höll, ok fremstr at öllo.*

II. 12. Haf-glóð hilmir sáði hialdr-ríkr ok gaf skiǫldo,   45
stétt-hrings stǫfnom veitti stikka, vǫpn ok skikkjor :
stór-ráðr steinda knǫrro stillir fekk, ok ekki
hildings hœfði mildi.—*Hann var ríkstr konung-manna*
13. Húns-nótt hverja knǫtto hirð-menn konungs spenna
gylld horn grædiss meldrar ; glaðr vísi drakk þaðra :   50
víð-frægr velja tœði vín hús-kǫrlom sínom
all-valdr einkar-mildom.—*Óláfr und veg sólar*
14. Morð-linnz mǫrgo sinni móð-þrútinn bió úti
(húfr svall, hrannir féllo) hvessi-meiðr á skeiðom :
gyllt hlýr (gnǫpðo skalptar) gunn-fíkinn lét blíkja   55
her-ruðr hǫfnom fiarri.—*höll, ok fremstr at öllo.*

III. 15. Ör-rióðr átta skeiðom efsta sinn ok þrinnom
(byrr varð) beita þorði (brýnn) or Þróndheims mynni :
Ormr skreið (árar kníði) ǫlna-vang inn-Langi
(hirð prúð) hilmir stýrði.—*Hann var ríkstr konung-manna*
16. Raun-skiótt ræsir hitti [rít] (vara friðr at líta)   61
[sól rauð Svolniss éla] senn dœglinga þrenna :
Fimmtán fiǫrniss mána fleygjendr at gram rendo
Ekkils ýti-blǫkkom.—*Óláfr und veg sólar*
17. Grár reif [gœerðo drífo] (gall brandr við slǫg) [randa]
troll-marr trýni sollinn [tveir nafnar] hræ iafnan :   66

---

houses of offering. He had the heathen gods broken up, then he taught
the people the true God. Three folklands and twain he christened, this
is the blessing he wrought. He got Iceland christened, Greenland and
the Isles too. He bettered the faith of the Shetlands and of the men
of Norway.

He scattered gold and gave gifts of shields, and bestowed weapons
and mantles, he gave away the painted ships ; no one could outvie his
largesse. Every winter the king's henchmen handled the gilded horn ;
when the merry king was drinking he gave his henchmen wine. Yet
many a winter he lay out at sea in his galley.

Last he clave the sea from Throndham's mouth with eight
galleys and three. The Long Serpent furrowed the main, the king
steered her. Soon he fell in with three princes. The enemies set upon
him with fifteen ships of war. The two namesakes fought [Olaf of

---

38. hildings, Cd.   4 f. Read, hátt-brögð ?   58. Or, Svoldrar mynni, B.

Svænskr herr sigri þorrinn; sverð beit; enn fló peita;
hríð óx ; hœlðar flýðo.—*höll, ok fremstr at öllo.*

IV. 18. Aur-bragðz ærir lœgðo ann at sinn at Linna
(grimmt varð Gœndlar borða gnaust) sex tigom flausta : 70
Danskr herr dýran harra, drótt hné mœrg, þar-er sótti
(hirð féll, hrafnar gullo).—*Hann var ríkstr konung-manna*

19. Strœng varð (stálin sungo) sterklig iœfurs merki.
gramr skaut, gœrðisk rimmo gangr um Orm-inn-Langa :
Nýtr herr Nóregs gætiss nær vasa trauðr at særa, 75
orð-prúðs, Ióta ferðir.—*Óláfr und veg sólar*

20. Myrkt hregg mækiss eggja mein-illa gekk Sveini ;
drótt hné dreyra þrútin ; Danir skundoðo undan :
Tandr beit (tyggi renndi tveim dœglingom) Skœglar ;
hans vœrn hefðisk firnom.—*höll, ok fremstr at öllo.* 80

V. 21. Ítr iarl einkar snarla endr fimm skipom renndi
þrek-mannz þriðja sinni þremja storms at Ormi :
Ben lét (bœrðosk ýtar) bryn-skíðs viðom svíða
Hyrningr heiptar-giœrnom.—*Hann var ríkstr konung-
manna*

22. Rán-síks remmi-lauka róg-svellir bað fella 85
(styrr þreifsk) stœri-aska stangr á Orm-inn-Langa :
átt-stórr ella mátti Eirikr í dyn geira
of-Linn aldri vinna.—*Óláfr und veg sólar*

23. Hvast skaut (hlífar brusto) hildingr or lyptingo
[síðan sýnt nam eyðask] sókn-strangr [Ormr-inn-Langi] :
unn-elldz yppi-runnom engi kann svá en lengra 91
'hegio' hilmiss segja.—*höll, ok fremstr at öllo.*

III. SLŒMR.

24. Hiœr-flóðs hnykki-meiðom her er um SLÆM at dœma,
hnig-reyrs, harða stóran ; hefi-ek þar lokit stefjom :

Norway and Olaf of Sweden]. The Swedes were reft of the victory.
The battle-storm raged high, the warriors fled.
  A second time the Serpent was set upon with sixty ships of the
Danish hosts; much people fell in that onslaught. The strong stave
bore the king's banner. There was a fierce attack made upon the Long
Serpent, the mighty men of the King of Norway were not slack in wound-
ing the Jutes. Sweyn fared very ill in the fray, the Danes fled away.
Our king's defence is renowned among men : he put two kings to flight.
  A third time the Serpent was attacked by the bold Earl [Eric]
with five ships. Hyrning's blows were sore. The Earl [Eric] ordered
huge ash beams to be cast upon the Long Serpent, or else Eric would
never have won the Serpent in the fray. The king kept shooting sharply
from the forecastle. At last the Long Serpent was being fast cleared of
its crew. No man after that can tell farther of the king.
  III. THE END-PIECE. Now men must listen to the *End-piece*, for I have

---

73. Read, stöng bar?   91. en sva, Cd.   92. Read, heggj-orð?

Ið-vandr aðrar dáðir ek fýsomk nú lýsa   95
gný-bióðs geysi-tíðar geira hóti fleiri.

25.   Tvær senn tiggja vinnor tel-ek (þær-er ek veit færi
gný-linnz Gœndlar runna, gramr iþróttir framði):
hyr-Baldr hvítra skialda hand-sœxom lék vandla
(flein-rióðr flestra dáða frár) ok gekk á œrom.   100

26.   'Val-stafns vætki rofna:' viti menn at ek frá tvenna
haus 'mannz' hringi liósom hirð-meðr konungs veðja :
(her-mart) hiœrva snyrtir hvárr lézk grams í hamri
(styr-remðr stillir framði stœra) œðrom fœri.

27.   Annarr œðlings manna ókvíðinn réð síðan   105
(stígr varð stála sveigi strangr) í biarg at ganga :
Hátt fiall hvárki mátti (hans var líf þrotið) klífa
eld-ruðr œlna foldar upp eða niðr frá miðjo.

28.   Hilding hvasst frá-ek ganga (hann réð prútt) eptir manni
[ráð-vandr hilmir rendi ríp] í bratta gnípo :   110
þrek-leyfðr þengill hafði (þat var endr) und hendi
[sigr-þoll svá barg stillir] sínn dreng, ok gekk lengra.

29.   Dreyr-serks dýrðar-merki dáð-minnigs skal-ek inna
ský-bióðs skelfi-hríðar Skœglar-borðz in fiorðo :
harð-leygs hrinda frœgom hvat-lyndom Þórkatli   115
styr-lund stríðra branda storms fyr borð á Ormi.

30.   Spell vann (sparðit stillir) spiót-runnz (skaða-bótir)
mein-garðr margra iarða mikit dýrligrar skikkjo :
goð-vefr gœrðisk iœfri, grœn ok skinn und hœnom,
senn á svip-stund einni síðan iafn eða fríðri.   120

31.   Ör-rióðr allra dáða iartegnir vann biartar
(Dvergs regn dreyra megnom dimmt) í sinn it fimmta :
sigr-giarn sólo vænni sénn vas skrýddr með prýddom
dœglingr Dróttins englom dýrðar-fúss í húsi.

---

finished the Staves. I will now hasten to speak of other exploits of the
king. *Two* of his feats that few beside could do, I will tell together: he
could play marvellously with daggers, and he could walk upon the oars.
I know a *third* miracle of his : two men betted, one a ring, the other
his head, as to which of them were the best cliff-climber. One of them
began to climb the rock, but he could not go on higher nor get down
again. When he was midway up his life was in danger. The king went
quickly after him on the steep cliff, caught his man in his arms and then
climbed higher still.
   The *fourth* deed of his I will set forth, how he threw Thorkettle
overboard out of the Serpent. He spoilt his precious cloak, yet in the
twinkling of an eye the king made the fine cloth and the grey fur
lining as fair or fairer than before.
   A *fifth* time he wrought a bright token: he was seen brighter than the
sun, compassed about with glorious angels of the Lord within a house.

---

101. Read, varr-skíðs verk it þriðja.   frá] sá, Cd.   110. Thus B ; ræsir
ɯendi, Cd.   113. dáð-styrks . . . dolgminnigs, B.   120. sion-fagr svip-stund
ɯina, B.

32.   Hring-skóðs herði-meiðar hvar viti þann, er anni   125
ellz-vellz annan stilli óð-ríkr frama slíkom:
gunn-elldz geymi-runnom Gœndlar fýstr sem ek lýsta
(hirð var hans at morði hrygg) arf-þegi Tryggva?

33.   Þengill þróttar-strœngom þeim bauð Kristr af heimi
byr-tiallz (bœzto heilli bragningi Goð fagni):   130
ygg-laust alla þiggi eljon-fimr á himnom
Óláfr œzta sælo ítr-bóls með gram sólar.

34.   'Her-mart "hví kvæðom" orti' hug-dyggs of son Tryggva
hand-báls hnykki-lunda hreins, ok flokka eina:
Hallfrœðr Hœrða stilli hríð-œflgom vann smíðat;   135
hiœr-gráps, hugða drápo hróðrar-giarn ok Biarni.

35   Eigi einkar lága ek fæ ena þriðjo
hyr-niœrðr hróðri stœrða hóps TVÍSKELFÐA DRÁPO.
Slíkr háttr, svá mun-ek vátta, siall-stundom verðr fundinn!
Herr prúðr hœrvi kvæða hafi gagn!   Enn ek þagna.   140

A LOVE-SONG (Edda and Skalda).

1.   HOLM-LEGGJAR viðr hilmir hring-sköglar mik þöglan.
2.   Sval-teigar mun seljo saltz Viðblinda galtar
raf-kastandi rastar reyr-þvengs muna lengi.
3.   þú munt fúrs sem fleiri flóðs hirði-sif tróðor
grönn við gæfo þínni, griótz Hiaðninga, briótask.   5
4.   Mens hafa mildrar Synjar miúk-stallz logit allir
(Siá höfomk velti-stoð stilltan straum-tungls) at mer draumar.
5.   Ek hefi óðar lokri öl-stafna þer skafna,
væn mörk skála, verki vandr, stef-knarrar branda.

ON SKALD-HELGI? (from Lauf. Edda).

1.   HART fló hvast um snerto (hregg magnaðisk) bragna   10
bókar sól þar es búkar (ben-vargs) hnigo margir.
2.   Flaug (enn firna biúgir) foldar negg at seggjom
(fiarð-elldz fleygi-nirðir fello skiótt at velli).

Who knows of such miracles as those of Tryggwi's heir which I
have now set forth, wrought by any other king? Christ, the king of
Heaven, called him from this world. May God welcome him with joy!
May Olaf partake of every joy in heaven with the Lord of the Sun!
  Epilogue. Many men have wrought mere lays and Short-Songs to the
son of Tryggwi, but Hallfred made an Encomium on him and so did
Biarni. And now I have the third encomium on him. May the noble
company profit by my TWO-STRESSED *Song of Praise.* Such a metre
as mine I know well is seldom to be met with. Now I will be silent.

THE Lady's lovely hue [a pun, Dwarf=Litr] makes me silent. I shall
long remember her. Thou, like other women, wilt struggle against thine
own luck. All my dreams of her have deceived me; she has beguiled me.
I have, lady, with my tongue carved thee a nice dwarf-ship [poem].

STONES flew, and the men fell apace . . . .

125. vita, Cd.   131. þiggr, Cd.   133. Read, hyggjomk orto, *or* hykk
at orti?

IOMSWIKINGA-DRAPA, by BISHOP BIARNI.

BISHOP BIARNI, of the Orkneys, was the son of Kolbein Hruga (the Cobbie Rowe of Orkney popular tradition), a hospitable man and the friend of such Icelanders as Bishop Paul, the son of John Loftsson, and of Raven Sweinbiornsson, 'as may be known from the tokens that Bishop Biarni . . . . sent him, a finger-ring of gold, that weighed an ounce, and was engraved with a raven and his name upon it, so that he might use it as a seal. A second time the bishop sent him a good saddle, and a third time some dyed cloth.' See Sturl. ii. p. 277.

In 1195 Biarni went with Earl Harold Maddadson to Norway to deprecate the wrath of the terrible Swerri, who was angry with the Western Islanders being found in the ranks of his foes. He had defeated them with a fearful overthrow on Palm Sunday, April 3rd, 1194, and now he was threatening 'to carry the war into Africa,' after the example of Harold Fairhair when he had beaten the Western Wickings at Hafrsfirth.

The Bishop's nephew, Thorkettle Walrus, has dealings with Snorri c. 1202. See Sturlunga, vii. ch. 30. According to the Annales Regii and Obituary (Sturlunga Saga, vol. ii. p. 369) Biarni died Sept. 15th, 1222. Sturla, indeed, makes Biarni to have been present at the Great Council at Bergen, 1223; but in writing this passage in Hakon Hakonsson's Life, he was, we take it, copying a list of contemporary bishops, and overlooked, if he ever knew it, that Biarni died a few months before.

The poem we here deal with is manifestly composed for *recital at entertainments*, see ll. 1–4, and contains references to the author's luckless love for the daughter of an Orkney gentleman—all circumstances more appropriate to Biarni's earlier years, say before 1200. It is well composed, has a certain quiet strength, which recalls Thiodwolf's Haustlong, and contains a minute and faithful account of the famous defeat of the buccaneers of Iom, as Biarni received the two-hundred-years old tradition.

In one respect the bishop adds to our knowledge of the battle, by his account of Arnmood, and his exploits and death; which seems to come from a Western version of the story, and to be well worthy of credit. This Arnmood we know as the progenitor of almost the whole Norwegian nobility, as may be seen from the famous pedigree of the *Arnmodlings* in Fagrskinna (Cod. B, § 215), which gives his origin thus:—'There was a man called Finwood the Foundling, he was found in an eagle's eyrie, wrapped up in a silk swaddling-cloth, and no man knows his family; from him is come the whole house which is called the house of the *Arnungs*. His son was Thorarin Bull-back, the father of Arnwood, the father of Arnmood [our hero], from whom is come all that house which is called the *Arnmodlings*.' The account of Finwood recalls William of Malmesbury's Nesting, whom King Alfred found. Bishop Biarni himself was a descendant of Arnmood; see Orkney Saga, Rolls Series, vol. i. Table iv. B.

The *text* rests on the Codex Regius of Snorri's Edda, the last three leaves of a sheet, which a fresh hand has filled up with Iomswikinga-Drapa (defective at the end), and Malshatta-kvædi (see Book ix, § 2). The ink is faded and dim, and the writing hard to make out. It was first correctly copied by Mr. John Sigurdsson, who first observed verse 2 written in the margin underneath the text. It has since (1880) been edited by Mr. Petersen, of Lund.

The *structure* is still clearly shown, though some stanzas at the end are lost. These we can only partly supply from the citations found in O. T. Saga, but they are taken from a worse text than ours. The whole poem would have stood thus:—$14 + 1 + (5 \times 4) + 15 = 50$. Peculiar to its internal shape is the 'cloven burden' (imitated by Snorri), which, with its broken love lament, runs, like a thread of gold on the dead dark iron of an Indian bracelet, through the Epic of war. The *metre* is so carefully observed, that from the two hundred pairs of contrasting vowels we can gather a fair view of the internal phonetic phenomena of the Orkney speech in the Bishop's day.

The *Malshatta-kvædi*, which we would ascribe to Bishop Biarni, will be found in Book ix.

BUA-DRAPA is one of the latest insertions in the great O.T. Saga. It is in Egil's rhyming-metre, and by an unknown poet, Thorkel Gislason, of the same age as Biarni, whom, indeed, he seems to imitate. Only part of it has been preserved. It is almost entirely made up of the worst and latest 'vulgus-phrases' of the school of Einar and the last court-poets. Two lines only present any interest,—l. 27, where it is said that 'Every hail-stone weighed an ounce!' and 31-32, 'The loathsome ogress shot sharp arrows from her fingers.' These exaggerations are duly inserted into the text of the later edition of the Kings' Book. Ari tells the tale simply according to the older and undecked traditions.

I.

1. ŒNGAN kveð-ek at óði órom malma-rýri
    (þó gat-ek hróðr of hugðan) hlióðs at ferðar prýði:
    Framm mun-ek fyr ⱥldom Yggjar biór um fóera
    ef einigir ýtar ætt-góðir mer hlýða.

2. Varka-ek fróðr und forsom; fór-ek aldregi at gⱥldrom; 5
    hefka-ek   .   .   .   .
    ⱥllungis nam-ek eigi Yggjar feng und hanga
    .   .   .   .

3. Hendir enn sem aðra úteitan mik sútar;
    mer hefir harm á hendi hand-fⱥgr kona bundit: 10
    þó em-ek óð at auka óerit giarn at hvⱥro;
    miⱥok em-ek at mer orðinn úgæfr um fⱥr vífa.

4. Dreng var dátt um svarra dorgar-vangs fyr lⱥngo,
    því hefir oss um unga elld-reið skapi haldit:

I. OPENING. *Prologue.* Of no prince [ring-breaker] do I demand a hearing for this song that I have made at this worthy assembly. If but any of you gentlemen will hearken to me, I will set forth my poesy before men. I did not get my knowledge beneath waterfalls [like Woden], I have never given myself to enchantment, I have never . . . . It was not beneath the gallows that I learnt the gift of song.

His love. Joyless grief has overtaken me like other men; a fair-handed damsel has loaded me with sorrow. Evil has been my fate in my dealings with women. Yet I am ready to trick out my poem for her. I have doted on her a long while, and this passion for her has

---

4. ef . . . hlýða] emend.; þoat . . . hlyði, Cd.   6 and 8 blotted out.

þó hefi-ek ort um ítra all-fátt miaðar þello,   15
vel samir enn um eina œl-seljo mer þylja.

5.   .   .   .   .
annat þarf at yrkja all-stórom mun fleira
.   .   .   .   .   greppr of snerto :
(þat berom upp fyr ýta) óhlióð (sœgo-kvæði).   20

6. Suðr frœgo ver sitja (seima-guðr) at Iómi
(fœgr rænir mik flaumi) fimm hœfðingja snemma :
vel samir víst at telja vinnor hreysti-manna,
þar er um malm-þings meiða merkiliga at yrkja.

7. Hver-vetna frá-ek heyja Harald bardaga stóra,   25
þeir ruðo bitra branda bœð-giarnastir niðjar :
siá knœtto þar síðan sið-fornir glym iarna,
þótti þeim at efla þœrf Véseta arfa.

8. Geta skal hins hverr hvatra hœfðingi var drengja,
sá gat sigri at hrósa sniallastr at gœrvœllo :   30
hverr var hóti minni hreysti-maðr at flesto
heldr í herði-raunom hauk-lyndom syni Áka.

9. Sigvaldi hét seggja snar-fengra hœfðingi ;
ok réð þar fyr þegna Þorkell liði sniœllo :
Bui var at hverjom hialdri harð-ráðr með Sigurði ;   35
frœgom Vagn at væri víst ofr-hugi inn mesti.

10. Héldo dreyrgra darra Danmarkar til sterkir
(þeim gafsk rausn ok ríki) rióðendr skipom síðan :
ok auð-brotar erfi ógn-rakkastir drukko
(þeim frá-ek ymsom aukask annir) feðra sínna.   40

11. Enn vildo þá einkom œldor-menn at skyldo
(slíkt ero yrkis-efni) ágæta ser leita :
ok haukligar hefja heit-strengingar gœto ;
eigi segi-ek at ýta œl-teiti vas lítil.

---

endured within me. But though it had well beseemed me to praise her,
few indeed are the songs that I have made upon her. For I have been
bound to deal with other and mightier themes . . . . din of war, and such
is the Epic that I shall now set forth to men.
The vows of the Iomwickings. My fair lady robs me of happiness !
South in Iom, they say, there sat five noble captains. Right seemly
it were to tell their deeds, for mighty men they were to sing of.
Everywhere, they say, Harold fought great battles ; the war-loving
kinsmen reddened their bitter brands ; as heathens they loved to look
on the shock of iron ; they held it their work to help Weseti's son
[Bui].   I will tell who was the noblest captain of them all, he that was
ever blest with victory. No warrior was more dauntless in trial or danger
than Aki's hawk-hearted son.   There was a captain named Sigwald,
and Thorkell held command there too, and Bui the Stern, and Sigurd
with him, and Wain, men say, the loftiest heart of all.   They sailed to
Denmark, and drank the arval there over their fathers.   Fit matter 'tis
for song !   They wished to show their prowess, and began to make their

---

17. Torn off.   21. Suðr frágo] . . . gv, Cd. (torn off).   32. Read, höldr ?

12. Heit-strenging frá-ek hefja heipt-mildan Sigvalda;   45
     Bui var ærr at efla órœkinn þrek slíkan:
     hétosk þeir af hauðri Hákon reka (fíkjom
     grimm vas frægra fyrða fíón) eða lífi ræna.
13. Bui lézk barr at fylgja bæð-mildom Sigvalda
     til hiær-þrimo harðrar hug-prúðr vera síðan: 50
     hafa kvazk Hávarð vilja hranna-briótr at gunni,
     ser kvað hann eigi ílla Áslák í fær líka.
14. Vagn kvað hitt enn hrausti, Hamðis gunnar tæmðom
     sá lézk frœknat fylgja fald-ruðr Bua skyldo:
     þá réð heit til hvítrar hringa-meiðr at strengja   55
     (mér kemr harmr at hendi hættr) Þorketils dóttor.

II. STEF.

15. Ein drepr fyr mer allri—Útrauðr á læg skeiðom
     ærr þengill bað ýta—ítr mannz-konan teiti:
     Góð ætt of kemr grimmo—Gekk herr a skip darra
     hinn er kunni gný gœrva—gœðings at mer stríði.   60
I. 16. Sagt var at sunnan héldo snyrti-menn um hrannir
     (kaldr dreif marr á meiða morð-báls) skipa-stóli:
     Læmðo heldir húfar (hríð kannaði lýðr);
     [gnúði svalr á sýjo sær] ísogar bæror.
17. Sagt vas at rauðra randa reynendr flota sínom   65
     Ióla-nótt at Iaðri Iómsvíkingar kœmi:
     Vǽro heldr á harðan hernoð firar giarnir;
     rióðendr buðo ríki rand-orma Geirmundi.
18. Þá buðo þeir á móti þeim er sunnan kvómo
     til geir-hríðar greppom gœrla Nóregs iarlar: 70
     þar var mestr á mæli (morð-remmandi) skæmmo
     (margr var at laufa leiki) land-herr saman fundinn.

vows. It was no small feud I ween. Sigwald, they say, began the
vowing; Bui was eager to second his task. Cruel was their hate!
They vowed to drive Hakon from his land or take his life. Bui swore
to follow Sigwald to the fray: he said that Haward and Aslac should be
his fellow-warriors. Wain said that he was minded to follow Bui, and
made a vow touching that white maid, the daughter of Thorkettle.

II. THE STAVES. Refrain: The noble's daughter, she alone, kills all
my joy; the scion of a great house is she that works me sore distress.
The gathering. The gallant prince bade them launch their ships, he
went aboard. From the south they sped in their galleys: the icy
billows smote the big-bellied hulls, the cold sea brine splashed upon the
strakes. It is told that at Yule-night the wickings of Iom came with
their fleet to Iader. They were very eager for the fray: they did
violence to Geirmund. Then the earls of Norway called out their
spearmen to meet the Southerners; that was the biggest host that ever
was gathered at such brief summons.

63. I. e. hveldir, see p. 189, l. 7.   68. Geirmundi] om. Cd.

19. *Ein drepr fyr mer allri*—Eldr gnauðaði víða
　elri skœðr um eyjar—*ítr-mannz konan teiti*:
　Góð ætt of kemr grimmo—Gauss upp logi or húsom;　75
　griðom rænti sá gumna—*gœðings at mer stríði*.

II. 20. Ok hœfðingjar hraustir heyra menn at væri
　(þat hefir þióð at minnom) þrír með flokki hvœrom:
　þar-er hregg-viðir hittosk hialma-skóðs á víðom
　(fundr þótti sá fyrðom frægr) Hiœrunga-vági.　80

21. Hauðr frá-ek Hákon verja hart svá at eigi skorti;
　Eirikr hefir eggjar ótrauðr verit rióða:
　ok sœgðo þar ýtar Arnmóð vera síðan
　(sá var greppr við gumna glaðr) odd-vita inn þriðja.

22. Lœgðo heiptar-hvattir herði-menn þar-er bœrðosk　85
　(herr var hauðr at verja hund-margr) saman randir:
　ok víkingom vœro (varð raun at því) einom
　[þat kveða eigi aukit] ýtar fimm at móti.

23. *Ein drepr fyr mer allri*—Atróðr mikinn greiðo
　. . . . . *ítr-mannz konan teiti*:　90
　Góð ætt of kemr grimmo—Glygg magnaðisk eggja
　. . . . . *gœðings at mer stríði*.

III. 24. Sigvaldi bað sína sókn-stranga vel ganga
　(hann vara samr á sáttir) sveit Hákoni á móti:
　Haraldz arfi klauf hialma hildar-œrr ok skiœldo;　95
　framm gekk hann fyr hlífar hart nakkvara snerto.

25. Þar gekk framm í folki frán-lyndr Bui síno
　(þess kveða verða visso vánir) hart með sveina:
　ok geir-viðir gœrðo grimma hœggom rammir
　(gengo þeir at gunni geystir) vápna-bresto.　100

26. Klauf með Yggjar eldi ólmr Gull-Bui hialma,

Refrain. Wide raged the fire over the islands; the flame gushed up
from the houses.
The Norwegian leaders. We have heard that there were three
doughty captains in each host when the warriors met on broad
Hiorunga Bay. That was a meeting men thought worth the telling.
Hakon that never flinched, Eric the Dauntless, and Arnmood the third,
—a gladsome wight among men was he! Angrily they dashed their targets together; great was the host that stood to guard the land. There
were five men to every one of the wickings: that is no multiplied
count.
Refrain. Mighty was the onslaught . . . . High rose the noise of the
swords . . . .
The attack. Sigwald bade his men meet Hakon boldly. Harold's heir
clove helms and shields in the battle-storm. Bui the eager-hearted went
forward in the ranks with his following. The weapons were fiercely
knapped by their stout blows. Bui o' the Gold clove helmets in his

---

83. Armod, Cd.　　86. Read, garpr.　　89. gniðo? Cd.　　90, 92. Torn off.
100. Emend. ; geysta, Cd.

niðr lét hann í herðar hring-serkja bœl ganga:
hart nam hœgg at stœra Hávarðr liði fyrða,
við hefir illt at eiga Áslák verit fíkjom.

27.　Ein drepr fyr mer allri—Él gnúði miœk stála;　105
almr spann af ser odda—ítr-mannz konan teiti :
Góð œtt of kemr grimmo—Gripo þeir í bug snœrom
gunn-rakkastir gumnar—gœðings at mer stríði.

IV. 28.　Þá frá-ek vápnom verjask (Vagn felldi lið) þegna;
hann klauf breiðra brúna borg hundroðom mœrgom :　110
grimmr var snarpra sverða sœngr; burgosk vel drengir;
vann arf-þegi Áka œs; féll blóð á kesjor.

29.　Vagn hefir orðit ýtom œr-fengr at bœð strangri;
með full-huga frœknom framm gingo vel drengir:
þar-er í Yggjar éli Áka sunr enn ríki　115
brátt frá-ek hann at hlœði hug-prúðom Arnmóði.

30.　Hver-vetna frá-ek hœlda (herr œxti gný darra)
fyr hregg-viðom hiœrva hrœkkva gunnar rœkkom :
áðr í œrva drífo ýtom grimmr at blóta
(framm kom heipt en harða) Hákon syni tœki.　120

31.　Ein drepr fyr mer allri—Ylgr gekk á ná bolginn;
þar stóð ulfr í œto—ítr-mannz konan teiti :
Góð œtt of kemr grimmo—Gein vargr of sal mergjar;
gráðr þvarr gylðiss ióða—gœðings at mer stríði.

V. 32.　Þá frá-ek él ít illa œða Hœlga-brúði,　125
glumði hagl á hlífom harða grimmt or norðri:
þar-er í orm-frán augo ýtom skýja grióti
(þá knátti ben blása) barði hreggi keyrðo.

33.　Þá var þœrfom meiri þrek-fœrloðom iarli

---

fury : down to the shoulders he drove his blade. Haward dealt out
many a great blow : it was ill to cope with Anslac in the fray.
　Refrain. Stern grew the fight, the bow sped the arrows, the warriors
drew their bow-strings tight.
　The battle. When the weapons crossed, Wain brought down a host of
men, cleaving the broad skulls of hundreds. Cruel was the song of the
sharp swords! The blood dripped on the javelins! Brave was the
defence. Aki's heir [Wain] made a havoc. Wain cheered his men to
fiercer fight. Brave was the attack! when in the fray Aki's mighty
son struck down the stout-hearted Arnmood. On every side the foe
gave way before them in the fight, till the cruel Hakon offered up his
son in the midst of the battle.
　Refrain. The she-wolf was crammed with carrion, the he-wolf stood
on his prey.
　The storm. It was then, they say, that the Bride of Holgi [Thorgerd
Hakon's patroness] raised a dreadful storm ; right cruelly the hail out of
the north clattered down upon their bucklers, what time the tempest-
driven stones of the clouds beat into the snake-keen eyes of the
wickings. That was too hard a proof for the failing earl [Sigwald]

---

116. Armóði, Cd.

(braut hygg-ek hann at héldi) hug-raun (flota sínom) :   130
snara bað segl við húna Sigvaldi í byr kœldom ;
gnúði hœrð á hlífom hríð ; féll byrr í váðir.

34. Þar lét Vígfúss verða veg-rœkinn Ásláki
(þann era þœrf at segja þótt) hel-farar veittar :
Þórleifr of vann þiokkva þrek-stœrðom Hávarði   135
(hart lét hann) með kylfo hœgg-ramr brotið leggi.

35. *Ein drepr fyr mer allri*—Andat folk at sandi
straumr dró út of eyjar—*ítr-mannz konan teiti* :
Góð œtt of kemr grimmo—Gífrs hesta brá fœsto
gný-miklandi geira—*gœðings at mer stríði.*   140

III. SLŒMR.

36. Bað fyr borð at skyldi bœð-svellandi allir
(þá frá-ek vápnom verjask Vagns lið) Bua þegnar :
áðr hregg-boði hiœrva hraustr með þungar kistor
(sá var illr af aurom) útrauðr á kaf réði.

37. Nam eld-broti Yggjar ýgr fyr borð at stíga ;   145
út bar hann af húfom, hraustr Gull-Bui, kistor :
ok optliga eptir óblauðir þar síðan
knego lýðir líta langan orm á hringom.

38. Skeið frá-ek vallt at verði Vagn með sína þegna ;
œll vóro þá þeira þunn skip hroðin œnnor :   150
upp nóðo þar eigi Eiriks menn at ganga ;
ofan réðo þeir œfga Eiriks vini keyra.

39. Upp stóðo þar eptir ungra snyrti-drengja
(sveit fylgði vel Vagni væn) þrír tigir einir :
allz œnga frá-ek aðra iafn-marga svá burgosk   155
(áðr létti dyn darra) dreng-menn hugom stranga.

---

he and his fleet put out of the battle.   Yea, Sigwald bade his men hoist
the sails in the cold gale, and the wind smote the canvas.   The storm
was beating hard upon their bucklers.   It was there that Wigfus sent
Anslac on the path of death (no need to tell of that), and the hard-
hitting Thorleif broke stout Haward's legs with his club.
Refrain. The stream drove the dead from the islands on to the
sand, the wolves broke their fast on the slain.

III. CLOSE. *The victory.* Wain's crew fought on! Bui called on
all his men to leap overboard, and then he plunged with his heavy chests
into the sea ; he would not part with his money.   He carried his chests
up from the hold, the bold Bui o' the Gold, and leapt overboard [with
them] ; and often since good men have seen the long snake lying there
over the rings.   Wain and his men, they say, kept their galley well.
All the other ships were cleared by this time.   Eric's men could not
board her, for they drove the friends of Eric backward down her sides.
Wain's crew followed him well, till the battle ceased.   At last only
thirty men were still afoot : I have never heard of so few men making

---

143. áðr] emend. ; ok, Cd. (cp. the following subjunctive).

40. Réð með Danska dolga drengr á land at ganga;
    roðin frá-ek dœrr í dreyra; dauðr lá herr á skeiðom:
    Vagn kvað eigi ýtom undan ráð at skunda;
    saman gœrðo þeir s   160
    . . . .

41. Þar lét Eirikr œndo átián þegar týna
    (heldr frǽgom þá þverra) þegna (lið fyr Vagni):
    mælto hraustar hetjor (haukligt var þat síkjom)
    (þau hafa þióðir uppi) þróttar-orð (með fyrðom).

42. Ok með fiorniss sǽlo fór Þorketill Leira,   165
    þá-er men-broti mælti man-sœng um Gná hringa:
    gœrðisk hann at hœggva hauk-lyndan sun Áka;
    Vagn gat heldr at háonom heipt-œrr vegit fyrri.

43. Viltu, kvað hringa hreytir hyggjo-gegn at Vagni,
    él-svellandi, yðvart, Yggjar, líf of þiggja?   170
    Eigi mun-ek nema efna (ungr) þat-er heit namk strengja
    (svá kvað Ullr at iarli egg-hríðar) fiœr þiggja.

44. Grið lét œrr ok aura Eirikr gefit stórom
    (miœk leyfa þat þióðir) þegnom tolf með Vagni.

45. Þá gekk Ullr at eiga œr-lyndr primo randa   175
    (menn fýsto þess) mæta (margir) Ingibiœrgo.

BÚA-DRÁPA.

1. BÁRO á vali víka (vel frá-ek þeim líka
   seggjom snarræði) sverð ok her-klæði.

2. Knúði hvast harða (hlíópo marir barða)
   hregg á hefils spiöllom á humra-fiöllom:
   blá þó hrönn hlýrom; hraut af brim-dýrom   5
   (kili skaut œst alda) uðr in sval-kalda.

3. Báro rökn rasta rekka grið-fasta
   (þröng at rym randa) til ræsis landa:

---

such a sturdy defence. Wain took counsel with the Danish foemen
[wickings] to try and land; he said it was no use for them to fly. The
darts were dyed with gore: the host was lying dead on board the
galleys. They .... together ....

Execution. Eric took the lives of eighteen there; Wain's crew was
running short. The bold heroes spoke words of prowess, which men
have held in memory ever since. They were as bold as hawks ....
Thorkettle [the headsman] swung his axe, when the captain [Wain]
sung a love-song to the lady [Thorkettle's daughter]. He was minded
to cut down the hawk-souled son of Aki, but Wain the Brave wrought
so, that he was beforehand with him and slew him .... 'Wilt thou,'
said the prince [Eric] to Wain, 'take thy life of me?' 'I will not take
my life unless I may fulfil my oath;' thus said the young lord to the
earl. The gallant Eric gave quarter to twelve men besides Wain ....
Then the bountiful hero [Wain] married the fair Ingibiorg; it was a
joy to many a man.

---

160. Here Cod. breaks off. The following fragments are from O. T. (AM. 61).
171. nam, Cd.

           við nam viði mörgom (vápn ero grimm törgom)
           (nýtr gaf nest hröfnom) Nóregr skip-stöfnom.   10

4.   Herr bar hátt merki; á Hamðis serki;
           grimt kom él eggja; at gekk lið seggja:
           meiddo fiör flotna (flest varð hlíf brotna)
           [glumðo gráir oddar] griót ok skot-broddar.

5.   Hruto fyr borð bæði (brusto her-klæði)   15
           höfoð ok hendr manna; hræ nam vargr kanna.

6.   Neytti herr handa; hríð var snörp branda;
           fúst var fár randa til fiörniss landa :
           féllo flein-börvar; flugo af streng örvar;
           sungo hátt hiörvar við hlífar gœrvar.   20

7.   Gullu hræss haukar; hvassir ben-laukar
           skýfðo liðs leggi; lamði griót seggi:
           gnusto gráir malmar (gengo í sundr hialmar);
           [hauks vara friðr fiöllom] í fiörnis stöllom.

8.   Bua frá-ek greitt ganga (gladdisk svanr hanga)   25
           [vökt var göll geira] gegnom lið þeira.

9.   Hagl vá hvert eyri; hraut á lög dreyri
           (blóð þvá bens árom) or bragna sárom :
           þar féll valr víða (vé sá gylld ríða)
           [barðisk sveit snarla] á snekkjom iarla.   30

10.   Örom réð snörpom (slíkt var raun görpom)
           flagð ið for-lióta af fingrom skióta :
           gœrðisk grimmt fíkjom at gumnom ríkjom
           (gnýr var hár hlífa) hregg ok lopt-drífa.

11.   Felldi Vagn virða (valði of nái stirða   35
           hrafn enn hvass-leiti) hrunði á borð sveiti :
           þá réð þess dála (þrymr var hár stála)
           eyðis unn-glóða Eirekr skip hrióða.

KONUNGA-TAL ; OR, GENEALOGY OF THE KINGS OF NORWAY.

INTERESTING as the last of a series, of which the first, Ynglinga-tal, preceded it by at least two hundred and fifty years, it completes its predecessor and model by continuing the royal line down to Swerri, who became sole king in 1184. The account it gives of the first ten kings, including Magnus the Good, is founded on the work of Sæmund the Historian (see ll. 159–60). Indeed it is in honour of John Loftsson, Sæmund's grandson, that it was composed, and during his life-time, which would place it about 1190, for John died 1st Nov. 1197 (born 1125). John's father, Loft Sæmundsson, married Thora, the natural daughter of King Magnus Bareleg, so that it was natural for this panegyrist to run over the roll of the race of kings to which his patron belonged. The number of royal names as in other 'Tals' is meant to be thirty.

In *form*, the poem is in strict stanzas, and in three parts or strophes $(2+38)+(32)+(10+1)=83$. The introduction, in which the author compares himself to a prudent whaler gradually closing upon his game, is fresh and original. In phrase and style, as far as he can, he copies Thiodwolf and Eywind (cp. ll. 125, 207, 259, 264). We have noted the most pronounced parallelisms in the foot-notes. The *author* is not named, but we would ascribe the poem to the monk Gunnlaug, author of Merlinus-Spá, the style and fashion of which it falls in with.

The error which led to the mistaken title in Flatey-bok—'Here begins the generation of the Kings of Norway which Sæmund the

Historian made'—arises from a misunderstanding of verse 40. All copies are derived from the unique MS. Flatey-bok text, cols. 581-2 (vol. ii. pp. 520-8). There are a few misreadings of the copyist, as we have learned to expect from the way in which all the verse is given in this MS.

One great merit of this poem lies in its having preserved Sæmund's chronology, which is, in one instance at least, more correct than Ari's, and is not given elsewhere so completely.

There was another Konunga-tal, called ODD-MIOR, of which there remains one morsel in the abridgment of the Kings' Lives, now known as Ágrip, where the following passage occurs:—

"After Halfdan, Harold took the kingdom that his father had held, and he won for himself a greater kingdom withal, inasmuch as he was a man of early ripeness and of mighty growth, so that he fought battles with the neighbouring kings and overcame them all, and came to be the first sole King of Norway when he was twenty years of age; and the last battle he fought was against a king called Sceidar-Brand [Galley-Brand] in Hafrs-firth, off Iadar, and Brand fled to Denmark and fell in battle in Wend-land, as it is said in the Lay that is called Odd-mior [Fine Point], which deals with the Generations of Kings in these words:—'The Shielding drove,' &c."

This is plainly a tradition of the great Hafrsfirth Fight. We find Brand nowhere else. There is a curious echo of the passage in Arnor's Hryn-henda Encomium on Magnus (see p. 186, vol. ii. ll. 19-20). Are we to account for it by supposing that the author of Odd-mior has borrowed the phrase and used it in a new sense?

I.

1. ÞAT verðr skylt, ef at skilit yrkja,
   greppom 'þeim,' at þeir gleði fyrða :
   allra helzt ef ero færi
   virðar þeir an verit hœfðo.

2. Roa skal fyrst fiarri reyði,   5
   ok koma þó niðr nær áðr lúki :
   þar hefi-ek hugt hróðri þessom
   orðom þeim eptir at mynda :—

3. Þar vil-ek fyrst, ef firar hlýða
   minni mærð, til máls taka :—   10
   Hug-prúðr HALFDAN SVARTI
   erfi-vœrð átti frœknan.

4. Tók kapp-samr við konungs-nafni
   HARALDR brátt inn HÁRFAGRI :

THE COUNT OF KINGS. I. *Prologue*. It becomes a poet, if he knows his work, to entertain men, all the more if good poets be fewer than has been. One must at first row farther from the whale, and then draw nearer and nearer to the end. According to this example I have thought to order the words of my song.

I will first take up my parable here, if men will give heed to me: HALFDAN THE BLACK had a noble heir. HAROLD FAIRHAIR early took

---

1. skilum, Cd.   2. Read, hveim or góðom?   7. Read, hródrar þessa
orðom því?   9. virar, Cd.

þá-er Halfdan hafði drukknat   15
   í hæings hallar næfri.
5. Ok er hann í haug lagiðr
   á her-ská Hringa-ríki :
   enn barn-ungr burr Halfdanar
   tók fram-lyndr við fæðor-arfi.   20
6. Eigi hann þat eitt eiga vildi
   er hans lang-feðgar leifðo hánom :
   svá var ríkr ræsir Sygna
   ok ágiarn við auð-gefendr :
7. At allt land Elfar á milli   25
   ok Finn-merkr fylkir átti :
   náði hann fyr Nóregi
   ꜹllom fyrst einn at ráða.
8. Átti gramr, sá-er giafar veitti,
   barna mart þeir-er biðo þroska :   3ꝋ
   því kemr hvers til Haralldz síðan
   skiꜹldungs kyn ins Skarar-fagra.
9. Réð þriá vetr Þundar beðjo
   siklingr snarr ok siau tigi :
   áðr an lofðung lífi at ræna   35
   Ása-dolgs kom einga-dóttir.
10. Þá var haugr eptir Harald orpinn
   reisoligr á Rogalandi :
   þess mun æ uppi lengi
   hildings nafns Halfdans sunar.   40
11. Tók EIRIKR við iꜹfurs nafni
   BLÓÐ-ŒX brátt sem buendr vildo :
   var víg-fimr vetr at landi
   Eirekr allz einn ok fióra.
12. Áðr an vin-sæll vestan kœmi   45
   AÐALSTEINS einga-FÓSTRI :

---

upon him the royal title, when Halfdan was drowned in the thatch of the
salmon's hall [ice] ; yea, he is laid in his barrow in war-wont Ring-rick,
but the ambitious young son of Halfdan took up his father's heritage.
He would not be content to own merely what his ancestors left him : the
Sygns' lord was so mighty and grasping towards his neighbours, that he
got hold of all the folklands between the Elbe [Gaut-Elbe] and Finmark. He was the first of all to reign alone over Norway. This king
had many children who grew to manhood ; so every king's family since
comes back to Harold Fairhair. He ruled three-and-seventy winters over
the land, before Loki's only daughter came to take his life. Then there
was a lordly barrow cast up over Harold in Rogaland. The name of
Halfdan's son will ever endure in the land. ERIC BLOOD-AXE forthwith
took the name of king as the franklins wished ; he was one-and-four
winters in the country before the only beloved FOSTER-SON of ÆTHEL-

---

17. haug] om. Cd.   30. Read, þau er.   36. Emend. ; audlings, Cd.

Ok Hákon halfrar allrar
bróðor sínn beiddi erfðar.

13.   Enn Eirikr undan flýði
heiptar-giarn ok hans synir :   50
kom harð-ráðr ' hersa' mýgir
aptr í land aldri síðan.

14.   Réð kapp-samr fyr konung-dómi
Hákon einn hríð nokkora :
var sex vetr samt at landi   55
tírar-giarn ok tuttogo.

15.   Háði gramr gunni á Fitjom
við Eiriks erfi-vœrðo :
varð í hœnd hilmir skotinn
þá-er folk-meiðr flótta kníði.   60

16.   Þat hygg-ek brátt til bana leiddo
lítið sár lofðung snaran :
þar-[er] ávallt er vísi dó
hella kennd til Hákonar.

17.   Enn í haug Hœrðar lœgðo   65
sikling þann á Sæ-heimi :
hurfu ' hryggvir' frá Haraldz arfa
frœknir menn fiœrvi ræntom.

18.   Þá hefi-ek heyrt at Haraldr tœki
ú-ár-sæll iœrð ok ríki :   70
réð Gráfeldr Gunnhildar son
nio vetr fyrir Nóregi.

19.   Áðr an Gorms-son ok Goll-Haraldr
nafna sínn at nái gerðo :
var siklingr suðr á Halsi   75
lífi ræntr í Lima-firði.

20.   Tók harð-ráðr ept Harald fallinn

---

stan came from the West. Yea, Hakon required half of all the inheritance from his brother. And the revengeful Eric and his sons
fled away; the stern oppressor of his barons [brothers?] never came
back to the country again. The glory-loving Hakon ruled alone over
the kingdom for some time : he was six-and-twenty years altogether in
the land. He fought a battle with Eric's heir at Fitia, and was shot in
the arm while he was chasing his flying foes. This little wound soon
brought him to his death, I ween ; ever since the king died the slope is
called after Hakon. And the Hords laid him in a barrow at Seaham ;
they turned sorrowfully away from the dead heir of Harold. After
this I have heard that Harold the famine-cursed took the land and
sway. Greyfell Gundhildsson ruled nine years over Norway, ere that
Gormsson and Gold-Harold made his namesake a corpse ; yea, the
king was reft of his life at Halse on Limbfirth in the south. The

---

51. Read, hlýra ?   60. knaði, Cd.   61. leiddi, Cd.   65. haudar,
Cd.   67. hryggvir] emend. ; svá, Cd.   74. gerði, Cd.

        HÁKON IARL við Hárs vífi:
        sá réð tiggi ok tuttogo
        þrettán vetr Þundar beðjo.   80
21.   Urðoa góð í Gaular-dal
        ævi-lok Eiriks fæðor:
        þá-er Karkr þræll knífi meitti
        hattar stall af Hákoni.
22.   Misti lítt, sú-er lægom stýrði,   85
        rekka kind ráðs ins bazta:
        þá-er norðr í Nóregi
        Kristinn mann til konungs tóko.
23.   Ok ÓLÁFR ARFI TRYGGVA
        tók lið-driúgr lænd ok þegna: 90
        hinn er fimm á fáom vetrom
        lofða vinr lænd kristnaði.
24.   Var Óláfr allz at landi
        fimm at eins faðmins galla:
        áðr Eirikr með ofr-liði   95
        ræsi þann rómo beiddi.
25.   Sú var allz, áðr Ormr hryðisk,
        hrotta hríð hæorð ok lengi:
        þar hefir æld er Óláfr féll
        Svoldrar-vág síðan kallat.   100
26.   Réð tolf vetr tíri gæofgaðr
        EIRIKR IARL fyr Yggs mani:
        áðr an lofðungr or landi fór
        vestr um haf, sá-er vini gœddi.
27.   Þá var úfr Eiriks skorinn   105
        áðr an Rúm-fæor ræsir hœfi:
        ok blóð-ræos til bana leiddi
        vitran iarl vestr með Englom.
28.   Talði land ok lausa-fé

---

stern EARL HAKON took the land after the dead Harold; one-score-and thirteen years he ruled the country. The end of the life of Eric's father in Gaula-dale was not a good one, where Cark the thrall slit the throat of Hakon with a knife. The men of the land, who swayed the provinces, did not fail to take the best of counsel, when they took a Christian man for king north in Norway. And OLAF, HEIR OF TRYGGWI, with his powerful guard, took land and lieges; he that christened five folk-lands in a few years. Olaf was altogether five winters only in the land, before Eric, with overwhelming odds, offered him battle. That battle-storm was fierce and long ere the Serpent was cleared. Men have since called the bay where Olaf fell Swold. EARL ERIC ruled twelve winters over the land, before he went away west over sea. Eric's tonsils were cut before he started on his pilgrimage to Rome, and the hæmorrhage brought about his death west among the English. SWAIN

---

81. urðu ei, Cd.   97. ryddiz, Cd.

sína eign SVEINN ok HÁKON : 110
ok tvá-vetr, at tali fyrða,
Eiriks arf iarlar hœfðo.

29. Áðr í land með lítinn her
konung-maðr kœmi vestan :
ok Óláfr iarli mœtti 115
í Sauðungs-sundi miðjo.

30. Varð Hákon þá hilmi at sverja
eiða þess, er Óláfr beiddi :
at folk-baldr flýja skyldi
óðul sín til aldr-slita. 120

31. Bauð Óláfr austr fyr Nesjom
snarpa sókn Sveini iarli :
varð lið-fárr lœnd at flýja
sigri sviptr sonr Hákonar.

32. Fékk lof-sæll lœnd með hringom 125
ÓLÁFR einn allt inn DIGRI :
réð hróð-mœgr Haralldz ins Grœnska
fimmtán vetr folldo grýttri.

33. Bar kapp-samr Knútr inn Ríki
biartan seim und bœndr marga : 130
sparði lítt við lenda menn
auð til þess at þeir iœfur vélti.

34. Reisto her hilmi á móti
kynjaðir vel Kalfr ok Þórir :
þar var feldr fylkir Þrœnda 135
sem -staðir Stikla- heita.

35. Þá bar raun, at ræsir var
Kristi kærr, um konung helgan :
stendr í Kristz kirkjo miðri
heilagt skrín yfir Haralldz arfa. 140

---

and HAKON [brother and son] claimed land and treasure for themselves,
and held Eric's inheritance for two years by the common reckoning,
till one of royal race came from the West with a small force, and Olaf
met the earl [Hakon] in the midst of Sauthung-Sound. Hakon was
obliged to swear the oath that Olaf gave him, to fly from his native land
till his death-day. East by Nesia Olaf gave sharp battle to Earl Swain ;
reft of victory, followed by few, Hakon's son was turned to flight. The
renowned·OLAF THE STOUT took land and treasure to himself alone :
the famed son of Harold of Gren-land ruled the land fifteen years.
Cnut the Mighty bestowed the bright ore upon many a franklin ; he did
not begrudge the liege lords his wealth to get them to betray their king.
The well-born Calf and Thori raised an army against their lord ; the
prince of the Thronds fell at the place called Stickle-stead. Then was
it made manifest of the holy king that he was dear to Christ. A holy
shrine stands over Harold's heir in the midst of Christ Church. Then

---

125. = Y. 85. hringom] rinum, Cd.

36. Þá réð Sveinn sonr Alfífo
    snáka stríð sex fyr landi:
    áðr an Knútz sonr af konungdómi
    vina-lauss varð at flýja.

37. Kom ágætr austan or Gœrðom   145
    einga-son Óláfs konungs:
    fekk Magnus, ok mikit ríki,
    óðals-iœrð alla sína.

38. Var tál-laust tólf vetr konungr
    mœnnom þarfr Magnus Góði: 150
    áðr í sótt Sygna dróttinn,
    afreks-maðr, andar misti.

39. Varð harm-dauðr hverjom manni
    fylkir fœrðr þars hans faðir hvílir:
    sá var norðr í Nóregi   155
    Kristz at kirkjo 'konung maðr' grafinn.

40. Nú hefi-ek talt tio landreka
    þá-er hverr var frá Haraldi:
    innta-ek svá ævi þeirra
    sem Sæmundr sagði inn Fróði.   160

II.

41. Þó er þess máls, er ek mæla hygg,
    meiri hlutr miklo eptir:
    Nú skal þann þóott of greiða
    iœfra kyns er enn lifir.

42. Þat er mer sagt at Sigurðr Hrísi   165
    Haraldz sonr héti forðom:
    var Halfdan Hrísa arfi,
    enn Sigurðr Sýr son Halfdanar.

Swain Alfgifuson ruled six years over the land, till Cnut's son had to fly friendless from his kingdom. There came from the East out of Garth [Novgorod territory] the only son of King Olaf; yea, Magnus took a mighty realm, all the lands of his heritage. Magnus the Good was doubtless king for twelve winters, ere he, the lord of the Sygns, lost his life in sickness. All men held it a sorrowful death: he was borne where his father rests; he was buried north in Norway at Christ Church in Cheaping.

Now I have told up ten kings, each of whom descended from Harold. I have gone over their lives, according to the words of Sæmund the Historian.

II. But yet by far the greater part of the discourse which I am minded to deliver, remains. Now I will set forth orderly that branch of the royal race that is still living. It was told me that of yore there was a son of Harold [Fairhair], named Sigurd the Bastard. Halfdan was

---

156. Read, í Kaupangi?   163. Emend.; því þaðan af, Cd.   165. risi, Cd.

43. Þá gat son Sigurðr ok Ásta,
     þann-er Haraldz heiti átti: 170
     sá réð einn all-vitr konungr
     víðri foldo vetr tuttogo.

44. Áðr her-fœr hilmir gerði
     til Englandz með of-stopa:
     felldo vestr í vápn-þrimo   175
     Enskir menn Óláfs bróðor.

45. Tók friðsamr til fœðor-leifðar
     ok ár-sæll Óláfr Kyrri:
     sá réð gramr grýttri foldo
     sam-fast vetr siau ok tuttogo.   18c

46. Kom of brátt œndo at ræna
     mikil sótt Magnuss fœðor:
     sá var enn œðlingr grafinn
     Kristz at kirkjo í Kaupangi.

47. Enn Óláfr átti enn Kyrri   18:
     frœknan son ok fiár góðan:
     réð Magnus fyr mani Yggjar
     tio vetr at tali fyrða.

48. Frá-ek Berfœttr bœrn at ætti
     Magnús mœrg þau-er metorð hœfðo: 19(
     vóro þess þengils synir
     fremdar-fliótz fimm konungar.

49. Fór mál-sniallr Magnus konungr
     til Írlandz ungr at herja:
     varð ágætr Eysteins faðir   19
     fleina flaug felldr í 'þeiri.'

50. Þat er þá sagt, at saman réði
     þióð-konungar þrír fyrir landi:
     þat hefi-ek heyrt at hafi varla
     fremri brœðr á fold komit.   2c

Bastard's heir, and Sigurd Sow the son of Halfdan. Sigurd begat a so
on Asta, who had the name of Harold. That wise king ruled th
land alone for twenty winters, till in his pride he made an expedition t
England. The English feiled Olaf's brother west in the battle [Stamfor
Bridge]. The peaceful and season-blessed Olaf the Quiet took u
his father's estate. He ruled the land seven-and-twenty winter
through. Too soon came a mighty sickness to stop the breath c
Magnus' father. The king was buried at Christ Church in Cheapin
But Olaf the Quiet had a noble and generous son. Magnus ruled th
land ten years, as men tell it up. I know that Bareleg had man
glorious children of his blood: five of his sons became kings. Kin
Magnus went to Ireland in his youth to harry. Yea, Eystan's fathe
was stricken down in battle there. It is told that three fellow-kin
ruled the land together. I have heard that three nobler brothers neve

---

179. ræðr, Cd.   196. Read, í fl. fl. f. þaðra?

51. Varð Óláfr ungr inn góði
lof-sæll fyrstr líf at missa:
móotto þess Magnúss sonar
skamma stund skatnar nióta.

52. Gerði flest þat er frama gegndi   205
innan-landz Eysteinn konungr:
unz hiart-verkr hilmi frœknan
brigða brátt til bana leiddi.

53. Þeir ero brœðr báðir lagðir
norðr í grund á Níðar-bakka: 210
þar stendr hátt í hœfuð-kirkjo
Óláfs skrín yfir altari.

54. Enn Sigurðr sýno lifði
þeirra lengst þriggja brœðra:
hinn er út til Iórsala   215
frægsta fœr fór or landi.

55. Réð ágætr ok ellifo
sextán vetr Sigurðr fyr ríki:
áðr mann-skœð Mœra dróttins
bana-sótt brygði lífi.   220

56. Þess er austr í Oslo bœ
lofðungs lík lagit í kisto:
nú grœr iœrð yfir iœfurs beinom
at Hallvarðz hárri kirkjo.

57. Enn bil-trauðr bæði lifði   225
eptir Sigurð sonr ok dóttir:
þess mun enn þokkom síðar
dóttir nefnd Dœla hilmiss.

58. Nú er heldr svá at halla tekr
ævi-lok iœfra at telja: 230
hét Magnus mœgr Sigurðar
heiptar-giarn, enn Haraldr bróðir.

walked the earth. First of them, Olaf the Good lost his life in his
youth; the people had but a short while to profit by *the rule of* Magnus'
son. Eystan did all that was good within the land [at home], till in
a short while spasm of the heart brought about his death. Both
these brothers are laid in the ground north by the banks of Nith,
where Olaf's shrine stands high above the altar in the cathedral church.
But Sigurd lived far the longest of the three brothers,—he who made
the very famous journey out of the country away to Jerusalem. Now
Sigurd ruled the realm sixteen-years-and-eleven, till a murderous mortal
disease [mania] cut off his life. This king's body is laid in a coffin east
in Oslo-by [Christiania]; the grass is growing over his bones by the lofty
church of *St.* Hallward. But a son and daughter both outlived Sigurd.
This daughter of the king of the Dales I will shortly speak of later
on. And here this count of the kings' deaths [necrology] is sad for me
to tell. Magnus was the name of Sigurd, but Harold was his

207. = Y. 173.   223. = Book vi, No. 54.

59. Þeir miæk róg-samt ríki hœfðo
nánir frændr í Nóregi:
allt fór verr an vera skyldi   235
(þess galt margr) á meðal þeira.

60. Unz Magnus misti beggja
sæmdar-laust sigrs ok heilso:
þat veit hverr, at HARALDR GILLI
var sex vetr sam-fast konungr.   240

61. Áðr an lofðung af líf-dœgom
tírar-laust tóko fyrðar:
Sá er í Kristz kirkjo iarðaðr
í Biœrgin bróðir iœfra.

62. Frá-ek land-vœrn ept liðinn ræsi   245
Sygna grams at synir tœki:
var EYSTEINN Inga bróðir
sóknar-giarn, enn SIGURÐR annarr.

63. Náði frægt í friði at standa
þeygi lengi þeirra ríki: 250
þvi-at þeir brœðr, er bruto sœri,
bana-spiót bœrosk eptir.

64. Varat saklaust þá-er Sigurð hœfðo
frœkinn mann fiœrvi ræntan:
sá er í fold hiá feðr sínom   255
í Biœrgin buinn at liggja.

65. Var Eysteinn austan-Fiarðar
lífi ræntr af liði Inga:
nú er sá gramr grundo ausinn
andar sparr austr at Forsi.   260

66. Stóð einart INGA ríki
áttián vetr ok aðra siau:
unz Hákon með her-liði
austr í Vík Inga felldi.

---

brother. These kinsmen had a reign of sore feud in Norway. Everything went worse between them that should have been; many a man
had to pay for it; till at last Magnus miserably lost both victory and
virility. Every one knows that Harold Gillie-[Christ] was king six
years together, till men ingloriously took his life. He is laid in the
earth at Christ Church in Bergen. I know that after the king's death
his sons took charge of the land—EYSTAN and SIGURD, the brothers of
INGI. Their rule did not long endure peacefully, for the brothers
broke their oaths, and took up the spear of deadly strife. It was not
guiltlessly that Sigurd was robbed of his life; he was duly laid by his
father in Bergen. Eystan was robbed of his life by Ingi's following
east of the Firth [of Christiania]. He lies lifeless with the earth heaped
above him east by Force. Ingi's sway endured eighteen winters and
seven to boot, till HAKON with his army struck him down east in

250. lengr, Cd.   259. =Y. 175.

67. Sá er gunn-diarfr gramr í Oslo   265
     hauðri hulðr at hæfoð-kirkjo :
     enn HÁKON hlaut at ráða
     lítla stund landi ok þegnom.

68. Því-at Erlingr átti inn Skakki
     vænan son ok vel borinn :   270
     gáfo landz-folk eptir liðinn Inga
     konungs nafn Kristínar bur.

69. Ok MAGNUS á Mœri norðr
     fremðar-giarn felldi Hákon :
     sá var vin-sæll vígðri moldo   275
     ræsir hulðr í Raumsdali.

70. Var sókn-diarfr SON KRISTÍNAR
     siautián vetr í samt konungr :
     unz ágætr austr í Sogni
     frœkinn gram felldi Sverrir.   280

71. Nú er gunn-diarfs í grœf lagit
     Magnúss lík í musteri :
     í Biœrgin, þar-er buit golli
     stendr skraut-gœrt skrín Sunnifo.

72. Nú er þat sýnt at SVERRIR ræðr   285
     ógnar-œrr einn fyr ríki :
     œllo því, er átt hefir
     Haralldz kyn Halfdans sunar.

III.

73. Þó skal-ek enn þokkom fleira
     frá Berfœttz bœrnom segja :   290
     œðlings þess, er aldregi
     elld né iarn óttask hafði.

74. Hét ein dœglings dóttir ÞÓRA,

the Wick. He is shrouded in mould at the cathedral church at Oslo.
Albeit Hakon was fated to rule land and lieges but a little while, for
Erling Shank had a fair and well-born son, and the people of the land
gave the name of king to Christina's child after Ingi's death. Yea, this
MAGNUS struck down Hakon north in More. The beloved king
[Hakon] was shrouded with hallowed dust in Ream's-dale. CHRIS-
TINA'S SON [Magnus] was king seventeen winters in all, till the re-
nowned Swerri felled him in Sogn in the east. Magnus' body is now
laid in the grave in the minster at Bergen, where stands the inlaid gold-
decked shrine of Sunweva. Now it is well known that the warrior
SWERRI rules alone over the whole realm that Harold, Halfdan's son,
held of yore.
III. Now I am going to speak more at length of the children of
Bareleg, the Etheling that never shrunk from fire or sword. One of his
daughters was named THORA. She was given in marriage to a noble-

---

265. =Y. 175.   280. gramr, Cd.

sú var gipt gæofgom manni :
allra helzt, sú-er IOAN fœddi ;   295
var son-sæl systir iæofra.

75. Kom ráð-væond ræsiss dóttir
til Næfr-landz-nykra-borgar :
gæofog-lynd góðrar tíðar
allra helzt Íslendingum.   300

76. Þvi-at hug-rakkr henni at fylgði
einga-sonr iæofra systor :
hiarta-prúðr, sá-er hefir allra
ýta vinr orð-lof fira.

77. Þat er víst at Ioans verða   305
metorð mest mistar runna
einarð-lyndz, þar-er eigosk við
merkis-menn mæolom skipta.

78. Nú vill kappi við konungs frænda
afreks-maðr engi deila :   310
gipto-driúgr, sem glíkt er,
verðr vin-sæll vella deilir.

79. Þótti æorr ok ósvikall
faðir hans flestom mæonnom :
vissi LOPTR und laufi skýja   315
óvin sínn engan fœddan.

80. Enn SÆMUNDR sína vissi
SIGFÚSS SONR snilli iafnan :
faðir Loptz, sá-er firom þótti
hæofoðs-maðr um hluti alla.   320

81. Þat hefir ætt Odda-verja
iæofra-kyns alla prýdda :
dóttor-son sá-er dæogom optar
fremsk marg-nýtr Magnuss konungs.

82. Nefnda-ek áðr nær þriá tigi   325
tignar-menn tíri gœdda,

---

man. She was blessed in her sons, especially in giving birth to JOHN.
This king's daughter came to the land of the Roof of the Nixie's town
[i.e. Iceland] in a good hour, especially for the Icelanders. For her
only son came with her, the courteous one, who has a good report of all
men. It is certain that John is the highest in rank of all men, foremost where men of mark take counsel together [at the Moots]. No
one will vie with this kinsman of kings, for he is much beloved, as is
most natural. His father LOFT was deemed gallant and guileless by
all : he had no enemy beneath the foliage of the clouds [under heaven]
And SÆMUND SIGFUSSON, the father of Loft, was unequalled in wisdom,
and was deemed foremost in everything. But the pride of the Ordwara
family (see Sturl. ii. 487) is the famous son of the daughter of King

---

þræto-laust enn þeir eru
Ioans ættar allir iæfrar.

83. Nú bið-ek Krist, at konungs spialli
hafi þat allt er hann œskir sér,   330
gipto-driúgr af Goði siœlfom
allan aldr, ok unaðs nióti.

ODD-MIOR.

SCIOLDUNGR rak með skildi Skeiðar-brand or landi,
réð sá konungr síðan sniallr Nóregi œllom.

---

§ 7. SCRAPS OF COURT POETRY.

THIS poem might have appeared with the other poems of Harold
Fairhair, but that one has no means of knowing whether Iorun was
contemporary with the events she describes or no. All we can with
certainty say is, that Ari has drawn from it one particular in his text
of Harold's life, the quarrel between father and son, where he mentions
'Thorsbiorg' within Cape Stad, and 'Rein-slétta,' place-names drawn
from this poem, either from the pure text (for ours is over-painted and
polished) or from lost verses. If Iorun were not earlier, we should fancy
that she was a contemporary of St. Olaf, but the few lines remaining of
her have been so metamorphosed that it is hard to judge. There are a
score of Ioruns in Landnama-bok, but none that one could fix on.
The place 'Rein-slétta' seems to have stood in l. 11, where the
MSS. have 'raun,' but beyond this we cannot mend the verses much.
The story of the incident related, touching Sindri the poet, has been
given, vol. ii. p. 29.
We take what is left to be a strophe of a longer poem, which dealt
with more than our tale, perhaps a poem of Embassies, which indeed in
Ireland formed one class of stories, just as cattle-spoils, elopements,
banquets, etc. did. The words of Harold's Saga, 'According to this tale
Iorun the poet-maiden (Skald-mær) made a certain section of Sendibit,'
evidently refer to a poem of which the 'erendis' were many and
various. A Saga of the poetess would have been a welcome thing, but
we are doomed to rest ignorant about this unknown lady.

WORM STEINTHORSSON. A poet whose age is also unknown (probably
of St. Olaf's time). He has left an unplaceable scrap, a beginning of an

---

Magnus [John]. Now I have named near three tens of famous princes:
they are all without gainsaying of the family of John.
Epilogue. Now I pray Christ that this companion of kings may have
all that he desires, life-long prosperity from God himself, and enjoy
. life of bliss.

ODD-MIOR. The Shielding with his shield drove Galley-Brand out
of the land. The gallant king ruled all Norway after this.

Encomium, and a piece of a Dirge on his dead lady, which ought to have been preserved whole: it is touching, and unlike other dirge-poetry. The metre is rough and 'docked,' feeling its way towards eight-measure. That Worm had made satires, a hint in l. 1 shows.

IORUN THE POETESS (SENDIBIT).

(Lines 1, 2 from Lives of Kings; 3–12 from St. Olaf's Saga in AM. 75 c. 4to.; 13, 14 from Edda.)

1. HARALD frá-ek Halfdans spyrja herði-brægð (enn lægðiss
      sýnisk svart-leitr reyni siá bragr) enn Hár-fagra:
    Þvi-at ríkr konungr rekka reyr und-lagar dreyra
    morðz þá-es merkja þorðo magnendr hófsk at fagna.

2. Hvar viti einkar ærvir ær-veðrs frama gœrvan   5
    tingl-rýrondom tungla tveir iæfrar veg meira?
    an geð-harðir gœrðo gollz land-rekar þollom
    (upp angr um hófsk Yngva óblindr) fyr lof Sindra.

3. Hróðr vann 'Hringa stríðiss' harm fyr-kveðinn ramman;
    Goðthormr hlaut af 'Gauti' góð laun kveðins óðar: 10
    'raun-framla' brá rimmo runnr Skiældunga 'gunnar'
    (áðr biósk herr til hiærva hreggs) dœglinga tveggja.

4. Bragningr réð í blóði (beið herr konungs reiði)
    [hús luto opt fyr eiso] óþióðar slæg rióða.

DIRGE BY ORMR STEINÞORSSON (Edda).

1. SEGGIR þurfot ala ugg (ængo sný-ek í Viðriss feng
      háði) [kunnom hróðr-smíð haga] of mínn brag.

2. Þvi-at hols hryn-báls hramma, þatz ek ber framm
    Billings á 'burar' full biarkar hefi-ek lagit mark.

3. At veri borit biórs bríkar ok mítt lík   5
    (rekkar nemi) dauðs (drykk Dvalins) í einn sal.

Sendibit. I have gathered how Harold Fairhair heard of Halfdan's venturous plots, and this behaviour seemed to him black-hued. The great king went forth to war against his son. Who has ever heard of more glorious honour granted to any man than this which the Two Kings bestowed on Sindri for his song? Open strife had arisen between the two princes. The poet's song prevented a great calamity. Guth-thorm gat from the king of the Ring-folk a good largesse for the poem he delivered; yea, the poet clearly stopped the battle between the Two Kings, when both armies were in array for the fight at Rein-slade within *Cape Stad.* The prince reddened his shafts in the blood of the wicked.

Worm Steinthorsson. A Dirge on his Lady. Prologue. Men need not fear my song, I put no spite in it; I know the poet's craft [I am not writing satire now]. But when I deliver the cup of Billing's maid [the poem], I put the mark of a fair lady on it [dedicate it to her]. Would that my dead body and hers were laid in one grave. Let men hear this Dwarves' draught of mine! The lady was clad in clean white raiment,

---

9. fyr-] emend.; fram kveðinn, Cd.   11. Read, Rein-slétto? ... fyrir
Stað ... innan.   4. Read, brúðar? i. e. Gunnlad.

4. Skorða vas í fæt fœrð fiarð-beins afar-hrein;
    nýri slœng nadd-Freyr nisting um miaðar-Hrist.
5. 'Hróðrar' nióti funa Fríðr! fundins mærða-ek salar grund;
    fastan lagða-ek flagðs gust fiarðar á brímis garð.   10

From another Song in different metre (Ups. Edda).

Ek hefi orð-gnótt miklo (opt finnom þat) minni
[fram bar-ek leyfð fyr lofða] liós, an ek munda kiósa.

Réð-ek þenna mæg manni   .   .   .   .
.   .   .   .   .   Vind-svals unað blindom.

EILIFR KULNA-SVEINN.

EILIF KULNA-SWAIN must be distinguished from Eilif Gudrunson. Of this man we know no more than we can gather from the scraps of his scattered in Edda. They seem to belong to an Encomium on a Saint (ver. 3). Two of the lines refer to a scarcity of hay caused by ice and snow (ver. 4). It is not impossible that the Saint referred to may be Bishop John of Holar (d. 1121), whose holy prayers and vow of the founding of Thing-ore church brought about a miraculous thaw after a terrible winter and long frost, whereby a 'hay-famine' had begun. The story, as given in the Bishop's life, runs—

"When St. John had been but a short while in his see, men fell into great straits, they were visited by mighty storms and cold weather, so that the ground was not green at the spring-moot-tide. The holy bishop John went to the spring-moot [in May] which was held at Thing-ore; and when he got there, he made a vow for a good season, with the consent of the whole people, promising that they would rear a church and glebe-farm there, and that each should do his share till the place was finished. After the vow, the holy bishop John took off his mantle, and himself marked out the foundation walls for the church; and so swiftly were men's condition bettered, that in the same week all the ice was gone, whereby the famine for the most part had risen, so that it could be no more seen anywhere; and the earth began to yield so fast, that there was well-nigh plenty of pasture grass for sheep within a week's time." This church and glebe became famous soon after, from the completion of the bishop's plan, by the founding of a Benedictine cloister at Thing-ore (1133), in which several learned Icelanders have lived; Abbot Karl, the author of Swerri's Saga; the two monks Odd and Gunnlaug; and, if we may guess, perhaps Eilif himself.

There is a curious play on the word 'vond-ol,' 'vond' being supplied by its equivalent 'torráðin' [this grammatical pun makes it unlikely

---

the needle-man sewed up her body in a new garment. May she enjoy the earth [rest in peace]. I have ended my song of praise. I have set my mind on . . . .

Beginning of an Encomium. My word-store is lower than I would. I deliver my Song of Praise to the Prince . . . . I was a blind man this . . . . son of Windcold [winter] . . . .

---

8. song, W.   9. Read, hauðrs?   11. mikla, Cd.

indeed that it could be by his tenth-century namesake, Eilif Gudrunson].
Verses 1–3 appear to be a variation of the burden.

ON BISHOP JOHN (?).

(Verses 1–4 from Edda; verse 5 from Skalda.)

1. HRÓTZ lýtr helgom crúci heims ferð ok lið beima,
   sœnn er enn œll dýrð œnnor ein Mário sveini.
2. Hirð lýtr himna dýrðar hrein Mário sveini;
   mátt viðr mildingr dróttar (maðr er hann ok Goð) sannan.
3. Máttr er an menn of hyggi mætr Goðs vinar betri; 5
   þó er Engla gramr œllo œrr helgari ok dýrri.
4. Himins dýrð lofar hœlða (hann er allz konungr) stilli.
5. Vóro vœtn ok mýrar [verðr hitt at þau skerða]
   (svell var áðr) of alla [œl tor-ráðin] hóla.
6. Báro mæta móti malm-þings viðir palma 10
   (sveit hrauð) seggja bœti (sorg) er hann kom til borgar:
   svá laðar siklingr skýja sín, hiarta, til, biartir
   þá er fyrða gram fœra fœgr verk með trú sterkri.

UNCLASSED FRAGMENTS OF ENCOMIA, ETC.

MOSTLY anonymous, drawn from later parts of Edda, and from
Skalda. They appear to have been overlaid, and some of them are
undoubtedly old. Even those scraps which have a name appended are
by poets not in Skalda-tal, so we cannot class them, and have
preferred to set them together here in such rough arrangement as
was feasible, under the heads MYTHICAL, HISTORICAL, PERSONAL,
SATIRICAL, LEGENDARY.

There is not much to be got from them apparently, but one or two
are certainly interesting. *Haflida-mal* was probably a satirical Dialogue.
Gudbrand, Skraut-Odd, Thorolf, Thord More's poet, Erringar-Stein (Brawl
Stone), *Gamli Gnævada-scald, Hall,* and *Harold, etc.* are the poets whose
names have been preserved. The fragment (9) is on Cnut the Great,
or St. Cnut; the No. 17 on Magnus the Good, or Magnus Barefoot.
There are bits of poems on *Kugi* and *Swala,* and two pieces called *Strid-
kera-visor* (cf. p. 336, § 7, No. 6) and *Morgin-sol* (Morning Sun) which
look genuine.

There is a bit on the Wolsung cycle, a scrap on the Hagbard-Haki
legend, and a bit from a Drapa on Asmund o'Gnod. Verses II. 6 and 6 *b*

Burden. The host of heaven and the company of mankind bow to
the Holy Rood. There is no greater glory than that of the only son
of Mary. The army of heaven bow to the pure son of Mary. Wide
is his fame, he is God and Man.

The friend of God's mother [Bishop John] is mightier than men think,
but the Lord of all angels is holier and nobler than all. The angels
praise the Lord, the King of All.

The waters were over all the marshes and hills, but before this there
was ice, hence it came about that hay-cocks were getting scarce.

Joyfully they carried precious palms to meet the Saviour when He
rode into the city: thus the Lord of Heaven welcomes those of pure
heart who bring him good deeds with strong faith.

look as if they came from a poem of the same class as Islendinga-Drapa, Book x, § 5. The Charlemagne legend is referred to in IV, No. 16: cf. Bp. Biarni's Proverb-Song. Einar Skulason's hand seems to be felt in several of these scraps. There is a marked difference in Skaldscapar-mal between the early good quotations, the middle citations of whole poems (unworked material collected by the first editor perhaps), and the mass of later and balder and drearier verse (much by Einar himself) in the end part, which is unfinished.

I. MYTHICAL.

1.   Á ÐR diúp-hugaðr dræpi dolga ramr með hamri
       gegn á græðiss vagna gagn-sæll faðir Magna.

2.   Áðr grimm-hugaðr gengi af Griót-móða dauðom.

Hafliða-mál.   3.   Rístu nú, Fála, farðú í búð hinig,
                        þo es mals-gengi mikit.

4.   Reið Brynhildar bróðir bort sá-er hug né skorti.

5.   Haki var brendr á báli þar er brim-slóðir óðo.

6.   þorði Idja orða   .   .   .   .   .

II. HISTORICAL.

(From Edda ; verses 8, 10, 20–24 from Skalda.)

þorðr Mæra-skald.   1.   S ÉR á seima rýri sigðiss látrs at áttom
                              hrauns glóð-sendir handa hermóðr föður góðan.

2.   Óð (enn œrno náði ims sveit freka hveiti),
     [gera öldra naut gyldir] gialpar stóð í blóði.

Erringar-Steinn.   3.   Enn þótt ófrið sannan al-þióð segi skaldi,
                            hlöðom Geitiss mar grióti (glaðir nenno ver) þenna.

Gamli Gnævaðar-   4.   Öðlingr drap ser ungom ungr nagl-fara tungor
skald.   inn-borðz ok orða afl-fátt meðal-kafla.

Haraldr.   5.   Grund liggr und bör bundin breið holm-fiöturs leiðar,
                  hein-landz hoddom grandar Höðr eitr-svölom nöðri.

I. MYTHICAL. *On Thor.* Ere the victorious father of Magni struck .... with his hammer.

On Thor and Rungni. Ere the fierce one [Thor] left Stone-heart [the giant Rungni] dead.

Haflidi's lesson. Arise, O Fala, and come into the booth; there is a great talk going on there.

From a strophe or burden on the Wolsung cycle. Brunhild's bold brother rode away.

The death-pyre of Haki, Hagbard's brother, on board a ship launched aflame on the sea. Haki was burned on a bale fire where the surges were washing.

II. HISTORICAL. *Thord Mora-scald.* It is manifest that we had a noble father [king].

A battle scrap, perhaps by Thord. The wolf waded in gore, etc.

Erringar-Stein. Though all men report war from the south, yet let us fill our bark with stones.

Gamli Gnævad's poet. The young king struck with his hilted brand.

Harold's obscure verse, Hall's battle lines, Atli's Arnor-like scrap on the burning and harrying of some land, and Leidolf's bit of eulogy follow.

Hallr.	6.	Heiðingja sleit hungri, hár gylðir naut sára, granar rauð gramr á fenri, gekk ulfr í fen drekka.
Atli.	7.	Œx rýðsk (eisor vaxa) all-mörg, [loga hallir; hús brenna; gim geisar; góð-mennit fellr] blóði.
Leidolfr.	8.	Niörðr bar goll or garði grams þess er verðung framði.
Anonymous.	9.	Allvalda kann-ek aldar austr ok suðr of flausta (Sveins es sonr at reyna) setr (hveim gram betri).
„	10.	Skíð gekk framm at flœði flóðs í hreggi óðo.
„	11.	Svá skaut gegn í gœgnom garð stein-farinn barða (sá vas gný-stœrir geira gunnar hæfr) sem næfrar.
„	12.	Erom á leið frá láði liðnir Finnom-skriðno; austr sé-ek fiöll af flausta ferli geisla merloð.
„	13.	Ör-gildiss var-ek eldi áls Fiörgynjar mála dyggr sé heiðr ok hreggi ' hryn boðs ár' steðja.
„	14.	Hregg-skornis vil-ek handa háleitan miöð vanda.
„	15.	Ganga él of unga Ullar skips með fullo þar er sam-nagla siglor slíðr-dúkaðar ríða.
„	16.	Ógn-rakkr skalat okkra, almr dyn-skúrar malma, (svá bauð lind í landi líns) hug-rekki dvína.
„	17.	Eldr brennrat siá sialdan (svíðr dyggr iöfurr bygðir) [blása rönn fyrir ræsi reyk] es Magnús kveykir.
„	18.	Boði fell á mik bráðla, bauð heim með ser Geimi, þá ek eigi löð lægiss . . . . .
„	19.	Hrauð í himin upp glóðom hafs; gekk sær af afli; borð hygg-ek at ský skorði; skaut Ránar vegr mána.
„	20.	Hring-lestir gekk hraustan hverjom kunnr at gunni.
„	21.	Fór hvat-ráðr hilmi at finna áðr siklingr til sætta gekk.
„	22.	þat hef ek sagt er sialfr vissak dulðr fer-ek hins er drengr þegir.

ANONYMOUS FRAGMENTS, 9–24. *On one of the Canutes.* I know all the kings east and south of the sea, and the son of Sweyn is the best of all his line.
A gale. Magnus' home-coming, or the like. The ship ran out to sea in the mad gale.
An archer-hero. He shot through the painted shield as though it were lime-bark.
Home from Finland. We are speeding away from the Scrid-Fins' land. I see in the east from the sea the sun's beams glancing back from the glittering hill-tops.
The faithful poet. I was faithful . . . .
Prologue of a poem. I will raise high the mead of . . . . [poesy].
Two obscure fragments (15, 16). *The first talks of* 'broad canvassed sails.'
On a King Magnus. They are not far between the fires that Magnus kindled.
Peril at sea. The billow fell upon me. Ocean bade me home to him, but I did not accept his welcome.
The storm. The embers of the deep [foam] surged up to heaven, the sea rose very mighty; I think that the ship was tossed up to the clouds;

Anonymous.	23.	Sá er af Íslandi arði barði.
„	24.	Hve's ef ek hleyp at cruci . . . .

III. PERSONAL, SATIRICAL.

(From Skalda, v. 5 from W. App.; vv. 8, 10 from Lauf. Edda ; v. 9 from AM. 748.)

Anonymous.	1.	H RŒKK at Hauga-brekko[m] hótz meir an til gátom fyrir hiör-gœði hríðar Halldórr í bug skialdi.
„	2.	Framm þraukoðo fákar fiórir senn und henni, þó gat þeim in háva þrym-göll hlaðit öllom.
„	3.	Heill kom-þú handar svella hlynr, kvaddi svá Brynja.
„	4.	Her liggja brot beggja, brúðr, strykvinna súða.
Morginsól.	5.	Hefka ek opt (enn ævi á-ek flióðs lofa góða) enni-leiptr af unnar eld-spöng degi löngom.
Anonymous.	6.	Aura stendr fyrir órom eik fagr-buin leiki.
Kúga-drápa.	7.	Megin-hræddir ro menn við Kúga, meiri ertu hverjom þeira.
Stríðkera-vísor.	8.	þess sit-ek þægra hnossa þrúðr avalt in prúða hverjom leik á hráka hnuggin Gleipniss tuggo : at urð-hœings iarðar ýtendr fyrir mer nýtir, greipar svellz ins gialla gefn, Stríðkera nefni.
Guðbrandr on Svala (poem).	9.	Upp dregr mökk inn mikla móð-stallz veröld alla.
Gnoðar Ás-mundardrápa.	10.	Megn í gegn glyggvi (kvað grefja tyggvi) [halft nam hann þat liúga] hrafnar títt fliúga.
Skraut-Oddr.	11.	Ef væri bil báro brunnins logs sú-er unnom (opt gœrig orða skipti einrœnliga) á bœnom.
The same.	12.	Böls munat bör at dylja Bergþórs nösom órom.
Anonymous.	13.	Rann hræddari hranna hyr-briótr frá styr liótom.
„	14.	því hefek heitið mey mætri mest nema hamlan bresti.
„	15.	Vætti ek harms nema hitta höfoð-gollz naim Fullo.
„	16.	Blés um hvápta hása höfoð skrípa-mannz pípa.

the streamers of Ran (see Balder's Doom, l. 49, vol. i. p. 183) [foam-sheets cut off by the wind] were flung against the moon.

The rest are in old-metre or mere phrases (20–24) referring to war (20, 21), to the poet's heroes (22, 23), and to some ecclesiastic figure (24).

III. PERSONAL. *On a certain Haldor.* At Howe-brinks [a play-moot place mentioned in Eyrbyggia, ch. 40] Haldor squatted behind the bend of his shield rather more than we guessed he would.

On a big bell being drawn to its steeple. Four horses plodded along together under her, but yet the big bell was a load for them.

A greeting. Hail, O man . . . . thus the giantess [lit. Brindle, a cow's name] greeted me.

Of his poem. Here lie the mortals of the ship *of the Dwarves*, lady ! *Morning Sun. A love-song.* The live-long day I could not lift mine eyes from her.

A lover's pain. The lady so fairly arrayed stands between me and joy. *On Kugi.* All are afraid of Kugi, thou outdoest them all.

The rest (8–16) are scarcely translateable or worth translating; to the satirical ones we have not the key. In No. 8 there is a pun, the slaver of the Wolf = Van = Ván, hope. No. 16 is a satire on a flute-player.

IV. Legendary.

1. FORK lætk æ sem orkar at glamrandi hamra
     á glot-kylli gialla Geirhildar hví meira :
     iarn-stafr skapar œrna (ero sollin rif trolli)
     hár á Hialta-eyri hríð, kerlingar síðo.—*Landn.* iii. ch. 14.

2. Einn byggi-ek stöð steina, stafn-rúm Atals hrafni ;
     ' erat ' of þegn á þiljom þrœng, bý-ek á ' mar ' ranga :
     rúm er böð-vitrom betra (brim-dýri kná ek stýra)
     [lifa man þat með lýðom lengr] an íllt of gengi.—*Landn.* ii. ch. 6.

3. Sniallr á haug á hello, Hialdr á búð til kalda
     —vekit ér í dag dreyra drótt, nú er sigr á spiótom !—   10
     valdr man hitt at Hildar hlæjandi rauð-ek blæjo
     (skiöld nefni-ek svá) sköfnom skióma fyrstr at rómo.
     Mín stóð búð sízt brœðra brandz gekk hvárr fyr annan
     ' holl ok heldom sniallir her fellom þa velli '
     hrósar ' hug fyrir vísa ' Hialdr, ero víg til sialdan ;
     gleðr oss þat er val Viðri veit ek þik gefa teitan.—
                                                    Landn. Hauks-bok, App.

4. Mælti dögla deilir dáðom rakkr sá-er háði,
     ' biartr ' með bezto hiarta, ' ben-rögn,' faðir Högna :
     heldr kvazt hialmi faldinn hiör-þiljo siá vilja
     vætti stafr enn vægja Val-freyjo stafr deyja—   20
     V. st. d.—   *Niala,* ch. 79.

5. Mundit mello kindar miðiungs bruar Iðja
     gunnr um geira senno galdrs brá-regni halda :
     er hræ-stykkis hlakka hraustz síns vinir mínir
     (tryggvi ek óð) ok eggjar und-genginn spor dundo.—*Niala,* ch. 131.

6. Vissa-ek Hrafn, enn Hrafni hvöss kom egg í leggi,
     hialt-uggoðom hœggva hryn-fiski mik brynjo :

IV. Legendary. *Epigram on Stanfred the brave blacksmith, who, with his tongs and bars, fought a witch in the shape of a cow.* The fork hammers about the back of Geirhild as hard as it can, the iron staff beats a loud tattoo on the old wife's side. The fiend's ribs are broken at Hilt-ore.

Asmund's cry from his burial-chamber in the ship, he wants the thralls buried with him to be taken away. I would fain be alone in my stone house. There is an ill crew on the decks of my ship. To a brave man room is better than bad company. I can steer my bark . . . .

Cairn-songs of two old heroes in a howe at Glammstone in Halland, heard by Sigfred the White and Biorn-buck, King Harold Hardrede's men. Snell has a howe on the cliff, Heald has a hilly dwelling. Wake men to a day of blood, there is victory now on your spear-points . . . . My booth is furthermost . . . . Hiald and Snell smile . . . . Wars are too few. We are glad that ye give slain to Woden. *Heald and Snell were the sons of Watnar, a king from whom many famous families sprang.*

Gunnar of Lithend. The bold-hearted father of Hogni, he that had the bright halbert, spoke; he said he would rather die than give in. *The verse of Skarphedin, which follows, is quite dark to us.*

Gunlaug's ghost sings. Raven cut me with the fin-hilted fish [sword] . . .

---

1. lætr, Cd.   5. Read, ill er.   6. Read, má?   14. Read, hell
Hialdr . . . Snialli.   15. Read, hugborð?

þá er 'hræ skærri' hlýra (hlaut fen ari benja)
klauf gunn-spióti gunnar Gunnlaugs höfuð nunna.

6 b. Roðit sverð, enn sverða, sverð-rögnir mik gerði,
vóro reynd í röndom rand-galkn fyr ver handan :   30
blóðog hygg-ek í blóði blóð-gögl of skör stóðo ;
sár-fíkinn hlaut sára sár-gammr en á þramma.—
Gunnlaugs S., ch. 13.

7. Var-ek þar er bragnar börðosk, brandr gall á Írlandi ;
margr, þar-er mœttosk törgor, malmr gnast í dyn hialma :
svipan þeira frá-ek snarpa ; Sigurðr féll í dyn vigra,
áðr tœði ben blœða ; Briann fell ok hélt velli.—*Niala*, ch. 148.

8. Vas-ek þar er fell af fialli flóð-korn iotuns móðir
hám Berg-risa or himni heiðins 'á na leiðar'
gœrr fárr iotunn fleiri 'fold ivinga moldo'
'homlo heiðar þumla' ham-váta mer báta.—   40
Landn. Hb. ii. ch. 7.

9. Hrœng er þarz hávan þöngul heldek . . . . fiör seldak ;
'sýn er at sitk' at Ránar, 'sumir ro í búð' með humrom :
lióst er lýso at gista, land á-ek út fyrir ströndo,
þar sit-ek bleikr í brúki, blaktir mer þari um hnakka.—
Haralds S., Hulda.

10. Högg-orma mun hefjask herði-þundr á landi,
siá mego menn á moldo margar heila-borgir :
nú vex blárra brodda beysti-sullr í fiöllom ;
koma mun sumra seggja sveita-dœgg á leggi.—*Niala*, ch. 134.

11. Víst er at allvaldr austan eggjask vestr at leggja
mótz við marga knúto (mínn snúðr er þat) prúða :   50
þar á val-þiðorr velja (veit hann œrna ser beito)
steik af stilliss haukom stafns ; fylgi ek þar iafnan.
Skœð lætr skína rauðan skiöld, er dregr at hialdri ;
brúðr sér Aurniss ióða óför konungs gœrva :
sviptir í svarðar-kiœpta svanni holdi manna ;
ulfs munn litar innan óðlát kona blóði—o. h. b.

In the same complicated metre is Raven's verse, not worth translation.
A ghost tells of Brian's battle. (7) I was where men fought. The sword
was whistling in Ireland. Sigrod fell in the rattle of spears, Brian fell
but kept the field.
The giant that wrecks ships. (8) I was where the . . . . Few giants have
pulled down more ships.
A sea-giant. (9) There is boisterous mirth where I wield the tall tangle-
root. . . . The sun shines where I sit at Ran's. It is blithe summer where
the lobsters dwell. There are bright guest-quarters with the pike. My
estate lies far from the shore; there I sit wan in the sea-weed, with
the tare-weed waving over my head.
The giant's prophecy of war, a dream before the Althing battle. (10) Then
shall be . . . . in the land. Men shall see many a skull upon earth. There
s a plague of spears preparing in the mountains. Blood shall flow to
men's knees.
Portents before Stamford Bridge. (11) Gurth's dream. It is true my lord
s going east to meet many knots there [a pun on Knut the name]. There
will be plenty of prey for the wolves and me.
Thord's dream. She hoists a red shield ready for the king's unlucky
voyage. She sweeps men's flesh into the wolf's mouth.

---

41. hefek, Cd.   42. sumor ro blíð?   44. því, Cd.

Gramr vá frægr til fremðar flestan sigr inn Digri ;
hlaut-ek, því at heima sátom, heilagt fall til vallar :
leggi-ek œfst ráð tiggja, yðr mon feigð of byrjoð ;
trollz gefit fákom fyllar fíks ; veldrat Goð slíko.—   60
                                  Haralds S., Hulda, ch. 114.

12. Of-fiarri stendr errinn (Ormr brunar dökkr at nœkkva)
     hárr með hyggjo stóra hlýri minn ok vinnor :
     ef værim her hárir Harðráðs synir báðir
     (Snákr skríðr þar-er brim blíkir) brœðr tveir, ne vit þá flœðim.
     Leika barðz á borði byr-hreins fyrir þer einom
     (gramr mun á foldo fremri fár) sex-tigir ára :
     mer leikr einn ok annarr öldo sveipr í greipom,
     því verð-ek barðz á borði bæginn fyrir vægja.—
                                  O. T., ch. 212 (see Reader, p. 215).

13. Hildr stendr hverjan morgin hialdrs und rauðom skialdi,
     nú hafa sigr-meyjar settan sverð-leik Dönom harðan :   70
     ' eigom víga veigi vil-baldrs föðor illan '
     ' Oðinn hörðr sem allir óliósan val kiósa.'
     Lætr-eigi mik lýtir lið-brandz sá er her grandar
     (reiðr em-ek stála stýri) Styrbiörn vera kyrran . . . .—
                                  Flatey-bok, ii. pp. 71, 72.

14. Hvarf inn hildar diarfi, (hvat varð af þorgarði ?)
     villo-maðr á velli víg-diarfr refil-stíga :
     farit hefir gautr at gríóti gunn-eldz inn fiöl-kunni,
     síðan man hann í Heljo hvílast stund ok mílo —
                                  Flatey-bok, i. 214.

15. Hér liggr skald þat-er skalda skörungr var mestr at flesto ;
     nadd-veiti frá-ek nýtan níð Hákoni smíða :   80
     áðr gat œngr né síðan annarra svá manna
     (frægt er orðit þat fyrðom) fé-rán lokit hánom.—
                                  Flatey-bok, i. 215 (see Reader, p. 146).

Olaf's appearance. The stout king [I myself] fought and won till his
death-day. I got a holy death in battle, for I died at home. I fear ye
must be death-doomed on your last journey. God does not order such
an enterprise.

Thor's son, Main, overtaken by Olaf Tryggvason at sea. My brother,
good in thought and deed, is too far off to-day. The black Serpent is
overtaking my boat. If both of us, the sons of stern Thor, were here,
we would not fly. The Snake is creeping up, where the sea is whitened
[by her oars]. Sixty oars [thirty a side] are playing before thee at thy
ship's side. One and a second [two] play in my hands at my ship's side,
so I must yield to the king.

*Woden appears before Fyris-valla fight, and prophesies the result of the
fray.* Monster : The Maids of War stand red-shielded every morning,
the ladies of victory have set a hard sword-game for the Danes . . . .
Woden: Styrbiorn will not leave me in peace. I am wroth with him . . . .

Earl Thorleif. Vanishing of a ghost over the sea or into the earth.
Thorgard disappeared, what became of him ? Up Refil's path the ghost
went. The wizard has gone into the earth, for he will rest in hell for
ever and a day [lit. an hour and a mile].

The ghost-poet. Here lies a poet, the best of poets, who made a
lampoon on Hakon. It has become famous. Never before or after
did a man so well avenge his loss of plunder.

16.   Hneggi ber-ek æ ugg ótta, hlýði mer drótt!
      Dána vek-ek dular mey drauga á kerlaug :
      drápo læt ek or Dvalins greip dynja meðan fram hrynr
      (rekkom býð-ek Regins drykk rettan) á bragar stétt.—
                                          Flatey-bok, i. 582.

VERSES OF THE SAGA EDITORS.

WE have spoken elsewhere of the verses put by thirteenth and four-teenth-century editors into the texts of the Sagas, and noticed how it is quite impossible to suppose them to be of earlier date. We have printed here a few of those which, for one reason or another, are worth special notice. To print the whole would be to try English readers overmuch, though it might be worth doing some time, as an illustration of a phase of Icelandic culture.

Of the whole number (some 1700 lines) those in *Gisli Sursson's Saga* are the only really poetic verses, and present a curious problem, to which we may suggest a possible solution. At first view one is struck with the definite marks of patchwork and late date; e. g. 'Hneiter,' the name of St. Olaf's sword, is used as a common sword-synonym; the kennings are ill-adapted, ponderous, long-drawn, the whole work is clumsy and botched. But, on the other hand, there are archaic words and poetic phrases, as in ll. 6, 10, 12, 20, 25, 31, 44, 63, 82, and there is a real beauty and power of romance running like a vein of silver through this dull formless block of lines. The case would seem to be, that the versifier, to whom we owe the composition as it now stands (he is, we think, the editor of our Saga withal), knew a snatch or two of some of the finest old poetry in the style of the Helgi-Poet, which referred—a. to a Walkyria coming to her lover before the battle in which he died, showing him his last resting-place, and giving him counsel; and b. to a Flyting Scene (our 6): that he took these genuine old-metre verses and worked them up into bastard court-metre stanzas, and used them to ornament his edition of the Gisli Saga. It may well be that in the few lines he knew (some score in all one might guess) there was no hero's name given, but we cannot help suspecting that if we had more, we should find some allusion which would fix them to Kara and her lover. See Book iii, § 1.

Parallels to Helgi-Poet are ll. 25, 45–56, 82, 91.

For Gisli Saga see Prolegomena, § 9. There are two vellums, Cod. AM = A, Cod. Reg. = B; which latter in the verses is preferable.

The two *American verses* by Thorodd of Wineland, which may or may not have something genuine in them, are given here from *Eric the Red's Saga*, as noteworthy.

Heidarviga Saga is full of verse, but we have only taken two as specimens: ll. 5–6 are cited in Codex Wormianus *from a written Saga*, we take it (perhaps even the very same now extant). The rare word þisl (our thill or phill), an old word, is a reminiscence of some genuine verse of older date.

From *Bandamanna* (a Saga which we have in its primitive state with-out later interpolations) we have two verses in the old metre.

In *St. Olaf's Saga*, AM. 61, there are two more in the same measure.

In the verses from *Gretti's Saga*, probably by Sturla, we have some

---

The bewitched king. The Charlemagne story transferred to King Harold Fairhair. I am waking the dead lady . . . .

old-metre stanzas which are remarkable for their word-plays, quite in the half-humorous taste of the thirteenth century.

A verse from *Egil's Saga* in Rhyme-metre (Rím-henda), attributed there to Egil's grandfather, Kveld-wolf, is an undoubted anachronism.

I. Gisli Sursson's Saga.

1. BETR hugðak at brygði (bíðkat-ek draums ins þriðja
   slíks) af svefni væktom sár-teina Vésteini :
   þá-er vér í sal sátom Sigrhaddz við miæð gladdir
   (komsk ei maðr á miðli mín né hans) at víni.

2. Hylr á laun und líni linn-vengis skap kinna   5
   Gríðar less or góðom Gefn él kerom svefna :
   eik berr angri lauka eirekks brá geira
   bróðor dœgg á bæði blíð ændugi síðan.

3. Hrynja lætr af hvítom hvarm-skógi gná bauga
   hrænn fylvingom hyljar hlátr-bann í kné svanna :   10
   hnætr less (enn þreyr þessom þægn at mærðar rægni
   snáka túns) af síno sión-epli bæl-gróno.

4. Teina sé-ek í túni Tál-gríms-vinar Fálo,
   Gautz þess es geig um veittag gunn-bliks, þá-mikla :
   nú hefik gunn-stœri geira, Grímo-þrótt, um sóttan ;   15
   þann lét-ek lund of lendan land-kost-ár branda.

5. Gatat sál-fastrar systir sveigar mín at eiga
   gætin Giúka dóttor Guðrúnar hug-túnom :
   þá-er log-sága lægiss lét sinn af hug stinnom
   (svá rak hon sniallra brœðra) 'saur freyjan' ver deyja. 20

6. Mondot þau á Þórsnesi
   mála-lok á minni sæk :

Gisli on the death of his friend Westan, stabbed in his sleep. Westan had a bitter waking. When we two sat merrily over wine on the benches in Sigrhard's hall there was no empty space between us, i. e. *we sat close together*.

Aud, Gisli's wife and Westan's sister, silently weeping. The lady hides her grief behind her head-rail, gathering the showers of her cheeks from the rain-cups of dreams [her eyes], and in her mourning for her brother the dews are on the high seat of her brows [her face]. She shakes the shower of the filberts of woe [tear-drops] from the thicket of her brows to her knees, and catches the nuts [big tears] from the sorrow-laden apples of her eyes.

Gisli confesses his foe's slaughter. I see the deep furrows in the howe of the Mask of the Giantess' foe [i.e. Thor-grim]. I set upon him [Grimo-þrott = Thorgrim]. I sent him to the god of good seasons [Frey].

Gisli's sister, Thordis Thorgrim's widow, overheard and interpreted his verse and betrayed him. My sister had not the steadfast soul of Gudrun,

---

5. qvinna . . . leggs, A, B.   6. avl kerum, A, B.   12. A ; sion
hersis, B.   15. Thus B.   16. landkostuðar, B.   20. Thus A, B.

ef Vésteins væri hiarta
Biartmárs sonom í bríóst lagit.
Þá glúpnoðo er glaðir skyldo   25
móðor-brœðr mínnar kvánar:
sem eyðendr eggi væri
fiarðar dags fúlo lostnir.

7. Fold kom-ek inn þar-er eldar unn-fúrs í sal brunno
(eir órom þar aura) einn ok sex (at meini):   30
sá-ek blíðliga báðar bekk-sagnir mer fagna
(hróðr-deilir bað heilan hvern mann) í því ranni.

8. Hyggit at, kvað Egða ann-spilli vár banda,
mildr, hve margir eldar, malm-runnr, í sal brunno:
svá áttu, kvað bil blœjo biargs, ólifat margan,   35
veðr-skiœldunga valdi, vettr; nu er skamt til betra.

9. Gœrskattu næmr, kvað nauma, nið-leiks ara steikar
œrr, nema all gótt heyrir iðja galdrs at skaldom:
fátt kveða fleina brautar fúr-þverranda verra,
randr logs ins renda runnr, an illt at kunna.   40

10. Vald eigi þú vígi, (vertu ótyrrinn) fyrri
morðz við mœti-mœrðo [mer heitið því] sleito:
baug-sendir hialp-þú blindom; Baldr hygg-þú at því skialdar;
fllt kveða háð at hœltom; hand-lausom Tý granda.

11. Heim bauð með ser sínom saum-Hlœkk gróm blakki   45
(þá var brúðr við beiði blíð) lof-skreyti at ríða:
má-grundar kvazt mundo (man-ek orð um þat skorðo)
hneigi-sól af heilo (horn-flœðar) mik gœða.

12. Dýr lét drápo stióra dís til svefns um vísat
lægiss eldz þar er lágo (lítt týni-ek því) dýnor: 50
ok með ser in svinna saums leiddi mik nauma,
sákat ek hol í hvílo, hlaut skald sæing blauta.

Giuki's daughter, who put her terrible husband to death to avenge her
gallant brothers; i. e. *Thordis slays her brother to avenge her husband.*
Gisli's dead friend. My suit at Thorsness would not have ended so if
Westan's heart had been in Biartmar's sons' breast.   My mother's
brothers whimpered, as though they had been children hit by a foul egg,
when they should have been merry.
The fair Dream-Lady. Gisli's vision of the seven fires. I came into a
hall where seven fires were burning.   I saw the men off both benches
welcome me thither.   Lo, said the Dream-Lady, as many fires as burn
in this hall, so many winters hast thou to live! Do not take up witchcraft, said she, nought is worse for a man than to know evil!   Do not
be the first to wake slaughter, help the blind, mock not the lame, hurt
not the handless Tew [the handless man]!
The fair Dream-Lady has prepared a place of bliss for him. The lady bade
me ride with her on a grey steed, promising me loving entertainment.
She took me to sleep whereon down cushions lay, and led me to a bed,

---

33. Agða, A; Agdi, B.   49. B; sess, A.   52. B; lagði heil í hvílo, A.

13. Hingat skaltu, kvað hringa hildr at óðar gildi,
fleina-þollr, með fullo fiall-heyjaðr deyja :
þá muntu Ullr ok øllo ísungs fé þvísa 55
(þat hagar okkr til auðar) orm-láðs, ok mer ráða.

14. Villa oss ef elli odd-stríðir skal bíða,
(mer gengr Siæfn í svefna sauma) mínir draumar : . . . .

15. Eigi verðr (enn orða oss lær um þat) [skorða
gefn drepr fyrir mér glaumi] gótt or hverjom draumi : 60
Kemr þegar ek vil blunda kona við mik til fundar,
oss þvær hon unda flóði øll í manna blóði.

16. Skuloð it ei, kvað skorða skapt-kers, 'saman' verja
svá hefir ykkr til ekka eitrs goð-munar leitað :
All-valdr hefir aldar erlendis mik senda 65
enn or œðra-ranni annan heim at kanna.

17. Hugða-ek þvá mer þrúði þremja linnz or brunni,
Óðins elda lauðri, auðs, mína skær rauða :
ok hyr-kneifar hreifa hænd veri því blandi
báls í benja éli blóð-rauð vala slóðar. 70

18. Hugða-ek geymi-gøndul gunn-elda mer falda
um rak-skorinn reikar rúf dreyrogri húfo ;
væri hendr á henni í hiær-regni þvegnar ;
svá vakti mik Sága saums or mínom draumi.

19. Vissa-ek fiándr at fundi (fekk-ek) innan (lið minna) 75
ár þótt ek eigi væra andaðr at mer standa :
(gætt var verr) enn væri (val-tafn í mun hrafni)
fríðr í fægro blóði faðmr þinn roðinn míno.

20. Hugða-ek blóð um báðar, baug-Hlín, granar mínar
harðar hvæsso sverði hræ-netz regin setja : 80
ok val-mærar væri Vár af miklo fári
(líkn reynomk sú lauka) lífs vánir mer grónar.

and laid me therein. Hither shalt thou come after death, of a truth, and
then thou shalt possess me and all this wealth.
  The dark Dream-Lady prophesying woe. My dreams belie if I am to live
to an old age. A lady appears to me in my dreams; my dreams are
bodeful of no good. As soon as I fall asleep a woman visits me,
washing me all over in blood. Ye two shall not, she said to me, wed
one another or live in bliss together; so the word of doom has
decreed. Woden has sent me from his High Hall to this world. Then
I dreamed that she washed my ruddy hair with the lather of Woden's
fires [blood] and her hands were dabbled with blood. I dreamed that
she covered my close-cropped head with a gory cap, her hands were
laved in blood. Then my Lady (his wife) woke me from my dream!
  His last dreams told to his wife. I thought my enemies had compassed
me about here, and that thy bosom was dyed with blood . . . . I dreamed

56. ok mer] A ; fyrir, B.   63. B ; vera, A ; read, líni verja.   64. goð-
runar, A.   65-66. A ; þik sendan einn or yðro ranni, B.

21.　Hugða-ek hlífar flagða hristendr af mer kvista
　　(stór fengom ben) brynjo báðar hendr með vendi:
　　enn fyrir mækiss munni minn hugða-ek, Syn tvinna,　　85
　　(oss gein hiœrr um hiassa) hialm-stofn ofan klofna.

22.　Hugða-ek Siœfn í svefni silfr-bandz at mer standa
　　(Gerðr hafði sú garða) grátandi (brá váta):
　　ok eld-Niorunn œldo all-skyndila byndi
　　(hvat hyggr-þú mer in mæra?) mín sœr er þá vœro.　　90

23.　Fals hallar skal fylla fagr-leit sú er mik reitir
　　rekki-lát at rækkom regns sínom vin fregna:
　　vel hygg-ek, þótt eggjar ítr-slegnar mik bíti;
　　þá gaf sínom sveini sverðz minn faðir herðo.

II. ERIC RED'S SAGA.

1.　HAFA kváðo mik meiðar malm-þings er ek kom hingat
　　(oss samir lítt fyrir lýðom lasta) drykk inn bazta:
　　Bíldz hattar verðr bytto beiði-týr at reiða;
　　heldr er hitt at ek krýp at keldo; komat vín á grön mína.

2.　Förom aptr þar er órir ero, sand-himins, landar,　　5
　　látom kenni-val kanna knarrar skeið in breiðo:
　　meðan bil-styggir byggja bellendr þeir-er hval vella
　　laufa veðrs, þeir er leyfa lönd, á Furðo-ströndom.

III. HEIÐARVIGA SAGA.

1.　LÁGO lýðar frægir lögðis skeiðs á Heiði
　　(lind sprakk í rym randa rauð) ellifo dauðir:
　　hitt var áðr en auðar (ógnar gims) í rimmo
　　(iókom sókn við sœki) sár-þíslar fekk Gísli.

2.　Styrr lét snarr ok Snorri sverð-þing hait verða,　　5
　　þa er gný-viðir gerðo Gíslungom hlut þungan:
　　enn varð eigi en minna ætt-skarð þat er hió Barði
　　(féll geysla lið Gísla) gunn-nórunga sunnan.

---

that my beard was dripping with gore, and that I had scant hope of life.
I dreamed that .... and that my head was cloven by the mouth of the
sword. I dreamed that my lady [the fair Dream-Lady] stood over me
weeping, and bound up my wounds.

His death-verse. The fair lady that charms me will ask for her lover.
I am glad of heart, though the keen sword-edges have bitten me! Such
endurance my father gave his son.

II. THORODD. *The old heathen in Wine-land.* I used to have the best of
drink, but now I have to wield the bucket and stoop to the well; wine
does not come between my lips! Let us go back whence we came,
while they stay here boiling the blubber down at Ferly-strand.

III. *Eric-Widsea on the fight.* There lay eleven dead on the Heath,
but ere that Gisli was touched by the wound-shaft [sword]. Styr and
Snorri made a hard lot for the Gislings, and no less havoc did Bard
wreak upon the Southerners. Gisli's men fell headlong.

---

90. er þá váro] thus A.

IV. Bandamanna Saga, AM. 132.

1. ILLT er ýtom elli at bíða,
   tekr hun seggjom frá sión ok vizko:
   átta-ek næsta val nýtra drengja,
   nú er ulfs hali einn á króki.

2. Brá-ek or slíðrom skalm ný-brýndri,   5
   þeirri lét-ek Mávi á maga hvatað:
   unna-ek eigi arfa Hildiss
   fagr-vaxinnar faðm-lags Svölo.

V. Olafs Saga, AM. 61.

1. FYLL horn, kona! féll af hesti
   Rannveigarson þar er riðo drengir:
   kunno eigi Sygnir á söðol-dýrom
   full-vel fara.   Fœr mer of ker!

2. Fyll horn, kona! frá-ek at belldi   5
   Óláfr konungr undri miklo:
   þa er hann söðlaði sínom mági
   bukk at ríða.   Berr mer of ker!

VI. Grettis Saga.

1. MITT var gilt gæfo-leysi
   Marþaks í miðjom firði:
   er gamlir grísir skyldo
   hladast mer at höfuð-beinom.

2. Sögðo mer, þau er Sigarr veitti,   5
   mægða-laun margir hæfa:
   unz lof-groinn laufi sæmðar
   Reyni-runn rekkar fundo.

3. Monda ek sialfr í snöro egnda
   hœlzti brátt höfði stínga: 10
   ef þorbiörg þesso skaldi
   (hon er all-snotr) ekki byrgi.

4. Mik bað Hialp handa tveggja

IV. *Bandamanna Saga. Ofeig's regret.* It is ill to come to old age.
Eld takes men's eyesight and wisdom away. I had many a good follower, but now one wolf's tail is left alone on the hook, [the shark of
ill-luck has snatched away the rest.]
Ospac's Boast. I plucked my fresh-whetted sword from the sheath,
and ripped open Mew's belly, for I could not grant him the fair
Swala's embraces.

V. *The boy St. Olave to Halldor Ranweigsson, who fell off his horse
in hunting.* Fill the horn, lady, Ranweig's son fell off his horse, the
Sogn-folk cannot sit the saddle-beasts. Bring me the cup.—*Halldor
answers:* Fill the horn, lady, Olaf did a marvellous thing when he
saddled a he-goat for his step-father to ride. Bear me the cup.

VI. *Gretti's adventures in Icefirth, when Thorbiorg saved him from
the galleys.* Wonderful was my ill-luck on the firth of the sea-thatch
[Icefirth] when the old hogs [churls] took me by the neck. They said
that the reward Sigar's brother-in-law got [hanging] was what I
deserved, till they met the noble Rowan-grove [Thorbiorg] with its
foliage of fame. I should have had to lay my head too early into

---

V. 4 and 8. emend.; fær *and* ber mer ok þer, Cd.   VI. 4. halda, Cd.

Sifjar-vers með ser fara:
sú gaf þveng-þundar-beðjo   15
góðan hest er mik gœddi friði.

5. Ætla-ek regns í raun-ketil
    steypi niðr fra Stór-Frerom:
    þar man Hængr hitta grundar
    Lítinn-stein ok land-hnefa.   20

6. Var þorfinnr þundar sessi
    aldar alinn oss til hialpar:
    þa er mik víf í val-skorom
    lukt ok læst lífs um kvaddi.

7. Var Stór-skip Stál-goðs-bana,   25
    Rauða-hafs ok Regin-skáli:
    er Byleistz bróður-dóttur
    manna mest mer varnaði.

8. Þótti þá þengils mönnom
    eigi dælt við oss at sóknom: 30
    er Hlíbarðr hlífar eldi
    bragða borg brenna vildi.

9. Varð í Veðra-firði vápn-sóttr í byr þróttar
    (œst fór Arfs-ok-Gneista-afl) fang-vinr Hafla:
    nú er ósiötlað Atla and-rán þat er var hánom   35
    (dauðr hné hann fyrr at fríðri fold) makliga goldit.

VII. EGILS SAGA (ch. 27).

NÚ er hersiss hefnd við hilmi efnd
    gengr ulfr ok örn of Ynglings börn:
flugo hœggin hræ Hallvarðz of sæ,
'grár slítr ari' undir Snarfara.

---

the noose, if gentle Thorbiorg had not rescued me. The help of Sif's husband's two hands [i. e. the rowan = Thorbiorg] bade me come with her. She gave the Thong of Woden's wife [i. e. earth-serpent = Grettir] his life.

Grettir is going to meet Giant Hallmund. To the kettle of the lava [cave] on Bald-glacier I am bound, where I [earth-fish = Grettir] shall meet the pebble of the hand [i. e. Hallmund].

Grettir in peril in Norway, rescued by Thorstan Dromund. It was Thorfin who was my saviour, when the cavern-locked beldame [Hell] craved my life. The great buss of the Red Sea and the Giant-killer's Dwarf-hall [i. e. Thorstan Dromund] did most of all men save me from Hell. The king's men thought it no easy game to set upon me, when Leopard [Beorn] wanted to burn my mind's abode [body].

Grettir slays Thorbiorn Ox-main in Ramfirth. The might of Arf and Gneist [Ox-main] was slain in Wether-firth [Ramfirth]; the unatoned murder of Atli has now been avenged on him.

VII. Qweld-wolf's verse on the death of Hallward-hardfarer and Sigtrygg-snarfari. Now the baron's revenge is wreaked on the king. Wolf and erne prowl over the king's sons. Hallward's hewn carcase is floating on the sea and .... the grey erne is tearing at Snarfari's wounds.

---

17. run ketil, Cd.   20. I. e. Hallmund.

BOOK IX.

EPIGONIC POETRY.

An after-math of verse on *legendary* or *didactic* subjects, not old enough to be put into the first volume. Most of the stories are late continuations of the epigonic stories of the Sigfred cycle in Book v; the link that binds them to this cycle being the birth of a daughter, Anslaug-Crow, to Sigfred and Brunhild (an incident by no means akin to the spirit of the older lays).

In SECTION 1 are the Kraku-mal and other verses on the Ragnar cycle, together with other fragments of poems on later epic or pseudo-epic subjects, some in *Turf-Einar metre* (continuing Book vi, § 2), some in *Epic metre* (like Book iv).

SECTION 2 contains the Orkney Bishop's *Proverb-Song*, and the *Runic verses*.

§ 1. THE RAGNAR CYCLE.

KRAKU-MAL.

WE have two texts of this well-known poem, Magnus Olafsson's copy (of 1632) of a lost vellum (B) given to Ole Worm, who published it in his Literatura Runica (1651) in Runic characters under the heading 'Biarkamal sem orti Ragnarr Lodbrok,' and the fourteenth-century vellum, Royal Library, Copenhagen, No. 1824 (A), which contains the unique Wolsunga Paraphrase, and Ragnar's Saga, followed by 'Kraku-mal;' but the last leaf, with the end of the poem on it (from l. 108), is lost in this copy. Two verses in Ragnar's Saga are duplicates of vv. 26 and 25.

The *story* of the poem is the one legend which has survived in Norway of the great movement which led to the conquest and settlement of half England by the Danes in the ninth century.

It is found in Saxo, in Ragnar's Saga, and in the short 'þáttr af Ragnar's Sonum' of Hauks-bok, which last gives one the idea that it is founded on parts of the lost Skioldunga Saga. Besides this, it occurs in the Turf-Einar-metre scraps of a long poem, scattered through the Saga and Thattr (see below, p. 345).

From the Thattr we hear that while Ragnar is away fighting in the Baltic, his sons Eric and Agnar are slain by Eystan Beli, king of the Swedes. Before he returns home, his wife and sons have avenged their deaths and slain Eystan. He is angry that they have not waited for his help, and when he comes home he tells his wife Anslaug (his first wife Thora, whom he won from the dragon, is dead) "that he will do as great a deed as his sons have done. 'I have now brought under me nearly all the realms my ancestors owned, save England only, and now I have had two busses built at Lithe in Westfold (for his realm stretched from Doverfell to Lidandis-ness).' Answers Anslaug: 'Many a long-ship thou mightest have built with what those busses cost, and thou knowest that it is not good to sail to England in big ships, because of the tides and shallows, and thou hast not planned wisely." But he set out with his two ships and five hundred men and was wrecked on the English coast. He and his men got safe to land, but were cut off and slain to a man by the ferocious Northumbrian king Ælla, save Ragnar, who was kept from hurt by his magic shirt. But Ælla put the Northern king into a pit full of serpents. This is the moment chosen by our poet, who supposes him to have sung a death-song in his torments, like an Indian bravo, in which he tells over his feats, and invokes vengeance on his foe. His son Iwar (the Inwær of our Chronicle) and his brothers arrive in England and avenge him, taking Ælla and cutting the 'blood-eagle' on his back ; (see Book viii, § 2, p. 135.) Two base-born brothers of Iwar, Yngwar and Hubbo [our chronicler's Hingwar and Hubba], put the holy king Eadmund to death at Inwær's orders, and reign in his stead. The brothers harry far and wide over the world, and set up kingdoms: Inwær ruling in Northumberland; Biorn Ironside in Upsala; Sigfred Snake-i'-th'-eye, who had married Blæja daughter of Ælla, in Selund, Sconey, Halland, Wick, Agdir to the Naze, and most of Upland; Whitesark in Reed-gothland and Wendland.

Inwær died childless in England of old age, and was laid in a barrow there, where Harold Hardrede saw his ill-omened ghost. Sigfred fell in Frankland with Godfred the Dayling, fighting against the Emperor Arnulf, in a battle in which one hundred thousand Northmen and Danes fell. There is a curious genealogy [1] drawn from Sigfred and Blæja, connecting their descendants with the Danish house; and it is said that Ethelmund, the brother of Eadmund the sainted East-English king, ruled after Iwar, 'and took scat off Northumberland because it was then heathen.' His son Ethelbriht, a good king and old, reigned after him, and fought against Gorm's sons at Cleveland and Scarborough.

The age of the poem is limited by the pronunciation of the language, i. e. the lost *h* in the 'hr' and 'hl' words, which here occur in alliterative syllables, ll. 27, 29, 34, 43, 143; the várum for órum, l. 55, a peculiar change which (see Dict. s. v. várr, p. 686) in Iceland does not occur till the end of the twelfth century, in Norway and the Orkneys the change may be a little earlier. Nor do we expect to find such words as palmr, messa (mass), asni (ass), kápa, etc. in very early poems. Looking to the language, metre, and character of the poem, we should be disposed to put it c. 1150–1200, and fancy the author an Orkneyman. The proverbs in the last lines remind one of Bishop Biarni.

The *metre* is the Turf-Einar metre, and the poem is divided into stanzas of five lines, the first line of each, save the last epilogue verse, beginning with the burden which fills half a line. Stanzas 1-21 are a business-like, prosy roll or list of battles fought in the Baltic, or on the British coasts and the Mediterranean. The latter stanzas (22–29) are by far the finest, and it is those that have made the poem famous. There is a wild savagery about them that is really striking. The earlier verses of the poem (if indeed they are not a later filling up or accretion by another hand), with their ingenious variations of the everlasting theme of bloodshed, would not alone have made much impression. The funny mistake which led Bishop Percy and his copiers down to this very day to entertain the belief that 'the Heroes hoped in Odin's hall to drink beer out of the skulls of their slain foes,' has its origin in a misinterpretation of the phrase 'biug-viðum hausa' l. 122, by Ole Worm, who says: 'Sperabant Heroes se in aula Othini bibituros ex craniis eorum quos occiderant.'

There is a spirited version of the poem by Professor Aytoun.

---

[1] Sigfred Snake-i'-th'-eye, Ragnar's son,   Ring a Dayling, descendant of Day,
      m. Blæja, Ælla's daughter   m. Thora, mother of Heroes (Hyndl. l. 71)

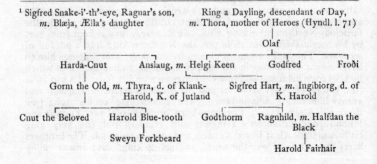

I.

1. *HIOGGO ver með hiörvi.*—Hitt var æ fyr löngo
er á Gautlandi gengom at graf-vitnis morði :
þá fengo ver Þóro, þaðan héto mik fyrðar,
—þa-er lyng-ál um lagðag—LODBRÓK, at því vígi ;
stakk-ek á storðar lykkjo stáli biartra mála.   5

2. *Hioggo ver með hiörvi.*—Heldr var-ek ungr þá er skífðom
austr í Eyra-sundi undurn frekom vargi ;
ok fót-gulom fogli fengo ver, þar-er sungo
við há-seymða hialma hörð iarn, mikils verðar ;
allr var ægir sollinn ; óð ramn í val-blóði.   10

3. *Hioggo ver með hiörvi.*—Hátt bárom þá geira
er tvítogir tölðomz, ok tír ruðom víða ;
unnom átta iarla austr fyr Díno-minni ;
gera fengom þá gnóga gisting at því vígi,
sveiti fell á sollinn sæ ; týndi lið ævi.   15

4. *Hioggo ver með hiörvi.*—Heðins kvánar varð auðit
þá-er ver Helsingja heimtom til heim-sala Óðins :
Lögðom upp í Ívo, oddr náði þá bíta ;
öll var unda gialfri á sú roðin heito,
greniar brandr við brynior benshilldr, klufoz skildir.   20

5. *Hioggo ver með hiörvi.*—Hygg-ek engan þá frýðo,
áðr an á heflis hestom Herrauðr í styr félli :
klýfr ei Egils öndrom annarr iarl in frægri
lindar völl til lægiss á lang-skipom síðan ;
sá bar sikliugr víða snart fram í styr hiarta.   25

6. *Hioggo ver með hiörvi.*—Herr kastaði skiöldom,
þá-er ræ-gagarr rendi ræstr at gumna brióstom ;
beit í Skarpa-skerjom skæri-bildr at hialdri ;
roðinn var randar-máni áðr Ramn konungr félli ;
dreif or hölða hausom heitr á brynjor sveiti.   30

7. *Hioggo ver með hiörvi.*—Hátt grenjoðo hrottar
áðr an á Ullar-akri Eysteinn konungr félli ;
gengo golli fáðar ' grundar vals at bryndom,'
ræ-kyndill smaug rauðar rítr at hialma móti ;
svíra vín or sárom sveif of hiarna kleifar.   35

I. WE hewed with the brand! It was ever-so-long ago when we went
to Gautland to the slaying of the snake. Then I won Thora ; hence
they called me Lodbrok [Shaggy-breech] because of that battle, when
I pierced the serpent. I struck through the monster with my bright
inlaid steel. We, etc. I was very young when we made a breakfast for
the wolf, east in Ore-sound. We, etc. We bore our spears high, when
we were twenty years old, and reddened our sword far and wide. We
overcame eight earls in the east at the Dwina's mouth. We, etc.
Hedin's wife [war] was fated when we sent home the Helsings to
Woden's hall. We laid our ships up at Iwa's mouth [East Baltic].
We, etc. No one, I think, questioned our courage, before Herraud fell
on his ships in the fray. We, etc. The host cast away their shields
when the sword bit at Skarpa-reef [Scarborough]. The shield-moon
was crimsoned ere King Raven fell. We, etc. The swords screamed
shrilly before King Eystan fell in Wuldur-acre. We, etc. At Enderis-

1. æ] ei, Cd.   10. ran, Cd.   16. heidins, A.   18. Ívo] B ; modo, A.
20. Read, . . . ; ben-síldr klufo skioldo ?

8.   *Hioggo ver með hiörvi.*—Hafa gáto þá ramnar
fyr Eynderis-eyjom œrna bráð at slíta ;
fengom Fálo hestom fullan verð at sinni ;
' íllt var eins at gæta,' með upp-runa sólar,
streng-völor sá-ek stíga ; stakk malmr á skör hialmi.   40

9.   *Hioggo ver með hiörvi.*—Háðom rendr í dreyra,
þá er ben-starra bræddom fyr Borgundar-holmi,
regg-ský slíto ringar ; ratt almr af ser malmi,
Vulnir fell at vígi ; varat einn konungr meiri ;
Val rak vítt um strandir ; vargr fagnaði tafni.   45

10. *Hioggo ver með hiörvi.*—Hildr ver sýnt í vexti
áðr Freyr konungr félli í Flæmingja-veldi ;
náði biárr at bíta blóði smeltr í gylltan
Högna kofl at hialdri harðr ben-grefill forðom ;
mær grét, morgin-skæro, mörg, þá-er tafn feksk vörgom.   50

11. *Hioggo ver með hiörvi.*—Hundraðom frá-ek liggja
á Eynefis öndrom, þar-er Engla-nes heitir ;
sigldo ver til snerro sex dœgr áðr lið félli ;
áttom odda messo við upp-runa sólar ;
varð fyr várom sverðom Valþiófr í styr hníga.   55

12. *Hioggo ver með hiörvi.*— Hrunði dögg af sverðom
brýn í Barða-firði, bleikan ná fyr hauka ;
umði almr, þá-er oddar all-hratt slíto skyrtor
at slíðr-loga senno Svolnis hamri þœfðar ;
rendi ormr til unda eitr-hvass drifinn sveita.   60

13. *Hioggo ver með hiörvi.*—Héldom Hlakkar tiöldom
hátt at Hildar leiki fyr Héðninga vági.
Siá knátto þá seggir, er sundroðom skiöldo
at hræ-sílna hialdri, hialm ' slitnaðar ' Gotna ;
varat sem biarta brúði í bing hiá ser legeja.   65

14. *Hioggo ver með hiörvi.*—Hörð kom hríð á skiöldo ;
nár féll niðr til iarðar á Norðymbra-landi ;
varat um eina ótto öldom þörf at frýja
Hildar-leik, þar-er hvassir hialm-stofn bito skiómar ;
böð-mána sá-ek bresta ; brá því fira lífi.   70

15. *Hioggo ver með hiörvi.*—Herþiófi varð auðit
í Suðreyjom sialfom sigrs á várom mönnom ;
varð at randar regni Rögnvaldr fyrir hníga ;
Sá kom hæstr of hölða harmr at sverða gusti ;
hvast kastaði hristir hialms streng-lögar palmi.   75

ore [?] the ravens soon got plenty of carrion to rip. It was ill at
sunrise. We, etc. We blooded the shields when we battened the
ravens at Bornholm. Woolner fell at the battle. We, etc. The fray
was fast growing ere Frey fell in the land of the Flemings. Many a
maid wept. The weapons bit in the morning. We, etc. They lay by
hundreds on their war-ships at the place called Angel-ness [Cape An-
gelico]. We held a mass of spears at the rising of the sun. Waltheow
fell by our swords in the struggle. We, etc. The dark blood dripped
off our swords in Bard-firth [?]. We, etc. We hoisted high the tent of
Hlank [shield] in the game of Hild [war] off Hedninga-bay [Hedinse by
Swold]. It was not like laying a fair lady by one's side, when we were
splitting men's helms. We, etc. Hard was the shower that fell on the
shield; the corse fell to earth in Northumberland; the battle in the
morning watch could not be gainsaid. We, etc. Hertheow was fated
to win a victory over our men. Regnwald sank in the shield-rain [war-

39. Some name ?   50. B ; skaru, A.   70. bænmana, A.   75. Read, streng-flaugar.

16. *Hioggo ver með hiörvi.*—Hverr lá þverr of annan;
glaðr varð gera bróðir gáti við sóknar læti:
Let eigi örn né ylgi, sá er Írlandi stýrði,
(mót varð malms ok rítar) Marsteinn konungr fasta,
varð í Veðra-firði val-tafn gefit hrafni.   80
17. *Hioggo ver með hiörvi.*—Hund-marga sá-ek falla
morgin-stund fyr 'meiði' menn at odda senno:
syni mínom hneit snimma slíðra-þorn við hiarta;
'Egill' lét Agnar ræntan óblauðan hal lífi;
Glumði geirr við Hamðiss grán serk; bliko merki.   85
18. *Hioggo ver með hiörvi.*—Hald-orða sá-ek brytja
ekki smátt fyr ulfa Endils niða bröndom:
varat á Vika-skeiði sem vín konor bæri;
roðinn var Ægiss asni ófárr í dyn geira;
skorin var sköglar kápa at skiöldunga hialdri.   90
19. *Hioggo ver með hiörvi.*—Háðom suðr at morni
leik fyr Lindis-eyri við lofðunga þrenna:
Fár átti því fagna (féll margr í gin ulfi)
[haukr sleit hold með vargi] at hann heill þaðan kœmi;
Íra blóð í ægi œrit féll um skæro.   95
20. *Hioggo ver með hiörvi.*—Hár-fagran sá-ek hrœkkva
meyjar dreng at morni ok mál-vini ekkjo:
vara sem varmar laugar vín-kers Niörun bæri
oss í Íla-sundi, áðr an Örn konungr félli;
vara sem unga ekkjo í öndugi kyssa.   100
21. *Hioggo ver með hiörvi.*—Há sverð bito skiöldo,
þar er goll-roðinn glumði geirr við Hildar-næfri:
siá mun í Önguls-eyjo of aldr mega síðan
hverso at lögðiss leiki lofðungar fram gengo;
roðinn var út fyr eyri ár flug-dreki sára.   105

II.

22. *Hioggo ver með hiörvi.*—Hví sé drengr at feigri,
at hann í odda éli öndurðr látinn verði?
opt sýtir sá ævi er 'aldregi' nistir:

tempest]. We, etc. Marstan, the king who ruled Ireland, let neither eagle nor she-wolf starve. A sacrifice of the slain was given to the raven in Wetherford. We, etc. I saw many hundred fall that morning in the Mouth in the battle. The sword cut my son to the heart: yea, Eystan slew Agnar. We, etc. On Wick-field it was not as when women are serving the wine. We, etc. South we held a game [of war] with three kings at Lindis-ore of a morning. The blood of the Irish fell into the ocean in the dawn. We, etc. I saw the fair-haired damsel's son quail in the morning, and the gallants gave back in the battle. It was not as if the damsel were setting a bath for us in Ila-sound ere King Erne fell. It was not as if one were kissing a young girl in the high-seat. We, etc. Ever after it will be seen in Anglesey, how the kings stormed forth to the sword-play. The dart was dyed on the Ore, early in the morning.

II. *Henceforward the poem is of a nobler type, and we translate more fully.* We hewed with the brand! Why should a man be nearer to death, though he be placed in the van in the tempest of spears? He who has never fed the she-wolf will often bemoan his lost life. Hard is

77. getu, Cd.   80. A om. stanza 16.   82. Read, Móðo?   84.
Read, Eysteinn?   88. -skæði, B; -skerði, A; read, Vikrar-skeiði?   95. Read,
Engla?   98. niurn, A.   99. Íla-sundi] B; Ala-sundi, A.   108. sýtir]
here A ends. Read, ylgi ne nistir?

Illt kveða argan eggja æorom at sverða leiki;
hug-blauðom kemr hvergi hiarta sítt at gagni.   110
23.   *Hioggo ver með hiörvi.*—Hitt tel-ek iafnt at gangi
at sam-togi sverða sveinn í móti sveini:

.   .   .   .

hrækkvat þegn fyr þegni; þat var drengs aðal lengi;
æ skal ást-vinr meyja einharðr í dyn sverða.   115
24.   *Hioggo ver með hiörvi.*—Hitt sýnisk mer raunar
at forlægom fylgjom: Fár gengr of skæp Norna:
eigi hugða-ek Ello at aldr-lagi míno,
þá-er ek blóð-vali bræddak, ok borð á læg keyrðak;
vítt fengom þá vargi verð í Skotlandz-fiærðom.   120
25.   *Hioggo ver með hiörvi.*—Hitt hlœgir mik iafnan,
at Baldrs feðrs bekki búna veit-ek at sumblom:
Drekkom biór at bragði or biúg-viðom hausa
(sýtira drengr við dauða) dýrs at Fiolniss húsom;
eigi kem-ek með œðro orð til Viðriss hallar.   125
26.   *Hioggo ver með hiörvi.*—Her vildo nú allir
burir Áslaugar brændom bitrom hildi vekja,
ef vandliga vissi of við-farar ossar,
hve úfáir ormar eitr-fullir mik slíta;
móðerni fekk-ek mínom mægom sva-at hiærto duga.   130
27.   *Hioggo ver með hiörvi.*—Harðla líðr at ævi;
grimmt stendr grand af naðri. Goinn byggir sal hiarta:

---

it to egg on a coward to the brisk play of the sword. The heart of the
coward will never stand him in good stead.

We hewed with the brand! I count it fair that man should meet
man when swords are drawn. Let not thane flinch before thane. That
was never the way of the brave. The darling of the maidens should
ever be dauntless amid the clatter of swords.

We hewed with the brand! Of a truth methinks we must follow our
fates: no man can overstep the decree of the Fates. I never thought
that Ella would be my death, when I gorged the blood-hawks and drove
my ships through the water, what time we gave the wolves a quarry in
the firths of Scotland [the West coast].

We hewed with the brand! It is ever my joy, that I know that the
benches are decked for a banquet at Balder's father's. We shall soon
be quaffing ale out of the crooked skull-boughs [horns] in the splendid
house of Woden. The brave man does not quail before death. I shall
not come into Withri's [Woden's] hall with a word of fear.

We hewed with the brand! All the sons of Anslaug would be waking
the battle here with their bitter blades if they but knew of my plight,
how a multitude of venomful serpents are rending me. Good kin on the
mother's side I gave my sons, so that their hearts will hold.

We hewed with the brand! My life is well-nigh past. Cruel is the
pang that the adder gives. Goin [the snake] has housed himself in my

---

113. A line missing here.   122. feðrs] emend.; feðr, B.   131. Emend.;
arfi, R.

vættom hins at Viðriss vœndr í Ello standi;
sonom mínom mun svella sínn fœðor ráðinn verða;
ei muno snarpir sveinar sítt kyrt vera láta.   135

28.   *Hioggo ver með hiörvi.*—Hef-ek fimm-tigom sinna
folk-orrostor framðar flein-þings boði ok eina;
minzt hugða-ek manna, at mer vera skyldi
(ungr nam-ek odd at rióða) annarr konungr frægri.
Oss muno Æsir bióða. Era sýtandi dauði.   140

29.   Fýsomk hins at hætta. Heim bióða mer Dísir,
sem frá Herjans hœllo hefir Óðinn mer sendar:
Glaðr skal-ek œl með Ásom í œndugi drekka.
Lífs ero liðnar stundir. Læjandi skal-ek deyja.

RAGNAR LODBROK, ANSLAUG, AND RAGNAR'S SONS.

THE Wolsunga vellum, No. 1824, supplies the text for these verses,
the Hauks-bok (AM. 544) gives a few stanzas in parallel text (vv. 10,
16–20, 32). All but a few are, unfortunately, hopelessly corrupt. The
metre is that of Turf-Einar. They seem to have been pieces of a poem
on Ragnar and his Sons, inserted piecemeal into a diluted amplification
of a piece of the lost Skioldunga Saga. The *age* of these verses we
should put to the end of the eleventh century. They are more simple
and genuine than many of those of the same metre, such as Kraku-mal;
nor is there anything in their language which forbids them to have been
made so early. The curious statement in Skalda-tal, part of the original
draft of that list, 'King Ragnar Lodbrok was a poet, and so were Anslaug
his wife and their sons,' seems to refer to the very verses we have, or
at all events to the best of them, and would testify to their existence as
early as the beginning of the twelfth century.

The story tells first of Ragnar's earliest feat, the winning of Thora
by slaying a dragon that guarded her (an early myth transferred to
the popular hero). Then comes the pretty tale of Crow, the
maiden in mean attire and low estate, who is seen by the king's men.
After a trial of wits—(copied perhaps from the well-known Irish tale
of Diarmaid and Graine, see Atlantis, where the same incident of the
net in which the lady is neither clad nor unclad is met with)—Ragnar
marries the fair one, who turns out to be Anslaug, a princess, daughter of
Sigfred and Brunhild. Four sons are born to the king and queen, and
these, because of the king's breaking the hallowed 'three nights' absti-
nence,' which we meet with in other old Teutonic stories, are each

---

heart's core. I hope that Woden's wand [the sword] shall one day
pierce Ælla. My sons will swell *with wrath*, when they find their
father has been *thus* betrayed. The brave lads will not rest in peace
withal.

We hewed with the brand! I, the harbinger of war, have fought fifty
pitched battles and one. My least thought was that any king should
ever prove my better. Young was I when I betook me to the reddening
of spears. The Anses will welcome me. Death is dreadless.

I am willing to depart. They are calling me home, the Fays whom
Woden, the Lord of Hosts, has sent me from his hall. Merrily shall I
drink ale in my high-seat with the Anses. My life days are done.
Laughing I will die.

distinguished by some physical peculiarity; the eldest, Inwær, is born without bones in his legs, but his cunning and speech-craft make up (as Æthelred and Alfred found out at Nottingham) for his bodily weakness; Sigfred has the likeness of a snake, as it were, coiled in the pupil of his eye, whence he was called Snake-i'-th'-eye. Biorn is called Ironside, no doubt from some mark on his body, but the legend or the exact meaning of his nickname and that of his brother White-sark, whose real name has perished, is not given us. After these children are grown up, Eric and Agnar, Ragnar's elder sons by Thora, fight against Eystan Beli, the king of the Swedes (and friend of poets according to Skalda-tal). Agnar is slain, and Eric is taken and allowed to choose his death. Eric chooses to be impaled on sharp spears fixed in the ground.

In the next scene Ragnar is setting out for England. Anslaug, presaging evil, gives him a charmed coat, which preserves him even in the snake-pit into which he is cast by Ælla, king of the Northumbrians, till the enchantment is suspected and it is torn from him. The two death-song stanzas are finer here than in Kraku-mal.

Then follows an account of the four brothers, their avenging their father, and their wicking exploits; on one of which Whitesark was taken, and, Tamerlain-like, chose for his death to be burnt alive on a pyre made of the heads of the foes he had slain.

A kind of epilogue to the whole is furnished by the story of the two huge men who came into the hall where a young king and his men were drinking the arval. They can empty the biggest horn at one draught, and were so big that the two together filled five men's places. They begin questioning each other in a surly mood, but soon recognise each other as former companions-in-arms, old sea-dogs of Beorn's and Ragnar's. This episode reminds one of the verses ascribed to Egil and the lady, Book vi, § 2, No. 6, which are probably parts of the same poem. Were they in better state we should be able to give some verdict on their age, for there is something genuine about them.

The continuation of verse 23 is probably to be found in the lines from Arrow-Ord's Saga, Book ix, § 1, No. II, p. 355.

I.

Ragnarr:

1. HÆTT hefek leyfðo lífi, lit-fægr konan vitra,
  (vá-ek at foldar fiski) fimtán gamall, míno:
  'hafa skal-ek bæl nema bíti bradrakin mer dauða'
  heiðar lax til hiarta 'hringleyginn vel' smiúgi.

II.

Kráka:

2. Þorig eigi boð brióta er báðot mik ganga,   5
  né ræsiss kvæð riúfa, Ragnarr, við þik stefno:
  mangi er mer í sinni, mitt er bert hærund eigi,
  'fylgi hefi ek full-gott, ferr-ek ein saman míno.'

I. *Ragnar on his fight with the Dragon.* I risked my life when I was fifteen years old . . . . I pierced the coiled serpent to the heart.

II. *At their meeting. Crow:* I dare not break the command ye laid upon me, nor the order ye gave me, Ragnar. There is no one with me; my body is not bare; *I have smelt but at a leek;* I am come alone.—*Ragnar:*

Ragnarr :

3.   'Sú mundi víst ef væri vorðr foður iarðar'
       'mætr á mildri snóto á mer taka hœndom.'   10

Kráka :
       Vammlausa skaltu, vísi, ef viltu griðom þyrma
       (heim hœfom hilmi sóttan) heðan mik fara látið.

Ragnarr :

4.   Viltú þenna þiggja, er Þóra Hiœrtr átti,
       serk við silfr of merkðan? sama all-vel þer klæði:
       fóro hendr hvítar hennar um þessar gœrvar,   15
       sú var buðlungi bragna blíðom þekk til dauða.

Kráka :

5.   Þorig eigi þann þiggja, er Þóra Hiœrtr átti,
       serk við silfr of merkðan; sama ælig mer klæði:
       því em ek Kráka kœlloð í kol-svœrtom vœðom,
       at ek hefi griót of gengit, ok geitr með siá reknar.   20

Kráka :

6.   Þriár nætr skolom 'þessar ok þo' saman byggja
       'hresvar nætr' í húsi, áðr vit heilog goð blótim:
       þó muno mein á mínom megi til lœng um verða;
       heldr ertu bráðr at byrja þann-er bein hefir eingi.

III.

Ragnarr :

7.   Sigurðr mun sveinn of heitinn, sá mun orrostor heyja,   25
       miœk glíkr vera móðor 'ok' mœgr fœðor kallaðr:
       sá mun Óðins ættar yfir-bátr vera heitinn,
       þeim er ormr í auga 'er annan lét' svelta.

8.   Brynhildar leizt brœgnom brún-stein hafa fránan

The king [I] would fain lay hold on the maid with my hands ....—
Crow: Thou shalt let me go hence unshamed, O king, if thou wilt keep
thy covenant.—*Ragnar:* Wilt thou take this sark, silver-broidered, that
Thora Hart had? It will befit thee well; her white hands often touched
this raiment. She was blithe to her husband till she died.—*Crow:* I dare
not take the silver-broidered sark that Thora Hart had, it will not befit
me. I am called Crow because in coal-black raiment I have tramped
over the pebbles and driven the goats along the shore.
Crow, after their wedding, to Ragnar. Let us wait three nights, nor lie
together, till we have sacrificed to the Holy God. There shall be a
blemish on my son for many a day. Thou art too eager to beget him
that shall have no bones.
III. *Ragnar on the birth of his son, naming the child.* Let the boy be
called Sigfred, he shall fight battles and be like his mother's father,
[*Sigfred*]. He shall be called the noblest of Woden's race, there is a
serpent in his eye .... Brunhild's dear daughter's son has a keen eye

---

21. Read, þreyja ok þeygi s. b.   22. Read, hý-nætr?   23. þó] þa, Cd.
26. Read, miok gl. mögr móðor-foðor kallaðr.   28. Read, er örn léta svelta?

dóttor-mœgr inn dýri, ok dyggvast hiarta :   30
sá berr alla ýta unn-leygs boði magni
Buðla niðr, er baugi, bráð-gerr, hatar rauðom.

9.   Siá er engi sveini nema Sigurði einom
í brún-steinom   .   .   .   .   'lœgða :'
siá hefir dagr enom dýra (dælt er hann af því kenna)   35
hauss í hvarma túni hrings myrk-viðar fengit.

IV.

Eirekr :

10.   Vil-ek eigi boð fyrir bróðor, ne baugom mey kaupa,
(Eystein kveða orðinn Agnars bana) heyra :
grætr eigi mik móðir, mun-ek œfstr á val deyja,
ok 'geir-tre' í gœgnom gœrr látið mik standa.   40

11.   Munat eins konungs efni, sva-at ek vita dœmi,
á dýrra beð deyja til dœgurðar hrafni :
mun blóði þá bróðor ok brátt yfir gialla
'hirðr veggja slita' blár þó at illa launi.

12.   Hlakkar hrafn of hœfði 'her minna nu sinna'   45
krefr unda-valr augna   .   .   .   .   minna :
veiztu, ef, hrafn, or hœfði hœggr brún-steina mína,
launar unda-valr Endils illa marga fylli.

13.   Þat berit orð it œfsta (ero austr-farar liðnar)
at mær hafi mína mió Áslaugo bauga :   50
þá mun mest af móði, er mik spyrja dauðan,
mín stiúp-móðir mildom mœgom til segja.

Aslaug :

14.   Hvat segit ér or 'yðro ero Sviar í landi'
'eða elligar úti all-nýtt konungs-spialli :'

and a doughty heart. He shall surpass all other men in might, he, the scion of Budli, that hates the red rings. There is a serpent in no other child's eyes save Sigurd's alone. This prince has a snake in his eyeball.

IV. *Eric fixes his own doom, and gives his last words to Starkad.* I will not take atonement nor rings as ransom for my brother's death. Eystan [Beli] is Agnar's slayer. No mother weeps for me. I shall die last; let the spears pierce me. No prince, that I know, shall die on a costlier bed for the raven's feast. The raven shall soon be screaming over my blood, requiting me ill for *my care for him.* The raven is screaming over my head, he is asking for the eyes out of my head. Know, O Raven, if thou tearest the eyeballs out of my head, that thou wilt be repaying me ill for many a fill I have given thee.

To a messenger. Carry my last words, now that the Eastern journeys are come to an end. Let my step-mother Anslaug have this ring of mine. She will be wroth when she hears of my death, she will egg her gallant sons on to avenge me.

Anslaug to the messenger. What say ye, are the Swedes in the land ?

35. enom] yfir, Cd.   49. þau . . . in ofri, Cd.   52. mogum sinum ti
segia, Cd.   54. Read, hvat . . . nýtt . . . spialla ?

fregit hef-ek hitt at fóro, enn framarr vitom eigi   55
(ok hildingar hæfðo hlunn-roð) Danir sunnan.

Sendimaðr :

15.   Þer segjo ver þína (þat er nauð) kona dauða
'elli einkar manni' ærlæg sonom Þóro:
œng spiæll vitom ænnor enn nýjari an þessi;
nu hefig fram komit 'fægrom flaug ærn of ná dauðan.'   60

Aslaug :

16.   Eigi mondi yðarr, ef ér dœið fyrri,
eitt misseri eptir óhefnt vera brœðra :
(lítt ráðomk því leyna), ef líf hafa knætti
Eirekr sitt ok Agnarr óbornir. mer niðjar.

Sigurd Ormr-i-auga :

17.   Þat skal þriggja nátta, ef þik tregar móðir,   65
(leið eigo ver langa) leiðangr buinn verða :
skal Uppsælom eigi, þótt ofa-fé bióði,
ef svá duga dísir, Eysteinn Beli ráða.

Biorn Iarnsíða :

18.   Duga mun hugr ok hiarta í hauk-snæro briósti,
þótt minnr um þat mæli. manni innan rifja :   70
eigi es oss í augom ormr né fránir snákar,
'brœðr glæddo mik mínir,' man-ek stiúp-sono þína.

Hvitserkr :

19.   Hyggjom at áðr heitim, at hefnt megi verða,
látom ymso illo Agnars bana fagna :
hrindom húf á hrannir, hœggom ís fyrir barði,   75
siám á hitt hve snekkjor ver snemst faim búnar.

Ivarn Beinlausi :

20.   Hafið ofr-huga œrinn ok áræði bæði,
þess mundi þá þurfa at 'þrá' mikit fylgði :

I have heard that the Danes have come from the South, and I know
that the kings had a sacrificial-launch.—*The messenger :* I tell thee, lady,
of Thora's sons' death. There is no news fresher than this, I have just
come from where the ravens were flying over their dead corses.
The egging words of Anslaug to her sons. Ye would not have been left
one year unrevenged of them, if ye had died first, if Eric and Agnar, no
sons of mine, were living.
The brothers answer one by one. Sigurd Snake-i'-th'-eye : The levy
shall be ready within three nights. Eystan Beli shall not rule Upsal
long though he offer us weregild, if the goddesses help us. — *Biorn
Ironside :* The heart may be steadfast in a man's breast, though he speak
little. I have no snake in my eye .... I will remember thy step-sons.
—*Whitesark :* Let us look ere we vow, that our revenge be feasible!
May every ill befall Agnar's slayers. Let us launch our barks on the
wave! Let us cleave the ice with our prows! Let us make ready our ships
as soon as may be!—*Inwar the Boneless :* Ye have spirit enough and dash
to boot, yet ye lack foresight. Ye must bear me with you in the van;

---

59. þung spioll, Cd.   72. Read, minjom.

bera mun mik fyrir bragna beinlausan framm verða,
'þó gat ek hænd til hefnda at ek hváriga nýta.'   80

V.

Ragnarr :

21.   Spari mangi ræf Rínar, ef rœskva vill her menn;
        verr samir horskom hilmi hringa fiœlð an drengja:
        'íllt es í borg lið bauga brandrauðum framm standa'
        'all-marga veit-ek iœfra þa-er . . . . lifir dauða'

22.   Hvat er þat 'baugs' or biœrgom 'bríót' heyrig nú þióta
        'at menn mundils mar svan drafnir hafna'   86
        þo skal-ek þeirra ráða 'þann bil' ef goð vilja
        'Egils alun leygjar' ókvíðandi bíða.

Aslaug :

23.   Þer ann-ek serk inn síða ok saumaðan hvergi,
        við heilan hug ofinn or hár-síma garni: 90
        mun eigi ben blœða, né bíta þik eggjar
        í heilagri hiúpo, 'vas hon þeim' goðom signoð.

VI.

Ragnarr :

24.   Orrostor hefi-ek áttar þær-er ágætar þótto
        (gœrða-ek mœrgom manni mein) fimm tigi ok eina:
        eigi hugðomk orma at aldr-lagi míno;   95
        þat verðr mœrgom manni er minzt varir sialfan.

25.   Gnyðja mundo grísir, ef galtar hag vissi;
        mer es 'gnot' at grandi, grafa inn rœnom sínom:

---

though I can use neither hand, yet I shall take my share *of the revenge*
with you.

V. *Ragnar setting out on his foray to England.* Let not a man spare
gold if he will gather warriors about him; a great treasure beseems
a king less than a company of heroes. *A fort cannot be held by rings.*
Many a king I know of that is dead *when he might have lived but for his
meanness.*

Ragnar will not listen to the evil omens. What is this murmuring I hear
from the hills? Nevertheless, I shall abide without fear what shall
happen, if the gods will it so.

Anslaug gives her lord a magic shirt. With a whole heart I give thee
this long shirt, not sewn, but woven of hair-fine yarn. Wound shall not
bleed on thee, nor weapon-edge bite on thee in this holy surcoat, that
was blessed by the gods.

VI. *Ragnar in the Serpent-pit.* I have fought battles fifty and one. I
never thought that serpents would be my death. What he least
looked for befalls many a man. The porklings would grunt if they knew
of the old boar's need. The serpents gnaw me to death, they are eating

---

80. hreifa at h. neytki, A.   95. hugða ek mik, Cd.   96. miok morgo
s uni, Cd.

ok harðlíga hrína, hafa mik sogit ormar;
nú mun-ek nár af bragði ok nær 'dyrom' deyja.   100

VII.

Biorn Iarnsiða :

26.   Her flygr hverjan morgin hress of borgir þessar;
    læzk heill muno hungri heiða valr of deyja :
    hann fari suðr um sanda 'seggi hvar ver letom'
    þar fær hann dauðs mannz dreyra dœgg or skýli-hœggom.

27.   Þat var fyrst er fórom Freys leika tók-ek heyja   105
    'þar er einiga allum old' í Róma-veldi:
    þar lét ek of grœn grána (gall œrn of val-falli)
    at 'mann skelko' morði mítt sverð dregit verða.

28.   Upp hrundo ver ópi ár 'bito meir an þeira'
    (satt man-ek til þess segja) sverð í Gnípa-firði: 110
    knátti hvar er vildi fyrir Hvítabý útan
    (ne sitt spari sveinar sverð) mannz bani verða.

Aslaug :

29.   Kaga léto mik mínir .... synir lœngom
    ér erot .... heiman .... meðal-fœrir,
    Rœgnvaldr tók at rióða rœnd í gumna blóði,   115
    hann kom yngstr til Óðins ógn-diarfr sona minna.

30.   Sonr beið einn sá-ek átta í Austrvegi dauða,
    Hvítserkr var sá heitinn hvergi giarn at flýja;
    hitnaði hann af hœfðom hœggins vals at rómo,
    kauss þann bana þengill þróttar-sniallr áðr félli.   120

31.   Hœfðom lét of hrundit hund-mœrgom gramr undir
    'í feiga bý foska fingi ivir syngja'
    hvat skyli beð inn betra bœð-heggr und sik leggja

---

into me, and they hiss cruelly, draining my blood. I shall soon be a dead man. *The verses which once followed here seem to have been used to make the final part of Kraku-mal.*

VII. *Biorn Ironside on the brothers' forays.* Here flies every morning a raven over the fort, he is hungry for carrion; let him go south of the sand where we fought, there he may slake his thirst in the wounds of the dead. When I first set Frey's game going in the Roman empire [Italy], I was eighteen years old. There .... my sword was drawn.

Biorn Ironside. Let us raise a mighty war-whoop in Gnip-firth [Scarbay = Scarborough?]. Let every one slay his man outside of Whitby.

Anslaug [now called Randalin] egging her sons to avenge Rognvald. My sons have left me sorrowing. Ye are aye laggards all of you. Rognwald the brave was wont to dye his target red in men's blood, he came first of all my sons to Woden.

The death of Whitesark, burnt on a pile of dead men's heads. One son I had that died in Eastway—Whitesark was his name—that never sought to flee. He was burnt on a pile of the heads of the slain, this was the

---

102. mun af, Cd.   109. hrunda var, Cd.

'illa deyr við orðztír allvaldr iofurs falli.'

32.   Sitja 'veiði-vitjar vals' á borgar halsom,   125
bǫl er þat'r hefir um hafnat hrafn Sigurðar nafni:
blási 'nýti niótar nás' í spǫn at hánom!
of snemma lét Óðinn alf valmeyjar deyja.

VIII.

1st. 33.   Seg þú frá þegn-skǫpom þínom; þik rǽðomk ek spyrja:
hvar sáttu hrafn á hríslo hrolla dreyra fullan?   130
optar sattu at ǫlðrom í ǫndugi fundinn
an þú dreyrog hræ drǿgir í dal fyrir val-fogla.

2nd. 34.   Þegi-þu heim-dragi heitinn! hvat er þik 'vesal látan!'
hefir-þú aldregi unnit þess es ek mega þrotna
feit . . . . sverð . . . . s. l.   135
gaftattu hafnar hesti (hvat rǿkir þik) drykkjo.

1st. 35.   Hafs létom ver hesta hlýr-stinna brim renna,
meðan á biartar brynjor blóði dreif um síðor:
ylgr gein oldor-monnom 'eyra' grár of svíra
harð-meldri   .   .   .   .   roðna.   140

2nd. 36.   Allz engi sa-ek yðarn þar-er upp lokinn fundom
'heila varg' fyr hvítom hesti máva rastar:
'ok við lasi luðrar' fyrir landi ver undom
.   .   .   . miǫllo hrafns fyrir rauðom stafni.

1st. 37.   Samira okkr at ǫlðrom of ǫndugi þræta   145
'hvarr okkar hefir unnit hvaðarr' framar ǫðrom:
þú stótt þar es bar bára branda-hiǫrt at sundi,
enn ek sat þar es 'rá reiddi' rauðan stafn til hafnar.

---

death he chose ere he fell. There were hundreds of heads piled beneath
him . . . . What better bed could a king spread for himself! . . . .
Sigurd Snake-i'-th'-eye's death. Lo, the ravens perched on the pin-
nacles of the burghs. The doom has overtaken Sigfred's namesake.
Blow, gentle winds, on the chips of his funeral pile. Woden made the
Walkyrie's darling die too soon.

VIII. *First Champion :·* Tell thy feats, I bid thee. Where hast thou
seen the blood-sated raven perched on the bough? Thou wert oftener to
be found in the high-seat than dragging their food to the eagles.—*Second
Champion:* Hold thy peace, thou stay-at-home. What hast thou, thou
wretch? Nought hast thou wrought wherein I should fall short. Thou
hast never slaked the wolf's thirst.—*First Champion:* We made the
prow-strong sea-horses speed through the brine. The grey wolf yawned
over the dead . . . . golden beacon heads.—*Second Champion:* I did not
see thee where we saw the white waves gaping for the ship . . . . and
the sea . . . . furiously before the red prow.—*First Champion relenting :*
Let us not quarrel in the high-seat which of us two has done the
greatest deed of daring. Thou didst stand where the billow floated
the ships, and I was sitting on the ship as she touched the harbour.—

---

131. þattu at oðom, Cd.   [142. Read, Heita vang.   145. öndugi]
read, önd? *or* anddyri?

2nd. 38.   Fylgðom Birni báðir í branda gný hverjom,
(vóro reyndir rekkar) enn Ragnari stundom: 150
var ek þar-er bragnar bœrðosk á Bolgara-landi
því berr-ek sár á síðo. Sittu innarr meirr, granni!

LAST FRAGMENTS.

IN the Legendary Tales, of which we have spoken in § 34 of Prolegomena, and which are chiefly to be found in the Fornaldar-Sögur,
Copenhagen, 1829, there are about seventeen hundred lines.
This mass falls into three categories, which we must treat separately.
First there comes a small number of verses in *Turf-Einar Metre*, more
or less poetic in character, and with *no direct* imitation of earlier poetry
or subject. The second group contains lines in the *Epic Metre*, dealing
with popular traditions of a more or less *mediæval* character. What is
noteworthy out of these two groups we have printed here. But the
third group is of a different character. It consists of a number of poems
in *Epic Metre*, by a late versifier, *directly* imitated from the old genuine
poetry, which he must have had access to in book-form. Three of
these poems, all of which may be by the same hand, of the same type, as
the Saxo Starkad-Lay, but not imitated from it, are the Death-Song of
Arrow-Ord, the Life of Rook sung by himself in the hall of Hake, and
the Wikar's-balk of Starkad in the hall of Alric. There are more
pieces, but of an inferior interest. We need not believe that more than
one person was concerned, and we have no proof that he knew more
about songs or traditions of old days than we do now. He knew the
poems of the Helgi and Heroic group, perhaps also those of the lost
sheet, for he may even have used our MSS. The Editor has long suspected
that the Fornaldar-Sögur, as we have them, were edited in the east of
Iceland, where there is some reason to suppose that the ' Edda ' MSS.
were lurking all along till the seventeenth century. The stiff, prosy,
monotonous vein of this set of poems betrays their wholly artificial and
book character; and when we take Gunnlaug's Merlinus-Spa, a poem
written at a time *between* them and the old poems they imitate, we can
see how great a difference there is between a man at home in the
old metre and to a certain extent inspired by noble models, and a mere
dilettante, forging verses for amusement, without a spark of real fancy
or any true comprehension of the spirit and melody of his originals.
These poems, of which the only use or worth can be that they contain
a few direct citations from the old poems, we cannot print here. They
are at best but appendage-matter. They are as much book-poetry as
forged eighteenth-century ballads; but, as far as space allowed, we have
given them in an appendage, that readers may see their nullity plainly
set out in black and white, and judge the question for themselves.
It should be noticed that the MSS. on which Fornaldar-Sögur occurs
are all of late date. The Editor's hypothesis as to the composition of
these tales will be found in Prolegomena, § 34.
Of the former two groups of verses, which we give below, we have
set first those in TURF-EINAR METRE.
I. The first set of lines in this metre belongs to the story of Asbiorn
the Proud. It was from part of this piece that we took the List

---

Second Champion: We both followed Biorn or else Ragnar to battle.
I remember how we followed men in the Bolgars' land [Bulgaria].
There I got a wound in my side. Come and sit here inside next me!

of Champions, No. III, printed in Book v, § 6. The maker knew Kraku-mal.

II. The next, from the tale of Arrow-Ord, the Northern Odysseus or Philoctetes. These lines would seem rightly to form a part of the verse in Ragnar's Saga, ver. 23, p. 350.

III. The third from the story of *Fridtheow*, well known by the poem of Tegner, of which it is the foundation. There are one or two antique touches in this verse, the parting of the ring, for instance, and the magic tempest. There are phrases resembling those of Kraku-mal I. and Egil's verse.

IV. The fourth set is modern in spirit, but really poetic. One or two verses of those we give are probably the best known lines in Iceland of all ancient poetry. The Saga in which they are found is purely fictitious, and worthless in itself, though the verse is so pretty. Metre, modernised court-metre.

V. The ditties which follow might perhaps have stood in Book vi, § 2. They are really popular in spirit; they are found in the late and manu-factured Saga of Bard the Snow-fell spirit, which is curious as containing several bits of native folk-lore.

The second group (vi–xi) in EPIC METRE, or other short metre, is arranged next in order.

VI. The first is taken from the end of Ragnar's Saga (the first few lines being also found in a different and, we take it, wrong connection in Half's Saga), where the prose runs—'There was a certain Ogmund called Ogmund the Dane, he was once coming with five ships and lay to off Samsey in Munarvoe.' The story goes, 'that the meat-swains landed to get meat, and that others of the men went into the woods to amuse themselves, and there they found an ancient wooden man, forty fathoms high and moss-grown; but yet his face could still be seen. And now they fell to reasoning among themselves, who could have worshipped this great god.' Then the wooden man spake—'It was, etc.'

The final lines of his speech remind one of pieces in the anthologies. The first line is the same favourite 'folk-phrase' we have in King Harold and the Fisherman, Book viii, § 3.

VII. The next set refers to the presages which foretell the fates of the kings in Half's Saga. They all occur in the first chapters of that Tale, from whence we have taken Nos. 4, 5 for Book vi, § 2; and

VIII. Here we, for the first time since Book iv, § 3, and the Ditty, Book vi, No. 13 *a*, meet with a scrap in DIALOGUE METRE. It is a bit of a song composed on an amusing half-allegoric folk-tale. A king (Gaut) is out hunting and loses his way, and comes to a hut in which he gets shelter; the household are strange folk, and one of the women explains their ways and doings to the wondering guest. 'My father is *Shabby*, my mother is *Tatter*, my brothers are *Curlew, Sea-urchin*, and *Drone*[1]. My name is *Gentle*, my sisters are called *Hetter* and *Fetter*. There is a cliff near our house called *Gilling's cliff*, and a steep thereon called the *Family-steep*; over it we throw ourselves if any misfortune falls upon us, and so we go to Woden.' The old people first kill themselves, and then the young do likewise, as one after another they are afflicted by some small piece of ill-luck. The daughter Gentle bears a child to the king, who grows up to be the famous prince Gautric the Munificent.

IX–XI. The next extract, from Rolf-Kraki's Saga, refers to the story of

---

[1] Norse Skafnortungr, Tötra, Fiolmod, Imsigull, Gillung, which last we would read 'Geitung;' the sisters Snotra, Hiotra, and Fiotra; the cliffs Gillungs-hamar and Ætternis-stapi.

two orphan princes, who, according to the prophecy in the Mill Song (l. 80), were to avenge Frodi. They escape their foes as the two young princes in the Lancelot story do, in spite of the witch, who discovers them. In the same Saga there are two other scraps referring to the two brothers who are deformed by enchantment and recognise each other, and to King Eadgil's recognising his old champion who visits his court with Rolf. There are two verses (cited in Edda) in this Saga which are older and genuine; these we have printed in Book iii, § 2, vol. i, p. 190.

XII. The next scrap, from Bard's Saga, tells of the heroine's home-sickness.

XIII. The last bit, in *rhyme metre*, is found in Fridtheow's Saga. It deals with a storm-scene, and is ascribed to Biorn, one of the characters in the Saga, though, of course, it would suit any hero in the same circumstances.

I. (From Flatey-bok.)

1. SAGÐI mer á seiði sœngom þat lœngom,
    at ek feigom fœti fœrag norðr á Mœri :
vætki vissi vœlva, vera man-ek enn með mœnnom
glaðr í Gauta-veldi. Gramir eigi spár hennar!

2. Segit þat mínni móðor, man hon eigi syni kemba 5
svarðar láð á sumri, Svanhvít í Danmœrko :
hafða-ek henni heitið, at ek heim koma mundag,
nú mun segg á síðo sverðz-egg dregin verða.

II. (From Arrow-Ord's Saga.)

SERK of frá-ek or silki í siau stœðom gœrvan :
    ermr var á Íra-landi, œnnor norðr með Finnom,
slógo Saxa meyjar, enn Suðreyskar spunno,
vófo Valskar brúðir, varp Oþióðans móðir. 4

III. (From Fridtheow's Saga.)

1. SYNDA lét-ek or Sogni (enn snótir miaðar neytto)
    bræddan byrjar sóta (í Baldrs-haga miðjom):

I. *Asmund the Proud defies the Sibyl's prediction, and resolves to explore the cavern and fight the Giant.* Long ago the Sibyl told me in her enchanted song that I should go north to More on doomed feet. The Sibyl was wrong, I shall live merrily among men in the realm of the Gauts. The fiends take her forebodings!

Asmund is caught by the Giant and tortured to death; he sings at the stake. Tell my mother, Swanwhite, in Denmark, that she will never comb her son's hair again this year. I promised her that I would come home, but now the sword-edge shall be drawn over my side.

II. *Arrow-Ord has a magic shirt given him by the fairy-maidens, who sing as they hand it to him.* That silken shirt was wrought in seven places, one arm in Ireland, the other north among the Fins, the Saxon maids beat *the flax*, the South-Island [Hebudes] damsels spun it, the ladies of Gaul wove it, the heathen mothers [of Wendland] warped it.

III. *Fridtheow in the storm which is raised by witchcraft against his good ship Ellida.* I put my black bark out of Sogn, while the ladies were

---

1. ok song um, Cd.   4. Read, Oþióðar = Vinda? Cp. p. 187, l. 35.

nú tekr hregg at herða ; hafi dag brúðir góðan
þær-er oss vilja unna, þótt Elliða fylli.

2. Miœk tekr siár at svella, svá er nú drepit skýjom, 5
því ráða galdrar grimmir at gialfr or stað fœrir:
eigi skal við ægi í ofviðri berjask,
látom Sólundir seggjom svell-vífaðar hlífa.

3. Helgi veldr at hrannir hrím-faxaðar vaxa,
era sem biarta brúði í Baldrs-haga kyssim. 10

4. Eigi sér til alda, erom vestr í haf komnir,
allr þykkir mer ægir sem í eymyrjo sæi:
hrynja haf-báror, haug verpa svan-flaugar;
nú er Elliði orpinn í œrðugri báro.

5. Her varð svarf um siglo, er sær á skip hrunði, 15
ek varð err við átta innan-borðz at vinna:
dælla var til dyngjo dœgurð konom fœra
an Elliða ausa í œrðugri báro.

6. Brusto báðir halsar í báro hafs stórri,
sukko sveinar fiórir í sæ ógrunnan. 20

7. Þann skal hring of hœggva, er Halfdanar átti,
áðr oss tapar Ægir, auðigr faðir rauðan:
siá skal goll á gestom, ef ver gistingar þurfom
(þat dugir rausnar rekkom), í Ránar-sal miðjom.

8. Sigldo ver or Sogni, svá fóro ver næstum, 25
þá lék eldr it efra í óðali váro:
enn nú tekr bál at brenna · Baldrs-haga miðjan,
því man-ek vargr í véom, veit ek þat munk heitinn.

---

boiling the mead in the midst of Balder's-Haye. The gale is rising, may
the ladies that love us fare well, though Ellida fill. The sea is swelling,
the air is thick with clouds; it is through wicked charms that the surges
are stirred. Who can fight against ocean in tempest? Let us seek
shelter behind the Solunds. It is Helgi that makes the rime-maned
billows swell. It is not as when we were kissing the fair maidens in
Balder's-Haye. We cannot see the .... We are driven westward on
the main. All ocean looks to me like glowing embers [all a-fire]; the
billows of the deep are crashing down upon us; the swan-meads [waters]
are cast up in high barrows ; Ellida is plunging into the ramping billow.
There was havoc in the waist when the sea clashed over the ship; I had to
do eight men's work in the hold. It was sweeter work to bring the
ladies their breakfasts in this bower than to be baling Ellida in the
ramping billows. Both neck-boards broke in the big sea-wave, four lads
sank to the bottom of the sea.

*He cuts his ring up and divides it among his men, believing that the
ship must founder.* Let us cut up the ring that Halfdan's father owned,
before ocean wrecks us, so that gold shall be seen on us as befits gentlemen if we must needs be guests in Ran's hall.

Having avenged his wrong and burnt Balder's-Haye, Fridtheow sails off.
We sailed out of Sogn, that was our last voyage ; the flame was playing
then over our heritage, but now the flame is blazing in the midst of
Balder's-Haye. I shall be called a 'Wolf in holy-places' for this, I know.

IV. (From Wiglund's Saga.)

1. EIGI má ek á ægi ógrátandi líta,
   sízt mál-vinir mínir fyr mar-bakkann sukku:
   leiðr er mer sióvar sorti ok súgandi bára
   (heldr gœrði mer harðan harm) í unna farmi.

2. Trúði malm-þings meiðir mar-glóðar þer tróða;   5
   hugða ek sízt at hefði hring-lestir þik festa:
   eigi tiáðu eiðar oss eða margir kossar,
   seint er kvenna geð kanna; kona sleit við mik heitum.

3. Stóðu vit tvau í túni; tók Hlín um mik sínum
   hœndum haukligt kvendi hár-fœgr, ok grét sáran: 10
   títt flugu tár um tróðu; til segir harmr um vilja;
   strauk drif-hvítum dúki drós um hvarminn liósa.

4. Skamt leidda ek skýran skrauta-niœrð or garði,
   þó fylgði hugr mínn hónum 'hverskyns konar' lengra:
   skylda-ek leitt hafa lengra, ef land fyrir lægi væri,   15
   ok ægis-mar yrði allr at grænum velli.

5. Laug-auðig strauk lauðri lín-eik um skœr mína,
   því er mer enn til annars úbrátt hœfuð-þváttar:
   œllungis skal engi auði glœst it næsta
   ein á aldri mínum ask-laugar mer vaska.   20

6. Sé-ek á fiall þat-er fiœtra fram-lunduðust sitr undir,
   þó renn ek til hennar hug-rekk vinar-augum:
   þá brekku kveð-ek mer þekka þrúðr er þar stendr hiá prúðri
   hlaðs sem hlíðar aðrar hug-þekk er mer nokkut.

IV. *Kettlerid believes her lover Wiglund to be drowned and weeps for him.* I can never look on the sea without weeping, since my love sank in the deep water. I hate the blackness of the sea and the sucking surges of the heaped waters. Cruel is my grief therefore.

Wiglund's reproach to his mistress. I trusted thee, lady; least of all did I think that another should have espoused thee. Vain were oaths and kisses many. It takes a long time to fathom a woman. My lady has broken her vow to me.

Wiglund on parting with his mistress. We stood together in the court, the fair-haired lady clasped me in her arms and wept sore, thick fell the tears upon her. Sorrow witnesses to love. She wiped her bright eye-lashes with her snow-white kerchief.

Kettlerid's farewell. I did not go far with thee out of the court, yet my heart followed thee ever farther. I would have gone farther with thee if the sea were land, and ocean's mere were all green fields.

Kettlerid is washing Wiglund's head. My lady has rubbed the lather into my hair. It will be long ere I have another head-washing. No other lady shall ever lave my hair as long as I live.

Wiglund looks back at the hills, where his lady lives, as he sails away. I look at the hills my love lives under, casting loving eyes towards her. Dearer to me than any other hillside is the brink of the hill where she

7.   Lióst er út at líta lauka-reið yfir heiði,   25
sól gengr síð und múla, slíkt langar mik þangat:
fiœll eru mer þekk af þellu (því er-ek hlióðr, valin tróða)
[víf á-ek vænst at leyfa val-grund] er þar sitr undir.

8.   Ketilríðr bað ei kvíða karlmann í fœr sniallri
ungan þótt œldor gangi iafn-hátt skeiðar stafni: 30
enn er á orð at minnazt (verum hraustir nú Trausti)
[verð ek af harmi hœrðum hríð-lundr] Ketilríðar.

V. THE GIANTESS AND THE FISHER (Barðar Saga).

1.   R OA skaltu fiall firðan fram í lœg stirðan,
       (þar mun gœr glitta) ef þú vill Gríms-mið hitta:
þar skaltu þó liggja; 'Þórr er víss til Friggjar;'
roi norpr inn nef-skammi Nesit í Hiúk-hvammi!

2.   Út reri einn á báti Ingialdr í skinn-feldi;   5
týndi átián œnglum Ingialdr í skinn-feldi,
ok fertogu fœri Ingialdr í skinn-feldi,
aptr kom aldri síðan Ingialdr í skinn-feldi.

VI.   (From Ragnar's Saga and Half's.)

1.   Þ AT var fyrir lœngo er í leið megir
       Hœkings fóro 'hlum tunglom:'
sigldo um salta slóð birtinga,
þá varð-ek þessa þorps ráðandi.

---

lives. It is light above the mountain tops, the sun is setting late behind the
Mull, would I were there! Dear to me are the hills because she lives
beneath them, that is why I am silent. Mine is the fairest of ladies.

Wiglund in the gale to his brother Trust. Kettlerid bade me never flinch,
though the waves rose as high as the bows of the bark. Now let us be
mindful of her words. Let us be bold, Trust. I am heart-sore with
my bitter sorrow.

V. *The giantess Hetta, wishing to lure Ingiald to death, shows him the
marks of a fine fishing bank.* Thou shalt row till the mountain shows low,
out in the high sea, where the wild fowl are glittering, if thou wilt light
on Grim's bank. There shalt thou lie . . . . Row till Andwerd's-ness
shows into Sleet-dell, and shiver there Snubbie!

*Ingiald rows out to the bank and is persuaded by an evil spirit in guise of
a fisherman to wait there, till he was caught in a terrible gale. While the
storm was raging his household, sitting at supper, hear a hollow voice
chanting at the window.* Out he rowed alone in his boat, Ingiald in his
sheep-skin coat. Eighteen hooks he lost and forty fathoms of line; he
will never come back again, Ingiald in his sheep-skin coat. *But Bard,
a friendly mountain spirit, saved him, and he came home alive to his
frightened household.*

VI. *The wooden image.* It was a long while ago, when the sons of
Hocing went forth . . . . on the salt sea-trout's path. It was then that I

---

2. Hæklings, Cd.

2.　Ok því setto ' sverð-merðlingar '　　　　5
　　suðr hiá salti synir Loðbrókar :
　　þá var-ek blótinn til bata mœnnom
　　í Sámseyjo sunnan-verðri.

3.　Þar báðo standa meðan strœnd þolir
　　mann ' hiá þyrni ' ok mosa-vaxinn :　　　　10
　　nú skýtr á mik skýja gráti,
　　hlýr hvárki mer hold né klæði.

VII. (From Half's Saga.)

1.　GAKK-ÞÚ frá brunni!—glottattu við mer—
　　　þræll herfiligr, þíns inniss til!
　　man-ek senda þer sveiðanda spiót
　　þat-er gyrja mun granar þínar.

2.　Veita gœrla víf þitt, konungr,　　　　5
　　hvat hnekkja mun hennar sælo :
　　' ver verðom þer ' . . . . .
　　' Hildr Hiœrleifi, haltu nær loga.'

3.　Ek se Hringjo haug um orpinn,
　　enn Hera hníga hvatinn spióti :　　　　10
　　sé ek Hiœrleifi hapt-bœnd snuin,
　　enn Hreiðari hœgginn galga.

4.　Ek sé lýsa langt suðr í haf,
　　vill Danskr konungr dóttor hefna ;

became ruler of this thorp. And the sons of Lodbrok .... set me up in the south, hard by the salt sea. It was then I was worshipped for the saving of mariners, southward in Samsey. They bade me stand there a wooden and moss-begrown man while the strand endures. The tears of the clouds fall upon me, neither flesh nor clothes cover me.

VII. *Hiorleif's men go to draw water at a spring in Finland, that fell from a rock ; there they saw a Burn-soiler (one of the Fox's names, here used of a goblin). When they told the king, he heated a spear-head in the fire and shot at the spirit, crying,* Go from the brook, thou filthy slave, to thine own place. Never make mows at me ! I will send thee a hissing spear that shall gore thy lips. *But the monster bolted into the rock, and afterward answered the king back.* Beware of thy wife, king, she will put an end to thy luck. We warn thee, O king, ... near the fires. *But Hiorleif threw a spear which put out his eye. Again, Hiorleif lay in a calm in the Jutland main, and at sunrise he saw in the north a man-mountain rise out of the sea, that spoke to him.* I see a barrow cast over Hringia [thy love] ; I see Heri [thy son] sink spear-smitten. I see the shackles twisted for Hiorleif, and a gallows cut for Reidhere [thy kinsman]. *Again, the fisherman caught a merman and brought him to Hiorleif, who let him go on condition of his prophesying his fate.* I see a gleam far south in the sea, the Danish king will avenge his daughter ; he has out ships untold ; he bids Hiorleif to a tryst of war. Keep thee if thou canst ! I will go back

---

7. Emend.; bana, Cd.　　10. Read, háþyrnis?　　1. gletta littu við mik, Cd.
10. Bugge; hingat, Cd.　　12. Bugge; huginn, Cd.

hann hefir úti ótal skipa, 15
býðr hann Hiœrleifi holm-stefno til,
varastu víti ef þú vill; vil-ek aptr í siá!

5. Sœgo kann-ek segja sonom Háleygja
vilgi góða, ef ér vilit heyra:
her ferr sunnan 'Svarðar' dóttir 20
um drifin dreyra, frá Danmœrko.

6. Hefir ser á hœfði hialm upp spentan,
her-kuml harðligt 'Heðins of létta'
skamt man sveinom 'sé þat sem er'
hildar at bíða her á ferli. 25

7. Bresta mun baug-rœst, brá mær augom
um heruð 'hingað Hœgna til þegna'
'hafa skal hverr drengr hiœr-niótz mœrg spiót'
'áðr komi mikil fram malm-hríð siðan'
'þó man, ef þat er satt þá ferr illa hafa' 30
'ýtar al keypt ár þá er kemr var.'

8. Minnistu, Hreiðarr, hverr Hera felldi;
vá vaktist þar fyrir vestr-durom:
enn man in svinna til sala þinna
byr-sæl koma; bíð-þú enn konungr! 35

VIII. (From Gautrick's Saga.)

1. SKUA tvá er mer Skaf-nœrtungr gaf,
þvengjom er hann þá nam:
illz mannz kveð-ek aldri vera
granda-lausar giafir.

2. Heimskliga veik-ek hendi til 5
er ek kom við kinn kono:
lítil lyf kveða hœfð til lýða sona;
af því var hann Gautrekr gœrr.

to the sea! I çan tell ye Haloga-men a tale if ye will hearken. Hither
comes from the south Hedin's daughter [war] blood-besprent out of
Denmark. She has on her head a helm .... stout war-tokens. It will
not be long waiting for war. The shield shall break, she is turning her
eyes into this quarter. Let every man take his sword and spear ....
yet shall .... if it be true .... *There was a voice heard crying,* Let
Reidhere remember who slew Heri. Woe was awakened at the west
doors. Nevertheless the Wise maiden shall come to thy hall. Wait
awhile, king!

VIII. *Gaut on the stinginess of Shabby.* The two shoes that Shabby
gave me he took the thongs out of. An ill man's gifts are never lucky.
*Gentle persuades her brother Drone that she is with child through his
having touched her face with his hand. Drone cries out:* Fool that I was to
touch her cheek with my hand. How little goes to make a man! That
is how Gautric was begotten.

20. Read, Heðins? 30. Read, þat er sák. 32. Thus Bugge; minstu ...
hvar H. feldut, Cd. 34. Bugge; hun sinna ... kona, Cd. 1. Read, Skaf-
nyrflungr? (nyrfill).

3. Svartir sníglar áto steina fyrir mer,
    nú vill oss hvat-vetna hata :   10
    snauðr mun-ek snópa, þvi-at sníglar hafa
    goll mitt allt grafit.

4. Þat var spell er spœrr um vann
    á akri Ims-iguls :
    axi var skatt, or var korn numit,   15
    þat mun æ Tœtro ætt um trega.

5. Ungr sveinn drap oxa fyrir mer;
    slíkt eru ban-væn bysn!
    mun-ek aldregi eiga iafn-góðan
    þo ek gamall verði.   20

IX. (From Rolf Kraki's Saga.)

1. ÖLL er orðin ætt Skiœldunga
        lofðungs 'lundar' at limom einom :
    brœðr sá-ek mína á berom sitja,
    enn Sævils rekka á sœðloðom.

2. Tveir 'ro inni, trúig hvárigom,   5
    þeir er við elda ítrir sitja :
    þeir í Vífilsey vóro lengi,
    ok héto þar hunda nœfnom,
        Hoppr ok Hó.

3. Sé-ek hvar sitja synir Halfdanar,   10
    Hróarr ok Helgi, heilir báðir,
    þeir muno Fróða fiœrvi ræna.

4. Ötul ero augo Hams ok Hrana,
    ero œðlingar undra diarfir.

Curlew seeing that two snails have scrabbled upon his gold slabs, cries, Two
black snails have eaten my slabs, everything is going against us. I shall
have to slink along in beggary, now those snails have eaten all my gold.
So he throws himself over the rock. Sea-urchin sees that a sparrow has eaten
an ear of his corn and laments : It was a destruction that the sparrow
wrought in Sea-urchin's acre, the ear was spoilt and one grain taken.
Tatter's race are doomed to woe! So he threw himself over also. Drone
saw the boy Gautric kill an ox, and called out, The boy kills an ox before
mine eyes, an awful business. I shall never have such a jewel of a beast
again however old I grow. And he followed his brethren.

IX. Signy's lament at her brothers' low estate. The Shielding race,
the kingly branches, have all shrunk to mere shrub twigs. I have seen
my brothers riding bare-backed horses while Seavil's men were sitting
on saddles. The sibyl Heid betrays the princes' presence. There are two
in the house, sitting by the fire, neither of whom I trust. They were
long in Weevilsey and were called by dog's names, Hop and Ho. And
again she says, I see where Halfdan's sons, Rodhere and Helgi, are
sitting safe and sound; they shall rob Frodi of his life, save they be quickly
sent away, and that will not be, says she; and she sung on, Keen are the

9. svartir] stuttir, Cd.   20. Corrupt text and metre.

5. Reginn er úti ok rekkar Halfdanar   15
    snœfrir andskotar, segit þat Fróða:
    Varr sló nagla, ok Varr hœfðaði,
    ok Varr vœrum var-nagla sló.

          X. (From Rolf Kraki's Saga.)
Elg-Fróði: GRENJAR skalm, gengr or sliðrom,
              minnisk hœnd hildar verka.
Thori: En ek læt viz á vegom
              œxi mína iafnt hlióð bera.

          XI. (From Rolf Kraki's Saga.)
Aðils: DALR er í hnakka, auga er or hœfði,
          œrr er í enni, hœgg ero á hendi tvau.

          XII. (From Bard's Saga.)
SÆL væra-ek ef ek siá mætta
    Búrfell ok Bala, báða Lón-dranga,
Aðalþegns-Hóla ok Öndurt-nes,
Heiðar-kollo ok Hregg-snasa,
Dritvík ok mœl fyrir durom Fóstra.

          XIII. (From Fridtheow's Saga.)
ERA sem ekkja á þik vili drekka,
    biœrt baug-vara biði nær fara:
sœlt ero augo sukkoð í laugo,
bill sterka arma, bítr mer í hvarma.

---

eyes of Ham and Rani, the Ethelings are wonderfully bold! *King Frodi
hears the voice of Regin the smith, outside, saying,* Regin is outside, and the
champions of Halfdan, bitter foes. Tell this to Frodi. Ware struck
the nail, Ware headed it, and Ware struck a ware-nail [bilge-plug] for
the wary.

X. *Two brothers meet in the fight and recognise each other by their strokes.
The one says,* The sword howls as it is drawn from the sheath, the hand
is mindful of the toil of war. *The other answers,* But far and wide on
the ways I make my axe match *thy sword* in noise.

XI. *Eadgils recognises the old champion Sweep-day by his wound-marks.*
There is a trench on the nape of the neck, an eye out of the head, a
scar on the brow, two cuts on the hand.

XII. *Helga, set afloat by her brothers in play on a piece of ice, drifts
to Greenland, where she is kindly lodged, but she cannot forget her home, and
laments:* Happy were I if I could see Burfell and Bole, and the two
Lon-drengs, Athelthane's hill and Andwordness, Heath's-knoll and
Sleet-peak, Dirt-wick and Shingle, before my foster-father's doors!

XIII. *Fridtheow and Biorn in the gale. Biorn says,* It is not as when
a maid is bidding one to drink with her, or a ring-decked damsel asking
one to draw nearer to her! The salt sea is in mine eyes, the brine
is washing into them. My strong arms are aching, my eyelids are
smarting!

§ 2. PROVERBS AND SAWS.

THE PROVERB-POEM.

FOLLOWING Iomswickinga Drapa, at the end of Codex Regius, comes this piece, which we, like Möbius, are inclined to ascribe to the same *author*—Bishop Biarni. It was first really read by Mr. John Sigurdsson, a most painstaking and successful reader of faded MSS., who spent a good deal of time and care over it; for, though the whole poem is on the vellum, it is almost illegible in many places. But the first and last words (containing no doubt the title and perhaps the name of the author) are either torn off or unreadable, and words and names here and there are still unsafe. Dr. Möbius published it from Mr. Sigurdsson's copy in 1873.

Its subject is 'forn ord,' old saws, and it contains about one hundred and twenty *saws* and *proverbs*, besides *allusions* to the exploits and fortunes of well-known *heroes :* Biarki; Starkad; B...; 'Bronting who slept himself to death;' ... Romund Gripson; Eleazar, the valiant Maccabee, who 'put himself in jeopardy, to the end he might deliver his people, and get him a perpetual name,' and slew the mighty elephant of the army of Antiochus Eupator (1 Macc. vi. 43–47); Nidiung the dwarf that carved the horn of the howe; Sörli the lover; Asmund that broke Gnod, his famous 'sea-steed,' to the waves; and Gizur that set the kings at variance. There are also *allusions* to sundry *gods* and *goddesses :* Frigg and her famous son, snatched away suddenly to the Hell's Hall; 'Eliudnir' [Sleet-den], wept for by all, and sought in vain by Hermod (that Northern Hermes) ; Thiazi and his golden speech; the Bond that bound Fenris; Woden's beer (the gift of song); and Mardoll's tears

It is in Drapa form, $10 + 1 + (3 \times 3) + 10 = 30$, with a *burden*, drawn from the late tale of Harold Fairhair's love-craze for the dead Finnish witch (a legend best known in connection with Charlemagne), the king's foolish passion being likened to his own fond love for a faithless 'pigsney' Randwey. The *metre* is eight-measured Rhyme metre. The poem was obviously composed for recitation at entertainments, where its variety and irony would render it amusing.

It is to be observed that all the feminine rhymes are ◡ ◡, never – ◡; in the masculine rhymes five in – occur to every one in ◡.

Dr. Egilsson cites it as 'Mansongs kvædi;' the Editor quotes it in the Dictionary as Malshatta kvædi, which is perhaps most convenient, in the absence of any definite hint as to its true title.

I.

1. . . . . . þegir: Dylja má þess er einn-hver segir;
. . . . eitt brigzt hóti síðr :
Fǿra ætlom forn orð saman : Flestir henda at nœkkvi gaman :
Gleði minnar veit geipon siá : Griplor er sem hendi þá.
2. Ekki hefi-ek með flimtan farit : full-vel ætla-ek til þess varit;

I. INTRODUCTION. .... One man's word may be denied .... I mean to set OLD SAWS together. Most men have some hobby, my pleasure is chattering odds and ends just as they come to hand. I have never

5. ætta-ek, Cd.

yrkja kann-ek váno verr : vita þykkisk þat maðrinn hverr :   6
Stolit væri mer 'ekki' or ætt : iafnan þótta-ek kveða slétt ;
(Roa verðr fyrst á it næsta nes) nokkuð ætta-ek kyn til þess.
   3. Þióð spyrr allt þat-er þrír menn vito : þeir hafa verr er trygðom
slito.
Ekki er því til eins mannz skotið : ymsir hafa þau dœmi hlotið.   10
Hermðar orð muno hittask í : heimolt á-ek at glaupsa af því.
Nokkuð varð hon sýsla of svik : svín-eyg drós hve hon fór með mik.
   4. Ró skyldo menn reiði gefa : Raun-lítið kemsk opt á þrefa.
Gagarr er skaptr því at geyja skal : Gœra ætla-ek mer létt of tal.
Verit hafði mer verra í hug : var þat nær sem kveiso flug.   15
Iafnan fagnar kvikr maðr kú : Kennir hins at ek gleðjomk nú.
   5. All-lítið er ungs mannz gaman : Einom þykkir daufligt saman.
Óvinar barn er sem ulf at friá : Óð-fúss myndi blindr at siá :
Dýrt láta menn dróttins orð : Drekarnir rísa opt á sporð :
Öðlingr skyldi einkar-ræskr : Œpa kann í mœrom fræskr.   20
   6. Fylki skal til frægðar hafa : Fregna eigom 'langt til gafa :'
Oddar gœrva iarli megin : Út-sker verða af bærom þvegin :
Ymsir bióða æðrom fár : Ormar skríða or hamsi á vár :
Vel hefir sá er þat líða lætr : Langar eigo þeir bersi nætr.
   7. Biarki átti hugar-korn hart : Her-lið felldi Stœrkoðr mart :   25
Ekki var . . . í hvíldom hœgr : Hrómundr þótti Grips-son slœgr :
Ókat þeim ne einn á bug : Eliazar var trúr at hug,

---

meddled with lampoons; my lay is well meant. I understand how to
compose, as every one knows, or else I take not after my family. My
verse is thought to run smooth, there is some touch of poet-craft in
my blood. We must first row to the nearest ness! (Begin with the
beginning.)
   Every one knows what three men know! Ill do they that break their
troth. (This woe of mine is not mine only, such fortunes have befallen
many a man. Angry words may be found in my song, I have something
to snap for; that pigsney when she dealt with me, it was not wholly
without guile.) One should let one's anger wait. Little things make
great quarrels. A dog was made for barking. (I will unburden my mind.
There have been worse things in my heart, they were just like shooting
pangs. A live man is sure to get a cow—it may be seen that I am
getting merrier now.) Very little amuses a boy. It is dull for a lone
man. A foe's child is a wolf to cherish. The blind would be very glad to
see. Precious are the master's words. Snakes often rise up on their tails.
An etheling should be a brave man. The frog will croak in the marsh.
Glory for a king! . . . . The spears make the earl's might. The seaward reefs are washed by the wave. There are ups and downs in every
fight. Serpents cast their sloughs in spring. Blessed is he that can bide
his time. The bear's night is a long night. Biarki had a steadfast heart.
Starkad killed a mort of men, ... was not a gentle . . . . . Romund
Gripsson was thought to be a cunning man : no one could make them

---

6. Read, váno ver?   7. Read, ella.   9. = Guest's Wisdom, 279 ; = Old Play of
Wolsungs, 259.   12. sik, Cd.   13. = Atlam. 280.   16. = Guest's Wisdom, 14.
18. Annars, Cd. ; = Old Play of Wolsungs, 311.   26. garpr z, Cd.

Fílinn gat hann í fylking sótt: full-stræng hefir sú mann-raun þótt.
  8. *Bana* þóttusk þeir bíða vel : Brandingi svaf loks í hel :
Mardallar var glysligr grátr : Gleðr sá menn er opt er kátr :   30
Ásmundr tamði Gnóð við gialfr : Golli mælti Þiazi sialfr :
Niðiungr *skóf af* haugi horn.—Hœlzti ero þau minni forn.
  9. Friggjar þótti svipr at sveini : sá var tældr af Mistilteini ;
Hermóðr vildi auka *hans* aldr : Eliúðnir vann solginn Baldr :
Öll gréto ' þau ' eptir hann ; auðit var þeim hlátrar bann ;   35
heyrin-kunn er frá hónom saga.—Hvat þarf-ek um slíkt at jaga !
  10. Sítt mein þykkir sárast hveim : Sættar-gœrð er ætloð tveim :
Odda-maðr fæsk opt inn þriði ; iafn-trúrr skal sá hvárra liði :
Engi of dœmir sialfan sik ; slíkt ætla-ek nú hendi mik :
Ýta lið þótt allt fari byrst : engi læzk því valda fyrst.   40

II.

  11. STEFJOM verðr at stæla brag :—stuttligt hefig á kvæði lag—
ella mun þat þykkja þula ; þannig nær sem ek henda mula :—
  Ekki verða fróðom farald : Finnan gat þó œrðan Harald.
  Hónom þótti sól-biört sú : Slíks dœmi verða mörgom nú.

1. 12. Skips láta menn skammar rár : ' Skatna ' þykkir hugrinn
        grár :   45
Tungan leikr við tanna sár : Trauðla er gengt of ís á vár :
Miæk fár er ser œrinn einn : Eyfit týr þótt skyndi seinn :

---

give way. Eleazar was true of heart, he set upon the elephant in the
fight, that was thought a mighty deed of daring. They thought B . . . .
waited well. Bronting slept to death at last. Mardoll's tears were bright
to see. A merry man makes others glad. Asmund broke Gnod [ship]
to the waves. Thiazi spoke gold. Nidiung carved the horn o' the howe ;
old indeed these memories be. Frigg's boy was snatched away, he was
done to death by Mistiltoe. Hermod tried to prolong his [Balder's] life.
Sleet-den [Hell's Hall] swallowed Balder down. All things wept for
him ; laughter's ban [sorrow] was fated to them. Widely known is the
story of him, why should I keep harping on it? Each man's own sorrow
is the sorest. It takes two to an agreement. There is often a third, an
odd man, he should be equally fair to each. No one condemns himself ;
so . . . . . When every one's back is up, no one says it is his fault.

  II. STAVES. I must inlay my song with a *burden*, or else it will be
thought a list, as if I had been picking up crumbs ; for my lay is made
up of odds and ends.

  Refrain. The wise man seldom goes astray, yet the Fin-woman could
craze Harold ; she seemed to him as bright as the sun. So it is with
many a man now.

  Scant of space are ships' cabins. The fox he has a crafty mind. The
tongue plays on the broken tooth. 'Tis unsafe to walk on ice in spring.

---

32. See Christian Wisdom, App. 11, 12.   33. Emend., syni, sá var taldr af
miklu kyni.   35. Read, þing, *or* regin, cp. vol. i, p. 124, l. 6.   aukit (auþit),
Cd.   43. Ekki varð at forðum, farald, Cd.   45.=Mythical Ensamples,
l. 43.   Read, Skolla ?   47.=Guest's Wisdom, 163.

Gœfgask mætti af gengi hverr : Gœrva þekki 'sut' hve ferr.
13. Afli of deilir sízt við siá : Sœrli sprakk af gildri þrá :
Stundom þýtr í logni lá : Litlo 'verr at ek ráða fá :'   50
Mœrgom þykkir full-gótt fé : Fræno-skammr er inn deigi lé :
Kvæðit skal með kynjom allt : Konungs morgin er langr ávallt.
14. Bráð-geð láta bœrnin opt : ' Bregðr at þeim er heldr a lopt :'
All-margr er til seinn at sefask : Svá kalla menn ráð sem gefask :
Ekki verða fróðom farald : Finnan gat þó œrðan Harald.   55
Hónom þótti sól-biört sú : Slíks dœmi verða mörgom nú.

II. 15. Auðigr þykkir ser œrinn hvar : Annars ræðir margr of far.
Ör-grannz erom ver lengst á leit : ' Lund-værr þykkir baztr í sveit.'
Skamm-æ þykkja ofin œll : Ekki mart er verra an troll.
'Eigi' spillir hyggins hiali : Hefkat-ek spurt at bersa kali.   60
16. Engi þarf at hræðask hót : Heldr kemr opt við sáran fót.
. . . .   Hlut-giarn ferr með annars sœk.
Nœkkvi ríkstr er heima hverr : . . . .
. . . . . ta-ek um at síðr : Orðin fara þegar munninn líðr.
17. Varla sýnisk allt sem er : ýtom   65
Eigi at eins er í fœgro fengr : Fundit mun þat er reynt er lengr.
Ekki verða fróðom farald : Finnan gat þó œrðan Harald.
Hónom þótti sól-biört sú : Slíks dœmi verða mörgom nú.

III. 18. Efnom þykkir bezt at boa : Brœgðótt reyndizk gemlo foa.
Margar kunni hon slœgðir ser : Slíkt nœkkut gafsk Rannveig mer.
Illa hefir sá er annan sýkr : Eingi veit áðr hefndom lýkr.   71

Few be they that can stand alone. A laggard's haste is little speed.
A man is famed by gaining [nothing succeeds like success] . . . . Never
try to match the sea. Sorli broke his heart for love. Sometimes the
sea will moan in a calm; . . . . Many think too much of money. A soft
scythe is soon blunt; . . . . The king's morning is very long. A child's
patience is soon worn out; . . . . aloft. Men are slow to be soothed
down. Call counsel good as it turns out.—*R*. The wise man . . . . .
The rich man thinks he can stand alone. Most men are busy over their
neighbour's concerns. Little things are the last to be found. A mild
man is the best mate. Violent delights are short-lived. Nothing is
worse than the devil [Troll]; *Anger* spoils the wise man's talk. I never
heard of a bear being frost-bitten. Pay no heed to angry words [hard
words break no bones]. A sore foot is sure to be trod on ; . . . . The
meddlesome man takes on himself his neighbour's business. A man is
king at home if anywhere ; . . . . Words have wings when they slip
the lips. Things are not always what they seem ; . . . . Fair-to-see is
not the only thing worth seeking. You will find it if you seek long
enough.—*R*. The wise man . . . . .
Happy he who lives according to his estate. The vixen outwitted the
old ewe; many were the sleights she knew. (In just such way has
Randwey served me !) It is an ill deed to betray one's neighbour. No

---

49. = Sona-torrek, 33 ff.   52. = Sighvat, xi. 38.   53. Emend.; brað-sett
. . . bragnar, Cd.   57. Cp. Christian Wisdom, 69.   œrinn] einn (erin), Cd.
59. = Sturl. ii. 276.   63. = Guest's Wisdom, 82.   69. bua—fua, Cd.

Bráð-fengr þykkir brullaups frami : Brigða-lengi er hverr inn sami.
  19. Lýtin þykkja skamm-æ skarar : 'Skrautlig kꜵllom ver nafnit
    farar.'
Trautt kalla-ek þann valda er varar : Verða 'menn' þeir er uppi
    fiarar.
'Úgipt verðr í umbúð skiót :' Elin þykkja mꜵrg um liót.   75
Engi of sér við ꜵllom rokom : Iafnan spyri menn at lokom.
  20. Ást-blindir ero seggir svá : sumir at þykkja miꜵk fás gá.
(Þannig verðr um man-sꜵng mælt) : Marga hefir þat hyggna tælt.
  Ekki verða fróðom farald : Finnan gat þó œrðan Harald.
  Hónom þótti sól-biört sú : Slíks dœmi verða mörgom nú.   80

III.

  21. Yndit láta engir falt : All-opt verðr í hreggi svalt :
Andaðs drúpa minnjar mest : Magran skyldi kaupa hest.
Œrit þykkir við-kvæm vá : vin-fengin ero mis-iꜵfn þá.
Fast-halldr var á Fenri lagðr ; fíkjom var hann mer ramligr sagðr.
  22. Grand-varr skyldi inn góði maðr : Gizurr varð at rógi saðr ;
etja vildi hann iꜵfrom saman : Ekki er mer at 'sturv' gaman :   86
Kunna vilda-ek siá við snꜵrom : Sialdan hygg-ek at gyggi vꜵrom :
Vel hefir hinn er sitr of sítt ;—Svart-flekkótt er kvæði mítt.
  23. Iafnan segir inn ríkri ráð : Rꜵskir menn gefa ꜵrnom bráð :
Upp at eins er ungom vegar : Engi maðr er roskinn þegar :   90
Fallz er vꜵn at forno tré : Fleira þykkir goll an sé :
Auð-sénna er annars vamm : Engi kemsk fyr skapa-dœgr framm :
  24. Enginn krettir um annars mein : Alldri læt-ek at munni sein.

---

one knows when the day of reckoning will come.   The bridal glory
blazes high for a day.   A man takes a long time to change.   Foul-cut
hair will soon grow straight ; . . . .   He that has warned one goes blameless ; . . . . ; . . . . ;   There is many a storm in a man's lifetime.   One
can't keep out every splash.   Men should look to the end.   Some
men are so blinded by love that they heed nought.   Love-songs tell many
such tales : many a wise man has been so beguiled.—*R.* The wise man . . . . .

III. END-PIECE. No one will willingly part with a pleasure.   It is
often cold in a gale.   Dead men's leavings wither away.   Buy a horse
when it's lean.   A sorrow is sore to touch ; friendships often fail one
then.   Holdfast was bound round Fenri [the Wolf], it was wonderful
strong they tell me.   The righteous man should be spotless.   Gizur was
proved to have sown discord ; he wished to set the kings at variance ;
. . . . I would be ware of snares ; the wary man seldom has a mis-
chance.   Well fares he that sits quiet with his own.   Chequered is my
song !   The stronger must rule.   Gallant warriors feed the eagles.   Up-
ward runs the young man's path.   No one is full-grown at once.   An old
tree may fall at any time.   More things seem gold than are.   [It's not all gold
that glitters.]   Other men's faults are sooner seen *than one's own.*   No
man can outlive his death-day.   No one dies of another man's wound.
I never found the tongue too slow.   The world, they say, is always

---

Heimi heyri-ek sagt at snui : Sumir einir hygg-ek at mer trui :
Ervitt verðr þeim er 'flla' kann : 'engan þarf at hiúfra mann ;' 95
þannig hefir mer lagzt í lund : Lang-viðrom skal eyða grund.

25. Sialdan hittisk feigs væk frœrin : Flióðin verða at ælðrom
kiœrin.

Lengi hefir þat lýst fyrir mer- : Lítinn kost á margr und ser :
Sagt er frá hve namn-lauss narir : Nú verðr sumt þat er manngi varir :
væri betr at ek þegða þokks : Þat hefir hverr er verðr er loks. 100

26. Þrýtr-at þann er verr hefir 'vallt : Verða kann á ymsa hallt :
Mis-iafnir verða blindz mannz bitar : Bœlit kœllo ver illt til litar :
Eik hefir þat af 'æðrom' skefr : Ekki mart er slœgra an refr :
Iafnan verðr at á-flóð stakar : Auð-fengnar ero gelti sakar.

27. Goll-ormr á ser brenn-heitt ból : Biartast skínn í heiði sól :
Undrom þykkir gagn-sætt gler : Glymjandi fellr hrœnn of sker : 106
Allar girnask ár í siá : Ekki er manni verra an þrá.

Fýsa man-ek ins fyrra vara : Flestr mun sik til nokkurs spara :

28. Geta má þess er gengit hefr : Gœrir sá betr er afund svefr.
Veitkat-ek 'víst' hvat verða kann : Véla er dælst of heimskan mann :
Flá-ráðom má 'sízt' of trua : 'Til sín' skyldi ino betra snua. 111
Hugga skal þann er harm hefir beðit : Hœlzti miæk er at flimti
kveðit.

29. Orða er leitað mer í munn : mælgin verðr oss heyrin-kunn.
Yggjar biórs hverr endir muni : ósýnt þykkir lýða kyni.

---

turning. Some will believe me, I think ; it is hard for him ; . . . . ; . . . . ;
so has my mind foreboded. Storm after storm will destroy a land. A
doomed man's ice-hole is never frozen. Ladies are chosen partners at
merry-makings. This 1 have long known, how small many a man's
mettle is. It is said that the nameless man lingers his life out. The
unlooked-for will sometimes happen. It would be better for me to stop
now! Every one gets his due at last. The wrong man doesn't always lose.
Each man gets the worst in turn. The blind man's bits are not all the
same size. Woe makes a wan face. The oak has what is scraped from
its neighbour. Nothing is slier than the fox. The stream makes one
stagger. A fat hog's guilt is soon proved. The gold-snake has a fiery lair.
The sun shines brightest in a clear sky. Glass is wondrous easy to see
through. The billows fall roaring on the reef. All the rivers make for
the sea. Nought is worse for a man than hope deferred. Fore-warned
is fore-armed. Every man is afeard of something. Tell the story as
it happened. Blessed is the peace-maker. . . . . A fool is soonest
caught. The fool will trust the fiend himself ; . . . the better part.
Comfort the afflicted. Most lampoons are much too strong.

I have been called on to speak, but I shall be called a babbler. Men
are looking out for the end of my song and see it not ; . . . . ; . . . . ; so

---

95. Read, ungan . . . hiuka?   99. Emend. ; = Alexander Saga, where
nennolaus, wrongly ; neflauss, Cd.   100. I. e. þokks betra, *much better*.   101.
= Lesson of Loddfafni, 61.   103. Read, annarri, cp. Hbl. 66.   108. Cp.
ii. 177, verse 15 : Arnor, iv. 18.   109. afund] annan, Cd.   110. villa, Cd. ?
111. Read, má sízt trolli trua, cp. Book vi, § 1, n. 2.   112. flestu, Cd. ; = Christian
Wisdom, 107.   114. endir] eiga, Cd. ?

Eyfit mun sú at-frétt stoða: 'All-miok ero ver lynd til hroða.'   115
Þeygi var siá aflausn ill: Eiga skal nú hverr sem vill.
    30. Stiórn-lauso hefi-ek slungit saman: s . . . . *gaman*

. . . .

. . . . 120

THE SONG OF THE RUNES.

(A Runic Fuþork or a b c.)

FOUND on a fly-leaf of a Norse Law Codex and copied by Ole Worm in the seventeenth century, whose copy, since the vellum is lost, we depend on for a text. However, Worm did not know Old Norse, and moreover thought right to put it into Runes when he published it, so that there are many corruptions and mistakes, some of which defy all resti- tution. It is evidently not older than the twelfth century, as the dropping of 'h' before 'r' shows, and it is possibly derived from *Old English* models, in imitation of such poems as that in the Exeter book. Where the Norse and English words do not correspond, the author has taken the Old English name unaltered, and seized upon the nearest Norse equivalent word of the like sound, e. g. the English 'Cǽn,' a torch, is made into the Norse 'Kaun,' a kind of blain which breaks out on children; and 'Ōs,' a god, Anse, is metamorphosed into 'Oss,' an oyce or river mouth.

The author alludes to Christ, the creation, the sacrament or halidom; and to the stories of Frodi and his generosity, of Loki and his contriving a net to catch Andware, of Regin and his sword.

Concerning the Runes, their character, origin, and extent, a brief account is given in the Icelandic Reader, pp. 444–458.

A RUNIC FUÞORK.

ᚠ   Fé veldr frænda rógi: Fǿðisk ulfr í skógi.

ᚢ   Úr er af eldo iarni: Opt sleipr rani á hiarni.

ᚦ   Þurs veldr kvenna kvelli: Kátr verðr fír af elli.

ᚱ   Óss er flestra ferða: Enn skalpr er sverða.

I have done my task, let him have it who will. I have put together a rudderless *dwarves' ship* [piece of verse] for entertainment.

Money (Fee) makes strife between kinsmen: The wolf is bred in the wood.
Steam comes from hot iron: The ice on a slope is often slippery.
'þ' causes hysterics: Old age seldom makes a man cheerful.
Every firth has an *Oyce* (mouth): And every sword a scabbard.

---

2. Ur er af ellu iarni opt sleipur Rani a hiarni, Worm.   3. kvillu . . . ellu, Worm.   4. Oys er flestra ferða, Worm.

ᚱ Reiᚦ kveða rossum nesta: Regin á sverðit bezta   5
ᚴ Kaun er bági barna: Bǫl gœrir 'neor fiolvarna.'
ᚼ Hagl er kaldast korna: Kristr skóp heim inn forna.
ᚾ Nauᚦ gœrir nappa kosti: Naktan kelr í frosti.
ᛁ Ís kǫllom brú breiða: Blindan þarf at leiða.
ᛅ Ár er gumna gróði: Get-ek at œrr var Fróði.   10
ᛍ Sól er landa liómi: Lútig at helgom dómi.
ᛏ Týr er ein-hendr Ása: Opt verðr smiðr at blása.
ᛒ Biarkan er lauf-grœnst lima: Loki brá flærðar síma.
ᛚ Lögr er þat er fellr or fialli: Fœst en goll ero halli.
ᛘ Maᚦr er moldar-auki: Mikil er greip á hauki.   15
ᛦ Ýr er vetr-grœnst viða: Vant er þar er brennr at svíða.

The *Cart* comes next the horse: Regin had the best of swords.
A *Blain* is a baby's ailment: Bale makes the colour wan.
Hail is the coldest of grain: Christ made the ancient world.
Need gives little choice: The naked man is bitten in frost.
Ice we call the broadest of bridges: The blind man must be led.
A good *Harvest-season* is an increase for men: Frodi was open-handed
I know.
The *Sun* is the earth's torch: I bow to the halidom.
Tew is the one-handed Anse: A smith has often got to blow.
The *Birch* has the greenest-leaved branches: Loki braided a coil of
falsehood.
The *Loch* falls from the mountain: Gold is set with gems.
Man is a heap of dust: The hawk's clutch is broad.
The *Yew* is the most winter-green of trees: Smart is wont to follow
scald.

5–6. Ridhr kvæða rossum vesta Raghn er sverðit bradesta.   Kaun er beggia
barna Böl giorer near folvarna, Worm.   13. Loki bar flærdar tima, Worm.
14. Fost en gul eru nalli, Worm.   15.=The Sun Song, l. 60, and the Waking of
Angantheow, l. 38.   16. Yr er urtur gronst viða, Worm.

BOOK X.

MEDIÆVAL AND BOOK POETRY.

THIS Book forms a necessary conclusion to the foregoing series. In it are gathered such pieces of genuine worth as may illustrate earlier poetry (sections 1, 5, 6, 7); and such notable and representative pieces as may show how Mediæval Influences affected Northern poetry, and led the way to fresh and distinct kinds of composition, the full history and development of which lie beyond the scope of these volumes (sections 2-7).

In SECTION 1 is Merlinus-Spá, a translation of Geoffrey of Monmouth's *Vaticinatio Merlini*, made by Gunnlaug, the Thing-ore monk, about the beginning of the thirteenth century.

SECTION 2 contains several satirical poems which close the series of genuine *old-metre verse.*

SECTION 3 comprises a collection of *Dance-burdens.*

In SECTION 4 are set the two oldest *Rimur,* followed by a collection of *Ditties* and *Impromptus* in the same metre.

SECTION 5 contains what is left of *Index-poems* by scholars on early topics.

In SECTION 6 are given the *Thulor,* mnemonic verse-graduses of high value, as illustrating the early poetry from which they were compiled.

SECTION 7 completes the whole with *Skalda-tal,* the old *prose-roll of court-poets.*

The verse in this Book is as a rule inspired by either foreign mediæval example or by antiquarian zeal, and is thus in spirit and style distinct from the poetry of earlier days.

§ 1. MERLINUS-SPÁ; OR,
THE PROPHECY OF MERLIN.

AN early versified paraphrase of Geoffrey of Monmouth's well-known prophecy, the text of which is freely treated and amplified by one who knew some, at least, of the old Heroic Lays, as we can see by the stray imitations and phrases cited from the Volo-spá, the Lays of Helgi, the Waking of Angantheow, Lay of Gripi, the old Wolsung Play with its insertions, etc. This is especially remarkable, as we have but few other proofs of these poems being known in Iceland during the Middle Ages.

Merlinus-Spá is only found inserted in the Hawks-bok text of Breta-Sögur, written in the delicate hand of Hawk himself (who died at a high age in 1334), with the heading ' Hér eptir [Merlin's words] hefir Gunn-laugr munkr ort kvædi þat er heitir Merlínus-Spá.' But in the other better text of Breta-Sögur we find the fuller statement, ' on which is formed the greatest part of the poem which is called the Prophecy of Merlin, which Gunnlaug Leifsson the monk made, and many men know that poem by heart.' This MS., however, omits the poem.

Bishop Bryniolf (died 1675), finding the ink of the text of Hawks-bok faded and yellow, handed it over to the clever penman Sigurd Johnsson, the Lawman (died March 4th, 1677), to be freshened up by inking it over with black ink. Sigurd has only added to the difficulty of reading the poem, for he often makes mistakes in running the letters over again. Many of these errors were corrected by the late Mr. John Sigurdsson, who was particularly keen-sighted and correct in the reading of such difficult manuscripts, in his editio princeps of Breta-Sögur, 1849. A few further emendations we have been able to supply (as in l. 440). The poem is in two sections or books.

Gunnlaug, a literary man of note in his day, was a Benedictine monk of Thingore in North Iceland, and died at a high age in 1219. (See Prolegomena.) Whence he got his early copy of Geoffrey of Monmouth we do not know, the one which comes last in Geoffrey's book, and refers to the future, standing first. Maybe that, like his older contemporary Bishop Thorlac, he had travelled and studied in England; if so, his journey would fall in c. 1170–1180. His paraphrase is a proof of the wide popularity of Geoffrey's romantic book.

I. FIRST SONG.

RÁÐOMK segja sunn-báls viðom
   spár spakligar spá-mannz göfugs,
þess er á breiðo Bretlandi [sat] ;
hét Merlinus marg-vitr gumi.
Sagðr var lýðom ok land-rekom
myrk at ráða mörg rök fyrir ;
kærr var hann Kristno kyni þióðar,
varað á moldo maðr vitrari.
   Leitiga ýtom orð at vanda
(viti flotnar þat) frœðiss þessa :   10

heldr fýsomz nú fornra minna
miðsamlig rök mönnom segja.
Liós man lýðom lióð-borg vera
þó er í frœði flest at ráða
þat-er fyrir ' iöfurr öldo ' sagði
Brezkri þióðo.—Nú skal brag kveða.

   Vaxa í víðri Vintonia
(þat er borgar nafn) brunnar þrennir :
þeir muno láði lœkjom skipta

þrír úlíkir í þriá staði. 20
Einn er brunna baztr at reyna,
eykr auð-stöfom aldr ef drekka :
né sótt höfug sœkir hölða
þá er bergt hafa beisko vatni.
Illr er annarr, allir svelta
þeir-er af bekkjar bergja drekko ;
þó er enn þriðja þyngst at reyna ;
deyja þeir allir er þar drekka af,
né hræ guma hyljask foldo.
Vilja hölðar hylja brunna 30
þá er flestom hal fiör-spell gœra ;
enn þat lýðir á lög bera ;
allt verðr at öðro an áðr sé,
grund at grióti, griót at vatni,
viðr at ösko, enn aska at vatni.
Farið er at meyjo marg-fróðastri
í kapps-auðga Knutz-skógar-borg,
at hon lækningar leiti fyrðom
ok hon firri menn fári slíko.
Tekr hon at reyna ok at ráða fiölð, 40
tekr hon íþróttir allar fremja ;
andar síðan snót á brunna
ok þá bruð-þurra báða gœrvir.
Hon þá drekkr et dýra vatn,
ok máttr við þat magnask brúðar,
berr hon í hœgri hendi sinni,
kyn-stór kona, Calidonis skóg ;
enn í lófa man Lunduna-borg.
Gengr hon síðan gótt frón yfir,
svá at sporom snótar sprettr upp logi 50
með römom reyk Rutheneos ;
sá vekr ok ' verkn ' ver-þióðo gœr.
Gœrisk ógorligt óp í landi,
er goll-skögul grætr há-stöfom ;
ok þióta tekr þióð með henni
innan um alla ey með hringom.
Hiörtr drepr hána, hinn er tvenna fimm
' hræs ' á hausi horn-kvisto berr ;
hafa korono kvistir fiórir,
enn sex aðrir sialfir verða 60
at vísundar verstom hornom ;
þeir þiótandi þriár um rœra
búnir at berjask Bretlandz eyjar :
þá mun vakna viðr enn Danski
ok mannz röddo mæla sialfri :
Kom þú Cambria með Corn-Bretom,
segðu Vintoni völlr þik um gleypir ;
fœrðu hirðiss siót hinig er leggja
lung at láði ; munu liðir allir
höfði fylgja ; þat er hialp guma. 70
Enn sæti hans sund-dýr fagna,
hans mun stóll vera yfir stöðom tvennom ;

þó hefir gumnom grandað mörgom
hvítrar ullar hvers-kyns litir.
Borg mun falla, veit-ek bana þióðom,
því-at hon eið-rofa áðr um gœrðisk :
munu grið-bítar gœrla drepnir ;
geldr Vintona vándra manna.
Mun biarn-ígull borg upp gœra,
smíðar hæsta höll land-reki : 80
hána mun remma ríkr odd-viti
fimm hundroðom fagra turna.
þat Lundunom líkar ílla,
eykr hon þrem hlutom þiokka veggi,
kostar hon keppa við konung iðnir,
ferr suðr um Fiall frægð af smíði ;
enn Tems um borg tekr at geisa.
Enn it horska dýr hlezk aldini
harðla góðo því-er hilmr velr ;
koma foglar þar fliúgandi til 90
af vám víða vitja epla.
Enn biarn-ígull býr um vélar,
leynir hann eplom Lundunom í ;
grefr í grundo götor háligar.
fýstr til fengjar, flá-ráðogt dýr.
þá mun or moldo mæla steinar
ok ver-þióðar væl upp koma ;
ey man víðaz, enn Valir skialfa,
ok siór saman sœkja fíkjom,
svá at millim landa mál um heyri. 100
Kemr or skógi Kalaterio
fogl fliúgandi, sá-er fira villir ;
flýgr um nóttom, nýsir gœrla,
kallar hegri hvern fogl til sín ;
er um tví-vetri tál-ráð samið ;
flykkja fuglar, fara þeir í sæði,
eyða þeir ökrom ok aldini ;
sultr verðr ok sótt, sé-ek mart fyrir.
mann-dauðr mikill, mein gengr um þióðir.
Enn fogl eptir þat ferr vestr í dal, 110
þann er Galabes gumnar kalla ;
hann mun hefja í eð hæsta fiall,
ok þar verpr í eikr-limom
hreiðr hegri, hræ-fogla verstr ;
þriá klekr hann unga því hreiðri í,
eigi er hegra kyn hug-þekkt firom :
þar er vargr ok biörn, ok at víso refr
slœgr ok ' sínom ' sialdan er alinn.
Vaxa þar ballir upp brœðr saman,
erat giarnir þeir gótt at vinna : 120
refr á móðor ræðr grimmliga,
tapar henni sá týnir sauða ;
er gren-bui giarn á ríki.
Brœðr vill hann sína beita vélom,
tekr ors-höfuð hildingi á sik ;

22. = Old Play of the Wolsungs, l. 294. 35. at osko vatn, Cd. 56.
ringom, Cd. 65. = Lay of Gripi, l. 67. 85. keppir, Cd. 91. Emend. ;
vagom, Cd.? 98. viðar, Cd. 108. = Volo-spá, l. 128. 113-114. þar
verpr . . .] thus emend. ; Cd. faded and uncertain. 119. allir, Cd. 125. ors-]
emend. ; hors-, Cd.

enn hodd-skata hræðaz báðir :
flýja barmar brott or landi.
Í suðr skal sveitar leita,
vekr vargr ok biörn villi-galta ;
enn galti þeim gengi síno   130
heitr hvatliga, því-at hann hug truir.
þeir snarliga sund-rökn bua ;
dragaz lítinn þeir land-her saman ;
gnýr of marr, gengr lið roa,
hylr Högna siöt herr Corn-Breta.
Halda þeir sunnan um svalan ægi
Bretlandz á vit, buaz til rómo :
enn refr hinig með rekka lið
ferr fráliga fold at verja.
Hríð gœriz hialma, hlífar klofna,   140
ero ramliga randir kníðar ;
gnesta geirar, er guðr vakin,
verðr víða lið at vall-roði :
dregr él yfir ógnar-liǫma ;
gœrir driúgan dyn dýrra malma ;
gnýrr er á glœstom Göndlar himni ;
ok i hörðom hlam Hlakkar tiöldom ;
erað skiól-samar sköglar treyjor ;
hrýtr hagl boga hlífar gegnom ;
grenja gránir garmar sliðra ;   150
bítr fránn freki ferð hels-gerðar ;
rýr gramr guma gollar-hallir ;
bregðr ben-logi bygðom hiarna ;
ero brotnar miök borgir heila.
Sé-ek vé vaða, verðr flýtt skaða,
syngr sára-klungr snyrti-drengjom :
enn á leið fara læ-giörn ara
ióð ok ylgjar enn til sylgjar ;
hrapa hræ-giörn heiðingja börn.
Enn refr gerir ráða á galta,   160
því-at hann reisa máat rönd við hánom ;
svá lætr döglingr sem hann dauðr sé ;
erað lík hulið lofðungs Breta.
Enn galti þat gerrat reyna,
blæss hann í andlit ok í augo gram ;
enn refr við þat ræðr á galta ;
fær hann af hánom fót enn vinstra,
hlust ina hœgri ok hryðjar-nes ;
enn í fialli felz fá-dyggt höfuð,
hyggr kærr iöfurr kyn at œxla :   170
Enn villi-göltr vargi ok birni
segir sárliga sorg ok misso :
enn hraustir brœðr hugga galta,
kveðaz sár muno sialfir grœða ;
fara skulom báðir fótar at leita
hlustar ok hala þer. Her bíðtu, galti !
Enn refr ofan renn or fialli,
ferr fár-hugaðr finna galta ;

hann býðr sættir af svikom einom,
kvezt hann mart við svín mæla vilja :   180
Heyrðu mer, galti, (ek mun heill vera,
svík-ek aldregi svín í trygðom) :
fund skulom leggja ok frið gera,
skaltú einn gera okkar í millom.
Er fundr lagiðr, ok friðr samiðr,
koma mildingar mál-stefno til :
enn á fundi þeim flærðir reynaz,
banar hertoga Brezkr land-reki ;
ok á sialfan sik síðan festir
leparðz höfuð lofðungr at þat :   190
ræðr hann lýðom ok lofða fiölð,—
þar þrýtr þessa þengils sögo.

Ok svíns [líki] á sik h. . . .
bregðr, ok brœðra bíðr slœgliga :
Enn er þeir koma kosti at fœra
bítr hann báða tvá ok banar hlýrom.
Er á hans dögom högg-ormr alinn,
sá-er fyrðom vill fiör-spell gœra :
svá er hann langr, at um Lundunir
heiðar hvalr hring of mælir ;   200
ok svá öðr, at urðar-lindi
um-líðendr alla gleypir.
Hann Cambrie kallar sveitir
ok Norðhumro nánar hiarðir,
ok ú-trautt Tems at þurro
drengs dolg-þorins drekka lýðir.
Verða síðan et sama ár
lœpartar tveir linni bornir :
þeir hafa brúsa böl-giörn höfoð,
ero dáð-lausir döglings synir :   210
þeir flestar taka fliöða sveitir,
her-vígs ramir, ok hóra mengi ;
ok sam-eignat sínnar kvánar
gœra geir-vanir ; geigr er í slíko.

Langt er at tína þat-er lofða vinr
um aldar-far ýtom sagði :
er fæst í því fagrt at heyra ;
læt-ek liða þat, ok lok segja.
Verðr á foldo, (kvað enn fróði halr)
styrjöld mikil, stórar ógnir,   220
víg ok vélar, varg-öld, ok köld
hrimi hvers-konar hiörto lýða.
þá muno gleymaz gálausir menn,
ok sæl-lifir seggir drekka,
leita at-fanga, ok við fé una,
vell at œxla ok vegs-muni :
hagr gœriz hölða hættr í mörgo,
munað fyrða ráð fagrt at reyna ;
dyljaz driúgom draums ívaðendr,

---

134. gnyr er meirr, Cd.   135. Corn-Breta] her korn skipa, Cd.   141.=
Hlod and Angantheow Lay, l. 60.   144.=Helgi and Sigrun, l. 81 ; the Western
Wolsung Lay, 70.   147.=Gretti, l. 1.   153.=Helgi and Sigrun, l. 213.   155.=
The Lay of Darts, l. 24.   159. her numin hvartveggi, Cd.   161. mott, Cd.   164.
gerrat] thus Cd.   170. Or kœnn?   181. Trúðu, Cd.   186.=Helgi and Sigrun,
l. 49.   221-2.=Volo-spá, l. 133.   225. at fagna, Cd.   229. drams, Cd.

við sialfa sik, siask ekki at. 230
Verst er í heimi, veitað sun föðor,
slíta þeir sifjom svá synir við feðr:
kannaz engi[r] við kuńna menn,
né nána frændr, nirðir bauga.
Höfugt er at heyra þatz um her gœriz;
lifa fénaðar fyrðar lífi;
hyggja á þenna þrá-giarnan heim,
ok hvers-konar hafna gœezko.
Mun eð hvíta silfr höldom granda,
ok goll gœra gumna blinda; 240
himni hafna, enn á hauðr siá,
svíkr of-drykkja ýta mengi.
Lifir in Danska drótt at holdi,
gœrir eyvið ser öld at móti:
því muno en tígno tíð-mörk himins
liósi síno frá lýð snua.
enn grund eptir þat gróða hafnar,
né skúr ofan or skýjom kemr;
sól ok máni sialf annan veg
fara fagr-sköpuð an þau fyrr hafi: 250
ok þar á hlýrni heiðar stiörnor
má marka því moldar hvergi;
sumar fara öfgar, sumar annan veg
af enni gömlo göngo sinni;
sumar sœkjaz at, enn sumar firraz,
bregða liósi ok litom fögrom;
berjaz vindar,—þau ero veðr mikil,—
ok hlióm gœra meðal himin-tungla.
Geisar geimi, gengr hann upp í lopt,
slíkt er ógorligt ýta börnom; 260

slíkt er ógorligt upp at telja;
mun en forna mold firir-verða.

Væri mart mönnom kynna
or folk-stafs forno kvæði;
ek mun þó þeygi fleira
þróttar-þings-þollom segja:
þó hefi-ek sagt seggja kindom
slíkt er bók brögnom kynnir:
nýti ser niótar stála
slíka sögn, ok sésk fyri! 270
siá við synð ok svika ráðom
ok allz kyns illom verkom!
drýgjom dáð, Dróttinn elskom!
hriudom ört illo ráði!
Skriúpt er líf lýða barna
undir hregg-ská heiðar tialdi;
enn lífs laun líða eigi,
góð eða íll, gumna mengiss.
Gleðjomk öll í góðom hug,
ok við ván vegs ok dýrðar; 280
gætom góðs, gleymom illo,
eflom opt andar prýði:
biðjom opt bragna stilli
œztan eflð öllo hiarta;
ok víð-frægr virða stióri
dœgr ok dag dróttar gæti!
Ok her-þarfir hrindi gœrla
gumna-liðs grandi hverjo:
svá at til lífs leiði gœrva
þióðar vörðr þetta mengi! 290

II. SECOND SONG.

Nú skal-ek flotnom þat-er forðom var
(hlýði fróðir mer fyrðar!) segja:—
At buðlungr sat Bretlandi at;
hét vell-skati Vortigernus.
Iörð var forðom fyrr-kend Bretom,
sú-er Englom er eignuð síðan;
þvi-at en Enska þióð áðan vélti
breks ósama Brezka hali;
ok láð þeirra með liði miklo
sialf eignaðisk í sögom fornom, 10
ok þar-er Kristnir kœnir byggja
áðr tók heiðin þióð hallir smiða.
Er átt-bogi Enskrar þióðar
Saxneskr sagaðr í sögom fornom:
þaðan eflðosk þeir til þrimo geira
landi at ræna lofðung Breta.
Enn hers-iaðarr halda máttið
Brezkri iörðo né bauga fiölð;
allt fór enn heiðni herr eð eystra
eldi ok iarni eylandz iaðar. 20

Enn hertogi bœliss leitar,
gœrisk traustan turn tiggi at smíða;
ok þangat til þeirrar gœrðar
samnar mörgom mildingr smiðom.
Kómo til smiðar spakir völundar
(þat-er ýtom sagt) uppi í fialli:
enn þat er drengir á degi gœrðo
sá þess engan stað annan morgin.
Kalla lét fylkir fróða seggi;
frá gunn-þorinn gramr hvat voldi, 30
er gœrla hvarf grund-völlr sá
brott sem grund gomol gleypði steina,
eða ham-loðin . . . . . . eldi.
Einn var maðr sá-er myrkva frétt
fyr skatna skýrom skynja kunni,
hét Yngva vinr Ambrosius;
ok enn ágæti öðro nafni
Merlinus sá maðr kallaðiz.
þat kvað valda ver-dags hötuðr
at þar undir var úlítið vatn. 40

---

232. = Volo-spá, l. 131. 248. né] ok, Cd. 251. = Volo-spá, l. 176. 259.
= Volo-spá, l. 177. 260. = Lay of Darts, l. 35. 262. firir-verða] affirum, Cd.
287. = Vellekla, l. 85. 17. = Western Wolsung Lay, l. 56.

Bauð grund grafa gumna stióri;
reyniz spaklig spá-mannz saga.
Ok enn fróði halr frétti lofða
hvat undir vatni væri niðri;
ok er engi þat annarr vissi
sagði fylki flein-þollr 'spökom:'—
　Sofa þar í dimmo diúpi niðri
tvennir ormar tveimr hellom í;
þeir ero lindar landz óglíkir,
sé-ek rauða seil rás ok hvíta.　　50
Láttu grund grafa, gœra skorninga,
(sagði Merlinus menja deili),
veitið vatni,—ok vitið síðan
hvat spáð hafi spillir bauga,
þat er nýlunda—niðr or fialli.
Gœrðo greppar þat er gumnom bauð;
varð vatni niðr veitt or fialli;
ok seim-gefendr snáka þekðo
trygðar lausa, sem týr firom
hafði Hristar hug-spár sagat.　　60
Ok driúgligir drekar vöknoðo,
gœrðoz báðir brott or rúmi;
rennask síðan snart at móti
fróns fá-sýnir frœknir baugar;
gœriz sókn mikil snáka tveggja,
gapa grimmliga grundar belti;
höggvar hæknir hauðrs girðingar,
blásask eitri á ok blám eldi.
For-flótti var fránn enn rauði,
bar enn liósi hann liðr at bakka;　　70
enn hann hagliga hrœkkr at móti,
elti hann enn hvíta hug-trúr dreka:
þeir víg gœra vatz far-veg í,
ok lengi hvatt linnar berjaz;
mega ormar þar ymsir meira,
ok ymsir þeir undan leggja.
Segðu, Merlinus, (kvað men-broti),
ertu fróðari fyrðom öðrom:
hvat tákna man tveggja orma
úgœrligt víg aldar-börnom.　　80
Grét gumna vinr, er hann greiða bað
þengill göfogr þessa hegjo;
ok eptir þat aldar snytrir
rök-stælta spá rekkom sagði:—
　Táknar inn rauði rás fagr-sili
(kvað bjóðr bragar) Brezka lýði;
enn inn hvíti naðr þá ena heiðno þióð,
er byggja man Brezkar iarðir.
Er harmr mikill höldom segja;
segi-ek sigr hafa snák enn hvíta;　　90
láð mun leggjaz ok lýða fiölð,
muno dreyrgar ár ór dölom falla;
faraz mun Kristni, kirkjor falla,
(sá er harmr höfugr); herr er í landi;
þá man enn eflaz en auma þióð,
áðr er harðla hnekkt hennar kosti.

Muno þar í líki lofðungar koma
(sá er vegligastr) villi-galtar;
hann full-tingir fáráðom her,
ok und fótom treðr ferðir Saxa;　　100
fersk undir hann foldo grœnni
ok eyja fiölð í út-hafi,
Íra ok Engla ok út-Skota,
víðom löndom Valskra þióða,
Noregs síðo ok Norðr-Dana;
ok Rúmverjar ræsi ugga,
megoð reisa þeir rönd við stilli.
Mart veit-ek annat um men-brota,
enn ek óglœggt ség œrlög konungs;
hann muno tigna tungor lýða,　　110
sá mun gramr vera gumnom tíðastr;
ey man uppi öðlings frami,
ok hans hróðr fara með himin-skautom.
Ok áttungar sex ens ítra grams
laða at lofðungi landi ok þegnom:
enn eptir þat orms ens hvíta
verðr meira vald an verit hafði;
hónom falltingir Fenrir sióvar,
þeim er Affricar útan fylgja;
verðr Kristni-brot um kyni þióðar;　　120
þó muno sialfir síðar nœkkvi
Enskir lýðir allir skíraz.
Liðr stóll Lundunom or
í ena breiðo borg Cantara,
ok langa tígn Legionum
taka mun en mœta Menevia.
Stór verða rök; rignir blóði;
hár snarpr at þat sultr mannkyni.
Enn inn rauði snákr efliz síðan,
fær hann af miklo mátt erviði;　　130
liðr nauð yfir naðr inn hvíta,
er hans kyn kvalið ok konor ristnar,
ræntr er hann borgom ok bui mörgo,
fé hvers-konar, foldo grœnni,
ero grimmliga gumnar drepnir.
Hníga fyr Brezkom braguinga kon
siklingar siau sigri numnir;
ok heilagr verðr herja deilir
einn af Enskom öðlingom siau.
Sá er slíkt gœrir mun sialfr taka　　140
eir-mann á sik aldar stióri;
ok of há hlíði hilmir síðan
eir-hesti á ítarligr sitr,
gætir Lunduna lof-sæll konungr.
þá gœrvisk þat um þióð Breta,
er þeim enn hefir áðr um grandat,
at þeir sialfir sízt sáttir verða,
deila þeir um veldi ok um víða fold,
ero kapp-samar kindir Brezkar.
Kemr bardagi buðlungs himins　　150
ákafr um her, ári steypir;
kvelr enn harði hel-verkr fira,

---

46. Read, spakr.　　49. ulíkir, Cd.　　113.= Lay of Gripi, l. 40.　　114.
sex] om. Cd.　　127.= The Lay of Darts, l. 2.　　149. -samir, Cd.

megoð dauðan her dróttir hylja,
liðr sultr ok sótt at sigr-viðom,
missir manna, mörg stríð höfug.
Láð muno láta, þeir-er lifa eptir;
ferr en þing-diarfa þióð or landi;
býr blezaðr gramr (sá er Brezkr iöfurr)
skip sín á brott, ok hann skiótla verðr
taliðr tír-göfugr tolfti í Höll   160
sæll með sælom settr Goðs vinom.
Svá tœmiz láð lýða börnom—
drífr hryggr heðan herr or landi :—
at skógar þar skiótla vaxa
er ár-samir akrar vóro
fyrr með fyrðom á fold Breta.
þá mun enn hvíti hiarl-þvengr fara,
snót Saxneska snar-ráðr laða,
ok með miklom mann-fiölða kemr
fiarð-byggs-Skögul fold at byggja.   170
Man sáð koma sinni öðro
útlent yfir óra garða ;
enn ' sumt yfir ' á svölom barmi
eylandz þrumir ormr enn rauði.
Fær hann lítið af landino ;
þá korónask kapps hvít-dreki,
ok Saxneskir seggir ríkja ;
enn eir-iöfurr ofan at stíga
verðr af bröttom borgar armi.
Ero lauf-viðar liósom fiötri   180
tak-mörk gefin í tali ára ;
munað hann ríkja um en römmo sköp,
né því eno fagra fróni ráða.
Vera mun ára í aga miklom
fimtán tigi foldar belti ;
enn tí-rœð tíri göfgaðr
hundruð þriú hann mun sitja
Lundunom at ok lýða fiöld.
þá man gumnom ganga at móti
land-nyrðingr hvass lundar fiötri,   190
ok blóma þá á brott reka
er vestrœnir vindar grœddo.
Mun goll gloa Goðs húsom á ;
enn lögðiss veðr lægr þeygi,
man trautt taka tál-samr dreki
híð sín mega, þvi-at honom nálgaz
víti fyr vélar þatz hann verðr bera.
Fá mun hann uppgang afar-lítla stund,
hnekkir honom hring-serkjat lið ;
kœmr sunnan sú sveit um ægi,.   200
er hann ríki mun ræna miklo.
Sá mun lofðungr, er liði stýrir,
brátt Brezkom her byggja iarðir ;
mun sáð tekit snáks ens hvíta
endr or ófám aldin-görðom.
þá mun hann gialda grimmra ráða,
er hans tiundað tál-aukit lið ;
verðr hann grœnni grund at vinna,

ok hann upp frá því aldri ríkir ;
tekr hann svá fyr svik sárar hefndir. 210
Ríkja enn at þat ormar tvennir,
missir annarr þar aldr fyr skeyti,
enn annarr mun aptr um hverfa
und skugga nafns, at sköpom vinna.
þá mun ríkja réttlætiss dýr,
þat er Eyverskir ormar hræðaz,
ok fyr sunnan sæ sialfir ugga
viz ramligir valskir turnar.
þá mun goll snarat af grasi mörgo,
flýtr ór klaufom kalfs-ættar silfr ;   220
ero fagr-buin flióð í landi,
verðrat snótom sið-bót at því.
Sprett er í miðjo mót penningom,
mun gœrst gleði, glataz ránsemi,
tennr muno gylð:ss trausti numnar,
ok leo-varga verða at fiskom,
hvassir hvelpar hval-túnom í.
Verðr meinliga mæki brugðit,
sé-ek blóði ben blása móðor ;
liðr mart höfugt yfir lýða kyn ;   230
rýðr varðar blóð Venedociam,
ok síðan sex snarpir lifra
kyns-menn drepa Corineus.
þá muno gumnar gráta á nóttom ;
ok þióð gœra þægjar bœnir ;
þá muno höiðar til himins kosta,
fá eð langa líf lofðar nýtir.
Enn muno í skógi skœðir síðan
vargar vakna, veiða í borgom ;
þeir muno sína sialfir dolga   240
fella eðr fiötra ; fair muno verða
þeir-er treystaz þeim ' telja ' at móti.
Einn sitr nýtastr Nevstrie or
Englandi at auðar skelfir ;
þó [ro] siklingar sunnan komnir
finnm eða fleiri foldo at ráða.
Sία biartar brýtr borgir Íra
ok foldar til fellir skóga ;
gœrir ræsir eitt ríki margra,
tekr leonis lávarðr höfuð.   250
Er í reiðingo ráð þióð-konungs
enn fyrra hlut fylkiss ævi ;
enn inn œfri aldr auð-varpaðar
líkar helgom himin-stilli vel.
Mun hann byskopa borgum skrýða,
ok helgan stað hefja margan,
tígnar borgir tvær pallio ;
gefr hann þjóom Kristz þægjar hnossir.
Verðr af slíko sverð-éls hötuðr
himna-ferðar hug-þekkr grami ;   260
ok at þetta líf þing-diafr konungr
taliðr er tígja tungls með englom.
Glíkt mun gaupo grams ióð vera ;
vill hann sínni þióð sialfri steypa ;

---

160. í tolfta, Cd.   162. tœmir, Cd.   173–4. = Waking of Angantheow, l. 66.
202. = Helgi and Sigrun. 226. -vargar, Cd. 231. = Sun Song, l. 108. 263. gaupa, Cd.

enn af þeim sökom þermlaz hann
bæði Íra ok Engla auðgrar iarðar,
Nevstria ok numinn tígnom.
Enn eptir þat óðals á vit
fara fráliga fyrðar Brezkir ;
þó er illa áðr ært í landi,　　　　270
ero úsáttar Enskar þióðir.
Riðr enn prúði til Perironis ár
hvítom hesti hvatr öldor-
maðr, ok hvítom þar hann markar staf
aldræn yfir á-kvernar hús.
Kalla mun Conan Cadwaladrus
ok skilfinga Skotlandi af ;
rœkkr at grimmo Göndlar éli ;
verðr eð mikla malm-þing l áit ;
svífr eð hvassa hagl tviviðar　　　　280
(hnígr hölða lið) hart af strengjom ;
enn geyst þingat gaflok fara,
megoð Sköglar ský við skotom halda ;
bresta brynjor, bíta malmar ;
ero dreyr-fáðir dörr á lopti ;
fleinn á flaugom, folk í dreyra,
bildr í benjom, broddr á skildi,
hialmr á höfði, hlíf fyr briósti,
geirr á gangi, guðr í vexti :
hittiz targa ok enn togni hiörr,　　　　290
hialmr ok hneitir, hlíf ok örvar,
brynja en Brezka ok brandr roðinn,
mannz máttog hönd ok meðal-kafli,
hvít-mylingar ok hölða bríóst.
Hrapa hrafna gœr, hátt gialla spiör,
er malm-þrima mest á hiarli ;
verðr einn við einn val-köstr hlaðinn,
muno blóðgar ár af biöðom falla ;
enn víg-roða verpr á hlýrni :
falla fyrðar í flein-drífo,　　　　300
verðr Enskri þióð aldr-spell skipat ;
er völlr roðin, enn víg boðin ;
hlýtr hávan sigr helmingr Breta.
Yppir fiöllom fliót Val-breta,
muno Brutus þau bera kórono ;
grœnaz öfigar eikr Corn-Breta,
fagnar slíko fús Cambria.
Eyðiz eyjar ið Enska nafn,
mun hon Anglia eigi kölloð,
hlýtr hon at halda heiti eno forna,　　　　310
kennd er við Brutum Britannia.
Mun villi-göltr víg-diarfr koma
or kyn-stórri Conanus ætt ;
sá víg-tönnom Valskar hœggr
Yngva son eðr or skógi,
þó mun hilmir hollr snlá-viði.
Muno Rábítar ræsi ugga

út í heimi ok Affrikar ;
för mun vísir víð-lendr gœra
á eð ýtra œgr Ispaniam.　　　　320
Sitr eptir hilmi hafr at löndom,
hans erat skilja skap frá vífni ;
berr hann á höfði horn ór golli,
er skegg skata skapat or silfri.
Blæss ' mistar vinr or nösom tiossa '
þoko því-líkri at þekr um ey ;
friðr [mun] um fylkiss fas'r líf-daga,
brestr eigi þá ár í landi.
þá muno [um] foldo fögr víf draga,
blístrar meyjom metnoðr í spor ;　　　　330
muno kvensemi castra smíðoð,
svíkr gumna vin girnd en ranga.
Verðr at blóði brunnr enn fagri,
þó er á grundo gnótt hvers-konar ;
enn á holmi hildingar tveir
berjaz um brúði biart-haddaða,
sú er í víðri Vadbaculi :
siá þessi rök þrennar aldir ;
þó er lýða ráð liótt fyr Dróttni :
unz land-rekar Lundunom í　　　　340
grafnir or grundo gumnom vitraz.
Kœmr ár-galli enn inn mikli,
ok meinliga mann-dauðr um her,
Eyðaz borgir við bragna tión,
er auðn mikil ítra manna ;
flýr margr á brott maðr or landi.
Kœmr kaup-skapar kapps-góðr þinig
villi-galti virðom samna,
þeim-er af fróni flýðo áðan,
lætr hann byggja þá Brezkar iarðir,　　　　350
borgir eyddar, ból góligost.
Mun hans bríóst vera brögnom fœzla
þeim er fátt hafa fiár með höndom ;
ok en tál-lausa tunga hilmiss
slœkkvir þorsta þióðans liði.
Falla or orða al-mœrri vök
dynjandi ár dróttar stýriss ;
þær muno dœggva dýrar iarðir
geðs í glœstom gollor-heimi,
ok þurrar kverkr þióðar margrar.　　　　360
Upp renn síðan (sé ek þat fyrir)
traust í turni tré Lunduna ;
þrír ero kvistir þeim lundi á ;
enn hann laufi þekr land með hringom.
Kœmr þar af lægi land-nyrðingr hvass,
lýstr hann íllom byl eik af stofni ;
þeir muno kvistir er þruma eptir
þess rúm taka.　þat sé-ek gœrla.
Hylja þeir alla ey með laufi
unz annarr þar öðrom bægir,　　　　370

---

278. rykr af, Cd.　　285. = The Lay of Darts, l. 8.　　dorir, Cd.　　295.
hræva, Cd.　　299. = Helgi and Sigrun, l. 127.　　302. = The Lay of Darts,
l. 34.　　320. hispanian, Cd.　　325. Corrupt.　　336. = Lay of Gripi,
l. 131.　　337. I. e. vado baculi = Stafford.　　345. nytra, Cd.　　356-8. = Some
lost Song ?　　364. = Konunga-tal.　　ringom, Cd.

ok hann eyðir hans öllo laufi;
tekr hann þriú rúm þrek-stórr hafa;
ok hann síðan þekr þiokko laufi
einn um alla ey-barms fiöro:
megoð þá fliúga fuglar í landi, [sín
þvi-at hann œgir þeim, enn hann enn til
laðar fogla fliótt ferð útlendra.
þá man illingar-asni ríkja,
sá er fliótr taka fé goll-smiða;
er lofða vinr latr at hefna 380
gylðiss barna gramr ránsemi.
Ok á hans dögom harðla brenna
ofs-ramligar eikr ór skógom;
enn á lítlom lindar kvistom
vex örliga akarn í lundi.
Ok Ránar vegr renn um ósa
Sabrinus sjau, sé-ek þat fyrir:
enn Óskar-á (þat er undr mikit)
man mánoðr siau máttog vella;
gœrviz fiskom fiör-tión at því, 390
er or sialfom þeim snákar verða.
Muno Badonis-borgar verða
(líðr mart yfir) laugar kaldar;
ok hennar vötn, heil-næm firom,
gœra þá dauða driúgt man-kyni.
Verðr tuttogo tión þúsunda
lióna ferðar Lundunom í;
þeir muno drengir drepnir allir;
gœrir karla tión Tems at blóði.
Muno kofl-mönnom kván-föng boðin,
ero ekkjor þar orðnar margar; 401
enn á köldom kall þeira mest
menn Mundio-montom heyra.

Hér mun-ek létta lióð at semja,
ok spá-sögo spilliss bauga;
þó ero fleiri orð ins fróða mannz;
hefi-ek sumt af þeim samit í kvæði.
þau ero önnor lióð upp frá þessom;
ylfiz eigi auðs ben-draugar
(bið-ek þióðir þess) við þenna brag, 410
þo-at ek mynt hafa mál, at hætti
þeim-er spakr fyrir spiöll um rakði
malm-þings hvötuðr, í mörgom stað.
Viti bragnar bat, þeir er bók lesa,
hve at spiöllom sé spá-mannz farit,

ok kynni þat kalldyrs viðom
hverr fyrða sé fram-sýnna háttr
mál at rekja, þau-er men vitoð.
Lesi Salma spiöll, lesi Spá-manna;
lesi biartar þeir bœkr ok Röðla; 420
ok finni þat, at enn fróði halr
hefir horskliga hagat spá-sögo,
sem fyrir hónom fyrðar helgir.
Virði engi þat vit-lauso,
þótt hann hodd-skötom heiti gæfi
viðar eða vatna, eðr veðrs mikils,
eða allz-konar orma ok dýra;
táknar eðli talðrar skepno
spiör-ráðanda spiöll eða kosti.
Segir Daniel drauma sína 430
marg-háttaða merkjom studda:
kvezt hann driúglig siá dýr á iörðo,
þau-er táknoðo tiggja ríki,
þau-er á hauðri hófoz síðan.
Rekr enn dýri Davíð konungr
marg-falda spá, ok mælir svá:
Fiöil mono fagna ok enn fríði skógr,
enn skœðar ár skella lófom,
ok dalar ymna Dróttni syngja.

Hirtisk hölðar at hæða bœkr, 440
nemi skynsemi, ok skili gœrla
hvat táknað man í tölo þessi.
Eráð enn liðin öll spá-saga;
þó ero mörgom myrk mál propheta.
Frétti fyrðar, þeir-er á fold bua
enn at óra ævi liðna,
hvat um her gœriz ok huga leiði,
beri en nýjo spiöll við spá-sögo;
sé síðan þat hve saman falli.
Varð sú en Enska ætt fyr stundo 450
veldiss missa; nú er Valskr konungr.
þó er þeygi enn þeirra 'hætti'
liðit af láði, né lýðs Breta
hvössom mæki hiarl eignaðiz.

Heilir allir, þeir er hlýtt hafa,
flein-varpaðir frœði þesso!
Gœri gótt gumar, enn glati íllo,
bíði bráða bót af-runa!
Hafi hylli Goðs ok Himin-ríki!

---

374. = Waking of Angantheow, l. 66.　386. asa, Cd.　400. kapps-, Cd.
404. = Western Wolsung Lay, l. 45.　409. Emend.; alviz, Cd.　412. spakr]
spar, Cd.　435. Emend.; enn dýra dom, Cd.; ' ðō '='.ðð.'　437. = Ps.
xcviii. 8.

§ 2. LAST POEMS IN OLD METRE.

WE have noticed in the preceding Books the old metre employed by writers of pseudo-epics and imitations of old poems, as it has been down to our own days. But the old metre was not quite forgotten by the people, and it was put to fresh use by popular singers at the very time when the book-poets were using it for their closet-poetry.

The last *popular* compositions in the Old Metre fall under two heads, *Satire* and *Fairy* or *Folk-lore verse*.

Under the former category, which we shall take first, came the FŒRSLA POEMS at merry-makings, representing a thing *passed* from hand to hand of the present guests, each being bound in turn to say a verse, somewhat after the fashion of Welsh *penillion* singing. These compositions are quite sui generis in Northern verse, where they are the sole remnants of a class of poetry well represented in Greek and Latin literature.

There are remains of two of these poems. At the end of St. Olaf's Life in Flatey-bok (cols. 483–85, vol. ii, pp. 331–35) is placed a Thattr which turns on a curious legend of Phallus-worship in the heathen days of Norway, derived from a piece of verse VOLSA-FŒRSLA, parts of which are cited. It begins with the proper formula, 'There lived in A. a man, etc.,' and is of course in dialogue, touching the Handing on of the Phallus (whence the title), each person in turn taking the emblem and passing it on, till the king casts it to the dog Leri, to the no small consternation of the good-wife. At this point the daughter recognises the king, and—here the piece breaks off incomplete. We have transposed ll. 9–11 to the end, where they ought rightly to come. This half-comic and wholly Aristophanic piece no doubt furnished a model for the humourous treatment of an incident in Gretti's career which was the subject of the next piece.

In Gretti's Saga, ch. 52, it is told that Gretti, after a long career of outlawry, was caught by some farmers who bound him to keep him safe till Wermund, the local chief, should come home and settle his fate. But the question arose, Who should have the care of the redoubtable prisoner? One after another, Helgi of Lauga-boll, Thorkell of Giorwe-dale, Thoralf of Eyre, refuse to take him, and in their puzzlement the worthy churls settle that the only way out of the hobble is to get rid of their prisoner by hemp-solution. Luckily for Gretti, Thorbiorg of Waterfirth (see p. 336) rode up as they had got the gallows ready, and offered to take charge of the luckless prisoner. They gladly closed with her offer, and Gretti was not ill-pleased. 'And,' says one of the editors of Gretti's story, 'on this parley and debate of theirs merry men have made the poem called GRETTIS-FŒRSLA ["the Handing on of Gretti"], and dressed it up with merry words for folk's amusement.' Indeed, the story in the Saga is, we take it, drawn from the poem.

At the end of the AM. 556 vellum of Gretti's Saga, occupying part of three pages, and written in the same fifteenth-century hand as the Saga, is the poem itself. But some 'unco guid' person, offended probably by some too free expressions, has scraped it all out, so that in spite of some trouble and care the Editor was (in 1861) unable to read more than the first line (whereby metre and kind were discovered), and to catch a word here and there, pointing to the drift of the whole.   It would have been about sixty verses or two hundred and forty lines long.

As the last editor of Gretti's Saga could remember Lawman Sturla, the poem can hardly be later than 1300, and, if our guess that it was directly modelled on Volsa-fœrsla be correct, a fair date would be c. 1200.   The verses that follow it at the end of chapter 52 in Gretti's Saga (see above, p. 336) *are not* part of this poem, but, we believe, of Sturla's composition.

There is a third poem in old metre, belonging to the SATIRIC DIVISION, which is worth giving here as a specimen of its class, and as the work of Einar Fostri, whose amusing *Skida-rima* we give below.   It is called SKAUF-HALA-BALKR, 'Sheaf-brush-piece,' and is found on a leaf of AM. 603, a sixteenth-century vellum of Rimur, etc.   Its *authorship* is testified to by Biorn of Skardsa, who gives lines from it, and attributes it to Einar.   It is of the same *metre*, but of even simpler character than Volsa-fœrsla, and begins in the orthodox way : 'An old grey brush had long lived in his earth,' etc.   The word 'balkr' seems to have been the technical name for this sort of composition.

The poem is almost perfect, as the hero is on his death-bed in the last stanza we have; but Biorn of Skardsa knew the last few lines, which are now lost.   The *story* is of an old fox, who, driven out by his vixen wife to get store for the empty larder, meets with an accident on his foray, whereon he returns, and feeling himself on the point of death proceeds to relate the story of his life to his six last cubs.   Uncle Remus will bear faithful testimony to most of Brer Fox's doings.

The poem, which almost deserves a glossary of its own, is full of curious words of life in the author's days on a country farm, the cooking, work, etc., that are not found elsewhere, and gives a good picture of the mediæval Iceland homestead.   It proves the early use of many modern words, and confirms the Editor's guess in the Dictionary (1872) as to 'Tóa'='Tófa,' Brush, Reynard's nickname, and 'yrlingr'='yrmlingr.'   The *date* would be about 1450.

The first edition is that by Mr. Kölbing in 1876, and the few citations in the Dictionary are from memory and not exhaustive, as the Editor had no copy at hand.

VOLSA-FŒRSLA.

(The persons are, a heathen good-man and good-wife, their son and daughter, their man-servant and maid-servant; and as guests in disguise, St. Olave and his two trusty men.)

1.   KARL hefir buit ok kona öldrut
       á andnesi eino hverjo :
    átti son við seima bil
    drengr ok dóttor driúg-skýrliga.

Here the Play begins.

The Thrall 2.   Her megot siá heldr röskligan   5
to Bondmaid :   vingol skorinn af viggs föðor :
             þer er, ambótt, þessi Volsi
             all-ódaufligr innan læra.

---

2. ein hverjo, Cd.   5. megit, Cd.

Good-wife :   3.   Aukinn ertu, Volsi, ok upp um tekinn,
                      líni gœddr, enn laukum studdr :—   10
                      þiggi Mörnir þetta blœti !
                      Enn þú, bóndi sialfr, ber-þú at þer Volsa !
Good-man :   4.   Mundi eigi, ef ek um réða,
                      blœti þetta borit í aptan :—
                      þiggi Mörnir þetta blœti !   15
                      Enn þú son bónda sé-þú við Volsa !
Son :   5.   Berið ér beytil fyrir brúð-konor,
                      þær skulo vingol væta í aptan :—
                      þiggi Mörnir þetta blœti !
                      Enn þú, dóttir bónda, drag-þú at þer Volsa !   20
Daughter :   6.   Þess sver-ek við Gefjon ok við goðin önnor
                      at ek nauðig tek við nosa rauðom :—
                      þiggi Mörnir þetta blœti !
                      Enn þú, þræll hióna, þríf-þú við Volsa !
Thrall :   7.   Hleifr væri mer halfo sœmri,   25
                      þiokkr ok œkkvinn, þrunginn sáðum,
                      an Volsi þessi á verk-dögom :—
                      þiggi Mörnir þetta blœti !
                      Enn þú, þý hióna, þrýstu at þer Volsa !
Bondmaid :   8.   Víst eigi mætta ek við um bindask   30
                      í mik at keyra, ef við ein lægim í andketo :—
                      þiggi Mörnir þetta blœti !
                      Enn þú Grímr gestr vórr, gríp-þú við Volsa !
1st Guest :   9.   Legit hefek víða fyrir andnesjom,
                      snæfgom höndom segl upp dregit :—   35

                      .   .   .   .   .   .
                      þiggi Mörnir þetta blœti !
                      Enn þú, Grímr griði minn, gríp-þú við Volsa !
2nd Guest :   10.   Sá-ek eigi forðom, þó hefig farit víða,
                      flennt reðr fyrri fara með bekkjom :—   40
                      þiggi Mörnir þetta blœti !
                      Enn þú, Aðal-Grímr, tak enn við Volsa !
The King :   11.   Verit hefik stýrir ok stafn-bui,
                      ok oddviti allra þióða :—

                        45
                      þiggi Mörnir þetta blœti !
                      Enn þú, hundr hióna, hirtu bákn þetta !
Good-wife :   12.   Hvat er þat manna mer ókunnra
                      er hundom gefr heilagt blœti ?
                      hefi-ek mik um hiarra ok á hurð-ása !   50
                      vita ef ek borgit fæ blœti 'no helga.
                      Legg niðr, Lærir ! ok lát mik eigi siá,
                      ok svelg eigi niðr, sár-tíkin rög !
The Daughter 13.   Ek sé goll á gestom ok goðvefjar skikkjor,
recognising   mer fellr hugr til hringa ; heldr vil ek ' bing en linga ;'   55
the guests :   kenni ek þik, konungr minn ; kominn ertu, Óláfr.
(The rest missing.)   .   .   .   .

                      GRETTIS-FŒRSLA.

K   ARL nam at búa, beint má því lýsa,
       .   .   .   .   .   í afdali
.   .   .   .

26. þrunginn sáðom] ok þó víðr, Cd. = Lay of Righ, ll. 13, 14.   34. víða]
read, opt ?   36. A line or two missing.   45. Here a line is missing.
48. = Balder's Doom, l. 17.

SKAUFHALA-BALKR, by Einar Fostri.

HEFIR í grenjum gamall skaufali
    lengi buit hiá lang-hölo;
átt hafa þau ser allz upp talda
átián sonu ok eina dóttur.

2. Því vóru nítján niðjar skaufala, 5
hundz iafningja, heldr en tuttugu:
þat sannaðiz fyrða forn-mæli,
at Opt verðr örgum eins vant á tög.

3. Þá vóru burtu börn skaufala
flest öll farin úr föður-garði, 10
þó vóru eptir þeim til fylgdar
þrír yrmlingar ok þriar dætr.

4. Mælti gor-tanni við gren-lægju:
Hvat skulum vinna ver til þarfa?
vit erum orðin veyk-lendut miök, 15
hrygg-snauð harla, en halar rotnaðir.

5. Svarar grenlægja gömul á móti:
Nú eru á burtu börn okkur roskin,
enn þau ung sem eptir sitja,
ok enn ekki á legg komin. 20

6. Þú munt heiman halda verða,
ok afla bráða til búss okkars;
væri þat til vinnu at leggja
sem virðum má verst gegna.

7. Mælti þannin móðir drattala: 25
Matr er eigi meiri mer í höndum,
hala-rófu-bein ok hryggr or lambi,
bóg-leggir þrír, ok bana-kringla.

8. Svó er nú liðit,—segir lág-fæta,—
loð-bakr minn, langt á tíma, 30
vón er upp heðan veðra harðra;
enn at höndum kominn haust-þústr
mikill.

9. Betra er nú bráða at leita,
en þá fyrða fé sítt geyma;
liggja með brúnum lömb hver-vetna, 35
enn á fialli feitir sauðir.

10. Sá er nú tími,—segir rebbali,—
sem seggir munu at sauðum ganga;
víst er allstaðar vón um hunda;
mun á fiöllum nú mann-ferð mikil. 40

11. Vissa ek eigi víst,—segir tófa,—
at þú huglaust hiarta bærir;
þú vilt bölvaðr til bana svelta
afkvæmi þitt ok okkr bæði.

12. Þú skalt ráða,—segir rebbali,—
við man ek leita vista at afla; 46
þó hafa nornir þess um mik spáð,
at mer gömlum glæpaz mundi.

13. Fór heiman þá fliótt drattali,
ok ætlar ser afla at-fanga; 50
fann skiótliga finntán sauði,

ok einn af þeim all-vel feitan.

14. Þat var geldingr gambrliga stór,
grá-kollóttr, gamall at aldri;
vendir skolli víst at hónum, 55
ok með tönnum tók í lagða.

15. Svó lauk skiptum skolla ok sauðar,
at grá-kollr gekk frá lífi;
bióz drattali burtu heim þaðan,
hafði sauð fengit ser til vista. 60

16. Nú skal segja nokkut fleira
frá ferðum hans fyrst at sinni:
heim kom síðla sauð-bítr gamall,
svangr ok sofinn svó til grenja.

17. Kallar kámleitr á konu sína 65
heldr hvass-eygðr hundz iafningi:
má-ek segja þer frá ferðum mínum
heldr hrakliga, sem mer hugr sagði:—

18. Þat var morgin þá ek heiman fór,
hafða ek fengit mer feitar bráðir, 70
bundit bagga, ok á bak mer lagðan,
hugðumk heim flytja hann til bygða.

19. Þá varð mer litið í lág eina
hvar há-fættr maðr hlióp kallandi,
fór með hónum ferlíki mikit, 75
kol-svart at lit; kenda ek hunza.

20. Rétti hann trýni, en rekr upp
siónir,
ok kendi þegar hvar ek keifaða;
mer kom heldr í hug 'hvat ek mundi
vilja,'
vatt-ek af mer vænni byrði. 80

21. Hann tók á skeiði skiótt eptir mer,
skundar hvatliga ok skrefaði stórum;
hlióp ek fráliga heldr undan;
leitaða ek við lífi at forða.

22. Fóru vit lengi um fiallz-hlíð eina
upp ok ofan svó undrum gegndi, 86
hitta ek hamra-skarð ok holu eina,
hlaut ek í hána hræddr at smiúga.

23. Var gren þetta grióti um hvorfit,
mátti hundr þar hvergi inn komaz; 90
gó hann grimmliga, þá hann gat ekki,
garpr gin-mikill, gripit mik tönnum.

24. Þar húkta ek, þó mer íllt þætti,
heldr hund-eygðr ok hræddumk dauða;
hlióp hinn há-fætti fyrir holu-munna, 95
hafði staf stóran ok stakk inn til mín.

25. Mer kom á síðu mikill stafs endir,
mátta-ek hvergi undan hlíða;
þá brotnuðu þegns fyrir skapti
um þvert þungliga þriú rifin í mer. 100

26. Víða er ek þó sárr vorðinn
stráks af stingjum ok stafs-enda;

<hr>

12. þeirra do:tir, Cd.   15. -lendit, Cd.   39. heðan, Cd.   78. kendi] þekti, Cd.

her kom þó at lyktum, at hann heim leitaði,
ok hafði bagga minn burt görvallan.

27. Svó hafa aldri, sízt ek leitaða við,
mer svó tekizt mínar ferðir ;　　106
þat er hug-boð mitt at heðan man ek eiga
skiótt skapliga skamt ólifað.

28. Hef-ek margan heldr hala-feitan
sauð serliga sviptan lífi,　　110
tínt kiðlinga, enn týnt lamb-gymbrum,
gripit geldinga ok gamal-rollur.

29. Hefik með ströndu strokit iafnliga
ok heima um hauga iafnan snudrat,
bitið hef-ek álar, bellt klýpingum,　　115
rifit af þönum rétt húð hverja.

30. Hef-eg optliga óþarfr verit
bænda folki í bygð þessi ;
skoðat iafnlega skreið í hiöllum,
riklinga rár, ok rafa-belti.　　120

31. Hef-eg í-hentað mer hákalz-lykkjur,
ok höggit mer hvinna snepla :
eiga mer allir, ef ek dyl einskis,
ýtar optlega íllt at launa.

32 Forðazt kunna-ek vélar görvallar,
þótt fyrðar þær fyrir mik setti ;　　126
þurfti eingi þess at leita,
þvi-at ek vissa ' vélar görvallar.'

33. Fannzt sá eingi fyrr né síðar
hundr há-fættr eðı hestr í bygðum,　　130
at mik á hlaupi hefði uppi ;
var ek frára dýr en flest öll önnur.

34. Nú tekr elli at mer sækja ;
má-ek allz ekki á mik treysta ;
farinn fráleikr, fit-skór troðnir,　　135
tenn slióvgaðar, enn toppr úr enni.

35. Mun-ek til rekkju reika verða ;
mer tekr verkr at vaxa í síðu ;
svó hef-ek ætlat, siá mun dagr koma
mer yfir höfut minn enn síðazti.　　140

36. þat hlægir mik, þó mun her koma
ór ætt minni annarr verri ;
hann mun mann gera margan sauð-lausan,
ok aldri upp gefa illt at vinna.

37. Bióst þá skolli í ból sitt fara,　　145
beit hann hel-stingi hart til bana :
þar mun hann verða þiófr af-gamall
líf at láta.　(Here the vellum breaks off,
some ten lines missing.)

.　　.　　.　　.　　.　　.　　.

.　　.　　.　　.　　.　　.　　.

38. Hefir balk þenna ok barn-gælur
ort ófimlega Einarr Fóstri.　　150

FAIRY METRE.

EVEN when the time of the 'fœrsla' and 'balkr' had gone by, and all forms of composition were in the Rima Metre, this old metre, or a modification of it, was still employed in pieces relating to the supernatural, especially those dealing with fairies.

The fairies or 'good people' are called in Iceland 'the darlings' (liúflingar), and there are of course many stories about them. One runs thus—A girl had a child by a fairy, and one day the baby was fretful and she could not still it, and the household folk spoke so unkindly of her and the child, that the poor girl sat down heart-broken and burst into tears. Then there came a sweet voice through the window above her, singing a lullaby, and calling down good luck on her child. This song was long remembered, and the more so, that all the blessing it had spoken of came to pass. When the baby-boy was grown up, he and his mother disappeared, and it was said that she had gone off with her fairy lover.

A poem on this story in Epic Metre, supposed to be the very Lullaby of the Fairy, 'Liúflings-Odr,' is to be found in a paper MS. in the AM. collection c. A.D. 1650–1700. There are numerous later copies with many additions, as the piece has always been very popular. From it the Epic Metre has for the last three centuries been commonly known in Iceland as the Fairy Metre, 'Liúflings-Lag.'

Kötlu-draumr, another well-known poem of the same type and cast, tells of a woman, named Katla, who is carried off by a fairy named Kári, who treats her with magnificence, but still she pines to come back, and at last rejoins her husband on Reykholar, much to the sorrow of her fairy lover. After her return she bore a child, who grew up like his father Kári, and became a famous man.

Besides these two, there are many more on kindred subjects, such as Sniors-kvædi, Kringil-nefju-kvædi, Mardallar-kvædi, Wambar-liod,

Thoru-liod, Bryngerdar-liod, and the New Hyndlu-liod. None of the MSS. of these go back 'to vellum,' i. e. beyond the Reformation-time. The poems are of the last years of the Middle Ages, and stand in the same relation to popular stories and folk-lore as the Rímur do to the Book-stories and romances.

After the Reformation the metre was used for other ends, e. g. POETICAL BIOGRAPHY. *Einar the Priest* (1540–1627) reviews his long life in *Æfi-quædi*, and *John the Learned* (1575-1655) does the like in *Fiolmod* (the Curlew).

After them the metre is somewhat neglected, till the Learned Revival when the Eddic Poems came to be known, and many poems to be written in imitation of them. But even in later times the cadence and harmony of John Thorlaksson's translation of Milton, and Grondal's version of Pope, are rather those of Liúflings-lag than Kvido-hattr, and smack rather of the mediæval than the early poetry they were professedly modelled on. Such lines as

> O gef þú góðan mer,
> eður allz öngan hróður,

are far too stiff and monotonous to be like 'Eddic' verse, but exactly fit the popular sixteenth-century metre.

In his contributions to K. Maurer's Islandische Volk-sagen, and in his preface to John Arnason's Icelandic Folk-tales (1862), the Editor has touched on the subject of the Fairy-poems and cited scraps of popular verse of the kind.

===

§ 3. DANZ OK VISUR.

AFTER the Icelandic Saga-time, there comes a blank of some seventy years (1030–1100) before the next literary development, the Biographic Sagas. This interval is an important epoch in Iceland's history, and at the end of it we find ourselves in a different social and political atmosphere from that of the old days: mediæval influence and culture have come in and made many changes. We are here more especially concerned with a new form of popular entertainment, which had been introduced and grown into high favour by the end of the eleventh century—the 'danz.'

Of this amusement we have a description in the Life of Bishop John (d. 1121). When speaking of his patron's strict piety the biographer says, "It was a customary pastime, and not a seemly one, for people to recite, man to woman and woman to man, wanton and ridiculous and improper verses, and this he did away with and forbade altogether. Love-lays and verses he would not hear sung or allow to be sung, yet he could not altogether accomplish this." A parallel MS. reads, "There was a favourite pastime before St. John became a bishop [1106-21] for the man to sing to the woman *in dance* soft and lustful lays, and the woman to the man love-verses; this pastime he did away with and strictly forbade." A third fifteenth-century version of the passage from a later MS. runs, "It was the custom at that time, which was very unseemly, to carry on *botatilldi* [a corruption from some English word, perhaps botafyld, butt-filling or gild-feast], when the man sings to the woman and the woman again to the man wanton and improper verses with allusions and filthy words of love-lays." We have been particular to cite these passages, as their scope and bearing have frequently been misapprehended as if Eddic songs were meant.

Again, in the Life of Bishop Thorlac (b. 1133), ch. 16, it is said of him that in his youth "he took pleasure in tales and poems, and all harpings and carpings and wise men's counsels and dreams, and everything that gentlefolk amuse themselves with, *except songs* ['leikr' here being 'danz']."

And of Bishop Arni (b. 1237) in his youth it is told, ch. 2 of his Life, how, "when his father, Thorlac, went away from Redleek, he made merry with every one, and joined in the popular merry-makings, and this was his way of life till he was at Scal, and then he went with other men to a 'scinnleic' [lit. a *hide-play*, possibly some kind of mumming in which the 'capul-hide' was used to deck out and disguise the players]. At that same play he struck one of his knees down on the hearth-slab in the big room, so that it was badly put out, and he lay in bed nigh a week of it. And after that he was never present at any play of this kind, or dance neither before or after [sic], for he felt that this was a judgment on such unseemly amusements."

In another story in Bishop John's Saga, the *singing of dances* at plays and mummings is indicated. "There was a man named Thori, a house-man of the blessed John, watcher of the sheep at the bishop's dwelling. He was a young man, reckless, little watchful of his words, not regular at service, though he lived in the bishop's house, and Bishop John often admonished him to do better .... It was on a certain holiday, while my lord bishop was at evensong and all decent folk were standing at the service, this man Thori was in the big room after his naughty custom, and fell to *playing* and wrestling with the boys. He was told that the service was over, but he paid no heed to it. And thereupon a sudden punishment overtook him for breaking the bishop's orders, for he fell in the play, and that very tongue of his which he kept so little watch over, was between his teeth and got a sore hurt." The mention of the *tongue* shows that there was singing at all events in the 'play.'

In the Islendinga Saga, ch. 81, where the wanderings of the exiled Bishop Gudmund and his rabble are told of, it is said that at one farm where he was stopping in the North (1229) "when the bishop was gone to bed of an evening, and those who chose had gone to the bath [evidently it was one Saturday], that there was a dance struck up in the big room. Canute the priest sat on the dais, and the room was lighted from above. In came John Birneson from the bath with his bath cap and linen clothes on," etc.

Another mention of dances and plays and amusements is in Thorgil's Saga, ch. 10, where, speaking of the famous banquet at Reek-hill (1119), the author says, "There was now mirth and much merry-making and good entertainment and many kinds of *plays*, both *dance-plays*, wrestling, and telling of tales." So in Islendinga Saga, ch. 295 (1255), "In Wood-wick there was much merry-making and good cheer, plays, and a great company gathered together. One Lord's day there was a *great dance* and many people came to it. Hammond, the priest of Holar, had sung the mass that morning at Mickleby in Osland's-lithe, and he rode into Wood-wick for the dance, and was in the play, and people thought a great deal of his dance. But when he came to Holar the bishop drove him out of the church with contumely, and would not see him." Again of Thorgils Scardi's last night at Ravengill, Jan. 21st, 1258, Sturla says, Islendinga, ch. 314, "He was asked to choose what pastime he would have, Tales or *Dance*, that evening. He asked what choice of Sagas they had there. They told him that they had in hand the Life of Archbishop Thomas, and he chose that because he loved him more than all the other saints."

We hear also of a man nicknamed from the dance, Danza-Berg.
The word 'danz' is used as synonymous with the older words
'nid' and 'flim,' which sufficiently indicate its character as *satirical*
or *amorous*, and we have two scraps of danz verse which illustrate this.
The first, dating from 1221, shows the answering couplet, one line sung
by the man, the other by the woman. It is No. 1 below. The other, of
1264 (No. 2 below), was cited by Thord Andrewsson as he was riding to
his death. He and his brothers had been inveigled into Gizur's power,
seized, disarmed, and forced to accompany the earl to Thrand-holt.
Arni, the son of the good-man of Audkoll-stead, was riding by him
and talking to him. "Said Thord to Arni, 'What thinkest thou the
earl will do concerning the case of us brothers?' Arni said he thought
that he would deal well with them, and put them up at some gentlefolk's
houses for the winter. But Thord said that it would not go off so. 'What
thinkest thou will happen then, good-man?' says Arni. 'I shall be slain,'
says Thord, 'but my brothers will get quarter.' And with that he spurred
his horse under him, and sung this *dance*—

'My sorrows are heavy as lead!'"

Poor Thord's forebodings proved right, and he was beheaded next
morning at the earl's orders, by Geirmund thief, ' with the axe that was
called Gilt,' two days before Michaelmas [Sept. 27th, 1264].

Three hundred years later, at the time of the Reformation, we have a
third scrap of 'danz,' when John Arason, the Northern catholic bishop,
had taken prisoner the Southern protestant bishop Martin. "He was
brought north to Maddersfield to Ari [John's son]. Ari kept him well,
and often had him at drinking-bouts, when folk came together, and Ari
was host. Once upon a time Ari was the host, and Bishop Martin was
sitting facing him at the table, and Ari drank to the bishop and sung the
old stave—

'So gay at heart and glad am I, all for thy sake,
Out in the grove I fain would be, with thee, fair make!'

The bishop took the stoup and answered him back in the same verse,
turning the words a little—

'So ill at heart and sad am I, all for thy sake,
Out in the grove I would not be, with thee, fair make!'

Then Ari grew angry and said, 'Back, back, into the bag, the bag, as the
Eyfrith men used to say!' and Martin got up from the table and went
away." [See our No. 3.]

In his preface to the First Reformation Hymn Book of 1589, good
Bishop Gudbrand gives testimony to the *Dance* of his day, in his own
earnest and racy words, to the following effect[1]:—

"For after the manner of drunkards, drenched in wine and beer, these
men keep up in their midst foul talk of fleshly and devilish defilement
and other uncleanness, singing and bellowing like cattle or calves, playing
and dancing, and carrying on other naughty behaviour and wantonness,

---

[1] We subjoin his own vigorous text:—

því at líka svó sem þeir drykkju-dárar, sem-að drekka vín og bjór, þeir hafa sín
á milli slæmt skraf um holdliga og diöfulliga saurgan og annan óhreinleika, syngja
og baula sem naut og kalfar, spila og danza, og fremja annað vondsligt atháefi eða
gáluskap, og láta opt af ser koma guðlastarnir og önnur ónytsamleg orð.

Að síðustu, til þess að af mætti leggjast onytsamlegir kveðlingar um Tröll og

and putting forth continually blasphemies and the like unprofitable words." *And again—*

"And lastly *I have made this book* to the end that men might be able to put away unprofitable songs of Ogres and of the Heathen of old, Rímur, naughty love-songs, amorous verses, sonnets of lust, verses of mockery and malice, and other foul and evil poesy, ribaldry, wantonness, and lampoonery and satire, such as are loved and used by the commonalty of this land to the displeasure of God and his angels, and to the delight and service of the devil and his messengers, more than in any other country, and more after the fashion of pagan men than Christian folk, for on Wake-nights *or* Vigils and other gatherings of men, and likewise at feasts and banquets, hardly anything else is heard by way of entertainment and merry-making than such vain poesy,—God a' mercy!"

And in the 'man-song' or prologue of a Ríma of the same century[1] we find—

'With holy writ they mock and play, to pious folk's displeasure;
And sacred song and wanton lay mix in the self-same measure.'

And—

'The gospel song and Bosi's screed are mingled up in one.'

The final account of the 'danz' is given by Eggert Olafsson (who was born 1726), in his Travels, 1772, when he says, § 520, "Entertainments or merry-makings are now held in the winter not nearly so often as of old. In these something or other is represented and always the same in each mumming. For example, a hart decked up with lights, a knight riding a horse, a procession of amazons or shield-maidens, and the like. During the show the guests that are bidden hold a Week-wake, that is a kind of song between men and women paired off together. They hold each other by the hands and sing verses touching each other, or on the common circumstances, to different tunes. Here it is an advantage to have a good memory and be able to bring out of one's head the prettiest verse that will suit best. And while they sing in this way they bow the body slightly backwards and forwards, stepping on the right leg, though without changing place. For the beginning and the refrains, the leader sings a verse in a loud voice, and some of the company sing with him and the others respond. Week-wakes have been known from old days, and are called in some places 'Dans,' which word in our old Northern speech does not properly mean a moving of the body, but a concert or song, sung by many people, so arranged as to set forth some occurrence or other."

In 1746 there was a decree put forth by the bigot King Christian VI of Denmark, against such popular mumming and merry-making, threatening transgressors with the pillory; and before the end of the century

---

Fornmenni, Rímur, illir Mansöngvar, Afmors-vísur, Bruna-kvæði, Háðs og Hugmóðs-vísur; og annar liótur og vondr kveðskapr, keskni, klám, og níð, og háð, sem her hiá Alþýðu-fólki er elskað og iðkað, Guði og hans Englum til stygðar, Diöflinum og hans árum til gleðskapar og þiónustu, framar meir enn í nokkru landi, og meir eptir plagsið heiðinna manna enn Kristinna; á Vöku-nóttum og öðrum manna-mótum, ok sömuleiðis í veizlum og gesta-boðum heyrist valla annað til skemtunar haft og gleðskapar enn þessi hegómlegi kvæðaskapur,—sem Guð náði.

[1]   Flíka þeir svo með fræðin góð : að frómum þykir að vansi;
       heilög kvæði og hindur-lióð : eru höfð í einum danzi.

And—

       Guðspiöllum og Bósa-brag : er blandað saman í einu.

Compare the language of W. Baldwin, 1549, with reference to his 'Canticles or Balades of Solomon,' which were to 'drive out of office the baudy balades of lecherous love.'—*See J. Ritson.*

the practice had entirely died out, so that people born in 1762 and 1775 in the West of Iceland knew nothing of such entertainments. Not that the worthy king's edict had so much to do with it as the deep distress caused by the appalling natural visitations to which Iceland was a victim during a score of years after Eggert wrote.

Still the prejudice of the more serious part of the community was deep-rooted against these mummings with their light songs, as the evidence of the Icelandic folk-tales illustrates. There is a story of a priest and all his congregation setting up a dance one Yule-night at service-time in the churchyard. The priest's old mother, terribly scandalised, ran out to stop it, and remonstrated with her son three times to no avail. The third time, at midnight, she saw a man among them who sang with a hollow voice—' My turn is come! These good folks have sung all round.' The good-wife took the priest's horse and rode off for help, for she saw that her son and the whole congregation had all gone mad. When she came back with the priest of Waltheowstead, they found that the congregation had sunk down wholly into the earth, and the priest and clerk were half covered, but they were able to rescue them. Long afterwards the noise of the merry-making of the dancers could be heard under the ground.

Another version lays the scene at Hruna, names the priest's mother Una, and makes the verses run—

'The song in Hruna sounds so gay,
The people flock to join the play;
The dance shall din in such a way
They shall not soon forget the day.
                    All save Una!'

One gathers from the above quotations that these 'danz,' which had lasted six hundred years, must have been very like the French 'jeu-partis,' and those twelfth-century songs in which there is a change of persons and a refrain or *chorus* to be sung by the company. This was the origin of our English 'jig' or 'ballad,' in which the leader sung the refrain first, then verse by verse was sung, sometimes by two persons, but afterwards, as the song became less lyrical and satirical than of an epic or narrative character, by one person, the whole company singing and stamping the chorus. Our mummeries, too, are just what Eggert describes as 'the show' St. George and the Dragon, Bessy (a late and uncouth Amazon), Jack-in-the-Green, and the like.

We have unluckily no full text of a Week-wake song, but we know many of the verses which, *being favourite and well known and setting the tune*, were used as refrains for the 'Visur' on epic subjects, which in the seventeenth century seem to have been known in Iceland, but which were, down to recent times, the staple popular poetry of the Faroese and Orkneymen. From a selection of their burdens, which we give below, a good idea of the mediæval 'Danz' may be gathered.

It will be manifest that the *Dance* may be clearly marked off from the *epic* VISUR, to which some modern writers have given the name 'fornkvædi.' These never had a deep popularity in Iceland. We have only one collection, that gathered and composed by Gizur, the brother of Bishop Bryniolf (b. 1603, d. 1681), priest and poet of Alpta-Myre. They represent a great variety of composition, adaptations of foreign (Danish, Swedish, Norse, Faroese) book-tales, and though a few have Icelandic names, they have not the flavour of the soil. One doubts indeed whether they were anything more than an attempt on the part of Gizur and his friends to imitate the ballads of the Continent or the British Islands. There was no necessity or place for them really in Iceland, where the pungent satire and love-poetry of the Week-wake were still enjoyed; while the alliterative 'Rimur' completely satisfied the appetite for epic narrative. The numerous Danicisms, the foreign form of the epic 'Visur,' suffice to prove their origin. Some (55 out of a hundred) have been edited by Sigurdsson and Grundtvig under the title ' Islenzk Fornquædi;' some 50 still remain in paper MSS., the Brit. Mus. 11,177 of the end of the seventeenth century containing about 75 Icelandic Visur, derived from Gizur's collection. The ballad is in fact an exotic in Iceland. The ballads of the Faroese are, on the other hand, good and fine of their kind; their subjects were, as we noticed in Prolegomena, mostly taken from one or two Saga-vellums which came from Iceland at the end of the Middle Ages, the contents of which can be gauged from the stories chosen by the poets of the ' Visur.'

The Orkney ' Visur' are almost entirely lost, a few fragments alone surviving to show the existence of a former school of ballad-poetry having flourished there also, the last leaf of the poetic stock which had borne such wonderful fruit there six centuries earlier.

Both the 'Danz' and the 'Visur' are distinguished from other Icelandic poetry by the frequent lack of alliteration. This lack was less felt because they were *sung* and *stepped to*, the metre being thus clearly and unmistakably marked out. But the absence of alliteration no doubt prevented the epic ' Visur' from ever competing successfully with the Rímur.

The ultimate French origin of this whole class of poetry is unmistakable, especially in the best ' Danz' fragments, which have quite the ring and tone of such lines as —

'Or ne hais rien tant com lou iour
Amis, ke me depart de uos.'—*Gaces Brulez.*

The article ' Danz' in the Dictionary was written Dec. 1867, and may be supplemented by this notice.

The Faroese ballads, which they themselves call 'Ruimur' (though they are not at all what are called in Iceland ' Rimur '), and which are, of all the Northern Ballads, nearest to the ' Danz' verses we have been speaking of, were first collected by F. C. Swaboe in 1781-1782, and remain for the most part unpublished in the Royal Library, Copenhagen. Selections have been published by H. C. Lyngbye, 1822, at Randers, and by V. V. Hammershaimb (in Icelandicised spelling), Copenhagen, 1851-55.

The earliest collection of Danish ballads is not older than 1548, to wit, the Folio of Karen Brahe in the Odense Library in Funen (a Royal wedding of 1548 is the subject of one of the ballads in it). Next comes that of the historian Swaning (b. 1503, d. 1584). There are other MS. collections, but all later. The first *printed* collection is that of 100 ballads by Andres Sörensen Wedel, Swaning's son-in-law, the translator of Saxo, which came out in 1591, and was dedicated to the reigning queen. A century later Peter Syv, the collector of Danish proverbs, republished this collection, adding a second hundred.

The first printed collection of Norwegian ballads is that of Landstad the priest, the famous Norse hymn-writer, taken down from *viva voce* recitation in Thelemark, printed in 1853 at Copenhagen. Landstad died at a high age in 1880.

The Swedish collections are late, those of Arwidson 1834, Afzelius 1814.

The palm of Northern Ballad Collections is due to Swen Grundtvig's huge work, Danmark's Gamle Folkeviser, 1853-81, a vast store of ballads and ballad-lore, especially interesting to Englishmen and Scots.

It would be very interesting if some good observer would give a careful account of the ballad-singing of the Faroese in the present day, for it is only there that the old way of performing *ballads* and *jigs* has survived in unbroken continuity from the Middle Ages.

I. ICELANDIC DANZ FRAGMENTS AND REFRAINS.

* 1. L OPTR er í Eyjom, bítr lunda bein,
     Sæmundr er á heiðom, etr berin ein.

* 2. Mínar ero sorgir þungar sem blý.

3. Svó er mer glatt ok gleðisamt,—því veldr þú—
mik langar út í lundinn með þá jungfrú.

Svó er mer íllt ok angrsamt,—því veldur þú—
mik langar ekki í lundinn með þá jungfrú.

4. Fagurt syngur svanrinn um sumar-langa tíð,
þá mun lyst at leika ser, mín liljan fríð.

5. Skínn á skildi sól ok sumarið fríða,
dunar í velli er drengir í burtu ríða.

6. Einum unna-ek manninum á meðan þat var,
þó hlaut ek minn harm at bera í leyndum stað.

7. Blítt lætur veröldin; fölnar fögur fold,
langt er síðan mítt var yndið lagt í mold.

8. Ungan leit-ek hofmann í fögrum runni,
skal-ek í hlióði dilla þeim mer unni.

9. Fagrar heyrða-ek raddirnar við Niflunga heim,
ek má ekki sofa fyrir sönginum þeim.

10. Mein-bugir bægja mer frá brúði,
sorgin mik lúði, sorgin mik lúði.

11. Ein ber hon angur fyrir þann öðling.

12. Sá er einginn glaður eptir annan þreyr.

13. Svó linna tregar sem tíðir,
allir dagar eiga kveld um síðir.

14. Fölnar fold, fyrnist allt ok mæðist,
hold er mold, hverju sem þat klæðist.

15. Leggjum land undir fót á Dana-mot
ok danz vil hun heyra.

16. Væntir frúin þín,
við Lundunaborg þar bíðr hún mín.

17. Út ertu við æginn blá, eg er her á Dröngum,
kalla eg löngum, kalla-eg til þín löngum.

18. Þeim var ekki skapað nema að skilja.

19. Þó er hinn sami vilinn minn til hennar.

20. Ekki er dagur enn! Vel danza vífin!

II. FAROIC 'VUÍGENGUR,' OR BURDENS.

1. V EL er mer ansad, her vil eg á golfið fram danza,
þo at þu vilt mitt líf í vanda, vel er mer ansad.

---

* Nos. 1 and 2 repeated here for completeness sake from Book vi, No. 70.

2.   Gefið hlióð fruvor, karl er kominn í danz,
     Guð láti engi iomfrúna gialda hans.

3.   Stígum fastara á fiol! sporum ei vorn skó!
     Guð mun ráða hvar ver drekkum onnur Iól.

4.   Hvað skal mer harpan undir mina hönd,
     vill ekki frægur fylgja mer á onnur lond?

5.   Orlof biðjum ver erlegir menn,
     danz skolum ver hefja, er ekki dagur enn.—Cf. I. 20.

6.   Glymur danzur í holl, slaið ring,
     glaðir ríða Norðmenn til Hildurs thing.

7.   Noregis menn danza vel í friðom:
     stillið yður alla riddara! Noregis menn. d. v. i. fr.

8.   Látum danz dynja, drengir, stoltsliga stígum í ring.
                                        Stendur hun vel fruva.

9.   Gyltan spora við minn fot eg spenni
     svo temi eg minn gangara goð og læt renna.

10. Mer stóð hugur á vænu mey, kann eg hana fá.

11. Olafur kongur herjar hann mót trollum.

12. Frœðið er komið fra Islandi, skrifað í bók so breida.

§ 4. R I M U R.

BESIDES the 'danz' songs, there is another type of poem, which was
adapted by Icelandic poets under the influence of French models. This
is the 'Ríma,' the very name of which points to its foreign origin.
The first of these is the *Olafs-rima* by Einar Gilsson, which is printed
below; it may be dated about 1360. The next that we know of is the
Skida-rima of Einar Fostri, c. 1450, which follows it; and the great
Wolfen-buttel Cod. and AM. 604, of about 1500. We have in Prolegomena, § 25, given a fairly complete list of those Rímur which are
found in *vellums*, i. e. older than the Reformation.

But besides these, there is a continual succession of Rímur down to
the present day, of which huge collections exist in paper MSS., not
to speak of those which have been printed. They are mostly book-
poetry, the earlier ones founded on the stories found in the Romantic
Sagas and the Bible; the later also based on foreign novels, and now and
then, though a less favourite theme, on the Kings' Lives and Islendinga
Sögur, etc. There are Rímur of all types,—religious, satiric, historical,
and romantic. Though popular, their poetical standard is low. A curious
story, to be found in the first volume of John Arnason's Icelandic Folk-
tales, pp. 196–7, will illustrate this:—A party of men lose themselves on
the mountains and take shelter in a cave, where they agree to while
away the time in reciting poetry. One wishes for 'Hallgrim's Hymns,'
but another calls for 'Andra-rímur,' one of the coarsest of these poems.
When this Ríma was being recited a deep voice was heard out of
the depths of the cave, 'Now I am pleased, but my wife is not.' Now
they changed the chanting, and Biorn, the best reciter of the company,
struck up Hallgrim's Hymns, and again the deep voice was heard,
'Now my wife is pleased, but not I.' When Biorn had done, the same

voice called out, 'Wilt have a lick of my ladle, poet Biorn?' and a
wooden trough full of porridge was handed out of the cave-depths to
the hungry men. The giant of the cave had evidently a Christian wife.
The Hallgrim of this story is the author of the beautiful Passion-
hymns, commonly called Hallgrims-salmar, sung at family worship, the
best and most popular of post-mediæval poems. There is some account
of Hallgrim Petersson in the Reader.
There are many varieties of metre employed in Rímur. The early
and original one is commonly called '*square verse*,' 'fer-skeytt-visa,'
from the alternate rhyme, the model being the well-known mediæval
hymn-measure used, for example, in—

'Mihi est propositum : in tabernâ mori,
Vinum sit appositum : morientis ori,' etc.

Both strict alliteration and rhyme are necessary in every variety of Rímur.
In imitation of the Drápa, the regular Rímur have a kind of introduction called 'man-song,' a dedication, as it were, addressed to some
lady, and sometimes an epilogue. These have no necessary connection
with the body of the poem, and are often in different metre. Several
metres are also often employed in the different 'fyttes' of the body of
the poem.
There are, besides long poems, heaps of ditties and epigrams in Rímur-
metre. The Rímur, to mediæval and modern Iceland, have replaced
the Saga as the *natural* artistic mode of expression and subject of
entertainment.

OLAFS-RIMA, by EINAR GILSSON.

At the head of Flatey-book, following Geisli and before Hyndlu-liod,
and written like them, by the second scribe of that volume, about 1380,
on an extra sheet affixed to the body of the big book, comes Olafs-
Ríma, the first, as far as we can tell, of its class.
Its *author*, Einar Gilsson, is named in Icelandic documents, which prove
his being in Shaw-firth in 1340 and 1353, his holding the post of Sheriff
in Hunawater Bailiwick in the North, and his filling the office of Lawman from 1367–1368. He is the author of poems in court-metre on
Bishop Gudmund (see Biskopa Sögur, vol. ii, pp. 1–184), and he was, we
believe, the scribe or owner of the great Saga-vellum, AM. 61.
The *contents* of Olafs-Ríma touch on the Battle of Sticklestead, the
Death and Translation of St. Olaf according to tradition and the church
legend. The poem has no historical worth, but, though not very melodious (the metre was new as yet), it is interesting as showing the
relations of the new mediæval poetic school to the old court-poetry.

1. OLÁFR kongur œrr ok fríðr : átti Noregi at ráða ;
gramr var æ við bragna blíðr : buinn til sigrs ok náða.

2. Dœgling hélt svá dýran heiðr : dróttni himna hallar ;
engi skýrir œrvar meiðr : œðlings frægðir allar.

3. Milding hafði mentir þær : er mestar vóro í heimi ;   5
hvergi frægra hilmi fær : hvórki af gleði né seimi.

4. Fimm hefir kongur kristnað lœnd : kann-ek œll at nefna ;
gramr vill iafnan rióða rœnd : ok rangan úsið hefna.

5. Rán ok stuldi refsti hann : ok ræktar stiórn í landi ;
hilmir lagði á heiðni bann : ok hefndi stórt með brandi.   10

6. Gramr nam lœgmál setja svá : at seggir þoldu valla;
dáligan lét hann dauða fá : dróttins svikara alla.

7. Rekkar ýfðuzt ræsi á mót : ok rétti harðla sœnnum;
vóru kongi heimsklig hót : hafin af sialfs síns mœnnum.

8. Hárekr var fyrir brœgnum bystr : buinn at stríða stilli;   15
Þórir hundr er þann veg lystr : þriði var Kálfr enn illi.

9. Kálfr var fyrst með kongi sá : kærr í œllum ráðum;
nú er hann horfinn hilmi frá : heiðri sviptr ok dáðum.

10. Þrændir gengu Þóri á hœnd : þeim var liúft at herja;
Háleysk þióð vill ríóða rœnd : ok ríkit kongi verja.   20

11. Fylkir ríkur, frægr ok mildr : fréttir safnað þenna;
þá vill hilmir hraustr ok gildr : hvergi undan renna.

12. Bragning lætur byrja ferð : bónda múg í móti;
hann vill iafnan hræra sverð : ok herða skot með spióti.

13. Sikling hafði safnað þá : sínum gœrpum sniœllum;   25
lofðungs kann-ek lýði at tiá : langt bar gramr af œllum.

14. Hlýri kongs var harðla iungr : hann vil-ek fyrstan nefna;
víst nam Haraldr þykkju þungr : Þrændum stríð at hefna.

15. Get-ek ei hrotta hœggit rœnd : (Haraldr talar við garpa);
bindit mér við mína hœnd : mæki þann inn snarpa.   30

16. Rœgnvaldur var mildr ok merkr : með þeim kongi góða;
Brúsason nam brigða sterkr : brand í dreyra at rióða.

17. Finnr Arnason frækn ok hraustr : fylgir iœfri sterkum;
Biœrn stallari tryggr ok traustr : trúr vel ræsi merkum.

18. Sá var annarr Árna mœgr : ýtar Þorberg kalla;   35
hann lét stálin stinn ok fœgr : í sterkum hlífum gialla.

19. Þormóðr var við Kolbrún kendr : kongsins skaldit dýra;
sá bar hvassar hyggju strendr : hvar sem garpar stríða.

20. Náðuzt menn í niflungs flokk : nær sem risar at líta;
þeir hafa bragnar brynju rokk : brandi skorit enn hvíta.   40

21. Gengu fram fyrir kongsins kné : ok kvœddu stilli enn teita;
buðu þeir bæði fylgð ok fé : frægum sióla at veita.

22. Gramr réð spyrja garpa þá : Gœrit mér heiti at inna;
trú skulu greina seggir svá : at satt megi til þess finna.

23. Opt hafa þegnar þriózku hefnt : þat mun engi lasta;   45
Gauka-Þóri hafa gumnar nefnt : glaðan ok Hafra-fasta.

24. Treystum vér á mátt ok megn : er margan riddara prýðir;
œngva hafa af Ásum fregn : okkrir sterkir lýðir.

25. Taki-þér heldr helga trú : himna kongs með blóma;
virðar kastið villu nú : ok verit með oss í sóma.   50

26. Lýðir gerðu lykt á þí : at leysa þenna vanda;
skírnar brunn fara skatnar í : ok skynda Guði til handa.

27. Þrek-stórr kom til þengils maðr : þann frá-ek Arnliót heita;
tók hann skírn ok gekk þó glaðr : grams í flokkinn teita.

28. Garpar fleiri at fylki renn : enn fyrðar mega þat telja;   55
siklingur nam sæmðar menn : sér til liðs at velja.

29. Kálfur hafði múga mann : merkta vœllu víða;
níðingligt var ‘næsta’ hans : niflung þeim at stríða.

30. Bialfa klæddizt hœrðum Hundr: ok hans sveitungar margir;
þat hafa geysi-grimmligt undr: gert Bú-Finnar argir. 60
31. Ræsir talar við Þorgils þá: —þat var mest af prýði—
Þér vil ek silfr í sióði fá: þú seð með auma-lýði.
32. Þorgils hugsar þengils mál: þér innit framar hóti;
Gef fyrir þeirra garpa sál: er ganga oss í móti.
33. Herrinn drífr á hilmis fund: at heyja imon stranga; 65
svá var þrútin þeirra lund: at þraut varð fram at ganga.
34. Múginn þessi geysizt gegn: gram með sárum vilja;
lœgðu á orku ok allt sitt megn: iœfur við land at skilja.
35. Á Stikla-stœðum var róman remd: ríkum kongi í móti;
þar vóru skœpt með hœndum hremd: ok hœrðu kastað grióti.
36. Hárekr eggjar her-lið sítt: heitir mœrgum sóma: 71
Lúki garpar geysi-strítt: gram-fyrir harða dóma.
37. Góða sverðit Hneitir hét: hafði gramr til víga;
þar fyrir margan þengill lét: þegn at iœrðu hníga.
38. Gumnar hlaupa geystir fram: grams fyrir merkit væna; 75
reisa þannig randa glam: ok rista skiœldu græna.
39. Gellini tók at geysazt hart: ok gerði rómu stranga;
sannliga lét hann seggja mart: sáran dauða fanga.
40. Árna-synir sínn unda naðr: einart drógu af magni;
kendiz ei svá klókur maðr: kæmi hlíf at gagni. 80
41. Þormóður nam brytja bráð: bleikum fálu hesti;
varði kong með dygð ok dáð: darra él hann hvesti.
42. Þórir Hundur þrautar gildr: þreif sítt spiótið snarpa;
laga var hann ok hœggva mildr: við harða kongsins garpa.
43. Þorsteinn hét sá er Þóri viðr: þar nam fram at ganga; 85
sá var kendur Knarrar-smiðr: kominn í villu stranga.
44. Kongrinn hió til Þóris þá: þat frá-ek undrum sætti;
ekki beit hans biálfann á: brátt sem grióti mætti.
45. Biœrn stallari bystr ok reiðr: barði Hund í móti;
síðan hné við sannan heiðr: seggr á Þóris spióti. 90
46. Þorgeirr vóð í randa regn: ræsi náði at finna;
snarr réð kongur þriózkum þegn: þessi orð at inna:
47. Þeygi gerir—þú Þórir rétt: at þreyngja mœnnum mínum;
lypta-ek þér af lágri slétt: lokit mun sigri þínum.
48. Kongrinn hió með Hneiti þá: svá hrauð af eggjum báðum;
Þorgeirr dauðr á lyngi lá: lífi sviptr ok dáðum. 96
49. Þorsteinn réð á þengils kné: þunnri œxi at smíða;
síðan lét hann fiœr með fé: ok féll í ánauð stríða.
50. Biœrtum varp sér brandi frá: buðlungs hœndin mæta;
sióli bað með sœnnu þá: siálfan Guð sín gæta. 100
51. Þórir lagði í kongsins kvið: kœldum snótar ráðum;
hilmis sál tók hæstan frið: himna grams með náðum.
52. Kálfur hió til bragnings bystr: batt sér þungan randa;
ramliga var hann á reiði lystr: ræsi þeim at granda.
53. Myrkri sló yfir menn ok hiœrð: við mildings dýran dauða;
litu þá hvórki lœg né iœrð: lýð aflar þat nauða. 106

54. Þá kom Dagr með drengi sín : darra þing at heyja ;
margur hlaut við mikla pín : maðr af sút at deyja.

55. Æsilig var odda hríð : undrum frá-ek þat gegna ;
mátti ekki meira stríð : af málma leiki fregna.   110

56. Hræðilig var hiœrva gnauð : harðar brynjur sprungu ;
drengir fengu dapra nauð : dœrr á hlífum sungu.

57. Stórt var þetta manna mót : mest kom hialp til bragna ;
dauðir fengu ok blindir bót : biúgir heilsu fagna.

58. Þorgils geymdi þengils lík : þat fór heldr af hlióði ;   115
maðr tók sýn fyrir merkin slík : af mætu kongsins blóði.

59. Fróni er huldur fylkir mætr : firður nauð ok grandi ;
líkami kongs var mildr ok mætr : mánuðr tólf í sandi.

60. Þeim kom virðum vondzlig þraut : at vísis fengu reiði ;
geislar skinu um grund á braut : grams af dýru leiði.   120

61. Lýðir tóku upp líkama hans : lutu þá kongi sniœllum ;
hár ok negl var heilags manns : hátt at vexti œllum.

62. Hildings taka þá helgan dóm : halir í skrín at leggja ;
nú er Kristz et biarta blóm : ok blíðust miskunn seggja.

63. Dróttni færði œðlingr œnd : ýtum líkam seldi ;   125
nú er hann Guðs á hægri hœnd : himins í æzta veldi.

64. Buðlungs heiðr er biartr ok ríkı : bæði um lœnd ok geima ;
fæddizt engi fylkir slíkr : fyrri norðr í heima.

65. Reiðzt-þú ei þó, þengill þér : þyrða-ek vísu at bióða !
Biðr ek Óláf biarga mér : við bragning allra þióða !   130

SKIDA-RIMA, by EINAR FOSTRI.

THE original vellum of this poem, which is from its subject, age,
and humour worthy of separate notice, is unfortunately lost. We have
nothing but a paper copy (AM. Additamenta) by Erlend Olafsson,
brother of the well-known John Olafsson, c. 1730. It is glossed with
proposed alterations (substituting coarse and common words for the
mock-heroic epithets and style of the original) between the lines, and is
a little difficult to deal with. The Editor copied it in 1862 and gave the
copy to Dr. Maurer, who published it in 1869. It has since been reprinted by Dr. Cederschiöld, who, in a few cases, has bettered the order
of the stanzas.

Biorn of Skardsa (c. 1633) mentions the poem, and describes its contents,
naming Einar Fosterer as its author; and we have no reason to doubt
this ascription, which may well have been on the vellum itself from
which Erlend copied it. The only point to settle is the date of Einar.
Biorn's words are, in his Greenland's Annals, talking of Biorn of Vatns-
firth, the Crusader, " With him on his journey was Einar Fostri, his poet
and entertainer, who used to amuse him every Sunday, Tuesday, and
Friday, whenever he wanted amusing. Wise men say that Einar made
Skida-Ríma for pastime one day when his turn came to entertain the
crew, as is indeed expressly mentioned at the end of his poem : ' Here
shall the poem wait till Sunday.' Einar also composed Skauf-hala-balkr

---

117. Read, sætr ?

and Barngœlur, as he says at the end of the 'balk.' This piece and lullaby-song Einar made without art, i.e. not in court-metre." But Biorn seems to have been mistaken in his dates, for misled by the words 'sfovar-rok,' a tradition had no doubt grown up taking Einar on the pilgrimage with Biorn, who is last mentioned about 1415, and was a little king in North-west Iceland in his day. However, Erlend Olafsson knows Einar as the poet of Lady Olaf, the wife of Biorn, the grandson of this Crusading Biorn, and this is perhaps the most likely. The phrase 'sea-drift of the dwarves' is a mere synonym for 'poetry,' and does not refer to a sea-journey at all. The metre and character of the poem would rather require more than less years between it and Olafs-Rfma, and had we not known Biorn's tradition, Erlend's date would readily have been accepted. At any rate, it has all the test-marks of a pre-Reformation poem: the end measure is always trochaic – ᴗ, never ᴗ ᴗ, which in a poem of four hundred lines cannot be a mere chance. Hence at the time of its composition quantity was still observed in speech. Further, the forms of the rhyme-words—vódinn (peril), svó, vórr, for the later vodi, svo, vor; the inflexive r is not syllabic before a pause (in the fourth measure), but in other places is syllabic now and then; strange foreign words, as jungr for ungr (the poet seems but half aware that jung and ung are the same word, for he calls the *old* beggar 'young' in v. 199, though that may be half for fun, perhaps, as the wooer of Walhalla), and so on. Neither date is impossible, 1400 or 1450.

The internal evidence of the poem points to the fact that it was intended for entertainment on Sunday evenings, the recognised time for dancing and music as in our Book of Sports, and that it was the work of a man who knew the Medalfell-Strand Headlands in Broadfirth, North-west of Iceland, thoroughly well; the journeys of his hero Skidi and the locale of the poem are there. Geirmund Hellskin, Skidi's patron in Walhalla, was the first settler of this peninsula.

The name 'Fostri' may allude to some connection between the poet and the Biorns. Was he the older Biorn's foster-son or the younger Biorn's fosterer?

The *story* of Skida-Rfma is based on an incident in the life of Sturla, Snorri's father, and is told in his Saga (Sturlunga, i. p. 69), but without the name of the hero, the beggar Skidi, which suggests that the author Einar got his story from an earlier and fuller life of Sturla than the abridged one which we possess. Skidi, the sturdy beggar, has been going his rounds in the North-west of Iceland, and comes to the house of Thorgils Oddason at Stadarhold, where they are just killing a fat ox from Stagley; he begs enough leather for two pairs of brogues out of the raw hide, and trudges over the ridge to Hvamm, where Sturla lives. Here he gets a steel knife and scrip, and goes on to Hit-dale to the homestead of Thorleif, no friend of Sturla's. Thorleif, finding out whence he has come, will not give him a meal, so when he has cut him the brogues out of his piece of hide, he trusses his pack on to his shoulders, and lying down with the other beggars in the porch falls fast asleep. So far the Saga has given material, but now follows the poet's own creation, Skidi's dream. In comes a big man with a great iron hammer and says that he is come from Woden to take him to Asiaham (on the Black Sea) to settle the disputes of the heroes. Off goes Skidi with Thor the messenger: crossing Iceland, they wade over to Norway from Cape Horn, the sea hardly covering their shoes. The first person they meet in Norway is Olmod, 'sitting out' working sorcery. He and Skidi quarrel, and Skidi breaks the rivet-band of his staff. But they cannot stay; on they trudge, down the whole length of

Norway, through Denmark, and ever on till at last they reach the god's hall in Asiaham. Thor acts as guide to Skidi, and points out the heroes in order to him, where they sit round the hall below Woden and the twelve Anses. Woden welcomes Skidi, and asks about the different Icelandic noblemen. Skidi praises Thorgil and Sturla. He then begs for a new rivet-band and his pig full of butter, which he gets; and Woden gives him a wife withal, the beautiful Hild. But Skidi crosses himself and so rouses the ill-will of the Anses, and Heimdal strikes him with his horn. A terrible conflict now takes place, in which mock-heroic exploits are performed of a Gargantuan character. At last Sigfred takes up the 'christian' Skidi and hurls him out of Walhall, but the beggar has left his butter-pig behind him and calls lustily for it. Asmund hurls it down to him, and it strikes him in the mouth and wakes him up again—in Hitdale. He is wounded and battered, four of his teeth are knocked out, he has been laying about him in his blind sleep-fury during the night and has killed five of his fellow beggars. The proof of the truth of the story is that Skidi's two new pairs of brogues are trodden to pieces, his staff is bound with an iron band weighing pounds and pounds, his pig is full of butter (which is given to the dogs and kills them), and lastly, in his wallet is found a tooth of one of the heroes, so huge that the 'best crozier north in Holar' was made out of it. Skidi was long ill, 'and I fear he will never thrive as long as he uses such bad language and refuses to wash on Saturdays.'

There is a fine Rabelaisian tone about Skida-Ríma, and the realism of its vocabulary, with the keen observation of life it implies, is quite akin to the French master's

'Nouvelles des diables et des damnés'

told by Epistemon when he came back from the Elysian fields, Pant. Book II, ch. 30 ; and give the poem a high place among the productions of Icelandic humour.

As verse it is extremely melodious and pleasing to the ear; after copying it out for the first time, many years ago, the Editor found that he had got it by heart, a test which Olafs-Ríma, or even Einar's own Reynard's Lay (Skauf-hala-balkr), utterly fails to bear.

An additional argument in favour of the later Biorn as Einar's patron is the poet's apology for not putting in a 'man-song' or introductory envoy. This framing of the later Rímur had clearly not been thought of in the days of Olafs-Ríma.

The list of heroes named in it gives an insight into the literature of Einar's day—Hilditann, King Halfdan the Generous, Iwar, King Alf the Strong, King Rolf Kraki, Haki, Hagbard, Starkad the Old, Arngrim's Sons, Blot-Harold, Thrain-o'-Howe, the Wolsungs, Widolf Mit-stang, Edgar the Giant and Aventrod, Wikar, Sorli the Strong, Gnod-Asmund, Ivar Widefathom, Sigurd Ring and Ragnar, Ali the Keen, the Ragnarssons, Earl Andri, Isung's Sons, Regin and Fafni, Dwarves, twelve Bearsarks, Rolf Ganger, Rolf Gautrick's son, Thori Ironshield, Hogni and Gunnar, Ubbi the Frisian, Sigurd Swain, Rook the Black, Utstan, Agnar, Biarki, Bruin and Brusi the Bearsarks, Earl Halfdan—and last not least, the Icelandic settler Geirmund Hellskin, the founder of the farm where Biorn and Lady Olaf resided, the only *unromantic* person of the list.

I. The Beginning.

1.   MER er ekki um Mansæng greitt : minztan tel-ek þat greiða; því mér þykkir öllum eitt : af því gamni leiða.

2. Yngis-menn vilja ungar frúr : í aldin-gardinn tæla ;
feta þar ekki fræðin úr : flest er gœrt til væla.

3. Ef koma upp nœkkur kvæðin fín : hiá kátum silki-hrundum ; 5
kalla þær sé kveðit til sín : af kærleiks elsku-fundum.

4. Ekki sómir afmors vess : œllum bauga skorðum ;
gengur mœrgum gaman til þess : at gylla þær í orðum.

5. Látum heldur leika tenn : á litlum ævintýrum ;
þá munu geta vór góðir menn : hiá gull-hlaðs skorðum dýrum.

6. Fiœlniss átti-ek fornan bát : sem flaut í óðar ranni ;   11
þar var skrifuð á skemtun kát : af Skíða gœngu-manni.

7. Hann ólzt upp í Hítardal : hár á ungum aldri ;
þat er hvórki skrum né skial : skráð af menja Baldri.

8. Manna hæstur, miór sem þvengr : miklar hendr ok síðar ; 15
þó var upp úr kryppu kengr : ok krummur harðla víðar.

9. Skeggit þunt ok skakkar tenn : skotit út kinnar-beinum ;
diarf-mæltur við dándis-menn : drengrinn hvass í greinum.

10. Skreppu átti hann Skíði sér : ok skó-nál harðla prúða ;
þar með enn, sem innt er mér : allan skreppu-skrúða.   20

11. Hér með á hann stóran staf : ok stæltan brodd með hólki :
Maðrinn kunni matar skraf : mis-iafnt kendraf fólki.

12. Hús-gang réð um allan aldr : ævi sinnar þreyta ;
enga menn fann auðar-Baldr : í orðum sínum neyta.

13. Hirzlu átti halrinn sér : heldur innan feita ;   25
úr máta stór ok mikil er : má hún því Smiœr-svín heita.

14. Er hun gœr sem annat svín : innan hol sem kista ;
Greland dvergr úr garði sín : gaf hónum þá til vista.

15. Hleypr á millum horna lands : halrinn búinn til pretta ;
getit er Skíða gœngu-manns : um gœrvalt landit þetta.   30

16. Nú hefir kempan kappi hœrð : kannat Vestur-sveitir ;
aptur kominn yfir um Fiœrð : ok þar Saurbær heitir.

17. Stóð þar bær, er Staðar-hóll hét : stefnir þangat Skíði ;
þenna frá-ek at þekkjast lét : Þorgils bóndinn fríði.

18. Odda-son til afreks vendr : ýtum stýrði fínum ;   35
þar var Skíði af skœtnum kendr : ok skemti af ferðum sínum.

19. Segist drengrinn sótt hafa heim : seggi vestr um Fiœrðu ;
' Brenni allr á baki þeim : beininn, sem mér gœrðu.'

20. Þorgils tekr úr seggnum sult : sá kann drengnum hiúka ;
mat-svín hans var meir enn fult : at morni vill hann striúka. 40

21. Árla dags er uppi sá : sem á fyrir mœrgu at hugsa ;
seggir fóru at slátra þá : ok slógu Stagleyjar-uxa.

22. Þorgils talaði þýðr ok glaðr : þá við drenginn fína :
' Hvat vill Skíði húsgangs-maðr : hafa fyrir skemtan sína ?'

23. Á skæðum kvað sér skiótast þœrf : því skó-laust gengi lœngum ;
margur hefir sá meiri svœrf : er minna treystir gœngum.   46

24. Skæðin vóru úr skarpri húð : skorin með hvœssum knífi ;
þau vóru ekki þynnri enn súð : þá var gaman at lífi.

---

46. svörf] þörf, Cd.

25.   ' Renna mundi rausn af þér : fyrir rekka harðla fróða,
      ef þú gæfir ønnur mér : af uxanum þeim inum góða.'   50

26.   ' Sker þú siálfur, Skíði minn : skæðin svó þér líki l '
      ' Ofrligt er um ørleik þinn : ørva lundrinn ríki l '

27.   Ristir hann ofan af mølunum mitt : mikla lengju ok síða ;
      hafði hann á því hvers manns kvitt : at hann mundi aldri ríða.

28.   Alt var senn í einum klið : upp vatt trúss meðal herða ;   55
      seggi biðr hann sitja í frið : svó er hann búinn til ferða.

29.   Asólfs-gøtu ok austr um Skœrð : ætla ek drengrinn þrammi ;
      þar til kempan kappi hœrð : kemur niðr at Hvammi.

30.   Sturli hét sá stýrði þar : staðnum þeim inum fríða ;
      sæmd ok heiðr af seggjum bar : siálf-boðit lét hann Skíða.   60

31.   ' Hefir þú kannat héruðin vestr ? (hátt réð Sturli at mæla) ;
      hverr er þar skatna skørungr mestr ? skylt er því at hæla.'

32.   ' Þorgils er þar bóndinn beztr : baugum kann at gæða,
      var-ek hans í gær-kveld gestr : hann gaf mér tvenn pør skæða.'

33.   Sturli gaf hónum stæltan kníf : stóra skreppu ok miúka ;   65
      siálfan Guð bað signa hans líf : ok svó er hann búinn at striúka.

34.   Drattar hann á Svín-biúg suðr : ok svó með Hítar-vatni ;
      í hónum gørðist illur kuðr : aldri trúi-ek hann batni.

35.   Beiskjaldi í Belgja-dal : byrðum trúi-ek at safni ;
      þenna þegninn þýða skal : Þorleif øðru nafni.   70

36.   Hónum var ekki hiúkat þar : heldur tók at nátta ;
      fram í stofunni frá-ek hann var : þá fólkit skyldi hátta.

37.   Hann vilja ekki hœldar siá : hvórki at mat né drykkju ;
      hann Leifi kvað ei liggja á : um lítil-mennis þykkju.

38.   Hann skefr þá ofan af skæðum sín : ok skóna gørði fióra ;
      (þat kom rétt í reikning mín) : hann rekr í þvengi stóra.   76

39.   Býr um skó á belti sér : enn bindr upp á sik aðra ;
      þat hafa seggir sagt fyr mér : at slíkt eru brøgðin þaðra.

40.   Setr hann fyr sik svínit frítt : ok síðan bregður kreppu ;
      fiska-stykkit fagrt ok hvítt : frá-ek hann hefði í skreppu.   80

41.   Seggrinn tæmdi svínit hálft : ok siau grunnunga barða ;
      við-bit hlýtr at synja siálft : setr nú at hónum kvarða.

42.   Kastar sér í krók-pall niðr : kænn til húsgangs-ferða ;
      svínit bindr hann síðu viðr : enn setr upp trúss meðal herða.

43.   Drengrinn frá-ek í lopt upp lá : lítið varð af søngum ;   85
      fátækt fólkit hvíldi hiá : ok hræddist strákinn løngum.

44.   Ekki frá-ek hann signdi sik : (seint tók gleðin at rakna) ;
      ei mun brátt, þat uggir mik : af íllum draumi vakna.

45.   Síðan fór at sofna brátt : segginn engi geymdi ;
      ferlig undrin fram á nátt : frá-ek hann Skíða dreymdi.   90

II. The Dream.

46.   Inn kom maðr í stofuna stórr : með stæltan hamar í hendi ;
      þat var enn illi Ása-Þórr : er Óðinn kóngur sendi.

47.   Orðum hagaði þanninn Þórr : þegar hann finnur Skíða :
      ' Óðinn kóngur, yfirmann vórr : yðr bað til sín ríða.'

48. 'Frétt hefir hann, at fremdin þín : ferr um heiminn víða ; 95
hann vill alla hafa til sín : sem heimsins lystir fríða.'

49. 'Lánað er þér list ok vit : lukkan hefir þik fangat :
því hefir sióli sent þér rit : at sækja austur þangat.'

50. 'Kom þar til með kóngum tveim : í kveld, þeir skyldu hátta ;
Óðinn gefr þér auð ok seim : ef þú gœrir þá sátta.' 100

51. Réttast gœrði raumrinn stirðr : ok réð þá fyrst at hrækja :
'Ei er milding minna virðr : mun-ek á fund hans sækja.'

52. Skíði frá-ek at skauzt á fætr : ok skundar út með Þóri ;
ekki frá-ek at lítit lætr : laufa-viðrinn stóri.

53. Arka þeir á iœkla austr : Ása-Þórr ok Skíði, 105
leiðsœgu-maðrinn lukku-traustr : ' læst þar ei þó ' bíði.

54. Austr af Horni ok út á haf : álpuðu þeir frá landi,
Nóreg frá-ek þeir næði af : nærri Þrándheims sandi.

55. Þó bylgjur rísi á brœttum sió : bragna gœrir þat káta ;
aldri tók þeim upp yfir skó : ok ei frá-ek þá váta. 110

56. Fundu þeir í fiœrunni mann : frá-ek hann Ölmóð heita,
úti-setuna eflir hann : ok ætlar spádóms leita.

57. Ölmóðr heilsar þegar á Þór : 'Þú munt kunna at skýra :
hverr 'r sá maðr er með þér fór : eðr mun hann lukku stýra ?'

58. Þor. 'Skíða Norðmann skulum vér hann : at skírnar-nafni kalla ;
hefr í briósti hreysti-mann : heims náttúru alla.' 116

59. Olm. 'Mér lízt ekki " meiri " kraptr : mens yfir þessum lundi ;
hitt mik uggir, hann komi ei aptr : heill af ykkrum fundi.'

60. Sk. 'Spáðu mér engra, Herjans hœttr ! hrak-falla ! (kvað Skíði)
ellegar skal-ek, þinn digri drœttr ! dubba þik, svó svíði.' 120

61. Olm. 'Hvórki er þat hól né skrum : hafi þik Æsir fangat ;
þér mun kostr at káklast um : komist þú austur þangat.'

62. Fliótliga leiddist Skíða skraf : skap-illr trúi-ek hann þekki,
laust til Ölmóðs lœngum staf : lítt kom við eðr ekki.

63. Skíði datt, þá skyldi hann : skiótt á þaranum ganga ; 125
hólkinn misti húsgangs-mann : af harkinu því inu langa.

64. Virðum gengur varla í hag : víst, ef fleiru týna ;
Ölmóðr hafði annan dag : iárnit þetta at sýna.

65. Austr af Nóreg ýtar tveir : áttu fyrst at ganga,
drukk-langa stund dratta þeir : fyrir Danmœrk endi-langa. 130

66. Svó var brautin breið fyrir þeim : sem borgar-stræti væri ;
ýtar kómu í Ásia-heim : Óðins hœllu nærri.

67. Þá vóru skórnir Skíða í sundr : skipti hann um þá síðan ;
enn ina fornu laufa-lundr : lagði í klas-sekk víðan.

68. Borgar-turnar glóa sem gull : glymr í hverju stræti, 135
heimsins er þar hegðan full : ok hæversk œnnur læti.

69. 'Hverr á þessi húsin stór ?' (hátt réð Skíði mæla)—
'Þetta er hún Valhœll vór : sem víss er í auðr ok sæla.'

70. Skíði spurði at þessu Þór : 'Þú munt kunna at skýra,
hvar kempur sitja ok kóngur vórr : ok kappa-sveitin dýra.' 140

---

96. prýða, Cd.   106. Somehow wrong.   117. Thus.   120. minn, Cd.

71. *Þor.* ' Óðinn sitr ðar inzt í hæll : ok Æsir tólf á stóli ;
glóar hun øll af greipar-miøll : ok grettis rauðu bóli.

72. Horfðu beint á Hilditønn : ok Hálfdan kóng enn Milda ;
þér mun virðast saga mín sønn : slíkt tel ek kapp gilda.

73. Ívarr sitr þar inzt í hæll : ok Álfur kóngr hinn sterki ; 145
Hrólfur Kraki ok hirð hans øll : hraðr at snildar-verki.

74. Haka líta ok Hagbarð má : hiá hónum Starkað Gamla ;
Arngríms-synir þar útar ífrá : ekki lítit bramla.

75. Blót-Haraldur býr þar næst : beint ok Þráinn í haugi ;
við þá líkar fyrðum fæst : flagðs er litr á draugi. 150

76. Vølsungur með " vísis " þjóð : ok Vídólfr Mittum-stangi,
Eddgeirr Risi ok Aventróð : alt er á reiði-gangi.

77. Hér er Geirmund Heljar-skinn : ok hiá hónum kappinn
Víkar,
Sørli hinn Sterki sezt þar inn : slíkt eru kempur ríkar.

78. Ásmundr sitr þar yzt við gátt : er sá mesti kappi ; 155
garprinn sá, sem Gnóð hefr átt : gørir sér flest at happi.

79. Enn Víðfaðmi Ívarr sitr : inztr á pallinn langa ;
hundrað kónga, herrann vitr : hvern dag með hónum ganga.

80. Sigurðr Hringur sitr þar hiá : ok sonr hans kóngrinn Ragnar ;
Áli hinn Frækni útar ífrá : eru þat røskvir bragnar. 160

81. Ragnars-synir reiknast þá : rétt hiá Andra ialli ;
Ísungs-synir útar ífrá : ekki smáir á palli.

82. Regin ok Fófni rekkrinn, siá : rétt fyrir norðri miðju,—
átián dvergar útar ífrá : allir hagir í smiðju.

83. Hér næst sér-þú hølda tólf : heldr í vexti gilda ; 165
garprinn, þekktu Gøngu-Hrólf : ok Gautreks arfa hins Milda.

84. Þóri Iárn-skiøld þekkja má : þar með Høgna ok Gunnar ;—
Ubbi hinn Fríski útar ífrá : " ei mun betra " sunnar.

85. Yzt við gátt er Sigurðr Sveinn : settr af gørpum sniøllum ;
fyrrum vann hann Fófni einn : frægstr af kóngum øllum. 170

86. Heldr hann øllum hræddum hér : hirðir orma-setra ;
Óðinn setr hann ei hiá sér : autt rúm þykkir betra.

87. Þar er á stóli Freyja ok Frigg : ok fara með hvíta glófa ;
enn er hin þriðja þorna-vigg : þat er hún Hildr in Mióva.

88. Heðinn vill giarna Hildi fá : enn Høgni stendr á móti ; 175
fyrir þat magnast málma þrá : múgrinn kastar grióti.

89. Hér felst undir auðnan þín : ef þú gørir þá sátta ;
ellegar verðr þat ýta pín : innan þriggja nátta.'

90. Því næst gékk í Háva-hæll : halrinn kanpa-síði ;
hirðin tók at hlæja øll : ' Hvat mun vilja hann Skíði ?' 180

91. Skíði heilsar Fiølni fyst : ok féll þat ekki úr minni ;
hann sá alla heimsins lyst : í húsi þessu inni.

92. Herra Óðinn hreyfði sér : ' Heill ok sæll, minn Skíði !
siálf-boðinn skaltu í sess hiá mér : seima-lundrinn fríði !

93. Hér er sá maðr mik hefir lyst : marga stund at finna ; 185

---

151. vísis] thus.   163. sá, Cd.   168. Some name?

þú skalt segja mér fréttir fyst : ok far-lengd þína inna.'

94. *Sk.* ' Frétta-laust er í ferðum mín : Fátt er kyrru betra ;
nálgast hef-ek á náðir þín : nú er-ek sex-tigi vetra.'

95. Óðinn spurði aptur nú : er þat minni vandi :
' Eru margir meiri enn þú : menn á Ísalandi ?'   190

96. *Sk.* ' Á Ísalandi eru margir menn : mis-iafnt nøkkut ríkir ;
þó eru ekki allir enn : oss at mentum líkir.

97. Þorgils er þar bóndinn beztr : á bygðum vestur-sveita ;
sá kemr engi gøngu-gestr : at greiða vili neita.

98. Ei er ek vanur (aulinn kvað) : í orðum menn at gylla ;   195
þó vil-ek sýna þér svínit það : er seggrinn réð at fylla.

99. Annat er þar ágætt líf : ætla-ek hann heiti Stulli,
mér gaf þenna mæta kníf : maðrinn sæmda-fulli.'

100. *Oð.* ' Fyr þá neyð, þú fékkt af mér : at fórtu úr landi þínu,
kiør-grip skaltu kiósa þér : karl ! úr ríki mínu.'   200

101. *Sk.* ' Herra, gef mér hólk á staf : hann vil-ek giarna þiggja ;
trúa mín veit, ek týndi hónum af : tel-ek við Nóreg liggja.'

102. Røgnir kallar Regin til sín : ' Rammliga skaltu smíða
stinnan hólk úr stáli fín : á staf míns herra Skíða.'

103. Hann kvaðst mundu hraðr at því : ok hefr sik út í smiðju,
hálfan fiórðung hafði í : hæst var rønd í miðju.   206

104. *Sk.* ' Góði herra ! gef mér smiør : greitt í hirzlu mína !'
Bænin sú féll beint í kiør : biðr hann Freyju sína.

105. *Fr.* ' Vista-fátt mun verða þér : víst, ef játar flestu ;
sá kostnaðrinn sezt at mér : smiørlaus er-ek at mestu.'   210

106. *Oð.* ' Laufey mín skal láta í : enn Loki eptir hlaupa.'
Fr. ' Mér sýnist engi sæmd at því : ef smiør þarf út at kaupa.'

107. Fárbauti lét fylla svín : ok færa þat heim til hallar.
Oð. ' Farðu ok geym þat, Freyja mín : ok fá hónum, þegar
hann kallar !'

108. Þar kom innar áfengt øl : Óðinn drakk til Skíða :   215
' Þú skalt hafa hiá mér dvøl : ok hvergi í kveldi ríða.'

109. Halrinn þakkar herra vín : ' Hafi-þér Guðs-laun, Óðinn !'
Enn hann greip fyr eyrun sín : sem at hónum færi vóðinn.

110. *Oð.* ' Hann skaltu ekki í húsum mín : hirða þrátt at nefna ;
ellegar tapast auðnan þín : sem áður hef-ek þér gefna.   220

111. Kvón-fang skaltu kiósa þér : kann-ek fleira at greina,
flióðin læt-ek føl huà mér : nema Freyju mína eina.'

112. *Sk.* ' Þýða kýs-ek þorna brú : þat er hún Hildr in Mióva ;
mér lízt engi ønnur sú : iafn-vel kunni hófa.'

113. *Oð.* ' Hægni ræðr hverr hana á : því hún er hans einga-dóttir ;
ei mun Heðni hugnast þá : ef hér eru menn til sóttir.'   226

114. Skíði veik at Hægna hér : ok hóf svó ræðu sína :
' Hvat skal ek leggja í lófann á þér : þú leifir mér mey svó fína ?'

115. Hægni segir, at Heðinn má : Hildi siálfur gipta :
Sk. ' Hvergi kýs ek hærra á : því hér er við dreng at skipta.'   230

---

116.   'Alt í heimi ynni-ek til : at þit Hꜵgni sættist.'
        Heð. 'Þeygi gengur þetta í vil : þó vit Hildur ættimst.'
117.   'Mágur þinn ek verða vil :' veik svó Skíði at Hꜵgna.
        Sk. 'Verið kátir ok víkið til : víst við kónginn Rꜵgna !'
118.   Hꜵgni segir, at mágr hans má : mikit um þetta ráða.   235
        Sk. 'Séu þit kvittir ok sáttir þá ! signi Guð ykkr báða !'
119.   'Illa er talat, (kvað Ása-Þórr) : afreks-maðrinn fríði !
        fyrir þat tapast vináttan vór : vendu þik af því, Skíði !'
120.   Óðinn spurði unga frú : orð þarf sízt at teiga :
        'Er þér viljugt, vella-brú : vaskan dreng at eiga ?'   240
121.   *Hi.* 'Heðni hef ek heitit því : hans ek skylda bíða ;
        en ef hann faðir minn fæst þar í : forsmái-ek ekki hann Skíða.'
122.   *Oð.* 'Hilditꜵnn skal hafa fyr vátt : ok Hálfdan kóng hinn Snialla ;
        vér skulum drekka brúðkaup brátt : við bragna þessa alla.'
123.   Skíði rétti skitna hꜵnd : skyldi hann fastna Hildi ;   245
        Óðinn gaf honum Ásia-lꜵnd : ok alt þat hann kiósa vildi.
124.   Kappinn þar með kóngs-nafn hlaut : kænn ok ꜵrr í stríði ;
        stungu sumir at stála-gaut : 'strákligr lízt mér Skíði !'
125.   Skíði gꜵrði skyndi-kross : skiótt með sinni loppu ;
        sú hefr fregnin flogit at oss : fékk hann hꜵgg á snoppu.   250
126.   Heimdall gaf hónum hꜵggit það : horns með stúti sínum.
        'Hví búi þér (hann Hꜵgni kvað) : svó hart at mági mínum ?'
127.   *Heimd.* 'Hann hefr fært þau fyrn at oss : fleina-lundrinn stælti !
        gꜵrði hann fyrir sér gamlan kross : ok "gꜵrvꜵll" orðin mælti.'
128.   Skíði gꜵrði at skylmast þá : skiótt á lítlum tíma,   255
        Heimdall sló svó hꜵfuðit á : at hann lá þegar í svíma.
129.   Hilditꜵnn réð hlaupa upp þá : ok hristi á sér biálfann :
        'Hverr veit, nema hrottinn sá : hꜵggvi kónginn siálfan.'
130.   Hió til Skíða hꜵggin þriú : hér var yss á fólki :
        skrꜵkva-ek ekki, at skræfan sú : lét skella í stæltum hólki 260
131.   Hlióp upp Geirmundr Heljar-skinn : ok hefr upp ꜵxi breiða :
        'Lemdu hann ekki landa minn : lítinn tel-ek þat greiða !'
132.   Remmi-gýgi rekr hann þá : rétt at Haraldi miðjum ;
        grimmliga lætr garprinn sá : sem geysist leon í viðjum.
133.   Mikit var um þá Haraldr hné : heita mátti ýki ;   265
        rétt sem stykki af stofni tré : stóra heyrði dýki.
134.   Ubbi hinn Fríski atgeir rak : ótt at Heljar-skinni ;
        ꜵfugr féll hann aptr á bak : ei varð dýkrinn minni.
135.   Hálfur kóngur hlióp upp þá : ok hreyfði brandi sínum :
        'Þann skal líf-tión leggja á : sem lemr á frænda mínum.' 270
136.   Ubbi fékk af Álfi slag : útan á kinnar-vanga ;
        þat má kalla keppa sag : er kratins-synirnir danga.
137.   Óvit beið þá Ubbi á sér : Ívarr réð svó mæla :
        'Maðr mun fást í móti þér : minst er oss um þræla.'
138.   Starkaðr Gamli stꜵkk á fætr : ok sterkliga tók at emja : 275
        'Ekki hirði-ek hvat Ívarr lætr : ei skal hann Skíða lemja.'

---

265. ynki, Cd.   266. dynki, Cd.

139. Ívarr fékk í augat slag : af Starkaði Gamla ;
ógurligt var eggja sag : engi mátti hamla.

140. Hálfi kóngi var haldit þá : svó hann mátti ekki stríða ;
alla lét hann eitthvat fá : sem ýfa vildu Skíða. 280

141. Hrókr hinn Svarti ok Útsteinn iarl : at Ubba sóttu báðir ;
skýzt í leikinn Skelja-karl : skœtnum gefr ei náðir.

142. Ubbi feldi átián menn : afbragðs-kempur stórar,
Skíða sló á skoltinn enn : svó skruppu úr tennur fiórar.

143. Áli hinn Frækni á þat spiót : sem ýta kann at dubba ; 285
rennur fram at randa briót : ok rekr í gegnum Ubba.

144. Ubbi féll þá út um dyrr : með átián hundruð sára ;
lét hann ekki lífit fyrr : enn lungun féllu um nára.

145. Sverði brá þá seima-viðr : sá var nefndur Agnarr ;
hann klauf Ála í herðar niðr : hann sezt niðr ok þagnar. 290

146. Eddgeirr Risi til Agnars hió : ofan kom mitt í skalla ;
seggrinn œngu svaraði ok hló : síðan gœrði at falla.

147. Arngríms-synir í œrva seim : ætla þegar at stríða,
enn Vœlsungar vœrðu þeim : ok veita þóttust Skíða.

148. Víkarr kóngur varðist þá : vakrt á hallar-gólfi ; 295
Sœrli hinn Sterki sverði brá : ok sótti at Gœngu-Hrólfi.

149. Mittum-stangi manaði Hrólf : mættust þeir ok Biarki ;
at hónum sóttu ýtar tólf : ei var lítill harki.

150. Varð þat loks at Víðólfr féll : veittist sigrinn Hrólfi ;
hundrað rasta heyrði smell : þá halrinn datt at gólfi. 300

151. At Skíða sótti mengit mest : margur varð at falla ;
heyrði þangat hávan brest : í hólkinum lét hann gialla.

152. Fyrðum þótti ferlig undr : fliúga um heiminn þaðra ;
hverr klauf annan hœlda í sundr : hverir drepa þar aðra.

153. Ógurlig var odda-skúr : undur mátti kalla ; 305
engi gœrðist œðrum trúr : ymsir réðu falla.

154. Sló til Gunnars Sigurðr Hringr : sá var arfi Giúka,
augna-brúnin á hónum springr : ei mun góðu lúka.

155. Svó hió hann til Sigurðar Hrings : at sverð stóð fast í
tœnnum ;
hér hefr næsta komit til kings : með kœrskum frægðar-
mœnnum. 310

156. Sveitin gœrðist sár ok móð : sumir af mæði sprungu ;
upp tók þar í œkla blóð : œxar ok kesjur sungu.

157. Eddgeirr Risi ok Aventróð : æða fram at Skíða ;
Blót-Haraldur berst af móð : búinn við Þráin at stríða.

158. Þórir Iárn-skiœldr þreif upp stein : þat má undur kalla ; 315
keyrði á Haralds kinnar-bein : svó kappinn varð at falla.

159. Þráinn er sterkur, þat er ei undr : því hann er trœll at mætti,
Risana báða reif í sundr : ok rak þá út um gætti.

160. Berserkr einn, er Brúni hét : barði Þráin til heljar,
enn í því hann lífit lét : liótliga í hónum beljar. 320

161. Ormrinn Fófnir eitri spió : ok æðir fram at Skíða ;
hrœkk hann útar at hurðu þó : hvergi var fritt at bíða.

162. Skíði rak sinn fastan flein : í Fófnis triónu lióta ;
trøllslig var sú tønnin ein : er tók úr hónum at hrióta.

163. [Starkaðr Gamli stóð þá upp : ʻok stillti næsta Brúna ʼ] ;
Ormrinn rak upp bølvat bupp : þá ball hónum høggit núna. 326

164. Skíði lét í skreppu sín : skák-manns efnit detta ;
løng var sú hin lióta pín : lifir hann enn við þetta.

165. Fófnir í sitt forna híð : fór nú heim at sinni ;
Starkaðr gørði stála hríð : um stund er løgð í minni. 330

166. Ása-Þórr at ýtum gengr : ok innir til við Skíða :
ʻMuntu ei ætla at lemja oss lengr : fyr løngu er mál at ríða.ʼ

167. ʻ Ei er vón, (kvað Ása-Þórr) : at Óðinn muni þér lúta ;
heldur mun fyr høggin stór : þinn hrottinn verða at stúta.ʼ

168. ʻEf þú vilt, ek ei þik slá : ofan í pønnu þína, 335
leggstu niðr ok lút mér þá : Lítt skulu høggin dvína.ʼ

169. Miølni spenti hinn máttki Þórr : af megni sló til Skíða ;
hér kom á móti hólkrinn stórr : heyrði bresti víða.

170. Starkaðr hió til Þóris þá : þat kom framan í enni ;
allan kviðinn ofan ífrá : ætla-ek sverðit renni. 340

171. Berserkr einn, er Brúsi hét : bregður kylfu sinni,
Starkað Gamla stúta lét : styrr varð ekki at minni.

172. Ragnar kóngr ok rekkar hans : réðu at Gautrek Milda ;
Ketill ok Hrólfr í kappa dans : kómu með drengi gilda.

173. Heyrði til þar hetjan fór : høggr hann Iøtuninn Brúsa; 345
féll hann dauðr á fætur Þór : flestir urðu at dúsa.

174. Þá varð Álfr í þessu lauss : ok þrífr upp kappann Víkar ;
færði ofan í Fiølnis haus : svó fiándliga Óðni líkar.

175. Þat sá hún Freyja, Fiølnis víf : at fast tók Óðni at svíða ;
støkk hun upp með stæltan kníf : ok stakk í nefit á Skíða. 350

176. Høgni þreif upp Hálfdan iall : hann var frægstur gotna,
rak hann niðr svó rammligt fall : at rifin gørvøll brotna.

177. Allir réðu Æsir þá : einni røddu at kalla :
ʻHrekið hann Skíða, hverr sem má : Hann mun drepa oss alla !ʼ

178. Flestir urðu fúsir þess : fékk hann høgg við vanga ; 355
þá var mikit þausnar vess : þriá-tigi at hónum ganga.

179. Hann barði í hel þá Baldr ok Niørð : bæði Loka ok Hæni ;
fimmtán lét hann falla á iørð : enn fleygði tólf í mæni.

180. Til orða tók þá Sigurðr Sveinn : er sá hann brynju ristna :
ʻ Mér lízt nú sé margr um einn : manninn þann inn Kristna. 360

181. Greyliga tókst þér gangan, Þórr : þú gintir hingat Skíða ;
sýndr er hónum siðrinn vórr : sá mun spyrjast víða.ʼ

182. Sigurðr tók þá sverðit Gram : ok sveiflar til með afli ;
allir þeir, sem oddrinn nam : innar hrukku at gafli.

183. Hnykti hann Skíða um hallar-dyrr : enn hlióp þar siálfr í
milli ;   365
lúinn ok móður lá hann þar kyrr : lítit varð af snilli.

184. Heyrði hann inn í Háva-høll : hark ok styrjøld bæði ;

---

325. This line is maimed or else in a wrong place.

borgin var sem bifaðist öll : beint ok léki á þræði.
185.   Skiótliga kallar Skíði inn : þar skatnar lágu hneptir :
       'Sæll ok liúfur Sigurðr minn : svínit lást mér eptir!   370
186.   Nefna mundi ek nafnit þitt : nistill silki-treyju,
       ef þú, Sigurðr, svínit mitt : sæktir inn til Freyju.'
187.   Gnoðar-Ásmundr gærði þá : gilda atsókn ok stríða ;
       svínit tekr hann seggjum frá : ok sendir út til Skíða.
188.   Þat kom framan í fræða sal : frá ek at aulinn vakni ;   375
       Nú er hann heima í Hítardal : Hildar trúi ek hann sakni.

III.   The End.

189.   Yzt við gátt at aulinn lá : ekki er trútt at hniósi ;
       þeir stæktu vatni strákinn á : ok styrmðu yfir með liósi.
190.   Þorleifr talar við þegninn brátt : 'Þú hinn vóndi slangi!
       ærst hefir-þú í alla nátt : ok einart verit á gangi.   380
191.   Fátækt hefir hér fólkit mart : fengit sárar nauðir ;
       ymsa hefr-þu beyst ok bart : svó bragnar fimm eru dauðir.'
192.   Á stafnum sáu þeir stóran hólk : stóð hann merkur átta ;
       hér hefr meizlin fátækt fólk : fengit af stórum hrótta.
193.   Troðnir í sundur tvennir skór : tel-ek þat ei með listum ; 385
       ærkumlaðr var aulinn stórr : upp vóru hinir á ristum.
194.   Fiórar tennur framan úr haus : fallnar vóru á Skíða ;
       enn hin fimta er orðin laus : í hána kvað sér svíða.
195.   Bráðliga segir hann brægnum frá : hvat bar fyrir hann í
           svefni ;
       margur setr í mikla skrá : minna yrkis-efni.   390
196.   Skatnar hugðu at Skíða brátt : ok skoðuðu hann uppi ok
           niðri ;
       hans var víða holdit blátt : enn hárit líkast fiðri.
197.   Hirzla hans af hagleik gær : hun var tóm at kveldi,
       þar var komit í þrí-fornt smiær : þat var úr Ásia-veldi.
198.   Hældar gáfu hundum smiær : úr hirzlu-tætri Skíða,   395
       þeir létu sitt hit leiða fiær : ok lágu dauðir víða.
199.   Fundu þeir í trússi hans tænn : tuttugu marka þunga ;
       Nú má heyra at sagan er sænn : seima þollsins iunga.
200.   Þeir grófu hána með fagran flúr : af fremstu meistara tólum,
       bragnar gærðu bagalinn úr : sem beztr er norðr á Hólum. 400
201.   Lengi vetrar lá hann siúkr : lítit batnar Skíða,
       flagnaði hans hinn fúli búkr : féllu á sárin víða.
202.   Aldri trúi-ek ærmum þriót : mun illra meina batna,
       fyrr enn lofar at leggja af blót : ok Laugar-nætr at vatna.
203.   Ei hef-ek heyrt hver ævi-lok : urðu Norðmanns Skíða. 405
       Hér skal Suðra siávar-rok : Sunnudagsins bíða.

ONE HUNDRED RHYME-DITTIES.

THERE are heaps of Rímur of the fifteenth century on vellum, of the sixteenth and seventeenth centuries on paper MSS., and of the eighteenth and nineteenth partly in print, rivalling the chansons de geste themselves in quantity, but very few among them are worthy of being dragged from their limbo.

But by far the best verses in Ríma-metre are the *Improvisations* and *Ditties*, of which there are hundreds known, some composed by well-known persons, some by farmers or labourers; for your Icelandic yeoman will often turn a Ríma-verse as neatly as a Welshman an 'englyn.' Many of these couplets are of great sweetness and deep melody; and coming from the mouths of the people, whose fine ears have instinctively picked out and remembered the best of them, a pretty collection might be formed illustrative of nearly every phase of Iceland's life and thought.

The one essential in a good ditty is that it charm the *ear*, and it is on this quality that its preservation as a live thing in the people's memory depends. Indeed to Icelanders for many generations the melody of the Rímur has supplied the place of vocal and instrumental music, and in consequence the harmonious qualities of the popular verse are notable. In the present day the imitation of foreign poetry and music has dulled the feeling for alliterative verse-melody, for tune and word-rhythm are two things.

They are roughly cast together as they came into the mind; and, being easy to make out and really rather illustrative matter than of the substance of the book, not translated. Their authors are in great part unknown, though some are by well-known poets, and no doubt many of the best now nameless verses are their work also.

Chief among authors of these pieces and ditties is *Hallgrim Peterson* (d. 1674). Of him many stories are told, and he has become the typical poet in the popular mind. It is told how he made his first couplet, when he was yet a child, on the cat; how he once abused his gift and lost it for a time by singing a fox to death by his curse; how he asked his little Steinun, a girl three years old, as to her creed, and how she, having inherited her father's powers, answered him in verse (she died aged 3½). There are stories, too, of incidents attached to the composition of his different hymns, and it is said that, like Thormod of old, he died with an unfinished verse on his lips.

Of his beautiful Passion-Psalms and their great popularity we have spoken in the Reader. Here we must notice the well-known *Rules of Life*, which every child learned, and which takes the place of the old mediæval Disticha, and the inimitable Skegg-karls-visor, *Beardie-verses* on the stone-ware Jug, a model of that pious humour which died, in England, with Fuller. Hallgrim's poems have never been completely edited. His Passion-Psalms were indeed printed in his life, 1666 (though the best edition is of 1693), but when there was a collection of his poems made in 1777 by Halfdan Einarson, the religious poems were all given, but the secular ones omitted. Thus there are many of his best couplets that have never been printed at all, and many a nameless ditty now passing from mouth to mouth may be his, its sweetness and sound melody its only remaining marks of parentage.

In the next generation after Hallgrim, many good ditties were improvised by such men as *Stephen Olafsson* (d. 1688), *Paul Widalin* (d

1727), *John Sigurdsson Dala-skald* (drowned 1720), and other less prominent contemporaries of Arni Magnusson (d. 1730), who is even
recorded to have made a couplet himself as an epitaph on a Norwegian friend of his. Paul Widalin's verses have a special interest
from their sweetness of flow and clear thought. Indeed it was at this
period (1650–1730) that the best couplets were made; their melody and
simplicity has never since been reached. There is a MS. collection of
Widalin's ditties in the Bodleian Library, though not complete, for
many of his good ditties are missing.

Eggert Olafsson (1726–1768, of whom there is some mention in the
Prolegomena), the most notable Icelander of last century, is the author
of some very beautiful Improvisations. Of his lyrics we give the bright,
grateful verses which he made on his last voyage back to Iceland in
1766, wherein he speaks of the gentle gale, the glad screams of the gulls,
the porpoises playing round the good ship, and finally of the glorious
greeting of flame from Hecla.

'Such welcome ne'er got I before, to mine own native land.'

Eggert's, too, are the verses, Heimildar-skrá, which give the now classical picture of a winter's night on an Icelandic farm, with the women
working and listening to the reading of Sagas and reciting of Rímur till,
when 'the star is past its middle height,' the night is brought to an end,
as in Burns' masterpiece, by prayer and psalm. Of such happy evenings
in his youth the Editor has lively recollections.

When Eggert was engaged in his five years' tour of Iceland (1752–57),
making the observations which were wrought into his well-known
'Travel Book,' he passed the winters at the little island Widey, near
Reykiavik, in the house of Sculi, a fine yeoman of the old type, and
there he wrote a set of verses, on the fly-leaf of a child's book, which
he gave to Sculi's daughter Oddny, whom he calls his sister 'little
Bunchie.' Oddny grew up and married, we can (though inquiring)
learn nothing more of her. Some of the verses we give below.

Eggert'ʳ ᵤtties are always melodious and clear. We have picked a
few lines of his best, which will give a fair example of his style when
he followed his own bent, for he tried to revive old Eddic and Court-
poetry—in vain one is glad to say.

In later days still, there are good racy couplets by John Thorlaksson,
the translator of Milton (1744–1819), a humorous man and good
scholar; Sigurd Petersson (1759–1827); Benedict Grondal (1763–1825);
Sigurd of Broadfirth, the Rímur writer who had lived in Greenland
(1799–1845); and Sweinbiorn Egilsson (1791–1852), who made the fine
prose version of Homer. But their ditties are the aftermath.

Our collection is fairly representative of all that is best among these
Ditties. Every verse of it (with but few exceptions) has been picked out
of a mass of verse which the Editor learnt as a child (age 8–12) by ear,
not by book, spontaneously and *not* as a task[1]. A verse which one picks
up in childhood, and which clings to one through life, must at all events
be really good in rhythm and clear in expression. The subjects are very
various. Thus, there are couplets on the *poet's changeful moods* and
passing feelings, his *passions*, and his *prayers*. Then there are numbers
of verses on the *daily farm-life*, the weather, the hayfield (one on a

---

[1] Capping verses in pairs was a favourite pastime of his youth; the rule was that
the second player should go on with a verse beginning with the *last letter* of the
verse the first player had cited; the first player again had to follow the cue given by
the second player's verse, and so on.

mouse killed by a mower recalls the occasion of Burns' ode), the household stock, the pet pony's death, the busy smith, the hard-working boat-builder, the household intrigues and quarrels even; but the prettiest of home-life verses are those on *children*, the little girl taught how to sit at meat, the child frightened by the cat, the little girl's catechism, the sampler, the boy in the dairy, the children being taught to read and write, etc. There are many lines on *travelling* too, of travellers on the coast or in the desert, of hospitality and inhospitality, of benighted wayfarers shouting to wake the household, of the priest who lost his horse and had to come afoot to church in his vestments. Then there are the *epitaphs*, often humourous or satirical, on well-known characters, poets and others. There is also no lack of those which deal with the *supernatural*, with ghosts, and fiends, and omens, and the like; amongst others, the story of the murdered love-babe's reproach to its mother (recalling our touching Northern ballads); and the *dream-verses* spoken by the spirits of those who have been lost at sea, or on the ice, or in the snow, and who appear in the visions of the night to their best-beloved and tell their fate. Ditties on fairies and ogresses there are too (as in England and Wales).

There are couplets on celebrated *adventures* or *incidents*, for instance, on the outlaw who fought himself free and got away though his leg was smitten off.

There are other ditties of a mere *didactic* character, triads, saws, riddles, and many *anagrams, rebusses* and *word-plays* of various kinds. There are some by *scholars*, the trying of the pen, the funny satire on the commentator by himself (Biorn of Skardsa's mentioned above).

The reader will get a better idea of the character of these ditties from reading two or three than from any definition we could give. Their essence lies in the simplicity of the *thought*, which must be so clear and naive that a child could have thought it; in the *cleverness* of the wording, which secures it popular favour in the first place; and (most vital of all) in the *melody* of the *sound*, which enables it to keep alive from generation to generation. No man could sit down to write such ditties, and no man but a born poet could write one that would outlive himself.

Hallgrim Petersson, *d.* 1674, Nos. 1, 2, 10, 13, 54, 67, 75 : Eggert Olafsson, *d.* 1768, Nos. 3–5 : Stephen Olafsson, *d.* 1688, Nos. 21, 22, 31, 34, 35, 38, 39, 81, 96, 99 : Paul Widalin, *d.* 1727, Nos. 12, 18, 20, 24, 36, 37, 40, 41, 58, 72, 93 : John Gudmundsson, lærði, *d.* 1655, No. 51 : Biörn Skarðsá, *d.* 1656, No. 71 : Bishop Stein, *d.* 1739, No. 65 : John Sigurdsson, Dala-skald, *d.* 1720, Nos. 69, 100 : Arni Magnusson, *d.* 1730. No. 71 : Gunnar Paulsson, *d.* 1792, No. 68 : Sigurðr Pétersson, *d.* 1827, Nos. 47 b, 73 b : Benedikt Grondal, *d.* 1825, No. 23 : John þorlaksson, *d.* 1819, Nos. 75 b, 79, 80, 82, 84, 86, 87 a, 88–91 : Sigurd Breidfiord, *d.* 1845, Nos. 25, 64 : Sveinbiörn Egilsson, *d.* 1852, No. 17 : Jakob Samsonson, No. 8.

1. *The Child's Rules.*

UNGUM er það allra bezt : að óttast Guð sinn herra ;
þeim mun vizkan veitast mest : og virðing aldrei þverra.
Foreldrum þínum þéna af dygð : það má gæfu veita,
varastu þeim að veita stygð : viliröu gott barn heita.
Hugsaðu um það helzt og fremst : sem heiðurinn má næra,
aldrei sá til æru kemst : sem ekkert gott vill læra.
Lærður er í lyndi glaðr : lof ber hann hiá þióðum ;
enn hinn er ei nema hálfur maðr : sem hafnar siðonum góðum.
Opt er sá í orðum nýtr : sem iðkar mentan kæra ;
enn þursinn heimskur þegja hlýtr : sem þriózkast við að læra.
Litilátur, liúfur, og kátur : leik þér ei úr máta ;
varastu spiátur, hæðni og hlátur : heimskir menn svo láta.

Vertu dyggur, trúr og tryggur : tungu geym vel þína,
við öngan styggur né í orðum hryggur : athuga ræðu mína.
Víst ávalt þeim vana halt : vinna, lesa og iðja,
um framm allt þú ætíð skalt : elska Guð og biðja.—[H. P.]

2. *The Beardie-jug.*
Skyldir erum við Skegg-karl tveir : skamt mun ætt að velja ;
okkar beggja er efni leir : ei þarf lengra að telja.
Við höfum það af okkar ætt : efnið slíkt eg þekki,
báðum er við broti hætt : byltur þolum ekki.
Ílát vínsins athuga vönd : erum við þess á milli,
og þurfum báðir hentuga hönd : svo hvorugur sínu spilli.
Það er annað ættar-mót : af okkar hætti réttum,
við höfum báðir valtan fót : vitum ei nær við dettum.
Einn eg mis-mun okkar fann : ef áföll nokkur skerða—
eg á von en aldrei hann : aptur heill at verða.—[H. P.]

3. *A Winter Night at Home.*
Fyrst að blaðið autt var eitt : og eptir stund af vöku,
vilda eg heldur en vinna neitt : vefa þar á stöku. . . .
Þegar hiá þeim húmar að : og hiarnar liós í ranni,
mart þær raula rímu blað : og reka hrygð frá manni.
Drósir iafnt með dygð og ást : dýrum hlýða sögum,
að feðra vorra frægðum dást : sem fyrri vóru á dögum.
Má þá snóta marka þel : máli birt í lausu,
illa líkar eða vel : eptir hverja klausu.
Sauma, greiða, karra, kliá : kappið sagan eykur,
spinna, prióna, þæfa þá : það er eins og leikur.
Á þeim hvergi svefninn sér : seggir tíðum heyra,
lesarinn þegar letjast fer : 'lestu núna meira.'
Siö-stiörnu spyr einginn að : inn í bóndans garði,
hún er komin í hádegis-stað : hálfu fyrr en varði.
Þegar háttum þokar nær : þrátt eg heyra kunni,
bezt er að fara, birta þær : að bæta ser í munni.
Slík þó sýnist vinna væn : við það öllum semur ;
iðju dagsins endi bæn : áður svefninn kemur.
Skamm-dægrin með svoddan sið : sem þær löngu nætur ;
vetrar þrek og þorra grið : þannig stytta sætur.—[E. O.]

4. *Homeward Bound,* 1766.
Heldur löng var Hafnar dvöl : hitinn ekki minni,
glaður læt eg flióta fiöl : fram í átta sinni.
Linast siónin lestrum af : lífið deyfist síðan,
af því skal eg um Íslandz haf Ægis hesti ríða. . . .
Akurinn hef-eg yrkt og sáð : aðrir gróðann taka,
hyggjan orðin því er þiáð : þungum vagni að aka.
Þó mitt hiarta þryti á ný : og þorna loksins tæki,
hver veit nema eg Ísland í : annað hiarta sæki.
Ég hefi fengið iómfrúr-byr : iafnan, hægan, blíðan,
öngan svo eg átti fyr : æskilega þíðan.
Náttúran er söm að siá : sækist skipa vegur,
leiðar-steinninn fiöllum frá : flaust að landi dregur.
Allar skepnur yndis-hót : inna að mínu geði,
höfrungarnir hlaupa á mót : hefja danz og gleði.
Landsins fugl um fiska tún : finnur hrelling öngva,
hleypur mót oss hafs á brún : hefja kvak og söngva.
Skipurum nóttin birtu bió : brá ei vanda sínum :
Hekla lýsti langt á sió : lauka-fáki mínum.
Hátt í loptið hvergi kyr : hygg-eg liósin brynni,
svoddan kveðju eg fekk ei fyr : á fóstur-iörðu minni.—[E. O.]

5. *Written on the Fly-leaf of a Child's Book.*

Oddný lítla bað um bók : bróðir hennar af því tók,
brátt hann Oddný kysti í krók : kverið fekk, það yndi iók.

Ef þú værir eins og brúð : undir borði nett og prúð,
handa-fipl og gumpa-giögt : gætir af þer vanið snöggt.

Eitt er það sem enn eg tel : ef hún nenti að prióna vel,
ekki þyrfti að óttast par : andann, myrkrið, grýlurnar.

Oddný falleg þætti þá : þá hún skyldi í kaupið fá,
bæði sykur, bók, og skrín : Böggull væri systir mín.

Oddný gáðu glöggt að því : görðu þig ekki svoddan bí,
að þú görir ílla litt : eða rífir kverið þitt.—[E. O.]

6. *Wet Weather.*

Nú er úti veðrið vott : og veykur manna hugur;
á morgun kann að gefa gott : Guð minn almáttugur.

7. *Evening and Sunset.*

Kvölda tekur, sezt er sól : sígur þoka á dalinn;
komið er heim á kvía-ból : kýrnar, féð, og smalinn.

Kveld-ulfur er kominn hér : kunnigur innan gátta,
sólin rennur, sýnist mér : senn mun mál að hátta.

Senn er komið sólar-lag : sezt á norður-fiöllum;
líður á þenna dýrðar dag : Drottinn hiálpi oss öllum.

Senn er komið sólar-lag : sezt á norður-heiði;
líður á þenna dýrðar dag : Drottinn veginn greiði.

Senn er komið sólar-lag : sezt á norður-tindi,
líður á þenna dýrðar dag : Dróttinn stýri vindi.

Senn er komið sólar-lag : sendi oss Drottinn friðinn;
og svo gefi annan dag : eptir þenna liðinn.

8. *Sunrise.*

Lifnar hagur nú á ný : nýr skal bragur spunninn;
dýr og fagur austri í : upp er dagur runninn.—[I. S.]

9. *The Calendar.*

Tólf á ári tunglin greið : til ber að þrettán renni;
sólin gengur sína leið : svo sem Guð bauð henni.

10. *The Catechism.*

Father : Hver hefir skapað þig skepnan mín? skýrðu mér það núna,
hver leið fyrir þig harða pín? hver hefir gefið þér trúna?

Child : Guð Faðir mig görði um sinn : Guðs Son endur-leysti;
Guðs fyrir Andann gafst mér inn : góður trúar neisti.—[H. P.]

11. *Prayer at rising.*

Nú er eg klæddur (or klædd) og kominn á ról : Kristur Jesus veri mitt skiól;
í Guðs ótta gef þú mér : að gangi í dag svo líki þér.

12. *The little Girl's Sampler.*

Niu vetra nú í vor : næm er á íþróttir,
hefir saumað hvert eitt spor : Hólmfríður Páls-dóttir.—[P. W.]

13. *The Child and the Cat.*

I huganum var eg hikandi : hart nær svo sem fallinn,
kattar róan kvikandi : kom hér upp á pallinn.—[H. P.]

14. *Capping Verses.*

Kondu nú að kveðast á : kvæðin okkar stór og smá,
eitt-hvat það sem ekki er last : eigum við að skanderast.

14 b. Kondu nú að kveðast á : karl minn ef þú getur,
láttu ganga lióða-skrá : lióst í allan vetur.

15. *Reading and Writing.*

Lesa og skrifa list er góð : læri það sem flestir,
þeir eru haldnir heims hiá þióð : höfðingjarnir mestir.

Or, Skrifaðu bæði skýrt og rétt : svo skötnum þyki á snilli,
Orðin standa eiga þétt : enn þó bil á milli.

Or, Skriptin mín er stafa-stór : og stýlað ílla letur,
það er eins og kattar klór : eg kann það ekki betur.

16. *The Boy in the Dairy.*
Drengur einn með dalli rann : drift-hvítur á hár og skinn,
litlar flautir fyrir sér fann : fingri drap í munninn sinn.

17. *Father teaching a Child to eat.*
Borðaðu með mér blautan fisk : brosleit hringa reinin,
tæri-látust tins af disk : taktu útúr þér beinin,—[S. E.]

18. *Melancholy.*
Ærið liggur illa á mér : ekki eru vegir fínir ;
heilir og sælir séuð þér : snió-titlingar mínir.—[P. W.]

19. *Hope in Distress.*
Látum líða og bíða, börn : befölum Guði tíma,
þegar eg kemst yfir þessa tiörn : þá er mér ráðin glíma.—[P. W.]

20. *The Poet's Farewell.*
Ó hvað tíminn er að siá : undarlega skaptur !
hvað mun dagurinn heita sá : að hingað kem-eg aptur ?—[P. W.]

21. *Three Things to cherish.*
Vand-farið er með vænan grip : votta eg það með sanni—
siðuga konu, siálegt skip : og samvizkuna í manni.—[S. O.]

22. *Love Repaid.*
Faðirinn bar mín æsku-ár : innst í skauti sínu,
geymi eg hans hin gráu hár : gott er í horni mínu.—[S. O.]

23. *Hardships make the Man.*
Flest er sagt í veröld valt : vondt hins góða bíður ;
hollt er að þola heitt og kalt : hiá meðan æskan líður.—[B. G.]

24. *Fate.* Forlög koma ofan að : örlög kríngum sveima,
álögin úr ymsum stað : enn ólög fæðast heima.—[P. W.]

25. *Changeful Moods.*
Eg er einsog veröldin vill : velta, kátur, hlióður,
þegar við mig er hún ill : ekki er eg heldur góður.
Þegar við mig hún er hlý : og hugann eitt-hvað gleður,
eg er léttur einsog ský : sem ýtir af sólu veður.
Þá heimur um dyrnar hrindir mér : hattinum af eg lypti,
og til hinna hnatta fer : holl eru mér þau skipti.—[S. B.]

26. *Sorrow after Joy.*
Sumarið þegar setur blítt : sólar undir faldi,
eptir-á með sitt eðlið strítt : andar veturinn kaldi.
Felur húm hið fagra liós : frostið hitann erfir,
væn að dupti verður rós : vindur logni hverfir,
Lýðum þegar lætur dátt : lukku-byrinn mildi,
sínum huga í sorgar átt : sér-hver renna skyldi.

27. *The Three Greatest Pleasures.*
Held ek mestu heimsins lyst, : hesti að ríða bráðum,
sofa hiá ungri seima rist : sigla byr í náðum.

28. *The Good-man's Wealth.*
Niu á-eg börn, enn nítján kýr : nær fimm-hundruð sauði,
sex ok tuttugu söðla dýr : svo er háttað auði.—[Esp. 1584.]

29. *The Boat-builder.*
Hundrað eitt með höfuð sveitt : blunna-birni fríða,
þriá-tigi tvenn og átta enn : eg hefi gört að smíða.

30. *The Grand New Ship splits on the Old Rock.*
Ýtar sigli austur um sió : öldu-iórnum káta.
Skipið er nýtt enn skerið er hró : skal því undan láta.

31. *The Pet Pony Dead.*
Mér réð falla fákurinn : framm úr öllum máta,
þar fór allur auður minn : ekki skal þó gráta.—[S. O.]

32. *The Busy Smith.*
Vili nokkur fá þinn fund : og frétti þinnar iðju,
allir svara á eina lund : 'Eyjolfur i smiðju.'

33. *The Mower.*
Griót er nóg í Gnípu-tótt : glymur iárn í steinum,
túnið er ekki á Tindum miótt : tefur það fyrir einum.

34. *The Fox's Doing.*
Grá-hnýfla er gengin af : eg get hana hvergi litið,
ærnar tölta tvær við staf : hún tóa hefir þær bitið.—[S. O.]

35. *The Trusty Friend.*
Nú vill ekki standa um stafn : stöðugan vin að fanga,
þó allir beinist að þér, Rafn : undan skal eg ganga.—[S. O.]

36. *Short-lived Peace.*
Þó þú lofir fögru, flióð : fer það sem er vani,
sættin verður á Svenskan móð : sem þeir giöra við Dani.—[P. W.]

37. *The Lawsuit over at last.*
Hross-skinns-lengjan er nú elt : allt fór það með stilli,
hún hefir lengi legið melt : Lögmannanna á milli.—[P. W.]

38. *The Mower and the Mouse.*
Í höggi einu hió eitt sinn : hér á grundu vallar,
undan fiórum maður minn : mýslum fætur allar.—[S. O.]

39. *Spade and Hoe.*
Sé eg við bæinn systkin þörf : er seint um matinn breka,
þokka-hiúin hent við störf : heita páll og reka.
Henni saurinn hrín opt á : enn honum er griót að meini,
hún vill þvott og hreinsun fá : enn hann fægist á steini.—[S. O.]

40. *Teaching a Boy to ride.*
Þó slípist klár og slitni giörð : slettonum ekki kvíddu,
hugsaðu hvorki um himin né iörð : enn haltu þér fast og ríddu !—[P.W.]

41. *The Fool in the Judgment Seat.*
Í dómara sæti seggurinn sitr : svo sem aða í leirum,
sé-eg að halurinn sýnist vitr : sér, enn ekki fleirum.—[P. W.]

42. *The Dead Poet's Work.*
Sigurður Gísla-son kvað mart : sá var skáld í Dölum—
sumt var gaman, sumt var þart : sumt vér ekki um tölum.

43. *The Outlaw's Escape on one Leg.*
Hiartað mitt er hlaðið með kurt : hvergi náir að skeika,
með fótinn annan fór eg á burt : fair munu eptir leika.

43 b. *Halt and Happy.*
Þó eg fótinn missi minn : mín ei rénar kæti,
hoppað get-eg í himininn : haltur á einum fæti.—[S. P.]

44. *Lost in the Ice.*
Enginn veit um afdrif hans : utan hvað menn sáu,
skafla-förin skeif-berans : skör til heljar láu.

45. *Weather-bound in a Cave.*
Leiðist mér að liggja hér í liótum helli :
betra er heima á Helga-felli : hafa þar danz og glímu-skelli.

46. *The Priest afoot.*
    Furðar mig á fréttum þeim : fót-gangandi var hann,
    þegar hann kom til Hóla heim : hempuna sína bar hann.

47. *Weather-bound in the Waste.*
    Biskups hef-eg beðið með raun : og bitið lítinn kost,
    áður eg lagði á Ódáða-hraun : át eg þurran ost.—[Esp. 1616.]

48. *For a Fair Wind.*
    Kristur minn fyrir kraptinn þinn : kongur í himna-höllu,
    gefðu þann vind á græðis hind : at gangi í lagi öllu !

49. *The Girl's Wish.*
    Eina vildi eg eiga mér : óskina svo góða,
    að eg ætti synina siö : við Sæmundi hinum Fróða !

50. *What the Raven bodes.*
    Hrafn situr á hárri stöng : höldar mark á taki,
    ei þess verður ævin löng : sem undir býr því þaki.

51. *The Fairies.*
    Hafa þeir bæði heyrn og mál : hold og blóð með skinni,
    vantar ei nema siálfa sál : sá er hluturinn minni.—[I. G.]

52. *Gryla the Bogie and her Children.*
    Grýla kallar á börnin sín : þegar hún fer að sióða,—
    komi þið hingað öll til mín : Leppur, Skreppur, Langleggur og Skióða !

53. *The Ghost of the Man who was buried Upright.*
    Köld er mold á kór-bak : kúrir þar hann Jón Flak ;
    ýtar snúa austur og vestur : allir nema Jón Flak.

54. *The Poet's Curse on the Fox.*
    Þú sem bítur bóndans fé : bölvuð í þér augun sé,
    stattu nú sem stofnað tré : steina-dauð á iörðunne.—[H. P.]

55. *The Murdered Babe and its Mother.*
    Móðir mín í kví, kví : kvíddu ekki því, því !
    Eg skal liá þér duluna mína að danza í.

56. *The Thief and the Moon.*
    Thief :   Viltu tungl, þér í munn : þenna bita feitan ?
    Moon :   Viltu, hvinn, þér á kinn : þenna lykil heitan ?

57. *A Ghost seeking his Stolen Skull.*
    Gengið hef-eg um garðinn móð : gleði-stundir dvína,
    haus-kúpuna, heillin góð : hvergi finn eg mína.

58. *The Wailing of the Ghosts.*
    Svo var röddin drauga dimm : að dunaði í fialla-skarði,
    heyrt hef-eg þá hlióða fimm : í Hóla kirkju-garði.—[P. W.?]

59. *Dream Verses :—Drowned at Sea.   The Dead Man's Wife Dreams.*
    Gakktu framm á Gygjar-stein : görðu svo mín kvinna,
    liggja þar mín látin bein : lióst muntu þau finna.
    Gakktu framm á Gygjar-stein : giótan er þar furðu-mió,
    bar mig þangað báran ein : biargaðu mér undan sió.

60. *Another.*
    Við höfum fengið sæng í sió : sviptir öllu grandi,
    höfum þó á himni ró : hæstan Guð prísandi.

61. *Dead in the Snow :—The Dead Man's Sister Dreams.*
    Einginn finna okkur má : undir fanna hiarni,
    dagana þriá yfir dauðum ná : dapur sat hann Biarni.

62. *Another.*
    Frost og fiúk er fast á búk : frosinn mergur úr beinum,
    það finst á mér sem forn-kveðit er : að Fátt segir af einum.

63. *Dying in the Fire.*
Rauð-litaður er ræfill minn : af rauna-baði hörðu ;
um litinn skiptir Lausuarinn : á lifandi manna iörðu.

64. *The Benighted Traveller's Shout.*
Hér sé Guð á góðum bæ : gestur er á lióra !
andsvörin eg engin fæ : ekki vaknar þóra.—[S. B.]

65. *Shaving has come in.*
Hér kemur maður og heitir Steinn : hefur skegg á grönum,
hann mun vera eptir einn : ekki er rakað af hönum.—[S. I.]

66. *The Good-wife's Generous Greeting.*
Gaktu í ána, góðurinn minn : það görir biskups hesturinn.

67. *A Pretty Speech.*
Held eg nú í höndina á þér : hana og fyrir mér virði ;
engi er sú sem af þér ber : í öllum Borgar-firði.—[H. P.]

68. *No Answer.*
Þó eg hrópi þrátt til þín : þú kant ekki að heyra,
þuríður ! þuríður ! þuríður mín ! þykkt er á þér eyra.—[G. P.]

69. *An Anagram.*
Öfugur smiður arkar sá : sem ýtti Dverga liði,
bindur skyndi-enda á : Allir lifi í friði !—[I. S. D.]

70. *The Commentator.*
Mín ei þykir mentin slyng : mætri að hlýða dróttu—
eg var að ráða árið um kring : það Egill kvað á nóttu.—[B. I.]

71. *An Epitaph.*
Mun hans uppi minning góð : meðal Noregs lýða,
meðan í Biörgvin byggir þióð : og bárur á víði skríða.—[A. M.]

72. *The Miser's Death.*
Sínum örfum sinti ei par : sálugi Gvöndur ríki,
auður í Brokey eptir var : þá öndin skrapp úr líki.—[P. W.]

73. *Epitaph on Biorn the Chemist, died* 1798.
Apotekarinn andaðist Biörn : öllum varð þá þungt um ;
sálin hans fló einsog örn : í upp-hæðirnar, Punktum.

73 *b. A Poet's Epitaph.*
Enginn grætur og einginn hlær : og öngum stofnast vandi,
þegar sálar sínum rær : Siggi kugg úr landi.—[S. P.]

74. *A Riddle : the Rainbow.*
Hver er sá vegur víður og hár : vænum settur með röndum,
grænn og rauður, gulur og blár : giörður af meistara höndum ?

75. *Hallgrim's Portrait of Himself.*
Sá sem orti Rímur af Ref : reiknast má hann glaður,
með svartar brýr og sívalt nef : svo er hann upp málaður.—[H. P.]

75 *b. John Thorlaksson.*
Seggurinn hefir söðul-nef : sem er hátt að framan,
mælir opt frá munni stef : svo mörgum þykir gaman.—[I. Þ.]

76. *Trying a Pen.*
Þessi penni þóknast mér : því hann er úr hrafni ;
hann hefir skorið geira grér ; Gunnlaugur að nafni.

77. *Upside-down Land.*
Fiskurinn hefir falleg hlióð : finnst hann opt á heiðum ;
ærnar renna eina slóð : eptir siónum breiðum.
Séð hef-eg köttinn syngja á bók : selinn spinna hör á rokk,
skötuna elta skinn í brók : skúminn príona smá-bands-sokk.
Séð hef-eg merina eiga egg : alptina folalds siúka,
úr reyknum hlaðinu vænan vegg : úr vatninu yst var kiúka.

78. *The Cow-boy mocks his angry Master.*
Rollant hió með Dýrumdal : driúgum vakti hildi,
bardagann í baulu-sal : byrja aldrei vildi.
Þórður Hræða þegna vo : þessi bió á Ósi,
breytti aldrei bóndinn svo : hann berði menn í fiósi.
Karla-Magnús keisarinn dýr : kendi trúna hreina.
aldrei hann fyrir aptan kýr : orrustu háði neina.

79. *The Love-child.*
Á Bæsá ytri borinn er : býsna valinn kálfur,
vænt um þykja mundi mér : mætti eg eiga hann siálfur.—[I. þ.]

80. *The Poet's little Nephews and Nieces on his Knees.*
Nú er komið full-mart fé : og fólkið nóg að vinna,
sitt á hvoru situr hné : systkinanna minna.—[I. þ.]

81. *Old and Young.*
Við höfum lengi sveizt hér saman silki-hlín ;
þú ert ung, enn eg er gamall, Eyvör mín.—[S. O.]

82. *A Poor Poet's Thanks.*
Guð launi ykkur góðu hión : giöfina nú og fyrri ;
fyrir kerta giöf og grión : gamli þakkar Bæsár-Jón.—[I. þ.]

83. *A Poet's Lameness.*
Hæði-þið ekki Herrans þión : um heltina þó eg kvarti,
hægri fóturinn heitir Jón : hitt er hann Kolbeinn svarti.—[I. þ.]

84. *The Greeting of the Lame Poet and his Pony.*
Yðar kærum ekta-maka og öllu kyni,
heilsið þér frá halta Jóni : Humrum-rumrum segir Skióni.—[I. þ.]

85. *The Poet's Pleasure.*
Að yrkja stöku ólán bió : eptir flestra sögu,
enn gaman er að geta þó : gert fer-skeytta bögu.

86. *The Purring Cat.*
Monsónia malar vel : með svo löngu skapti,
enn þó kennur aldrei mél : útúr hennar kiapti.—[I. þ.]

87. *Coming Down in the World.*
Minn var faðir Monsiur : með það varð hann Séra,
síðan varð hann Signiur : og seinast tómur þorlákur.—[I. þ.]

87 b. *How to address a Bishop.*
Sælið verið þér Séra minn : sagði-eg við biskupinn ;
ansaði mér þá aptur hinn : þú áttir að kalla mig Herra þinn.

88. *Luna Latrata.*
Margur rakki að mána gó : mest þá skein í heiði ;
enn eg sá hann aldrei þó : aptra sínu skeiði.—[I. þ.]

89. *How Big Folks are Fed.*
Ef að dauður almúginn : allur lægi á Fróni,
mætti ske að mör-vömbin : minkaði í honum Jóni.—[I. þ.]

90. *The Population Question Solved.*
Margur fengi mettan kvið : má því nærri geta,
yrði fólkið vanið við : vind og snió að éta.—[I. þ.]

91. *The Bursten Tub.*
Tunnan valt, og úr henni allt : ofan í diúpa keldu,
skulfu lönd, enn brustu bönd : botn-giarðirnar héldu.—[I. þ.]

92. *How not to behave.*
Þakkaðu aldrei þegnum mat : þegjandi burtu skunda,
ávalt settu ask ok fat : ofan á golf til hunda.

93. *A True Tory.*
Vili nokkur segja þeim satt : svara þeir allir á einn veg—
hann faðir minn sæli—og sé honum glatt : sá hafði það einsog eg.—[P. W.]

94. *A Dangerous Silence.*
Margir héldu mig málugan mann : mælti kerling orðs-kvið þann,
þagað gat-eg þó með sann : þegar hún Skálholtz-kirkja brann.

95. *The Cries of the Beasts.*
Hani, krummi, hundur, svín : hestur, mús, titlingur—
galar, krunkar, geltir, hrín : gneggjar, tístir, syngur.

96. *Name in Runes.*
Einn piltur að hné : í blautan snió sté,
ós, lögur, ár, fé : úr, reið,—hans nafn sé.—[S. O.]

97. *Hard Rhyme : Capping Verse with the Devil.*
Devil : Allt er runninn út í botn : áttungur með hreina vatn—
Man : Öll er náð hiá einum Drottn' : á hans náð ei verður siatn.
Devil : Líttu í þessa egg, egg : undir þetta tungl, tungl !
Man : Steypi-eg þér með legg legg : lið sem hrærir unl, unl.

98. *Palindromes.*
Forward. Dóma grundar hvergi hann : hallar réttu máli,
sóma stundar aldrei ann : illu pretta táli.
Backward. Táli pretta illu ann : aldrei stundar sóma,
máli réttu hallar hann : hvergi grundar dóma.

99. *Rhymes in Complex Metres.   On a Horse.*
Bylur skeiðar virta vel : vil-eg þar á göra skil,
þylur sanda, mörk og mel : mylur griót enn syndir hyl.—[S. O.]

And— Hialla fyllir, fenna dý : falla vill ei kári,
valla grillir Ennið í : alla hryllir menn við því.—[Hreggviðr.]

In Consonantic Line-rhyme.   The Bad Pen.
Blekið lekur bók-fell á : bítur lítið penni,
heldur veldur höndin smá : henni menn um kenni.

100. *Tíma-Ríma :* Mansongur.
Opt eru kvæða efnin rýr : ekki á stundum parið,
eg á skrýtið ævintýr : í þó lítið varið.
Mart er sér til gamans gert : geði þungu að kasta,
það er ekki einskis vert : að eyða tíð án lasta. . . .
Beri maðr létta lund : linast rauna tetur,
eigi hann bágt um eina stund : aðra gengur betur.
Sumir hlióta sæmd og vin : sorg í annan tíma,
eptir biarta blíðu skin : brunar dökkva gríma.
Hverfult lukku-hiólið er : hamingju einn þó næði,
ámóta fyrir augum mér : og það léki á þræði.
Kalla eg hræri kroppinn önd : kortur máti sléttur,
eins og sker-borð reist á rönd : rambar þar til dettur.
Sól og máni sýnir öld : sama vitnar manna geð,
allir dagar eiga kvöld : inn til þessa svo er skeð.
Held eg liðið heims á dag : Herrann þó það viti,
sigur undir sólar-lag : sýnist bregða liti.
Þeir sem vilja vakna í söng : og vondar kvalir flúa,
undir nótt þó ei sé löng : eiga sig að búa.
Teygir ei dauðinn tíma vorn : þá tíð er burt að halda,
það eru á oss álög forn : allir skuld þá gialda.—[I. S. D.]

§ 5. INDEX POEMS.

ISLENDINGA-DRAPA, by HAWK THE SON OF WALDIS.

On the fly-leaf at the end of Cod. AM. 748, covering two pages and going on to a leaf or leaves which have now perished, stands this poem, which contains a series of brief notices of Icelandic heroes, forming a kind of Index to the Sagas known to the author. Judging from the precedence and disproportionate space he allots to the heroes of the East, he must have been of Eastern Iceland, but neither of him nor his mother Waldis do we hear aught elsewhere. One would take him to have lived about the middle or third quarter of the thirteenth century. We have made use of this poem in the Prolegomena as a base for certain calculations with respect to the number of Sagas *lost* since Hawk's day, etc. It is in regular stanzas, but not strophic, unless we allow it to have been of greater length than is likely. We have marked the heroes of Sagas alluded to, in distinctive type, noting in the margin the Saga presumably alluded to, whether lost or extant. Hawk (verse 1) has borrowed words and images from Egil's Arinbiorn Lay, l. 24, and from Haleygatal, ll. 1 and 34 (from the citations in Edda and the Lives of Kings).

From a similar poem by *Thorkil Elfara-skald*, no doubt, comes the stanza on Gunnar, our No. II. *Thormod Olafsson* seems to have written a poem of the same kind from which one stanza survives, our No. III. Thormod is mentioned in the Annals, signature N. s. a. 1338. 'The Krafsi sailed from Deerfirth to Norway. Priest Thormod Olafsson was a-board her. The ship was wrecked on the North of Norway, but men and cargo were saved.'

Other *Kappa-kvædi*, or songs about Champions, were written, perhaps all founded on the prototype by Eywind Poet-spoiler, which is now lost. Such is our No. IV, which is the beginning of such a poem, but we do not think, as some have thought, that it is to be ascribed to Eywind.

In the Stockholm MS. 22, of the fifteenth century, is a poem dealing with the heroes of the Romantic cycles, etc.

Poems of the same class continued to be written after the extinction of traditions in Iceland, taking subjects from the Sagas known to us, for example, one by Thord of Striug, at the end of the sixteenth century.

It is interesting to compare this class of composition with the old catalogue poems of the earlier type, and with the Thulor-Lists of Sea-kings and Gods.

I. Islendinga-drapa, by Hauk Valdisarson.

Introduction.   BERA skal lið fyr lýða Lóðors vinar, glóða
            hrafna-víns nema hafni hneigendr Dvalins veigom :
reyndir bið-ek at randa runnar hlusta-munnum
hausa harða liósan hasl-rekka miöð drekki.
            2. Hvals- mun-ek hvassa telja -húð-lendinga búðar   5
hamra vífs þá er höfðo hodd-lógendr byr gnógan :
meðan til þess, (enn þessum þögn veiti hlyn peitu
garða grundar nirðir) geð deilizt mer (seilar).

1. *Vapnfirðinga S.*   3. Hverr gekk hræddr við örvan Hundings á Snæ-grundu
(verses 3–5).   árr til odda skúrar elg-rennir *Brodd-Helga :*   10
áðr grunnungi gunnar *Geitir* réð at beita
(askr féll alms inn röskvi örlyndr *föður Sörla.*

---

4. hasl-] hals, Cd.

25. getu, Cd. 26. -völu, Cd.

xi. *Thorleif Iarla-*   18. þorði þorleifr herða þing all-snarpra hringa,
skald.   óð sá-er iarli heiðnum ófríðan réð smíða :   70
     vega kváðu því þióðir þann ok Óláf annan
     (bræðr váru þar báðir) Berserk (at því verki).

xii. *Gauk Trand-*   19. Sniallr frá-ek opt at olli *Ormr Skógar-nef* rógi ;
ilsson (lost S.).   örr var sá til snerru snarr hlióm-boði darra :
     Ok geir-raddar gladdi *Gaukr Trandils sun* hauka ;   75
     (geig vann heldr) at hialdri (hann ófám manni).

xiii. *Gunnar S.*   20. Varðizt göndlar garða *Gunnarr* snörum runnum
(Niala).   greitt, enn Gizurr sótti garp ákafa snarpan :
     niörðr lét sextán særða snarr hlióm-viðu darra
     (sárt lék halr við hölða) hiör-regns, enn tvá vegna.   80

xiv. *Miðfirth*   21. Hvast frá-ek hialms at æsti hregg *Miðfiarðar-Skeggi*
Skeggi (lost S.)?   (drengr rauð opt inn ungi ulfs munn) fyr haf sunnan :
     gekk í haug at hnykki hræ-klungrs ept Sköfnungi
     hríð-gervandi hiörva hild-frækn Kraka ins milda.

xv. *Síðu-Hall*   22. Hélt til fullz, sá-er fylla fúr-runna lög kunni   85
(lost S.?).   (sén raun var þess) sónar, *Síðu-Hallr* við alla :
     átti él-bióðr hrotta ágætr sonu mæta ;
     dýrr skóp himna harri höfuðs-manni veg sannan.

xvi. *þorstein Hall-*   23. Hallz arfa frá ek hollan hyr göllungum styrjar,
son's S.   þann er óligast, unnar, ill-mælis rak, tælir :   90
     valdr lét fimm of fellda fleins á morni einum
     (þá vá *þorsteinn* hávan þórhadd) viðu nadda.

xvii. *Bersi* (lost   24. Kunnr var mörgum manni marg-þróttr ' leizt sá ' dróttum
S.?).   vægðar-trauðr at vígum, vers, *Holm-göngu-Bersi :*
     hinn er of hlakkar runna harð-glóðar sté móði   95
     bliks með bruma ekka borðz halfan tog fiorða.

xviii. *Kormaks S.*   25. Kendi *Kormakr* stundum kyn-stórr viðum brynju
     (opt brá hann við heiptir hrafns sút) í gras lúta :
     ok almr sá-er hlaut hilmis hald blóðugra skialda
     (höld frá-ek hræðazt aldri) hug-prúðr á sik trúði.   100

xix. *Thorarin Stein-*   26. Felldi horska hölda hialdr-örr, ok vann sialdan
arsson (lost S.).   (malmr beit hlíf) á holmi happ, *þórarinn kappi :*
     ne þrym-nirðir þorðu þeim í gegn (enn seima-
     lundr hió stórt) at standa *Steinars syni,* fleina.

xx. *Starri* (lost S.).   27. Víst seim-farra snerru snarr *Holmgöngu-*[*Starri*]   105

. . . .

II. þorkell Elfara-skald (from Niala).

SPURÐU vér hve varðiz víg-móðr kialar slóða
     gný-stærandi geiri *Gunnarr* fyrir Kiöl sunnan :
sókn-ryrir vann sára sextán viðris mána
hríðar herði-meiða hauðr-mens en tvá dauða.

III. þormoðr Olafsson (from Niala).

ÖNGR var sólar slœngvir sand-heims á Íslandi,
     (hróðr er af heiðnum lýðum hægr) *Gunnari* frægri :
Niörðr vann hialma hríðar hlíf-nunna tvá lífi ;
sár gaf stála stýrir stórum tolf ok fiórum.

IV. By an unknown Author (from Skalda).

UT réð Ingolfr leita ógn-reifr með Hiörleifi.

. . . .

§ 6. RHYMED GLOSSARIES.

THULOR.

To the chief MSS. of the Edda of Snorri there are affixed certain *collections of words*, either in prose or verse, which are of high interest both for philology and mythology. These lists of words were thrown together as a kind of poetical word-book, a 'gradus,' in which the poet would find choice of terms gathered from all sources. When these lists are in verse they are known as *Thulor*. The MSS. containing them may be divided into two classes, A and B; the A-class best and fullest, consists of AM. 748 and 757; but the latter is in so deplorably rotten and bad a state that it is of little use, and ends at line 594. The B-class comprises Cod. Regius, which has hitherto been made the basis of editions, though it is imperfect and inferior to 748, and leaving out Kings' names, dwarves, trees, Woden's titles, and ending altogether at line 502. Of the B-type is AM. 1 e β.

The value of the Thulor will appear when it is stated that in these seven hundred odd lines in *old metre*, some three thousand primitive words and names are found. The arrangement has a rough symmetry of its own. Beginning with some sixteen sections relating to PERSONS MYTHICAL and POETICAL, titles of gods, and terms of kinship and the like, we next come to a section on *battle, arms and armour*, man's belongings, which make up the first part. This is followed by a fresh part treating of PHYSICAL OBJECTS and the like: the *Ocean* with its *Rivers*, the *fishes*, *whales*, and *ships* that occupy them, with a final vocabulary touching the various *parts of a ship;* next comes *Earth* with the animals that dwell thereon, from *oxen* to *wolves;* then the *Heavens* with its population of *moon, sun, stars, skies*, and *tempests:* after *Air* comes another set of animals, *serpents, horses, birds* of various kinds. Another section, somewhat out of place, deals with *female* names, the hart, fox-names, and *Walkyria-names*. The Third part seems of a MIXED cast. It gives lists of *Islands, Firths, Seeds*. To these we have added a little morsel (ll. 691-718) printed in the editions of Edda as prose. It is found in all the MSS., but it is derived from an older MS., as there is the same omission of the last line but one in all.

The question now arises, whence and when were these verse-lists compiled. For a variety of reasons we are inclined to think that they were put together in the West about the age of Bishop Biarni. The number of foreign words and places forbid a very early origin, and would make it subsequent to the Crusades, by which time Latin and Byzantine Greek words would have crept in and reached the North in the mouth of sailors and pilgrims. The number of foreign birds, many of which the Editor, when writing the Lexicon, was only enabled to identify from Bewick, and of which the names are not known to Icelanders or Norwegians, as well as the positive indications offered by such Old English words as 'sicul-görd,' sail-yard, would point rather to the Western Colonies than to Iceland or Scandinavia proper. In the section on Rivers, which contains one hundred and twenty names, when the sprinkling of classic and scriptural streams (such as Euphrates, Tiber, and Jordan) are taken out, the remainder are almost all *British Rivers*, an observation which startled the Editor as he was looking over a map in the Oxford City Library many years ago (Oct. 1866). These rivers belong to the river-system of the North-East of Scotland and of the Northumbrian coast. It is evident that when one can once identify certain of those rivers as British and nothing else, then those river-names which may be found existing in Norway as well as in Great Britain must refer to British, not Norwegian streams. This cannot be wholly accidental; this section at least must be by some one who knew, or was working for those who knew, these coasts and streams. Smaller indications point the same way, the occurrence of grain and trees, not grown in Iceland or Norway, but common in Great Britain; the knowledge of ship-building and rigging, which would never suit an Icelander, but is singularly appropriate to those favourite Wicking haunts, the Orkneys and North-Scotch coasts. A Gaelic word here and there tells the same tale. With regard to the Islands (ll. 650 ff.), so distinctly a feature of the Norwegian and Danish coasts, they are mostly Scandinavian, and it is not surprising that they should be so, the Wickings came precisely from those Norwegian skerries and island-bound coast-counties, and they gave the old names to some of the islands in the West; but still, of these there are some twenty which can only belong to the West, of mostly Gaelic origin. There is an evident intention on the compiler's part to put round numbers, especially 120 and 60, the hundred and half-hundred, whenever he could, which will account for a few synonyms to eke out the long lists. They must have been made by one who used *writing*, one would fancy.

We have also *Thulor in court-metre*, some of them attributed to Einar Skulason, who may indeed have been the author of all such lines, they would suit his time and cast of thought. They are evidently less important than the others, and the difficulty of the internal rhymes would not tempt many men to try such a task.

We have added a few more in court-metre, of *grammatical* bearing, etc., found in Edda MSS. (Cod. Ups.) and AM. 778, by the same Einar and others.

I. *Mythical, Personal.*

1. *Sea-kings.* ATLI, Fróði, Áli, Glammi,
            Beiti, Ati, ok Beimuni,
Auðmundr, Guðmundr, Atall, ok Gestill,
Geitir, Gauti, Gylvi, Sveiði,
Goir, Eynefr, Gaupi, ok Endill,
Skekkill, Ekkill, Skævill, Sǫlvi,
Halfr ok Hemlir, Hárekr ok Gorr,
Hagbarðr, Haki, Hrauðnir, Meiti,
Hiǫrolfr, ok Hrauðungr, Hǫgni, Mýsingr,
Hundingr, Hvítingr, Heiti, Mævill,   10
Hialmarr, Moirr, Hœmir, Mævi,
Róði, Rakni, Rær, ok Leifi,
Randverr, Rǫkkvi, Reifnir, Leifnir,
Nævill, Rǫfill, Nóri, Lyngvi,

Byrvill, Kilmundr, Beimi, Iorekr,
Ásmundr, Þvinnill, Yngvi, Teiti,
Virvill, Vinnill, Vandill, Sǫlvi,
'Gaverr,' ok Húnn, Giúki, Buðli,
Homarr, Hnefi, Hurfi, Surfi.—
Sékat-ek fleiri S.Æ-KONUNGA.   20

2. *Kings.* Man-ek HAUK-STALDA heiti segja:—
allvalldr, fylkir, ok afraki,
bragningr, æðlingr, buðlungr, dæglingr,
æðlingr (!) ok gramr, iæfurr, ok tiggi,
hildingr, ok harri, ok hertogi,
mæringr, hilmir, mildingr, ok nor,
lofðungr, niflungr, ok landreki,
þengill, vísi, þióðan, konungr:
sinnjor, siklingr, sióli, ræsir,
Skiældungr, Skilfingr, skyli, ok Yngvi,   30
Ynglingr, Ylfingr—Ero nú talið
HÖFUD-SKIOLDUNGA HEITI nækkur.

3. *Dwarfs.* Tel-ek Motsǫgni ok Miǫklituð,
Miðvið, Munin ok, Miǫðvitnir,
Blin[d]viðr, Burinn, Bumborr, Nýi,
Bivorr, Bavorr, Blainn ok Norðri (!),
Grímr, Nár, Niði, Niðǫttr, Dvalinn,
Nainn, Nefr, Nefi, Nifengr, ok Dolgr,
Nýraðr, ok Nýr, Norðri ok Suðri,
Skaverr, Skaviðr, Skirvir, Virvir,   40
Alþiofr, Austri, Aurvangr, ok Dúfr,
Ae, Andvari, Önn, Draupnir,
Dori ok Dagfinnr, Dulinn ok Onarr,
Alfr ok Dellingr, Oinn ok Durnir,
Vindalfr ok Vitr, Vivir, Ori,
Varr, Gull, Mevill, Viðr, ok Ölinn,
Ginnarr ok Þrórr, Gandalfr, Þorinn,
Þekkr, Þrár, Þulinn, Þrasir ok Fullangr,
Fainn, Fárr, Fili, Fiǫlsviðr, Gloinn,
Fiðr, Hár, Farli, Frosti, ok Tigve,   50
Hanarr, Forve, Hepti, Fili (!),
Heri, Hǫg-stari, ok Hænbui,
Hlioðolfr, Kili, Hildingr, ok Litr,
Rað-spakr, Lofarr, Reginn, ok Liomi,
Ráð-sviðr, Loinn, Rekkr ok Eitri,
Toki, Eggmoinn, Eikin-skialdi.

4. *Giants.* Ek man IÖTNA inna HEITI—
Ymir, Gangr, Mimir, Iði ok Þiazi,

---

15. bilmundr, 1 e β. 16. íosmundr, 1 e β. 18. Gautrecr? 36. blavorr,
Cd. 44. ok] or, Cd. 56. Cd. 757; íaki, Cd.

Hrungnir, Hrimnir, Hrauðnir, Grimnir,
Hveðrungr, Hafli, Hripstuttr, Gymir,　　60
Harðverkr, Hrǫkkvir, ok Hástigi,
Hræ-svelgr, Herkir, ok Hrim-grimnir,
Hymir ok Hrím-þurs, Hvalr, Þrí-geitir,
Þrymr, Þrúð-gelmir, Þistil-barði,
Geirrǫðr, Furnir, Galarr, Þrifaldi,
Fiǫlverkr, Geitir, Flegr, Blap-þvari,
Forniótr, Sprettingr, Fialarr, Stígandi,
Sómr, ok Svásuðr, Svarangr, Skratti,
Surtr, ok Stórverkr, Sækarls-muli
Skærir, Skrymir, Skerkir, Salfangr,　　70
Öskruðr, ok Svartr, Önduðr, Stumi,
Alsvartr, Aurnir, Ámr ok Skalli,
Kǫttr, Ösgrui, ok Alfvarinn,
Vind-svalr, Viðarr, ok Vafþrúðnir,
Eldr, Aur-gelmir, Ægir, Rang-beinn,
Vindr, Víðblindi, Vingnir, Leifi,
Beinviðr, Biǫrgolfr, ok Brandingi,
Dumbr, Ber-gelmir, Dofri ok Miðiungr,
Nati, Sǫkk-mimir, ...
Enn ero eptir Iötna heiti :—　　80
Eim-geitir, Verr, Imr, Hring-vǫlnir,
Viddi, Viðgripr, Vandill, Gyllir,
Grimnir, Glaumvarr, Glámr, Sam-endill,
Vǫrnir, Harð-greipr, ok Vagn-hǫfði,
Kyrmir, Suttungr, ok Kalld-grani,
Iǫtunn, Oglaðnir, ok Aur-grimnir,
Gyllingr, Gripnir, Gusir, Ófoti,
Hloi, Gang-lati, ok Hel-reginn,
Hross-þiófr, Durnir, Hund-alfr, Baugi,
Hrauðungr, Fenrir, Hroarr ok Niði—　　90
. . . . . Nú ero upp talið
amatligra Iötna heiti.

5. *Giantesses,*　Skal-ek Troll-kvenna telja heiti :—
Ogresses.　Gríðr, ok Gnissa, Grýla, Bryia,
Glumra, Geitla, Gríma, ok Bak-rauf,
Guma, Gestilja, Grottin-tanna,
Gialp, Hyrokkin, Hengi-kœpta,
Gneip, ok Gnepja, Geysa, Hála,
Horn, ok Hrúga, Harð-greip, Forað,
Hryða, Hveðra, ok Hǫlga-brúðr,　　100
Hrímgerðr, Hæra, Herkja, Fála,
Imð, Iarn-saxa, Ima, Fiǫlvǫr,
Mavrn, Iviðja, Amgerðr, Simul,

---

62. hriki, 1 e β.　　66. Fleckr, 1 e β.　　79. sægrimnir, 1 e β.　　91.
þa er nú lokit þursa heitum, 1 e β.

Svivǫr, Skríkja, Sveipin-falda,
Öflug-barða, ok Iarn-glumra,
Imgerðr, Ama, ok Iarn-viðja,
Mar-gerðr, Atla, Eisor-fála,
Leikn, Munn-harpa, ok myrk-riða,
Leirvǫr, Lióta, ok Loðin-fingra,
Kráka, Varð-rún, ok Kiallandi,　　　　110
Vigglǫð, Þurr-bǫrð—viljom nefna—
Rygi, síðast, ok Rivin-geflo.

6. *Woden's names.*

Nú skal yppa ÓDINS næfnom :—
Atriðr, Auðunn, ok Allda-fǫðr,
Gizurr, Kialarr, Gautr, Viðrimnir,
Gollorr, Grimnir, Ginnarr, Hnikoðr,
Fiǫlnir, Dresvarpr, Fengr, Arn-havfði,
Fráriðr, Al-fǫðr, ok Farma-týr,
Herjan, Fiǫl-sviðr, Hnikarr, Fornǫlver,
Hróptr, Hialm-beri, Hǫrr, Fiall-geigoðr,　　120
Grímr, Gap-þrosnir, Gangraðr, Svipall,
Glapsviðr, Ganglær, ok Ganglæri,
Her-teitr, Har-barðr, ok Hropta-týr,
Geigoðr, Gǫllnir ok Geir-loðnir,
Hlæfoðr, Hávi, Hagyrkr, Sviðoðr,
Síð-hǫttr, Svafnir, Sig-fæðr, Þrasarr,
Hrami, Hiarrandi, ok Hengi-kœptr,
Hrosshárs-Grani, Hriótr, Tví-blindi,
Þroptr, Her-blindi, ok Herja-fæðr,
Hvat-móðr, Hlé-freyr, Hveðrungr, Þriði,　　130
Gǫllungr, Bileygr, ok Geirǫlnir,
Vávǫðr, Val-fæðr, Vingnir, Rǫgnir,
Sviðurr, ok Skollvaldr, Sig-gautr, Viðurr,
Sviðrir, Báleygr, Sigþér, Brúni,
Sigmundr, Svǫlnir, Síð-skeggr, ok Niótr,
Ölgr, Biblindi, ok Enni-brattr,
Bǫlverkr, Eylúðr, Brunn, Sann-getall,
Þekkr, Þuðr, Ómi, Þrundr, ok Ofnir,
Uðr, Iǫlnir, Vakr, Ialkr, ok Lang-barðr,
Grímr, ok Lǫðungr, Gestum-blindi,　　　140
Sigtryggr, Iǫrmunr, Saðr, Gunn-blindi,
Iafn-harr, Óski, Iǫlfoðr, ok Þrór,
Yivngr, Skilfingr, Óðinn, Tveggi,
Vera-týr, Sigþror, Val-gautr, ok Yggr.

7. *Sons of Woden.*

BURIR TO ÓDINS :—Baldr, ok Meili,
Viðarr, ok Nepr, Vali, Áli,
Þórr, ok Hildolfr, Hermóðr, Siggi,
Skiǫldr, ok Öldnir, ok Itreks-ióð,
Heimdallr, Sæmingr, Hæðr, ok Bragi.

8. *Thor.*

Heitir Atli, ok Enni-langr,　　　　　150

Þórr, Eindriði, ok Ása-bragr,
Biorn, Hlorriði ok Harð-veorr,
Vingþorr, Sǫnnungr, Veoðr, ok Rymr
Ása-hetja . . . .

9. *Names of* Enn skal telja Ása heiti :—
the Anses. Þar er Yggr, ok Þórr, ok Yngvi-Freyr,
Viðarr, ok Baldr, Vali, ok Heimdallr ;
þá Týr, ok Niǫrðr, tel-ek næst Braga,
Hœðr, Forseti ; her er œfstr Loki.

10. *Goddesses.* Nú skal Ásynjor allar nefna :—   160
Frigg, ok Freyja, Fulla, ok Snotra,
Gerðr, ok Gefjun, Gná, Lofn, Skaði,
Iǫrð, ok Iðunn, Ilmr, Bil, Niǫrunn,
Hlín, ok Nanna, Hnoss, Rindr, ok Siǫfn,
Sól, ok Sága, Sigyn, ok Vǫr.
Þá er Vár, ok Syn, verðr at nefna ;
enn Þrúðr ok Rán er þeim næst talið.

11. *Names of* Grét ok at Óði golli Freyja :
Freyja. heiti ero hennar : Hǫrn, ok Þungra,
Sýr, Skialf, ok Gefn, ok it sama Mardǫll.   170
Dœttr ero hennar : Hnoss, ok Gersemi.

12. *Walkyries.* Enn ero aðrar Óðins meyjar :
Hildr, ok Gǫndul, Hlǫkk, Mist, Skǫgul,
þá Hrund ok Eir, Hrist, ok Skuld, talið.
Nornir heita þær er nauð skapa.

13. *Women.* Nipt ok Dísi nú mun-ek telja :—
Snót, brúðr, svanni, svarri, sprakki,
flióð, sprund, kona, feima, ekkja,
rýgr, víf, ok brúðr, ristill, sæta,
svarkr, drós, ok man, mær, ok kerling.   180

14. *Men.* Mál er at segja Manna heiti :—
Greppar ok gumnar, gumar ok drengir,
gotnar ok rekkar, garpar, seggir,
sveit, snillingar, ok sælkerar :
bragnar, þegnar, beimar, hǫldar,
firar, ok flotnar, fyrðar, ...
fœroneyti, drótt, flokkr, harð-menni,
kniar, ok kappar, kenpor, nautar,
Öld, ok ærir, ok afar-menni,
liðar, ok lofðar, lýðr, ok sagnir,   190
lióðr, of-látar, liónar, ok ferðir,
mildingr, ok mæringr, mann-baldr, spekingr.

---

153. Vingþorr . . . Veoðr] Vingþær . . . Vingþor, Cd.   159. œfstr] 1 e β ;
nest, Cd.   174. Eir] add. 1 e β.   178. kona] add. 1 e β.   179. bruðr]
1 e β ; dros, Cd.   sæta] 1 e β ; hneita, Cd.   185. hauldar, A.

Þá er glœsi-maðr, ok goll-skati,
snyrti-menn, ok sælingar,
auð-kýfingar, ok oflátar (!),
herr, ok helmingr, ok hœfðingjar :
Folk, ok fylki, fundr, almenningr ;
er þrœng, ok þyss, þorp, auð-skatar,
drótt, ok syrvar, dunn, prýði-menn,
sœgn, ok samnaðr, seta, sterti-menn,   200
fiorr, ok brionar . . . .

15. Company   Enn ero eptir ALDAR-HEITI :—
and Kindred.   hirð, ok gestir, ok húskarlar,
inn-drótt, ok hión,—ef ek allt segi—
rúni, ok þopti, ok ráð-giafi :
Inn-hýsingar, alda-þoptar,
sessi, ok máli, sœrlar, fylgðir :
þá ero félagar ok frændr saman,
vinir, einkili, verðung, halir :
Ai, ok áttungr, arfi, sonr,   210
faðir, bróðir, barmi, blóði, ok lifri,
ióð, burr, nefi, ok arfuni :
þá eru hlýrar, ok hœfuð-baðmr,
niðr, hleyta-maðr, niðiungr, ok barn,
konr, ok kyn-kvísl, kundr, ætt-bogi,
mœgr, málo-nautr, mágr, ok spialli,
ætt-barmr, ætt-slóð, of-skœpt, ok sveinn :
sesso-nautar, ok sifiungar,
af-spring er þá, ok ætt-stuðill.

16. Household. Þá ero ráðo-nautar, ok ráð-giafi,   220
þiónar, ok þrælar, þírr, œnnungar,
verk-menn, kefsir, ok víl-megir.

17. Battle.   ORROSTA heitir :—hialdr, ok rimma,
giǫll, geira-hǫð, ok geir-þrivul,
róg, ok róma, rand-gríð, ok storð,
svipul ok snerra, sig, folk, iara ;
sókn, morð, ok víg, sóta, dolg, ógn,
dynr, gnýr, tara, drima, imun ;
þá er orrosta, ok ǫrlygi,
hríð, ok etja, her-þœgn, þrima.   230

18. WEAPONS.   Ek man segja SVERDA HEITI :—
Swords.   hiœrr, ok Hrotti, hǫguðr, Drag-vandill,
groa, gramr, gillir, giallarr ok neðan-skarðr,
sigðr, ok snyrtir, sómi, skiómi ;
skalkr, skerkir, stúfr, Skrýmir, Laufi,

---

201. fiorr ok br.] add. 1 e β.   210. arfi] 1 e β; avi, Cd.   213. -bað-
mar, Cd.   223. Orrosta heitir] þau ero heiti, Cd.   227. sóta] sotti, Cd.
230. etja] B ; ætna, Cd.

ǫltír, langbarðr, ok orm-þvari,
Legg-bítr, kyr, galmr, ok leifnis-grand,
her-beri, Hneitir, ok hræ-frakki,
lotti, hrǫnduðr, lǫgðer, mækir,
mǫðuðr, mundriði ok Mistil-teinn,   240
malmr, þrór, ok marr, ok mið-fainn,
fet-breiðr, grind-logi, ok Fiær-svafnir,
vægi, leiptr, vægarr, valangr, ok brandr,
verulfr, valnir, vinn-biartr, ok kol,
askr, angr-vaðill, eggjom-skarpi,
svipuðr, ok svipa-liótr, salgarðr, hnefi;
hvati, hæfuð-hvessingr, hausa-mælvir,
hræva-gautr, her-brai, ok hold-mímir,
ben-sægr, brigðir, brimarr, huðlognir,
skyggþer, skryver, skarði, grindlogi,   250
Mimungr, fellir, ok mál-vitnir,
taurar, hrævaðr, trani, vind-þvari,
liðnir, Kvern-bítr, liómi, herðir,
vitnir, yfri, vægja-lestir:
skelkingr, fillingr, flæmingr, skerðingr,
skotningr, skilvingr, Skǫfnungr, rifiungr,
brotningr, hvítingr, Bæsingr, Tyrvingr,
hækingr, ok hringr; hittaz man nættingr:
logi ok mund-giallr, langr, hvass, ok eldr,
avrn, ok ægir, 'ok' naglfari,   260
brigðir, maurnir, blær ok skerðir,
hyrr, ok helsingr, hríðir, átti:
fellir, fǫlvir, Fáfnir, raufnir,
imir, eimnir, afspringr, þinurr,
siglir, snyrtir, svælgr, skar, ok nár,
goinn, gest-moinn, ok gramr, þrimarr, niðhæggr.

19. *Parts of*   Oddr, blóðvarta ok ben-knuar,
the sword.   blóð-refill, blóð-varp, ok blóð-iða,
blóð-vaka, liúgfengr, ok blóð-hnefi,
iðvarp, ok brandr, egg-teinar, folk,   270
emjar, þremjar, ok ǫlrúnar-nautr,
merki, vett-rim, ok missi-fengr,
onn, ok skafningr, undir-dregningr,
vargr, kall-hamarr, valbæst ok herðr:
sverð, ok gelmingr, ok sam-nagli,
hugró, sigr-hnoð, hialt, ok tangi,
mundriði, hægg-fáðr, ok meðal-kafli.

---

238. hræ-f.] 1 e β; hafraka, Cd.   240. munduðr, 1 e β.   242. 1 e β; fiǫr-
soðnir, Cd.   244. verulfr] 1 e β; verr vifr, Cd.   kol] kvol, 1 e β.   248.
her-brai] huglognir, 1 e β.   255. filbiungr, 1 e β.   269. -vaka] r; -varta,
Cd.   271. r; olræða-, 1 e β.   274. kalld hamar nautr, 1 e β.   277.
1 e β; hogg staðr, Cd.

20. *Axe.*   Œx, iarð-hyrna, . . . s[parða]
skiava, ok skeggja, skráma, ok genja,
regin-spǫrn, gnefja, ok gygr, fála,   280
snaga, ok bulda, barða, vígglǫð,
þveita, ok þenja; þá er arg-hyrna ;
hon er œfst talið œxar-heita.

21. *Spear.*   Darr, spiót, ok myt, dœf, lenz, ok vigr,
snata, fleinn, ok svaf, sviða, hræ-mæki,
geirr, spiœr, nata, gefja, kesja,
gaflak, frakka, Gungnir, peita.

22. *Arrows.* Örr er ok, akka, oddr, hvít-mylingr,
fenja, drífa, flaug, dynfara,
bǫsl, bǫl, bílda, broddr, ok hremsa,   290
gǫgn, flaug, ok þrǫs . . ., ok skapt-snœr,
flug-glavð, ok flug-svinn, fiva, ok skeyti :
Geta ṣkal, Fennu ok Gusis-smíðis,
Iolfs-smíði, hon er œfst þura.

23. *Bow.*   Almr, dalr, bogi, ýr, ok tvíviðr,
sveigr, glær, ok þrymr, [sómr], scal, gelmir :
Enn kveð-ek heita ǫll vápn saman ;—
iarn, ǫr, ok spiœr, ísarn, slǫg.

24. *Shield.* Skioldr, þrungin-salr, skaun, salbendingr,
bugnir, hlébarðr, ok buklari, ·   300
vettrimi, targa, veðr-glaðr, ok hlíf,
við-bleiknir, rít, víg-glaðr, ok lind,
giallr, dogg-skafi, ok gunn-skylir,
bœð-liós, grýta, ok bœð-skýlir,
svalinn, ok randi, saurnir, borði,
skutfingr, barði, skirr, tví-byrðingr,
yrlygr, ok svarmr, eilifnir, heiðr,
baugi, fagr-blainn, bera, mið-fornir.

25. *Helmet.* Hroptz hattar skal-ek heiti segja :—
hialmr, goll-fainn, hraur, val-hrimnir,   310
hall-hrimnir, skǫlkr, ok hlífandi,
fiǫrnir, þoki, ok fisk-moinn,
hildi-gœltr, kellir, her-kumbl, ok velgr,
gríma, ægir, glæver, stefnir.

26. *Coat of* Brynja, kund, hialmgǫll, hvǫð ok nan,
Mail.   kœld, Finnz-leif, bœðfara, þyn, syn, bloð-leika.

II. *Physical.*

Water.   SÆR, silægja, salt, Ægir, haf,
1. *The Sea :—*   lœgr, sumr, lœgir, laga-stafr, ok vágr,

---

284. myt] naut, 1 e β.   293. Fenna, B.   Gusisnauta, 1 e β.   299. Read,
salpenningr.   315. hrǫð ok nati, 1 e β.

giallr, gnap, geimi, gnarr, svifr, ok marr;
súgr, sog, sami, svelgr, ræst, ok fiœrðr;   320
sund, œgr, velfærr, sǫni, víðir,
hríð, verr, breki, húm, flóð, ok brim,
græðir, glýjoðr, Gymir, ok vægir,
gniðr, ok oror, gialfr, fen, snapi:
gnat, vœr, vika, vǫzt, hóp, ok mið,
vatn, diúp, ok kaf, vík, tiœrn, ok sík,
stormr, díki, hylr, straumr, lœkr, ok bekkr,
áll, bruðr, kelda, iða, fors, ok kíll:
hefring, alda, hvítingr, ok lá:
hrœnn, Rán, kolga, ok himin-glæva,   330
dræfn, uðr, ok 'solmn,' dúfa, bylgja,
boði, ok bára, blóðug-hadda.

2. *Rivers*   Gœll, Glit, Gera, Glǫð, ok Valskialf,
(*geograph.*):— Van, Við, Vimur, Ving, ok Ysa,
Sið, Suðr, Freka, Sekin, Einstika,
Elf, Ro, Ekla, Ekin, Rennandi:
Þyn, Rin, ok Nið, Þǫll, Rymr, Ysia,
Dun, Ofn, Dyna, Dyn, Hǫll, Fara,
Orun, ok Bro, Auð, Skialg, Lodda,
Myn, Merk, Riða, Mein, ok Sax-elfr: 340
Tifr, Dyrn, Vina, Tems, Vind, ok Strind,
Mavrn, Moða, Þrym, Morn, ok Gaut-elfr,
Alin, Uðr, Kolga, ok Evfrates,
Ogn, Eiðr, Eimir, ok Apardion:
Rǫgn, Hrǫnn, ok Rǫnn, Raum-elfr, Hnipul,
Hnǫpul, Hiǫlmunlá, Humra, Vina,
Vil, Vin, Vella, Valin, Sǫmd, Salin,
Nepr, Drǫfn, Strauma, Nis, Mynd, Gnapa.
Gilling, Nilus, Ganges, Tvedda,
Luma, Ver, Vóða, Leira, ok Gunnþró,   350
Ið, Svǫl, Vegsvinn, Yn, Þioðnuma,
Fiǫrm, Strǫnd, ok Spæ, ok Fimbul-þul:
Nyt, Hrǫnn, ok Nauð, Nǫt, Slíðr, ok Hríð,
Kǫrmt, Leiptr, ok Örmt, ok Kerlaugar tvær,
Gǫmul, Sylgr, ok Yn, ok Geir-vimul,
Ylgr, Vǫð, ok Flóð,—Iordan er á lesti.

3. *Fishes*:—   Lax, ok langa, lýsa, brosma,
birtingr, hæingr, bust, ok hrygna,
humarr, hrognkelsi, hveðnir, flóki,
ǫlunn, aurriði, ok andvari: 360
síld, seiðr, skata, síl, reyðr, ok ǫgr,
skreiðungr, ok síkr, skalgi, ok flyðra,
fyldingr, styrja, ok fuðryskill,

---

hámerr, steinbítr, ok háskerðingr :
fiœrsungr, þrœmmungr, ok fengrani,
hamarr, sand-hverfa, ok horn-gæla,
mar-knútr, glǫmmungr, ok mar-þvara,
sílungr, skel-fiskr, sverð-fiskr, ok lýr:
þyrsklingr, ufsi, þorskr, vartari,
grunnungr, gedda, giǫlnir, keila,   370
áll, ok karfi, krabbi, geir-síl,
hár, ok guðlax, horn-síl, igull.

4. *Whales :*—   Hafr-hvalr, geir-hvalr, ok haf-gufa,
hnísa, haf-strambr, ok hnýðingar,
reyðr, reyðar-kalfr, ok rauð-kembingr,
bruungr, rostungr, ok blæjo-hvalr :
norð-hvalr, ok búr-hvalr, ná-hvalr, ok leiptr,
skeliungr, fisk-reki, ok skúto-hvalr,
sletti-baka, skiald-hvalr, ok sand-lægja,
hross-hvalr, and-hvalr, hrafn-reyðr, ok vǫgn.   380

5. *Ships :*—   Nú man-ek skýra of SKIPA HEITI—
œrk, ára-kló, askr, sess-rúmnir,
skeið, skúta, skip, ok Skíð-blaðnir,
nór, Nagl-fari, nǫkkvi, ok snekkja :
byrðingr, buza, barð-kaldr ok hreinn,
bakki, hǫmlungr, hélug-barði,
rǫst, bátr, ok regg, rǫð, Hringornir,
lung, kióll, lang-skip, leifnir, karfi,
hringr, Gnóð, freki, hrǫð, móðrói,
hemlir, barði, ok hylbauti,   390
ugla, leðja, ok askvitill,
kœna, kǫtla, kati, reið, ok skalpr :
knǫrr, kuggr, knui, keipull, eikja,
dreki, Elliði, dromundr, ok prámr,
fura, vigg, galeið, ferja, skalda,
fley, flaust, ok_þækr, far, tíðr, ok lið.

6. *Parts of a*   Segl, skœr, sigla, sviðvís, stýri,
    ship :—   sýjor, saum-fœr, súð, ok skaut-reip,
stag, stafn, stiórn-við, stuðill, ok sicul-giœrð,
snotra, sól-borð, sess, skutr, ok strengr,   400
sœx, ok stœðingr, sviptingr, ok skaut,
spíkr, siglo-tré, saumr, lǫk-stolpar,
laukr, siglo-toppr, lína, eyro,
flaug, flaugar-skegg, ok far-nagli :
húnn, hún-bora, ok hialmun-vœlr,
húfr, hlýr, hrefni, ok hals-stefni,
hefill, hals, hanki, ok hœfut-hendor,

---

376. bunungr, 1 e β.   388. karfi] B ; barði, Cd.   390. homlu-barði?
407. hnacki, 1 e β.

háir, hæll, hamarr, hialp-reip, ok lík,
rá, rakki, rif, rengr, ok hǫmlur,
vind-áss, vengi, vǫndr, lang-nefjur, 410
vǫlt, beiti-áss, varta, brandar,
bitar, bóg-lína, bulka-stokkar :
barð, kné, byrði, bellti, ok kinnungr,
kiǫlr, borð, keili, ok kiǫl-sýja,
kraptar, kerling, klœr, ok þoptor,
kal-reip, þrimir, klofar, ok þiljur,
drengir, drag-reip, dœla, árar,
ak-taumar, rœr, arinn, ok nálar,
aur-borð, kialar-hæll, ok akkeri,
hnakk-miði, aust-ker, ok hún-spænir. 420

7. EARTH :— Iǫrð, fiǫrn, rofa, eskja, ok Hlóðyn,
gyma, Sif, fiǫrgyn, grund, hauðr, ok rǫnd,
fold, vangr, ok Fif, frón, hiarl, ok barmr,
land, biǫð, þruma, láð, ok merski,
hollt, hals, ok fiǫll, hlíð, ok leiti,
hóll, heiðr, ok hvilft, hváll, ok brekka,
hró, dalr, ok vǫllr, hvammr, ok tunga,
mold, flag, rimi, mór, laut, ok sandr.

8. *Trees and* VIDR, yllir, tág, víðir, selja,
Plants :— pors, mœrk, ǫlviðr, plóma, spíra, 430
biǫrk, við-vindill, beinn, fiall-rapi,
buss, hlynr, ok bók, beinviðr, mǫpurr :
hasl, heggr, hallarr, hagþorn, reynir,
rǫ, almr, ok rót, reyrr, askr, fura,
apaldr, ǫsp, laurus, ulfviðr, lykkja,
eik, einir, píll, elri, palmar :
lind, lág, ok linnr, lyng, skíð, pera,
þǫll, ok þyrnir, þinurr, storð, ok klungr,
mǫsurr, grœn, mistil-teinn, ok mar-hrísla,
ilstri, vín-viðr, iolstr, cipressus. 440

9. ANIMALS. Ek man skýra fyr skatna mengi
Oxen :— all-ramligra **yxna heiti** :—
arvǫrðr, drioni, ok iǫrmun-rekr,
simi, Freyr, Reginn, Smiðr, eyþvari,
rauðr, ok rekningr, ok rǫkkvi-liðr,
viggi, bautaðr, Vingnir, stióri,
Himin-hriótr, simarr, ok harð-fari,
hæfir, dignir, hiǫllorr, simull :
hliðr, stúfr, ok litr, hriðr, forsimi,
arfr, iǫrmuni, ok eiki-smiðr, 450

---

411. varta] vortur, 1 e β. 426. heiðr] B ; heill, Cd. 427. hró] B ;
bro, Cd. ; hrof, 1 e β. 439. Emend. ; grön tvenn, Cd. 440. iolstr] iostr, Cd.
448. B ; hæfir, dirnir, kiollor, Cd. ; digni, 1 e β (better).

gneisti, apli, gollin-horni,
auðr, kvígr, æ014-18ldungr, ok ǫrfuni,
griðungr, ǫlgr, gellir, glymr, ok hreði,
tíðungr, boli, tarfr, aur-gefinn.

10. *Cow:*— Kÿr heitir : skirja, kvíga, ok frenja,
ok Auðumbla,—hon er ellzt kua.

11. *Ram:*— Hrútr, ofr-hyrningr, hornum-skali,
gumarr, horn-gloinn, ok giald-hroinn,
hveðruðr, horn-glói, hallin-skíði,
berr, horn-hroinn, ok heimdali,   460
bekri, miðiungr, blær, mærðr, ok veðr.

12. *He-goat:*— Hafr heitir, grímnir, ok geirælnir,
Tann-gnióstr, kiappi, ok Tann-grisnir,
skæmotr, ok brúsi, bukkr, grímr taliðr.

13. *She-goat:*— Geitar-heiti : Heiðrún, haðna, ok kiðlingr ;
er ok kol-múla, ok kið saman.

14. *The Bear:*— Biörn, bersi, bolmr, bera, elgviðnir,
blá-iaxl, ísolfr, ok breiðvegi,
bestingr, bassi, ballti, hlæbarðr,
ulfr, frekr, vilnir, Iǫrekr, mosmi,   470
fetviðnir, húnn, fress, vetr-liði,
iug-tanni, ialfuðr, ifiungr, vil skarpr.

15. *The Stag:*— Hiörtr, Dura-þror, hliðr, eik-þyrnir,
Dúneyrr, Dainn, Dvalarr, motroðnir.

16. *The Boar:*— Göltr, valglitnir, gríss, irminir,
svín, tarr, runi, Sæ-hrímnir, bærgr,
rai, valbassi, roðr, dritroði,
þrór, viðrir, skrumpr, þrǫndr, vaningi.

17. *The Wolf:*— Vargr, ulfr, Vitnir, ilmr, skǫll, Geri,
hvinnir, ok grá-dÿri   480
Hati, Hróðvitnir, ok heiðingi,
freki, kinni, víðnir, Fenrir, hlæbarðr,
goti, gildir, glammi, gyldir, imarr,
imr, egðir, ok skolkini :
Enn heitir svá :—ylgr, vargynja,
bokn, ok ima . . . svimul.

18. Heavens:— Nio ero heimar á hæð talið :—
veit-ek inn neðzta, sá er vind-blainn,
þá er heiðornir ok Hregg-mimir :
annarr heitir andlangr himinn,   490
(þat máttu skilja), þriði víð-bláinn ;

---

464. skimuðr, 1 e β.   467. bolmr] 1 e β ; blomr, Cd.   474. Dainn]
1 e β ; dalarr, Cd.   479. Ylgr vargr vitni, Cd.   480. hvinnir, ok grá-dÿri]
add. 1 e β.

víð-feðmi kveð-ek vera inn fiorða;
hrióðr, ok hlýrni, hygg enn sétta;
grímr, vett-mímir:—get-ek nú vera
átta himna upp um talða:
skatyrnir stendr skýjom œfri,
hann er útan alla heima.

19. THE SUN:— SUNNA, sýni, SÓL, fagra-hvel,
    hrióðr-leika, lík, skin, ræðull,
    leiptr, if- rœðull, ok liósfari,   500
    drífandi, alf-ræðull, ok Dvalins-leika;
    al-skír, geisli ok ey-gloa.

20. THE MOON:—MÁNI, 'miðgarðr,' mulin, tungl ok glámr,
    skyndir, ok skin, skrámr, ártali,
    ný, skialgr, luna, nið, fengari.

21. Day and   DŒGR, hlyrn, ok rœkr, dies, ok lýsing,
    Night:—   dagr, nótt, svefn-gaman ok draum-niǫrun,
               nox, nis, gríma, niol, myrkfara,
               óliós, draum-vǫr, emisperium.

22. The Heavens Heimr, hregg-mimir, himinn, skatyrnir,   510
    (repeated):— víð-bláinn, andlangr, ok vætrimnir,
               gimir, vindblainn, víðfeðmir, hrióðr,
               hlýrnir, leiptr, ok heiðornir.

23. Wind and   VEÐR, byrr, væonsuðr, vindr, él-reki,
    Weather:— glygg, blœr, ok gustr, gráp, logn, þoka,
               regn, úr, rota, ríð, miorkvi, él,
               fiúk, fok, mugga, frost, kári, hregg:
               'gǫnsurr,' gráði, gol, of-viðri,
               giósta, grindill, gæla, ok ólióðr,
               gneggioðr, gǫnsuðr, gę, dyn-fari,   520
               hlǫmmuðr, ganrekr, hús-briótr, ok þiótr.

24. Fire:—   GIMS heiti vil-ek greppum segja:—
               Ægiss-bróðir ok él-reki,
               eldr, eimr, usli, úði, herkir,
               'hrǫtuðr,' ok hrót-gandr, Hrimnir, eimi:
               leygr, Vafr-logi, linnr, ok farri,
               brandr, fýrr, túsi, brimi, nertill,
               viti, eimyrja, vellan-fasti,
               funi, hýrr, fœðir, fúrr ok eisa:
               freki, ǫlgr, seti, feykir, ysja,   530
               hrǫðuðr, ok hǫrvir, harkr, for-brennir,
               hrapi, myln, logi, hripuðr, aldr-nari,
               kyndr, bál, væginn, kveykir, ok busi:
               brísingr, brenna, blossi, gneisti,

---

gnipall, glǿðr, dúni, geiri, tandri,
dunsuðr, dini, dusill, ok snæra :—
Nú er sex-tigir seyðiss heita.

25. ANIMALS   Skal-ek eitr-fá ORMA telja :—
again.   óinn, ok ofnir, ǫlirr, iapra,
Serpents :—   furr, flug-dreki, Fáfnir, ori,   540
fræningr, ok áll, feginn, ok ornir :
grafvitnir, fánn, goinn, holt-skriði,
grafningr, grettir, grá-bakr, trani (!),
grímr, ok graf-þvengr, gargan, eitrungr,
hringr, holdvarinn, haugvarðr, dreki :
Níðhǫggr, náinn, niðr, holdvari,
langbarðr, lyðer, linnr, heiðbui,
strykr, steinbui, stýrir, svafnir,
snákr, scorpion, sneldingr, naðra :
liðr, iapr, bráinn, linni, stefningr   550
snillingr, viðnir, særfr, ok vinduðr,
ráðr, rabia, reimir, seimir,
moinn, dalginna, ok Miðgarðz-ormr.

26. Horses :—   Glaðr, Glær, Gyllir, Gollin-faxi,
glitnir, Goll-toppr, Gisl, skeiðbrímir,
Silfr-toppr, Simir, Sleipnir, Skævoðr,
Goti, Skin-faxi, Grani, Stúfr, ok Skær :
fákr, Léttfeti, fiǫr-svartnir, Valr,
fengr, Falhofnir, fet-móðr, ok lungr,
Vakr, viglitnir, vindr, Tialdari,   560
veðr, viðir, vigg, ok veg-draupnir :
vegbiartr, Hǫlkvir, Ving-skornir, Hrafn,
Alsviðr, allvarr, Árvakr, Drasill,
Blakkr, bǫlþvari, bráinn, Há-stigi,
marr, iór, bautuðr, mór, iormuni :
Moinn, hestr, fiǫtri, móðnir, róni,
alsvartr, apli, askr, mál-feti,
Blóð[ug]-hófi, Ham-skarpr, brúnn, Hóf-varpnir,
vigr, Skinfaxi (!), Virvill, Hrím-faxi.

27. BIRDS.   HAUKR, hamðer, harmr, Hábrók, tregi,   570
The Hawk :— heiðér, heim-þér, hrimnir, kolking,
ginnar, gandir, ok geirloðnir,
gǫllungr, ginnungr, ok gagl-hati :
yrlygr, ymir, und-skornir, valr,
ifiungr, ifli, ifill, veðr-fǫlnir,
Forseti, viðnir, fiǫrsungr, þrǫmmungr,
ǫlgr, mútari, ǫglir, sauðnir.

28. The Raven :— HRAMN, holdbori, Huginn, óværi,
blæingr, liti, borgin-móði,

horn-klofi, viti, kloakan, krákr, 580
drukr, Muninn, corvus, geri (sic),
krummi, krumsi, korpr, boringi,
spori, Ártali, ok ár-flognir.

29. *The Cock:*— Fegringr, HANI, Fialarr, ok áslákr,
kokr, Sal-gofnir, kambr, viðofnir,
gylmir, gallus, ok gallina:
HŒNA, keila, Hábrók, skaða.

30. *The Eagle:*—Örn, gallofnir, ok Andhimnir,
Hræ-svelgr, ok hregg-skornir,
egg-þér, kumarr, ari, blindviðnir, 590
arnkell, Gemlir, ok aquila.

31. *Birds:*— Gamr, gripr, gaukþior, gaukr, sviplækja,
grá-gás, heim-gás, gagl, ok helsingr,
geir-fugl, geitungr, glæða, doðr, kvisa,
ari, nagr, arta, alpt, már, ok haukr:
Óðins-hani, alka, ønd, hrossa-gaukr,
hramn, hœns, himbrin, hryggjar-stykki,
héri, hani, hœna, ok hilduri,
úfr, valr, smyrill, ugla, skurfir:
svørr, storkr, súla, svarr, skiór, sparr-haukr, 600
stelkr, spørr, svala, stein-delfr, spiki,
skúfr, spói, sæðingr, skarfr, ok svart-bakr,
skeglingr, skíði, skiøldungr, pái:
kárn, igða, kialar-fogl, kráka, dúfa,
þrøstr, þiðorr, þerna, þeisti, dunna,
trana, tialdr, titlingr, tyrðil-múli,
lómr, lævirki, ok leðr-blaka:
langvę, lundi, lóa, fiøl-móði,
fýling, ló-þræll, Friggjar-elda,
rindill, þvari, líri, riúpa, fiall-rota, 610
iarpi, ertla, ok iaðrákarn,
akri, doðka, æðr, ok nætingr,
kreppingr, flóð-skítr, 'kiar-filki,' spætr,
mæisingr, ýfingr, mýri-snípa,
rytr, hængi-vakr, rivann-skinna:
hrókr, gióðr, hegri, ok haf-tyrðill,
brand-gás, hróð-gás, brimm-orri, márr,
sendlingr, skrýtingr, snæ-fogl, skári,
vakr, valr, dúfa (!), vallofr, starri.

III. *Sundries.*

1. *Goddesses* Þessi skal kenna KELLO-HEITI: 620
again:— Sága, Sigyn, Sif, Þrúðr, Iðunn,
Frigg, ok Bestla, Fulla, ok Nanna,
Gefiun, Horn, Gerðr, ok Laufey.

2. *Females
again :—*

Reið, selja, strind, rein, skorð, ok fiǫrn,
biœrk, veig, ok þœll, brík, þopta, Gefn,
lág, grund, ok lið, lodda, broka,
fit, norn, . . . , fold, þirr, ok lind.
Sól, fiœtra, spœng, Siœfn, Nauma, Rindr,
Eir, þella, list, Ilmr, troða, dís,
Niǫrn, Vǫr, ok Fríðr, nipt, Rán ok Bil,   630
Líkn, Hlín, ok Syn, Lofn, ok Gná.

3. MIND AND
HEART :—

Móðr, hiarta, negg, munr, hugr, sefi,
geð, heil, siafni, gollorr, ok eljun.

4. *The Fox :—*

Skolli, slapparðr, ok skaufali,
skollr, mel-rakki, skaufi, grýla :
enn er refr, ok skrǫggr, ǫldungr, dainn,
laufa-fettir, foa, brunn-migi.

5. THE HAND:— HEITI ero HANDAR :—hrammr, dýr, ok ravkn,
greip, mund, ok spœnn, gaupn, ok hreifi,
ulfliðr, ok fingr, armr, lǫggr, ok bógr,   640
lámr, hnefi, lófi, loppa, krumma.

6. THE WAL-
KYRJAS :—

Man-ek VALKYRJOR Viðris nefna :—
Hrist, Mist, Herja, Hlǫkk, Geiravǫr,
Gǫll, Hiǫr-þrimul, Guðr, Her-fiǫturr,
Skuld, Geir-œnul, Skœgul, ok Rand-gnið,
Ráðgríð, Gœndul, Svipul, Geir-skœgul,
Hildr, ok Skegg-old, Hrund, Geir-driful,
Rann-gniðr, ok Þrúðr, Reginleif, ok Sveið,
Þǫgn, Hialm-þrimul, Þrima, ok Skalm-œld.

7. ISLES :—

Ey, Ömð, ok Örmst, Öllum-lengri,   650
Horn, Hrund, ok Hugl, Herðla, Ivist,
Hveðn, Hrafnista, Hísing, Skrofa,
Mǫn, Mǫst, Hasley, Myl, Stolm, Bataldr,
Selja, Sólrœnn, ok Sortoland,
Sigg ok Salarey, ok . . . . .
Sága, Láland, Salbiǫrn, Leka,
Skíð, Strind, ok Vigr, Solm, ok Aldi :
Krít, Kipr, Lygra, Kǫrmt, Rǫð, Biarkey,
Hæring, Gylling, Hugró, Varða,
Lauga, Lygra, Lag, ok Gizki,   660
Þriðna, ok Þiótta, Þruma, Kinn, ok Hrótt :
Nǫs, Dyn, Nauma, Nala, Nǫrva,
Fólskn, Frigg, Fætilǫr, Fenring, ok Mǫn,
Bolm, Bokn, Raufa, Bǫnn, Sekk, ok Vǫrl,
Alǫst, ok Storð, Iala, Tiǫr, Veey :
Aurn, Íl, ok Rist, Ira, Lodda,

Soland, Siri, Solskel, Miǫla,
Hlesey, Veðrey, Hitra, Frosta,
Loǫnd, Vikna, Lág, Syllingar:
Fión, Fiǫlbyrja, Frikn, ok Senja,　　　　670
Selund, ok Dimun, Sæla, Þumla,
Usna, Sióland, Askræð, ok Síld,
Ála, Borgund, Erri, Torgar,
Hæl, Rǫkstr, ok Falstr, ok Helliskor,
Asparnir, Hin, Iolund, ok Hanki,
Marsey, Sámsey, Mystr, ok Vingi,
Hlesey (rep.), Heðinsey, ok Hnotirnar.

8. FRITHS:—　FIÖRÐR: Sogn, Iali, Folld, Ófóti,
Angr, Harmr, Tregi, Eitri, Vefsnir,
Harðangr, Stafangr, Heyangr, ok Glaumr,　　　　680
Goðmarr, Harðsær, Grenmarr, Hroði.

9. SEED:—　　Akr, ax, sæði, ǫgn, barr, ok halmr,
Áll, efsta-kné, eigin, skotblað,
blað, kné, ok rót, bygg, rugr, ok sáð,
korn, gin-hafri, korki, barlak,
grión, ok val-bygg, groska, dumba,
hveiti, hirsi, hialmr, skrúf, ok miǫl,
bendill, heslar, bundin, sáð-korn,
flúr, ǫmstr, þrefi, fræ-korn, gnioði.

10. NUMBERS:—

Maðr heitr einn fyrir ser—
Tá ef tveir ero,　　　691
þorp ef þrír ero,
fiórir ero færo-neyti,
flokkr eru fimm menn,
sveit ef sex ero,
siau fylla sǫgn,
átta bera ámælis-skor,
nautar ero nio,
dunn ef tiu ero:
ærir ero ellifo,　　　700
tog-loð ef tolf ero,
þyss ero þrettán,
ferð ero fiortán,
fundr er ef fimtán hittaz,

seta ero sextán,
sókn eru siautián,
œrnir þykkja óvinir þeim er
átián mœtir,
neyti hefir sá er nítián menn
(fylgja),
drótt ero tuttugu,
þióð ero þrír tigir,　　　710
folk ero fiórir tigir,
fylki fimm tigir,
samnaðr sex tigir,
svarfaðr siau tigir,
ǫld ero átta tigir,
[1] . . . ero nio tigir (blank),
herr er hundrað.

---

[1] Some word on *n*.

APPENDIX.

THULOR IN COURT-METRE.

SEA-KINGS:—

E KILL. Eitill, Skekkill, Emmir, Gestill, Remmir,
Heiti, Hœkingr, Meiti, Heimi, Mýsingr, Beimi,
Randverr, Róði, Mundill, Rœkkvi, Solsi, Nœkkvi,
Hemingr, Hagbarðr, Glammi, Haki, Beimuni, Rakni.

Kvenna heiti okend :—

Braut er svanni ok sæta, sveimar rýgr ok feima,   5
brúðr er í fœr með flióði, fat-ek drós ok man kiósa,
þekki-ek sprund ok sprakka; sparik við hæl at mæla,
firrumk-ek snót ok svarra; svífr mer langt frá vífi.

Blíð er mær víð móður; mála drekkr á ekkjo
kvíðir kerling eiðo; kveðr dóttir vel beðjo;   10
opt finnr ambótt hæpto; æ 'r frilla græm sværo;
kiljar kván ok elja; kann nipt við snœr skipta.

The Mind (from Cod. Ups.):—

Stendr þat er stórom grandar, *sterk-viðri* mer *Herkjo*,
í hnegg-verøld hyggjo hefi-ek stríð borit víða,
þar kemr enn, ef unna ítr vildi Bil skaldi,   15
at blíðr grœr *Gríðar glaum-vindr* í sal þindar.

Islands :—

Bókn, Kormt, Brising, Vikna, Brua, Hírar, Dun, Síri,
Sotr, Þœmb, Selja, Hítrar, Sigg, Rótt, Bataldr, Þiótta,
Vigr, Storð, Vǫrl, Rǫð, Lygra, Veig, Fenring, Tiǫr, Senja,
Hveðn, Vað, Hísning, Friðnar, Hœð, Borgund, Smyl, Torgar.

The Sea-girt Isles by Einar Skulason :—

1. Brattr er baldrekr Þiótto; berr vindr Raðar linda,   21
    við-gyrðill þýtr Vœrðo, veltr Fenringar belti;
    ygliz umgiœrð Huglar; olmr er grá-sili Stolmar;
    fleygir Bolmar baugi; brakar Lygro men nakvat.

2. Blár er baldrekr Síra; Brú gyrðill þvær fyrðom;   25
    sundr springr Lygro lindi; Leko velt af þræm belti;
    kiœl skolar Karmtar helsi; klýfr stiórn sila Þiórnar;
    bœrð skera Gizka girði; grafaz borð í men Storðar.

3. Stórt fellr gyrðill Garta; grefr vindr Þrumo linda;
    þýtr sval-fiœturr Seljo; svellr undrom men Hrundar;   30
    allt skelfr Brimlar belti; brestr ern sili Hernar;
    œst ferr umgiœrð Hristar; olmr er hringr Þrimlinga.

---

5. sæta] sværa, Ups.   28. Edda Lauf. enters these three following stanzas
under the name of Einar Skulason.

4.   Barð rístr Gælo girði ; grefr saum fiæturr Tauma ;
geist ferr umgiæorð Ostrar ; opt er men klofit Senjo ;
brand þvær Bolmar lindi ; bifaz stinnr sili Kinnar ;   35
hringr þýtr Hveðno læongom ; hart veltr Glanar belti.

The Daughters of Ran :—
Œsir hvasst at hraustom *Himinglæva* þyt sævar ;
Glymr *Unnar* vex grenni Gæondlar skúfs, ok *Dúfa ;*
Brædd strykr *Blóðughadda ;* brim-solginn fellr *Kolga ;*
hlýr skylr *Hefring,* stœérir haf-lauðr of við rauðan.   40

Another Version :—
Dröfn skylr stál þar er stafni straum-fylgin þvær *Bylgja ;*
Hefring brestr, enn hristir *Himinglæva* mar Vimrar ;
Hrönn dregr græonn or grunni ; gadd svelr *Blóðug-hadda ;*
elg venr *Uðr* ok *Kolga* egg-húfs við glym *Dúfo.*

Grammatical (from Skalda, of later date) :—
1.   Því veldr *ár* at *aerir* akr bú-manna spakra ;   45
aera verðr með *árum* undan dolga fundi,
rǽða gengr af *róða* rúna systir olystug
órar dregr af *ærum* ýtum skemda flýtir.
2.   *Ǽli* telsk þat er *óli* úsnotran mann gotnar ;
aelir vatn þar er *álar* all-strangir fram hallazt ;   50
heitir *lǽr* á *Lœru ; laeringar* kenningar ;
kallazt *mœr* á *Mœri ; maeringr* ef giæof tærizt.
3.   *Haetta* verðr á *haettu ; hǽting* ef bæol rœétisk,
ást er *naer* at *naera,* nú er vær konan færi ;
skeind tekr *aeðr* enn œéðazt ; *œði* deyr þá er br . . .   55
. . . .

Hair by Arni the Benedictine :—
Skafa sveinar klif krúno ; kveðr eik meðan reikar ;
biúgr þyrnir hnígr hiarna ; haf-skíða stafar ríða ;
þola hlusta kæol kvistir ; kná skalla ráó falla ;
æolr kringiz vel vanga ; venz skarði græon svarðar.

Einar :—
Hrynja lét in hvíta haus-mioll ofan lausa   60
strind æorriða strandar stallz af skarar-fialli.

Snorri :—
Kom ek inn þar er sat svanni svanna vænstr í ranni ;
gerðr leysti siá svarðar svaið-akr raðar garði.

Olaf :—
Hæog leit hvarma skógar hlað-norn við mer stiæornom.
                                          Cd. Worm., App.

_____

35. Herðar, Cd.   41. From 748.   55. Read, þat er bræði ?

§ 7. SKALDA-TAL.

THIS interesting Roll of Poets has reached us from two sources. A, the Kringla MS., c. 1264, which, the vellum having perished, we have in Arni Magnusson's autograph copy, AM. 761. B, the Codex Upsalensis of Snorri's Edda, c. 1300, in which this table appears side by side with other additimenta of interest. The Kringla text is the best, but the other is the more complete, adding to the lists of Kings and Earls and their poets, lists of lesser noblemen, etc., and their poets. From these two our text is composed.

The date to which the table reaches in its fullest text is about coeval with that of Codex Upsalensis itself, but Skalda-tal itself, we think, bears traces of earlier origin than even Kringla. Skalda-tal is in *two parts*, the first entitled 'Scalda-tal Dana kononga oc Svia;' the second 'Her *hefr* up Scalda-tal Noregs kononga.' But these titles do not correspond to the present contents, for in both our MSS. the order now is: Title I, a beginning of Danish list to the word Boddason, followed by a list of Swedish kings and earls. Title II, a Norwegian list, followed by the rest of the Danish list. The original order plainly was, Title I, Danish list, Swedish list; Title II, Norwegian list; and this would suggest that the table was first drawn up at a time when the memory of the great Danish kings' hegemony was not faded out of men's memories. In Ari's days the tongue was still called 'Danish,' and the Danish (Canute's) empire was vividly remembered, and we should be disposed to put the original table about 1130.

The *origin* and grounds of the list are for the most part unknown. There are some pieces of information in the short glosses, e. g. on Erpr Lutandi and Ulfr hinn Oargi, which are not found elsewhere. The list of poets of Eystan Beli looks as if it were derived from a verse.

The first edition of Skalda-tal is that of Ole Worm ; the first trustworthy edition is that of Text B, by Möbius, 1856, at the end of his useful Catalogue, and both texts were given by Mr. John Sigurdsson in the third volume of the AM. edition of Edda, 1880.

I. SKALDA-TAL DANA KONONGA OK SVIA.

STARKAÐR INN GAMLI var skald: hans kvæði ero fornuzt þeirra er menn kunno nu; hann orti um Dana kononga. Ragnarr konongr Loðbrók var skald, ok Áslaug kona hans, ok sœnir þeirra.

Ragnar konungr Loðbrók :
　Bragi skalld inn Gamli Bodda son.

SWEDISH KINGS :—
　Eysteinn Beli :
　　Bragi inn Gamli.
　　Grundi Prúði.

Erpr Lútandi.
Kalfr þrœnzki.
Refr Ruzci.
Ormr Oframi.
Olvalldi.
Oc enn Ölvalldi.

Avalldi.
Fleinn Skalld.
Rognvalldr.

Biorn at Haugi:
Bragi inn Gamli.
Erpr Lútandi vá víg í véum ok var
ætlaðr til dráps; hann orti drápo
um Saur konongs hund, ok þá
höfut sítt fyrir.

Eirekr Refils son:
Alfr iarl inn Lítli.

Styrbiörn Sterki:
Ulfr Súlo iarl.

Eirekr Sigr-sæli:
Þorvalldr Hiallta son.

Óláfr Sœnski:
Gunnlaugr Orms-tunga.
Rafn Önundar son.
Óttarr Svarti.
Gitzorr Svarti.

Önundr Olafs son:
Sigvatr skald Þórðar son.

Ingi Steinkels son:
. Marcus Skeggja son lögsogo-maðr.

Sörkvir Kols son:
Einarr Skúla son.
Halldórr Skvalldri.

Knútr Eireks son:
Hallbiörn Hali.
Þorsteinn Þorbiarnar son.

Sörkvir Karls son:
Sumarliði skalld.
Þorgeirr Dana-skalld.

Eirekr Knutz son:
Grani Hallbiarnar son.

Ion Sorkvis son:
.. ..

Eirikr Eireks son:
Óláfr Þórðar son.

SWEDISH EARLS :—
Ion iarl Sorkvis son:
Einarr Skúla son.
Halldórr Skvalldri.

Soni iarl Ivars son:
Halldórr Skvalldri.

Karl iarl Sóna son:
Halldórr Skvalldri.

[Birgir iarl Magnus son :]
[Sturla Þórðar son [1].]

II. HER HEFR UPP SKALDA-TAL NOREGS KONONGA.

ÞIOÐOLFR INN HVINVERSKI orti um Rognvald Heiðom-hæra Ynglinga-tal, brœðrung Haraldz ins Hárfagra, ok talði þriá tigi lang-feðra hans. Hann sagði frá dauða hvers þeirra ok legstað.

NORSE KINGS :—
Haraldr Hár-fagri:
Auðon Illskælda.
Þorbiorn Hornklofi.
Ölver Núfa.
Ulfr Sebba son.
Þiodolfr or Hvini.
Gothormr Sindri.

Eirekr konungr Blóðœx:
Egill Skallagrims son.
Glúmr Geira son.

Halfdan Svarti:
Guthormr Sindri.

Hákon Góði:
Eyvindr Skalda-spillir.
Gothormr Sindri.

Haraldr Gráfelldr:
Glúmr Geira son.
Kormakr Ögmundar son.

Óláfr Tryggva son:
Hallfrœðr Vendræða-skald.
Biarni skald.

Óláfr inn Helgi:
Sigvatr Þórðar son.
Óttarr Svarti.
Bersi Torfo son.
Þórðr Kolbeins son.
Þorfinnr Munnr.
Þormóðr Kolbrúnar-skald.
Gitzorr Gullbrá.
Hofgarða Refr.
Skapti Þóroddz son.
Þórðr Siarreks son.

Magnús Góði:
Sigvatr skald.
Arnórr Iarla-skald.
Oddr Kikina-skald.
Refr skald.
Þióðolfr skald.

Haraldr Sigurðar son:
Þióðolfr Arnórs son.
Bölverkr bróðir hans.
Valþiófr.
Oddr Kikina-skald.

---

[1] The lines in [ ] add. Cod. Ups.

Stúfr Blindi.
Arnórr Iarla-skald.
Illugi Bryndœla-skald.
Grani skald.
Snöglo-Halli.
Þórarinn Skeggja son.
Valgarðr af Velli.
Halli Stríði.
Steinn Herdísar son.

Óláfr Kyrri :
Steinn Herdísar son.
Atli Lítli.
Vilborg skald.

Magnus Berfœttr :
Þorkell Hamar-skald.
Ívarr Ingimundar son.
Biorn Kreppil-hendi.
Bárðr Svarti.
Gísl Illuga son.

Sigurðr Iorsala-fari :
Einarr Skúla son.
Ivarr Ingimundar son.
Halldórr Skvaldri.
Þórarinn Stutt-feldr.
Þorvaldr Blöndo-skald.
Arni Fiöro-skeifr.

Eysteinn Magnus son :
Ívarr Ingimundar son.
Einarr Skúla son.

Haraldr Gilli :
Einarr Skúla son.
Halldór Skvaldri.
Hallr Munkr.

Magnus Blindi :
Einarr Skúla son.

Sigurðr Slembir :
Ívarr Ingimundar son.

Ingi Haraldz son :
Einarr Skúla son.
Þorvarðr Þorgeirs son.
Kolli skald.

Sigurðr Haraldz son :
Einarr Skúla son.
Böðvarr Ballti.
Þorbiörn Gauss.

Eysteinn Haraldz son :
Einarr Skúla son.
Sigurðr Skrauti.

Magnus Erlings son :
Þorbiörn Skakka-skald.

Súgandi skald.
Hallr Snorra son.
Markus Stephans son.
Þórðr Hallz son.
Skald-Máni.

Hakon Herdi-breiðr :
Þorbiörn Gauss.

Sverrir konungr :
Ásgrímr Ketils son.
Þorstein Þorbiarnar son.
Sumarliði.
Arnórr Saxa son.
Hallbiorn Hali.
Blakkr skald.
Unas Stephans son.
Liótr skald.
Bragi.
Snorri Sturlo son.
Sigvatr Egils son.
Snorri Butz son.
Þorbiorn Skakka-skald.

Hákon Sverris son :
Liótr skald.
Bragi Hallz son.

Ingi Barðar son :
Snorri Sturlo son.
Liótr Sumarliða son.
Iatgeirr Torfa son.
Höskullr Blindi.
Runolfr.

Hakon konongr Hákonar son :
Snorri Sturlo son.
Óláfr Þórðar son.
Sturla Þórðar son.
Iátgeirr Torfa son.
Gitzorr iarl.
Arni Langi.
Óláfr Leggs son.
[Guthormr Kortr [1].]

Hakon son Hakonar ins koron-
    aða konongs :
Óláfr Þórðar son.

[Magnus Hákonar son :]
[Sturla Þórðar son [1].]

[Eirikr Magnus son :]
[Þorsteinn Orvendils son.]
[Þorvaldr Helga son.]
[Ion Murti Egils son.]
[Þorsteinn Ingialdz son.]
[Guðmundr skald [1].]

---

[1] The lines in [ ] add. Cod. Ups.

EYVINDR Skalda-spillir orti um Hakon inn Ríka kvæði, þat er heitir Háleyja-tal, ok talði þar langfeðga hans til Óðins, ok sagði frá dauða hvers þeirra ok legstað.

NORSE EARLS :—
Hakon iarl Griótgarðz son :
  Þióðolfr or Hvini.
Sigurðr Hlaða-iarl :
  Cormakr Ögmundar son.
Hakon iarl inn Ríki :
  Eyvindr Finnz son.
  Einarr Skála-glamm.
  Tindr Hallkelz son.
  Skapti Þóroddz son.
  Þórolfr Munnr.
  Eilífr Guðrúnar son.
  Þorleifr skald.
  Hvannar-Kalfr.
Eirekr iarl Hakonar son :
  Hallfrœðr Vendræða skald.
  Gunnlaugr Orms-tunga.
  Þórðr Kolbeins son.
  Halldórr Úkristni.
  Eyiolfr Daða-skald.
  Skúli Þorsteins son.
  Þórðr Siarreks son.
Sveinn iarl Hakonar son :
  Bersi Torfo son.
Hakon iarl [Eiriks son] :
  .. ..
Ormr iarl Eilifs son :
  .. ..
Hakon iarl Ivars son :
  .. ..
Sigurðr iarl Havarz son :
  .. ..
Erlingr Skakki :
  Þorbiörn Skakka-skald.
Eirekr iarl Sigurðar son :
  .. ..
Philippus iarl Birgis son :
  .. ..
Hákon Galinn :
  Snorri Sturlo son.
  Steinn Ófeigs son.
  Liótr skald.
  Þorsteinn Eyiolfs son.
Skúli hertogi :
  Snorri Sturlo son.
  Óláfr Þórðar son.
  Iátgeirr skald.
  Liótr skald.
  Alfr Eyiolfs son.
  Sturla Bárðar son.
  Guðmundr Oddz son.

Teitr skald.
  Roðgeirr Afla son.
  Þóralfr prestr.
Knútr Hákonar son :
  Óláfr Þórðar son.
DANISH KINGS :—
Sveinn Tiúgo-skegg :
  Óttarr Svarti.
Knútr inn Ríki :
  Sigvatr skald.
  Óttarr Svarti.
  Þorarinn Lof-tunga.
  Hallvarðr Háreks-blesi.
  Bersi Torfo son.
  Steinn Skapta son.
  Arnórr Iarla-skald.
  Óðar Keptr.
Sveinn Alfifo son :
  Þórarinn Lof-tunga.
Sveinn Ulfs son :
  Þorleikr Fagri.
  Þórðr Kolbeins son.
Knútr Helgi :
  Kalfr Mána son.
  Skúli Illuga son.
  Markus Skeggja son.
Eirikr Sveins son :
  Markus Skeggja son.
Eirikr konongr Eimuni :
  Halldórr Skvaldri.
Sveinn Svifandi [1] :
  Einarr Skúla son.
Valdimarr Knútz son :
  Þorsteinn Kroppr.
  Arnhallr Þorvallz son.
Knútr Valdimars son :
  Þorvarðr Þorgeirs son.
Valdimarr Gamli :
  Óláfr Þórðar son.
  Iátgeirr Torfa son.
  Þorgeirr Dana-skald.
  Suguvalldi.
DANISH EARLS :—
Strút-Haraldr iarl :
  Þióðolfr or Hvini.
Sigvaldi iarl :
  Þórðr Sigvalda-skald,
Haraldr Þorkels son :
  Þióðolfr Arnórs son [2].

[1] Read, sviðandi.   [2] Arna son, Cd.

Cod. Ups. adds the following :—

ENGLISH KINGS :—

Aðalsteinn Engla konungr :
Egill Skallagrims son.

Aðalráðr konungr :
Gunnlaugr Orms-tunga.

ULFR HINN OARGI var hersir ágætr í Noregi í Naumodali, faðir Hallbiarnar Half-trollz, foður Ketils Hæings. Ulfr orti drápo á einni nótt ok sagði frá þrek-virkjom sínom. Hann var dauðr fyrir dag.

NORSE NOBLES :—

Þorleifr Spaki :
Þióðolfr or Hvini.

Arinbiorn Hersir :
Egill Skallagríms son.

Þorsteinn Þóro son :
Egill Skallagrims son.

Erlingr Skialgs son :
Sighvatr Skald.

Guðbrandr í Dolum :
Óttarr Svarti.

Ívarr Hvíti :
Sighvatr Skald.

Hárekr or Þiótto :
Refr Gestz son.

Einarr Fluga :
Refr skáld.

Kalfr Arna son :
Biarni Gullbrá-skald.

Ulfr stallari :
Steinn Herdísar son.

Eysteinn Orri :
Þorkell Hamar-skald.

Viðkunnr Ions son :
Áso-Þórðr.

Gregorius Dags son :
Einarr Skúla son.

Nikulas Skialdvarar son :
Súgandi skald.

Eindriði Ungi :
Einarr Skúla son.

Ívarr Selki :
Arnórr Kalfs son.

Sigurðr munkr :
Arnórr Kalfs son.

Arnbiorn Ions son :
Óláfr Herdísar son.

Gautr á Meli :
Steinvör Sighvaz dóttir.
Óláfr Herdísar son.
Dagfinnr Guðlaugs son.

EXCURSUS I.

ON THE FIGURES AND METAPHORS (KENNINGAR) OF OLD NORTHERN POETRY.

WITH SOME REFERENCE TO THE ANCIENT LIFE, THOUGHT, AND BELIEF AS EMBODIED THEREIN.

INTRODUCTION.

JUST as Snorri dealt with the question of Metre, founding a system upon an analysis of the elaborate and artificial verse of his day, so has he handled the subject of Metaphor, Trope, and Synonym, which forms so prominent a feature of Northern poetry; basing his classification and treatment upon the highly rigid and conventional phrasing of his own time. In fact, he began at the *wrong end*, and he has led the tribe of commentators after him. They have no excuse. He is justified by his object, which was not the study of the old poets' minds and feelings, but simply the production of a handy 'Gradus.' Thus he culls his first metaphor from Arnor, and, though he certainly knew Egil's poems, Wolospa and Ynglinga-tal, makes little use of them, but gathers the bulk of his examples from such men as Einar Sculason and his compeers and models. True, he uses Bragi and the Shield poems; but it is rather because of his intense appreciation of the humorous Thor stories, after all, than the striking and complex metaphorical phrases in which they abound.

So again Snorri, treating first of the favourite style of Synonym in his day (for which the technical word 'kenning,' description, recognition, was invented, and to which it fitly- applies), relegates the earlier *pro-nominal terms* to the end of his unfinished treatise, where they remain huddled together under some half-dozen heads.

Yet they are the germ from which the whole later many-branched and far-spreading growth has sprung. They are examples of the primitive observations out of which language itself has sprung; they are 'crystallised thinking;' looking through them, as it were, we can see the world as the early poet saw it,—nay more, we can even find out what he thought of himself, and how he supposed himself to think. To call the flesh the *locker of the bones*, the bone-box, as it were; to think of the breast as the *abode of thought*, for thought came not from the brain, but from the heart, to the man of old time; to speak of the ship as the *steed of the waves*, or the hair as the *sward of the head*, exhibits quaint primitive ways of thought, which are not only common to old Northern and old English poetry, but would readily occur to early poets of all times. In Egil's vigorous and concise figures we have the noblest example of this kind, often as deeply thought out and as ruggedly true and bold as the tropes of Æschylus himself. Yet Snorri knew

Egil's three poems in their pure form, and could have preserved for us the true text of these marred and ruined lines and dark blanks, every one of which marks the lost thought of a true poet, gone beyond recovery; for it is rarely that one can hope to get back such a metaphor as '*the cauldron of tears*,' which we have been able to restore to the text. One can only hope that, had Snorri ever lived to finish his incomplete Treatise (for Skaldskapar-mal is not only incomplete as regards the *citations*, which very probably are added by a later hand, but actually unfinished in substance, e.g. giants and giantesses are wholly omitted), he would have filled up many of the blank spaces from the works of the poet on whose homestead he dwelt and whose office and blood he inherited.

Later than these early metaphors we have been speaking of, are those Synonyms which are based on early beliefs respecting Cosmogony and the Supernatural World in its lighter and darker aspects—myths of the Creation, of the Monsters and Powers of Evil, of the Blessed Gods, and of the Holy Draught that inspires men to sing of things past and to come. Later than these, again, are those which witness to heroic exploits, to the warring and sea-roving of wicking-leaders, and the offerings and dooms of heathen tribal kings. We can in the case of this class, 'myth-figures,' as we might call them, often almost detect the poet who set the fashion of a particular kind of synonym. Thus we have a large number of expressions derived from sea-kings' names (as the lists in the Thulor drawn from actual poetry show). Many of these names in the later poetry are *manufactured*, drawn from analogy of names which really existed; for instance, one whole set of names ending in -ill looks very suspicious, as they exactly fit the requirements of the court-metre and are none of them hinted at in real tradition. Later poets, who were not fanciful enough to invent, actually use the names of such well-known persons as Atli, Budli, and others, which well fit their verses, as if these 'tyrants of the steppes' had been North-Sea rovers of Alfred's or Ecgberht's days. Of the names of Woden many are founded by analogy upon real old titles, and among those of the Dwarves, Giants, etc. there are similar instances. By noticing such points it is possible to form a rough classification, sufficient to give basis for a psychological study of the early poetry.

Snorri of course makes no distinction between the different strata of synonym, though the difference is so patent to us. Such an expression as the *Meed of Woden* for *Poetry*, enwraps a deep and sacred sense, while to invent a new synonym for Walcyria or Ogress, by which to vary the everlasting sameness of the later poets' metaphors for *Shield* or *Wolf*, is merely a trick of song-craft. Some other arrangement of matter and subject than that which suited Snorri's purpose is evidently required to exhibit the growth, development, and inward thought-life of these metaphors.

There are several other points to be noticed; for instance, there is an evident reason for the extreme development of the 'kenning' in Northern poetry in the very make of the verse. The simplicity of syntax and the dependence on the root-syllables for *the* rhythmic element—alliteration—both necessitated a variety of *expression*; hence comes the strict rule (hardly ever violated) against repetition of a stressed word; hence, too, the pleasure felt at the recurring though appearing each time in a fresh and varied raiment. Greater complexity of verse-structure, the increased necessity for strict line-rhythm and regular measure, which characterise the court-poetry, imply, or necessity, a singular syntax, still more restricted form and subject, and a more lavish use of synonyms, for without them the verse could not be constructed: so it comes that the ornament, which Bragi and Thiodwolf wisely restrict to the main subjects of their poem, their ingenuity on it *there*, is now spread over every noun in every line, till the hearer gives up all idea of tracking the poor little thought under its gorgeous garniture, and is content to listen to the babble of sweet sound.   The type and plan of the court-poem might be represented in six lines:—

Introduction.   The Poet brings the King a poem.

Body × n. { The King launched his ship. } Historical fact.
             { He met his foes at N. }
             { He battened the wolf, } Embellishment.
             { And quenched the raven's thirst. }

End.   The King will reward the Poet.

And every subject and object throughout every poem is put into a more or less dark and rigid dressing of metaphor.

It is but fair to observe that the *sameness* of metaphor is far more marked in the court-poems, as we have them, than it would have been could we have heard them in their original state ; for, as has been shown in this volume, *the whole of the court-poetry from 970–1070 bears evident marks of corruption and overworking by some twelfth-century poet.*   The best example of the way in which this 'restorer' worked (whom the Editor has guessed to have been Einar Sculason) would be to say that he has swept away the *historical clause* which told *where* the king met his foes, *whom* they were, *what* counties he ruled over, etc., and replaced it by such stock phrases as 'he clove the shields and dyed his blade in blood;' where metaphors of little meaning but of pleasing sound take the place of the historical, but less euphonious, names of men, islands, rivers, and towns which give their real value to the lists of exploits in the Panegyrics of the Court-poets (as Ari well says).

The examination of the synonyms of the Early Poetry is extremely interesting in the results it yields.   The justice of our classification of these older poems is confirmed by it, and a very marked distinction is made manifest between the terminology of the different groups.   Thus the rich, bright Homeric metaphors of the Helgi-poems are quite distinct from the myth-figures of the Didactic and the Aristophanian lays. The synonyms of the Hymi-lay show affinities with the more developed metaphor-system of Thiodwolf's Ynglinga-tal, while the poems of Book v, so strong in description—note the ornate embroidery scenes, so characteristic of them—but so strikingly bare of these figures of speech, recall the style of many of our Old English Poems.   The contrast between Atla-mal, with its one or two 'kennings,' with its citations or imitations of the Atla-kvida phrases, and the wealth of free primitive figures in the Helgi trilogy, is very noteworthy.   Again, the coincidence between the terminology of these latter and of the Waking of Angentheow and that of Wolospa is marked.

The data gleaned by a careful investigation of these points are to be depended on, for one must not forget that the terminology is here a faithful mirror of the poet's thoughts, feelings, and ways.   How eloquent in its witness to the Helgi poet's ideas is his beautiful metaphor for Sleep, 'the Parliament of Dreams,' bringing one back to Job, shrinking from the awful gathering of 'the Visions of the Night,' and Homer's fancy of the shadowy figures that people Dreamland, thronging out through the horn and ivory gates.   How vividly such a word as

Bragi's 'sal-penningr' calls up the picture of the long smoke-darkened wooden hall, set round with tables and benches, crowded by a goodly crew of merchant-adventurers, and filled by the merry sounds of the clinking can, blithe talk, and laughter, while the light of torch and hearth plays upon the long row of glittering brazen targets that deck the walls above their owners' heads. Again, how deep is the thought that is expressed by that tragic figure of the 'cauldron of tears,' which we noticed above. No one who has not seen, as Egil saw, the hot spring of volcanic Iceland, the cup-like pools in which the boiling water slowly wells up in a strange weird way, can fully realise the force of the old hero's setting forth in his own way the 'divine mystery of tears.'

Many more examples might be given did space permit, but these will suffice to show how much there is of interest in these figures, many of which seem at first so strange and barbarous to a modern reader. What we have tried to do in the following pages, is to exhibit, as clearly as may be, a view of the metaphors and synonyms of Northern Poetry. We have been careful not to smother the varied and primitive examples beneath the rank and weedy crop of the spurious and imitative metaphors of the court-poem, while at the same time including the striking and evidently genuine phrase of Sighvat or Arnor or Cormac in its due place. The arrangement adopted has been to begin with the most primitive type of synonym, then to put the vast class of phrases derived from cosmogonic and classic myths, which are followed by those terms that bear witness to later states of society, the home-life of the franklin, the warring of the noble, the sea-life of the wicking, the sacrifice and the rule of the heathen tribal king, and finally, the curious group of figures which witness to the poet's acceptance and conceptions of the New Faith. To each class is prefixed a short introduction pointing out briefly the main features; a general index concludes the list.

It may be well to note that a careful comparison of our lists with the Thulor and Snorri's collection will be by no means unfruitful. The sources from which the Thulor drew are *in the main* those which are still happily preserved to us. Many of Snorri's later and less valuable sources have perished.

In the course of working at the text and going through the metrical and metaphor systems of the different poems a fresh sheaf of emendations and corrections has been gathered. These have been printed in such-wise that the reader may be able at once to enter them in the text of the poems, each in its proper place. In the references which occur in the following tables, we shall always quote from the corrected text.

The *metrical* use and *technical* history of the 'kenning' have been given in the Excursus on Metre. The following pages are concerned with its *interpretation*. With their help the reader may be able to get a *literal word for word* rendering of any uncorrupt passage in the foregoing poems; indeed they form a little 'poetic lexicon,' and may be looked on as a supplement to the Editor's Dictionary.

§ 1. PHYSICAL.

I. THE BODY.

THE chief interest in this first group is the insight it gives into the life and ways of thinking of the early Northmen. Thus taking the BODY first, the *Breast* and upper trunk is looked on as the most noble and worthy part, and styled 'the mind's house, memory's sanctuary, the lurking-place of thought, the shore of the mind, the bark of laughter, the hall of the heart;' while the *Heart* is conceived to be 'the acorn of courage, the life-clod, the pebble *or* stone of the will.' Such terms conform to the ideas of most primitive peoples, and we still talk, like Jews and Greeks of old, as if the bowels were the seat of pity and sympathy, and the heart the organ of courage and will.

The *Head* is treated with far less respect by Northern poets; its worth to them lies in its proving a fit support for a helmet, and as containing *eyes, mouth, and ears,* the importance of which they fully recognise. Egil is the fountain-head of many curious phrases for the head. His humourous lines on his own high craggy forehead and huge grey jutting brows will be remembered. He held strength and solidity the most desirable attributes for the head, and of this point of view typical expressions are—'helm-stock, helmet-block, the rock of the shoulders, the peak of the hair.' More descriptive are, 'brain-roof, field of the brows,' for the *skull;* and more fanciful 'the bolster's fellow' for the whole head. The metaphor 'Heimdal's sword' refers to a lost myth in which the god chooses his weapon like Samson. The *brains* are seldom noticed, and simply described as 'the ocean of the brain-pan;' and not connected with *thought,* which in obedience to a legend now perished is held to be an afflatus, 'the storm *or* gale of a giantess,' tearing through the breast and stirring it.

The *eye* is the 'moon *or* star of the brows, the light *or* levin of the forehead, the cauldron of tears, the pledge of Woden,' shining out from under the 'crags *or* steeps of the eye-brows;' striking and vigorous similes. The remarkable brightness of the eyes of Walcyria-born heroes is noticed, and they are likened to those of a hawk or snake. The eye is also known as the 'sight-apple;' *tears* are 'the cob-nuts *or* filberts that roll from the forest of the eyelid;' they are also the 'rain of the cheeks, the ban of laughter,' while the eyelids are poetically styled the 'cups of sleep.'

Next in rank comes the *mouth,* 'the temple of speech, the city or song, the cave of the voice, the ice-hole of words [a fisherman's metaphor], the croft of the teeth,' and even in humourous vein 'the purse of the grinders.' The *teeth* are the 'pales of this temple, the fence of this sanctuary.' The *tongue* is the 'steelyard of song, the plane of poesy' (with which compare Richard Fitz-Neal's image of the *dolabrum prudentioris architecti* working on the rough-hewn, axe-squared timber to fit it for building a royal palace), and quaintly 'the talking-pin' (for so we read Egil's simile in Arinbiorn's Lay).

From another point of view the head is 'the field' on which grows the crop of *hair,* 'the harvest of the skull, the forest *or* scrub of the brain-pan,' and the *beard* 'the shaw *or* thicket of the chin.' On the head too are set the *ears,* 'listening mouths, tents or awnings of hearing, pails of hearkening,' and the like. In the case of animals the head may be, like the neat's head with which the giant fisherman, Hymi, baits his hooks, the lofty 'acropolis of the horns.' Of the *horns* themselves we shall speak below.

The *limbs* are not forgotten. *Arms* and *legs* are looked on as 'boughs' of the human trunk, branching out hands and feet. So the *toes* are the 'twigs of the footsole,' and the *arms* the 'crooked limbs of the shoulders.' But the *hand* has many uses, each of which yields its stock of metaphor. It is the 'perch *or* field *or* crag *or* croft of the hawk,' a mark of the love of hawking in the North recalling the early scene in the Tapestry where Harold rides down, hawk on fist, to the sea. The hand and wrist is also 'the gallows of the gold rings,' which are the faithful henchman's guerdon and wage from generous kings. In sterner aspect, the hand is the 'quivering field of the yew, the tongs of the bow, the seat of the buckler, the haunt of the spear.' The *back* is the 'staple *or* stall of burdens,' the *spine* the 'keels of the ship of laughter.' The *feet* are aptly described as the 'snow-skates of the heels.'

THE BODY :—

The Breast.—Mun-tún, Wak. 71; mun-vangr, Lokas. 206 ; mun-strönd, Höfuðl. 2 ; munar-grunnr, 67 ; hugar-fylgsni, Sonat. 4 ; hyggjo-staðr, 6; minnis-knörr, Höfuðl. 4 ; minnis-vé, Lokas. 206 ; hug-tún, Gisli, 18 ; hug-borg, Gkv. 54 ; vilja-byrgi, Yt. 17 ; hlátra-hamr, Höfuðl. 72 ; hlátr-elliði, þd. 56 ; geð-mörk, Husd. 2 ; Boðnar-smiðja, ii. 80. 32 ; hiarta-hrót, ii. 79. 14.

The Heart.—Móð-akarn, Helgi, i. 23; diúp-akarn, þd. 37; hug-steinn, Hyndl. 138 ; þróttar-steinn, þd. 40; fiör-segi, W. W. L. 46; hugar-korn, Malsh. 25.

The Head.—Hattar-staup, Ad. 28 ; hattar-fell, ii. 74. 13 ; hattar-steði, 80. 32 ; hialm-stofn, Hym. 120; lesnis-stofn, ii. 79. 12 ; svarðar-stofn, 91. 28 ; herða-klettr, Lokas. 231 ; skarar-há-fiall, Hym. 90; brá-völlr, ii. 36 29 ; brúna brims himin, 64. 9 : hiarna mœnir, Haust. 74 ; hlusta-grunn, Húsd. 20 ; heila himin, Geisli 236 ; ár-síma grund, ii. 72. 7.

Bólstr-maki, Ad. 21.

Mythical.—Heimdals hiör, ii. 114. 10.

The Brains.—Hiarna ægir, Yt. 1.5.

The Mind. *Mythical.*—Brý-vindr, Sonat. 50; Iarnsöxo veðr, ii. 211 ; Griðar byrr, 223. 23 (cp. ii. 440. 13–16).

The Eye.—Enni-máni, Ad. 19 ; ennis inn-máni, Husd. 13; enni-tungl, Bragi, 43 ; enni-leiptr, ii. 327 ; brá-tungl, Ad. 17 ; brá-tíror, 29 ; brúna brim, ii. 64. 9 ; brá-máni, id. ; hvarma skógar-stiörnor, 441.

Tára vellir, Hofuðl. 74; svefna ker, Gisli, 6 ; sión-epli, 12 ; brún-steinar, ii. 348. 34.

Vagna várar, Hofuðl. 74.

Tears.—Hvarma skógs fylvingar, Gisli, 10 ; kinna él, 6; brá-dögg, 8 ; brá-drift, ii. 271. 4.

Hlátr-bann, Málsh. 35.

The Eyelashes.—Hvarma skógr, Gisli, 9 ; ii. 441.

The Eyebrows.—Hvarms gnípor, ii. 72 ; hvarma hvít-völlr, 73. 27 ; brúna mið-stallr, 72. 12 ; ár-síma grundar gerði-hamrar, 7.

The Mouth.—Orð-hof, Sonat. 19 ; bragar-tún, Ad. 95 ; bragar-stóll, Geisli, 269 ; lióð-pundara lopt-vætt, Sonat. 2 ; galdra flés, ii. 48. 12 ; radd-kleif, Haustl. 2 ; orða vök, Merl. 356.

Tanna-hverfi, ii. 80. 27 ; iótrs bi-gyrðill (við-gyrðill ?), þd. 68.

The Teeth.—Góma sker, ii. 62. 18.

The Tongue.—Omon-lokarr, Ad. 57 (ii. 300. 8) ; lióð-pundari, Sonat. 2 ; mál-þorn (-priónn ?), Ad. 93 ; óðar-ár, Geisli, 160; orða-hlýða, 102 ; mál-tól, 76 ; bragar-tól, 198.

The Hair.—Skalla rá, ii. 73. 28 (cp. p. 441, l. 58) ; reikar rúfr, Gisli, 72 ; haus-miöll, reikar eik, hiarna þyrnir, hlusta kvistir, vanga ölr, svarðar grön, svarð-akr, ii. 441.

The Comb.—Svarðar raðar garðr, ii. 441.

The Beard.—Kinn-skógr, Hym. 38.

The Ears.—Hlusta-munnar, Ad. 24 ; hler-tiöld, 34 ; heyrnar-spann, 74.

Head of Beast.—Horna há-tún, Hym. 73.

LIMBS:—

Hand and Arms.—Alin-munnr, Husd. 26; herða biúg-limir, ii. 49. 1; axl-limar, 68. 111.

Seat of Hawk.—Hauk-strönd, Höfudl. 60; hauka-fiöll, ii. 36. 26; heiðis stallr, 54 3; heidis land, 68. 112; hauk-mœr, 64. 19.

Seat of Ring.—Hringa há-ferill, ii. 167. 18.

Seat of Bow.—Dal-töng, ii. 56. 25; ýs bif-vangr, Korm. 14; baug-set, Hofuðl. 47; baug-vangr, ii. 76. 10; at-geirs toptir, Ad. 84.

The Nailed Fingers.—Ýfs ár, ii. 142. 88.

The Back.—Byrðar stallr, Bk. vi. 30; hlátr-elliða kiölr, þd. 56.

The Feet.—Hæls hleypi-kiólar, ii. 207. 61.

The Toes.—Il-kvistir, Am. 233.

Nakedness.—Fótar bergis borr, ii. 73. 29.

Claws.—Il-þorn, i. 372. 20.

II. THE HOME.

Turning from the man to his HOME and work-a-day life, one finds the *house* looked on as the place for cooking, eating, drinking, and sleeping, and described as the 'mead-hall, the ship *or* keep of the hearth, the fire-ship, the bark of the beds.' One learns the look and build of the old Northern hall from such phrases as 'the ship of the toft, the bear of the walls, Bruin with the floors,' the latter simile being followed up in the description of the *pillars* as the legs of this bear-like mass of timber and thatch, with its rough-rounded, turfed or shingled back, its twin gable-ends like ears and snout, and feels that the comparison is by no means so extravagant as at first sight it appears. Indeed modern English instances of like metaphors applied to buildings might be given. The word *window*, 'eye of the wind,' is a Norse loan-word, which explains the use of the old dead-lights that ventilated the hall; curiously enough, it is not found in any of our poems. The *door* is alluded to, but the passage is too corrupt for one to gather any facts regarding it therefrom. The *hearth* is the central and most important part of the house, it is called 'the fire-table' on which burnt the 'waster of the wood, the murderer of the lime-tree, the dread of the birch-tree;' the glowing *fire* itself, feeding on the wood-fuel and boiling the *cauldron* that hung over it, a vessel which (as the emblem of hospitality, in which ale was brewed, fish and meat boiled) was held in due respect and honour by the poets and their patrons as the 'ale-barge, liquor-boiler,' etc. *Sausages* of sheep's flesh, which were favourite viands in Iceland, are associated with the cauldron too, and merrily termed by Cormac 'the snakes of the kettle.' From the cauldron to the *horn* or *cup* was the first journey of the ale or mead when it was brewed, and the poet's fancy lingers round these. The horn he tells of as the 'spear *or* blade *or* pike *or* dirk of the ox;' the *cup* is 'the argosy of wine, the ale-box,' and the like; while the *liquor* itself, mead, beer, or wine, is termed 'the wave *or* stream *or* lake *or* waterfall of the horn, the lake *or* pool of the mash-tub.'

Of *food* less is said than of drink, as was to be looked for, but the 'mill-grit' of the *quern* and the *grain* are spoken of. In the poems hams, flitches, and joints are mentioned.

The flocks and herds are not forgotten. The *oxen* are the 'reindeer *or* bears of the yoke, whales of the harness, steeds of the giant;' the *goat* is 'the champer, the deer of the birch-buds, the shackled team-beast of Thor.' The *horse* is 'the pad-horse, the saddle-beast, the war-horse,' used only for riding, as it seems; his *bridle* 'head-fetter, the riding trappings;' his food the *hay* is 'Slipner's banquet' (Slipner being Woden's steed, best of all horses).

The broad plain of EARTH which lay beneath the covering vault of heaven was called the 'floor beneath the wind-cup, the bottom of the bowl of the showers.' It was also, in a higher aspect, the 'seat of mankind,' the sacred 'τέμενος of man.' It was also 'the evergreen,' fresh and beautiful to look on, with its clothing of sward and forest, which are likened to 'the hair or waving locks of Sif, Europa, mother Earth,' or, in sailor-phrase, as the 'sea-weed of the mountain sides.' But the waste places and *deserts* of earth are not forgotten; they are the 'patrimony of the wolf, the home of the reindeer.' The *hart* is hardly spoken of, because he was not found in Scandinavia in olden times; only in the Helgi-poet and his western compeers, who had seen the red-deer in Ireland and Scotland, we meet with glorious similes wherein the hero is likened to a great hart in his pride. The *snake* is well known and aptly described as the 'thong *or* necklace of the woods, the fish of the heather *or* the vales;' his *venom* is the 'draught the Wolsungs quaffed.' The wild shore by the sea too is the haunt of wild *birds*, such as the *osprey*, 'fish-hunter,' whose *pinions* are 'oarage,' and whose *claws* are 'foot thorns.' The birds' skins are 'feather cloaks *or* pelts' (bialbi is a trade word).

The *fox* is well known in the later poems: 'sheaf-tail, long-brush, low-foot, shaggy-back' they call him from his looks; 'lair-lurker, den-holder, and gory-tooth' from his habits. Of his victims the *geese* are mentioned, but not in metaphor. The *mouse* is 'the spoiler of old walls.' And the *cock*, 'gold-comb,' that crows and wakes the sleepers in the hall, is not met with after the earlier poems, from which the names given in the Thulor are taken.

The *tools* mentioned are mostly the simple implements of the smith or husbandman: the *tongs*, 'the lifter of the lump, the bar of the forge;' the *hone*, the 'pumice of the steel, the rust-medicine;' the iron-shod *walking-staff*, 'the broken branch of the tree of the wood;' the *hay-fork*, 'pitching-staff.' *Cord* was spun of goats'-hair, as the term 'she-goat's heir-loom' proves.

More poetical, though not perhaps of such psychological interest, are the *metaphors* of *observation* applied to NATURAL OBJECTS, as when the *sky* is called 'the world above, the field of heaven, the fair-roof, the seat *or* hall *or* path *or* pavilion of the sun or moon, the sun's helmet; the cup *or* vault *or* dome *or* bason of the winds, the vault *or* hall *or* basket of the clouds, the hall *or* cup of the rain, the path of the birds.'

(Helgi's poet once calls air the '*sea of the Walcyria Mist*:' by an extension of this idea, his magnificent picture of the shield-maidens appearing on their steeds high above the heroes' ships in the midst of the storm, works out this fine thought.) Last of all, the half-Christian Wolospa calls heaven 'the gods' home.'

Wind is the 'death *or* destroyer of ships, the roarer, the waster of the woods, the wolf of the forest.' *Calm* is 'the cheery warmth, the lull of the wind, the sweetness of the day.' *Hail* is the 'gravel of the clouds,' *rain* the 'tears of the sky.' The *clouds* are the 'wind-floe, the dark helm, the shower-harbinger.' The *rainbow* is the 'sky-bridge, the fiery *or* flickering league,' or (if we read Bifrost) the 'swaying *or* rocking mile.' Then the *sun* is the 'target of heaven, the loaf of the sky, fair-wheel, ever-sheen, eye-glow;' the *moon* is the 'year-teller, the warping *or* changing wheel.' *Night* is the 'lightless one, the dreams' joy, lady of dreams;' and *sleep* the 'moot of dreams.' A charmed slumber is 'the thorn or stave of sleep;' worked by magical staves or characters put into the ears.

The *seasons* are also characterised: *summer* is the 'joy of the serpent,' and *winter* 'the snake's dread, horror, and death, the bear's night;' *autumn* is the 'hemp-cutter.' The *sea*, as one would guess, is very fully treated. It is the 'blue-moor,' —a term still used in Norway—'the glittering land.' Then it is the 'home of the eels, the hall of the whales, the pike's meadow, the road of the cod, the path *or* the moor of the sea-mew, the path of ships;' it is the 'shackle *or* fetter *or* girdle of islands, the band of the land, the necklace of the earth:' so the *ice* is the 'heaven *or* roof of the deep,' etc. Its *billows* are the 'mountains of the main, the steeps of the sea;' its *coast* is the 'sea-bed, the islands, the studs of the sea.' The *rock* or boulder of the coast is the 'bone *or* apple of the sea, the heart of the ocean;' *pearls* are the 'kidney of the sea.'

Of the SEA-BEASTS and FISHES, the porpoises are of course the 'swine of the waves,' the *herrings* the 'arrows of the sea, the darts, the tail-barbed arrows of the deep.'

SHIPS are characterised by a host of metaphors; the 'tree *or* beam, the sled, the car, the beam *or* timber of the waves;' or as the 'steeds, deer, hart (only in Helgi-lays, Ragnar's verses, and in one of Harold Hardrede's lines), dragons, goats, bears *or* boars *or* elk *or* hinds *or* reindeer of the main:' and again, by an instructive series of synonyms, as the 'steeds of the helm, oars, mast, sail-yard, sails, prow-heads, prows, stems, tiller, steer-withy [stior-vid], seams, keel,' and the like. The *sails* are called the 'mast-scroll, the sheet the ladies spun;' the *oars* the 'square sea-grippers, wave-sweepers, the feet of the ship;' the *anchor*, 'cold-neb;' the *fishing-lines*, 'sea-thread *or* ribbon;' and the *hook* the 'gallows of the bait.'

In later times by a metaphor, dear to the court-poets, the *sea* is treated as the sea-kings' realm, 'the track of Frodi, the road of Enkil, the moor of Ialk [?], the way of Geiti, the land of Leif, the tracks of Glammi and Budli, the path of Rakni, and the huge-ground of Wandil.'

The SHIPS that traverse the sea are, in consonance with this fancy, called 'the cars, sleds, snow-skates, or beams of a host of sea-kings, Ræ, Shield, Endil, Atal, Glammi, Ati, Eynefir;' and by another figure, the steed, riding-horse, deer, reindeer, of Gylfi [sic], Rokkvi, Thwinnill, Sweidi,' see p. 458.

THE HOME :—

The House. *As ship.*—Brand-nór, Yt. 113 ; árin-kióll, 21 ; toptar nökkvi, 115 ; leg-vers-knörr, Ad. 82.

As animal, steed.—Golf-hölkvir, Bragi 30 ; hvíl-beðjar hölkvir, Akv. 120.

As bear.—Veggja viðbiörn, Biark. 22 ; flet-biörn, Þd. 66.

The Bed.—Hvíl-beðr, Akv. 120 ; leg-verr, Ad. 80.

The Drinking-hall.—Miöð-rann, Akv. 39.

The Pillars.—Flet-biarnar fót-leggr, Þd. 66 ; bratt-steinn, Hym. 111 (of a cave).

The Window.—Vind-auga.

The Door.—Hallar hlunn-blik, Brunh. L. 278.

The Hearth.—Birkis-ótta-bióðr, Ad. 64.

The Fire.—For-brennir, Alvm. 103 ; lindar váði, W. W. L. 72 ; lindar bani, Grip. 59 ; viðar herr, Brunh. L. 324 ; elris grand, Mark. 57 ; aura-mein, Gisli, 30.

The Cauldron.—Öl-vellir, Hornkl. 23 ; lög-vellir, Hym. 21 ; öl-kióll, 127.

Sausages.—Ketil-ormar, Bk. vi. No. 62.

The Horn *or* Cup.—Vín-ferill, Hym. 121 ; vín-gnóð, ii. 48. 6 ; öl-karmr, 79. 11 ; (hrosta) karmr, id. 4 ; öl-stafn, ii. 113. 3.

The Horn.—Hiarðar mækir, Yt. 83; sveiðoðs mækir, 80; svigðis geirr, 3; ok-hreins lögðir, 82; hæfis hiörr, 92; brúna hörgr, 90; farra trióno fræningr 87; hausa biúg-viðir, Krákom. 123.

Ale.—Hrosta fen, ii. 192. 2; [hrosta tiörn, Egil]; horna fors, ii. 62; horn-straumr 26. 5; hver-lögr, Hlt. 3; ker-straumr, i. 371. 3; svigðis geira vágr, Yt. 4 hreina-lögr, Alvm. 135.

Wine.—Vín-gnóðar austr, ii. 48. 6.

The Mill.—Griótz griá, Grott. 6; ákvernar hús, Merl. 275.

Grain.—Laga-stafr, Alv. 127.

BEASTS :—

Oxen.—Ok-hreinn, Yt. 82; ok-biörn, Haust. 22; þrym-seilar hvalr, 18; renni rökn, Bragi, 42.
Iötuns eykr, Yt. 86.

The Goat.—Tann-gnióstr (see Thulor and Edda); birki-brums hind, ii. 37. 42 skökuls skær (Thor's), Hym. 143.

The Horse.—*Saddle-horse.*—Hnakk-marr, Yt. 57; söðul-dýr, Old G. L. 11. *War horse.*—Víg-blær, Helgi, i. 282.

The Bridle.—Hnakk-mars hofuð-fetlar, Yt. 57; eykja görvi, 59.

Hay.—Sleipnis verðr, Yt. 47.

LAND, EARTH :—

The Earth.—Vind-kers botn, Ad. 72; él-kers botn, Mark. 4; glyggs varð-ker botn, ii. 137. 15.
Alda vé, i. 22. 47; manna siöt, Bragi, 62; í-grœn, Alvm. 39.

The Wood, Forest.—Vallar-fax, Alv. 109; fagr-limi, 111; hlíð-þang, 110, Y 114; iarðar haddr, Biark. 23.

The Deserts.—Varga-leifar, Old G. L. 36; hreina stöð, Helgi, i. 168.

The Hart.—Dýr-kalfr, Helgi, i. 290.

The Wolf.—Hrís-grisnir, Hlt. 26; hræ-gífr, Old G. L. 99.

The Fox.—Skauf-ali, lang-hali, rebbali, loð-bakr, gor-tanni, gren-lægja, lág-fæta Skaufh. ii. 383–84; gren-bui, Merl. i. 123.

The Mouse.—Aldinna veggja vælir, Biark. 22.

The Snake. *As thong.*—Holt-vartari, ii. 62. 11; lyngva men, 37. 40. *As fish.*—Dal-fiskr, i. 377. 34; lyng-fiskr, Old G. L. 126; heiðar-lax, foldar fiskr, i 346; storðar lykkja, Krak. 4.
Mythical.—Volsunga drekko hrœkkvi-áll, Bragi, 56.

Venom.—Volsunga drekkja, Bragi, 56.

The Osprey.—Fiska veiðir, Vsp. 184.

The Cock.—Sal-gofnir, Helgi, i. 318; gollin-kambi, Vsp. 122.

Bird's Plumage.—Fiaðrar leik-blað, Haust. 47; hauks bialbi, 46; fiaðr-ham þrym. 11.

TOOLS, ETC. :—

Hammer.—Trióno troll, Haust. 68.

Smith's Tongs.—Sio lyptir, þd. 62.

A lump of Iron.—Töngo segi, þd. 59; tangar rauð-biti, Husd. 25; esjo áss, þ 63; sio lypti-sylgr, 62.

A Woof.—Rifs reiði-ský, Darr. 2.

The Hone.—Stála vikr, Haust. 76; ryðs heili-böl, 78.

The Hay-fork.—Sleipnis verðar slongo þref, Yt. 47.

The Walking-staff.—Skógar hóg-brotningr, þd. 74.

The Gallows.—Varg-tré, Hamð. 81; hörva sleipnir, Yt. 71.

The Halter.—Hagbarðz höðnoleif, Yt. 74.

The Hanged.—Virgil-nár, Hávam. 57; tröno hvöt? Hamð. 83.

SKY AND WEATHER AND SEASONS:—

The Heavens.—Vind-ker, Ad. 72; él-ker, Mark. 4; glyggs varð-ker, ii. 137. 15; vind-hialmr, Helgi, i. 317; glygg-rann, ii. 239. 102; vinda mund-laug, Bragi, 62; röðuls tiald, Wak. 101; heims tiald, ii. 224. 1; vagn-braut, ii. 55; mána salr, Helgi, i. 12; mána vegr, Haust. 56; sólar siöt, Grip. 208; él-siöt, Bk. vi. 1; fialla salr, ii. 171; sólar hialmr, 197. 78; sól-tiald, 194. 19; dags grund, 197. 76; ský-rann, 194. 8; skyja laupr, Kont. 315; hauks holms hialmr, ii. 74. 5.

Vind-ofnir, fagr-ræfr, upp-heimr, driúpan-salr, Alvm. 46–48.

Ragna-siöt, Vsp. 114; fogl-vegr, Helgi, i. 316; Róða (wind's) braut, 315; Mistar-marr, Helgi, i. 192; himin-vangr, 60.

The Wind.—Dyn-fari, Alvm. 79; súða bani, Sonat. 34; vandar iötunn, ii. 72. 22; seljo gandr, 73. 24.

The Clouds.—Skúr-ván, vind-flot, veðr-megin, hialmr huliðs, Alvm. 70–72.

The Rainbow.—Vindhialms brú, Helgi, i. 317; Bil-röst or Bif-röst, Wols. Pl. 119, i. 77. 4.

Hail.—Skýja griót, Jomsv. 127.

Rain.—Skýja grátr, ii. 359. 11.

Calm.—Vind-slot, of-hlý, dag-sevi, dags-vera, Alvm. 86–88.

The Sun.—Himins hleifr, Bk. vi. No. 1; himin-targa, þd. 13; Ey-gló, fagra-hvel, al-skír, Alvm. 63–64.

The Moon.—Ár-tali, Alvm. 56; hverfanda hvel, 54.

The Night.—Svefn-gaman, draum-niórun, óliós, Alvm. 119–120.

Sleep.—Blund-stafir, Wols. Pl. 203; draum-þing, Helgi, i. 301.

The Summer.—Dal-fiska miskun, i. 373. 34.

The Winter. Snake's death.—Orms-fellir, ii. 196. 60; naðra deyðir, ii. 264. 87; Sváfnis böl, Vellekl. 2; faðmins galli, Kont. 94; snáka stríð, 142.

Bear's night.—Húns nótt, Rekst. 49, cp. Malsh. 24.

The Autumn.—Hör-meitiðr, Hym. 152.

SEA AND SHIPS:—

The Sea.—Sílægja, laga-stafr, ál-heimr, diúpan mar, Alvm. 86–88; blá-mær, ii. 35. 6; glæ-heimr, 103. 13.

As girdle.—Hauðr-men, ii. 57. 44; þangs þialmi, 230. 21; skers glym-fiöturr, 239. 4 (cp. ii. p. 440); landa band, ii. 165. 10.

Land of sea-beasts.—Má-skeið, Ad. 89; máva mær, Bragi 58; lýr-gata, ii. 137. 7; augrs búð, 26. 9; hval-mœnir, 167. 20; hvals rann, 239. 2; lýso vangr, 148. 2; sæðings slóð, 165. 3.

Land of ships.—Fleyja flat-völlr, ii. 17; borða-braut, borð-heimr, 168. 27; haf-slóðir, 239. 3; stafn-klif, 159. 15.

Land of fishing.—Dorgar vangr, Jomsv. 13.

Land of sea-kings.—Vandils iörmun-grund, ii. 81. 54; Ekkils braut, 56. 24; Ialks mær, id.; Rakna rym-leið, 35. 7; Róða rein, 127. 6; Róða röst, 49. 4; Geitis vegr, 17; Leifa land, Bragi 30; Glamma slóð, ii. 218. 17; Rakna stígr, 219 5; Buðla slóðir, 10; Fróða flat-slóð, 170; Sveiða vangr, 103. 4; Sveiða tröð, 162. 4; Sölsa bekkr, 5.

The Waves.—Siá-gnípa, ii. 167. 23; mar-fiöll, 239. 98; húna gnípor, 239. 2.

The Ice.—Ál-himin, ii. 37. 58 ; hæings hallar næfr, 311. 16; elgjar galgi, Sonat. 58.

Rocks and Stones. *Bones of the sea.*—Lagar hiarta, Yt. 119 ; lagar bein, 151; sævar bein, Hlt. 11 ; fiarð epli, þd. 57. *Of earth.*—Foldar bein, Yt. 127 ; Hlóðynjar bein, ii. 62. 20 ; foldar negg, ii. 300. 10 ; Hergautz vino herði-mýll, Bragi, 34 ; hvél-volor, þd. 23 ; mœrar leggr, 58 ; Feðjo steði, 54.

Pearls and Gems.—Haf-nýra, Husd. 23 ; iarkna steinn, Ordeal 30, Gkv. 71.

Caves and Caverns.—Holt-riða hver, Hym. 105 ; undir-fialbr, þd. 74; gialbra fialbr, Haust. 69 ; regns hraun-ketill, ii. 337. 17.

The Coast, Beach.—Sævar-beðr, i. 126. 7; mar-beðr, 135. 14; ey-barmr, Wak. 66.

The Ship. *Tree or car.*—Sæ-tré, W. W. L. 27 ; sæ-skíð, ii. 159 ; varr-viðr, 136. 23. *As sea-beast, steed, horse.*—Gialfr-marr, Wak. 102 ; gialfr-dýr, Helgi, i. 118 ; brim-dýr, 205 ; vág-marar, W. W. L. 26 ; stiórn-marr, Helgi, i. 114; segl-vigg, W. W. L. 25 ; hlunn-vigg, 30; hlunn-goti, Hym. 76 ; lög-fákr, 103 ; lög-sóti, ii. 37. 43 ; rá-fákr, 80. 29 ; lauks hestr, 165. 4; sæðings slóð-goti, id.; sólborðz góti, id. ; byrjar drœsull, Bragi, 8; haf-sleipnir, Husd. 11 ; stiór-viðjar skær, ii. 54. 1 ; blámœrar skær, 35. 6 ; sikol-giarðar harð-vigg, 161. 2; varrar málfeti, 81. 41; barms vigg, 103. 16; hremnis stóð, 9; skorðo drasill, ii. 167. 27 ; siá-gnípo sleipnir, 23 ; hranna há-dýr, 29 ; stafn-klifs stóð, 159. 15; landa bandz iór, ii. 165. 10. *Bear.*—Rastar vetr-liði, ii. 239. 1 ; hvals-rannz iúgtanni, 2 ; skorðo bersi, flóðs biörn, id. ; festa biörn, 167. 21 ; skaut-biörn, 168. 26. *Boar.*—Brim-svín, Hym. 104 ; brim-göltr, ii. 159. 11. *Hind.*—Segl-hind, ii. 200. 12. *Buck.*—Flot-brúsi, Hym. 100. *Elk.*—Hranna elgr, ii. 169. 7 ; œði-veðrs elgr, 188. 51. *Reindeer.*—Hlýrs hreinn, 170. 18; hún-ferils hreinn, 219. 15 ; byr-hreinn, 330. 65 ; hún-lagar hreinn, 101. 7 ; Sölsa bekkjar hreinn, 162. 5 ; hlunnz hreinn, 155. 10. *Serpent.*—Fiarð-linni, ii. 239. *Hawk.*—Krapta valr, ii. 170. 32 ; stafn-valr, 80. 19; sval-heims valr, 159. 19. *Hart.*—Rakka hirtir, Helgi, i. 199; branda hiörtr, ii. 352. 147 ; vengis hiörtr, 228. 6.

Steed and car of Sea-kings.—Refils hestar, W. W. L. 23 ; Rokkva stóð, Ad. 90; Ræs reið, Bragi, 40 ; Eynefis öndurr, 48 ; Endils öndurr, ii. 49. 10 ; Ála öndurr, 169. 10; Glamma skíð, 168. 25 ; Atals dýr, 40. 44; Atals grundar skíð, 81. 37 ; Sveiða hreinn, 162. 4 ; Gylva hreinn, 81. 42 ; þvinnils dýr, 80. 35 ; Gylva rastar glaumr, 165. 2 ; Róða rastar rið-marar, 49. 4 ; Skialdar viðr, ii. 196. 56.

The Sail.—Hún-skript, ii. 199. 5 ; skaut þat er drósir spunno, 155. 10.

The Anchor.—Kald-nefr, ii. 230. 9.

The Oars.—Fer-kleyf sæ-föng, ii. 209. 11, 13 ; öldo-sveipr, 330. 67 ; lög-sóta fœtr, 37. 4.

The Fishing-line.—Mára mœrar mió-tygill, Bragi, 58 ; sæ-þráðr, ii. 212. 14.

The Hook.—Agn-galgi, ii. 148. 4.

Hooked Fish.—Agn-galga hangi, ii. 148. 4.

Herring.—Sævar mæ-örvar, ii. 37. 49 ; iokla akkar (?), id. ; sp . . . þornar, id.

Porpoises.—Unn-svín, ii. 37. 46.

§ 2. MYTHOLOGICAL.

I. WODEN.

The Northern Mythology, like that of the Greeks, is very complex and heterogeneous, and historical analysis alone can help us to get order and reason out of the tangled strata. Thus we have two distinct layers or deposits, the older, with many marks of its primitive origin, with a simple cosmogony; gods who are evidently personifications of natural forces, 'powers of might, the mighty ones,' or deified heroes, 'the blessed gods, the chosen gods;' regular practices of sacrifice and feasting, such as other early religions can parallel; and a profound belief in ghosts, who lived in their barrows a second life, and who were the objects of the family and clan worship. These features of the older faith we have, in part, sketched in the first volume; they are just those which, from our knowledge of other parallel Aryan systems, we should expect to find. But this primitive bed of faith is overlaid in places by wholly new and strange beliefs, the key to which is not, as has lately been proposed, to be sought in book-reminiscences of Greek and Roman classic mythology, but rather in the Christian Churches of the East and West, whose beliefs, reaching the Northmen of the Wicking Age (oftenest in somewhat distorted shape), coloured his ideas, and gave rise in the imaginative brain of two or three foremost poets to a system and view of mythology very different to the old simple faith of their forefathers. In this system Woden became king of the Slain in Battle, head of a royal race of Anses, a Charlemain of the Empyrean with a splendid hall, a host of handmaidens, a chosen guard of the fallen kings and heroes of all generations, who feast on roast pork and mead, and spend the day in warlike sport, just as their earthly types did. Then there is a great Last Battle to be fought by the Warrior-Angels and the Elect against the Beast and the Dragon—and the Demons of Fire, an eschatology the origin of which is very plain. The old myths again are twisted into new forms; the ancient Prometheus story of the wise man enduring pain for knowledge, the idyllic weeping for Balder, the Northern Adonis are coloured, as we have them in the Edda, with the hues cast by the dawn of the New Faith upon the last hours of heathendom.

This Wicking religion, with its half-Mahomedan fatalism, its belief that death in battle was a victory, its material paradise of fighting and banqueting, its Warrior-gods and Amazon-angels, is a new and striking phenomenon in the history of the Teuton peoples. But it has been somewhat unduly treated. It was never the accepted faith of the Northmen, Danes, or Swedes. Some of its most famous myths, such as that which transformed the Gallows-tree *Ygg-drasill* to a Tree of Life, the Rood itself, may never, most probably, have travelled beyond the single poem in which it was wrought out by a master-mind. Its striking shape, the disproportionate part which it plays in the later scholars' mythic system and in Snorri, and its systematic form, artificial as Hesiod's own, have all helped in leading people to think that what was the lightly-held if enthusiastic creed of three generations of Wickings, was the arch-belief time out of mind of the whole Teuton-stock. Nay, there have been those who have not been afraid to hint that Christianity was hardly needed by men who knew of the Self-Sacrifice of Woden, of the Sorrowing for Balder, of the Judgment Day, or Twilight of the gods as it is erroneously named; who in short already held the more important truths of revelation,—a wholly false and unhistoric view it is needless to say.

The case of WODEN is one of the best examples of the way in which the new ideas have wrought upon the old in Northern mythology. In the præ-wicking days he is the God of the Heaven, nay the Heaven itself, 'Earth's love and lord,' Ouranos. Then the process went on, which tended to blend into one god's personality the attributes and adventures of many gods, to hang many myths upon one peg as it were. Among the separate figures that have been fused into the one many-sided god, are a god of Poetry, of Wisdom, of the Holy Draught; a god of magic and sorcery; a war-god, patron of the Gauts, the deity that the Deacon tells of. Each of these had his own gear of myths and legends, and they will not always fit together congruously, so that we can with some certitude decompose the compound, and gain some knowledge of the various parts. It was upon Woden as the *god of war*, the adventurous god, that the Wicking fancy chiefly dwelt, and it is in this capacity that he was made the warrior king of a host of heroes, prince of the Anses, with such state of palace and service as befitted a warlike monarch of the ninth and tenth centuries.

Among the first in order (taking Woden's several aspects one by one) is that of the *Heaven*, 'husband of Earth, father of Gods and Men:' by that primal wedlock he acquires the titles, 'Blessed Father, Sire' (so we take Gautr). To him, as the Heaven, belongs the myth which explains why the sky has only one eye, by the tale that there *were* two, but that one was pledged to the 'Giant of the Abyss' [Sokk-mimi] for a draught of the deep well of wisdom,—a myth of the earliest type. To Woden as the *Creator*, who with his fellow-gods made earth, sky, and sea out of the Giant's body, and who (according to the myth in one half-Christian lay) made man and woman out of trees, Ash and Emble, belong the epithets 'friend of Loft, Loder, and Hœni.'

As *God of War* he bears the names 'Sire or lord of hosts, lord of spears, father of victory *or* battle, master of victory, wielder of Gungnir [his magic spear], the Gauts' god;' for in this capacity they worshipped him as their 'confederate or ally,' while the Swedes worshipped a patron god whom they called Frey, another Woden.

As the *God of Wisdom* Woden is hymned in early poems, 'the Sage of the Powers, the Councillor of the Gods;' Hroptr is probably his right title in this capacity. How he got this wisdom is told in several myths: the chiefest of these are connected either with a Prometheus legend of privation and pain gone through to win the secrets of knowledge, of long fasting, and strange penances, prevailing in the end; or the legend takes another turn, and tells how, by wiliness and Ulysses-like patience, and even perjury, the Soma-draught was stolen by the god from its foolish or wicked possessors—to be a gift and joy for men.

Woden is taunted in one early poem with having won his wisdom by magic, with sitting under waterfalls, and speaking with the dead; here he is the *Wizard-God* consulting the omens of the ravens, and haunting the gallows upon which his victims are offered to him; 'raven-consulter, raven-flamen, companion of the ravens,' he is called, and the ravens are his 'swan *or* hawks *or* mews.'

The *gallows* is Woden's 'steed *or* tree,' and he is the 'lord of the gallows, the god of hanging.' Most famous of the myths of lift-offerings to him are the stories of Sigere and Hagbard, and of King Wikere and Starkad, which also furnish metaphors for the accursed tree, 'Sigar's steed, Signy's husband's horse.' The connection between the ∏-shaped gallows and the horse, and between gallows and cross, is common to English poetry, and late in the Middle Ages the cross is spoken of as 'Christ's palfrey.' Whether it is as God of Heaven or as God of War that the gallows belongs to Woden is not quite clear.

Woden's adventures are hinted in such phrases as Way-wont *or* Traveller, Wide-beard, and the like; and the stories of the one-eyed, cowled, long-bearded old sage who tells King Olaf tales of old days, witness to the late belief in his wanderings among men.

Most striking of all his adventures are those which have to do with the *Soma*, when he became the guileful 'lover of the Soma-giant Sup-tung's daughter Gundfled,' and stole the precious draught, which is known as his 'wine, his mead, his ale, his toast, his stream, pool, sea, liquor, his theft, and his find.' He was held to have swallowed the Soma when he flew home in eagle-plumage; hence poetry is the 'billows of Woden's breast, the stream of the lipbeard of Woden,' and bad verse is the 'ancient eagle's leavings.'

Earlier probably are the myths which connect the *Inspiration* of *Poesy* ('Mood-raiser') with the *Dwarves*, and give rise to the expressions, 'Dwarves' cup, the Dwarf's ship (which is met first in Bragi, but now a popular and hackneyed synonym), Quasi's blood, the ransom of Gilling, and the weregild of Woden.' The archaic metaphors, 'Soma's blood, Soma's seed, Bodn's billow,' denote the drink itself rather than (as Snorri and the later poets say) the cups in which the mystic drink was kept. 'Quasi's blood' refers to a sacrifice or covenant between the two tribes of the gods.

The *Giants* succeeded to the precious possession according to Snorri's tale, but it is evident that this was originally a separate myth. It has given rise perhaps to the curious phrase for *Mind* or *Thought* noted above, and has certainly supplied many a quaint figure for poetry; such as the 'beer of the Rock-dwellers, the Boulder-men's ransom (referring to the tale told by Snorri), the cup of the Rock-Saxons, the foaming *or* fermenting Rhine of the lady of the crags.'

So the *Poet* is looked on as 'brewing Woden's mead,' as 'bearing his cup;' and his *Song* is the 'poet's brew, the wine' he bears.

We may here put Woden's *genealogy*, as the poets give it us; it is doubtless early and traditional, and seems to belong to the war-god of the Goths and Gauls. He is 'son of Bestla *and* Bor, brother of Wili and Wil, husband of Frigg,' the lover of Hlodyn *or* Fiorgyn [Firgen, O. E.], that is of Dēmētēr. He is head of the Anse clan, of the gods, 'father of Balder' and many sons more.

In the later poets, when Woden is a mighty monarch, the old Liths-shelf—the watch-tower of his mountain-fort (the window of heaven of the old fairy tales, as Grimm points out)—is heard of but little more. His *dwelling* is now a magnificent hall, thatched with shields, pillared with pikes, lit with swords for torches, with pit and gallows at its west door, like a Frank noble's castle. In this Walhall are banquetings and the joy of song; thither are the Elect gathered, in readiness for that great day, the Crack of Doom, when Woden shall go forth to meet the Beast (whose 'foe *and* enemy' he is), and steadfastly undergo the doom that shall fall upon all, gods and men. The authors of Eiriks-mal and Haconar-mal, both, we know, popular poems, no doubt did much to spread these conceptions, the originals of which are to be found in the beliefs of the early Christian Churches. It is a view of Woden's power and position peculiar to one branch, the colonial, of the Western Scan-dinavian tribes, but its poetry and fire have preserved it in the minds of the court-poets, from whose verses Snorri derives his account.

WODEN:—

Father of Gods and Men.—Sig-tivi, Lokas. 4; Sig-föðr, 236; Her-föðr, Vsp. 82; Herja-föðr, 132, Hyndl. 4, Grimn. App. 6; Alda-föðr, Bragi, 45; Val-föðr, Vsp. 3, 93; goða iaðarr, Sonat. 87 (goð iarðar, v. l.).

Lord of Soma, God of Wisdom, Charms, and Poetry.—Míms vinr, Sonat. 88, ii. 62. 17; galdrs faðir, Doom 10; Sónar sylgs sið-reynir, Husd. 9; Rögna hroptr, Hávam. 31; Hropta-týr, 112, Hakm. 38, Husd. 8; forns hrosta hilmir, Sonat. 76.

Lord of the Ravens.—Hrafn-áss, Haust. 14, ii. 167. 10; hrafn-freistaðr, Husd. 6 ; hrafna sig-reynir, 9 ; hrafna-blœtr, ii. 97. 19.

Lord of the Gallows.—Galga-farnir, Hlt. 4; farma-týr, 37 ; galga valdr, ii. 79. 8 ; hanga-goð, 76. 2 ; hanga-týr, 75. 35.

As Creator.—Lóðors vinr, Hlt. 34; Loptz vinr, Vellekl. 17 ; Vagna rúni, Sonat. 84.

Giver of Victory.—Sigr-höfundr, Sonat. 85 ; geira dróttinn, 83 ; her-þrimo gautr, þd. 3 ; Her-týr, ii. 48. 5.

Friend of the Gauts.—Gauta spialli, Sonat. 69 ; Gauta eið-svari, þd. 29 ; Gauta týr, Hakm. 1 ; Her-gautr, Sonat. 4, Bragi 34; Val-gautr, ii. 167. 11.

His Adventures.—Val-tamr, Doom 21 ; Veg-tams sonr, id. ; Síð-grani, Alvm. 22 ; Ulfs bági, Sonat. 90; Vitnis váði, ii. 168.

His Kinship.—Bestlo sonr, ii. 48. 7 ; Börs sonr, Vsp. 13 ; Bors arf-þegi, Hyndl. 123; Bors burr, ii. 250; Vilja or Vilis bróðir, Yt. 11, Sonat. 86; Friggjar-angan, Vsp. 164 ; Fiörgynjar faðm-byggvir, Hornkl. 83 ; Gunnlaðar arma farmr, ii 62. 22 ; Baldrs faðir, Hyndl. 123.

Seat of.—Hliðskialfar gramr, ii. 51. 7 ; Hliðskialfar harri, ii. 96. 9.

Wielder of the spear.—Gungnis vávoðr, Bragi, 63.

His Steed, Sleipni.—Gungnis vávaðar lung, Husd. 63.

The Sun, his Eye.—Valföðrs veð, Vsp. 97 ; vagna veð, Alvm. 11 ; Vagna várar, Hofuðl. 74.

Walhall.—Heilagt vé, Hyndl. 4 ; Svafnis salr, Hornkl. 79 ; Svelnis salr, Bragi, 21 ; Viðris höll, Krak. 125; Herjans höll, 142 ; Fiolnis hús, 124 ; Val-höll, Eiriksm. 2, Hakm. 4, Hyndl. 4, Grimn. 26, Vsp. 105 [of a king's hall Akv. 55].

Anses.—Hroptz megir, Lokas. 182 ; Hroptz gildar, Husd. 12 ; Ás-megir, Doom 27; Ása synir, Lokas. 11, 227, 258; Sigtiva synir, 4, ii. 76. 28; Óðins ætt, ii. 96. 11, 17 ; Niarðar niðjar, 18 ; Friggjar niðjar, Sonat. 7.

Einherjar.—Sigr-þióð, Helgi, i. 318 ; Ás-liðar, Skirn. 138 ; Einherjar, Vþm. 160, Grimn. 136, App. 4, 22, Eiriksm. 3, Hakm. 46, Helgi i. 160.

The Walcyries, the Maids of Woden.—Herjans dís, Tale of G. 73 ; Oðins meyjar, ii. 427. 172 ; Valkyrjor, Eiriksm. 5, Hakm. 26, Husd. 9, Hornkl. 5 ; cp. ii. 75. 17–23, Helgi i. 158.

The Earth. *As Woden's leman.*—Valtýs brúðr, Hlt. 48 ; Hergautz vina, Bragi, 34 ; Báleygs brúðr, 95. 5 ; Yggjar brúðr, ii. 51. 3 ; Svelnis Vár, 37. 41 ; Svelnis ekkja, Haust. 60; Rindar elja, ii. 205. 10. *Sister, daughter of.*—Óds systir, ii. 95. 10 ; Ónars dóttir, 4 ; Ánars mær, 205. 11.

The Gallows. *Woden's Steed.*—Yggdrasils askr, Vsp. 50, 139, Grimn. 88, 96, 144 ; Vinga meiðr, Havam. 9, Hlt. 18. *Steed of Hagberd.*—Sigynjar vers hestr, Yt. 53; Sigars iór, Hlt. 15 ; Sigars hestr, ii. 139. 28 ; Sigars fiánda grand-meiðr, 269. 9.

POETRY :—

Soma, *the holy drink.*—Sónar dreyri, Hyndl. 156, Old G. L. 123; sónar sáð, ii. 51. 9 ; hapt-sœni, Korm. 16 ; heið-sœni, Hlt. 23 ; Boðnar bára, ii. 48. 1 ; Óðrerir, Havam. 21 ; Óðreris alda, ii. 48. 12 ; drykkr ausinn Óðreri, Old Ritual. 21 ; Kvásis dreyri, ii. 48. 3 ; dia fiörðr, Korm. 9 ; Hagbarðz véa-fiörðr, ii. 80. 28 ; Iolna sumbl, Hlt. 52 ; Viðris veig, ii. 49. 3 ; Viðris þyfi, Sonat. 3 ; Friggjar niðja (vas) fagna-fundr, 7 ; Viðris mun-strandar mar, 2 ; (Woden's) geð-markar lá, Husd. 1 ; Galga farms hver-lögr, Hlt. 3 ; Mims vinar straumr, ii. 62 ; Gautz giöf, Bk. vi. No. 1 ; Grimnis giöf, Husd. 2 ; hapta beiðis (Woden's) gildi, ii. 39. 1 ; Alföðrs hrosta fen, 194. 2 ; Grimnis gran-straumr, þd. 11.

Woden's cup, *mead.*—Óðins miöðr, Sonat. 6 ; Óðins ægi, 68 ; Hárs lið, Hlt. 1 ; Hrafn-ásar full, ii. 167. 10 ; Viðris full, Ad. 50 ; Yggs full, 23 ; Yggjar miöðr, Ad. 27, ii. 48. 10 ; Yggs öl, Bk. vi. 1 ; Yggs biór, Malsh. 114 ; Vitnis váða vín, ii. 168; Valgautz veig, 167. 11; Hertýs vín-gnóðar flausta austr, 48. 5.

The mead of Giants.—Gillings giöld, Hlt. 2 ; bauga biórr, Hofuðl. 73 ; fialla fiolnis full, Bragi, 65 ; Forniotz (?) hrosti, Sonat. 76 ; Hrimnis horn-straumr, ii. 26. 5 ; fiarð leggjar fyrða brim, 48. 4 ; fen-tanna Sýrar iast-Rin, Korm. 2 ; Berg-mœra bára, ii. 166. 2 ; griót-aldar gildi, 1 ; Berg-saxa fley, 48. 2 ; berg-iarls brúðar sollinn vindr, 62. 23.

The mead of Dwarves.—Dvalins hallar full, ii. 54. 1 ; Dverga grunn-lá, 48. 14. *Dwarves' ship.*—Víðurs skip, Bk. vi. No. 1; Dverga skip, ii. 62. 23 ; cp. Skíða R. 1. *Poets' liquid.*—Greppa aurr, Korm. 2.

Bad poetry.—Ins gamla ara leirr, ii. 252. 10.

The Poet. *Bearer of Woden's mead. Soma inspired.*—Yggs öl-beri, Bk. vi. No. 1; Óðs skap-móði, id. ; Hagbarðz vea-fiarðar sann-reynir, ii. 80. 27. *Brewer of the divine draught.*—Bragar hag-smiðr, Bk. vi. 1 ; Viðurs skip-smiðr (Dwarf ship-wright), id. ; Gautz giaf-rötuðr, id.

II. THOR.

WIDE is the contrast between Woden and Thunder in the lays of the earlier poets. Thor is a less complex divinity, with a well-marked and individual character; the friend of man, the husbandman's god, whose wrath and anger are ever directed against the evil powers that injure mortals and their possessions, whose bolt destroys the foul thick blights that betray the presence of the wicked ones, and smites through the huge cloud-masses that seem to be crushing the earth. Thus we see him ever associated with *Earth*, who bore him to *Heaven* (Woden in his Ouranos character); her proudest titles are the ' mother of the Giant-killer, the mother of the Ill-dam's foe.' So also he is ' husband of Sif,' the golden-haired goddess [the cornfield, Ceres].

When the mythology was worked up into a system, Thor, as ' Woden's heir *or* comfort,' of course is treated as one of the heavenly family, and the poets give him such titles as ' brother of Meili *or* of Balder, brother-in-law of Wuldor,' and the like. There is a curious set of legends which tell of his adventures in Giant-land, and amours with giantesses, by whom he is the father of such half-allegoric beings as Main and Mood and Might, huge Æschylean creations. Of his deal-ings with the giants we shall have examples below.

Among his noblest titles are those of ' champion of the gods, the mighty one of the gods, hallower *and* sanctifier of earth, friend of man, patron of the people.' ' Wing-Thor ' is obscure to us (the Heaven-Thunderer ?). His goat-drawn *car*, whose rumbling wheels scare the giants, makes him ' the car-god, the wain-wight, the lone-rider, the captain of the keel *or* boat-shapen car, lord *and* owner of the goats.' The unexplained but frequent title ' Hlor-ridi ' doubtless belongs to this category.

Thor also owns the *mittens* and *belt of strength*, but it is as the Lord of the *Hammer* or Thunderbolt (' the Pick-headed ogress, the bane of Hrungni, the hammer of Might ') that he has won his chief claim to men's gratitude, as the ' adversary, foe, crusher, feller, life-despoiler, death-dealer, awe, dread, down-healer, mauler, and destruction of the giants and ogresses.'

The poets know of his dealings with that devil's dam *Mella ;* with *Hrungni*, who is the moon's foe, the ravisher of Thor's daughter, Might ; with *Garfred*, the giant smith, the god of the bellows [?], the metal-wright [?] ; with the Nimrod-like *Thiazzi*, the ' foul foe of the Anses *and* Thor, the clansman of Hymi, the son of Olwald [Orwandil, Orion ?], the haunter of Giant-land, the Nidad [king] of the rocks, the winged being, the hunter-god, the father *or* foster-father of the Snowskate goddess *or* of Morn the ogress, the brother of Idia and Orni,' whose speech or mouthful is a synonym for *gold*, from the legend that Thiazzi and his brethren divided their hoard, in barbarous and uncouth fashion, by each filling his mouth with as much as it could hold. From these exploits Thor is called 'Mella's foe, Hrungni's head-crusher.' He is also the 'adversary' of far more formidable beings than these rude Titans, 'Frost-giants and Mountain-giants,' whom he journeys over Ocean and through icy torrents to seek out and destroy,— for he is the deadly enemy of Loki [Wloki] and his brood. His famous fishing-expedition at Hymi's is fondly dwelt on by the early poets, who held this deity in peculiar veneration ; and the later eschatologic fancies make Thor 'the god that shall in the Doomsday slay with his unaided might the Leviathan that girdles earth deep in the ocean stream.'

The homely features of Thor's character mark him out for humourous treatment, and the anonymous Aristophanes of the West, and Snorri himself, deal so with him. Alone of all the gods we find his image carved on stocks and stones, a long-bearded face with the hammer hung beneath ; and the hammer itself, a primitive stone-headed short-hafted instrument, is found separately as a charm. The 'Anse,' *or* 'the God of the Country,' *or* 'the Mighty God' in the old carmina of oaths and vows, always refers to Thor. It is curious to notice how ill the sturdy farmer's friend suits the new Walhall. The poets get out of the difficulty by making him stay away fighting giants; his uncouth might is scarcely needed when Woden has a host of chosen warriors ever ready to defend himself and his friends.

THOR :—

> *His kinships.*—Iatðar burr, þkv. 4 ; Iarðar sonr, Haust. 55 ; Hlóðynjar mögr, Vsp. 199 ; Fiörgynjar burr, 171 ; grundar sveinn, Haust. 74 ; Óðins burr, 76 ; Óðins sonr, Vsp. 170, Hym. 135 ; Viðriss arfi, Bragi, 47 ; Alda föðrs son, 45 ; þrúðar faðir, 9 ; Magna faðir, Harb. 138, Husd. 47 ; Móða faðir, Hym. 130 ; Meila bróðir, Harb. 23, Haust. 56 ; Baldrs barmi, 61 ; Ullar mágr, 57, ii. 27. 7 ; Ullar gulli, þd. 67.
>
> *His wife.*—Sifjar verr, þkv. 100, Hym. 11, 132 ; Sifjar rúni, ii. 26. 24 ; þröng-var langvinr, þd. 62.
>
> *His home.*—Bilskirnis gramr, ii. 27. 8.
>
> *Champion of the gods.*—þrúðvaldr goða, Harb. 24 ; Vingþórr, þkv. 1, Alvm. ; Vingnir, Vþm. 205.
>
> *The Car-god.*—Einriði, Lokas. 242, Haust. 76 ; Hlórriði, Lokas. 219, 222, þkv. 26, 29, 59, 126, Hym. 15, 61, 101, 110, 142 ; kióla valdi, 75 ; reiði-Týr, Haust. 88 ; hóg-reiðar huf-regin, 59 ; vafreyða (lightning's) húf-stióri, þd. ; vögna váttr, Haust. 64.
>
> *Lord of the goats.*—Hafra dróttin, Hym. 76 ; hafra niótr, Bragi, 54.
>
> *Hallower of earth.*—Miðgarðz veorr, Vsp. 172 ; Veorr, Hym. 43, 64, 83, 151.
>
> *Friend of man.*—Verliða vinr, Hym. 43 ; folka reynir, Husd. 16 ; banda vinr, 14 ; Land-áss, ii. 72. 16.
>
> *The slayer of monsters.*—Orms ein-bani, Hym. 85 ; allra landa endi-seiðs eygir, Bragi, 50 ; Hrungnis haus-sprengir, 52 ; Loka böl-kvettir, þd. 15.
>
> *The foe of giants and ogresses.*—þurs ráð-bani, Hym. 72 ; hröðrs andskoti, 42 ; Iötna ótti, Haust. 53 ; Iötna dolgr, ii. 36. 31 ; Belja verðungar fiör-spillir, Haust. 69 ; mello dolgr, 28 ; gygjar grætir, Hym. 53 ; mello mög-fellandi, ii. 81. 40 ; kveld-runninna kvenna þröngvir, 24. 24 ; gnipo hlœðr, þd. 52 ; stop-hníso steypir, 36 ; Berg-Dana bríótr, Haust. 67, 72 ; fiall-gautz fellir, Husd. 17 ; urðar-þriotz stökkvir, þd. 20 ; steins Ello aldr-minkandi, 76 ; Ivo-nesja dróttar kneyfir, 45.
>
> *Owner of the belt of strength.*—Giarð-vendir, þd. 7 ; niarðgiarðar niótr, 26 ; himin-sióli, 34.

Lord of the hammer.—Trióno trollz rúni, Haust. 68.

The Hammer.—Hrungnis bani, Lokas. 247; þrúð-hamarr, 229, 245, 254; trióno-troll, Haust. 68; gliúfr-skeljungs grand, ii. 27. 9.

Earth, *Thor's mother.*—Iötna dolgs móðir, ii. 36. 31; mello dolgs móðir, 28; Fiorgyn, Vsp. 171, Harb. 144; Hlóðyn, Vsp. 199.

Giant Hrungni.—Mána sak-dolgr, Haust. 61; þrúðar þiófr, Bragi, 2.

Giant Thiazi.—Ása ósvifrandi, Haust. 20; Hymis átt-rúni, 34; Iötun-heima reimoðr, 27; Ölvalda sonr, Harb. 50; Öndor-goðs fóstri, Haust. 26; Öndor-dísar faðir, Bragi, 62; Morna faðir, 22, 48; skotgiarn (?) iotunn, Hyndl. 127; Vagna Ving-rögnir, Haust. 15; griót-niðoðr, 36; leiðblaðs regin, 47.

Gold.—þiaza þing-skil, Biark. 18. See below.

Giantess Skaði.—Öndor-goð, Haust. 26; Öndor-dís, Hlt. 12, Bragi, 62.

The Constellations, *Castor and Pollux.*—Ölvalda sonar (þiaza) augo, Harb. 50. *Rigil in Orion.*—Orwandil tá, Edda.

Giant Garfred (Geirrod).—See þd. and ii. 212. 4-8.

Giant Thrym.—þursa dróttinn, þkv.

Thialvi, *Thor's page.*—Roskvo bróðir, Husd. 27.

III. MINOR GODS.

THE other gods are not such favourites with the poets, and, as the figure of Woden gradually grows larger and more striking, the other divinities fade out of mind; indeed, most of their attributes have been absorbed by him, as it were. An ancient god is Heimdall, from whom the Amals spring. There are strange lost myths connected with him; his struggle with Loki for the Brisinga necklace; the fight in which they fought in the shape of seals. He is 'the gods' warder,' dwelling on the gods' path, the Rainbow. There he sits, 'the white god,' 'the wind-listening god,' whose ears are so sharp that he hears the grass grow in the fields and the wool on the sheep's backs, with his Blast-horn, whose trumpet-sound will ring through the nine worlds, for in the later legends he has some of the attributes of the Angel of the Last Trumpet. His teeth are of gold; hence he is 'stud-endowed.'

Curious genealogical myths attach themselves to him. He is styled son of nine mothers; and as Rig's father, or Rig himself, the 'walking or wandering god,' he is the father of men, and the sire of kings, and of earls and ceorls and thralls alike. His own name is epithetic, perhaps the World-Bow. The meaning of Hallinskidi is obscure.

Frey means simply 'Lord,' and is used in the early poems of Woden the chief god, 'the Anses' king.' It is the epithet of Yngwi (Tacitus' Inguio). But later on it becomes the special title for a god, whose attributes are marked off to some degree, as 'patron of the Swedes, harvest-god, slayer of Beli (a monstrous Titan).' He is the 'lover of Gerd,' the giant Gymi's daughter and maiden. He is the 'Wanes' god,' of a different gens or clan from the Anses, 'the son or heir of *Niorth*' (Nereus) sea-god of riches, and his consort *Skadi* the giantess, 'Thiazi's daughter, the god's bride, the snow-skate nymph, *or* goddess, huntress,' like a Finnish amazon; and brother of the lady *Freyia*, the 'Wanes'-maid, Syr, Mardoll [an unexplained epithet], the leman and maid of Od,' whom she seeks, weeping tears of gold [Mardoll's tears] all over the world, like a northern Isis. Her boar-steed 'Gold-bristle, War-swine, the Chosen-boar,' is brought into Hyndla-liod. Her neck-lace or cestus is the 'Brising's necklace.' By late poets she is given as Hnoss and Gersime, 'Jewel' and 'Necklace,' law-terms for paraphernalia or women's ornaments. *Gefion,* a giantess with a mighty plow, is the Old English Geofen, an ocean goddess. She is 'Woden's love.'

Frigg is a repetition in more human form of Mother Earth. As one would expect, she is ' Woden's wife, and Earth's daughter.' She weeps for *Balder*, her son and Woden's. Balder, which, like Frey, is an impersonal name, meaning lord or king, is in early times the genealogic head of a whole Teutonic clan, of whose legend we know nothing. In later times the story of his hapless death, wrought by Loki's treachery, is the most pathetic of all the northern myths. It is deeply coloured, as we have it, by the Christian Gospel stories which had won their way among the Northmen. He is the ' Bloody victim, *or* Sacrifice.' *Höd*, Balder's innocent slayer, is entitled ' the adversary, the bane of Balder,' the ' greatest coward of the Anses.' There must have been at least one beautiful and famous poem on the Balder story to have given the legend its peculiarly impressive form. *Nand*, Balder's wife, the image of constancy, is merely by etymology—maid, like *Full*, etc.

The other gods and nymphs are to us names and naught else, the poets have not even noticed the legends at all. Bragi, the poets' god of Snorri, is simply the king ('brago' in Old English poetry), and meant Woden himself in the earlier poetry; but when Woden was turned into the image of a human king, with palace and train, he must have his poet and counsellor ('Thyle' or 'Þulr'), and accordingly he is cut in two, and his finest attributes, song and wisdom, go with the name Bragi, to make a fresh god, who henceforth is looked on as a separate being, ' husband of Idwyn' and servant of Woden, of whose hall he is an ornament, 'bench-adorner.'

Heimdall.—Goða vörðr, Lokas. 195, Grimn. 47, Skirn. 111 ; ragna rein-vári, Husd. 22 ; Hallin-skíði, ii. 40. 39.

Einnar ok átta mœðra mögr, Husd. 24; cp. Hyndl. 147–156. [See **Head** above.]

Human-kind.—Meiri ok minni megir Heimdallar, Vsp. 2.

Frey.—Yngvi-Freyr, Hlt. 44; Ingunnar-Freyr, Lokas. 172 ; Niarðar son, 160, Skirn. 171 ; Niarðar bur, i. 75. 26 ; Niarðar aðull, ii. 97. 21 ; goða folkvaldi, Skirn. 9 ; Ása-Bragr, 133.

Belja bani, Vsp. 163 ; Belja dolgr, Hlt. 22 ; Vaningi, Skirn. 156 ; Vanr, ii. 166. Landkost-árr, Gísli, ii. 332. 16.

Gerðr.—Gymis dóttir, Lokas. 168 ; Gymis mær, Skirn. 48.

Skaði.—Goð-brúðr, ii. 166 ; Öndor-dís, Hlt. 12 ; Öndor-goð, Haust. 26.

Freyja.—Óðs vina, Hyndl. 177 ; Óðs mær, Vsp. 73 ; Niarðar dóttir, þkv. 91 ; Vana dís (Edda) ; Vana brúðr, ii. 271. 7.

Freyja's Boar.—Val-svín, Hyndl. 22, 25 ; Gollin-bursti, Hildi-svíni, 26, 27.

Hnoss, her Daughter.—Sýrar mær, ii. 96. 6 (cp. ii. 271).

Frigg.—Fiorgyns mær, Lokas. 104.

Gefion.—Diúp-röðuls glöð, Bragi, 41.

Balder.—Oðins sonr, Doom 35, Skirn. 80, Husd. 3 ; Friggjar sveinn, Malsh. 33; bloðogr tivor, Vsp. 98.

Höð.—Baldrs bani, Doom 40 ; Baldrs andskoti, 44; hræddastr Ása, i. 124. 10.

Bragi.—Bekk-skrautoðr, Lokas. 59 (cp. Eiriks mal).

IV. GIANTS, DWARVES, ETC.

WITH regard to the cosmography, the ideas of the poets seem to have been somewhat of the following kind;—for we must remember that the striking figures of the Tree that reached all worlds, and the ideas of the nine heavens tier above tier, are clearly of foreign and Christian origin, and confined to a few poems. The general idea was, that the flat earth-plain, on which mankind dwelt, 'Mid-Yard,' was ringed round by Ocean, along whose shores lay gloomy caves, beetling cliffs and huge mountains, rocks and wastes, the home of the GIANTS, 'the Etyns' land;' the 'ways, the garths, the dwelling-places of the Giants, the paths *or* stairs *or* causeways of the giantesses;' the huge beings themselves being called the 'hill-folk, the mountain-dwellers, the crag-men, the cave-men, the dwellers in the waste,' and more fancifully the 'whales of the wilds, the seals of the surfing caverns, the folk of the beach;' with greater loathing they are styled 'the foes of earth, the mighty enemies;' and by a quaint conceit, for which Eilif Gudrunsson is responsible, copying perhaps from the hints in Haustlong and Hymisquida, the giants are marked out as the 'Danes of the reefs, the Jutes of the outlands, the Cumbrians of the caverns, the Scots of the White Sea, the Brets of . . ., the Gauts and Fins of the cliffs, the Weal Rugians that dwell in the Strand [county of Norway, List] of the whale's litter.' They are also called 'the people of Cold-Sweden (Scythia), the folk of the reefs of Iva's nesses' [off the Baltic coast]; and single giants are termed 'the Ælla of the boulders, the Forniot of the steeps, the Woden of the Outland.' A *giantess* is mentioned as the 'lady of the hills, the maid of the caverns, the nymph of the teeth of the tarns [rocks], the dolphin of the precipices.'

One or two giants have a regular habitation in the poets; Suptung, the father of Gundfled, lives at 'Hnit-hill' or Hnit-cliff; Thiassi's house is Thrum-ham at the edge of the world.

Under-ground, but upon Mid-Yard, live the DWARVES, beings not wholly baleful. Of their habits but little is told in the poets' phrases, which are chiefly concerned with their pedigrees: they are the 'Stone *or* Boulder-folk, lords of the Stone-wall, sons of Durnir, kinsmen of Dulsi;' their king is the 'Warden of the dwarves' hall' [i. e. of the stone]. Of particular Dwarves, Atlantes, etc., and of particular giants, we have spoken above.

Far away somewhere the earlier poets placed an *abyss*, 'Abaddon,' 'the hall of the giant of the pit, the deep dale of Swart,' a place which Woden once visited in search of wisdom.

The *Ogresses* are not akin to either of these races, though they are often confounded with giantesses: they are pictured as cruel demonic women riding on wolves [see p. 482] in the night, or cowering in dark forests, working their unhallowed spells, 'night-riders, fence-riders, corse-greedy monsters, Wicked Ones.' Evil *ghosts*, fiends, cairn-abiders are also known, and the *barrows* are called ghost-houses.

GIANTS.—Hraun-bui, Hym. 147; berg-bui, 6; hraun-drengr, Haust. 67; gilja grundar gramr, 71 ; biarga gætir, 65 ; hellis burr, 54 ; gialbra fialbrs (caverns) bolmr, 70; fiöro-þióð, þd. 43. *Rock-beasts.*—Hraun-hvalr, Hym. 140; gliúfr-skeliungr, ii. 24. 17; iötna átt-niðr, Hym. 31; herjo heim-þingoðr, Haust. 73.

As *the Adversaries.*—Iörmun-þriótr, Haust. 72 ; vallar dolgr, 23 ; tál-hreinn, 9 ; urðar-þriótr, þd. 20; Belja böl-verðung, Haust. 70.

By *proper names.*—Gandvíkr Skottar, þd. 7 ; helliss Kumrar, 50; flóð-rifs Danir, 47; harð-gleipnis borðz Hörðar, 42; Skyld Bretar, 44; Ivo nesja-fiés-drótt, 46; Kolgo-Sviþióðar drótt, 45; hval-láttrs Lista Val-Rygir, 75; steins Ella, 76; flug-stalla Forniótr, 1; útvés Iolnir, 48; fiall-gautr, Husd. 17; fialla Finnr, Haust. 51; berg-Danir, Hym. 67.

Giantess.—Iarn-saxa, ii. 211; hellis sprund, þd. 56; fialla Hildr, Husd. 11; fen-tanna (rocks) Sýr, Korm. 1; stop-húsa, þd. 36. See above, **Mind.**

DWARVES.—Dulsa konr, Yt. 8; Durnis niðjar, Yt. 6; Durnis niðja sal- (rock) vörðuðr, id.; veggbergs vísir, Vsp. 1,6.

Atlas-borne Heaven.—Austra erviði, ii. 73; Norðra nið-byrðr, 94. 96.

Night-hags —Myrk-riðor, Harb. 60; kveld-riða, Hrimg. 16; hála ná-gráðug, 17, Svipd. and M. 53; kveldrunnar konor, Husd. 26; tún-riðor, Havam. 84; íviðja, Hyndl. 183, Vsp. 7.

Evil Ghosts.—Dolg-megir, Helgi i. 321.

Cairns.—Draug-hús, Helgi i. 319.

V. COSMOGONIC BEINGS.

THE *Cosmogony* of the poets is full of beautiful and fanciful figures, which sometimes have a deeper meaning than perhaps those who made them knew. The *creation-myth* of the *world-giant* Ymir or Hymir is witnessed to by such phrases as make the *hills* ' Ymi's-bones,' the vault of the *sky* his 'skull,' the *sea* his 'blood,' the *clouds* his ' brains.'

The firmament is figured as a huge skull or head, revolving every day, with but *one* eye; and why *one?* because Woden (here Ouranos) had for a draught of his well pledged his other eye to Mimi the Titan of the Deep, the Bourn of Mimi or Sunken-bench.

Quaint is the idea of the *firmament* being upheld by such pillars as the Dwarves of the Airts, North, South, East, and West, whose 'burden' or 'labour' the heavens are. Early too is the idea of the *world-giant* Forniot *or* corse-swallower sitting at the world's end in the shape of a huge eagle, flapping the tempest out of his wings.

Of the *Sun* there are mythical names; 'Mundilfori's daughter (i.e. the daughter of the Fire-Auger, the holy Drill by which some Teutonic Prometheus first woke the elemental flame), the Moon's sister, the Dwarves' play, the Wheel of the Elves,' and, as noted above, ' the Pledge of Woden.' The Sun comes and goes through doors in the East and West, as if from another world. The *Day* is Delling's son, child of Heaven; and the *Night* is 'the kinswoman of the Dark-moon, Niorvi.'

Other notable myths are those of *Ocean*, which figure him as a huge giant, ' Eager, Hler, Gymi, brother of the Wind *or* Rodi,' whose *daughters* are the Billows, whose *song* is the roaring of the surf, whose *wife* is the cruel net-wielding goddess Ran (Ἀράχνη, as we take the etymon to be), who weaves destruction for sailors, and takes the drowned to her hall. Then Eager is the ' brewer of the gods,' or 'the giant-miller Hamlet' (Amlodi), whose ' quern' is the sea, and whose ' flour' is the sand. Hence we get such phrases as ' Ran's heaven, Amlodi's mill.' The hall of Eager is lit by *gold*, which recalls to one the golden sands, and those secrets of the deep that Clarence saw, ' wedges of gold, . . . heaps of pearl, inestimable stones, unvalued jewels, all scattered in the bottom of the sea.' So the northern poets term *gold* 'the gleam of Ocean, the fire of Oran (a Scottish stream), the sun of the deep *or* the rivers.'

The Pantheon would be incomplete without the dim mysterious Three, the *Weirds* or *Fates*, who speak men's doom, or spin on magic web the changeful pattern of his earthly life. We have several pictures of these goddesses in the old poems. One, familiar to us all from the fairy tales, is that of the Midwife Norns coming to the hero's cradle to predict his fate (like the Wise-women who, in those days, went round prophesying). Another is the dream of them sitting far away in their *Paradise* or Hesperian Garden, ' the paths of bliss, the Brook of Weird, Bee-hive's-by,' the ' Garden of the Norns' [Neorxna wang], as the Old English poet has it. Again, we find them metamorphosed into Walcyries in the later wicking-days, but still retaining their character as weavers of the web of fate, in the powerful and terrible vision that is set forth in the Lay of Darts. The Norns or Fates are called 'the maids of Mögthrasi,' and one evil Fate is called the ' Weird of kings, the sister of Night.' Their decree or doom is called the ' Word of the Fates, the Norns' decree *or* design.'

The *Walcyries*, as we have them, belong to the later stage of Northern Religion; they are the creatures of the Wicking-Age. In early belief they are of the tribe of the Norns, or Weird sisters; thus the old German charm speaks of the 'fairies twisting bonds,' and we have the names ' Shackle' and ' Fetter of the Host' applied to Walcyries in Norse songs, which Grimm connects with the *War-chain* of the early German armies. They also have a spiritual affinity to the spirits of slaughter and doom, κῆρες or badbs, such as howled over Cuchullin's head on the day of battle, in the older faith. As they are depicted by the Helgi-poet they are half-human, half-unearthly *Amazons*, whose love brings death and glory to their love : only in one passage does he talk of the Walcyries as associated with the Einheriar; indeed he uses the word as one of reproach. He is indeed halting between the old and the new ideas. His heroine goes into the grave (according to the old beliefs) with her lover; but again, like the armed angels of later times, she soars through the air. The author of Erics-mal has, on the contrary, made them merely the handmaids of the king of the Heavenly Hall, hardly to be distinguished from the noble captive maids that were wont to hand round the ale-horn for the earthly conquerors, of whose court Woden's was but the idealised copy. Eywind imitates Erics-mal, but he has on this point inspired himself, we take it, from the Helgi Lays, when he makes Woden send his angels horsed and helmed with spear and shield to bid the dying king to the banquet in Wal-hall among the Elect. The human element is gone here entirely, and it is in no barrow-chamber, but on the 'starry threshold of Ygg's court,' that the poet leaves his war-weary hero. This is the view that subsequent poets took up, it was in consonance with the rest of the wicking-creed, and in the 'kennings' of the late court-poets it is as the messengers of Woden, the patronesses of war, that the Walcyries figure.

The old word ' vittr,' ' wight,' used in the technical sense of *fairy*, is only used in compounded or metaphoric form to denote Walcyries; in its proper meaning it is suited to such beings as the *swan-maidens* of Weyland's Lay, Melusina-like nymphs who sit spinning by the side of the lake in the wood, like the 'good people' of later days, who however have shrunk in size in most countries.

The names of the Walcyries are to be found in the Thulor. The Helgi-poet's metaphors for his heroines are ' helm-fairies, all-fairies [the one epithet common to the Swan-maidens and the Walcyries, if the readings be right], the winged wound-fairies, tribe- *or* host-fairies.' The 'lady of the Kings, of the Shieldings, the maid of the Wolfings' refer to the heroic amazon rather on her human side. Later poets use the term ' maid of Woden.' The origin and meaning of the word Walcyrie is discussed below.

COSMOGONIC GIANTS:—

Giant Ymi.—Ymir, Vþm. 77–84, Vsp. 9. v. l.; Bergelmir, Vþm. 112.

    Heaven.—Ymis hauss, Vþm. 79, ii. 196. 57; Hymis hauss, Hornkl. 8.

    Earth.—Ymis hold, Vþm. 77.

    Mid-yard.—Ymis brár, Vþm. l. c.

Rocks.—Ymis bein, Vþm. l. c.

Clouds.—Ymis heili, Vþm. l. c.

Sea.—Ymis blóð, Vþm. l. c., ii. 55. 1.

Soma Giants.—Suptungr, Less. 54; Baugi, Höfuðl. 73; Suptungs synir, Skirn. 138; Sœkk-mimir, Grimn., App. 47.

Frost Giants.—Hrím-þursar, Less. 52, Skirn. 120, 137, Vþm. 127.

Rock Giants.—Berg-risar, Harb. 105, Grott. 41, 89.

Mud Giants.—Miskor-blindi, Hym. 6; Mökkor-kalfi, þd. 74 (?), Edda; Aurgelmir, Vþm. 114.

Prometheus.—Mundil-föri (i. e. Pramantha), Vþm. 189 (father of the Sun and the Moon).

Giant Okeanos.—Ægir, Gymir, Lokas., Skirn. *The brewer.*—Allra tíva ölsmiðr, Sonat. 30. *As the island grinder.*—Ey-lúðr, ii. 54. 4; Ey-mylrir, 55. 8; Skerja grotti, 54. 3; Amlóða lið-meldr, 55. 6.

The Surf.—Gymis lióð, Yt. 122.

The Sea-Ogress.—Rán, Sonat. 25; Róða vá-brúðr, 31; Ægis man, 32; Gymis völva, ii. 167. 72; Rán-himin = sea, Haust. 62.

The Okeanid Billows.—Ægis dœttr, ii. 54. 2; Hléss dœttr, 4; Eylúðrs nio brúðir, 4; Ægis dóttir, Helgi i. 113; kolgo systir, 109.

The Wind Giant.—Forniótr, þd. 1, ii. 54. 1; Forniótz synir (the gales), id.; Hræsvelgr, Vþm. 143.

Chaos.—Gap Ginnunga, Vsp. 12.

Ether.—Ragna siöt, Vsp. 114; ginnunga vé, Haust. 78.

The Deep, The Pit.—Mimis brunnr, Vsp. 91; Hver-gelmir, Grimn. 83; Sökk-mimis salr, Yt. 9; Surtz sœkk-dalar, Hlt. 4.

Caves and Rock-Hollows.—Iotna vegir, Less. 42; Suptungs salir, 34; Hnit-fiöll (Hnit-biorg), Hlt. 24 (Edda); Hallvarps hlíf, Yt.145; Iötna garðar, Less. 49.

Night.—Niörva nipt, Sonat. 95, Vþm. 98.

Day.—Dellings sonr (son of Heaven), Vþm., cp. Dellings dyrr = the east doors (opp. to Vestr dyrr), Riddl. i. 88. 30 ff.

Winter.—Vindsvals mögr, ii. 323. 9.

The Sun.—Glens beðja, ii. 102. 13; Mána systir, W. W. L. 36; Dvalins leika, Alv. 62; Valföðrs veð,Vsp.97; Vagna veð, Alv.11; Mundil-föra dóttir,Vþm.90.

The Powers.—Regin, Vsp.; val-tivar, Hym. 1, Vsp. 195; ginnheilög goð, Vsp.; ginn-regin, Alvm. 78, 118, Havam. 30 (cp. i. 29. 3), Hym. 14, Haust. 49; ginnungar, 58; upp-regin, Alvm. 40.

The Norns.—Mögþrasis meyjar, Vþm. 195; Nera nipt, Helgi i. 15; öðlinga urðr, Gkv.

Fate, Weird.—Norna dómr, Wols. Pl. 101; Norna sköp, W. W. L. 78; Urðar orð, i. 100. 237; Norna kviðr, Hamð. 135.

The Wolves.—Norna-grey, Hamð. 129.

Heavenly Abodes.—Goð-heimr, Sonat. 69; bý-skips-bœr, 73; Urðar-brunnr, Vsp. 54; Havam. 2, ii. 22. 1; mun-vegar, Sonat. 39; Gim-lé, Vsp. 200.

Fays, Fairies (see Valkyrjas).—Hialm-vittr, Helgi i. 224; al-vittr, 240; fluga sárvittr, 226; folk-vittr, W. W. L. 71; lofða dís, Helgi i. 344; Ylfinga man, iii. 18; Skioldunga dís, i. 330; Her-fiotur, ii. 438.

VI. THE DEMONS.

BESIDES the monstrous beings that dwelt in the waste places of the earth by the Ocean-stream, there were also distinct powers of evil, the foul brood of *Loki* (i. e. Wloka). This god is shown as 'the friend of Woden and Honir,' in the days of yore ere trouble began, and called 'the Raven-god's friend and counsellor, the colleague and fellow of Honi.' Of Loki's kinship mention is made: he is 'the son of Farbaut and Laufey' (names as yet unexplained), 'the brother of Byleist, the husband of Sigyn.' His evil deeds and adventures are also sung of; he is 'the mischief-maker, the thief of the Brising's girdle, the dog or wolf that stole Idwyn, the adversary of the Anses, the contriver of Balder's death.' But it is as the father of the Evil Ones that he is most notorious. He is 'father of the Beast, and of Leviathan, and of Hell,' fit children of the chained Titan whose throes cause earthquakes.

Hell, the first-born, is known as 'Loki's only daughter, the maid of the Hwethrung' (for Loki's race sprung from Ogress Hwedra), 'the sister of the Wolf and Nara, the nymph of Glitni (wolf?), the lady of the cavern.' From a lost song, quoted by Snorri, we get a good picture of her dread abode. Her hall is Sleet-den; despair, the porch; stumbling stone, the threshold; pale woe, the door; Gilling, the precipice, the key; falling peril, the hangings; carebed, the couch; lazy, the latch; hunger, the dish; famine, the knife; starvation, the spoon, etc.

The *Wolf*, the mighty monster, the 'Wolf of Fenri, the child of Fenri, the son of Loki,' is less mentioned by the poets than the *Serpent*, which they believed to lie wound round the earth beneath the sea, 'earth's girdle, or net-rope, or ring, the monster-snake, the fish of earth, the fast brother of the Wolf.' With these we may couple the other monsters and demons that will join in the final *Catastrophe*, the Doom of Gods and Men, such as the *Wolves of the Eclipse*, 'the gripper and tearer of the moon, the swallower of the loaf of the heavens, the destroyer of the sky's light,' and the *Flying Dragon*, the wicked, venomous 'tearer' of corses (Nið-hogg), and lastly, the *Fire Fiends* that shall gather to the *Wreck of the World* [Mu-spilli, older Mut-spilli = Mund-spilli?], 'sons of Treason,' 'the demons or sons of the Destruction, Monster-demons, Destroyers of the Doom's day.'

LOKI.—*As Lodor. Friend of*—Hrafn-ásar (Woden's) vinr, Haust. 14; her-þrumo Gautz geð-reynir, þd. 3; Hœnis vinr, Haust. 28; Hœnis hugreynandi, 46; hvatz m . . . málo-nautr, 32.

As father of monsters, etc. Son of—Laufeyjar son, Lokas. 208; Fárbauta mögr, Haust. 17, Husd. 22. *Brother of*—Byleistz bróðir, Yt. 150, Vsp. 154, Hyndl. 136. *Father of*—Vulfs faðir, Lokas. 37, Haust. 30; lög-seims faðir, þd. 2. *Husband of*—Sigynjar arma farmr, Haust. 25.

His evil deeds.—Ása dolgr, Kont. 36; bölva smiðr, Lokas. 167; Brísings girði-þiófr, Haust. 36; snótar (Idwyn's) ulfr, 5; öl-gefnar hundr, 42; her-fangs hirði-týr, 24; Hveðrungr, Yt. 156, Vsp. 167.

Hell.—Loka mær, Yt. 40; Byleistz bróðor mær, 150; Hveðrungs mær, 156; Ása dolgs einga-dóttir, Kont. 36. *Sister.*—Nara nipt, Höfuðl. 36; Vulfs lifra, Bragi 12; Ulfs ok Narfa iodis, Yt. 37; Glitnis (Wolf's?) gná, 36; hall-varps (abysms) hlífi-nauma, 145.

Hell's Abode (from a lost song).—*Hall*, Él-iúðnir; *porch*, yglöð; *curtain*, fall-anda forað; *bed*, kör; *pillow*, kör-beðr; *threshold*, brota-böl; *key*, gillingr; *door*, blíkjanda böl; *latch*, lati; *hangings*, forað; *dish*, hungr; *knife*, knifr, sultr; *spoon*, affeldr; *chest*, frost-ofna; *acre*, hnipinn; *dog*, vaningi; *horse*, . . .?; *cock*, . . .?; Cd., AM. 748 at the end (Edda ii. p. 494).

The Wolf.—Hveðrungs mögr, Vsp. 167; hróð-vitnir, Lokas. 156; Fenris úlfr, Hakm. 64; Ulfr-inn-hösvi, Eirm. 26; Fenris kind, Vsp. 111; Fenris ulfar, Helgi i. 164.

The Serpent.—Ulfs hnit-bróðir, Hym. 91; Iormun-gandr, Vsp. 148, Bragi 48; allra landa um-giörð, Hym. 87, ii. 26. 1; mold-þinor, Vsp. 186; iarðar seiðr,

Bragi 6; allra landa endi-seiðr, 50; Iarðar reistr, 46; lög-seimr, þd. 2; barða brautar hringr, Bragi 51; brattrar brautar hringr, ii. 26. 8; hraun-galkn, Hym. 92; storðar men, Husd. 14; storðar-leggs stirð-þinoll, 15; grundar fiskr, ii. 27. 9.

The Dragon.—Nið-höggr, Vsp. 215, 221, Grimn. 117.

The Demon World-destroyers.—Muspellz synir, Lokas. 170; Muspellz lýðir, Vsp. 151; Mims synir, 135; Fífl-megir, 153; (ragna rök) riúfendr, Doom 7.

The Crack of Doom.—Ragna rök, Doom 7, Vsp. 129, Lokas. 159, Vþm. 221, Atlam. 78, Helgi i. 303; alda-rof, 307; alda rök, Vþm. 154; Muspell, Lokas. 170, Vsp. 151.

§ 3. POLITICAL.

THE FAMILY.

THE ties of FAMILY were looked on with great respect by the heathen Northmen, and it is possible, by an analysis of the terms ap-plied to the family and its members in the old poets, to throw some light upon the matter, though the subjects with which the poets were chiefly concerned did not permit the introduction of a very full voca-bulary on this head. Still, what they have given is of high worth, and one can trace the transformations which came upon the family system of the North in successive generations; the old-fashioned patriarchal life of the præ-wicking days, with its unvaried course, as shown in Havamal; the change of manners which, as in Rome after the Punic war, and Hellas after the Persians' defeat, followed the growth of luxury and the importation of - captive slavery into Northern chiefs' households. The contrast between the wild gallant and his brother the stay-at-home yeoman is, as we noticed, well shown in the pictures of Woden the wicking and Thunder the worker in Harbard's Lay. The increase of polygamy, of a new and lower type than the patriarchal, influenced even the religious views of the wicking and post-wicking days among the upper classes (for the lower rank would cling perforce to the old ways, they could not afford captive slaves), which in the end had its effect; as Norway became united, and the chiefs from all quarters brought under the influence of the head-king's court, the tone of the higher families relaxes, especially in those reigns in which wicking ex-peditions occur, till at last the royal race ends in a slough of bastards and pseudo-bastards, and the great Houses wore themselves out in low drunkenness and debauchery or fell in the unglorious slaughter of those civil wars which in the twelfth and thirteenth centuries killed off well-nigh all the nobles and gentlemen of Iceland and Norway. There are among our poems some which must be carefully studied for their evidence on the old Teutonic family; those of Egil himself, a patriarch with strong and pious family feeling, Thryms-kvida with its wedding scene, Gudrun's ordeal, a tale of an injured and righted wife. The Icelandic Sagas of the Patriarchal time, too, afford some beautiful pictures of family life and affection: the union of Nial and Bergthora, faithful unto death, is the noblest example, the one blot on that picture being the episode (for it is no more) of the concubine[1] and her son.

---

[1] This however may well be an addition of a late Editor; it is a doubling of the other Hoskuld, who is really essential to the plot, and it does not bring out any special traits of Nial's character: though even allowing it to remain, it is but the kind of connection which was accounted lawful in patriarchal times.

Wholly different to these are the Helgi poems, with their wild, furious, romantic love, the most heart-stirring of all Northern stories, akin to the boiling passion of the court-poets' lives, and the deadly love of Gudrun Oswif's daughter. The individual is all in all here; the man or woman stands alone; the old family tie, which had forced all personal feelings to bow to its supreme claims, is gone; the wandering wicking, the captive lady are left to work out their life's struggles as best they can, with the keen sense that sudden death might at any moment cut the knot.

The court-poets again are outside the family ties in great measure. They are the slaves of love in their lives, but they ignore it in their works (Cormak's fragments have been so 'over-laid,' that one hardly knows whether they be true or false; and real songs, such as those in Book ix, are mediæval, inspired by troubadours, and late), save in the coarse satire where it is used to point an insult. They are proud of their pedigrees too, but they have their fortunes to make, and are ready, the noblest of them, to become Northmen at heart in their love for their patron, caring little to look back to their old homes, and this is more the case as poetry becomes a profession.

To take the evidence of the poets in order, and begin with their conception of the *family* itself. In the earliest metaphors one sees the family conceived as a *fence* of pales or stocks, the 'garth of kinsmen,' and one of the individuals composing it is the 'family-ash, the family stake *or* stock *or* prop' (the word ' ætt,' lit. 'ought,' with that mixed idea of property and blood-community which 'familia' bore in Rome). Again, the family is likened to the 'ring of stakes and cords' which always enringed the temple and the hallowed court or lists, the members being the 'family bonds *or* cords *or* staves.' In another metaphor the family is a 'shield-wall *or* phalanx' against foes, and its members the 'family shields' locked in united strength. An archaic term is that which points to the family *sacra* and *sortilege*, and calls the members sortilege-men' (hleyti - menn). The 'att-rúni' of Haustlong would seem to be the family-friend or kinsman. Egil's 'kynwid' [O. H. G. 'Chuni-wit'], the fruit-tree, we take it, is to be noticed. The terms 'heritage-taker, heritage-warden' (like the old London charter's yrf-numa) are to be observed. Of the word 'avenger,' as applied to the next of kin after the head of the family has suffered violent death, we have spoken elsewhere: the feud or blood-revenge, of course, like were-gild and inheritance, descended as part of the universitas familiae. The *patrimony* is called the 'family's-leaving, the kindred's-leaving,' and the technical word 'leif' appears in such compound names as Anleif, Thorleif, and in such images as homera-laf, darrada-laf, in Old English poetry. 'Head-tree' is the title of the caput-familias, and hints that the law of descent was reckoned as in England and Germany, by the joints beginning from the neck downwards. 'Ættar-scati,' which we find in a corrupt line in Egil's Arinbiorn's Lay, very likely means 'head of the family;'· 'scati,' an obscure word, not yet fully traced, seems to have 'stock *or* pale' as its primitive meaning. Hence the image of the tree is constantly applied to man throughout the poems of the court-poets, and gives rise to such expressions as 'offshoot, scion' [nid-quisl], and to various names for men and women.

The family is founded on the union of blood or kinsmen, begot in lawful marriage, when we get our first view of Scandinavian life in the poems (not earlier than 800). *Husband* is 'wer' [vir], *wife* is 'quán' [γυνή] or 'worð,' 'ward.' In Iceland as in England 'bondi' and 'husband' and 'hús-freyia,' 'housewife,' have replaced those in ordinary use. The 'man of the house' [husguma] is once used in the Rigs-mal. 'Frum-wer' [O. E. fruma-were], 'foremost man,' is found in the sense 'lawful husband.'

The recognised *concubine*, Lat. pellex, or secondary wife, the captive lady, whom the king or chief brings home as his *choice* from the booty, is the '*alien* woman,' 'elja,' and with more contempt the 'bond-maid,' 'man' [mancipium]; for foreign slaves were bought from the merchants who followed the track of conquest. There is a large class of words, sprung from the secondary meanings of this word, which is always associated with lustful love, e. g. 'love-matters, love-wiles, love-meeting [congressus], love-songs,' etc. But the most remarkable terms in this connection are those compounds of 'osk,' 'osk-wif,' 'osk-kwan,' 'osk-mær,' and the like, used rightly with a genitive of the possessor, Woden's wish-wife and the like. These words we take to refer to *chosen captives*, the chief's share of the spoil, as Briseis, *or aliens chosen for wives and then captured*, as Helen, looked on with pride as the spoil of the bow and the spear (the trace perhaps of an early system of exogamous marriage), and the evidence of the superiority of the conquering race. These words may be paralleled by a word hitherto unexplained, 'wal-cyria,' which the Editor believes to mean simply '*chosen alien-woman*,' that is, 'captive' [wal = osk and cyria standing for some foreign word for woman, κόρη, or the like, in which case it would mean a Greek bond-woman, brought to the North through Russia]. In Hornklofi's Raven-song figure captives or bondmaids 'from the East;' money, swords, and *maids from the East* are the king's guerdon to his valiant men. When we first meet Walcyries they are distinctly the attendants, wine-bearers, etc. of Woden, part of the riches and glory of his golden Wal-hall, as they were of the timber-palaces of earthly pirate-kings. The gold-decked maid slaves which Angantheow offers his brother, the gold-decked woman who sank on Sigfred's pyre were such as these, noble captive ladies who by the fortune of war fell into captivity, as we are told in the Lay of Gudrun. The idea of an Amazonian guard and of warring women seems to have been partly derived from the general feeling that even Woden's bondmaids must be armed; his hound is the wolf, his hawk is the raven, his hat is the helmet, his staff the sword, his bondmaids must be clothed as he is, preside over the swaying fight, and bring home the war-weary champions to their master's banquet. The fact that there were Amazon sea-queens in the wicking days, such as the Ingen Ruadh, would necessarily add touches of truth and force to the idea. Then the noble or dire features of the Destinies that weave men's fates, the Norns that sit by the Well of Paradise, and the Holy Three, Divae Matres, who give men bliss and wealth, and the War-Fairies, are borrowed and attributed to the Walcyries, in such poems as the Web of Darts, the Helgi Lays, and the like.

The marriage-union was sacred and respected, but the loose bonds of concubinage with foreign-born slave-women, dependent on their master's passion and goodwill, have given rise to such terms for *paramour* as the 'burden of a mistress's arms or embrace,' or most expressive of them all, 'he whose head is buried in his mistress's tresses.' The position of the bond-woman is shown by the phrase applied to her, 'she that whispers in her lover's ear.' The shame and secrecy of more unbridled lust, *chance-love*, are shown in the phrase 'secret-meeting' for an intrigue, and in the words for the offspring of such amours, the 'wood-child, the nook-child, the captive's son or love-child, the straw or bast - child (our " bastard "), or stall-child, the son of secrecy, the secretly-begotten one [1].'

THE FAMILY. As fence.—Frænd-garðr, Sonat. 22 (cp. frænd-balkr).

Single Member. As tree.—Ættar askr, Sonat. 70; kvánar kynviðr, 71; ætt-stafr, Helgi i. 223; átt-stuðill, ii. 48. 15; ætt-baðmr, ætt-bogi, kyn-kvísl, 428. 215-219; nið-kvísl, Yt. 169; af-springr, 60; höfuð-baðmr, Ad. 69, Hlt. 23; ættar-skati, [Ad. 48].

As kinsman.—Átt-konr, Yt. 141; átt-niðr, Hym. 31; átt-rúni, 77.

As shield.—Ættar-skiöldr, Sonat. 40.

As bond.—Ættar-þáttr, Hamð. 17, Sonat. 28; ættar-bönd, 27.

As sharer in sacrifice.—Hleyti-menn, þul. 224.

Son, Heir.—Erfi-nyti, Brunh. L. 102; erfi-vörðr, Tregr. 25.

Avenger.—Hefnir, hefnandi,—Blóðöxar hefnendr, ii. 35. 1; Hákonar hefnir, 29. 60; Skialgs hefnir, 137. 14; Áláfs hefnir, 188. 47; Haraldz hefnendr, 211. 4.

Husband.—Frum-ver, Brunh. L. 242, ii. 96. 14; angan . . .? Vsp. 164; hús-gumi, Rigsm. 103.

Wedded Wife.—Hús-kona, Rigsm. 105; hús-freyja, Atlam. 9; varð-rún, ii. 192. 18; vörðr, Ord. 12, þkv. 54, Lokas. 217, Thulor 166.

Concubine (pellex).—Ósk-kván, Bragi 1, ii. 31. 28; ósk-víf, 157. 12; ósk-mær, Vols. S. ch. 1; eyra-rúna, Less. 15, Vsp. 215; elja, ii. 440.

Paramour.—Faðm-byggvir, Hornkl. 83; arma farmr, Haust. 25, ii. 62. 21; lokka lyf-svelgr, 102. 41.

Amour.—Man-kynni, Harb. 97; man-þing, ii. 200. 28; man-vélar, Harb. 60; laun-þing, 95.

Bastard.—Hornungr, Hamð. 75; hrísungr, Yt. 126; bæsingr (see Lex.); ósk-mögr, Lokas. 63.

Patrimony.—Ætt-leifð, ii. 144. 11; œðli, Bragi 41.

People.—Ver-þióð, Lokas. 98; ver-liðar, Hym. 43; yr-þióð (=ver-þióð), Ad. 66, Vell. 62; al-þióð, Ad. 62.

Household.—Varð-drótt (?), Less. 24; sal-drótt, 28; drótt-megir, Atlam. 231.

Thralls.—Víl-megir, Biark. 2, Less. 96, Skirn. 144.

Farmer.—Bundin-skeggi, Breið-skeggr, Rigsm. 90-92.

Bondmaid.—Ökkvin-kalfa, Arin-nefja, Gengil-beina, Tötrug-hypja, Eikin-tiasna, Rigsm. 46-50, Helgi i. 280.

A Captive Slave-woman.—Her-gopa, Hornk. 89.

MAN AND WOMAN.

THE place of *women* in the late poetry is not high, it does not deal with the noblest women of old, the wise prophetesses whose words could stop the Roman legions and sway the national will (the last of whom are finely sketched in such sagas as Eric the Red), nor even with the honoured and respected housewife. The court-poet only sees or notices in his verse two kinds of women, the Queen and her damsels, gold-decked and silent, living apart, and the train of fair captive-women who bear the wine at the king's banquet. Hence for the former we get such metaphors as exhaust the list of ornaments and goddesses and nymphs, e. g. Gefn of the necklace, Gna of the broidery, Gund of the gems, Wrind of the head-band or golden snood, Wor of the gold, and

---

[1] The Norse 'bæsing' [from bás-s] and the Normannic 'bastard' [from the elder form banst-s] are cousins, as we have observed in 1867 in Icel. Dict. s. v., p. 92, and six years later, p. 771, bottom.

the like. And as Wrind is Earth, the later poets will use all the synonyms of earth to swell out their verse, calling their mistresses the ground of gems, the field of gold *or* of the veil *or* linen (if married, for Northern matrons, like English ones, ' went under the linen,' and covered their heads after the bridal).

From the other class of women came the terms, ' the nymph *or* goddess—Thrud, Freyia, Gefn, Hlokk, etc., of the horn *or* beaker *or* cup, *or* wine, *or* ale, *or* mead,' and the like. That once-found word ' laukalind,' leech-lady, *may* refer to the office of nurse to the wounded, and the leek-broth and leech-craft, which women occasionally at all events exercised, as the Kings' Lives testify. The later half of the ' kenning' —the nymph's name—might be replaced by the name of any feminine tree, ' linden, oak, fir-sapling, birch,' and so on. These frigid and pedantic metaphors are even used in the few genuine love-verses that remain.

As regards *Man*, we have already noticed the appellations proper to chiefs and kings, but some of more general type must be added here. As the pronouns must never be used in court-poetry, we shall of necessity find many varieties of equivalents to ' he ' and ' him,' but they may be reduced to very few categories. Man, as member of a family, is a *stock*, as we have seen; so we have many compounds, one member of which is ' stock,' e. g. ' the pillar of war, the stock of the helmet, the staff of wealth.' Then we have the names of masculine trees coupled with the like attributes of *war* or *wealth*, e. g. ' elm, ash, plane-tree of the gold, apple-tree of war.' Sea-life has given the ' steersman ' as a synonym for man. But for the court-poets the noblest work for man is to be the *wolf's butcher* and the *raven's brewer*, which culminates in Earl Rognwald's, in Snorri's and Sturla's compositions, and is shown in its worst form in the latter-day wicking-poets of the twelfth century. Such compounds are the ' feeder, hunger-queller, steward, provider, battener, meal-maker, etc. of the wolf,' and the ' thirst-quencher, slaker, drink-giver of the raven or eagle.' We have rarely been able or cared to translate these terms save by the simple pronouns ' he ' or ' him,' the repetitions would have been too tedious and coarse for most people now-a-days to take pleasure in or even tolerate. As a specimen, the first part of Kraka-mal, which is the best of its kind, will show the reader the kind of impression which the originals of the greater part of the panegyrics, if translated verbally, with their useless fill-gap phrases wholly made up of such images of the shambles, would produce. The importance of ' war' in the poets' metaphor system will be noticed below.

Woman. *Goddess of jewels and trinkets.*—Menja mörk, Brunh. L. 189; gollz Vár, 295; men-Skögul, 159; hör-gefn, W. W. L. 74; goll-hrings Fríðr, Korm. ii. 64. 11; auð Frigg, 111; hringa Hlín, 12; baudz Rindr, 14; sörva Rindr, 142; hodda fægi-Freyja, 28; erma Ilmr, 22; báro logs Vár, 131; sundz sól-Gunnr, 32; silki-Sága, 144; sörva-Gunnr, 52; men-Gefn, 109; földo hald-Eir, 129; gollz Eir, 43; steina Gná, 49; borðz Gná, 50; borðz Skögul, 143; gims Gerðr, ii. 49. 1; hördúks Rindr, 97; geira Syn, 73. 26; linn-vengis, Bil. 79. 10; borða Bil, ii. 112. 32; flóð hyrs fold, id. 31. *From trees.*—Men-reið, Korm. 2; auðar-þella, 29.

Ale-server.—Öl-Sága, ii. 64. 25; ölkarma Lofn, 79. 11; horn-þeyjar Freyja, Korm. 105; vín-Gefn, 112. 30; hvítinga Hlökk, 102, 4.

Needle-work.—þráða þrúðr, Korm. 119.

Healing.—Sára öl-gefjon (=Gro), Haust. 77; lauka lind, i. 373. 32; lauka Hrist, ii. 64. 10.

Men. *From trees.*—Hildi-meiðr, Helgi ii. 23; hialm-stafar, Wols. Pl. 55; auð stafar, 294; ognar lióma almr, Helgi i. 34; róg-apaldr, ii. 23; vápna hlynr, Wols. Pl. 245; Hárs drífo askr, ii. 167. 6; börr, 56. 25; þollr, 95. 1; runnr, 56. 19; draugr, id. 9; lundr, 95. 2; viðr, 92. 63; hlynr, 103. 6; þorn, 191. 58, etc. etc.

From gods.—Áss, ii. 58. 10; árr, ærir, 140. 53; niörðungr, 56. 14; tívar, id. 21; Höðr, 325, bottom; Ullr, 113. 5; Niörðr, 97. 26; Óðinn, 39. 25; Baldr, 208. 5; Freyr, 39. 11; reginn, id. 19; rögnir, 45. 33; Týr, 176. 27; Þróttr, 194. 18, etc. etc.

Wolf and carrion-bird feeder.— -greddir, ii. 95. 23, 244. 9; -grennir, 269. 1; -brynnir, 218. 3; -bræðir, 103. 18, 223. 24; -fœðir, 61. 4; -alandi, 240. 1; -hungr-deyfir, 93. 69; -hungr-þverrir, 244. 19; -lif-giafi, 267. 8; -feitir, 101. 3; -gœlir, 210. 2; -teitir, 52. 8; -nistir, 245. 9; -nistandi, Geisli, 99; ulfs tann-litoðr, i. 373. 33; hrafns munn-litoðr, ii. 267. 2; -gran-ríóðr, 267. 4; -munn-ríóðr, Geisli 53; -fióðri-ríóðr, ii. 186. 16; -fet-ríóðr, 194. 6; -il-ríóðr, 263. 61; etc. etc. ad nauseam !

War-waker.—Hildar hvessir, ii. 223. 22; gunnar herðir, 222. 3; herðandi, 273. 11; hildar haldboði, Vell. 42; hialdrs vekjandi, 208. 93; hialdr-vitjoðr, 206. 34; sókn-stœrir, 202. 67; ógn-stœrir, 159. 26; bragna fallz beinir, 197. 68; morð-kennir, 195. 31; morð-kannaðr, 62. 9.

The steerer of a ship.—Skeiðar stýrir, ii. 187. 28; unnar skið-rennandi, Geisli 161; -rennir, ii. 419. 10.

KING AND FOLK.

THE epithets applied by the poets to the king furnish a fair view of the royal duties, claims, and rights in their day; and show the various stages between the early conception of a half-heroic god-begotten tribal priest and general to that of a national ruler keeping order, upholding law, and preserving his land and people.

In the early poets the *divine origin* of kings is dwelt upon, ἐκ δὲ Διὸς βασιλῆες. Yngwi, also called the Lord-Yngwi [Yngwi-Frey], is the ancestor of that royal race which tradition brought from Upsal to reign in Norway. Tacitus' Ingaeuones point to the Yngwi genealogy. Hence come such titles as 'the scion, the offspring, the descendant of Yngwi *or* the God [Tyr], the branch of Woden's own race.' So the Lay of Righ brings all kings from Rig [Heimdal].

Another early and widespread set of metaphors refers to the *priest-hood* of the king. As head of the race, the duty of worship is incumbent on him. He is the 'Warden of the holy Temple *or* the holy altar, the prophet of the hallowed twigs of divination.' We should have had many more of these epithets but for Christianity.

As old as either of these is the idea of the king as *lord of his comitatus.* The *comitatus* is called the household (hird), the in-service (inn-drott), the guard (verdung), the soldiery (heid-), the following (fylgia), and the men composing it the housecarls (húskarlar), the young men (drengs), the lads (haukstaldar, a word borrowed from hagestalder), men of valour (itr-menn), braves (herdi-menn), gallants (snyrti-menn), sword-bearers (sverd-berendr), wage-takers (heid-þegar=solidarii), and the king is 'their patron, lord, chief,' etc. These mighty men were often, like David's guard, foreigners, and there were certain special champions among them, who in Harold Fairhair's case were called 'Wolf-hoods' and 'Bear-sarks,' as being fur-clad, according to what appears to have been an old custom. The whole band ['weorode' O. E.] formed a guard, paid, drilled, and disciplined, over whom the king had power of life and death, according to 'Thingmen's Law' [the guards' custom]. A good comitatus was the king's pride and security, and warlike princes surrounded themselves with as large and well-drilled guard of gentlemen adventurers as they could support. Young men of good family served for a time in the comitatus of a great king, learning by obedience then how to rule when it came to their turn to command.

It is no doubt in this connection that the frequent phrases touching the *king's liberality* arose; for instance, 'ring-breaker, lord of treasure, necklace-sharer, gold-divider, spoiler of neck-rings, gold-minisher, wage-giver, guerdon-dealer,' and the like.

As *supreme general* in war, leader of the battle-wedge, the king is the 'first man of the host, lord of the host,' and 'destroyer of the host' [her = invading army]. In more peaceful aspect the king is the 'establisher' or 'settler of the land,' a fit name for colonising princes; and in some early poets he appears as the *patron and defender of the people*, he is the 'feeder of his folk (ποιμὴν λαῶν), captain of the tribe, warden of the country, or the patron, lord, *or* director of men.'

His *political status* and the means by which tribal kings became head-kings are shadowed forth in such terms as the 'ruler of barons, foe of earls, the sole slayer of earls, and the crusher of dukes,' and 'head-king,' 'national-king' (þiod-konungr). The king is the *supreme judge*, 'settler of disputes,' as in Hesiod's well-known verses :—

οἱ δέ νυ λαοὶ
πάντες ἐς αὐτὸν ὁρῶσι διακρίνοντα θέμιστας
ἰθείῃσι δίκῃσιν.

It is not till Sighvat's day however that he has become a 'terror to evil-doers,' such as Henry I, Leo Justiciae, or Henry II, who would have loved to be sung of as the 'minisher, *and* crusher, *and* scorner, *and* disappointment of thieves, malefactors, and pirates;' so had times changed since Angantheow (in the Waking) could be praised as 'patron of wickings.' Sighvat also calls the king 'Moot-keeper.'

There is a good deal of history to be gleaned from the terms applied to particular kings: thus in Norway the recent rise of the *overlordship* and head kingship of Harold Fairhair is witnessed to by the persistence of *tribal-names*, by any of which the 'King of the North-men' or 'Lord of the East-men' (as the Western colonists styled him) might be fitly called. So we find Norwegian monarchs addressed as 'princes *or* kings of the Dalemen, Egdes, Fils, Firth-folk, Grans, Halogers, Hades, Heins, Hords, Hrings, Holm-Rugians, Mores, Œnes, Reams, Rugians, Renes, Sognfolk, Throwends, Thiles, Worses,' the original tribes which settled in Norway. So the Danish king is called 'Lord of the Danes, Jutes, Ey-Danes, Way-Jutes, Sconians, Scots, English, Cumbrians,' and the Swedish monarch 'Prince of Gauts and Swedes.' So the Earl of the Orkneys is known as 'Prince of the Shetlanders, lord of Tyree' (if we guess right), and the like.

In Denmark the famous old settlements and sanctuaries at Lund and Lethra have given the terms 'Lord of Lund, Sitter at Lethra, Holder of Frodi's throne.' Had we Swedish poems, no doubt 'Upsal's Lord' would be a standing phrase also.

Particular kings are spoken of as 'Norway's king' (late), 'lord of Humberland or Yorewic-land' (Eric Bloodaxe), 'head of Randwe's race' (Eormanric). Akin to these are the Eastern-looking expressions which point out a king by means of his relations, often insignificant persons; thus, Harold Hardrede is called 'Olaf's brother;' Earl Eric, 'Heming's brother;' and there are many such phrases which must have been picked out and used by Ari to construct his genealogies. The bombastic phraseology applied to the Orkney Earls, 'furtherer of Turf-

Einar's kin, Rognwald's son, Heiti's kinsman, head of Endil's race,' should be noticed here. One phrase, ' the avenger,' coupled ever with the name of a *slain* king, points to the duty of blood-revenge as felt by princes, and, as we have noted, settles the chronology of an interesting verse of Thiodwolf's at Stamfordbridge. See vol. ii. p. 211.

Another more curious instance of hereditary feud is seen in the epithets derived from *national hate:* to call the Swedish king the foe of the Ests, the Northern king ' enemy, and destroyer, and dread of Danes;' to call the Danish king ' crusher, and foe of the Wends *or* Frisians,' or to style either 'the ravager, and waster, and turner-to-flight of Scots, Brets, English, Saxons, *or* Irish.'

The *Pope* and the *Greek Emperor* receive special attention: the former is the 'lover of Christ,' the latter 'throne-king, preserver of the Greeks.'

The *countries* best known to the poets receive characteristic epithets. England is the ' patrimony of Ælla's race,' Norway is ' Harold's hawk-island' (Harold Bluetooth's tributary land, the annual payment of which was in hawks), Sweden is ' Gylwi's heir-land,' Greece the 'mould of monks,' Zealand the ' prey won from Wenner' or 'the eking of Denmark,' from the old story told in vol. ii. p. 8. Iceland, whose name lends itself to the wildest fancies of the court-poets, is the ' land of the sea-sky *or* sea-floor [ice], the country of the elks' gallows [ice, from the way in which elks were hunted over water-holes],' and the 'land of the roof of the Nixies' hall.'

KINGS:—

God-born, especially the King of Upsal.—Yngva konr, W. W. L. 16; Yngva ætt, Hakm. 3; Yngva þióðar allvaldr, Yt. 39; Yngva aldar allvaldr, Korm. 14; Yngva ætt-stafr, Helgi i. 229; Yngvi-Freys ætt, Hlt. 44; Freyss áttungr, Yt. 104, Hlt. 30; Freyss afspringr, Yt. 60, Korm. 5; Týss áttungr, Yt. 86, Hlt. 43; Freyss vinr, Brunh. L. 97; Ylfinga niðr, Helgi i. 17. iii. 31; Fiölnis niðr, Yt. 34; Skilfinga niðr, 91; lofðunga niðr, Wak. 104; Lofða kyns átt-konr, Yt. 141; þróttar burs nið-kvísl, 108.

Goð-konungr, Yt. 132; Austr-konungr, 84, Hlt. 14.

Pontiff of temple worship, of the King of Upsal mainly.—Vé-tiallz (vé-stallz) vörðr, Yt. 62; vé-frömoðr, 100; Rögna hrœrs frömoðr, 128; valteins spak-frömoðr, 44; vés valdr, Korm. 7; val-sœfandi, Yt. 66; reyks lauðoðr, 152; skiald-blœtr, Hlt. 7.

Lord of the guard.—Verðungar vísi, Hakm. 15; verðungar gramr, Brunh. L. 170; gumna stióri, Grip. 3; dróttar stióri, ii. 93. 90; inn-dróttar geymir, 197. 74; verðungar vörðr, Sighvat.

Pay-master of the guard.—Baug-broti, Helgi i. 70; hring-broti, 184, Oddr. 83; hodd-freyr, Höfuðl. 58; goll-miðlandi, Brunh. L. 327; sörva deilir, 122; men-glötoðr, Yt. 16, Hlt. 16; vell-vönoðr, Ad. 91; hramm-þvita bióðr, Höfuðl. 57; heið-frömoðr, Ad. 40; haukstalda vinr, Oddr. 21; haukstalda gramr, Brunh. L. 75; haukstalda konr, ii. 212. 10.

Defender, protector.—Land-vörðr, ii. 36. 21; foldar-vörðr, 40. 42; folk-vörðr, Old G. L. 18; iarð-byggvir, Vell. 91; land-reki, Helgi i. 127, v. l., Hlt. 41; flotna-vörðr, Mark 4; folk-nárungr, ii. 56. 3; þióð-skati, Hofuðl. 48; folk-hagi, 61; lióð-frömoðr, Ad. 14; lofða holl-vinr, i. 315. 16; þióðar þengill, Grip. 164; aldar ástvinr, Mark 61; folka treystir, 62.

War-captain, conqueror.—Hers oddviti, Grip. 161, 205; folks oddviti, Helgi ii. 39, iii. 45; sigr-höfundr, Yt. 160; her-baldr, Brunh. L. 75; her-konungr, Yt. 160; þióð-konungr, 146; hers-iaðarr, W. W. L. 56; folks iaðarr, Helgi i. 311; egg-leiks hvötoðr, Old G. L. 109; hiös-leiks hvati, Hofuðl. 48; her-glötoðr, Short Brunh. L. 20, 71; bryn-jalfr, Yt. 148; sverð-alfr, Hlt. 47; her-megir, Helgi iii. 20; hildi-meiðr, W. W. L. 55; Víkinga vinr, Wak. 10; Víkinga niðr, 90.

Hersa valdi, Yt. 73; hersa dróttinn, Sighvat; iarla bági, Hlt. 21; iarla ein-
bani, Hakm. 11.

Enemy of aliens.—Ála dolgr, Yt. 108; Eistra dolgr, 125; Ióta dolgr, 27;
Ey-Dana œgir, Hakm. 13; Skota fár-bióðr, Höfuðl. 35; Vinda myrðir, ii.
91. 31; Breta stríðir, 92. 41; Frísa dolgr, 102. 7; Dana grandaðr, 36. 16;
Engla œgir, 226. 40.

Justice.—Sök-miðlandi, Yt. 144; [víg or vé?] miðlungr, 175; rógs hegnir,
Mark 50; þinga kennir, ii. 132. 91.

Foe of thieves.—þiófa rýrir, ii. 132. 87; þiófs véltir, 147. 61; hlenna hneigir,
125. 17; hlenna þreytir, 188. 56; hlenna dolgr, 58; hlenna þrýstir, id.;
svik-folks eyðir, Mark 12.

A Christian King.—Vísdóms grœðir, Mark 66.

A tyrant.—Lofða stríðir, ii. 51. 15; folk-mýgir, 16.

King of the Norwegians, Lord of the various tribes or folks.—Dœla-, Egða-,
Fila-, Firða-, Græna- (ii. 91. 38), Haða-, Háleygja-, Heina-, Hörða-, Hringa-,
Holm-Rygja-, Mœra-, Œna- (101. 5), Rauma-, Rygja-, Rena-, Sygna-,
þrœnda-, þila-, Vorsa-, dróttinn, gramr, konungr, etc., pass., and Norðmanna-
dróttinn, Hornk. 18; Austmanna iofur, 69.

Noregs konungr, ii. 39. 14.

King of the Danes.—Dana, Ióta-, Ey-Dana-, Skánunga-dróttinn . . ., pass.;
Hleiðrar at-seti, ii. 224. 11; Fróða stóls stillir, Mark 17; Lundar allvaldr,
ii. 203. 28.

Greek Emperor.—Stól þengill, ii. 205. 21; Girkja stillir, 24; Mikla-garðz
konungr, Geisli.

Bear-sarks, Wolfcoats. — Berserkir, Hyndl. 96, Hornkl. 44, 71, i. 161. 14;
Ulfheðnar, Hornkl. 47, 72.

Wickings.—Víkingar, Wak. 10. 90, Helgi i. 105, Brunh. L. 298, 330.

Henchmen.—Inn-drótt, ii. 197. 74; heið-þegar, 128. 24; lióð-megir, Hakm. 17;
hilmis fylgja, Old G. L. 51; hús-karlar, Atlam. 101, pass.

Nobles.—Herðimenn, Jomsv. 85; snyrti-drengir, 153; ítr-menn, 138; gœðingar, id.

Evil-doers.—Laga heptendr, ii. 56. 15; auði-menn, 29; grið-bítar, 28.

Traitor.—Vár-liúgr, Ad. 50; vára vargr, Wols. Pl. 259; drottins sviki, pass.

The Divining Rods.—Val-teinn, Yt. 4; hlaut-viðr, Vsp. 196; hlautar-teinn, Vell.
44; teinar, Hym. 3; hlaut-spánn (?), id.; spá-gandar, Vsp. 83; blót-spánn,
Ari [see Excursus to vol. i. p. 411].

Temples.—Einriða hofs-lönd, Vell. 82; banda vé, id.; hapta vé, 88.

COUNTRIES:—

Zealand.—Venis valrauf, Bragi 44; Danmarkar auki, 42; Sel-meina tríóna (Selund),
ii. 31. 6; Svana dökk-sala dalr, 159. 25.

Sweden.—Gylva œðli, Bragi 41.

Norway.—Haraldz hauk-ey, Sighvat ii. 148. 76.

Icelanders.—Ál-himins-lendingar, ii. 37, 48; elgjar galga alþióð, Sonat. 58;
Nykra borgar næfr-land, Kont. 298.

Greece.—Munka veldi, Mark 32; munka mold, ii. 162. 11.

England.—Ello ættleifð, ii. 162. 8.

WAR, WEAPONS, GOLD.

WAR was the most honourable occupation of a king in his own eyes,
and the court-poets, whose business is purely to recount in sounding
verse the victories of their patrons, in as unvarnished but more inflated
strain than the Assyrian chroniclers of old, are full of metaphorical expressions relating to this all-absorbing subject.

The *battle* itself is spoken of as the 'moot of swords, the game of
iron, the play of edges, the assembly of blades;' or, more poetically, as

the 'gale of spears, the shower of arrows, the tempest of darts;' or, again, as the 'din *or* the sweeping of swords, the clatter of edges, the clash of brands, the song *or* hum of the bows, the ring of metal' [black-metal is iron and yellow-metal bronze].

Later terms, derived from myths, were favoured, and the court-poets abound in such expressions as the 'storm, the gale, the drift of Woden *or* of the Walkyries, Hild, Hlank, Shackle, Gondul.' In Hornklofi's phrase we take 'Frey' to have the primitive sense of 'Lord,' and to stand for Woden, *the* Lord. In later times the famous heroes and sea-kings are pressed into the composers' service, and one gets 'Hedin's gale' and 'Ali's [Anilas] shower' as synonyms for the tempest of war.

The *sword* is by far the favourite weapon of the Northman, as it was of the Roman of old, and it is fully dealt with. It is the 'leek of war, the wand of wounds.' Its brightness (so remarkable to those who had been used to 'fallow blades' of bronze) provokes the titles 'wound-fire *or* flame;' its power and uses supply the terms 'the destroyer of the shield, the saddle of the hone, the graver *or* chisel of wounds, the shearer [justice, doomer] of man.' From myth and legend come such names of the sword as 'Woden's wand *or* flame; the work of the Dwarves; the bane of Hialmar *or* of Fafni.'

The *spear* is less often noticed, but it is called the 'wound-thorn,' and may be meant (rather than the sword) by the phrase 'the plug *or* gag of Fenri's lips,' a synonym derived from the well-known story of the Beast and the Gods.

Arrows are spoken of as 'wound-bees, corse-ogres;' or else they are 'Gusi's *and* Iolf's craft' (two kings of Fins or the Dwarves); or 'the tribute *and* the craft of the Fins' (who appear to have been skilled in making spears and to have paid their Scandinavian neighbours dues in arrow-heads as well as skins. Fin and archer are almost synonymous terms, and the bow, save in myths such as that of Egil, is hardly a regular Northern weapon. (Gunnar's defence, half legendary in its de-tails, perhaps derived from that of Egil, will scarcely weigh much on this point.) Arrows are also the 'hail-shower of Egil's hands,' or, more fancifully, 'the swift-herrings' of the same great archer: they are also the 'barley of Woden *or* the wheat of Woden,' a comparison drawn from the evident likeness between the haulm and ear of those grasses and the shaft and head of the arrow.

The *axe* is the most curiously treated; it is called the 'ogress of the woods *or* the shields.' This personification of the axe may date back far (the axe is mountain-born, like giantesses, being of stone or metal). It is 'battle-ogress, shield-crasher, helm-cleaver.' We hear much of the axe in the Sagas, but on the other hand it is curious that the axe is so rarely mentioned in the poems, late or early. The later celebrity of S. Olaf's axe in monument and story makes the axe famous as Norway's emblem, and a well-chosen one it is for a nation of 'woodsmen.' The witness of Wace and Giraldus is conclusive as to its efficacy in defence.

Of defensive weapons the first place belongs to the *shield*, in whose honour famous bards in the North, as among the Greeks of old, wrought elaborate lays. The phrases applied to it by the early poets are varied and striking, and have some reference to its round target shape, the brazen rings which surround it, the linden wood of which it is com-posed, and the bosses that adorn and strengthen it; or to its uses, to be hung up round the hall above the guests like pictures in a College Hall: such are the 'penny of the hall [see above, p. 450], the quivering ring-cliff (or perhaps flag-stone), the cloud with the rims.' Later singers prefer to call it, from its battle uses, the 'ness of the sword, the floor of the spear-heads, the field of the pikes, the sky of darts.'

Many are its mythical names, some derived from the story of the god Wuldor, as 'Wuldor's ash or boat;' some from Hrungni's adventure, 'the giant's foot-bridge;' others (mostly of later type) concerned with Woden or the Shield-maidens, e.g. 'the bark, flake [shingle] of Walhall; the plank or garth or thatch or toft of Woden; the cloud or gate or wheel or board or τέμενος or wall or cliff of Skogul, Hild, Gondul, or Gund.' Later the sea-kings are drawn upon, and the buckler is called the 'roof of Reifnir, the cliff of Gestil,' etc. Last of all in point of time are the metaphors drawn from the rows of shields that ran round the waist of a war-galley, glittering in red and gold—the 'moons of Ræ's car; the foliage of Leif's land; the lee-board moons of the steeds of the boat-house or dock.'

The *helmet* is spoken of in early days with reference to some such belief as is witnessed to by Latin writers, who tell of the Teutonic custom of wearing a boar or other image on the helm, which was supposed to charm the wearer and terrify the foe; the 'boar-helm' of Beowulf is one of the best instances of this in Teutonic poetry. In the Western Scandinavian tribes, the giant sea-god Eager is especially associated with the helmet, and takes the place elsewhere filled by the patron, Lord or god (called Frea, Woden, or Gaut as it may be). Hence the phrases, 'helm of awe, Eager's helm [Ocean's helm?],' and the fascination of the look of a warrior is called the 'eye of the serpent.' The helmet is also 'Woden's hood or hat.'

The *mail-coat* is the 'raiment of war, the ring-kirtle or skirt, the dart-web.' It is also, from the legends of charmed armour, the 'kirtle of Hamtheow, the shirt of Sarila, the raiment of Hagena.' The Walkyries ride panoplied like their master Woden, and so the later poets talk of the mail-coat as the 'trapping of Spear-Rota, the awnings or pavilion of Hlank, the sark of Gund,' and the 'weeds or grey-coat of Woden.'

The right array of chosen champions was the hide of a wolf or bear (an old Teuton custom borrowed by the Romans in the case of their standard-bearers); this raiment is called the 'wood-boar's sark' (the wolf here, as usual, being the wood-beast par excellence).

The delight in battle and bloodshed, which is noticed as a marked feature of the early Teuton warrior, is well brought out by the poets in the endless series of synonyms and metaphors which speak of *wounds* and *blood* and *carrion*, and the *beasts and birds of prey* that haunt the battle-field. The Helgi lays have several such metaphors, though in the later court-poets this mode culminates. So pleasing was it to their patrons and so deeply interesting to themselves, that there is no difference between Christian and heathen poets in this respect; indeed the 'Christians' here make the saddest show, and down to the last the fashion is kept up, even by clerks like Sturla, a man of peace and letters, who had no love for battle or slaughter, but who, nevertheless, in his poems has to follow the set fashion, employing such forced imagery as to call the shield the 'heavenly vault of the Walkyries, underneath which the lightnings, i. e. the swords and missiles, gleam forth '— poor and borrowed conceits.

Wounds are the 'footprints of the dirk, of the sword-edge;' the *scar* is the 'mark of war.' Blood is the 'gash-shower, the wound-dew, the ocean or lake of the sword, the river or stream of the blade, the beer or mead of the raven.'

Carrion is the 'wolf's dainty, the raven's barley, the eagle's supper, the sword's harvest or swath.'

Of *birds of prey*, the hawk is the 'falcon's son,' and is never spoken of as a carrion-bird, but the *raven* and *eagle* are ever the 'haunters of the battle-field.' The former is called the 'rover of the sky, the eagle's sworn brother, the partridge, mew *or* hawk of the wounds, the crane of battle, the blood-drinker.' But the raven is also the 'wise bird, the companion of Woden, and the follower of the Walkyries,' hence he is called 'Woden's swan, hawk,' etc., and the 'goose *or* hawk *or* mew of Gund.' The *wolf* is known as the 'corse-greedy beast, the greyhound of Woden, the steed of Leikni, Grith,' and many another 'night-riding witch-wife.'

GOLD is one of the most frequently mentioned objects in the court-poets, who have repeated occasion to mention it when talking of the king's generosity, the poet's guerdon, or the lady's ornaments. Several of its synonyms have already been alluded to, such as 'Freyia's tears, Sifia's tresses, the roof of Holgi's barrow, Thiazi's speech, Glasi's leaves, Draupni's sweat,' which all refer to mythologic incidents. There is an equal wealth of these which touch on heroic legends, such as that of the *Hniflungs*, from whence are formed such phrases as 'the Hniflung [Niebelung] hoard, the Hniflung heirloom, the Weregild of Otter, the Earth of Fafni, the burden of Grani, the discord-breeder of the Hniflungs, the red ore of Rhine.' The idea of serpents lying on treasure, which appears in the Sigfred and Beowulf stories, is wide-spread among the poets, and gives rise to the terms, 'Snake's meadow, serpent's bed, the downy couch *or* the litter of the snake.' Another story, that of the *Mill that ground Gold*, gives the metaphors, 'Frodi's flour, the meal ground by Frodi's bondmaids, Fenia's grits, Menia's meal.' The story of Hrolf Craci has produced the phrases, 'Craci's barley, the sowing of Yrsa's child, Craci's glistening seed, the seed of Fyris-field.' More general terms are the vivid 'metal of strife, foreign metal.' Commonest and most prosaic and far-fetched are such as refer to personal adornment, e. g. 'the fire of the elbow, the pebbles of the wrist, the meal of the hand, the lady's snood.'

WAR, ARMOUR, WEAPONS:—

Battle.—*Moot.*—Hiör-þing, Helgi i. 217; val-stefna, 76; hiör-stefna, 50; bryn-þing, W. W. L. 85; brímis dómar, Helgi i. 147; Fiolnis þing, ii. 56. 23.

Play.—Egg-leikr, Old G. L. 109; ísarn-leikr, Höfuðl. 30; Freys leikr, Hornkl. 22.

Din, rattle.—Geira veðr, Helgi i. 46; nadd-él, Grip. 92; sverða svipan, Wols. Pl. 44; malm-hríðar spá, Höfuðl. 16; hiörva glöm, 13; dolga dynr, Helgi i. 79; randa rymr, 68; alma þrymr, 67; víg-þrima, 27; egg-þrima, Eirm. 31; vigra seiðr, i. 373. 36; egg-roð, Short Br. L. 36; egg-tog, Höfuðl. 62.

Storm.—*Of Woden.*—Hárs veðr, Hlt. 25; Óðins veðr, i. 266. 15; Viðris vandar veðr, ii. 76. 2. *Of Walkyries.*—Hlakkar drífa, ii. 70. 6; Sköglar veðr, 266. 14; Göndlar flaumr, 76. 50; Göndlar þeyr, 105. 2. *Of sea kings.*—Heðins drífa, ii. 76. 48; Ála él, 75. 40.

The Sword. *As wand.*—Imon-laukr, Helgi i. 28, ii. 36. 35; ben-vöndr, Short Brunh. L. 73; sár-laukr, ii. 102. 10. *As fire.*—Ben-logi, Helgi i. 213; ben-eldr, i. 266. 9; bauga tuss, Eywind 265. 5; víg-nesta böl, Helgi iii. 33; hein-söðull, Höfuðl. 27; ben-grefill, 28.

Mythical.—Dverga smíði, Wak. 57; Fáfnis bani, Grip. 60; Hialmars ban

(Tyrfing), Wak. 77, 107; mannz miötuðr, 109; Fiolnis fúrr, ii. 49. 2; Gautz eldr, Korm. 11; Viðris vöndr, ii. 75. 28.

The Spear.—Sára-þorn, ii. 56. 1; Fenris varra sparri, 36. 17.

The Axe.—Rimmo-gýgr, Niala; nausta blakks hlé-mána gífr, ii. 165. 3; hlýr-sólar hála, 271. 14; fiornis (helmet) gríðr, 24, cp. id. 16.

Arrows.—Unda bý, Hofuðl. 51; hræ-skóð, ii. 94. 5; flug-glöð, flug-svinn, Thulor 292; hvít-mylingar, ii. 242. 52, Merl. 294, Thulor 288.

Mythical.—Egils vápna (gaupna) hryn-gráp, ii. 96. 16; Egils gaupna hlaup-sildr, 37. 50; Yggjar val-bygg, ii. 208. 83; Herteitz hveiti, id.; Iolfs smíði, Thulor 294; Gusis smíði, 293.

Historical.—Finna giöld, ii. 206. 47.

The Shield.—Baugs bif-kleif, Haust. 52; randar himin, i. 266. 13; sverða-ness, id. 11; brodd-flötr, Höfuðl. 47; geir-vangr, 18. *From the hall.*—Svelnis sal- (Walhall's) penningr, Bragi 21; Svafnis sal-næfr, Hornkl. 79. *From ships.*—Ræs reiðar máni, Bragi 40; Leifa landa lauf, 30; nausta blakks hlé-máni, ii. 165. 12. *From Giant Hrungni.*—Fialla finnz ilja brú, Haust. 51. *From Wuldor.*—Ullar askr, ii. 95. 1. *From Walkyries.*—Sköglar ský, ii. 51. 6; Hildar veggr, 114. 2; Hildar borð, 57. 31; Gunnar ræfr, 28; Gondlar grind, 74. 13; Hildar vé, Haust. 4; Högna meyjar hiól, Bragi 4. *From Woden.*—Viðris balkr, ii. 114. 5; Svolnis garðr, 56. 21; Gautz þekja, 60, 68; Hroptz toptir, 103. 27. *From Sea-kings.*—Reifnis ræfr, ii. 102. 5; Gestils kleif, 75. 42.

The Helmet. *Boar's head.*—Hildi-svíni, Hildi-göltr, Edda and Hyndl. (see also Thulor).

Helm of terror.—Ygrs hialmr, Ad. 13; ægis-hialmr, Wols. Pl. 121; holm-fioturs hialmr, Vell. 27; holt-vartaris enni-tingl, ii. 62. 11. *Woden's hood.* —Hanga-týs höttr, iii. 75. 35.

The Mail-coat. *War-woof.*—Víg-nest, Helgi iii. 36; víg-nisting, i. 23; darraðar vefr (spear woof), Höfuðl. 17 (cp. Lay of Darts); hring-skyrta, ii. 91. 40.

Legendary.—Hamðes skyrta, ii. 96. 16; Sörla föt, 17; Högna váðir, 95. 12. *From Walkyries.*—Geirroto götvar, ii. 95. 13; Hlakkar tiald, 114. 1; Gunnar serkr, 57. 30. *From Woden.*—Váfaðar váðir, i. 265. 2; þundar grá-klæði, 57. 34.

A Wolf's or Bear's Coat.—Hrís-grisnis serkr, Hlt. 26: cp. Ulf-heðinn, Ber-serkr, p. 480.

Wound.—Dolg-spor, Helgi i. 313; eggja spor, Death Song 36; her-kuml, i. 192. 36.

Blood.—Sár-dropi, Helgi i. 314; val-dögg, 330; harm-dögg, 334; hiör-lögr, Wols. Pl. 115; Sár-gymir, i. 266. 11; fleina flóð, odd-lá, mækis-straumr, Eywind 266. 11-16; mækis á, Höfuðl. 15; odd-breki, 39; hræ-sær, Hornkl. 44; hræ-sollr, Bk. vi. § 2. 6; Farma týs svana biór, Hlt. 36.

Carrion.—Ulfa krásir, Helgi i. 50; Hugins barr, 227; ara náttorðr, Höfuðl. 36; hræs lanar, id., etc.

Raven and Eagle.—Arnar eið-bróðir, Hornkl. 14; hræ-sævar bergir, 44; ben-þiðorr, i. 373. 41; ben-már, Hofuðl. 38; hialdr-tranar, 37; hræva nagr, ho!unda valr, i. 372. 12. *Raven, Woden's bird.*—Farma týs svanr, Hlt. 35; Óðins haukr, Helgi i. 324. *From Walkyries.*—Gunnar systra gögl, Helgi iii. 26; Gunnar haukr, ii. 56. 4.

Wolves.—Hræ-gífr, Old G. L. 99. *Woden's hounds.*—Viðris grey, Helgi i. 52. *Witch steed.*—Flagðs goti, Höfuðl. 35; Gríðar sóti, ii. 163; kveldriðo stóð, 94. 18; Leiknar hestr, 16.

GOLD :—*Sun, light, fire of the deep.*—Diúp-röðull, Bragi 41; Oranar eldr, Biark. 16; ógnar-liómi, W. W. L. 70, Helgi i. 32, 82; elfar alf-röðull, ii. 36. 31; Rínar röf (amber), 350. 81.

From Myths.   *Freyja.*—Mardallar tár, Biark. 15; Freyjo tár, ii. 102. 12
(cp. Thulor 168 and Malsh. 30).

From Sif.—Sifjar svarð-festar, Biark. 15; Fullar brá-vallar fall-sól, ii. 36. 29.

From King Holgi.—Hölga haug-þök, ii. 102. 6.

From Giant Thiazi.—þiaza þing-skil, Biark. 18; Iðja glys mál, 16, cp. Bragi
66 (cp. Malsh. 31).

From the Tree of Wealth.—Glasis barr, Biark. 11.

From the Wonder-ring.—Draupnis dýr-sveiti, Biark. 12; Draupnis drog, ii.
55. 10; Draupnis dögg, 167. 15.

From heroic *legends.   Niflungs.*—Hniflunga arfr, Akv. 42, 107; Hniflunga
hodd, 103; Hniflunga róg, Biark. 19; Rínar rauð-malmr, id.; Rínar malmr,
Brunh. L. 66; Otrs giöld, Biark. 15; Fáfnis miðgarðr, 10; Grana byrðr,
11; Grana hlíð-farmr, Oddr. 79; linn-vengi, 120; orm-beðr, Tale of G. 103;
Grafvitnis dúnn, Biark. 12; lyngva mens láttr, ii. 37. 40.

As Frodi's Meal.—Fenjo forverk, Biark. 10; Fenjo meldr, ii. 177. 68; Menjo
neit, Brunh. L. 110; Fróða þýja meldr, ii. 36. 27; Fróða miöl, Höfuðl. 59
(cp. Runic Song 10).

From King Craki's Story.—Fyris-valla fræ, ii. 36. 26; Kraka barr, 208;
Kraka drífa, 218. 9; Yrso burðar (Craki's) örð, 208. 88.

As the metal of strife.—Róg-malmr skatna, Akv. 106; Vala malmr, Hyndl. 32.

From the hand.—Ölna bekks eldr, Bragi 64; Ölna griót, ii. 71. 29; hauk-
strandar möl, Höfuðl. 60.

Gems.   *Pearls.*—Haf-nýra, Husd. 23; iarkna-steinn, Volkv. 99, Gkv. 71, Ordeal
30; Hallin-skíða (Heimdal's) tannir, ii. 40. 39.   *Necklace.*—Hals-baugr,
Bragi 8; Hildar svíra hringar, 17.

CHRISTIAN SYNONYMS.

Christianity, as it induced the poets to write of sacred subjects
and make Drapas to saints, obliged them to make fresh similes for sacred
things and persons, when they were obliged to speak of them; the
court-poetry was however dying at heart when these terms were
made, and (save one or two) they are all imitations of long-used epic
formulas, but they are often ingenious, and show the thoughts of the
makers on religious matters.   The *second Person* of the Trinity is called
the ' Lord and friend of the monks, the King of heaven, the Lord of the
sun.'   He is also the ' King of the monks' land [Rome], the Lord of
Jordan, the King of Greece, the Warden of the Greeks and Gard-
folk [Russians or Byzantians].'   The Brook of the Fates was supposed
to be at *Rome* and to be ' God's seat.'   In exact consonance with the
royal state as it was before their eyes, the poets make heaven a more
glorious Wal-hall, with *angels* for henchmen, *saints* for heroes and
champions.   The saints are also ' Christ's limbs, Christ's knights, the
Saviour's friends, God's crew, the beams *or* rays of God's hall, the
pillars *or* studs of book-speech ' [i. e. the Gospel or Evangel].   The
Virgin Mary is called the ' Star of the Sea,' a phrase translated from
the Latin hymn.   A *priest* is the ' bell-warden ' (a name well suited to
the early Irish missionaries), or ' God's thrall ' (Culdee), *The Pope* ' lover
of Christ;' the *heathen* are the ' host of the high places.'   The *church* is
the ' ship *or* nave of the services.'

Epistles or Letters, which may be mentioned here, are called by
Sighvat ' searching birds of love,' in reference to their passing between
friends.

Illuminating, ' staining,' books is recorded by a twelfth-century poet.

Christ.—Munka reynir, ii. 54. 2; Munka dróttinn, 115. 21; Gríklandz gætir, 160. 32; Iordanar gramr, 148. 77; Grikkja ok Garða vörðr, Arnor.; heiðis foldar hallar dróttinn, ii. 54. 3; munka mold-rekr, ii. 161. 11; banda [angels] gramr, 22. 4.

Heaven.—Munka mold-reks vald, ii. 162. 8.

The Virgin.—Flæðar stiarna, Geisli 8.

Angels.—Heims hrótz (heavens) ferð, ii. 324. 1; himins dýrð, 7; himna dýrðar hirð, 3.

A Saint.—Bóka máls regin-nagli, ii. 161. 38; miskunnar sólar geisli, Goðs hallar geisli, Goðs liðr, Kristz limr, Goðs ríðari, Lausnara spialli, þegn-prýði, etc., Geisli passim.

A Church.—Tíða flaustr, Mark 68.

A Shrine.—Borðvegs sæing, ii. 161. 23; Glæ-logn, i. e. Glæ-lung, id.

The Pope.—Kristz unnandi, Mark 37.

Priest.—Biöllo-gætir, ii. 51. 39; Goðs þræll, Geisli.

Pagans.—Hörga herr, Mark 46.

Rome.—Munka veldi, Mark 32.

Letter.—Smoglir ástar foglar, Sighvat ii. 144. 3.

Stone, i. e. colour for illustrating, ' staining,' books.—Bókar Sól (Book Sun), ii. 300. 11, Hallarstein.

EXCURSUS II.

ON CHRONOLOGY.

THE ideas of time and reckoning of dates which prevailed among the early Teutons seem to have been of the most primitive kind. Genealogies soon lose themselves among gods and heroes and giants: thus Iordanis takes only seven steps between Heimdall the god and Hermanric [1], the famous king of the Goths; and the similar genealogy in the imperfect Lay of Righ would probably have had even fewer steps. Such long genealogies as that of Ynglinga-tal are merely artificial. Ari's longest pedigrees, such as Bodwere the settler [2], do not reach a dozen names. No other mode of reckoning save by pedigrees was known. Three generations prove *allodial* possession; the man who, like Nestor of the Iliad, has seen three generations is the 'ancient witness' (our 'oldest inhabitant'). Eternity was for great men's fame; 'his renown shall endure while mankind endureth upon earth' and the like phrases are used with a childlike faith in the certainty of remembrance, which is touching and all unconscious of Ulysses' baser worldly wisdom:—

> 'Time hath (my Lord) a wallet at his backe,
> Wherein he put almes for oblivion :
> A great-siz'd monster of ingratitudes :
> Those scraps are good deedes past, which are devour'd
> As fast as they are made, forgot as soon
> As done.'

There is no reckoning of numbers, backward or forward, and the past, 'times of yore,' is a region in which Attila, Theodric, Sigfried all appear on the same plane with complete absence of historic perspective;

---

[1] " But of these heroes, as they tell in their own stories, the first was Gaut, who begat Haimdal, but Haimdal begat Rigis, Rigis begat him who is called Amal, from whom also the beginning of the Amals comes. Which Amal begat Isarna, who begat Ostrogotha, who begat Hunwine, who begat Athal, who begat Athiwolf and Oduwolf; but Athiwolf begat Ansila and Ediwolf, Wuldwolf and Hermanarig. Now Wuldwolf begat Walraven, who begat Winethari, and he begat Wandalari, who begat Theodmir and Walamir and Widimir. Theodmir begat Theodric, Theodric begat Amalswinth, who bore Athalric and Mathswinth to Eadric her husband, who by family kinship was related to her, as will be seen. For the aforesaid Hermanric, Athwolf's son, begat Hunmund, who begat Thorismund, who begat Bearmund, who begat Widric, who begat Eadric. . . . Athalric dying in childhood, Mathswinth was married to Witgar, by whom she had no children . . . . and Witgar dying, Germanus the Patrician, brother's son of the Emperor Justinian, took her in wedlock, and got her the rank of patrician: by him she had a son, who was called Germanus."— *Iordanis*, ch. 14 (Holder's edition).

[2] The steps are given at p. 490. In England there are only seven names between Woden and Æthelberht of Kent, Augustine's friend ; and from Eadwine of Deira, Æthelberht's son-in-law, to Woden, twelve.

see, for instance, the rolls of heroes in the Lay of Hyndla. Just as Gildas and Nennius reckon by great *battles*, so there is a rough popular chronology by *famines*, *fire-raisings*, and *Mickle-Moots* noticed by Ari. Thus there was a famine "in the year when Islaf was hallowed bishop by Albert of Bremen in the days of King Harold Sigurdson." And "eighty years before" there had been a still worse famine "at the time when King Harold Greyfell fell and Earl Hakon took the sway of Norway."—[Landnama-bok, Appendix.]

The first man who had a sense of the necessity of an exact reckoning for historical purposes was the historian Ari, who was the sixth in degree from Anlaf Feilan, one of the Western settlers; born thirty-seven years after the close of the heroic period of Icelandic history (1030, 1067), of a famous family, in the most central and wealthiest district of the land. He not only collected historical information, but he put it in good order; and though in his complete isolation he has made some mistakes (for he knew no neighbouring nation's chronicles—ours of Winchester would have saved him much labour), it is easy to put these right, and so to avail oneself of the vast stores of fact which he has painfully saved for ever from the Ogre Time.

His scheme of chronology hinges upon the one well-known date A.D. 1030, the death of S. Olaf. This year 1030 is a memorable one; it is the last of the Saga Age, and in it there died a famed King of Norway and a famed Law-speaker in Iceland. The great eclipse fixes it for certain. It is the only year of the ancient Saga Age where the A.D. is absolutely certain. From it he reckons the dates backward according to the years of the *Law-speakers in Iceland* and the *Kings in Norway*, to two other points which he makes to coincide in 930:—

Iceland.	Years		Norway.	Years	
	27	Skafti.		15	S. Olaf.
	2	Grim.		14	The Earls.
	17	Thorgeir.		5	Tryggwason.
	15	Thorkel Moon.		19	Earl Hakon.
	20	Thorarin.		16	Greyfell.
	20	Raven.		26	Hakon the Good.
				5	Eric Blood-axe.

101 — 1 years	=	100 years

Thus he brings his history of Iceland back to the foundation of the Althing (for he has evidently counted in the year of the foundation), and that of Norway to the death-year of Harold Fairhair. His Icelandic chronology he rests on the authority of Mark Skeggison the Law-speaker, who had the authority of his brother Thorarin, who got it from his father, whose father could remember Thorarin the second Speaker and the six who followed him, remembrance not implying here more than contemporaneity.

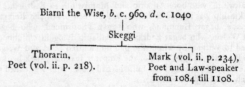

Biarni the Wise, *b*. c. 960, *d*. c. 1040

Skeggi

Thorarin,   Mark (vol. ii. p. 234),
Poet (vol. ii. p. 218).   Poet and Law-speaker
                             from 1084 till 1108.

Beyond this second stage, 930, Ari goes back, in a great stretch of sixty years, to a third and final fixed point, 870, which (having, as he tells us, access to a Life of S. Edmund) he marks as the year of that king's martyrdom, reckoning thus:—

Iceland.	930 A.D.	Norway.	930 A.D.
	60 years of settlement		60 years of Harold's reign
	870 A.D.		870 A.D.

When we come to test these schemes, which bear evident marks of arrangement, first by independent chronology, and then by Ari's own witnesses the pedigrees, an aberration of about thirty years is revealed, which only requires to be corrected, when the discrepancies between his scheme and the true year at once disappear.

Taking the external evidence first. Othere's account of Halogaland is given to King Alfred some time after 880, probably nearer 890. But neither Othere nor his fellow-voyager says anything about the discovery of the great island far in the West, nor of the stir of emigration which by Ari's chronology must have been convulsing the Norwegian coast-counties. Othere's chief merchant-station is Sciring-heale in Westfold, the very cradle of the Northern kingdom and of Fairhair and his race ; yet Othere speaks of no rising kingdom there, which he could hardly fail to do if he had really been a contemporary of Harold Fairhair. Rather, Othere's whole narrative, the more valuable on this account, is a picture of a peaceful land, resting between the adventurous career of Godfred, Charlemagne's foe, and Harold the founder of the Norwegian kingdom. It is a record from the very eve of the discovery of Iceland.

Again, Ethelstan is spoken of as the contemporary of Harold Fairhair, whose son Hakon he fostered; but, by Ari's chronology, the Northern king would be 76 when Ethelstan began to reign, and would have only reigned three or four years more, decrepit and failing.

Almost immediately after Hafursfirth battle, say 877, a settler goes to Iceland; but his son fights at Brunanburh in 937, as a young man beginning his career. This is in the highest degree improbable.

According to Ari again, King Eric Blood-axe was five years king and then went to the West in 935, but the English Chronicles give his coming many years later, 951; and it is certain that 935 cannot be right, there was no place for him in the West at that time.

How can all this be set right ? One must suppose that the dates of the first Settlement and of Harold's accession have been *antedated* by Ari about thirty years; that Iceland began to be colonised and Harold to reign about 900. Harold probably survived till at least 940. If this be accepted, all will fall in with what we know from Irish and English Annals. Eric's wife Gundhild, Harold Bluetooth's sister (as we have seen), becomes his contemporary, instead of being too late for him.

Ari has made Harold Fairhair's reign too long, and also lengthened the years of Hakon the Good; in fact the whole century from 870 to 970 has been *stretched*, as it were, out of seventy years.

To come to the equally conclusive evidence of the Landnama-bok. When the Editor was writing Tima-tal (an Essay on Early Icelandic Chronology) in 1854–55, purely from the parallelism of dozens and dozens of pedigrees recorded by Ari, he arrived at the conclusion that the bulk of the Settlers came, not from Norway direct, but from the Western Islands, and that they did not begin to come to Iceland till about 892 at earliest : and this coincides with all that is to be gleaned from foreign sources. As the Editor at that time placed implicit faith in any direct statement of Ari on chronological matters, he was compelled to except from the mass of Settlers a few expressly dated by his author, and place them in a *first period of settlement* by themselves. But this position gave rise to immense difficulties which he could not solve; and a glance at the accompanying table of genealogies will show how, though extraordinary circumstances might account for a single instance, the consensus of cases forbids such an explanation, and forces one to the conclusion that Ari has antedated the Beginning of the Settlement by nearly thirty years.

We have taken below a number of the most prominent Icelandic families, and given the steps from the *Settlers* to the contemporaries of S. Olaf, and side by side with them are placed the chief Norwegian families with their pedigrees, from Harold Fairhair to the generation of the sainted King (marking the Icelandic series by a, b, c ..., the Norwegian by A, B, C ...). There can be no doubt about the ancestries of these genealogies of men of mark; they are the faithful record of family traditions, without any trace of being 'made up' to suit a chronological theory; indeed it is through them that the need of some correction of Ari's date is so clearly seen.

By way of illustration to the list below:—a. 2, first settler's grandson, held office till 985;—b. 2 (also in second degree) was in the year 1000 'baptized in his old age;'—c. 3 and h. 3 died, one in 1031, one in 1030; —d. 3 fought at Swolder, a young man of twenty, in 1000;—e. 3 slain in 1029 [vol. ii. p. 170];—f. 2 baptized in 1000, then an old man;—i. 3 survived year 1034;—k. 2 a missionary in year 1000; his son, Iceland's first bishop, consecrated in 1056, died in 1079;—l. 3 fought at Clontarf 1014[1];—g. 4 died about 1025; whose great-grandson Bishop Ketil, Ari's friend, died in 1145;—n. 3 a young man in Tryggwason's reign, 995-1000;—o. 3 (father to l. 3) baptized in 999, a founder of the Mission;—m. 3 survived into S. Olaf's reign; his daughter, Ari's great-grandmother, lived much beyond 1030; her nephew Wulf [vol. ii. p. 232] died in 1066.—In Norway, A. 1 (Harold Fairhair's son) died in 954; another son survives to c. 965; Tryggwason, Fairhair's great-grandson, dies under forty in 1001; S. Olaf, in fourth degree, in 1030, he, too, under forty; King Harold, in same degree, in 1066, aged 51;— C. 3 (well known from the English Charters and Chronicles) died an old man c. 1023;—D. 3 fell at Clontarf in 1014;—E. 3 (the Conqueror's grandfather) died 1026;—F. 1 lived in 950;—F. 3 died in 1028 [ii. p. 137]; —G. 1, Egil's friend [i. p. 271], died in 976.—All is in good concordance if we accept the year 900 as the starting-point. On the other hand, there are several impossibilities if we follow Ari's choice of 870, e. g. in B. 1 Earl Sigrod survives his father by some ninety years[2].

---

[1] We give here Bodwere's pedigree back to the heroes; as one of Ari's longest, it may compare with that of Theodric, p. 487:—'Bodwere the White was the son of Thorlaf Midlung, the son of Bodwere Snow-thrum, the son of Thorlaf Whale-gull, the son of An, the son of Erne Horn, the son of King Thori, the son of Swine-Bodwere, the son of King Kaun, the son of King Solgi, the son of Rodwulf o' Rock.'—*Landn.* IV. 7.

[2] It may be noted here that there are but two sources for the older Icelandic genealogy, Ari's works and the genealogies of Nial's Saga, which belong to a different source of tradition. The later mediæval genealogies of Iceland must be sought in Sturlunga Saga and the Bishops' Lives. For the continental Northern genealogies Ari (resting on tradition and poems) is the fountain-head, though there are a few items to be gathered from other less trustworthy remains.

ICELANDIC SETTLER FAMILIES.

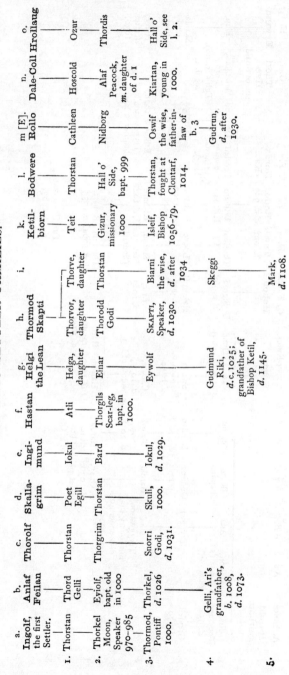

NORSE ETC. KINGS, EARLS.

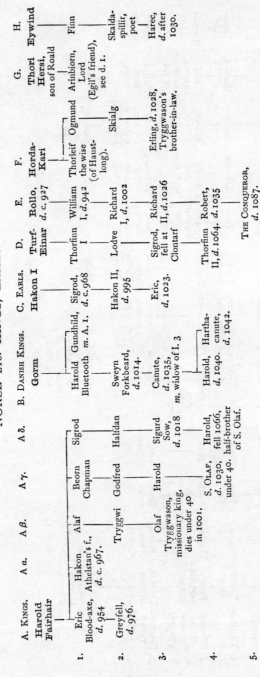

	A. KINGS.	A α.	A β.	A γ.	A δ.	B. DANISH KINGS.	C. EARLS.	D.	E.	F.	G.	H.
	Harold Fairhair	Hakon Athelstan's f., d. c. 967				Gorm	Hakon I	Turf-Einar	Rollo, d. c. 927	Horda-Kari	Thori Hersi, son of Roald	Eywind
1.	Eric Blood-axe, d. 954		Alaf	Beorn Chapman	Sigrod	Harold Bluetooth, Gundhild m. A. 1.	Sigrod, d. c. 968	Thorfinn I	William I, d. 942	Thorleif the wise (of Haustlong).	Arinbiorn, Lord (Egil's friend), see d. 1.	Finn
2.	Greyfell, d. 976.		Tryggwi	Godfred	Halfdan	Sweyn Forkbeard, d. 1014.	Hakon II, d. 995	Lodve	Richard I, d. 1002	Ogmund		Skalda-spillir, poet
3.			Olaf Tryggwason, missionary king, dies under 40 in 1001.	Harold	Sigurd Sow, d. 1018	Canute, d. 1035, m. widow of I. 3	Eric, d. 1023.	Sigrod, fell at Clontarf	Richard II, d. 1026	Skialg		Harec, d. after 1030.
4.				S. Olaf, d. 1030, under 40.	Harold, fell 1066, half-brother of S. Olaf.	Harold, d. 1040. Hartha-canute, d. 1042.		Thorfinn II, d. 1064.	Robert, d. 1035	Erling, d. 1028, Tryggwason's brother-in-law.		
5.									The Conqueror, d. 1087.			

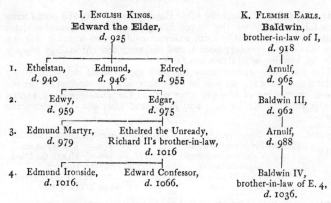

I. ENGLISH KINGS.

Edward the Elder,
d. 925

1. Ethelstan,   Edmund,   Edred,
   d. 940   d. 946   d. 955

2. Edwy,   Edgar,
   d. 959   d. 975

3. Edmund Martyr,   Ethelred the Unready,
   d. 979   Richard II's brother-in-law,
                     d. 1016

4. Edmund Ironside, Edward Confessor,
   d. 1016.   d. 1066.

K. FLEMISH EARLS.

Baldwin,
brother-in-law of I,
d. 918

Arnulf,
d. 965

Baldwin III,
d. 962

Arnulf,
d. 988

Baldwin IV,
brother-in-law of E. 4,
d. 1036.

It will be seen that one cannot differentiate the Settlers, to whom Ari expressly gives a date, from the others; they were evidently all contemporaries, many of those to whom Ari does not assign any definite date being among the settlers of *Waste-land*, and could not therefore have been late-comers, for the land was very soon parcelled out in great 'claims,' and the later immigrants were forced to 'take land' of those whom they found already in occupation. Broadly speaking, one hundred years back our great-grandfathers were ado, bustling and busying, at a similar age as their living great-grandsons. In modern life, with its late marriages, there will be exceptions; less so in old times, especially so in the stir and perils of the Wicking Age, when men aged fast, married early, died young. Now in rank 3 of our list is the generation between 1000 and 1030, so that we should give 900–930 for the Settlers and Kings and Earls (printed in thicker type) at the head of each file. For, taking those men as a contemporary generation, we must either imagine that they were as far in time from their grandsons as Chatham and Frederick the Great's generation is from us living in 1882, or we must throw over Ari's scheme, and shorten the time he allows by about thirty years, at a distance of time which is as that of Washington and the younger Pitt to us. This change will fill up an otherwise unexplained blank in Icelandic history, between 930 and 960 of Ari's chronology, and will bring the history as related by Ari into exact conformity with the ascertained chronology of the ninth and tenth centuries, with the statements of the English Chronicles, and with ordinary human experience.

We may note that the Editor's conclusion as to Rollo, drawn in 1855 from the Pedigrees, "that all that was said of him in the foreign annals before 912 is nothing but moonshine," has lately been independently confirmed by Mr. H. Howorth in a conclusive Essay on Dudo [Archæologia, vol. xlv] based on a study of the continental annalists [1].

The amended chronology exactly fits in too with the position which, judging from internal evidence, one would assign to Hornklofi's Raven-

---

[1] The following are the dates which he has established:—

> 921. Rollo settles with his men in the dioceses of Rouen, Seez, Lisieux, and Evreux, and makes peace with Charles.
> 924. He is granted Bessin and Maine.
> 925. He is defeated (and, according to Richer, slain) at Eu.
> 927. His son William does homage to Charles.

Song, to Ynglinga-tal, and the other Court-poems. A.D. 870 would have been far too early for the Raven-Song, 920 is a most probable date. Again, it was impossible from external evidence to imagine that we have many ninth-century poems, and the amended chronology happily does not require us to strain our faith.

The following scheme gives the best approximate dates for Early Iceland and Norway. It will be seen that one can depend on the received chronology of Norway after 976, as the *great famine*, a known date, is rightly given by Ari; and in Iceland after 960 Ari's dates are true:—

Iceland.		Norway.	
c. 900	Discovery.	c. 900–45	Harold Fairhair.
960	Settlement over, and	c. 945–50	Eric Blood-axe.
	Constitution settled.	950–67	Hakon the Good.
	Saga-tide begins.	967–76	Greyfell.
998–1000	Mission-tide.	1001	Fall of Tryggwason.
1030	Saga-tide ends.	1030	S. Olaf's death.

The millenniums of Iceland and Harold Fairhair are therefore *yet to come*, and there is yet time for further progress ere the first thousand years of the colony and mother country's history are completed.

Some other single errors in Ari's chronology may be noted here. The Jomswicking battle is somehow post-dated about ten years, the expedition of Otto II to Denmark post-dated about ten or twelve years, while Sweyn's conquest of England is ante-dated about five or six years. This discrepancy between the taking of Christendom in Iceland and the death of Olaf Tryggwason, and the Editor's view as to the right date, are noticed in vol. ii, as years ago in Tima-tal.

The difficulty which Ari met in putting events into a strict system of chronology is far greater than we can easily allow for now-a-days. Years, when past, are *so* apt to run into clusters or nebulæ, even those of one's own life. And when one had got a clear starting-point, to convert it into the year of Christian era was no small perplexity. The very notion was in Ari's days unusual or all but unknown. Even two generations later a contemporary of S. Thorlac and Bishop Paul, writing 1200–15, adopts an inexplicable system, which we have elsewhere called the *Thingore system* of chronology, the peculiarity of which is that Christ is supposed to have been born in the year 7. It is followed in the Bishops' Lives, in Hungrvaka, Bishop John, and in the Life of Swerri, an evidence that our A.D. system was, even at that late date, not yet established. Here there is no insecurity about the right year, for the dating of the Bishops' Lives is largely helped by the fact noticed by the Editor (in 1856–58, whilst editing the whole series), that every Icelandic bishop whose consecration-day is known (and there are some nineteen so given) was consecrated on a Sunday. We can even sometimes get the exact date, elsewhere lost, of a Norwegian prelate who happened to be hallowed along with an Icelandic bishop.

One more chronological point must be considered from its bearing on the date and condition of one poem, the *date* of the *General Moot* or Althing, and the final establishment of the Icelandic constitution. Here we must first hear Ari's testimony:—" And when Iceland was already widely settled, an Eastern-man [Norwegian] first brought a Constitution out hither from Norway—so Teit told us,—and it was called the Constitution of Wolfliot. And it was for the most part set according to the then Constitution of Gula and according as the counsel of Thorlaf the Wise, Horda Kari's son, ran, with regard to what should be added thereto or taken away or changed therein." [Libellus.] Now the Constitution of Gula was fixed and founded by Hakon the Good and Earl Sigrod, therefore not before 950; and as we must allow some years for knowledge of this Constitution and its benefits to reach Iceland, the Constitution of Wolfliot must be postponed from 930 (Ari's date) to, say, 960.

That a suit of Egil at Gula-Moot is mentioned in Egil's Saga, ch. 57, cannot be a valid objection. A thirteenth-century story-teller is a small authority for a lawsuit three centuries earlier. He will of course tell his story in the best way for his audience; he does not seek out legal antiquities, or care to enquire whether there was a Gula-Moot or Gula-Law in King Eric or Fairhair's day. His audience knew there was such a court in Norway in their day; that was enough. No legal argument can be founded on such a statement; it is as if one were to seriously try and get at old Kweld-Wolf's style of clothing from the thirteenth-century foreign dress of Bolle in Laxdola Saga.

The other difficulty is more important; it is that of Wolfliot's age. Landnama-bok is very puzzling on this head, and cannot be taken as authoritative where it contradicts the pure and certain mention of him in Libellus as a *Norwegian*. The references in Landn. iii. ch. 16, iv. 17 are on the face of them false glosses, which have crept into the text. On the other hand, the statement that Wolfliot was son of Thora Horda-Kari's daughter, and therefore nephew of Thorleif the Wise, King Hakon's friend and adviser, is probably true. It must always be remembered that Landnama-bok in our MSS. is not Ari's text pure and simple—glosses and mistakes must have crept in. There is no necessity to suppose that Wolfliot ever lived in Iceland more than a year or so. He vanishes after the settling of the General Moot.

It is interesting to find in Libellus and the fragment (as we take it) of the lost Liber some account of the earlier striving after a Constitution and General Moot. Ari says, "The General Moot was set, by counsel of Wolfliot and all the folk of the land, where it now is. And before this the Moot was at Keelness, which Thorstan son of Ingolf the Settler, the father of Thorkell Moon the Law-speaker, hallowed, he himself and those chiefs who were banded with him." [Libellus, ch. 3.] And again, "Thorstan, Ingolf's son, first of men, set up a Moot on Keelness ere the General Moot was set up, according to the counsel of Helgi Beolan and Œrlyg o' Esia-hill, and other wise men. For which reason the hallowing of the General Moot follows that priesthood [that of Thorstan's family]. Thorkell Moon the Law-speaker [a. 2 of the pedigrees above) was the son of Thorstan, Ingolf's son; Thormod the son of Thorkell was the Priest of the Whole Congregation when Christendom came to Iceland." [From the lost Liber?]. We have even notice of the oath by which the Moot at Keelness, and afterwards at Axewater, was hallowed: "So said the sage Thormod, who was Priest of the Whole Congregation when Christendom came to Iceland, that with these words and Moot-marks his forefathers were wont to hallow the General Moot all their days—." Here the foolish copyist has left out the carmen which, as the oldest instance of the Opening of a Teutonic Court and the heathen prototype of our House of Commons' 'prayers,' would have been highly instructive[1].

---

[1] Alþingi vas sett at ráði Ulfliótz ok allra landz-manna þar es nú es. Enn áðr vas þing á Kialarnesi þat es þorsteinn Ingolfs son landnáma-mannz, faðir þorkels

Other reminiscences of the præ-Wolfliot days are preserved in the gloss of Hen-Thori's Saga, ch. 14, "And the Moot was at that time under Arman's fell;" i. e. at its present site, the explanation meaning, "It was after the days when the Moot was at Keelness[1]." The remains of the booths of the old Keelness Moot could still be seen in the days of the author of the fabricator of Kialnesinga, who at all events knew the geography of his district[2]. The old Moot seems to have been deserted when the General Moot was set up, and there is a notice, we believe, of a Spring-Moot held at Axewater.

The history of the General Moot may thus be summed up in a few lines: In the midst of the seething life of the sixty years of settlement, a little knot of the earliest, most reputable, and noblest settlers banded together for law and order, and held a League-Moot, as we might call it, at Keelness; their influence spread, till probably they were joined by most of the chiefs in the South-west and South[3].

At last a general feeling, fostered by their success and peace, arises elsewhere as to the desirability of a General Moot and one Constitution for the whole country. Wolfliot the Northman is the link by which the new and good Constitution of Gula, which has become famous, is brought out to Iceland with necessary modifications. Then a compromise is effected: the League of the Moot at Keelness is enlarged into a General Moot, and the locale changed to the more central and convenient Moot at a specially chosen Mootstead at Axewater. The link between the two was the Keelness priesthood, which now rises to the more glorious dignity of the Priesthood of the Whole Congregation, a noble compensation to the Keelness family for their early efforts in behalf of a settled government. And it is pleasant to know that the Priesthood of the General Moot, the Chaplaincy of the Icelandic Parliament as it were, remained in their hands as late as the Sturlung-Time[4].

Mána lögsögo-mannz, hafði þar, ok höfðingiar þeir es at því hurfo.—*Libellus*, ch. 3.

Þorsteinn Ingolfs son lét setja fyrstr manna þing á Kialarnesi áðr Alþingi vas sett, við ráð Helga Biólo ok Œrlygs at Esjobergi, ok annarra vitra manna. Ok fylgir þar enn sökom [þess] því goðorði Alþingis helgon. Þorkell Máni Lögsögo-maðr vas son Þorsteins Ingolfs sonar. Þormóðr vas son Þorkels, es þá vas allz-herjar-goði es Kristni kom á Ísland.—*From Islendinga-bok.*

Enn þá es Ísland vas víða byggt orðit, þá hafði maðr Austrœnn fyrst lög út hingat or Noregi, sá es Ulfliótr hét.—Svá sagði Teitr oss—ok vóro þá Ulfliótz-lög köllöð. Enn þau vóro flest sett at því sem þá vóro Golaþings-lög, eða ráð Þorleifs ens Spaka Horða-Kára sonar vóro til, hvar við skyldi auka eða af nema, eða annan veg setja.—*Libellus*, ch. 2.

Svá sagði vitr maðr Þormóðr, es þá vas allzherjar goði es Kristni kom á Ísland, at með þessom orðom ok þing-mörkom helgoðo lang-feðgar hans Alþingi alla ævi (carmen unfortunately lost).—*Ari* (in Landn. Append.)

[1] Enn þingit vas þá undir Ármannz-felli.—*Gloss in Hen-Thoris Saga*, ch. 14.

[2] Enn sér stað búðanna.—*Kialnes. S.*, ch. 2.

[3] Thus Raven of Wrangwater was the first Speaker of the General Moot, and we might well suppose that, like the Keelnesing Moot-priest, he was chosen to hold this office because he had already filled it in the League-Moot.

[4] We may here, to save further discussion, record our adherence to the views, as to the Moot-stead, accepted and confirmed by Dr. Kaalund, and put forth fully in an Excursus to vol. ii of Sturlunga Saga, for the following reasons:—(1) There is no mention whatever in the old authorities of the Moot-stead being on the *east* of the river. (2) There are no remains such as would mark a Moot-stead on the east of

Anything relating to Thorlaf the Wise, who with Hakon and Earl Sigrod made the Gula-Moot and Frosta-Moot Constitutions, is of high interest to us, because of his connection with the early poets, whose patron he was; for instance, Ynglinga-tal, Haustlong; and even to know his date would be a step towards fixing the date of Hyndluliо̃, a poem which Ari never knew. In the Prolegomena we have already given a brief view of the origin and growth of Northern Law in Norway and Iceland; this it is not necessary to recapitulate here, but it is necessary to sketch the true position in which Thorlaf, the creator of the Gula-Moot, stood to Harold Fairhair, the founder of the Northern monarchy. In considering these questions, it is most needful here to state once more clearly that the view of even the best and most learned continental writers on these matters is biased radically by their inveterate conception of Law as a Code, of Law-makers as Parliamentary Orators and Bureaucrats,—Statesmen of modern days, everlastingly proposing, emending, and digesting statutes. Law in old times is Custom, the Legislator is the man who makes or mends the necessary machinery for getting this Custom-Law observed. What the chiefs of Iceland wanted from Wolfliot was not a Code,—they knew the law of weregild, of inheritance, and the like; what they did lack was means for having it enforced, and for putting an en 1 to the conflict of customs which inevitably arises when men of different districts are brought face to face. Wolfliot brings them over the plan of the machinery which Thorlaf had devised and set up; not a Code, but a Constitution. Englishmen and Americans can understand this easily enough; but, as they are liable to be misled in such matters

---

the river. (3) There is no 'berg' (rock or hill) there, as there was at the true spot. (4) There is no tradition, older than a hundred years, as to the Moot-stead being *east* of the river; for that the present 'tradition' is false and late, not indeed a tradition at all, is clear from direct statements of scholars of the seventeenth and eighteenth centuries. (5) The site of the 'pseudo-logberg' is well fitted for a place of defence or robbers' stronghold, but for a place of public assembly a more dangerous and ill-chosen spot could hardly have been found than a narrow tongue of land, surrounded by two deep and dangerous crevasses or rifts. Wherever the Moot-stead was, it was not at any spot east of the river, and certainly not where the pseudo-logberg (really Byrgi's booth) was placed by some imperfectly informed antiquary of the end of the last century. To call on local tradition to support such a theory is as if one were to try and find out whether Alfred founded the University of Oxford by questioning and collecting affidavits of the old women in Heading on Workhouse.

That the Law-hill was on some part of the lower brink of the Great Rift *west* of the river is supported (1) by its suitability for the purpose, it is a *brink* sloping down to the river—a true 'þing-brekka;' (2) by the traditions of the seventeenth and eighteenth centuries as to a Moot-stead west of the river, see Kaalund; (3) by the site of the Logretta during the Middle Ages down to 1800 west of the river; (4) by the testimony of Sturlunga to its being near Lathe-booth, the site of which is well known; this again is corroborated by Kristni-Saga; (5) by the very name Almanna-gia, i. e. the Rift of the Whole People. Every visitor is struck by the sight of Almanna-gia. It is the crown and glory of the whole place. One sees the whole people thronging together to listen to the Speaker; and one feels as if one were listening to his voice, echoed back, as in some ancient cathedral, from the walls of the Rift. During an earthquake in 1789 the lower brink sunk in places some eight to twelve feet, so in days of yore the place was even more impressive than it is now.

We have no doubt that the place could be ascertained within a few yards, by careful examination of the lower brink of the Great Rift, and it is to be hoped that this will ere long be carried out.

when they find eminent authorities and good scholars talking of Codes, and Law-making, and Legislative machinery and the like in this connection, we do not deem it out of place to give them a word of warning.

Another error connected with the subject is to suppose that Harold Fairhair was a mere tyrant, who put down the old Folk-Moots and crushed freedom out in Norway. On the contrary, he was the champion of the yeoman, the enemy of the wicking, the general whose victory brought law and order in his train. The impression left upon one's mind by reading the Book of Settlement and Fairhair's Battles is that before his day Norway was a land of loosely organised folk-kingdoms, an n-archy rather than even hept-archy; save in the South, where, as Ari tells us, under Halfdane the Black (perhaps even of earlier origin) there was a little well-organised nucleus, strong, compact, orderly, a small league we take it of folk-tribes round Heathsævi-Moot by the Wick [Frith of Christiania]. Harold Fairhair in fact starts as head of the best organised state in Norway, *the only compound state which was ruled by one king*, and he wins folk-kingdom after folk-kingdom, and governs them by his sons as other conquerors have done, but ever keeping a strict eye to their good rule and peace-keeping. The only time that Harold is in danger, through all his task of conquest, is when he meets the war-league of kings and Western wickings, which he beat at Hafrsfirth after a struggle of the most desperate kind[1]. But this victory was the key-stone of his power. His kingdom was never again in jeopardy, and he was able by his expedition to the West (Scotland and Orkney) to force great part of the Confederation that had fought against him at Hafrsfirth to leave the Western island for the Northern colony. Harold dies, but his kingdom survives the struggle for the crown among the sons of the dead conqueror, a struggle repeated so often in history, Eastern and Western; and after a brief interval Hakon comes in fresh from the teachings of Athelstan, whose task of uniting all England, Danes and English, under himself was the very prototype of his own policy, down to the details. The Three Laws of Hakon's day are to be compared to our Three Laws. Hakon, like the English kings, left each set of folks their own customs, but insisted upon unity and good law within these limits. Neither does Hakon try to make the West or North Norwegian tribes obey the Southern customs, he simply confederates them round two convenient central Moot-steads, Gula and Frosta. He has in each case the assistance of local magnates, Thorlaf the Wise for the West and Earl Sigrod for the North; who have the wisdom to see how far better it is to have folk-confederation with free law and good order under a head king, than to continue on in isolated tribal kingdoms each under its own dynasty in the midst of everlasting war. The Upland kings alone seem to have had the sense to make some sort of league, and accordingly they manage to preserve their independence long after the rest of Norway was under one head king.

The testimony of Ari is as follows[2]:—

" King Halfdane [Fairhair's father] was a great sage, and a man of verity and even-dealing, and he set laws and kept them himself and

---

[1] The Waking of Angantheow must be subsequent to this fight, if the allusion in l. 93 points, as we believe it must, to Fairhair.

[2] We here give only the translation; for the texts we refer the reader to Prolegomena, § 35, notes.

forced all men to keep them; and that violence should not beat down law, he himself made a Cause-List [Table of Crimes] and arranged weregilds for every man according to his birth and rank."—The very ideal of the early statesman ruling his confederate state wisely and well, and simplifying the variety of local customs.—And, "King Hakon [Athelstan's foster-son] was very wise, and gave much thought to making a Constitution (laga-setning). He made the *Gula-Moot Constitution* [in West Norway], according to the counsel of Thorlaf the Wise, and he made the *Constitution of Frosta-Moot* [in North Norway], according to the counsel of Earl Sigrod and other of the wisest men among the Thronds. But the *Heath-sævi Constitution* [in South Norway] Halfdane the Black had made, as was written above." And again of Hakon, "He made the Constitution of Gula-Moot and of Frosta-Moot, but Heath-sævi's Constitution [here is something dropped out; we read, *was made by Halfdane the Black*] first of all, but before that *every folk had its own Constitution*[1]."

Later on, the rest of the kingdom is finally brought into big Moot-districts by S. Olave, who "set up the Constitution which is called Sefs-Law, which has stood ever since over Upland and the east half of the Wick;" substituting the district-Moot under a head-king for a confederacy of kings.

The little confederacy in the South, ruled by the just Halfdane (for let us dismiss all thought of him or his son's having been a tyrant or a bad king), has thus formed a model for the organisation of all Norway and also for Iceland; for the All-Moot (Alþing) and Constitution there is copied, as we have seen, from the Moot and Constitution of Gula.

This organisation greatly furthered the legal acceptance of Christianity in Norway and in Iceland; for it must not be forgotten that Christianity was carried in Norway, no less than in Iceland, not by violence[2], but by Act of Parliament at the three Great Moots, by the free vote of each Moot in its turn, won over by the eloquence and wisdom and (last not least) by the spell the heroic missionary king threw over all that saw or heard him. And we shall get the best idea of the scenes of missionary work at the Moots of Gula and Frosta, Moster and Heath-sævi, where Olaf Tryggwason was, like Oswiu, the

---

[1] Years ago (Dict. p. 736, s.v. þing C, and p. 776 a) the Editor showed that 'Laga-setning' (Law-setting) in Ari's parlance and in its proper sense means Constitution-making, *not* Code-making, and in Prolegomena he again repeats the proofs. But apparently in vain, for in an Essay just to hand, an otherwise well-informed Scandinavian scholar is found talking of 'Gula-Code,' and supposing that this 'Code,' of which he quotes a paragraph, dates from 'the middle of the tenth century.' Law, like Religion, is too often supposed to lie not in Life, but in Books. It is all important that the terms which stand at the base of a great subject should be rightly and clearly understood: one such word misapprehended will bring down the whole structure it underlies. In modern histories, for instance, Fairhair is spoken of as if he had uprooted a model Commonwealth, and driven its members to carry off their precious organisation to a new asylum in bleak cold Iceland, whose Althing is supposed to be a reconstruction of the pre-Haraldic political life of Norway. As in most errors of this kind there is a grain of truth in the hypothesis—the Icelandic constitution contains elements of pre-Haraldic life, swept away as it seems in Norway—but that does not prevent the hypothesis itself being false, and indeed, as we have tried to show, the very reverse of the real state of the matter.

[2] The stories of Tryggwason's clubbing idols and torturing pagans are but idle gossip; see above, vol. ii, p. 83 sqq.

preacher of the word to his people, from the true and faithful record in Kristni Saga of what took place at the Icelandic General Moot, which was in fact a repetition of the same phenomena, only that in Iceland the king preached through the mouth of his delegate, though the charm of his person was even there at work. Moreover our records are fuller and purer with regard to Iceland than they are with regard to the Christening of Norway. In Law and in Religion Iceland is still a part of Norway, her General Moot is the last of the series of General Moots which began with Heath-sævi, her vote of acceptance of Christendom the last of the list of votes which had begun with the vote of Heath-sævi-Moot at the proposal of Olaf Tryggwason himself.

EXCURSUS III.

ON THE TRACES OF OLD HEROIC POEMS TO BE FOUND IN THE ICELANDIC FAMILY TALES (IS-LENDINGA SÖGUR).

It is a strange thing that one rich branch of Northern literature (the Islendinga Sagas[1]) has never been examined with a view to discover the echoes of old long-lost *Teutonic ballads* which are undoubtedly to be found there. The fact is that sufficient attention has not been paid to the comparative physiology and psychology of the Saga. The criticism of the last century, which took as literal truth all that was not absolutely miraculous in old literature, had survived far too long among scholars with respect to these epic tales, which from their very style and phrases are as clearly the creations of imagination as the Song of Roland or the ballad of Edom o' Gordon. They treat indeed of real personages, real events, real utterances, but the whole is seen in that golden 'light that never was on sea or land,' in fact, to coin a needful word, *epicised*. There was no Chinese wall between the Icelandic Sagas and the outer Teutonic world, the men that composed them had their heads full of older cycles of story and song, and is it not probable that they would weave much of their old stock of stories or incident here, a personage there, into the prose epics they were making?

1. *Gretti and Beowolf.*

The first instance which we may give of the survival of old Teutonic legend in the Islendinga Sagas is the notable one of the *Grettis Saga*. Here the most famous episode in the whole tale is undeniably an echo of a Beowolf poem or poems. A good farmer is living in a wild part of the country, which is haunted by an evil ghost named Glam, whose power waxes as the sun wanes, and is greatest at Yule-tide. Year after year the franklin's shepherd is killed, he can keep no servants, his cattle are maimed, his house is wrecked, benches torn up, panelling broken, roof-rafters crushed in, the whole place a scene of desolation. When things are at their worst and the poor farmer at his wits' end, Gretti the Strong, who has shown his prowess in many a fight, resolves to go to his help, against the counsel of his friends, who tell him that he is over-bold, that it is no common fiend he will have to overcome. Gretti however sets out, is welcomed, but the farmer has become hopeless, and though he thanks his guest, has not much faith in his success. The first night the ghost is pretty quiet, but the second evening he kills Gretti's horse, and on the third he boldly enters the hall, where the hero is lying on a bench

---

[1] The Islendinga Sagas are those which relate to Icelanders of the Heroic Age. See Prolegomena, §§ 8 and 9.

wrapped in a rug. Gripping the rug the fiend tugs against Gretti till
the coverlet is riven in twain between them, and he stumbles back with
the bit in his hands. The hero springs upon him, and a dreadful
struggle ensues. Up and down the hall they wrestle, every post and
pillar crashing and cracking as they dash against it, while the fearful
franklin is trembling in his cupboard-bed. At last Glam manages to get
Gretti to the porch, but at this supreme moment, for the fiend's power
would be resistless in the open air of the night, Gretti by a trick
contrives to bring down the fiend beneath him. They fall outside, and
as the hero grips his sword to cut off his head, Glam curses him with
haunting and ill-luck to the end of his days, warning him that he will
bring about his death. Gretti, at first horror-struck at his evil look
and words, recovers, and cutting off his head lays it at the corpse's
thigh[1]. · The farmer, over-joyed at his release, thanks Gretti, begifts
him with a horse, and praying him first in vain to abide longer with
him, dismisses him with high honour. Here the haunting, the broken
hall, the wrestling, the farmer's attitude, his gifts are all identical in
poem and tale; the riven coverlet is paralleled by the torn limb of
the fiend; only the curse is a fresh feature, and this may be a trait
of the original legend which our poem has not preserved. It is almost
needed as a thread to bind the whole life of Beowolf together[2].

But we have also the struggle with Grendel's mother in the mere-cave
in a subsequent chapter of the Saga. An ogress haunts at Yule-tide
a farm in the same way as Glam had done; the hero awaits her in
the hall, struggles with her at night, she drags him out of the house
to the edge of the cliff by the waterfall, where her abiding-place is,
but at last he manages to get his right arm free and cut off her right
arm; she looses her hold and falls headlong into the force out of
sight. Here is a certain repetition of the Grendel story. Shortly after
Gretti resolves to search the waterfall; he goes out with a companion
(who watches for his return, but deserts him just as the Danes do
Beowolf when the blood and gore comes up in the mere). Having
dived below the force, he gets into a cave, where he finds a giant,
whom he slays with a thrust of the famous short sword (hefti-sax,
Beowolf's hefti-mæci). He then plunders the cave, finding the bones
of two men, which he brings back with him, and gets back to the
farm. Here are the incidents of the Grendel's dam struggle with little
alteration,—the wound through the bowels, the weapon that inflicted
it, and the cave in the mere. The Saga also gives the very reason
why it localises the story in Bardsdale, viz. that there was a pillar
near the fall there, which was held to be a giantess turned into
stone by the sunlight falling on her ere she could regain her home
in the force.

The story in Gretti we take to be an echo, not of the present diluted
epic, but of the lays from which the epic was later made up. There
must have been such lays—one or two on Grendel and his dam, and one
on the Dragon fight, each, say, some 250 lines.

---

[1] This is the proper way to prevent the ghost from rising again.

[2] The childlessness of Beowolf, his devotion to others, and his Weird, all seem to
require some such explanation; the noteworthy speechlessness of Grendel would also
point to his speaking *once* to terrible effect. We may be allowed to repeat here what
we once said (Reader, p. 705):—' There is a deep tragic scene underlying the story—
Gretti rid the land of the monster, but like many great men, he does so at the cost
of his own happiness. His reward is, that he is a doomed man and an outlaw for
the rest of his life.'

The third part of the Beowolf legend, his Dragon fight, is not in the Saga, but the especial stress laid upon Gretti's prowess as a *strong swimmer* cannot, one would think, be wholly influenced by Beowolf's special glory for his feats of long swimming in the cold stormy sea[1].

The historical Gretti, the great outlaw, is given accurately in the brief lines of Landnama-bok, and especially in the purely native parts of the Gretti's Saga, his escape from hanging, his fellowship with the other outlaws, and his death. That the revenge-part of the end of the Saga is borrowed from a mediæval romance has long been known.

2. *Waterdales' Saga and the Lay of Ælfwine's Youth.*

We have noticed (Introd. § 7) that the story of the good faith of Thuriswend and the daring of Ælfwine is imperfect in the paraphrase of Paul the Deacon, and that the central epic link of the Ælfwine ballads is the revenge of the queen, the kinswoman of the man Ælfwine has slain. We can however supply what is missing from the legend given in the beginning of *Vatzdola Saga*. It runs thus:—

A mountain-path between Sweden and Norway suddenly becomes a pass of death. Travellers who start upon it never reach their goal, and no one knows how they disappear. Ketill the Ream, the chief who lives on the Norwegian side, is blamed for not freeing the road of danger, but he is old, and his son Thorstan is a lazy fellow, who lies at the fire and pays no heed to anything that is going on. "Young men were very different when I was young," the old father breaks out one day. "They used to go warring in their youth, earning riches and glory. You are old enough to be following your noble kinsmen's footsteps, and this is *Warriors' Law*[2], which I would have you to remember, that a young man cannot hold land or fee till he has proved his worth." The boy gets up angrily—"You have egged me enough!"—and goes forth secretly to the pass of death, resolved to meet the hidden peril. He finds in the wood a great desert house, well garnished with meat and drink; he hides till the owner comes in, a huge man, who seeks for the intruder, whom he feels certain is lurking about, but missing him falls asleep. Thorstan now gets up, and drawing a short sword drives it through the sleeping outlaw into the bedstead. The big man wakes with the deadly thrust, seizes the lad, and asks him his name, which Thorstan tells him truly. He then says, "I might slay you, but I give you your life, and I wish you to do as I tell you after my death. I am Iokle, son of Ingimund Earl of Gautland. Go to his hall and tell my mother Wigdis what has happened, and give her this ring as a token, and greet her from me, and bid her set the Earl at peace with you, and give you my sister Thordis in marriage. And if you two have a son, call him after me, that my name perish not utterly." Thorstan promised him to obey his will. Then at his bidding Thorstan plucked the sword out of his breast and he fell back dead. Thorstan sets off at once to Ingimund's hall, gets an interview with Wigdis, and showing

---

[1] In the English Poem of Eger and Grime in the Percy MS. there is an echo of the Beowolf story in the hand of Graysteel, the monster knight of the moor; and that 'noble brand Egeking' mentioned there, which King Fundus got from 'full far beyond the Greekes sea,' may be the last traditional descendant of the hefti-sax.

[2] The technical word for the Court-Law relating to House-carles and Kings' Guests, the Martial Law or Custom to which Ælfwine's father appeals.

her the token tells her the whole truth. "Thou art a bold fellow to come here with this tale. But since Iokle gave thee thy life, thou shalt have it. I will break the story and make thy peace with the Earl." So all falls out as Iokle wished. But there is a curse upon the marriage, springing from the bloodshed that lies between them. The dying man had said that tragic death (or, as Landnama puts it, "death by chance medley") should not cease out of his slayer's race. Here we have the missing links of the Ælfwine story: Ælfwine has been lying lazily at home till his father tells him "the Custom of the Lombards." (The next piece is missing in Paul's paraphrase.) He then must have gone forth secretly and slain in single fight Thurismund son of Thuriswend king of the Gefths. No doubt the dying hero bade him go to his father, ask him for knighthood, and for his sister or kinswoman in marriage. He obeys, and the story goes on as Paul gives it (Introd. § 7). The old father, for love of his dead son, carries out his last request and refrains from following up the blood-feud. The hero weds Rosamund, and to-seeming all goes well, but the curse (which in Paul's original was no doubt foretold in the dying Thurismund's words) after many long years awakes and brings about the tragedy of Ælfwine's death.

The hatred of Rosamund, roused by the sight of the cup made out of her father's skull, brings Ælfwine to an evil death, "to be slain like a coward in his own house." Of course the cup story is purely epic; the one Paul saw was probably one captured by Ælfwine from some Kaan of the Huns. For it was a Hunnish, not Teutonic, custom to make cups from enemies' skulls, as Mr. Howorth has noticed; the classic instance (among many others) being the skull-cup which Crum made out of the Emperor Nicephoros' head in 811. The real events which led to Ælfwine's death we shall never know, tradition has woven a dire tragedy out of it, and linked together his knighthood and his death by the epic motive of the curse of the blood-feud, which no forbearance can stay, and against which, as in Attila's case, not even the most sacred bond can hold[1].

3. Gunnar and Egil the Archer.

Our third instance of transferred tradition is from *Niala*.

A lady of Irish descent, of great beauty, with wonderful golden hair, but of evil nature, "with thief's eyes," marries in succession three husbands, each of whom in turn she provokes, by her elfish wickedness, to slap her in the face, and the blow in each case leads to her husband's death. But the tale of the death of the third husband Gunnar is to be carefully considered. He is beset by his foes in his house, but keeps them at bay with his unerring arrows, till one of them creeps up and cuts his bowstring. He turns round and begs his wife for a lock of her hair to replace the severed string. "Does your life lie on your getting a fresh bowstring?" says she with cruel mockery. "Of a truth it does." "Then die! You mind the slap on the face you gave me, I will repay you now." In vain the hero's old mother curses the

---

[1] The Frodi-peace, which is given to Eadgar among English kings, to Rollo of the Norman earls, etc., is ascribed by Paul to Ælfwine. For excellent examples of the mutation of myths from person to person, see Mr. Steenstrup's *Normannerne*, with regard to the stratagems of taking towns by birds carrying fire and by pretended burial-parties.

bad wife, she persists in her refusal, and Gunnar's foes, dreading his arrows no more, break in upon him and slay him at his wife's feet. Now this story is plainly legendary. Gunnar's real weapon was his famous bill, and though the real Hallgerd was married thrice, we may be quite sure that it was not because her husbands slapped her face.

In reading lately Professor Rhŷs' pretty little collection of Welsh fairy-tales on the Melusine or Lady of the Lake theme, the Editor was struck by the coincidence of the fairy water-maiden with long hair and tricksy disposition. She comes out of the lake and marries a Welsh gentleman, and brings him riches and luck, but she must not be struck. Her wayward humour and accident bring it so about that her husband strikes her with cold iron, whereon she gathers the beautiful water-cows of her dowry and goes back to the lake for ever. Her descendants, a famous family of Doctors, still survive. Here we have the skeleton of a legend which has clearly attached itself to Hallgerd. In the tragic death of Gunnar it would seem that we have the lost legend of Egil the archer and Alrune the daughter of Caer, the fairy bride whom he won from the lake, the second part of the trilogy of which we have one fragment in Weyland's Lay. On Mr. Franks' casket we see the death scene, the foemen besetting the house, the hero in the loft shooting, the woman spinning by his side [just as Gunnar in Niala]. How Egil outwits the king by his skill (parallel to Weyland's revenge on Nidad) we have in the Palnatoki (Tell) story. The story of Weyland's death, brought about no doubt by his fairy-wife too, we have not yet been able to trace; nor the story of the third brother Slag-Finn (whom we from the surname 'slag' take to be the *harper-hero*), unless the tragedy of Glas-Gerion be a last echo of the tale of his death, and the Magic Fiddler of Grimm's Märchen the legend of his outwitting the king. There is a foreign cast (Celtic we believe) about all the three stories[1].

4. Gunlaug and Waltharii Poema.

Again, in *Gunlaug's Saga* there is a legendary element which the Editor believes may be traced back, in part at least, to a scene in the Waldhere cycle. An Icelandic franklin, whose wife is with child, has a dream in which he sees a fair white swan on his house ridge. An eagle flies down to her and caresses her, but their love is broken upon by another eagle with whom the first one fights, till the two fierce birds have torn each other to death and fall lifeless together from the roof to earth. The swan sits disconsolate and forlorn till a little hawk flies up and wins her over to fly away with him. This dream is read as a prophecy of ill to the coming child, who, according to it, proves a girl. The franklin determines to expose the babe. She however is saved, grows up of wondrous beauty, and one day is made known to her father, who, seeing that fate is not to be fought against, takes her home to him. The rest of the dream is fulfilled: the first eagle is the true lover Gunlaug, who is tricked out of his wife by the second eagle Raven; they fight for her, and after a fruitless judicial duel in Iceland (an historic event) adjourn to Norway. Here the two rivals meet and

---

[1] The whole legend might be represented thus:—

The opening.	The brothers' deeds.	The curse works.
Capture of the Swan-maidens by three brothers.	Weyland outwits Nidad.	Weyland betrayed by (?).
	Egil „ a king.	Egil betrayed by his wife.
	Finn „ a king.	Finn betrayed by his servant.

fight again. Gunlaug wounds Raven's leg severely, but Raven wishes to go on with the fight; "If only I could get a draught of water I could fight on merrily." "I will get thee thy desire, if thou wilt not betray me," answers Gunlaug, and accordingly fetches his wounded foe the water in his own helmet. But Raven, despairing of success, cannot withstand the opportunity, and he treacherously smites his adversary a deadly blow on his defenceless head. "Thou hast betrayed me!" "I could not bear to think that Helga the Fair should lie in thine arms." So both the eagles fall, but Helga weds a third husband, and pines to death.

The unhistorical character of Gunlaug's Saga and the small foundation of fact which Landnama supplies have been noted (Introd. § 8, vol. i); but compare the last deadly duel with the final unfinished scene in the tenth-century Waltharius' legend, told in the Novalician Chronicle. Here Waldhere has carried off Hildegund from Attila's court; he is pursued by twelve champions headed by Hagan his old brother-in-arms. He turns upon his pursuers and discomfits them all save Hagan, and lies down to rest, but is awakened by the lady. "Hagan is upon thee!" "Him alone I fear, for he is my old comrade and knows all my feats of fence." They fight, and Hagan, exhausted, spies a keg of wine at the saddle-bow of Waldhere's horse[1]. Here the good monk, whose autograph we have, breaks off in the middle of his page and the rest of the story is lost. But can we not supply the end? Hagan prays for a drink, Waldhere gives it to him; Hagan, betraying the trust of his rival, smites him a deadly blow, but not before Waldhere has scarred him for ever by a stroke that puts out or blinds his right eye. True, the later Wilkina Saga (thirteenth century), founded on Saxon Lays, makes a comic incident of the loss of Hagan's eye, which Waldhere destroys by a blow of the flitch. The death of Waldhere by Gaudefer (a *Southern* Romance form of Waldfrid) is in Wilkina Saga obviously imaginary, and merely put in to finish off a prominent person who must be got rid of. The English fragment of a Waldhere Lay and the allusions to the story in the later German mediæval poems do not explain the story, nor tell of Waldhere's death. The 'moiniage' of a Waldhere in the other part of the Chronicle has in reality no connection with the Waldhere Saga.

5. *Laxdola and the Lays of Brunhild and Hamtheow, etc.*

In the *Laxdola Saga* we have historic personages shining with a light borrowed from the Sigfred story. Gudrun, whose pedigree and kindred are given from Landnama-bok (ii. ch. 17), married Thorrod, by whom she had two children; she married again Bolli Thorlac's son, by whom she had six children before he was slain by Kiartan Olatsson's brother, in revenge for Kiartan, who had been murdered by Gudrun's brethren a short time before. . Gudrun now married a third time, had two children, and one of her sons, Gelli, was born 1008, as the Editor pointed out in the Tima-tal (1855). So far the facts, which will not admit of being reconciled with the Saga; for we must allow two years at least between

---

[1] 'Occisis cunctis præter Regem [Gundharium] et Haganonem . . . contra quos ilico Waltharius quasi leo insurgens, armis protectus fortiter debellabat bellantibus sibi. Qui diu multumque inuicem pugnantes, ac præ nimia lassitudine et siti deficientes iam non ualebant uirorum fortissimum superare. Et ecce respicientes uiderunt a sagma Waltharii uasculum uini dependere.'—*Chron. Novaliciense*, lib. ii.

Gelli's birth and the death of Bolli, and six children who lived would, according to ordinary statistics, give ten years for the years of the second marriage. So that Kiartan could *not* have loved her as a single woman or as a widow during Tryggwason's reign (995–1000), and all the scenes abroad must be purely epic. The real facts have no doubt been epicised under the influence of some old Sigfred Lays. Kiartan is the blameless Sigfred, Bolli is Gundhere, the anger of Gudrun is exactly like that of Brunhild, the revenge and all the rest are parallel. There is also a purely unhistorical scene, when Gudrun, like her namesake in Hamtheow Lay, eggs on her sons to revenge Bolli, an evident echo of that old Lay. The Dream of Gudrun, as to her four husbands' fate, is a parallel to the Dream of a Lay in the Lacuna (which we have translated in the Appendix to vol. i, p. 392), and may even be borrowed from a parallel lost Lay, which the Wolsunga Compiler has not put in. The words of the Treg-rof, 'the hardest woe, the cruellest woe,' etc., are even paralleled in the fine dialogue between Gudrun and her young and best-loved son Bolli, where the famous phrase

' I treated him the worst I loved the most '

is far more poetic than the poetry from which it is borrowed. The passages of Laxdola referred to will be found in the Reader, pp. 43 and 81.

The scene in the Northern version of *Eiric the Red's Saga*, in which the virago Freydis snatches up a sword and dashes among the frightened Eskimo, reminds one of the view taken of Gudrun in the Atla-mal, ll. 164–172, and of the fierce Amazon Chriemhilt of the later German poem.

The Flyting scenes of Skarphedin in *Niala*, chaps. 120–124, are obviously an echo of ancient lays, in which these rough word-contests were favourite topics; e.g. the scenes in Helgi and Sigrun, and the Ælfwine Lay, in which some of the images are the very same.

The Dream-story of *Gisli's Saga* (as is pointed out on p. 336) is clearly an echo and imitation of an old poem, perhaps the lost Lay of Cara and Helgi.—Indeed the whole of the Islendinga Sagas should be carefully searched for such imitations and reflexions of the old Teutonic Heroic cycles. The bigger complex Sagas, which we have carefully examined, nearly all, as we have shown, bear evident traces of the existence of the old Teutonic traditions down to the time when the Sagas were put together.

The Latin Chronicles and the French Romances will also be found, when minutely searched, to contain many an incident which is derived from some of our old epic cycles. Thus in the first chapters of *Widukind of Corbey's* History of the Saxons there is a very full paraphrase of the story of Gizur Greotingalidi, 'who set the kings at odds.' Widukind's Iring replaces Gizur, and there are minor details which, as we should expect, differ (a wicked queen is brought in), but the main plot is exactly the same. The story is plainly unhistorical, an epic accretion which has grown round Theodric the Frank. Very likely, if we knew the poems that were sung in Ælfwine's hall, we should find some whose incidents were afterwards transferred to him. We cannot always, as is the case of Gudrun and Charlemagne, get behind the scenes and see how a History becomes an Epic.

A curious instance of a phenomenon, met with once or twice in *Saxo*, the same myth told of different heroes, is the parallelism of the Northern Biarka-mál and the Old English *Fin's Lay;* the fragments that survive of each running absolutely side by side.

There is in Deor's Woe a fragment of the Hiarrand cycle and a mention of Weyland's Nidad, and Widsith's Wanderings is a conspectus of the poems and heroic legends known to the author, amongst others that of Ælfwine. Some others of the Old English Poems also contain passages which run parallel to our Lays (see Introd. vol. i, § 7).

It may be worth while, in conclusion, to clearly disclaim holding any such theory as that of Finn Magnusen, that the Islendinga Sagas are derived from ballads or poems. It is by no means so in our opinion, What we hold is, that the Sagas are to be looked on as Epics, founded on fact, not as exact Histories: that in certain cases the historic nucleus has gathered round it old traditions, which have completely obscured and overshadowed the scant facts upon which they are strung. Some of these cases we have pointed out. It is very necessary, both from a literary [1] and from an historical point of view, that the true position of the Islendinga Sagas should be definitely ascertained, and as this question was intimately associated with other weighty questions referring to the poems of these volumes, we have thought it right to deal briefly with it here.

---

[1] That admirable and philosophic study of the *Saga-style* by Dr. R. Heinzel (Beschreibung der Isländischen Saga, Wien, 1880) should convince the most hardened patriot that the Sagas are not *literally* true. Niels Mathias Petersen, the Danish historian and Rask's friend, held a similar opinion, and used to tell me that the Sagas were 'Dichtung und Wahrheit,' Facts and Fancy woven together.—*The Editor.*

EXCURSUS IV.

THE CREATION-MYTH AND THE NORTHERN GENEALOGIES IN HYNDLA'S LAY, ETC.

It has always been a matter of puzzlement to the Editor, after reading the famous passage of the Germania in which Tacitus gives what he tells us was the very soul and essence of the Teutonic religion of his day, the divine origin of the pure German race, or after perusing the pedigree of Ermanaric in Jordanis, and the account of the way in which the Anses were linked by ancestral tie to the heroes of his history—to turn to the Eddic poems and find there so little answering to the old beliefs and songs of Tacitus' or even Jordanis' day, with reference to those ideas which lie at the core of our ancestors' religion— the origin of man, the faith that they are Heaven's chosen sons, a god-born race, like Homer's warriors and kings.

Yet, if we put aside the later poetical fancies that cluster round Walhall, Ygg-drasil, Doomsday, and are so attractive to the modern imagination, and look deeper for the older substratum of granite thought, we shall find it by no means inadequately set forth in two notable poems, the *Lay of Righ* and *Hyndla's Lay*. The importance of the first, which has hitherto been too lightly treated as a mere playful poet's dream, we have noted; the second however, mangled and misjointed as it is, must be our main authority. We have given it in vol. i. in its due chronological rank, with such mending and re-construction as we at first thought sufficient to show the reader some-thing of its true purport; but there is need of a more radical treat-ment, if its true scope and import are to be fully brought out, and this we must attempt here in connection with the very problem which the Lay is to help us to solve. Thus the right placing and under-standing of the lines on Heimdal is most vital and in reality the key to the right intent and scheme of the whole poem. Luckily we have the assistance of a (twelfth-century?) paraphrase of the genealogical part of the Lay (in Flatey-bok i. pp. 24, 25) from a fuller and better text than that which Flatey-bok supplies[1].

Before turning to the Lay of Hyndla it may be well to note that in the first passage from Tacitus we take *Tuisconem* to be the right reading; almost all the MSS. have *sc* or *st* (*t* and *c* being the commonest of

---

[1] That it is a paraphrase is indeed (though not stated) obvious from the wording, falling in places (as in Halfdane's marriage) literally in with our poem. The story in Snorri's Edda on Halfdane the Old is again manifestly merely an abridgment of our paraphrase, the date of which is thus thrown back to the twelfth century, most likely its earliest part, when the poem was still entire in men's memory.

confusions), and the archetypus no doubt read Tuisc. In Ulfila's and probably in Tacitus' days our Týr (Δίος, divus, divas) would have been nom. Tius, gen. Tiwis, whence the regularly formed adjective Tiwi-sc-s, Tacitus' Tuisco-, which in sense and use exactly answers to the 'Týs áttungr' of our poems. The word or the passage in Tacitus can never have been Theutonem, or Teutonem, etc. For, though Isidore (five hundred years after Tacitus) says that Spaniards and Gauls of his day call Germans Teutones, this use, we take for granted, was not so old as Tacitus; it only arose after the small German tribes had linked themselves together into leagues, Franks, Saxons, Wandils, and the like, against the common danger, the Romans in front and the Sclavs and Huns behind. In Tacitus' days, Thiudans would mean a king as it does in Ulfila and old English poetry. Besides, the context requires, not a mere eponym, but a significant word, pointing to the descent of the race from a God (Heaven) and Mother Earth, 'Mammun Ertham,' i.e. Terram Matrem, as we take Tacitus to have written (in accordance with Holder's and Holzman's view).

Now, turning back to our Lay of Hyndla, and its prose paraphrase— The paraphrast leaves out (1) the framework, or setting of the whole poem, and all that refers to Othere's claims, (2) the part touching Heimdal the god, and the links between him and Halfdane the Old: and on the other hand he extends the pedigrees, by drawing them all to Harald Fairhair, adding links which we have tried to weed out and mark off by []. To him Scandinavia is the cradle of all the royal heroic races of the οἰκουμένη, and he divides them into three groups: (a) the home-kings, Danish, Swedish, Norwegian; (b) the sea-kings, conquerors and colonists by sea; (c) the conquering kings of foreign lands, Saxony, Gaul, Hunland, whom he also draws from the Scandinavian stock—from Heimdal and Halfdane. This is the attitude of a Western man to whom the Teutoni-Celtic world is practically one.

As for the poem itself it may be analysed into—

1. Frame (Introduction and End): 'Flá estu Freyia, etc.' must be transferred to the end, Freyia having evidently said something to rouse the ogress' anger, as in the Doom.

2. The section on Heimdal, displaced in Fb. text: 'Vard einn borinn, etc.' is given twice over, 'Sifjaðan siotom gorvollom' (the gossip to all tribes) manifestly referring to Heimdal as Sire of gods and men. The links between Heimdal and Halfdane are lost, but from Half-dane one may guess Dane to have been one and perhaps Righ another, three would be quite sufficient (Righ, Dane, Halfdane).

3. The last section on Halfdane and his sons, which is the central part of the whole, is duly preserved in the paraphrast.

Halfdane the Old makes a sacrifice, begging the gods that a life of three generations may be granted him, but gets for answer, that a life of but one generation shall be vouchsafed to him, but that for three generations no one less than a king or earl shall spring from him, and no woman shall till then be born in his race.—Here we see the poet's hand. Unfortunately the Flatey-bok text leaves out these lines, remembering only the fragment on Halfdane's marriage.

This part seems to have been divided into three pieces: (a) Halfdane's two nines of sons, the first nine, dying in battle, childless, mere archaic names for kings, Iofur, Stillir, etc. (as one sees from the pedigree in Snorri's Edda); the second nine, founders of royal lines, ranked in three groups of three. (b) Great ladies, heroines of the past, descended from Halfdane—a very fragmentary morsel. There would have been always three generations of kings, and *no* ladies till, according to the oracle, the queens appear in the fourth and following generations. (*c*) Othere's own special pedigree, also very fragmentary[1].

According to this scheme the poem is to be *restored*, keeping continually in sight the better preserved morsels of the paraphrase, which again and again give help in interpreting and correcting and restoring or putting aright, like the potsherds of a broken vessel, the mutilated lines of the poem, which stands to the paraphrase as a B to an A text. So, for instance, it may be seen that ' Ali vas adr' comes from the *Day section;* 'þo war Frodi fyrr enn Kari' must be inserted in the *Audi section;* under 'hinn ellri war' lies 'Alrunar,' Cear's daughter (of the Weyland cycle). The lines on Haki, too, we can identify in the paraphrase; it is not a part of the Sibyl Songs (as we once thought), and so on.

There is much missing, perhaps the greater part; but the plan is clear; and it is a happy chance that what the poem gives best the paraphrast ignores or omits, and on the other hand, what the paraphrast preserves the poem has lost; the paraphrast cared but for the history, the poetical dress he discarded; the only really mournful loss is that of the Halfdane-Heimdal links. This is a more antique poem than Righ's Lay, more *aristocratic* in tone; the Lay of Righ is more democratic (and surely the later of the two). Righ is father of earl, churl, and thrall equally, and all men are in one sense brothers, though not peers; but Hyndla's Lay only concerns itself with nobles and gentlefolk, kings, earls, lords (hersar), and gentlemen (holdar, hold = hæled); the rest of mankind are beneath and beyond its notice, *turans* and *monkey-men* as the proud Eastern Aryans would have called them.

Both this Lay and Righ's are the latest descendants of those old *carmina* of which Tacitus had heard. Every Teutonic tribe, of course, had its own version of the subject, endless variation of the same *motive*, with its own *Anses* and heroes. No matter which version we take— Erdha, Tius, Mannus (Tacitus)—Gaut, Heimdal, Righ (Jordanis)— Heimdal [Dane], Halfdane (Hyndla-poet)—Heimdal, Righ, Kon (Righ Lay)—Odin, Niord, Yngwi-Frey (Ynglings)—Odin, Skiold, Frid-leif (Skioldungs), etc.—all are really one in character and meaning: Heaven and Earth, and the gods and the heroes sprung from them (the Anses), are the 'ultima fons et origo' of each tribe, of each pureblooded Teuton freeman. The *Anses,* deified heroes in the later links, are the 'sanctum divorum collegium,' 'gumnar goðom signaðir,' 'numero deorum recepti, collegio deorum ascripti,' as the good Adam repeats King Eric's phrases. When the old Northern poets speak of 'Ty's áttungr,' 'Freys áttungr,' 'Yngwa ætt-stafr,' and the like, they are alluding to this well-known and deep-set heathen belief,—one so human and so true, that Paul, far from refuting it, eagerly seized on it as a link between the New Tidings and the Old Faith. And have not we Teutons also, in the authors of these two Lays, 'certain poets of our own,' who, like Aratæus, witness that 'we too are His offspring?'

So also when Woden is called by our poets Al-fodr, Wal-fodr, Wera-Tyr, Aldin-Gautr, and by other such titles, or where Thunder is spoken of as Earth's Son, or even Sif's Goodman, the same beliefs are, we take it, witnessed to. We have a last echo of them in the Old English phrase 'Adam's grandmother' for Earth.

---

[1] We have transposed this piece; in the paraphrase it stands foremost, before Halfdane and his Nine Sons.

The LANGFEDGA-TAL or Generations[1] are artificially built up out of this basis of the divine origin of heroes and gods. Thus in the *Ynglinga* generation the first names, Woden, Niord, Yngwi-Frey, were held to be the Anses of the Swedish kings' race long ere Thiodwolf composed his poem. He may have worked upon an Old English model, the Pedigree of Ecgberht or Ethelwolf. His genealogic poem again was the model in form and style for many others; the *Haleygia* generation, with its Sæming (son of Saomi, the Finn which would seem to speak to a mixture of blood in the great Earl race), is the best known. There was, we might guess, a *Skioldunga* generation on the same model; the names down to Cnut the Great are just the right number, thirty; see Hauks-bok, AM. 415, and the early leaves of Flatey-bok.

The *Orkney Earls* have a genealogy made out for them, the early names of which are those of physical and metaphysical entities—the Elements (Fire, Wind), the Months (Thorri, Goi), and etymological inventions such as 'Nór,' an imaginary hero from which the name Nóregr is derived. This etymology, Nór's way, points to a date when the 'ð' of 'Norð-wegr' was lost, and perhaps the 'w' becoming vocalised, yet so that the meaning of 'way' still survived, while that of 'North' was gone. The long vowel in Nóregr is the compensation for the loss of the 'ð' and 'w'—Norð-wegr, Nór-wegr, Nóregr. The 'ð' was lost as early as the tenth century, as the Jellinge-stone (see Reader, p. 443, no. 8) shows; the 'w' probably vanished in the eleventh century, so that we have pretty certain proof of the lateness of this Orkney genealogy, even if the Story of the Tarbet did not fix its fabrication to the days of Magnus Barefoot.

There are two genealogies given for the *Dublin Kings:* one (Laxdola) taking them up to the Skioldungs and connecting them with the Danish kings; the other (Ari in Libellus) linking them with the Ynglings. It would almost seem as if Ari at different times in his life had had varying information through song or tradition, and had given both, once in his *Liber* whence Laxdola draws, the other in his later *Libellus*[2].

With regard to the Upsala Kings' generation it is necessary to walk circumspectly, as the road is full of pit-falls. The Ynglinga Saga makes the true Ynglings to have been driven by Ingwar Wide-fathom from Upsala to Norway, where alone they were to be found[3], and Hervarar Saga mentions also a further conquest by the Sons of Ragnar[4]. Here we have Norwegian and Danish views. The proud Swedish kings would never have accepted such traditions, or acquiesced in an inferior position to their younger neighbours. But in the Fridgerd Story (an episode now of St. Olaf's Life, dramatised in Snorri's finest vein) we hit upon the true old Swedish version of their pedigree, taken from some lost bit of Ari, one would think. Says the Swedish king: "I am the tenth Upsala king, every one of whom hath taken the realm after his kins-

---

[1] We use 'generations' in the sense of Matt. i. 1 in the Authorised Version: it answers to Icelandic 'langfeðga-tal,' to which else there is no good equivalent in English.

[2] The Laxdola pedigree as it stands is plainly wrong somehow; see II. Skioldungs.

[3] 'Eptir Ingialld Illrada hvarf Uppsala veldi or ætt Ynglinga, þat er Langfeðgum mætti telja.'—*Yngl. S.* ch. 45.

[4] 'þeir synir Ragnars konungs lögðu þá undir sik Swia-weldi, en eptir dauða Ragnars konungs tók Biorn sonr hans Iarnsíða Swia-weldi.'—*Hervarar Saga.* And from Biorn the present race is derived! The list in Hervarar Saga is wholly worthless, only Eric the Victorious and perhaps his father and grandfather are really historical persons. See Thorgny's speech in the Reader, p. 178.

man, and hath been sole lord of the Swedish realm and many other mighty lands, and hath been suzerain of all other kings in the Northern Lands[1]." And further on, speaking of his daughter's birth, he boasts that "she is of kingly birth in every branch of the race of the Up-Swedes, which is the most worshipful in all the Northern lands, for this race is sprung from the gods themselves[2]."

A king of Norway—again says the Swede—is far below the king of Sweden, which he thus proceeds to prove in grand logical style. "Blue-tooth slew Grayfell when he ventured to rise against him, and my uncle Styr-biorn beat and overcame Blue-tooth; yet my father King Eric overcame Styr-biorn and slew him when he rebelled against him[3]." All which is in direct contradiction to the Norwegian theories of Ynglinga-tal.

We take the 'ten kings' to be the intervening links—Anses, heroes, and men—between the Swedish king Olaf and his divine ancestor Frey; Jordanis has just as many steps from Ermanric to the God. The Swedish king in poetry is called 'Týs áttungr' and 'Freys áttungr,' 'son of the God' and 'son of the Lord.' What were the first steps down from the gods? Not improbably, if one might guess, the per-sonifications which Theodwolf has borrowed for the early part of his poem—Dom-here [the Judge], Dom-waldi [the Justiciar], Wís-bur [the Priest],—names suitable to the most legal and priestly of all Northern kings, the guardians of the greatest Treasury and Temple of the whole of Scandinavia[4].

Men have laughed—as indeed Snorri's fine irony incites one to do—at the proud vaunting of the Swede; but we must sympathise with him too; he was of an old stock and a good stock, and, just as Mr. Carlyle says that Henry of Anjou felt big with something great he knew not what—American colonies, Indian empires, British commerce and constitutions, so we may say of Olaf that he too felt big with future glories—King Göstaf the Liberator, Gustavus Adolphus, Charles XII, Linnæus, etc. Cnut's mighty empire has long ago passed like a dream of the morning, but without Gustavus, the true avenger of Widukind, freedom and science and letters would have been swept out of Germany, and the labours of lesser and later statesmen could never have been begun.

We may be very sure that the lost pedigree of the Up-Swedes was no

---

[1] því at ek em enn tiundi konungr at Uppsölum, sva at hverr hefir eptir annan tekit várra frænda, ok verit einvaldz konungr yfir Svia-veldi, ok mörgum öðrum stórum löndum, ok verit allir yfir konungar annarra konunga á Norðr-löndum.—*S. Ol. S.* ch. 54.

[2] Er hon konung-borin í allar kvíslir of Upp-Svia ætt, er tignust er á Norðr-löndum, því at su ætt er komin frá goðunum sialfum.—*S. Ol. S.* ch. 54.

[3] Gunnhildar synir vóro af lífi teknir þegar er þeir görðuz úhlýðnir Dana konungi, lagði þá Haraldr Gorms son Noreg við sitt ríki ok skatt-gildi, ok þótti oss þó Haraldr konungr Gormsson vera minni fyrir ser en Uppsala konungar, því at Styrbiorn frændi várr kúgaði hann, ok görðiz Haraldr hans maðr, enn Eirikr inn Sigrsæli faðir mínn steig þó yfir hofuð Styrbirni þá er þeir reyndu sín á milli.—*S. Ol. S.* ch. 71 (*Kr.*)

[4] In Beowolf are pedigrees of the *Scylfings* of Sweden (from Scylf through (?) Angantheow, Ohthere, to Eadgils); of the *Scyldings* of Denmark (from Sceaf through Scyld, Beowolf, Healf-dene, Hálga, to Hrodwolf [Hrólf Craci]); of the *Weder-Geatas* of Gaut-land (from Swerting through Hreðel, Hygelac, to Heardred); of the *Angles* (through Garmund or Wærmund, Offa, to Eomær); of the *Heath-Bards* or *Wickings* (Froda, Ingeld); of the *Wolsungs* (Wæls, Sigemund, Fitela); besides notices of the *Wolfings, Mere-Wioings, Healmings, Folcwaldings* of Friesland, and *Brondings.* Widsith, too, gives some of the names that occur in Beowolf and Hyndla's Lay.

mean one, and certainly it has been worthily vindicated by the royal line of Sweden.

To this brief Excursus we subjoin the etymology of Edda and Anses.

THE WORD EDDA.

THE first point to settle is, how this word came into the Lay of Righ; no solution, which does not account for this part of the problem, can be correct. The poet makes *Edda* the ultimate ancestress, grandmother, first mother, from whom, by Righ, the earliest race of mankind sprung. Tacitus tells us how the old poems of the Germans of his day make ' Terra mater ' the mother of ' Tuiscon,' whose son is ' Man.' And he gives the German name of Terra Mater—Mammun Ertham. Here, between the *Ertha* of Tacitus and the *Edda* of the Lay, there is a twofold identity, viz. the common *notion* of MOTHER, and the *resemblance* of both words in form and sound. In the days of the Righ Lay, the Low German form of earth would still have been ' Ertha,' as in Tacitus' time, while the High German (even Frankish?) would be ' Erda ;' the Old English ' Eorthe ' weakened ; the Old Northern ' Eorth ' monosyllabic. Both words Earth and Edda are, we take it, etymologically identical, Edda being a poet's adaptation of the foreign bisyllabic form, by him aptly designed as great-grandmother. The High German form meets all requirements. According to the regular Northern formula, ' zd ' becomes ' dd ' (thus the old ' hozd-' becomes ' hodd-,' the old ' hazd-' becomes ' hadd-,' and so on). The Old Northern tongue had no *rd*, only *rth;* the nearest sound to a German or foreign *rd* would thus in fact be the assimilated *dd.*

It is not hard to fancy how it came about. Let us suppose that a western man has learnt a snatch of a High German song on that favourite subject with all Teutons, the *Origin of Mankind* and *Mother Earth,* from a Southern trader or comrade (there were Germans and Southlings in Orkney and Scandinavia in the tenth and eleventh centuries as we know from history and Saga). In this song the word ' Erda ' (or *Grandmother Erda*[1]) occurs ; he puts it into his own tongue as neatly as he can, and the result is ' Edda.' Or, if he himself did not make the change, the minstrel would have done so, who sung it after him, for the Lay had passed through many Northern mouths before it got written down in our Codex. There are other foreign words half understood, half unchanged in the poem, such as Righ, in which the notion of the Celtic ' ri ' is intermingled with the Old Teutonic hero-god, Jordanis' ' Rigis.' And even ' afi' and ' amma ' are loan words ; ' ai,' too, is the vocalised High German ' ano' (whence Modern German ahnen, ancestry).

From the Lay of Righ the word Edda passed into that curious List of Synonyms, ' okend heiti,' which is the base of the Thulor Collections and of Poetic Gradus, such as Snorri's. Thus the name got applied to Snorri's book ; for it is probable, though not absolutely demonstrable, that this older draught of Scaldscapar-mal was *headed* by our Lay of Righ, being in all likelihood called forth by that very Lay. From it the text in Cod. W is derived, for the List of Synonyms, at the end of the MS. of Snorri's unfinished work, contains the words ' móðir heitir, ok amma, þriðja, Edda.' Hence it follows that the author knew the Lay.

From Snorri's work, as we have elsewhere shown, the word came into general use as expressing the very spirit and essence of the Court-poetry with all its intricate synonyms and figures. Thence, by false and misleading application of the scholars

---

[1] An A. S. poet, as noticed above, calls Earth Adam's *grandmother*, in fact, his *Edda*.

of the Icelandic revival, it got transferred to the old heroic epic Lays, the 'Eddic' poems of our first volume.—The word has had a strange history.

In Wolospa, as we should expect, there is another version of the myth of the Creation. Three gods wandering like Righ on earth, breathe life into two stocks, 'Ask' and 'Embla,' Ash and Elm [Emla for Elma]. In the initials of these two stocks it must be more than a coincidence to find the initials of 'Adam' and 'Eve[1].' The Sibyl-poet treats the subject in his own half-mystical, philosophic, semi-Christian way, and has managed by the force of his genius to impress it on his hearers, so that this late and wholly individual conception has swallowed up, in the minds of modern readers and commentators, the old primæval and popular version which we have endeavoured to bring to light again in these pages.

THE WORD ANSE.

Disguised in its Northern form, owing to the vocalisation of *n* before *s* [as in gás, Gans, Greek χην-]; hence the forms áss, æsi, æsir, ásu; it is a u-stem; its Gothic form would be ansus. The Northern vocalised form has been very mischievous, for from Ari down to a quite recent date it was the fashion to derive it from Asia, the gods having immigrated to the North from the far East. In our days the *ns* root has demolished that etymology. Throughout the Teutonic world, ancient and new, it is frequent enough as a prefix to proper names, e. g. Anscar (in A. S. even in Bede's time the *an-* is vocalised and the vowel rounded into *o*, Osfrid, Osred, Osric, Os-thryd, Oswald, Oswini, Oswulf), but as an appellative it is, excepting Jordanis' famous passage, not found outside Scandinavia. What then is the true etymon of Anses? We have tried to show that it means *ghost, ancestral spirit* of such kind as the Di manes of the Romans. This leads one to the etymology from the root AN, to breathe, whence an-i-m-us, ἄνεμος, an-d-a, as well as, we should say, an-s-u-s, the word thus simply meaning *spirit*. Whether the German *ano*, *ahnen* (ancestors), be related to it we leave undecided.

One wonders not to find a household word like this in Tacitus' Germania; but is it not there after all? In ch. 43 we read—'Apud Nahanarvalos antiquae religionis lucus ostenditur; praesidet sacerdos muliebri ornatu; sed deos interpretatione Romanâ Castorem Pollucemque memorant; ea vis numini, *nomen Alcis;* nulla simulacra; nullum peregrinae superstitionis vestigium; ut fratres tamen, ut juvenes venerantur.' Is not Tacitus here speaking of the *Anses*-worship of the Germans, and is not *Ansis* (not Alcis) the word? Munch has indeed suggested as much. The Germania has come down in a single MS., a now lost archetype of the eighth or ninth century, written therefore seven or eight hundred years after Tacitus, and, however good this copy may have been, yet in so long a time, a slip between cup and lip is not to be wondered at.

I. THE LAY OF HYNDLA.

Reconstructed from the Paraphrase (A) and the Text in Fl. (B).

Introduction.

[*Freyja q.:*]

VAKI mær meyja! vaki mín vina!
  Hyndla systir es í helli býr!
Nú es rœkkr rœkkra; ríða við skolom
til Valhallar ok til véss heilags.

Biðjom Herja-föður í hugom sitja;
hann geldr ok gefr goll verðungo:
gaf hann Hermóði hialm ok brynjo,
enn Sigmundi sverð at þiggja:
gefr hann sigr sonom, enn sinnom aura,

---

[1] The expression 'son of Adam,' derived probably from the Hebrew through the Latin, is common enough in the Irish poems, as a synonym for 'human being.'

mælsko mögom, en man-vit firom;
byri gefr hann brögnom; enn brag
  skaldom;
gefr hann mansemi mörgom rekki.
Þór mun-ek blóta; þess mun-ek biðja,
at hann æ við þik einart láti.
Þó es hónom ótítt við Iötuns brúðir.
Nú taktú ulf þín ein af stalli;
lát hann renna með rúna mínom.
'Seinn es' göltr mínn Goðveg troða;
vil-ek á mar þínn mætan hlœða.
Sennom við or söðlom! sitja við skolom,
ok um iöfra ættir dœma:
gunna þeirra es frá goðom kvómo.
Þeir hafa veðjat Vala-malmi
Óttarr inn ungi ok Angantýr.
Skyllt es at veita, sva-at skati enn ungi,
föður-leifð hafi eptir frændr sína:
Hörg hann mer gœrði hlaðinn steinom;
nú es griót þat at gleri orðit;
rauð hann í nýjo nauta-blóði;
æ trúði Óttarr á Ásynjor.
  Nú láttu forna niðja talða,
ok upp bornar ættir manna:—
Hvat es Skiöldunga? Hvat es Skilfinga?
[Hvat es Öðlinga]? Hvat es Ylfinga?
Hvat es hölð-borit? Hvat es hers-borit—
mest manna-val und Miðgarði?

Genealogies.
  Hyndla:
Varð einn borinn í árdaga
ragna reinar ramm-aukinn mögr
nio báro þann nadd-gofgan mann
Iötna meyjar við iarðar þröm:
Hann Gialp um bar, hann Greip um bar,
hann bar Eistla ok Eirgiafa,
hann bar Ulfrún ok Angeyja,
Imðr ok Atla ok Iarn-saxa:
Sá vas aukinn Iarðar megni
sval-köldom sæ ok Sónar dreyra.
þann kveða stilli stórúðgastan
s . . . sifjaðan siótom gœrvöllom:
Mart segjom þer ok munom fleira:
Vorömk at viti svá: viltu enn lengra?
  [*Here are lost the links between Heim-*
dal and Ha!fdane, upon which the poet
proceeds to Halfdane and his nine sons.]

Halfdan fyrri hæstr Skiöldunga;
fræg vóro fólk-víg þau es frama[1] gœrðo,
hvarfla þótti hans verk með himin-
  skautom.
Eflðisk hann við Eymund iöfur Austmanna[2]
enn drap Sigtrygg svölom eggjom
eiga gekk Alvigo[3] œzta kvinna,
ólo þau ok átto áttián sono:
. . . .[4]
Alla senn borna arfa, nio[5]:
þengill, Gramr, Gylfi, Ræsir,
Hilmir, Iöfurr, Tiggi, Harri, Skyli
Engi þeirra . . . börn . .
fello allir senn í orrosto.
  Enn átto þau aðra sono,
héto, Hildir ok Auði, Hnefill ok Skelfir,
Buðli ok Dagr, Bragi ok Lofði[6],
þaðan ero Skioldungar, þaðan ero Siklingar
þaðan ero Ödlingar þaðan ero Ylfingar,
[þaðan ero Bragningar þaðan ero Bud-
  lungar]
[þaðan ero Hildingar þaðan ero Hnif-
  lungar]
[þaðan ero Döglingar . . . . ?]
[þaðan ero Lofdungar . . . . ?]
þaðan hölð-borit, þaðan hers-borit
mest manna val und Mið-garði.
Mart segjom þer ok munom fleira:
Vöromk at viti svá: viltu enn lengra?

  I. *The Daylings:*
Dagr átti Þóro Drengja-móðor:
ólosk í ætt þar œztir kappar:
Áli, Amr, Iösur[7], Már,
Arngrimr[8] . . . Alfr inn Gamli,
Fraðmar, Gyrðr ok Frekar báðir.
. . . .
  Áli vas áðr öflgastr manna
. . . .
  Enn Arngrími óro bornir
arfar tolf ok Eyfuro:
Hervarðr, Hiörvarðr, Hrani, Angantýr,
Bui ok Brami, Barri ok Reifnir,
Tindr ok Tyrfingr, Tveir Haddingjar.
Brœðr Berserkja í Bolmi austr

---

[1] frama] emend.; framir, Cd. [2] iöfur Austmanna] emend.; see A, ' or Holmgarði.'
[3] Alvig, A. [4] Lost line. [5] See A. [6] See A. [7] Iöfur, Cd. [8] í Bolmi.

um lönd ok um lög sem logi fóro.
Allt es þat ætt þín, Óttarr Heimski.
II. *The Bragnings.* [Blank.]
III. *The Skilfings.* [Blank.]
IV. *The Hildings.* [Blank.]
V. *The Siklings.* [Blank.]
VI. *The Lofdungs.* [Blank.]
VII. *The Ethelings, Othlings:*
. . . Fróði foður Kiars . . .
föður Ölrúnar, es vas Agli gefin (?).
VIII. *The Budlungs.* [Blank.]
IX. *The Hniflungs:*

. . . .
Gunnarr ok Högni Giúka arfar,
ok it sama Guðrún systir þeirra,
þeygi vas Guthormr Giúka ættar,
þó vas hann bróðir beggja þeirra.

Ladies:
[Iosurr Már, Alfr inn Gamli . . .][1]

. . . .
Haraldr Hilditann, borinn Hrœreki
Slœngvan-bauga, sonr vas hann Auðar,
Auðr Diúp-auðga Ívars dóttir,
Enn Raðbarðr vas Randvéss faðir.
Gunnar Balkr, Grímr Arðskafi,
Iarnskioldr þórir, Ulfr Gínandi.
þeir vóro gumar goðom signaðir . .
Vóro þeir í hirð Hrolfs ins Gamla
' allir bornir ' frá Iörmunreki,
Sigröðar mági—hlýð þu sögo minni—
folkom grimms þess es Fafni vá.
Sá vas vísir frá Volsungom [2],
enn Hiordís frá ' Hraudungum,'
enn Eylimi frá ' Öðlingom.'

. . . .
Var Hildigunn ' hennar ' móðir
Svávo barn ok Sækonungs [3]

. . . .
Othere's Genealogy:
Haki vas Hroðmars son Hrodgeirs burar,
enn Hrodgeirr var Haka borinn [4].

. . . .
þú ert, Óttarr, borinn Innsteini;
enn Innsteinn var Alf enom Gamla;
Alfr vas Ulfi; Ulfr Sæfara;

enn Sæfari Svan 'nom Rauða.
Móðor átti faðir þinn menjom göfga,
hygg-ek at hon héti Hlédís gyðja;
Fróði vas faðir ' þeirrar,' enn ' Friaut '
móðir;
öll þótti ætt sú með yfir-mönnom.

. . . . . .
Ketill vas vinr þeirra, Klypps arf-þegi;
vas hann móðor-faðir móðor þínnar.

. . . . . .
Nanna vas næst þar Nœkkva dóttir,
vas mœgr hennar mágr þíns föðor.
Fyrnd es siá mægð. Fram sé ek lengra :
kunna ek báða Brodd ok Horfi—
Allt es þat ætt þín, Óttarr Heimski.
Ísolfr ok Ásolfr Ölmóðs synir,
ok Skúrhildar Skekkils dóttor.
Skaltu til telja skatna margra—
Allt es þat ætt þín, Óttarr Heimski.

End of the Poem.

H. Flá ertu, Freyja, es þú freistar
mín,—
vísar-þú augom á oss þanog,—
es þú hefir ver þinn í val-svíni,
Óttarr inn unga Innsteins bur.

Fr. Dulið ertu, Hyndla, draums ætlig
þer—
es-þu kveðr ver mínn í val-svíni,
þar-es göltr gloar Gollin-bursti,
Hildi-svíni, es mer hagir gœrðo
dvergar tveir Dainn ok Nabbi.

H. Hleypr þú, Óðs vina, úti á nóttom,
sem með höfrom Heiðrún fari :
Rannt at Óði ey þreyandi,
skutosk þer fleiri und fyrir-skyrto.

Fr. Ber þú minnis-öl mínom gelti,
sva-at hann öll muni orð at tína
þessar rœðo á þriðja morni,
þa-es þeir Angantýr ættir rekja.

H. Ber-þu Óttari biór at hendi
eitri blandinn miok illo heilli.

Fr. Orð-heill þín skal œngo ráða,
þóttú, brúðr Iötuns, bölvi heitir :
Hann skal drekka dýrar veigar ;
bið-ek Óttari öll goð duga !

---

[1] A corrupt line repeated by mistake from the Daylings I.   [2] Volsungi, Cd.
[3] Hildigund is the daughter apparently of Swava and Hedin, Helgi's brother ; see
p. 527.   [4] See A.

VÖLOSPA IN SKAMMA; or, The Short Sibyl's Prophecy.

A Scene of Necromancy.   Woden and a Sibyl.

To this poem may possibly belong many of the fragments embedded in the Lay of Volospa in the MSS. Such as those numbered II and i. 23, Bk. ii, § 1, on Dwarves, Fates, and Walkyries. These bits are Western, as is proved by the word 'Durinn,' Welsh 'Dwryn.' II and I has a double text and is very corrupt.

Sibyl:
Snúðo braut heðan, sofa lystir mik
fær-þu fátt af mer fríðra kosta.

[*Woden*]:
Ek slæ elldi of Iviðjo
sva at þú . . . ú braut heðan.

Sibyl:
Muno¹ ellifo Æsir talðir
Baldr es hnígr við bana þúfo ;
þess læzk Vali ' verðr' at hefna,
síns um bróðor slær hann handbana.

. . . .
Ero Völor allar frá Víðolfi,
Vitkar allir frá Vilmeiði,
Seið-berendr frá Svarthöfða,
Iötnar allir frá Ymi komnir.

. . . .
Heiðr ok Hross-þiófr Hrimnis kindar.

. . . .
Freyr átti Gerði, hon vas Gymis dóttir,
Iötna ættar ok Aurboðo.

Ól Ulf Loki við Angrboðo,
enn Sleipni gat við Svaðil-fora :
Eitt þótti skars allra feiknast
þat vas bróðor frá Byleistz komit.
Loki ' af hiarta lindi brendo '
' fann hann half-sviðinn hugstein koma :'
varð Loptr kviðogr at kono íllri,
þaðan es á foldo flagð hvert komit.

. . . .
Haf sé-ek brenna enn hauðr loga,
verða flestir fiör-lausn þola.

Haf gengr hríðom við himin sialfan,
líðr lönd yfir ; enn lopt bilar,
þaðan koma snióvar ok snarir vindar,
þá es ráð ok regin þrióta².

þá kœmr annarr enn máttkari ;
þo þoriga-ek þann at nefna :
Fair siá nú framm um lengra
an Óðinn mun Ulfi mœta.
. . . .

THE PARAPHRASE OF HYNDLA'S LAY (Fl., vol. i. pp. 24–26).

Þeirra son var Halfdan Gamli : ok þa er hann tók konungdóm gœrði hann blót mikit at miðjom vetri, ok blótaði til þess, at hann skildi mega lifa þriú hundruð vetra [three generations] í konungdómi sínom, sem sagt var at lifað hefði Snærr hinn Gamli. Enn fréttin sagði hánom svá, at hann mundi lifa ekki meirr en einn mannz-aldr ; enn þat myndi vera þriú hundruð vetra [three generations?] at eingi myndi vera útiginn maðr í hans ætt, ok engi kona. Hann var hermaðr mikill ok herjaði víða um Austrveg, þar drap hann þann konung er Sigtryggr hét í ein-vígi : hann gekk at eiga Alveigo³ dóttir Eymundar konungs or Holmgarði :—

a. þau átto nio sono :—hét einn þengill, er kallaðr var Manna-þengill, Ræsir, Gramr, Gylfi, Hilmir, Iöfurr, Tiggi, Skyli, ok Harri—þessir nio er sagt at allir væri iafn-gamlir⁴, ok urðo svá ágætir, at í öllom frœðom ero þeirra nöfn höfð fyrir tignar-nöfn ok konunga nöfn. Svá er sagt, at eingi þeirra ætti börn, ok féllo allir senn í orrosto.

β. Enn átto þau aðra nio sono : héto þeir Hildir, Hnefill⁵, Auði, Skelfir, Dagr, Bragi, Buðli, Lofði, Sigarr.—Hildir, Sigarr ok Lofði vóro allir *her-konungar :* Auði, Buðli ok Hnefill vóro *sæ-konungar :* Dagr, Skelfir, ok Bragi *sáto at löndom* [i. e. remain in Scandinavia, the other six being ex-Scandinavian].

---

¹ Emend.; Vóro . . . hneig—lezt—sló, Cd.   ² í ráði at regn um þrióti, Cd.
³ Alfnyju, Cd.; cf. Almveig Ed.   ⁴ nio sono, alla senn borna, Edda.   ⁵ Næfill, Cd.

HOME KINGS:—

I. DAGR átti þóro Drengja-móðor, ok átto þau nio sono.—Hét einn *Áli*, Annarr *Ámr*, þriði *Iofurr*, fiórði *Arngrimr*. [*Rest lost here.*]

a. *Áli* var faðir Dags, föðor Oleifs, föður Hrings, föður Oleifs, föður Helga, [föður Sigurðar Hiartar, föður Ragnhildar, móður Haralldz ins Hárfagra] *b and c lost.* . . . . . .

d. *Arngrímr* átti Eyfuro. þeirra son var Angantýr Berserkr. *e, f, g, h, and i lost.* . . . . . .

Sú ætt [Haralldz] var kölluð DÖGLINGAR.

II. BRAGI Gamli var konungr á Valldresi: Hann var faðir Agnars, föður Alfs, föður Eireks [föður Hildar, móður Halfdanar ins Milda, föður Goðrœðar, föður Halfdanar Svarta, föður Haralldz ins Hárfagra]: þessi ætt [Haralldz] heita BRAGNINGAR.

III. SKELFIR [1] var konungr á Vörs: Hans sonr var Skioldr, faðir Eireks, föður Alreks, föður Eireks ens Málspaka, föður Alreks ins Frœkna, föður Vikars, föður Vatnars, föður þeirra Hialldz ok Sniallz [2] [*links here lost*], [ok Eireks, föður Gyðo, er átti Haraldr inn Hárfagri]. þat heitir SKILFINGA ÆTT eðr SKIOLDUNGA ÆTT.

CONQUEROR KINGS:—

IV. HILDIR var enn fiorði sonr Halfdanar gamla [3]: Hann var faðir Hildibrandz, föður Höðbrandz [4], föður Hilldiss ok Herbrandz [föður Haralldz ens Granrauða [5] föður Áso innar Stórráðo, móður Halfdanar Svarta, föður Haralldz ins Hárfagra]. (þat heitir HILDINGA ÆTT.)

V. SIGARR var faðir Siggeirs, er átti Signýjo, dóttor Volsungs konungs: Sigarr var ok faðir Sigmundar er átti Hildi, dóttor Griótgarðz konungs af Mœri, hans son hét Sigarr, faðir Signýjar; hann lét hengja Hagbarð. þat heitir SIKLINGA ÆTT.

VI. LOFDI var konungr mikill. þat her-lið er hónom fylgði ero Lofðar kallaðir. Hann herjaði á Hreð-Gotaland [6], ok varð þar konungr: Hans synir vóro þeir Skekkill sæ-konungr ok Skyli, faðir Egðiss, föður Hialmþérs, föður Eylima, föður Hiördísar, móður Sigurðar Fáfnis-bana [föður Áslaugar, móður Sigurðar Orms-í-auga, föður Áslaugar, móður Sigurðar Hiartar, föður Ragnhildar, móður Haralldz ins Hárfagra]. þessir [ætt-menn Haralldz] ero kallaðir LOFDUNGAR.

SEA KINGS:—

Auði ok Buðli vóro sæ-konungar ok fóro báðir saman með her sinn; þeir kómo með liði síno til Saxlandz ok herjoðo þar víða; lögðo undir sik Valland ok Saxland, settozk þar at löndom.

VII. AUDI hafði Valland, ok var faðir Fróða, föður Kiars, föður Ölrúnar. þat ero kallaðir ÖDLINGAR.

VIII. BUDLI hafði Saxland; hann var faðir Attils, föður Vífils, föður [Læ]fa, föður Buðla, föður Sörla eðr Serla, ok Atla [ok Brynhildar, móður Áslaugar]. Ok er sú ætt [Haraldz ins Harfagra] kölluð BUDLUNGAR.

IX. HNEFILL konungr var faðir Heimars, föður Eynefs, föður [Ra]kn, föður

---

[1] Edda Sk. has Yngvi for Skilfir, and calls the family Ynglingar, and Ylfingas a little below.   [2] Imaldz, Cd.   [3] Halfdanar gamla] Dags, Cd.   [4] Höðbrandz] Vigbrandz, Cd.   [5] Granrauða] Grenska, Cd.   [6] Reiðgota-l., Cd.

Giúka, föður þeirra Gunnars ok Högna, Guðrúnar, Guðnýjar ok Gull-
randar.

Ok er þat kölluð **Hniflunga ætt.**

QUEENS OR LADIES :—

Nú ero taldar konor þær er fyrst kómo í ætt Halfdanar Gamla.—Enn þá er
in fyrsta kona kom í ættina, var liðit þriú hundruð vettra [three genera-
tions ?] frá blótino er Halfdan blótaði til aldrs ser ok ríkiss :—
Alfr konungr inn Gamli [1] réð fyrir Alfheimom. Hann var faðir Alfgeirs, föður
Gandalfs, föður ALFHILDAR. Alfhildr var móðir Ragnars Loðbrókar, föður
Sigurðar orms-i-auga, föður ÁSLAUGAR, móður Sigurðar Hiartar [föður
RAGNHILDAR, móður Haralldz Hárfagra].

Haraldr inn Gamli, son Valdars hins milda Hroars sonar, átti HERVÖRO
Heiðreks dóttur konungs, þeirra son var Halfdan Snialli, faðir Ívars Víð-
faðma, föður AUDAR innar DIÚPAUDGO ; hána átti Hrœrekr Slœngvan-
baugi ; þeirra son var Haraldr Hilditann.   Síðarr átti Auði Raðbarðr
konungr : þeirras on var Randvér, faðir Sigurðar Hrings, föður Ragnars
Loðbrókar [föður Sigurðar, föður ÁSLAUGAR, móður Sigurðar, föður Ragnhildar, móður Haralldz ins Hárfagra, er fyrstr var einvalldz konungr yfir
Noregi].

[Finnalfr inn Gamli fekk SVANHILDAR er kolluð var GOLLFIÖÐR ; hon
var dóttir Dags Dellings sonar ok Sólar, dóttor Möndilfora.]

OTHERE'S PEDIGREE :—

. . . .

Sonr þeirra var Svanr inn Rauði, faðir Sæfara, föður Ulfs, föður Alfs, föður
þeirra Innsteins ok Utsteins [2] . . . .

Höðr átti þar ríki er kallat er Haðaland ; hans son var Höðbroddr, faðir
Hrolfs, föður Hrómundar berserks, föður þeirra Hámundar [3], Haka, ok
Gunnlaðar, móður þeirra Útsteins ok Innsteins [4].

Hámundr var Hörða-iarl ; hann var faðir Hróks ins Svarta ok Hroks ins
Hvíta.

Haki var faðir Hroðgeirs, föður Hroðmars, föður Haka Berserks.—Gunnlöð var
dóttir Hroks ins Svarta, enn móðir Hrómundar Grips sunar [5].

[Haddingr son Rauma átti Haddingja-dal ok þela-mörk ; hans son var
Haddingr, faðir Haddings, föður Högna ins Rauða.   Eptir hann tóko
ríki Haddingjar þrír, ok var hverr þeirra eptir annan.   Helgi Hadd-
ingja-skaði [6] var með einum þeirra.   Hringr son Rauma átti Hringa-
ríki ok Valldres, hann fekk dóttor Vífils Sækonungs.   þeirra son var
Halfdan Gamli, etc. *ut supra* [7].]

---

[1] Is he Dag's son?   [2] Ingimundar ok Eysteins, Cd.   [3] Hámundar] Hag-
bardz, Cd.   [4] This should be Ingimund and Eystan probably.   [5] Gunnlöð, Grip's
wife, seems here confused somehow with the Gunnlöð above, who ought to be
the daughter of Hromund Bearsark.   [6] -skaði] -skati, Cd.   [7] The latter part
of this Paraphrase should be compared with Appendix A 1, the Helgi Prose pieces.

LANGFEDGA-TAL, OR GENERATIONS.

Of the *Ynglings* and *Skioldungs* preserved in three MSS.—

1. The Hawk's-book, Arna-Magn. 415 (containing, beside Annals, Lists of the Firths in Iceland, Sturl. ii. p. 474, and the Fylki or Shires of Norway, Lists of Bishops, etc.) This is the best text: here also we have the pedigrees superscribed 'langfedga-tal,' a word we know from Ari's Preface, as one of his authorities, so it must needs be old. Cod. 415 contains the Skioldung and Yngling generations.

2. The Flatey-book, in its first two leaves [vol. i. pp. 26, 27], along with the Lay of Hyndla and the Paraphrase thereof given in Appendix below. It is superscribed 'ættar-tolor,' and contains a double text of the Skioldungs (whereof we give the best), one text of the Ynglings, and one of the Orkney Earls.

3. Cod. Resenianus, destroyed in the fire of 1728, but used by Torfæus in Series Regum Daniæ, 1702, contained Skioldungs and Ynglings, in a text similar to AM. 415.

All the texts of the Yngling Generations are drawn from Theodwolf's poem I. 243. The confused state of the Skioldung pedigree is perhaps a proof that it never passed through any genealogical poet's hand.

Next comes the *Haleygia-tal*, preserved in Torfæus, Hist. Norw., and in AM. 22, chart., drawn, as it seems, either from a lost leaf in Fagrskinna, Cd. B = Noregskononga-tal, or from the lost Cod. Resen. Compared with Flatey-book i. 25, where the last six links have been preserved. Many of the earlier names are evidently pure inventions of Eywind.

Lastly, we subjoin the *Orkney Earls' Pedigree* and that of the *Dublin Kings*.

I. THE YNGLINGS (from Flatey-book, vol. i. p. 26).

Burri hefir konungr heitið er réð fyrir Tyrklandi; hans son var Burs, er var faðir—

Óðins Ása konungs, föður	Ana ens Gamla, er ver kollom Aun,
Freys, föður	er nio vetr drakk horn fyrir elli
Niarðar, föður	sakir áðr hann dó; Ann var faðir
Freys, föður	Egils Tunna-dolgs, föður
5. Fiolnis, föður [1]	Óttars Vandils-kráko, föður
Svegðis, föður	20. Aðils at Uppsölom, föður
Vanlanda, föður	Eysteins, föður
Visburs, föður	Yngvars hins Hára, föður [3]
Dómalda, föður	Braut-Onundar, föður
10. Dómars, föður	Ingialldz ens Illráða, föður
Dyggva, er ver kollom Tryggva, föður	25. Áláfs Trételgjo, föður
Dags, föður	Halfdanar Hvítbeins, föður
Agna Skialfar-bonda, föður	Eysteins, föður
Alreks, föður	Halfdanar ens Milda ok Matarilla, föður
15. Yngva, föður	Goðroðar Veiði-konungs, föður
Iormun-Fróða [2], er ver kollom Iörund, föður	30. Halfdanar Svarta, föður [4]
	Haraldz ens Hárfagra.

---

[1] From here cf. Yt.   [2] Only found here.   [3] Lines now missing in Yt. may have given his surname as also that of Onund and the two Halfdans.   [4] Anlaf Geirstada-alf is here omitted before Halfdane.

Another Text from AM. 415.

Langfeðga-tal fra Yngva til várra konunga.

. . . Vóden þann kollvm ver Oðen. Frá hánom ero komnar flestar konunga ęttir í Norðr-afluna heimsins. Hann var Tyrkja konungr ; hann flýði fyvir Romverjum norðr hegat :—

Oðen	Agni Skialfar-boandi	Braut-Onundr
Niörðr í Noa-túnum	Alrekr	Ingialdr Illráði
Yngvi-Freyr	Yngvi	Olafr Tretelgja
Fiolnir	Iorundr	Haldan Hvitbeinn
5. Vallandi	15. Avnn hinn gamle	25. Eysteinn
Visburr	Egill Tunna-dolgr	Halfdan Milldi
Domalldr	Óttarr Vendil-kraca	Goðrœðr Gavfoglati
Domarr	Adils at Uppsolum	Halfdan Svarti
Dyggvi	Eysteinn	Haralldr Harfagri
10. Dagr	20. Yngvarr	

II. THE SKIOLDUNGS (from AM. 415).

Oðinn	Hrœrekr Hnœggvan-baugi Ingiallz s.
Skioldr h. s. [=his son]	Froðe hans son [3]
Friðleifr h. s.	20. Halfdan h. s.
Friðfroðe h. s.	Hrœrekr Slavngvan-baugi h. s.
5. Friðleifr h. s.	Haralldr Hillditavnn h. s. ok Randver
Havarr Handrami h. s.	bróðir hans [4]
Froðe h. s.	Sigurðr Hringr Randvers s., Raðbarz
Vermundr Vitri h. s.	sonar bróður Haraldar Hildi-tannar ;
Oláfr lítiláti h. s.[1]	þeirra móðir var Auðr Diuphvgða,
10. Danr Mikillati [h. s.]	dottir Ivars Víðfaðma, sonar Halfdanar
Froðe Friðsami h. s.	snialla, sonar Valldars Milda, Hroars
Friðleifr	sonar, Halfdanar sonar [bróður Ingi-
Froðe Frœkni h. s.	alldz Starkaðar fostra] [5]
Ingialldr Starkaðar-fostri h. s.	Ragnarr Loðbrok sun Sigurðar Hrings
15. Halfdan bróðir hans [2]	25. Sigurðr Or ŗ-í-auga h. s.
Helgi ok Hroarr hans synir	Hörða-Knútr h. s.
Rolfr Kraki Helga son	

III. HALEYGJA-TAL (derived from Eywind's poem I. 251).

I. KINGS :—

1. Oðinn [and Skaði giantess]
2. Sæmıngr [6]
3. Goð-hialti
4. Sverð-hialti
5. Höðbroddr
6. Himinleygr
7. Veðr-hallr
8. Havarr Handrami

9. Godgestr
10. Heimgestr Huldar-bróðir
11. Gylaugr
12. Goðlaugr [7]
13. Mundill Gamli

II. EARLS :—

14. Hersir
15. Brandr iarl

---

[1] Olof, hon var moðir Froða ins friðsama, Fl. (badly).　[2] Fl. drops this and the following two (badly).　[3] Om. Fl.　[4] ok . . . hans] add Fl.　[5] In the margin in later hand.　[6] Hlgtal.　[7] Hlgtal.

16. Bryniolfr
17. Bárðr
18. Hergils
19. Havarr
20. Haraldr Trygill
21. þrondr

22. Haraldr [1]
23. Herlaugr
24. Griótgarðr
25. Hakon [Urna iarl]
26. Sigrœðr Hlaða-iarl
27. Hákon Hlaða-iarl.

IV. THE ORKNEY EARLS.

(From Flatey-book i. 21 and Orkn. S. ch. 3, Rolls Edit.)

FORNIOTR (father of the winds)

Hler.   Logi.   Kári
                  Iokull
                  Snær Gamli
                  þorri

Nór   Gói   Gor
(father of land kings). (daughter). (father of sea kings)

| Sea King Empire |
Heiti   Beiti [2].
Sveidi, sea king
Halfdan Gamli
Ivarr Upland Earl [3]
Eystein Glumra
Rögnvald the Old
TURF-EINAR.
(See vol. ii. p. 183.)

V. THE KINGS OF DUBLIN (tacked to the Ynglings or Skioldungs).

α.

YNGLINGS (Libellus)
  Halfdan Hvítbeinn
  Godroðr [4]
  Anlafr
  Helgi
  Ingiald, daughter's son of Sigurd
    Snake i' th' eye
  Anlafr Hviti (Anlaf White, king of
    Dublin).

β.

SKIOLDUNGS (Laxdola)
  Froði Frœkni (whom the Swartings
    slew)
  Ingiald Starkaðar-fostri
  Anlaf White.

---

[1] Given henceforward in Fl. and calls Thorfin 'Heiti's kinsman.'
[2] Arnor makes Rognwald a 'scion of Endill,'
[3] The historic pedigree begins here.
[4] Not Charlemain's foe, but a brother to Eystan.

APPENDIX.

A. *In Prose.*

1. *The Prose Pieces from Cod. R.*—In former editions they are printed with the Songs themselves, but we have weeded them out, and set them together here, marking their place in every instance.

2. *The Wolsunga Paraphrase of the Lacuna Lays*, translated in vol. i. p. 391 sqq. As it contains several poetical words and phrases we here give the text.

2 *b. The same text from the Interpolated Sigfred Saga in Edda*, Cod. *r* and 1 e β; the latter MS. begins in the middle of the bathing scene. The author has known and used the Western Wolsung Lay [i. 155], and, of the Lacuna-Lays, that on the Bathing in the River, which is here more powerful than in the Wolsunga paraphrase; maybe, this poem was by the same hand as the Wolsung Lay [Helgi-poet]. The Lays of the Tapestry-poet our paraphrast has despatched in a few lines; perhaps he knew them not, only the subject thereof.

3. From the same source we subjoin the *Story of Hamtheow*, drawn, as one sees, from Hamtheow's Lay and Bragi's Shield Song, the Saga man using both poems in a better state than we now have them.

4. *The final portion of Edda's Scaldscapar-mal*, from Halfdane the Old towards the end. This was apparently once a *detached independent Essay*, the first draught of our present Edda, older than Snorri, whether Icelandic or not it is hard to say. It is a parallel piece to the Thulor. The author knew the Lay of Righ, and more bits of songs one would think. His vocabulary is interesting; mostly poetical or satirical. He winds up with *puns*. Citations of verses from the poems are not wanting. The text is taken from AM. 748 (except the beginning from 1 e β), but mended in a few instances from the other vellums, *r* and 1 e β.

4 *b. The same in a briefer text from Cod. Worm.* from the leaf which followed the Lay of Righ [see Introd. § 6, p. xliv]. At first the text runs much like 748, though somewhat briefer, but soon takes a more independent turn, containing many new words, mostly however slangy.

This Essay being headed by and drawn from the Lay of Righ, we take it, got the name of the 'Edda-book,' and from it the name 'Edda' was transferred to Snorri's later and bigger work.

5. *A curious glossary*, in AM. 748, following after the Thulor, and only found here. The words in Cod. are written above the line, mostly only the initial letter, so that the sense is not always clear. Many of the words are met with nowhere else.

1. THE PROSE PIECES FROM R.

(See Introduction, § 10, p. lxxii.)

I. BEFORE THE LACUNA.

To Grimnis-mal. (Bk. ii, § 1.)

Synir Hravdungs konungs. Hravdungr konungr átti tvá sono, het annarr Agnarr, en annarr Geirravðr. Agnarr var tio vetra, enn Geirravðr átta vetra. Þeir rero tveir á báti með dorgar sínar at smá-fiski. Vindr rak þá í haf út.

Í nátt-myrkri bruto þeir við land ok gengo upp, fundo cot-bónda einn. Þar vóro þeir um vetrinn. Kerling fóstraði Agnar enn karl fóstraði Geirroð ok kendi hónom ráð. At vári fekk karl þeim skip. Enn er þau kerling leiddo þá til strandar þá mælti karl ein-mæli við Geirrœð. þeir fengo byr, ok kvómo til stǫðva föður síns. Geirrœðr var framm í skipi; hann hlióp upp á land, enn hratt út skipino ok mælti: Farðu nú þar er smyl hafi þik! Skipit rak í haf út. Enn Geirrœðr gekk upp til bœjar; hónom var þar vel fagnat, enn faðir hans var þá andaðr. Var þá Geirrœðr til konungs tekinn, ok varð maðr ágætr.

¹ Óðinn ok Frigg sáto í Hliþskialfo ok sá um heima alla. Óðinn mælti: Sér þú Agnar fóstra þinn, hvar hann elr bǫrn við gygi í hellinom; enn Geirrœðr fóstri minn er konungr ok sitr nú at landi? Frigg segir: Hann er mat-níðingr sá, at hann kvelr gesti sína, ef hónom þikkja of margir koma. Óðinn segir at þat er in mesta lygi. þau veðja um þetta mál. Frigg sendi eski-mey sína Fullo til Geirrœðar. Hon bað konung varaz at eigi fyr-gerði hónom fiol-kunnigr maðr sá er þar var kominn í land; ok sagði þat mark á, at engi hundr var svá olmr, at á hann mundi hlaupa. Enn þat var inn mesti hégómi at Geirrœðr koungr væri eigi mat-góðr. Enn þó lætr hann hand-taka þann mann, er eigi vildo hundar á ráða. Sá var í felldi blám ok nefndiz Grimnir, ok sagði ekki fleira frá sér, þótt hann væri at spurðr. Konungr lét hann pína til sagna, ok setja milli elda tveggja, ok sat hann þar átta nætr. Geirrœðr konungr átti þá son tio vetra gamlan ok hét Agnarr eptir bróður hans. Agnarr gekk at Grimni ok gaf hónom horn fullt at drekka, ok sagði at faðir hans gœrði illa, er hann píndi þenna mann saklausan. Grimnir drakk af. þá var eldrinn svá kominn at felldrinn brann af Grimni. Hann kvað.—Grimnis-mál. Heitr ertu, etc.

At the end.—Geirrœðr konungr sat ok hafði sverð um kné ser ok brugðit til miðs. Enn er hann heyrði at Óðinn var þar kominn, þá stóð hann upp ok vildi taka Óðinn frá elldinom. Sverðit slapp or hendi hónum ok visso hioltin niðr. Konungr drap fœti ok steyptiz afram, enn sverðit stóð í gœgnom hann, ok fekk hann bana. Óðinn hvarf þá. Enn Agnarr var þar konungr lengi síðan.

To Western Aristophanes Lays. (Bk. ii, § 2.)

For Skirnis.—Freyr sonr Niarðar hafði einn dag setzk í Hliþskialf ok sá um heima alla. Hann sá í Iǫtun-heima ok sá þar mey fagra þá er hon gekk frá skála fǫður síns til skemmo. þar af fekk hann hug-sóttir miklar. Scirnir het skó-sveinn Freyss. Niǫrðr bað hann kveðja Frey máls. þá mælti Skaði.

After line 41.—Skirnir reið í Iötunheima til Gymiss garða. þar vóro hundar olmir ok bundnir fyrir skíð-garðz hliði þess er um sal Gerðar var. Hann reið at þar er fé-hirðir sat á haugi ok kvaddi hann.

After line 164.—þá reið Skirnir heim. Freyr stóð úti ok kvaddi hann ok spurði tíðenda.

Harbarz lioð.—þórr fór or Austrvegi ok kom at sundi eino; ǫðrom megom sundzins var ferjo karlinn með skipit. þórr kallaði. Hverr er sá . . .

Fra Egi ok Goðom.—Egir, er ǫðro nafni hét Gymir, hann hafði buit Ásom ǫl, þá er hann hafði fengit ketil inn mikla, sem nú er sagt. [*Lay of Hymi has just preceded.*] Til þeirrar veizlo kom Óðinn ok Frigg kona hans. þórr kom eigi, því at hann var í Austr-vegi. Sif var kona þórs. Bragi ok Iðunn kona hans. Týr var

---

¹ This is a parallel or pendant to the Deacon's well-known story.

þar, hann var ein-hendr. Fenriss-ulfr sleit hond af hónom þá er hann var bundinn. þar var Niorðr ok kona hans Skaði. Freyr ok Freyja. Viðarr hét son Óðins. Loki var þar. Ok þiónosto-menn Freyss Beyggvir ok Beyla. Mart var þar Ása ok Alfa. Egir átti tvá þiónusto-menn, Fima-fengr ok Ellder. þar var lýsi-gull haft fyrir elldz liós. Sialft barsc þar ǫl. þar var griða-staðr mikill. Menn lofoðo miok hverso góðir þiónusto-menn Egiss vóro. Loki mátti eigi heyra þat, ok drap hann Fima-feng. þá scóco Æsir skioldo sína ok œpðo at Loka, ok elto hann braut til skógar, enn þeir fóro at drekka. Loki hvarf aptr ok hitti úti Elldi. Loki kvaddi hann.—Loka-senna. Segðu þat Elldir, etc.

After line 20.—Síðan gekk Loki inn í hǫllina. Enn er þeir sá er fyrir váro, hverr inn var kominn, þǫgnoðo þeir allir.

After line 40.—þá stóð Viðarr upp ok scǫncti Loka ; enn áðr hann drycci kvaddi hann ásona.

After line 211.—þá gekk Sif framm, ok byrlaði Loka í hrím-calci miǫð ok mælti . . . Loki tók við horni ok drakk af.

After line 228 —þá kom þórr at ok kvað.

At the end.—Enn eptir þetta falz Loki í Fránangrs forsi í lax líki. þar tóko Æsir hann. Hann var bundinn með þǫrmom sonar síns Nara [read Vala], enn Narfi sonr hans varð at vargi. Skaði tók eitr-orm ok festi upp yfir annlit Loka ; draup þar ór eitr. Sigyn kona Loka sat þar ok helt munn-laug undir eitrið. Enn er munn-laugin var full, bar hon út eitrið. Enn meðan draup eitrið á Loka. þá kiptiz hann svá hart við at þaðan af skalf iorð oll. þat ero nu kallaðir land-skialptar.

Wayland Lay. (Bk. iii, § 2.)

Fra Volundi.—Niðuðr hét konungr í Sviðióð, hann átti tvá sono ok eina dóttor, hon het Bavdvilldr. Brœðr váro þrír synir Finna konungs, hét einn Slag-Fiðr, annarr Egill, þriði Vǫlundr. þeir skriðo ok veiddo dýr. þeir kvómo í Ulfdali ok gerðo ser þar hús. þar er vatn er heitir Ulf-siár. Snemma of morgin fundo þeir á vaz-strondo konor þriár ok spunno lín, þar vóro hiá þeim alptar-hamir þeirra. þat vóro Valkyrjor. þar vóro tvær dœttr Lavðvess konungs, Hlaðguðr Svanhvít, ok Hervor Alvitr, en þriðja var Alvrún Kiars dóttir af Vallandi. þeir hǫfðo þær heim til skála með ser. Fekk Egill Avlrunar enn Slag-Fiðr Svanhvítrar, enn Vǫ-lundr Alvitrar. þau bioggo siau vettr. þa flugo þær at vitja víga ok kvómo eigi aptr. þá skreið Egill at leita Avlrúnar, enn Slag-Fiðr leitaði Svanhvítrar, enn Volundr sat í Ulfdǫlom. Hann var hagastr maðr, sva at menn viti í fornom sǫgom. Niðuðr konungr lét hann hondom taka. Svá sem her er um kveðit.—**Fra Volundi ok Niðaði.** Meyiar flugo, etc.

After line 64.—Niðuðr konungr gaf dóttor sinni Bǫdvilldi gull-ring þann er hann tók af bastino at Volundar; enn hann sialfr bar sverþit, er Vǫlundr átti. Enn dróttning kvað.

After line 69.—Svá var gort at skornar váro sinar í kness fotom, ok settr í holm einn er þar var fyrir landi er hét Sævar-staðr. þar smíðaði hann konungi allz kyns gorsimar. Engi maðr þorði at fara til hans nema konungr einn. Vǫlundr kvað.

Helgi and Swava. (Bk. iii, § 1.)

Fra Hiorvarði oc Sigrlinn.—Hiorvarðr hét konungr. Hann átti fiorar konor. Ein hét Alfhilldr, son þeirra hét Heðinn ; onnor hét Sereiðr, þeirra son hét Humlungr. In þriðja hét Sinrioð, þeirra son hét Hymlingr. Hiorvarðr konungr hafði þess heit strengt at eiga þá kono er hann vissi vænsta. Hann spurði at Svafnir konungr átti dóttur allra fegrsta, sú hét Sigrlinn. Iðmundr hét iarl hans. Atli var hans son, er fór at biðja Sigrlinnar til handa konungi. Hann dvalðiz vetr-langt með Svafni konungi. Fránmarr het þar iarl, fóstri Sigrlinnar; dóttir hans hét Álof. Iarlinn réð at meyjar var synjat, ok fór Atli heim. Atli iarls son stóð einn dag við lund nokkorn, enn fugl sat í limonom uppi yfir hónom ok hafði heyrt til, at hans menn kolloðo vænstar konor þær er Hiorvarðr konungr átti. Fuglinn kvakaði, enn Atli lýddi hvat hann sagði. Hann kvað. Sattu Sigrlinn, etc.

After line 16.—þetta var áðr Atli fœri. Enn er hann kom heim ok konungr spurði hann tíðinda, kvað hann.

After line 21.—Konungr bað at þeir skyldo fara annat sinn. Fór hann sialfr. Enn er þeir kómo upp á fiall, ok sá á Svava-land landz bruna ok ió-reyki stóra. Reið konungr af fiallino fram í landit, ok tók nátt-ból við á eina. Atli hélt vorð ok fór yfir ána. Hann fann eitt hús. Fugl mikill sat á húsino ok gætti ok var sofnaðr. Atli skaut spióti fuglinn til bana; enn í húsino fann hann Sigrlinn konungs dóttor ok Álofo iarls dóttor ok hafði þær báðar braut með ser. Fránmarr iarl hafði hamaz í arnar líki ok varit þær fyrir hernom með fiolkyngi. Hroðmarr het konungr biðill Sigrlinnar. Hann drap Svava konung, ok hafði rænt ok brent landit. Hiorvarðr konungr fekk Sigrlinnar, enn Atli Álofar. Hiorvarðr ok Sigrlinn átto son bæði mikinn ok vænan. hann var þogull; ekki nafn festiz við hann. Hann sat á haugi. Hann sá ríða Valkyrjor nio, ok var ein gofogligozt. Hon kvað.

After line 37.—Eylimi het konungr; dóttir hans var Svava; hon var Valkyrja ok reið lopt ok logg; hon gaf Helga nafn þetta, ok hlífði hónom opt síðan iorrostom. Helgi kvað . . .

After line 45.—Hiorvarðr svarar, at hann mundi fá lið Helga, ef hann vill hefna móður-foður síns. þá sótti Helgi sverðit, er Svava vísaði honom til. þá fór hann ok Atli ok feldo Hroðmar ok unno morg þrek-virki. Hann drap Hata iotun, er hann sat á bergi noccoro. Helgi ok Atli lágo skipom í Hatafirði. Atli hélt vorð inn fyrra lut nætrinnar. Hrimgerðr Hata dóttir kvað. [*Follows Lay of Atli and Rime-gerð.*] Helgi konungr var all-mikill hermaðr; hann kom til Eylima konungs, ok bað Svavo dóttor hans. þau Helgi ok Svava veittoz várar ok unnoz furðo mikit. Svava var heima með feðr sínom, enn Helgi í hernaði. Var Svava Valkyrja enn sem fyrr. Heðinn var heima með foður sínom Hiorvarði konungi í Noregi. Heðinn fór einn saman heim or skógi Ióla aptan, ok fann troll-kono. Sú reið vargi ok hafði orma at taumom ok bauð fylgd sína Heðni. Nei, sagði hann. Hon sagði : þess skaltu giallda at Bragar-fulli. Um kveldit óro heit-strengingar; var fram leiddr sónar-goltr. Logðo menn þar á hendr sínar, ok strengðo menn þá heit at Bragar-fulli. Heðinn strengði heit til Svavo Eylima dóttor, unnosto Helga bróður síns, ok iðraðiz svá miok, at hann gekk á braut villi-stigo suðr á lond, ok fann Helga bróðor sinn. Helgi kvað : Kombu heill Heðinn . . .

After line 66.—þat kvað Helgi, þviat hann grunaði um feigð sína, ok þat, at fylgjor hans hofðo vitjað Heðins, þá er hann sá konona ríða varginom. Alfr het konungr son Hroðmars, er Helgi hafði voll haslaðan á Sigars-velli a þriggja nátta fresti. þar var orrosta mikil ok fékk þar Helgi bana-sár.

At the end.—Helgi ok Svava er sagt at væri endr-borin.

Helgi and Cara (see Translation, Introd. § 11). (Bk. iii, § 1.)

Fra Vavlsungom.—Sigmundr konungr Vavlsungs son atti Borghilldi af Brá-lundi; þau heto son sinn Helga, ok eptir Helga Hiorvarðs syni. Helga fostraði Hagall. Hundingr hét ríkr konungr. Við hann er Hundland kent. Hann var hermaðr mikill, ok átti marga sono þa er í hernaði vóro. Ófriðr ok dylgjor voro á milli þeirra Hundings konungs ok Sigmundar konungs; drápo hvárir annarra frændr. Sigmundr konungr ok hans ætt-menn héto Volsungar ok Ylfingar. Helgi fór ok niósnaði til hirðar Hundings konungs á laun. Hemingr son Hundings konungs var heima. Enn er Helgi fór í brot, þá hitti hann hiarðar-svein ok kvað. Segðu Hemingi . . . Hundingr konungr. Hamall hét son Hagals. Hundingr konungr sendi menn til Hagals at leita Helga. Enn Helgi mátti eigi forðaz annan veg enn tók klæði ambáttar ok gekk at mala. þeir leitoðo, ok fundo eigi Helga. þá kvað Blindr inn Bol-vísi. Hvoss ero . . . mondul tre. Hagall svaraði ok kvað. þat er .l. vá . . . man. Undan komz Helgi ok fór á her-skip. Hann felldi Hunding konung, ok var síðan kallaðr Helgi Hundings-bani. Hann lá með her sinn í Bruna-vágom ok hafði þar strand-hogg, ok áto þar rátt. Hogni hét konungr; hans dóttir var Sigrún; hon var Valkyrja ok reið lopt ok log. Hon var Svara endr-borin. Sigrún reið at skipom Helga ok kvað. Hverir láta flióta . . . Enn Havgna mer kennir. Granmar hét ríkr konungr, er bio at Svarins-haugi. Hann átti marga sono. Havð-broddr, annarr Guðmundr, þriði Starkaðr. Hoðbroddr var í konunga stefno, hann fastnaði ser Sigruno Hogna dóttor. Enn er hon spyr þat, þá reið hon með Val-kyrjor um lopt ok um log at leita Helga. Helgi var þá at Loga-fiollom ok hafði bariz við Hundings sono. þar felldi hann þa Alf ok Eyjolf, Hiorvarð ok Hervarð, ok var hann all-víg-móðr ok sat undir Ara-steini. þar hitti Sigrún hann, ok rann á hals hónom ok kyssti hann, ok sagði hónom erendi sitt. Svá sem segir í Volsunga-kviðo inni Forno. Sótti Sigrun . . . Helgi samnaði þá . . . trega þer at segja. [For the following see vol. i. p. 376, Text B.]

From the end of Helgi i.—(Við himin sialfan) Havgr var gorr eptir Helga. Enn er hann kom til Valhallar þá bauð Oðinn hónom ollo at ráða með ser. Helgi kvað. þú skalt Hundingr . . . sofa gangir. Ambátt Sigrúnar gekk um aptan hiá haugi Helga ok sá at Helgi reið til haugsins með marga menn. Ambótt kvað. Hvárt ero þat svik . . . heim-for gefin. Heim gekk ambótt ok sagði Sigrúno. Út gakk þu S. . . . svefja skyldir. Sigrún gekk í hauginn til Helga ok kvað. Nu em ek s. fegin . . . hia oss liðnom. Sigrún bio sæing í hauginom. Her hefi ek þ. H. . . . sigr-þióð veki. þeir Helgi riðo leið sína, enn þær fóro heim til bœjar. Annan aptan lét Sigrún ambótt halda vorð á hauginom. Enn at dag-setri er Sigrún kom til haugsins kvað hon. Cominn v. nú . . . um daga liósa. Sigrún varð skamm-líf af harmi ok trega. þat var trua í forneskjo at menn væri endr-bornir, enn þat er nú kolloð kerlinga villa. Helgi ok Sigrún er kallað at væri endr-borin. Hét hann þá Helgi Haddingja-skati [*read* -skaði], enn hon Kára Halfdanar dóttir, svá sem kveðit er í Káro-lióðom, ok var hon Valkyrja.

Frá dauða Sinfiotla.—Sigmundr Vavlsungs son var konungr á Frakklandi. Sinfiotli var ellztr hans sona, annarr Helgi, þriði Hamundr. Borghildr, cona Sig-mundar, átti bróðor er hét [blank]. Enn Sinfiötli stiup-son hennar, ok [blank] báðo einnar kono báðir, ok fyr þá sok drap Sinfiotli hann. Enn er hann kom heim, þá bað Borghildr hann fara á brot, enn Sigmundr bauð henni fé-bœtr, ok þat varð hon at þiggja. Enn at erfino bar Borghildr ol; hon tók eitr, mikit horn fullt, ok bar Sinfiotla; enn er hann sá í hornit, skilði hann, at eitr var í, ok mælti til Sigmundar. Giorottr er drykkrinn, ai! Sigmundr tók hornit ok drakk af. Svá er sagt, at Sigmundr var harð-gorr, at hvarki mátti honom eitr granda útan né innan; enn allir synir hans stóðoz eitr á horund útan. Borghildr bar annat horn Sinfiotla ok bað drekka, ok fór allt sem fyrr. Ok enn ið þriðja sinn bar hon hónom hornit, ok þó ámæliss orð með, ef hann drykki eigi af. Hann mælti enn sem fyrr við Sig-mund. Hann mælti. Láttu gron sía þá, sonr! Sinfiotli drakk, ok varð þegar dauðr. Sigmundr bar hann langar leiðir í fangi ser, ok kom at firði einom mióvom ok lǫngom, ok var þar skip eitt lítið, ok maðr einn á. Hann bauð Sigmundi far of fiǫrðinn. Enn er Sigmundr bar líkit út á skipit þá var bátrinn hlaðinn. Karl mælti at Sigmundr skyldi fara fyr innan fiǫrðinn. Karl hratt út skipino ok hvarf þegar. Sigmundr konungr dvalðiz lengi í Danmork í ríki Borghildar, síðan er hann fekk hennar. Fór Sigmundr þá suðr í Fraccland til þess ríkiss er hann átti þar. þá fekk hann Hiordísar dóttor Eylima konungs. þeirra son var Sigurðr. Sigmundr konungr fell í orrosto fyr Hundings sonom. Enn Hiordis giptiz þá Alfi syni Hialp- reks konungs. Óx Sigurðr þar upp í barnæsko. Sigmundr, ok allir synir hans, vóro langt um fram alla menn aðra um afl ok voxt ok hug ok alla atgervi. Sigurðr var þó allra framastr, ok hann kalla allir menn í forn-frœðom um alla menn fram, ok gǫfgastan her-konunga.

Gripir hét son Eylima bróðir Hiordísar ; hann réð lǫndom ok var allra manna vitrastr ok framvíss. Sigurðr reið einn saman ok kom til hallar Gripiss. Sigurðr var auð-kendr. Hann hitti mann at máli úti fyr hǫllinni, sá nefndiz Geitir. þá kvaddi Sigurðr hans máls ok spyrr, Hverr byggir her . . . [The Lay of Gripi follows, Bk. v, § 1.]

The Old Play of the Wolsungs.

Sigurðr gekk til stóðs Hialpreks ok kauss ser af hest einn, er Grani var kallaðr síðan. þá var kominn Reginn til Hialpreks, sonr Hreiðmars ; hann var hverjom manni hagari ok dvergr of voxt ; hann var vitr, grimmr ok fiolkunnigr. Reginn veitti Sigurði fóstr ok kenzlo ok elskaði hann miok. Hann sagði Sigurði frá forellri síno, ok þeim atburðom :—At Óðinn ok Hœnir ok Loki höfðo komit til Andvara- fors, ok í þeim forsi var fioldi fiska. Einn dvergr hét Andvari, hann var longom í forsinom í geddo líki ok fekk ser þar matar. Otr hét bróðir várr, er opt fór í forsinn í otrs líki. Hann hafði tekit einn lags ok sat á ár-bakkanom ok át blund- andi. Loki laust hann með steini til bana. þóttoz Æsir miok heppnir verit hafa, ok flógo belg af otrinom. þat sama kvelld sótto þeir gisting til Hreiðmars ok sýndo veiði sína. þá tóko ver þá hǫndom, ok lǫgðom þeim fior-lausn at fylla otr- belginn með gulli ok hylja útan oc með rauðo gulli. þá sendo þeir Loka at afla gullzins. Hann kom til Ránar ok fékk net hennar, ok fór þá til Andvara fors, ok kastaði netino fyrir geddona, enn hon hlióp í netit. þá mælti Loki. Hvat er þat fiska . . . leiða limar. Loki sá allt gull þat er Andvari átti. Enn er hann hafði fram reitt gullit, þá hafði hann eptir einn hring, ok tók Loki þann af hónom. Dvergrinn gekk inn í steininn ok mælti. þat skal gull . . . nióta. Æsir reiddo Hreiðmari féið ok tráðo upp otr-belginn ok reisto á fœtr. þá skyldo Æsirnir hlaða upp gullino ok hylja. Enn er þat var gort, gekk Hreiðarr fram, ok sá eitt grana- hár ok bað hylja. þá dró Oðinn fram hringinn Andvara-naut ok hulði hárit. þá kvað Loki. Gull er þer nú r. . . . heim heðan. Fáfnir ok Reginn krǫfðo Hreið- mar nið-gialda eptir Otr bróðor sínn. Hann kvað nei við. Enn Fáfnir lagði sverði Hreiðmar fǫðor sinn sofanda. Hreiðmarr kallaði á dœtr sínar. Lyngheiðr ok L. v. m. l. f. . . . þíns harms reka. þá dó Hreiðmarr, enn Fáfnir tók gullit allt. þá beiddiz Reginn at hafa fǫðor-arf sínn ; enn Fáfnir galt þar nei við. þá leitaði Reginn ráða við Lyngheiði systor sína, hvernig hann skyldi heimta fǫður-arf sínn. Hon kvað. Brúðar kveðja . . . fiár. þessa luti sagði Reginn Sigurði. Einn dag er hann kom til húsa Regins var hónom vel fagnat. Reginn kvað. Cominn er h. . . . ǫrlog simo. Sigurðr var þá iafnan með Regin, og sagði hann Sigurði, at Fáfnir lá á Gnita-heiði ok var í orms líki. Hann átti ægis-hialm, er ǫll kvikvendi hræddoz við. Reginn gerði Sigurði sverð er Gramr hét. þat var svá hvasst, at hann brá því ofan í Rín, ok lét reka ullar-lagð fyrir straumi, ok tók í sundr lagðinn sem vatnið. því sverði klauf Sigurðr í sundr steðja Regins. Eptir þat eggjaði Reginn Sigurð at vega Fáfni. Hann sagði. Hátt muno hlæja . . . hefnd fǫður. Hialprekr konungr fekk Sigurði skipa-lið til fǫður-hefnda. þeir fengo storm mikinn ok beitto fyrir bergs-nǫs nacqvara. Maðr einn stóð á bergino ok kvað. Hverir ríða þar . . . far vil ek þiggja. þeir viko at landi, ok gekk karl á skip, ok lægði þá veðrit. Segðu mer þ. Hnikarr . . . hrapa. **Capitulum.** Sigurðr átti orrosto mikla við Lyngva Hundings son ok brœðr hans. þar fell Lyngvi ok þeir brœðr. Eptir orrosto kvað Reginn. Nu er bl. orn . . . huginn gladdi. Heim fór Sigurðr til Hialprecs. þá eggjaði Reginn Sigurð til at vega Fáfni. Sigurðr ok Reginn fóro upp á Gnita-heiði ok hitto þar slóð Fáfniss þa er hann skreið til vaz. þar gorði Sigurðr grof mikla á veginom ok gekk Sigurðr þar í. Enn er Fáfnir skreið af gullino, blés hann eitri, ok hraut þat fyrir ofan hǫfuð Sigurði. Enn er Fáfnir skreið yfir grofna, þá lagði Sigurðr hann með sverði til hiarta. Fáfnir hristi sik ok barði hǫfði ok sporði. Sigurðr hlióp or grofinni, ok sá þá hvárr annan. Fáfnir kvað.

Frá dauða Fafniss.—Sveinn ok sveinn . . . hiarta hiorr. Sigurðr duldi nafns síns, fyr því at þat var trua þeira í forneskjo, at orð feigs mannz mætti mikit, ef hann bolvaði óvin sínom með nafni. Hann kvað. Gofugt dýr . . . meira megin. Reginn var á brot horfinn meðan Sigurðr vá Fáfni, ok kom þá aptr, er Sigurðr strauk blóð af sverðino. Regin kvað. Heill þú nú. S. . . . hvaz hugar. þá gekk Reginn at Fáfni, ok skar hiarta or hónom með sverði er Riðill heitir, ok þá drakk hann blóð ór undinni eptir. Reginn kvað. Sittu nú S. . . . at hendi kœmr. Sigurðr tók Fáfniss hiarta ok steikði á teini. En er hann hugði at full-steikt væri, ok freyddi sveitinn or sárino, þá tók hann á fingri sínom ok skynjaði, hvárt full-steikt væri. Hann brann, ok brá fingrinom í munn ser. Enn er hiart-blóð Fáfniss kom á tungo hónom, ok skilði hann fugls rǫdd. Hann heyrði at igðor klǫkoðo á hrísino. Igðan kvað. þar sitr Sigurðr . . . avnnor kvað . . . in iii kvað . . . In iiii kvað . . . In fimta kvað . . . fara til heliar heðan. Sigurðr hió hǫfuð af Regin, ok þá át hann Fáfnis hiarta, ok drakk blóð þeirra beggja Regins ok Fáfniss. þá heyrði Sigurðr hvat igdor mælte : Bitt þú Sigurðr . . . skǫpom Norna. Sigurðr reið eptir slóð Fáfniss til bœliss hans, ok fann þat opit, ok hurðir af iarni ok gætti: af iarni voro ok allir timbr-stokkar í húsino, enn grafit í iorð niðr. þar fann Sigurðr stór-mikit gull, ok fylldi þar tvær kistor. þar tók hann ægis-hialm ok gull-brynjo, ok sverðit Hrotta, ok marga dýr-gripi, ok klyfjaði þar með Grana. Enn hestrinn vildi eigi fram ganga fyrr en Sigurðr steig á bak hónom. Sigurðr reið upp á Hindar-fiall, ok stefndi suðr til Frakklandz. A fiallino sá hann liós mikit, svá sem eldr brynni, ok liómaði af til himins. Enn er hann kom at, þá stóð þar skiald-borg ok upp or merki. Sigurðr gekk í skialld-borgina, ok sá, at þar lá maðr, ok svaf með ǫllum her-vápnom. Hann tók fyrst hialminn af hǫfði hónom. þá sá hann at þat var kona. Brynjan var fǫst sem hon væri holld-groin. þá reist hann með Gram frá hǫfuð-smátt brynjona ígognom niðr, ok svá út ígognom báðar ermar. þá tók hann brynjo af henni. Enn hon vaknaði, ok settiz hon upp, ok sá Sigurð ok mælti. Hvat beit brynjo . . . blunn-stǫfom. Sigurðr settiz niðr ok spurði hána nafns. Hon tók þá horn fullt miaðar, ok gaf hónom minnis-veig. Heill dagr . . . meðan lifom. Hon nefndiz Sigrdrífa, ok var Valkyrja. Hon sagði, at tveir konungr bǫrðuz ; hét annarr Hialm-gunnarr, hann var þá gamall, ok inn mesti her-maðr, ok hafði Oðinn hónom sigri heitið. Enn Annarr hét . . . þiggja. Sigrdrífa felldi Hialm-gunnar í orrostonni. Enn Óðinn stakk hána svefn-þorni í hefud þess, ok kvað hána alldri skylldo síðan sigr vega í orrosto, ok kvað hána giptaz skylldo. Enn ek sagðak hónom, at ek strengðak heit þar í mót, at giptaz ongom þeim manni er hræðaz kynni. Hann svarar ok biðr hána kenna ser speki, ef hon vissi tíðindi or ollom heimom. Sigrdrífa kvað. Biór fœri ek þer . . .

II. AFTER THE LACUNA.

[N. B. For the paraphrase of the Lays in the Lacuna see next page.]

At the end of the Short Brunhild Lay.—Innan fáðar. **Frá dauða Sigurðar.** Her er sagt í þessi kviðo frá dauða Sigurðar, ok víkr her svá til, sem þeir dræpi hann úti. Enn sumir segja svá, at þeir dræpi hann inni í rekkjo sinni sofanda. Enn þyðverskir menn segja svá, at þeir dræpi hann úti í skógi, ok svá segir í Guðrúnar kviðo inni Forno, at Sigurðr ok Giúka synir hefði til þings riðit, þá er hann var drepinn. Enn þat segja allir einnig, at þeir sviko hann í trygð, ok vógo at hónom liggjanda ok óbúnom. Guðrún sat yfir Sigurði dauðom. Hon grét eigi sem aðrar konor; enn hon var buin til at springa af harmi. Til gengo bæði konor ok karlar at hugga hána, enn þat var eigi auð-vellt. þat er sogn manna, at Guðrún hefði etið af Fáfnis hiarta, ok hon skilði því fugls rodd. þetta er enn kveðit um Guðrúno. **Guðrúnar kviða.** Ar var þatz Guðrun . . .

At the end.—(Er hon sar um leit a Sigurði.) Guðrún gekk þaðan á braut til skógar á eyði-merkr, ok fór allt til Danmarkar, ok var þar með þóro Háconar dóttor siau misseri. Brynhildr vildi eigi lifa eptir Sigurð; hon lét drepa þræla sína átta ok fimm ambóttir. þá lagði hon sik sverði til bana. Svá sem segir í Sigurðar kviðo inni Skommo.

The Long Lay of Brunhild, after line 287.—Eptir dauða Brynhildar vóro gor bál tvau, annat Sigurði, ok brann þat fyrr, enn Brynhildr var á oðro brennd, ok var hon í reið þeirri er guðvefjom var tiolldoð. Sva er sagt, at Brynhildr ók með reið-inni á Hel-veg, ok fór um tún þar er Gygr nokkor bió. Gygrin kvað. Scaltu í gognom, etc.

Dráp Niflunga.—Gunnarr ok Hogni tóko þá gullit allt Fáfniss arf. Ófriðr var þá í milli Giúkunga ok Atla; kenndi hann Giúkungom vold um andlát Brynhildar. þat var til setta, at þeir skyldo gipta hónom Guðrúno, ok gáfo henni óminnis-veig at drekka áðr hon iátti at giptaz Atla. Synir Atla vóro þeir Erpr ok Eitill, enn Svanhilldr var Sigurðar dóttir ok Guðrúnar. Atli konungr bauð heim Gunnari ok Hogna, ok sendi Vinga eða Knefrœð. Guðrún vissi vélar, ok sendi með rúnom orð, at þeir skyldo eigi koma. Ok til iartegna sendi hon Hogna hringinn Andvara-naut, ok knýtti í vargs hár. Gunnarr hafði beðit Oddrúnar systor Atla, ok gat eigi. þá fekk hann Glaumvarar, enn Hogni átti Kostbero; þeirra synir vóro þeir Sólarr ok Snœvarr ok Giúki. Enn er Giúkungar kómo til Atla, þá bað Guðrún sono sína, at þeir bæði Giúkungom lífs; enn þeir vildo eigi. Hiarta var scorit or Hogna, enn Gunnarr settr í orm-garð. Hann sló horpo ok svæfði ormana; enn naðra stakk hann til lifrar. þióðrekr konungr var með Atla, ok hafði þar látið flesta allam enn sína. þióðrekr ok Guðrún kærðo harma sín á milli. on sagði hónom ok kvað. Mær var ek meyja . . .

The Ordeal of Gudrun.

Herkja hét ambott Atla; hon hafði verit frilla hans. Hon sagði Atla at hon hefði séð þióðrek ok Guðrúno bæði saman. Atli var þá all-ókátr. þá kvað Gúðrun. **Kviða Guðrunar.** Hvat er þer Atli . . .

Lamentation of Ordrun.

Fra Borgnyjo ok Oddrúno.—Heiðrekr hét konungr. Dóttir hans het Borgný.
Vilmundr hét sá er var friðill hennar. Hon mátti eigi fœða born áðr til kom
Oddrún Atla systir ; hon hafði verit unnosta Gunnars Giúka sonar. Um þessa sǫgo
er her kveðit. Heyrða ek . . .

The Lay of Atli.

Dauði Atla.—Guðrún Giúka dóttir hefndi brœðra sínna svá sem frægt er orðit.
Hon drap fyrst sono Atla, enn eptir drap hon Atla, ok brendi hollina ok hirðina
alla. Um þetta er siá kviða ort. **Atla quiða in Grœnlenzca.** Atli sendi . . .
At the end.—Enn segir gleggra í Atla-málom enom Grœnlenzkom.

The Chain of Woe and Hamtheow Lay Medley.

Guðrún gekk þá til sævar er hon hafði drepit Atla. Gekk hon út á sæinn ok vildi
fara ser. Hon mátti eigi sœcqua. Rak hána yfir fiorðinn á land Ionakrs konungs ;
hann fekk hennar ; þeirra synir vóro þeir Savrli ok Erpr ok Hamþer. þar fœddiz
upp Svanhildr Sigurðar dóttir, hon var gipt Iormunreck enom ríkja. Með hánom
var Bicci. Hann réð þat, at Randvér konungs son skyldi taka hána [blank]. þat
sagði Bicci konungi. Konungr lét hengja Randvé, enn troða Svanhilldi undir
hrossa fótom. Enn er þat spurði Guðrún, þá kvaddi hon sono sína. **Guðrunar
hvavt.** þá fra ek senno . . .
At the end of Hamtheow Lay.—þetta ero kolloð Hamþiss mál in Forno.

III. LAY OF RIGH (in Cod. Wormianus of Snorri's Edda).

Svá segja menn í fornoms ǫgom, at einn hverr af Ásom, sa er Heimdallr hét, fór
ferðar sínnar ok framm með siovar-strǫndo nokkorri ; kom at einom húsa-bœ, ok
nefndiz Rígr. Eptir þeirri sǫgo er kvæði þetta . . .

2. WOLSUNGA PARAPHRASE OF THE LACUNA LAYS.
(Englished on pp. 391–399, vol. i.)

SIGURÐR ríðr nú þar til er hann kemr at einum miklum bæ ; þar réð fyrir einn
mikill hofðingi sá er Heimir hét ; hann átti systur Brynhildar, er Bekkhildr hét,
því at hón hafði heima verit, ok numit hannyrðir, enn Brynhildr fór með hialm ok
í rynju, ok gekk at[1] vígum ; var hón því kolluð Brynhildr. Heimir ok Bekkhildr
áttu einn son er Alsviðr hét, manna kurteisastr. þar léku menn úti ; ok er þeir siá
reið mannzins at bænum, hætta þeir leiknum ok undraz manninn, því at þeir
höfðu engan slíkan sét ; gengu í mót hónum ok fögnuðu hónum vel. Alsviðr býðr
hónum með ser at vera, ok af ser at þiggja slíkt er hann vill ; hann þiggr þat.
Hónum er ok skipat vegliga at þióna ; fiórir menn hófu gullit af hestinum, enn
fimti tók við hónum. þar mátti siá marga góða gripi ok fá-séna : var þat at
skemtan haft, at siá á[2] brynjur ok hialma, ok stóra hringa, ok undarliga mikil gull-
staup, ok allz konar her-vápn. Sigurðr dvelz þar lengi í mikilli semð ; spyrz nú
þetta fregðar-verk um öll lönd, er hann hafði drepit þann inn ógurliga dreka. þeir
undu ser nú vel, ok var hvár öðrum hollr. þat höfðu þeir at skemtan, at bua vápn
sín, ok skepta örvar sínar, ok beita haukum sínum.

---

[1] at] á, Cd.   [2] siá á] sia, Cd.

þá var komin til Heimiss Brynhildr fóstra hans; hón sat í einni skemmu við meyjar sínar. Hón kunni meira hagleik, en aðrar konur; hón lagði sínn borða með gulli, ok saumaði á þau stór-merki er Sigurðr hafði gört, dráp ormsins, ok upp-töku fiárins ok dauða Regins. Ok einn dag er frá því sagt, at Sigurðr reið á skóg við hundum sínum ok haukum, ok miklu fiölmenni. Ok er hann kom heim, fló hans haukr á hávan turn ok settiz við einn glugg. Sigurðr fór eptir haukinum: þá ser hann eina fagra konu; ok kennir, at þar er Brynhildr. Hónum þykkir nú um vert allt saman, fegrð hennar ok þat er hón görir; kœmr í höllina ok vill önga skemtan við menn eiga. Þá mælti Alsviðr: Hví eru þer svá fálátir? þessi skipan þín harmar oss[1] þína vini, eða hví máttu eigi gleði bella[2]? Haukar þínir hnípa, ok svá hestrinn Grani[3], ok þessa fám ver seint bót. Sigurðr svarar: Góðr vin, heyr hvat ek hugsa! minn haukr fló á einn turn, ok er ek tók hann, sá ek eina fagra konu, hón sat við einn gulligan borða ok las þar á mín liðin ok fram komin verk. Alsviðr svarar: þú hefir sét Brynhildi Buðla dóttur, er mestr skörungr er. Sigurðr svarar: þat mun satt vera; eða hversu [longu] kom hón her? Alsviðr svarar: þess var skamt í milli ok þer kvómut. Sigurðr segir: þat vissu ver fyrir fám dögum; sú kona hefir oss bezt sýnz í veroldu. Alsviðr mælti: Gef ekki gaum at einni konu, þvílíkr maðr; er þat íllt at sýta er maðr fær eigi. Hána skal ek hitta, segir Sigurðr, ok gefa henni gull, ok ná hennar gamni ok iafnaðar þokka. Alsviðr svarar: Engi fannz sá enn um aldr, er hón léði rúms hiá ser eða gæfi öl at drekka; hon vill sik í herskap hafa ok allz konar frægð at fremja. Sigurðr mælti: Ver vitum eigi hvárt hón svarar oss eða eigi, eða lér oss sess hiá ser. Ok annan dag eptir gekk Sigurðr til skemmunnar, enn Alsviðr stóð hiá skemmunni úti, ok skepti örvar sínar. Sigurðr mælti: Sit heil frú! eða hversu megi þer? Hón svarar: Vel megum ver; frændr lifa ok vinir; enn háttung er í hverja giptu menn bera til síns enda-dags. Hann setz hiá henni. Síðan ganga þar inn fiorar konur með stórum borð-kerum af gulli, ok með inu bezta víni, ok standa fyrir þeim. þá mælti Brynhildr: þetta sæti mun fám veitt vera, nema faðir mínn komi. Hann svarar: Nú er veitt þeim er oss líkar. Herbergit var tialdat af ínum dýrstum tiöldum, ok þakit klæðum (?) allt golfit. Sigurðr mælti: Nú er þat fram komit, er þer hétuð oss. Hón svarar: þér skoluð her vel komnir. Síðan reis hón upp, ok fiórar meyjar með henni, ok gekk fyrir hann með gull-ker, ok bað hann drekka. Hann réttir í mót höndina kerinu, ok tók hönd hennar með, ok setti hána hiá ser; hann tók um hals henni, kyssti hána ok mælti: Engi kona hefir þer fegri fæzt. Brynhildr mælti: Vitrlegra ráð er þat, at leggja eigi trúnað sínn á konu vald, því at þær riúfa iafnan sin heit. Hann mælti: Sá kœmi beztr dagr yfir oss, at ver mættim niótaz. Brynhildr svarar: Eigi er þat skipat at vit buim saman: ek em skiald-mær, ok á ek með her-konungum hialm; ok þeim man ek at liði verða; ok ekki er mer leitt at berjaz. Sigurðr mælti: þá frioumz ver mest, ef ver buum saman, ok meira er at þola þann harm, er her liggr á, en hvöss vápn. Brynhildr svarar: Ek man kanna lið her-manna, enn þú mant eiga Guðrúnu Giúka dóttur. Sigurðr svarar: Eigi tælir mik eins konungs dóttir, ok ekki lér mer tveggja huga um þetta; ok þess sver ek við guðin, at ek skal þik eiga, eða enga konu ella. Hón mælti slikt: Sigurðr þakkar henni þessi ummæli, ok gaf henni gull-hring; ok svörðu nú eiða af nýju; ok gengr hann í brott til sínna manna, ok er þar um hríð með míklum blóma. [ch. xxiii, xxiv.]

. . . Eitt sinn segir Guðrún meyjum sínum, at hón má eigi glöð vera. Ein kona spyr hána, hvat henni sé at úgleði. Hón svarar: Eigi fengu vér tíma í draumum; er því harmr í hiarta mer; ráð drauminn þar er þú fréttir eptir. Hón svarar: Seg mer

---

[1] ok add. Cd.   [2] bella] halda, Cd.   [3] A verse unchanged.

ok lát þik eigi hryggja, því at iafnan dreymir fyrir veðrum. Guðrún svarar: þetta er ekki veðr: þat dreymði mik, at ek sá einn fagran hauk mer á hendi, fiaðrar hans vóru með gulligum lit. Konan svarar: Margir hafa spurt af yðrum vænleik, vizku ok kurteisi; nökkurs konungs son mun biðja þín. Guðrún svarar: Engi hlutr þótti mer haukinum betri, ok allt mítt fé vilda ek heldr láta enn hann. Konan svarar: Sá er þú fær, man vera vel mentr, ok muntu unna hónom mikit. Guðrún svarar: þat angrar mik, at ek veit eigi hverr hann er; ok skulum ver hitta Brynhildi; hón mun vita. þær biogguz með gulli ok mikilli fegrð, ok fóru með meyjum sínum, unz þær kómu at höll Brynhildar; sú höll var buin með gulli, ok stóð á einu bergi. Ok er sén er ferð þeira, þá er Brynhildi sagt, at margar konur óku at borginni með gyltum vögnum. [Brynhildr svarar:] þar mun vera Guðrún Giúka dóttir; mik dreymði [1] hána í nótt ok göngum út í mót henni, ekki sækja oss fríðari konur heim. þær gengu út í móti þeim, ok fögnuðu vel; þær gengu inn í þá ina fögru höll. Salrinn var skrifaðr innan ok miök silfri buinn; klæði vóru breidd undir fætr þeim, ok þiónuðu allir þeim. þær höfðu margs konar leika. Guðrún var fá-orð. Brynhildr mælti: Hví megi þer eigi gleði bella? ger eigi þat; skemtum oss allar saman, ok ræðum um ríka konunga ok þeirra stór-virki. Gerum þat, segir Guðrún; eða hverja veiztu fremsta konunga verit hafa? Brynhildr svarar: Sonu [Hamundar] Haka ok Hagbarð [2]; þeir unnu mörg frægðar verk í hernaði. Guðrún svarar: Miklir vóru þeir ok ágætir, enn þó nam Sigarr systur þeirra, enn hefir aðra inni brennda [3], ok eru þeir seinir at hefna. Eða hví nefnðir þú eigi bræðr mína, er nú þikkja fremstir menn? Brynhildr segir: þat er í góðum efnum; enn eigi eru þeir enn miök reyndir; ok veit ek einn miök af þeim bera, en þat er Sigurðr son Sigmundar konungs; hann var þá barn er hann drap sonu Hundings konungs, ok hefndi föður síns ok Eylima móður-föður síns. Guðrún mælti: Hvat var til merkja um þat? segir þú hann borinn þá er faðir hans fell? Brynhildr svarar: Móðir hans gekk í valinn, ok fann Sigmund konung sáran, ok bauð at binda sár hans; enn hann kvezt of gamall síðan at berjaz, enn bað hána við þat huggaz, at hón mundi œztan son ala; ok var þar 'Spá spaks geta.' Ok eptir andlát Sigmundar konungs fór hón með Alfi konungi, ok var Sigurðr þar upp fæddr í mikilli virðingu, ok vann hann mörg afreks verk á hverjum degi, ok er hann ágætastr maðr í veröldu. Guðrún mælti: Af ást hefir þú fréttum til hans haldit; enn af því kom ek her at segja þer drauma mína, er mer fengu mikillar áhyggju. Brynhildr svarar: Lát þik eigi slíkt angra; ver með frendum þínum, er allir vilja þik gleðja. þat dreymði mik, sagði Guðrún, at ver gengim frá skemmu margar saman ok sám enn mikinn hiört; hann bar langt af öðrum dýrum; hár hans var af gulli; vér vildum allar taka dýrit, enn ek ein náða; dýrit þótti mer öllum hlutum betra; síðan skauztu dýrit fyrir kniám mer; var mer þat svá mikill harmr, at ek mátta trautt bera; síðan gaftu mer einn ulf-hvelp, sá dreifði mik blóði bræðra mínna. Brynhildr svarar: Ek mun ráða sem eptir man ganga: Til ykkar mun koma Sigurðr, sá er ek kaus mer til mannz; Grímhildr gefr hónum mein-blandinn miöð, er öllum oss kemr í mikit stríð; hann muntu eiga ok hann skiótt missa; þú munt eiga Atla konung; missa muntu bræðra þínna; ok þá muntu Atla vega. Guðrún svarar: Of-harmr er oss þat, at vita slíkt.—Ok fara þær nú í brott ok heim til Giúka konungs. [ch. xxv.]

Sigurðr ríðr nú í brott með þat mikla gull; skiljaz þeir nú vinir; hann ríðr Grana með öllum sínum her-búnaði ok farmi; hann ríðr þar til er hann kom at höll Giúka konungs, ríðr nú í borgina. Ok þat sér einn af konungs mönnum, ok mælti:

---

[1] dreymði um, Cd., = dreymðomk of the Lay.   [2] ss. haka ok hagbarð, Cd.
[3] This is doubtful, probably corrupt, but we know not the clue to it.

þat hygg ek, at her fari einn af goðunum; þessi maðr er allr við gull buinn, hestr hans er miklu meiri en aðrir hestar, ok afburðar-vænn vápna-burðr; hann er langt um aðra menn framm, enn sialfr berr hann þó mest af öðrum mönnum. Konungrinn gengr út með hirð sína, ok kvaddi manninn, ok spyrr: Hverr ertu, er ríðr í borgina, er engi þorði nema at leyfi sona mínna? Hann svarar: Ek heiti Sigurðr, ok em ek son Sigmundar konungs. Giúki konungr mælti: Vel skaltu herr kominn með oss, ok þigg her slíkt sem þú vilt. Ok hann gengr inn í höllina, ok vóru allir lágir hiá hónum, ok allir þiónuðu hónum, ok var hann þar í miklu yfirlæti. þeir ríða allir saman, Sigurðr, ok Gunnarr, ok Högni, ok þó er Sigurðr fyrir þeim um alla atgervi, ok eru þó allir miklir menn fyrir ser. þat finnr Grímhildr, hvé mikit Sigurðr ann Brynhildi, ok hve opt hann getr hennar; hugsar fyrir ser, at þat væri meiri gipta, at hann stað-festiz þar, ok ætti dóttur Giúka konungs; ok, sá at engi mátti við hann iafnaz; sá ok, hvert traust at hónum var, ok hafði of [1] fiár, miklu meira, en menn vissi dæmi til. Konungr var við hann sem við sonu sína, enn þeir virðu hann framarr en sik. Eitt kveld er þeir sátu við drykk, ríss dróttning upp ok gekk fyrir Sigurð, ok kvaddi hann ok mælti: Fögnuðr er oss á þínni her-vist, ok allt gótt viljum ver til yðar leggja. Tak her við horni, ok drekk! Hann tók við ok drakk af. Hón mælti: þinn faðir skal vera Giúki konungr, enn ek móðir, bræðr þínir Gunnarr ok Högni;

ok allir ér eiða vinnit [2].

Ok munu þá eigi yðrir iafningjar fázt. Sigurðr tók því vel. Ok við þann drykk mundi hann ekki til Brynhildar. Hann dvaldiz þar um hríð. Ok eitt sinn gekk Grímhildr fyrir Giúka konung, ok lagði hendr um hals hónum ok mælti: Her er nú kominn inn mesti kappi er finnaz mun í veröldu; væri at hónum mikit traust; gipt hónum dóttur þína með miklu fé, ok slíku ríki sem hann vill, ok mætti hann her yndi nema. Konungr svarar: Fá-títt er þat, at bióða fram dætr sínar; enn meiri vegr er at bióða hónum, en aðrir biði. Ok eitt kveld skenkir Guðrún. Sigurðr sér, at hón er væn kona, ok at öllu en kurteisasta. Fimm misseri var Sigurðr þar, sva at þeir sátu með frægð ok vingan, ok ræðaz konungar nú við. Giúki konungr mælti: Mart gótt veitir þú oss, Sigurðr, ok miök hefir þú styrkt várt ríki. Gunnarr mælti: Allt viljum ver til vinna, at þer dveliz her lengi, bæði ríki, ok vára systur með boði, er [3] eigi mundi annarr fá þótt bæði. Sigurðr svarar: Hafit þökk fyrir yðra sæmd, ok þetta skal þiggja. þeir sverjaz nú í bræðra-lag, sem þeir sé sam-bornir bræðr. Nú er ger ágætlig veizla, ok stóð marga daga, drekkr Sigurðr nú bruðlaup til Guðrúnar, mátti þar siá margs konar gleði ok skemtan, ok var hvern dag veitt öðrum betr. þeir fóru nú víða um lönd ok vinna mörg frægðarverk, drápu marga konunga sonu, ok engir menn gerðu slík afrek sem þeir; fara nú heim með miklu her-fangi. Sigurðr gaf Guðrúnu at éta af Fáfniss hiarta, ok síðan var hón mikla grimmari en áðr ok vitrari. þeirra son hét Sigmundr. Ok eitt sinn gekk Grímhildr at Gunnari syni sínum ok mælti: Yðart ráð stendr með miklum blóma, fyrir útan einn hlut, er þer erut kván-lausir; biðit Brynhildar, þat er göfgazt ráð, ok mun Sigurðr ríða með yðr. Gunnarr svarar: Víst er hón væn, ok eigi em ek þessa ófúss. ᴜk segir nú feðr sínum ok bræðrum ok Sigurði, ok eru allir fýsandi. þeir bua nú ferð sína listuliga; ríða nú fiöll ok dali til Buðla konungs, bera upp bónorðit; hann tók því vel, ef hón vill eigi níta, ok segir hána svá stóra, at þann einn mann mun hón eiga vilja, er hón vill. þá ríða þeir í Hlymdali. Heimir fagnar þeim vel. Segir Gunnarr nú erendin. Heimir kvað hennar kiör vera hvern hón skal eiga; segir þar sal hennar skamt frá, ok kvazt þat hyggja, at þann einn mundi hón

---

[1] ofr, Cd.   [2] A verse line.   [3] er] en, Cd.

eiga vilja er riði eld brennanda, er sleginn er um sal hennar. þeir finna salinn ok eldinn, ok siá þar borg gulli byrsta, ok brann eldr um útan. Gunnarr reið Gota, enn Högni Hœlkvi. Gunnarr keyrir hestinn at eldinum, enn hann hopar. Sigurðr mælti: Hví hopar þú, Gunnarr. Hann svarar: Eigi vill hestrinn hlaupa þenna eld, ok biðr Sigurð liá ser Grana. Heimilt er þat, segir Sigurðr. Gunnarr ríðr nú at eldinum, ok vill Grani eigi ganga. Gunnarr má nú eigi ríða þenna eld. Skipta nú litum, sem Grímhildr kendi þeim Sigurði ok Gunnari. Síðan ríðr Sigurðr, ok hefir Gram í hendi, ok bindr gull-spora á fætr ser. Grani hleypr fram at eldinum er hann kenndi sporans. Nú verðr gnýr mikill, er

eldrinn tók at æsaz, en iörð tók at skialfa,

loginn stóð við himin. þetta þorði engi at gera fyrr, ok var sem hann riði í myrkva; þá lægðiz eldrinn, enn hann gekk af hestinum inn í salinn. Svá er kveðit [Eldr nam at æsaz . . . Reginn átti, see Fragment, Book v, § 3, pp. 314, 315]. Ok er Sigurðr kom inn um logann, fann hann þar eitt fagrt herbergi, ok þar sat í Brynhildr. Hón spyrr hverr sá maðr er. Enn hann nefndiz Gunnarr Giúka son, ertu ok ætluð mín kona með iá-yrði feðr þíns—ef ek riða þinn vafor-loga—ok fóstra þíns með yðru atkvæði.—Eigi veit ek gerla hversu ek skal þessu svara. Sigurðr stóð réttr á golfinu ok studdiz á sverðz hiöltin ok mælti til Brynhildar: þer í mót skal ek gialda mikinn mund í gulli ok góðum gripum. Hón svarar af áhyggju af sínu sæti, sem alpt af báru, ok hefir sverð í hendi, ok hialm á höfði, ok var í brynju: Gunnarr, segir hón, ræð ekki slíkt við mik, nema þú sért hverjum manni fremri, ok þá skaltu drepa er mín hafa beðit, ef þú hefir traust til. Ek var í orrostu með Garða konungi, ok vóru vápn vór lituð í manna blóði, ok þess girnumz ver enn. Hann svarar: Mörg stórvirki hafi þer unnit; enn minniz nú á þat þessi eldr væri riðinn, at þer mundit með þeim manni ganga er þetta gerði. Hón finur nú her sönn svör ok merki þessa máls; stendr upp ok fagnar hónum vel. þar dvelz hann þriár nætr, ok bua eina rekkju; hann tekr sverðit Gram, ok leggr í meðal þeirra bert. Hón spyrr hví þat sætti. Hann kvað ser þat skapat [1], at svá görði hann brúðlaup til konu sínnar, eða fengi ella bana. Hann tók þá af henni hringinn Andvara-naut, er hann gaf henni; enn fékk henni nú annan hring af Fáfniss-arfi. Eptir þetta ríðr hann brott í þann sama eld til sínna félaga, ok skipta þeir aptr litum, ok ríða síðan í Hlymdali, ok segja hve farit hafði. þann sama dag fór Brynhildr heim til fóstra síns, ok segir hónum af trúnaði, at til hennar kom einn konungr, Ok reið mínn vafor-loga, ok kvazt kominn til ráða við mik, ok nefndiz Gunnarr; enn ek sagða, at þat mundi Sigurðr einn gœra, er ek vann eiða á fiallinu; ok er hann mínn frum-verr. Heimir kvað nú svá buit vera mundu. [Brynhildr mælti: Dóttur okkar Sigurðar, Áslaugu, skal her upp fæða með þer [2].] Fara konungar nú heim;—enn Brynhildr fór til föður síns.—Grímhildr fagnar þeim vel, ok þakkar Sigurði sína fylgð. Er þar buizt við veizlu; kom þar mikill mann-fiöldi; þar kom Buðli konungr með dóttur sína, ok Atli son hans, ok hefir þessi veizla staðit marga daga. Ok er lokit er þessi veizlu, minnir Sigurð allra eiða við Brynhildi, ok lætr þó vera kyrt. Brynhildr ok Gunnar sátu við skemtan ok drukku gótt vín. [ch. xxvi, xxvii.]

þat er einn dag, er þær gengu til árinnar saman at þvá ser. þá óð Brynhildr lengra út á ána. Guðrún spyrr hví þat gegndi. Brynhildr segir: Hví skal ek um þetta iafnaz við þik, heldr en um annat; ek hugða, at mínn faðir væri ríkari enn þínn, ok mínn maðr unnit mörg snildar-verk, ok riði (!) eld brennanda; enn þínn bóndi var þræll Hialpreks konungs. Guðrún svarar með reiði: þá værir þú vitrari ef þú þegðir, en lastaðir mann mínn; er þat allra manna mál, at engi hafi slíkr komit í

---

[1] Emend.; skipað, Cd.   [2] [ ] an interpolation.

veröldina fyrir hvers vetna sakir; ok eigi samir þer vel at lasta hann, þvi at hann er
þínn frum-verr, ok drap hann Fáfni ok reið váfur-logann, er þú hugðir Gunnar
konung; ok hann lá hiá þer, ok tók af hendi þer hringinn Andvara-naut; ok máttu
nú her hann kenna. Brynhildr sér nú þenna hring ok kennir; þá fölnar hón, sem
hón dauð væri. Brynhildr fór heim, ok mælti ekki orð um kveldit. Ok er Sigurðr
kom í rekkju, spyrr Guðrún: Hví er Brynhildr svá úkát? Sigurðr svarar: Eigi
veit ek glöggt, enn grunar mik at ver munum vita brátt nökkuru görr. Guðrún
mælti: Hví unir hón eigi auð ok sælu ok allra manna lofi, ok fengit þann mann
sem hón vildi? Sigurðr mælti: Hvar var hón þá er hón sagði þat, at hón þœttiz
enn œzta [ver] eiga, eða þann er hón vildi helzt eiga. Guðrún svarar: Ek skal
eptir spyrja á morgin, hvern hón vill helzt eiga. Sigurðr svarar: þess let ek þik; ok
iðraz muntu, ef þú gœrir þat. Ok um morgunininn sátu þær í skemmu sínni, ok var
Brynhildr hlióð. þá mælti Guðrún: Ver kát, Brynhildr; angrar þik okkart við-
tal? eða hvat stendr þer fyrir gamni? Brynhildr svarar: Illt eitt gengr þer til
þessa, ok hefir þú grimt hiarta. Virð eigi svá, segir Guðrún, ok seg heldr. Brynhildr svarar: Spyr þess eina, at bezt sé attú vitir; þat samir ríkum konum; ok er
Gótt góðu at una, er yðr gengr allt at óskum. Guðrún svarar: Snemt er því enn
at hæla, ok er þetta nokkur svá [1] for-spá; hvat reki [2] þer at oss? ver görðum yðr
ekki til angrs. Brynhildr svarar: þess skaltu gialda, er þú átt Sigurð, ok ek ann
þer eigi hans at nióta né gullz ins mikla. Guðrún svaraði: Eigi vissa ek yður ummæli, ok vel mætti faðir mínn siá ráð fyrir mer, þóttú værir ekki at hitt. Brynhildr
svarar: Ekki höfum vit laun-mæli haft, ok þó hofum vit eiða svarit, ok vissu þer
þat, at þer véltuð mik; ok skal þess hefna. Guðrún svarar: þú ert betr gefin en
makligt er, ok þínn ofsi man ílla siatna, ok þess munu margir gialda. Una mundu
ver, segir Brynhildr, ef eigi ættir þú göfgara mann. Guðrún svarar: Áttú svá
göfgan mann, at úvíst er, hverr meiri konungr er, ok gnótt fiár ok ríkiss. Brynhildr
svarar: Sigurðr vá at Fáfni, ok er þat meira vert, enn allt ríki Gunnars konungs.
Svá sem kveðit er: Sigurðr vá at ormi . . . yfir stíga. Guðrún svarar: Grani rann
eigi eldinn undir Gunnari konungi, enn hann þorði at ríða, ok þarf hónum eigi hugar
at frýja. Brynhildr svarar: Dyljumz eigi við, at ek hygg Grímhildi eigi vel. Guðrún svarar: Ámæl henni eigi, því at hón er til þín sem til dóttur sínnar. Brynhildr
svarar: Hón veldr öllum upphófum þessa böls er oss bítr; hón bar Sigurði grimt öl,
sva at eigi mundi hann mitt nafn. Guðrún svarar: Mart rangt orð mælir þú, ok
mikil lygi er slíkt. Brynhildr svarar: Nióti þer svá Sigurðar, sem þer hafit mik [3]
svikit, ok er yðar sam-veldi [4] úmakligt, ok gangi yðr svá sem ek hygg. Guðrún
svarar: Betr mun ek nióta en þú mundir vilja, ok engi gat þess, at hann ætti of
gótt [5] við mik ne eitt sinn. Brynhildr svarar: Illa mælir þú, ok er af þer rennr,
mantú iðraz; ok hendum eigi heipt-yrði. Guðrún segir: þú kastaðir fyrri heiptar-
orðum á mik; lætr þú nú sem þú munir yfir bæta, enn þó býr grimt undir. Leggjum
niðr ónýtt hial, segir Brynhildr; ek þagða lengi yfir mínum harmi þeim er mer bió
í brósti; enn ek ann þínum bróður at eins; ok tökum annat hial. Guðrún segir:
Langt sér hugr þínn um framm.—Ok þar af stóð mikill ófagnaðr er þær gengu á
ána, ok hón kenndi hringinn; ok þar af varð þeirra viðræða. [ch. xxviii.]

Eptir þetta tal leggz Brynhildr í rekkju. Ok kómu þessi tíðendi fyrir Gunnar
konung, at Brynhildr er siúk. Hann hittir hana, ok spyrr hvat henni sé, enn hón
svarar engu ok liggr sem hón sé dauð. Ok er hann leitar eptir fast, þá svarar hón:
Hvat görðir þú af hring þeim er ek selda þer, er Atli [6] konungr gaf mer at efsta

<hr />

[1] svá] su, Cd.   [2] =ræki?   [3] eigi, add. Cd.   [4] Thus?   [5] Thus,
corrupt.   [6] Atli] emend.; Buðli, Cd.

skilnaði, er þer Giúkungar kómuð til hans, ok hét ek at herja ok brenna heldr en þer næðit mér[1]. Síðan leiddi hann mik á tal, ok spyrr hvern ek kœra af þeim sem komnir váru ; enn ek buðumk til at verja landit ok vera höfðingi yfir þriðjungi liðs. Váru þá tveir kostir fyrir hendi, at ek munda þeim verða at giptaz sem hann vildi, eða vera án allz fiár ok hans vináttu ; kvað þó sína vináttu mer mundu betr gegna en reiði. þú hugsaða ek með mer hvárt ek skylda fella val, ok drepa margan mann[2]; ek þottumk van-fær til at þreyta við hann. Ok þar kom at ek hétumk þeim er riði hestinum Grana með Fáfnis arfi, ok ridi mínn vafur loga, ok dræpi þá menn er ek kvað á. Nú treystiz engi at ríða nema Sigurðr einn ; hann reið eldinn, þvi at hann skorti eigi hug til ; hann drap Orminn ok Regin ok fimm konunga, enn eigi þú, Gunnarr, er þú fölnaðir sem nár, ok ertu engi konungr né kappi ; ok þess strengða ek heit heima at feðr míns, at ek munda þeim einum unna, er ágætztr væri alinn ; enn þat er Sigurðr ; nú erum ver eið-rofa, er ver eigum hann eigi, ok fyrir þetta skal ek ráðandi þíns dauða ; ok eigum ver Grímhildi íllt at launa, henni finzt engi kona 'huglausari[3]' né verri. Gunnarr svarar, svá at fáir heyrðu : Mörg flærðar-orð hefir þú mælt, ok ertu ill-úðig kona, er þú ámælir þeirri konu, er miök er um þik fram, ok engi mann tók hon undir ver sínn[4], svá sem þú görir, eða kvaldi dauða menn, ok engan myrði hón, ok lifir við lof. Brynhildr svarar : Ekki höfum ver laun-þing haft né óðáðir gert, ok annat er várt eðli, ok fúsari verim ver at drepa yðr. Síðan vildi hón drepa Gunnar konung ; enn Högni setri hána í fiötra. Gunnarr mælti þá. Eigi vil ek at hón bui í fiötrum. Hón svarar : Hirð eigi þú þat, þvi at aldri sér þú mik glaða síðan í þínni höll, eða drekka né tefla, né hugat mæla, né gulli leggja góð klæði, né yðr ráð gefa. Kvað hón ser þat mestan harm, at hón átti eigi Sigurð. Hón settiz 'upp ok sló sinn borða svá at sundr gekk, ok bað upp luka[5] skemmu durum[6].' Ok langa leið mátti[7] heyra 'hennar' harma-tölur. Nú er harmr mikill ok hreimr[8] um allan bæinn. Guðrún spyrr skemmu meyjar sínar, hví þær sé svá úkátar eða hryggvar.—Eða hvat er yðr ? Eða hví fari þer sem vitlausir menn ? Eða hverr geiski[9] er yðr orðinn ? þá svarar hirð-kona ein er Svafrlöð hét : þetta er ótíma-dagr, vár höll er full af harmi. þá mælti Guðrún til sínnar vin-konu : Stattu upp ! ver höfum lengi sofit ; vek Brynhildi ; göngum til borða ok verum kátar. þat göri ek eigi, sagði hón, at vekja hána, né við hána mæla ; ok mörg dægr drakk hón eigi miöð né vín, ok hefir hón fengið goða reiði. þá mælti Guðrún til Gunnars : Gekk at hitta hána, eða hennar fé at skipta[10]. þó ferr Gunnarr at hitta hána, ok leitar marga vega málsenda við hána, ok fær ekki af um svörin, gengr nú á brott ok hittir Högna, ok biðr hann finna hána ; enn hann kvezt vera ófúss, ok ferr þó, ok fekk ekki af henni. Ok er hittr Sigurðr ok beðinn at finna hána. Hann svarar engu ; ok er svá buit um kveldit. Ok annan dag eptir, er hann kom af dýra-veiðum, hitti hann Guðrúnu ok mælti : þann veg hefir fyrir mik borit, sem þetta muni til mikils koma, hrollr siá, ok mun Brynhildr deyja. Guðrún svarar : Herra mínn, mikil kynsl fylgja henni ; hón hefir nú sofit siau dœgr, svá at engi þorði at vekja hána. Sigurðr svarar : Eigi sefr hón ; hón hefir stór-ræði með höndum við okkr. þá mælti

---

[1] Emend. ; ok hétuð at herja eðr brenna nema þer næðit mer, Cd. [2] Emend. (cp. Long Lay of Brunh. l. 150) ; hvart ek skylda hans vilja eða dr. m. m., Cd. [3] Thus, corrupt. [4] Emend. (see Introd. § 14, p. lxxxix) ; ok eigi yndi hón ver sínu, Cd. [5] Read, bað-at upp lúka ? [6] This passage is quite corrupt. From the context we see that Brunhild shut herself up in her room (like Egil in his sorrow ; the colouring of the Saga may be taken from here), and no one dared to approach her ; 'hennar harma tolur' is certainly wrong : Brunhild's grief is silent, sullen, brooding ; the wailing all refers to her household. [7] ok . . . mátti] at . . . mætti, Cd. [8] Emend. ; Nú er harmr mikill ok heyrir, Cd. [9] gyzki, Cd. [10] Something wrong or missing.

Guðrún með gráti: þat er mikill harmr, at vita þínn bana. Far heldr ok finn hána, ok vit, ef siatni hennar ofsi; gef henni gull, ok mýk svá hennar reiði.

Sigurðr gekk út, ok fann opinn salinn, hann hugði hána sofa, ok brá af henni klæðum, ok mælti: Vaki þú, Brynhildr, sól skínn um allan bæinn, ok er ærit sofit, hritt af þer harmi ok tak gleði. Hón mælti: Hví sætir þín dirfð, er þú ferr mik at hitta; mer var engi verri í þessum svikum. Sigurðr spyrr: Hví mælir þú eigi við menn, eða hvat angrar þik? Brynhildr svarar: þer skal ek segja mína reiði. Sigurðr mælti: Heilluð ertu, ef þú ætlar grimman minn hug við þik, ok er siá þínn maðr, er þú kaust. Nei, segir hón, eigi reið Gunnarr eldinn til vár, ok eigi galt hann mer at mundi feldan val; ek undruðumk þann mann er kom í mínn sal, ok þóttumk ek kenna yður augu, ok fékk ek þó eigi víst skilit fyrir þeirri huldu, er á lá á mínni hamingju. Sigurðr segir: Ekki erum ver göfgari menn en synir Giúka, þeir drápu Dana-konung, ok mikinn höfðingja, bróður Buðla konung. Brynhildr svarar: Mart íllt eigum vér þeim upp at inna, ok minn oss ekki á harma vára; þú, Sigurðr, vátt Orminn, ok reitt eldinn, ok of mína sök, ok váru þar eigi synir Giúka konungs. Sigurðr svarar: Ekki varð ek þínn maðr, ok þú [eigi] vartu mín kona; ok galt við þer mund ágætr konungr. Brynhildr: Eigi sé ek svá Gunnar, at mínn hugr hlæja við hónum, ok grimm em ek við hann, þótt ek hylma yfir fyrir öðrum. þat er ógurligt, segir Sigurðr, at unna eigi slíkum konungi; eða hvat angrar þik mest? mer sýniz sem hans ást sé þer gulli betri. Brynhildr svarar: þat er mer sárast mínna harma, at ek fæ eigi því til leiðar komit, at bitrt sverð væri roðit í þínu blóði. Sigurðr svarar: Kvíð eigi því, skamt man at bíða áðr bitrt sverð man standa í mínu hiarta, ok ekki muntu þer verra biðja, því at þú munt eigi eptir mik lifa; munu ok fair várir lifs-dagar heðan í frá. Brynhildr svarar: Eigi standa þín orð af lítlu fari[1], síðan þer svikuð mik frá öllu yndi, ok ekki hirði ek um lífit. Sigurðr svarar: Lif þú, ok unn Gunnari konungi ok mer, ok alít mítt fé vil ek til gefa at þú deyir eigi. Brynhildr svarar: Eigi veizt þú görla mítt eðli; þú berr af öllum mönnum; en þer hefir engi kona orðit leiðari en ek. Sigurðr svarar: Annat er sannarra; ek unna þer betr en mer, þótt ek yrða fyrir þeim svikum, ok má því nú ekki bregða; því at ávalt, er ek gáða míns geðs, þá harmaði mik þat er þú vart eigi mín kona; enn af mer bar ek sem ek mátta, þa er[2] ek var í konungs höll, ok unda ek því þó, at ver várum öll saman; kann ok vera at fram verði at koma þat sem fyrir er spát, ok ekki skal því kvíða. Brynhildr segir: Of seinat hefir þú at segja at þik angrar mínn harmr, enn nú fám ver enga líkn. Sigurðr svarar: Giarna vilda ek, at vit stigim á einn beð bæði, ok værir þú mín kona. Brynhildr svarar: Ekki er slíkt at mæla, ok eigi mun ek eiga tvá konunga í einni höll, ok fyrr skal ek líf láta, enn ek svíkja Gunnar konung. Ok minniz nú á þat er þau funduz á fiallinu ok sóruz eiða, Enn nú er því öllu brugðit, ok vil ek eigi lifa. Eigi munda ek þítt nafn, segir Sigurðr, ok eigi kenda ek þik fyrr en þú vart gipt, ok er þetta enn mesti harmr. þá mælti Brynhildr: Ek vann eiða, at eiga þann mann er riði mínn vafur-loga, enn þann eið vilda ek halda, eða deyja ella. Heldr en þú deyir, vil ek þik eiga, enn fyrirláta Guðrúnu, segir Sigurðr.—Enn svá þrútnuðu hans síður, at í sundr gengu brynju-hringar.—Eigi vil ek þik, sagði Brynhildr, ok öngan annarra. Sigurðr gekk í brott. Svá segir í Sigurðar-kviðu: Ut gekk Sigurðr andspilli frá . . . Ok er Sigurðr kom í höllina, spyrr Gunnarr hvárt hann viti, hverr mun-tregi[3] henni væri, eða hvárt hón hefir mál sítt. Sigurðr kvað hána mæla mega.

Ok nú ferr Gunnarr at hitta hána í annat sinn, ok spyrr hví gegndi hennar mein, eða hvárt nökkur bót mundi til liggja. Ek vil eigi lifa, segir Brynhildr, því at

---

[1] Corrupt passage.   [2] þat er, Cd.   [3] mein-tregi, Cd.

Sigurðr hefir mik vélt, ok eiði síðr þik, þá er þú lézt hann fara í mína sæing. Nú vil ek eigi tvá menn eiga senn í einni höll, ok þetta skal vera bani Sigurðar eða þínn eða mínn, þvi at hann hefir þat allt sagt Guðrúnu, enn hón brigslar mer. Eptir þetta gekk Brynhildr út ok sezt undir skemmu-veg sínn, ok hafði margar harma-tölur, kvað ser allt leitt, bæði land ok ríki [Here falls in a bit of the Old Brunhild Lay]. . . . Gunnar segir Sigurð deyja skulu, eða man ek deyja ella. Hann biðr Brynhildi upp standa ok vera ká'a. Hón stóð upp, ok segir þó at Gunnarr mun eigi koma fyrr í sama rekkju henni, en þetta er fram komit. Nú ræðaz þeir við bræðr. Gunnarr segir, at þetta er gild bana sök at hafa tekit meydóm Brynhildar, ok eggjum Gutthorm at göra þetta verk. Ok kalla hann til sín, ok bióða hónum gull ok mikit ríki at vinna þetta til. Þeir tóku orm einn ok af vargs holdi ok létu sióða ok gáfu hónum at eta, sem skaldit kvað : 'Sumir viðfisk toku, sumir vitnis hræ-skifdu . . . ok marga hluti aðra í tyfrum' [verse corrupt]. Ok við þessa fæzlu varð hann svá æfr ok ágiarn, ok allt saman ok fortölur Grímhildar, at hann hét at gera þetta verk. Þeir hétu hónum ok mikilli sæmd í móti. Sigurðr vissi eigi ván þessara vélræða, mátti hann ok eigi við sköpum vinna né sínu aldrlagi, Sigurðr vissi sik ok eigi véla verðan frá þeim. Gutthormr gekk inn at Sigurði eptir um morgininn, er hann hvíldi í rekkju sínni. Ok er hann leit við hónum, þorði Guthormr eigi at veita hónom tilræðit ok hvarf út aptr ; ok svá ferr í annat sinn. Augu Sigurðar vóru svá snör, as fár einn þorði gegn at siá. Ok et þriðja sinn gekk hann inn, ok var Sigurðr þá sofnaðr. Gutthormr brá sverði, ok leggr á Sigurð, svá at blóðrefillinn stóð í dýnum undir hónum. [Here old Brunhild Lay resumes again.] [ch. xxix.]

2 *b*. THE SAME TEXT FROM THE INTERPOLATED SIGFRED SAGA IN EDDA.

Sigurðr reið þaðan, ok kom til þess konungs er Giúki hét ; kona hans er nefnd Grímhildr ; börn þeirra vóro þau Gunnarr, Högni, Guðrún, Guðný. Gotthormr var stiúp-sonr Giúka. Þar dvalðiz Sigurðr langa hríð, þá fékk hann Guðrúnar Giúka dóttor, enn Gunnarr ok Hogni sóruz í fóstbræðra-lag við Sigurð. Því næst fóru þeir Sigurðr ok Giúka synir at biðja Gunnari konu til Atla Buðla sonar, Brynhildar systur hans. Hón sat á Hindar fialli ; ok var um sal hennar vafur-logi ; enn hón hafði þess heit strengt, at eiga þann einn mann, er þorði at ríða vafur-logann. Þá riðu þeir Sigurðr ok Giúkungar—þeir eru ok kallaðir Niflungar—upp á fiallit, ok skyldi þá Gunnarr ríða vafrlogann. Hann átti hest þann er Goti heitir ; enn sá hestr þorði eigi at hlaupa í elldinn. Þá skiptu þeir litum, Sigurðr ok Gunnarr, ok svá nöfnum, þvi at Grani vildi undir engum manni ganga nema Sigurði. Þá hlióp Sigurðr á Grana, ok reið vafor-logann. Þat kveld gekk hann at brúðlaupi með Brynhildi. En er þau kómo í sæing, þá dró hann sverðit Gram or slíðrum ok lagði í milli þeirra. En at morni þá-er hann stóð upp ok klæddi sik, þá gaf hann Brynhildi at lín-fé gull-bauginn, þann er Loki hafði tekit af Andvara, enn tók af henni annan baug til minja. Sigurðr hlióp þá á hest sínn ok reið til félaga sínna. Skipta þeir Gunnarr þá aptr litum, ok fóru aptr til Giúka með Brynhildi. Sigurðr átti tvau börn með Guðrúnu, Sigmund ok Svanhildi.

Þat var eitt sinn at Brynhildr ok Guðrún gengu til vatz at bleikja hadda sína. Þá er þær kvómu til árinnar, þá óð Brynhildr út á ána frá landi ok mælti, at hón vildi eigi bera í höfuð ser þat vatn, er rynni or hári Guðrúnu, þvi at hón átti buanda hugaðan betr. Þá gekk Guðrún á óna eptir henni, ok sagði, at hón mátti fyrir því þvá ofar sínn hadd í ónni, at hón átti þann mann er ekki uggði[1] ok engi annarr í veröldu[2] var iafn frækn, þvi at hann vá Fáfni ok Regin, ok tók arf eptir þá báða.

---

[1] ekki uggði] emend. ; ᴠɢ, Cd. [2] Cd. ɪ e β begins here.

þá svarar Brynhildr: Meira var þat þó vert at Gunnarr reið vafur-logann, enn Sigurðr þorði eigi. þá hló Guðrún ok mælti: Ætlar þú at Gunnarr riði vafur-logann! sá ætla ek at gengi í rekkjo hiá þer er mer gaf gull-baug þenna; enn sá gull-baugr, er þú þátt at lín-fé, hann er kallaðr Andvara-nautr, ok ætla ek at eigi sótti Gunnarr hann á Gníta-heiði. þá þagnaði Brynhildr ok gekk heim. Eptir þat eggjaði hón Gunnarr til ok Högna at drepa Sigurð. Enn þvi at þeir vóru eið-svarar Sigurðar, þá eggjoðu þeir til Gutthorm bróður sínn at drepa Sigurð, ok Gutthormr lagði Sigurð sofanda sverði í gegnum. Enn er Sigurðr fékk sárit, þá greip hann sverðit Gram ok kastaði eptir hónum svá at sundr sneið manninn í miðju. þar dó Sigurðr ok sonr hans þré-vetr er Sigmundr hét, hann drápu þeir. Eptir þat lagði Brynhildr sik sverði í gögnum, ok var hón brennd með Sigurði, enn Gunnarr ok Högni tóku Fáfnis arf ok Andvara-naut, ok réðu löndum.

3. THE HAMTHEOW STORY FROM EDDA.

(See for earliest traces of this story the notes to Hamtheow Lay, vol. i.)

Eptir þat snœri hón til siófar ok hlióp á sióinn ok vildi drekka ser; enn hána rak yfir fiörðinn, ok kom hón þá á þat land or átti Ionakr konungr. Enn er hann sá hána, tók hann hána til sín ok fékk hennar. þau áttu þriá sonu er svá heita, Sörli ok Erpr ok Hamðér; þeir vóru allir svartir sem hrafn á hárs lit, sem Gunnarr ok Högni ok aðrir Niflungar. þar fæddiz upp Svanhildr dóttir Sigurðar Sveins, ok var allra kvenna fegrst. þetta spurði Ermenrekr konungr inn ríki; hann sendi son sínn Randvé at biðja hennar til handa sér. Enn er hann kom til Ionakrs borgar, þá var Svanhildr selld í hendr Randvé at færa hána Ermenrek konungi. þá sagði Bikki iarl, at þat væri betr fallit at Randvér ætti Svanhildi, er hann var ungr ok bæði þau, enn Ermenrekr var gamall. þetta ráð líkaði þeim vel enum ungum mönnum. því næst sagði Bikki iarl konungi þetta. þá lét konungr leiða son sínn til galga. þá tók Randvér hauk sínn ok plokkaði af fiaðrarnar, ok bað senda heim feðr sínum. Ok síðan var hann hengdr. Enn er Ermenrekr konungr sá haukin, þá kom hónom í hug hvat hann hafði gört, at svá sem haukrinn var ófleygr ok fiaðr-lauss, svá var ok ríki hans ófært er hann var gamall ok sonlauss. þat var eitt sinn er Ermenrekr konungr reið or skógi frá veiðum, at Svanhildr dróttning sat at hadd-bliki. þá riðu þeir á hána ok tráðu undir fótum til bana. Enn er þetta spurði Guðrún þá eggjaði hón sonu sína til hefnda eptir Svanhildi. Enn er þeir bioggoz til ferðar, þá fekk hón þeim brynjur ok hialma svá sterka at eigi mátti iarn á festa. Hón lagði ráð fyrir þá, at þá er þeir kæmi til Ermenreks konungs, skyldu þeir ganga um nótt at hónum sofanda, skyldu Sörli ok Hamðer höggva af hónum hendr ok fætr, enn Erpr höfuð. Enn er þeir koma á leið, þá spurðu þeir Erp bróður sínn, hver liðsemd þeim mundi at hónum vera þá er þeir hitti Ermenrek konung. Enn hann segir, at hann mun veita þeim því líkt sem hönd fæti. þeir segja, at þat var allz ekki er fótr studdiz við hönd. Enn svá vóru þeir reiðir móður sinni er hón hafði þá heipt-yrðum út leitt, at þeir vildu göra þat er henni þætti verst, ok drápu þeir Erp bróður sínn, því at hón unni hónum mest. Lítlu síðar þar sem Sörli gekk, skriðnaði hann öðrum fæti, ok studdi hann sik með hendinni. þá mælti hann: Betra væri nú at Erpr bróðir okkarr lifði, því at veitti nú höndin fætinum. Enn er þeir kómu til Ermenreks konungs of nótt þar sem hann svaf, þá hioggo þeir af hónum hendr ok fætr, ok við þat vaknaði hann, ok kallaði á menn sína, ok bað þá vaka. þá mælti Hamðer. Af mundi nú höfuðit ef Erpr bróðir okkarr lifði. þá stóðu upp hirðmenn ok sóttu at þeim, ok fengu eigi með vápnum sótt þá. þá kallar Ermenrekr at þá skyldi með grióti berja.

Ok svá var gört. þar féllu þeir Hamðir ok Sörli. þá var ok dauð öll ætt ok afkvæmi Giúka.—því er brynja kölluð klæði eða váðir Hamðiss ok Sörla. Her eptir kvað Bragi skalld. . . .

4. THE FINAL PORTION OF EDDA SKALDSKAPAR-MAL.

(Paraphrase of Hyndla's Lay and List of Synonyms.)

Einn konungr er nefndr Halfdan Gamli; hann var ágætr konungr. Hann gœrði blót mikit at miðjum vetri, ok blótaði til þess, at hann skyldi lifa í konungdómi sínum .ccc. vetra. Enn hann fekk þau andsvör, at hann mundi lifa ekki meir en mikinn einn mannz-aldr; enn þat mundi þó vera .ccc. vetra, at engi mundi vera í hans ætt ótiginn maðr, né kona. Hann var hermaðr mikill, ok fór víða um Austr-vegu. þar drap hann í einvígi þann konung er Sigtryggr hét. þá fekk hann þeirrar konu, er hét Alvig in Spaka, dóttir Eymundar konungs or Holmgarði, ins Ríka. þau áttu áttián sono, ok vóru niu senn bornir. þeir hétu svá—Einn var þengill, er kallaðr var Man-þengill, annarr Ræsir, þriði Gramr, fiórði Gylfi, fimti Hilmir, sétti Iöfurr, átti Skyli eða Skúli, niundi Harri eða Herra.—þessir niu bræðr eru svá ágætir í hernaði, at í öllum fræðum síðan eru nöfn þeirra haldin fyrir tignar-nöfn, svá scm konungs nafn eða iarls nafn. þeir áttu eingi börn, ok féllu allir í orrostum [1].

Enn áttu þau Halfdan ok Alvig niu sonu, er svá hétu.—Einn var Hildir, er Hildingar eru frá komnir; annarr Næfir, er Niflungar eru frá komnir; þriði Auði, er Öðlingar eru frá komnir; fiórði Yngvi, er Ynglingar eru frá komnir; fimti Dagr, er Döglingar eru frá komnir; sétti Bragi, er Bragningar eru frá komnir—þat er ætt Halfdanar Milda; siaundi Buðli, er Buðlungar eru frá komnir—ok af þeirri ætt er komin Atli ok Brynhildr; átti Lofði, hann var her-konungr mikill; hónum fylgði lið þat er Lofðar vóru kallaðir—hans ætt-menn eru kallaðir Lofðungar; þaðan er kominn Eylimi móður-faðir Sigurðar Fáfniss-bana; niundi Sigarr er Siklingar eru frá komnir: þat er ætt Siggeirs er hengi Hagbarð.—áf Hildinga ætt var kominn Haraldr inn Granrauði móður-faðir Halfdanar Svarta. Af Niflunga ætt var Giúki. Af Öðlinga ætt Kiarr. Af Ynglinga ætt Eirekr inn Málspaki.

þessar konunga ættir eru miök ágætir.—Frá Yngva, þaðan eru Ynglingar komnir. Frá Skildi í Danmörku, þaðan eru Skiöldungar. Frá Völsungi í Frakk-landi, þaðan eru Völsungar. Skelvir hét enn her-konungr, ok er hans ætt kölluð Skilvingar; sú kyn-slóð er í Austr-vegum—þessar ættir, er nú [2] eru nefndar, hafa menn sett svá í skáldskap, at halda þessi heiti öll fyrir tignar nöfn [3].

Skáld heita greppar, ok er rétt í skaldskap, at kalla svá hvern mann er vill. Rekkar vóru kallaðir þeir menn er fylgðu Halfi konungi, ok af þeirra namni eru kallaðir her-menn, ok er rétt at kenna svá alla menn. Lofðar heita ok menn í skaldskap, sem fyrr er ritað. Skatnar vóru þeir menn kallaðir er fylgðu Skata konungi, þeim er Skati inn Mildi var kallaðr; af hans nafni er Skati kallaðr sá er mildr er. Brag [4] nar héto þeir er fylgðu Braga konungi hinum Gamla. Virðar heita þeir menn er meta mál manna. Fyrðar ok Firar [ok] Verar heita landvarnar-menn. Víkingar ok flotnar, þat er skipa-herr. Beimar, svá hétu þeir er fylgðu Beimuna. Gumnar eða Gumar heita þeir menn er flokki stýra, svá sem gumi er kallaðr í brúðför. Gotnar eru kallaðir af heiti konungs þess er Goti er nefndr, er Gotland er við kennt; hann var kallaðr af nafni Óðins—Gautz; því at Gautland ok Gotland var kallat af nafni Óðins, enn Sviþióð af nafni Sviðors—þat er ok Óðins heiti.

---

[1] To here from 1 e β; the following mainly according to AM. 748.   [2] nú] enn, Cd.   [3] So far paraphrase of Hyndla's Lay.   [4] Here W. begins.

Í þann tíma var kallað allt meginland, þat er hann átti, Reið-Gotaland, enn eyjar allar Ey-Gota-land. Þat er nú kallat Dana-velldi ok Sviaveldi. Drengir heita ungir menn ok búlausir meðan þeir afla ser fiár eða orðztír; þeir far-drengir er milli landa fara; þeir konungs drengir, er höfðingjum þióna; þeir heita ok drengir er þióna ríkum mönnum; drengir heita vaskir menn ok batnandi. Seggir eru ok kallaðir, kniar ok liðar, þat eru fylgðar-menn. Þegnar ok havlldar ok höldar, svá eru ok bœndr kallaðir. Liónar heita þeir menn er ganga um sættir manna.

Þeir eru enn er svá eru kallaðir: kappar, kenpur, garpar, snillingar, hreysti-menn, avar-menni, hetjur. Þessi heiti standa her í mót, at kalla mann, blauðan, veykan, þirfing, sleyma, blota-mann, skauð, skræfu, skriáð, vák, vám, lóra, sleyma, teyða, dugga, dirokr, dusil-menni, ölmusa, avvirð.—Örr maðr heitir, mildingr, mæ-ringr, skati, þióð-skati, gull-skati, mann-baldr, sælingr, sæl-keri, auð-kýfingr, ríkmenni. Her í mót er svá kallað, hnøggvingr, gløggvingr, mælingr, vesalingr, fé-níðingr, giöf-lati.—Heitir spekingr, ráð-valdr. Heitir óvitr maðr, fífl, ok afglapi, gassi, ok gin-nungr, gaurr, ok glópr, snápr, fóli, œrr, óðr, galinn.—Snyrti-maðr, ofláti, drengr, glæsi-maðr, sterti-maðr, prýði-maðr.—Heitir ok hraumi, skrápr, skrokkr, skeið-klofi, flangi, slinni, fiósnir, slöttr, slápr, dröttr.—Lýðr heitir land-folk, lióðr.—Heitir þræll ok kefsir, þiónn, önnungr, þirr.

Maðr heitir einn fyrir ser [see vol. ii, p. 439, ll. 690-717].

Enn er þau heiti, er menn láta ganga fyrir nöfn manna; þat köllu ver viðr-kenn-ingar, eða sann-kenningar, eða for-nöfn.—þat eru við-kenningar, eða sann-kenn-ingar, at nefna annan hlut réttu nafni, ok kalla þann er hann vill nefna, eiganda; eða svá, at kalla hann þess, er hann vildi ok nefndi, föður, eða ava, ái heitir hinn þriði[1]. Son heitir arfi ok arfuni, barn, ióð ok mögr[2], erfingi. Heitir ok bróðir, blóði, lifri, barmi, hlýri. Heitir ok niðr, nefi, áttungr, konr, kundr, frændi, kyn-kvísl, ætt-barmr, ætt-stuðill, ætt-bogi, af-kvæmi, af-springr, of-sköpt; Heita ok mágar, sifjungar, hleyta-menn. Heitir ok vinr, ráðu-nautr, ráð-giafi, máli, rúni, spialli, allda-þopti, einkili, sesso-nautr, sessi: þopti er half-rýmiss-félagi. Heitir óvin, dolgr, andskoti, fiándi, sœkkvi, skaða-maðr, bana-maðr, þrængvir, sœkkvir, osvifruðr. —þessi heiti köllu ver viðr-kenningar, ok svá þo at maðr sé kendr við bœ sinn eða skip sitt, þat er nafn á, eða eign sína, þá er einkar-nafn er gefit.—þetta köllu ver sann-kenningar, at kalla manninn, speki-mann, eða ætlanar-mann, orð-speking eða ráð-speking, ráð-snilling, auð-milding, óslækinn, gæi-mann, glæsi-mann.—þetta eru for-nöfn.

Þessi eru kvenna heiti ókend í skaldskap:—víf, ok brúðr, ok flióð heita þær konur er manni eru gefnar[3]. Sprund ok Svanni heita þær konur er miök fara með dramb ok skart. Snótir heita þær konur er orð-næfrar eru. Drósir heita þær er kyrrlátar eru. Svarri ok Svarkr, þær er hávaða-miklar eru. Ristill er kölluð sú kona, er sköruglynd er. Rýgr, sú er ríkust er. Feima[4] er sú kölluð er ofröm er, sem meyjar ungar eða þær er ódiarfar eru. Sæta heitir sú kona, er buandi hennar er af landi farinn. Hæll heitir sú kona, er bóndi hennar er veginn. Ekkja, er sú kona, er bóndi hennar varð sótt-dauðr. Mær heitir fyrst hver, er ung er, enn Kerlingar, er gamlar eru.—Enn eru þau kvenna heiti, er til last-mæliss eru, ok má þau finna í kvæðum, þótt þat sé eigi ritað. Þær konur heita eljur, er einn man eigu. Snor heitir sonar-kvæn, enn Sværa vers móðir. Heitir ok Móðir, Amma, þriðja Edda[5]. Eiða heitir

---

[1] From the Lay of Righ. [2] From the Lay of Righ. [3] From verse Thulor. [4] A.S.-Latin word: O.F. femue, fenme. The word 'kenpur' above is the A.S. form 'cempa,' and for-nöfn appears to be a gloss translating 'prænomen.' [5] From Lay of Righ.

móðir; heitir ok, Dóttir, ok Barn, ok Ióð; heitir ok, *dóttir*, Dís, Ioð-dis. *Kona* er ok kölluð beðja eða mála bónda síns,—ok er þat viðr-kenning.

Höfuð heitir á manni. Þat skal svá kenna, at kalla þat, erviði hals, eða byrði; land hialms, ok hattar, ok heila, ok hárs, ok brúna, svarðar, eyrna, augna, munnz. Heimdallar sverð, ok er rétt at kenna til sverðz heita, við hvert er vill, ok kenna við eitt-hvert nafn Heimdallar. Höfuð heitir ókennt, hauss, hiarni, kianni, kollr.—*Augu* heita, sión, ok lit, eða viðr-lit[1], aurmiótt. Þá má svá kenna, at kalla, sól, eða tungl, skiöldu, ok gler, eða gim-steina: eða stein brá, eða brúna, eða enniss.—*Eyru* heita, hlustir, ok heyrn; þau má svá kenna, at kalla land, eða iarðar heitum nökkurum, eða munn eða rás, eða sión, eða augu heyrnarinnar, ef ný-görvingum er ort. —*Munn* skal svá kenna, at kalla hann, land, eða hus tungu, eða tanna, orða, eða góma, varra, eða þvílíkt: ok er ný-gervingar eru, þá kalla menn skip munninn, enn varrarnar borðin.—*Tunga* ræðit, eða stýri.—*Tennr* eru stundum kallat, griót, eða sker, orða eða tungo: tunga er opt kölluð, sverð máls, eða munnz.—*Skegg*, barð, eða grön; kanpar, er stendr á vörum.—*Hár* heitir lá; haddr þat er konur hafa; skopt heitir hár. Hár er svá kennt, at kalla skóg eða viðar heiti nokkuro; kenna til hauss, eða hiarna, eða hofuðs. Skegg skal kenna við höku, eða kinnr, eða kverkr.—*Hiarta* heitir, negg, eisköld, göllorr: þat skal svá kenna: kalla korn, eða stein, eða epli, hnot, eða myl, eða þvílíkt, ok kenna við brióst, eða hug; kalla má þat ok, hús, eða iörð, eða berg hugarins.—*Brióst* má svá kenna, kalla, hús, eða garð, eða skip hiarta, anda, eða lifrar, eða eljunar; land hugar ok minniss.—*Hugr* heitir, sefi, ok siafni, vili, munr, ást, elskugi. Huginn má svá kenna, at kalla hann, vind troll-kvenna, ok er rétt at kenna til ok nefna hverja er vill, ok svá at nefna iötnana, eða kenna þá til konu, eða dóttur.—þessi nöfn eru sér. Hugr heitir, ok geð, ok þokki, eljun, þrekr, nenning. minni, vit, skap, lund, trygð. Heitir ok hugr, reiði, fiánd-skapr, útrygð, geðleysi, þunn-geði, gæsni[2], ováeri.—*Hönd* má kalla, mund, lám, arm, hramm. Á hendi heitir, alnbogi, arm-leggr, ulfliðr, liðr, fingr, greip, hreifi, nagl, gómr, iaðarr, kvikva, vöðvi, afl, æðar, sinar, knui, ok kögglar: hönd má kalla, iörð vápna eða hlífa, við axlar ok ermar, lófa, ok hreifa; gull-hringa iorð, ok vals, ok hauks, ok allra hans heita; ok í nýgervingum, fót axlar, bog-nauð.—*Fœtr* má kalla, tré ilja, eða rista, eða leista, eða þvílíkt; renni-fleina brautar, eða göngu, fetz: kalla má fótinn, tré, eða stoð þessa. Við skíð ok skua eru fætr kendir ok brækr. Á fæti heitir, lær, kalfi, kné, bein, leggr, rist iarki, ökla, il, tá. Við allt þetta má fótinn kenna, kalla hann tré, ok kalla rá, ok siglu fótinn, ok kenna við þessa hluti.

Mál heitir, orð, ok orð-tak, snilli, saga, senna, tala, þræta, söngr, galldr, kveðandi, skial, bifa, ok hialdr, hial, skval, glaumr, þiarka, gyss, þrapt, skalp, hól, dælska, lióðæska, skraf, hégómi, afgelja: Heitir ok, röJd, hliómr, rómr, omun, þytr, göll, gnýr, glymr, rymr, brak, svipr, svipon, gangr.

Svá skal *orrostu* kenna, við vápn ok hlífar . . .[3]

Vit heitir, speki, minni, ætlan, hyggjandi, ráð, skilning, tölvísi, lang-sæi, bragð-vísi, orð-speki, skorungskapr :—Heitir *undir-hyggja*, væl-ræði, flá-ræði, brigð-ræði.

Puns.—'Læti' er tvennt: læti heitir rödd eða ólund. 'Reiði' er ok tví-kent: reiði er þat, ef maðr er í illum hug: reiði er ok fargervi skips eða hross. 'Fár' er ok tví-kennt: fár er reiði: far er skip.—þvílíkt orðtak hafa menn miök til þess at yrkja folgit, ok er þat kallat miök ofióst. 'Lið' kalla menn á manni er leggir mætaz: lið heitir skip: lið heitir mannfolk: lið heitir öl: lið er þat ok kallat, er maðr veitir öðrum lið-sinni: 'Hlið' heitir á garði: ok hlið kalla menn uxa: enn hlíð kalla menn

---

[1] Undoubtedly a corrupt form for wlit, the sole remnant of *wl.* [2] Hence modern 'keskni?' [3] Thus, only the beginning of the clause.

brekku.—þessar greinar má setja svá í skaldskap, at gera oflióst, at vant er at skilja, ef aðra skal hafa greinina, en áðr þykki til horfa in fyrri vísu-orð. Slíkt hit sama eru ok mörg önnur orð, þau er margir hlutir eigu heitið saman. *Hereupon follows the Thulor,* vol. ii, p. 423 sqq.

4 b. The List of Synonyms from Wormianus.

... nar hetu þeir menn er fylgðu Braga konungi hinum Gamla. Virðar heita þeir menn er meta mál manna; firar ok verar heita landvarnar-menn; víkingar ok flotnar, þat er skipa-herr; beimar heita þeir menn er fylgðu Beima konungi; gumnar ok gumar heita folk-stiórar, sem gumi heitir í brúðför. Gotnar heita af Gota konungi, er Gotland er við kennt; hann heitir af nafni Óðins, ok dregit af Gautz nafni. þeir heita drengir, er millum landa fara; þeir konungs drengir, er þeim þióna eða öðrum ríkis-mönnum; þeir heita vaskir menn, er batnandi eru; seggir heita ok kniar; liðar eru fylgðar-menn; þegnar ok höldar, þat eru bændr; liónar heita þeir er um sættir ganga.

Kappar heita ok, kempur, garpar, snillingar, hreysti-menn, harð-menni, afar-menni, hetjur.—þessi eru þar í mót, kalla mann, blauðan, þirfing, blota-mann, skauð, eða skræfu, vak, vam, lok, leymu, daasa, drok, dusil-menni.

Örr maðr heitir, mildingr, mæringr, skati, þióð-skati, gull-skati, mann-baldr, auð-kýfingr, sæl-keri, rík-menni. Her í mót er svá kallat, hnǫggr, glǫggr, mælingr, smæ-lingr, vesælingr, giöf-lati, þiófr, hvinn, hlenni.

Spekingr, ráð-valdr, snyrti-maðr, of-laati, glæsi-maðr, sterti-maðr. — Raumi, skraumi, skrapr, slokr, skrokkr, skeið-klofi, slinni, flangi, fiosnir, trúðr, lokr, kyrpingr.

Svá heita,—höldar, halr, drengr, holdr, þegn, smiðr, breiðr, bóndi, bundin-skeggi, bui, ok boddi, bratt-skeggr [1].

Kauði, fnauði, fóli, fifli, flangi, gassi, gokr, gromr, gogr, gaurr, hriki, glopr, gopi, glonn, glanni, slaani, slappi, strundi, smortr, stortr, hrokr, hrotti, þumr, þriotr, þrapr, totr, tangi, motti, vaamr, daar-bekill, gaaði, ginnungr, gap-þrosnir, gunnungr.— þræla heiti standa í Rígs-þulu.—Lini, staf-klapr, ǫnnungr, lydda [2].

Maðr heitir einn hverr, etc., *leaving out one or two passages, we subjoin*—

Heitir, ái [3], arfi, sonr, arfuni, arf-þegi, mǫgr, niðr, sefi, erfingi, konr, hefnir, burr.

Heitir bróðir [4], blóði, barmi, hnefi, hlýri, lifri, sifr, kundr, kyn-stafr, niðjungr, ætt-stuðill, ætt-baðmr, kyn, af-kvæmi, af-springr.

Heita ok, maagar, sifjungar, svilar, hleytar, spiallandi, þopti, kompann [5], félagi, fóstri, vinr, vanda-maðr, frændi.—Heitir, dolgr, andskoti, sœkkvi, þrǫngvir, skaða-maðr, usvifrungr, baagi, andskoti (rep.), úvin.—þetta köllu ver *sann-kenningar*, at kalla, at maðr sé hraustr, harðr, hagr, horskr, kænn, kuðr, ríkr, rǫskr, reiðr, rammr, ráðugr, sniallr, snarpr, snotr, sterkr, stór-vitr, vaskr, vænn, varr, voldugr, blíðr, biartr.

þetta kollu ver *tví-riðit;* her fylgir *stuðning sann-kenningu,* ef maðr er kallaðr al-röskr, ofr-hugaðr, full-hvatr, veg-sæll,—ok á marga vega er sann-kenningum breytt, ok heyja þær mest orða-fiǫlða í skaldskapnum, ok fegra mest kveðskapinn, ... kallaðir eru menn niorðungar, eða nárungar, miðjungar, eða strengjandi víga eðr verka, ... maðr er kenndr, fleygir eða fergir: heitir ok, hreytir, mygir ok meiðir, sækir, ok særir, sǫkkvir ok slǫngvir, vælir ok veitir .... [6].

---

[1] = Lay of Righ.   [2] A verse from the same Thulor.   [3] ai heitir, Cd.
[4] bróðir heitir, Cd.   [5] A Roman word.   [6] These words all run in alliterative couples.

5. THE GLOSSES FROM MA. 748.

Frá híbýlum Heljar [1].—'Eljúðnir' heitir salr hennar; 'gillingr' lykill hennar; 'hungr' diskr; 'sulltr' knífr; 'affelldr' spǫnn; 'hnipinn' akr; 'ganglati' þræll; 'ganglǫt' ambátt; 'víð-opnir' garðr; 'giallandi' grind; 'lati' láss; 'blíkjanda böl' hurð; 'brota-böl' þreskǫlldr; 'forað' tiald; 'fallanda forað' forfall; 'kǫr' rekkja; 'kǫr-beðr' dýna; [blank] hani; 'frost-opna' kista; 'vaningi' göltr; 'hryggr' hestr; 'gráfętr' hundr; 'yglöð' ǫnd [2].

Dresses.—**Klæða heiti.**—'Einhagi' (sleða); 'helfni' (vefjar upp-hlutr); 'tasla' (tyglar); 'fang' (kyrtill); 'siðerni' (serkr); 'ripti' (s.); 'veipa' (s.); 'lina' (s.); 'skeptingr' (hofuð-dúkr); 'motr' (h.[3]); 'meðja' (h.); 'vimpill' (h.); 'iflugr' (h.); 'loð-dúkr' (h.); 'stafn' (h.); 'sveipr' (h.); 'ísungr' (h.); 'skúfr' (hk.[4]); 'vísl' (hk.); 'dolpr' (k.); 'giarða' (i.); 'fallda' (k.); 'skypill' (h.); 'veipr' (h.); 'ferma' (f.); 'iotr' (iaxl); 'vǫf' (hringar); 'vartari' (þvengr [5]).

Sundries.—'Iǫln' (goð); 'brý' (troll); 'eiða' (móðir); 'nipt' (systir); 'baðmr' (viðr); 'miǫtuðr' (bani); 'glý' (gleði); 'slæki drengr' (?): 'sarkat' (roðit).

Stones.—**Steinn**, sindr, steinn, sisisill, bivivill, bleikr, kǫgðir, mǫgðir, gyfingr.

Nail, peg.—**Nagli**, darraðr, ialfaðr, aurmulinn, eyþolinn (i. k. [6]), mellingr, blindingr, þolinmóðr (í knífi), fríðr;—hniflungr, regin-gaddi, far-nagli, stag-nagli, varnagli, veraldar-nagli; eymylinn (i. t.[7]); sam-nagli (i. s.[8]); fast-haldr (i. st.[9]); þolinn (ra); blóðvarinn (sior); ið-mǫlinn.

---

[1] See Excursus I to vol. ii, p. 471.
[2] Emend.; vaningi hvndr, g'fętr hryggr hæstr, yglöd ǫnd, Cd.; 'g'fętr' stands above the line, by which word the wolf is no doubt meant (cp. Norweg. 'graabeen'); he is the *dog* of Hell, and so vaningi must mean something else. Here the Thulor 478 yields the clue; vaningi is Hell's boar 'goltr,' from its leanness called waster or vanisher. The poet makes the inmates of Hell, like those of Walhalla, to have their boar to feed on. Hell's *ale* has slipped out of the glosses,—'tears,' a bitter brew!
[3] (h.), here and in the next following, means 'hofuðdúkr.'
[4] 'hk.'=hofuð-klæði?   [5] The English 'garter.'   [6] i. k. = í knífi?
[7] i. t.= í tré, peg in the wooden handle of the quern.   [8] i. s.= í skipi, in a ship.
[9] i. st. = í stokki, in a stock.

SPURIOUS EPIC POETRY.

B. *Poetry.*

THE following pieces are given, as promised (p. 353), that the reader may have all the evidence before him. Their intrinsic value is small indeed, but they sometimes give the last reflexion of a dying tradition, like the broken bits of glass on a wall glittering in the sunset. The *first* is Starkad's Death Song from *Gautric's Saga*, Cod. Holmensis. The type is such as the Songs which Saxo knew. The end, ll. 113–128, is the best.

Next comes a group of pieces from *Arrow-Ord's Saga*, Cod. Holmensis, etc. The *first*, a scene in the hall where Ord is bragging against two other heroes. The *second*, Ord's Death Song, with touches borrowed from Hialmar's Death Song, etc. *Third* and *fourth*, fragments from different parts of the Saga. One verse gives the foreign Cloak o' Beards tradition of the Mabinogion, which had no doubt filtered through the Arthur cycle of Romance to Iceland. There is also a dialogue between Ord and a priestess.

The succeeding set is from *Half's Saga*. *First*, a dialogue between Half and Instan, one of his famous champions, who warns the king not to go forth, for he has had evil dreams—echoes of the Atli poems. *Second*, Instan's last words. *Third*, the challenge etc. of Utstan, Half's champion after his master's death. *Fourthly*, the Death Song of Rook the Black, who, aged and in a stranger's hall, is crooning over the triumphs of his youth. All these we hold to be by the same man, all founded on the prose of the Saga, and all seemingly produced from an idea that, as there had once been Lays on the subject of Half and his champions which had perished (as we think there were), their places must accordingly be thus supplied for the reader's satisfaction.

The next piece comes from *Herraud and Bosi's Saga*, the curse of Busla on King Ring. There are echoes from old poems in this poor screed.

A few remaining pieces—*Star-Ord's Dream*, which may be by Lawman Sturla, from a separate Thattr published by the Editor with Bardar Saga, 1860; a bit from *Gang-Hrolf's Saga;* a bit from *An the Bowman Saga;* a bit from *Fridtheow's Saga*, out of the scene where the witch-whales have raised the magic storm.

A group of verses from *Ketil Hæng's Saga* and *Grim Hairy-cheek's Saga* follows— dialogues and flytings between the hero and ogresses, giants and a Finnish king, etc. It is poor stuff, imitating however and echoing the Dialogue-metre Flytings of the old poems.

The Editor, as early as May, 1854, made a collection of these poems, and prepared a text, but afterwards gave up the project. It has however been so far useful that here and there better readings have been got at than the editions give. The MS. authority, as far as is needful, is given with each piece.

1. STARKAD'S DEATH-SONG from GAUTREK'S SAGA.

(AM. 590 chart.; copy of a fourteenth-century vellum.)

Þá var ek ungr er inni brann
  frekna fiölð með feður þióð,
'nerungi' fyrir þrumu innan
her 'hrauðuðr' Haraldz ens Egöska,
ok men-brota mágar vélto
Fiori ok Fyri Freka arf-þegar,
Unnar bræðr, eiðo minnar.

þá er Herþiófr Harald um vélti
ser óiafnan sveik í trygðum,
Egða dróttinn öndu rænti,   10
enn hans sonum hapt-bönd sneri.
þrévetran mik þaðan af flutti
Hrosshárs-grani til Hörðalandz,
nam ek á Aski upp at vaxa

sákat niðja á niu vetrum.
Afl gat-ek ærit, uxu tiálgur,
langir leggir ok liótt höfuð,
enn hímaldi 'af hagsi sat'
'faaz' forvitni í fleti niðri.
Unz Víkarr kom frá vita innan, 20
gísl Herþiófs gekk inn í sal,
hann kendi mik, hann kvaddi mik
upp at standa ok andsvara;
hann mælti mik mundum ok spönnum,
alla arma til ulfliða,
vaxit hári á höku niðri.
þá safnaði Sorkvi ok Gretti [see vol. i,
   p. 355].
þá vóru ver þrettán samam,
fær varliga friðri drengi.
Svá kómu ver til konungs garða, 30
hristum grindr, hiuggum gætti,
brutum borg-lokur, brugðum sverðum,
þar er siau tigi seggir stóðu
kostum grimmir fyrir konungi,
þó var um aukit öllum þrælum,
verka-lýð ok vatn-drögum.
Var Víkari vant at fylgja,
því-at fremstr ok fyrstr í flokki stóð
hiuggum hialma með höfuð-gnípum,
brynjur sníddum, ok brutum hialma. 40
Var Víkari vegs um auðit,
en Herþiófi herfur goldnar,
særðum seggi, enn suma drápum,
stóðkað ek fiarri þá er féll konungr.
Vart þú eigi með Víkari
austr í Væni ár-dag snemma,
þá er sóttu ver Sisar á velli,
þat var þrek-virki þokkz megnara.
Mik lét sverði hann sárum högginn
skarp-eggjuðu skiöld í gegnum, 50
hialm af höfði, enn haus skorat,
ok kinn-kialka klofinn í iaxla,
enn it vinstra viðbeina látið;
ck á síðu sverði beitti
mer öflugr fyrir miöðm ofan,
enn í aðra atgeir lagði,
köldum broddi, svá at á kafi yddi,
þau sér þú merki á mer groin.
Sneidda ek hónum síðu aðra
brott með brandi um búk þveran, 60
svá ek af heiptum hiörvi beittag
at allz megins áðr kostaðik.
Lét þreksamr þriðja sinni
Hildar leik háðan verða,
áðr Upplönd unnin yrði
ok Geirþiófr um gefinn helju.
Átti sér erfi-vöiðu
tírsamr tvá tiggi alna,
hét hans son Haraldr enn ellri,
setti hann þann at þela-mörku. 70
Var sink-giarn sagðr af gulli

Neri iarl nýtr í ráðum,
Víkars sonr vanr í sóknum,
sá reið einn Upplendingum.
   Réð Friðþiófr fyst at senda
heiptar boð horskum iöfri
hvárt Víkarr konungr vildi gialda
hilmi skatt eða her þola.
Réðum lengi orðum við ekki dælir,
þat kaus herr at konungr skyldi 80
ríkr með her rómu knýja.
Réð Ólafr austr inn Skygni
sældar gramr fyrir Svia-ríki,
hann bauð út almenningi,
mikill var hans helmingr talinn.
Gengum framm í glam vápna
konungs menn kappi gnægðir,
hió ek brynju-lauss báðum höndum.
Réð Friðþiófr friðar at biðja, 90
þviat Víkarr vægði ekki,
ok Starkaðr Stórverksson
almátt framm allan lagði.
   Mer gaf Víkarr Vala malm,
hring inn rauða er ek á hendi bur,
mer þrímerking, enn ek þrumu hónum,
fylgða-ek fylki fimtán sumur.
Fylgða ek fylki þeim er framast vissag
þá unda ek bezt ævi minnar,
áðr fóru ver, enn því flögð ollu, 100
hinzta sinni til Hörðalandz:
þess eyrendis, at mer þórr um skóp
níðings nafn, nauð margs konar,
hlaut ek óhróðigr íllt at vinna.
Skylda ek Víkar í viði háfum
Geirþiófs-bana goðum um signa,
lagða ek geiri gram til hiarta,
þat er mer harmast handa-verka.
Þaðan vappaða ek viltar brautir
Hörðum leiðr með huga illan, 110
hringa vanr ok hróðr-kviða,
dróttinn-lauss, dapr allz hugar.
   Nú sótta-ek til Svíþióðar
Ynglinga siöt til Uppsala.
Her láta mik, sem ek lengi mun,
þöglan þul þióðans synir.
Her settu mik sveina milli
holdar hæðinn ok hvít-brán,
skelkja skatnar ok skaup draga
oss óframir at iöfurs greppi. 120
Siá þikkjast þeir á sialfum mer
iötun-kuml átta handa,
er Hlórriði fyrir Hamar norðan
Hergríms-bana höndum rænti.
Hlægja rekkar, er mik siá,
liótan skolt, langa triónu,
hanga tiálgur, hár ulf-grátt,
hriúfan hals, húð iótraða. 128

---

2. ARROW-ORD.

I. The Scene in the Hall. (From Holm. 7. 4to.)

Sg. = Sigurðr, Si. = Siolfr, O. = Oddr.

Si. ODDR klauftu eigi at orrosto
(hrökk hialmat lið) Hamðis skyrtor:
guðr geisaði, gekk eldr í bæ,
þá er af Vindum vá sigr konungr.
Sg. Oddr vartu eigi at egg-roði
þá er seggi allvaldz svelta létum ;
bar-ek sár þaðan sex ok átta,
enn þú með bygðum batt þer matar.
O. þið skuluð hlýða hróðri mínum,
Sigurðr ok Siolfr, sessu-nautar :   10
ykkr á-ek at gialda greypan verka,
hróðr harð-snuin huglausum tveim.
þú látt, Siolfr, soð-golfi á
dáða vanr ok dýrs hugar :
enn ek út með Akvitanum
fióra menn fiörvi næmdak.
Si. þú hefir, Oddr, farit með ölmusum,
ok bitlinga borit af borði :
enn ek einn af Ulfs-fialli
höggvinn skiöld í hendi bark.   20
Sg. Oddr, vartu eigi út með Girkjum
þá er á Serkjum sverð vár ruðom :
gerðum harðan hlióm ísarna,
féllu fyrðar í folk-roði.
O. Siolfr . . . við meyjar mal-þingsamr
meðan loga létum leika um konung,
unnum harðan Hilding drepinn,
ok hans félögum aldrs of synjat.
Enn þu látt, Sigurðr, í sal meyja
meðan við Biarma börðumz tvisvar :   30
háðum hildi heldr snarliga
enn þú, seggr, í sal svaft und blæju.
Si. Oddr, vartu eigi á Atals-fialli
þá er fen-loga fengit höfðum :
ver berserki binda knáttum,
þá var af kappi konungs lið drepit.
O. Siolfr, vartu eigi þar er siá knátti
brynjur manna blóði þvegnar :
hrukku oddar í iarn-serkjum,
enn þú höll konungs heldr kannaðir.   40
Sigurðr, vartu eigi þar er sex hruðum
há-brynjuð skip fyr Holms-nesi :
vartu ok eigi vestr með Skolla,
þá er Engla gram aldri næmdum.
Siolfr, vartu eigi þar er sverð (ruðum)
hvoss á hiarli fyrir Hléseyju :
enn þú hallaðist heima milli
kynmála-samr kalfs ok þýjar.
Sigurðr, vartu eigi þar er á Sælund
feldak
bræðr böl-harða Brand ok Agnar,   50
Ásmund, Ingiald, Alfr var inn fimti,
enn þú heima látt í höll konungs

skrökmála-samr, skauð her-numin.
Siolfr vartu eigi suðr á Skíðu
þar er konungar kníðu hialma,
óðum dreyra, sva at í ökla tók,
víg vakta-ek, vartu eigi þar.
Sigurðr, vartu eigi þar í Svia-skerjum
þa er Haldani heiptir guldum :
urðu randir róg miklaðra,   60
sverðum skornar, en hann sialfr drepinn.
Hvar vóru þið þa vesalar snýtur
er ver héldum aski í Elvar-sund :
teitir ok reifir at Trönu-vágum.
þar lá Ögmundr Eyþiófs-bani
trauðastr flugar á tveim skipum.
þar letu ver lindi börðu
hörðu grióti, hvössum sverðum :
þrír lifðu ver, enn þeir niu,
hrókr hernuminn, hví þegir nú ?   70
Siólfr vartu eigi Sámseyju í
þar er við Hiörvarð höggum skiptum :
tveir vóru við, enn þeir tolf saman,
sigr hafðak, saztu kyrr meðan.
Gekk ek um Gautland í grimmum hug
siau dægr saman áðr ek Sævi fyndak,
knáttak þeira áðr ek þaðan færa
fimtán liða fiörvi ráða.
Enn þú giögraðir, gárungr vesall,
síð of öptnum til sængr þýjar.   80
þið munuð hvergi hæfir þikkja,
Siolfr ok Sigurðr, í sveit konungs
ef Hialmars get ens Hugum-stóra
þess er snarligast sverði beitti.
Gekk skarpr þórðr fyrir skiöldu framm
hvar er orrostu eiga skyldim :
hann lét Halfdan hníga at velli
fræknan stilli ok hans fylgjara.
Vóru við Ásmundr opt í bernsku
fóstbræðr saman báðir litnir :   90
bar ek fyrir stilli stöng Darraðar
þars konungar kappi deildu.
Hefi ek á Saxa ok á Svia herjat,
Frísi ok Frakka ok á Flæmingja :
Íra ok Engla ok endr Skota,
þeim hef ek öllum óþarfr verit.
Nú hefi ek dýra drengi talda
þá er forðum mer fylgdu úti :
munu engir verða síðan
frægri fyrðar í folk-roði.   100
Nú hefi ek órar iðnir taldar
þær er forðum ver framðar höfðum :
opt gengu ver til öndvegis
sigri fegnir. Látum Siolf mæla.

II. Ord's Death-Song.

(AM. 343 and 471.)

HLÝÐI seggir, enn ek segja mun
vígs-valdendum frá vinum mínum;
seint er at dylja, sé ek eigi mátti
skokks skæ-stafr við sköpum vinna.
Var mer fóstr tekit at föður ráði,
brátt vöndumk því, á Beru-ríóðri;
var mer ekki vant til sælu
þess er Ingialdr átti kosti.
Uxum báðir á Beru-ríóðri
Ásmundr ok ek upp í bernsku,   10
skófum skeyti, skip sníðuðum,
görðum örvar okkr at gamni.
Sagði mer Völva sannar rúnir,
enn ek vætki því vilda hlýða,
gat ek fyrir ungum Ingialdz syni
at ek föður-túna fýstumk vitja.
Búinn lézt Ásmundr opt meðan lifði
málþings vanr mer at fylgja,
sagða ek karli at ek koma mundak
aptr aldregi ; nú em ek orð-rofi.   20
Létum beiti á brim þrauka,
stóð hörr dreginn höndum fiarri,
kómum at eyju utan-verðri
þar er Grímr fyrir garða átti.
Sá ek blíðliga, er til bæjar kom,
bekk-sagnir mer báðar fagna,
víst mátta ek með vinum mínum
gulli skipta ok gaman-málum.
Varð ek at vári víss at gærðuz
bryn-þings boðar Biarma at sœkja,   30
síðan kvaddak Sigurð ok Guðmund,
vilda ek með fræknum til farar ráðaz.
Vóru horskir á her-skipum
frændr mínir tveir at for-ráði,
vildu hásetar horskir eignaz
tak þat er áttu Tyrfi-Finnar.
Vér kaup-skipi kómum heilu
at þar er Biarmar bygðir áttu
eyddum eldi ættir þeirra,
fengum löskvan láðmann tekinn.   40
Hann lézt seggjum segja kunna
hvar til hodda var hæft at ráða,
hann bað oss ganga götu lengra
ef vér vildum fé fleira eiga.
Réðu Biarmar brátt at verja
haug her-mönnum ok hamalt fylkja,
létum þegna, áðr þaðan færim,
ofa-marga öndu týna.
Réðum skunda til skipa ofan,
þá er flótti var á fen rekinn,   50
mistum bæði bátz ok knarrar,
auðs ok ýta, er ver ofan kómum.

Skióтt nam kynda í skóg þykkvum
háfan uppi hrót-garm viðar,
svá við lopti létum leika.
Sám skiótliga skynda at landi
skeiðr vegligar ok skraut-menni,
fegnir urðu þeir er fyrir vóru
frændr mínir er finnaz görðum.
Létu skeika at sköpuðu   60
drengmenn snarir í drifa-veðri,
sýndiz seggjum sandr á þiljum,
landz vón liðin ; lá ek eigi þar.
Kómum at eyju útan brattri
sumar síðla, þá var segl rifit,
görðu fyrðar flestir allir
skipum til hlunnz skiótt at ráða.
Slógum tiöldum, en sumir fóru
biörnu at veiða, þeir er boga kunnu,
réðum í eyju upp at kynda   70
bál brenniligt, stóð biörn fyrir.
Kvóðuzt fiall-buar flytja mundu
oss úr eyju, nema útan færim,
þótti eigi rekkum rómr at heyra
hógligr sa er var hraun-skiöldunga.
Ugðum ekki, sízt eyjar til,
vópns vígligir viðir kómo ;
hlóðu bragnar fyrir biarg framan
vegg sterkligan ; var ek enn at því.
Réð ek at ganga með Gusis-nauta   80
beggja á milli biargs ok esjo,
skaut ek í auga einum þursi
ok í brióst framan biarga Freyju.
þar fekk ek heiti þat ek hafa vilda,
er mik or fiöllum flögð kölluðu,
kvóðuzt Oddi-Örvar vilja
byr bráðliga á burt gefa.
Búnir létumk á burt þaðan
brátt or eyju þegar byr fengi,
heilir kómum heim úr þeirri,   90
görðu fagna frændr holl-vinum.
Vórum allir vetr þann saman
gulli gladdir ok gaman-málum,
drógu fyrðar þegar frerum létti,
heldr skrautligar skeiðr at vatni.
Sigldum síðan suðr með landi
tál-laust skipum tveimr ok einu,
vænto fengjar þeir er fyrir vissu
skiótt ef Elvar-sker könnuðum.
Fundum um síðir fyrir í sundi   100
þegna nýta þórð ok Hialmar,
fréttu fyrðar, þeir er fyrir vóru,
hvórt ver vildim frið eða á för halda.
Báru rekkar ráð sín saman,

þótti eigi fyrðum fé-vón mikil,
kiöru Háleygir kost inn vildra,
réðum leggja lag vórt saman.
Héldum allir úr höfn skipum
þegar full-hugar fengjar væntum,
hræddumz ekki meðan höfðingjar   110
heilir réðu fyrir her-skipum.
Vórum reiðir þá er rand-berendr
horska hittum fyrir Holms-nesi,
réðum eignaz allar gerðar
snyrti-drengja af sex skipum.
Vórum allir vestr með Skolla
þar at landi sat lýða dróttinn,
báru bragnar blóðgar randir
sverðum meiddir, enn ver sigr þaðan.
Höfðu iarls liðar út-nes hroðit   120
róg-þings vanir, sem refar hundum,
unnum vit Hialmar, er hinnig fórum,
eldi ok usla eytt lang-skipum.
Frétti Guðmundr ef ek fara vilda
heim at hausti, ok hónum fylgja,
sagða-ek svinnum at ek siá vilda
norðr aldregi niðja mína.
Mæltum allir mót at sumri
austr í Elfi til út-farar,
vildi Hialmar hinn hugum-stóri   130
sveit mína suðr með ser hafa.
Fóru teitir tveggja vegna
bryn-þings boðar þegar byrir fenguzt
sigldum síðan Svíþióðar til,
sóttum Ingva til Uppsala.
Mer gaf Hialmarr inn hugum-stóri
fimm ból-staði á fold saman,
unda ek auði meðan aðrir mik
hringum kvöddu ok heils friðar.
Funduzt allir á fegins dægri   140
Svenskir seggir ok Sigurðr norðan,
ræntu ýtar eyjar-skeggja
auði öllum, enn þeir eldz bíða.
Létum vestr þaðan vandar fáka
Írlandz á vit öldur kanna,
höfðu þeira, er þangat kómum,
drengir ok drósir drifit or húsum.
Rann-ek at viðri vagns slóð-götu
unz ek streng-völum stríðum mætta ;
munda ek Ásmund auði mínum   150
aptr ódáinn öllum kaupa.
Sá ek um síðir hvar saman fóru
karlar röskvir ok konur þeirra,
þar lét ek fióra frændr Ölvarar
egg-leiks hvata öndu týna.
Réð mik úr vagni víf at hefja,
ok þær hoddum mer hétu góðum,
bað mik snót koma sumar hit næsta,
lézt þá launum leita mundu.
Varat sem brynja eðr blair hringar   160
ísköld um mik áðan félli,

þá er um síður silki-skyrta
gulli saumuð gekk fast ofan.
Fórum vestan fengjar vitja
sva at bragnar mer bleyði kendu,
unz á Skíði Skatnar fundu
bræðr böl-harða ok at bana urðu.
Sóti ok Hálfdan í Svía-skerjum
mörgum manni at morði varð,
unnum þeirra, áðr þaðan færim,   170
hundrað skipa hroðit með stöfnum.
Fundum þegna, er þaðan fórum,
teita ok sleitna í Trönu-vógum,
var eigi Ögmundi and-rán togut,
kómumz þrír þaðan, en þeir niu.
Knátta ek ban-orði fyrir bröngnum hrósa
snotra seggja, er ek til siófar kom,
höfðum við Hialmar haldit illa
þá er Glámi stóð í gegnum spiörr.
Fórum heim þaðan horskir þegnar,   180
enn haug þórði háfan urpum,
maðr engi þorði oss mót göra,
var oss vettegis vant ins góða.
Vóru við Hialmarr hvárt dægr glaðir
meðan her-skipum heilum réðum,
unz í Sámseyju seggi fundum
þá er ben-logum bregða kunnu.
Lét ek falla und fætr ara
tírar-lausa tolf berserki,
þá varð ek skiljazt á skapa-dægri   190
við þann inn mesta minn full-trúa.
Hafða ek ei á aldri mínum
höfuð hraustara hvergi fundit,
bar ek mer á herðum hialmum grimman
ok til Sigtúna síðan hafðak.
Lét ek eigi þess langt at bíða
at ek Sæundi at siónum varð,
unnu skatnar skip mín hroðin,
enn ek siálfr þaðan sundz kostaðik.
Gekk ek um Gautland í grimmum hug
sex dægr í samt áðr ek Sæund fyndag,
lét ek hans liða hiörvi mæta   202
sex ok átta með siálfum gram.
Lét ek suðr um haf langt um farit
at ek grunn-sævi gildu mættag,
varð ek einn saman, en annan veg
gumna mengi gekk hel-vegu.
Enn kom ek þar er Akvitania
bragna kindir borgum réðu,
þar lét ek fióra fallna liggja   210
hrausta drengi. Nú em ek her kominn.
þat var fyrr er ek fór senda
ok öllum þeim orð in mestu
niðjum mínum á Norðr-vega,
varð ek svá feginn fundi þeirra
sem hungraðr haukr bráðum.
Brögnum þremr buðu skatnar
margir síðan metorð þaðra

---

183 = Vspá 32.   187 = Helgi i. 323.   215, 216 = Helgi i. 213.

enn ek þeygi þat þiggja vilda,
urðu báðir þar bræðr eptir.　　220
Réð ek skunda frá skatna liði,
hittak breiða borg Iórsala,
réð ek allr í á fara,
kunna ek þá Kristi at þióna.
Veit ek at forsum falla lét
Iordan um mik fyrir utan Girki,
hélt enn þó, sem hverr vissi,
ítr-gör skyrta öllum kostum.
Mætta ek gammi gliúfrum nærri,
flaug hann með mik fiarri löndum,　　230
þar til háfa hamra fundum,
lét mik hvílazt þar í hreiðri sínu:
Unz mik Hildir hafði áburtu,
risi ramligr, á róðrar-skútu,
lét mik veitir Vimrar elda
tolf mánaði með ser hvílazt.
Þýddumk ek hiá Hildi horska ok stóra
raun-siáliga risa dóttur,
ok við henni heldr sterkligan
ítran son eiga görðak　　240
ok ólíkan ossum niðjum.
þann drap Ögmundr Eyþiófs-bani
í Hellulandz hrauns óbygðum,
enn ek félaga hans fiörvi næmdak,
hefi-ek ei víking verra fundit.
Fleiri hefir mína fóstbræðr drepit
Garðar ok Sirni, gekk skegg af flagði,
var hann þá öngum líkr at yfir-liti,
kallaðr síðan Kvillanus Blesi.
þótta ek hæfr at hiör-regni,　　250
þá er vér börðumk á Brávelli,
bað Hringr þá hamalt fylkja

Odd hinn Víðförla at orrostu.
Hitta ek eptir á hug-snara
lofðunga tvá lítlu síðarr,
veitta ek öðrum vígs um gengi
ungum iöfri arfs at kveðja.
Kom ek um síðir þar er snarir þóttuzt
Sigurðr ok Siólfr í sveit konungs,
réð oss skatna lið skotz at beiða　　260
ok skialdar fimi við skatna mengi:
Skaut ek ei skemra en skilfingar,
var létt skafin lind í hendi,
réðum síðan sundz at kosta,
lét ek þá báða blóði snýta.
Var mer skiald-meyiu skipat it næsta
þa er orrostu eiga skyldum,
veit ek at ýtar í Anþekju
and-rán biðu, enn ver auð fiár.
Sóttum sverði seggja kindir,　　270
ok tré-goðum týndum þeirra,
barða ek Bialka í borgar-hliði
eiki-kylfu, sva at hann önd um lét.
þá var mer Hárekr hollr full-trui
er hann festi mer fóstru sína,
átta ek horska hilmis dóttur,
vel réðum snót saman sigri ok löndum.
Sat ek at sælu síðan minni
vilgi lengi, sem ek vita þóttumz.
Fiöldi er at segja frá förum mínum,　　280
snotrum seggjum siá mun in efsta.
þer skuluð skynda til skipa ofan
heilir allir ; her munum skiljazt,
Berið Silkisif ok sonum okkrum
kveðju mína. Kem ek eigi þar.

III. Ord and Priestess.

(From Holm. 7.)

Alf Bialki :
Hverr veldr eldi hverr orrostu,
hverr iarls magni eggjum beitir ?
hof sviðnuðu, hörgar brunnu,
hverr rauð eggjar á Yngva nið ?
　O. Oddr brendi hof ok hörga braut,
ok tré-goðum týndi þínum,
görðu þau ekki góðs í heimi
er þau ór eldi ösla ne máttu.
　Pr. þess hlægjumz ek at hafir fengna
Freys reiði þú fári blandna.　　10

Hialpi Æsir ok Ásynjur,
görvöll regin gyðjum sínum !
Eða hverr eggjaði þik austan hingat
fræknan fella ok fláráðan ?
　O. Hirði ek eigi þótt heitir þú,
fárgiarnt höfuð, Freys reiði mer,
íllt er at eiga þræl at einka-vin,
skoloð eigi ér skratta blóta.
Veit ek í eldi Ásu brenna,
tröll eigi þik ! truig guði einum.　　20

IV. The Cloak o' Beards.

Ogmund says :
Nú mun ek kasta verða kápu mínni
þeirri er gör var af grön iöfra
en hlað-buin á hliðar báðar,

mun ek hennar móðr miök missa verða ;
þeir elta mik all-sýsliga
Oddr ok Sirnir orrosto frá.

---

241 = Helgi iii. 43.

3. HALF SAGA.

(From Cod. Reg. 2845.)

I. *Innstan and King.*

In. Upp mundu ver allir ganga
skatna beztir af skipum vórum,
láta brenna bragninga sveit
ok Ásmundar lið aldri týna.
Ki. Ver skulum halfir herjar þessa
sáttir sækja frá sió neðan;
Ásmundr hefir oss um boðna
hringa rauða sem hafa viljum.
In. Sér ei þú allan Ásmundar hug,
hefir fylkir sá flærð í bríósti,   10
mundir þú, þengill, ef ver því réðim,
mági þínum miök lítt trúa.
Ki. Ásmundr hefir oss um unnit
margar trygðir, sem menn vitu;
mun ei góðr konungr ganga á sættir,
né gramr annan í griðum væla.
In. þer er orðinn Oðinn til gramr,
er þú Ásmundi all-vel truir,
hann mun alla oss um væla
nema þú víti við-siár fáir.   20
Ki. Æ lystir þik æðru at mæla,
mun ei sá konungr sættir riúfa,
gull eigum þar ok gersimar,
hringa rauða frá hans búum.
In. Halfr dreymði mik, hygðu at slíku,
at logi léki um liði vóru,
íllt væri þar or at leysazt;
Hvat kvað þú, þengill, þann draum vita?
Ki. Hrynja um herðar þeim er hamalt fylkja
grams verðungu gyldnar brynjur,   30
þat mun á öxlum öðlings vinum
lióst at líta sem logi brenni.
In. Enn dreymði mik öðru sinni,
hugðak á öxlum elda brenna,
gruna tek ek nokkut at þat gott viti,
Hvat kvað þ. þ. þann draum vita?
Ki. Gefa mun ek hverjum hialm ok
brynju
frækna drengja er fylgja mer,
þat man at líta sem logi brenni
skiöldungs liði of skarar fiöllum.   40
In. þat dreymði mik þriðja sinni,
at ver í kaf niðr komnir værim;
eiga mun all-stórt um at væla.
Hvat k. þ. þ. þ. draum vita?
Ki. Full-langt er siá fífl-skapr talaðr
vera kvað ek ekki undir slíku:
seg þú enga svá at heyri
drauma þína í degi síðan.
In. Hlýði Hrókar ok her-konungr
orðum mínum, Útsteinn þriði!   50
göngum allir upp frá ströndu,

kunnum ekki konungs mál um þat.
Konung látu ver keppinn ráða
fyrir fólki um farar vórar;
hættum, bróðir, svó hónum líki,
fiörvi okkru með frömum vísi.
Hlýtt hefir fylkir í förum úti
mínum ráðum mörgu sinni,
nú kveð ek öngu er ek mæli
hlýða vilja sízt hingat kómum.   60

II. *In the Hall.*

In. Rýkr um hauka í höll konungs,
vón er at riúki vax af söxum;
mál er gulli ok gersemum,
hialmum skipta með Halfs-rekkum.
Hins fýsi ek nú at Halfr vaki,
er ei af eklu eldar kyndir,
áttu, men-bríótr, mági þínum
grimm-lunduðum giafir at launa.
Hrindum heilir hallar bióri,
nú taka súlur í sundr þoka: 10
æ man uppi meðan öld lifir
Halfs-rekka för til hertoga.
Hart skulum ganga, ok hlífa ekki við,
verðr vísis lið at vega með söxum;
þeir skulu sialfir á ser bera
blóðgar benjar áðr braki létti.
Snuizt snarliga, snyrti-drengir,
út ór eldi með auð-brota;
enginn er ýta sá er æ lifir,
mun ei baug-broti við bana kvíða.   20
Her sá ek alla einum fylgja
iafn-röskliga öðlings vini;
hittumzt heilir þá heðan líðum,
er ei léttara líf enn dauði.
Hrókr er fallinn með hertoga
fræknn á fótum fólks oddvita.
Eigum Óðni íllt at gialda
er hann slíkan konung sigri rænti.
Ek hefi úti átián sumur
fylgt fullhuga flein at ríóða;   30
skal ek eigi annan eiga dróttinn
gunnar-giarnan né ganaall verða.
Hér mun Innsteinn til iarðar hníga
horskr at höfði hers oddvita.
þat munu seggir at sögum giöra
at Halfr konungr hlæjandi dó.

III. *Útstan and Ulf and Eystan.*

Út. Hitt hlægir mik helzt í máli,
mun eigi Ásmundi öll vá sofa;
þrír eru fallnir af því liði
Eynefs synir, enn einn lifir.
Upp skulum rísa ok út ganga

ok ramligar randir knýja,
hugg ek við hialmum hingað komnar
til Dannerkr dísir várar.

Ul. Yðr munu dauðar dísir allar, 9
heill kveð ek horfna frá Halfs-rekkum ;
dreymði mik í morgin at megir vórir
efri yrði hvar er ver mættumz.

Út. Sigrs vænti ek mer sýnu betra,
enn Ulfr vili æskja Steini,
yðr mun snimma at sverð-togi
hauss um högginn, enn hals roðinn.

Ul. Munu þeir efri verða Ulfs synir,
Oddr ok Ornolfr, Atli inn Svarti,
Börkr ok Brynjolfr, Bui, Harðskafi,
Rauðr inn Rammi, ef þú reynir til. 20

Út. Mundi eigi Steini né Stara þikkja
ógn at etja við Ulfs-sono,
því at eigi var vórum bróður
við drit-menni þitt dramb at etja.

þótti eigi Hrókum né Halfdani
raun at berjaz við rag-menni,
þá er fiórir ver falla létum
átta iarla fyrir Annis-nesi.

Fari Ulfs synir út at berjaz
átta drengir við eitt höfuð, 30
mun ei stökkva, þótt Steinn hafi
færa nökkut í flokki lið.

Halfr dreymði mik hvati at ek berðumz,
ok kvaz mer frækn konungr fylgja
skyldu,
hefir mer gramr verit góðr í draumi
hvar ver orrosto eiga skyldum.

Nú er ek inn kominn Ulfi at segja,
at hans synir höggnir liggja,
nú fari Eysteinn ef þer vilit
fleiri at freista við fleina við. 40

Ey. Sialft mun letja slíks at freista
Halfs eru rekkar hverjum meiri ;
þik veit ek manna miklu fremstan,
einn sniallastan er þú átta vótt.

Út. Alla munda ek Eysteins liða
sverði beita at sömu hófi.
Ef mer þarfir þess verks sæi,
eðr íllt með oss áðr um væri.

Magni fýsir engi við mik at deila,
því at mer var ungum aldr skapaðr : 50
ek hefi hiarta hart í bríósti
sízt mer í æsku Óðinn framði.

IV. *Hrók the Black.*

Nú mun segja sonr Hámundar
hvert eðli var okkart bræðra :
minn var faðir miklu fremri
haukr görr at hug, enn Haki yðvarr.
Vildi engi við Vífil iafnaz

þó at Hámundar hiarðar gætti,
sá ek öngan þar svína-hirði
huglausara enn Heðins arfa.

Mín var ævi miklo æðri,
þá er Halfi konungi horskum fylgðum ;
bárum allir eitt ráð saman 11
ok herjuðum hvert land yfir.

Höfðum ver allir hauk-manna lið
hvar sem fróð-hugaðr frama kostaði,
gengum ver í gögnum með grá hialma
full-stór öll fóstr-lönd niu.

Half sá ek höggva höndum báðum,
hafði eigi hilmir hlíf-skiöld fyrir ser,
finnr engi maðr, þótt fari víða,
hæfra hiarta ok hug-prúðara. 20

Mæla virðar, þeir er vitu eigi,
at Halfs frami heimsku sætti,
kann eigi sá konung Háleyskan
er heimsku þrótt hónum eignaði.

Það hann ei við dauða drengi kvíða,
né æðru-orð ekki mæla,
engi skyldi iöfri fylgja
nema forlög um fylkis héldi.

Skyldu ei stynja, þótt stór hlyti
sár í sóknum, siklings vinir, 30
né benjar ser binda láta
fyrr enn annars dags iafn-lengd kæmi.

Það ei hann í her höptu græta,
né mans-kono mein at vinna,
mey bað hann hverja mundi kaupa,
fögru gulli, at föður ráði.

Vóru ei svá margir menn á skeiðum,
at ver á flótta fyrir héldim,
þó at miklu lið minna hefðim,
svá at ellifu einum gegndi. 40

Höfðum ver allir enn efra hlut
hvar sem Hildar [él] hlífar knúði :
einn vissa ek iafn-sniallan gram,
Sigurð konung at sölum Giúka.

Margir vóru menn á skeiðum
góðir ok fræknir með gram sialfum.
Börkr ok Brynjolfr . . . .
. . . .
Fáir mundu þeim fylkis rekkum
hæfir þykkja or Haka veldi.

Hvergi þótta ek í því liði 50
opt aukkvisi annar monnur;
mik kvóðu þeir manna snarpastan,
því at hvárr öðrum hróðrs leitaði.
. . . .
fylgði sínu sá framligast
lofðungr liði meðan-lifa mátti.

Naut eigi svá aldrs sem skyldi
frækn landreki við frama dáðir,
tolf vetra nam tiggi at herja,
enn þá var þengill þritugr er dó.
Slíkt kennir mer at sofa lítið 60

---

6. Hlod and Angantheow, l. 60.   9. Atlamal 94.   47. See vol. i, p. 355.

marga grímu ok miök vaka,
er bróðir minn brenna skyldi
kvikr í eldi með konungs rekkum.
Sá hefir dagr um mik daprastr komit
miklu í heimi, sva at menn viti;
muna þikkjumk ver allir síðan
at fylgja máttum fræðum hollum.
Allz mundi mer angrs léttara,
ef ek Halfs konungs hefna mættak,
svá at Ásmundi egg-fránan hiör   70
brúna ' baugspiot ' bríóst raufgaðak.
Hefnt mun vera Halfs ins frækna,
því at þeir göfgan gram í griðum vældu,
olli morði ok mann-skaða
Ásmundr konu; gr íllu heilli.
þá mun reyna ok raun gefa,
ef vit Sveinn komum saman í rómu,

hvárir í vígi verða hæfri
Hámundar burr eða Haka þegnar.
Segi ek svá kveðit snotru vífi,   80
at ek Brynhildar biðja mundak,
ef vita þættumz at vildi hón
Hróki uuna Hámundar bur.
Vón væri mer vitra manna
snarpra segja, ef ver saman ættim,
því ek fann ei mey marg-svinnari
hvergi landa, en Haka dóttur.
Fann ek aldri, þó hef-ek farit víða,
hugg-þekkri mey, en Haka dóttur.
Her þykki er nú í Haka veldi   90
hornungr vera hverrar þióðar,
eigu allir innar at sitja
. . . enn Halfs-rekkar.

4. BUSLU-BÆN, from BÓSA SAGA.

(From AM. 577, 343.)

HER liggr Hringr konungr hilmir Gauta
ein-ráðastr allra manna,
ætlar þú son þinn sialfr at myrða,
þau munu fá-dæmi fréttaz víða.
Heyr þú bæn Buslu, hun mun brátt
sungin,
sva at heyraz skal um heim allan,
ok óþörf öllum þeim er á heyra,
en þeim fiándlegust sem ek vil fortala :
Villiz vættir, verði ódæmi,
hristiz hamrar, heimr sturliz,   10
versni veðrátta, verði ódæmi—
Nema Hringr konungr Herrauð friði
ok Bögo-Bósa biargir veiti.
Svá skal ek þiarma þer at bríósti
at hiarta þitt högg-ormr gnagi,
en eyru þín aldri heyri,
en augu þín út hverf snuiz—
Nema þú Bósa biörg um veitir
ok Herrauði heipt upp gefir.
Ef þú siglir, slitni reiði,   20
en af stýri stökkvi krókar,
rifni reflar, reki segl ofan,
en ak-taumar allir slitni—

Nema þú Herrauði heipt upp gefir,
en Bögu-Bósa biðir til sætta.
Ef þú ríðir, raskiz taumar,
heltiz hestar, en hrumiz klárar,
en götur allar ok gagn-stígar
traðiz tvefaldar í tröll-hendr fyr þer—
Nema þú Bósa   30
Sé þer í hvílu sem í halm-eldi
en í hásæti sem á haf-báru,
þó skal þér síðar sýnu verra
ef þú vilt við meyjar mans gaman.
villr ertu vegarins. Viltu þulu lengri ?
Troll ok alfar ok tavfra nornir
buar, berg-risar brenni þínar hallir,
hati hrím-þursar hallir þínar ;
strain stangi þik ! stofnar angri þik !
verði þer vei, nema þú vilja minn görir.
Komi her seggir sex, seg þú mer nöfn
þeira   41
öll óbundin, ek skal þer sýna ;
getr þú eigi ráðit sva rett þiki,
þá skulu þik hundar í hel gnaga
ok sál þín sœkkva í víti.

5. STAR-ORDI'S DREAM (AM. 555, chart.)

(Drauma vitranir, edit. 1860.)

VÓRU austr á Ioru-skógi
barmar tveir böls um fyldir,
ok til fiár fyrðar næmdu
við morð-ráð mörgu sinni.
Enn sá gramr er gera bræðir
hefir tír-giarn tindótt hiarta,

ok böð-frækn báða felldi
Garp ok Gný Geirviðr konungr.
Réð iafn-giarn auði at skipta,
Roðbiartz sonr rekka mærði   10
af því fé fyrða kindir
er svik-menni safnat höfðu.
Lét gunn-diarfr gefna hringa
seggja ætt siklingr Gauta,

svá at hirð-menn höfðu allir
hauka stóls hengi-skafla.
Mun Dagfinnr dýrra mála
við lofs-orð lúka kvæði,
nióti vel vegs ok landa
gramr göfugr Gauzkrar þióðar !   20

6. *From Gongu-Hrolf Saga* (AM. 343).

Gleðzt Hreggviðr af góðri för
Hrólfs ins hugdiarfa hingat til landa,
mun rekkr sá ræsis hefna
á Eireki ok öllum þeim.

Gleðzt Hreggviðr af Gríms dauða,
þórðar ok þar með þrióta lífs-stundir,
mun flokkr sá fiánda minna
fyrir Hrolfi hníga verða.

Glezt Hreggviðr þá Hrolfr fær
ungrar meyjar Ingigerðar,   10
mun Hólm-garði hilmir stýra
Sturlaugs sonr.   Standi kvæði !

7. *Ans Saga* (AM. 343).

Vel þer, selja, stendr þú sió nærri
laufguð harðla vel . . . .
maðr skekr af þer morgin-döggvar,
enn ek at þegni þrey nátt sem dag.

þat muntu finna er þú flór mokar,
at þú eigi ert Án bog-sveigir,
þú ert brauð-sveigir heldr en bog-sveigir
osta-sveigir, en eigi alm-sveigir.

Meyjar spurðu er mik fundu
hvít-haddadar, Hvaðan komtu fer-faldr?
Enn ek svaraða silki-gunni   11
heldr hæðinni: Hvaðan er logn úti?

8. *Fridthiow Saga* (see Bk. ix).

Sé ek troll-konor tvær á báru
þær hefir Helgi hingat sendar,
þeim skal sníða sundr í miðju
hrygg Elliði áðr af för skríðr.
Heill Elliði ! hlauptu á báru,
brióttu í troll-konom tennr ok enni,
kinnr ok kialka í konu vándri
fót eða báða í flagði þessu.

þurfið ei drengir dauða at kvíða
verit þióð-glaðir þegnar mínir,   10
þat of vita vórir draumar
at ek eiga mun Ingibiörgu.

Ek bar upp til eld-stóar
dæsta drengi í drífu-veðri,
nú hef ek segli á sand komit,
ei er við hafs megin hægt at reyna.

Menn sé ek ausa í megin-veðri
sex á Elliða enn siau róa,
þat er gunn-hvötum glíkt í stafni,
Friðþióf Frækna er fram fellr við árar.
Taktu af golfi, gang-fögr kona,   21
horn holfanda, hefik af drukkit,
menn sé ek á mar þá er munu þurfa
hregg-móðir lið áðr höfn taki.

. . . . . .

Drukkum fyrr á Framnesi
fræknir drengir með föður mínum,
nú sé ek brendan bæ þann vera,
á ek öðlingum íllt at launa.
Einn mun ek ganga inn til bæjar,
þarf ek lítið lið lofðunga at finna,
varpið eldi í iöfra bæ   30
ef ek kem eigi aptr at kveldi.

Taktu við skatti skatna dróttinn
fremstu tönnum, nema þú framar beiðir,
silfr er á botni belgjar þessa
sem vit Biörn höfum báðir ráðit.

Kysta ek unga Ingibiörgu
Bela dóttur í Baldrs-haga,
svá skolu árar á Elliða
báðar bresta sem bogi Helga.

þá hét ek Friðþiófr, er ek fór með vík-
öngum,   40
enn Herþiófr, er ek ekkjur grætta,
Geirþiófr, er ek gaflokum fleygða,
Gunnþiófr er ek gekk at fylki,
Eyþiófr, er ek út-sker rænta,
Helþiófr, er ek henta smá-börnum,
Valþiófr, þá ek var æðri mönnum.
Nú hef ek sveimat síðan með salt-körlum
hialpar þurfandi áðr ek hingat kom.

9. KETIL HŒNG'S SAGA (AM. 343 and 471).

I. *Bruni and Ketil.*

Bruni.   HEILL kom þú, Hængr, her skaltu þiggja,
allan vetr með oss vera
þer mun ek fastna, nema þú fyr látir,
dóttur mína áðr dagr komi.

Ketil.   Her mun ek þiggja, hygg ek at valdi   5
Finnz fiölkyngi feikna-veðri,
ok í allan dag einn iós ek við þriá,
hvalr kyrði haf, her mun ek þiggja.

II. *Ketil and Gusi the Finn King.*

Ketil. Skríð þú af kialka, kyrr þú hreina
seggr síð-förull, segðú hvattú heitir.
Gusi. Gusi kalla mik göfgir Finnar,
em ek oddviti allrar þióðar.
Ketil. Hængr ek hetti kominn or Hrafnistu,
hefnir Hallbiarnar, hygg ek ei friðar biðja,
frið-mælum mæla, mun ek ei við Finn ragann,
heldr mun ek boga benda þann mer Bruni gaf.
Gusi. Hverr er á öndrum öndverðan dag
giarn til gunnar í grimmum hug,   10
við skulum freista flein at rióða
hvórr at öðrum, nema hugr bili.
Ketil. Hæng kalla mik hálfu nafni,
mun ek veita þer viðnám heðan,
skaltu víst vita áðr vit skiljum
at bú-körlum bíta örvar.
Gusi. Bústu nú við bitri egg-þrimu,
haf þú hlíf fyrir þer, hart mun ek skióta,
þer mun ek bráðla at bana verða
nema þú af auði öllum látir.   20
Ketil. Mun ek af auði eigi láta
ok fyr einum þer aldri renna,
fyrr skal höggin hlíf fyrir bríósti,
en fyrir siónum svart at ganga.
Gusi. Skaltu ei gulli ok gersemum
með heilum hag heima ráða,
kemr þer bani brátt at höndum,
ef vit skulum úti oddum leika.
Ketil. Mun ek ei gulli við Gusi skipta
né fyrri friðar mæla,   30
mer er bráðr bani betri miklu
en hugleysi ok héðan-kváma.
Feigr er nú Finnr inn ragi,
at hann fót-treðr flein sinn rangan.

III. *Ketil and Ogre.*

Ogre. Hvat er þat býsna er ek á biargi sé
ok gnapir eldi yfir?
bú-sifjar okkrar hykkat ek batna munu,
líttu á lióð-vega ª.
Hvat er þat manna er mer í móti ferr,
skríðr þú sem vargr af viði,
æðru skaltu mæla . . . . . .
þrysvar í þrumu firði (!).
Ketil. Hialmr ok Stafnglámr, hlifið ykkr báðir,
gefið rúm gömlum at ganga framar hóti.   10
Fliúga folk-nöðrur, frækn er Dala-kappi,
liótr er leikr eggja, litað er skegg á karli,
skrapa skinn-kyrtlar, skialfa iárn-serkir,
hristazt hring-skyrtur, hræðizt biðill meyjar.

IV. *Ketil and Ogre.*

Ketil. Hvat er þat flagða er ek sé á fornu nesi
ok glottir við guma,

___

24. Hialmar's Death Song, l. 22.   ª These are echoes from old poems in
dialogue-metre mixed up with the spurious, and are in the following lines :—III. 1-8 ;
IV. 1-4, 8, 9, 17, 25-30, 36-39, as well as in V.

at upp verandi sólu? hef ek önga fyr
    leiðilegri litið.

Ogre. Forað ek heiti, fædd var ek norðarla
hraust í Hrafnseyju, hvim-leið bú-mönnum
ör til áræðis hvatki er íllt skal vinna.
Mörgum manni hefek til moldar snuit
    þeim er til fiskjar fóro (!)
hverr er siá hinn kopur-máli er kominn er í skerin?   10

Ketil. Hæng kalla mik hálfu nafni.

Ogre. Hollara væri þer heima í Hrafnisto,
en dratta einum til út-skerja

Ketil. Einhlítr ek þóttumk . . . .
hvat er flögð mæla
lasta ek dreng dæsinn, drep ek á vit fanga.
Hykkat ek fyrir vinnast hvat er Forað mælir,
nauðir mik hvöttu, nánum átti ek biarga,
hætti ek eigi á holm til sela,
ef í eyju heima ærnir væri.   20

Ogre. Synja ek þess eigi, segir hin víð-förla,
at þú líf hafir langt um menn aðra
ef þú fund okkarn fyrðum segir,
sveinn lítill, sé ek þiun hug skialfa.

Ketil. Ungr var ek heima, fór ek ein saman,
    opt í út-veri,
marga myrk-riðu ek fann á minni götu,
hræddumk ek aldri . . . .
    flagða friósan.
Langleit ertu fóstra, ok lætr róa hefit,   30
ei hefik flagðit ferligra litið,
eða hvert hefir þú förina görva?

Ogre. Gang hóf ek upp í Angri, eigraða ek til Steigar,
skalm . . . . ek til Karmtar,
elda mun ek á Iaðri ok á Útsteini blása,
austr skal ek við Elfi, áðr dagr á mik skíni
með brúðguma . . . . ok bráðla gefið iarli.

Ketil. Seyði þínum mun ek snua, en sialfum þer gnúa,
    unz þik gríðr grípr.

. . . .
Örum trui ek mínum, en þú afrendi þínu,   40
fleinn mun nú mæta nema þú fyrir hrœkkvir.

Ogre. Flög ok Fífu hygg ek þer fiarri vera,
hræðumk ek eigi Hremsu bit.

V. *Böðmóð and Ketil.*

Böðmóð. Hverr er sá inn hári er á haugi sitr
    ok horfir veðri viðr?
frost-harðan mann hygg ek þik feiknum vera,
    hvat þer hvergi hlyr?

Ketil. Ketill ek heiti kominn or Hrafnistu,
    þar var ek upp um alinn,
hug-fullt hiarta veit ek hlífa mer,
    þó vildag gisting geta.

Böðmóð. Upp skaltu rísa ok ganga haugi af,
    ok sækja mína sali   10
máls-efnis ann ek þer margan dag,
    ef þú vilt þiggja þar.

---

26. Guest's Wisdom, l. 97.

Ketil. Upp mun ek rísa ok ganga haugi af,
    allz mer Böðmóðr býðr,
    bróðir minn þætt sæti brautu nær
    mundi eigi betr um boðit.
Böðmóð. Reyndr ertu fóstri at ganga her-vígis til
    ok berjazt við Framar til fiár
    á léttum aldri gaf honum Óðinn sigr,
    miök kveð-ek hann vígum vanan.   20
Ketil. Óðinn blóta görða ek aldregi,
    hefig þó lengi lifat,
    Framar veit ek falla munu
    fyrr en þetta it háfa höfuð.

VI. Framar and Ketil.

Framar. Veifir þú vængjum, vópnum mun ek þer heita,
    vafrar þú nú, víð-flögull, sem vitir mik feigan,
    villr ertu víg-starri, við munum sigr hafa,
    hverf þú at Hængi, hann skal nú deyja.
Ketil. Dregzt þú nu Dragvendill við . . . arnar,
    mætir þú mein-göldum, máttu ei bíta,
    mik þess ei varði at hrœkkva mundi
    eggjar eitri herðar, þó at Óðinn deyfði.
    Hvat er þer Dragvendill? hví ertu slær orðinn?
    til hef ek nú höggit, tregt er þer at bíta,   10
    hliðar þú at hiör-þingi, hefir þer ei fyrr orðit
    bilt í braki malma, þar er bragnar hiugguzt.
Framar. Skelfr nú skegg á karli, skeika vápn gömlum,
    frýr hann hiör hvòssum, hræðizt faðir meyjar,
    brýnduz ben-teinar svá at bíta mætti
    höldum hug-prúðum, ef þer hugr dygði,
Ketil. Ei þarftu oss at eggja, eiga mer sialdan
    fyrða flaug-trauðir frýja stór-höggva ;
    bít þú nú, Dragvendill, eða brotna ella,
    horfin er heill báðum ef bilar hinn þriðja.   20
    Hræðizt ei faðir meyjar meðan heill er Dragvendill,
    vita ek víst þikjumk, verðr honum ei bilt þrysvar.
Framar. Hugr er í Hængi, hvass er Dragvendill,
    beit hann orð Óðins sem ekki væri,
    brást nú Baldrs faðir, brigt er at trúa hónum,
    nióttu heill handa, her munum skiljazt.

10. GRIM SHAGGY-CHEEK'S SAGA.

Grim and Ogress.

Gr. HVAT heita þær hrauns íbúur
er skaða vilja skipi mínu,
ykkr hef ek einar sénar,
amátligstar at yfir-litum.
Og. Feima ek heiti, fædd var ek norð-
    arla
Hrimnis dóttir í Háfialli,
her er systir mín halfu fremri
Kleima at nafni komin til sióvar.
Gr. Þrífizt hvergi þiazza dóttir,
brúðir vestar, brátt skal ek reiðazt,   10
rétt skal ek ykkr áðr röðull skíni
vörgum senda víst til bráðar.
Kleima. Þat var fyrr at faðir okkar
burtu seiddi báru hiarðir,

skuluð aldregi, nema sköp ráði,
heilir heðan heim um komazt.
Gr. Skal ek ykkr báðum skiótla heita
oddi ok eggju í upp-hafi,
munu þá reyna Rögnis mellur
hvórt betr dugir broddr eða krumma.   20

Gr. Hér höfum fellt til foldar
tírar-lausa tolf berserki,
þó var Sörkvir seggja þeira
þroska mestr ok þrostr annarr.
Fyrst mun ek líkja ept fóður mínum
skal eigi mín dóttir, nema skör höggviz,
nauðig gefin neinum manni.

APPENDAGE TO INTRODUCTION.

(Page xxvii, note 4.)

I. Rímur in vellum, from the year 1450 to 1550.

Leikr enn hrygð í lióða sal : lítið kann eg spektar tal ;
hef eg ei *Eddu* heyrt né séð : hún hefir öðrum meira léð.—
Sigurðar þögla Rímur, AM. 604.

Óðrinn skal nú eigi myrkr : orða er þat minni styrkr ;
skaldin munu þá skiala betr : ef skiölum ver ekki um *Eddu letr*.—
Sturlaug Starfsama R., AM. 603.

Eigi nennig *Eddu klifun* í orðum hylja ;
gleðinnar brögð fyrir gumnum dylja : gaman er ekki myrkt at þylja.—
Áns R., *Cod. Wolph.*

Bragarins smíð um bauga hlíð skal brögnum sent,
þó *Edda* hafi mer ekki kent : orða fiöld eða kvæða ment.
And— Akta kann eg enga sorg í *Eddu greinum.*
And— *Eddu lát* með orðin kát : ýtar fylla mærðar bát ;
sónar gamm skal setja framm : ok selja út á orða damm.—*Jarlmanns R.*

Þó er mer ekki þat svó kært : at þylja vísur hreinar,
aldri hef-ek *Eddu* lært : orða-dygðir neinar.—*R. af Ill Verra ok Vest.*

Aldri hef ek úr *Eddu* nein : afmors brögð eða kvæða grein,
berst eg því sem brim við stein : þá blíða nefni-eg lauka rein.—
Konrads R., AM. 604.

Ekkert fæ eg af *Eddu* lið : að auka þenna mála klið ;
þýkir hún sumum þung-skilin : því komst ekki í huga minn.—
Dinus Drambláta R.

Svó er mer *Edda* orðin leið : hiá öðrum fræðum kátum ;
nú hefig ekki um nokkurt skeið : nýtt af hennar látum.—*Reinallz R.*

II. From the year 1550 to 1650 (on Paper MSS.: Arna-Magn. 521, 606, 609, 611,
615, 4to ; and 132, 139, 141, 143, 145, 8vo).

Edda görir mer öngan styrk : orða vals í smiðju
því er mín ekki mælskan myrk : mærðar tals við iðju.—*Pontus R.*

Hárs eg fiaðra hreggið tel : heimskra manna fræði ;
skatnar hyggnir skilja vel : *Skáldu* og *Eddu* bæði.—
Valdimars R. [*Þórðr á Striúgi*].

Eddu króka aldri mig : ætla-eg við að styðja
og engan nema einsaman þig : sem allir eiga at biðja . . .
And— Víst munu skaldin virða mer : til vórkunnar þá gæta að sér,
þeir sem *Eddu* iðka fín : á henni líma kvæðin sín.
And— Sannleik allan segi eg þer : og satt með-kenni,
allt eins fer fyrir *Eddu* og mer : eg áles henni.—
Siö Meistara R. [*Biörn Sturluson,* 1621].

Ekki hefi-eg á *Eddu* stoð : né orða dýrum greinum,
má eg því ekki mærðar boð : meyjunum færa neinum.—
Þorsteins Bæjarmagns R.

Margir yrkja mærðir vel í minnis ranni
lióða smiðir lióst af munni : lítið þó í *Eddu* kunni.
And— Frosta lögur fremur sögur um frúr og sveina,
bernsku bögur margir meina : málin fögur *Eddu greina.*—*Rollants R.*

Af *Eddu* fekk eg engan snert : um efnið þykir meira vert.—*Esthers R.*

Onga hef-eg af *Eddu* ment : orða snild að vanda,
veit eg mer því varla hent : Viðris drykk að blanda.—*Tobias R.*

Edda er sögð ein ágæt bók : öllum sem hana stunda,
mörg og fögr á kenning klók : ef kappar að því grunda.—*Vilmundar R.*

Minzt er eg við mentan kringr : mærðir saman að reyra,
allra sízt í *Eddu* slingr : öldin má þat heyra.—*Ulfars R.* (Jón í Vattarnesi).

Nýtum ýti eg Norðra priám : ef nú vill hlýða mengi,
Ekki fekk eg *Eddu* nám : óðs við lióða strengi.—*þialar Jóns R.*

Margir brúka í mansöng fyrst : *málin Eddu* diúp og há,
þessa ekki lasta eg list : þó langt sé eg henni burtu frá.

And— Eg hefi sízt við *Eddu* tök . . .—*Ambales R.*

Hvernig má sá heimskur er : hrundum færa mansöngs kver,
ef hann ekki *Eddu* ber : og engin hennar dæmin sér.

And— Engin hef-eg á *Eddu* skil : né ungri skemta menja bil,
þó vil eg siötta sónar spil : sögunnar verða að hverfa til.—*Hermóðs R.*

Skil eg mig við skalda lög og skikkan *Eddu*,
aldrei er, ef að því grundið : efni þyngra í mærðir bundið.—*Moyses R.*

Eddu greinir engar þyl : er þær bágt að skilja,
leirinn arnar læt eg til : lasti hann þeir sem vilja.—*Álaflekks R.*

Ei skal þurfa öldin her við *Eddu* að hnýta,
hennar orð og hagleg fræði : hafa skal ekki í mínu kvæði.—*Egils R.*

Lítið hefeg lært að stunda lagið á kvæðum,
Eddu kann eg ekki af ræðum : sem efni hefir af mörgum gæðum.

And— *Eddu kenning* ekki þykir öllum bata.—*Flovents R.*

Önga lærði eg *Eddu* ment : sem iðkuðu skáldin forðum,
því er mer ekki í hróðri hent : að haga miúkum orðum.—
R. *of Lykla Petri* [Hallgr. Peterson].

Áður hefir sú *Edda* þént : afmórs lióða greinum,
því skal heðan af þessi ment : þióna Guði einum.

And— Er mer tregur *Eddu* vegur : orða snild að hrósa.—*Syraks* Ʀ.

Ment úr *Eddu* mín er krenkt : mála lengð að hrista,
ervidið skal þó yður sent : eftir frægra lista.

And— Náttúru fer nægðin ser : numin af ríkum anda,
námið *Eddu* annað er : Ónars miöð að vanda.—*Magnus Olafsson in* 1609.

það mega sanna sprundin spök : er spektin menta náði ;
að eir.gin hef-eg á *Eddu* tök : og aldri hennar gáði.

And— Lítil hef-eg á lióðum tök : lagða eg sízt við *Eddu* mök,
diúp-fundin að dikta rök : dugir sialdan mentin lök.

And— þau orðin spök og *Eddu* rök : ekki margir skilja . . .

And— Edda studdi flesta fast : í fraða smiði kláru.—*Króka Refs R.*

And— því skal ráða þióð við mig : í þessu orða sæði,
hún nam *Edda* hvíla sig : heima og *Skálda* bæði.—
Apollonius R. [Biörn of Skarðsa].

Efnið þarf í orða starf : allt þó sett í gætur,
Eddu-magr, illa hagur : aldri kemst á fætur.—*Gríshildar R.*

Vinst þeim ekki að vanda brag : sem veit ei *Eddu króka*,
og aldrei lærði á sínn dag : orð-gnótt fræði-bóka.—*Grettis R.*

Allir fá í *Eddu* séð : æ fallvaltan þenna heim,
vanmátt Ása og virðing með : hún veltur á þessum hiólum tveim.—
Jón Lærði, 1641 [Cod. Holm. 38].

Lastly in Liuflingslag—
Ekki siást her *Eddu kenningar*,
útan sam-fellur sagna minna.—*Kötlu-draumr.*

NOTES.

BOOK VII.—*Bragi*, (p. 6.)

In the Mabinogion, Creiddylad, daughter of Lludd of the Silver Hand or Llyr, is the Hilda of Everlasting Battle, taking place every first day of May between Gwynn [Finn] ap Nudd and Gwythyr mal Greidiawl. Yet, she is genealogically the sweet gentle Cordelia of Shakespeare's Play—what a strange metamorphose! The Greek form of the legend is the tale of Eriphyle, who is bribed by the Belt of Beauty to fight at Thebes. Chaucer knows this story—

> Eriphile, that, for an ouche of gold,
> Hath privily unto the Greeks told
> Wher that hir husband hid him in a place,
> For which he had at Thebes sory grace.

line 5 can now be restored; in oskrán we espy ósk-kván (see Excursus, vol. ii, p. 474); and 'Heðins' in 'þeris,'—Heðins ósk-kván = Hilda, Heðin's captive wife. The sense remains as in the translation.

l. 12. Valgifris is suggested by the A.S. wælgifre; the alliteration then requires 'wulfs,'—a notable fact, showing that in Bragi's day the *w* before *u*-vowel was still heard, Wodin, wull, wulf.

l. 19. Heðin was the son of Hiarrand (Heorend the Harper). Here the prose in Edda yields the true reading.

l. 21. sal-penningr, hence is the corrupt 'sal-bendingr,' Thulor, l. 229.

l. 29. öl-skálir; the Lay of Hamtheow yields this emendation.

l. 31. gœrðan = gory (?), a rare word, see however Dict. s. v. gyrja, and vol. ii, p. 359, vii. 5.

l. 41. Geofen's ground or path is the Ocean in Beowolf.

l. 42. Read, 'renni-röknom,' cp. Helgi, i. 209.

l. 44. The name of the lake is Vænir (rather than Venir), Yngl. S. ch. 33; we surmise either 'Vænis of víðri,' or perhaps an older gen. Væneris, like vartaris (p. 62, l. 12), mutaris, Sighvat x. 64.

l. 46. Read, Iarðar.

l. 66. vazta undir-kúlo (stone's) Ála (giant's) rödd (gold)—unless the whole phrase be over-daubed by the restorer.

Haustlong, (p. 14.)

l. 2. The addition 'raums þa er rekka sæmi' is only found in paper copies of the middle of the eighteenth century, a mere modern fill-gap. Mark in this poem the numerous blank first halves, and, though rarer, consonance instead of rhyme in second half, for instance, l. 4.

l. 9. tál-hreinn, a *decoy reindeer;* it recalls 'stæl hrán' of King Alfred, which after all may be simply the Norse word thus transformed into English, for tál (bait) is a well-known Icel. word, whilst 'stæl' (stale) in English is so near in sound.

l. 28. Read, hollz.

l. 34. One would prefer átt-konr, cp. Yt. 141 and Mark 31 (the *kinsman* of

Hymi). On the whole, 'runnr' is in all such instances doubtful; the change was, on account of the rhyme, tempting to a later 'remanieur.'

l. 43. veoðr, here = veorr.

ll. 61, 62. We read berg-folginn (crag-entombed, rock-pent), a fit epithet for a giant.

l. 63. Construe, Haka myrk-reinar (sea's) bein (stone's) mœtir (giant).

ll. 66, 67. Construe, imon-dísir, the war-fairies. One would prefer trióno trolli; bíða höggs frá hörðo trióno trolli (wait for a stroke of the Hammer).

l. 72. þriótr was once a law term, a defaulter, 'bankrupt.'

Eilif's þors-drápa, (p. 19.)

l. 5. Gamm-leið (vultures' path), a pun: lopt (the air) = Loptr, one of Loki's names.

l. 7. giarð-venðir (Thor), from his Belt or Girdle.

l. 18. þrym-seil, the team or harness-pole.

l. 23. We prefer hreggi höggna as epithet to möl: bor (the borer)—the clattering files (staves) rattled against the tempest-beaten gravel.

l. 24. Feðja, the Norwegian island of that name. The poet uses by preference images drawn from proper names of places or people, see Excursus, vol. ii, p. 467.

l. 44. The Shield Britons.

l. 45. Kolgo Svíþioð = Svíþioð in Kalda = Scythia.

l. 53. fylvingar vallar, the filberts of the field, i. e. stone, cp. fiarð-epli below.

l. 55. vafreyði = vaforlogi.

l. 59. tongo segi, see p. 456.

l. 74. Under 'bliku kalfa' we surmise 'Mokkor-kalfa,' Muck-calf, the Mud monster; a name known from the story in Edda; this phrase would then be Snorri's authority for it. Alfheim's mokkor-kalfi is an apt denomination for a giant.

l. 75. Listi, a county in Norway; Rygir, Rugians, a Norwegian folk; Ella, the English king. Construe, hval-láttrs Lista Rygja (gen. pl.), the denizens of the whale-littering coast, an apt denomination for Giant-land, sited at the outskirts of Earth, where the whales litter.

Wolf's House Lay, (p. 23.)

ll. 1–2. The Cod. r reads geð-niarþar, corrupted for geð-markar (the soul's abode, the breast). We have the second part of the image in l. 1, for under 'hoddmildom hildar' must be concealed a genitive, denoting a name of Woden, Woden's breast's liquor, the poetry, the sacred Soma. Wolf the poet manifestly modelled his lines after Egil's Head Ransom, ll. 1, 2. Construe, ek té Áleifi [Woden's] geð-markar lá.

l. 8. Under sigrunni svinnom we surmise sáð-reyni Sónar sylgs (dat.), i. e. Woden, cp. a parallel, p. 80, l. 33; Sónar sylgs sáð-reynir = the searcher of the Soma drink, the Soma-inspired god; 'heilags tafns' would stand in apposition to it, meaning the holy offering.

l. 10. We take hrót to be the word; the figures were painted or carved on the roof of the hall; 'minni' are the old tales represented thereon.

l. 19. The fording of the river Wimmer, see above, pp. 17, 18. Thor's grasping the rowan tree is not now preserved in the poem, cp. Iliad xxi. 242.

l. 29. Over-daubed, underneath which we once more espy Egil's Head Ransom, l. 69, Wolf's model here as elsewhere in this song: 'Here the river reaches the sea' is a proverb, preserved here and p. 54, l. 8—a favourite phrase, it seems, to end a song.

Vetrliði, (p. 27.) 'Starkad' is here the eight-handed giant—Sá maðr bió við Aloforsa er Störkoðr hét; hann var kominn af þursum ... Starkaðr hafði átta hendr, ok vá með fiórom sverðum í senn—He abducts Alfhilda whilst she is reddening the altar at a sacrifice; her father Alf invokes Thor, who then slew the giant [Hervar Saga]. This passage is only found in a late paper MS.; we take it to be drawn from a lost leaf of Skioldunga.

Thorbiorn, p. 27. These verses were known to the Thulor compilers, see p. 424.

Glymdrapa, (p. 29.)

This poem is so completely restored that hardly an original word or sentence remains; yet Ari must have known it in its pure state, and even now the names he records can ever and anon be recognised underneath.

Ari says—þess getr Hornklofi í Glymdrápu at Haraldr konungr hafði fyrr barzk á 'Uppdals-skógi við Orkndœli.' 'Heiði' represents the place; under 'œski meiða' we recognise 'Orkndœli.'

vv. 3 and 8. The history underlying these verses must be sought in the Irish and Welsh Annals.

l. 10. Hunþiófr er nefndr konungr, sa er réð fyrir Mœra-fylki. Sölvi Klofi hét son hans, ... en sá konungr er réð fyrir Raumsdal er nefndr Nokkvi [l. 10], hann var móður-faðir Sölva. (They rise against Harald) ok hittask þeir við Sólskel. Farther on Ari relates, Harold fought Arnwid, King of Southmore, and Eadbeorn of the Friths, and there a second battle was fought at the Isle of Solskel—of which names we find Nökkvi, l. 10; the place, Solskel, we catch hidden under 'dyn skotom,' l. 14. In l. 17 we recognise—Ok at lyktum varð Haraldr svá reiðr, at hann gekk fram á 'rausn' á skipi sínu ... leitoðo þá menn Arnviðar konungs á flótta, enn hann sialfr fell á skipi sínu, þar fell ok Auðbiörn konungr, en Sölvi flýði,—citing verse 5 as his authority.

vv. 6, 7 refer to a battle in the Gotha River. In line 23 we recognise—'stikuðu' Gautar Gautelfi ... Haraldr konungr hélt skipum sínum upp í Elfina 'ok lagðizk við stikin.' Farther, Haraldr konungr fór víða um Gautland herskildi, ok átti þar margar orrostor tveim megin Elfarinnar, ok fekk hann optast sigr; Enn í einhverri orrosto fell Hrani inn Gauzki, which last name lurks probably underneath l. 25.

v. 8 is cited by Ari as authority for the harrying of the West, in the Hebrides, the Isle of Man, Scotland, in one of which battles Earl Iwere was slain. One fancies to discover 'Manverja' in l. 27 (men-fergir); 'sandi Manar' (beach of the Isle of Man) under 'sandmens,' l. 28 [cp. Sandwad, Manx Chron. 1098]; under 'læbrautar' some place is hidden.

Guthorm Sindri, (p. 30.)

These verses are in just as bad a plight.

v. 1 is cited as authority for a raid of the Danes in the Wick; the king chases them, some back to Halland [ialfaðar, l. 3], some to Jutland, whither the king follows them, overtakes and beats them [l. 2].

v. 2. The king with two ships fights three Danish galleys in Zealand, in Ore-sound. In 'Selmeina' is hidden Selund, here as a pun (seal-wound, Sel-und).

v. 3. Eptir þat herjaði Hákon konungr víða um Selund, rænti mart folk, enn drap sumt, enn sumt her-tók hann, ok tók giöld stór af sumum ... Síðan fór Hákon konungr austr fyrir Skáneyjar-síðu, herjaði allt, tók giöld ok skatta af landinu, enn drap alla víkinga hvar sem hann fann, bæði Dani ok Vindr [l. 10]; fór hann allt austr fyrir Gautland [l. 11] ok herjaði þar, ok fekk stór giöld af landinu. Hákon konungr fór aptr um haustit ... hann sat um vetrinn í Víkinni við áhlaupum, ef Danir eða Gautar görði þar.

v. 4 refers to King Tryggvi, Olaf Tryggvason's father—þat sama haust kom Tryggvi [l. 14] konungr Óláfsson or vestr-víking, hann hafði þá herjat um Írland ok Skotland [l. 15]; um várit fór Hákon norðr í land, ok setti Tryggva konung, bróður-son sínn, yfir Víkina [l. 14].

vv. 5, 6. A battle in the Isle of Karmen (Kormt), on Agwaldsness, where King Gudrum (Gorm), Bloodaxe's son, fell. The king chases the flying host to West Agde, and hence to Jutland. Every word and fact is here blurred and blotted out.

v. 7 relates to the Battle on Rastar-kalf; names of places are, Stað (Cape Stadt), Fræðar-berg, Féeyjar-sund. Notable events—Egil Woolsark is slain; the stratagem of the Ten Banners; King Gamli, the son of Eric Bloodaxe, is slain. This is all dramatically told in Ari, who, besides the poem, seems here to have had popular tradition (or, even, a scrap of a song?); the cairns, too, were still visible in his day as standing memorials. It is around old Egil Woolsark that the tradition wove its tale. In l. 25 we seem to espy 'fyrir Fræðar-bergi;' in l. 26, 'Ullserkr ... tio merkjom;' in l. 27 'Gramr,' read 'Gamli;' 'oðskvanar' [l. 28] must be 'ósk kvánar,' the leman of Woden = the land which Hacon won.

Cormac's Sigrod Drapa, (p. 33.)

But fragments, in part sadly over-painted, though ever and anon whole lines and phrases remain intact. One would like to know what is hidden under lines 9, 10; does 'ennidúkr' mean the kerchief worn by the sacrificing priest? if so, it would be the only instance where anything like Lat. vittæ is mentioned; however, the clue to the whole is wanting.

l. 10. Cod. has Rindar.

l. 15. Cod. r and 1 e β read, Sigraðar; though erroneous (the poem is on Sigrod Hacon's son, not on Hacon his son), yet the form Sigrod is notable, being only met with here, else the scribes have throughout turned it into Sigurd. Haleygiatal, l. 35.

Eywind's Improvisations, (p. 35.)

l. 2. hefnendr, the sons of a slain father, see Excursus, vol. ii, p. 475.

l. 17. Fenriss varra sparri, F.'s lip-bolt; see in Edda how the Bound Wolf was gagged with a sword.

l. 24. The spear-sheath and the deep edges of the broad-bladed javelin are noticed here: it is seldom one gets a detailed account of the weapons in a Court-poem.

l. 25. imon-lauks, drawn, we think, from the Helgi poet, where (Helgi i. 28) we hence mend the erroneous 'itr-lauk.' Eywind knew the Helgi line in this shape. We have elsewhere noticed how a few other phrases and words in Eywind were actually drawn from the Helgi Lay.

vv. 7, 8. The poet's lament, telling how in Hacon's days every man wore his gold and paraphernalia, whilst now that we have fallen on evil times, people have to hide their treasures in the earth.

l. 34. A saw. *Eld bears hard on the soldier.*

v. 10 is clearly corrupt; Eywind had to pay, as fine, a ring, an old heir-loom— Eyvindr átti gollhring mikinn ok góðan er kallaðr var Moldi; hann hafði verit tekinn löngu áðr or iörðu. [Hkr. p. 112, Unger.] This must be drawn from this very verse; under 'foldar' we recognise the name 'Moldi;' under 'þursaby' may be hidden the name of the *place* where the ring had been dug up; indeed, a 'Thursaby' is found in South-east Norway.

l. 42. birki brums hind (a goat), see Excursus, vol. ii, p. 456.

On the Famine and the Herrings and the gift of the brooch, the Kings' Lives, drawing from our verses, record—Svá kom um síðir, at náliga misti landz-folkit víðast korns ok fiska. Á Hálogalandi var svá mikill sultr ok seyra at þar óx náliga ekki korn, 'enn sniór lá þá á öllu landi at miðju sumri, enn bú allt var inni bundit at miðju sumri.' Svá kvað Eyvindr skálda-spillir, hann kom út, ok dreif miök . . . Eyvindr orti drápu um alla Íslendinga ; enn þeir launuðu hónum svá, at hverr bóndi gaf hónum skatt-penning, sá stóð þriá penninga silfrs vegna, ok hvítr í skor. Enn er silfrið kom fram á Alþingi, þá réðu menn þat af, at fá smiðo til at skíra silfrið ; síðan var gorr af feldar-dalkr, enn þar af var greitt smíðar kaupit ; þá stóð dalkrinn fimm tigi marka ; hann sendu þeir Eyvindi. 'Enn Eyvindr lét höggva í sundr dalkinn, ok keypti ser bú með.' þá kom ok þar um vár við útver nokkur broddr af síld ; Eyvindr skipaði róðrar-ferjo húskörlum sínum ok landz-buum, ok reri þanog til sem síldin var rekin. Hann kvað [v. 12] . . . ok svá vendiliga var upp gengit allt lausa-fé hans, at hann keypti síldina til borðz ser með boga skoti sínu. Hann kvað [v. 13].

l. 44. spa-þernom, corrupt ; the exact word uncertain, the image is throughout an *arrow*, spá-þornom must mean the *thorns of the sea?* In the next line read, okkor, plural from ' akka,' a (barbed?) arrow, Thulor 288 ; ' mutor iokla ' is corrupt, (*the sea?*), and we know not at present how to restore it.

l. 46. Read, rönom sínom (raunom), *with their snouts;* cp. 'It is said that they (the porpoises) often descend to the bottom in search of shrimps, sand-eels, and worms, which they root out of the sand with their snouts, much in the manner of hogs when seeking food in the fields. The porpoise, indeed, is known by the title of *herring hog*, etc.'—*Leisure Hour*, Oct. 1882.

l. 150. A proverb. *Hunger is a great king.* 'Au mandement de Messer Gaster tout le ciel tremble, tout la terre bransle. Son mandement est nommé, *Faut le faire sans delai ou mourir.*'—Pant. 4. 57.

Glum Grayfell's Praise, (p. 39.)

v. 2. Here either Skáneyjar (Denmark) or Skotlandi (Scotland) must need be wrong ; if it be a foray in Gautland and Schonen, read 'Hallandi' for 'Skotlandi' [Hak. S. ch. 5].—In the Saga the warfare in the West is thus mentioned : Tóku þá Eireks synir undir sik Hialtland ok Orkneyjar ok höfðu skatta af, enn fóru í vestr-víking á sumrum ok herjuðu um Skotland ok Írland. þess getr Glúmr Geira-son [vv. 2 and 4].—Their Eastern Foray : Sumir Eireks synir fóru í hernað, þegar er þeir höfðu aldr til, ok öfluðu ser fiár, herjuðu í Austrveg. þeir vóru snemma menn fríðir, ok fyrr rosknir at afli ok atgörvi enn vetra tali. þess getr Glúmr Geirason í Gráfeldar drápu [v. 6]. Eiriks synir snerosk þá ok með herr sínn norðr í Víkina ok herjuðu þar, enn Tryggvi konungr hafði her úti ok hélt til mótz við þá, ok áttu þeir orrostor margar, ok höfðu ymsir sigr ; herjuðu Eiriks synir stundum í Víkina, enn Tryggvi stundum um Siáland ok Halland. [Hak. S. ch. 10.]

v. 7. The Arctic Foray in Permia—Haraldr Gráfelldr fór á eino sumri með her sínn norðr til Biarma-landz ok herjaði þar ; hann átti orrosto mikla við Biarma á Vino-bakka, þar hafði Haraldr konungr sigr, ok drap mart foik, herjaði þá víða um landit, ok fekk ofa-mikit fé. þess getr Glúmr Geirason [v. 7].

v. 8. Gull-Haraldr kom til 'Hals í Lima-firði,' bauð hann þegar Haraldi Gráfeld til orrosto : enn þótt Haraldr hefði lið minna, þá gekk hann þegar á land, ok biósk til orrosto [ll. 27–32]. Enn áðr fylkingar gengi saman, þá eggjar Haraldr Gráfeldr hart lið sítt, ok bað þá bregða sverðom [l. 27], hlióp þegar framm í öndurða fylking, ok hió til beggja handa. þess getr Glúmr Geirason í Gráfeldar-drapu [v. 8]. þar fell Haraldr konungr Gráfeldr. Svá segir Glúmr Geirason [v. 10].

l. 29. We suggest, hvárir-tveggjo Haraldar.

l. 38. The two remaining brothers were Reginfred and Godfred.

l. 40. See vol. ii, p. 227, for parallel passages on gifted kings.

Wellekla, etc., (p. 44.)

Ruins of a once fine poem.

vv. 1, 2. Hákon iarl hélt Þróndheim með styrk frænda sínna ' Þriá vetr ' svá at Gunnhildar-synir fengu engar tekjor í Þróndheimi ; hann átti margar orrostur við Gunnhildar sonu, ok dráposk marga menn fyrir. Þess getr Einarr Skálaglam í Velleklu, er hann orti um Hákon iarl [vv. 1–3]. Enn getr Einarr hvernig Hákon iarl hefndi föður síns [vv. 4, 5]. Enn er Þat spyrr Hákon iarl, Þá samnar hann liði at ser ok hélt suðr á Mœri ok herjar Þar. Þá var Griótgarðr föður-bróðir hans Þar ok skyldi hafa landvörn af Gunnhildar sonum, hann bauð her út svá sem konungar höfðu orð til sent ; Hákon iarl hélt til fuudar við hann ok til bardaga, ' Þar féll Griótgarðr ok tveir iarlar með hónum ok mart lið annat.' Þessa getr Einarr Skálaglam [v. 6]. To which Fagrskinna adds—Hákon iarl hafði Þá rekit sínna harma, fyrir Því at af hans ráðum var drepinn Haraldr Gunnhildar sonr, sem Einarr Skálaglam sagði [v. 7].

vv. 1–11. The expedition against Kaiser Otho is in the Saga told at some length —Ótta keisari dró saman her mikinn ; hann hafði lið af Saxlandi ok Frakklandi, Fríslandi, ok Vindlandi. Keisari hafði riddara-her mikinn ok miklu meira fótgöngo lið ; hann hafði ok af Holtseta-landi mikinn her. Haraldr konungr sendi Hákon iarl með Norðmanna her, Þann sem hónom fylgði, suðr til Dana-virkiss at verja Þar landit. Svá segir í Velleklu [v. 11]. Ótta keisari kom með her sínn sunnan til Dana-virkiss, enn Hákon iarl varði með liði sínu borgar-veggina. Þá varð orrosta mikil . . . Féll Þar mart af keisara liði, enn Þeir fengu ekki unnit at borginni [vv. 8–11], all of which is painted over in our text, see Introd. § 13 ; in l. 30 we surmise that Holsatia is meant ; in l. 38 is hid the emperor's name ; in ll. 35, 36 the people in the Kaiser's army ; here we miss the *Saxons,* which name would be hidden in l. 36. But what is 'Hagbarða,' l. 32 ? 'Langbarða' is a guess of ours, sup-posing that the Kaiser is here the subject-matter. ' Heath-beards ' would suit the verse, but the term is perhaps too archaic. The dauber's big brush has destroyed all.

vv. 12–14. Siglir iarl Þá austr í gegnum Eyrarsund ; herjar hann Þá á hvártt-tveggja land ; síðan siglir hann austr fyrir Skáneyjar síðu, ok herjaði Þar hvar sem hann kom við land. Enn er hann kom austr fyrir Gauta-sker [l. 44], Þá lagði hann at landi, görði hann Þá blót mikit ; Þá kómu fliúgandi hrafnar tveir ok gullu hátt [ll. 42, 43] ; Þá Þykkisk iarl vita at Óðinn hefði Þegit blótið, ok Þá mun iarl hafa dagráð [l. 42] til at berjask. Þá brennir iarl skip sín öll, ok gengr á land upp með liði sínu, ok fór allt her-skildi. Þá kom á móti hónum Óttar iarl, hann réð fyrir Gautlandi ; áttu Þeir saman orrostu miklu, fær Þar Hákon iarl sigr, enn Óttar iarl fell, ok mikill hluti liðs með hónum. Hákon iarl ferr um Gautland hvárt-tveggja, ok allt her-skildi, til Þess er hann kemr í Nóreg, ferr síðan landveg allt norðr í Þróndheim [this march overland is hid in lines 45-48]. Frá Þessu segir í Velleklu [vv. 12, 13].

Fagrskinna sums it up somewhat briefer and better :—Þá er Hákon kom austr fyrir Gautland, Þá felldi hann blót-spán, ok vitraðisk hónum svá sem hann skyldi hafa dagráð at berjask ; sér á hrafna tvá, hversu gialla ok fylgja liðinu svá sem her segir [v. 12]. Þá lét Hákon spilla skipum sínum, gekk upp á land með öllu liði sínu, fór her-skildi yfir allt Gautland, ok brendi bæi ok rænti hvar sem hann kom. Þá kom í mót hónum Óttarr, iarl Gauta ; börðosk Þeir ; ok lauk svá at hann flýði, enn drepinn inn mesti hlutr liðs hans, enn Hákon tók mikit fé at her-fangi, fór hann um Smálönd ok allt til Vestr-Gautlandz, skattar allt folk, ok kom við svá buit í Noreg. Svá sem her segir [vv. 13, 14].

There is little doubt that all this was contained in our poem, the *sacrifice* at Gauta skerries, the *fight* with the Earl, the *burning* of the ships, and the long *march* back to Norway. As the poem now reads, all is painted out and defaced. In l. 50 we seem to see the *Earl's name*; in ll. 45–48 the wonderful march; whereas the sacrifice, the ravens, the chips, we can in the main restore, ll. 41–44.

vv. 15–23. The two encounters with Reginfred, Gundhild's son, must have been a somewhat serious piece of business. The story is told, Hkr. 17, 18, whereof we only subjoin a few sentences—Hélt Ragnfröðr þá norðr um Stað, ok herjaði um Sunn-mæri . . . Battle on Southmore—Hélt Hákon þegar til orrosto, hann hafði lið meira ok skip smæri, . . . þeir börðusk um stafna sem þá var siðr til, straumr var í sundinu ok hóf öll skipin inn at landinu [l. 70] . . . Battle not decisive—Hélt Ragnfröðr liði sínu suðr um Stað . . . Ragnfröðr konungr hafði þá allt fyrir sunnan Stað, Firða-fylki, Sogn, Hörðaland, Rogaland . . . Hákon iarl bauð liði út þá er váraði; hann hafði lið mikit af Hálogalandi ok Naumudali, svá at [read, svá ok?] allt frá Byrðo [Lat. 65°] til Staðs [Lat. 62°] hafði hann lið af öllom siá-löndom; hónom drósk herr um öll þrœnda-lög, svá ok um Raumsdal; svá er at kveðit, at hann hefði her af fiórum folk-löndum [l. 61]; hónom fylgðu siau iarlar [l. 64], ok höfðu þeir allir ógrynni hers. Svá segir í Velleklu [vv. 18–20]. Hákon iarl hélt liði þessu öllu suðr um Stað. Þá spurði hann at Ragnfröðr konungr með her sínn væri farinn í Sogn; sneri hann þá þannug sínu liði, ok verðr þar fundr þeirra Ragnfröðar. Lagði iarl skipum sínum at landi, ok haslaði völl Ragnfröði konungi, ok tók orrosto stað. Svá segir í Velleklu [v. 21]. Þar varð all-hörð orrosta, hafði Hákon iarl lið miklu meira, ok fekk sigr. Þetta var á þinga-nesi [l. 65] þar er mætisk Sogn ok Hörða-land. Ragnfröðr konungr flýði til skipa sinna, enn þar fell af liði konungs þriú hundruð manna [l. 72]. Sva segir í Velleklu [v. 22]. Eptir orrosto þessa flýði Ragnfröðr konungr or Noregi, enn Hákon iarl friðaði land [ll. 75, 76].

All this is mangled in our text, with a bit of the torn web left here and there.

vv. 23–29. Hákon iarl lagði þá land allt undir sik [l. 75] ok sat þann vetr í Þróndheimi. Þess getr Einarr Skálaglam í Velleklu [v. 23]. Hákon iarl, er hann fór sunnan með landi um sumarit, ok landz-folk gekk undir hann, þá bauð hann þat um ríki sítt allt, at menn skyldo halda upp hofum ok blótum, ok var svá gört. Svá segir í Velleklu [vv. 24–27]. And again [Hkr. ch. 50]—Hákon iarl réð Noregi allt it ýtra með siá ok hafði hann til forráða sextán fylki [*sixteen folklands* or *shires*]. Enn síðan er Haraldr inn Hárfagri hafði svá skipat, at iarl skyldi vera í hverjo fylki, þá hélzk þat lengi síðan. Hákon iarl hafði sextán iarla undir sér [l. 52]. Svá segir í Velleklu [v. 29]. Meðan Hákon iarl réð fyrir Noregi, þá var góð árferð í landi ok góðr friðr innan-landz með bóndom [ll. 89, 90]. Or, as Fagrskinna says—Hákon iarl var ríkr, ok tók at efla blót með meiri freku enn fyrr hafði verit; þá batnaði brátt árferð, kom aptr korn ok síld, grœr iörðin með blóma. Svá segir Einarr [v. 27]. Þá var friðr góðr með árinu, sem enn segir Einarr [v. 28]. Í annari drápu segir Einarr á þessa lund [see p. 48, v. 9]. Her má heyra at synir Eireks brutu niðr blótin, enn Hákon hóf upp annat sinn.

In v. 25 the extent of Hacon's dominion is given; the *southern* boundary is Wick (the Bay).—Cp. here Eywind's Haleygiatal (ll. 49, 50) as restored in the notes to vol. i, reading ' Eiða ' for the evidently false ' Egða.' The *northern* boundary we hold is hidden in l. 80; in Halogaland there is an island Vedrey [Lat. c. 65°].— Later, in Earl Eric's day, the boundary in the north is Vægja or Veggi-staf [Lat. c. 69°]. In S. Olaf's day (as we conclude from a corrupt verse, vol. ii, p. 155, l. 65) it was still expanded, extending from the Eid Forest, west of Gotha River, to Gandwick or the White Sea. ' Between Gotha River and Finmarken,' says the author of Konunga-tal, c. 1190. Snorri, in 1222, gives the marches as the Gotha River and the White Sea, including Finmarken.

The other Drapa contains, beside vv. 2, 9, 10, no facts whatever; most of the fragments are from Edda (Sks.), and the whole may, for ought we know, be a fabrication of Skalaglam's namesake Skulason. Mark the genealogical touch, v. 8, Hacon's descent from Harold War-tusk.

In Tind's poem the battle in Godmar [l. 40], a bay or estuary on the east side of Christiania frith, is notable.

Red-cloak's son. Who the *nine* princes were [p. 51, l. 4], whom Hacon sent to Woden (*slew*), we are nowhere told. Earl Othere, the Gunhildsons, Gritgard, and the two other earls make some six or seven.

Eilif (p. 51), l. 10, note. Sónar sád (the Soma seed), with which cp. Husd. 9 (as above) and p. 80, l. 33.

Banda-drapa, etc., (p. 51.)

Ari relates how the earl, age ten or eleven, on Mori fought Tiding-Skopti, the earl—Sva segir Eyjolfr Daðaskald í Banda-drápo [v. 1]. The poem must have contained Skopti's *full* name, so, l. 8, we read and restore, opt *Tíðinda* Skopta, hid under ' blóðvolum ' (the usual *bloody* image the remanieur delights in)—l. 5, at móti, read á Mœri?—l. 6, we have Utver, an isle off Sogn.

The next spring the *Danish* King makes Eric earl in South Norway—Eptir um várit sendi Dana konungr Eirik norðr í Noreg, ok gaf hónum iarldóm ok þar með Vingul-mörk ok Rauma-ríki til yfir-sóknar með þeim hætti sem fyrr höfðu haft skatt-konungar. Svá segir Eyiolfr [v. 1]. In ll. 1, 2 one espies ' ellifo ' vettra; and in l. 4 one espies ' Hleiðrar ' mildingr under ' hildar,' viz. the *King of Lethra*, the Danish King.

Olafs S. (Hkr.), ch. 96, 97, narrates the battles in the Baltic—Hann helt fyrst til Gotlandz [l. 15] ok lá þar við lengi um sumarit, ok sætti kaup-skipum er sigldu til landzins, eða víkingum; stundum gekk hann upp á landit, ok herjaði þar víða með siánum. Svá segir í Banda-drápu [v. 4]. Síðan sigldi Eirekr suðr til Vindlandz, ok hitti þar fyrir Staurinum Víkinga skip nokkur . . . ok drap Víkingana. Svá segir í Banda-drápu [l. 5].

l. 17. Read, stýrir gumna . . . (the earl) sigldi í Austrveg. Enn er hann kom í ríki Valdimars konungs, tók hann at herja ok drepa mann-folkit ok brenna allt þar er hann fór, ok eyddi landit; hann kom til Aldeigio borgar [ll. 31–33] ok settizk þar um þar til er hann vann staðinn, drap þar mart folk, enn braut ok brendi borgina alla, ok síðan fór hann víða her-skildi í Garða-ríki. Svá segir í Banda-drápu [v. 9]. Eirikr var í þessum hernaði öllum samt fimm sumur. Enn er hann kom or Garða-ríki, fór hann her-skildi um alla Aðal-sýslu [l. 29] ok þar tók hann fiórar víkinga skeiðr af Donom [l. 24] ok drap allt af. Svá segir í Banda-drápu [vv. 7, 8]. Upon which he returns to Denmark and marries the king's daughter—Eirikr iarl var á vetrum í Danmörk enn stundum í Svia-veldi, enn í hernaði á sumrum.—' Eyrar-sundi,' l. 23, is probably not the right place, some other sound in the East Baltic being meant.

Sailor Poets, etc., (p. 54.)

From the Sailor Poets (p. 53 sqq.) we have in Excursus I extracted the mythical figures as far as they can be made out.

In Snowbiorn's poem, l. 2, mend ' skæ ' for ' sæ,' and construe, buðlunga máli (king) lætr húflangan stiór-viðjar skæ (*steerwithy steed*=ship) styðja hlemmi sverð við harðri dúfo; stiórn-við, Thulor 399. Ey-lúðr=*island bin*, Ey-mylrir, *id.*

ll. 5, 6. Construe, þær es fyr löngo mólo Amlóða meldr-lið, *who in ages past ground Amlodi's meal-vessel = the ocean.* The occurrence of Amloði (Hamleth) as Ocean Giant is noticeable; observe the figure of speech preserved in Saxo who calls the sand 'The meal ground by the gales.'—Orm's epithet recalls William's line, ' Our Sire in his see above the Seven Stars.' R. R. 352.

Romund, (p. 56.)—Only the first three verses are fine, and they alone may be genuine.—v. 3 gives the proverb of predestination.—vv. 4-11 are all more or less commonplace.

l. 10. áðr ne gorr, cp. Hamtheow Lay, l. 134.

The Mewsider's verses, (p. 58.)—l. 13. sóttomk heim, cp. heim-sókn, a law term.

l. 24. dœmi-salr dóma, corrupt, but refers to the 'Door Doom,' whereof the Saga speaks—Eptir þat setti þorbiorn dura-dóm, ok nefndi sex menn í dóm, síðan sagði þorbiorn fram sökina á hendr þórarni um hrossa-tökuna. þá gekk Geirríð (Thorarin's mother) út í dyrnar, etc. [Eyrb. ch. 18.]

l. 28. Fróða-vellir? Fróðá, i. e. Froða á (*Froði's water*), is a farm on the inmost side of the creek; Enni, l. 38, a big headland on the outer side.

l. 55. A proverb: *Storm often comes out of a sultry sky.*

l. 63. Note the older uncontracted form Arnketill.

Illuga-drapa, (p. 61.)—Á þessu þingi deildu þeir þorgrímr Kiallaksson ok synir hans við Illuga Svarta um mund ok heiman-fylgju Ingibiargar Ásbiarnar dóttur, konu Illuga, er Tinforni [l. 64] hafði átt at varð-veita ... enn Kialleklingar gengu at dóminum ok vildu upp hleypa; var þá þröng mikil [l. 1], áttu menn þá hlut í at skilja þá. Kom þá svá at Tinforni greiddi fét at tölum Illuga. Svá kvað Oddr skald í Illuga-drápu [v. 1]. ... Snorri goði bað ser þá manna til meðal-göngu, ok kom á griðum með þeim. þar féllu þrír menn af Kialleklingum [l. 67] enn fiórir af Illuga, etc. [Eyrb. ch. 17.]

l. 6. Read, þremja svellz.

l. 12. holt-vartaris, *the holt-garter,* i. e. *a snake.* Observe 'vartari,' which word occurs only here and thrice besides; Thulor, l. 369 (of some fish); Edda in the story of Loki, whose mouth was sewed together with a thong called vartari; and lastly, in the List, Edda 748, our vol. ii, p. 546. The etymon of this word has never been observed; it is indeed the Engl. *garter,* which thus turns out to be a good, sound Teutonic word; French *jarretier* we are inclined to take as a popular etymology, the identity in sense and the resemblance to the Teutonic word are too striking to be but casual. Construe, holt-vartaris enni-tingl = ægis-hialmr, an ornament particular to serpents, cp. Old Wols. Play, ll. 121, 125.

l. 13. Read Fyris-valla, the banks of the River Fyri (*short* vowel, not Fýri), the river near Upsala, now Föret: the banks of that river, famous in ancient history and legends, are Fyris-vellir.

l. 16. King Eric the Victorious, mentioned in Thorgny's speech, Reader, p. 178.

Sibyl Stein.—l. 16. Míms vinar, cp. Sonat. 89; fundr þundar, cp. Sonat. 7.

l. 17. Glaumberg, a place?

l. 25. Bárröðr, the uncontracted form, later Bárðr, earlier Bar-fred.

Cormac's Improvisations, (p. 63.)—The first ten or twelve verses are the best; indeed, the greater part of the rest is very doubtful, yet we have drawn hence the synonyms of women, Excursus, p. 476.

Noticeable is the carved pillar, representing Hagbarð, the Danish prince, the lover of Signy. Hagbarð and Signy are the Romeo and Juliet of Northern tales, of whom

Saxo tells a story. Note also v. 7, wherein he values Stangerd's eyes and locks; and, v. 8, her whole body, which he puts at seven countries, indeed at the whole world known to him.

In l. 32, we mend Svia; still we miss Norway, which we take to be hid in l. 30.

l. 54. By guess, though we have not seen this image used elsewhere.

l. 60. The Saga names a brother of Cormac named Froði; here, however, it is rather himself that is meant; maybe Froði was Cormac's Norse nickname.

l. 74. Stangerd's husband was surnamed Tin-teinn [*tin-wire, tin drawer*]; he was Eystan's son, of a family called the Skidungs [from Skíða in Norway?].

l. 82. fioll fiarðar kelli, corrupt = the *tents*? the white towering rime-mantled awnings.

l. 88. Thorkettle's daughter, Stangerð.

l. 100. Solunds, isles, Norway off Sogn.

v. 31. *This* verse is sure enough to be genuine; the image was a favourite in old Lays of the Aristophanes type, cp. p. 81, v. 12.

l. 149. dalkr, an Irish loan word, *dealc* = a *brooch*. Mend Dict. s. v. accordingly.

Bersi.—l. 11. toro-gætr, older form for 'tor-gætr,' an old literative proverb.

l. 16. Þorröðr, the old form for Thord; Thoríred is the still older form.

l. 16. vinon [read vinoð?], an else unknown word for vinátta; Egil uses vinað, Hofuðl. l. 84.

Egil, (p. 72.)—l. 7. Metaphor from lifting a shutter-door, of Egil's *craggy* eyebrows.

v. 4. For the raising of the Nith pole (Libel pole) and the carmen, see Egil's S. ch. 60.—Hann tók í hönd ser hesli-stöng, ok gekk á bergs-nös nökkura þa er vissi til landz inn; þá tók hann hross-höfuð ok setti upp á stöngina. Síðan veitti hann for-mála ok mælti: 'Her set ek upp níð-stöng, ok sný ek þessu níði á hönd Eireki konungi ok Gunnhildi dróttningu.'—Hann sneri hross-höfðinu inn á land: 'Sný ek þessu níði á landvættir þær er þetta land byggja, sva at allar fari þær villar vega, ok engi hendi né hitti sítt inni [cp. Havam. v. 18] fyrr en þær hafa rekit ór landi Eirek konung ok Gunnhildi.' Síðan skýtr hann stönginni niðr í biarg-rifo, ok lætr þar standa; hann sneri höfðinu inn á land: enn hann reist rúnar á stönginni, ok segja þær formála þenna allan. [Eg. S. ch. 60, cp. Excursus to vol. i, p. 419.]

l. 25. vrungo, an archaic form, an evidence that Egil pronounced *wr* (owing to his long sojourn in England?).

l. 27. hvarma hvít-vellir, *the hoary white brows.*

v. 9. Undoubtedly genuine, but in part obscure: to the first we have not found a clue; it may refer to his tottering *gait*. Follomk rá skalla, restored from the ditty of Arni the Monk, vol. ii, p. 441. rá (*shrub*), neuter, as it seems, is a rare word, occurs else, in Havam. l. 70, ef mik særir þegn á rótom rás viðar (by carving charms thereon); cp. Lay of Skirni, l. 130, where we read, til holtz ek rann ok til rás viðar, *I ran to the holt, to the shrubwood I wended my way;* once in Hallfred, p. 91, l. 30; twice in Merlin Spa, ii. 50, 85. We subjoin the readings of the existing MSS., Worm., Arna-Magn. 748, 4to, and 132 fol.:—

W.	Vals hefi ek vafur helsis val fallz enn ek kalla
	blautr em ek bergis fótar berr enn hlust er þorrin.
748.	Vals em ek vavar helsis vafallr em ec skalla
	blautr em-ek bergis fótar borr enn hlust er þorrin.
132.	Vafs hefi-ek vafor hessis vafallr em ek skalla
	blautr erumz bergi þota borr enn lust er þorrin.

v. 9. fótar bergi, *the thigh;* 'borr' cruris perforaculum, i.e. membrum virile. This is undoubtedly the sense; cp. Piers Plowman, Pass. xx, on his old age. The compiler of Egil's Saga has defiled the image, which in the poet's mouth is serious and not impure.

Glum, (p. 74.)—l. 3. hróðr-skota, a verb here, and ἅπ. λεγ.

l. 6. firin-dísi, *a mighty fay;* dóms í draumi, ll. 7 and 16, is dubious.

l. 10. A proverb.

l. 20. goð-reið, *a troop of spirits.*

l. 21. of Fiörð tveggja vegna, *on both sides of the Frith,* thus emendated.

l. 25. van-talið, as seen from the words of the Saga—þar hygg ek at, hvat hónum þykkir *van-talið* í einni vísu.—Gluma, ch. 24.

ll. 26, 27. Cp. the old Warrior-law, Excursus III, vol. ii.

l. 42. Read, Gestils kleif, *the cliff of Gestil* = the shield; the MS. has klauf.

Vigfus.—Construe, ver skeytum spiör meðan hæla bossi neytir hlýs und vörmum vífs bœgi.

Satires, (p. 77.)

v. 1. Read and construe, nú hefi ek ristið (her) skopt á bœkis hepti míno.

l. 6. unnar, i.e. önnar, part of the sword; else only found in Helgi ii. 35 and Thulor 273.

l. 7. Ásmóðar, i.e. þór-móðar.

l. 13. A saw—Woe makes a man wan, cp. p. 369, l. 6, and Proverb Song, l. 102.

l. 16. hlaut-teins hreytir, the *priest,* from *casting the divination chips,* cp. Excursus to vol. ii, p. 480, and vol. i, p. 411.

l. 20. fiall-rœnt, cp. haf-rœnn, of the wind; words modelled by analogy after austr-œnn, etc. In all the words of a genuine formation there is a radical *r,* as in souther-n, easter-n.

l. 21. Áss ríkr = Thor.

l. 23. Read, ein-hendis (one word).

l. 25. firin-argr, very '*arg,*' monstrously foul, a word of deep abuse or abhorrence.

l. 26. rigna here seems to mean *to blaspheme.*

v. 8. Construe, tekkat ek við tanna hverfs (mouth's) hleypi-skarfi (the fly), and Hagbarðz (Woden's) vea-fiarðar (poetry's) sann-reynir = the poet; I will not take his (the poet's) fly; I'll not be his fool; not gulp his bait.   l. 30. Read, gína.

v. 9. A very obscure verse; all interpreters have widely missed the mark.   Our clue is the *parallelism* between the two halves.   In 'ryð-' we surmise 'róðo' (the rood), róðo reynir (the priest), *the man of the rood:* in 'bœði' we surmise 'blóðs,' Boðnar blóð (poetry), Boðnar blóðs smiðja = the poet's breast.   Of the parallelisms between the two halves, mark—róðo reynir and sónar sáð-reynir; Boðn and Són; sig-tól and morð-hamarr; smiðja and steði; Boðnar blóð and Sónar sáð.   Of this verse we have two recensions, one, purer, in Kristni Saga, the other in Olaf's Saga (Fms. ii), remodelled, with the parallels blotted out.

v. 12. Cp. the lampoon in Cormac above.   Here the king's treasurer is the mare, pursued by the king as stallion, both speeding toward the Arctic regions.

v. 14. An interesting verse; new words are, iörmun-grund, ur-grandari.   Construe, Vandils Iörmungrundar (sea's) reið (ship's) viðor (a sailor): folginn (cp. Lat. se-*pultus*) is here in the primitive sense.   Note the dat. þaim-si = þessom.   In l. 4 *w* alliterates with a vowel, being sounded, we presume, as a half-vocalised English *w*.

BOOK VIII.

§ 1. KING TRYGGVASON, etc.

Hallfred, etc., (p. 90.)

I. l. 1. Observe the simile. The author of Theodric's Saga has entered this verse into his preface—Enn þat skaltu skilja, at sú auða sé vorðin mest af ríkis-manna falli ok af því at engir eru þeirra iafningjar eptir. Svá sem stendr í Norðmanna lofkvæðum. Svá segir Hallfredr [v. 1]. Eigi var svá sem hann sagði at auð væri öll Norðrlönd þótt Oláfr væri fallinn, enn þat fœrði hann til lofs við konung, at engi þvílíkr maðr væri eptir á Norðrlöndum sem Ólafr Tryggvason—*a prosy Commentator Wisdom!*

l. 2. flug-styggs, cp. Helgi i. 137, 222, 230.

l. 14. The Saga says—Konungr stóð í lyptingunni við þessa tíðinda sögn, ok mælti til sínna manna : Látit síga seglit sem skiótast, enn sumir leggi árar á borð, ok taki skriðinn af skipinu, ek vil giarna berjaz heldr en flýja, ek hefi enn aldri flýit í orrosto, ráði Guð lífi mínu, enn aldri skal ek á flótta leggja . . . *and,* tengi menn saman skipin, ok bui menn sik til bardaga, ok bregði sverðum. Ekki skolo mínir menn hyggja á flótta. þess getr Hallfreðr Vandræða-skald [v. 2].—Ol. S. ch. 249 (*dramatised*). Tryggvason's last orders, 'Never to think of flight,' recall the Elizabethan days, when Grenville, like the Northern hero and Judas the valiant Maccabee before him, preferred death to flying, like others, before overwhelming odds. See Raleigh's Account, and 1 Macc. ix. 10. Parallel passages here are, Grayfell's Drapa, v. 8, and Eywind's on Stord, v. 4.

v. 3. þess getr Hallfreðr, at Ólafr konungr missti þess liðs, er frá hónum hafði siglt, ok hónum aflaði þessi bardagi mikillar frægðar. Her segir svá [v. 3].

l. 24. Read, Dönum vardizt; or, if, as Steinar says, the Swedes ran the first onslaught, 'Sviom varðizk.'

l. 30. hold-barkar ('flesh-bark'=the mail-coat), its rá (*wand*)=the sword.

l. 35. We surmise líf-skiörr (life-scaring), epithet to lög; the simile appears to be drawn from the Speaker reading the law from the Tinwall or Hill of Law.

vv. 10, 11. Herein are concealed the topographical details of the battle, hidden to Ari himself. The battle took place off Stralsund, near Hiddinse, which got its name from a current or *swelchie*, called in the native tongue of the Slavonic Wends 'reca' [our friend Mr. Morfill's communication]. We meet the word in l. 47, 'Hedins Rekka,' *Hiddin's Race*, or *Stream*, by whose broad bank, in the lea-water between the shore and the race, the battle was fought. The place is again, l. 46, called 'the Wide Sound of Hiddinse.' The Norse word *swolð* is in fact the Norwegian or the Danish rendering of Wendish *reca*. Adam, in his curious account of Olaf, has mistaken the place, as he has the meaning of the nickname which he gives to the king. Cracaben [cracabben] must mean, not Raven-seeker, but 'Long-shanks,' a fit name for such a tall man as Anlaf or our Edward. Cp. vol. ii, p. 83.

l. 44. fyrir *or* frá Skylja, here is hidden the name of some place, *off the headlands* . . .

l. 59. Read, húf-iöfnom (even-hulled), a Homeric epithet, νῆες ἐῖσαι : hefnir Hákonar, see the tale of Hacon's tragic death given in the Reader, p. 152 sqq.

The following verses, as well as the burdens at the beginning, are the best preserved parts of the poem.

l. 65. Trani (masc.), this is the original gender as used in Tryggvason's day. The verse has been misinterpreted, as if Thorkettle had jumped *overboard;* Hallfred says nothing of the kind, but that he never left the battle in his galley till it was hopelessly lost [as if somebody else had left earlier ?].

l. 70. Construe, Heita dýr-bliks dyn-sæðinga hungr-deyfir, see Excursus II, vol. i, p. 457.

l. 73. Name of some person, Hallfred's authority hidden here.

l. 79. Some *treason* here alluded to.

l. 88. veifanar orð (idle rumours, tattle?).

v. 20. The allusion looks as if the Thronds had led the attack; or are we to read, þrœnda gramr sótti, meaning Earl Eric?

l. 92. A proverb.

l. 93. Skalmöld, can this be an echo from Volospa, l. 133? Note also v. 25.

l. 96. orðin seems here to mean *lost*, perhaps from the phrase verða dauðr (*to die*).

II. (p. 94.) The other poem is a mere bald jingle-register of battles and peoples. Here is the fashionable course of a Norse Wicking starting from the East, tending westward. We note l. 19, which has puzzled editors; it is corrupt, the sense requires a name, and ' Val-Bretar' seems to be the word. Cp. the early use of this word in the York or Exeter Ode to King Æthelstan after Brunanburh, 'Constantinus rex Scottorum et Uealum-Bryttonum,' for so we must read it. Nero, . ii. 7. 89.

l. 26. týr Tiorva looks as if some local name were hidden, Tyree?

III. Hallfred's Saga tells us that Hallfred made a poem on Earl Hacon; that, however, is very problematic. The impression one gathers from Tryggvason's Saga is, that King Olaf was Hallfred's *first* master. We are here told how the king sent Hallfred on a message to Earl Ragnwald at Skara, West Gothland (who later married the king's sister). The poem, bald enough, speaks of a prince 'in the east.' Mr. Sigurdsson once suggested to the Editor that these fragments were on Earl Ragnwald. They are all taken from Edda, and are in Einar Skulason's vein, factless [are not they of his manufacture too?]. Curious are the repeated variations on the land as Woden's Bride, as if composed from a written ' Edda.'

V. (p. 96.) The *improvisations* are better. l. 2. akkeris frakki, ' anchor-frank' (?), *Anchor Jack* (?), is this what is meant? hnakk-mið (the anchor-buoy) also met with in Thulor, l. 420: l. 3. drengr is perhaps here a nautical term, Thulor, l. 417.

vv. 3-7 are important on account of the poet's state of mind towards the new Christian faith; somewhat conservative, grumbling at the turn things have taken. They have often been cited, and are most undoubtedly genuine. v. 7 looks like a paraphrase of Ps. ii. 12. l. 17. láta fyrir róða, *to throw to the winds*, still in use, but in mod. Icel. falsely spelt, leggja fyrir óðal (!): aðul (son), see Lay of Righ, l. 164. We have used these verses in Excursus I, vol. ii.

v. 8. The sword story: iarðar-men, a pun = svörðr (sward), which means also *leather*.

vv. 9-11. Hallfred's death-verses, a notable utterance of the dying poet; Dr. Johnson's very words, ' Hell, sir.' Dauðr verðr hverr is the proverb, Deyja skal hverr um sinn, see Reader, p. 259, No. 27.

Halldorr ukristni, (p. 100.)—l. 5. Œna, else called Eynir, one of the many tribes whereof the Throndheim ' lagu' was composed: the Ænen of Widsith, l. 71.

l. 13. fiord, Dan. *ifior* (year gone).

l. 16. Holmi, some ' holm' near to where the battle was fought, cp. Hallfred, l. 45.

Skuli, (p. 102.)—' Fyrir Swolð' (off Swold) and ' fyrir Swoldar mynni' (off Swold's mouth) prove clearly that Swold was a *stream* [reca], not an *isle*, as the Saga has metamorphosed it. Note the beautiful scene of the ' Passing of Tryggvason's fleet,' given in the Reader, p. 167.

l. 6. Helga haug-þök; this remarkable image is only met with here. Skuli (the

poet) would have learnt this story from his master Earl Eric, whose family patroness
Thorgerd Holgi's Bride was. Edda says—Sva er sagt at konungr sá er Holgi er
nefndr, er Hálogaland er við kent, hann var faðir þorgerðar Hölga-brúðar, þau
vóru bæði blótuð, ok var haugr Hölga kastaðr, onnur fló af silfri eða golli—þat
var blótfeit—enn önnor fló af moldo ok grióti. Svá kvað Skúli þorsteinsson
[ll. 5, 6].

l. 14. We follow Cod. W., grán mána setr ofan (impers.); gran serks ofan
mána, r.

Thorod—I. Eireks-drapa, (p. 102.)

Poem in a fearfully mangled state.

l. 1. vík-buendr, as the better MSS. have it. The word 'Wick,' as well as Tind's
song, indicates that the Iomswickings first made a raid on the Wick, then, running
northwards, met the earl coming from the north; both met on More, where the
battle was fought, and the Wickings driven back: The later story of a sudden
inroad in depth of winter at Yule-tide is manifestly a fable.

l. 17. œfri vard, an emendation evident enough.

l. 19. A proverb. Cp. Proverb Song, 101 and 23.

l. 22. kómo, pret. infin., a form met with here for the first time; it occurs ever
and anon in the following Court-poets. In prose we only know it from the words
skyldo, mundo.

l. 29. We here recover a fresh word, 'svárr,' Germ. schwager = brother-in-law;
it should hence be entered into Dict. 607 b [unknown to us in Jan. 1872]. Hyrning, a noble of Wick, South Norway, married Tryggvason's sister [see Ol. S.], and
was one of the king's spokesmen on the Moot of Heithsewa in the memorable
year of that Moot. It appears that he fell at Swold—ἀπέθανεν εὐγενῶς, or 'fekk
gótt orð,' is the epitaph the poet gives him. Some remarkably heroic feat must have
been told of him, now dimly seen through a story given in the Saga, how he repelled
Earl Eric's first attempt at boarding the Serpent.

v. 9. Manifestly records the division of Norway, and the earl's share thereof.
The Saga [Ari] says—Enn Eirikr iarl hafði fiogur fylki í þróndheimi, Hálogaland,
ok Naumodal, Fiorðo, ok Fialir, Sogn, ok Hörðaland, ok Rogaland, ok Norðr-Agðir
allt til Líðandisness. This is a paraphrase of our poem's 'frá Vægi-staf suðr til
Agða,' i. e. the whole western coast-land of Norway [Vægi-staf, see note to Vellekla,
p. 569]. Lines 33 and 34 seem to be the record of Earl Swein's share—þá hafði
Óláfr Svia konungr fiogur fylki í þróndheimi, ok Mœri hvára-tveggi, ok Raumsdal,
' ok austr Ránríki frá Gaut-Elfi til Svína-sundz, þetta ríki fekk Óláfr í hendr Sveini
iarli' með slíkum formála sem fyrr höfðu haft skatt-konungar eða iarlar af yfir-
konungum. Under the commonplace touches of the remanieur we can espy 'Svína
sundz' in l. 33, though a literal restoration is now quite unfeasible.

l. 35. We have shifted this line; it is clearly enough a bit of the stanza relating
to the earl's marriage into the Danish Royal House.

v. 11. Relates how all the barons but Erling submitted to the foreign rule—a fact
not to be forgotten in view of Erling's subsequent fate. In l. 37 one seems to see
names of places, i. e. all the barons from N. N. to N. N. submitted to the earls, save
Erling alone. There is a 'Farsund' near Cape Naze (hidden under 'farland'). Then
we miss the north boundary; here there is a peak 'Fastlandstind,' c. Lat. 67° (hidden
under 'fastaty?')=all western Norway from Fastland Peak to Farsound (Lat.
58°–67°), that is to say, all the western coast from one end to the other. Cp. O. H.
(Kringla), ch. 21, and Sighvat's verse. The requirements of rhyme would make the

poet select places for their sound which the hearers knew and which were not far off the march.

vv. 12–17. This passage seems to point to the events mentioned in the following passage of the Peterborough Chronicle, 1013 : And on ðam ilcan geare to-foran þam monðe Augustus [correct *spring-tides* of translation, the date is obscure in l. 46] com Swegen cyning mið his flotan to Sandwic and wende swyðe raðe abutan East Englum. into Humbran muðan. and swa úppweard andlang Trent þet he comt to Gegnes-burh. [l. 48 *may* refer to the coasting voyage when they had left the Thames mouth ; if so, we must seek some other word than *Sturry* for the enigmatic ' átt stórr,' and read ' eyrar Gegnes,' Gainsborough.] And þa sona abeah Uhtred eorl, and eall Norðhymbra to him. and eall þet folc on Linde-sige. and siððan þet folc of Fif-burhingan. and raðe þæs eall here be norðan Wætlinga stræte. and him man sealde gislas of ælcere scire. [Can the *joyful meeting at W . . .* , which ll. 51, 52 speak of, be the meeting of Uhtred and Cnut ? or is it, as is more likely, the first meeting of Eric and Sweyn at the Thames mouth ? if so, these lines should rather follow l. 44.] Syððan he undergeat þet eall folc him to ge-bogen wæs. þa bead he þet man sceolde his here metian and horsian. and he þa gewende syððan suðweard mid fulre fyrde [ll. 51, 52]. and betæhte his scipa and þa gislas CNUTE his sunu. and syððan he com ofer Wætlinga-stræte. hi wrohton þet mæste yfel þe ænig here don mihte. wende þa to Oxnaforda, and seo burhwaru sona abeah and gislode. and þanon to Winceastre. and þet ilce dyðon. [Was there a fight at Oxford before they made peace, and is Oxford, or some other place on their path, the obscure G . . . by ?]. Wendon þa þanon eastward to Lundene. and mycel his folces adranc on Temese. forðan hi nanre brycge ne cepton [this disaster appears to have been unnoticed by the poet]. Ða he to þære byrig com þa nolde seo burh-waru bugan ac heoldan mid fullan wige ongean. forðan þær wæs inne se cyning Æðelred. and þurkil mid him [also Wolfkettle the Brisk, as we learn from l. 60, who seems to have led a sally at some place, the name of which is hidden under l. 59]. If v. 17 refers to any event related in our chronicles it may be the fight, ' innan East Seaxan æt þere dune þe mann hæt Assandun,' four years later, where Eric had the satisfaction of seeing his old foe Wolfkettle slain, ' and eall se dugoð on Angelcinne.' The poem is so fragmentary that it is only by guess one can fix the order of the verses, and fit them to their corresponding passages in the Chronicles, which must be our main authority.—W . . . lade (varr lad), l. 51, is possibly Whap-lode in Lincolnshire.

II. (p. 105.) þeir Grímr ok Óláfr gengu báðir í mót Gunnlaugi einum, ok lauk svá þeirra við-skiptum, at hann drap þá báða. þetta sannar þórðr Kolbeinsson í kvæði því er hann orti um Gunnlaug Ormstungo.—*Gunl. S.* ch. iv.

III. Biorn is Thorrod's guest one winter at Hitarness ; he is suspected of cuckold-ing his host, and setting the household [sixteen souls] all at loggerheads ; mark the bad *meal;* for at this place there grows *wild corn* [mel] : the trunk traffic, vv. 3, 4, is also to be noticed.

l. 22. hlyrn, see Thulor, ll. 506 and 493.

v. 6. After Biorn's death, Ordny, who for her loveliness was surnamed the ' Candle of the Isle,' pined away—Henni þótti ser þat helzt ró, at hon sat á hest-baki, enn þórðr (her husband) leiddi undir henni aptr ok fram [Biarn. S. p. 66] ; a gentle, little trait of old life, like wheeling a sick person about for the sake of air and exercise : under merki-skin is hidden her surname : fiargvefiar, l. 30, probably corrupt from fiargviðraz, which means *to fondle, pet;* Eggert uses it of birds love-pairing —giptuz iurtir ok fóru að frævast : fiarg-viðrast dýrin sein og þung.

The Lithsmen Song, (p. 106.)

The following passages from the Peterborough Chronicle are the best comment and explanation (year 1016) : þa comon þa scipo to Grenawic to þam gang-dagum [May 7]. and binnon lytlum fæce wendon to Lundene. and dulfon þa ane mycele díc on ða suðhealfe and drogon heora scipa on west healfe þære brycge. and be-dicodon syððon þa burh uton þet nan mann ne mihte ne inn ne út. and oft-rædlice on ða burh fuhton. ac hi heom heardlice wið-stodon.

þa wæs Eadmund cyng ær þam ge-wend út, and ge-rád þa West Seaxan. and him beah eall folc to. and raðe æfter þam he gefeaht wið þone here æt Peonnan wið Gillinga. and oðer ge-feoht he ge-feaht æfter middan sumera æt Sceorstane. and þær mycel wæl feoll on ægðre healfe. and þa heres him sylfe to-eodon on ðam ge-feohte. and Eadric ealdorman and Ælmær deorlingc wæron þam here on fultume ongean Eadmund cyng. And þa ge-gaderode he iii siðe fyrde and ferde to Lundene. eal be norðan Temese. and swá ut þuruh Clæig-hangran. and þa burhware ahredde. and þone here aflymde to scipon. And þá wæs ymbe twa niht þet se cyning ge-wende ofer æt Brent-forda. and þá wið þone here ge-feaht and hine aflymde. and þær adrane mycel Ænglisces folces on heora agenre gymeleaste. þa ðe ferdon beforan þære fyrde. and fang woldon fon. And se cyning wende æfter þam to West Seaxan. and his fyrde ge-somnode.

þa ge-wende se here sona to Lundene. and þa burh utone be-sæton. and hire stranglice wið-feaht ge be wætere ge be lande. ac se Ælmihtiga God hi ahredde.

Se here ge-wende þa æfter þam fram Lundene mid heora scipum into Arwan. . . . Then come the harrying of the Marchland by the Host and their return to the Medway, Edmund's foray into Kent, and the flight of the Northmen to Sheppey. A second harrying of Essex and the Marchland is followed by the fight at Assandun and the consequent peace of Olney. Se here ge-wende þa to scipon mid þam þingum þe hi ge-fangen hæfdon. and Lundene-wæru griðede wið þone here. and heom frið ge-bohtan. and se here ge-brohton heora scipa on Lundene. and heom wintersettle þær inne namon.

v. 4. Thorkel's men seem to be mentioned as a distinct body of troops here. The Chronicle tells how in 1017 the old I[oms]wicking is given the Earldom of East-England, and after in 1021 Cnut cyng to Martin'mæssan ge-út. lagode þurkil eorl; but in 1023 þurcil and he wæron ánræde. and he betæhte þurcille Denemearcan and his sunu to healdenne. and se cyning nam þurciles sunu mid him to Engla-lande.

v. 10. The common comparison of the luckless hero with the lucky stay-at-home, which is found several times in these satirical ' man-songs.'

Sighvat's Praise of Olaf, p. 125, should be compared with this song and the Chronicle, it makes his *sixth* and *seventh* battles, the fights at the ditch by London and at Ring-mere heath, the *eighth* is at Canterbury and New-mouth.

Biorn, (p. 108.)

I. Genuine, no doubt, but coarse.—þess er getið, at hafnar-mark fanz í landi Þórðar [mended, cp. Atli and Rimegerd, l. 81] . . . þat vóru karlar tveir, ok hafði annarr hött blán á höfði; þeir stóðu lútir, ok horfði annarr eptir öðrum. [Biarn. S. p. 33.]

II. þá hafði Biörn eigi miklo áðr ort flim um þórð, ok var þá œrit heyrin-kunnigt nökkorom mönnum ; enn þau vóru efni í, at Arnóra, móðir þórðar, hefði etið þann fisk, er hann kallaði grámaga, ok lét sem hann hefði fundiz í fiöru, ok hefði hón af því áti hafandi orðit at þórði, ok væri hann ekki dála frá mönnum kominn í báðar ættir. Enn þetta er í fliminu.—[Biarn. S.]

[vv. 1–3.] Both pieces are interesting enough as specimens [genuine] of ancient 'nith' (libels) : the 'flytings' in vol. i. are similar in kind. 'slíkr' we here take to be = *sleek*. 'einagi,' a piece of *dress*, occurs else only in the word-list, AM. 748, our vol. ii, p. 546 ; einhaga ylgr, an offensive kenning.

l. 11. Alliteration at fault. 'þömb' can hardly be adjective ; þömb means *guts*, used for bowstrings, hence þambar-skelfir (gut-shaker), a surname of a great archer : the error lies in 'heldr,' for which read 'elði' (*fœtus*), varð elði í þömb, *the babe was kindled in her womb*.

Gunlaug, (p. 111.)—vv. 5–9 are the best and least corrupt, note, l. 33.

l. 38. Allvangs eyrr ; the wagers of battle were fought in a 'holm' on the banks of the river Axewater ; Allvangr = the Tyn-wall.

l. 45. lítil . . . líta (i. e. wlíta) is perfectly right. It may be that Gunnlaug, who had been in England, was not quite a stranger to the sound of *wl*. See an interesting essay of Grimm, Kleinere Schriften, vol. vi, p. 277, reproving modern critics for cancelling such lines as false (as commentators have done to this line), and showing how little good poets avoided such rhymes, when the words (as lítill and wlíta) were *different in sense*.

Gretti, (p. 114.)—höggazk til skeggjom and halda saman nefjom are comic proverbial phrases : construe, Hlakkar tialda (mail-coat's) hefjendr *and* Hildar veggs (shield's) hregg (battle's) Nirðir (men).

l. 10. Heimdala hiör = *the head* [see Excursus I, vol. ii, p. 452] is of old poets only found here. Read *so I guard my life*.

Gest.—It is more than problematic whether these lines be genuine.

Thormod.—In a coarse vein ; only noticeable for the names of places [see Eyrb.] : note the pun, Gifrs (ogress') grand (Thor's) ness = *Thorsness*, where the moot was held. Snorri's character could certainly not be gathered from this poem.

Skapti.—Notice the belief of the old neophytes, that Christ built Rome.

§ 2. KINGS ST. OLAF AND KNUT.

Sighvat, (p. 124.)

I. It may be doubted whether this poem is not by some common-place poet, and not Sighvat ; for it has none of his characteristic marks.

l. 9. Herdalir, mod. Herjedalen, North Sweden ? Balagarðz síða = Aland Sker-gaard, Finland.

l. 18. Kinmaria *or* Kinheim (see mediæval maps), = the sea side of Holland.

l. 24. Note the long vowel in Súðvirki, mod. *Southwark*.

l. 32. *Port reeves*; the commentators, not knowing English, have made a strange mess of this sentence.

vv. 12–14. These places, mostly on the Loire [l. 51], one should think, we have not been able to identify ; they are all more or less corrupt : Warrand (Guérande) is near the sea, hence read, sió *nerri*.

v. 15. For notes to this verse see under Othere ; we have put it in brackets, for it can be none of Sighvat's, rather from one of Othere's poems. Our poem seems to have been composed not earlier than in 1014, perhaps even in England. It is a young or else poor poet's work, a mere register ; between it and No. II there is a great leap.

II. (p. 127.) Sighvatr skald var þar í orrosto, hann orti þegar um sumarit eptir flokk þann er Nesja-vísor ero kallaðar, ok segir þar vandliga frá þessum tíðendum. [S. Ol. S.] Nesia is midway between Laurvig and Skien ('east of Agde,' l. 10).

v. 3. Óláfr konungr hafði þat skip er kallat var Karlhöfði [Carle-head, from her figure-head], þar var á fram-stafni skorit konungs höfuð; hann sialfr hafði þat skorit : þat höfuð var lengi síðan haft í Noregi á skipum þeim er höfðingjar stýrðu. [S. Ol. S. l. c.] The figure-head was carved by the king's own hand (who was a skilled craftsman at carving), and was for long afterwards used on the ship where the king was on board [as an admiral's flag].

l. 14. kvistungar (*saplings*).   *The men were cut down as saplings.*

l. 21. The golden banner staff occurs here for the first time, afterwards frequent in battles fought in Great Britain, as in Arnor's songs.   The poets called it 'stong' or 'wé.'

l. 33. þá færðu konungs-menn stafn-liá á skeiðar-kylfurnar, ok héldu þeim svá ; þá mælti iarl, at stafn-buar skyldu af höggva kylfur [S. Ol. S.] ; hence, for 'harðliga' read 'stafn-bua.'

l. 36. Read, 'haldit . . . leám skeiðar stafna' (*we having grappled their stems with our hooks*).

l. 38. Note the Homeric simile, Od. i. 9.

v. 13. The Uplanders and Heathmark folk (Central Norway) were the chief stock of Olaf's host.   On the Earl's side, Einar the Archer, his sister's husband, was the chief baron.   In Olaf's last battle at Stiklastead, fifteen years and four months later, the same Uplanders were on the king's right hand, and stood true to him to the last.

III. *The Eastern Travel,* (p. 129.)—Is not so much overpainted, but the text is in a poor state and disjointed in the same manner as the 'Eddic' poems.   It has given a good deal of trouble : the 'plan' of Sighvat's journey having been somewhat of a puzzle.   The Saga has made confusion still more confounded by misdating and misplacing (as it seems), making Sighvat go to *Skara,* or even *Upsala,* leaving Novogorod (Garda) out of sight altogether.   We have here endeavoured to reconstruct the poem.   The marking points in Sighvat's journey are : the Strind Sea in Throndheim [l. 14] ; the Lister Sea [l. 15], west off South Norway ; Eikunda Sund [l. 16], or Eker Sound, though concealed, but pretty certain ; Eygotaland [l. 18], restored, but absolutely certain, meaning Isle of Gothland ; and lastly, Gardar [l. 75, cp. l. 92], Novogorod.   Hence it appears that the eastward journey was *by sea,* from Throndheim, via Gothland, to Ladoga.   The ride in vv. 6–8 would then be the ride from the shore up to Ladoga, the earl's residence.   Lastly, the account, vv. 9–18, can only be the journey *homeward back* across Sweden : ll. 35, 36, the recrossing the Baltic to East Gothland.   Still there are hitches and puzzles left, especially the Eida-skog, the word 'norðan,' l. 40.   We leave the matter in part unsolved to the fitter hands of Swedish scholars, who may possibly unearth some new names of places underneath the palimpsest text, should they deem it worth their while.   It is a strange freak of history, that the most hospitable of European countries here enters, as it were, on the scene as the very home of inhospitality—poor poet Sighvat !   But mark the *tone* of the poem : Sighvat, like a Norwegian, is all prejudice against the Swedes.   Christianity was still backward in Sweden, the country yet half heathen [vv. 13, 14].—All this is very interesting.   There is a fine vein of humour and fun running through the poem.   The Sagas call Earl Ragnwald 'Ulfsson;' Sighvat [l. 67] seems, if we interpret him aright, to call him 'Saxason' (and he must have known), and 'Ulf's brother's son' [l. 84] : who is this Ulf, the wise counsellor? [l. 85].   The two earls, Eilif and Ulf, who, according to English sources, fought in 1026 at the Holy River, were they not Ragnwald's sons?   When Sighvat made his journey, the earl had left Sweden for Novogorod (Ladoga), whether as the Swedish king's friend or not we cannot tell; the Sagas represent him as an exile: vv. 21, 22 would explain much, could we but put them aright and interpret them.

l. 17. Some name of place, Skioldungs ey = Zealand?

l. 18. Eygotaland is the ancient name of the Isle of Gothland, occurring, besides, in Thattr of Ragnars sons and in Sogo-brot, both parts of the lost Skioldunga.

l. 20. Misbracketed; construe, hlýtk at ríða *and* tékk ekkjom ymissar iðir.

l. 23. knörrom, emend. for 'Donom,' which gives no meaning. The Saga represents this as a ride up to Skara [now a Bishop's see in West Gothland, on the south border of Lake Wener]—Enn er þeir riðo upp um Gautland [from the sea, the Cattegat] kvað Sighvatr vísor þessar [vv. 4, 5]. Enn er þeir riðu upp um Gautland síð um aptan kvað Sighvatr [v. 6]. Þá ríða þeir í kaup-staðinn á Skörum ok um strætið fram at garði iarls. Hann kvað [v. 7].

l. 26. Rognvalldz býr, i. e. Ladoga *or* Aldeigia?

ll. 35, 36. Construe, svan-vangs (sea's) öndrum (ships).

l. 41. valtan karfa, and, ver stilltum til glœps á báti : vatr (wet?), or vatr (water)?

l. 44. Read 'húms' for 'heims?' húms hrútr (a clumsy smack or punt).

l. 56. alfa-blót, a sacrifice to the Elves or Dii Manes, see Excursus. Here we meet for the first time the word 'ótwín,' the stress on the second half; since met with several times in the poets of the following reign, when it disappears; probably foreign, English or French ; even the sense is not quite clear. Cp. Thiodolf, i. l. 62 ; p. 225, l. 25 ; p. 231, l. 13.

l. 59. grefs gætir, *keeper of the delve, pickaxe-man, labourer ;* 'gerstr,' cp. Germ. 'garstig.'

l. 61. Misbracketed ; construe, heinfletz þollar bella þeygi tíri.

l. 70. Eiða-skógr, so called from the many lakes or lochs, with their countless necks, 'eið ;' usually of the big forest, west of the Gotha River.

vv. 19 sqq. Partly obscure : l. 75, deila e-n málom harða mörgum, a necessary emendation.

l. 78. nefi iarla, the earl's *nephew ;* the relationship is not clear ; cp. iarla frændi, l. 83 ; Ulfs bróðor son = Ragnwald?

l. 92. Austr-vego, Grano salti are names that only can apply to the East Baltic, not to an earl residing in Skara.

This embassy of Sighvat seems to have purported what a modern scribe would call a commercial treaty with the earl in Novogorod. There must have been in St. Olaf's days an extensive traffic from Norway in the East Baltic; King Olaf himself dealt in trade as partner in Greenland, Iceland, England, and the Baltic.

IV. *Western Travel*, (p. 133.)—These verses too are in a poor state, though not so much through overpainting.

Sighvatr kom þat sumar til Englandz vestan af Rúðo á Vallandi, ok sá maðr með hónum er Bergr hét, þeir höfðu þangat farit kaup-ferð it fyrra sumar. Sighvatr orti flokk þann er kallaðr var Vestr-farar-vísor, ok er þetta upphaf [v. 1].—S. Ol. S. ch. 156 (Kringla).

l. 4. 'melld' (*locked*), mello lás (*a latch*), cp. Dict. s. v. malla and mella : þá var herbergit *læst,* ok stóð hann lengi úti [the paraphrase in S. Ol. S.].

l. 5. ber ek opt á armi iarn-stúkor is a wretched piece of restoration, but what once stood we cannot make out.

l. 7. 'Allt hefir sá er' . . . úti, maimed; the sense is that Cnut is raising a large levy of ships ; cp. Enn er Sighvatr varð þess varr at Knútr konungr býr herferð á hendr Ólafi konungi, ok hann vissi hversu mikinn styrk Knútr konungr hafði, þá kvað Sighvatr [v. 3].—S. Ol. S.

l. 8. Read, konungs, but the clause is, maybe, but the editor's work.

l. 10. Some proverb, but we have been unable to find the clue to it.

v. 4. Maimed text; barely the sense seems to gleam through.

l. 16. Húnn, *a young bear*, a play on his fellow poet's name.

l. 19. Cf. Peterborough Chr. 1031, and þy ilcan geare he for to Scotlande. and Scotta cyng him to beah Mælcolm. and twegen oðre cyningas. Mælbæþe. and Iehmarc.

v. 7. Enn er hann kom í Noreg, fór hann þegar til fundar við Oláf konung ok hitti hann í Borg; gekk fyrir konung þá er hann sat yfir borðum; Sighvatr kvaddi hann. Konungr leit við hónum ok þagði. Sighvatr kvað.—S. Ol. S.

v. 9. In a very poor state, two proverbs discernible; Eigi varðar einn eiðr alla: the second, l. 34, we cannot make out. Construe, esa gengit fyrir mál þat.

v. 11. Obscure; we read and construe, hám (not hás) himni, and diúpan eld; *Traitors* (the poet says) *barter away a place in the high heaven for a deep fire* (in hell).

v. 12. Obscure; the Saga says by way of paraphrase—Opt var sú umrœða þar í munni höfð, hversu illa þat samði Hákoni iarli, at fœra her á hendr Óláfi konungi, er hann hafði hónum líf gefit, þá er iarl hafði á hans vald komit. Enn Sighvatr var inn mesti vinr iarls. Ok þá enn er Sighvatr heyrði iarlinum ámælt, kvað hann. Perhaps the bearing is, The earl's complicity is but a foul charge, let us sweep before our own door.

v. 14. Very obscure and mangled; there are two proverbs discernible—Hverr verðr með sialfom ser lengst at fara (hverr þegn skal hafa sik sialfan miklo lengst), *and*, Upp koma svik um síðir (upp hvolfra svik). The first two lines are quite dark.

V. (p. 135.) ll. 1, 2. Mark the mid. form Jorwik.

l. 12. at 'há' (or, at heyja), name of some place?

l. 14. mar-beðjom, cp. vol. i, p. 126, l. 7.

ll. 15, 16. Mangled beyond recovery.

l. 24. Read, varr glœstr, varr (acc.), *across the sea*.

l. 30. The proverbial phrase, láta af étask (image from two animals at the manger).

l. 36. 'Suman,' we surmise 'Cumbra.'

l. 37. May refer to Cnut's meeting the Emperor Conrad in St. Peter's Church at Rome; Clús-Petrus (*Key Peter*) = the Pope.

VI. (p. 137.) *Dirge on Erling.*—Very much overpainted.

ll. 1, 2. The 'palimpsest' sense of which (for what we now read is manifestly a false and empty common-place) we take to have been,—that Erling, while scouting on his swift, famed galley, fell unawares in with the king, his small craft was over-powered, his crew to a man cut down or surrendered, and he himself slain by the hand of his own kinsman Anslac (a disappointed man, why, we are not told), who was with the king. The account in the Saga, making Erling to have had a fleet ready, and to have gone in pursuit of the king, is manifestly epicised. The season—depth of winter—τὰ πράγματα (in Polybius' parlance) speak against it. The account of Erling's last moments, when the king is said to have stabbed his prostrate foe, then gray with age [1], in the cheek (a thief's punishment), is not to be lightly

---

[1] Erling's age, say 55; married in 996, then apparently a young chief, Tryggvason's sister, died Dec. 21, 1028. Munch has overstated his age. O. H. L. says that his head was turning gray; which may be tradition or mere 'epic,' though in those days men lived fast, and the wrong side of fifty then made one an old man; three score and ten was with the Norsemen (the men) quite an exception.

credited. Sighvat supplies no hint of all this; on the contrary, Anslac is with him the felon and murderer. No exact record, even in modern life, can fairly be expected of a sudden fray like this; yet the story in Agrip, which puts down to Anslac both the stab and the death-blow, is to be preferred. Genuine is the exchange of words between the king and Erling, but this is rather a mark of sympathy than of deadly hate. Sighvat, who seems to have loved Erling—he must often have been his guest—gives the date at Iólom [l. 30], the day, Thomas messa [palimpsest in l. 21] [1]. The *place* is over and over again marked out [ll. 6, 7, 9, 10, 20]: Erling's reply to the king's call [ll. 17–20]; Sighvat absent [l. 29] in Wick, says the Saga—paraphrasing the words of our poem when still in a pure state—which we take to be underneath l. 30 ('sa er réð Iaðri' is too poor and common-place; besides, Erling's rule was wider by far).

l. 14. Skialgs hefnir, Erling's father had been slain; from a romanticised story in Ol. Tr. S. we learn that he perished by fire.

l. 15. Construe, glyggs varð-kers (heaven's) víð-botn (earth).

l. 18. The proverb, öndurðir skolo ernir kloazk, Reader, p. 240, No. 40. Saxo, too, has this saw.

vv. 9–11 treat of Erling's power and the extent of his dominion. In the earlier portions of S. Olaf's Saga we recognise statements drawn from Sighvat's words. Thus, ch. 21 (Kringla)—þá er Oláfr Tryggvason réð fyrir Noregi, gaf hann Erlingi, mági sínum, halfar landskyldir við sik, ok at helmingi allar konungs tekjor milli Líðandisness ok Sogns [Lat. 58°–61°]. Oláfr gipti aðra systur sína Rögnvaldi iarli Ulfs syni [v. 9]. Sighvat says, ' Ulfs *feðr* ' (Wolf's *father*); is this an error for ' nið,' or did Ari here make a slip? See above, the notes on the Eastern Travel. Farther, ch. 122— Erlingr Skialgsson hélt ríki síno svá, at allt ' norðr frá Sogn-sæ ok austr til Líðandis ness ' réð hann öllu við bœndr. Still closer, however, to our text is ch. 180, Var þat í heitom við Erling af hendi Knútz konungs, at hann skildi hafa land allt til forráða *milli Staðar* [Lat. 62°] *ok Rygjar-bitz* [east of Naze, near Christiansand],— the very words which we espy underneath ll. 38–40. Characteristic and true are the remarks O. T. ch. 64—þá bauð konungr [Tryggvason] at gefa Erlingi iarldóm. Erlingr svarar svá: hersar hafa verit frændr mínir, vil ek ekki hafa nafn hærra en þeir; upon which the king enfeoffs him with the land between Firth of Sogn and Naze.

ll. 33, 34 seem to refer to this very enfeoffment of Tryggvason. Under ' svá at œgði' we read ' at Agðom,' or the like.

v. 11. A comparison between Erling and Gudbrand of the Dales, of whom we else know little, for the comical story in S. Ol. S. is but a fable. The two, Erling and Gudbrand of the Dales, were in the days of the two Olafs the two great barons of Norway.

VII. *Olaf's Dirge*, (p. 138.)—Fearfully overlaid. Verses 1, 3, 4–6, 24–30, though not immaculate, have escaped the remanieur's scathing hand; vv. 2 and 7 will not fit well in with the rest; we take them to be none of Sighvat's, but perhaps Othere's.

l. 7. The received version is, that the Upland kings were *five;* here they are ' eleven ;' but the verse is wholly corrupt, ' eleven ' and all. In Fb. ii. 67 we read—Svá segir Styrmir inn Fróði, at Oláfr konungr hafi tekið ríki af ellifu konungum . . . ok er þat lög-tekið er hann hefir saman sett. But in Styrmi's days the poems were just as we have them now; *his* authority, therefore, as to the facts of that king's life, is of small value.

l. 21 is maimed. The verses 4–6 are very momentous, and substantially clear.

---

[1] Some MSS. read ' tapaðr slico,' which is nearer.

The king is here the Leo justitiæ. The preceding rule of the Earls appear to have been licentious in the extreme—no king in Israel—and the people demoralised. The Saga, ch. 192 (Kringla), draws substantially upon our verses. Ari perhaps knew more. The cutting off the *hands* and *feet* of thieves and robbers (but the *head* of Wickings that broke the king's peace) is here recorded for the first time in Northern history; so also the enforcement of one law on poor and great alike.—Here indeed we have the *key* to the rising against St. Olaf. Sighvat has proved a true historian to his master.

v. 8 tells of the king's legislation, as if the poet were addressing the *living* Olaf; perhaps this is no part of the Dirge. Construe, eiki-hliðs (ship's) lopt (castle) byggvir (king); but very likely the clumsy 'kenning' is merely a retouch, some law phrase buried underneath.

vv. 9–23. The account of the battle is mangled, 'from head to heel;' we have to turn to the prose of the Saga, and thence glean out the sense that once was here: unfortunately, the Saga's account too is, even in our O. H. (Kringla and Cod. Holm.), a mere agglomeration of incident.

l. 31. Þórðr Fólason [hidden in l. 32] bar merki Ólafs konungs. Svá segir Sighvatr skald í erfi-drápu þeirri er hann orti um Olaf konung, ch. 224 (Kringla).

l. 35. The king stands next to his banner. This is epicised in ch. 218; but the best account is in ch. 216. There were three banners: (1) the king in the centre with the *chosen men;* (2) Day, the South Norwegians, and the Uplanders on his *right* hand; (3) the Swedes, auxiliaries, on his *left* hand. The Swedes had an evil report as to their faith, so the poet (and the traditions after him) represents Norsemen and Swedes like the sheep and goats in the Gospel, the Christian (Norse) host on the right, the heathen (Swedes) on the left. The number of the king's army was thirty divisions (folcs[1]), each folc counting forty, geographically ranked, as in a modern army. We have in the Saga *double versions*, one historical, one legendary; ch. 216 represents the *historical*, ch. 218 the *epic poetic account:* there are many more such *doublets* in S. Ol. Saga. All this we can still see through a thickly over-daubed coat of silly remaniement, cp. lines 35–45. There follows an account of the *Bonders'* battle array [ch. 233 of the Saga]: they, too, had three banners; (1) Kalf (the chief) in the *centre* with his house-carles, Thori Hound there too; (2) the Thronds and Haleygs (so we read the sense) on the *right;* (3) the Rugians, Hords, Sognfolk, and Frithmen on the *left.* The Uplanders and the Wickmen, being true to the king, are not mentioned as of the Bonders' party. A bit of a stinted, mangled account of all this is still visible in ll. 49, 50. The Bonders were 'halfo fleiri,' twice as many [l. 47]; better, thrice as many, for 'halfo' is a vague term, by *half* or *more*. The aggregate number of both is, we believe, hidden in l. 48; 'hundrað folk' (120 × 40) roughly, yet certainly overstated; the aggregate number being (30 × 40) + (90 × 40) = (120 × 40): l. 40 contains the number of the king's men—

Folk . . . fylkir . . . þriá togo hafði.

l. 48 that of the Bonders; underneath 'fry ek' we espy 'folk:' read—

hundroð töld at hildi hvár-tveggja folk váro.

The legendary S. Ol. S. is partly right here—Buendr hafa þriu merki ok tuttogo ok hundrað manna liðs undir hverju; svá er sagt at konungrinn lét iamn-mörg bera í móti, ok 'fiora tigo manna undir hverjo merki.'—O. H. L., ch. 30.

---

[1] Cf. Thulor, l. 711, folk er fiorir tigir: 'folc'='forty' is, we believe, drawn from a ship's crew; the early battles were fought on the shore, the men drawn up, crew by crew; a sixteen or twenty-seated galley would then be the average ship.

vv. 19, 20 are devoted to Thori Hound's striking at the king; v. 21 to Biorn the Marshall's death, 'at the king's head.'

vv. 24-26. Most interesting, on the worship of the Saint in its infancy. ll. 88, 89. Misbracketed. Construe, Lýg ek nema Álafr eigi hár-vöxt *ok* ýfs árar (*nails*) sem kvíkvir tivar? ek gœði í hróðri *helgi* konungs ; and ll. 90, 91, construe, enn helzk svörðr á liósom hausi, þeims seldi son Valdimar (dat.) í Görðom; hann [i. e. the Saint] fékk læss lausn; '*læ*' means here a *corruption* in N. T. sense. Former commentators (even Egilson) have misconstrued and misunderstood these lines.

v. 28. The king had held Sighvat's daughter under the font; the story is given in the Reader, p. 113. The Christian terms are most interesting; the neophyte Christian Sighvat struggling for utterance as he speaks of sacred subjects in a heathen tongue.

v. 30. On the eclipse we have spoken elsewhere; Sighvat's words do not strictly speak to a *contemporaneity* of battle and eclipse. l. 106. 'furða' is a heathen word, here used in a Christian sense, the ecclesiastical wonder, a token of the king's sanctity, wrought by God—no longer the work of the Wolves trying to swallow the Sun Goddess as in heathen days of yore. [See cut in 'Old Stories from British History,' by the Translator, 1882, p. 11.]

VIII. (p. 143.) These verses have mostly escaped overhauling.

ll. 3, 4. Overlaid. 'Sult' we take to be, not appellative, but to denote the *place*: it was at Sult, present Sylte at the bottom of Storfiord [Lat. 62° 50'], that King Olaf abandoned his ships early in 1029, leaving the country for the East. Sighvat appears to say, *I started on my pilgrimage what time the king from Sult left his ships and his kingdom.* Did the poet (then in Wick) have a last interview with Olaf? was the gold-hilted sword the king's parting gift?

v. 2. Sighvatr skald hafði farit til Rúms þá er orrosta var á Stikla-stöðum, enn er hann var sunnan á leið, spurði hann fall Óláfs konungs [whilst crossing the Alps?]; var hónum þat inn mesti harmr, hann kvað þá [v. 2]. Sighvatr gekk einn dag um þorp nokkut, ok heyrði at einn hverr hús-boandi veinaði miök, er hann hafði misst kono sínnar, barði á brióst ser, ok reif klæði af ser, grét miök ok sagði, at hann vildi giarna deyja. Sighvatr kvað [v. 3]. Sighvatr kom heim í Noreg, hann átti bú ok börn í þróndheimi, fór hann sunnan fyrir land á byrðingi ; enn er þeir lágu í Hillar-sundi [near Mandal], þá sá þeir hvar hrafnar margir flugo. Sighvatr kvað [v. 4] . . . þat var einn dag at Sighvatr gekk úti á stræti, ok sá hvar konungs menn léku. Sighvatr kvað [v. 5]. Síðan fór hann til búss síns ; hann heyrði marga menn ámæla ser, ok segja, at hann hefði hlaupizk frá Óláfi konungi. Sighvatr kvað [v. 6]. Sighvatr unði illa heima ; hann gekk úti einn dag, ok kvað [v. 7].— Kringla Magnus Saga, ch. 2.

l. 11. sá er varð (*lost*) drottinn, see note on Hallfred, p. 575.

l. 12. víg-tár, a word coined by Sighvat, or an echo from the Helgi poet; it calls to mind Helgi i. 355.

ll. 19, 20. We must mend this; read and construe—

Minnomk ek hve manna míns dróttins lékk sinnom
opt á óðal-toptom orð-sæls es vas forðom.

I. e. *I remember how I in times past oftentimes used to play at the home of my beloved lord:* lékk = lék ek ; then a coherence is between the first and second half. The poet does not mean to say the king was playing; *his* mind was of a stern pensive cast, little given to play, his life was all work and no play—he was essentially a lawyer and constitution-maker : óðal-topt, a law term = óðal torfa, of the Tapestry poet.

l. 21. Hvíta-Kristr, a new-coined word for Christ.

l. 23. vatn-œrin, a law term, ᾅπ. λεγ.: í haska, in jeopardy (from illness?).

l. 25. há, höll klif, *the high, sloping cliffs*.

l. 26. Knörrum ; what place is meant we know not.

l. 28. varð ek, lost?

l. 29. Read, ungs drengs ; refers to the boy-king, not to the poet himself, who by this time was no longer young.

l. 32. There are various readings ; this one we take in preference.

IX. (p. 144.) Sighvat travelled east to Sweden to St. Olaf's Dowager Queen Anstrid : Sighvatr spurði optliga, er hann fann kaupmenn, Holmgarðz-fara, hvat þeir kynni segja hónum til Magnúss Óláfs sonar.   Hann kvað [ix. v. 1].

ll. 3, 4. Somewhat obscure, a kind of apology for not being able to put in an appearance at the moot at Hangra [Sweden] convened by Queen Anstrid, where she pleaded her step-son's case before the Swedes.

l. 7. þings beið herr ; one should prefer ' þing bauð.'   The sense must be, that a moot of many Swedes convened at Hangra, or, that a host of Swedes gathered thither.

l. 9. ' hætna,' heitom?

v. 5. Hann kvað þá þetta er þær Ástríðr dróttning ok Alfhildr konungs móðir höfðu skotizt á orðum nokkorom.—Magn. S., ch. 10.

X. (p. 145.) Text not much overpainted, yet in parts very unsafe from the poor MSS., for many of the verses are only preserved in the third hand of the Flatey-book. The commentary in Hulda (Fms. vi), ch. 22, is feeble, and cannot be from Ari's hand.

The rising of the Bonders, headed by Atli the Speaker (a Norse Thorgny), or Tribune, has left but few echoes behind.   The Kringla, or Book of Kings, does not even mention it ; did Ari overlook it?   The Agrip (ch. 29) transfers it to Throndham—Hann [the boy-king Magnus] átti þing í Niðarósi ok reisti með freko sakargipt við þrœndr alla ok *stungu allir nefi í skinn-felld ok veitto allir þögn* en engi andsvör [clearly an echo of ll. 67, 68].   Stóð upp þá maðr, Atli at nafni, ok mælti eigi fleiri orð en þessor : svá skorpnar skór at fœti mer at ek má eigi or stað komask. Enn Sighvatr kvað þar þegar víso þessa [v. 17].   The Norwegian Gula Law-book has a more marked notice—Nú höfum ver land-vörn vára á skrá setta, ok vitom eigi hvárt þat er rétt eða rangt.   Enn þo at ragnt (!) sé þá skolom ver þat logmál hafa um útgerðir várar, er fyrr hefir verit, ok *Atli taldi fyrir mönnum í Gula*, nema konungr várr vili oss öðrum iátta, ok verðim ver á þat sáttir allir samt [ch. 314].

v. 1. Text unsafe ; under ' lattan' we espy ' Atli,' and ' hvatta ' (egged) under Sig ' *hvatr ;*' the rest is twilight.

l. 6. We have restored this line ; Cnut's sons, Hardicnut and Harald, were then alive.   The poet, threatening the young king, says—*I will leave, I shall go to either of them, I knew their father* (Cnut) : ' *I was then altogether beardless* ' (quite a youth) does not refer to his meeting with Cnut (that meeting in 1027), but, ' I have earned my bread by my tongue (poet craft) ever since I was a beardless boy.'

v. 3. In a very poor state, well-nigh blotted out.

ll. 15, 16. Two proverbial sayings, which we have tried to restore.   The image is drawn from wattling, ' *though none of the biggest, yet I ever filled my place, there was no gap where I stood.*'   There is an Icelandic proverb—Eigi fyllir annars rúm. Construe, þiökkva (wattle) skal hrœsinn húsa-við með hrísi.   In Dict. p. 740 b we once tried another explanation.

vv. 5, 6. In a wretched plight; what the poet really did say has evaporated.

vv. 7–8 are better; it is a warm appeal to the happy reign of Hacon the Good and the two Olafs: lauk-iafn, a word of the poet's coinage? justice, *upright as a garlic*, unbiassed righteousness, without bend or break.

l. 36. All this is very unsafe; 'Skiri-nafni' (I, your godfather), for Sighvat chose the name of the baby Magnus. In l. 37, perhaps, 'skorpnar skrift skíri-nafna,' though the rhyme requires another word; 'nafni' would by Sighvat be sounded 'namni,' the sound *bn* being quite modern. See the words skræma, skræmi, skrimd, denoting *scare, scaringly, ugly*.

l. 38. Quite corrupt.

l. 43. We read, ætti drengir dýrðar dróttinn, ef sonr yrði feðr glíkr.

l. 46. 'á svik,' or as some have, 'á svig;' fara á svig við e-n is an Icelandic phrase, and 'svigr-mæli,' garbled utterances, imputations; but we prefer the stronger 'svik,' for Sighvat was no tale-bearer; conspiracy, words breathing treason, he would report to his master.

l. 50. Construe, þat orð ryðr til dýrðar dróttins.

l. 57. Read, bú þegna, in two words.

l. 60. Construe, véltir þiófs, see Excursus, p. 450: Stytta skal hönd í hófi is a proverb.

l. 63. A proverb, Vinr es sá vörnuð býtr, cp. Guest's Wisd., l. 172.

l. 64. mútaris, a French word, the *moulting hawk*. Note, Sighvat heard no *l;* mark also the genitive on *-is*, as in vartaris, note p. 571; and perhaps Væneris in Bragi's line.

v. 17. Very corrupt. Underneath 'ætla' we surmise 'Atla;' barely the drift of the sense is here attainable.

ll. 67, 68. See above.

l. 70. öfgast, not verb, but adjective to orð.

l. 71. Read rán, and construe, seggr hinn er selr út sína föður-leifð konungs greifom at flaums felli-dómi, mun telja rán í því.

l. 73. A proverb.

l. 76. We read, 'varða þu,' *guard thou! be thou the guardian of Norway!* The poet's farewell words, or final address, winding up the poem; for Norway, as Harold Bluetooth's 'hawk isle' in the reign of the Gundhildsons, we are told how King Forkbeard charged King Olaf with, er hann hafði sezk í skattland hans Noregsveldi, er Haraldr, fadir hans, kallaði 'haukey sína,' Fms. x. 341. (Odd Monk's Ol. S.)

XI. (p. 148.) The fishing anecdote is given in the Reader, p. 111; the verses are obscure and corrupt.

l. 21. gör-bœnn, *solicitous, importunate*.

l. 23. We read, lýra láð (sea's) þaks (ice's) veri (the Icelander); construe, veittu lýra láð-þaks veri (dat.) landaura, mörk halfa, af knerri (give him up the half-mark, for I have none to spare myself): bracket the intercalary clause.

l. 25. The story given in the Reader, pp. 112, 113.

v. 8. Perhaps none of Sighvat's [of Othere's?].

v. 9. Men were finding fault with his poetry: ll. 35, 36 a proverb.

l. 38. A proverb. The verse seems to be an address to the king when alive: the text is unsafe. Selja is a little isle near cape Stadt (close up to the neck Dragseið), famed from its Saints, 'the Men of Selja ' (8th of July).

Othere the Black, (p. 150.)

I. A bald poem and much overlaid, but never of high worth.

l. 11. Sallt [Salt-ið-Eystra in Arnor's song], *the Baltic*.

l. 17. The Isle of Gothland is meant [Gautzkr, *of the Gauts*].

v. 7–10. All overdaubed most miserably, 'stained' means dyed with colour, especially with red.

The following extracts from the Peterborough Chronicle will show the relation of the poem, as far as can be made out, to the history of the Danish invasions:— 1009. 'Ða æfter S. Martinus mæssan. þa ferdon hi [the invading host] eft ongean to Cent. and namon him wintersettl on Temesan. and lifedon of East Seaxum. and of ðam scirum þe þær-nyxt wæron on twam healfe Temese. and oft hi on þa burh Lundene ge-fuhton. Ac si Gode lof. þet heo gyt ge-sund stent. and hi þær æfre yfel geferdon.' [After a raid in the beginning of 1010 through the Chilterns to Oxford, which they burnt, they got back to Kent by way of 'Stane' (Kingston), and passed the spring mending their ships.] 1010. Her on ðissum geare com se fore-sprecenda here ofer Eastron to Englum. and wendon up æt Gipes-wic. and eodon an-reces þær hi ge-axodon Ulfcytel mid his fyrde. Ðis wæs on þam dæg prima ascensio Dñi. and þa sona flugon East Engla. þa stod Grantabrycg scir [ana] fæstlice ongean. þær wæs of-slægen Æthelstan þes cynges aðum. and Oswi and his sunu. and Wulfric Leofwines sunu. and Eadwig Æfice's broðor. and feala oðra godra þegna. and folces unge-rím. þone fleam ærest astealde þurcytel Myran-heafod. After this Ringmere heath fight follows a terrible harrying of fifteen shires, and a second wintering at the ships. In 1011, betwix Natiuitas S. Marie and S. Michaeles mæssan hi ymbesætan Cantwaraburh. and hi þær into comon þurh syre-wrenceas. for þon Ælmær hi be-cyrde Cantwaraburh þe se arcebiscop Ælfeah áer ge-nerede his life. And hi þær þa genaman þone arcebiscop Ælfheah. and Ælfword þæs cynges ge-refan. and Leof-wine abbot. and Godwine biscop. And Ælmær abbot hi lætan aweg. and hi þær genaman inne ealle þa gehadode menn. and weras. and wif. þet wæs un-asecgendlic ænigum menn hu mycel þæs folces wæs. and on þære byrig siððon wæron swa lange swa hi woldon. and þa hi hæfdon þa burh ealle asmeade. wendon him þa to scipon. and læddon þonne arcebiscop mid him. After a poem on this terrible blow, which concludes the story of 1011, the Abingdon chronicler goes on to speak of the Dane-geld of our v. 10. 1012. Hér on þissum geare com Eadric ealdorman. and ealle þá yldestan witan géhadode and læwede Angelcynnes. tó Lunden-byrig to foran þam Eastron. þa wæs Easter dæg þa on þam datarum Idus Aprilis. and hi ðær þa swá lange wæron oþ þat gafol eal gelæst wæs ofer ða Eastron. þat wæs ehta and feowertig þusand punda.

Æthelred's flight from Wight to Normandy in 1013 in Thorkettle's fleet is not noted by Othere, but his return *in Olaf's ships* (a new fact for English history) is only briefly noted thus in the Abingdon Chronicle: ðá com Æthelred cyning innon ðam Langtene hám tó hís agonre þeode. and hí glædlice fram him eallum onfangen wæs. Olaf seems to have turned to the English side after the archbishop's death, as did Thorkettle.

vv. 13–15. Arrival in Norway. This is very much overpainted. Ari knew the lines in their purity, see S. Ol. S., ch. 27 (Kringla)—Óláfr konungr lét þar eptir vera lang-skipid, enn bió þaðan knörro tvá [l. 43]. ok hafði þá tuttugo menn ok tvau hundruð albrynjaða [this must have been in the verse], ok valit miök. Hann sigldi norðr í haf um haustit, ok fengo ofviðri mikit í hafi [ll. 45–48] svá at mann-hætt var; enn með því þeir höfðu liðs-kost góðan [l. 46] ok hamingju konungs, þá hlýddi vel. Svá segir Óttarr [vv. 13, 14]. Her segir svá, at Óláfr konungr kom útan at miðjom Nóregi [l. 50]; enn sú ey heitir Sæla, er þeir tóku land, út frá Staði [this is now lost]. We must here add the verse, p. 127, v. 15, which we think belongs here. It is all overpainted; the substance, and even the words, we gather from S. Ol. S., ch. 28

(Kringla)—thus, underneath 'strangr hitti' we surmise 'ströng heit.' The following words of praise surely refer to the young king Olaf, and by no means to the earls; we accordingly read, es varð *einna* œztr, etc.

l. 59. Under 'rióðr' we surmise the *number* of the exiled kings, *four* or 'þriá?'

l. 62. The Saga has here an atrociously cruel story of King Olaf—Hann lét blinda Hrœrek báðum augom, ok hafði hann með ser, enn hann lét skera tungo or Goðröði Dala-konungi, enn Hring, ok aðra tvá lét hann sverja ser eiða, at þeir skyldo fara brott or Nóregi ok koma aldri aptr [ch. 74] (Kringla). We suspect our old acquaintance the clerical legend manufacturer who libels Tryggvason to have had his hand in the pie—the Book of Joshua being his model. There is also a long dramatic story on King Hrorek, ch. 82–86, true in substance: Old Hrorek *was* blind, but through no act of St. Olaf. As for the poems, l. 62 is the only apparent authority, yet the sense we take to be merely, *Ye put a stop to his evil tongue*. From other sources we learn that in fact the kings went into exile. The whole story of the Upland kings is dramatised in Snorri's best vein, long political speeches in Thucydidean style [S. Ol. S. (Kringla), ch. 30–36, 72, 73, 82–86]. Notice that the faithfulness of the Uplanders to St. Olaf in his hour of need at Sticklestead speaks loudly against any such things as his having cruelly maimed the Upland kings. The Wick and Central Norway stood by him, or at least were neutral.

l. 64. Notice here the *five* kings, which puts at rest the *eleven* of p. 583.

ll. 65, 66. The extension of the king's dominion, now the lord of Norway, from one end to the other, is in the south-east 'Eiðar,' so called from the *necks* and tarberts between the lochs of Wermland. We miss the boundary towards the north, hidden, we take it, in 'Gondlar,' i. e. Gandvík (víkr Ganda). 'He rules the land between the Elbe (Gotha River) and Gandwick,' says Snorri in Hattatal, verse 1.

l. 69. King Fairhair had, in times past, subdued the Isles, but no Norse king ever since.

II. *Cnut's Praise,* (p. 155.)

l. 6. lið-ván (levy?).

l. 14. Proverbial; reka e-m íllan þveit = liósta einn illom steini, p. 207, l. 67.

vv. 6–11. Very thickly overpainted, see Saxon Chronicle.

l. 27 apparently refers to some skirmish not mentioned in the Chronicle. The lines originally may have run—*The deep dyke was filled with the bodies of dead Northumbrians.* The fight must therefore have taken place between Uhtred's treaty with Eadmund and submission to Cnut. 'Sverd castala verða' is quite enigmatic. 'Hazelworth' is a mere guess. The whole of vv. 6–11 seems to be covered by the year 1016. (For English account of which, see p. 578.) Names certainly found in them are:—Lindesey, l. 17; River Ouse, l. 20; Norwich, l. 22; Thames, l. 26; Tees, l. 27; the Northumbrians' Dyke, l. 28; Sherstone, l. 30; Brentford, l. 32; Assington, l. 36; Forest of Dean, l. 38.

v. 12. A-in-Helga, Holy River, South Sweden; this battle is noticed in the Peterborough Chronicle, 1025. [The true date is 1026.]

III. (p. 157.) Utterly bare of facts, looks much as if it had been manufactured by Einar Skulason.

IV. (p. 157.) ll. 1, 2. Cnut's titles in these songs confirm Steenstrup's remarks as to the extent of his empire *never* including Sweden.

l. 4. víðari, Norwegian form for víðara.

l. 7. A proverb, Miór er mikils vísir, Reader, p. 264, No. 204, still in use in Iceland.

v. 3. Note the tapestry work of Sigfred in Canute's day: l. 12, cp. West. Wols. Lay, ll. 43, 44. A Swedish Rune-stone has the roasting-scene of l. 4 carved upon it.

Thorarin Praise-tongue (p. 159), etc.

I. *Stretch Song.* Note how Canute, setting out for Norway, starts from Limfrith, Jutland. In King Forkbeard's and Cnut's days [and earlier as well] the Limfrith was open towards the west; in fact, a sound or strait cutting clean across Jutland. Here the Danish fleet, bound for England, used to gather [see Knytl. S., year 1087]. Cnut, coming from England to Denmark, lands at Limfrith [Sighvat, vi. 28]. Mark the points in Cnut's northward route, leaving Limfrith, Agde (Naze), Listi (Lister), Highdoor (Haadyr, south of Jæderen), Ekersund, Hornelen (off Nordfiord), Cape Stadt, Stemshesten [Lat. 63°], River Nith [Nidaros, Throndheim].

l. 23. nefi, here sister's son, Earl Hacon Eric's son: Veg-Iótar [from A. S. *wæg* = sea], this folk-name also occurs in Vellekla, l. 83; but is else unknown. Cf. the Holm-Rygum of Widsið and Sæ-Geatas of Beowulf, the last of which is an exact parallel, it means the Island or Sea-Jutes. By the *son* [l. 84] Hardicnut is meant.

l. 25. dœkk-sala svana (sea) dalr, *the sea-dale*, that is, Denmark. Did not the poet say 'Dana-mörk?' it sounds better so, else the Icelandic Sagas only know the docked form *Dan-mörk*, but in Cnut's day, we surmise, the full form was still heard.

l. 30. For the long-fetched kenning see Excursus, vol. i, p. 457.

III. (p. 160.) This ecclesiastically interesting poem we have been able to partially restore. The title we take to be = 'Glœ-lung' (*the transparent vessel, the shrine*).

l. 2. The name of Earl Harald, son of Thorkettle the Tall, is, we believe, hidden under these words, he is *the Earl*, cp. þá hafði Knútr konungr gefit iarldóm í Dan-mörku Haraldi syni þorkels Háva [S. Ol. S. (Kringla), ch. 194]: underneath 'upp-*hafi*' we recognise '*Havi.*'

l. 13. kvikva settr (*enshrined*), of saints, cp. mod. kvik-settr (*buried alive*).

ll. 15, 16. Síðan fluttu þeir þorgils líkit upp með ánni ok grófu þar niðr á sand-mel þeim, er þar verðr [S. Ol. S., ch. 251]; a statement drawn, we think, from this very line whilst unadulterated.

l. 17. var þá líkami konungs borinn inn í Clemenz-kirkjo ok veittr umbúnaðr yfir há-altari [S. Ol. S. ch. 258]; derived, we take it, from our song; the MSS. leave here a blank: the 'high altar' is implied in l. 26.

l. 23. borð-vegs sæing, *the shrine*.

l. 27. Emendated, 'Cristi þæg' = cisto k'gs of the Archetypus. The sense is indubitable: it was over the high altar that the candles burnt above the king's coffin.

l. 31. 'kryppr' = kryppill—certainly so, a *noun*, not a *verb;* so also [l. 33] þióðan (*the king*), not þióðar; cp. Enn svá sem þórarinn segir, at til ins helga konungs kom herr mannz, *haltir* ok blindir, eða á annan veg siúkir, enn fóro þaðan *heilir.*—[S. Ol. S., ch. 259.]

l. 35. 'þinnar;' some MSS. 'sínnar,' i. e. the land he once ruled. In after days St. Olaf was the perpetual suzerain; indeed, the St. Peter of Norway. That, how-ever, is an interpretation appropriate only to later days, in Archbishop Eystan's and Magnus Erlingson's reign: it would be an anachronism—even though we accept the reading 'sinnar'—to urge any such meaning.

l. 38. bóka-máls (Holy Scriptures) regin-nagli, *the Scripture's holy peg* = *Saint:* 'regin-nagli' is a term borrowed from the heathen temple. See Excursus I, vol. ii, p. 403.

Hallward, (p. 161.)—l. 2. sikolgiorð is simply the sigel-gyrd, *sail-yard.*

l. 6. Fleet, the Humber; Ello ætt-leifð = England.

l. 11. munka-mold (Palestine) rekz (King's = God's) valld (heaven).

Biarni Goldbrow, (p. 163.)—l. 1. Harold's heir, i. e. St. Olaf.

ll. 7, 8. Underneath we read, Rygja ræsir, *and* land-vörðr Egða, of Erling. His enemies used to call him 'the King of the Rugians'—vera kann þá, at ek hafa ekki varliga mælt, ef þú ert systur son konungsins Rygjanna [Hkr., p. 353, Unger]. Sighvat calls him 'Vörðr Hörða,' *the Warden of the Hords.*

l. 22. We read, satt er at setja knáttir Svein ; the poet addresses his patron in the 2nd person—thou made Sweyn put up with Denmark alone ; didst dismiss him to Denmark.

l. 26. Read herr in its old bad sense, cp. öfundmenn in line below.

ll. 31, 32. Very corrupt. It refers to the battle at Redburgh, where Calf, siding with Earl Thorfin, his brother-in-law, beat Earl Rognvald.

The Rood Song, (p. 165.)—The last burden of this encomium most probably referred to the Rood, and gave it its name. Sigg, a peak on the Isle of Bommel, West Norway : Kormt (Karmen) and Aumar, isles off Rogaland (Stavanger).

II. *On Thoralf,* (p. 165.)—Fitjar, a farm on the Isle of Stord, west of Hardanger, where King Hacon the Good fell : for kenning, l. 3, see Excursus, vol. i, p. 457.

III. *An unknown song.*—Mythical phrases, cp. Atlam., l. 282, vol. i, p. 76, l. 42.

Ref. (p. 166.)—I. 'griótaldar ;' one should prefer a name of Woden ('Gautz alldins ' = Woden's breast liquor = poetry) : the image is modelled from the one in Egil's Head Ransom, l. 2.

II. Hrafn-ásar (Woden's) heilagt full, *holy toast,* poetry, and Valgautz veigar, *id.*

III. Mark the 'kennings ' of a ship, see Excursus, vol. ii, p. 458.

Bersi, (p. 169.)—hróðrs hag-kennendi = *a poet :* v. 3 apologizing for his not being willing to desert his old master, the earl, in his need and defeat : the Bison, St. Olave's ship, with a bison figure-head [Carlhead was his ship at Nesia].

Iokle.—Sult, now Sylte, a harbour in Valdal, Söndmör, Norway. Here St. Olaf left his ships, see Sighvat viii. 3.

Harek.—Læbaugs-ey, a pun = Veðr-ey (Weather Isle), an island in Cattegat. Vettalandir, an estate, county, Ranríki, on the east side of Christiana fiord.

Tryggvi's verses.—l. 51. This is the first time we meet a *week-day ; since* frequent in poets of the following reign [see especially Arnor].

St. Olaf.—l. 162. Gramr ok brattir hamrar, a pun = Ingi-gerðr.

l. 66. Ein glop (fem.) sœkir iarl hvern, a proverb. Icelanders now say, eiga eitt glappa-skotið á ævi sinni.

Coalbrow's Poet, (p. 175.)—l. 18. Loftunga, i. e. Thorarin the Poet.

l. 18. Read hregg-land, cp. Sighvat, x. 40.

l. 26. skopt, cp. p. 79, l. 4; survives in mod. Icel. skott, *a scut* or *tail* (of dog, fox).

l. 33. Skopta ek, see Dict. 554 a ; mod. skotta : goð-fión (podex).

l. 37. brenna e-m illan díla, proverbial phrase : ' fröm,' l. 39, dele.

ll. 45, 46. Inney, Herbiorg, places in Inner Throndheim.

l. 59. Hring and Day, on whom see Flatey-book ii, p. 118.

l. 66. Necessary emendation. Dags hríð was the final charge at Sticklestead, where the king's right wing (Day and the Uplanders) was beaten after a hard fight. [The king in the contest was, it seems, killed ere the battle was lost.] We need not give credence to the story that Day came *too late ;* for that is in direct contradiction with Sighvat's exact statements, that the Norsemen (and who else could they have been ?) were on the king's right hand.

§ 3. KINGS HAROLD AND MAGNUS.

Arnor, (p. 186.)

I. This poem is but little meddled with. Specimens of the most marked 'kennings' are—*A King*, Ulfa ferðar (wolves') tungu-rióðr 14, Yggjar más (raven's) fiðri-rióðr 16, benja kolgo (blood's) blágamms (raven's) fæðir 17, ulfa gráðar eyðir 19, fengins gollz ótti 52, hlenna þrýstir 36, hlenna þreytir 56, hlenna dolgr 58, gotna spialli 20, iöfra bági 55 : *the ship*, geima valr 62, él-marr 30, skorðo skíð 24, þopto eiki 26, sævar skíð 59, hlunna reið 57 : *the wind*, fyris garmr 28 : *the sea*, meita hlíð 59 : *blood*, hræ-lögr 48, Hlakkar haukr 48 : *raven*, val-gammr 44, etc.

l. 2. Quite obscure and fragmentary.

l. 8. skrúð, here a nautical term.

l. 9. verða (bulwark) ; better 'varta,' Thulor 412, and a verse in Orkney S. (á úrga vorto), but not in this collection.

l. 10. Read 'hlér.'

l. 14. tírar-þing; perhaps the moot at Hangra (see Sighvat ix. 7) is here meant.

l. 32. Stefja mél—'mál' is a later form (stave division), see Excursus on Metric.

l. 35. óþióð (*un-people, un-folk*), the pagan Wends.

l. 39. River on the border of Sleswick and Jutland.

l. 45. með hringom (crew and all).

l. 47. Hefnir Áláfs, see above, p. 35, l. 2 ; 92, l. 59 ; 137, l. 14 ; 211, l. 4.

l. 48. Nú mun kvæðit *aukask;* the initial verse to the third part or *Slœm.*

II. (p. 189.) l. 7. Sallt, see p. 152, l. 11 : heltr, better 'helldr' =hvelldr, vocalising the *w*, cp. p. 304, l. 63 ; 270, l. 29.

l. 8. Sigtuna, the famed place near Upsala, see Ynglinga Saga, the first chapter.

l. 10. afkarr, cp. Atla kv. 150, and below, l. 17 : hence we believe comes mod. Engl. *awkward.* Cf. 'carhand' of the fourteenth-century North English poet.

l. 14. otvín, see Sighvat iii. 56 ; Thiodolf ii. 62.

l. 22. hallr (=steinn), the *stained*, red-painted sides.

l. 23. fetil-stingr, a sword or dirk.

l. 30. ámr (blackish), cp. p. 278, l. 8. 'Iom,' on the coast of Pommerania, where the Danish kings once founded the famous Iomswicking colony : in Arnor's days dissolved, and the place given over to the Wendish pagan.

l. 36. The Axe Hell. This is the first time we meet with the axe as a weapon instead of the sword : the axe was long the favourite weapon of the Norwegians and Danes ; see the English Chronicles, Giraldus, and Sturlunga.

l. 40. á-leggjar (stone's) Yggjar (giant's) víf- (giantess') marr (wolf).

l. 42. Helganess, a point on the eastmost point of Jutland.

l. 45. Reggbuss, a Wendish name, as it seems.

l. 46. róg-skýja (shield's) rygjar (axe's) regn (battle).

l. 49. Hneitir, St. Olaf's sword. Magnus had the father's three heirlooms, his ship (Bison), his axe (Hel), and his sword (Hneitir) ; of which sword, see the later fables in Geisli, vv. 43–50.

l. 51. Biorn, a famed Wicking, Sweyn Wolfsson's brother, known also from English Chronicles, 1050.

l. 62. Chronological fact ; the young King Magnus was now [1045] filling his 'second teen,' his twentieth year.

III. (p. 191.) l. 3. River Niz, Halland ; battle fought here in 1062.

l. 4. Note here Tyrfing, the famed sword of the Waking (Bk. iii, § 1) ; no other poet, though verily from no lack of opportunity, is found using this name.

l. 5. The Snake, Harold's ship, a successor to the Bison and Long Serpent.

l. 19.=Eymdit, from eyma ; cp. Dan. *ömme* sig ved noget.

IV. (p. 192.) In a sad state. l. 3. The English Chronicles tell of the battle at Fulford ; we recognise the name under ' fell at fundi,' and ' Dík Uso ' under ' togfusa.' The Saga, in conformity with the Abingdon Chronicle, states (from our poem ?) that the battle was fought on Wednesday before St. Matthew's day. Is this hidden in l. 4 ? Gauta = Woden.

vv. 5, 6. Very sadly overdaubed.

l. 24. The Saga says—Emma het brynja hans, hon var svá síð at hónum tók á mitt bein, ok svá styrk at aldri hafði vápn á fest—' Emma ' hidden under ' hlenna.'

vv. 9, 10. Mere blurred sentences.

V. (p. 193.) Both this and the following Lay are overpainted beyond mending.

l. 1. Deildiz af svá aldri ; see Dict. s. v. deila, III. 2.

l. 4. ' hegjo,' see Rekst., l. 92, and Merl. ii. 82.

l. 13. blézk, from blanda : saum-för, see Thulor, l. 398.

VI. (p. 194.) skelkingr, a sword, Thulor, l. 255.

l. 8. See Excursus on Metre, p. 454.

The Orkney Saga, ch. 22, founded on our poem, speaks of a Carl Hundason (a Scotch ' maormor,' we believe, and no *king* of Scotland) ; his nephew is Muddan or Mumtan. Earl Thorfin fights and beats Hundason [Mac-beath, *Dog's Son*, as Mr. Rhys most ingeniously puts it] at Deersness. Thorkel Fosterer, Thorfin's ally and friend, slays Muddan ; upon which Hundason gathers an Irish and Scotch host, fights, and is beaten again at Torfness, whereon the earl harries and burns North Scotland, having in one summer fought three battles.

l. 9. ' kyndom lofuð brynjo,' some name hidden here, (Hundason?).

l. 20. Sandwick, the second battle.

l. 21. Torfness, the third battle, on a Monday ; on a Friday (l. 35) ; on a Wednesday morning (l. 40). Arnor is fond of showing off his learning by marking the *week days*—of scant use to us now, as often we neither know the *place* nor the *year*.

l. 24. Skotlands harra, lord of Scotland, only a ' maormor ' may be meant.

l. 28. Lodwe's grandson, see pedigree, p. 183.

l. 30. Mark the reed or rush-thatched houses.

l. 33. Read ' Vestrfiorðr,' Westfirth, on the west side of the Isle of Skye ; see Hak. S., chs. 166, 327, Rolls' edit. The poem was, one can see, already ' tainted ' when the paraphrase in Orkn. S. was taken, for there too we read Vatzfiorðr.

l. 34. A Skíði, manifestly = in the Isle of Skye.

v. 11. Name of the place hopelessly gone (buried in l. 47 ?). The Orkney S., ch. 27 (Rolls' edit.), says—þat var á einu sumri at þorfinnr iarl herjaði um Suðreyjar ok vestan um Skotland ; hann lá bar sem Gaddgedlar heita (Galloway), þar mœtiz Skotland ok England—from a lost verse of Arnor ?

v. 12. The same defacement of place-name. The Irish annals might be of help.

v. 13. We guess ' Öngulseyjar sund ;' l. 45 fixes it as ' south of the Isle of Man.'

v. 17 has reference to the Redburgh battle.

l. 56. Skialdar viðr, the ship [from a now half dim myth].

v. 19. The extent of Thorfin's dominion (in imitation of Othere, p. 155, and Vellekla, l. 80). The Thurs Skerries are also mentioned in Hak. S., ch. 265, but are no longer known, being some reef off the north-eastmost point of Orkney or Shetland.

v. 20. þorfinnr iarl görði þat frama-verk í Orkneyjum, at hann veitti allri hirð sínni, ok mörgum öðrum ríkum mönnum, allan vetrinn gœgnum, bæði mat ok mungát, svá at engi maðr þurfti í skytning at ganga—svá sem konungum eða iörlum er títt í öðrum löndum, at veita um Iól hirð sinni ok gestum. Svá segir Arnórr [v. 20].—Orkn. S., ch. 23. *And*—Annat öndvegi var á inn úœðra pall, gegnt konungi; skyldi þar sitja inn œzti ráðgiafi konungs fyrir hans ádrykkju, ok þótti þat mest virðing at sitja fyrir konungs ádrykkju. Sem Arnórr Iarla-skáld segir [v. 21]. Her hrósar Arnórr því, at hann sat í úœðra öndugi fyrir ádrykkju þórfinnz iarls, þá er hann var með hónum í Orkneyjum.—*Hulda*, Olaf Quiet's S.

v. 22. Hence it appears Arnor had married some relation of the earl's.

v. 23. The dead earl's two sons, Erlend and Paul.

v. 26. Mark the echo from Volospa.

l. 75. gœðingr; in Orkney the nobles (the ' hersar' of Norway) were called ' gœðings,' or *good men*, ἄριστοι.

VIII. (p. 197.) We take this to be from the Dirge on Gelli, Ari's grandfather ; Gelli built a church at Holyfell. Niala, ch. 10—Hall says to Thangbrand the missionary, ' Í hverja minning heldr þú þenna dag ?' þangbrandr segir, ' Michael engill á daginn, segir hann.' ' Hver rök fylgja engli þeim,' segir Hallr. ' Mörg,' segir þangbrandr, ' hann skal meta allt þat er þú görir, bæði gótt ok illt ; ok er hann svá miskunsamr, at hann metr allt þat meira sem vel er gört.' Hallr mælti : ' Eiga vilda ek hann mer at vin.'

IX. (p. 197.) Gótt es at fylgja dróttni, a proverb.

Thiodolf Arnorsson, (p. 199.)

I. *Magnus Flokk.*—l. 18. Infin. pret.; with acc. see above.

ll. 22, 23. There are here *two* battles, for Lürschau (Hlýrskógs-heiðr) is on the southern, the Skotborg River on the northern border of Sleswick, distanced by a day's march or two.

l. 24. It is strange to call King Magnus ' Ello konr ;' yet, if true, it is a fingerpoint to his plans and claims on England ; see our remarks, p. 178.

l. 26. All the Norse poets of this date dub Sweyn the Danish King ' Earl.'

l. 28. Read, munðot, i. e. they remembered no greater fight.

vv. 9, 10. Observe the manner of battle, staff-slings, spears, stones, arrows ; ' snœri-dorr' (sling-darts) and ' skepti-flétta' would be identical ; böslar, *a quarrel* or *crossbow bolt*, besides in Thulor, 290, a M. Lat.-Rom. word, M. Lat. *bolsonem*, French *bozoun, boujon.*

l. 39. The poet present in the battle.

l. 47. þessi orrosta var Dróttins-dag næsta fyrir Iól.—Magn. S. (Hulda), ch. 38.

l. 50. Sveinn flýði þá yfir á Fión (leaving Jutland), ch. 38.—' Fion' underneath ' í folk,' l. 52.

l. 54. We surmise ' þriðjaby' = Oðinsve in Funen, see Thulor, 130.

l. 58. Helga-nes, see Arnor, i. 44.

l. 69. þrennin, tvennin *or* þrenni, tvenni, is an older form than þrenn, etc. ; to bear the higher shield is to ' carry it off triumphantly.'

II. (p. 201.) l. 4. Borrowed from Sighvat, ii. 38.

l. 11. We suggest ' Hnikars-lund,' *Woden's grove* = Oðinsve, see Thulor, 119.

l. 22. What place can this be ? We think some harbour in Zealand ? (Thulor, 325). In the following lines we espy places in Zealand—Andwerd-wood, l. 25 ; Ringsted, l. 26 ; Sorö, l. 26 ; Kiöge, l. 30. See the map of Denmark. Here and in the following lines the prose of the Saga yields no help whatever, yet the palimpsest nature of the text is unmistakeable.

vv. 10, 11. In Schonen ; but we have been unable to recover any of the names underlying the metamorphosed text.

III. (p. 204.) l. 9. Favourite simile, cp. Bk. vi, Ditty 33 ; vol. ii, p. 76, v. 2.

l. 10. ómyndr, a law term, *a marriageable lady*, 'sub mundio ;' an ἅπ. λεγ.

l. 19. höss, *gray*, cp. Eirm. 26, Hltal. 25 (Michael V. Kalaphastes, 1041-2).

l. 21. Stól-þengill, the Greek Emperor. For his story, see Gibbon, ch. xlviii, and Finlay.

l. 28. The poets all talk of the great *hoard* that Harold brought from the East.

l. 29. hléborð, lea-board, 'shelter board,' the side off the wind; 'larboard' is etymologically, though not in sense, identical.

v. 12. The ships were drawn up in a wedge [hamalt], the king's ship foremost ; a shield fence all around : but what of ' hömlur ?' See Steenstrup's Danelag.

l. 42. hremsa, *arrow*, see Thulor, 290. Finna-giold, Excursus, vol. ii, p. 481.

l. 50. Read, Sveinn . . . suðr at gunni ; svá er sagt at konungr hefði með sér til orrosto sex iarla, var einn af þeim Finnr Árnason.—Har. S., ch. 78.

l. 59. Eiga auðan plóg, a fearfully realistic phrase ; 'plow' was originally, as here a wheeled vehicle.

l. 60. A proverb = to run as if chased by the Fiend. In the translation v. 20 follows here, but the text seems right.

l. 65. hrót-garmr = hrót-gandr (house-devourer), Thulor, 525.

l. 66. gagn, *gain, crop;* ' glóð,' glede or glowing ember.

l. 68. Liðar, the menn of Liðir or Lier, near Drammen?

l. 69. Halfs galli (fire), synonym drawn from King Half's story, cp. Yt. l. 132.

l. 71. færa starf til króks, metaphor from anchorage : friðr namsk at hvarfi (*peace ensued?*), cp. at-hvarf, hverfa at.

l. 73. A proverb.

l. 76. A proverb = *to lie as one has made his bed.*

l. 88. Yrso burðr = Rolf Craki, Yrsa's son ; cp. Mill Song, 79. See l. 69 above.

IV. (p. 208.) l. 8. It was merely on account of the 'ungr allvaldr' (l. 8) that we put these verses under the year 1048; we now simply read 'yngvi' (yngvi en árar drengja allvalldz í sió falla). The Saga distinctly states that shortly before the battle at the River Niz, King Harold had a great Dragon built on the River Nith (of 35 rooms = 70 oars, modelling her upon Tryggvason's Serpent).—þann vetr er Haraldr sat í Níðarósi, sem fyrr er ritað, lét hann reisa skip mikit ; þat var skeið ; var þat gört eptir vexti Orms-ins-Langa, ok vandat at öllu sem mest ; var dreka-höfuð á framm, enn aptr krókr, ok vóro svírar allt golli búnir. þat skip var half-fertogt at rúma tali, ok mikit at því, ok var þat it fríðasta ; lét konungr allan búnað vanda til skipsins, bæði segl ok reiða, akkeri ok strengi . . . Enn er váraði . . . lét Haraldr konungr setja út á ána skip þat it mikla ; síðan lét hann upp setja dreka-höfuðin. þá kvað þiodolfr [verse 1]. Síðan er skip þetta it fríða var buit, þá hélt konungr því út eptir ánni. Svá segir þióðolfr [v. 2]. þá var vandaðr miök róðr á drekanum. Svá segir þióðolfr [v. 3].—Har. S. (Hulda), ch. 76. In this ship we may take it for granted Harold went to England a few years later, in 1066; and the very building thereof is a silent witness to the plans he was maturing while waiting for King Edward's death.—This is the finest of Thiodolf's poems ; one more evidence for the *later* date.

l. 9. rœði, here the *oar ;* verri, the *wake* of oar or rudder.

l. 11. fer-kleyf sæ-fang (pl.), the *square-loomed oars.*

l. 13. Corrupt ; sarglar vítt? the sound of the oar sweeping through the water? sæ-fang is suspicious here ; the law against repetition is rarely if ever violated : ' ekkjan,' in l. 15, is also very doubtful.

l. 15. heglda, the stream *beaten* by the swift stroke, as by hail.

l. 16. So Homer calls the oars the *wings* of the ship, Odyss. xi. 125.

V. (p. 209.) Hléseyjar hlym-garðr = the Cattegat.

VIII. (p. 210.) l. 2. hæll, Thulor, 408.

l. 9. Sýstot suðr, probably thus.

v. 5. Pretty clear as to the sense, though the text is not quite safe; miðla mál, *to mediate.*

l. 21. Read, Hitt hefi-ek heyrt; and l. 22, góð sýsl es þat, *this is a blessed piece of work.*

l. 23. Construe, þeir, ok öll ferð, haldi svá sœrom í fullom friði (friði fullom?).

IX. (p. 211.) l. 1. hefnendr (l. 4) evidences that the verse was made *after* the king's death; hence we have to read either, 'fallinn siá til vallar,' *or*, 'þótt sé fylkir fallinn sialfr til vallar.'

l. 4. True hawks, cp. Arnor, i. 5.

X. (p. 211.) l. 3. Iarislaf of Novgorod, King Harold's patron during his exile after Sticklestead.

l. 7. aka e-m í öngan krók, a proverbial phrase, to drive one into a corner.

l. 8. Læsir, the Lech, a Slavonic people: Liðsmenn (cp. þingamenn), cp. svá segir í flokki þeim, er þá var ortr af Liðs-mönnum, Skiold. S. (Knytl.), ch. 14; the Lithsmen's Song, p. 106. In both instances Lithsmen is a technical word.

XI. (p. 212.) The story in Edda, translated above, pp. 18, 19, of Garfred the Blacksmith Giant. The King and his poet see a Tanner fighting a Blacksmith.— Says the king, 'Make a song on them, one to be Giant Garfred and the other Thor' [v. 2]. And again, when the verse was made, 'Well done,' says the king. 'Now make one Sigfred the slayer of Fafni and the other Fafni the Serpent, and name each from his craft.'—Har. S., ch. 101. The poet makes a comic transposition in his epithets, calling,—þórr smið-belgja = Garfred, and, Iötunn hafra-kiötz = þórr: húða hrœkkvi skafl = brák. Read, Geirröðar, and construe, Smiðbelgja þórr (the giant) varp eldingom (fire) or þræto-þorpi (mouth) at hafra kiötz Iötni (Thor): and, heiða hrœkkvi-skafls glaðr (the Tanner = Thor) tók hlióð-greipum (*with his mouth*) við þeiri sio smiðjo Geirröðar [of the *Smithy-Garfred* = the *Blacksmith*]:

And v. 1. Sleggjo Sigurðr (*Sledge-hammer* Sigfred = the *Blacksmith*), and, brákar Snákr (the Serpent of the brakes, id., see Dict., p. 77 b): leista heiði (the *leather* heath = Gnita heath of the myth): il-vegs (foot's) kiljo (*brogues'*) Ormr (the *Tanner*); nauta leðrs naðr (*neat leather's Serpent*, id.); Tangar konungr (the *King of the Tong* = Garfred the Smith).

l. 8. Read, Geirröðar.

XII. sæpráðr, read 'sí-þráðr,' qs. síð-þráðr, *oakum*, for caulking; see Nicolaysen's Wicking Ship; bits of it are found in the seams of the Wicking ship of 1880. (Hence mend Dict. 532 a, s. v. síðraðr.)

Minor Poets, (p. 212.)

Odd Kikina-scald, (p. 214.)—l. 3. þessi orrosta var Dróttins dag næsta fyrir Iól [Magn. S. (Hulda), ch. 38]. Under the impossible word ohlít*uleg* we surmise, óhlítin dag, and under 'sunnan,' Sunno, i. e. Sunday.

l. 17. langar limar leiða, metaph., cp. Old Wols. Pl., l. 16, where we should perhaps read, 'langar leiða limar.' The king's death has planted long, undying woe in my breast. Such mention of the bitter fruit of passion and its growth is very archaic, and no doubt a citation or imitation here (from O. W. L.?).

Bolwerk, (p. 215.)—l. 1. The king's action is not quite clear. One looks for something stronger in the verse.

l. 15. reið-mæltr, *ready spoken;* the poets are, for rhyme's sake, fond of 'reiðr,' meaning not = wroth, but *rathe,* prompt, cp. p. 219, l. 14; 224, l. 11.

l. 17. *The king stepped the mast in the heavy sea* (omitted in translation).

l. 18. Read miollo (?) for 'mioll á,' and construe, skúrr laust á dýra skiald-rim, miollo stokkinn skokks þröm (apposition).

l. 22. The emperor's name hidden here?

Walgard, (p. 216.)—l. 2. skipt, a Lat.-Byz. word, *excubium,* Byz. Gr. ἐσκύβιον. Ari explains that Harold got the usual largesse at an emperor's three times. If this be true and drawn from a poem, the dates would be April 11, 1034, after Romanos III ; Dec. 14, 1041, after Michael IV ; and April 21, 1042, after Michael V.

l. 3. Italy is meant; can there be any idea of Bruttium under 'breiðo?'

l. 8. stopðir [akin to stapi], bolt upright.

l. 12. Overlaid; we surmise, sviptir . . . Sigtúnom skript húna. Snorri calls the sail hún-skript. Hann sneri fyrst til Sviþióðar, ok lagði til Sigtúna. Svá segir Valgarðr af Velli.—[Har. S. (Hulda), ch. 17.]

vv. 9, 10. All overlaid. The king seems to have moored his ships at the mouth of Roskeld-fiord: names still unimpaired are, Selund (l. 20), Roskeld (l. 21): overlaid, but still recognisable, are, Helsinge (l. 23), Ramlöse (l. 24); the rest doubtful; perhaps Skioldelöv (l. 25): what more there were we are unable to disinter.

l. 33. beði (‿‿), impossible word; 'fyrir bardi?'

Illugi, (p. 218.)—Would we had the whole poem with its interwoven mythological sentences.

ll. 3, 4. Read hélt, cp. Old Wols. Pl., v. 44, which poet Illugi must have known, for 'eiskiald' (*heart*) is a direct loan.

l. 5 we have been unable to restore; if under duglom (an impossible word) lies 'deigla,' *gold,* the *hoard* Sigfred won from Fafni is meant.

Grani, (p. 218.)—Horn-skógr, a forest near Randers, Jutland: þiólarnes, Tiele, near River Gudenaa, Jutland. Mark the favourite Craki story. Cp. Thiodolf Arnorsson, iii, ll. 88, 90.

Thorarin, (p. 218.)—The blinding story again, cp. Thiodolf, iii, v. 5, above, p. 205, l. 22.

Thorleik, (p. 219.)—Much overlaid. '*North*' of Heathby; but *south,* Thiodolf, i. 22 : 'hauk*storða*' and '*norðan*' are both wrong.

l. 15. húnferils hreinar, *ships,* cp. p. 101, l. 7.

l. 23. þengils býr, some place?

v. 9. Sveinn konungr hélt flota sínom suðr undir Hléssey (or Sámsey) ok hitti þar siau skip af Norðmönnum, þat var leiðangrs lið ok bœndr ór Víkinni. þeir báðu griða, ok buðu fé fyrir sik. þess getr þorleikr [v. 9].—Har. S. (Hulda), ch. 53. 'Samsey' or 'Læssoe' and 'seven ships' must all have been in the unadulterated verse, and can even now be partly seen underneath.

Stuf Blind, (p. 222.)—Haraldr offraði til grafar Dróttins ok til kross ins helga ok annarra heilagra dóma á Iórsala-landi, svá miklo fé í golli ok görsimom, at torvelt er mörkum at telja. þá friðaði hann veginn allt út til Iórdánar, ok drap þar reyfara ok annat illþýðis-folk. Sem Stufr segir [v. 3]. Fór hann þá til Iórdánar, ok laugaðiz þar í ánni, sem síðr er til annarra palmara.—[Har. S. (Hulda), ch. 11.]

v. 9. Haraldr konungr, faðir hans, ok aðrir konungar fyrir hónum, vóru vanir at drekka af dýra-hornum, ok bera öl um eld, ok drekka minni á þann er gegnt sat; enn Óláfr konungr [his son] lét hvern drekka á þann sem vildi. Svá segir Stúfr skald [v. 9].—Ol. S. K. (Hulda), ch. 4. Refers to the change in Olaf the Quiet's reign of the old Norse hall (fires in the middle) to the Normannic hall, with the dais or high table at the end. See Reader, pp. 370–71.

Stein, (p. 223.)—l. l. 5. Ulfr, see p. 232.

l. 11. Mend interpolations, and construe, rísta þangs láð (acc.) and ' sunda mörom.

l. 20. Cp. Thiodolf, i, l. 33.

l. 26. linnz láttr (gold's) sveigjandi (king).

l. 30. Read, Selundar kon ? (the Danish King).

II. (p. 224.) This is the *last* of the restored court poems, and there is none of the whole list more corrupt.

l. 1. Construe, Ek kveð fyrr at brag þeima helgan heim-tiallz ræsi an fyrða (gen. pl., 'king' understood) : the King of Heavens first, the king of men next.

vv. 2, 3 refer to the battle of the River Niz (Olaf then a mere boy).

ll. 13, 14. Too bad, even for a court poet, out-Heroding Herod !

l. 21. í Flióti. By this the Fleet in the Humber is meant.

l. 40. Note the epithetal Engla œgir, *Terror of the English*, used of *this* king of all others just after Stamford Bridge ! This is court poetry with a vengeance !

Thorkettle, (p. 227.)—v. 2. Very fine and gentle; l. 5 is the only time that the Conqueror is named.

King Harold, (p. 228.)—l. 5. Mark the galley being called stag, ' hart.'

l. 7, etc. For ' renna ' read ' nenna,' *to travel, journey*, see Dict. s. v., p. 453 b.

l. 9. The four ' rooms ' in the waist of the ship.

v. 4. We only have left *six* out of the eight, cp. p. 276, v. 2, which is the better text and fuller of the two.

II. (p. 229.) lirla or 'lítla,' to dandle, a nursery word, gov. dat.

l. 10. iast-ostr, *a yeasting cheese*, some kind of fresh cheese : construe, ey-baugs þengil, the *sea-king* = Harold.

l. 19. Buttered brose or porridge was a favourite dish of the Norsemen.

l. 21. þangs þialmi, *the sea-weed's dyke*, i.e. the bond *or* wall of the coast = the sea, see Excursus, p. 457.

l. 23. House-carles, a king's or earl's picked body-guard.

l. 29. A proverb; read, Lítið er lauki gæft *til* auka.

III. (p. 231.) A bit of banter. l. 3. hrotti, qs. hrunti, cp. ' Hrunting ' of Beowolf.

l. 19. King Harold was *never* in any waters south of England ; neither the Channel nor the Bay of Biscay did he ever behold. We surmise Serkland and sveif, unless ' St. Angelo ' be meant.

Ulf, (p. 232.)—þinga-manni, thus (not þingmanni); ' þinga-manna-lið' is the true old form.

§ 4. KINGS ERIC AND MAGNUS BARELEG.

Mark.—I. *Eric's Praise*, (p. 235.)

We are now at the end of the overpainted court poems—henceforward, though the text be now and then faulty, it is never wilfully so—we shall therefore, though sparingly, give a few of the ' kennings.'

King : flotna vörðr 4, folk-vörðr 97, folka treystir 62, ástvinr aldar 61, herjar holl-vinr 67, vísdóms grœðir 66, hersa reyfir 64, hersa máttar reynir 89, harra spialli 72, sigrs valdari 21, fremdar ráða fœðir 6.—As *Vanquisher :* iöfra ríkir 84, iarla meiðir 96, Vinda fergir, rýrir 10, 18.—As *Justice :* svik-folks-eyðir 13, rógs hegnir 50, dolga steypir 93.

Waves: mar-fiöll 98.—*Earth:* él-kers (heaven's) botn 4. For the rest, see Excursus, p. 484.

l. 5. Cp. Sighvat, vi. 15.

ll. 12 and 41. 'hlýða,' a bulwark put up against the waves, a word not found in Thulor; it appears to be the same as 'varða' or varta, Arnor, i. 9.

l. 16. Read, 'hodda' slongvir?

l. 19. Cp. Sighvat, vii. 6.

l. 27. balkat, *fenced,* of the Lagoon City.

l. 31. átt-konr Yngva; we have here the true word; for 'átt-runn,' in Hym., l. 76, Yt. 114, we take to be but false forms: note, that Mark is a voice anterior to the remaniements.

l. 52. hömlo vígs *or* viggs, uncertain.

l. 72. láð-menn, an English loan word (láð = leið), *pilots,* lode-men.

l. 93. hryggva, verb impers.

IV. (p. 239.) Cp. Excursus, p. 458.

Gisl Illugason, (p. 240.)

'Kennings,' Ímðar faxa (wolf's) alendr (men): Báleygs vina (the earth).

l. 35. Lawman, King Godred Crowan's son, 1095–8 and 1103–8.

l. 40. Woden's wind-maker, King Magnus.

l. 52. hvít-mylingar, *arrows,* see Thulor, 288; cp. Biorn, v. 9.

vv. 14–16. The storm and the glorious ships are finely described.

l. 73. The black standard ' Hell' is worthily named.

II. l. 3. Two saws.

Biorn, (p. 243.)—Harmr, Frith of, see Thulor, 679. Biorn is a model annalist, brief and fact-ful.

l. 13. vall-baugs (snake's) vengi (earth = gold).

l. 25. Note, Sanntiri [Gael. *ceann tir* = Headland], hence it appears that the *n* was *still heard* in Bareleg's day; later on it was contracted into Sátiri.

Thorkel, (p. 245.)—l. 3. Skialg, Erling Skialgson's grandson, a picturesque 'maker.' Mark how he cites Egil's death-words, v. 2, and the king's order of the day, v. 5.

l. 4. A proverbial phrase; now, kasta steini um *megn* ser.

v. 4. A fine verse on the encounter with the earls.

II. For *swollen* read *cold.*

Stray verses, (p. 246.)—II. l. 1. Read vigg, i. e. of vigg tyggja.

l. 4. Note the height of the mast, ' seventy feet:' the alliteration is a warrant that only ' seventy' or ' sixty' can stand here: the ' seventy' of the MSS. of course is the right word.

III. (p. 247.) l. 5. Note the rhyme, hvat'r betra (what is better). In King Magnus' day one would think that the s was still sounded.

l. 9. varpa á glæ, a proverbial phrase, cp. Lay of Arinbiorn, l. 89.

l. 15. 'ingjan,' here an appellative (*lassie,* from Irish *inghean* = a daughter), cp. Bk. vi, Ditty 55 *a.*

Halldor Squaller, (p. 249.)—l. 23. ' af tig gamall,' *aged off teen,* cp. Lat. *un-de-viginti.* The Crusader King would in the year 1109 have been *nineteen* years old.

Thorwald, (p. 250.) In the superscription read ' Blondo skald.'

I. Note how the poet brings in the hero Sigurd to compliment his namesake.

II. (p. 250.) The son of Bor, Buri's son = Woden.

Curtcloak, (p. 250.)—I. *As men have heard, how, in time past, the race of kings followed the wise Craki* [Danish mythical king].

l. 27. kvik-sáttar; we have here the same word as above, p. 160, l. 13.

II. The men were Hacon Serksson, surnamed Mor-strútr, and Arni Fioro-Skeifr.

Einarr Skulason, (p. 252.)—l. 5. Construe, und sólar ranni, *beneath the sky.*

l. 15. hauka-setrs (hand's) leyg (gold's) hati (king).

l. 16. Note the Western form 'vatri' for the Norse 'vatn.'

II. l. 5. A proverb of the usual fatalistic kind.

§ 5. THE GILCHRIST POETS, (p. 261.)

Ivarr, (p. 261.)—l. 10. Dáfinns, a Norse imitation of Dávíð; Niala names a 'Dagvið' of Caithness; the famed 'Dagfinnr' in Hak. Saga is probably merely = David, and only apparently a Norse name.

l. 17. morð-als (sword's) metendr (men).

l. 48. roðo-veðr, *red weather* = foul weather.

l. 55. snekkjo sneisar, the *galley skewers* = the masts.

l. 72. For 'fall' read 'fylli?' The Elbe, here and l. 78, is the Gotha River.

ll. 90 sqq. Vágar, a fishing-place, North Norway [Lat. 66°]: Byrda [Lat. 65°], see p. 46, l. 63: Valsnes, North More: Kvildrom, on the south-east border.

Halldor Squaller, (p. 266.)—Eric II, the Danish King: Sarp, the great fall in the River Glommen (Sarpen).

l. 9. Sigars fiánda (Hagbard's) grand-meiðr = *the gallows.*

v. 4. This verse is in O. H. L. given as Sighvat's at Nesia; but on the face of it it cannot be his. The only place where, having regard to the context, we could place it is here: by the 'town' (l. 16) Bergen is meant.

Einarr Skulason, (p. 267.)

Pages 267-274, as well as Geisli, Rekstefja, etc., are all by the 'remanieur' or contemporaries. One blesses the fates for not having preserved more: though we may miss a few historical facts, in the lost poems.—I. We are here in the very thick of Einar's 'kennings:' seiðs (fish's) hryn leiðar (sea's) eldr (gold's) skerðir (king) 2; and gifr (ogress') skæs (wolf's) gran (lip) rióðr (king) 4; Ello (Engl. king's) geitunga (eagle's) líf-giafi (king) 8; svan-bekkjar (sea's) sól (gold's) þverrir (king) 12.

III. (p. 268.) Aberdeen, Hartlepool, Whitby, Langton are known, but not Pilwick and Sharpreef [Scarborough?]. These verses are imitated in Krakomal.

IV. (p. 269.) Gray Holm, in the mouth of Christiania Firth (here Sigurd Slembi was slain, Nov. 12, 1139). The Kinglets are the four Gilchristsons. l. 2 is misbracketed; read 'geir-þing,' and unbracket it.

l. 11. Harold Maddadson, Earl of Orkney.

v. 16. Son of Day = Gregorius Dagsson, a Norse baron: Simon Skalp slew Sigurd Gilchrist.

VI. (p. 270.) Snæ-grund; probably *Iceland* is here meant.—[Reader, p. 3.]

VII. (p. 270.) Fight in the mouth of the Gotha River, 1159.

VIII. (p. 271.) The 'kennings' on the axe are curious:—(1) He dubs the axe the *child of Freyja*, whose two daughters were Hnoss (Jewel) and Gersemi (Treasure), ll. 1, 5, 8. The axe is inlaid with *gold;* as *Freyja's tears*, Oðs beð-vino augna-regn 19, Freyjo hvarm-þeyr 12, Mardallar grátr 19, Freys niptar (sister's, Freyja's) brá-driptir 4; as *Fenja's meal* 29. (2) He calls *the axe an ogress:* fiornis (helmet's) griðr 24; hlýr-sólar (shield's) hála 13; iastar (willow's) herkja 16; lastly, as *plague*, Herjans (Woden's) hattar (helmet's) sótt 15.

l. 23. Construe, geima (sea's) eldr (gold), *and* sióðs snær (silver).—*Men:* Rævils fold (sea) viggs (ship's) ríðendr 25.

l. 31. Construe, Heita blakks (ship's) hlýr (shield's) skyldir (man); Beita borgar (sea's) bál (gold's) grimmr (*open-handed*); *and*, heims skála (sky's) vafur-logi (the sun), and so on—ad nauseam.

IX. (p. 272.) haus-miöll (hair): skarar fiall (the head): strandar aurriða (serpent's) stallz (gold's) strind (woman).

We cull a few of the 'kennings' of the 'poets,' pp. 272–274.—*Men*, arnar hungrs eyðendr, Thorbiorn 3; hlunnz hafreiðar (ship's) hlœðir, 5; flóðs hyrjar (gold's) stœkkvir, p. 274. 18: *battle*, tognings (sword's) veðr, p. 272. 10: *shield*, her-skript, Kolli 8: *sword*, sár-íss, Kolli 10: *ship*, vág-fylvingr, Thorbiorn 4; Hogna vagn, p. 274. 17; Geitis glaðr, and lesta hestr, Klœng: *wolf*, gríðar fákr, Thorbiorn 7; ulfs (ok) arnar barn, p. 273. 19: *shafts*, iarna þrumo miöll, p. 273. 14: *waves*, hlunnz heiða (sea's) fannir, p. 274. 18: *winter*, orms tregi, Asgrim 2.

Occasional verses, (p. 276.)

v. 1. márs mýrar (*mew's moors*, the sea): branda elgr (ship).

v. 2. Doll's Cave in the Isle of Dollsey, off Sondmore, Norway. Ragnwald entered the cave, as told in Orkney Saga.

v. 4. Ragna, a noble Orkney lady, her son Thorstan: grúpan, *a sausage;* 'Morlandi' was a sobriquet given to the Icelanders.

v. 5. aldr'=aldri is here=*ever*, not=aldrigi: read, frán-stall, *the head*, governed by 'féldo;' 'frán' has here reference to the *eyes:* hauk-strindar (hand's) Hlokk = Lady Ragna.

v. 6. For 'midævi' and 'Imbolum'—both imitations of Greek words—see Dict., p. 426 b: rengðiz, i. e. wrengðiz (*to writhe*): þengils mágr, Earl Erling, King Sigurd Crusader's son-in-law.

v. 7. Playing on the word Acre [Palestine], called Akrs-borg, Bk. vi, No. 54.

v. 8. The earl's narrow escape, see Orkney S. A story like this is told of William by Wace.

v. 9. The cry of distress and disgust of a court poet, his craft being out of fashion, cp. 21, 22 below.

v. 10. gyrða um svangann, *to buckle a belt round the waist* so as to keep hunger out (metaph.) l. 6. Mend and read, þoli or . . . víti fyr þat: Bakki, the Cloister Bank in Throndheim, Norway.

v. 11. Read, leikari; and límí barðan príma, the time being *beaten* by the rod.

v. 12. Read, ási (appell.), the *yard*.

v. 13. lang-viðris lengi, *long-weather-long*=for ever so long.

v. 14. víg-garðz (shield's) veðr (battle) eggjandi (man).

v. 16. Men of seven Norse counties.

v. 17. Róða (sea-king's) glym-vollo (sea). At this time—King Swerri's reign and for a while after—'súð' (see above) is a favourite name for a ship of war (Máriusúð, Óláfs-súð).

v. 18. hlýrs fagr-goti (ship); reyðar (whale's) rym-vollr (sea).

v. 19. 'fant' (Romance word), *a footman*, hence *tramp.*

v. 20. sólar þung-stóls (heaven's) konungr (God).

v. 22. Note 'umb;' in the twelfth century the *b* was sounded; the mod. sound is 'umm.'

v. 25. A metaphorical phrase ; Icelanders now say, það er komið annað hlióð í strokkinn.

v. 28. Sverris-borg = Swerri's Castle in Bergen.

vv. 30–34. Here the *steep* Sanda [of the northern Hebrides], but *flat* Sanda [the isle off Cantyre?], p. 244, l. 23 : hafnar mark, a pile or cairn raised, cp. vol. i, p. 154, l. 81. Eiði, Tarbert, a place in the western range of the Hebrides.

vv. 36–39. Gylva láðs (sea's) báls (gold's) hlynr (bishop), and, unnar elg (ship's) rennir, *id.*: himna prýði, the hosts of heaven? cp. p. 302, l. 2.

v. 43. Ígultanni = Biörn, also iugtanni, p. 239, l. 2.

v. 45. ölbærð = ölværð, i. e. al-værð, hospitality (*lb = lv*).

Geisli, (p. 284.)

The subject-matter of this and the following twelfth-century poems is given in the translation : we shall therefore treat it very shortly. The 'kennings' (not attended to in the translation) being characteristic, we cull the most representative, i. e. the most crabbed ones, leaving the rest to the reader's ingenuity :—

God, Christ.—*From sky and sun :* allz heims um-geypnandi (compasser of) 64, veðr-hallar vísi 6, dag-bóls konungr 20, byrjar vegs (sky's) tungla (sun's) lofðungr 254, tungla rannz lofðungr 183, sólar bóls siklingr 267, grundar sal-vörðr 74, vagn-ræfrs vísi 284, hauðr-tialda harri 75 : better are, aldar yfir-skiöldungr 260, heims dómari 165, heims læknir 228, réttlætis sunna 14, iarðar fyrða líf 11.—*Angels :* himnesk ferð 166, öðlinga döglings hirð 20.—*Virgin Mary :* flœðar stiarna 8.— *Heaven :* himna salr 263, Goðs höll 25, Kristz höll 42, allz ráðanda höll 18.

Saint : miskunnar sólar (Christ's) geisli 3, Goðs hallar (heaven's) geisli 25, röðuls tyggja vinr 35, tungla rannz lofðungs (God's) vinr 183, Lausnara langvinr 269, Lausnara spialli 117, himna-sal-konungs limr 263, Kristz limr 130, Goðs liðr, Goðs ríðari 71, fyrða fár-skerðandi 252, harm-skerðandi 150, þegn-prýði 41.

A man, from slaughter and gold, often applied to the saint himself : *from gold,* orms landa árr 92, lyngs hrœkkvi-baugs (snake's) láttr (gold's) stríðandi 62, snáka vangs slöngvir 152, brim-loga slöngvir 223, straums sólar sokkvir 109, vala strætis fasta týnir 97, linnz grundar lestir 125, gialfrs grundar nið (moon's) branda (gold's) skerðir 157, lagar eld-broti 210 : *from battle,* hræ-síks þrimo gœðir 280, grímo glaum-vekjandi 186 : *from shield,* víga-skýs veléndr 271, baug-skialdar beiðir 73 : *sword-reddener,* alm-reyrs litoðr 66, eggja marg-litendr 233 : *wolf-battener, raven-feeder,* Hugins munn-ríóðr 53, ulf-nistandi 99 : *from ships,* unnar skíð-rennandi 161, lög-skíðs syndir 80, Reifniss rökn stefnandi 194.

Battle, Hamðes klæða hríð 208, barð-rökn (ship's) röðuls (shield's) veðr 212 : *sword,* vettrima maðr 186, valbasta röðull 172, mundriða borgar (shield's) galli 190, gyldis kindar (wolf's) góm-sparri 192.

Gold, más iarðar eisa 197.

Eye, heil-himin-tungl 236, sión-braut 91 : *mouth,* bragar stóll 266 : *tongue,* orða-hlýða 102, óðar ár 160, mál-tól 76, bragar-tól 198 : *hand,* baug-nes 273, vala-stræti 98.

Epithets.—All are common-place; one notices only, hríð-blásin (of the sky) 27, tand-rauðr (of gold) 97, nagl-skaddr (of Christ) 270.

ll. 1, 2. Dubious. A poem, Líknarbraut (Introd., § 16), has imitated our passage :

Einn lúktu upp sem ek bœni : óðar rann ok gef sanna,

hence perhaps we may read, eins má óð, *sem ek bœni* (as I now pray).

l. 5. Read, húms?

ll. 9, 10. Also obscure ; construe, þat var auð-finnendom fyrir betra (liósi) annars ómióss röðuls.

v. 31. For the story, referred to by the poet, touching Guthorm, see Kings' Lives.

l. 37. Thus we understand this line.

l. 76. Construe, fyrr var hept skini sólar er . . .

l. 157. fyrir Skauti, some point on the Wendish coast, Stræti ? Strelitz ?

l. 178. Einriði, a Norse noble who travelled in the East c. 1149, and again with Earl Ragnwald of Orkney, year 1151–53.

l. 191. þátti, pret. from þekkja, cp. Oddr. 65, Haust. 64, Lithsmen's Song 15.

l. 231. A saying.

l. 235. Obscure ; construe, líknar lög ; but what means ' kröfð ?'

l. 241. Construe, lamiðs fótar, stýförar tungo, út-stunginna augna.

ll. 250–252. Citations from the Vulgate.

l. 268. Construe, hvarr er greiðir lof hilmis, taki ást ens hæsta . . . siklings.

l. 279. Construe, ek fæ holl laun göfugs óðar, Goðs blezon, ef . . . líkar.

Rekstefja, (p. 295.)

The metre is here the chief thing, we therefore give but the pick of the ' kennings.'

King, *man*, rand-hvels (shield's) remmi-þundr 2, skialdar linna (sword's) runnr 3, þróttar þing-Baldr 4, þróttar éla (battle's) blik (sword's) ruðr 8, hræ-linnz (sword's) hlióm-váttandi 11, göndlar gný-linnz runnr 97, ullar kióla (shield's) él (battle) Freyr 22, ölna foldar (hand's) eld-ruðr 108, Sköglar elda sker (shield's) Baldr 26, sigr-brandz her-lundr 36, göndlar þeyss éla skyndir 42, skialda hyr-baldr 99, morð-linnz hvessi-meiðr 54, fiornis (helmet's) mána (spear's) fleygendr 63, rán-síks (gold's) remmi 85, róg-svellir 85, unn-eldz yppi-runnr 91, sköglar borðz hríðar skelfir 114, branda storms (battle) leygs (sword's) styr (battle) lundr 116, gunn-ellz geymi runnr 127, hóps hyr-niorðr 138, hand-báls lundr 134, hring-skóðs (sword's) él- (battle) svellz (sword's) herði-meiðr 125, hior flóðs (blood's) hnig-reyrs (sword's) hnykki-meiðr 92.

Sword, Sköglar tandr (fire) 79 : *wolf*, troll-marr 66 : *ship*, frón-bandz (sea's) fœri-andrar 25, Ekkils ýti-blakkr 63 : *hand*, hauk-ióðs (hawk's) býr 30 : *poetry*, þund-regn (?) 50 : *winter*, húns nótt 49 : *sea*, ölna vangr 58, margra iarða mein-garðr 118.

l. 37. tvenni, older form than tvenn.

l. 55. Read, skolptar.

l. 67. peita, spear, a foreign word, Thulor, 287 : ' speat ' rather than ' spear.'

l. 92. ' Slœmr ' occurs here for the first time.

l. 110. ríp, acc. governed by renndi.

ll. 123, 124. The King seen among angels ; this story, given in the Reader, p. 163, is manifestly an echo from Adamnan's S. Columba, lib. iii, ch. 16 ; even the incidents are the same, the curious on-looker, the stole-clad angels, the promise never to tell it as long as the saint be alive : only in Tryggvason it is in a *house*, in S. Columba a *hill*, the Cnoc Angel (Angel's Hill), or Sithan more (the Great Fairy Hill), well known to all visitors of that lovely island.

l. 133. Corrupt text. Steinarr evidently wishes for the canonization of the elder Olave.

II. *Love Song*, (p. 300.)—Holm leggjar (stone's) hilmir (dwarf)—here a pun, litr meaning *colour* and *dwarf* :—*lady, from gold and gems*, flóðs-fúrs hirði-Sif, and Hiadninga griótz (gem's) tróða 5, straum-tungls velti-stoð 6, hring-skögul 1, reyr-þvengs rastar (gold's) selja 2.

A man, fiarð-ellds fleygi-Nirðir 13, Viðblinda (giant's) galtar (whale's or porpoise's) sval-teigar (sea's) raf (gold) kastandi 3 (fourfold kenning). Edda Skskm. says—Whales are called Withblind's hogs; he was a giant and fished for whales out in the deep as for fish.

Battle, ben-vargs (sword's) hregg 10: *tongue*, óðar lokarr 8 [from Egil's poems]: *stone*, foldar negg [hnegg=heart] 12, bókar sól 11 [image from book-illumination].

Iomsvikinga-drapa, (p. 302.)

Much finer than the preceding poem, which we are right glad to leave behind; only a few kennings, and these not complex ones, are here met with. It is from this Drapa that the Rimur composers get to know about Bui and Wain.

King, *man*, Hamðis fald (helmet's) ruðr 54, rand-orma riðöendr 68, morð báls-meiðr 62, hialma skóðs (axe's) hregg (battle's) viðr 79, geira gný miklandi 140, hiörva hregg-viðr 118, -boði 143, yggjar eld broti 145, egg-hríðar Ullr 172, yggjar él-svellandi 170, randa þrimo Ullr 175.

Lady, dorgar vangs (sea's) eld (gold's) reið 14.

Axe, fiörniss (helmet's) fála 165 : *sword*, hring-serkja böl 102.

Head, brúna borg 110: *bones*, mergjar salr 123 : poetical is only *hail*, skýja gríót 127.

A few of the *epithets* are noticeable—hand-fögr (of a lady) 10: hauk-lyndr 32, 167, frán-lyndr 97, veg-rœkinn 133, þrek-stœrðr 135, hugum-strangr 156 (of a hero): elri skœðr (of fire) 74: heldir (of ships) 63 : ísogr (of waves) 64 : haukligar (of vows) 43 : orm-frán (of eyes) 127 : sið-forn (of pagans) 27.

l. 2. at ferðar prýði, at this proud gathering.

l. 4. Necessary emendation (if but).

v. 2. Mythologically interesting. Here, and only here, is a notice of Woden getting wise by sitting underneath water-falls; cp. '*Fossegrimen*' and '*Nökken*' in modern Norse Tales: under hanga, under gallows, see Havam. and Yngl. Saga: unfortunately a line is here torn off, for one would like to know what stood there.

l. 9. úteitan (neut.)

l. 21. We guess 'suðr.'

l. 47. fíkjom ; he is fond of that word, cp. ll. 104, 163.

l. 160. Paper MSS., and hence editors, have filled up, ' sáttir á einni nátto,' but nátto (bisyll.) is a modern form, appearing first at the time of the Reformation.

Konungatal, (p. 310.)

A few kennings are worth noticing—*Earth* (Norway), þundar beðja 33, 80, Hárs víf 77, Yggs man 102, 187: *Hell*, Ása dolgs (Loki's) einga dóttir 36 : *ice*, hæings hallar (sea's) ræfr 16, nykra landz (sea's) næfr 298 : *sky*, skýja laupr (cloud-basket) 315 : *winter*, faðmins (snake's) galli 94, snáka stríð 142 : *head*, hattar stallr 84.

Epithets, none very striking ; the mention of the kings' graves is very interesting.

l. 1. Somehow wrong ; if 'skilit,' 'at ' must go out, cp. Hallfred, i. 44.

l. 25. Note the boundary of Norway ; see above, Ottar, i. 65.

l. 140. Read, háleitt ?

l. 163. Necessary emendations.

l. 295. The metre requires Ioan ; in the twelfth century ' John ' was bisyllabic.

l. 315. laupi, our 'lip,' as in 'seed-lip,' an easy and necessary emendation. Render, *the cloud-basket*.

l. 325. It is hard to see exactly how the *thirty* are told up.

Oddmior, (p. 321.) (Haraldr) hélt ina síðosto orrosto við konung þann er Skeiðar-

Brandr hét í Hafrs-firði fyrir Iaðri, ok flýði Brandr til Danmarkar, ok fell í orrosto á Vinnlandi, sem segir í kvæði því er heitir Oddmiór, er gört er um konunga tal, með þessom orðom [v. 1].—Agrip. ch. 2. Is not this a confused recollection of Arnor, i. 20? (the Wends come in just afterward in that poem too.) Can Odd-mior have been the traditional title of Arnor's Hrynhenda Drapa?

Iorun, etc. (p. 322.)

Overlaid fragments, thus earlier than Bareleg's or Olaf Quiet's time.

Konungr varð þesso ákafliga reiðr [ll. 1, 2], ok samnaði her saman, ok fór á hendr þrœndum; enn er þat spyrr Halfdan Svarti, þá býðr hann út liði ok skipom, ok verðr all-fiölmennr, ok lagði út til Staðs [Cape Staðt] fyrir innan þórsbiörg. Haraldr konungr lá liði sínu út við Rein-slétto [North—More north of Throndham's Firth].—Har. S. (Harf.), ch. 39.   The name is hidden in l. 11.

l. 9. fyr-kveðin (prevented), necessary emendation.

Orm, (p. 322.) *Lady*, fiarð-beins (stone's) skorða 7, fundins (dwarf's) salar (stone's) grund 9, fiarðar brímis (gold's) garðr 10, hramma (hand's) báls (gem's) biörk 4: *poesy*, Billings brúðar full 4 [cp. Wod. Love-Lesson 13] : *winter*, Vindsvals mögr 13.

Eilif.—Angels, heims hrótz (heaven's) ferð : himna dýrðar hirð 3, himnis dýrð 7. l. 9. The pun, ǫl tor ráðin = vönd-öl (acc.)

Unclassed Fragments, (p. 325.)

p. 325, v. 5. See Yngl. S., ch. 27.

p. 326, v. 12. Cp. Skrið-Finnar, so famed in the mediæval Latin writings, Papal Bulls, etc., but in Norse only preserved in this phrase; cp., however, Fiðr skríðr, in the law carmen (Excursus, vol. i, p. 438).

p. 327, v. 2. þrym-goll (a bell) ; to be inserted in Excursus, p. 486.

vv. 8–10. Riddles, the key missing.

p. 328, v. 1. glot-kyllir, of a skin-bag with water : Geirríðr hét fiolkunnig kona ok meinsöm ; þat sá ófreskir menn, at Steinröðr kom at henni (the witch) óvarri, enn hón brá ser í nautz-belgs líki vatz-fullz.   Steinröðr var-iarn-smiðr, hann hafði iarn-gadd í hendi. Um fund þeirra er þetta kveðit.—Landn. [An overlaid verse, once in epic metre, one should think].

v. 2. Ásmundr var heygðr þar, ok lagðr í skip, ok þræll hans með hónum sá er banaði ser sialfr ok vildi eigi lifa eptir Ásmund ; hann var lagðr í annan stafn skipsins.   Lítlo siðarr dreymði þóro, at Ásmundr sagði ser mein at þrælinum. þat heitir Ásmundar-leiði er hann er heygðr. Vísa þessi var heyrð í haug hans. Eptir þat var leitað til haugsins ok var þrællinn rekin or skipino [Landn.] : l. 4. rúm er betra en íllt gengi, a proverb ; mod., betra er autt rúm enn ílla skipat : l. 6. For 'erat,' read, *ill es* of þegn á þiljum þröng . . . má (mew) ranga.

v. 3. These are Hialdr and Sniall of the Lay of Hyndla (as reconstructed).   The verses here are mangled beyond recognition.

v. 4. ll. 4, 5. Obscure, a manufactured verse ; 'Valfreyjo stafr' is noticeable.

v. 5. Probably from a lost Islendinga Drapa.

v. 6. hialt-uggaðr, fit epithet to sword, to call it *fish*, and the hilt its fins.

v. 8. Enn er hann kom hiá Dröngom, sá hann troll-karl sitja þar á uppi ok láta roa fætr ok skelldi þeim saman svá at sió-drif varð af, ok kvað víso.—Landn. ii, ch. 7. ham-vátr, *skin-wetted* = drowned, cp. 'koll-votr' in mod. Icel. usage.

v. 9. Very corrupt ; Har. S. (Hulda), ch. 105—Mer þótti koma at mer maðr ógor-legr, hann var allr vátr, ok hafði í hendi þöngul mikinn ; hann kvað þetta fyrir mer : blurred in the MS. and overpainted, sýn (sun), Thulor, 498 ; see our translation.

v. 12. The Long Serpent had *sixty-eight* oars.

v. 14. refil-stigar, cp. Edda Gylva G., beginning.

v. 16. hneggi, *in my heart*, cp. Thulor, 632.

Verses of Saga Editors, (p. 332.)

I. l. 7. We read 'hauka,' and, l. 9, in hvíta . . . hvarm-skógs fylvingar (acc.), 'eyelash filberts' = *tears*, see Excursus, p. 452.

v. 4. Fálo (giantess') tál-vinar (Thor's) gríms = Thorgrim's; and þrótt-grímr, *id.*

l. 15. -ár, dat. = æri.

l. 20. saur, in the original lay probably sór (wounds).

l. 25. Cp. Old Wols. Play, l. 182.

l. 30. aura mein = *fire*: l. 31. bekk-sagnir, from the lost lay.

l. 44. handlausan Tý, from the lost lay.

l. 63. vera (◡◡), here impossible; hence 'verja,' which calls back the Eddic phrase 'líni verja,' 'líni' hidden in 'saman,'—an evidence that we have here a fragment of an old epic: 'goð munar,' too, is from the lost lay.

l. 83. An echo from the Helgi poet (Helgi, i. 299).

v. 23 is a manifest echo from the Helgi poet, the Walkyrja = fals hallar fylla.

V. (p. 336). ll. 4 and 8. Manifest emendation.

VI. Marþaks fiorðr = Icefrith; Reyni-runnr = þorbiörg; Sifjar vers (Thor's) beggja handa hialp, *id.*: þundar beðjo (earth's) þvengr and Grundar hængr = Grettir (Thulor, 543): Stór-frörar = Ball-iökull, etc.—all puns.

l. 34. = Ox-main, Thulor, 450, 451.

BOOK IX.—*Krakomal*, (p. 341.)

A few of the kennings from the bald former part will show best the character of this curious and notorious poem. The first score of verses are variations of the 'leit-motive,' 'We fought at Z early in the morning, A fell.'

Serpent, lyng-áll 4, storðar-lykkja 5, graf-vitnir 2.

Ship, heflis hestr 22, Eynefis öndurr 52, Egils öndurr 23, ægis asni 89.

Sword, ræ-gagarr (carrion dog) 27, ræ-kyndill 34, skeri-bildr 28, ben-grefill 49, slíðra þorn 83, sveita ormr 60, sára flug-dreki 105, biartra mála stál 5: *mail-coat*, Högna kofl 49, Sköglar kápa 90, Svolnis skyrta 52, Hamðis serkr 85, Hildar næfr 102: *shaft*, streng-völor 40, streng-lögar palmr 75: *shield*, regg-ský 43, böð-máni 70: *raven*, ben-starri 42: *blood*, unda gialfr 19, svíra vín 35: *sea*, lindar völlr 24.

Battle, oddá messa 54, Svölnis (Woden's) slíðr-loga senna 59, hræ-sílna (carrion herrings') hialdr 64, odda senna 82, logðis (sword's) leikr 104, sverða sam-tog 112, sverða gustr 74, Heðins kván 16.

Head, hialm-stofn 69, hiarna kleif 35.

Into the *geography*, which is modelled on the Drapas of Harold, Magnus, and Eystan, it is useless to enter, much of it is purely imaginary; indeed the really fine lines at the end contain none of this fictitious stuff.

l. 31. Read rottar; the poet (an Orkney man?) wavers between *r* and *hr*.

Ragnar Lodbrok, Anslaug, and Ragnarssons, (p. 346.)

v. 6. We surmise, hý-nætr, cp. Lay of Skirni, 177.

v. 11. Enn ek vil at spiót sé tekin sem flest, ok sé stungit spiótunum í voll niðr, ok þar vil ek mik láta hefja á upp.—Ragn. S., ch. 9.

l. 56. See Excursus, vol. i, p. 410.

l. 119. A Hunnish horror—Enn hann kaus ser þann dauð-daga, at bál skyldi gera af manna höfðum, þar skyldi hann brenna.—Ragn. S., ch. 19.

l. 127. Thoroughly modern in tone.

Last Fragments, (p. 355.)

I. gramir (fiends), see Harb. 151.

II. óþióðans, Wendish? cp. Arnor, i. 35.

III. svell-vífiðar? hrím-faxaðar (of the waves): l. 13. svan-flaug (waves).

IV. mar-bakki, the shed between the deep and shallow water: l. 20. ask-laugar?

V. l. 2. A favourite verse in Iceland. There are proverbs in ll. 8, 11.

VI. Hœking's sons, sea-kings :—bit of a true old song.

VII. þar sá þeir brunn-miga (fox, goblin, see Thulor, 637) ; síðan heitir konungr brodd-spiót í eldi ok skaut til hans, konungr kvað. . . . þá tóku þeir vatn, enn þursinn skauzt inn í biargit ; þá er þau sáto við eldinn kvað þursinn af biargi annat lióð . . . þá skaut Hiörleifr inu sama spiót í auga því trolli.—Halfs. S., ch. 5.

v. 3. Í Iótlandz-hafi lá Hiörleifr konungr í logn-rétt, ok er hann fór [a word missing] í sólar upp-rás, sá hann í norðr koma upp or siónum mikit fiall, ok iafnt vaxit sem mann ; hann kvað.—Half. S., ch. 7.

v. 8. Hiorleifr konungr var upp festr í konungs höll með skó-þvengjom sínom sialfs, millum elda tveggja [cp. Lay of Grimni] ar ráði Æso ; enn hirðin sat við drykkju. Á meðan vakti Hildr, ok iós mungáti í eldana, ok kvað Hiorleifi þat verra [thus mended] ; hon leysti hann svá, at hon hió með sverði skó-þvengina.— Half. S., ch. 8.—Part of a very ancient story. One should perhaps render ' harra,' king, not as a proper name.

VIII. (p. 360.) l. 1. Cp. nyrfill, nyrfla.

ll. 3, 7. Proverbs.

l. 7. lyf = φάρμακον.

l. 17. Ims-igull (ígull, urchin) ; 'im' = blackish, cp. imleitr.

IX. v. 5. Something archaic about this verse, or rather the phrase that underlies it.

Proverb Poem, (p. 363.)

For comparison with proverbs of other countries we have now neither space nor time. Cf. Craci's and Wogg's story with l. 17 and Barefoot's motto with l. 21.

l. 1. A law maxim : l. 4, ambiguous, for ' hendi ' may be either verb or dative case ; griplor (mittens) would fit in that case.

l. 6. Unsafe : l. 7, ' slétt ' or ' slœtt ? '

ll. 11, 12. Personal remarks of the poet ; svíneyg, cp. Engl. pigsney, and Od. viii. 319 : glaupsa (to vaunt).

l. 14. gagarr (dog), a Gaelic word. See Krakomal, 27.

l. 18. Emendated = skalat ulf ala ungan lengi, Old Wols. Pl. 311.

l. 20. We take this opportunity to mend an error in Dict. 171 a—read, frauðr, m. a frog, Old Swed. fraud, Dan. frö, dropping the d : ' frauð ' in the horse-hoof is of the same root, cp. Greek βάτραχος : mörom (from marr), meres, a word not in use in Iceland.

l. 21. Cp. Reader, p. 262, No. 117. (2) = spyrja er bazt til váligra þegna ?

l. 22. Cp. p. 75, l. 26 : löng er biarnar nótt (the bear's night = winter).

l. 26. Gripsson, thus, we think.

l. 27. Unsafe, perhaps þráni ?

l. 29. Unknown.

l. 32. Italics not safe.

l. 33. Thus restored; 'sá var taldr af miklu kyni' is palpably false and bald.

l. 35. 'þau' regin? öll greto regin eptir hann, cp. vol. i, p. 124, l. 6.

l. 37. odda-maðr = umpire, qs. 'numpire,' 'non-peer.'

l. 43. Thus mended, 'fróðom' for 'forðom.' Strange it is that Fb. i. 583 has the same error; did he (the scribe) draw from our vellum (Cd. 'r')?

l. 48. vex hverr af gengi, Snorri (Ht.).

l. 51. fræno-skammr = bit-skammr, ἅπ. λεγ.

l. 58. Unsafe.

l. 60. 'eigi,' read 'ergi' or 'reiði?' For the bear's warmth cp. biarn-ylr, Dict. s. v. Svá segja menn, at Oláfr hafi haft biarn-yl, þviat aldri var þat frost eða kuldi, at Oláfr færi í fleiri klæði en eina brók ok skyrtu gyrða í brœkr.—Háv. S., ch. 2.

v. 18. foa, Thulor, 637: sýkr = svíkr.

l. 95. Read, ungan þarf at hiúfra (hiúka) mann, *lullabies are sung for children?*

l. 97. From 'tvimenning,' men and women being paired off to dance.

l. 99. Undoubtedly so, cp. Alex. S., p. 100, where nennolaus = namnlauss?

ll. 100, 101. i. e. þokks betra, much better: valt = avalt is interesting, showing how the word was sounded, the *v* (of allt) makes alliteration.

l. 111. Unsafe; the *t* must carry the letter-stress.

Song of Runes, (p. 369.)

We have been able to restore many places, yet not all.

l. 3. 'kvelli,' cp. kvelli-siúkr, Dan. *kjæle-syge.*

l. 4. ferða = fiarða?

l. 5. 'Reid,' here the *cart:* Regin á sv. bezta, though it is a dubious emendation.

l. 6. Guessed, though not altogether safe. Cp. Proverb Song, l. 102, and Hallbiorn, p. 79, l. 13.

l. 7. Cp. St. John's Gospel, ch. 1, and the clause 'By whom also he made the world.'

l. 9. A riddle like the others in the O. E. Dialogues.

l. 11. Mark the *weak* form (lútig).

l. 13. 'brá,' from bregða, so undoubtedly (not 'bar'); flærðar síma must here mean a *net;* see Edda, how Loki, in salmon's shape, was caught in his own device, the net—Enn er hann (Loki) sat í húsinu, tók hann lín-garn ok reið á ræksna, svá sem net er síðan gort.

l. 14. fost en goll ero halli, guessed.

l. 15. The first saw is carved on the porch of Oriel Hall. The second occurs in the Dialogus de Scaccario, lib. 1, Ut pedes aquilæ, qui parva non retinent, et quos magna non effugiunt.

l. 16. A safe emendation, cp. Dan. *vinter-grönt* = ivy.

BOOK X.—*Prophecy of Merlin,* (p. 372.)

Gunlaug mainly gives a paraphrase, throwing in from time to time a series of lines of his own making, usually of a descriptive character, e. g. Canto i, ll. 1–16, 139–159, 215–219, 263–290; Canto ii, ll. 278–300, 403–459. It is in these interlarded verses that most echoes of old songs occur, as is noted underneath the text; a few words and phrases bear the mark of being from *lost* songs, perhaps one or two from songs once contained in the lacuna of R. We take down but the best of the 'kennings:'—

God, bragna stillir i. 283, virða stióri 285, þióðar vörðr 290, himin-stillir ii. 254.

Battle, ognar lióma (sword's) él i. 144, Göndlar él ii. 278, lögðis veðr 194, malm-þing 279, malm-þrima 286, malma dynr i. 145, flein-drífa ii. 300: *sword*, ben-logi i. 153, sára klungr 156, slíðra garmr 150, ógnar liómi 144.

King, land-reki i. 80, 188, odd-viti 81, hers iaðarr ii. 17, bragninga konr 136, herja deilir 138.

Men, auð-stafir i. 22, hodd-skati 126, folk-stafr 264, vell-skati ii. 4, ver-dags (gold's) hötuðr 39, auðar skelfir 244, men-broti 108, bauga spillir 54, 404, auð-varp-aðr 253, sigr-viðr 154, sverð-éls hötuðr 259, seim-gefendr 58 : *lady*, goll-skogol i. 54.

Arrows, boga hagl i. 149, tvíviðar [Thulor 295] hagl ii. 280 : *shield*, Göndlar himin i. 146, Sköglar ský ii. 283, Hlakkar tiöld i. 147, Sköglar treyja 148.

Serpent (characteristic here), heiðar hvalr i. 200 : as *belt* or *rope*, urðar lindi 201, landz lindi ii. 49, rás (rushwood's) seil 50, rás fagr-sili 85, foldar belti 185, hauðrs girðing 67, grundar belti 66, fróns baugr 64, hiarl-þvengr 167, lundar fiöturr 190, lauf-viðar fiöturr 188: *wolf*, heiðingja barn i. 159: *fox*, gren-bui i. 123.

Sea, hval-tún ii. 227, Ránar vegr 386, Hogna siöt i. 135: *luminary, stars*, himins tíð-mork i. 245 : *heaven, sky*, i. 276: *coast*, eylandz iaðar ii. 20, barmr 175: *gem*, fiarð-bygg ii. 170 : *ship*, sund-dýr i. 71, sund-rokn 132 : *gold*, sund-bál i. 1, ver-dagr ii. 39.

Song, lióð-borg i. 13 : *breast*, gollor-höll i. 152, geðs gollor-heimr ii. 359 : *head*, hiarna bygð i. 153, heila borg 154.

Canto i. l. 40. bruð-þurr, qs. brauð-þurr?

l. 52. Corrupt : gœr (bevy of birds).

l. 91. vám, i. e. vrám (nooks, corners), dropping the *r*, see Dict. 673 a (B. III. 3).

l. 125. ors = head of an ass.

l. 229. draums í-vaðendr? from a song.

Canto ii. l. 10. sagaðr = sagðr.

ii. l. 82. hegja, *fate*, cp. Arnor, v. 4.

ii. l. 230. varðar?

ii. l. 325. Unsafe ; perhaps drawn from Helgi i. 192.

ii. l. 409. auðs ben-draugar, somehow wrong.

ii. l. 420. Röðlar, *Saints*.

ii. l. 435. Ps. xcvii. Vulgate—Flumina plaudent manu, simul montes exaltabunt. But what of 'The valleys shall sing hymns to the praise of the Lord,' is this added by the poet, as is certainly the Epilogue which follows? Merlin's prophecies were the Sibylline Books of the Middle Ages, almost canonical, hence ll. 455 etc.

Note, lung (ship), i. 69, and biöð (land), ii. 288, are Irish words.

Volsa-færsla, (p. 381.)

The poems in this and the following sections it is not necessary for us to translate. 'Wolsi' is undoubtedly etymologically connected with *Phallus*. The transposition of v. 13 towards the end is necessary, and speaks for itself.

l. 10. Read, líni klæddr, and for 'studdr' read saddr, *wrapped in linen, and stuffed* or *fed with leeks (herbs)*.

l. 11. heilagt blœti (blót) seems to mean rather '*teraph*,' some object used for pagan worship, than '*idol*,' cp. vol. i, p. 408, foot-note; and Dict. p. 70 a, s. v. blót, I. 2.

l. 22. nosi, in mod. Icel. hnósi; enn á meðan önnur þeirra var að koma í lag hnósanum, Isl. þióðs. ii. 41.

l. 26. Echo from Lay of Righ, ll. 13, 14.

l. 30. andketo, obscene word, else unknown : l. 40 also obscene.

l. 50. Mark the alliterative hiarra ok hurð-ása. l. 55. 'bing en linga,' unsafe.

Sheaftail-baulk or *Fox Lay*, (p. 383.)

By way of a small glossary we subjoin a few words, as this poem was only partly used in the Dictionary :—

Fox, skaufali 1, 5, 9, dratt-ali 25, 49, 59, loð-bakr 30, gor-tanni 13, lang-hala 2, gren-lægja 13, 17, låg-fæta 29, rebbali (ref-hali) 37, 45, tófa 41, skolli 55, 57, 145, sauð-bítr 63 : *fox-cub*, yrmlingr (vermin) 12 : *sheep*, grá-kollr (grey humble sheep) 58 : *dog*, hunzi 76 : *horse*, viggs faðir 6.

l. 8. A proverb; nineteen is a favourite number in popular tales; a dangerous river has just taken 'nineteen' victims, and is waiting for the last; Mount Hecla has had 'nineteen' eruptions, and the like.

l. 15. veyk-lendut, *weak loined;* hrygg-snauð, *shrunk in the back, lean.*

l. 27. hala-rófu-bein, *tail bone of a tail,* superfluous, hala put in for alliteration's sake.

ll. 33–35. haust-þústr, *autumn gales,* 32 ; brúnum, *mountain brows,* 35.

l. 38. ganga at sauðum, i. e. to search the mountains for sheep in the autumn.

l. 53. gambrliga, *wantonly.*

l. 77. keifa, to walk wearily, as reeling under a burden. The fox is here represented as *carrying* off a sheep like a wolf or bear.

ll. 111, 112. lamb-gymbr, *ewe lamb;* gamal-rolla, old scabby ewe.

l. 115. klýpingar, better klippingar, a *shorn sheep-skin* for trade, an article of export from Iceland in the Middle Ages.

ll. 120–123. riklinga rár, *poles hung with wind-dried stripes of flounder,* see Dict. 497 b; skreið, *wind-dried fish;* rafa-belti, *the belt* or *round of the fins of flounders;* hákarls lykkjur, *the flesh of sharks hung and dried,* used for food—all which 'dainties' of his childhood are well known to the Editor: hvinna snepla = bitlinga, *stolen morsels.* Observe, the Icelanders of Reynard's day, as at present, could have had no poultry yards, otherwise our poet would not have omitted to notice his hero's devotion to Dame Partlet and her lord.

l. 127. Corrupt.

l. 141. Cp. Virgil's Exoriare aliquis nostris ex ossibus ultor, Æn. iv. 625.

l. 146. hel-stingi, death-pain.

The *Dance-Burdens* (p. 391) deserve attention from French and English scholars.

Olafs Rima, (p. 393.)

As to Grammar :—

Observe, (1) the dropping the nom. *r* in words on -ingr—milding 5, dögling 3, sikling 25, bragning 23. This is the common licence of all 'Rímur,' caused by the requirements of the rhyme; yet *bookish*, never in speech. The *r* was already beginning to become syllabic, and was inconvenient in these often repeated longish words. (2) Changing final *r* into *ur*, ever and anon, ll. 1, 31, 56, 57, 80, 83, 103, 108, but *never before the line-pause* or *at the end of a line.* (3) The contracted form kongr = konungr. At this date Icelanders said, svó, vótr, vóði, hvórki ; yet we find rhymes in the old style, as vv. 6, 22.

l. 27. iungr; the Rimur poets are fond of this foreign word, but it is purely *bookish*, and never obtained in speech.

l. 60. Bú-Finnar, the Border Laps that have taken to agriculture.

l. 91. vóð = óð, merely a book-form, like 'vorðinn, vurðu,' so frequent in the fourteenth-century MSS.

Skiða Rima, (p. 398.)

As to language the remarks upon Olafs Rima also apply here : *vá* sounded *vó*, in rhymes, vv. 47, 69, 70, 109, 119, 181 : *rl* sounded *ll*, Stulli, v. 99 ; iall, v. 176. Of the vocabulary we note the following :—

Foreign words—fínn (fine), ll. 5, 35, 43, 204, 228 ; afmors vers (love-song, Fr. vers d'amour), 7 ; pör (a pair), 64 ; panna (pan, skull), 335 ; lukka (luck), 97, 114 ; líf, of a person, 197 : foreign forms, mann = maðr, 116, 126.

The kennings are very plain, and often half comic—*lady*, bauga skorða 7, gull-hlaðz skorða 10, silki hrund 5, vella brú 240, þorna vigg 174, þorna brú 223 : *man*, menja Baldr 14, auðar Baldr 24, örva lundr 52, laufa viðr 104, stála gautr 248, randa briótr 286, silki-treyju nistill 371 : *poetry*, as *dwarves' ship*, Fiölnis (dwarf's) bátr 11, Suðra (dwarf's) siávar-rok 406 : *breast*, óðar rann 11 : *mouth*, fræða salr 375 : *gold*, greipar miöll 142, Grettis ból *id.* : *battle*, eggja sag, 278, örva seim 293. *Men, people*, dándis-menn (*gentlemen* translation of the Fr. *prudhommes*, Lat. *boni homines*) 18 : *abusive*, Herjans höttr 119, dröttr 120, auli 195, 375, kratins synir 272, slangi 379.

Skrúði = *tackle* 20, kuðr = kviðr? (*empty belly*) 68, við-bit (*a relish*, usually *butter*) 82, kvarði? (*the sense is that his stomach begins to heave*) 82 : álpa (*to walk*) 107, drukk-langr = drykk-langr 130, klas-sekk (*a trunk, bag*) 134, bramla (*to make a noise*, cp. Fr. *bramer*, cp. *brabble*) 148, í kiör (*to heart's content*) 208, danga (*to bang*) 272, bupp (*howl* as in our *butter-bump*) 326.

vv. 2, 3. The 'Dance' Song (Love-song) [see vol. ii, p. 385 sqq.], says the poet, is now the set fashion.

v. 6. The Dwarf-ship (Song) is riding at anchor in the poet's breast ; and yet he speaks of her as 'old' and 'written.' The fact is, the poet falls out of the metaphor (cp. Egil's Head Ransom, verse 1) : the reason being that the song is his own ; yet, at the same time, he is thinking of the old scroll, from which he drew his subject, viz. Sturla's Saga, in Sturl. II.

l. 26. The beggar's keg called Butter-pig, cp. 40.

l. 29. From one end of the country to the other.

l. 45. skæði, leather cut into squares for brogues : svörf, *to be exacting*.

l. 69. Thorleif Beiskialdi in Hítardal (hít, *a scrip*).

l. 75. To scrape the hair off the brogues with a blunt knife.

l. 79. bregða kreppu, *to stretch oneself*.

l. 83. The gaberlunzie man's character is sketched in a most masterly way here.

l. 85. lítið varð af söngum, his evening prayer was short.

l. 98. sióli (*king*), now frequent in Rimur, cp. Thulor 29 ; prob. a Celtic loan-word, Irish *siol* (race).

l. 99. kom þar til með kongum tveim, they came to quarrel.

l. 187. Fátt er kyrru betra, a proverb.

l. 206. The weight about five pounds avoirdupois.

l. 217. The phrase for returning thanks, mod. 'Guð-laun,' Shaksp.-Engl. God 'ild you. Í sveitum er það góð og gömul venja hér á landi, eða hefir verið, þegar ein-hverjum er gefið að borða, hvort heldr er gestr eða heima-maðr, að hann segir við þann eða þá sem veita hónum, áðr enn hann tekr til matarins : Gefðu (gefið þið) mer í Guðs friði matinn! Enn á eptir máltíð er sagt 'Guð-laun' eða ' Guðs ást fyrir matinn.'—Jon Arnason, ii. 527.

l. 251. Heimdall, elsewhere in þrymlur called Heimdæll.

l. 263. Remmi-gygr, properly Skarphedin's axe, known to us from Niala.

l. 282. Skelja-karl = Maugis—þar var karl einn gamall, hann var í fátækligum búningi, enn alla vega útan á hans tötrum var sem ekki væri nema kúfungar einir ok skeljar . . . Skelja-karl mælti.—Magus. S., ch. 12 (Ed. Cederschiöld).

vv. 162, 163. Here is some displacement. The *tooth* that was knocked out must have been *Starkad's;* the poet is too clever to miss *that.* The legend says that Starkad was doomed to receive a scarring wound in every battle. In one battle we are told he had a grinder knocked out, which was afterwards shown and used in a belfry string in a church in Denmark, weighing seven ounces.—Norna Gestz S., cp. Icel. Annals s. a. 1405, þar [in a place in Africa] var ok tönn, er sögð var or Starkaði Gamla, var hon þver-hendar á lengd ok breidd, fyrir útan þat er í höfdinu hafði staðit.

l. 350. This is mock imitation of Sturlunga, Bk. iii, ch. 31 [in Facsim., p. ccxix].

l. 370. svínit lásk mer eptir, *I forgot it, left it behind.*

l. 375. fræða salr, *the mouth.*

l. 386. All worn to pieces.

l. 398. 'iunga,' the German form, used mockingly of the *old* beggar.

l. 404. vatna = vatna-fasta.

l. 406. *Here let my song wait for the Sunday,* to be then used for entertainment.

The *Rhyme Ditties* (p. 410) we, of course, must leave unnoticed here. For Ballads, see vol. i, p. 501.

Islendinga-drapa, (p. 419.)

We subjoin some of the most crabbed 'kennings.'

Poetry, Lóðurs vinar lið 1, Dvalins veigar 2, hausa hasl [pun, hár is = *hair* and also Hár, i. e. Woden] rekka (Anses') miodr 4.

Icelanders, hvals búðar (sea's) húð (ice's) lendingar 5 : *poet,* ása öl-beinir 64.

Courage, hamra víís (giantess') byr 6, hraun-atla sprakka hregg 17 : *ear,* hlusta munnr 3 : *horn,* hæfis fleinn 64 : *earth,* þrós drós 68.

Axe, bruma ekki 96 : *sword,* gunnar grunnungr 11 : *raven,* sónar ofnir 20, styrjar göllungr 89.

Men, from *gold*—grundar seilar (snake's) garða niröðr 8, fiall-gestils (giant's) orðz beiðir 15, snáka stígs niörðr 31, arms fann-viðr 47, unnar hyr-tælir 90, linna foldar freyr 29, metins auðar niörðr 44: from *ship*—Hundings elg-reynir 10; fens elg viðr 21, ára elgs týr 32, flausta fylgi-meiðr 61, unnar hreina æsi-þróttr 58 : from *battle, sword,* etc.—sverða þrimo herðendr 22, sár-geima (blood's) iökuls (snow's) þrym (battle's) svellir 56, darra hlióm-boði 74, hrings há-raddar þollr 56, fleina þrym niörðr 103, bræ-klungrs (sword's) hnykkir 83, hrotta él-bióðr 87, hrafna víns (blood's) glóða hneigendr 2, hiör regns niörðr 79, fiolnis elda geymir 29, borðz (shield's) harð-glóðar (sword's) móði 95, hlakkar bliks runnr 95.

The contents of the poem—

Introduction—Give ear and listen to me whilst I tell up Icelanders that were men of courage :—

i. The slaying of Brodd-Helgi, in revenge for Geiti [4]. It was through no fault of Thorkel that he avenged not Geiti his father [5].

ii. Helgi Asbiornson slays Helgi Droplaugson, his namesake : Grim goes into the house, and stabs Helgi, avenging his brother.

iii. Thorolf falls in battle in King Athelstan's service, Egil was in the battle.

iv. Glum Geirason does battle at Fitja : gets speech out of a dead man (!).

v. Hallfred visits the king.

vi. Thoralf son of Skolm does battle with Hacon, Athelstan's foster-son.

vii. Finnbogi the Strong fights.

VIII. Orm Storolfsson, brandishing a pole, fought alone with twenty-four men.

IX. Biarni the poet struck Earl Hacon in the face with a horn.

X. Gretti to avenge his brother slew Thorbiorn.

XI. Thorleif, he that made a bad song on the earl, the brothers, he and Olaf, slew the Bearsark [Klaufi Boggvi].

XII. Orm Skógarnef did battle, and Gauk Trandilsson too.

XIII. Gunnar, attacked by Gizur, slew two and wounded sixteen.

XIV. Midfrith-Skeggi fought beyond the sea (in the Baltic), and fetched the sword Skofnung out of Craki's cairn.

XV. Hall o' Side held his own against all, and had valiant sons.

XVI. Thorstein Hall's son, angry at a libel, slew on one morning five men, Thorhard one of them.

XVII. Holmgang-Bersi slew thirty-five men, cp. p. 70, v. 5.

XVIII. Kormak, in the king's service, trusted in himself.

XIX. Thorarin Steinarsson, the champion, felled men in wager of battle, and dared any one to withstand him.

XX. Holmgang-Starri . . . [rest lost].

II, III (p. 421), parallel to I. xiii ; with IV compare Landn. i, chs. 5, 6.

The Thulor, (p. 423.)

It would be out of place here to give a complete commentary upon these interesting glossaries, well deserving of careful and minute treatment as they are; all that can be done is to point out the lines upon which such work should be done. With regard to their *chronology*, it is evident that they are not of high antiquity (though their prototypes may well have been the early didactic poems), for they are largely drawn from late sources, the crusading poets, and the like. Their composers certainly had before them much that is now lost, though it is difficult to estimate the exact proportion their material bears to that which is accessible to us. Certain sections, such as that of the *giants* and *giantesses*, appear to rest largely on early poems of the Thor cycle, though even lost Encomia would have supplied many names in their 'kennings' which are not included in the fragments now extant.

There are also curious omissions of terms met with in poems which we know, but which do not seem to have been utilized by the Thulor-composers, though here it is necessary to remember that there are indications of incompleteness and copyist's errors in our texts. Some words are apparently taken from prose, such as the Kings' Lives, or at all events, from late poems founded on prose texts, and many terms, which look at first as if they came from lost early poems, may no doubt be thus accounted for, so that one must not be too ready to suppose that any very great additions would be made to the known mass of Eddic poems if all the works known to the Thulor compilers were extant.

From a philological point of view the great number of *foreign words* is in some sections very notable, and supplies ample matter for the history of culture in the north.

The Thulor, like the other sections of that aggregate of literature which we know as the Prose Edda, show plain evidences of growth; they are not homogeneous productions of one man, or even of one generation ; marks of additions, changes, editorship are very apparent. Many sections are, as we have them, forced into a *numerical frame*: thus there are sections of twenty synonyms, e.g. *women;* thirty, *battles;* forty, *men;* sixty, *fish* and *fire;* seventy, *ships;* eighty, *sea;* a hundred (120), *rivers,* and so on; as noticed below, a circumstance which sometimes is a help to a critical treatment of the text.

In the Dict., owing to the disjointed state of the text, we entered the Thulor simply as ' Edda (Gl.) ;' they can now be cited by line. In the first sheets of the Dict. a few have slipped out.

I. 1. *Sea-kings.* When the number of -fi and -ill names, the creation (largely it must be) of late court-poets, is excepted, most of the rest are to be accounted for from extant sources.—Hyndla's Lay (in a more perfect text than ours, of the same type as that used by the Flatey-book paraphrast), Arnor, the Orkney pedigree (p. 183), and late court-poets; cp. the court-metre table (of 24 terms), p. 440.

2. The *Kings'* section is founded on a similar basis.

3. *Dwarves.* This list borrows largely from the Short Wolospa. It was apparently meant to contain 120 names.

4. *Giants.* A section of 70, to which a second list of 40 (imperfect) has been added. The earlier list is drawn from the Eddic poems to a great extent, though several names, e. g. Buzear, which one looks for, are missing; and there are others only met with here, part of which the Short Wolospa, when perfect, might have contained.

5. *Giantesses.* A perfect section of 60; late fairy-tales and poems may account for most of them which are not found elsewhere.

6. *Woden.* This list is helped out by the early Eddic name-lists; it must also be largely drawn from lost proems to Encomia, the very parts of those poems which were neglected by the glossators who used the fact-full verses of the middle sections to ornament the Kings' Lives.

7–12. *Gods, Goddesses, Walcyries* consist mostly of well-known and frequent names, from existing poems or paraphrases, in Gylfa-ginning and Scaldscapar-mal. Section 12 looks like a paraphrase of part of the Short Wolospa.

13. *Women.* A list founded on a better text of Righ's Lay than ours. Cp. Court-metre Thulor, p. 440: l. 179, for brúðr (bis) read ' hæll.'

14. *Men.* A section of 40 synonyms, founded apparently on the same sources as the early List printed on p. 542, as are also section 15, *kinships,* and section 16, *household.*

17. *Battle.* Founded on the court-poems.

18. *Swords.* A long list of 140 terms, preserving about 20 proper names of swords (such as Foot-broad) known from legend or history, and several names of fishes, snakes, wolves, etc. Cp. II. 3, 17, 25.

19. *Parts of a sword.* A curious section, much of which is purely enigmatical to us, and can only be interpreted by the help of such study as has produced M. Montelius' excellent monograph on sword-types in the Congrès International, Stockh. ii. p. 882 sqq. There are ten words or more in this section which rightly belong to the foregoing list, such as ' falk,' not ' folk,' l. 270 (Lat. *falc-s,* Fr. *fauchon*), sword, brand.

20. *Axe.* An incomplete but noteworthy list; ' scrama,' ' gygr,' and ' fala' are proper names of ogresses; cp. the whole list with the treatment of the same subject in the Axe-poem of Einar Skalason, p. 271.

21. *Spear.* Several loan-words from late court-poems: lenz, Lat. *lancea,* Fr. *lance;* spiör, Eng. spear; gefia, which we would read glefia, Fr. *glaive;* gaflak, Mod. Eng. gavelok, cp. Mod. Eng. javelin. This word slipped out in the Dict. p. 186 b; references—Fms. i. 311, 321, 330, vi. 77, viii. 76, and pass. in Romantic Sagas : frakka, Lat. *franca;* peita, cp. N. Eng. speat.

22. *Arrows.* Bösl, from Lat. *bolsonem,* Fr. *bosoun, boujon;* read böls, a *quarrel,* see p. 201, l. 34; akka, cp. *uncinata* tela, Bede i. 12; Gusis-smiði is clearly from Arnor.

23. *Bow.* The comparative neglect of artillery in Northern battles is well marked in the paucity of these words.

24. *Shield.* Drawn in part from the early Shield-poems, with their vigorous imagery. The court-poems prefer to use synonyms for the shield: buklari, Eng. *buckler*, and targa, Eng. *targe*, are late loan-words.

25. *Helm* and (26) *mailcoat* are also based on early sources, partly lost.

II. 1. *Sea* and *water.* A list of 80 words, derived very largely from the kennings for poetry, Woden's liquid, in the court-poet's poems; even the Holy Soma comes in here (l. 321). The last few lines are borrowed from verses of some early poet describing Eager's daughters; cp. the two verses, vol. ii, p. 440, ll. 37–44.

2. *Rivers.* A notable glossary, of which we have spoken above. The enormous proportion of British rivers with unmistakable Celtic names must be carefully noted. Most of these are from North Britain, a few are Irish. Besides these are a few from the late Crusading-Encomia, and a few from the early Eddic Lays.

It is quite useless to try to account for them by supposing that Norwegian streams of somewhat similar names can be meant. Not only is there a most striking absence of Norwegian geographical indications in the Old Northern poetry throughout, but, when all allowance has been made, there is an unmistakable residuum of British rivers which cannot be explained away.

3. *Fishes.* A list which should be studied by the biologist and philologist alike. It is full of most interesting and valuable information. Our English fish-names of to-day will account for a large proportion of the list, which is indeed based as far as can be seen on the ichthyology of the British Isles. The fluke, skate, syle, flounder [flyndra?], sword-fish, gurnard, gad, crab, eel, shell-fish, gar-fish [geir-sil], ling, are examples of these. We know others under different names, as steinbítr, the cat-fish; hámerr, the blue shark. See I. 18.

4. *Whales.* An imperfect section (once 24 or 30?); these names could probably be still in great part identified by a Shetlander or a Faroe-man. Reyðr and fisk-reki are *balæna physalis* and *balæna boops*, but others are known; see Dict. ss. vv.

5. *Ships.* Seventy interesting terms: ark, ship, buss, neak, boat, keel, cat, canoe, dromond, pram, galley, fly-boat [fley], smack, schuyt, ferry-boat, carvel, cog, skiff are among them, terms common in English books and speech. The Irish *lung* is also present; keipull is Adamnan's *caupallus;* we miss Irish *curac.*

6. *Gear and parts of a ship.* A rich list of words, each of which should be carefully considered. Many of them survive in full use, e.g. sail, stay, stem, seam, stern, sheet [skaut-reip], spike, sail-tree, sail-yard, stool, sheer, snotter, sewed, swifter, syphering, vang, leech, line, ear, hank, rib, windlass, bits, bowline, bulk-stocks, naval *hoods*, ro-bands, heel, hawse, wale, clove, or*lop*, knee, keel, board, carling, clews, oars, and anchor. The French *hune* is also amongst them, and among French naval terms one would expect to find some, which we have not been able to identify as yet. Useful guides are Falconer's quaint epic *The Shipwreck*, Southey's *Life of Nelson*, and Dana's *Manual.*

7. *Earth or land.* Many of these words still remain in use among us as common or place names: fold, land, ground, lathe, fell, lithe, leet, holt, heath, brink, dale, tongue, mould, moor, sand, marsh, earth. Some being really English, others, such as -wald, völlr, part of the legacy of Northern local nomenclature. Fibh and biodh are Celtic.

8. *Botany.* Here the English botanist should give some help. Most of the plants and trees are clearly not part of the Norwegian or Icelandic flora. Hazel, hawthorn, asp, apple-tree, elder, pear, bush, plum, elm are common English words; heggr looks like hedge or haye, beinn like bean. Píll is Lat. *populus*, wid-windle (the bind-weed) is in our glosses. Mark Bede's words of Britain—Opima frugibus atque arboribus insula.—H. E. lib. i. ch. 1.

9. *Oxen.* 10. *Cows.* A list containing many interesting words, showing that the mediæval system of naming oxen after saints is merely a survival of the heathen practice of giving names of gods and giants to the plough-steers. Some beautiful old epithetal names are among the others, taken, one fancies, from old lays such as Gefion's. Bull, quae, cow, heifer, steer are still English; tarbh [tarfr] is an Irish word.

11–13. *Ram and goat.* Some archaic epithets. Others are drawn, as it seems, from such realistic poems as Skiða-rima or Skaufhala-balkr.

14. *Bear.* A section largely drawn from the court-poets' kennings for ship.

15. *Hart.* A meagre list from the mythic poems—cervorum caprearumque venatu insignis, says Bede, H. E. i. 1, of North Britain; cp. Adamnan's Canons also.

16. *Boar.* Grice, swine, barrow-pig, with a few nicknames, speaking to the acquaintance of the composer or his authority with the Irish or British pig; l. 477. for 'rai' we must read 'rati' (of the Runic Stone).

17. *Wolf.* A gathering from the older poems. Grádýri is characteristically English; 'þæt græge déor, wulf ón wealde.' See also I. 18. Grey-Norna is omitted, perhaps once in l. 480.

18. *Heavens.* A quotation from a lost didactic poem.

19. *Sun,* 20. *Moon,* and 21. *Day.* Allwise Lay was known to the composer.

22. *Heavens.* The regular Thulor drawn from old sources.

23. *Wind and weather.* For this section the compiler is indebted to the Encomia kennings for battle, the 'storm of Hild or Woden or the Walcyries.'

24. *Fire.* Composed chiefly from the kennings for sword, the 'flame of the wound'—tusi Finnish or Chudic (used by Eywind).

25. *Serpents.* The kennings for 'gold,' as the 'serpent's bed' in the lost epilogues of court-poems, gave probably the chief stock of these terms. Some Latin Elucidarius has yielded such words as gargan, scorpion, rabia, iapr [vipr?]. See I. 18.

26. *Horses.* This section must be compared with the old lists, vol. i, pp. 78, 80; fake is found in N. Eng. poems. Alswartr and some more should be marked as proper names.

27. *Hawk.* Drawn from kennings for the raven,—Woden's hawk.

28–30. *Raven, Cock, Eagle.* Mark the foreign corvus, corpr; the Latin authority has also given gallus, gallina, aquila in the following sections. Cocr is English. The Raven-poem of Hornclofi and the mythic poems are laid under contribution.

31. *Birds.* Here again the British fauna is the main source of the compiler's long and remarkable list. For instance, smyrill, the lanner; stelkr, the spotted red-shank; iaðrakarn, the water-rail; rytr, the tarrock; spói, the wimbrel, are all characteristic Western birds. Even the sea-birds are such as frequent the British Isles. See Prolegomena, p. 188, and Dict. ss. vv. Mark what Bede says of Britain—avium ferax, terra marique, generis diversi; and, Piscium volucrumque venatu insignis.—H. E. lib. i. ch. 1. The last line is corrupt, valr, dúfa, repeated.

III. 1, 2. *Women and goddesses.* Evidently culled from court-poets' 'kennings,' which have preserved several interesting and enigmatic titles for us, and also a good many common names of trees both here and in II. 8 above. The section is an appendix to I. 10, 11.

3. *Mind and heart.* Curious old words illustrating early psychology. For negg read hnegg (prop. a sheaf, hence heart).

4. *Fox.* Chiefly gathered from some such poem as Skaufhala-balk.

5. *Hand, etc.* Noteworthy are mund (law word) *manus;* gaupn, *gowpen;* spönn, *span* (law words); lámr, Irish *lam;* and hnefi, lófi, which remain in our N. English *neif, loof;* rökn, Slavonic, a trade word from the Baltic, used as a measure, like gaupn.

6. *Walcyries.* The proper Thulor section on this head, from i. 12, is only a

citation from some lost authority. The sources here are the characteristic Walcyrie poems, Hacon's Dirge, Darrada-liod, and the like, as well as the court-poets. l. 648 is corrupt.

7. *Isles.* Mostly Norwegian and Danish islands, known from the court-poems on the naval exploits of the Norwegian kings. Crete and Cyprus figure by the side of the Celtic Scillies and Dimon, and the half mythic Samsey and Heðinsey. In l. 660 Lygra and Lag are by some mistake repeated from ll. 658, 669; l. 657 read 'Stolm ;' l. 667 read 'Solund ;' l. 776 read ' Vingr.' The list should be compared with Einar's list of 32 islands, and the anonymous court-metre verse containing 33 ; there are really three parallel authorities.

8. *Friths.* An index to early Norwegian geography and history, for all the national life is grouped round these firths.

9. *Corn.* Many of these words are not Scandinavian, for besides such common terms as acre, seed, awn, haulm, blade, shoot, root, thrave, meal, bere, bigg, barley, wheat, rye, haver, there are foreign words,—corci, Irish *carca ;* barley, flour. What is hirsi?

10. *Numbers.* A jingle based on the old legal names of organisations by number, crews, companies, courts, levies, and the like. A complete history of the words in it would give a large part of Old Teutonic constitutional history. ' Flokkr' is important as referring to the crews and battle array ; cp. note, p. 584, on the Sticklestead battle.

Thulor in Court-metre, (p. 440.)

'*Kennings*'—*Mind as the Gale of the Giantess,* Herkju sterk-viðri 13, Gríðar glaum-vindr 16: *Breast,* hnegg-veröld 14, þindar salr 16.

In ll. 21–36 note the synonyms for *belt* or *ring* (all variations on calling the sea the *belt* or *ring* of the isles): baldrekr 21, 25 ; lindi 21, 26, 29, 35 ; belti 22, 26, 31, 36; gyrðill 22, 25, 29; sili 23, 27, 31, 35; men 24, 28, 30, 34; helsi 27; girði 28, 33; fioturr 30, 33; um-giörð 23, 31, 34; hringr 32, 36.

Lady, strandar aurriða (snake's) stallz (gold's) strind 61.

Ship, egg-húfs (= skör) elgr 44.

Head, skarar-fiall 61 : *hair* (the wood of the skull), krúno klif 56, reikar eik 56, hiarna þyrnir 57, hlusta kvistir 58, skalla rá (neuter) 58; vanga ölr 59, svarðar grön 59, svarð-akr 63, haus-miöll (snow) 60 : *eyes,* hvarma skógar (eyelashes') stiornor 63 : *comb,* svarðar raðar (hair's) garðr 63.

ll. 1–12, 17–24 have been referred to above and compared with the earlier epic metre. Thulor on the same subjects : l. 20. read ' Hísing.'

Arni's verse, (p. 441.) The hair-cutting day in the old Benedictine cloister is visibly brought before the reader.

Einar's and Snorri's lines. Epigrammatic couplets on a lady with beautiful hair. The two fine-haired ladies of Iceland were, as Ari tells, namesakes—the wicked Hallgerd, and her namesake, vol. ii, p. 79. See Excursus, vol. ii, p. 505.

For list of *stones* and *gems,* see p. 546; many unintelligible to us, some even Slavonic. Britain is rich in stones and pearls, says Bede—Gignit et lapidem gagatem plurimum optimumque, est autem nigro-gemmeus et ardens igni admotus, incensus serpentes fugat.—H. E. i. 1. The Norse-Icelandic hégetill is but a corruption of gagates, as observed by Dr. Fritzner of Christiania. Mend Dict. 246 b, s. v. accordingly. Bivivil looks like beryllus or barillus ; Gyfingr may be a corruption of jacinthus.

For list of pieces of *lady's dress,* see also p. 546.

APPENDAGE TO THE NOTES.

A Brief Poetical Gradus of the Twelfth Century.

By way of summing up we here subjoin a condensed *Gradus*, a first draught, as it seems [older than Snorri?], to Skaldskapar-mál, hence it is not contained in the received texts of that work. This brief and quaint Gradus—showing as 'in a nut-shell' the Norse poetry of the twelfth century, in the lifetime of our 'Remanieur'—has come down in—

a. Two old vellums, Arna-Magn. 748 and 757; both are faulty copies of a lost archetype, AM. 757 being, on the whole, the better of the two. We have fused both into one. See Snorri, Edda, Ed. Arna-Magn. vol. ii, pp. 428–431 (Cd. 748), and pp. 511–515 (Cd. 757). Cp. List of Synonyms given above, pp. 542–545, and Excursus I, vol. ii, p. 447 sqq.

b. In Cod. Worm. App., the end-piece is preserved, partly in Magnus Olafsson's Copy. Both (*a* and *b*) speak to a common archetype.

a. Codd. Arna-Magn. 748 and 757.

Skaldskapr er kallaðr skip Dverga, ok Iǫtna, ok Óðins, ok fundr þeirra, ok drykkr þeirra; ok er rétt at kenna svá, ef vill, bæði skip ok drykk, sem annar-staðar í skúldskap, ok eigna þeim; enn *skip* má kalla dýra heitum, ok fugla, ok hesta, ok kenna við sió, ok allt reiði skips; enn kalla hesta heitum einum, ef við sæ-konunga er kennt. *Drykk* má kalla sævar heitum ǫllum, fiarða, ok bylgna, ok vatna allra, ok kenna til ǫl-kera, eða horna, munnz eða góma, tanna eða tungu. *Dverga* ok *Iǫtna* er rétt at kalla þióða heitum ǫllum ok sæ-konunga, ok svá gram ok vísa, ok slíkum ǫllum, ok kenna Dverga til steina eða urða, enn Iǫtna til fialla eða biarga. *Steina* má kalla bein iarðar, ok sióvar ok vatna, enn hús Dverga, enn grand þeirra Hamðiss ok Sǫrla.

Ekki skal kenna þat er sialfs síns nafni er nefnt; enn kenna allt þat er annars nafni er nefnt en sialfs síns.

Orrosto má kalla namni nokkurs háreystiss starksamligs, glaum eða hlióm; kenna við her-klæði, eða vápn, eða hlífar, ok því meirr at þá skal kenna við Óðin eða sæ-konunga ef vill—*Skiǫld* má kalla sólar heitum ok tungls, himins ok skýss; kalla má hann ok vegg, eða garð, balk ok brík, hurð ok gátt, þili ok grind, hleða ok segl, tiǫld ok refil, ok eigna ávallt orrostu eða Óðni eða sæ-konungum.—Öll *her-klæði* eru fǫt Óðins ok sæ-konunga.—Öll *hǫgg-vápn* má kalla elldz heitum eða annarrar birti, leiptr eða lióss, kenna við Óðin eða orrostu eða sæ-konunga, her-klæði eða hræ, ben eða blóð.—Öll *vápn* ero trǫll ok vargar ok hundar her-klæða ok hlífa; enn lag-vópn má kalla fiska heitum ok orma, ok kenna við her-klæði ok hlífar, sár eða blóð.—*Blóð* er kallað sióvar heitum ok vatna, ok kennt við hræ eða ben, sár eða undir.

Sió má kalla garð landa, ok men, band ok belti, lás ok fiǫtur, hring ok boga; kalla má hann ok heim sæ-kvikvenda ok hús, iǫrð ok gǫtu sæ-konunga ok skipa.— *Ormr* sá heitir Miðgarðz-ormr er liggr um ǫll lǫnd útan; því er rétt at kenna orma alla svá til landa sem sió, kalla band eða baug iarðar. Orma er rétt at kalla fiska heitum ok hvala, ef þeir eru kendir við nokkut láð, við eða hraun, gras eða griót, gliúfr eða heiðar.—Orma iǫrð er *gull*, rekkja þeirra ok gata. Gull skal kenna einn veg til handar ok sióvar, ok til vatna allra, kalla elld ok sól, ok tungl ok stiǫrnu, ok kyndil ok kerti, dag ok leiptr, geisla ok blik, ok alla birti; enda má gull kenna til snæss ok íss, ok kenna þá til handar: baugr er fiǫturr handar, ok hanki, ok virgill. Gull er korn, eða melldr Fróða konungs, enn verk ambátta hans tveggja, Fenju ok Menju; enn sáð Kraka konungs, ok fræ Fyrisvalla; byrðr Grana; haddr Sifjar; enn tár Mardallar; mál Iǫtna. Hringr hét Draupnir, fyrir því at ina niundu hverja nótt draup af hónum hringr iafn-hǫfugr hónum; því er gull sveiti hans.

Hǫnd er hauka iǫrð, grund ok gata þeirra, ok hestr, skip ok stallr; heitir hǫnd ok mund; hǫnd er bǫl eða nauð boga, eða tǫng; kalla má hána fót eða lim axlar; rétt er at kalla hǫndina heitum kvikvenda, ef þau eru kennd við ǫxlina; kalla má hǫndina ok tǫng axlar.—Svá má ok *horn* kalla triá heitum, ef þau eru kennd við drykkju eða þat sem þau vóxu af; horn ok ǫnnur ǫl-kerǫld má kalla siávar heitum, skip eða hús allz drykkjar.

Íss er himin eða hús sióvar ok allra vatna, ok hialmr þeirra.—*Hundr* er vargr eða trǫll beina. þess hlutar trǫll er allt sem þat má fyrir fara; *fé* er trǫll fóðrs síns: enn *elldr* er trǫll þess er hann eyðir, ok viðar: griót ok ryð (er trǫll) iarna: vǫtn iarðar ok elldz: regn eða skin snæss ok ísa: hríðir hiarðar.—*Nótt* er angr eða sótt allra fugla: *Snœrr* er sótt orma, ok vetr: *Vetr* er nótt biarnar: enn *sumar* er dagr hans.—Hestar trǫll-kvenna eru *vargar*, enn taumar þeirra eru *ormar*. Drykkr varga er *dreyri*. Haukar ok hrafnar eru hræ-fuglar, ok svá ernir; rétt er aðra *fugla* at nefna til, ok eigna Óðni, eða kenna við orrostu eða hræ eða blóð.

Hvern *karl-mann* má kenna fciti eða bræði hræ-fugla ok varga; svá il-rióð þeirra eða góm-lituð. Karla má ok kalla triá heitum karl-kendum, ok Óðins ok allra Ása, hvárt sem vill lofa eða lasta, ok kenna við her-klæði eða vápn, hlífar eða orrostu, skip eða gull. Enn ef ílla skal kenna, þá má hann kalla allra íllra kvikvenda nǫfnum karl-kendra, ok Iǫtna, ok kenna til fœðzlu nokkurrar; kalla má hann þá ok grenni svína ok allz fénaðar, svá hunda: kalla má hann ok konunga heitum, ok kenna við nǫkkurs konar verk-fœri, eða þat annat er hann er stýrandi; kalla lesti ok þverri allz gagns.—*Konu* er rétt at kalla triá-heitum kvenn-kendum, svá ok Ásynju heitum ok eyja ok landa kvenn-kendra; svá ok orrostu heitum, svá konunga heitum, gram eða ræsi, ok slíkum ǫllum, ok kenna avallt við gull eða glys þeirra, ok við allt þat er þær eiga í gripum, ok við hannyrðir þeirra, svá ok við ǫl-kerǫlld ok drykkju; kenna má þær ok við sió ok steina ef vill. Regin heita goð heiðin, bǫnd, ok rǫgn; kalla má konu þeirra heitum ok kenna. Enn ef ílla skal kenna, þá er hon kennd við hvet-vetna hervilekt, þat er hon er stýrandi, þvál ok sveipu, hryðu ok hland-ausu, skióðu ok skreppu allra ódáða. þess beðja er kona hver sem hána á.

Hár mannz má kalla viðar heitum ǫllum ok grass, þess er á iǫrðu vex; kenna við svǫrð, eða hvirvil, eða hnakka, eða enni; eða reik, eða vanga.—*Hauss* mannz er kallaðr hús heila, enn grund hialma.—*Eyru* mannz eru kǫlluð skip eða siálldr[1] kinna eða vanga, heyrn[ar] eða hlust[a]. Eyru mannz eru kǫllut hlustar augu eða siónir.—*Augu* mannz má kalla skiǫlld, eða skript[2], eða himin-tungla heitum eða annarrar birti; kenna við brýnn eðr hvarma, kinnr eða brár.—*Nef* mannz er kallað inni eða skip hors eða hnœra.—*Munnr* mannz er kallaðr inni eða skip allz fróðleiks.

---

[1] Thus both vellums; read sald? or tiöld. Cp. Lay of Arinb. l. 34.
[2] Thus W.; skip, 748 and 757.

—Svá er ok *brióst* kallað inni eða skip aldrs, ok hugar, ok hiarta, ok þess allz er innan rifja er holld-groit.—*Tenn* eru kallaðar góma-griót.—*Tunga* er kolluð ár eða stýri eða vápns heiti, ok kennd til orða, eða góma, eða tanna.—*Hiarta* er kallað steinn, eða korn, hnot, eða epli, enn kennt til hugar; hiarta heitir ok akarn ok eiskolld: gollorr heitir þat er næst er hiarta mannz: hnetr heita fylvingar.

Heimr er kallaðr hús eða ker veðra: enn *himinn* erviði Dverga fiogurra, þeirra er svá heita, Norðri, Suðri, Austri, Vestri: himinn er kallaðr hialmr eða salr landa, enn braut himin-tungla.—*Sól* er kolluð elldz heitum, ok kennd til himins . . . þat er rétt at kalla iorð hold Ymiss, enn sæ blóð hans, enn Miðgarð brár hans; enn ský heila hans.

b. From Cod. Worm.

. . . *Hofuð* heitir, hauss, kiannr, kollr, hiassi, hvirfill, hnakki: þat skal svá kenna, erviði ok byrði hals; land hialms, hattar, heila, hárs, brúna, svarðar ok heyrnar, augna ok munnz, ok alla þess er á hofði er; sverð Heimdalar; er ok rétt at nefna sverðs heiti, hvert er vill, ok kenna til nokkurs heitis Heimdallz: höfuð er kennt himin eða hús, holl eða snekkja heila ok allz þess er í hofði býr.—*Auga* heitir litr, sión, viðr-lit. þau má svá kenna, kalla sól ok tungl, skript eða skiolld, liós eða leiptr (lopt, Cd.), gler eða gim-steina, stein eða stiornor, goll eða geisla, ok alla birti, ok kenna til brá eða brúna, hvarma ok enniss.—*Brá* má kalla hrís eða gras hvarma eða augna.—*Grát* eða *tár* má kalla hagl eða él, regn eða dropa, skúrir eða forsar augna eða kinna, hlýra, eða brá, eða hvarma.—*Hár* heitir lá ok haddr, þat er konor hafa; hár er svá kennt, at kalla skóg, eða akr, eða gras, eða viðar heiti nokkuro, ok kennt til hofuðs eða hvirfils, hlýrs, eða vanga, hnakka eða reikar, svarðar eða enniss; kalla má ok snió eða mioll hauss eða svarðar . . . (*Here W. ends incomplete.* Cp. Introduction, § 6.)

THE PROPHECY OF THE THREE SIBYLS.

WOLOSPA RECONSTRUCTED.

I. *First Sibyl.—The Past.*

H LIÓÐS bið-ek allar helgar kindir,
meiri ok minni mǫgo Heimdallar :
vildo at ek, Valfǫðr, vel fyr teljak
forn-spiǫll fira þau-es ek fremst um mank.
Ek man Iǫtna ár um borna,   5
þá-es foiðom mik fœdda hǫfðo ;
nio man-ek heima, nio Íviðjor,
miǫtoð mæran, fyr mold neðan.

Ár vas alda þat-es ekki vas,
vasat sandr né sær, né svalar unnir,   10
iǫrð fannsk æva, né upp-himinn,
Gap vas Ginnunga, enn gras ekki.
Sól þat né vissi hvar hon sali átti,
Máni þat ne vissi hvar hann megin átti,
Stiǫrnor þat ne visso hvar þær staði átto.   15

.   .   .   .

Áðr Bors synir biǫðom um ypðo
þeir-es miðgarð mæran skópo,
sól skein sunnan á salta steina,
þá vas grund groin grœnom lauki.

The Sibyl begins to speak of the creation of all things—
I PRAY all holy beings, the children of Heimdall, both high and low, for silence.
Thou wouldst have me, O mighty Father, set forth in order the ancient history
of men, as far back as I can remember it.
I remember the Giants born of yore, that bred me up long ago :
I remember nine Worlds, nine Pythonesses, a blessed Judge beneath the Earth.

The Chaos—
There was a time of yore when nought was,
There was neither the sand, nor the sea, nor the cold billows,
There was no earth to be seen, nor heaven above,
There was a Yawning Gulf, but no grass at all :
The Sun knew not her inn,
The Moon knew not his dominion,
The Stars knew not their dwelling-place.

The Creation—
Before the sons of Bor raised up the land and made the blessed Mid-garth [Earth] . . .
The Sun shone from the south upon the salt rocks,
And the ground grew green with the leek.

Þá gengo Regin oll á rok-stóla,   20
ginn-heilog Goð, ok um þat gættosk.
Sól hvarf sunnan, sinni Mána,
handar innar hœgri til himin-dura.

.   .   .   .

Nótt með niðom nofn um gáfo,
morgin héto ok miðjan dag,   25
undorn ok aptan, árom at telja.

.   .   .   .

Fundo alandi, ómegandi,
Ask ok Emblo orloglausa :
ond þau ne átto, óð þau ne hofðo,
lát né læti, né lito góða :   30
ond gaf Óðinn, óð gaf Hœnir,
lát gaf Lóðurr ok lito góða.

.   .   .   .

Hittosk Æsir á Íða-velli ;
teflðo í túni, teitir váro,
þeir horg ok hof há timbroðo,   35
tangir skópo ok tól gœrðo,
afla logðo, auð smíðoðo
—vas þeim vettegis vant—or golli.
Unz þriár kómo þursa meyjar
amátkar miok or Iotun-heimom.   40

.   .   .   .

Þá gengo Regin oll á rok-stóla,
ginn-heilog Goð, ok um þat gættosk.

.   .   .   .

The Sun's and Moon's course fixed—
Then all the Powers, the most holy Gods, went forth to their judgment seats, and
took counsel together thereon—
The Sun, the Moon's companion, began to turn from the south ever to the right
hand toward the doors of heaven.

.   .   .   .

They gave names to the Night and to the Changes of the Moon,
They named Morning and Mid-day, Afternoon and Evening, for the telling of
the seasons.

Creation of Man—
(*Three Gods wandering along the shore.*)   They found Ash and Embla, outcast, helpless, and torpid,
They had neither the breath of life, nor had they the might of speech, nor carriage,
nor fashion, nor well-favoured looks.
Woden gave them the breath of life ; Hœne the might of speech ; Lodur carriage
and well-favoured looks.

.   .   .   .

Paradise—
The Anses met on the field of Ith,
They played at tables in the court and were merry,
They built up altars and temples, . . .
They made tongs and tools,
They set up a forge, and wrought treasures of gold, they lacked nothing :
Until there came out of Giant-land three ogress-maidens passing loathsome.
Then all the Powers, etc.

Ask veit-ek ausinn, heitir Ygg-drasill,
hár baðmr heilagr, hvíta auri :
þaðan koma dœggvar þærs í dala falla,   45
stendr æ yfir grœnn Urðar-brunni.
þaðan koma meyjar margs vitandi
þriár ór þeim sal es und þolli stendr ;
Urð héto eina, aðra Verðandi,
—skáro á skíði—Skuld ena þriðjo :   50
þær lǫg lǫgðo, þær líf kuro,
alda-bornom, ǫrlǫg segja.

Unz þriár koma ór því liði
ióð-dísir Ás-kungar . . . at húsi.

.   .   .   .

Hvers fregnit mik ?   Hví freistið mín ?   55
Allt veit-ek, Óðinn, hvar þú auga falt
í enom mæra Mímis-brunni :
á sé-ek ausask aurgom forsi
af veði Val-fǫðor.—*Vitoð ér enn eða hvat ?*
Veit-ek Heimdallar hlióð [horn] um folgit   60
und heið-vǫnom helgom baðmi :
or eno galla Giallar-horni
drekkr miǫð Mímir morgin hverjan.

—   þat man-ek frænd-víg fyrst í heimi
es Gráta-goð geirom studdo . . .   65
Ek sá Baldri, blóðgom tívor
Óðins barni, ǫrlǫg folgin :
stóð um vaxinn fyrir Valhǫll austan
miór ok miǫk ungr Mistil-teinn :
varð af þeim meiði, es mær sýndisk,   70

The Holy Tree—
I know an holy Ash called Ygg's steed, a lofty tree sprinkled with white ooze :
From it comes the dews that fall on the dales,
Ever green it stands over the Brook of Weird.
Three Wise Maidens [the Fates] came forth from the hall that stands beneath
the trunk of that tree, writing upon tablets.
The name of the one is Weird, the other is Becoming, Should is the third :
They lay down law, they forecast life, they decree fate for the sons of man.

.   .   .   .

But *other* three mighty beings, midwives, sprung from that race [Norns] come to
the house (*whenever a child is born*) . . .

.   .   .   .

Quoth the Sibyl—
Why do ye seek me ?   Why do ye enquire of me ?
Well I know, Woden, where thou didst hide thine eye, in the blessed Burn of Mim ;
I see a river pouring forth a stream of loamy water out of the pledge of the Lord
of Hosts.
I know where Heimdall's Horn is hidden under the shadowy Holy Tree :
Mim drinks out of the clanging Horn a *draught* of mead every morning *from
the Burn.*

The first crime, Parricide—
This is the first murder among kinsmen that I remember in the world,
When they foined at *Balder*, the God of Tears, with their spears.

.   .   .   .

I beheld the fate that was hidden for Woden's son, Balder the bleeding victim ;
Very slender and young stood Mistletoe growing east of Walhall :

harm-flaug hættlig, Hǫðr nam skióta: . . .
Enn Frigg um grét í Fen-sǫlom
vá Valhallar.—*Vitoð ér enn eða hvat?*

þat man-ek folg-víg fyrst í heimi . . .
Brotinn vas borð-veggr borgar Ása,   75
knátto Vanir víg-ská vǫllo sporna :
Fleygði Óðinn ok í folk um skaut . . .
Þá gengo Regin ǫll á rǫk-stóla,
ginn-heilog Goð, ok um þat gættosk :
Hvárt skyldo Æsir afrað gialda,   80
gíslar seljask eðr gildi eiga . . .
Á gengosk eiðar, orð, ok sœri,
mál ǫll meginleg es á meðal fóro.

Þá gengo Regin ǫll á rǫk-stóla,
ginn-heilog Goð, ok um þat gættosk :   85
Hverr hefði lopt allt lævi blandit,
eðr ætt Iǫtna Óðs mey gefna.
Þórr þar . . . þrunginn móði,
hann sialdan sitr es hann svik of fregn . . .

Hapt sá-ek liggja und Hvera brunni   90
Vila gǫrnom Vloka 'áþekkjan :'
þar Sigyn sitr of sínom veri
. . . 'vel glyjoð.'—*Vitoð ér enn eða hvat?*

From this shoot, that seemed so slender, grew a perilous dart, which Hoth shot. . . .
And Frigg [Balder's mother] wept in the Hall of Ooze over the woe of Walhall.

War in heaven, the first murder—
This is the first murder that I remember in the world . . .
The pale of the city of the Anses was broken ;
The Wanes tramped over the war-wasted field.

. . . .

And Woden shot a spear into the host :
Then all the Powers, the most holy Gods, went forth to their judgment seats,
and took counsel together,
Whether the Anses should pay ransom and give hostages, and make a league
[treaty] . . .

The Hostages are slain—
Then were broken all the oaths and the plighted words, and the sacred truths ;
and all the mighty covenants that had been between them.

The Rape of Freyia—
Then all the Powers, the most holy Gods, went forth to their judgment seats,
and took counsel together,
To know who had mingled the air with plague,
And given Od's maid [Freyia] to the kindred of the Giants :
Thunder alone was not there . . . in wrathful mood,
He will seldom sit still when treason is stirred *against the gods.*

The Loki Titan chained, and his wife Sigyn—
I saw Wloke lying a captive, bound with Wili's guts, beneath the Well of the
Cauldrons ;
Sigyn is sitting there sorrowful over her husband [holding a bowl in her hands].

II. *Second Sibyl.—The Future.*

1. *The Doom.*

HEIÐI hána héto hvars til húsa kom.
vǫlo vél-spá, vítti hon ganda,
seið hon kunni, seið hon 'leikin,'   95
æ var hon angan íllrar brúðar.

.   .   .   .

Ok í hǫllo Hárs hána brendo,
þrysvar brendo, þrysvar borna,
'opt ósialdan'—þó hon enn lifir.   100
'valdi' henni Her-fǫðr hauga [hanga?] ok . . .
fe-spiǫll spaklig ok spá-ganda,
sá hon vítt ok um vítt um verǫld hverja.
        Ein sat hon úti þá-es inn aldni kom
Yggiongr Ása ok í augo leit—   105
Fiǫlð veit-ek frá ða, fram sé ek lengra,
um Ragna-rǫk 'rǫm' sigtíva :—
Brœðr mono berjask, ok at bǫnom verðask,
mono systrungar sifjom spilla :
hart es í heimi, hórdómr mikill.   110
Skeggj-ǫld, Skalm-ǫld, skildir ro klofnir,
Vind-ǫld, Varg-ǫld, áðr verǫld steypisk.
Sól mun sortna, sœkkr fold í mar,
hverfa af himni heiðar stiǫrnor,
snýsk Iǫrmun-gandr í iǫtun-móði,   115
Ulfr knýr 'unnir, enn ari' hlekki,
'slítr nai nef-fǫlr,' Nagl-far losnar :

The dark Sibyl of Doom—
They called her Heithe, that equivocal sibyl, wherever she came to a house ;
She was acquainted with teraphim,
She knew enchantments,
She knew 'witchcraft,'
She was ever the joy of the wicked woman.

.   .   .   .

And they burnt [buried] her in the hall of the High One [?].
Thrice was she burnt, thrice was she born,
. . . and still she is alive.
The Sire of Hosts endowed her with . . . with wise spells to win treasures, and teraphim of prophecy ;
She could see far and wide over every world.
She was sitting out [over her enchantments] what time the old Gallows-god of the Anses came and looked into her eyes. *Quoth she—*
Many stories of old I know, far forward can I see. The Doom of the Powers . . . of the Blessed Gods.

Signs of the Doom—
Brothers shall fight together and slay each other ;
Sisters' children shall commit incest,
It shall be hard with the world, there shall be great whoredom,
An age of axes, an age of swords, shields shall be cloven,
An age of tempest an age of felons [wolves], ere the world falls in ruin.
The sun shall grow black,
The earth shall sink into the sea,
The bright stars shall vanish from the heavens,
Leviathan writhes in great fury,
The Snake's brother [Wolf Fenri] . . . and breaks his fetters . . .

griót-biǫrg gnata, enn gífor rakna,
troða Halir hel-veg, enn himinn klofnar.
    Geyr nú Garmr miǫk fyr Gnípa-helli,   120
festr mun slitna, en freki renna.
    Surtr ferr sunnan með sviga lævi,
skínn af sverði sól valtíva,
. . . Múspellz megir . . .

.   .   .   .   .

Kióll ferr vestan . . . Heljar   125
um lǫg . . . enn Loki stýrir,
fara fífl-megir með freka allir,
þeim es bróðor mær Bysleistz í fǫr.

.   .   .   .   .

Muno Heljar-sinnar heim-stǫð ryðja.
Hrymr ekr austan or Iǫton-heimom   130
. . . Hrim-þursar . . .

.   .   .   .   .

    Geyr nú Garmr, etc.
Hart es með Ásom; hart es með Alfom.
Hátt blæss Heimdallr, horn es á lopti
. . . . Æsir ro á þingi   135
Skelfr Yggdrasils askr standandi,
Ymr it aldna tré, ok or iǫrðo losnar.
Stynja Dvergar fyrir stein-durom
vegg-bergs vísir.—*Vitoð ér enn eða hvat?*
Mælir Óðinn við Mims hǫfoð,   140
'leika' Mims . . . enn miǫtoðr brynnisk
or eno galla Giallar-horni.
þá kœmr Heimdallr . . .
Enn bani Belja biartr at Surti:

. . . the [Hell] ship Nail-fare is loosened,
The granite rocks shall crash together,
And all gyves are unloosened.
All men shall tread the path of Death,
And the heavens be rent.

The array of the Evil Powers—
Swart shall come from the South with a plagueful staff of fire [in his hand],
A brightness as of the sun shines from the Demon's sword,
Muspell's sons follow him . . .
A ship shall sail from the West . . . the Hell's brood shall come over the waves,
and Loki shall steer her.
All the monster-brood (of the Deep) shall march with the Beast,
Byleist's brother's daughter [Hell] is with their company.
They that dwell with Hell shall lay waste the world whereon men dwell.
From the East, Rym shall drive out of Giant-land,
The Rime-ogres [Titans] follow him . . .
Garm, etc.

The great Terror—
It goes hard with the Anses,
It goes hard with the Elves,
Heimdall blows loud with his horn in the air,
The Anses gather at the Moot,
The towering Ash, Ygg's steed, is quivering,
The ancient tree is groaning, and is uprooted from the earth:
The Dwarves, that dwell in the rocks, are moaning before their doors of stone.
Woden takes counsel with Mim's head,
. . . and the judge [Mim] drinks out of the clanging Yell-horn.

Enn Óðinn ferr við Ulf vega, 145
þar man Friggjar falla angan:
þá kœmr inn mikli mǫgr Sigfǫðor
Viðarr vega at val-dýri,
lætr hann megi Hveðrungs mund um standa
hiǫr til hiarta. þá es hefnt fǫðor. 150

. . . . . .
þá kœmr inn mikli mǫgr Hlóðynjar,
Óðins sonr, við Orm vega,
drepr hann af móði Miðgarðz veorr;
gengr fet nio Fiorgynjar burr
neppr frá naðri 'niðs ókvíðnom.' 155

. . . . . .
Geisar eimr ok aldr-nari,
leikr hárr hiti við himin sialfan.

2. The Places of Bliss and Torment.

Sal veit-ek standa sólo fegra
golli þakðan á Gim-lé :
enn annarr stendr á Okolni 160
biór-salr . . . s; enn sá Brimir heitir :
stendr fyr norðan á Niða-fiǫllom
salr or golli ; enn sá Sindri heitir—
þar skolo dyggvar dróttir byggva
ok um aldr-daga ynðiss nióta. 165

Sal veit-ek standa, sólo fiarri,
Ná-strǫndo á, norðr horfa dyrr ;
falla eitr-dropar inn um lióra,
sá es undinn salr orma hryggjom.

The Gods marshalled to battle—
Then shall come Heimdall [to fight with Loki],
And the bright slayer of Beli [Frey] shall meet Swart,
And Woden go forth to do battle with the Wolf,
And there Frigg's love [Woden] shall die.
Thereupon Widar, the mighty son of the Father of Victory, shall come forward to do battle with the Beast [Wolf].
He shall thrust the sword with his hand into the heart of the son of Whethrung [Loki], and so shall he avenge his father.
Then shall *Thunder*, the blessed child of Hlodyn [Earth], the son of Woden, come against the Dragon.
The Holy One of Earth shall slay him,
Earth's son shall walk nine paces ere he fall dead from the venom of the Serpent.
[Ty fights with Garm and each slays the other.]

After the battle is over Swart sets fire to the world—
Smoke and fire shall gush forth,
The terrible flame shall play against the very sky.

The Three Places of Bliss—
I know a hall, fairer than the sun, thatched with gold, that stands on Fire-lea :
There is another, standing on Okoln, the glittering ale-hall that is called Brim :
Upon the North, on the hills of the moon, there stands a golden-built hall called Glede [Glowing-ember] :
There [in these three halls] shall the righteous nations dwell and rejoice in bliss for evermore.

The Three Places of Torment—
I know where a hall stands, far away from the sun, with its doors facing northward, on Corse-strand :

Á fellr austan um eitr-dala   170
sǫxom ok sverðom—Sliðr heitir sú :
Skolo þar vaða þunga strauma
menn mein-svara ok morð-vargar,
ok sa's annars glepr eyra-rúno ;

þar kvelr Níð-hœggr nái for-*dæða;*   175
slítr vára varga.—*Vitoð ér enn eða hvat ?*
þar . . . . dimmo díki . . . .
Naðr fránn . . . .
. . . . . fiǫtrom . . . .
níðinga nai.—Nú man hon sœkkvask.   180

III. *Third Sibyl.—The Regeneration.*

SÉ-EK upp koma ǫðro sinni
iǫrð or ægi iðja-grœna,
falla forsar, flýgr ǫrn yfir
sa es á fialli fiska veiðir.
Muno úsánir akrar vaxa,   185
bǫls mon allz batna, man Baldr koma,
bua þeir Hǫðr ok Baldr Hroptz sig-toptir,
vé val-tíva—*Vitoð ér enn eða hvat ?*
þá kná Hœnir hlaut-við kiósa
ok burir byggva brœðra tveggja   190
vind-heim viðan.—*Vitoð ér enn eða hvat ?*
Finnask Æsir á Íða-velli,
ok und mold-þinor máttkom dœma,
ok minnask þar á megin-dóma

Venom-drops fall in at its luffer, and the hall is wattled with the bodies of snakes.
. . . .
There is a river falls from the East over Venom-vales, full of knives and swords—
Slith is its name—and those of men that are man-sworn or murderers, and they that
put to shame the wives of others, shall wade through its thick waters.
. . . .
(*The third place of Torment, the Pit Hvergelmi*)—
There Felon-cutter (serpent) shall batten on the corses of wizards,
And tear the truce-breakers.
There in that dark pit . . . shall the cruel Serpent . . . in bonds . . . the corses
of the Nidderings.

The Sibyl sinks—
Now must she sink.

The Sibyl of the World to come—
I can see Earth rise a second time, fresh and green out of the sea,
The waters are falling, the erne hovering over them, the bird that hunts the fish
in [the streams of] the mountain.
The fields unsown shall yield their fruit,
All ills shall be healed at the coming of Balder,
Hoth and Balder shall repeople the blessed habitations of Hroft [Woden the Sage],
the holy place of the High Gods.
Then Hœne shall choose the rods of divination [again],
And the sons of the two Brothers [Hoth and Balder] shall inhabit the wide world
of the winds [heaven].
The Anses shall meet on the Field of Ith,
And do judgments under the mighty Tree of the World,

ok á Fimbul-týss fornar rúnar. 195
þar mono eptir undrsamligar
gollnar tǫflor í grasi finnask
þærs í árdaga áttar hǫfðo.

. . . .

VOLOSPÁ IN SKAMMA (Fragment).

Sib. SNÚÐO braut heðan ; sofa lystir
  mik !
Fær-þú fátt af mer fríðra kosta.
Wod. Ek slæ elldi of íviðjo
sva at þú . . . á braut heðan !

W. Hve skyldi Dverga drótt of skepja ?

. . . . 5
S. Or Brimiss blóði ok or blains legg-
  jom :
þar mann-líkon or mǫðkom gœrðosk :
Dvergar í iorðo . . .
þar vas Mótsognir mæztr um orðinn
Dverga allra, enn Durinn annarr . . . 10
Nýi ok Niði, Norðri ok Suðri . . .

. . . .
Mál es Dverga í Dvalins liði
lióna kindom til Lofars telja,
þeir-es sótto frá salar-steini
Aurvanga-siǫt til Ioro-valia . . . 15
þat man uppi meðan ǫld lifir
langniðja tal Lofars hafat.

[Sat þar á haugi oh sló hǫrpo

gygjar hirðir glaðr Egðer :
gól um 'hánom' í gagl-viði 20
fagr-rauðr hani sa es Fialarr heitir :
Gól um Ásom Gollin-kambi,
sá vekr hǫlða at Herja-foðor :
Enn annarr gelr fyr iǫrð neðan
sót-rauðr hani at sǫlom Heljar.] 25

Ól Ulf Loki við Angr-boðo,
enn Sleipni gat við Svaðil-fœra :
Eitt þótti skars allra feiknast
þat vas bróðor frá Byleistz komit.
Loki 'af hiarta lindi brendo' 30
'fann hann half sviðin hugstein komo :'
varð Loptr kviðogr at kono íllri—
þaðan es á foldo flagð hvert komit.

Ero Vǫlor allar frá Viðolfi :
Vitkar allir frá Vilmeiði : 35
Seið-berendr frá Svarthǫfða :
Iǫtnar allir frá Ymi komnir.
Heiðr ok Hross-þiófr Hrimnis kindar.

Freyr átti Gerði, hon vas Gymis dóttir,

And call to mind the dooms of might and the ancient mysteries of the Great God :
And after that the wonderful golden tables, which they had owned in the days of
yore, shall be found in the grass.

. . . .

THE SHORT SIBYL LAY.

The raising of the dead Sibyl. She speaks to Woden—
Get thee gone from this place, I would fain sleep !
Little good shalt thou get in thy dealing with me.
Woden answers—
I will cast fire about thee, thou evil witch !
So that thou . . . ere that I go home.
*Here is a great gap ; she tells of the Creation ; first of Audhumbla and the
Cosmic Titan, then of the creation of the Giants and the Dwarves from his body.*
W. How were the people of the Dwarves created ?
S. Out of the blood of Brimir [Ymi] and the legs of Blue,
And thereafter the Dwarves in the earth, that had been maggots before, took the
shape of men.
Mot-sogni was the mightiest of them all, and Dwryn the second, etc.
Now I will tell the Dwarves, of the race of Dwalin, back to Lofhere . . .
Those of them that came from the salt rocks to Mudfield's abodes in the Field
of Ooze.
The cocks of the four worlds, translated, vol. i, p. 198.
The formation of the Monsters of Evil.
Loki's brood, ll. 26-30, translated, vol. i, p. 232.

iǫtna ættar ok Aurboðo: 40
þá var þiazi þeirra frændi,
skot-giarn iǫtunn, hans vas Skaði dóttir.

Muno ellifo Æsir taldir
Baldr es hnígr við bana-þúfo,
þess læzk Vali ' verðr ' at hefna,   45
síns of bróðor slær hann hand-bana.

Austr býr in aldna í Iarnviði,
ok fœðir þar Fenris kindir;
verðr af þeim ulfom einn máttkastr
tungls tiúgari í trollz hami: 50
Fyllisk fiǫrvi feigra manna,
rýðr ragna siǫt rauðom dreyra

svǫrt verða sól-skin, né sumar eptir,
veðr ǫll válig . . .
Haf gengr hríðom við himin sialfan,   55
líðr lǫnd yfir, enn lopt bilar,
þaðan koma snióvar ok snarir vindar.
Haf sé-ek brenna, enn hauðr loga,
verða flestir fiǫr-lausn þola . . .
þa es ráð ok regin þrióta.   60

. . . . . .

þá kœmr annarr enn máttkari,
þó þoriga-ek þann at nefna.
Fair siá nú framm um lengra
an Óðinn man Ulfi mœta.

EXTRACTS FROM EDDA, OF PARAPHRASES BASED ON THE SIBYL SONGS AND OTHER POEMS.

a. = Paraphrase from the Long Sibyl Lay.   [a] = From the lost parts of Long Sibyl Lay.   b. = From the Short Sibyl Lay.   [b] = From the lost parts of Short Sibyl Lay.   c. = From Wafthrudni and other poems.

1. *Cosmogonic.*

FYRR var þat mörgum öldum en iörð væri sköput, er Niflheimr var gorr, ok í hónum miðjum liggr brunnr sá er Hver-gelmir heitir, ok þaðan af falla ár þær er svá heita . . .

[a] Fyrst var þó sá heimr í Suðr-halfu er Muspell heitir; hann er lióss ok heitr;

The generation of the Sibyls and Wizards, ll. 34–38, see vol. i, p. 232. *Balder's death*, ll. 43–46, see vol. i, p. 231.

The end of the World—
An aged giantess dwells in Ironwood, and there she gives birth to Fenri's race [Wolves]:
Among them one shall be the mightiest of the wolves; he shall be in the shape of an ogre, the pitch-forker of the moon.
He feeds on the lives of the dead, spattering the heavens with red blood.

Signs of Doom—
The sunshine shall wax dark, nor shall any summer follow, and all the winds shall turn to blight;
The sea shall rise in tempest against the very heaven and cover the land,
And the sky shall be rent, and out of it shall come snow-storms and mighty winds.
I can see the sea a-fire and the land in flames,
And every living thing shall suffer death,
When the . . . and the Powers shall perish . . .

The coming of Christ—
Then there shall come One yet mightier:
Though I dare not name him.
There be but few who can see farther forward than the day when Woden shall meet the Wolf.

PROSE PARAPHRASE.

The Yawning Gulf Muspell or the two Worlds of Fire and Ice—
It was many ages before Earth was shapen that the Cloud-world [Nifl-heim] was made, and in the midst thereof is the brook that is called Hwer-gelmir, and from out of it there fall the rivers that are called . . . [a] Yet first [of all] was the world in the south, which is called Muspell; it is bright and hot, flaming is it and burning,

logandi er hann ok brennandi, ok ófœrr þeim er þar eru útlendir, ok eigi eigu þar óðul. Sá er Surtr nefndr er þar sitr á landz enda til land-varnar; hann hefir loganda sverð, ok í enda veraldar mun hann fara ok herja ok sigra öll goðin, ok brenna allan heim með eldi.

c. Ár þær er kallaðar eru Éli-vágar, þá er þær vóru svá langt komnar frá uppsprettum, at eitr-kvikva, sú er þeim fylgði, harðnaði svá sem sindr þat er ferr or eldinum, þá varð þat íss; ok þá er sá íss gaf staðar ok rann eigi, þá heldi yfir þannig úr þat er af stóð eitrinu, ok frauss at hrími, ok iók hvert hrímit yfir annat allt í Ginnunga-gap. Ginnunga-gap þat er vissi til norðr-ættar fylldiz með höfugleik íss ok hríms; ok inn í frá úr ok gustr.

[a] Inn syðri hlutr Ginnunga-gaps léttisk móti gneistum ok siom þeim er flugo or Muspellz-heimi. Svá sem kallt stóð af Nifl-heimi, ok allir hlutir grimmir, svá var allt, þat er vissi námunda Muspelli, heitt ok lióst. Enn Ginnunga-gap var svá hlœtt sem lopt vind-laust.

[b] Ok þá er mœtti hríminu blœrr hitans, sva-at bráðnaði ok draup, ok af þeim kviko-dropom kviknaði, með krapti þess er til sendi hitann, ok varð mannz líkendi, ok er sá nefndr Ymir.

c. Enn Hrím-þursar kalla hann Aurgelmi, ok eru þaðan komnar ættir Hrim-þursa. . . . hinn gamli Hrím-þurs, hann köllum ver Ymi.

[b] Næst var þat þa er hrímit draup, at þar varð af kýr, sú er Auðhumbla hét; enn fiórar miolk-ár runnu or spenum hennar, ok fœddi hon Ymi; hon sleikði hrímsteina er saltir vóru; ok enn fyrsta dag er hon sleikði steinana, kom or steininum at

---

and not to be lived in by them that are aliens and have it not as their native land [lit. have no heritage there]. Swart is the name of him that stands at the border of that land to keep it; he has a flaming sword, and at the end of the world he shall go forth and harry and overcome all the gods, and burn the whole world with fire.

[c] The rivers that are called Sleet-billows, when they were come so far from their springs, that the poison-freshet that they bore hardened, like a cinder that is taken out of the fire, turned to ice, and when the ice stopped and ran no more, then straightway the fume that steamed out of the venom was mantled over and froze into rime, and the rime grew thicker, coat over coat, all along the Yawning Gulf. And that part of the Yawning Gulf, that looked towards the North, was filled with a heavy load of ice and rime; but farther in it [towards the centre] was fume and steam. [a] But the southern part of the Yawning Gulf was brightened by the fireflakes and sparks, that flew out of the world of Muspell. Just as cold and all sorts of horrors proceeded from Cloud-world, so was all that turned towards and came nigh to the world of Muspell hot and bright. But in the Yawning Gulf it was close and sultry like air when there is no wind.

The Giant Ymi.—[b] And when the waft of heat struck the rime so that it melted and dripped, then from out of the freshet-drops, by the power of him that sent the heat, there came a quickening, and it grew into the shape of a man, and this is he that is called Ymir. c. But the Rime-ogres call him Mud-gelmir, and from him are come all the generations of the Rime-ogres . . . the old Rime-ogre, we call him Ymir . . .

The Cow Audhumbla.—[b] After this it came to pass that from the dripping of the rime there grew the cow that is called Audhumbla, and four rivers of milk ran out of her dugs, and she suckled Ymi. She licked the lumps of rime that were salt, and the first day that she licked the stones, there came out of the stone by the evening the hair of a man, and the second day a man's head, and by the

kveldi mannz-hár; annan dag mannz höfuð; þriðja dag var þat allr maðr; sá er nefndr Buri; hann var fagr álitum, mikill ok máttugr; hann gat son þann er Borr er nefndr; hann fekk þeirrar konu er Bestla er nefnd, dóttir Bölþorns iötuns, ok gátu þau þriá sonu, hét einn Óðinn, annarr Vili, þriði Vé . . .

[b] Synir Bors drápu Ymi iötun; enn er hann féll, þá hlióp svá mikit blóð ór sárum hans, at með því drekðu þeir allri ætt Hrim-þursa:

c. Nema einn komsk undan með sínu hyski; þann kalla Iötnar Ber-gelmi; hann fór upp á lúðr sínn ok kona hans ok héllzk þar; ok eru af þeim komnar Hrim-þursa ættir . . .

c. þeir (Bors synir) tóku Ymi ok fluttu í mitt Ginnunga-gap, ok gǫrðu af hónum iörðinn, af blóði hans sæinn (etc. as in Vþm.)

[a] þá tóku þeir sior ok gneista, þa er lausir fóru, er kastað hafði or Muspellz-heimi, ok settu á himin, bæði ofan ok neðan, til at lýsa himin ok iörð.

a. þeir gáfu stað öllum eldingunum, sumum á himni, sumar fóru lausar undir himni, ok settu þó þeim stað, ok sköpuðu göngu þeim. Svá er sagt í fornum vís-endum, at þaðan af vóru dœgr greind ok ára-tal.

a. þá er þeir gengu með siávar-ströndo Bors synir, fundu þeir tré tvau, ok tóku upp tréin, ok sköpuðu af menn: gaf inn fyrsti önd ok líf; annarr vit ok hrœring; þriði ásiónu, mál ok heyrn ok sión; gáfu þeim klæði ok nöfn; hét karl-maðrinn Askr, enn konan Embla; ok ólsk þaðan af mann-kindin sú er iörðin var gefin undir Miðgarði.

[a] Í upphafi setti hann stiórnar-menn, ok setti þá at dœma með ser örlög manna,

---

third day it was a whole man; this is he that is called Buri, he was fair to see, big and strong, he begat a son who is called Bor; he took to wife a woman called Bestla, the daughter of Giant Bale-thorn, and they had three sons, one was called Woden, the second Wili, and the third Wé . . .

The Deluge; Rime-ogres drowned.—[b] Bor's sons slew Giant Ymi, and when he fell, so much blood ran out of his wounds that the whole generation of the Rime-ogres were drowned in it, c. save one that escaped with his household; him the giants call Ber-gelmi; he went into his ark *or* bin with his wife, and so they were saved therein, and from them are come the generations of the Rime-ogres . . .

Earth made.—c. [Bor's sons] took Ymi and cast him into the midst of the Yawn-ing Gulf and made the earth out of him, out of his blood the sea [etc., as in Vþm.]

Sun and Moon and Stars.—a. Then they took the flakes and sparks that were flying about, which had been cast out of the World of Muspell, and set them in the heaven, both above and below, to give light to the heaven and·the earth. And they appointed a place to each of the particles of fire, to some in the heaven, but some wandered about freely under the heaven, and to them they gave a place also and appointed their courses, as it is told in old song that in this way the day and night were marked off, and the seasons of the year also.

a. *The making of Man.*—And as they went along by the sea-shore, the sons of Bor found two trees, and they took them up and made men out of them; the first of them [Woden] gave them breath and life, the second [Wili] understanding and motion, the third [Wé] form, speech, hearing, and sight; they gave them also clothes and names; the man was called Ash and the woman Elma, and from them sprung mankind, to whom the earth was given upon Middle-garth.

The Golden Age—

In the beginning he set rulers and ordained them to give judgment along with

ok ráða um skipan borgarinnar; þat var þar sem heitir a. Iða-völlr í miðri borginni. a. Var þat it fyrsta þeirra verk at gœra hof þat er sæti þeirra standa í, tolf önnur en hásætið þat er Allföðr á; c. þat hús er bezt gort á iörðu ok mest, allt er þat útan ok innan svá sem gull eitt; í þeim stað kalla menn [c.] Glaðsheim. Annan sal gœrðu þeir; þat var a. hörgr er gyðjurnar áttu, ok var hann all-fagr; þat hús kalla menn [c] Vingolf. a. þar næst gœrðu þeir þat, at þeir lögðu afla, ok þar til gœrðu þeir hamar, ok töng, ok steðja, ok þaðan af öll tól önnur; ok því næst smíðoðo þeir malm, ok stein, ok tré, ok svá gnógliga þann malm er gull heitir, ok öll búsgögn höfðu þeir af gulli.—Ok er sú öld kölluð *Gull-aldr* :—a. áðr en spilltisk af til-kvámu kvennanna; þær kómo or Íötun-heimum.

    a. þar næst settusk guðin upp í sæti sín, ok settu dóma sína, ok mintusk,

    b. Hvaðan Dvergar höfðu kviknat í moldunni ok niðri í iörðunni, svá sem maðkar í holdi. Dvergarnir höfðu skipask fvrst ok tekit kviknan í holdi Ymiss, ok vóru þá maðkar; enn af atkvæði guðanna urðu þeir vitandi mann-vitz, ok höfðu mannz líki, ok bua þó í iörðu ok steinum. Móðsognir var œztr, ok annar Durinn.

    b. Enn þessir eru ok Dvergar ok bua í steinum, enn inir fyrri í moldu . . . b. Enn þessir kómu frá Svarins-haugi til Aurvanga á Iorovöllu, ok er þaðan kominn Lofarr.

    b. Gýgr ein býr fyrir austan Miðgarð í þeim skógi er Iarnviðr heitir; í þeim skógi byggja þær troll-konor er Iarnviðjor [read Iviðjor?] heita; en gamla gýgr fœðir at sonum marga Iötna, ok alla í vargs líkjum, ok þaðan eru komnir þessir ulfar. Ok svá er sagt, at af ættinni verðr sá einn máttkastr er kallaðr er [b] Mána-

---

him upon the fates of men, and to give counsel upon the constitution of the City [Ansegarth]. And this *court* was set at the place that is called a. the Field of Ith [Magh Ith] in the midst of a city. a. This was the first work they did, to make a temple for their seats to stand in, twelve of them beside the high-seat, which belonged to the All-father. c. This is the best built and biggest house on earth; it is all one mass of gold, as it were, both within and without, and this place is called c. Gladham. They made *also* another hall; it was a high-place [a harrow], which belonged to the goddesses, and it was very fair, and this mansion men call [c] Win-golf [Joy-room]. a. And the next work that they did was to lay down forges and make a hammer, and tongs, and stithy for it, and with these they wrought all other tools, and then they smithied metal and gems, and wood-work, and in great abundance the metal that is called gold, and all their household gear they had of gold; and that age is called the *Golden Age*, until it was destroyed by the coming of women from Giant-land.

    The Dwarves.—After this the gods sat down in their seats, and set the court and took counsel : b. Whence the Dwarves had come that had come to life in the mould and down under the earth, like maggots in flesh. The Dwarves had bred first and come to life in the flesh of Ymi, and at that time they were maggots; but by the word of the gods they had become endowed with the wisdom of man, and got the likeness of man; albeit they dwell in the earth and the rocks. Móð-sogni was the chief of them, and Dwryn the second. b. There are also Dwarves that dwell in the rocks, as the first do in the mould . . . b. but they [the third race] came from Swarin's howe to Loom-wang in Ior-weald, and from them came Lofar . . .

    The Monsters.—b. There is an ogress that dwells in the east of Mid-garth in the forest that is called Iron-wood; in that forest there live the giant-women that are called Inwiddas [witches], but the old ogress gives birth to many giant-sons, all of them in the shape of wolves, and thence are come these wolves [as spoken of]. And as it is said, out of this race comes one the mightiest of all, called the [b] Moon-hound; b. he is

garmr; b. hann fyllisk fiörvi allra þeirra manna er deyja; ok hann gleypir tungl; en stœkkvir blóði himin ok lopt öll. þaðan af týnir Sól skini sínu, ok vindar eru þá ókyrrir, ok gnýja heðan ok handan.

(þá mælti Gangleri: Hvar er höfuð-staðrinn eða helgi-staðr guðanna? Hárr svarar): þat er at Aski Ygg-drasils, c. þar skolo goðin eiga dóma sína hvern dag. a. c. Askrinn er allra treá mestr ok beztr; limar hans dreifask um heim allan; ok standa yfir himni þriár rœtr tréssins, ok halda því upp, ok standa afar-breitt; c. ein er með Ásum; enn önnor með Hrim-þursum, þar sem forðum var Ginnunga gap: En þriðja stendr yfir Nifheiᵐi; ok undir þeirri rót er Hvergelmir; enn Níðhœggr gnagar neðan rótina.

a. Enn undir þeirri rót er til Hrim-þursa horfir, þar er Mimis-brunnr, er spekð ok mann-vit er í folgit, ok heitir sá Mimir er á brunninn; hann er fullr af vísendum, fyrir því at hann drekkr or brunninum af horninu Giallar-horni. a. þar kom Allföðr ok beiddisk eins drykkjar af brunninum; enn hann fekk eigi fyrr en hann lagði auga sítt at veði.

a. þriðja rót Asksins stendr á himni; ok undir þeirri rót er brunnr sá, er miok er heilagr, er heitir Urðar-brunnr; þar eigu guðin dóm-stað sínn. c. Hvern dag ríða Æsir þangat upp um brúna Bifröst—hon heitir ok Ás-brú— . . .

(þá mælti Gangleri: Brennr eldr yfir Bifröst? Hárr segir): þat er þú sér rautt í loganum, er eldr brennandi, upp á himin mundu ganga Berg-risar, ef öllum væri fœrt á Bifröst þeim er fara vilja.

a. Margir staðir eru á himni fagrir, ok er þar allt guðlig vörn fyrir. þar stendr salr einn fagr undir Askinum við brunninn, ok or þeim sal koma þriár meyjar þær er

---

filled with the life of [he devours] every man that dies, c. and he shall swallow the Moon, b. and sprinkle heaven and the whole air with blood, and therewith the Sun shall lose her sheen, and the winds shall grow restless and blow hither and thither . . .

The Holy Tree. The Brook of Weird and of Mim.—a. (Then spake Gangler: 'Where is the chief abode or sanctuary of the gods?' The High One answers): c. It is at the Ash Ygg's steed, where the gods held their court every day. a. This Ash is the greatest and best of trees; its limbs spread over all the world, and three roots of it stretch across the heaven, and hold it up and stretch wonderfully far. c. One turns towards the Anses, the second towards the Rime-ogres, where once the Yawning Gulf was, but the third stretches over Cloud-world, and Hwer-gelme [Cauldron-Whelmer] is under this root, and Felon-cutter [the snake] gnaws the bottom of this root. a. But under the root that trends towards the Rime-ogres is Mim's Burn, wherein is wisdom and understanding, and he that owns the burn is named Mim; he is full of knowledge, because he drinks from the brook out of the Yell-horn. a. The Father of All came and asked him for one draught of the brook, but he could not get it till he had pledged his eye for it. a. The third root of the Ash stands upon the heaven, and under that˙ root is a very holy burn, called Weirds'-burn, where the gods have their moôt-stead. c. Every day the Anses ride up thither over the bridge Rocking-Race, which is also called the Anses-bridge [Spirit-bridge = Rainbow] . . .

Then spake Gangler: 'Is there fire burning along Rocking-Race?' Says the High One: 'That red flame which thou seest therein is a blazing fire. The mountain giants would get up into heaven if Rocking-Race were easy travelling for all that would go by it.'

a. There are many fair places in heaven, and it is all under the guard of the gods [a sanctuary under divine protection].

svá heita.—Urðr, Verðandi, Skuld—þessar meyjar skapa mönnum alldr, þær köllu ver Nornir.

a. Enn eru fleiri Nornir, þær er koma til hvers barns er borit verðr, ok skapa aldr, c. ok eru þessar goð-kungar, enn aðrar Alfa ættar, enn inar þriðju Dverga ættar. . . . [a] Góðar Nornir ok vel ættaðar skapa góðan aldr; enn þeir menn er fyr ósköpum verða þá valda því illar Nornir.

a. Enn er þat sagt, at Nornir þær, er byggja við Urðar-brunn, taka hvern dag vatn í brunninum, ok með aurinn þann er liggr um brunninn, ok ausa upp yfir askinn, til þess at eigi skolo limar hans tréna eða fúna; [a] enn þat vatn er svá heilagt, at allir hlutir þeir er þar koma í brunninn verða svá hvítir sem hinna sú er skiall heitir, er innan liggr við egg-skurn. [a] Sú dögg er þaðan af fellr á iörðina, þat kalla menn hunangs fall, ok þar af fœðask bý-flugur. [a] Fuglar tveir fœðask í Urðar-brunni; þeir heita svanir, ok af þeim fuglum hefir komit þat fugla kyn er svá heitir.

[a. b] Margir staðir ero þar göfugligir: Sá er einn staðr er kallaðr er Alfheimr, þar byggvir folk þat er Liós-alfar heita; enn Dökk-alfar bua niðri í iörðo, ok ero þeir ólíkir þeim sýnom, enn miklo ólíkari reyndum. Liós-alfar ero fegri en sól sýnom, enn Dökk-alfar ero svartari en bik.

Sœttir Vana ok Ása.—a. Óðinn fór á hendr Vönom með her; enn þeir urðo vel við, ok vörðo land sítt, ok höfðo ymsir sigr; herjoðo hvárir land annarra, ok gœrðo skaða á. Enn er þat leiddisk hvárom-tveggjom, lögðo þeir milli sín sættar-stefno, ok gerðo frið, ok seldosk gíslar; fengo Vanir sína ina ágætosto menn, Niörð inn

---

a. There stands a fair hall under the Ash over against the brook, and out of this hall there came three maidens, called Weird, Becoming, and Should. These maidens shape the fates of men, and we call them Norns. a. But there are other Norns, some of whom come to every child that is born and shape his fate, c. and these are of God-kind, but others are of the race of the Elves, and a third kind of the race of the Dwarves . . . [a] good Norns and well-born shape good lives; but those men, whose fate is ill, owe it to the evil Norns . . .

a. And it is said that those Norns that dwell by Weird's burn draw water every day from the burn, and the ooze with it that lies at the bottom of the burn, and sprinkle it over the Ash, that its branches shall never wither or rot. [a] And this water is so holy that everything that comes into this burn becomes as white as the film that is called 'sciall,' that lies inside the egg-shell. [a] The dew that falls from it upon the earth men call honey-dew, and the bees feed upon it. a. Two birds live in Weirds'-burn, they are called Swans, and from them are come all the race of birds that bear that name.

White and Black Elves.—[a. b] There are many noble places there; there is one called Elf-ham, wherein dwell the people that are called the Elves of Light; but the Dark Elves live down in the earth, and they are altogether unlike in look, and a great deal more unlike in reality; the Light Elves [Fairies] are fairer than the sun to look on, but the Dark Elves [Brownies] are blacker than pitch.

War with the Wanes.—a. Woden went with a host to fight the Wanes, but they made ready to meet them and defended their land, and the victory swayed between them, and each harried the other's land and wrought great destruction. And forasmuch as this was hurtful to both of them, they set an accord between them and made peace and gave each other hostages. The Wanes gave their best man Niord

auðga, ok Frey son hans; enn Æsir þar í mót þann er Hœnir hét, ok kölloðo hann all-vel til höfðingja fallinn; hann var mikill maðr ok vænn; með hónom sendo Æsir þann er Mimir hét; hann var inn vitrasti maðr: Enn Vanir fengo þar í mót þann er spakastr var í þeirra flokki, sá hét Kvásir. Enn er Hœnir kom í Vanaheim, þá var hann þegar höfðingi gerr; Mimir kendi hónom ráð öll, enn ef Hœnir varð staddr á þingom eða stefnom, svá at Mimir var eigi nær, ok kvæmi nokkur vanda-mál fyrir hann, svaraði hann æ ino sama :—'Ráði aðrir!' sagði hann. þá grunaði Vani, at Æsir mundo hafa falsat þá í manna skiptino, þá tóko þeir Mimi ok hals-hioggo, ok sendo höfuðit Ásom. Óðinn tók höfuðit ok smurði urtom þeim er eigi mátti fúna, ok kvað þar yfir galdra, ok magnaði svá at þat mælti við hann, ok sagði hónom marga leynda hluti. Niörð ok Frey setti Óðinn blót-góða, ok vóro þeir Diar með Ásom. Dóttir Niarðar var Freyja; hon var blót-gyðja, ok kendi fyrst með Ásom seið, sem Vönom var títt. þá er Niörðr var með Vönom, hafði hann átta systor sína—því at þat vóro þar lög; vóro börn þeirra Freyr ok Freyja ;—enn þat var bannat með Ásom at byggva svá nait at frændsemi.—[Yngl. S. ch. 4.]

[a] Guðin höfðu ósætt við folk þat er Vanir heita; enn þeir lögðu með ser frið-stefnu, ok settu grið á þá lund, at þeir gengu hvárir-tveggju til eins kers, ok spýttu hráka sínum í. Enn at skilnaði þá tóku goðin, ok vildu eigi láta týnask þat griða-mark, ok skopoðu þar or mann ; sá heitir Kvásir; hann er svá vitr, at eingi spyrr hann þeirra hluta at eigi kann hann órlausn. Hann fór víða um heim at kenna mönnum frœði: ok þá er hann kom at heim-boði til Dverga nökkura, Fialars ok Galars, þá kölluðu þeir hann með ser á ein-mæli ok drápu hann, létu renna blóð hans í tvau ker, ok einn ketil—ok heitir sá Óðrœrir, enn kerin heita Són ok Boðn—þeir bléndu hunangi við blóðit, ok varð þar af miöðr sá, at hverr er af drekkr, verðr skald ok frœði-maðr. Dvergarnir sögðu Ásum at Kvásir hefði kafnat í mann-viti, fyrir því at eingi var þar svá fróðr, at spyrja kunni hann fróðleiks.—[Edda, Skaldsk.-mál.]

Nú var Loki tekinn griða-lauss ok farið með hann í helli nokkurn; þá tóko þeir þriár hellor ok sett á egg, ok lustu rauf á hellunni hverri. þá vóru teknir

---

the wealthy and his son Frey, but the Anses in return gave him who is called Hœne, saying that he was well fitted to be a ruler of men. He was a big man and well favoured. With him the Anses sent a man called Mim, who was the wisest of men, but the Wanes gave in return the greatest sage of their company, whose name was Quasi. But as soon as Hœne came to Wana-land he was straightway made ruler, and Mim gave him counsel in all his designs. But when Hœne was sitting in council or court and Mim was not at hand and he could get no decision from him, he always answered in one way, 'Let others settle the matter,' said he. Then the Wanes began to suspect that the Anses must have deceived them in exchanging men, so they took Mim and cut off his head, and sent it to the Anses. Woden took the head and smeared it with such worts as might not let it decay, and spoke charms over it, and prevailed so that it spoke with him and told him many secrets. Niord and Frey Woden made priests, and they were the Anses' seers [Diar]. Freyja was Niord's daughter; she was a priestess, and she first taught the Anses enchant-ments after the manner of the Wanes. When Niord was with the Wanes he had his sister to wife (for that was their law); their children were Frey [Lord] and Freyja [Lady]. But it was forbidden among the Anses to marry within such kinship.

The same story from Edda, already translated, vol. i, p. 464.

Loki chained.—And now Loki was taken, no truce being granted him, and borne off to a certain cave, and then they took three flag-stones and set them up on edge, and struck a hole in each of these stones. Then they took the sons of Loki,

synir Loka, Vali ok Nari eða Narfi; brugðu Æsir Vala í vargs líki ok reif hann í
sundr Narfa bróður sínn. Þá tóku Æsir þarma hans ok bundu Loka með yfir þá
þriá-egg-steina—stendr einn undir herðum, annarr undir lendum, þriði undir knés-
bótum—ok urðu þau bönd at iarni. Þá tók Skaði eitr-orm, ok festi upp yfir hann,
svá at eitrið skyldi driúpa or orminum í andlit hónum. Enn Sigyn, kona hans, sitr
hiá hónum, ok heldr munn-laugu undir eitr-dropa; enn þá er full er munn-laugin,
gengr hon ok slær út eitrinu, enn meðan drýpr eitrið í andlit hónum; þá kippisk
hann svá hart við, at iörð öll skelfr—þat kalli þer land-skialpta. Þar liggr hann í
böndum til Ragna-rökkrs.

Arna-Magn. 748 and 757, *add this from Lost Memorial Verses on Loki*—
Am-svartnir heitir vatn, enn Lyngvi holmi í vatninu, enn Siglitnir hvóll í hol-
minum; enn þviti heitir hæll er stendr í hvólinum, enn Ginul (*or* gnioll) heitir rauf
er boruð er á hælinum; enn Hræða heitr festr er Fenris-ulfr er bundinn með, ok er
henni drepit í gögnum raufina; enn Gelgja heitir spýta sú sem fyrir er stungin.
Fiöturinn heitir Gleipnir, sá sem hónum heldr. Tveir fiötrar vóru gœrvir til hans,
þeir Drómi ok Lœðingr, ok hélt hvárrgi. Þá var gerr Gleipnir or sex hlutum—or
kattar dyn . . . [see vol. i, p. 16]; því er þat ekki eptir síðan at þat var þar allt til
haft. Ár tvær falla or munni hónum, heitir önnur Víl enn önnur Van; ok er þat
rétt at kalla vötn hráka hans, enn Giolnar heita granar hans.

THE WORLD-DESTRUCTION.

(Hver tíðendi er at segja um Ragna-rökr, þess hefir ek eigi fyrr heyrt getið?
Hárr svarar—Mikil tíðendi eru þaðan af at segja ok mörg: þau in fyrstu, at),
    b. Vetr sá kemr er kallaðr er Fimbul-vetr; þá drífr snær or öllom ættum; frost

---

Wali, and Nari or Narfi; they changed Wali into a wolf's shape, and he tore his
brother Nari. Then the Anses took his guts and bound Loki with them upon the
three-edged stones; one stone comes under his shoulders, another under his loins,
and the third under the tenons of his knees, and these fetters were turned into
iron. Then Scathe took a venomous snake and fastened it up above him, so
that the venom should drip down from the snake into his face. But Sigyn, his wife,
sits by him holding a hand-cup to catch the drops of venom, and when the cup is
full she goes and pours away the venom, and in the meanwhile the venom drips into
his face, then he writhes so hard with the pain that the whole earth quakes, and
that is called an earthquake, and there Loki lies in bonds till the Twilight [*better*
Doom] of the Gods.

Tawny is the name of the mere, and Ling the holm in the mere, and Marl
the knoll in the holm, and Thwaite the stake that stands upon the knoll, and Cleaft
the hole that is bored through the stake, and Scare is the cable that Fenris-wolf is
bound to, and it is reaved through the hole, and Gill-bone is the peg that is put
through the ear of the rope. The fetter that holds him is called Gossamer. There
were two fetters made for him, called Hobble and Coil, but neither of them held;
and then Gossamer was made out of six things, the din of the cat's tread, the birds'
milk . . .; and there is no more left of these things, for they were all used in the
making of it. Two streams fall from his mouth, the one called Wailing, the
other Wanhope, and it is right [for a poet] to speak of *water* as his spittle, and
his lip-bristles are called Gills.

Signs of the Doom.—Says Gangler, 'What tidings are there to tell of the Doom
of the Powers? I have never heard tell of it before.'
The High One answers, 'There are great tidings of it and many to tell withal,

eru þá mikil, ok vindar harðir ; ekki nýtr sólar. þeir vetr fara þrír saman, ok ekki sumar í millum. (Enn áðr ganga svá aðrir þrír vetr), a. at þá eru um allan heim orrostur miklar. þá drepask brœðr fyrir ágirni sakar, ok engi þyrmir föður eða syni í mann-drápum eða sifja-sliti. b. þá verðr þat er mikil tíðendi þykkir, at ulfrinn gleypir sólina (ok þykkir mönnum þat mikit mein) ; þá tekr annarr ulfrinn tunglit (ok görir sá ok mikit ógagn). a. Stiörnor hverfa þá af himni. a. (þá er þat tíðenda, at) svá skelfr iörð öll, at biörg ok viðir losna or iörðu upp, enn biörgin hrynja ; enn fiötrar allir ok bönd brotna ok slitna. a. þá verðr Fenris-ulfr lauss. þá geysisk hafit á löndin, fyrir því at þá snýzk Miðgarðz-ormr í iotun-móði ok sœkir upp á landit (þá verðr ok þat at) a. Naglfar losnar (skip þat er svá heitir ; þat er gœrt af nöglum dauðra manna, ok er þat fyrir því varúðar-vert, ef maðr deyr með óskornum nöglum, at sá maðr eykr mikit efni til skipsins Naglfars, er goðin ok menn vildu ógœrt [1] yrði). Enn í þessum sióvar-gang flýtr Naglfar :

a. Hrymr heitir iotunn er stýrir Naglfara. c. Enn Fenris-ulfr ferr með gapanda munn, ok er enn neðri kœptr á iörðu, enn inn efri við himni ; gapa mundi hann meira, ef rúm væri til. Eldar brenna or augum hans ok nösum. [a] Miðgarðz-ormr blæss svá eitrinu at hann dreifir lopt öll ok lög, ok er hann all-ógurlegr, ok er hann í aðra hlið Ulfinum.

a. Í þessum gný klofnar himininn ok ríða þaðan Muspellz synir ; Surtr ríðr fyrstr,

and the first tidings are—That a winter shall come that is called the b. Monster Winter, then shall the snow drive from every airt, great frost shall there be then and cruel winds, no light of the sun, three winters shall come together, and no summer between them. And before three other winters pass so, a. there shall be great wars all over the world, brothers shall slay each other for the sake of greed, and no man shall spare his father and son, (and there shall be) murders and incest. b. Then there shall come to pass what shall be thought great tidings, to wit, the wolf shall swallow the sun, and men shall count that a great loss, and the other wolf shall seize the moon and work great damage thereby, a. and the stars shall vanish out of heaven, a. and then this shall come to pass, that the whole earth shall quake so that the a. rocks and woods shall be loosened out of the ground, and the mountains shall quake, a. and every fetter and bond shall be broken and riven. [a] And the wolf of Fenri shall get loose withal, for the Leviathan writhes in giant rage, and the sea shall gush over the land, and therewithal it shall be that a. Nail-fare shall be loosened [from her moorings]. [That is the name of the ship that is built out of the nails of dead men, and therefore it is a forbidden deed for a man to die with unshorn nails, for such a man worketh mightily towards the building of the ship Nail-fare, which gods and men would never have built.]

The array of the Evil Powers.—And Nail-fare shall float upon this sea-flood. a. The giant that steers Nail-fare is named Rym. [b] And the wolf Fenri shall go with gaping jaws, and his nether jaw shall touch the earth, and his upper jaw the heaven, and he would gape wider still if only there were room withal. Fire shall blaze from his eyes and his nostrils. [a] The serpent of the earth shall [also] breathe venom so that the air and water shall be charged therewith, and he shall be awful to look on, and he shall stand on the other side of the wolf [2]. And with this crack [of Doom] a. the heaven shall be rent, and out of it there shall ride the sons of a. Muspell ; Swart shall ride first, and before him and behind him a blazing fire ; his

---

[1] Emend., seint a gert, Cd.
[2] Here is only the passage telling how the fiends were wakened.

ok fyrir hónum ok eptir eldr brennandi; sverð hans er gótt miök, af því skínn biartara en af sólu. c. Enn er þeir ríða Bifröst, þá brotnar hon (sem fyrr er sagt). c. Mus-pellz megir sœkja framm á þann vǫll er Vígríðr heitir. [a] þar kemr ok Fenris-ulfr ok Miðgarðz-ormr. þar er ok þá kominn Loki ok Hrymr ok með hónum allir Hrim-þursar; Enn Loka fylgja allir Heljar-sinnar; enn Muspellz-synir hafa einir ser fylking, ok er sú biört miök. c. Völlrinn Vígríðr er hundrað rasta víðr á hvern veg.

(Enn er þessi tíðendi verða) a. þá stendr upp Heimdallr, ok blæss ákafliga í Giallar-horn, ok vekr upp öll goðin, ok eiga þau þing saman. a. þá ríðr Óðinn til Mimis-brunnz ok tekr ráð af Mimi fyrir ser ok sínu liði. a. þá skelfr Askr Ygg-drasils, ok engi hlutr er þá ótta-lauss á himni eða iörðu. a. Æsirnir her-væða sik, ok allir Einherjarnir, ok sœkja framm á völluna: Ríðr fyrst Óðinn (með goll-hialm ok fagra brynju, ok geir sinn er Gungnir heitir), stefnir hann móti Fenris-ulf. Enn þórr framm á aðra hlið hónum, (ok má hann ekki duga hónum, því at) hann hefir fullt fang at berjask við Miðgarðz-orm. a. Freyr bersk móti Surti, ok verðr harðr sam-gangr áðr Freyr fellr (þat verðr hans bani, at hann missir þess ins góða sverðz er hann gaf Skirni). [a] þá er ok lauss orðinn hundrinn Garmr er bundinn er fyr Gnípa-helli; hann er ið mesta forað. Hann á víg móti Tý, ok verðr hvárr öðrum at skaða. a. þórr berr ban-orð af Miðgarðz-ormi, ok stígr þaðan brott nio fet; þá fellr hann dauðr til iarðar fyrir eitri því er Ormrinn blés á hann. c. Ulfrinn gleypir Oðinn, verðr þat hans bani. Enn þegar eptir snýsk framm Viðarr, ok stígr öðrum

---

sword shall be a right fair one, and the sheen thereof brighter than that of the sun [1]. c. And as they ride over the Rocking-Race [Rainbow] it shall break beneath them [as was said before]. c. Muspell's sons shall go forth to the field that is called the Links of Battle. Thither also shall come the [a] Wolf of Fenri and the Serpent of Earth. And thither shall Loki have come, and Rym, and with him all the Rime-ogres; but all the a. Hell-dead shall follow Loki, and a. sons of Muspell shall be a troop by themselves, very bright to behold. c. The field of the Links of Battle is a hundred miles every way.

The Gods marshalled to battle.—And when these tidings shall come to pass, there shall a. Heimdall [the World-bow] arise and wind the Yell-horn with mighty power, and awaken all the gods, and they shall hold a moot together. Then Woden shall ride to the Burn of Mim, a. and take counsel of Mim for himself and his company. a. And the Ash of the Steed of the Hanged One shall quiver, [a] and there shall be no part of heaven and earth that shall not then tremble for fear. [a] The Anses shall put on their harness, and all the Host of the Elect, and go forth to the field. a. Woden shall ride first with his gold helm and his fair mail-coat and his spear that is called Gungnir [Tusker], he shall challenge the Wolf Fenri, a. and Thunder next beside him, and he shall not be able to help him, for he shall have enough to do to fight with the Serpent of Earth. a. Frey shall fight against Swart, and there shall be a cruel battle between them before Frey falls, and the loss of the good sword that he gave Skirni shall be his death. [a] And the Hound Garm [Sarama?] that is bound before the Cave of the cliff shall have got loose too. He shall stand against Tew, and each of them shall be the other's death. a. Thunder shall get the better of the Serpent of Earth, and shall run back nine paces from him, and then fall dead to the ground by reason of the venom that the Serpent shall breathe upon him. c. The Wolf shall swallow Woden, and that shall be the death of him; c. and straightway Widar shall dash forward and step with one foot upon the nether

---

[1] Mention of Loki and his crew omitted by mistake.

fǿti í neðra kœpt Ulfsins (á þeim fǿti hefir hann skó þann er allan aldr hefir verit til samnat; þat eru biórar þeir er menn sníða or skóm sínom fyrir tám eða hæli; því skal þeim biórum brott kasta sá maðr er at því vill hyggja at koma Ásunum at liði). c. Annarri hendi tekr hann inn efra kœpt Ulfsins ok rífr sundr gin hans, ok verðr þat Ulfsins bani. a. Loki á orrosto-við Heimdall, ok verðr hvárr annars bani. a. því næst slyngr Surtr eldi yfir iörðina, ok brennir allan heim.

(Þá mælti Gangleri: Hvat verðr þá eptir er brendr er heimr allr, ok dauð öll goðin, ok allir Einherjar ok allt mann-folk; ok hafi þér áðr sagt at hverr maðr skal lifa í nokkorom heimi um allar aldir? þá kvað þriði: a. Margar eru þá vistir góðar ok margar íllar.)

a. Bezt er þá at vera á Gimlé[1], ok all-gótt er til góðs drykkjar, þeim er þat þykkir gaman, í þeim sal er Brimir heitir; hann stendr á Okolni. a. Sá er enn góðr salr er stendr á Níða-fiǫllum, gœrr af rauðu golli; sá heitir Sindri. Í þessum sölum skolo góðir menn vera ok siðlátir. a. Á Ná-ströndum er mikill salr ok íllr, ok horfa norðr dyrr; hann er ofinn allr orma-hryggjum: enn orma-höfuð öll vitu inn í húsit ok blása eitri, svá at eptir salinum renna eitr-ár, ok vaða þær ár eið-rofar ok morð-vargar. [a] Enn í Hver-gelmi er verst. [*Here a sentence seems missing.*]

(Þá mælti Gangleri: Hvárt lifa nokkur goðin þá, eða er þá nökkur iörð eða himin? Hárr svarar):

a. Upp skýtr iörðunni þá or siónum, ok er hon þá grœn ok fögr; vaxa þá akrar

---

jaw of the Wolf [and upon this foot he shall have the shoe that every age has gone to the making of, from the shreds that men pare off their shoes to shape the toes and heels withal, wherefore he that is minded to be of the company of the Anses must take heed to cast away those parings]. And with one hand he shall take hold of the upper jaw of the Wolf and rend his jaw asunder, and that shall be the Wolf's death. Loki shall battle with Heimdall, and each shall be the death of the other.

a. *Swart sets fire to the world.*—Thereupon Swart shall cast fire over the earth and burn the whole world.

Places of Bliss.—[Then spake Gangler, 'What will happen then when the whole world is burnt, and all the gods dead, and all the Host of the Chosen, and all mankind, for thou hast already said that every man shall live in one of the worlds through all ages?']

Then said Third, a. There shall be many good abodes and many ill. The best that shall then be is a Fire-lea, and there is a right good chance of good drink for them that take pleasure therein in the hall that is called a. Brim, which stands in Uncold. a. That is a good hall that stands on the Moon Hills, built of red gold; it is called Cinder. a. In these halls shall good and right-living folk abide.

Places of Torment.—a. On Corse-strand there is a great hall, and ill to boot, and the doors open northward; it is wattled with the bodies of serpents, and the heads of the serpents all turn inwards, and keep spirting venom into the house, so that rivers of venom run down the halls thereof, and oath-breakers and murderers shall be wading in these rivers. But in [a] Cauldron-whelmer it is worse, [for there Felon-cutter, the monstrous snake, feeds upon the living bodies of the worst of sinners.]

The New World.—[Then spake Gangler, 'Will any of the gods be alive then, and will there be any Earth or Sky?']

The High One answered, a. 'Earth shall shoot up out of the sea, and she shall be

---

[1] a himni, W.

ósánir.   c. Víðarr ok Vali lifa svá at eigi hefir siórinn ok Surta-logi grandat þeim.
a. Ok byggja þeir á Iða-velli, þar sem fyrr var Ásgarðr.   c. Ok þar koma synir
Þórs, Móði ok Magni, ok hafa þar Miollni.

a. Því næst kemr þar Baldr ok Hǫðr frá Heljar.   a. Setjask þá allir samt ok
talask við, ok minnask á rúnar sínar, ok rœða um ǫll tíðendi þau es fyrr höfðu verit,
um Miðgarðz-orm ok um Fenris-ulf[1].

a. Þá finnask þar í grasinu gull-töflur þær er Æsirnir höfðu átt.   c. Enn þar sem
heitir Hoddmimis-holt leynask menn tveir í Surta-loga, er svá heita, Lif ok Leif-
þrasir, ok hafa morgin-dœggvar fyrir mat.   Enn af þessum mönnum kemr svá mikil
kyn-slóð at byggvisk heimr allr.   c. Ok hitt mun þer undarligt þykkja at Sólin hefir
getið dóttur, eigi ófegri en hon er, ok ferr sú þá stigu móður sínnar.

(Enn ef þú kannt lengra framm at spyrja þá veit ek eigi hvaðan þer kemr þat,
fyrir því, at engi mann heyrða-ek lengra segja framm aldar-farit[2],—ok nióttu sem þú
namt!   Því næst heyrði Gaugleri dyni mikla hvern veg frá ser, ok leit hann út á
hlið ser; ok þa-er hann sésk meirr um, þá stendr hann úti á sléttum velli; sér hann
þá œnga höll ok œnga borg.   Gengr hann þá brott leið sína ok kemr heim í ríki
sítt, ok segir þau tíðendi er hann hefir séð eða heyrt.   Ok eptir hónum sagði hverr
maðr öðrum þessar sögur.)

---

green and fair then, a. And the fields shall bear all unsown.   b. Widar and Wali
shall be alive, since neither the sea nor the fires of Swart have harmed them, and
they shall dwell in the a. Field of Ith [Ida-field], where Anse-garth stood before.
a. And Mood and Main, the sons of Thunder, shall come there, and they shall have
Milner with them.   And afterward a. Balder and Hoth shall come thither also out of
Hell.   a. They shall all sit down together and talk to each other, and call to mind
their mysteries, and speak about all those things which have come to pass, about the
Serpent of the Earth and the Wolf of Fenri . . .

a. 'And in those days they shall find in the grass the gold tables that the Anses
had of yore.   c. But in the wood that is called Hoard-Mim's Holt two of mankind,
Simple and Life-stayer, with the morning-dew for their meat, shall have hidden
themselves from the fires of Swart.   And from these two there shall come such a
mighty kindred that they shall inhabit the whole world.   And it will seem wonderful to thee that the Sun should have borne a daughter, no less fair than herself,
and she shall journey in her mother's ways.'

Epilogue.—'But if thou art wishful to enquire further forth I know not whence thou
wilt get help, for I have never yet heard any tell further of the World-History,—and
may what thou hast heard profit thee!'   And with that Gangler heard a mighty
crash on every side of him, and looked about him, and while he was peering about
him as far as he could, he found himself standing in the open air upon a smooth
plain, he could see no hall and no stronghold.   Then straightway he set out upon
his way and came home to his kingdom and told all the tidings that he had seen
and heard.   And according to his account one man has handed on this tale to
another [down to our day].

---

[1] Here the paraphrast has misunderstood his text.
[2] This is a twofold echo, from Short Wolospa, last line, and Vsp. l. 3.   The
author says, The task of telling the History of the World (aldar-far), from its
Genesis to the Doom and Regeneration, is herewith finished.

NOTES ON WOLOSPA.

As has been noticed in the Introduction [§ 16], a wholly new way to a right treatment of the text of Wolospa was opened when, unexpectedly and at the eleventh hour, as it were, the proper conception of the value of the prose paraphrase of that poem in Snorri's Edda dawned upon our mind.   When once one got to understand that the paraphrase rested upon a purer, fuller, and earlier text than any other version preserved, it became possible to see one's way through and over dark places which one had been hopeless of being ever able to lighten.   It is the text reconstructed upon this new basis that we shall take as the foundation of our notes and critical treatment.

The state of the text of Wolospa may be best represented thus (a denoting the full, β the stinted, disorderly text):—

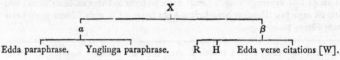

Edda paraphrase.   Ynglinga paraphrase.   R   H   Edda verse citations [W].

What may best be done with the materials is to put in correct order the verse-text as it exists.   To effect this it is necessary, *first* to sort out of the mangled mass of fragments, headed Wolospa in R, what really belongs to our chief poem, the Long Wolospa. In doing this we are helped by the reconstruction, which we have been able to make of Hyndla's Lay (vol. ii, p. 515).   From our work on that poem we know not only that a *Shorter Wolospa* existed, but are able to see something of its character, plan, and style, and it becomes very clear that it is precisely of fragments of this Shorter Wolospa that the greater part of the interpolation in the Wolospa mass comes.   The distinct character of the two poems affords a clear and ready test by which each line or verse may be tried.

The *Shorter Wolospa* is a poem of the old type, somewhat rough and coarse and material in character, didactic, genealogic, anthropomorphic, altogether more barbaric and indigenous, with a simple framework of archaic fashion.   The *Longer Wolospa* is, on the other hand, a poem which stands quite alone among the creations of Northern poets; it is spiritual, immaterial, philosophic, even mystical in its inspiration; perhaps nearer in cast and form of thought to one of Plato's dialogues than to any other extant composition.   Moreover, the peculiar metre and the melody of rhythm which distinguish it, are qualities which would serve to mark out its verses from those of any other Eddic poem whatever.   Its poet, whoever he was, is the 'Sweet Singer' of the Northern tongue.

Guided by such tests we may disentangle what remains of the Long Wolospa from the other pieces with which it has been so long mingled,—and now a *second* process is necessary, to wit, the right *ordering* and *rebuilding* of the precious fragments. Our toil must be that of the patient worker, who sits down with the broken bits of a Greek vase before him, and a rough idea of its form and subject in his head, to put it together and get at the details as far as they have been preserved.   After many mistakes and much care he is able to fit every little shard into its place, and the vase stands before him again in its original shape; but though the outline is true and the subject of the painting unmistakeable, how much has perished! A great crack here has scarred the finest figures, a hole there has broken away the name of the hero, a handle has gone, and a good deal of the border ornament is lost, though luckily enough remains to show the pattern. Such must be the state of Wolospa after all one's work.

The prose paraphrase is our chiefest help, both with regard to the order and to the text; and we by its aid are able to give a general plan and the proper sequence of the fragments, to tell not only where a gap occurs, but even to supply the contents of the missing lines, and so to form some rough idea as to the amount of the poem which is lost for ever. All this is an immense gain; and no one, who has read the poem in the old β text, will fail to see how far more clear, intelligible, and beautiful it becomes when rearranged and restored by the light of the α text of the prose paraphrase.

It is indeed a wonder that a poem of such spiritual and imaginative cast should have come down to us at all, through the three generations at least which must have intervened between its creation and the days of Ari. Its preservation is no doubt owing to the extraordinary sweetness of its verse, whose soft melody enchanted and attracted its hearers, and thus ensured its existence. Written or unwritten it was still mainly whole and sound when it reached the eye or ear of the Edda paraphrast, and the decomposition set in during the time intervening between α and β: and an evil fate has willed that β, not α, should survive in our present copies. Yet the frequent and scarring gaps which disfigure the β text are just what was to be looked for in the case of a poem dealing with such philosophic themes in so delicate a way.

The first part may have once contained 150 lines, the second about the same, the third some 50,—say 350–400 lines in all.

It is not possible here to go into the vast mass of detail which gathers about this poem; the notes below will touch upon such points as should be noticed in due order, but it is to the paraphrase that the reader must constantly look for the interpretation of what is vague, dim, and uncertain in the verse-text.

The now cancelled text of vol. i, pp. 193 sqq., has not been wholly useless; it has served us as a helpful base for further work. When it was made we were on the right track, though the Editor had not yet found the clue which has guided us in the setting forth of this the third and final text. It may remain for the present to show the reader the path by which we have arrived at the conclusions here set before him. The greater part of the original as it stands in R is given in vol. i, pp. 377–379. The second text is a stepping-stone, as it were, without which the transition to our final text would perhaps be too startling for the reader to easily accept.

As to the *plan* of the poem as now presented, it may be considered a kind of *trilogy*, the utterances of *Three Sibyls*, a 'Walna-spa' rather than Wolospa.

The *First Sibyl*, an aged giantess, is repeating the past history of the world to the gods and men who are gathered about her seat; she tells of the creation of the world (the first step in that passage from Chaos to Cosmos, which is the central idea of the poem), of the golden age, of the beginning of evil (a fragmentary and tantalising passage), of the first crime—brother slaying brother, the first murder—that of the hostage, the rape of the matron, the creation of man, the world-tree, the Holy Norns, the punishment of the criminal Titan.

The *Second Sibyl*, a darker figure, a witch 'sitting out' at her enchantments, is questioned by the unquiet Woden, who, like Saul, feels a presentiment of misfortune, and tells a sadder tale of the judgment to come;—the gathering of the fiends at the Crack of Doom, the muster of the gods at the blast of the warder's horn, the terrible and deadly conflict, and the whelming of the world. But her story is not entirely of horror—retribution will indeed fall upon the wicked, but the righteous must also meet with their reward, and the three heavens of Warmth and Light and Cheer are set over against the hells of the snake-wattled hall, the river of swords, the pit where the dragon tears the corpses of the nidderings.

The *Third Sibyl*, no doubt a purer and more celestial being than her two elder sisters, has but a brief message to men, but it is one of hope. The world shall be reborn, a new heaven and a new earth, the golden age shall come once more, never to pass away.

THE SHORTER WOLOSPA.—Something has already been said in the Introductions to Hyndla's Lay and Wolospa respecting this poem. Its *name* has never been wholly perished, though it had, as a separate creation, been entombed beneath the broken fragments of the two poems, from which we have at last extricated it. Its *double* character has led to its being saved and hidden away, its *necromantic* framework running parallel to Wolospa, Part II, while its *genealogic* contents led to its confusion with Hyndla's Lay. Yet it has a distinct individuality of its own, as can be perceived, now that it is possible to read it, though but a fragment, side by side with its sister poem.

The *framework* is unmistakeably a scene like that of the beginning of Menglad's Lay, where the wise woman is awakened from the dead and adjured to unveil her mysterious knowledge; or like the opening of Balder's Doom, where Woden awakens the dead witch. Of the contents, by far the greatest part has perished, and we cannot always fill the blanks. It was whole when in the hands of the Edda Paraphrast, hence it is easy to complete such pieces as those which detail the growth of the dwarves like maggots in the world-giant's flesh, or to guess that the story of the wonderful cow Audhumbla, a most Indian-looking figure, must have been drawn from *lost verses*. There are two or three morsels, such as that about the cocks of the four worlds, which may have belonged to any poet, and cannot be with certainty fitted in here; but such pieces as those which tell of the brood of Hell, or hint at the coming of Christ, we believe to be quite safely placed. The poet is distinctly a heathen, living in the last days of the old faith, but he is earlier in time and style than the composer of the Long Wolospa.

The text emendations rest chiefly upon the paraphrase, which must be carefully watched, both when it touches upon an existing verse and when it is narrating incidents taken from lost lines.

The Paraphrase Extracts.—The nature of this paraphrase must be carefully borne in mind before it can be safely and rightly used. It is not a mere prose version of the Long Wolospa, but rather a Diatessaron or Harmony of four or five poems, and therefore in its nature incomplete; for the paraphrast has, though basing his work most largely on the two Sibyl Songs *plus* Wafthrudni's and Grimni's Lays, not scrupled to omit or rearrange where it suited his purpose, though he has *not* falsified or defaced his authority. We have therefore in the text above taken care to mark by letters the pieces of different poems paraphrased therein, *a* marking the Long, *b* the Short Wolospa, *c* other poems, especially Wafthrudni's and Grimni's Lays: when the letter is bracketed, the citation is, we take it, from a part of our poems now lost.

The existence of this paraphrase raises many interesting questions. Was text *a*, Ari's text as we might call it, written or oral? We need only *one* copy to supply both Ynglinga, ch. 4, and Gylfa-ginning.

There are several indications that this a came from the West; it contains Gaelic words, rightly explained in the prose, which would hardly have been understood by an Icelander [e. g. gifr, Gael. *geimhlich*, Welsh *gefyn*], hence the Icelandic scribe, whoever he was, must have had some assistance from one who did understand those words; that is, a Western man.

The figures in *brackets* mark the lines of the old text, vol. i, p. 163.

WOLOSPA—

ll. 1–4. By 'Heimdall's children high and low' is meant the Human race, Human kind, Humanity, Earl and Ceorl and Thrall, figured as one great household. The 'Holy Kin' we hold to mean not so much the celestial gods as the departed Anses, *ancestral spirits*, dwelling in hills and howes, but invisibly present at the family gathering and sacrifices.

l. 3. 'vildu at ek Valföðrs vel' does not construe, is harsh, lacks the flow and grace so characteristic of the Song. It is of a surety corrupt; we expect an object to *tell*, a parallel to forn-spioll, the subject-matter of the Sibyl's tale, the World's Genesis and History. We have now, just in the last moment (too late for p. 621 of a preceding sheet), lighted on the word, viz. aldar-far; (valfoðrs and aldar-far have several letters in common, a distant similarity in *sound;* the error is here we think of the *ear*.) 'aldar-far' occurs (1) in Edda Gg. at the end (see p. 641, bottom), drawn throughout from this lay; nobody, he says, was ever heard to reckon the aldar-far beyond this. (2) In the Preface to Book of Settlement, where Ari renders Bede's Ætates Mundi by Aldafars-bók. (3) Merl. i. 216, echoed here too, we hold, from Vsp. We therefore now read and restore—

> Viljak aldar-far allt fram telja,
> forn-spiöll fira, etc.

I will recount the whole World-History, the old stories of men, as far back as I remember.

At great gatherings and feasts in the late autumn, an itinerant sibyl, seated on a throne, the household standing listening all around, used to forecast the course of the coming winter (ár-ferð, vetrar-far), the fortunes of those present, like gipsies in our days. Even how the spirits, invisibly present, were allured by the chant of the Wardlock Songs is told in the vivid picture, given in Eric the Red's Saga of such an incident; see Reader, pp. 126–128 and 378–380 [1]. In the Saga all is on the human scale, and deals with the little concerns of life; in the Poem all is superhuman, Titanic; the theme is the World's Genesis and Doom; the listening household is Human kind, the departed dead as well as the living, one undivided, all-embracing household.

ll. 5–8. íviðior (in R the abbreviation ∞ has been dropped at the end; the word

---

[1] The reader should peruse the classical scene in the Greenland Franklin's hall. Those who do not understand Icelandic may be directed to the translation of Eric the Red by Mr. Sephton of the Liverpool Institute.

As a last survival, I can well remember from my childhood (age eight to twelve) an itinerant pedlar prophet who used to call in the autumn and forecast the coming winter from inspecting the Milky Way (Winter-path). I can still see the fellow gravely gazing up at the sky, ponderously shaking his head; 'so and so looks the sky, so will Thorri and Goi be.' The greater or lesser brightness of the Aurora Borealis would in these high latitudes (65° 30′) affect the aspect of the Milky Way; striated narrow spots meant a hard winter, and pinched, straitened supplies of hay. It is but fair to add that the man was no quack, but honest enough in his belief. Such was my first lesson in astronomy.—[Editor.]

is rare) occurs besides in Sh. Sibyl Lay, l. 3; Heimdall's nine mothers would here be meant.

l. 8. miotoð, a well-known word in A.S. poetry, but strange to the Icelandic copyist, who fancied that it was connected with viðr (wood). In heathen days meotoð would have been a law term, meaning a *judge*, the *meeter* out of justice; it occurs again, l. 140; we hold Titan Mimi to be meant, the stern Rhadamanthus of the Sibyl's Hell.

From here we are assisted by the Edda Paraphrase.

ll. 9–15. The sequence of lines restored. We have, l. 9, chosen the reading of Cod. W; for the material, gross cosmogony from the Titan's flesh is alien to the spiritual metaphysics of the Sibyl. The lines of Aristophanes, Birds 693, 694[1], are of one stamp with the Sibyl's, both echoing still older songs or beliefs; cp. also Cædmon, Genesis, ll. 116–119.

l. 12. Ginnunga gap occurs only here; Haustlong 58 calls the ether ginnunga vé.

ll. 13–15 [19–21] are here restored to their right place in the Chaos section; some lines however seem lost.

ll. 15–26. *Cosmos rising out of Chaos;* the earth (biod, a Gaelic word) lifted out of the Tohu-bohu: salar-steina must mean the salt rocks; the earth, sparkling with brine, floating up out of the deep, all mantled with green herbs.

ll. 22–26 [17, 18, 24–26]. *The Sun and Moon's course settled; the seasons:* for 'varp' we read hvarf (archtype varf, v = hv), the technical word for the sun's *wheeling* round the heaven, cp. Vþm. 91: 'hendi hœgri' we take to allude to the sun's *rightward* course, and we propose to read handar innar hœgri, the genitive denoting *direction* (like Righ. 1, 5, etc.); himin iodur is suspicious, for ioður = iaðar is grammatically inadmissible; neither will io-dýr (horse-deer) nor ió-dyrr (horse doors) do: Sun-horses and Sun-wolves are alien to this Sibyl's cosmogony. In ll. 113, 114 the sun *darkens*, the phrase being identical with that of the Bible, Joel ii. 10, Rev. ix. 2. If we strike out 'io' (presumably borrowed, by scribe or minstrel, from the other lays), the line at once gains in ring and flow, and the sense becomes clear. The sun wheels round rightward to the *western door*, there vanishing, to reappear every morning at heaven's *east gate*.

l. 22. sinni, A.S. gesið: after l. 23 some lines seem to be missing, telling the moon's *leftward*, wither-shin course: nótt með niðom, perhaps better than ok, cp. Vþm. 96.

ll. 27–32 [43–48]. *Creation of man.* We follow the sequence in the Edda Paraphrase, where, after Sun and Moon being fixed and seasons and years regulated, man is created; upon which follow in succession, the Golden Age, the Holy Tree, the Norns, etc. In alandi (á landi of received text) we have long suspected hidden the old adjective, *alien*, outcast—the exact Norse form is not known (eliandi, ǫlandi?) —answering to Germ. *elend*, O.H.G. *elilenfi, ellendi* (see Grimm's Dict. iii. 410), a word all but forgotten in Icelandic (Dict. 34 b). The substitution into á landi necessitated lítt megandi for the more poetical and truer ó- megandi. By óð we understand *speech*, by lát and læti the *sensual* fleeting portion of the human soul, whilst önd and ód denote the higher, godly, undying *faculties*.

For Woden being akin to Lat. *vātes*, and Hœni to the Eros-Bird of Creation, we

---

[1] Wonderful how even the words coincide—Γῆ δ' οὐδ' ἀὴρ οὐδ' οὐρανὸς ἦν = Iorð fansk æva ne upp-himin; and yet who would assert that the Sibyl's prophet ever heard of Aristophanes' Birds?

have spoken elsewhere (General Introd. pp. cii, civ) [1]. So, too, Lóðorr, occurring only here and Hlt. 34, must spring from some Eastern word unknown to us.

ll. 33–40 [26–35]. *The Golden Age.* The sequence of the lines put right so as to rejoin the words 'smiðoðo' and 'ór golli,' vas þeim v. vant being an aside: Iðavollr occurs again, l. 192 (see Introd. p. cxxii, foot-note).

ll. 39, 40. *The Giant Maids*, how the life of the Golden Age came to an untimely end. The paraphrase, in our present text, here leaves us in the dark, giving just the two lines and no more: amatkar, *eldritch, weird, unearthly.*

Here follows the Creation of the Dwarves, which we have relegated to the Short Sibyl Lay.

ll. 43–52 [49–56]. *The Holy Tree.* We have followed W. in order not to lose 'heilagr;' yet, as askr *standandi* reappears in l. 136 (the high *towering* tree), the best perhaps would be to read—

> Ask veit ek standa—heitir Ygg-drasill—
> hár baðmr heilagr, ausinn hvíta-auri,

scanning ausinn slurred.

ll. 49, 50. The Norns we now take to be an integral part of the lay, only that 'skaro á skíði' is an *aside*, Norns represented writing on tablets the fate of mortal men.

l. 52. The reading varies (segja or seggja? segja too is ambiguous); we prefer taking it pres. plur. indic. = *they speak the fate*, cp. segja lög and lög-saga : the dat. alda bornom is governed by kœro.

ll. 53, 54 [41, 42] have been dislodged; they have no concern with the creation of man. Here the words, *come to the house*, exactly fall in with the Edda Paraphrase speaking of a *second race of Norns, who come to every house where a child is to be born.* The identity is clear; the lines belong to the section on the Norns. Now, too, we understand the phrase 'or því líði,' i. e. *from that kin proceed other Norns*, viz. the midwife Norns: mark, too, that the 'þriár' (feminine) is a survival of the old undefiled text [2]. Further, in ástkir we espy ás-kungar, an epithet given to the Norns, O. W. L. 111 : some vowel-word is required; finding none nearer, we have suggested ióð-dísir (midwives). The whole is fragmentary; the following lines would have given the substance of the paraphrase, how, for good and evil, the Norns shape the life of every mother's child.

ll. 55–63 [89–97] need not be an address to Woden; rather not. The Sibyl says, 'I know right well where Woden hid his eye:' þu, þitt, is superabundant; perhaps read—Allt ek veit hvar Óðinn auga fal sítt, whilst the words '*why do ye seek me, why do ye tempt me?*' are in keeping with the Sibyl seated on her high-seat, as depicted in Red Eric's Saga, the household one by one coming up to enquire of her. Woden is out of place. We have, in strict accordance with poetical requirement, rearranged the lines by help of the paraphrase : ll. 60–63 speak of the Horn, while the paraphrase tells us how Mim drinks wisdom from the Burn out of the Giall-Horn ; the one suite of lines treats of Woden's eye, the other of the Horn and Mim's draught.

ll. 64–73 [57, 58, 98–105]. *Balder's death, the Brother-murder.* The first two lines have been wrenched from the rest, and thrust in far away, so that no one has ever suspected their right berth or bearing. The *foining with spears* unmistakeably

---

[1] In foot-note, p. civ, 'hœni is a cognate word' has by inadvertence slipped in from p. cii, note 1.

[2] To alter it into þrír is one instance more of cheap emendations, see Introd. pp. l, lxxxix.

points to where they belong, viz. to Balder's clause; hence under 'gollveig' (an else unknown, impossible name) some title of Balder's should be hidden, a *g*-word it must needs be; the extracts in Edda Gg. preserve such a word, fitting in with the alliteration and metre of the line, viz. gráta-goð (taken, we doubt not, by the Edda Compiler from this very line when still in a pure state). Further, the theme being *brother*-murder, folc-víg (pitched battle) is here wholly out of place; frænd-víg, *paricide*, meets sense and alliteration (for an *f*-word it must be). Hence we learn that in the Sibyl's Creed Balder's death, like Abel's, lies in the *past*, not, as in the Doom and in the Edda legends, in the future just before the Final Catastrophe.

ll. 66 sqq. tívor, ἅπ. λεγ., A. S. *tibr*, still preserved in Germ. unge-*ziefer*.

l. 68. East of Walhall, says Edda; völlom hæri is a banal phrase; we read, fyrir Valholl austan, the letters are partly the same (v . . . ǫllom = Valhǫll). *Very young* is Edda's epithet to Mistletoe; miok fagr (fair to behold) is inappropriate and commonplace; it was a *tiny*, harmless-looking thing; so we restore and read miok ungr. Hauks-bók omits lines 66–73.

ll. 74–83 [62–69, 76, 77]. *War with the Wanes, the first Felony.* Here we are helped by the story in Ynglinga Saga, once copied, as we now can see, from the Sibyl Lay when whole. We have rearranged the lines, there being *three* stages — (a) ll. 74–77, the battle; (b) ll. 80, 81, the peace *after* battle; (c) ll. 82, 83, the breach of the truce and *slaying of the hostages:* folk-víg (l. 74) cannot be the right word, for, in ancient morals, simple killing was no murder. Here the theme is the *felonious* slaying of the hostages, a foul murder indeed; we suggest folg-víg, meaning *foul, secret murder;* a law-term which, though not occurring in the extant law remains, must once have existed, for in Sighvat (x. 45) we read folgin orð = *words of treason, conspiracy*, as it were, and so we recover an important law word. Several lines seem to be missing.

l. 76. We read víg-ská, formed like her-skár (see Dict. 259 a).

l. 81. The suffixed article speaks to a false reading; now the Saga tells us how the giving *hostages* (gisling) and the *league* (gildi) were the two cardinal points— Logðo þeir milli sín sættar-stefno (= gildi) ok gœrðo frið, ok seldosk gíslar; upon which base we have restored the text: it cannot be mere accident that both gíslar and gildi fit in with the alliteration.

ll. 86–89 [72–75] fragmentary: l. 88 we take to mean that Thor was absent, was *not* there; cp. the Hrungni story in Edda: for 'slíkt' we read svik; the same error we meet in O. W. Pl. 191 and W. W. L. 47.

ll. 90–93 [106–109]. *The Titan Wloki (Loki) chained.*

l. 90. lund (grove) is a most inappropriate place to keep the Volcano-Fire-Titan in; we read Hvera-brunni, *the Cauldron Pit* = Hver-gelmir or Tartarus, where Wloki is chained.

l. 91 is all awry, 'lægiarnliki' being a hybrid impossible vocable. We are in Edda (see pp. 636, 637) told how the Titan was chained with his son Wali's or Nari's *guts;* now in 'giarn' we detect 'gornom,' in 'læ' the son's name (Vala, Vila); Wali, Woden's and Wrind's son, is well known in the old eschatological legends, and it is not likely that two should be of the same name. We suggest that Loki's son was named Vili—vil (root vili) means *entrails* (see Dict. 705 b). The alliteration further speaks to Wloki; the line may be echoing a still older song, where *wl* was still sounded, and where vilja was merely an appellative (cp. Dict. 776 b): in 'aþekkjan,' some verb, meaning *chained* (hlekktan, if it might be), seems to be hidden. A line or more is missing, telling of the dripping venom, of Sigyn's bowl, and the Titan's writhing spasms; for there can be no doubt but that the whole scene was briefly set forth in the Sibyl's song. Cp. Æschylus' mighty lines in Prometheus Bound, where he describes the Titan 'withering in destin'd pain : '—

Καὶ νῦν ἀχρεῖον καὶ παράορον δέμας
κεῖται στενωποῦ πλησίον θαλασσίου
ἰπούμενος ῥίζαισιν Αἰτναίαις ὕπο·
κορυφαῖς δ' ἐν ἄκραις ἥμενος μυδροκτυπεῖ
Ἥφαιστος, ἔνθεν ἐκραγήσονταί ποτε
ποταμοὶ πυρὸς δάπτοντες ἀγρίαις γνάθοις
τῆς καλλικάρπου Σικελίας λευροὺς γύας·
τοιόνδε Τυφὼς ἐξαναζέσει χόλον
θερμοῖς ἀπλάτου βέλεσι πυρπνόου ζάλης,
καίπερ κεραυνῷ Ζηνὸς ἠνθρακωμένος.

Mark the identity even in phrase between the Greek and the Northern poems—
καὶ νῦν ἀχρεῖον καὶ παράορον δέμας κεῖται . . . ἰπούμενος ῥίζαισιν Αἰτναίαις ὕπο and Hapt sé-ék liggja und Hvera-*brunni*. The venomous snake and the Titan's wife holding the bowl are accretions absent in the Greek. But we see the full scene represented on the Gosforth Cross, Cumberland[1].

Note that Hauks-bók omits ll. 90, 91, substituting two lines manufactured from the Edda Prose—þar kná Vala víg-bönd snua | heldr voru harð-gor hopt or þormom, þar sitr, etc.—tasteless hackney versification, devoid of the harmony of true Wolospa lines.

The Second Sibyl—

ll. 64–105 [78–81, 59–61, 82–84]. *Introductory.* Heith, a favourite Sibyl name, see Landn. Bk. iii, ch. 2, Heiðr völva spáði þeim ollom at byggja á því landi es þá vas ófundit vestr í haf. Vatzd. ch. 10 calls her Finna and Volva.

l. 95. We read, vél-spá—

> And be these juggling fiends no more believ'd,
> That palter with us in a double sense ;
> That keep the word of promise to our ear,
> And break it to our hope.—*Macbeth*, v. 7.

l. 96. leikin, *witches* (?), cp. Thulor 108, an else unknown word.

ll. 98–100 [59–61]. In R and H tacked to the Balder lines, but can refer to but one thing, viz. the Sibyl herself: 'höll hars' is suspicious; the evil Sibyl was thrice born; see for a parallel the Long Br. Lay 185–187.

ll. 101–103. Obscure; we suggest hauga or hanga—Enn stundum vakði hann (Woden) upp dauða menn or iörðo, ok settisk undir *hanga* . . . Óðinn vissi um allt *iarð-fé* (= fé-spioll) hvar folgit vas, ok hann kunni þau lióð, es upp lauksk fyr hónom iörðin ok biörg ok steinar, ok *haugarnir*, ok batt hann með orðom einom þa-es fyrir bioggo, ok gekk inn ok tók þar slíkt es hann vildi [Yngl. S. ch. 9]— words, as we consider, copied from the Sibyl Song when it was still complete ; we suspect 'vakði' under '·valdi,' and 'hanga' under 'hringa.' The text, as it now stands, is ruined beyond recovery.

ll. 104, 105. The plot of this section is the 'úti-seta,' *a sitting out at cross-roads;* see Orkney Saga, ch. 70—Enn Sveinn brióst-reip [a wizard] gekk út, ok sat

---

[1] This most curious piece of Old English art has lately been unearthed, copied, and published by that enthusiastic indefatigable archæologist, Professor Stephens of Copenhagen. In drawing inferences, however, from this interesting find, we must never forget that both Cross and Poem are from a part of Britain which lies on the border-line of Irish, Northern, and English culture.

úti um nóttina eptir venjo sínni (Rolls Ed.): ll. 104–107 omitted in Hauks-bók: Yggiongr occurs only here.

ll. 106 sqq. *The Sibyl speaks and forecasts the impending doom.*

ll. 108 sqq. 'But when ye shall hear of wars and commotions, be not terrified . . . nation shall rise against nation, and kingdom against kingdom, and great earth-quakes shall be in divers places, and famine and pestilence, and great sights and great signs shall there be from heaven.'—Luke xxi. 9–11, Matt. xiv. 7.

ll. 113, 114 [175, 176]. Christian influence is here manifest; cp. 'I will cover the heaven, and make the stars thereof dark; I will cover the sun with a cloud, and the moon shall not give her light.'—Ezek. xxxii. 7, 8. And, 'The sun shall be turned into darkness, and the moon into blood, before the great and terrible day of the Lord come.'—Joel ii. 32. 'The earth shall quake before them; the heavens shall tremble; the sun and the moon shall be dark, and the stars shall withdraw their shining.'—Joel ii. 10, Is. xiii. 9, 10, xxxiv. 4.

ll. 115 sqq. Text in a parlous state, wide gaps, shattered shivers flung pell-mell up and down. We have, by help of the Edda paraphrases, attempted a partial restoration. The sequence of the events in the paraphrase is—

(*a*) The prognostics of the impending Doom, Crimes, Wars; all nature quivers with terror; the Fiends are unbound [ll. 108–119].

(*b*) The Fiends march up from South, East, West, (North.) Here are to be paired off—the Fire Demon Swart and the sons of Muspilli from the South, by air; Giant Hrym and the Hrim-giants (Titans) from the East, driving by land; Loki and the Fiends of Hell from the west, by sea in the ship Nailfare; from the North (?). Besides, the Serpent and the Wolf [ll. 122–130, fragment].

(*c*) The Anses (Gods) prepare for defence; they hold counsel under the Tree; Woden at the Burn inquires of Mim; Heimdall blows his horn for battle; the Anses march up; the battle-array [ll. 133–144, ruinous text].

(*d*) The Battle; the Anses are vanquished, and fall one by one, but are avenged by the slaughter of the Fiends; the Fire-demon Swart survives [ll. 145–155].

(*e*) World consumed by fire [ll. 156, 157].

(*f*) Three places of Bliss [ll. 158–165], and another three of Torment [ll. 166–180].

Even half-lines are wrongly pieced together; we can only touch on a few instances—

l. 115 [149] = þá verðr Fenris-ulfr lauss: in 'hlakkar' we surmise 'hlekki,' he breaks his *chains:* 'unnir' and 'ari' are senseless.

l. 118 [157]. The paraphrase says—'biörgin hrynja, enn *fiötrar* allir ok *bönd brotna ok slitna;*' here is the key to the 'gifr rata,' if we take gifr to be Engl. *gyves,* Welsh *gyvin;* in 'rata' we descry 'racna' (rata = rača), *to be unloosened,* see Dict. 481 b.

What is hidden under·'hefiz lind fyrir' [l. 147 old text] we cannot guess, perhaps = þá snysk Iormungandr í iotun-móði, ok *sœkir upp á landit;* if so, it should follow after l. 115.

l. 119. Enn himin klofnar = í þessum gný klofnar himininn, just preceding Swart and Muspelli's sons (?) marching up through the rent in the sky.

ll. 112–124 = Ok ríða þaðan Muspellz-synir, Surtr ríðr fyrstr, etc.: in R the sons of Muspelli have been put in a wrong berth, and are made to come *by sea*, Loki the steersman! palpably false.

l. 125. vestan: 'austan' is twice repeated; in one of the instances we have to substitute 'vestan;' the sea lies towards the North-west, whence comes Nailfare.

l. 128. We guess bróðor-mær, i.e. Hell, for Loki is mentioned two lines above.

l. 129 = Enn Loka fylgja allir Heljar-sinnar : Fifl-megir seems to denote the *monsters of the deep*, cp. *fifel-cyn*, Beow. 104, see also 420 ; fifel-streâm = *the ocean*.

l. 130. Here even the paraphrase is in error, ' Hrymr heitir lötunn es stýrir Naglfara.' In truth the Titans come *driving* (ekr) from the east; thus Thor always *drives* to Giant-land, cp. Haust. 55 : or Ioton-heimom we have added by guess.

l. 131. Hrim-þursar = Hrymr, ok með hónom allir Hrim-þursar. For Hrym the Titan cp. Gr. Κρόνος. Hrim-þursar, intentionally spelt so, not Hrím-, for it has probably nothing in the world to do with Icel. hrím (*rime frost*) ; the Hrim-ogres are the Titans of northern mythology : ' hrim ' here again was possibly akin to Gr. Κρόνος.

l. 133. The query Hvat es með A...., echoed from þkv. 22, does not fit in here ; we read Hart es ..., cp. þkv. 25.

l. 138. Enn iotunn losnar, R. ; but in the paraphrase we read—skelfr iorð oll, ok biorg ok viðir losna or iorðo upp. The Gods hold a meeting underneath the Tree, cp. Grimn. 95, 96, and Vsp. 193.

l. 141. ' kyndiz ' is senseless; we surmise ' brynnisk,' reflexive from brynna, see Dict. s. v., *to drink out of the burn;* if this is right, Miotuð and Mim are identical. All the next following lines, esp. 147–155, are more or less wrenched—in none is left the sweet easy flow of a true Wolospa line. The passage looks like shivered bits of some old glass window—alas, as Goethe says, Es giebt scherben.

l. 156. aldr-nari, an else unknown word; in Thulor 532 interpreted *fire* (copying from Vsp. ?) ; etymology not found : is it possible that we have here the last survival of *Neron* the Antichrist ? M. Rénan traces the word in the West-European churches down to Charlemagne. The poet of Vsp., if he used it, must have learnt it from Irish church tradition.

l. 158. Read, sólo nærri (?), cp. solo fiarri, 166.

l. 159. Gimlé, occurs only here (*gim* is probably a Lat. loan-word) ; unless a word be dropped, lé must be sounded bisyllabic, for a two-docked measure in the *latter* half-line is unwarranted : Gimlé is the heavenly meadow whereon the house stands, not the hall itself, unless we read, ' es á Gimlé heitir ;' yet ' á Gimlé ' is parallel to ' Náströndo á.' For the nine heavens, see Thulor 487 sqq.

l. 163 = Sá heitir Sindri.

ll. 164, 165 refer to all three places—Í þessom sölom skolo vera góðir menn ok siðlátir.

ll. 166–169. The first place of torment ; 170–174 the second; 175–180 the third : the paraphrase to the last is missing in our Edda texts—Enn í Hvergelmi er verst (*the rest missing*).

ll. 171 sqq. In which places of torment are felons, guilty of bootless crimes, not to be atoned for ; *mansworn* (mein-svarar), *murderers* (morð-vargar), *adulterers* (173) ; in ' framgengna ' we espy ' for-dæða,' i. e. *wizards;* in ' vargr vera,' ' vára-vargr,' *truce-breaker*, see O. W. Pl. 259 ; in ' nið-hœggr ' (repeated in R), ' niðinga,' *nidderings*, see Bk. vi, Ditty 59 ; we know not the exact law-bearing of this word, though it is a word of especial infamy[1]. We thus recover *six* specified crimes, all infamous and ' fee-less ' in the ancient heathen Canon of Morals. Yet, the text being defective, we scarcely have the full list, and so miss goð-vargr, *the blasphemer*, see vol. ii, p. 80,

---

[1] We here add the verse-line, inadvertently omitted vol. ii, p. 280—

Sœkjask ser um glíkir, saman skríða níðingar.

Hakon S., p. 123 (Rolls Ed.)

l. 25, and the argr, arga, the *craven, corpore infamis.* Filthiness or cowardice, not violence, is the essential aggravation in each of these crimes. Cp. O. W. Pl. vv. 4, 71.

ll. 177–180. 'Niðafiollom' is a foolish repetition from 162, where it is a place of bliss: berr ser í fiöðrom cannot be right; the damned souls are gorged by the dragon, Kveljask andir í orms *gini,* Bk. vi, Ditty 13 b, probably echoed from Wolospa when in a pure state.

The Third Sibyl—
The introduction is here missing, though the rest is in a much better condition than the preceding. Christian influence from the old Irish Church is here manifest.

ll. 181–185. Cp. Is. xi. 6 sqq., Rev. xxi. 1—'And I saw a new heaven and a new earth:' iðja- is only met with here.

l. 186. Böls man allz batna, cp. 'He will swallow up death in victory, and the Lord God will wipe away tears from off all faces,' Is. xxv. 8, Rev. xxi. 4.

l. 187. Better Hróptz (ó); what is the etymology of this word? akin to Lat. *cāsmen,* qs. Hórmtr, then through metathesis Hrómtr, Hróptr? at any rate, Hróptr, Hrópta-týr denote Woden as the *father of song.*

l. 189. Sacrificial rites resumed, see vol. ii, p. 480.

l. 193. Meetings in judgment beneath the World Tree are resumed. Here the paraphrase for once is in error—ok rœða . . . of Miðgarðz-orm : we read *und* mold-þinor (dat.): the World Tree is undoubtedly meant, under which the gods in times of yore assembled.

l. 195. Added by Hauks-bók, but seems to be genuine.

l. 196. Hauks-bók reads—þá mono Æsir . . . finna, perhaps better. The end of the Lay is missing.

The Short Sibyl Song.

A poem recovered from remnants—lines 1–4, 26–46, 55–64 being *embedded* in Hyndla's Lay (vol. i, pp. 226–234), and lines 5–25, 47–54 in Volospa (vol. i, p. 193 sqq.); cp. p. 518.

The *Title* has been preserved in Edda Gg., Sem segir í Volospa inni skömmo— Ero volor allar, etc.

ll. 1–4. *Introductory,* necromantic, the Witch Sibyl ghost raised (by Woden).

Between ll. 4 and 5 there would be many missing links; the tale of the Cow Auð-humbla we believe was once drawn from this poem—strange præ-Arian myths! May not Auð-humbla preserve some Pictish vocable? cp. Auðr (a bull), Thulor 452. Farther, we are told how that the Cow licked the salt stones, whence on the first and second day appeared, first the hair, then the *head,* and on the third day the whole man, 'and they called him *Buri,* whose son was *Bor,* whose son was Woden' (pp. 631–632); the Basque for head is *buru*—a strange coincidence; we take the word to have come to the poet from some Pictish source in the north of Scotland.

l. 6 = Dvergar höfðo kviknat í iörðunni svá sem 'maðcar í holdi,' under the corrupt 'morgum' we espy 'möðcom,' for the poet would not have omitted a fact so characteristic, and if he did, whence did the Edda paraphrast get it?

ll. 12–17. Genealogical, maybe part of some memorial poem; as also the *cocks* of the various dwellings, filed in ll. 18–25.

ll. 26–33 record the origin of Loki as the Sire of the Hell-brood: ll. 28–33 refer to lost myths of the birth of Ogress Hell; the roasted heart is elsewhere wholly unknown: the text of ll. 30, 31 corrupt; Loki is here represented as 'argr,' 'blaudr.'

ll. 34–38. Generations of Wizards and Ogres; seið-berendr, ἅπ. λεγ., and unsafe, for one says, efla, magna seið, never bera seið; must we read, seið-menn bornir frá S.? Svart-höfði strikes one occurring here in mythical garb; it is a pure and simple translation of Gaelic *Dubh-ceann*[1].

ll. 39–42. Memorial verses; one line has slipped out before 39—

Var Baldrs faðir Bors arf-þegi.

Balder's father (i. e. Woden) *was the son of Bor;* see the note above.

ll. 43–46 we have changed into future, mun, hnígr, læzk, slær; for only so can the lines have stood in the Sibyl Song, yet the preterite would well suit some memorial-didactic poem; the passage affords a parallel to Doom 41–45.

ll. 47–54. The paraphrase (p. 633) styles the ogress 'gygr,' Scot. *gyre*—Gygr ein býr fyrir austan Miðgarð, etc. Perhaps read—

Austr býr in aldna gýgr: í Iarnviði.

l. 49 = Af ættinni verðr sá einn máttkastr er kallaðr er Mána-garmr; a line must be missing containing Mánagarm's name, not found elsewhere.

l. 53 = þeir vetr fara þrír saman ok ekki sumar í millom.

l. 54. Read válynd (so R, H, W.)

ll. 53, 54 = þaðan af týnir sól skini síno, ok vindar ero þá ókyrrir ok gnýja heðan ok handan.

ll. 55–57 = þá drífr snær or öllom ættom, frost eru þá mikil ok vindar harðir; ekki nýtr sólar.

ll. 58–60. haf and hauðr, alliterative; hyr, Cd.

l. 60. Guess; ráð ok regin, cp. Hakm. 57; a word seems missing before þrióta.

ll. 61–63. Clearly an allusion to Christ. Thus in this fragment of song, Pictish, Norse, and Christian ideas are intermingled;—a weird amalgam of beliefs.

Hyndla's Lay.

[Vol. i, pp. 225–234. The present notes are written to the reconstructed text, vol. ii, pp. 515–517, see Excursus IV to vol. ii.]

ll. 1–36. Proem, Introductory[2].

l. 1. Mark the emphasising genitive, mær meyja, rœkr rokra.

l. 2. Hyndla, the little dog; or are we to read Hýnla, qs. Hunila?

l. 4. véss heilags we render *holy place, asylum, sanctuary,* epithet to Walhall (echoed from Rev. xxi. 2 ?).

l. 5. hugom sitja does not construe; hörgom (?).

ll. 6–12. verðugum (a quite modern word), svinnom, mörgom, by an easy emendation, verðungo, sinnom, mögom: mann-semi, an else unknown word, from man (bondwoman), not mann.

l. 13. Coaxing the giantess; we read mun-ek; she offers a safe-conduct, as it were, to Hyndla.

ll. 15–19. The wolf is the ogress' steed, the boar Freyja's.

---

[1] In the Book of Settlement (as we have lately become aware) Irish Gaelic influence is not confined to the actual Gaelic names (see Dict. last page), but beside these we find a whole regiment of names which are Norse in form, but really *translations* from Gaelic into Icelandic; one of these is Svart-hofði: further, Hundi and several others.

[2] The reader must please mark the number of lines 10, 20, 30, etc., omitted in the reconstructed text.

l. 20. sitja við skolom should be obelised; read,—

Sennom vit or soðlom, sáttar við skolom

of . . . iöfra ættir dœma.

Let us have a snug, peaceable chat about the ancient race of kings. Helgi i. 140–143 (in foot-note to vol. i, p. 136) presents a parallel.

ll. 37 sqq. *The central genealogical* part of the poem.

ll. 37, 38 we have tried to restore by help of Husd. 21, 22: in miok we suggest mög: under 'rogna kindar,' ragna reinar; Husd. styles Heimdall, ragna-rein-vári.

l. 39. nadd-gofgan; from the star-studded vault of heaven? we find the epithet in Swipd. M. 54.

l. 48. sif sifjaðan siötom gærvöllom, an apt epithet of Heimdall the Sire of the human race.

l. 52. þau es frama gœrðo = hann var hermaðr mikill.

l. 54. Under 'œztan manna' we detect Austmanna = hann herjaði víða um Austrveg, ok drap þar þann konung er S. het; the better form is Alvig, Alveig (Edda)— þá fekk hann þeirrar kono es kolloð es Alveig in spaka, dóttir Emundar konungs or Holmgarði ens ríka (Edda).

ll. 82–89. Arngrim's sons; under 'aní omí' we espy Arng'mi, i. e. Aungrimi, see Introd. p. lxxxix: í Bolmi austr, to be distinguished from Isle of Bolm, in Western Norway.

ll. 90, 91. faðir Fróða, föðor Kiars, foðor Ölrúnar.

l. 99. diúpúðga, diúp-hugða, p. 522; cp. Hygð the Queen in Beowulf.

l. 111. Hildigunn, of Waldere's Lay?

ll. 113, 114 = Haki var faðir Hroðgeirs, foðor Hroðmars, foðor Haka berserks.

l. 117. Sæfari, cp. Sæfred of Beowulf.

l. 123. Ketill, Klypp, Olmod, family names in the Horð-akara family.

ll. 134 sqq. The end of the poem. All the lines depicting the Sibyl as *angry* belong to the last stage; but her anger comes too late, she has been beguiled of all her wisdom.

l. 136. val-svíni, so we have mended the hopeless, impossible 'valsini.'

l. 147. minnis-öl, else minnis-veig.

YNGLINGATAL RESTORED, see Notes, vol. i, p. 514.

(The proem is lost. Maimed stanzas are marked ¹, ², ³, as they have lost one, two, or three line-pairs.)

i. *Yngwi-Frey strophe lost.*

ii. ³Varð fram-gengt þar es Fróði bió
feigðar-orð es at Fiǫlni kom :
ok sikling svigðiss geira
vágr vindlauss um viða skyldi.

iii. ²Enn dag-skiarr durniss niðja
sal-vǫrðoðr Svegði vélti :
þa-es í stein inn enn stór-geði
dulsa konr ept dvergi hlióp :
ok salr brattr þeirra Sǫkk-mimiss
iǫtun-bygðr við iǫfri gein.   10

iv. ²Enn á vit Vilja bróðor
vitta-vættr Vanlanda kom :
þa-es troll-kynd um troða skyldi
1 . . . Hulð lióna bága :
ok sá brann á beði Skúto
men-glǫtoðr es Mara kvaldi.

v. ²Ok Vísburs vilja byrgi
sævar niðr svelgja knátti :
þa-es mein-þióf markar ǫtto
Gísl ok Ondorr á sínn góðan
fǫðor :   20
ok allvalld í árin-kióli
glóða garmr glymjandi beit.

vi. ²Hitt vas stór firn es stalla ruðo
sverð-berendr sœni dróttins :
ok land-herr á lífs vǫnom
dreyrog vápn Dómalda bar :
þa-es ár-giǫrn Ióta dolgi
Svia kind um soa skyldi.

vii. ²Ok ek þess opt um Yngva hrœr
fróða menn fregit hafðak :   30
hvar Dómarr á dynjanda
bana Halfs um borinn væri :
nú ek víst veitk at verk-bitinn
Fiǫlniss niðr við Fyri brann.

viii. ²Kveðkat-ek dulnemaDyggva hrœr
glitniss gná at gamni hefir :
þviat ióð-dís Ulfs ok Nara
konung-mann kiósa skyldi :
ok allvald Yngva þióðar
Loka mær at leikom hefir.   40

ix. ¹Frá-ek at Dag dauða-yrðr
frægðar fúsom fara skyldi :

þa-es val-teins til Vǫrva kom
spak-frǫmoðr spǫrs at hefna :
ok þat orð á Austr-vega
' vísa ferð frá ' vígi bar :
at þann gram um geta skyldi
slœngvi-þref Sleipniss verðar.

x. ²þat tel-ek undr es Agna hrœr
Skialfar-vers at skǫpom fórot :
þa-es gœðing með goll-meni   51
Loga dís at lopti hóf :
hinn-es við Taur austr temja skyldi
svalan hest Signýjar vers.

xi. ²Fell Eirekr þars Alreki
bróðor vápn at bana urðo :
ok hnakk-mars með hǫfoð-fetlom
Dags frændr um drepask kvóðo :
frá-at maðr áðr eykja gœrvi
Freyss af-spring í folk hafa.   60

xii. ¹Ok varð . . . es Alfr um vá
vǫrðr vé-tiallz um veginn liggja :
þa-es dǫglingr drœrgan mæki
ǫfund-giarn á Yngva rauð :
vasa þat bært verk at Bera skyldi
vé-sœfendr vígs um hvetja :
þa-es brœðr tveir at bǫnom urðosk
óþurfendr um afbrýði.

xiii. ²Varð Iǫrundr inn Iǫrmun-fróði
lífs um lattr í Lima-firði :   70
þa-es há-brióstr hǫrva Sleipnir
bana Goðlaugs um bera skyldi :
ok Hagbarðz hersa valdi
hǫðno leif at halsi gekk.

xiv. Knátti endr at Uppsǫlom
Ána sótt Aun um standa :
ok þrá-lífr þiggja skyldi
ióðs aðal ǫðro sinni :
ok sveiðoðs at ser hverfði
mækiss hlut inn miávara :   80
ok ok-hreins áttunga rióðr
lǫgðiss odd sem lé-barn drakk :
máttit hárr hiarðar mæki
Austr-konungr upp um halda.

xv. ¹Ok lof-sæll or landi fló
Týss áttungr Tunna ríki :

ok flœming farra trióno
iǫtuns eykr á Agli rauð:
sa-es um Austmǫrk áðan hafði
brúna hǫrg um borinn lengi: 90
ok skíðlauss Skilfinga nið
hœfiss hiǫrr til hiarta stóð.

XVI. [1] Fell Óttarr und ara greipar
'duganligr' fyr Dana vápnom:
þann her-gammr hrægom fœti
viti borinn á Vendli sparn:
þau frá-ek verk Vǫttz ok Fasta
Sœnskri þióð at sǫgom verða,
þa-es Eylandz iarlar Fróða
Vandil-kráko um veginn hǫfðo.

XVII. [1] Þat frák 'undr' at Aðils fiǫrvi
vitta-vigg um viða skyldi: 102
ok s . . . af Slœngviss bógom
Freyss áttungr falla skyldi:
ok við aur ægir hiarna
bragnings burs um blandinn
varð:
ok í dísa-sal deyja skyldi
Ála-dolgr at Uppsǫlom.

XVIII. [1] Veit-ek Eystein endr um folginn
leikinn lævi á Lofundi: 110
ok sikling með Sviom kvóðo
Iótzka menn inni brenna:
ok bit-sótt í brand-noi
hlíðar-þangs á hilmi rann:
þa-es timbr-fastr toptar nœkvi
flotna fullr um fylki brann.

XIX. [2] Þat stœkk orð upp at Yngvari
Sýslo kind um soit hefði:
ok liós-hǫmom við Lagar-hiarta
herr Eistneskr at hilmi vá: 120
ok Aust-marr iǫfri Sœnskom
Gymis-lióð at gamni kveðr.

XX. [2] Varð Onundr Iónakrs bura
harmi heptr und Himin-fiǫllom:
ok of-væg Eistra dolgi
heipt hrísungs at hendi kom:
ok sá frǫmoðr foldar beinom,
haugi hrœrs um horfinn vas.

XXI. [1] Ok Ingialld Illráðan trað
reyks rǫsoðr á Ræningi: 130
þa-es hús-þiófr hyrjar leistom
Goð-konung í gœgnom steig:
ok siá yrðr allri þióðo
siall-gætast með Sviom þótti:

es hann sialf-ráði síno fiǫrvi
í fíknom fúr fara skyldi.

XXII. [2] Ok við vág Væniss Viðar-telgjo
hræ Áláfs hof-gylðir svalg:
ok glóð-fiálgr gœrvar leysti
sonr Forniótz af Svia iǫfri: 140
Svá átt-runnr frá Uppsǫlom
Lúfo kyns lang-feðgom hvarf.

XXIII. [2] Þat frá hrœr . . . at Halfdanar
sǫk-miðlendr sakna skyldo:
ok hall-varps hlífi-nauma
þióð-konung a þotni tók:
ok Skær-eið í Skirings-sal
um brynj-alfs beinom drúpir.

XXIV. [2] Enn Eysteinn fyr ási fór
til Bysleistis bróðor-meyjar: 150
ok nú liggr und lagar beinom
reiks lauðoðr á raðar broddi:
þars él-kaldr hiá iǫfors gǫtvom
Vǫðlo straumr at vági kœmr.

XXV. [2] Ok til þings . . . þriðja iǫfri
hveðrungs mær or heimi bauð:
þa-es Halfdan sa-es í Holtom bió
Norna dóms um notið hafði:
ok buðlung á Borroi
sigr-hafendr síðan fálo. 160

XXVI. [1] Varð Goðrœðr inn Gǫfogláti
lómi beittr, sás fyr lǫngo vas:
ok 'um ráð' at ǫlom stilli
hǫfoð heipt rækt at hilmi dró:
ok laun-svik inn lóm-geði
Áso árr at iǫfri bar:
ok buðlungr á beði fornom
Stiflo-sundz of stunginn vas.

XXVII. Ok nið-kvísl í Nóregi
þróttar burs um þroask hafði.
Réð Áleifr Upsa forðom, 171
Víði, Grœnd, ok Vestmarom:
unz fót-verkr við foldar þrǫm
víg-miðlung um viða skyldi:
Nú liggr goð-alfr á Geir-stǫðom
'her-konungr' haugi ausinn.

Strophes XXVIII–XXX *missing.*

þat veit-ek bazt und blám himni
kenni-nafn sva-at konungr eigi:
es Rǫgnvaldr inn Ráð-svinni
Heiðom-hárr þik heita réð: 180
ok mild-geðr Mœra dróttinn . . .
(*the end missing*).

HALEYGJATAL RESTORED, see Notes, vol. i, p. 523.

Viljak hlióðs kveðja at Hárs líði
meðan Gillings giǫldom yppik:
þviat hans ætt í hver-legi
Galga-farms til goða teljom.

. . . . . .

Hinn es Suptungs or sœkk-dǫlom
farma-goð fliúgandi bar:

. . . . . .

Hǫfoð-baðm þa-es heið-sœni
á f . . . Hnit-fiǫllom drýgði.

. . . . . .

þann skoll-blœtr at Skatvǫlom gat
Ása nið við Iarnviðjo: 10
þa-es þau meirr í Mannheimom
Skatna vinr ok Skaði bioggo:
Sæming einn ok sono marga
Ondor-dís við Óðni gat.

. . . . . .

Enn Goðlaugr grimman tamði
'við ofr-kapp' Austr-konunga
Sigars ió, es synir Yngva
men-glǫtoð við meið reiðo:
ok ná-reiðr á nesi drúpir
Vinga-meiðr þar-es víkr deilir: 20
þar-es fiǫl-kynt um fylkiss hrœr
steini merkt Straumseyjar-nes.

. . . . . .

þa-es út-rǫst iarla bági
Belja-dolgs byggja vildi.

. . . . . .

Ok sá . . . halr at Hárs veðri
hǫsvan serk hrísgrisniss bar.

. . . . . .

Varð Hákon Hǫgna meyjar
viðr vápn-bitinn es vega skyldi:
ok sinn aldr í odda gný
Freyss áttungr á Fiǫlom lagði: 30
Ok þar varð es vinir fello
magar Hallgarðz manna blóði:
Stafaness við stóran gný
vinar Lóðors vágr of blandinn.
Ok Sigrœð hinn es svǫnom veitti
hróka biór Haddingja vals:
Farma-týss fiörvi næmðo
iarð-ráðendr á Ogloi.
Ok ǫðlingr Yrna iarðar
'alnar orms' á Aurom varð   40
lífs of lattr þa-es landrekar
Týss áttung í trygðom sviko.

. . . . . .

þar varð minnztr mein-vinnǫndom
Yngvi-Freyss ættar ǫndurðan dag
fagna-fundr es flota þeysto
iarð-ráðendr at Ey-Dǫnom:
þa-es Sigvalldi sunnan kníði
lagar stóð at liði þeira.

. . . . . .

þeim es allt austr til Eiða-búss
brúðr Valtýss und bœgi liggr.   50

. . . . . .

Iólna sumbl, Enn ver yrkja gátom
stilliss lof sem steina-brú.

A few additional notes.

l. 1. Viljak hlióð is not idiomatic; viljak is to be scanned as slur, as in Vsp. 3;
therefore the first half has only one measure left; a word has been dropped out, viz.
kveðja; Jomsv. 1–3 presents an exact parallel to kveðja hlióðs at kvæði.

l. 2. hans; to substitute 'Hakonar' is on account of metre inadmissible; a line is
perhaps missing, giving the Earl's name, to which 'hans' refers; unless indeed the
poet said—þviat Háleygi í hver-legi | galga farms til goða teljom. Cp. the poem's
title Haleygjatal.

l. 25. sá halr, suspicious; ok sá to be scanned as slur, a measure is missing; is not
Wether-Hall's name (the seventh in the Haleygja generation) hidden underneath?

ll. 31, 32 are overlaid. The Saga, apparently Ari's sole authority for the Hacon-
Atli episode, says, ch. 13—þar fell Hákon iarl enn Atli iarl varð sárr til ólífis, ok
fóro menn hans með hann til Atleyjar ok andaðisk hann þar. Svá segir Eyvindr
Skalda-spillir. Earl Atli and his death must have stood in the poem. We suspect it
is hidden under hallvarðz, 'maga Atla,' or the like. The verses as they stand
are harsh, a sure indication of a decomposed text.

FINAL READINGS TO VOLUME II.

(See p. cxix of the Introduction, vol. i.)

Bragi—
line 5. ok um Heðins . . . ósk-kván at þat sínom.

Þórs-drapa—
l. 74. . . . alfheims mokkor-kalfa (?).

House Lay—
l. 2. (hann vilk at giof Grimnis) geð-markar lá (kveðja).
l. 9. þar hykk sáð-reyni Sónar sylgs Valkyrjor fylgja.
p. 48, l. 5. hlióta man ek (né hlítik) Hertýs (of þat frýjo).
p. 54, l. 11. hlemmi-sverð við harðri húf-langan skæ dúfo.
p. 79, l. 4. hauka skopt á hepti hlín ǫl bœkis mína.
p. 109, l. 11. ok aum í vǫmb, varð elði í þǫmb.
p. 246, l. 4. *for* swollen *read* cold.
p. 250, ll. 15, 16. *read,* As it is told that the kindred of kings sought service of yore with the wise Kraki.
p. 268, l. 10. *read,* the hound of the fir-wood, i. e. fire.
p. 327, l. 12. *read,* the morsels of the ship.
p. 545, note 5. *read,* a Romance word.

Sighvat—
ii, l. 36. . . . lét herr um haldit . . . skeiðar stafna.
v, l. 23. skreið vestan viðr vörr, glœstr sa's bar.
vii, l. 40. folk . . . fylkir . . . þriá togo harði.
vii, l. 48. hundrað tölð at hildi hvár-tveggja folk váro.
viii, ll. 19–20, see p. 585.
viii, l. 29. Alfífo mank ævi ungs drengs muna lengi.
x, l. 71. rán man seggr hinn es sína selr út í því telja.

Arnor—
vi, l. 33. Veit ek þar es Vestfiörðr heitir, etc.

Thiodolf—
iii, l. 78. . . . él-kers glötoðr hersa.
xi, l. 8. Glaðr við galdra smiðjo Geirrœðar sio þeiri.
xii, l. 3. snart við sið-þráð.
p. 263, l. 74, *read* hnigo hringviðir Hvinant-orða.
p. 264, l. 106, *read* Heðin harðmaga, etc.

Konungatal—
l. 315. Vissi Loptr und laupi skýja (*beneath the basket of the clouds*).

Gisli's Saga—
p. 323. hrynja lætr in hvíta hvarm-skógs gná bóga.

Olafs Ríma—
l. 124. Nú er hann Kristz et b. bl. etc.

Thulor—
l. 179. rýgr, víf ok hæll, ristill, sæta.
l. 477. rati, val-bassi, roðr, drit-roði.

LIST OF ABBREVIATIONS
USED IN THE INDICES AND IN EXCURSUS I, VOL. II,

Showing the volume and pages where the respective poems are to be found. The poems of the second volume are cited under the authors' names.

INDEX I. MYTHICAL.

Cited mostly by poem and line; I. or II. marks the volume, e. g. II. 4. 12 = volume, page, and line.

æ is treated as *e ;* œ and ö (ǫ) as o.

Vsp., Hyndl., Yt., Hlt., and Sonat. are cited from the restored texts.

[ ] mark lost poems and parts of poems.

n. marks foot-note or notes at the end of volume.

1. MYTHOLOGIC BEINGS.

Alda-föðr, Vþm. lines 15, 210, Bragi 45.

Alfar, Havam. 32, 111, Spell S. 25, Grimn. 10, Alvm. *pass.*, Lokas. *pass.*, Skirn. 27, 63, þkv. 22, Volkv. *pass.*

Alf-kungr, O. W. Pl. 111.

Alföðr (Woden), I. 80; Helgi i. 159.

Alf-röðull (sun), Vþm. 186.

Allvaldi, Harb. ; see Olvaldi.

Alrúnar (love runes), Spell S. 29, O. W. Pl. 216.

Alsviðr, Havam. 34.

Alsviðr (Sun's horse), Spell S. 11, Grimn. 118.

Alviss, Alvm. 9 sqq.

Amlóði (Giant Hamlet), II. 55. 6.

Amrar (dwarves ?), II. 54. 1.

Andhrimnir, Grimn. App. 1.

Andvara-nautr, II. 529.

Andvari (dwarf), O. W. Pl. 5, 9.

Angeyja, Hyndl. 43.

Angrboða, Sh. Vsp. 26.

Ár (rune), Run. 10.

Árvaka, Spell S. 11, Grimn. 118.

Ása (Anses), Hávam. 32, 111, Spell S. 25, Vþm. 151, Lokas. *pass.*, Alvm. 37, Harb. 78, Flyt. Iv. 5–15, þkv. 22.

Ása-Bragr, Skirn. 133.

Ása-dolgr, Kont. 38.

Ása-synir, Grimn. 132, Alvm. 64, Lokas. 11, 111, 214, 258, Skirn. 27, 63, 67 ; see Thulor 145–149.

Askr, Vsp. 28.

Ás-kungr, O.W.Pl. 111, Righ 3, Vsp. 54.

Ás-liðar, Skirn. 138.

Ás-megin, I. 127. 25, Hym. 119.

Ás-megir, Doom 27.

Áss = Thor, Grimn. 20, þkv. 8 ; II. 80. 22.

Ásynjor, O.W. Pl. 208, Lokas. 42, Doom 2, þkv. 57, Hyndl. 30.

Atla, Hyndl. 44.

Atriðr (Woden), I. 80, þþ. 10.

Auðr (Night's son), Hallfr. iii. 10.

Aur-boða, Sh. Vsp. 40.

Aur-konungr (Hœni), I. 575.

Aurnir, Grott. 40.

Baldr, Vþm. 216 *n.*, Grimn. 41, Riddl. 135, Lokas. 109 sqq., Flyt. Iv. 6, Doom 4 sqq., Sh. Vsp. 44, Vsp. 65 ; I. 126. 18 ; 369. No. 66.

Báleygr (Woden), I. 80.

Baugi (Soma giant), Hofuðl. 73 ; see I. 465.

Beli (Giant Belja), Vsp. 144, Hlt. 24, Kv. 3, Haust. 70.

Berg-Danir, Hym. 57, Haust. 72.

Bergelmir, Vþm. 112, 136.

Berg-rísar, Harb. 105, Grott. 42, 89.

Bestla, Havam. 19; II. 48. 7.

Beyla, Lokas. 225.

Biarg-rúnar, Spell S. 28, O. W. Pl. 222.

Biarkan (rune), Run. 13.

Biflindi, Grimn. App. 45.

Bil (goddess), I. 78. 19.

Bileygr (Woden), I. 80.

Billingr, II. 322. 4.

Biörn (constellation), Spell S. 14.

Blæingr (constellation), Spell S. 16 *n.*

Blóðughófi (horse), þþ. 9, Kv. 3.

Boðn, II. 48. 1 ; 80. 32.

Bók-rúnar, Spell S. 28.

Bolverkr, Love L. 53 ; I. 80.

Bolþorn, Havam. 19.

Bor (Buru), Vsp. 17, Sh. Vsp. (I. 231. 23); II. 250.

Bragar-full, Helgi ii. 52.

Bragi, Spell S. 14, Lokas. 44, Eirm. 12, Hakm. 38.

Brimir, Sh. Vsp. 6.

Brimir (sword), I. 77. 6.

Brim-rúnar, O. W. Pl. 226.

Brisinga-men (necklace), þkv. 52, 63, 76, Haust. 35, [Husd.]

Bruungr (constellation), Spell S. 15 *n.*

Buri, II. 250; see Bor.

Buzeyra (ogress), II. 27. 5.

Byggvir, Lokas. 180, 184, 225.

Byleistr, Sh. Vsp. 29, Vsp. 128, Yt. 150.

Dagr, O. W. Pl. 204, Vþm. 40, 95.

Dags synir, O. W. Pl. 204.

2. HEROIC BEINGS.

Vilmundr, Oddr. 21.
Vingi, Am. 13, 108, 139.
Ving-skornir (horse), W. W. L. 76.
Visburr, Yt. 17.
Vitri (ekename), Langft.
Volsungar, Helgi i. 217, Bragi 56, Hyndl.
Volsungr, W. W. L. 32, O. B. L. 2 sqq.
Völundr (Wayland), Volkv. 9 sqq.
Vöttr, Yt. 97.

Ylfingar, Helgi i. 17, 134, 346, iii. 31.
Yngvarr, Yt. 117, Thiod. iii. 88.
Yngvi, Helgi i. 215, Yt. 39, Hlt. 17.

Yngvi (king), Yt. 64.
Yngvi-Freyr, Hlt. 44.
Yrsa, Grott. 79.

þakkráðr, Volkv. 161.
þegn, þþ. 6.
þiaurikz = þióðrekr, I. 59.
þióðmarr (Theodrick's father), Ord. 11.
þióðrekr (Theodrick), Ord. 7, 17.
þóra, Drengja-móðir, Hyndl. 77.
þóra, hiörtr, II. 347.
þrá-mæli (poem?), Am. 384.
þvinnill (sea-king), II. 80. 35.

3. HEROIC AND MYTHOLOGIC GEOGRAPHY.

Alfheimr, Grimn. 15.
Algrœn (isle), Harb. 42.
Am-svartnir, II. 637.
Andlangr, Thulor 490.
Ara-steinn, Helgi i. 54.
Ár-heimar, Hlod A. 11.
Ása-garðr = Asgard, þkv. 16, 73, Hym. 24, Lokas. 149.
Ás-brú, Grimn. 89.
Ás-garðr, þkv. 73; II. 27. 3.
Aur-vangr, Sh. Vsp. 15.
Austr-vegar, Lokas. 239.

Barri, Skirn. 161.
Bil-röst, O. W. Pl. 119; I. 77. 4.
Bil-skirnir, Grimn. App. 14; Hlt. 27. 8.
Bolm (in the east, Sweden), Hyndl.
Borgundar, Akv. 74.
Braga-lundr, Helgi iii. 33.
Brá-lundr = Bragalundr, Helgi i. 4.
Brandey, Helgi i. 85.
Brá-völlr, Helgi i. 173.
Breiða-blik, Grimn. 41.
Brimir, Vsp. 161.
Bruna-vágar, Helgi iii. 25.
Brunn-akr, Haust. 35.

Danir, see p. 679.
Danmörk, see p. 679.
Daupar-staðir, Hlod A. 30, Akv. 19; cp. Righ.
Danskr, see p. 679.
Dún-heiðr (?), Hlod A. 85.
Dylgja (?), Hlod A. 85.

Éli-vágar, Vþm. 119, Hym. 17.
Eljúðnir, Malsh. 34; see II. 546.

Fen-salir, Vsp. 72.
Fiötur-lundr, Helgi i. 254.
Fivi (Fife), O. G. L. 55.

Folk-vangr, Grimn. 49.
Freka-steinn, Helgi i. 140, 219.

Gim-lé, Vsp. 159.
Ginnunga-gap, Vsp. 12.
Ginnunga-vé, Haust. 58.
Glaðs-heimr, Grimn. 25.
Glitnir, Grimn. 53.
Gnípa-hellir, Vsp. 120.
Gnípa-lundr, Helgi i. 118, 204.
Gníta-heiðr, Akv. 23, Volkv. 54, Grip. 42.
Glasis-lundr, Helgi ii. 4.
Goð-heimr, Sonat. 44.
Goð-vegr, Hyndl. 18.
Goð-þióð, Hamð. 59, Tregr. 32, Hlod A. 29, 50 sqq.
Gotnar, Hamð. 10, 84, 89, 106, 109, 132. Hlod A. 2.
Gotneskr, O. G. L. 56.
Grafar-óss, I. 352.
Gríótuna-haugr, Haust. 54.
Gýmis-garðar, Skirn. 29 sqq.

Harvaða-fiöll, I. 352.
Hata-fiörðr, Rimeg. 1.
Há-tún, Helgi i. 31, 97.
Háva-höll, Havam. 6, 125.
Heðinsey, Helgi i. 87.
Heiðornir, Thulor 489.
Hel (place and goddess), see p. 662.
Hel-grind, Wak. 86.
Himin-biörg, Grimn. 84.
Himin-fiöll, Helgi i. 2.
Himin-vangar, Helgi i. 31.
Hindar-fjall, W. W. L. 67.
Hlé-biörg, Helgi i. 245.
Hleiðrar-stóll, Grott. 73.
Hlessey (Learsey), Harb. 105.
Hlið-skialf, II. 51. 7, Hallfr. v. 9; see II. 525.
Hlym-dalar, L. B. L. 309, 313.

INDEX II. HISTORICAL.

1. NAMES OF PERSONS AND THINGS.

Þóra (King Bareleg's daughter), Kont. 293.
Þóra (girl), II. 282. 5.
Þóralfr Skolmson, Isldr. 50.
Þórarinn, kappi, Isldr. 102.
Þorbergr Arnason, II. 164. 25.
Þorbiörn, Svarti, I. 367. No. 54.
Þórðr Fólason, Sigh. vii. 31.
Þórðr, see Þórroðr.
Þorfinnr (Orkney Earl), II. 162. 31, Arnor vi. 59, 74.
Þorgils Oddason, Skíða R. 34.
Þórhalldr, Isldr. 92.
Þórir, þegjandi (Earl), Wick. 4.
Þórir (Baron, Arinbeorn's father), Ad. 58.
Þórir, Hundr, Sigh. vii. 65.
Þórir (Steigar-Þórir), I. 369. No. 63; II. 244. 7; 246. 10.
Þórir (of Garth), II. 114. 7.
Þórir, hvinan-torði, Ivar 75.
Þorkell, Fóstri, Ivar 5.

Þorketill, Leira, Iomsv. 56 sqq.
Þorketill (Earl), II. 107. 15; Iomsv. 34.
Þorketill (dyrðill), Hallfr. i. 68, Rekst. 115.
Þorketill (Steingerd's father), Korm. 88.
Þorketill, I. 363. No. 32.
Þorketill Geitisson, Isldr. 17.
Þorleifr (Baron, the wise), Haust. 2.
Þorleifr (poet), Isldr. 69.
Þorleifr, Skúma, Iomsv. 135.
Þorleifr, beiskjaldi, Skíða R. 70.
Þórrœðr (poet), II. 193. 3.
Þórrœðr (Sighvat's father), Sigh. viii. 8.
Þorsteinn Egilsson, II. 166. 1; 167. 4.
Þorsteinn (Siðo-Hallzson), Isldr. 92.
Þorvaldr Koðransson (missionary), I. 363. No. 31; 368. No. 57.
Þorvalldr Kiartansson, I. 369. No. 64.
Þórveig, Korm. 68.
Þrainn, I. 363. No. 27.
Þúfo-skítr (nickname), II. 280. 63.

2. NAMES OF PLACES, ETC.

Á-in-Helga, Ott. ii. 40.
Aðal-sýsla, II. 52. 29.
Aðalþegns-hólar, II. 362. 27.
Africa, Thiod. iii. 11.
Agðir, II. 104. 32; 165. 4; Sigh. ii. 10, Ivar 80.
Agna-fit, Hialm. D. 44.
Akr (Acre), II. 277. 25.
Akrs-borg, I. 367. No. 54; II. 252. 12.
Aldeiga, II. 52. 17.
Alfheimr, þd. 74.
Alkassi, II. 249. 11.
Alpta-fiörðr, II. 115. 10.
Alvangs-eyrr, II. 112. 38.
Andverðo-skógr, II. 25 n.
Apardian (Aberdeen), Einar iii. 12.
Árós, II. 214. 4.
Askr, I. 366. No. 49.
Ásolfs-gata, Skíða R. 57.
Assatún, Ott. ii. 36.
Aumar (Isles), II. 165. 2.
Aurar, Hlt. 40 n.
Aust-kylfor, Hornkl. 80.
Aust-menn, Hornkl. 69; II. 220. 29.
Aust-mörk, Yt. 89.
Aust-rœnn, Hornkl. 30.
Austr-vegr, Yt. 45, Sigh. iii. 92; II. 235. 8.
Austr-Vindr, Thiod. x. 7.

Bakki, II. 277. 7.
Balagarðz-síða, Sigh. i. 12.
Bali, II. 362.
Bár (Bari), Mark. 28.
Belgjadalr = Hítardalr, Skíða R. 67.
Biarkey, II. 246. 5.

Biarmskr, II. 39. 22.
Biörgyn, Einar v. 8; II. 267. 6; 276. 4.
Bitra, II. 115. 17.
Blá-land, II. 215. 16.
Blá-menn, II. 231. 15; 251. 16.
Bókn, Sigh. vi. 10; II. 163. 2.
Bolgara-land, II. 353. 151.
Bolgarar, Thiod. iii. 2.
Bolm (in the East, Sweden), Hyndl.
Bolm (Isle), Norway, Thulor 664.
Borg = York, Arnor iv. 10.
Borro, Yt. 159.
Brandfurða (Brentford), II. 107. 26 n. (?); Ott. ii. 32.
Bretar, Hallfred i. 41.
Bretzkr, II. 95. 27; Arnor vi. 27.
Búr-fell, II. 362. 26.
Byrða, Vell. 62, Ivar 93.

Cantaraborg, Sigh. i. 31, Ott. i. 30.
Clement-kirkja, Loft. iii. 17.

Dana-skógar, Ott. ii. 38.
Dana-veldi, Arnor i. 30, Thiod. ii. 44.
Danir, O. B. L. 330, Ott. iv. 1; II. 235. 1 pass.
Danmarkar-auki = Selund, Bragi 42.
Danmörk, O. G. L. 45, Wick. 50, Hild. 3; II. 81. 53; 235. 13; Sigh. v. 17, Ott. i. 8, Loft. i. 25.
Danska Tungo, Sigh. i. 58, Mark. 74, Geisli 104.
Danskr, O. G. L. 47, Hornkl. 86.
Díki, II. 108. 28; Sigh. i. 23.
Dinganes, Vell. 66 n.
Dœlir, II. 252. 17.

INDEX III. SUBJECTS.

Comprises the contents of both Volumes under the following *Sections :—*

The small roman numerals refer to the General Introduction.

1. Philological References.

af-karr, cp. E. car-hand, II. 592.
alandi = O. G. elilenti, II. 696.
aldar-far, II. 645.
aldr-nari, cp. nĕron, II. 651.
alfr, I. 419.
alh = al- = alch, I. 407.
-an, Gaelic names in, I. 531.
and-keto (?), II. 609.
and-uari (?), I. 469.
Anlaf = Olaf, spelling of, cx ; I. 524.
Anse, I. 413 ; II. 515.
arin-geypr, not arin-greypr, I. 473.
ármaðr, I. 417, 489.
article, en = hin [A. Kock], cx.
Ask and Embla, cp. Adam and Eve, II. 515.
ätt-högar, I. 416.
basmir [?], cp. E. baswa-stán, I. 567.
bear-sark, I. 425.
blóta, cp. fladmen [Bugge], I. 408.
Bor = Bask buru, II. 653.
böslar, *better* bölsar, Lat. bolso, II. 594.
braungo, I. 478.
bróc, see **Loan-words Gaelic**, lx.
Change of pronunciation etc. in the eighth century in Scandinavian tongue, lvii ; I. 441.
cracaben, long-shanks, II. 574.

dafar, I. 473.
Dagr, dative of, I. 492.
dalkr = dealg, II. 518.
-dédun, past suffix of weak verbs in Gothic formed by analogy, I. 572.
dís = E. ides, I. 419.
draugr, I. 419.
dual in O. N., I. 558.
dyngia, etymology [Grimm], I. 556.
Edda = erda, II. 514.
— use of the word, xxvi ; II. 560.
ekkja, I. 569.
fægi = fich = uicus, I. 537.
falk = falcem, II. 614.
for-doer, wizard, I. 408.
fóst-brœðr, I. 424.
frauðr = frog, II. 607.
freista, meaning, I. 412.
fretta, meaning, I. 412.
Genitive fem. in -oz, -or, -ur [Säve], I. 512.
— *masc. in* -is, I. 472.
Genitive, of emphasis, II. 643.
Gimlé, I. 496 ; II. 651.
glæfia = F. glaive, II. 615.
glæ-logn = glæ-lung, II. 590.
glissir, Guest's Wisd., I. 31.
glöă, cviii.

gœðing, cp. aristos, II. 594.
gofgir, gentlemen, I. 406.
Goi [?], I. 431.
Gŷmis, I. 487.
halir = E. hæleð, I. 420.
hána, spelling of, cix.
hand-laun = E. hond-lean, I. 514.
hégetill = gagatem [Fritzner], II. 617.
hegri = kirkē, I. 466.
heið-sifa, cp. eið-sifja, I. 424.
heill, I. 411.
hlaut, I. 408.
Hœni = kúknos, cii.
horg = E. hearg = harrow, I. 407.
Hrim, Hrymr = Kronos, II. 651.
hrista tein, I. 411.
hrœr, meaning of, I. 521.
Hróptr, cp. cäsmen, II. 652.
hrotti, cp. E. Hrunting, II. 598.
Hyndla = hunila, II. 653.
Iða-vollr, cp. Magh-Ith, cxxii.
ingjan = Ir. inghean, II. 599.
Ingunar-Freyr, I. 486.
Inn-drótt, I. 530.
Ionakr, I. 478.
iungr, lxx; II. 612.
ividja = E. inwidda, I. 496.
iþrótt, not íþrótt, I. 530.
kinga, I. 497, 519.
kírkē, I. 466.
klé = láia, I. 555.
kogur = E. cocur, I. 488.
kopir, Guest's Wisd., l. 25.
kvelli, II. 608.
leikin [?], II. 649.
leyðra, meaning of, I. 532.
lióða-hattr, true meaning of, I. 439.
Loan-words from English — buklari, greifi, hagestalda, penning, pundari, scilling, scattr, sigli, lix, lx, lxiv.
Loan-words from Greek—fengari, skipt, midhæfi, II. 597.
Loan-word from Basque — buru, II. 652.
Loan-word from Finnic—tusi, I. 533.
Loan-words from Slavonic—reca, rokn, II. 574, 616.
Loan-words from Gaelic—biodh, broc, carca, caupall, conn, cras, dealg, eth, fibh, fich, gagarr, inghean, lam, lind, lung, niol, sgeulache, siol, tarbh, tir, lx, lxx; I. 483, 518, 567; II. 537, 575, 599, 607, 611, 614–616.

Loan-words from Latin and Romance— akka, berillus, böslar, fant, frakka, glefja, lenz, lín, mútari, peita, targa, tresc, lx; I. 562; II. 587, 601, 615, 617.
miotoðr = E. meotuð, I. 558.
Mundil-fœri = Prometheus[Ward], I.479.
nadd-gofgan, lxviii; II. 654.
nór, meaning of, I. 523.
Nóregr, *historical* spelling of, II. 512.
óð-rĕrĭr, I. 466.
œrir, Guest's Wisd., l. 36.
ogur-stund [?], I. 497.
ó-freskr, I. 425.
ó-myndr, cp. in manu, II. 595.
ond, cp. Unnar-steinn [Rhŷs], cxxi.
ondvegis-súlor [1], I. 406.
Orkney dialect, II. 606.
orð, yrðr, uses of, I. 521.
Ösgrui, cp. gruva, I. 484.
otwin [?], II. 581.
pari-cida [2].
patri-monium = feðr-munir, I. 470.
Place-names in Western Isles, lxiv; I. 510.
port-greifi, cp. E. port-gerefa, II. 579.
Pronunciation, evidence of coins on, I.441.
Puns in the Old N. Poetry, I. 152, 484; II. 96, 172, 272, 300, 327, 329, 337, 362, 365, 501, 544, 606.
Quantity of inflexion -anda = ◡◡, cviii.
Quantity of words, vowel before vowel = ◡◡, e. g. bua, blyi, gloa, hloa, nio, sæing, skeom, soit, trui, veom, cviii.
Quantity of words with consonantic 'i' in final syllables, e. g. gleðja, miðjom, dynja = – ◡, cviii.
Quantity in Cædmon's metre, I. 435.
Quantity in Court-metre, I. 448, 449.
Quantity in Dialogue-metre, I. 439.
Quantity in Wolospa, I. 443.
ragna-rok, I. 486.
Rán = arachne = arānea, I. 491.
rim-henda, *not* run-henda, I. 451.
roðra, *not* róðra, I. 407.
rosmun-fiöll, I. 470.
Sága, *not* Saga, I. 480.
Sann-tiri = ceann-tir, II. 599.
scald = sgeulache, I. 567.
scalda-spillir, meaning of, I. 262.
scansion of weak preterites and comparatives, I. 497.
segl = Lat. săgulum, I. 491.
Sigfrœðr = Sigurðr, historic spelling of, cx.

---

[1] Professor Sayce notices that the Phœnician temples in Malta were furnished with two stone pillars close to the entrance.

[2] The first factor, 'pari,' so long unexplained, is solved by the gloss of Paul the Deacon, *fara*, kin (Langobardorum *faras*, hoc est generationes vel lineas) ; pari-cida therefore means *kin-killer, slayer within the family*, a consistent interpretation.

sil-, cp. Lat. sil-entium, I. 483.
sinnar = E. gesithas, I. 500.
skyldi, use of, I. 521.
sliðar = E. sliðe, I. 477.
soa, I. 408.
soma = sónar, I. 561.
sororium tigillum, I. 429.
Spelling in this Edition, cviii, cix.
Spelling of R, xliii.
-stafar, compounds of, I. 472.
suðrœni, curious use of, by Tapestry
    poet and Exeter-book, I. 557.
Suftung = Sumtung = Suntung, I. 466.
Suptung, etymology of, I. 561.
svæfa, I. 408.
svárr = G. schwager, II. 576.
Svart-hofði, cp. Dubh-ceann, II. 562.
Svold, cp. Slav. reca, II. 574.
tál-hreinn = E. stæl-hrán, II. 563.
tíra = G. zier, I. 538.
trani, gender altered, II. 574.
Val-Bretar, II. 575.
val-gifr = E. wæl-gifre, II. 563.
vár-liúgr = E. wær-loga, I. 539.
vartari, cp. E. garter, II. 571.

Vættlinga, I. 420.
vættr, l. 419.
vættrar-braut, I. 420.
vé, I. 407.
Veorr, I. 219.
vero, from verr, værr, I. 483.
-víg, compounds of, frequent in Helgi
    poet's Lays.
víg-roði, I. 491.
vika, Lat. uices [Jessen], I. 428.
Vili, cp. vil, II. 648.
Vitnir, cp. vit, I. 479.
vr = E. wr, often changed to 'hr' or 'r,'
    cix.
Woden = Lat. uātes, ciii; II. 647.
Wolsi = phallos, II. 609.
Wrind, *not* Rind, I. 485.
Ygg-drasill, I. 480.
þaðan, *better* þanan, I. 573.
þorri [?], I. 431.
þrasis, *not* þrásis, I. 479.
þulr, I. 24.
þwingor, imaginary word coined out of
    a misreading of the Tune-stone, as
    was also 'singoster,' I. 573.

2. Poetical Subjects, References to; see also 3. Critical Index.

Age, date, etc., see Introd., § 8, and
    Special Introductions and Notes.
Asides, intercalary phrases used by the
    Helgi poet, I. 489.
    by the Greenland Atli Lay, I. 330, 562.
Ballads, history and origin of, II. 389.
Classification of Poems, Introd. § 9,
    lxv–lxx.
Collections of Old Poems, now lost.
    Lost collections used by—
        Ari, lxxv.
        Saxo, lxxv.
        Snorri, lxxv.
    Lost collection of Danish Lays, lxxv.
Court-poetry, see **Metre**, Excursus
    on—
    its origin, lxxx; I. 433–435.
    its intent, lxxxi; I. 433–435.
    its composition and delivery, lxxxi;
        I. 540.
    its structure, I. 456.
Dramatic Poems, see Old Wolsung
    Play, I. 31.
    Dramatic frameworks to didactic
        poems, e. g.—
        Loddfafni's Lessons.
        Swipdag and Menglad.
        The Aristophanic Poet.
    Metres of dialogue-poems, I. 439–
        440.
Epigrams, I. 368.

Improvisation, II. 408.
    by Einar, II. 275.
    by Sighvat, II. 119.
Kennings or **Synonyms**.
    For general account of use in the
        older poems and list of kennings,
        see Excursus II, 449–486.
    Kennings in—
        Arnor, II. 592.
        Brunhild Lay, I. 557.
        Eilif, II. 605.
        Einar, II. 600.
        Geisli, II. 602.
        Gisli Illugison, II. 599.
        Islendinga-drapa, II. 612.
        Jomsvikinga-drapa, II. 606.
        Konunga-tal, II. 604.
        Krakomal, II. 606.
        Later Poems, II. 606.
        Love-song, II. 603.
        Mark, II. 598.
        Merlinus-spa, II. 608.
        Old Wolsung Play, I. 469.
        Orm, II. 605.
        Rekstefja, II. 603.
        Skaufhala-balk, II. 610.
        Skiða-rima, II. 611.
        Thulor in Court-metre, II. 617.
Lost Poems, see Index III. 4, **Saxo**
        and **Skioldunga**, and above.
        Balder's Burning, I. 126, 574.

---

[1] Add to the parallels given II. 573, Juvenal x. 205, Jacet exiguus cum ramice nervus.

4. Authorities Cited, Translated, or Paraphrased.

How Egil made his poem Sona-torrek, I. 541.

The poet Einar's shield, II. 42.

Eric the Red's Saga.
Freydis' character coloured from Gudrun's in the Greenland Lay, I. 338, 564.
The Sibyl-scene, II. 647.

Eyrbyggia Saga.
Ch. 10. Thor's stone of sacrifice, I. 409.
Ch. 4. Temple fittings of heathen days, I. 403.
Ch. 11. The dead feasting in the Holy Hill, I. 415.
Ch. 44. Devotion of enemy by casting a spear, I. 425, 567.

Fostbrodra Saga.
Thormod the poet and his two loves, II. 173.

Gisla Saga.
Paraphrases of lost Helgi Lay in poems by Editor of Gisla, lxvii; II. 331.

Gretti's Saga.
Gretti given Thor's exploits, I. 513.

Gunnlaug's Saga.
Gunnlaug's story coloured and imitated from Waldhere's story, I. 568.
Gunnlaug and King Sigtryg, II. 119.
Moot-stead of Egil's family, I. 551.
Thord's poem on Gunnlaug, II. 577.

Hall-o'-Side's lost Saga.
[Thidrand's Thattr] the goddesses, Disir, in arms, I. 419.

Hallfred's Saga.
Hallfred meets Tryggvason, II. 87.
Hallfred's death, II. 88.
Goodman sitting on a barrow near his house, I. 416.

Hen-Thori's Saga.
Old Moot-stead, II. 495.
Vow at toast of Woden, I. 423.

Hord's Saga, the omen of the broken necklace, I. 563.

Kialnesinga Saga.
Ch. 5. Temple furniture, I. 404.

Laxdæla Saga.
Olaf Peacock's new hall, II. 22.
Gudrun's Lays, echo of, I. 562.
Kiartan's character and adventures coloured from those of Sigfred and Waldhere, I. 565.

Nial's Saga.
Brian's battle, I. 281, 554.
Hallgerd's treachery to Gunnar (echo of Egil's story), II. 505.

Scald-Helgi's lost Saga.
Rimur on, I. 238.

Sighwat's lost Saga.
Morsel from, II. 121.

Vatzdæla Saga.
The boy Thorstan and the Outlaw (echo from Tale of Elfwine's Youth), II. 503.
The Yoke, going under it, I. 423.

d. **STURLUNGA AND LIVES OF BISHOPS.**

Islendinga Saga.
Dancing, II. 295, 386.
Sturla and King Magnus, II. 261.
Thord Anderson's death, II. 387.

Hrafn Sweinbiornsson's Life.
Bishop Biarni's gifts, II. 301.

Thorgils' Life.
The dance, II. 386.

Bishop Arni's Life.
On dancing and mumming, II. 386.

Bishop John's Life.
His objection to dancing and mumming, II. 385, 386.
His objection to heathen names of week-days, I. 428.
His objection to Ovid's Ars Amoris, II. 259.

Hungrwaka.
Bishop Cloing, II. 259.

Annals (Flatey-bok and Fragments).
Thormod Olafsson, death of, II. 419.
Starkad's tooth in Africa, II. 612.

e. **EDDA PROSE AND TRADITIONAL SAGAS.**
Snorri's real part in, lxxxvi, c.

Bragamal.
The Rape of Idwyn and Fall of Thiazi, II. 10.
The Weregild of Thiazi and Wedding of Scathe, I. 464.
The Guild-feast of the gods at Eager's, I. 463.
The origin and history of the Soma-drink, I. 464, 465.

Skaldskaparmal.
Eormanric's end, II. 5.
Everlasting battle of the Heathnings, II. 5.
Thor's wager of battle with giant Hrungnir, II. 11.
Thor's struggle with giant Garfred and his daughter, II. 18.
The Treasures of the gods, and how they got them, I. 481.
Paraphrase of *Hyndla's Lay*, II. 518.
Synonym List, I. 545.

Gylfa-ginning, II. 630.

Glosses following Thulor AM. 748, II. 546.

Gradus gleaned from Prose-Edda, I. 574.

---

[1] On this casket is not only a scene from Egil's story, but one from Weyland's—Beadhild before the smith, who has just slain her little brother. Weyland's escape through the air like Dædalus is sculptured on the base of the Leeds' cross.

p. **GREEK BOOKS.**
Aeschylus.
  Prom. The Titan chained, II. 604.
  Agam. 'Helen of Troy' described as
    a Walcyrie, a Brunhild, I. 562.
Arataeus.
  Cited by St. Paul, I. 511.
Aristophanes.
  Birds. Birth of Love, cii.
  —— Chaos, II. 646.
Herodotus.
  Psammenitos, xxiv.
Homer.
  Od. x [1].
  Od. viii. 319 ; II. 607.
  Od. xii. 414, 415 ; I. 531.
  Od. xx. 105 ; I. 499.
Pindar.
  Poetry, image drawn from nectar,
    and house-building, I. 540 ; II.
    712.

q. **BIBLE** (mostly eschatological).
  Old Testament—
  Leviticus iv. 17.
  Numbers xvii. 4, xix. 4, I. 411.
  Psalms xcvii, I. 609 ; cxxviii 3, I.
    550.
  Isaiah xiii. 9, 10, xxxiv. 4, II. 650.
  Ezekiel xxxii. 7, 8, II. 650.
  Daniel v, I. 477.
  Hosea iv. 12, I. 411.
  Joel ii. 10–32, II. 650.
  New Testament—
  Mark xiv. 7.
  Luke xxi. 9–11, II. 650.
  Hebrews ix. 3.
  Revelation xiii. 4, xxi. 2, II. 653.
Hegesippos.
  The kinsfolk of the Lord in the days
    of Domitian, I. 516.
Sibylline Books.
  Compared with Wolospa [Bang], lxvii.

5. Chronology, Pedigrees, and Calendar.

Ari, his chronology, II. 494.
Bæda, Ari's model, II. 645.
Birthdays, none kept in Iceland, I. 430.
Calendar.
  Old Teutonic and old Persian weeks
    of five days, cxx ; I. 428.
  Times of Sacrifices, I. 405.
  Times of work, I. 429.
  Reformers of Calendar, Thorstan, etc.,
    I. 429.
  Old heathen Calendar, I. 429.
  Difficulty in introducing the Roman
    Calendar into the North, I. 429.
Chronology of Northern History.
  Founded by Ari, II. 489.
  To be corrected, II. 490.
  Other sources, Niala, etc., II. 490.
  Of Thingore school of writers, II. 494.
Dates correctly given of—
  A-in-Helga battle, II. 589.
  Arnor's life, II. 184.
  Bishop Biarni of Orkney, II. 301.
  Bragi the poet, II. 1.
  Egil's Sona-torrek, I. 543 ; cp. II. 23.
  Einar-fostri, II. 397.
  Gunnlaug the monk, II. 372.
  Harold Fairhair, II. 494.
  Hornklofi the poet, I. 255.
  Krakomal, II. 340.
  Konungatal, II. 305.
  Norwegian early kings, II. 494.
  Olaf Tryggvason's life and death, II.86.

St. Olaf's life and death, II. 117.
Ragnar Lodbrok, II. 3.
Rollo [Howorth], II. 493.
Settlement of Iceland, II. 494.
Sighvat the poet, II. 119.
Thiodwulf and Ynglingatal, I. 243.
Icelandic Calendar at the present
  day, I. 429–431.
Moon, the year-teller, I. 431.
Night, reckoning by, among Teutons,
  I. 431.
Pedigrees.
  Angles, royal race of, II. 513.
  Ari to Rollo, II. 228.
  Arnmodling family, II. 301.
  Beowulf pedigrees in, II. 513.
  Bragi the poet, II. 2.
  Danish kings, II. 492, 513.
  Dublin kings of O. N. blood, II. 512,
    523.
  St. Edmund of E. England, II. 340.
  Egil, I. 542.
  English, royal race of Wessex, II. 493.
  Eywind, poet-spoiler, II. 34.
  Finwood, II. 301.
  Flemish earls, II. 493.
  Gaut, royal race of, II. 513.
  Gundhild Kings' mother, II. 37.
  Haleygja earls, II. 522.
  Heroes, pedigree of, II. 518–520.
  Horda-Kari family, II. 452, 512, 523.
  Lombards, royal race of, II. 513.

---

[1] The home-coming of Hymi is exactly like that of Polyphemos.

6. Historical References.

See INDEX II for List of NAMES and PLACES mentioned.

7. Law, Family and Constitutional.

8. Life of Warrior and Sailor.

9. Household Life in Old Days.

Accomplishments & amusements.
Accomplishments of a chief, I. 241, 242; II. 276, 299.
Capping verses [mod.], II. 412.
Chess-playing, II. 279.
Dance [med. and mod.], II. 412.
Dice-playing, I. 240, 257.
Jugglery and jesting, I. 255, 530; II. 279.
Mumming, II. 212.
Reading stories aloud, xxiii.
Tables, play at, I. 92, 194, 241, 342, 484.
Wakes, II. 412.

Agriculture.
Dunging land, I. 515.
Fencing, I. 515.
Horse-keeping, I. 369.
Plowing, I. 515.
Wood-cutting, I. 515, 524.
Sea-weed burning, II. 232.
Goat-herding, I. 37, 136.
Swine-tending, I. 136, 141, 236.
Goat-driving, I. 179, 220.
Hay-making, I. 246; II. 458.

Animals.
Beasts, wild, see *Thulor*.
Bear, black, I. 46, 58, 334, 362; II. 455, 458.
Bear, white, I. 334.
Buck, II. 458.
Deer, I. 328, 393 b.
Elk, II. 458.
Fox, II. 266–268, 383, 456; Index III. 10.
Hart and Hind, II. 456, 458.
Mouse, I. 189.
Wolf, I. 141, 335; II. 456.
Beasts, tame, see *Thulor*, and II. 454.
Cat, II. 407, 417.
Dog, I. 51, 135, 334, 348; II. 417.
Goat, I. 37, 136, 137; II. 456.
Greyhound, I. 141, 176.
Horse, I. 240, 350, 353; II. 456–458.
Oxen, I. 144, 179; II. 456.
Pigs, I. 191; II. 336, 366.
Reindeer, I. 15, 137, 247.
Sheep, II. 610.
Birds, see *Thulor*, II. 615.
Cock, II. 456.
Cuckoo, I. 185.
Eagle, I. 400, and often in Court-poetry.
Erne, I. 136, 334; II. 152, 218.
Geese, tame, I. 297.
Goslings, I. 568.

Hawk, I. 560, and often in Court-poetry.
Heron, I. 23.
Osprey, II. 456.
Puffin, I. 370.
Raven, I. 131, 256, 306; II. 56, 156, and often in Court-poetry.
Sparrow, tame, I. 246.
Swan, I. 318; II. 159, 265.
Wild fowl, I. 242; II. 358.
Fishes and sea beasts, see *Thulor*, and II. 457, 615.
Whale, see *Thulor*, and II. 172, 310.
Porpoise, I. 513; II. 32, 367.
Perch, II. 109.
Herring, II. 32.
Pike, II. 329.
Lobster, II. 329.
Urchin, II. 361.
Haddock, II. 231.
Ling, II. 231.
Other living things—
Snake, II. 456, 457.
Snail, II. 361.
Drone, II. 360.
Wasp, II. 267, 361.

Appearance and looks, in different classes of society, I. 515; II. 617.
Signs of anger, I. 298.
Dark hair, II. 64.
Curly hair, see Cormac's poems, II. 64.

Baby, fed in cradle from a horn, I. 523.

Beggar, II. 400.

Book.
Pen [mod.], II. 416, 418.
Illuminating, II. 300.
Scriptures, I. 209; II. 161.

Caricature, I. 374.

Carpentry and Carving, I. 138, 274, 310, 515, 539, 540; II. 589.

Colour, I. 57.
Black, I. 98, 138, 222; II. 159, 215, 271, 341.
Blue, I. 239; II. 136.
Green, I. 157, 264.
Grey, I. 53, 326.
Red, I. 135, 162, 326; II. 167, 220, 278.
Tawny, I. 240.
White, I. 258.

Costume, see Glosses in II. 546, and I. 51, 118, 515.
Brogues, I. 121; II. 611.
Clothes of different ranks, I. 515.
Cloak, I. 55; II. 251, 299.
Fur, I. 319.
Gems, I. 326; II. 485, 617.
Ladies' head-dresses, II. 276.

Butter-pig, II. 407.
Cups and cans, I. 221, 238, 240; II. 455.
Dish, I. 221.
Horn, II. 456.
Jug, II. 411.
Kettle, I. 221, 368 ; II. 455.
Weaving[1], I. 87, 91, 282, 319, 484.
Wedding, I. 82.
Wooing, I. 393.

Bridal procession, I. 350.
Wedding feast, I. 81, 178.
Work, Domestic, in old days.
Brogue-making, II. 611.
Singeing sheep, II. 227.
Autumn beast-killing, I. 333, 348.
Menial work, I. 136, 141, 236.
Woman's work, I. 325.
Washing head, II. 33, 357.
Washing clothes, II. 66.

10. Heathen Religion, Legend, and Ritual.

Altar.
Of sacrifice, I. 144, 245, 409.
Of the temple, I. 403.
Ancestor-worship, see Sacrifice, Dead. I. 413–422.
Augury and Divination, see Witchcraft.
From accidents, I. 563.
From animals, I. 34, 412.
From birds, I. 34, 412 ; II. 56.
From blade-bones, I. 412.
From divining-rods, I. 159, 220, 411, 413 ; II. 46.
From meteyard, II. 32.
From scales[2], II. 43.
Barrow of the dead, see Burial, I. 399, 417, 418, 524, 526.
Broken into, I. 418.
Grave-fires over, I. 166 ; II. 286.
Hills used as, I. 416.
Grave-stone, I. 8, 252, 371.
Beasts speaking and weeping.
Horse, I. 307, 317.
Pie, I. 144, 259.
Raven, I. 131, 305.
Beast-tales.
How the bear lost his tail, I. 462, 569.
How the hawk lost half his tail, I. 484.
Blood-eagle, see Sacrifice.
Burial[3] in heathen days, see also Barrow, I. 43, 347, 420, 421.
Bale-pyre, I. 303, 330; II. 325.
Cerecloth, I. 347.
Coffin, I. 347.

Corse buried in several pieces apart, I. 417.
Funeral-feast, I. 342–344, 349.
Cauldrons of stone[4], lxx.
Charmed weapons, I. 114, 162.
Children, unborn, I. 35.
Consecration.
By fire, I. 407.
By iron, I. 409, 425.
Curse, I. 116; II. 547.
Dead, spirits of the.
Ghosts, I. 142; II. 329, 330, 415.
Raising the dead, I. 227.
Dying into hills, I. 416.
Dead seen near or in their barrows, I. 415–416.
Worship of the dead, I. 414.
Dead called Elves and Disar, I. 405.
Death-songs, II. 547.
Demon, see *Excursus on Mythology,* and II. 471.
Demoniacal possession, I. 425.
Dreams and their Interpretation. I. 333, 347, 393, 413; II. 410, 547.
Dwarf, see *Thulor,* I. 244.
Turned to stone by the sun, see *Alvismal.*
Fairies [mod.], dwindled Elves, II. 385, 414.
Fate, strands of, see Norns, I. 131, 157.
Feast.
Temple feast, heathen, I. 403, 407.
Toasting Gods at, I. 404, 405.
Fetch, I. 335, 397.

---

[1] There is a coarse Lancashire broad-sheet song of this century, The Power Loom, which runs parallel to the Riddle of Heidrek on Weaving.
[2] Divination by scales is one of the regular legal ordeals of Ancient India.
[3] A burial in the Western Isles of a Northern wicking-smith with his tools, hammer, tongs, etc., precisely like that of Skallagrim, is described in Anderson's Pagan Scotland.
[4] Funeral urns of *steatite* (and sometimes of sandstone) are especially characteristic of wicking funerals in the Orkneys and in those parts of Norway from whence the wickings came and whither they went home to die; they are only met with in Norway *just at* the Wicking Period. See Anderson's Pagan Scotland, p. 78.

11. Christian Religion and Ritual [1].

---

[1] Anderson's Christian Scotland contains the best account of the old Scottish Church legends gathered from its surviving relics.

12. **Proverbs and Saws.**

See Proverb Song, II. 364 ; also Rune Song, II. 369.

In the Icelandic Reader, p. 259, will be found a collection of O. N. Proverbs from the Prose Sagas, etc. Saxo has in his earlier books full paraphrases of several proverb-poems now lost.

In Proverb Song, l. 26, one would read Ector var i hvildom hœgr, ' Hector was of gentle mood.' That true Trojan's courtesy being renowned from Homer's days to Eglinton's.

þeygi war siá aflausn ill,
Eiga skal nú huerr sem will.
                    The Proverb Song, 116.

THE ISLANDS.

Thulor 650-677 put into alphabetical order.

[N. B. = North Britain; S. B. = South Britain; D. = Denmark; the rest Norway.]

Ala.
Alldi.
Alǫst.
Askroð.
Asparnir.
Aurn.
Batalldr.
Biarkey.
Bokn.
Bolm.
Bǫnn.
Borgund.
Brising.
Brua.
Dimun. [Faro.]
Dyn.
Erri. [D.]
Ey. [N. B.]
Falstr. [D.]
Fenring.
Fiolbyrja.
Fión. [D.]
Folskn.
Fœtilǫr. [N. B.]
Friðnar.
Frigg.
Frikn.
Frosta.
Gartar.
Gizki.
Gylling.
Hanki.
Hasley.
Heðinsey. [Foreign.]
Hæl.
Hellis-kor.
Hæring.
Herna.
Hin.
Hirar (?).
Hísing. [Sweden.]
Hitra.
Hlessey. [D.]

Hnotirnar.
Hǫð.
Horn.
Hrafnista.
Hrott.
Hrund.
Hugl.
Hugro.
Hveðn. [D.]
Iala. [N. B.]
Il. [N. B.]
Ira. [N. B.]
Ívist. [N. B.]
Kinn.
Kipr. [Cyprus.]
Kǫrmt.
Krit. [Crete.]
Láland. [D.]
Laug.
Lauga.
Leka.
Lodda.
Loǫnd.
Lygra.
Marsey. [N. B.]
Miola.
Mǫn. [N. B.]
Mǫst.
Myl. [N. B.]
Mýstr.
Nála.
Nauma.
Nǫrva.
Nǫs.
Öllum-lengi [?].
Omð.
Ormst. [N. B.]
Raufa.
Rist.
Rǫð.
Rǫkstr.
Rott.
Saga.

Salarey.
Salbiǫrn.
Sámsey. [D.]
Seima (?).
Sækk.
Sæla.
Selja.
Selund. [D.]
Senja.
Sigg.
Sild.
Sióland. [D.]
Siri.
Skíð. [N. B.]
Skolm.
Skrofa.
Smyl.
Solrǫnn.
Solskel.
Solundir.
Sortoland.
Sotr.
Stolm.
Storð.
Strind.
Syllingar. [S. B.]
Tiǫr.
Torgar.
Usna.
Vað.
Varða.
Véey.
Veig.
Vigr. [N. B.]
Vikna.
Vingr.
Vǫrl.
Þiórn.
Þiotta.
Þǫmb.
Þriðna.
Þruma.

For British Rivers, Thulor 333-356, see Dict., last page.

AFTERMATH, *August*, 1883.

The Spirit-path. Wætlinga-braut (I. 420). This myth is aptly illustrated by Ovid—

> Est *via* sublimis cœlo manifesta sereno,
> *Lactea* nomen habet, candore notabilis ipso;
> Hac iter est superis ad magni tecta Tonantis
> Regalemque domum.—*Met.* **i.** 168–171.

It is indeed probable that (pace the compiler of Gylfa-ginning) the word Bil-rost or Bif-rost, which clearly indicates a *stream, path, road,* or the like, was originally applied to the Milky Way, for it was not till the arch-bridges of the Romans were known to the Teutons that they would think of the rainbow as an arch, bridge, or door, they would imagine it as a serpent perhaps (like the Bretons) or the bow of a mighty archer (as the Hebrews did), but certainly not as a Spirit-path. The etymology of Bil- or Bif- is unknown. Can Bil- be a parallel form of Gala-?

Ovid also gives a most interesting parallel to the 'aldar-far' etc. of the beginning of the Wolospa (II. 645), with which it should be carefully compared—

> Primaque ab *origine mundi*
> Ad mea perpetuum deducite tempora carmen:
> Ante mare et terras et, quod tegit omnia, cœlum
> Unus erat toto naturæ vultus in orbe
> Quem dixere *chaos*, rudis indigestaque moles,
> Nec quicquam, nisi pondus iners, congestaque eodem
> Non bene junctarum discordia semina rerum.
> Nullus adhuc mundo præbebat lumina Titan,
> Nec nova crescendo reparabat cornua Phœbe,
> Nec circumfuso pendebat in aëre Tellus
> Ponderibus librata suis, nec brachia longo
> Margine terrarum porrexerat Amphitrite.—*Met.* i. 3, 4.

There can be no question of the Teuton poet borrowing here; and it is, one would say, pretty clear that Ovid is writing from some lost original (probably Greek) which was like the Northern Lay, a Song of the Beginnings. The Wessobrunner Prayer supplies another parallel, Gill's Polynesian Collection includes others. The Latin text justifies the transposition which we have effected in the text of Wolospa.

The Tanner's epithet (II. 212), *for* 'skap-dreki skinna' *read* 'skaf-dreki skinna,' meaning the skin-scraper-monster.

Haleygja-tal (II. 657). There is still an emendation to be made in the last line —'stillis-lof' is not satisfactory; a more substantial word is wanted for the image. Now when we recollect Egil's 'hlóð ek *lof*-köst' we find the two similes identical, and the word *lof* in both; under 'stillis' some word, meaning *structure, tower, pillar,* must needs be concealed; 'studla,' we doubt not, is right, it has three letters in common with stillis. So we read—

> Enn ver yrkja gátom
> stuðla lofs sem steina-brú,

I have reared columns of praise lasting like a stone bridge (the 'bridge' here in the sense used in the Swedish Runic Stones), which completes the image properly; 'lasting' would have stood in the preceding lost line. If either poet borrows here, it is Eywind, whose poem is twenty years later than Egil's.

Kvási. The poem from which Kvasi's story (II. 636) is drawn having perished, we have no clue to the history of the word or legend. Is it possible that the word may be parallel to the Greek Βακχος, Kvah-[si = Bak-]chos, the termination alone differing?

At the end of *Hornklofi's Song,* read 'Dísar dramblátrar.'

ADDENDA AND CORRIGENDA.

A law-phrase in the Old Wolsung Play, line 262.   There is an Old Norse term, akveðins orð, okveðins orð, which (no doubt through the stage 'okvens ord') appears as the modern Danish ukvems-ord (*ns* = ms).   It means lampoon, libel, *scandalum* of the bitter kind, so greatly dreaded by the Old Irish and Old Northmen, who thought that such words of hate and cursing were bound to take effect, unless counteracted by proper proceedings on the part of the injured person.   As it stands, verse 68, O. W. Pl., makes no good sense at all.   Under 'opt kveðin orð' we intimate okveðin orð; 'verri' would be a gloss; we sound *word* for orð; 'an viti' may be a corruption for œr-viti, which occurs in this connection in Lokas, l. 82, and Helgi i. 271, Oddr. 1.   At any rate, okveðins orð is safe, and we read—

> þviat ósviðr maðr lætr ókveðin
> vorð . . . œr-viti,

for a fool in frantic mood may use cursing words.   The remainder of the lines contain the precautions to be adopted and the consequences which may come : 'Either thou must go to law, and that is risky, or thou must go to the sword, and that leads one into feuds.'   'Heimis-kviðr' is probably 'compurgation' by the fellow-township-men.